Autodesk Fusion Black Book (V 2701.1.18) Part I

By
Gaurav Verma
Matt Weber
(CADCAMCAE Works)

ISBN # 978-1-77459-204-5

DEDICATION

To teachers, who make it possible to disseminate knowledge
to enlighten the young and curious minds
of our future generations

To students, who are the future of the world

THANKS

To my friends and colleagues

To my family for their love and support

Table of Contents

Chapter 2 : Sketching

Chapter 3 : 3D Sketch and Solid Modeling

Chapter 4 : Advanced 3D Modeling

Chapter 5 : Practical and Practice

Chapter 6 : Solid Editing

Chapter 7 : Assembly Design

Chapter 8 : Importing Files and Inspection

Chapter 9 : Surface Modeling

Chapter 10 : Rendering and Animation

Chapter 11 : Drawing

Part II of this book covers

Preface

Autodesk Fusion is a product of Autodesk Inc. Fusion is the first of its kind software which combine 3D CAD, CAM, and CAE tool in single package. It connects your entire product development process in a single cloud-based platform that works on both Mac and PC. In CAD environment, you can create the model with parametric designing and dimensioning. The CAD environment is equally applicable for assembly design. The CAE environment facilitates to analysis the model under real-world load conditions. Once the model is as per your requirement then generate the NC program using the CAM environment.

The **Autodesk Fusion Black Book** (V 2701.1.18) is 9th edition of our series on Autodesk Fusion. The book is updated on Autodesk Fusion Student Version 2701.1.18 which is March, 2026 version of software. With lots of features and thorough review, we present a book to help professionals as well as beginners in creating some of the most complex solid models. The book follows a step by step methodology. In this book, we have tried to give real-world examples with real challenges in designing. We have tried to reduce the gap between educational use of Autodesk Fusion and industrial use of Autodesk Fusion. This edition of book, includes latest topics on Sketching, 3D Part Designing, Assembly Design, Sculpting, Mesh Design, CAM, Simulation, Sheetmetal, 3D printing, Manufacturing, and many other topics. Latest enhancements of the software have been added in this edition. The book covers almost all the information required by a learner to master the Autodesk Fusion. The book starts with sketching and ends at advanced topics like Manufacturing, Simulation, and Generative Design. Some of the salient features of this book are :

In-Depth explanation of concepts

Every new topic of this book starts with the explanation of the basic concepts. In this way, the user becomes capable of relating the things with real world.

Topics Covered

Every chapter starts with a list of topics being covered in that chapter. In this way, the user can easily find the topic of his/her interest easily.

Instruction through illustration

The instructions to perform any action are provided by maximum number of illustrations so that the user can perform the actions discussed in the book easily and effectively. There are about **2450** small and large illustrations that make the learning process effective.

Tutorial point of view

At the end of concept's explanation, the tutorial makes the understanding of users firm and long lasting. Almost each chapter of the book has tutorials that are real world projects. Moreover, most of the tools in this book are discussed in the form of tutorials.

Project

Free projects and exercises are provided to students for practicing.

For Faculty

If you are a faculty member, then you can ask for video tutorials on any of the topic, exercise, tutorial, or concept. As faculty, you can register on our website to get electronic desk copies of our latest books, self-assessment, and solution of practical. Faculty resources are available in the **Faculty Member** page of our website (**www.cadcamcaeworks.com**) once you login. Note that faculty registration approval is manual and it may take two days for approval before you can access the faculty website.

Formatting Conventions Used in the Text

All the key terms like name of button, tool, drop-down etc. are kept bold.

Free Resources

Link to the resources used in this book are provided to the users via email. To get the resources, mail us at ***cadcamcaeworks@gmail.com*** with your contact information. With your contact record with us, you will be provided latest updates and informations regarding various technologies. The format to write us mail for resources is as follows:

Subject of E-mail as ***Application for resources of ________ book***.
Also, given your information like
Name:
Course pursuing/Profession:
E-mail ID:

Note: We respect your privacy and value it. If you do not want to give your personal informations then you can ask for resources without giving your information.

About Authors

The author of this book, Gaurav Verma, has authored and assisted in more than 17 titles in CAD/CAM/CAE which are already available in market. He has authored **Autodesk Fusion PCB Black Book** for working on electronics design. He has authored **AutoCAD Electrical Black Books** which are available in both **English** and **Russian** language. He has also authored books on various modules of Creo Parametric and SolidWorks. He has provided consultant services to many industries in US, Greece, Canada, and UK. He has assisted in preparing many Government aided skill development programs. He has been speaker for Autodesk University. He has assisted in preparing AutoCAD Electrical course for Autodesk Design Academy. He has worked on Sheetmetal, Forging, Machining, and Casting designs in Design and Development departments of various manufacturing firms.

For Any query or suggestion

If you have any query or suggestion, please let us know by mailing us on ***cadcamcaeworks@gmail.com***. Your valuable constructive suggestions will be incorporated in our books.

Page left blank intentionally

Chapter 1

Starting with Autodesk Fusion

Topics Covered

The major topics covered in this chapter are:

- ***Overview of Autodesk Fusion***
- ***Installing Autodesk Fusion (Educational)***
- ***Starting Autodesk Fusion***
- ***Starting a New Document***
- ***File Menu***
- ***Preform***
- ***Undo and Redo button***
- ***User Account drop-down***
- ***Help drop-down***
- ***Data Panel***
- ***Simulation Browser***
- ***Navigation Bar***
- ***Display Bar***
- ***Customizing Toolbar and Marking Menu***

OVERVIEW OF AUTODESK FUSION

Autodesk Fusion is an Autodesk product designed to be a powerful 3D Modeling software package with an integrated, parametric, feature based CAM module built into the software. Autodesk Fusion is the first of its kind 3D CAD, CAM, and CAE tool. It connects your entire product development process in a single cloud-based platform that works on both Mac and Microsoft Windows; refer to Figure-1.

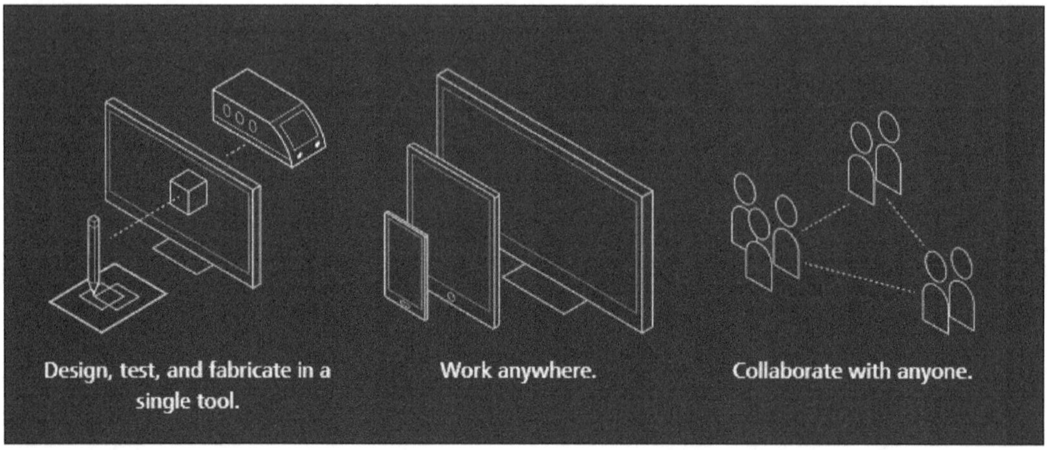

Figure-1. Overview

It combines mechanical design, collaboration, simulation, and machining in a single software. The tools in Fusion enable rapid and easy exploration of design ideas with an integrated concept to production toolset. This software needs a good network connection to work in collaboration with other team members.

This software is much affordable than any other software offered by Autodesk. To use this software, one need to pay monthly subscription of Fusion. You can work offline in this software and later save the file on Autodesk Server. User can access this software from anywhere with an internet connection. The user is able to open the saved file and also able to share files with anyone from anywhere as long as he/she has the software and good internet connection. Also, the pricing of this software is so effective that anyone can use it for manufacturing of tools and parts. Autodesk Fusion is build to work in multi body manner: both parts and assemblies build in a single file. The procedure to install the software is given next.

INSTALLING AUTODESK FUSION (STUDENT)

- Connect your PC with the internet connection and then log on to **https://www.autodesk.com/education/edu-software/overview** as shown in Figure-2.

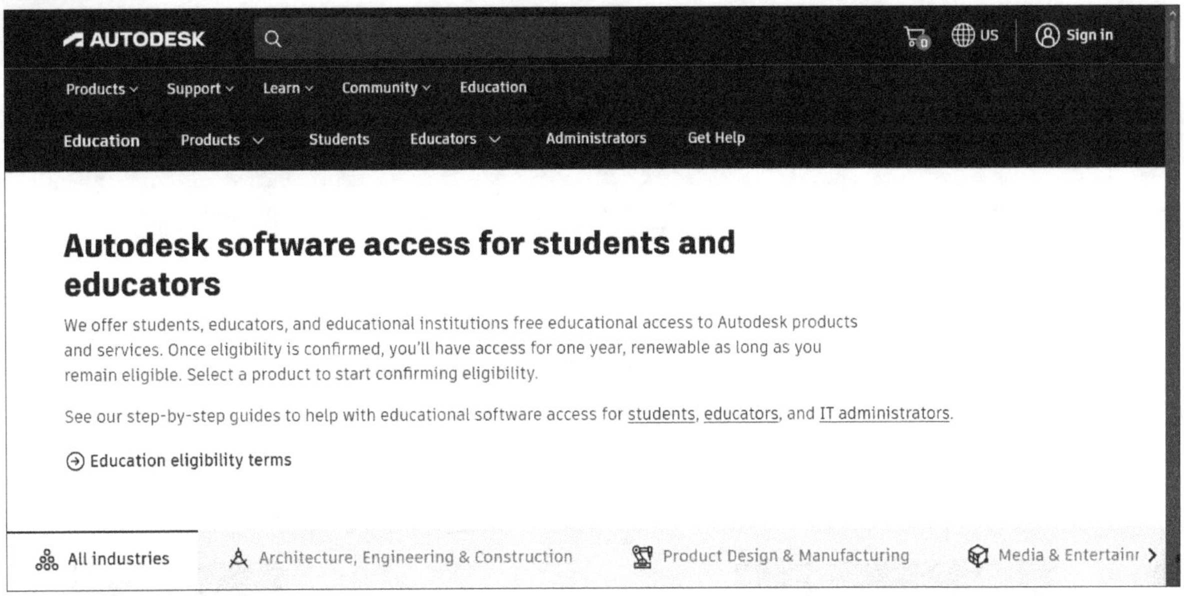

Figure-2. Autodesk website

- Click on the **Select** button for Fusion from the webpage. The web page to define your current role will be displayed.
- Click on the **Select** button for Student from the page. Click on the **Continue** button from the notification shown on web page. The **Sign up** page will be displayed; refer to Figure-3.

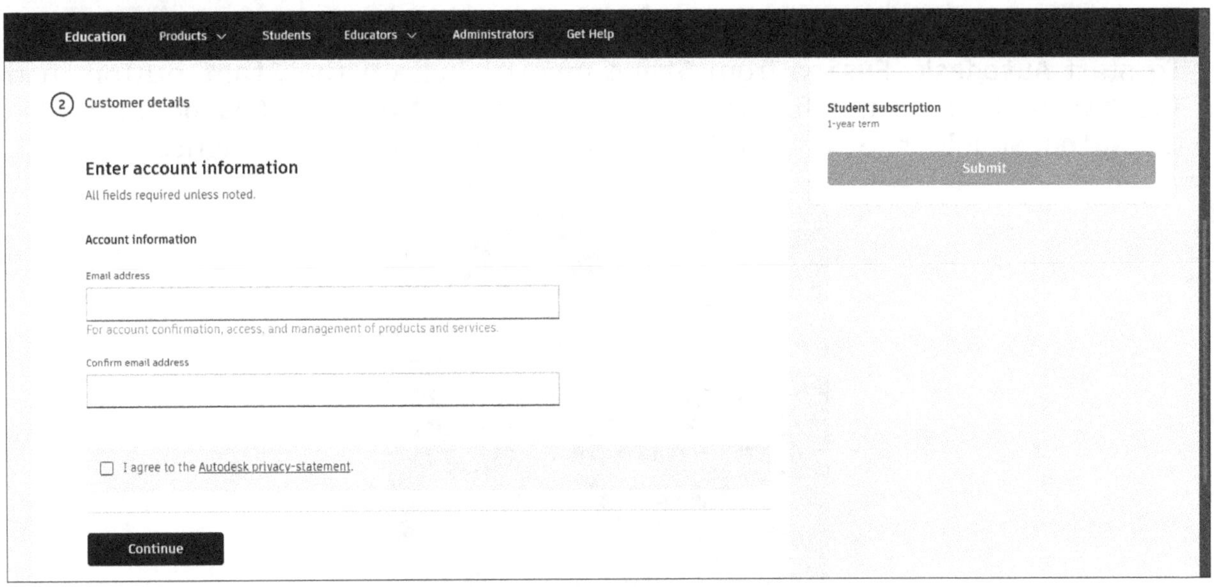

Figure-3. Sign up page

- Enter your student E-mail ID in the fields, select the check box, and click on the **Continue** button.
- Fill the other details as asked on webpage. After completion of these processes, you may be asked to upload your documentation like ID card scan or receipt to confirm your student status. Once your account is approved which can take up to 2 days, you need to sign-in to your Autodesk Account and search for the **Autodesk Fusion software**.
- Click on the **Get product** button below the software name. The **Access** button will become active; refer to Figure-4. Click on this button to download the **Autodesk Fusion software**.

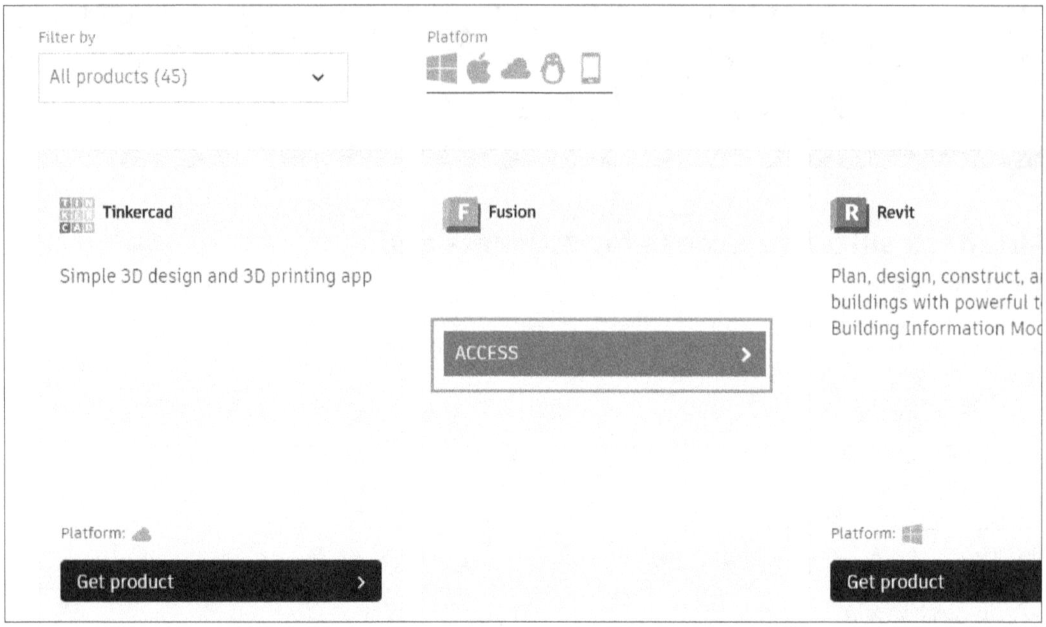

Figure-4. Access button

- Open the download setup file and follow the instructions as per the setup instruction.
- The software will be installed in a couple of minutes.

STARTING AUTODESK FUSION

- To start **Autodesk Fusion** from **Start** menu, click on the **Start** button in the **Taskbar** at the bottom left corner and then select **Autodesk Fusion** option from the **Autodesk** folder. Select the **Autodesk Fusion** icon; refer to Figure-5.

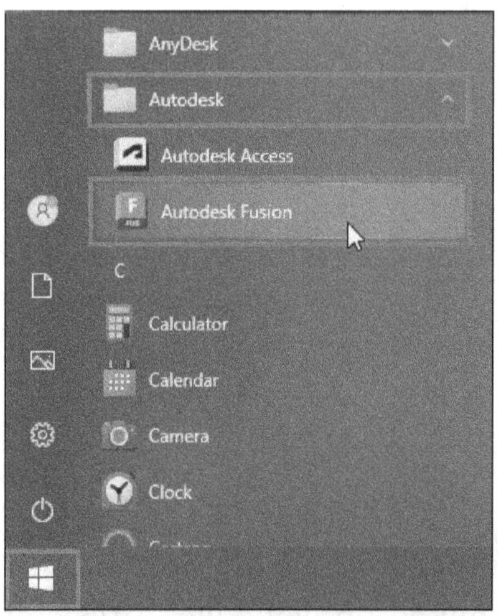

Figure-5. Start menu

- While installing the software, if you have selected the check box to create a desktop icon then you can double-click on that icon to run the software.
- If you have not selected the check box to create the desktop icon and want to create the icon on desktop now in Windows 10 or later, then drag the **Autodesk Fusion** icon from **Start** menu to Desktop.

After clicking on the icon, the Autodesk Fusion software window will be displayed; refer to Figure-6.

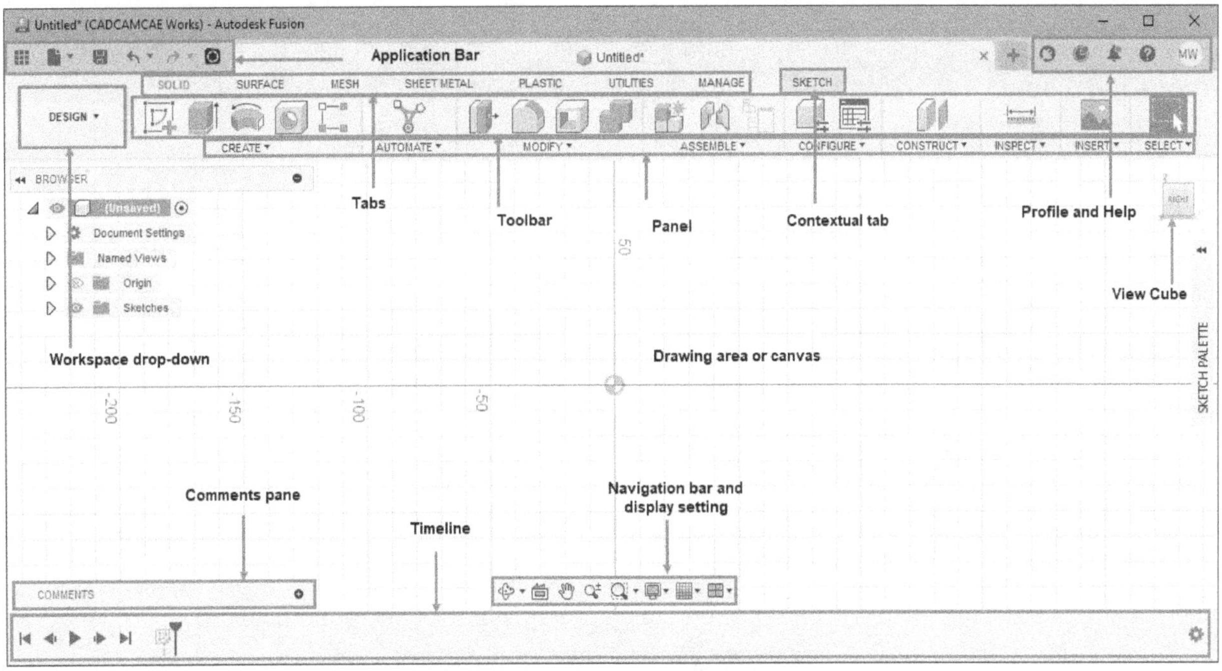

Figure-6. Autodesk Fusion application window

STARTING A NEW DOCUMENT

- Click on the **File** drop-down and select the **New** tool as shown in Figure-7. A dialog box to define which type of document is to be started; refer to Figure-8.
- Select **Part Design** button from the dialog box to start a new part design. Select desired button from the **Type** section to define document type and select desired unit system for the part.
- Click on the **Create New** button from the dialog box. A new document will open.
- Select desired workspace from the **Workspace** drop-down; refer to Figure-9.

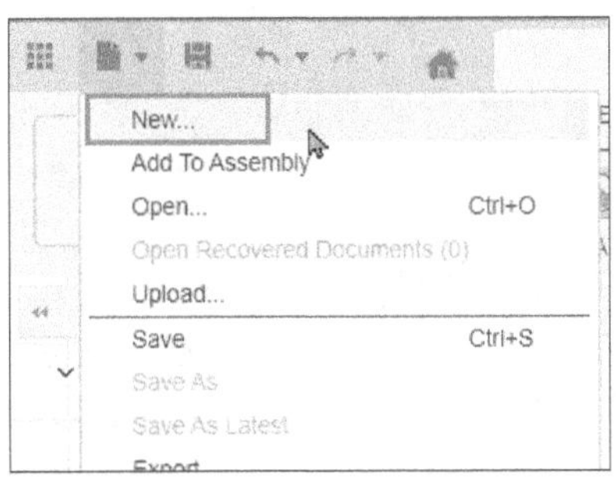

Figure-7. File menu

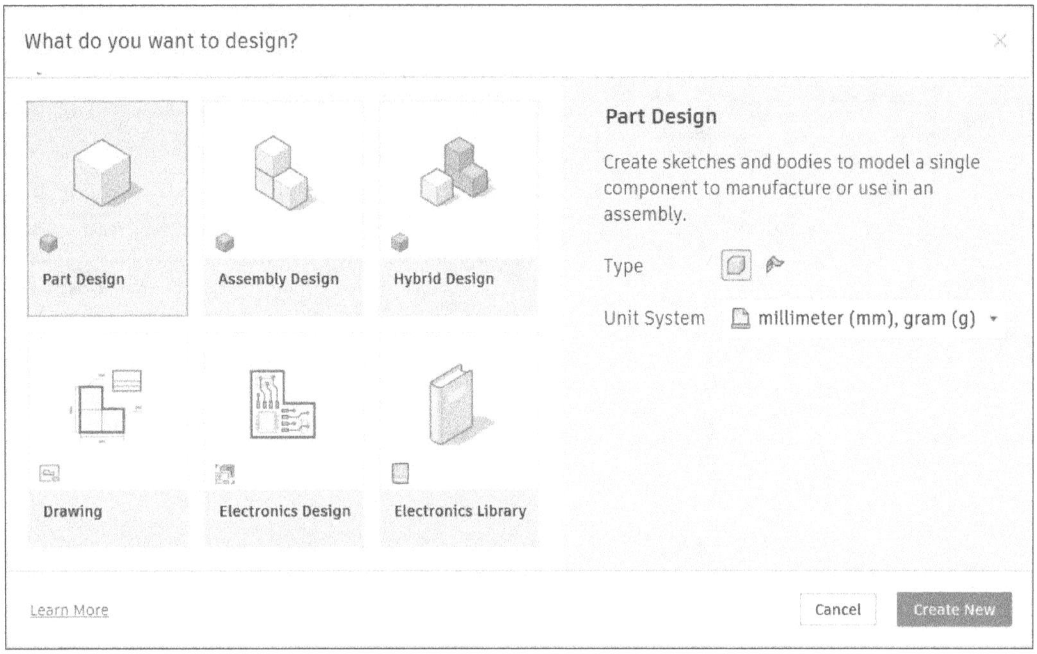

Figure-8. Options for starting new file

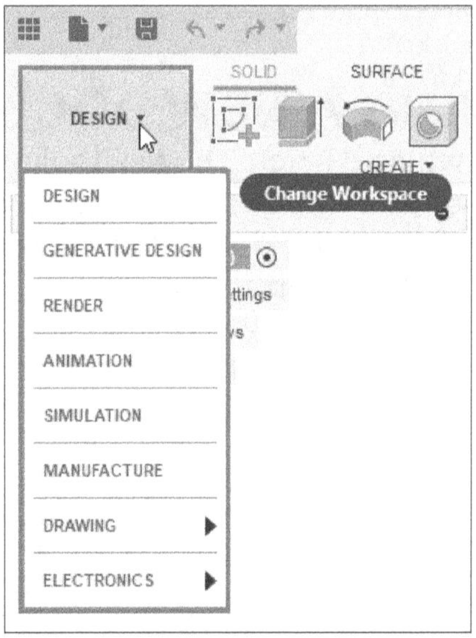

Figure-9. Workspace drop-down

- Various workspaces available in **Workspace** drop-down of Educational version are **DESIGN**, **GENERATIVE DESIGN**, **RENDER**, **ANIMATION**, **SIMULATION**, **MANUFACTURE**, **DRAWING** and **ELECTRONICS**.
- The **DESIGN** button is used to create solid, surface, and sheet metal designs.
- The **GENERATIVE DESIGN** button is used to create multiple designs that meet your geometric, performance, and manufacturing requirements.
- The **RENDER** button is used to activate workspace for rendering realistic model for presentation.

- The **ANIMATION** button is used to activate workspace for creating automatic or manual exploded views as well as direct control over unique animation of parts and assemblies.
- The **SIMULATION** button is used to perform Engineering Analyses.
- The **MANUFACTURE** button is used to generate G-codes for manufacturing processes like turning, milling, drilling, cutting, probing, and so on.
- The **DRAWING** button is used for generating drawings from model and animation.
- The **ELECTRONICS** button is used to create electronic designs.

You can learn more about these workspaces in our Autodesk Fusion Black Book.

FILE MENU

The options in the **File** menu are used to manage files and related parameters. Various tools of **File** menu are discussed next.

Add to Assembly

The **Add to Assembly** tool is used to add current model to assembly design model. On clicking this tool, a dialog box will be displayed asking you whether to add model to new assembly or an existing assembly; refer to Figure-10.

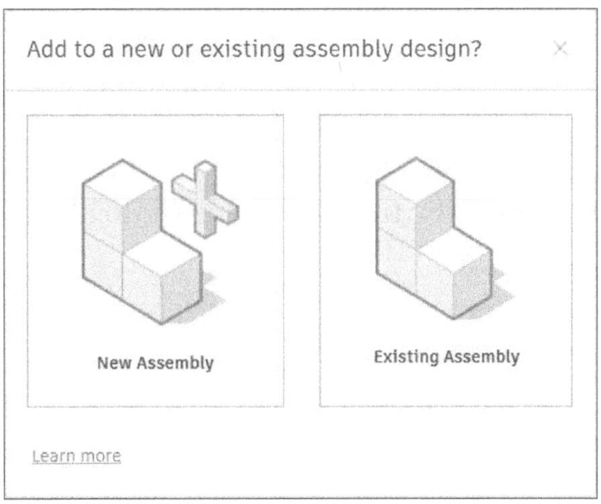

Figure-10. Add to Assembly dialog box

- Open desired component from the local directory which you want to insert into new or existing assembly and then click on the **Add to Assembly** tool from the **File** menu; refer to Figure-11. A **Save design required** dialog box will be displayed asking you to save the component; refer to Figure-12.

Figure-11. Component opened

Figure-12. Save design required dialog box

- Click on the **Save and Insert** button, the **Save** dialog box will be displayed to save the component; refer to Figure-13.

Figure-13. Save dialog box

- Specify desired name of component in the **Name** edit box and specify desired location of component in the **Location** area of the dialog box.
- Click on the **Save** button. The component will be saved and a dialog box will be displayed as shown in Figure-10.

- Click on the **New Assembly** button to create a new assembly design and insert the active component; refer to Figure-14.

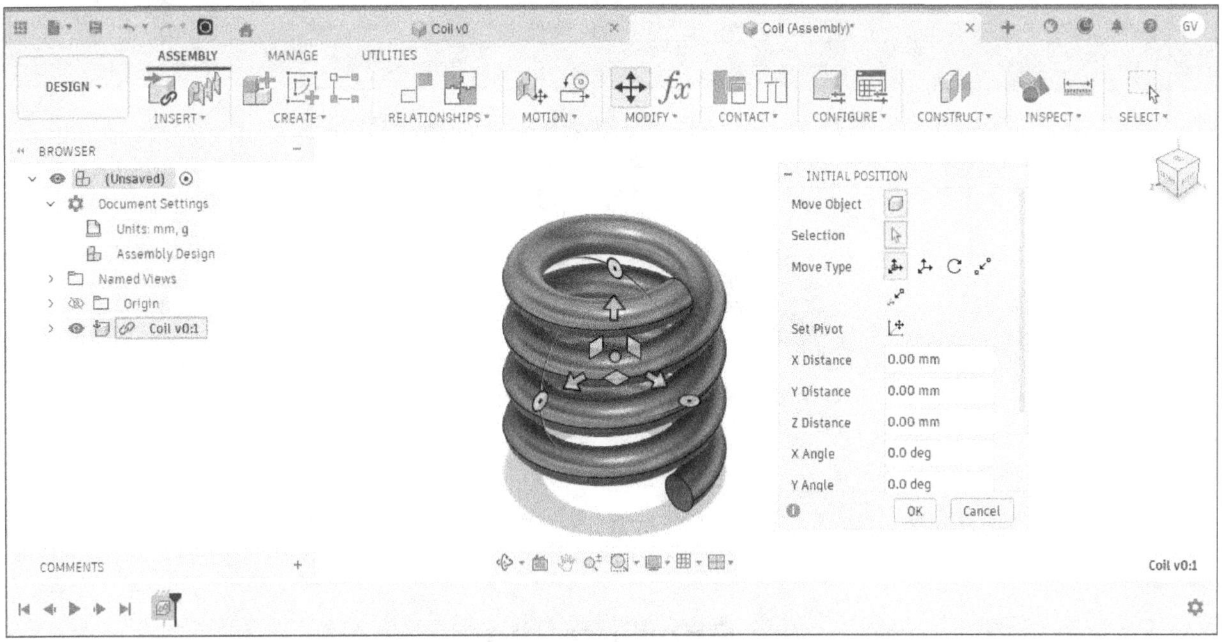

Figure-14. Component inserted in the assembly design environment

- And, click on the **Existing Assembly** button, the **Choose Assembly** dialog box will be displayed asking you to select desired existing assembly file; refer to Figure-15.

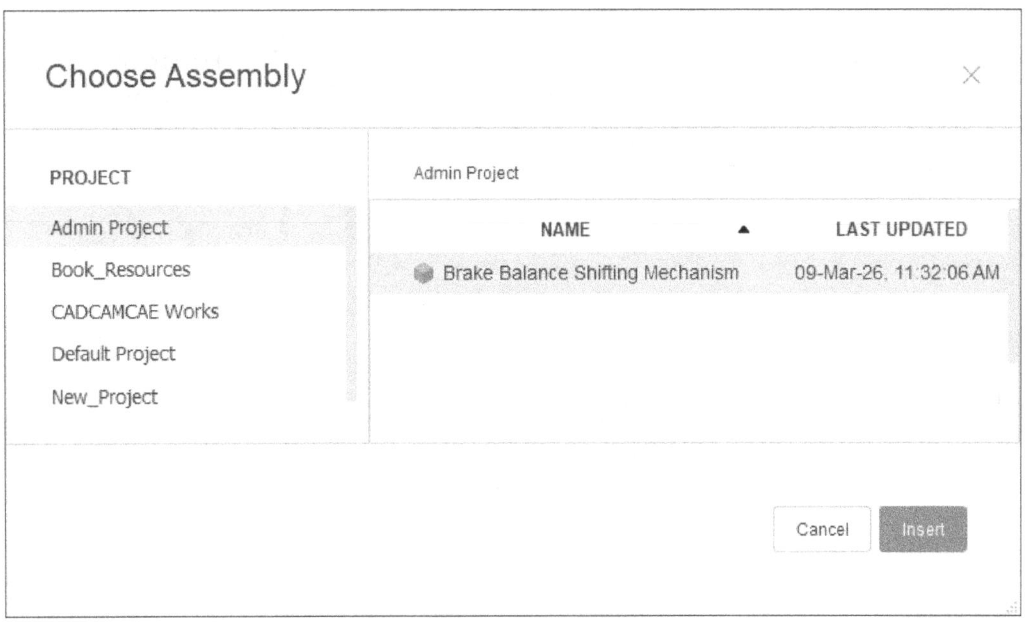

Figure-15. Choose Assembly dialog box

- Select desired assembly file from the dialog box and click on the **Insert** button. The inserted component will be displayed with the selected assembly file; refer to Figure-16.

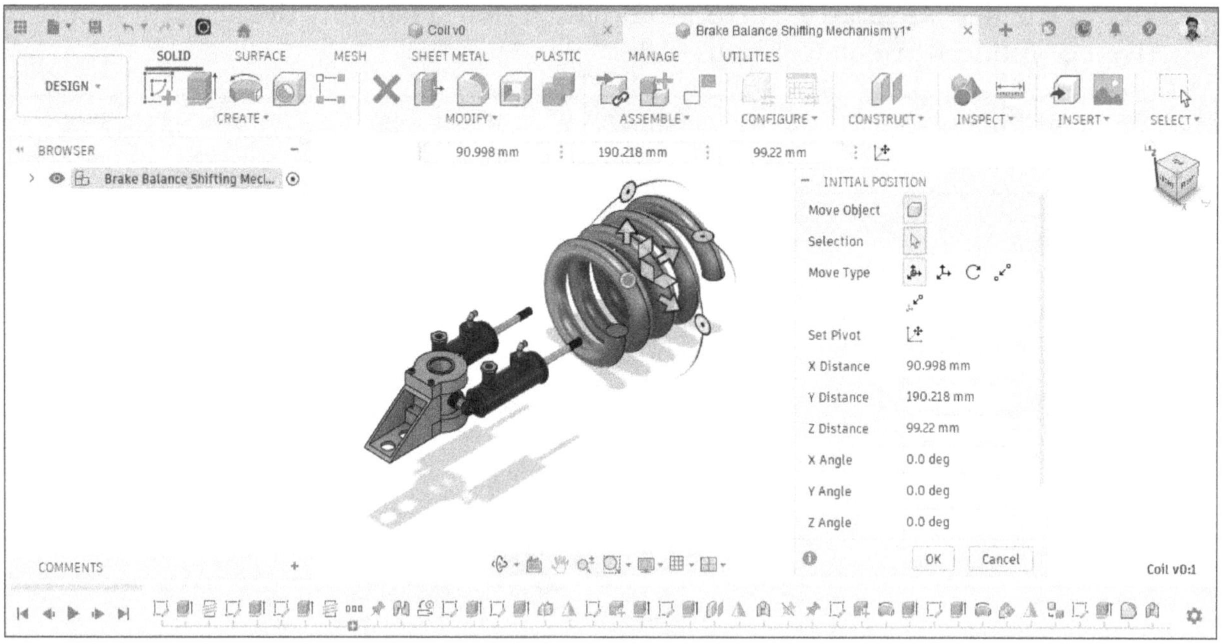

Figure-16. Component inserted with the assembly file

Opening File

The **Open** tool is used to open files earlier saved in cloud or local drive. You can also use this tool to import supported files of other software. The procedure to use this tool is given next.

- Click on the **Open** tool from the **File** menu or press **CTRL+O** from keyboard. The **Open** dialog box will be displayed; refer to Figure-17. Note that we are working in online mode of Autodesk Fusion.

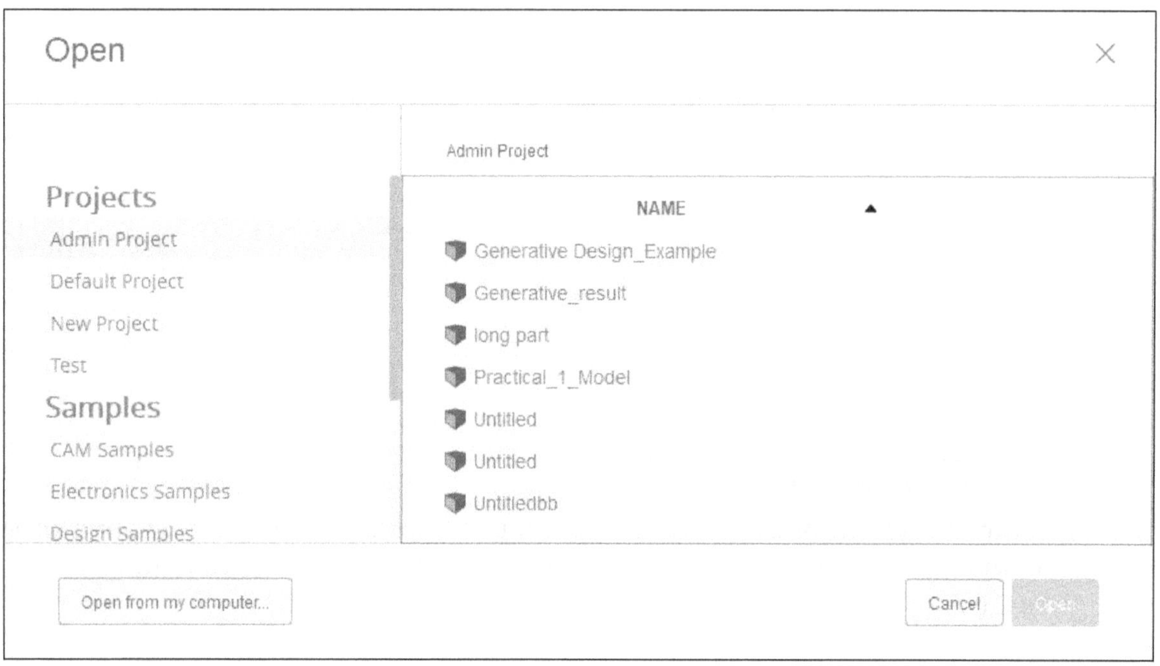

Figure-17. Open dialog box

- By default, files saved on cloud are displayed in the dialog box. Select desired file and click on the **Open** button. The file will open in Autodesk Fusion.
- If you want to open a file stored in local drive then click on the **Open from my computer** button. The **Open** dialog box will be displayed; refer to Figure-18.

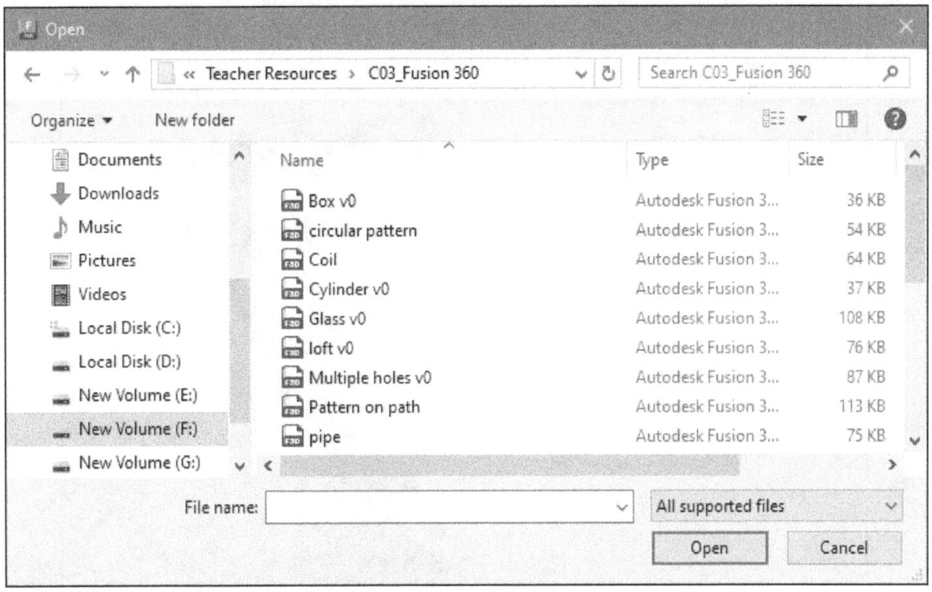

Figure-18. Open dialog box

- Select desired file and click on the **Open** button. The file will be displayed in the application window. If you have selected the file of different format from native format then the **Job Status** dialog box will be displayed notifying you the status of file import; refer to Figure-19.

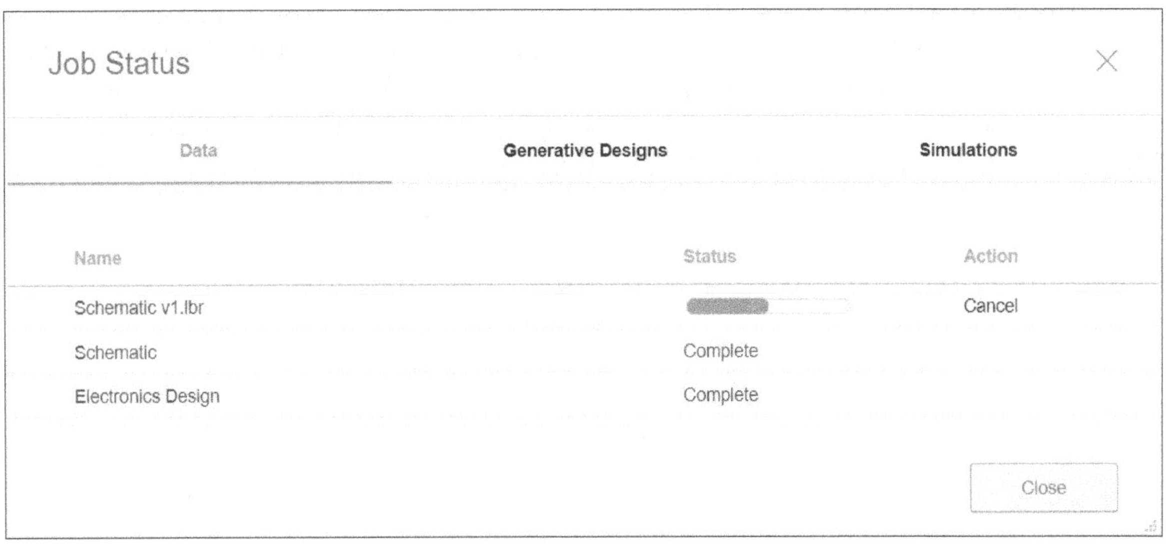

Figure-19. Job Status dialog box

- Once the status of import is complete then click on the **Open** button from the **Action** column in the dialog box. The model will be displayed; refer to Figure-20 (Creo Parametric file imported in Fusion).

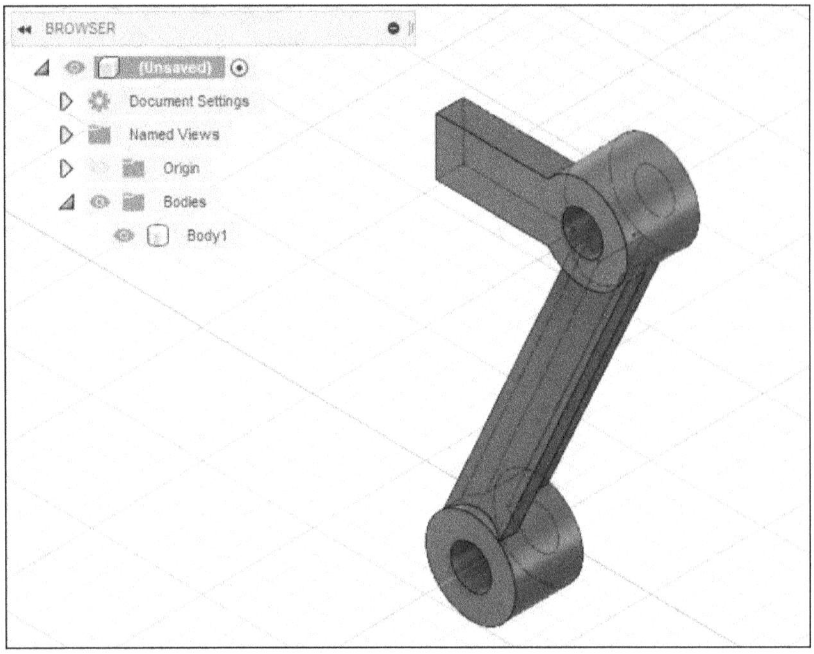

Figure-20. Model imported from Creo Parametric file

Recovering Documents

The **Recover Documents** tool is used to recover unsaved file versions which are created when software closes unexpectedly; refer to Figure-21. Note that there is an auto save feature in Autodesk Fusion which saves versions of file at a specific time intervals. If software has created the auto save version of your file then only you will be able to recover the file. By default, this time interval is 5 minutes and it can be changed in **Preferences** dialog box which will be discussed later. The procedure to use this tool is given next.

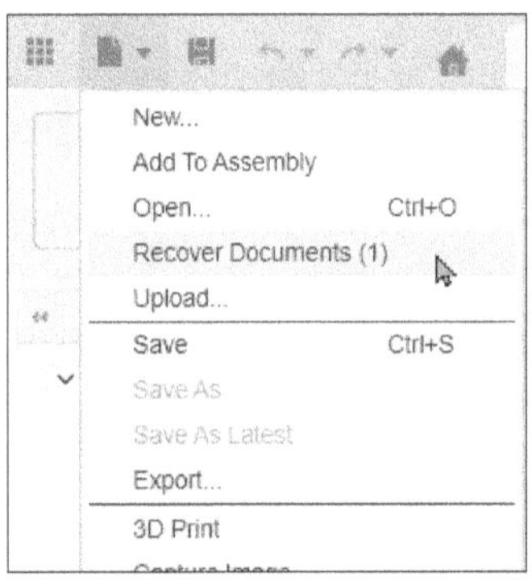

Figure-21. Recover Documents tool

- Click on the **Recover Documents** tool from the **File** menu. The **Recovered Documents** dialog box will be displayed where you need to select auto save version of your file; refer to Figure-22.

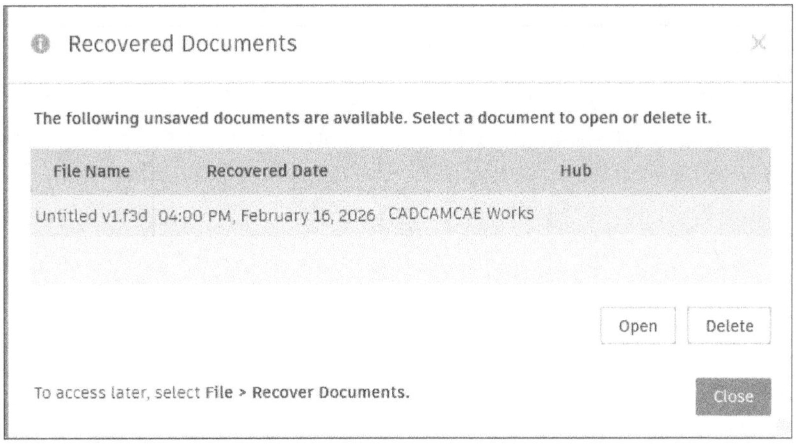

Figure-22. Recovered Documents dialog box

- Click on the file version that you want to be recovered and click on the **Open** button from the dialog box. The file version will open in **Autodesk Fusion**. If the opened version is as desired then save it otherwise close it and open the other version from the **Recovered Documents** dialog box. If the file version is not as desired then click on the **Delete** button from the dialog box to remove the selected recovered documents.

Upload

The **Upload** tool is used to upload files on cloud. The procedure to use this tool is discussed next.

- Click on **Upload** button from the **File** menu. The **Upload** dialog box will be displayed; refer to Figure-23. Click on the **Select Files** button or Drag & Drop the files to be uploaded in the **Drag and Drop Here** area of the dialog box.
- If you want to change the location where files will be uploaded then click on the **Change Location** button and select desired location from the **Change Location** dialog box; refer to Figure-24.

Figure-23. Upload dialog box

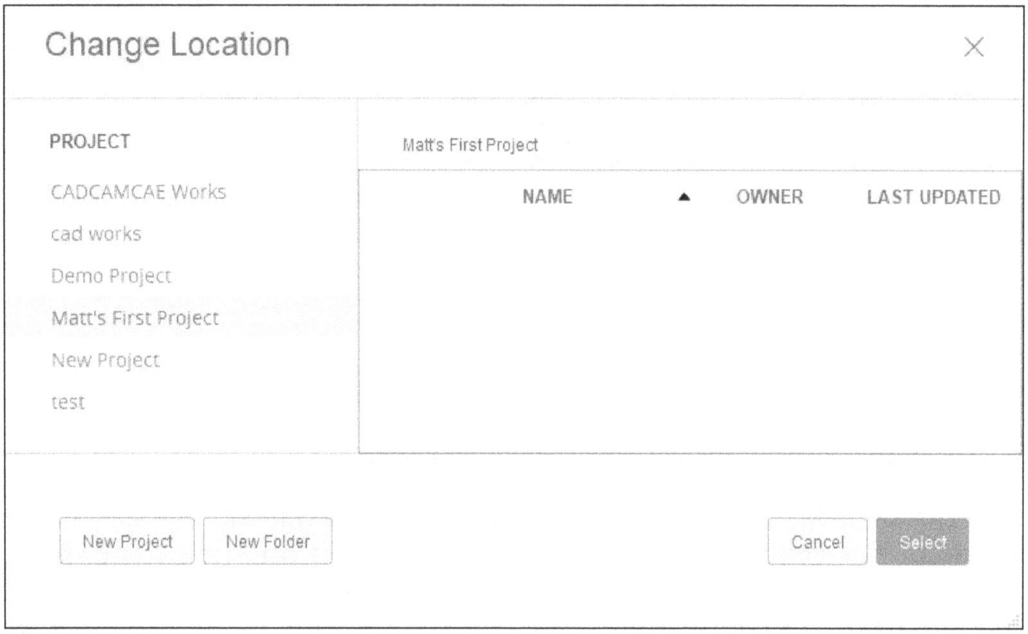

Figure-24. Change Location dialog box

- After selecting desired location, click on the **Select** button. You will return to **Upload** dialog box with updated location. Note that you can also create new folders and new locations by using the options in **Change Location** dialog box which will be discussed later in this book.
- Click on the **Select Files** button to upload files and select multiple files while holding the **CTRL** key from the **Open** dialog box displayed; refer to Figure-25.

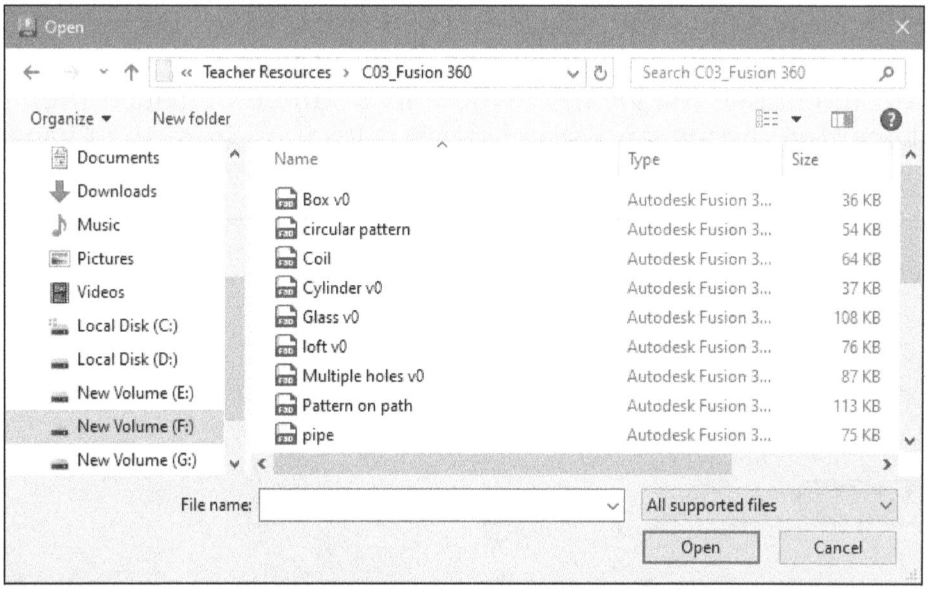

Figure-25. Open dialog box to upload file

- Click on the **Open** button from the dialog box to upload files. Or, drag the files in the dialog box and drop them. The options in the **Upload** dialog box will be updated; refer to Figure-26.

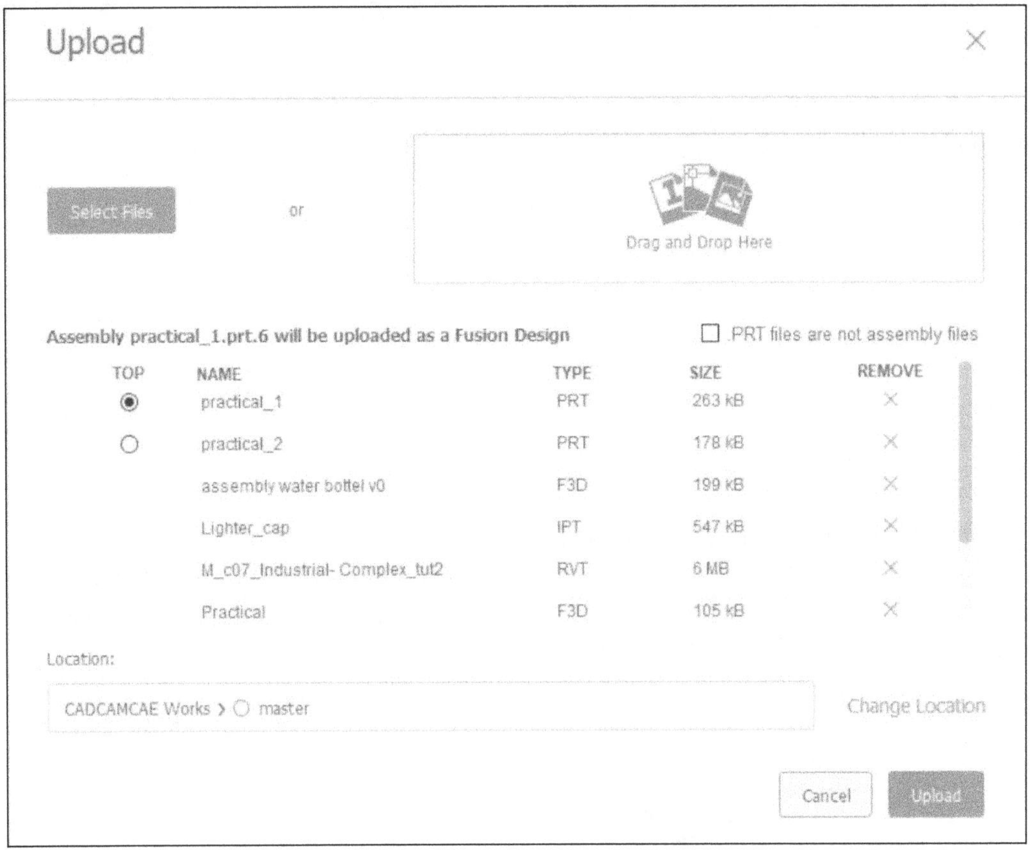

Figure-26. Updated Upload dialog box

- If you have selected a **.PRT** file of NX or Creo then select the **.PRT files are not assembly files** check box to explicitly tell software that these PRT files are not connected to any assembly.
- After specifying desired parameters, click on **Upload** button from **Upload** dialog box. Files will be uploaded and status will be displayed in **Job Status** dialog box.

Save

The **Save** tool is used to save the current file on cloud. You can press **CTRL+S** key from keyboard to save file. The procedure to save file is given next.

- Click on the **Save** tool from **File** menu or select the **Save** button from **Application bar** as shown in Figure-27. The **Save** dialog box will be displayed asking you to specify the **Name** and **Location** of your file; refer to Figure-28.

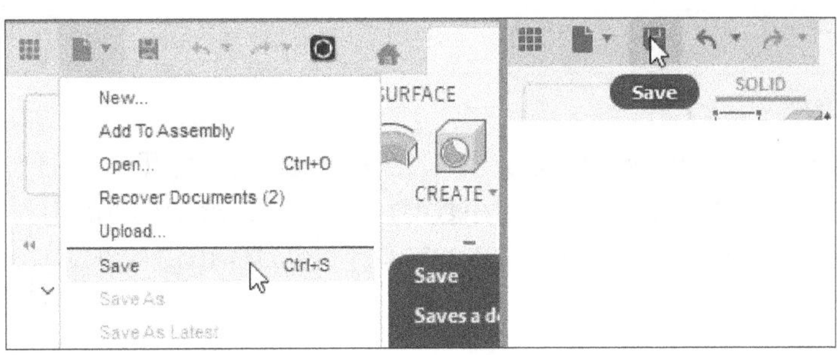

Figure-27. Save tool

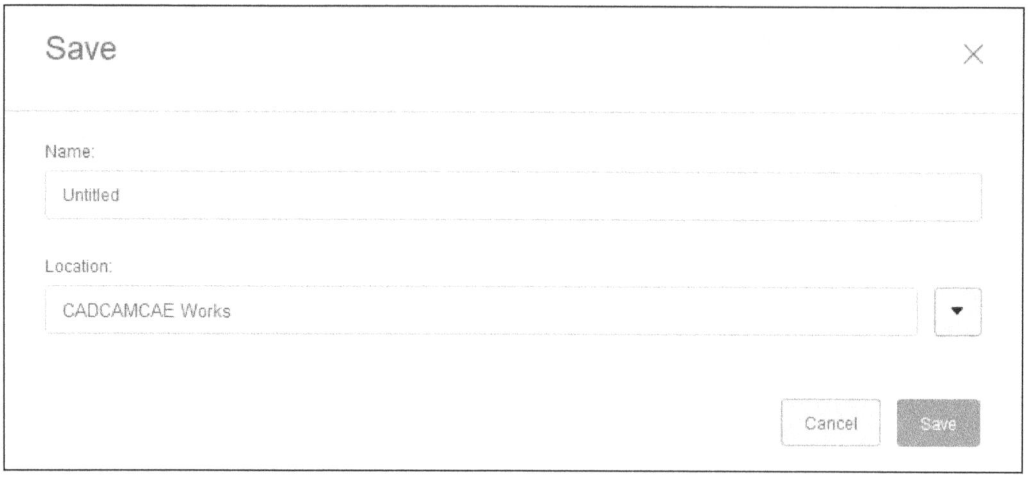

Figure-28. Save dialog box

- Specify desired name in the **Name** edit box.
- Click on the down arrow next to **Location** edit box in the dialog box if you want to select a different location on cloud. A list of locations created for/by you in Autodesk Cloud will be displayed; refer to Figure-29.

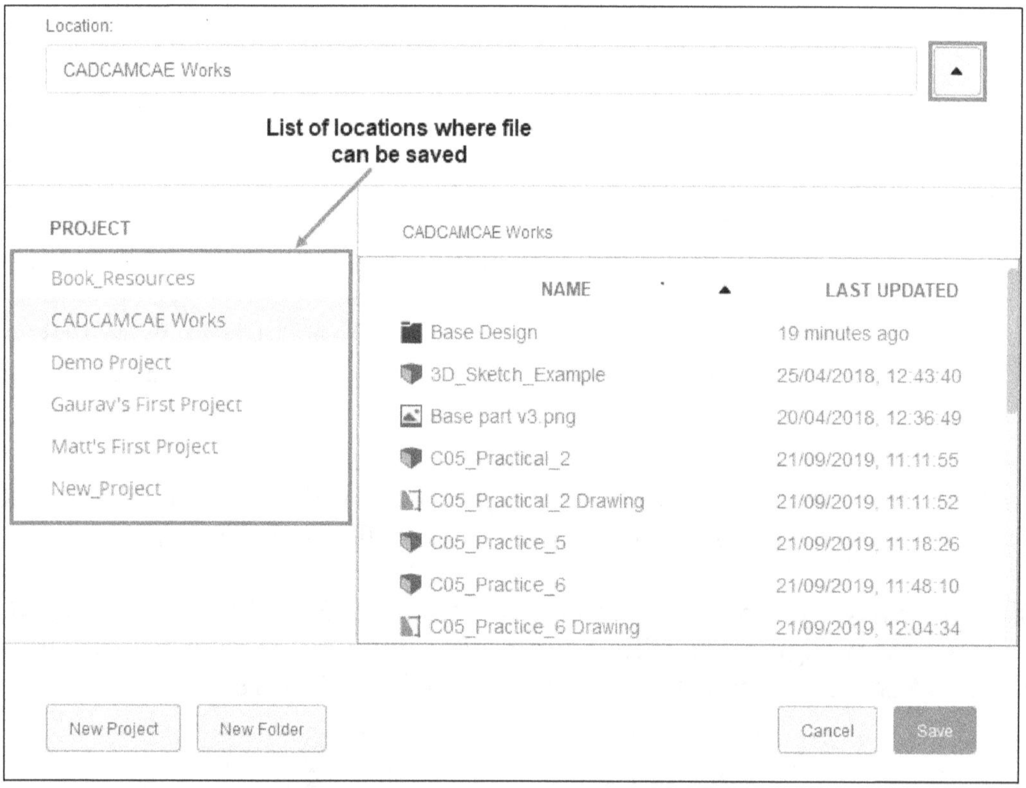

Figure-29. Locations to save files

- By default, Demo Project is added in the Project list. To add a new project, click on the **New Project** button at the bottom left corner of the dialog box. You will be asked to specify name of the new project; refer to Figure-30.

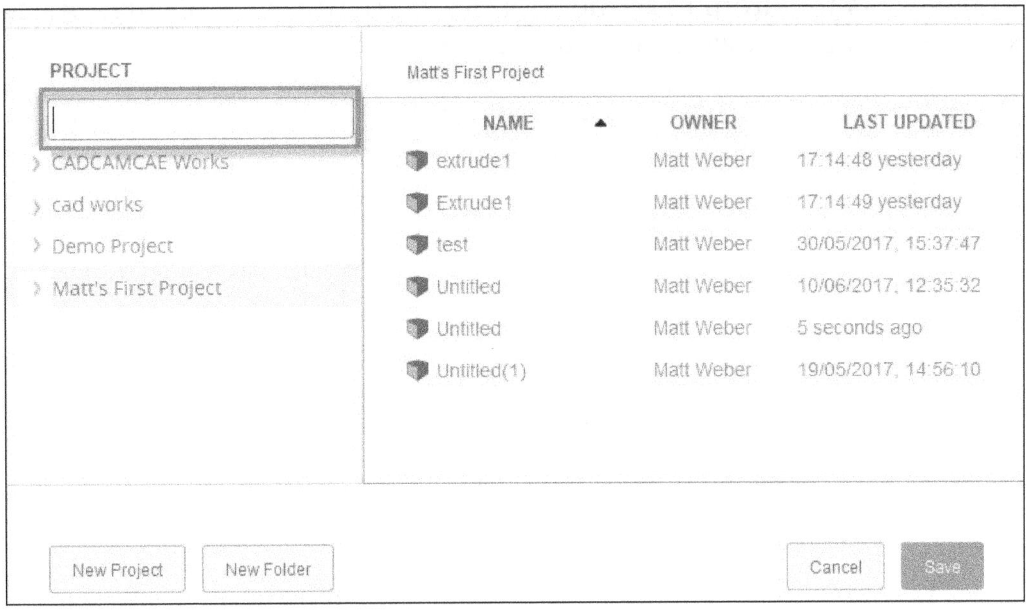

Figure-30. Specifying project name

- Specify desired name for the project in displayed edit box and click anywhere in blank area of the dialog box. The new location will be created. Select this new location to save the file; refer to Figure-31.

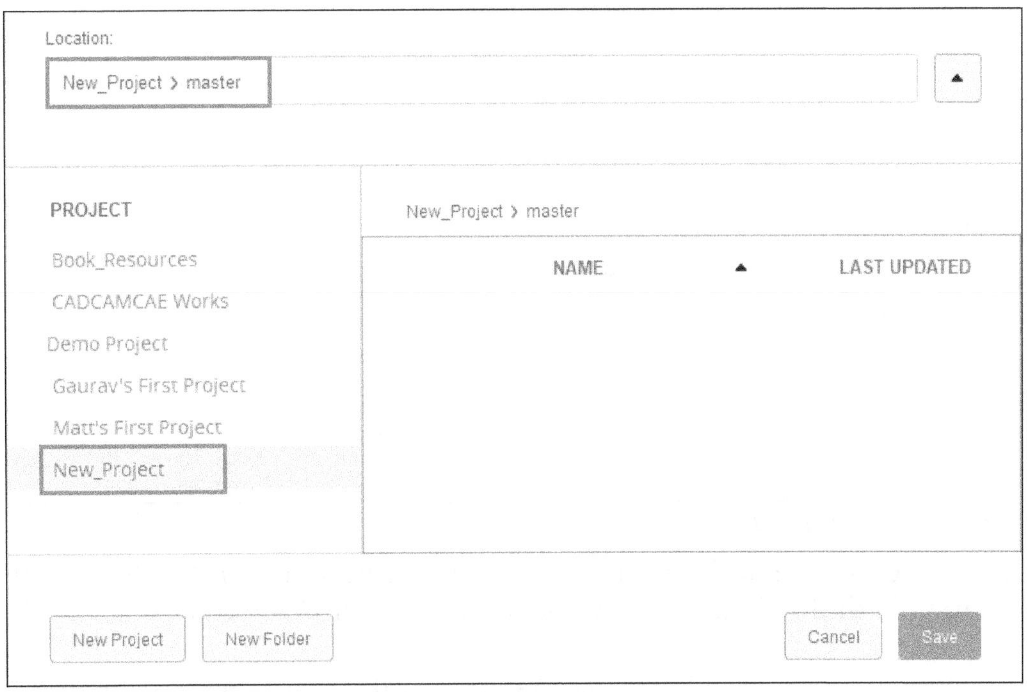

Figure-31. Location selected for saving file

- If you want to create folder in the project with desired name then click on the **New Folder** button from the dialog box. You will be asked to specify the name of the folder. Specify the name of folder and click in blank area of the dialog box.
- To save your file in the folder, double-click on folder name to enter the folder and then click on the **Save** button. The file will be saved at specified location.

Save As

Using the **Save As** tool, you can save the file with different name at different location. The procedure to use this tool is discussed next.

- Click on **Save As** tool from **File** menu; refer to Figure-32. The **Save As** dialog box will be displayed as shown in Figure-33.

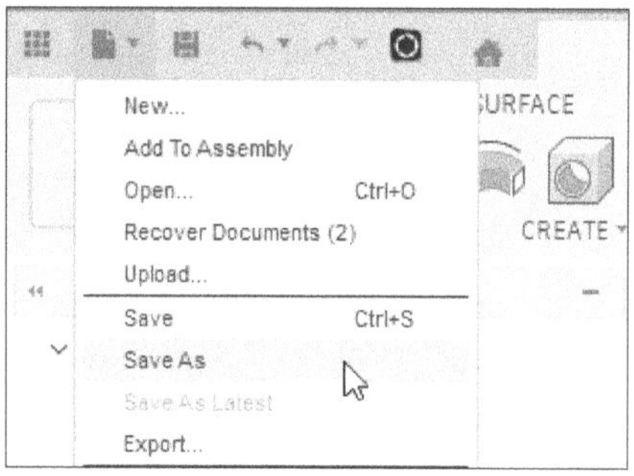

Figure-32. Save As tool

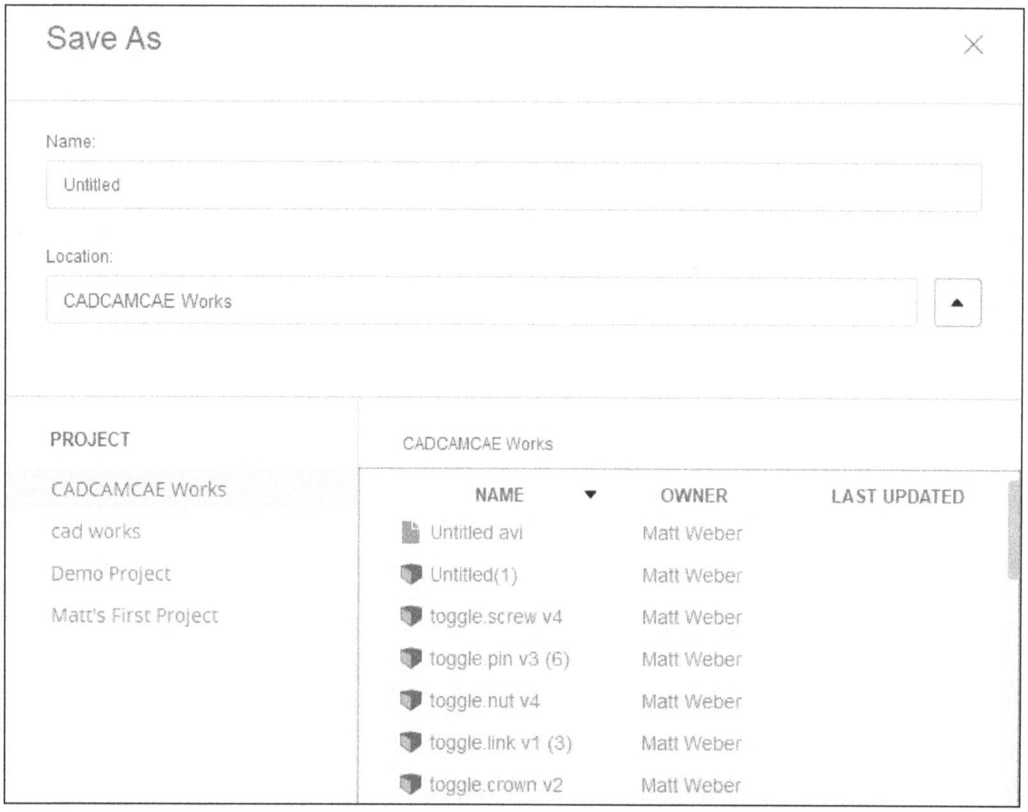

Figure-33. Save As dialog box

- Specify desired name and location for the file, and click on the **Save** button. The options in this dialog box are same as discussed in **Save** dialog box.

Save As Latest

When you are collaborating on a model with your team and after creating many versions of the model, you find that one of the previous versions is to be considered as final model for use. In such case, open the previous version file of Autodesk Fusion using **Open** tool; refer to Figure-34. The **Save As Latest** tool will be active in **File** menu to save this version as latest; refer to Figure-35. On clicking the **Save As Latest** tool, an information box will be displayed about the changes available in the model; refer to Figure-36. Click on the **Continue** button from the information box. The file will be saved as latest and uploaded on cloud.

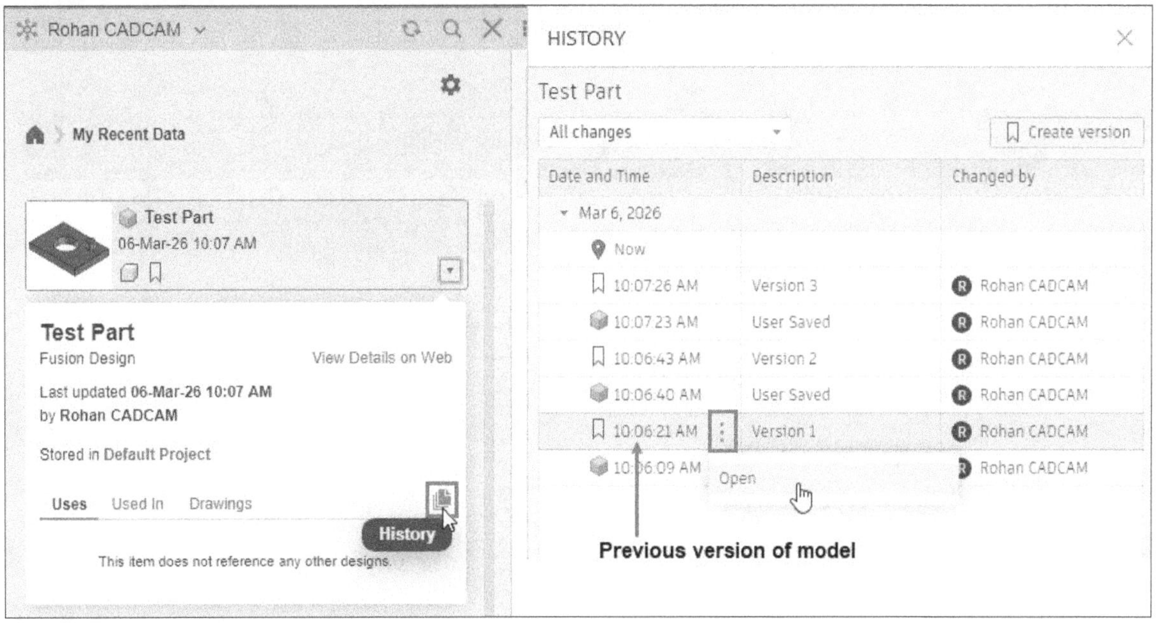

Figure-34. Previous version of model

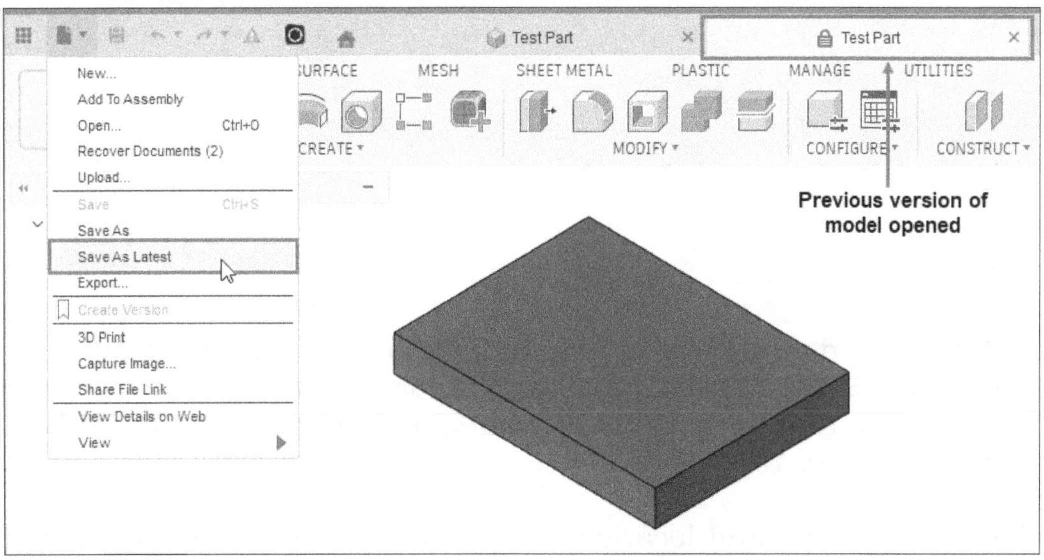

Figure-35. Save As Latest tool

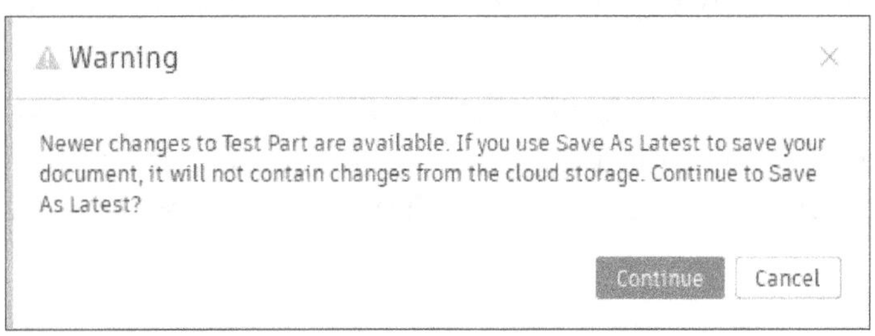

Figure-36. Information box for Save As Latest tool

Export

The **Export** tool is used to export the file in different formats. The procedure to use this tool is given next.

- Click on the **Export** tool from the **File** menu; refer to Figure-37. The **Export** dialog box will be displayed; refer to Figure-38.

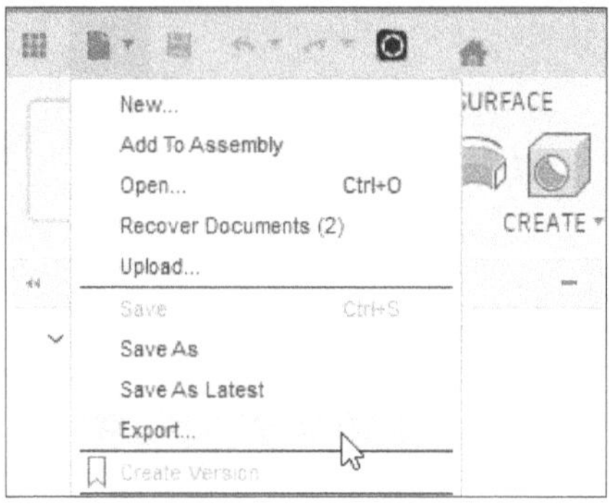

Figure-37. Export tool

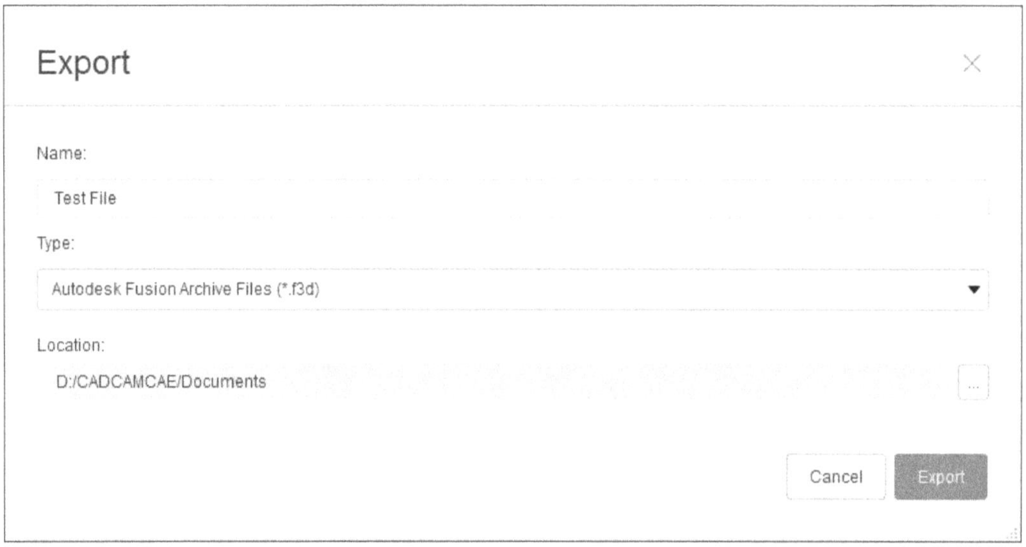

Figure-38. Export dialog box

- In the **Type** drop-down, there are various options to specify export format; **F3D**, **IGES**, **SAT**, **SMT**, **STEP**, **IPT**, **DWG**, **DXF**, and so on. Select desired format from the drop-down. Note that for some file formats, a cloud conversion will be required and take some time. You will be able to see progress of conversion in **Job Status** dialog box.
- Specify desired name and location for the file. Note that you can save the files only in the local drive by using this dialog box.
- Click on the **Export** button from the dialog box to save the file.

Create Version

The **Create Version** tool is used to save new version of a design file. This tool is available in commercial version of software. The procedure to use this tool is discussed next.

- Click on the **Create Version** tool from the **File** menu; refer to Figure-39. The **Create Version** dialog box will be displayed asking you to specify description for this new version of same file; refer to Figure-40.

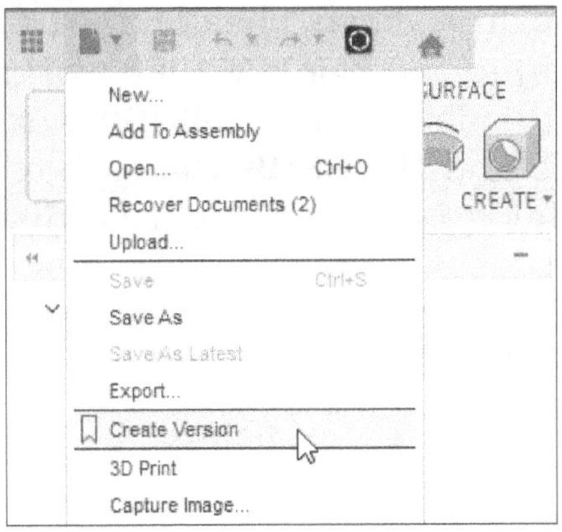

Figure-39. Create Version tool

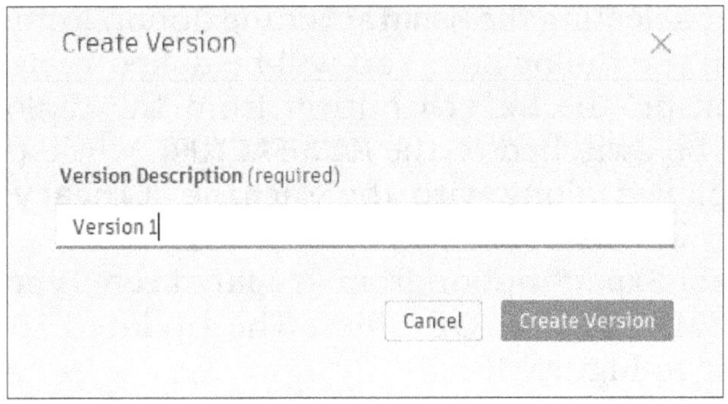

Figure-40. Create Version dialog box

- Specify a short description about what has changed in this version in the **Version Description** edit box and click on the **Create Version** button from the dialog box. The newer version of that file will be created. These versions can be accessed by **Data Panel** which will be discussed later.

3D Print

The **3D Print** tool is used to prepare and send current model for 3D printing. This tool convert the selected body to mesh body and sends the output to 3D-Print Utility or converts it to **STL** format. The procedure to use this tool is given next.

- Click on the **3D Print** tool from the **File** menu or click on the **3D Print** tool from the **MAKE** panel in the **UTILITIES** tab of the **Toolbar**; refer to Figure-41. The **3D PRINT** dialog box will be displayed; refer to Figure-42.

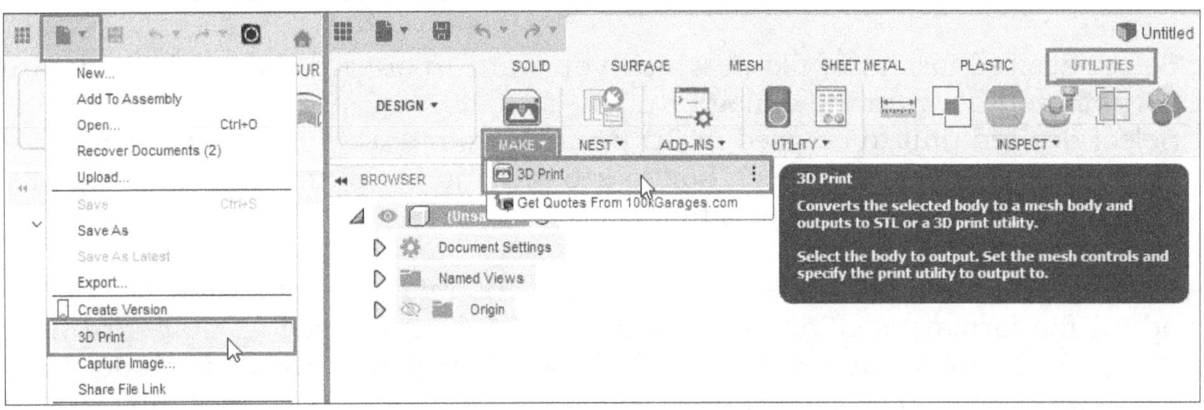

Figure-41. 3D Print tool

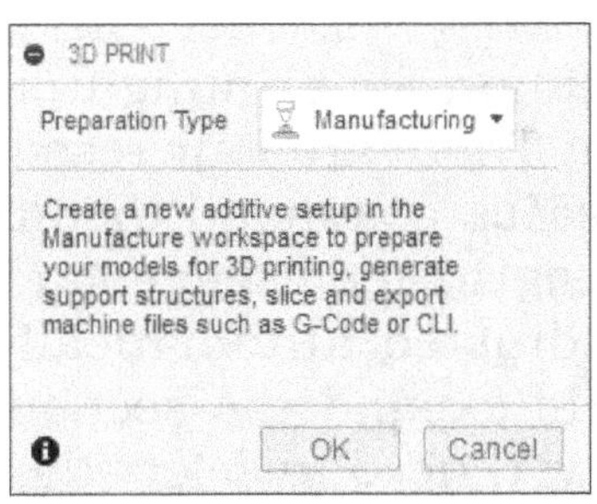

Figure-42. 3D PRINT dialog box

- Select **Manufacturing** option from **Preparation Type** drop-down to create bodies to be manufactured by desired 3D printer.

- After selecting the **Manufacturing** option from the drop-down, click on the **OK** button from the dialog box. You will be asked to switch to the **MANUFACTURE** workspace.
- Click on the **Switch** button from the dialog displayed. The **DESIGN** workspace will be switched to the **MANUFACTURE** workspace and the **SETUP** dialog box will be displayed along with the **Machine Library** dialog box which will be discussed later in this book.
- Select **Export** option from **Preparation Type** drop-down to export selected bodies as 3MF, STL, or OBJ files. The updated **3D PRINT** dialog box will be displayed; refer to Figure-43.

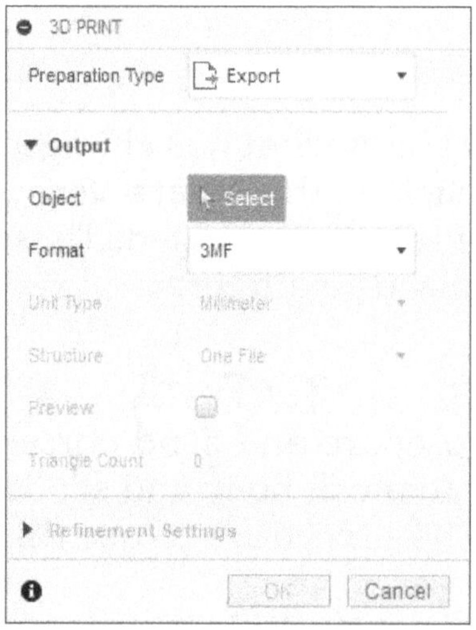

Figure-43. Updated 3D PRINT dialog box

- By default, the **Select** button is active in the **Object** area of **Output** rollout and you are prompted to select model to be 3D printed. Click on the model to be 3D printed.
- Select desired format of file in which you want to output the mesh model from **Format** drop-down in the dialog box.
- Select desired unit to be used in 3D printing from **Unit Type** drop-down.
- Now, select the **Preview** check box to see the number of triangles forming in the selected body when it converts to mesh.

If you don't know why it is previewed in mesh then you need to know full name of standard file format used for 3D printing. STL format is used as standard for 3D printing which abbreviates **Standard Triangle Language**. So, your model will be broken into very small triangles and then these triangles will be arranged in the shape of your model in layers.

- Select desired level of resolution for printing from **Refinement** drop-down in the **Refinement Settings** rollout. There are four resolution in this drop-down. If you select the **High**, **Low**, and **Medium** command then the **Surface deviation**, **Normal deviation**, **Maximum Edge Length**, and **Aspect Ratio** parameters in the **Refinement Settings** rollout will be adjusted automatically. (Click on the arrow before **Refinement Settings** node to expand the section.) If you want to adjust these parameters manually then you need to select the **Custom** option from **Refinement** drop-down; refer to Figure-44. Note that your 3D printing machine should be able to print the model at specified resolution. A higher resolution will take more time and power in 3D Printer. Unnecessarily high refinement should be avoided in 3D printing.

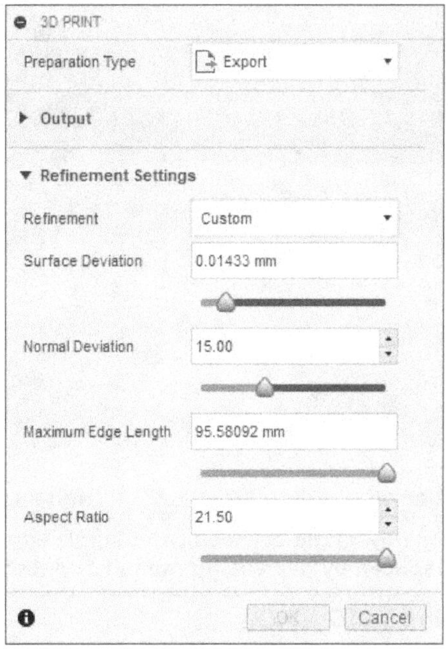

Figure-44. Refinement Settings

Now, for the technical stuff :

The **Surface Deviation** is difference between real surface of model and triangulated tessellation of model. In simple language, it drives the number of triangles to be generated along the surfaces/faces in mesh; refer to Figure-45. The value specified in **Surface Deviation** edit box will be taken as maximum deviation allowed, the software will process the deviation lower than specified value but it will not go higher.

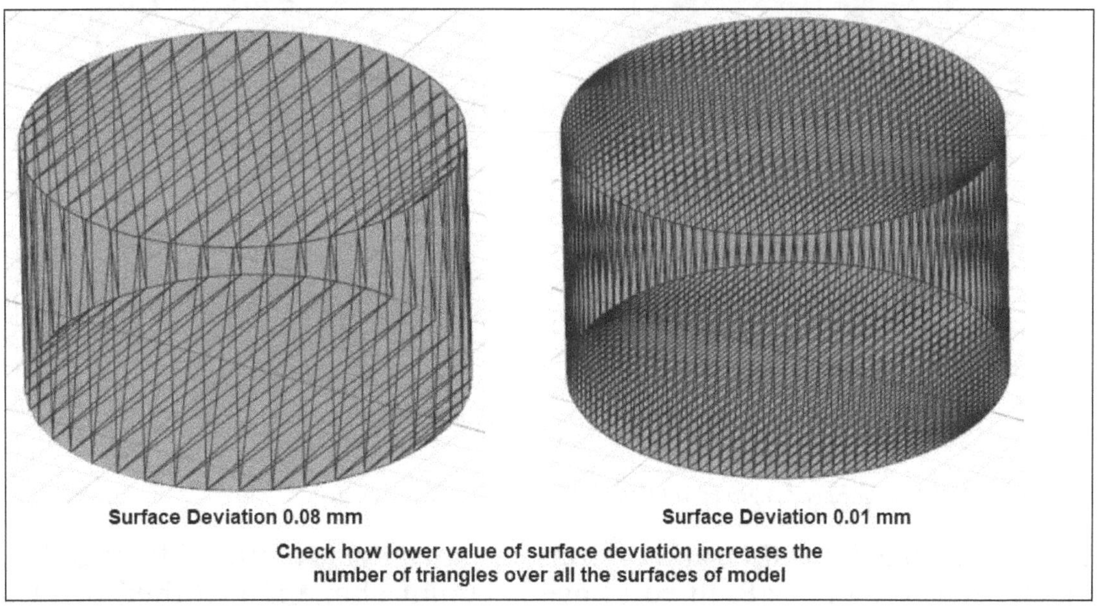

Figure-45. Surface Deviation in 3D Printing

The **Normal Deviation** is gap between two normals of consecutive triangles in tessellation. In simple words, a lower value of normal deviation will increase the number of triangles perpendicular to the edges of model in a given region; refer to Figure-46.

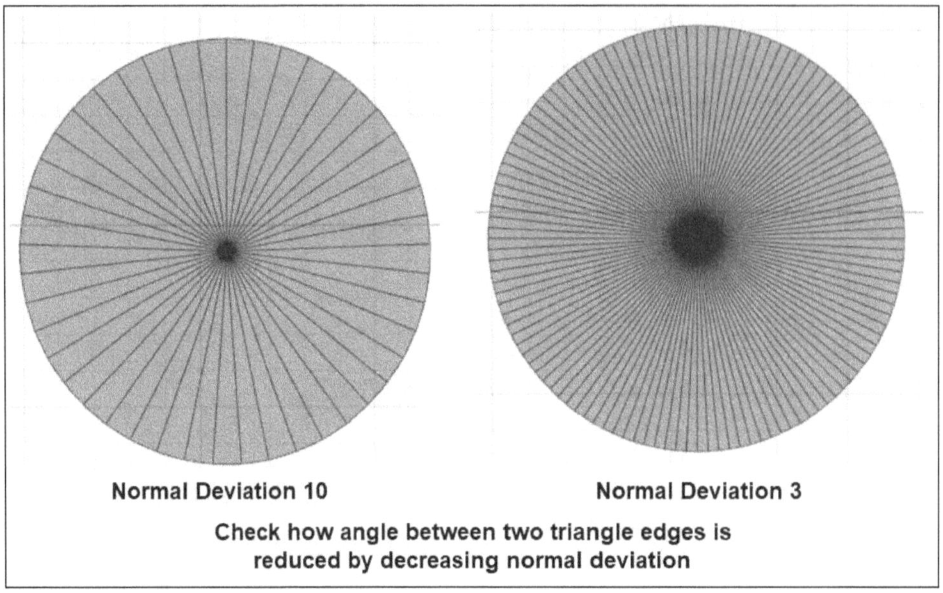

Figure-46. Normal Deviation in 3D printing

The **Maximum Edge Length** is used to define maximum length of triangle edges. If you decrease maximum edge length then more triangles of smaller edge length will be created in best possible orientations; refer to Figure-47.

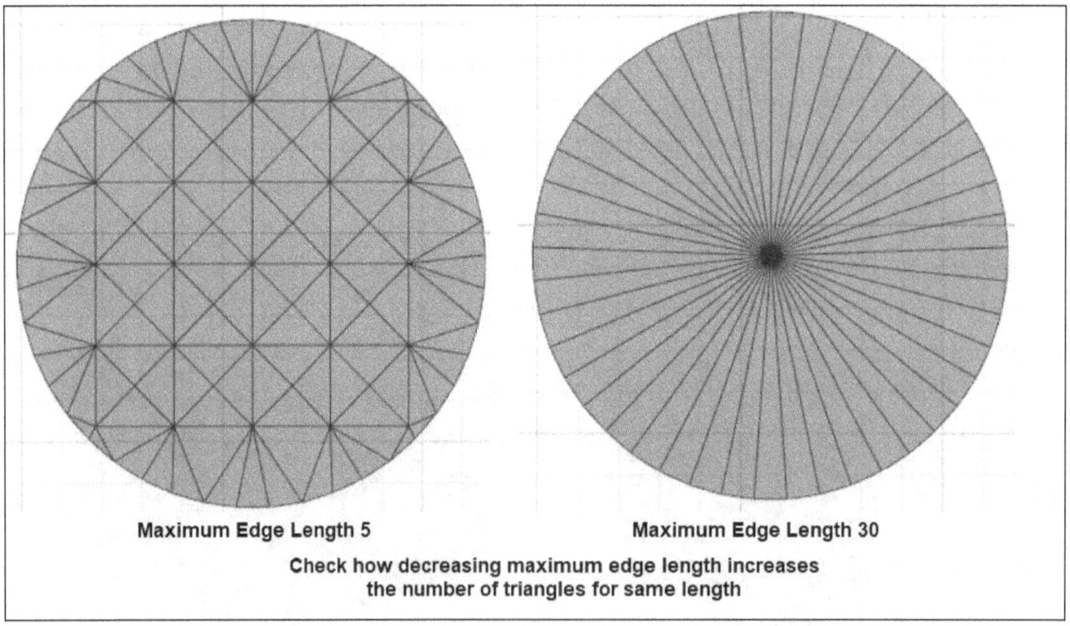

Figure-47. Maximum Edge Length in 3D Printing

The **Aspect Ratio** defines the ratio of number of triangles along width and height of the model; refer to Figure-48. (If you have irregular shape model then don't bother finding aspect ratio, your software knows better!!)

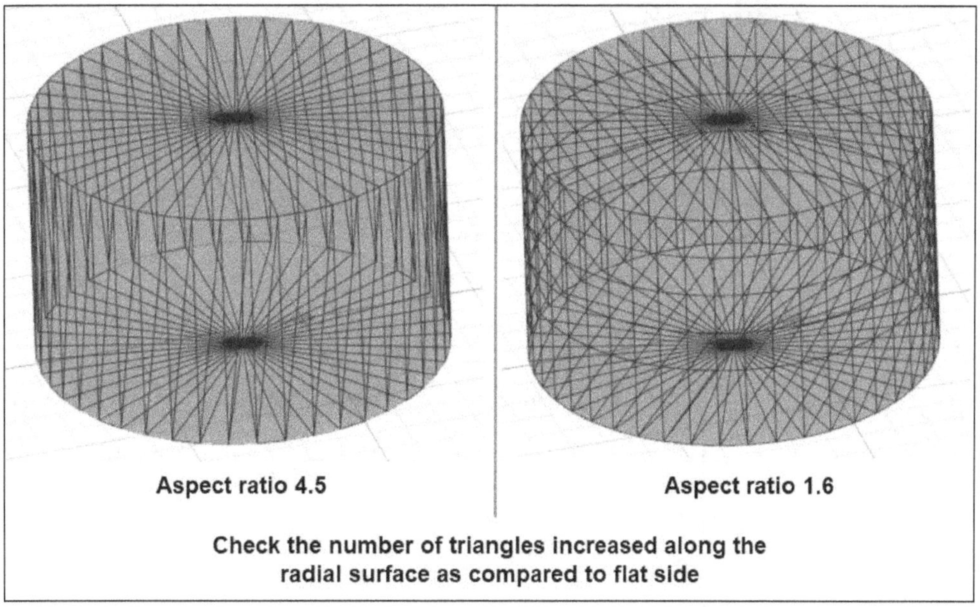

Figure-48. Aspect ratio in 3D printing

- Select **Print Utility** option from **Preparation Type** drop-down to export. The updated **3D PRINT** dialog box will be displayed; refer to Figure-49.

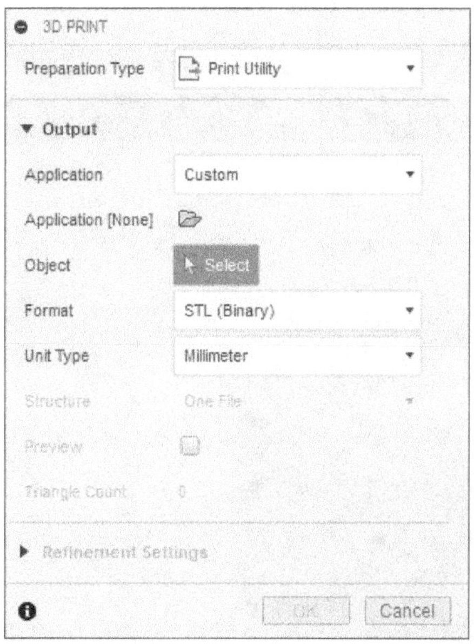

Figure-49. Print Utility preparation type

- Select desired 3D Printing utility from **Application** drop-down in the **Output** rollout. Select **Custom** option from the drop-down and click on the button for **Application** option; refer to Figure-49. The **Application** dialog box will be displayed to select the custom application and export the files directly to the application and 3D print them. Note that 3D printing utilities are not installed automatically during Fusion installation. On selecting the **Preform** option from **Application** drop-down, an option to download and install the utility will be displayed in the dialog box; refer to Figure-50. Download and install desired utility.

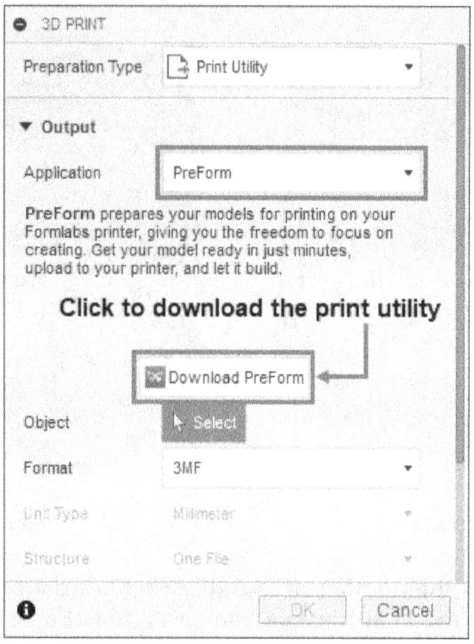

Figure-50. Option to download print utility

- In our case, we have selected **PreForm** option from the **Application** drop-down (Needless to say, we have installed it already). Click on the **OK** button from the dialog box. The **PreForm** application window will be displayed; refer to Figure-51.

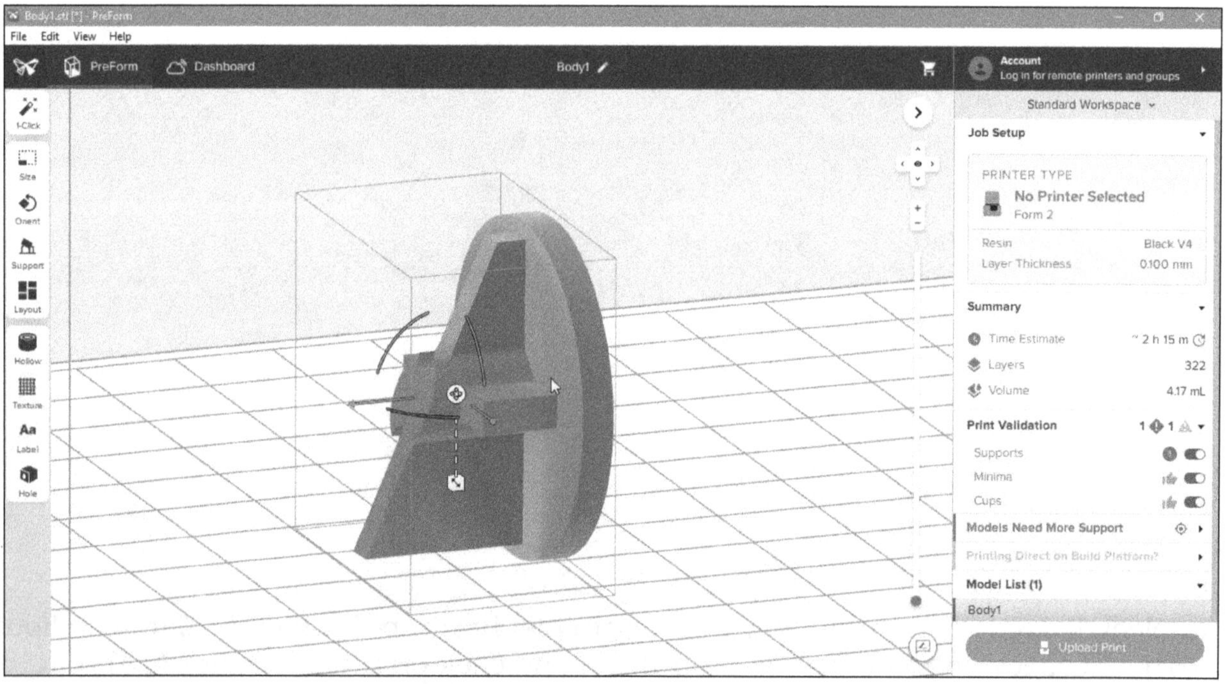

Figure-51. PreForm window

The tools of this application are discussed next.

PREFORM

Click on the **Apply** button from the **JOB SETUP** dialog box to enter the print utility, we will come back to these options later. On clicking **Apply** button, the model will be displayed in PreForm application window; refer to Figure-52.

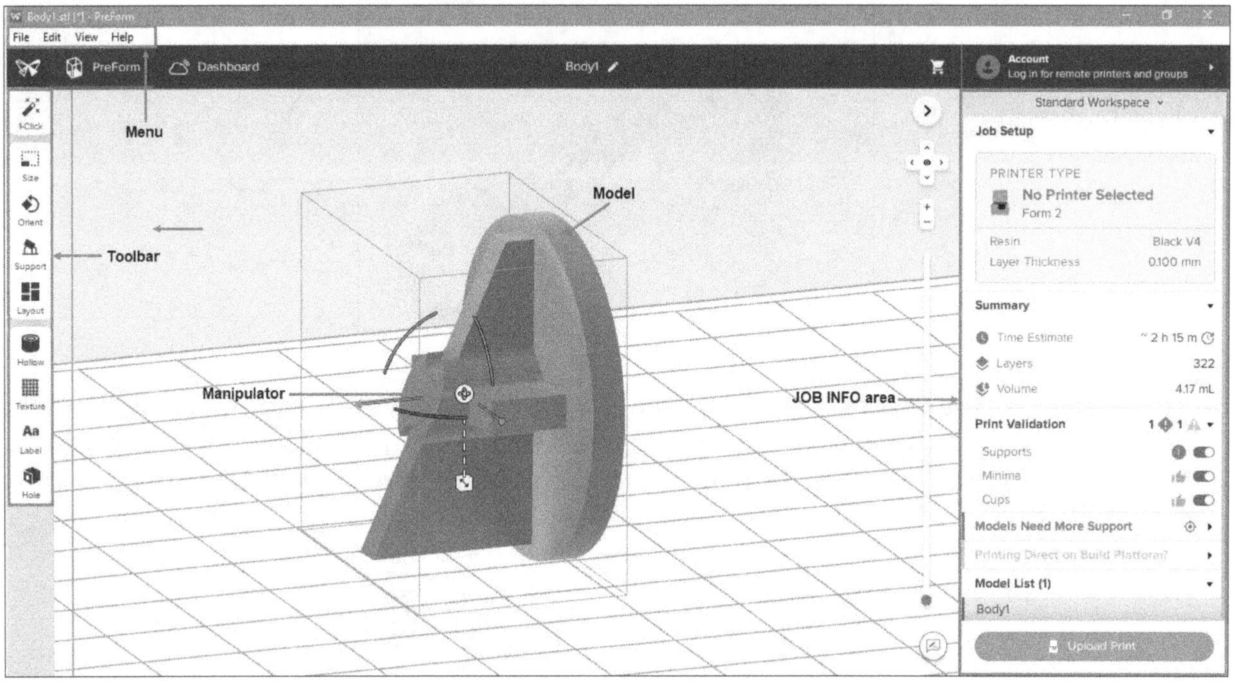

Figure-52. Interface of PreForm

Orienting the Model

There are two ways to orient a model in Preform, using **Orientation** tool from **Toolbar** or by using **Manipulator** displayed on the model. We will discuss both the ways here.

Orienting Model Using Manipulator

Click on the **Circle** handle in **Manipulators** for direction in which you want to rotate the model for orientation and drag the handle; refer to Figure-53. Note that software will automatically place the flat face of model on the bed of virtual machine.

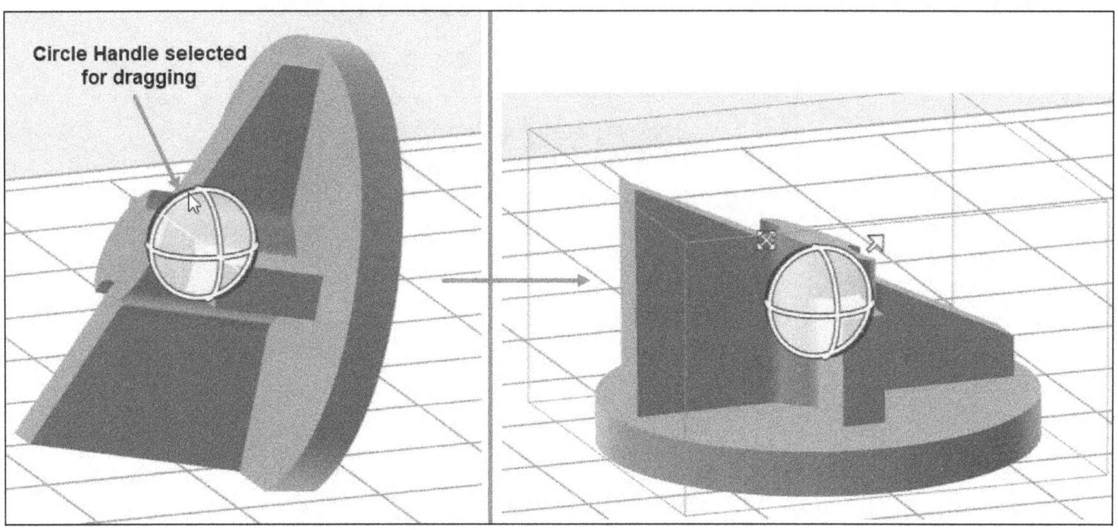

Figure-53. Orienting model using Manipulator

If you want to move the model at some other location then click on the **Move** handle in **Manipulators** and drag it to desired location; refer to Figure-54.

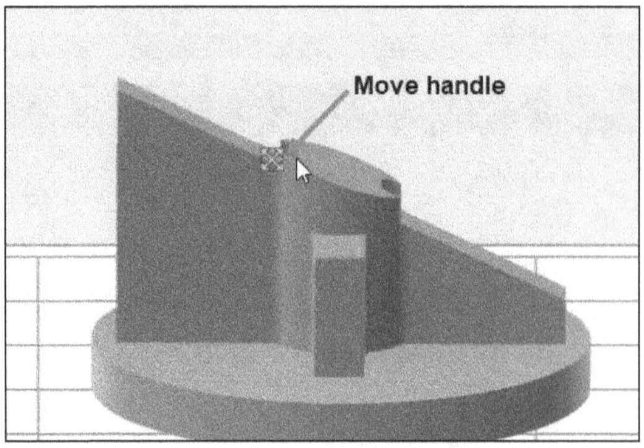

Figure-54. Move handle in Manipulator

Note that the **Manipulators** are displayed on model only when the model is selected. If the **Manipulators** are not displayed by default in your case or it is hidden then select **All** option from **Show Manipulators** cascading menu from the **View** menu; refer to Figure-55.

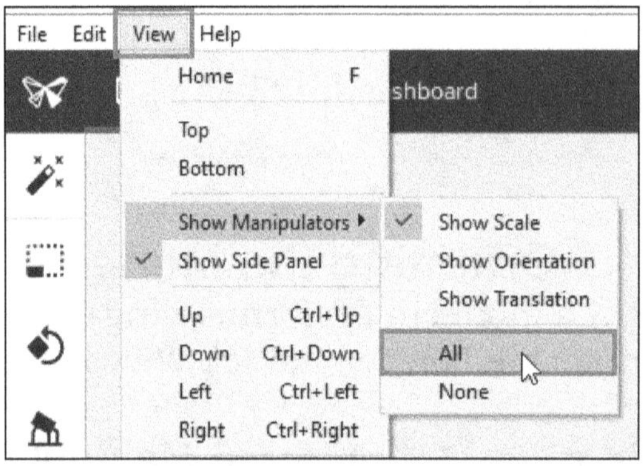

Figure-55. Show Manipulators options

Orienting Using Orientation Tool

- Click on the **Orientation** tool from the **Toolbar** at the left in application window. The **ORIENTATION** toolbox will be displayed; refer to Figure-56.

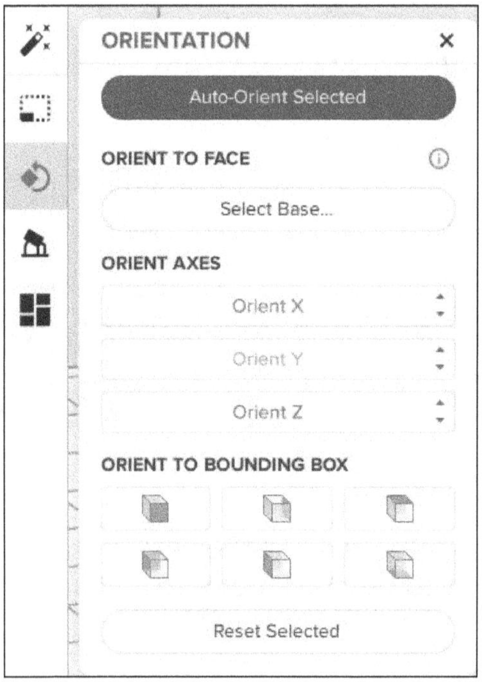

Figure-56. ORIENTATION toolbox

- Click on the **Auto-Orient Selected** button to automatically orient the selected model on bed. (Note: this option was clumsy while writing this book and could not generate a proper orientation so we do not recommend this tool.)
- Click on the **Select Base** button to define the face which will be placed flat on the bed. After selecting this button, click on the face to be used as base of model; refer to Figure-57. The model will be automatically oriented to bed. Click on the **Done** button from the information box displayed in top-left corner. (This is the most used and recommended method to orient the part.)

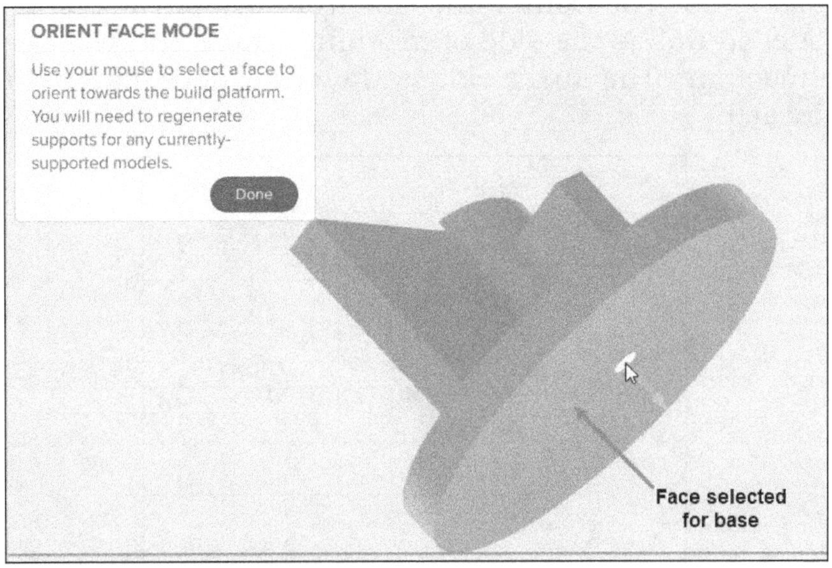

Figure-57. Selecting face for base

- You can use the spinners in **ORIENT AXES** area of the dialog box to define orientation angles for model. (These options are generally used to tweak the orientation; refer to Figure-58. You can also use handles in Manipulators to tweak the orientation.)

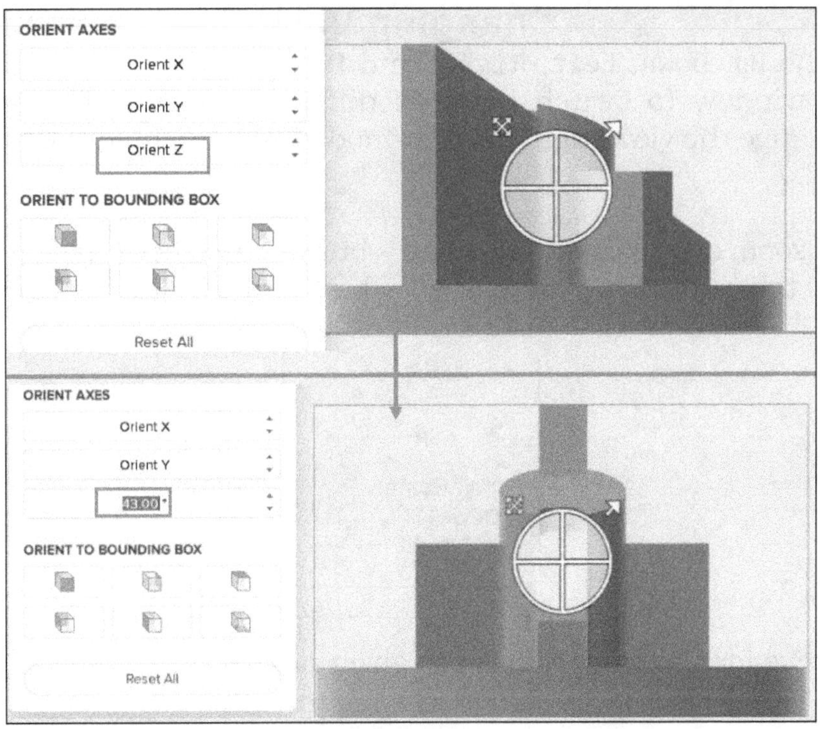

Figure-58. Tweaking the orientation of model

- The buttons in **ORIENT TO BOUNDING BOX** area of toolbox are used to orient the model along respective faces of the bounding box. (Bounding box is an imaginary cuboid which defines maximum length, width, and height occupied by the model.)
- At any time, you find that you have messed up the orientation then you can move back to original orientation by clicking on the **Reset Selected** button at the bottom in the toolbox.

Note that there are two sides of bed for 3D printing machine called FRONT and MIXER SIDE; refer to Figure-59. The front is the side from where you will be extracting the 3D printing model so this is the side of machine where you will be standing while controlling the machine. The Mixer side is the one where material cartridge of 3D printer will be located.

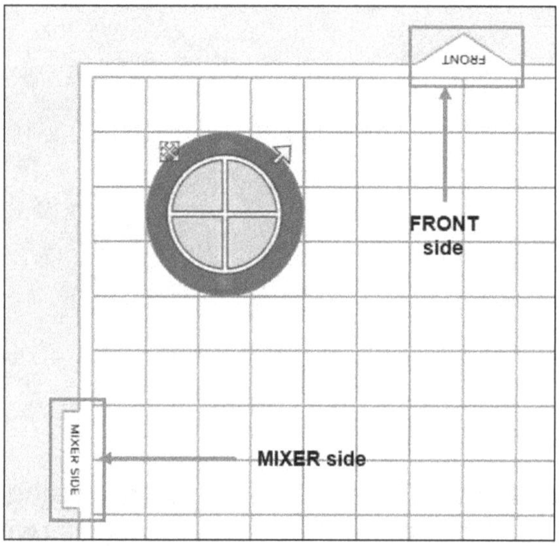

Figure-59. Sides of machine bed

Changing View

You can use the **Up**, **Down**, **Left**, **Right**, and **Home** buttons at the top-right corner of application window to switch between different views; refer to Figure-60. To dynamically change the view, right-click in modeling area, hold the button, and drag the cursor.

To zoom in and zoom out, click on the **+** and **-** buttons respectively which are available in the **View Switch** buttons or you can scroll up and scroll down with mouse.

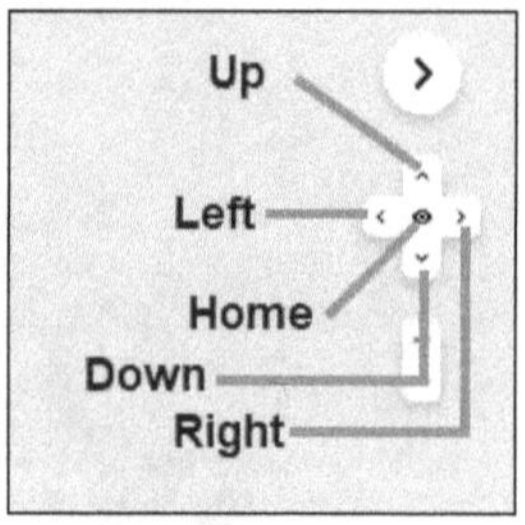

Figure-60. View Switch buttons

The shortcut keys for changing views are given next.

Up View	CTRL + Up key
Down View	CTRL + Down key

Left View	CTRL + Left key
Right View	CTRL + Right key
Home View	F
Zoom in	+ or Scroll up
Zoom out	- or Scroll down
Pan	SHIFT + Right-click drag
Dynamic View change	Right-click drag

Scaling Model

To scale up or scale down the model, click on the **Size** handle in **Manipulators**, hold the button and then drag in desired direction to scale up or scale down; refer to Figure-61.

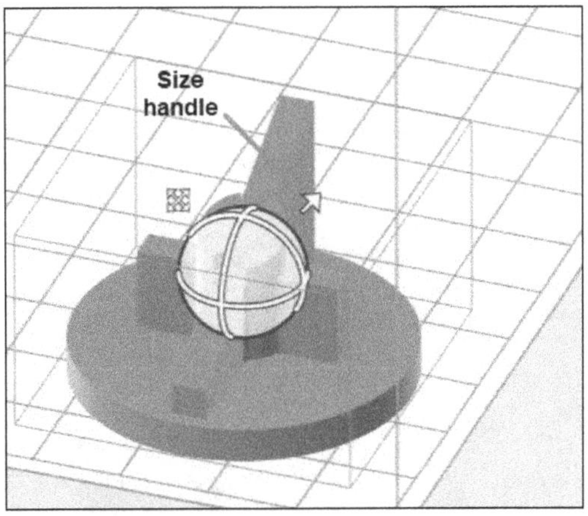

Figure-61. Size handle

OR

- Click on the **Size** button from the **Toolbar** at the left in application window. The **SIZE** toolbox will be displayed; refer to Figure-62.

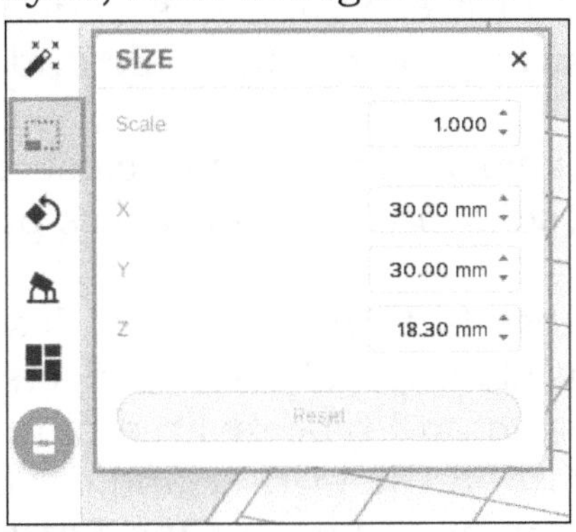

Figure-62. SIZE toolbox

- Specify desired scale value in the **Scale** edit box of toolbox or you can use the spinner to change its value.
- You can also use **X**, **Y**, or **Z** spinners to change the scale of model. Note that size of model will increase or decrease uniformly in all direction so it does not matter whether you use **Scale**, **X**, **Y**, or **Z** spinner.
- Click on the **Reset** button if you want to revert back to original scale. Close the toolbox after making desired changes.

JOB INFO Settings

The options in the **JOB INFO** area are used to set parameters related to printer. You can also check the warnings and details related to 3D printing process. Various tools and options are discussed next.

Job Settings

- Click on the **Edit Job Setup** button (**Printer Type** selection box) from the **JOB INFO** area at the right in the dialog box. The **Job Setup** window will be displayed; refer to Figure-63.

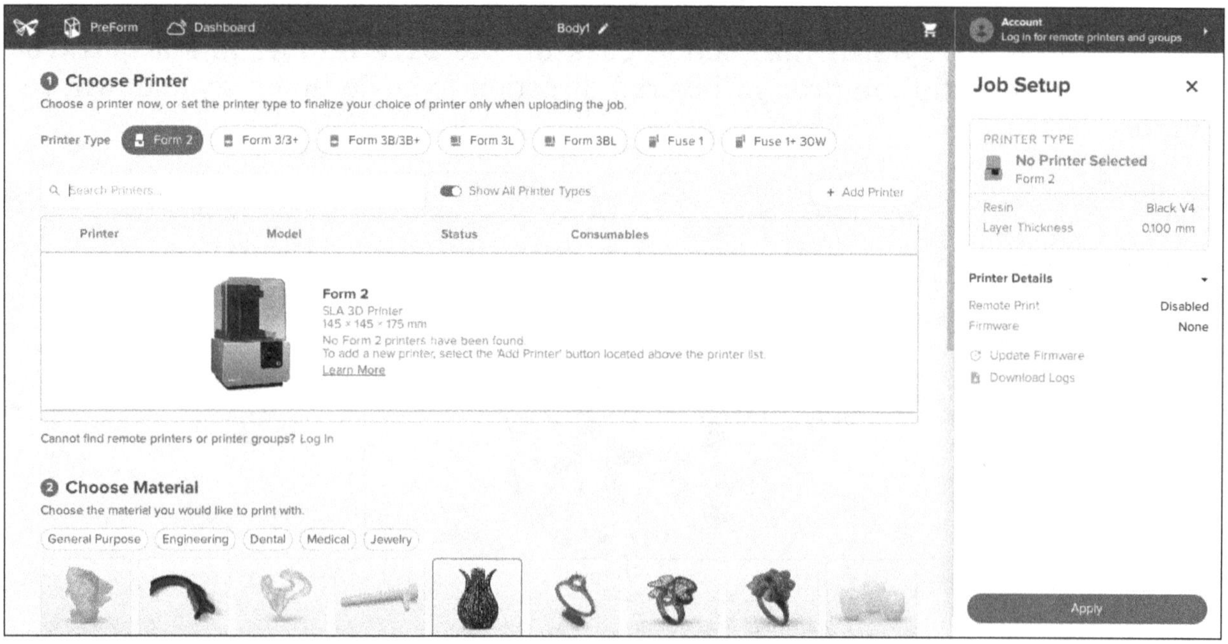

Figure-63. Job Setup window

- Click on the **Printer Type** button from left area of the window and select desired type of printer you want to use for printing.
- If you have selected a 3D printer which has options to select different types of materials then select desired type of materials and versions of resins you want to print with.
- Click on the **Layer Thickness** button and select desired thickness of layer to increase print speed or resolution. Thicker layers print faster and thinner layers print slower.
- Click on the **Print Settings** button and select desired print settings to control print speed, support print shape, and other aspects of print performance.
- Click on the **Job Name** button and type desired name in the **Job Name** edit box to help differentiate your print on the printer and dashboard.
- After specifying desired parameters in the **Job Setup** window, click on the **Apply** button to make the changes.

Job Details

Various details of the printing job will be displayed in the **DETAILS** rollout of the **JOB INFO** area like estimated printing time, number of layers in 3D printed model, and total volume of material used in 3D printing.

Print Validation Options

There are three options in the **Print Validation** rollout of **JOB INFO** area; **Minima**, **Cups**, and **Form Auto Release**. The **Print Validation** icon defines whether the model is good for printing, there are warnings for 3D printing, or there are errors stopping from 3D printing like in Figure-64, a warning is displayed telling you that you need to elevate the model and add some supports for proper extraction.

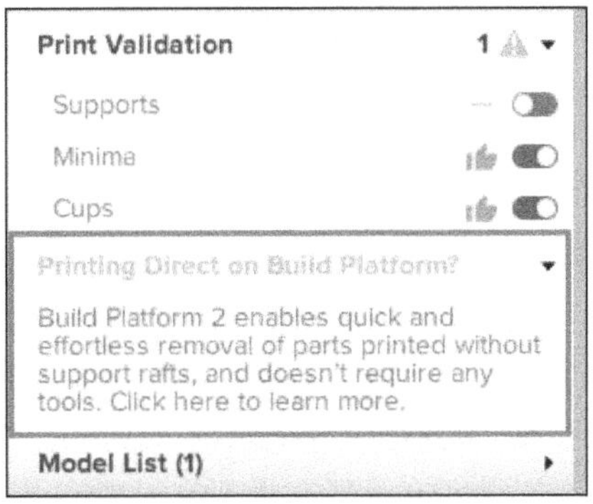

Figure-64. Warning for 3D printing

- Toggle the **Minima** button to display the unsupported areas of model if the model is not oriented correctly; refer to Figure-65.

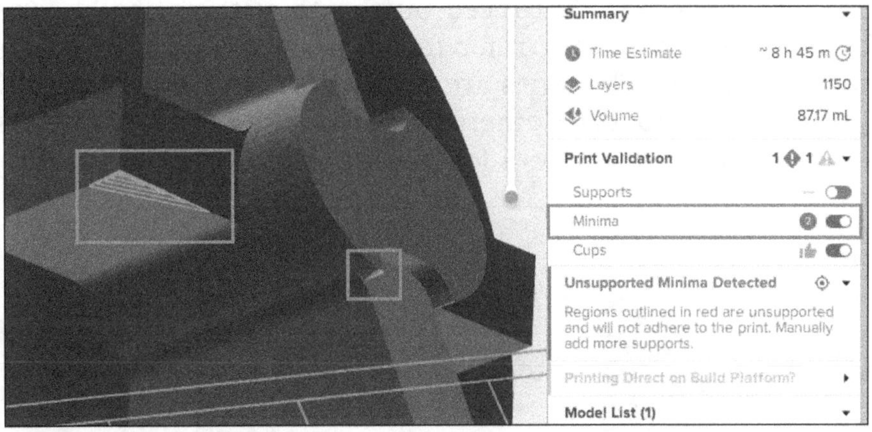

Figure-65. Unsupported minima areas of model

- Toggle the **Cups** button from the **Print Validation** rollout to display areas on model that can trap air while 3D printing. Most of the time cups are generated when there are holes/cuts perpendicular to base plane.

Adding Supports

The **Supports** tool in the **Toolbar** is used to add supports to the 3d printing object. Supports are used when the model is unstable or extraction of 3d printed model from base plate can cause damage to the model. The procedure to add supports is given next.

- Click on the **Supports** tool from the **Toolbar** or press **C** from keyboard. The **SUPPORTS** toolbox will be displayed; refer to Figure-66.

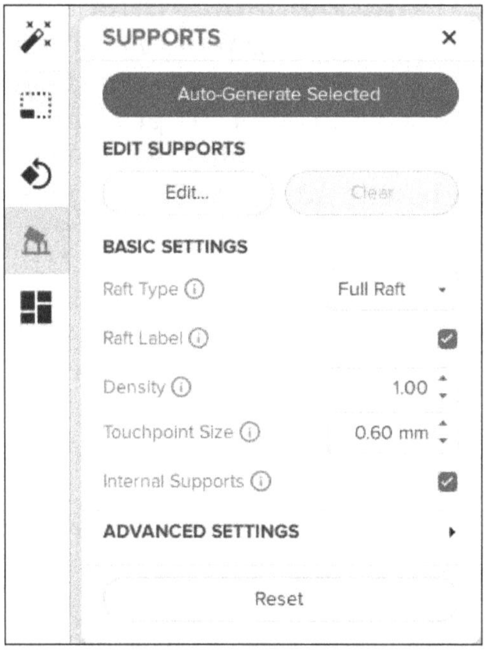

Figure-66. SUPPORTS toolbox

- Click on the **Auto-Generate Selected** button to automatically generate support features for the selected model; refer to Figure-67. Note that using this button, only positions of support elements are decided. It does not automatically decides the shape and size of support elements. So, you should click on this button after you have specified the parameters for supports in the toolbox.

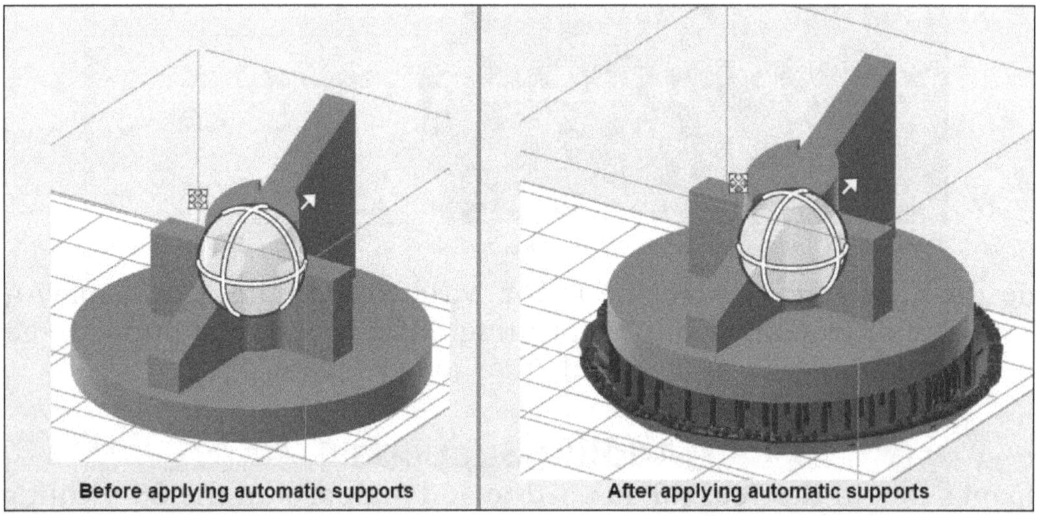

Figure-67. Applying supports

- Select the **Mini-Rafts** option from the **Raft Type** drop-down if you want to mini-rafts for supports; refer to Figure-68.

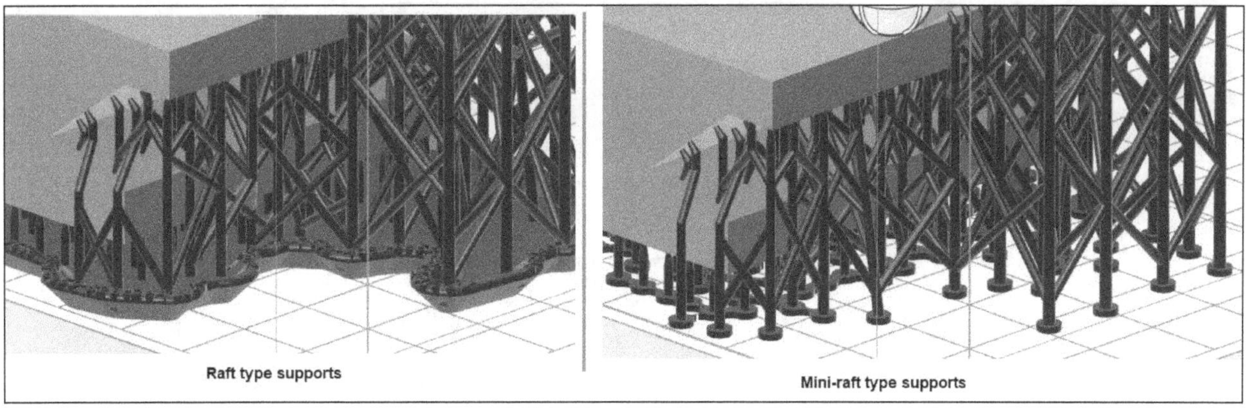

Figure-68. Raft types for supports

- Select the **Raft Label** check box if you want to 3D printing the name of file on the support raft.
- On selecting the **Breakaway Supports** check box, the breakaway support structures are easier to remove in pieces, but make a mess and do not perform well with high stresses like very long flat spans.
- Set desired density and touch point size in respective edit boxes in the toolbox. Density is the thickness of support base and touch point size is the thickness of upper section of support where it touches the model.
- Select the **Internal Supports** check box if you want to create internal supports whose start point and end point are on the model; refer to Figure-69.

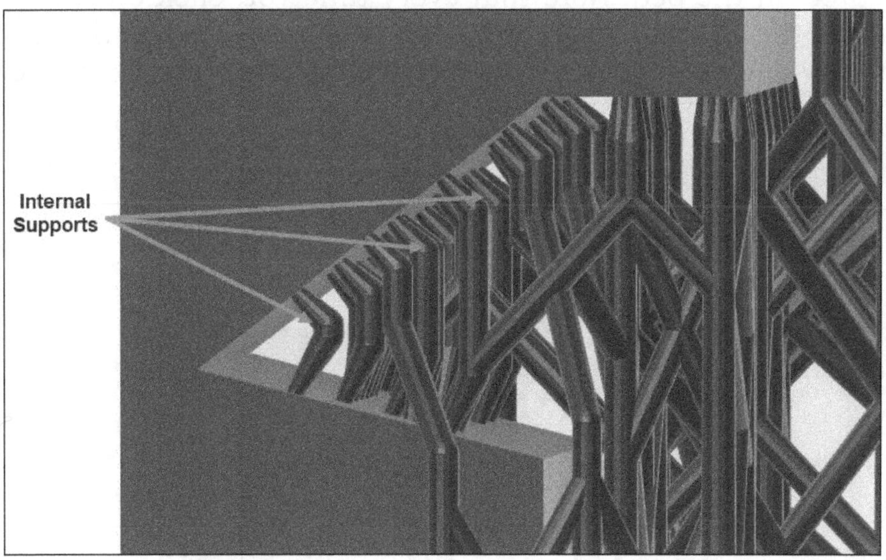

Figure-69. Internal supports created

- Specify desired parameters in the **ADVANCED SETTINGS** rollout of the toolbox if needed.

Creating Layout for Multiple Part Printing

- Click on the **Layout** tool from the **Toolbar**. The **LAYOUT** toolbox will be displayed; refer to Figure-70.

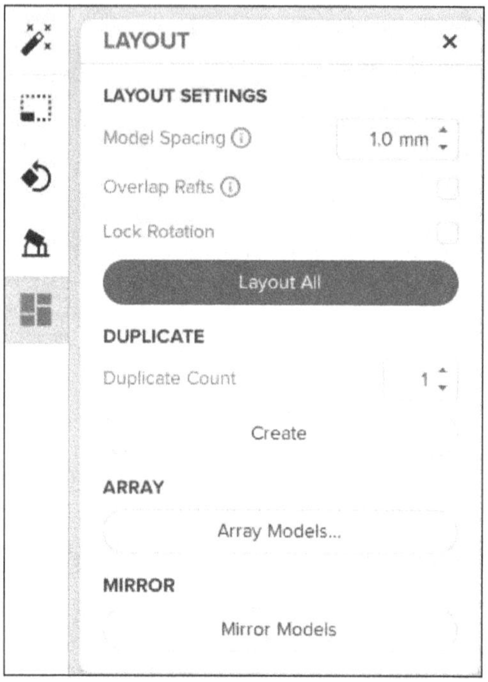

Figure-70. LAYOUT toolbox

- Set desired parameters like space between two instances of the model, raft overlap, rotation lock, and number of duplicate copies of model to be created on same bed.
- After setting desired parameters, click on the **Create** button. The copies of model will be created on the bed. Note that every time you click on the **Create** button, new copies of the model are created. So, it is better to set the duplicate count value carefully and then click on the **Create** button; refer to Figure-71.

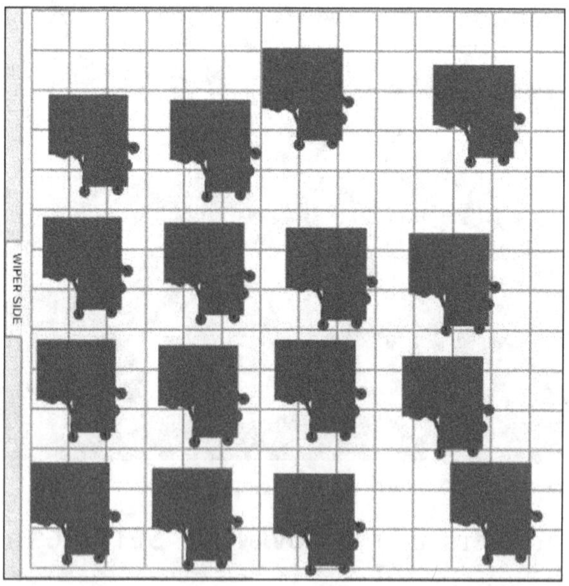

Figure-71. Duplicate copies of model

- Click on the **Layout All** button to arrange the copies of model in such a way that maximum number of copies can be accommodated on the bed; refer to Figure-72. Note that after using this tool, you might be able to add more copies of the model on bed.

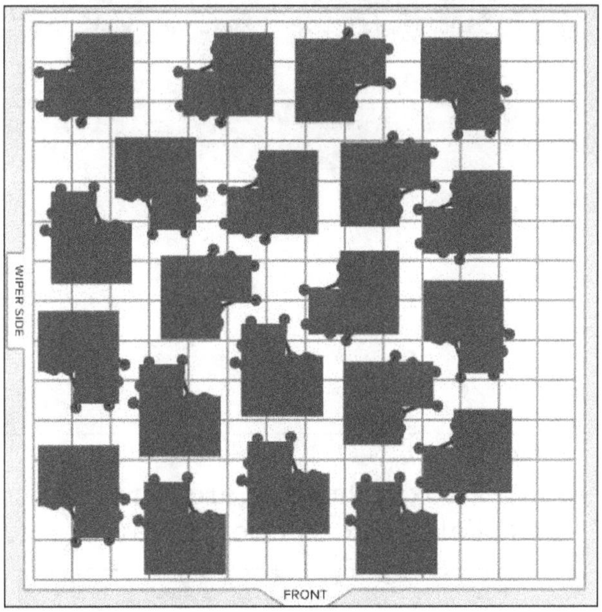

Figure-72. After using Layout All tool

- Click on the **X** button at top-right corner to exit the toolbox.

Creating Hollow model

Click on the **Hollow** tool from the **Toolbar**. The **Hollow** toolbox will be displayed to create hollow model to reduce material use and print time.

Applying Texture

Click on the **Texture** tool from the **Toolbar**. The **Texture** toolbox will be displayed to apply surface textures for a customized finish.

Adding Label

Click on the **Label** tool from the **Toolbar**. The **Label** toolbox will be displayed to add labels to parts for identification during post-processing.

Adding Hole

Click on the **Hole** tool from the **Toolbar**. The **Drill Hole** toolbox will be displayed to add vent holes to prevent resin during the printing process.

Printing

Now, we are ready to start 3D printing of model layout. If you have printer connected with your system then click on the **Print** tool from the **File** menu. The **PRINT** dialog box will be displayed; refer to Figure-73. Click in the **Job Name** edit box and specify desired name for print job. If you have 3D Printer connected then it will be displayed in the Printer list. You need to select the printer from the list. If your printer is connected to a network on FORMLABS then you need to specify account information or log in to your FORMLABS account. After setting desired parameters, click on the **Add to Queue** button. The file will be uploaded on FORMLABS account for printing.

Figure-73. PRINT dialog box

- Click in the **Select Printer** box of **Printer** area in the dialog box to select desired printer. The **DEVICE LIST** dialog box will be displayed; refer to Figure-74.

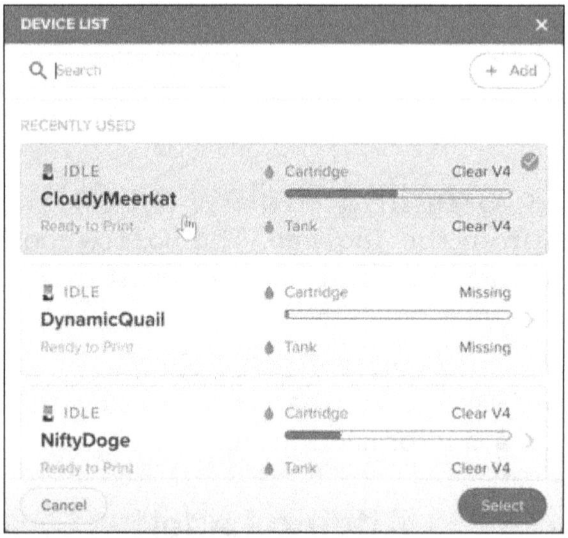

Figure-74. DEVICE LIST dialog box

- Select desired printer from the list and click on the **Select** button from the **PRINTER DETAILS** dialog box displayed; refer to Figure-75.

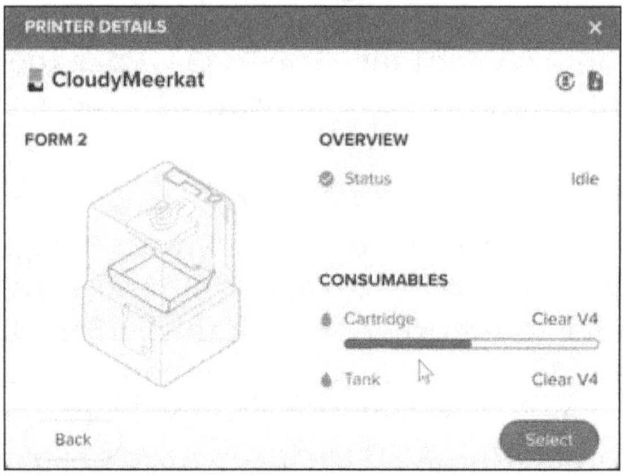

Figure-75. PRINTER DETAILS dialog box

- If you want to add a new printer in the list of **DEVICE LIST** dialog box, click on the **+Add** button from the dialog box. The **ADD DEVICE** dialog box will be displayed; refer to Figure-76. Specify the IP address of network printer in the **IP address** input boxes and click on the **Connect** button. The printer will be added in the list.

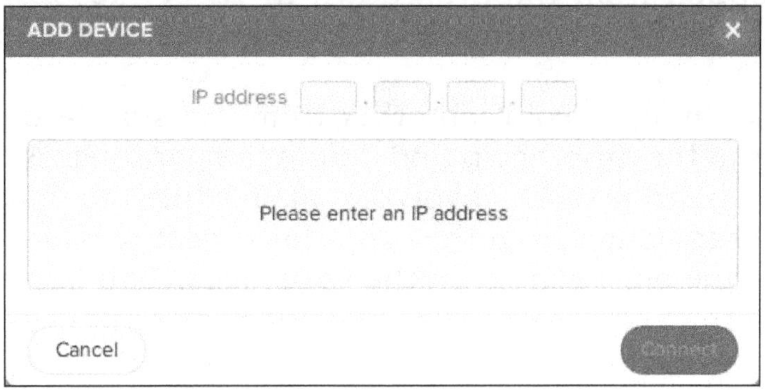

Figure-76. ADD DEVICE dialog box

After performing desired operations, click on the **Quit PreForm** tool from the **File** menu in the application window to exit the PreForm application.

Capture Image

The **Capture Image** tool is used to capture the image of model in current state. The procedure is discussed next.

- Click on the **Capture Image** tool from **File** menu; refer to Figure-77. The **Image Options** dialog box will be displayed; refer to Figure-78.

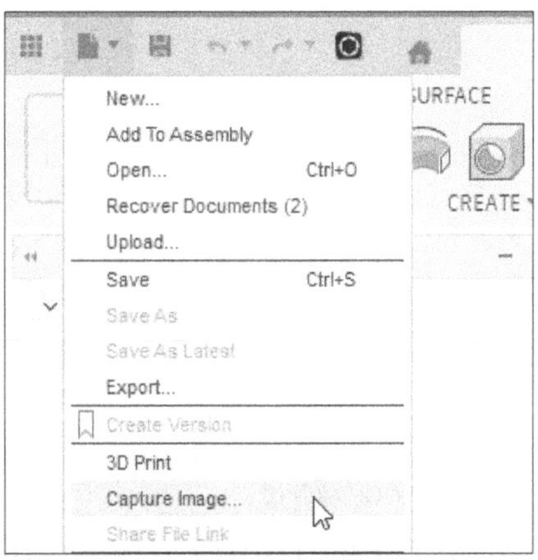

Figure-77. Capture Image tool

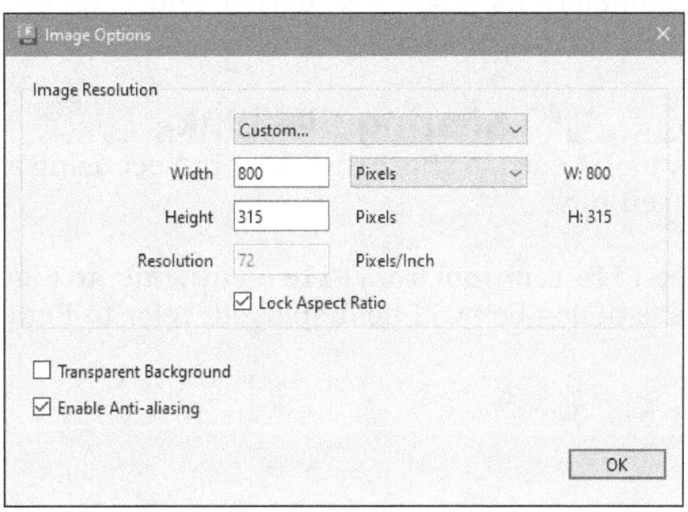

Figure-78. Image Options dialog box

- Select desired option from the drop-down in **Image Resolution** area to define size of image. All the other parameters of **Image Resolution** area will be defined automatically.
- If you want to set image resolution other than the standard one then select the **Custom** option from the drop-down and define the parameters. By default, you are asked to specify size in pixels but you can also define the image size in inches by selecting the **Inches** option from the drop-down next to **Width** edit box. Now, you will be able to define pixel density in the **Resolution** edit box manually. Clear the **Lock Aspect Ratio** check box to specify values of height and width individually.
- Select **Transparent Background** check box for setting the background of the image to be transparent.
- Select the **Enable Anti-aliasing** check box to smooth jagged lines or textures by blending the color of an edge with the color of pixels around it.
- After setting desired parameters, click on the **OK** button from **Image Options** dialog box. The **Save As** dialog box will be displayed; refer to Figure-79.

Figure-79. Save As dialog box for image capturing

- Select desired format from the **Type** drop-down for image. There are three formats available: PNG, JPG, and TIFF.
- Set the other parameters as discussed earlier and click on the **Save** button to save the image.

Sharing File Link

The **Share File Link** tool is used to share the file or project using a link. The procedure to use this tool is given next.

- Click on the **Share File Link** tool from **File** menu; refer to Figure-80. On selecting this tool, the **Share** dialog box will be displayed, refer to Figure-81.

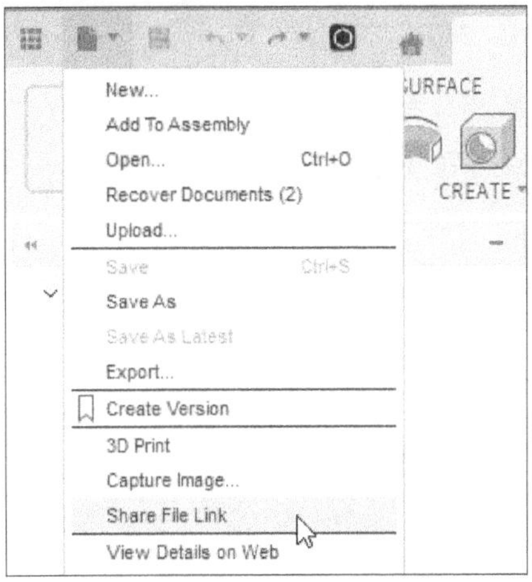

Figure-80. Share File Link option

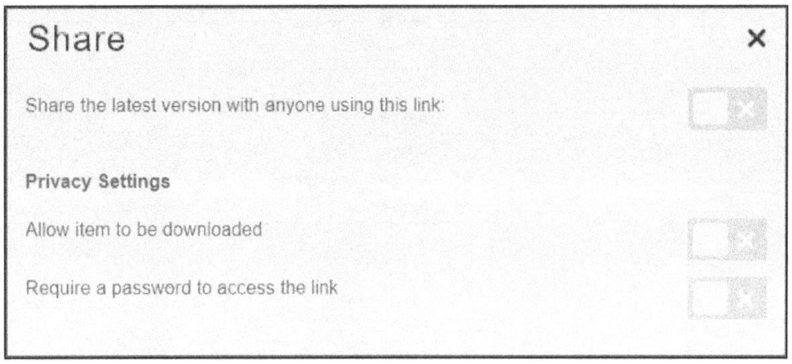

Figure-81. Share dialog box

- Click on the toggle buttons to activate or de-activate respective functions.
- After activating the sharing function, copy the link from **Copy** box and share the link via E-mail or other method with anyone. Set the **Allow item to be downloaded** toggle button to allow downloading of file.
- Activate the **Require a password to access the public link** option and specify desired password in the edit box displayed below it to secure your link with a password.

View details On Web

The **View Details On Web** tool is used to display the details of current file on Autodesk cloud in web browser; refer to Figure-82. You can use this option only after you have saved your file on Autodesk cloud.

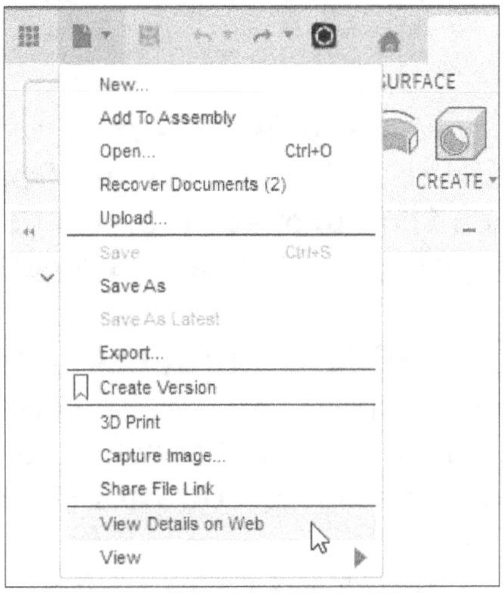

Figure-82. View Details on Web tool

View

The **View** tool is used to show and hide various elements of Fusion application window.

- Click on the **View** tool from **File** menu. The **View** cascading menu will be displayed; refer to Figure-83.

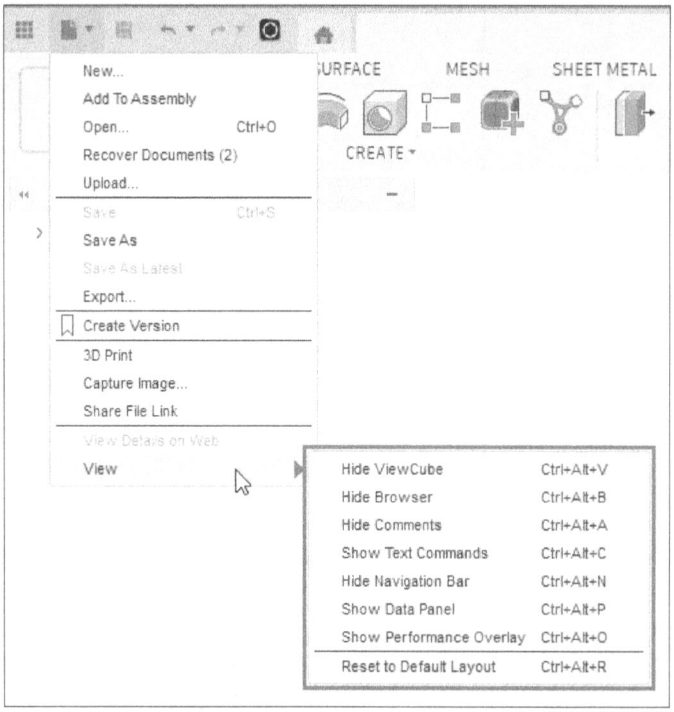

Figure-83. View cascading menu

Various tools in this cascading menu are given next.

Hide ViewCube

The **Hide ViewCube** tool is used to hide the **ViewCube**. If the **ViewCube** is already hidden then **Show ViewCube** tool will be displayed in place of it. On again selecting this tool, **View Cube** will be displayed. You can also show/hide **ViewCube** by pressing the **CTRL+ALT+V** keys.

Hide Browser

The **Hide Browser** tool is used to hide the **Browser** from the current screen. If the **Browser** is already hidden then **Show Browser** tool will be displayed in place of it. This tool can also be activated by pressing **CTRL+ALT+B** together.

Hide Comments

The **Hide Comments** tool is used to show and hide the **Comments** from Fusion software. If the **Comment** is already hidden then **Show Comment** tool will be displayed in place of it. This tool can also be used by pressing **CTRL+ALT+A** together.

Show Text Commands

The **Show Text Commands** tool is used to show **Text Commands Bar**. If the **Text Commands Bar** is already displayed then **Hide Text Commands** tool will be displayed in place of it. This tool can also be activated by pressing **CTRL+ALT+C** together.

Hide Navigation Bar

The **Hide Navigation Bar** tool is used to hide the **Navigation bar**. If the **Navigation Bar** is already hidden then **Show Navigation Bar** tool will be displayed in place of it. This tool can also be activated by pressing **CTRL+ALT+N** together.

Show Data Panel

The **Show Data Panel** tool is used to show the **Data Panel**. If the **Data Panel** is already showing then **Hide Data Panel** tool will be displayed in place of it. This tool can also be activated by pressing **CTRL+ALT+P** together.

Show/Hide Performance Overlay

The **Show/Hide Performance Overlay** tool is used to show or hide performance details of software like frames per second and video memory used by the software. This tool can also be used by pressing **CTRL+ALT+O** together.

Reset To Default Layout

The **Reset To Default Layout** tool is used to reset user interface to default settings. This tool can also be used by pressing **CTRL+ALT+R** together.

Scripts and Add-Ins

The **Scripts and Add-Ins** tool is used to run and manage **Scripts** and **Add-Ins** in Autodesk Fusion. The procedure to use this tool is discussed next.

- Click on **Scripts and Add-Ins** tool from **ADD-INS** drop-down in **UTILITIES** tab of **Ribbon**; refer to Figure-84. The **Scripts and Add-Ins** dialog box will displayed; refer to Figure-85.

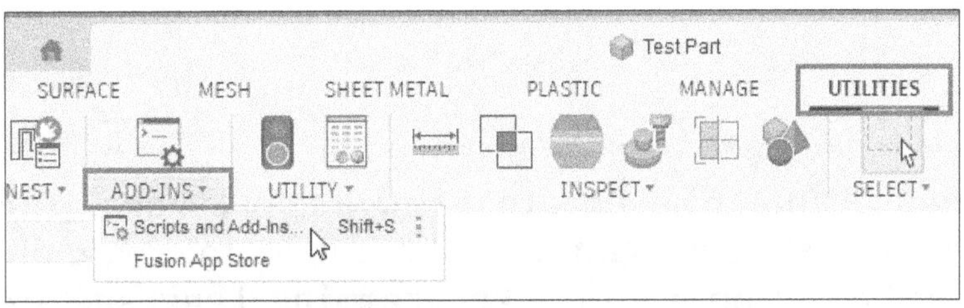

Figure-84. Scripts and Add-Ins tool

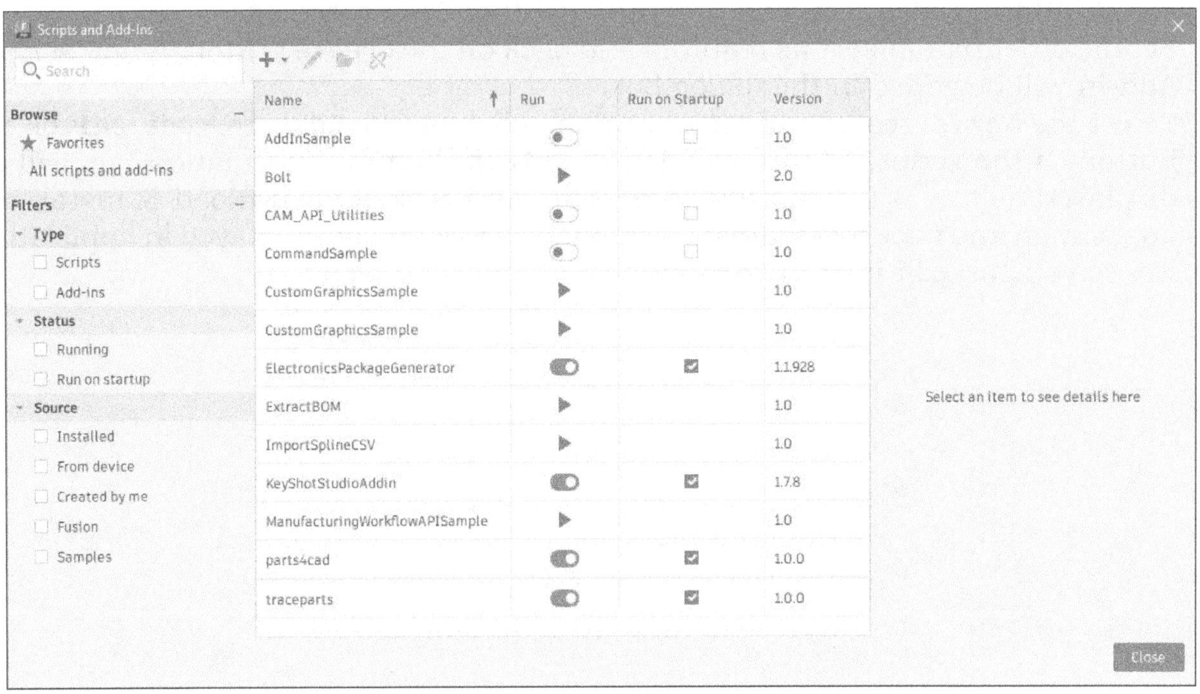

Figure-85. Scripts and Add-Ins

There are two tabs in this dialog box; **Scripts** and **Add-Ins**. Select the **Script** tab to run Python scripts in Autodesk Fusion. Select the **Add-Ins** tab to run the third party applications inside Autodesk Fusion.

Creating Script and Add-Ins

- To create a script or Add-Ins, click on the **Create script or add-in** button from drop-down in the **Scripts and Add-Ins** dialog box. The **New script or add-in** dialog box will be displayed; refer to Figure-86.

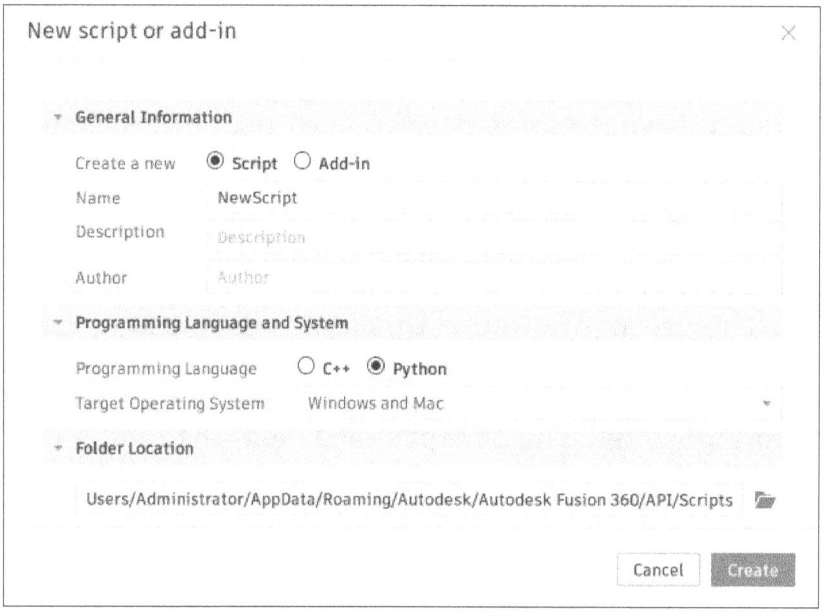

Figure-86. New script or add-in dialog box

- Select **Script** radio button from **Create a new** area of **General Information** rolloout to create a script or select the **Add-in** radio button to create an Add-In.
- Select desired radio button from the **Programming Language** area of **Programming Language and System** rollout to define the language in which you will be writing script/Add-in codes. You can program in either **C++** or **Python**.
- Set the other parameters as required and click on the **Create** button. A new script/Add-in will be added in the dialog box.
- Select the newly created script/Add-in and click on the **Edit in code editor** button. If the script/Add-in is coded in **Python** then an information box will be displayed asking you to download and install VS Code. Download & install the application and once installation is complete, codes will be displayed in application where you can edit it; refer to Figure-87.

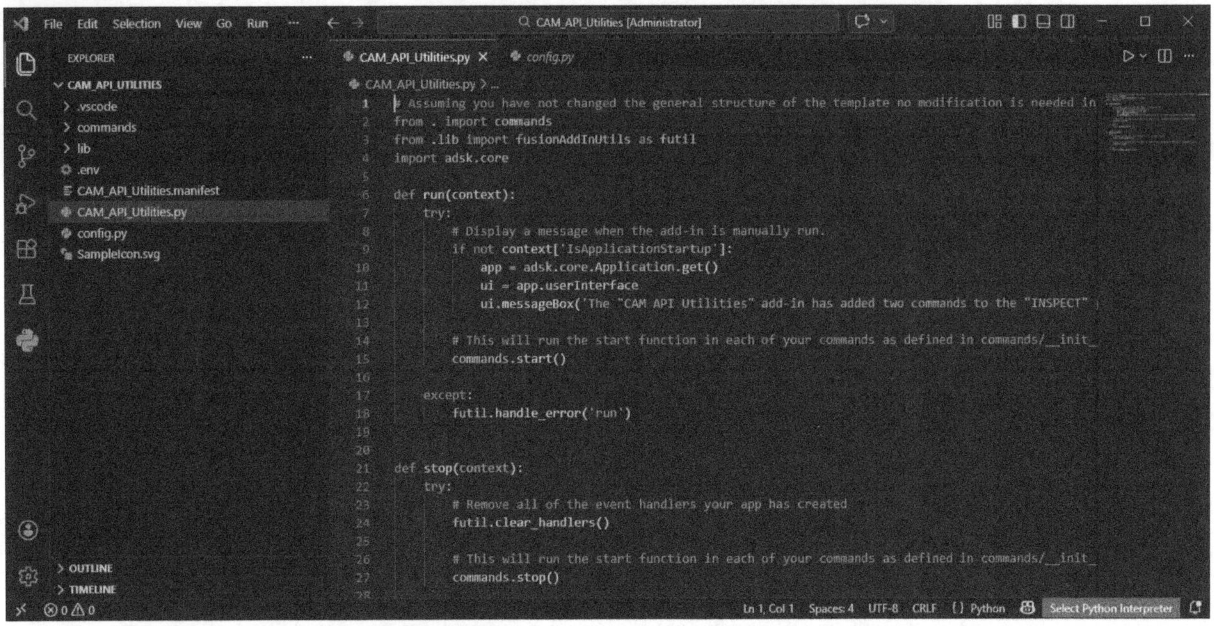

Figure-87. Visual Studio Code application window

- If you have opted for any other language then system will ask you for respective Programming software to display codes. If you like coding then you can check **Learning Python, 5th Edition by Mark Lutz** as reference book for Python programming.
- Click on the **Run** button from the **Scripts and Add-Ins** dialog box to run selected script.

Fusion App Store

The **Fusion App Store** tool in **ADD-INS** drop-down of **UTILITIES** tab in **Ribbon** is used to download and install third party Apps in Autodesk Fusion. On clicking this tool, a web page is displayed in your default web browser; refer to Figure-88.

Figure-88. Fusion Store webpage

- Login to your Autodesk account after clicking **Sign In** button at the top right in the web page.

- Select desired app, set the operating system option, and click on the **Download** button from web page; refer to Figure-89. The software will start downloading.

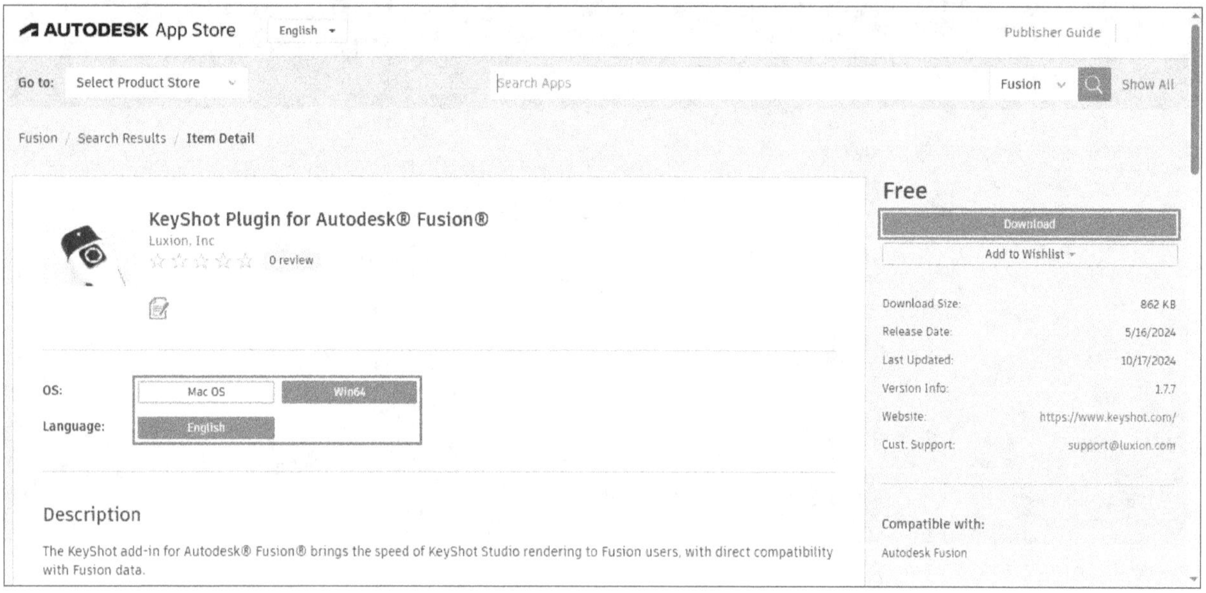

Figure-89. Downloading app

- Once downloaded, double-click on the setup file to install it and follow the instructions as displayed during installation.
- Once the app is installed, you can access it from **Scripts and Add-Ins** dialog box; refer to Figure-90.

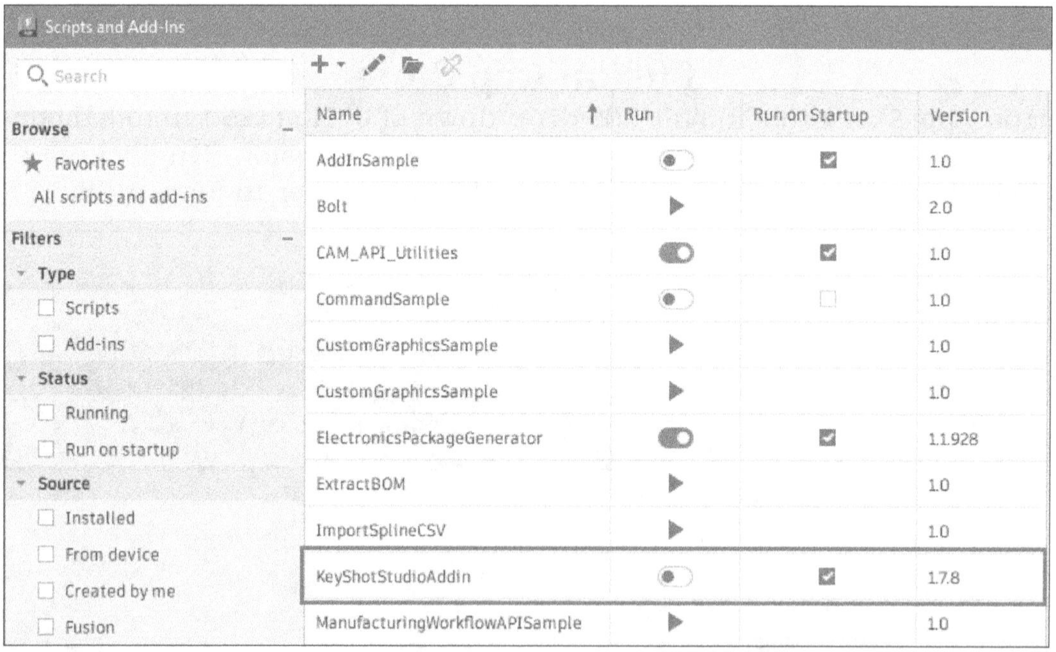

Figure-90. Installed app

UNDO AND REDO BUTTON

The **Undo** tool is used to revert back to condition before performing most recent action. The procedure to use this tool is discussed next.

- Click on **Undo** tool in **Application bar** or press **CTRL+Z** keys; refer to Figure-91.

- You can't undo some actions, like clicking commands on the **File** tab or saving a file.

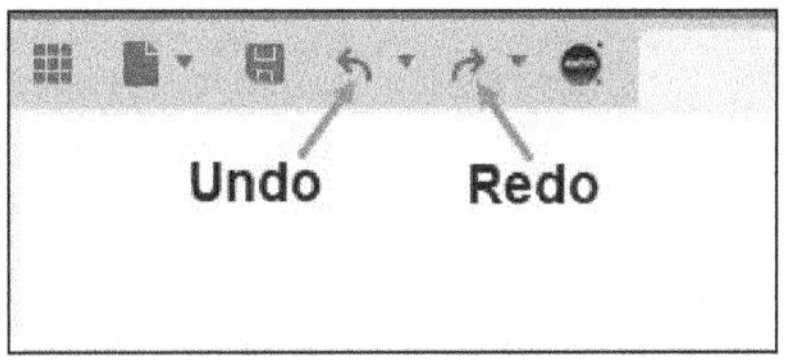

Figure-91. Undo And Redo Button

- The **Redo** tool is used to redo an action reverted by **Undo** tool. To use this tool, select the **Redo** button in **Application bar** or press **CTRL+Y** keys.
- The **Redo** button activates only after you have undone an action.

USER ACCOUNT DROP-DOWN

The tool in **User Account** drop-down are used to manage user account details and preferences for Autodesk Fusion; refer to Figure-92. The tools in this drop-down are discussed next.

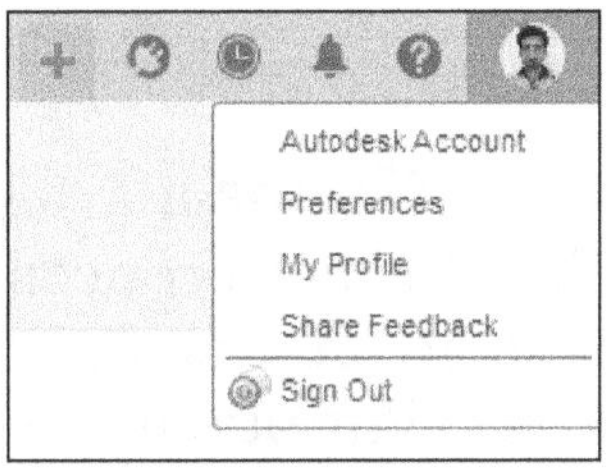

Figure-92. User Account drop down

Preferences

The **Preferences** tool is used to set the preferences for various functions of the software like you can set units, material libraries, display options, and so on. The procedure to use this tool is given next.

- Click on **Preferences** tool from **User Account** drop-down; refer to Figure-92. The **Preferences** dialog box will be displayed where you can specify various parameters for application; refer to Figure-93.

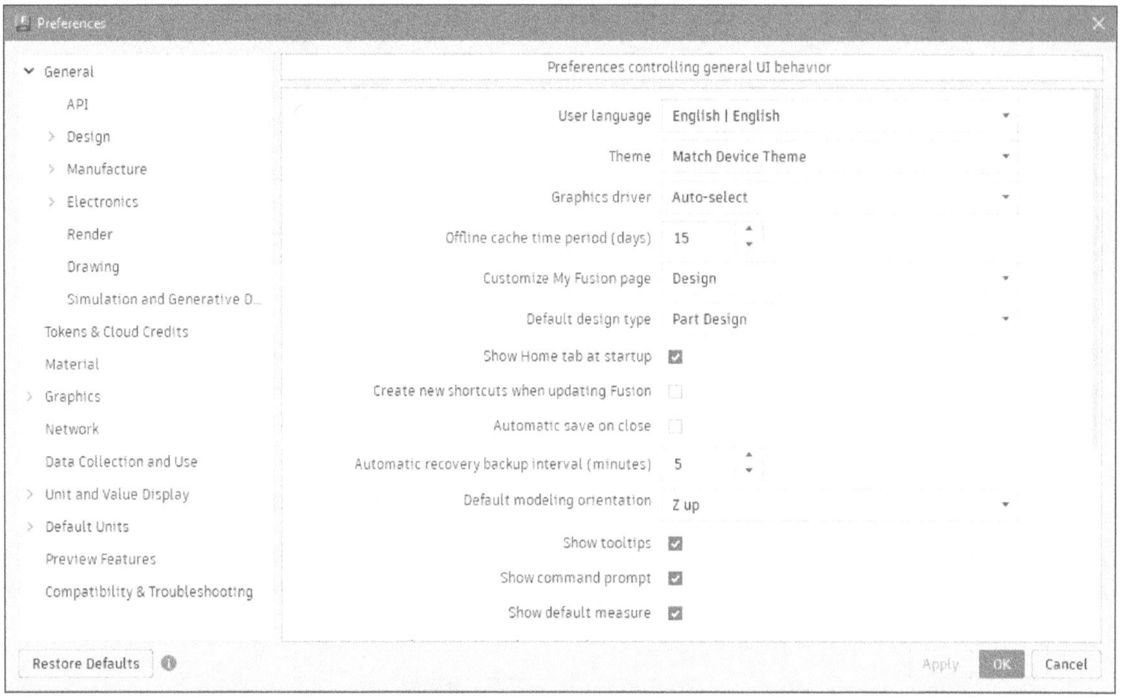

Figure-93. Preferences dialog box

General

In **General** node, you can specify the preferences for language, graphics, mouse functioning, default workspace, and so on. Click on the **General** node at the left in the dialog box to display general options. Various important options are discussed next.

- Click on the **User language** drop-down and select desired language for Autodesk Fusion interface.
- Select desired theme to be activated in the software from **Theme** drop-down.
- Click on the **Graphics driver** drop-down to select the graphics driver to be used by Autodesk Fusion.
- **Offline cache time period (days)** edit box/spinner is used to specify the number of days up to which your documents can be in the cache memory of Autodesk Fusion before you go back to online mode of Autodesk Fusion. If you specify high value then more local memory will be used by Autodesk Fusion to save temporary copy of your documents. If you specify a low value here then system will prompt you soon to go back online. The maximum number of days specified here can be 360 and minimum number of days can be 7.
- Select desired option from **Customize My Fusion page** drop-down to display the content of selected page in the **Home** tab of the software.
- Select desired option from **Default design type** drop-down to start a new design.
- Whenever Autodesk Fusion is updated, launch icons are created automatically in various locations.
- Select **Show Home tab at startup** check box to show the home tab at starting of the application.
- Select the **Automatic save on close** check box to automatically save the newer version of file when you close Autodesk Fusion.
- Specify desired time in minute after which a recovery copy of your model will be created automatically in the **Automatic Recovery backup interval (minutes)** edit box.

- Click on the **Default modeling orientation** drop-down and select desired direction option to define default orientation of model. In most of the CAD software, Z axis upward is the default orientation of model. To set the common orientation, select the **Z up** option from the drop-down.
- Select the **Show tooltips**, **Show command prompt**, **Show default measure**, and **Show in-command errors and warnings** check boxes to display respective interface elements.
- Select desired software style from the **Pan**, **Zoom**, **Orbit shortcuts** drop-down to define which software style for shortcuts of pan, zoom, and orbit should be used. If you are switching from Alias, Inventor, Solidworks, or Tinkercad to Autodesk Fusion then you can select respective option from the drop-down to use familiar shortcuts.
- Select desired option from the **Default Orbit type** drop-down to define the default orbit type for rotating model view. There are two options available for orbit; **Constrained Orbit** and **Free Orbit**.
- Select the **Reverse zoom direction** check box to reverse the zoom direction of mouse scroll and other zoom methods.
- Select the **Enable camera pivot** check box to display camera pivot point used as center for orbiting.
- Select **Use gesture-based view navigation** check box to use the gesture based navigation to view the components.
- Select **Use Windows touchpad for gestures** check box to activate the two-finger swipe and pinch-to-zoom touchpad gestures.
- Select **Spacebar repeats last command** check box to repeat the previously used command on pressing the **Spacebar** key from the keyboard.

Note that by default the pivot point is placed on center of mass point of model but if you want to change the position of pivot point then right-click in blank area of canvas and select the **Set Orbit Center** option. The green point will get attached to cursor and you will be asked to define the location of orbit point. Click at desired location to place the orbit center.

API Options

- Click on the **API** option under **General** node in the left of the dialog box and set desired parameters to define default location and language of scripts/Add-Ins.

Design Options

- Click on the **Design** option under **General** node in the left of the dialog box to set the parameters related to model creation. The options in the dialog box will be displayed as shown in Figure-94.
- Select the **Parametric Modeling** option from **Default Modeling Mode** drop-down if you want to keep detail of every operation you perform on the model in model history. If you want to save space or want to delete operation details while sharing file then create the model after selecting **Direct Modeling** option from the **Default Modeling Mode** drop-down. Select **Prompt** option from the drop-down to allow the user to select the modeling mode when creating a new document. Note that changes made in most of the options will be applied only after you have restarted Autodesk Fusion.

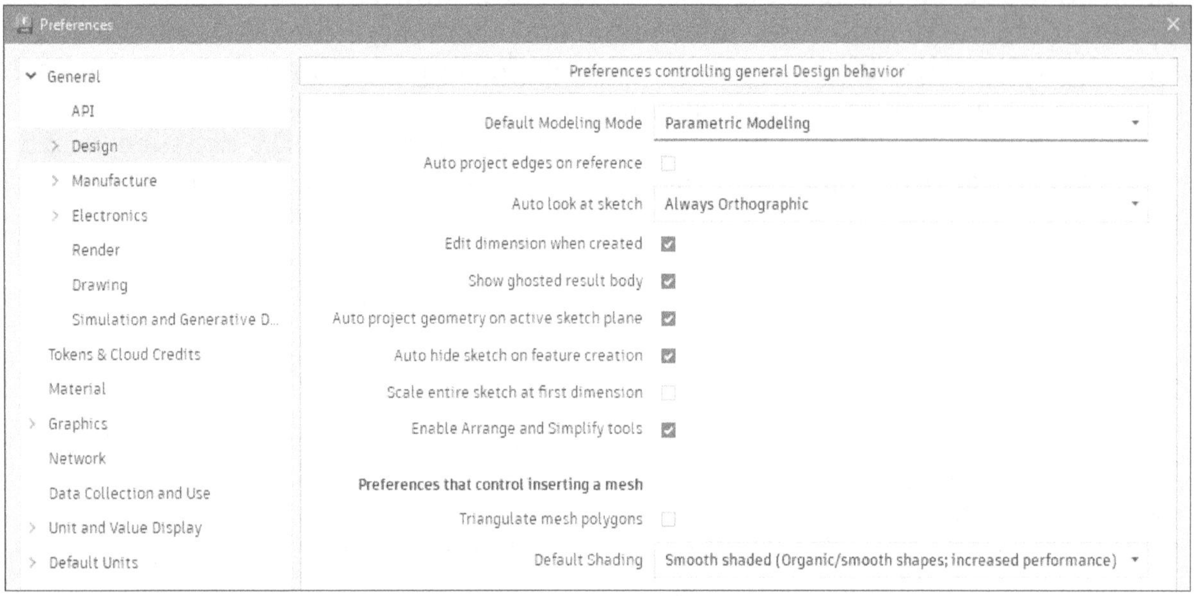

Figure-94. Design page

- Select the **Auto project edges on reference** check box if you want to automatically project edges of model when they are used as reference for dimensioning or constraining of other sketch elements. Refer to Figure-95.

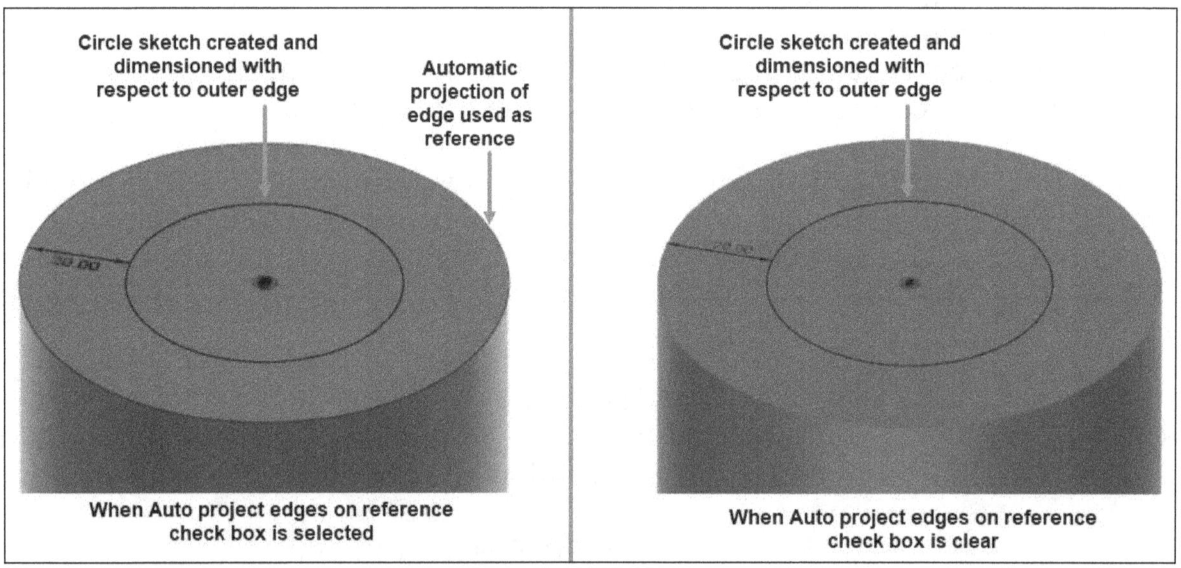

Figure-95. Use of Auto project edges on reference check box

- Select desired option from **Auto look at sketch** drop-down to automatically make sketching plane parallel to screen.
- Select the **Edit dimension when created** check box if you want to edit the values of dimensions when you are applying dimensions to objects.
- Selecting the **Show ghosted result body** check box will create a ghost image of model before a sculpting operation is performed on it. Note that the ghost image will be displayed while you are in sculpt mode; refer to Figure-96. When you exit the model after making changes then the ghost image will not be displayed.

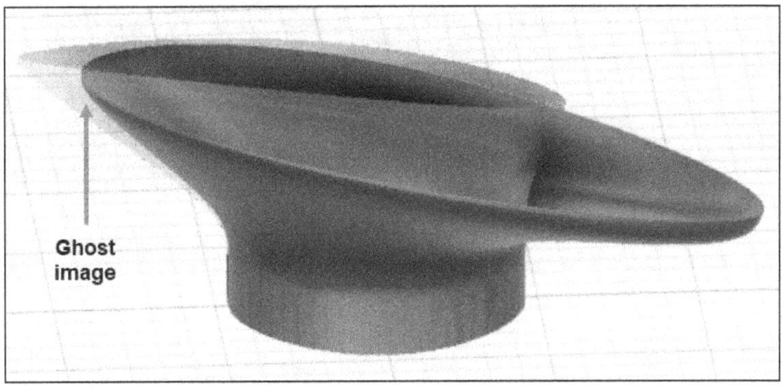

Figure-96. On selecting Show ghosted result body check box

- Select the **Auto project geometry on active sketch plane** check box if you want to project geometry on the sketching plane by default.
- Select the **Auto hide sketch on feature creation** check box to automatically hide the sketch after it has been used to create a feature.
- Select the **Scale entire sketch at first dimension** check box to automatically fit the sketch objects in view area with reduced dimensions after you specify first dimension of the sketch; refer to Figure-97. Note that all the other objects reduce in same ratio as the first dimension reduces its respective entity.

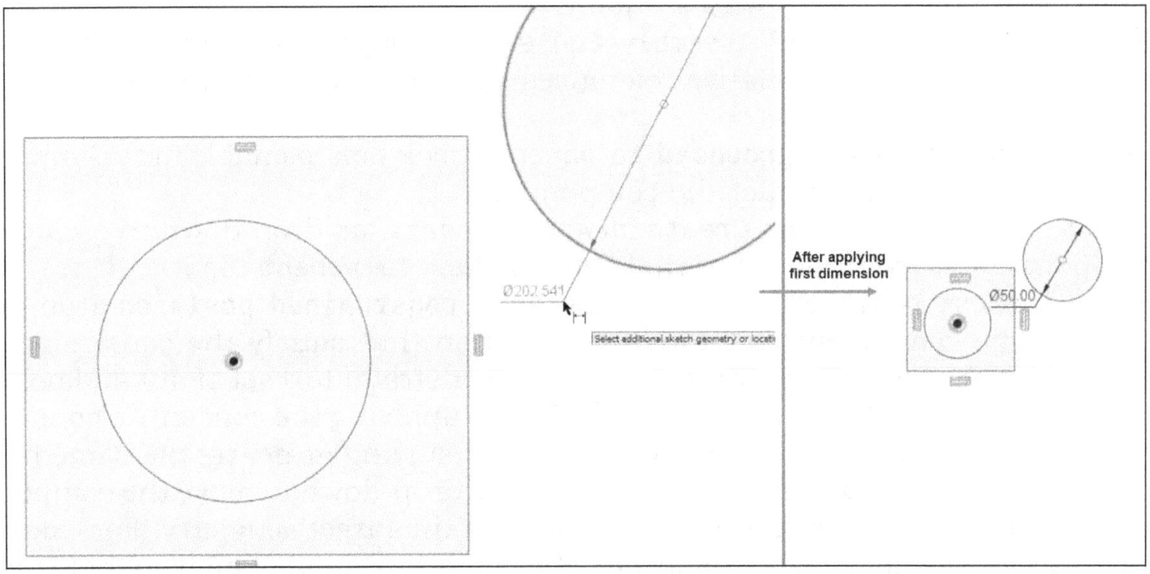

Figure-97. When Scale entire sketch at first dimension check box is selected

- Select **Enable Arrange and Simplify tools** check box to enable **Arrange**, **Remove Features**, **Remove Faces**, and **Replace with Primitives** tools to the **Modify** menu in the **Design** workspace.
- Select **Triangulate mesh polygons** check box from **Preferences that control inserting a mesh** area to convert polygon facets in the imported mesh to triangles.
- Select desired option from **Default Shading** drop-down to render the mesh as smooth shaded or flat shaded.
- Click on the **Assemblies** option from **Design** node of the dialog box. The options will be displayed as shown in Figure-98.

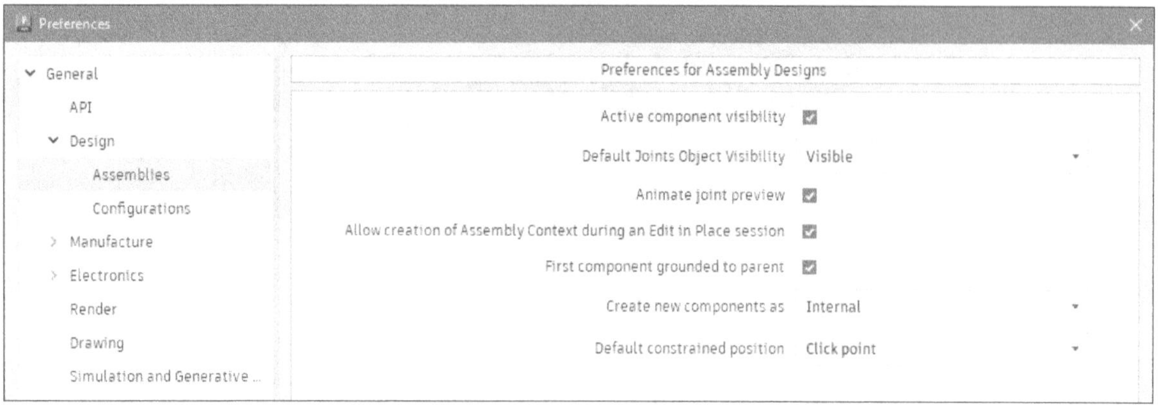

Figure-98. Assemblies options

- Select the **Active Component Visibility** check box to display only currently active component and hide rest of the components.
- Select desired option from **Default Joints Object Visibility** drop-down to show or hide the joints in the canvas.
- Select the **Animate joint preview** check box if you want to check small animation of how joint will work. The animation can give you clues about degrees of freedom which are constrained by selected joint.
- Select **Allow creation of Assembly Context during an Edit in Place session** check box to create associative references while editing external components in context.
- Select **First component grounded to parent** check box to enable first component as a ground to parent under the component.
- Select desired option from **Create new components as** drop-down to create new components as external or internal with the **New Component** tool.
- Select **Closest position** option from **Default constrained position** drop-down to move the component at the nearest location that satisfy the constraint. For example, when you are applying a concentric constraint to a set of nut and bolt and the bolt is floating **50**mm away from a hole. On applying the concentric constraint it will slide to align with the axis of hole while staying at nearly the same height as original. Select **Click point** option from the drop-down to move the component to the exact spot where your cursor clicked on the target geometry. For example, when applying a concentric constraint, the bolt jumps immediately to that specific point on the hole where you clicked rather than the nearest location of the hole.
- Similarly, set the other options as required on different nodes of the dialog box. We will work with options in this dialog box during rest of the book whenever a change in application settings is required.
- After setting the parameters, click on the **OK** button from the dialog box and restart Autodesk Fusion if needed.

Autodesk Account

The **Autodesk Account** tool in **User Account** drop-down is used to manage your Autodesk account profile in default web browser.

My Profile

The **My Profile** tool in **User Account** drop-down is used to manage your project data stored on cloud via web browser.

Work Offline/Online

The **Work Offline/Online** toggle button is displayed on clicking **Job Status** button at the left of **User Account** drop-down; refer to Figure-99. Click on this button to toggle between offline and online mode of Autodesk Fusion.

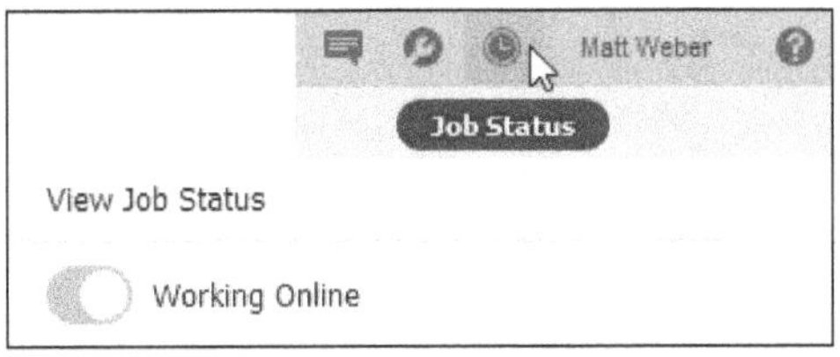

Figure-99. Work Offline Online

Extensions

The **Extensions** tool is used to display the list of current available extensions in the **Extension Manager** dialog box for adding more functionality to Autodesk Fusion. Click on the **Extensions** button from the toolbar; refer to Figure-100. The **Extension Manager** dialog box will be displayed; refer to Figure-101.

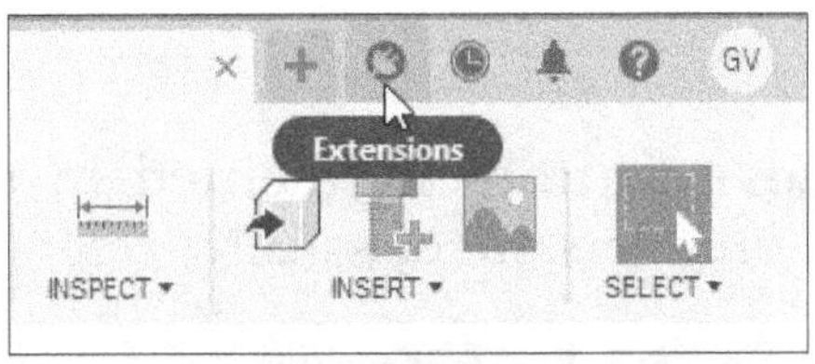

Figure-100. Extensions button

Figure-101. Extension Manager dialog box

- Select desired extension from the list to be activated. The extension details will be displayed; refer to Figure-102.

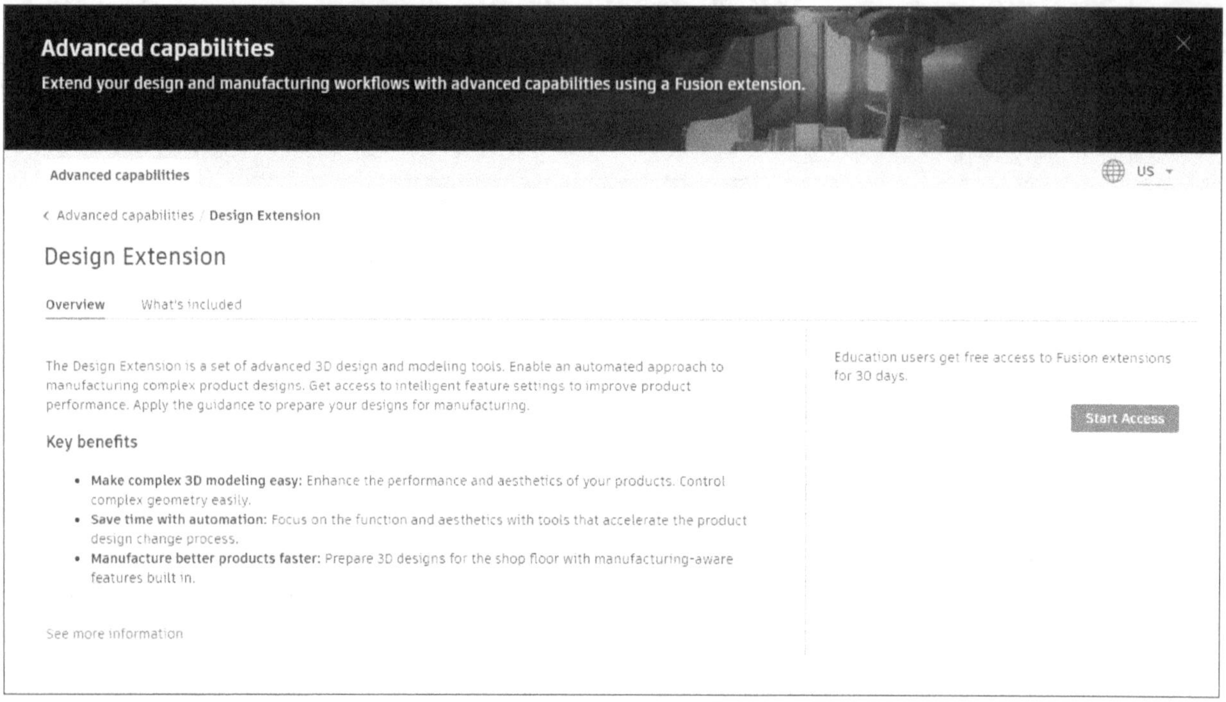

Figure-102. Extension details page

- Click on the **Start Access** button highlighted in the dialog box. The **Design Extension** access will be enabled successfully; refer to Figure-103.

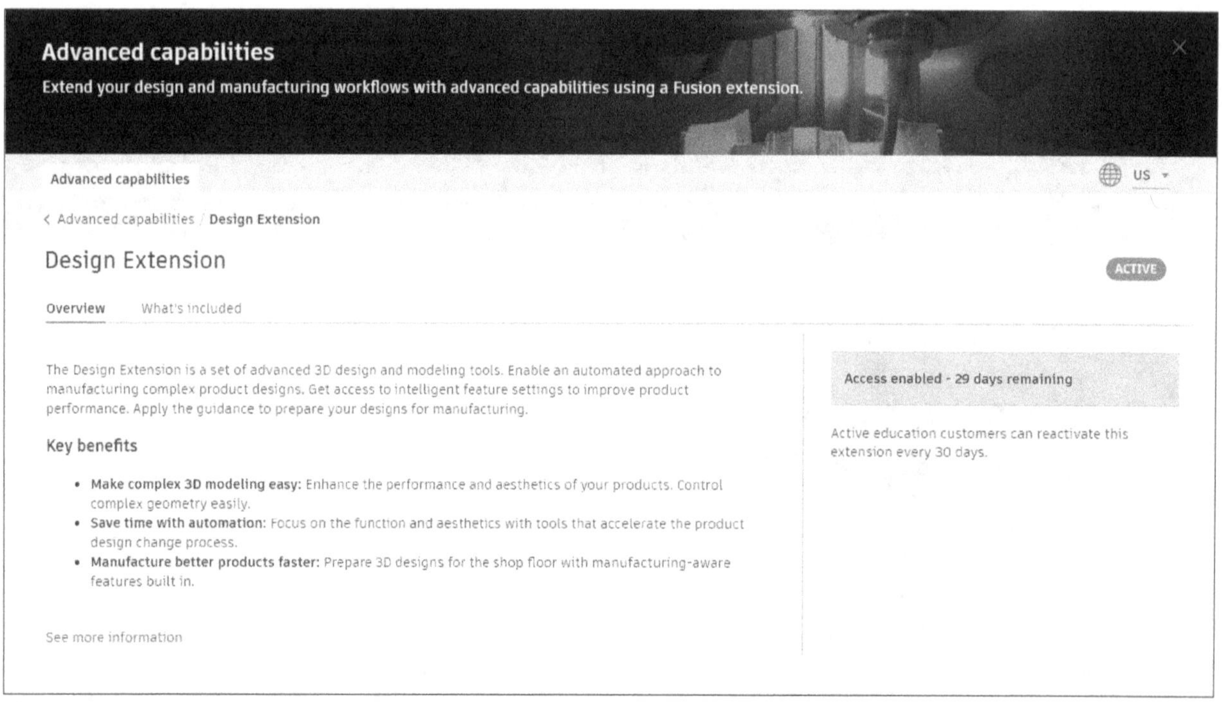

Figure-103. Design Extension access enabled

HELP DROP-DOWN

When you face any problem working with Autodesk Fusion, the tools in **Help** drop-down can be useful; refer to Figure-104. Tools in the drop-down are given next.

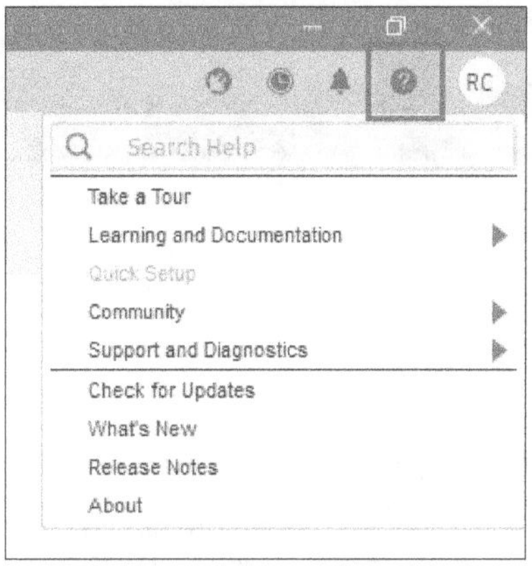

Figure-104. Help drop down

Search Help Box

When you are facing any problem regarding tools and terms in the software, then you need to type keywords for your problem in **Search Box** and press **ENTER** to find a suitable solution to your problems; refer to Figure-105.

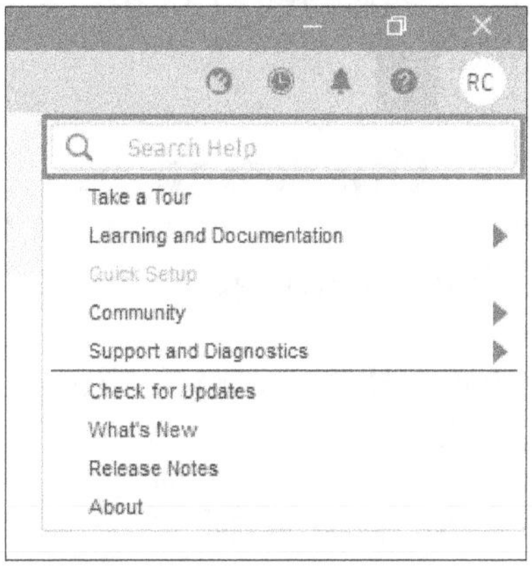

Figure-105. Search box

Learning and Documentation

The tools in the **Learning and Documentation** cascading menu are used to display video tutorials, help files, and Fusion api related content in web browser; refer to Figure-106. On clicking the **Self-Paced Learning** button in the **Learning and Documentation** cascading menu of **Help** menu, the website of Autodesk Fusion will be displayed; refer to Figure-107.

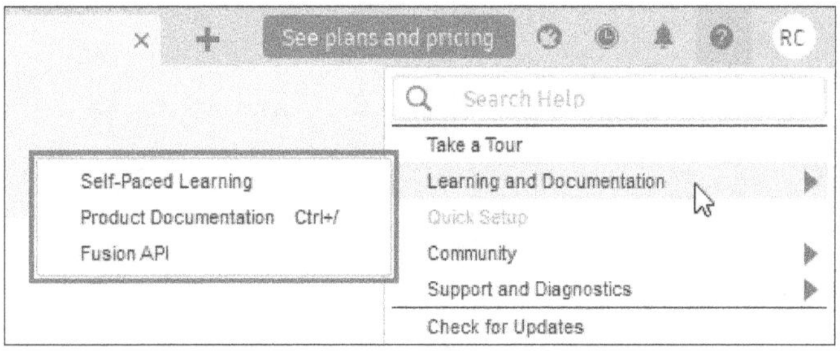

Figure-106. Learning and Documentation cascading menu

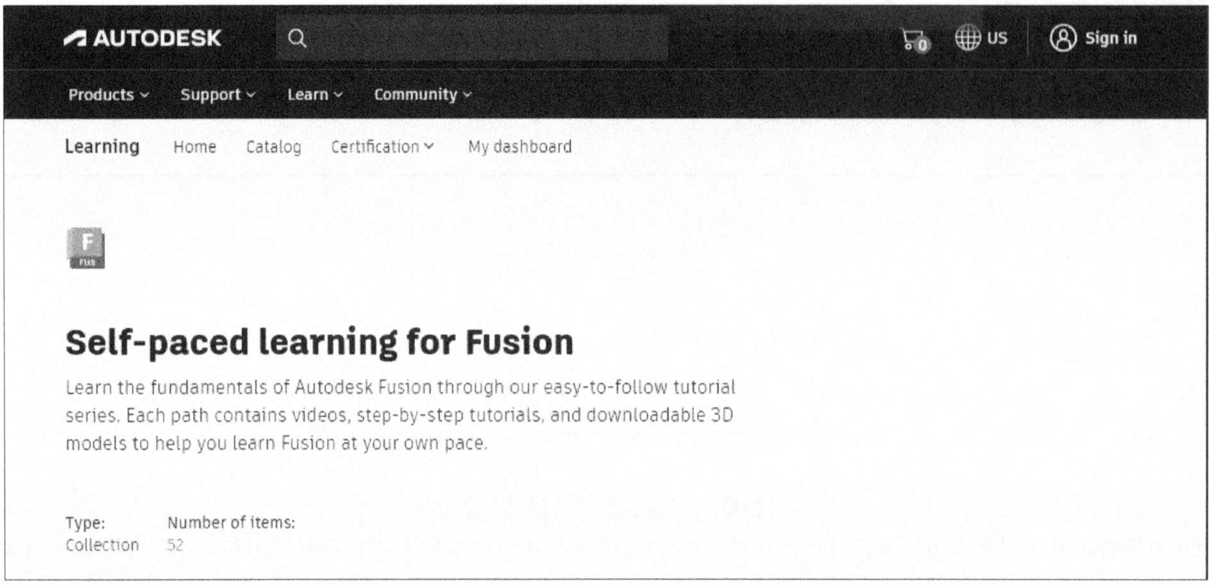

Figure-107. Fusion learning website

Similarly, you can use **Product Documentation** and **Fusion API** tools to learn about Fusion interface, design methodology, and APIs.

Quick Setup

When you are new to Autodesk Fusion then this tool will help you to understand this software terminology and basic settings.

- Click on **Quick Setup** tool from **Help** menu. The **QUICK SETUP** dialog box will be displayed; refer to Figure-108.

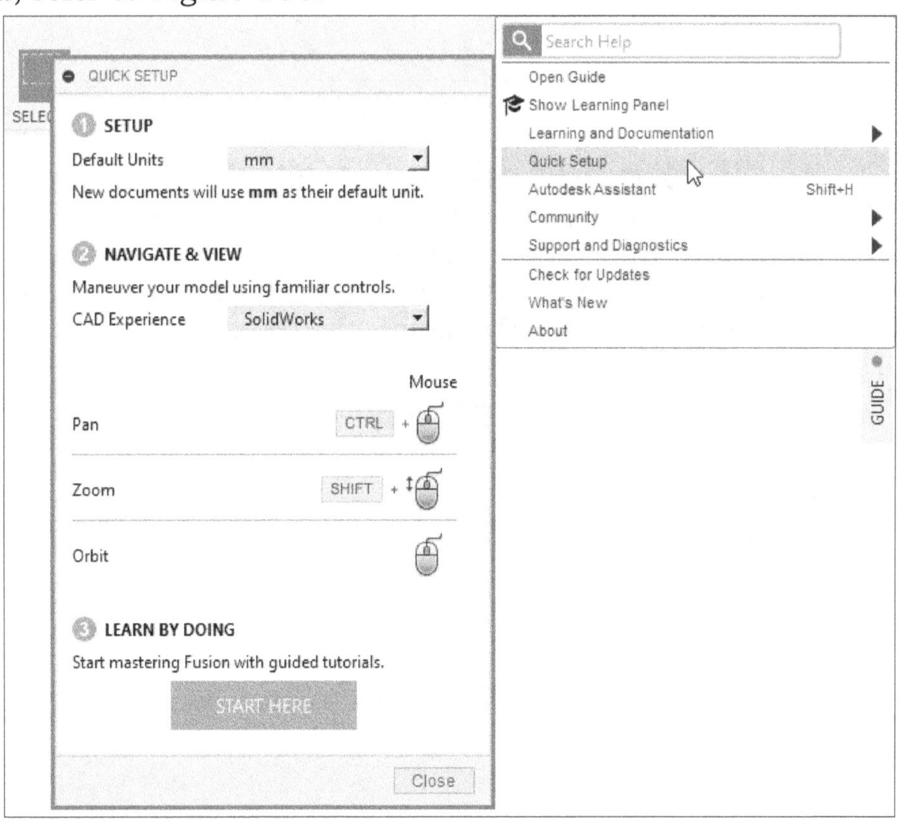

Figure-108. QUICK SETUP

- Set desired unit in the **Default Units** drop-down.
- The navigation functions of mouse can be set as per Autodesk Inventor, SolidWorks or Alias software by selecting respective option from the **CAD Experience** drop-down.
- If you are new to CAD then you can select the **New to CAD** option in **Cad Experience** drop-down. The mouse will function as per Autodesk Fusion.

Similarly, you can use **Forum, Insider Program, Blog** tool from **Community** cascading menu to get help from Autodesk Fusion users or provide feedback.

Autodesk Assistant

The **Autodesk Assistant** tool is used to get AI-powered support for the design problems while using the software or to connect with the support agent online. The procedure to use this tool is discussed next.

- Click on the **Find answers or connect with a support agent** button from the bottom right corner of the design environment. The **AUTODESK ASSISTANT** dialog box will be displayed; refer to Figure-109.

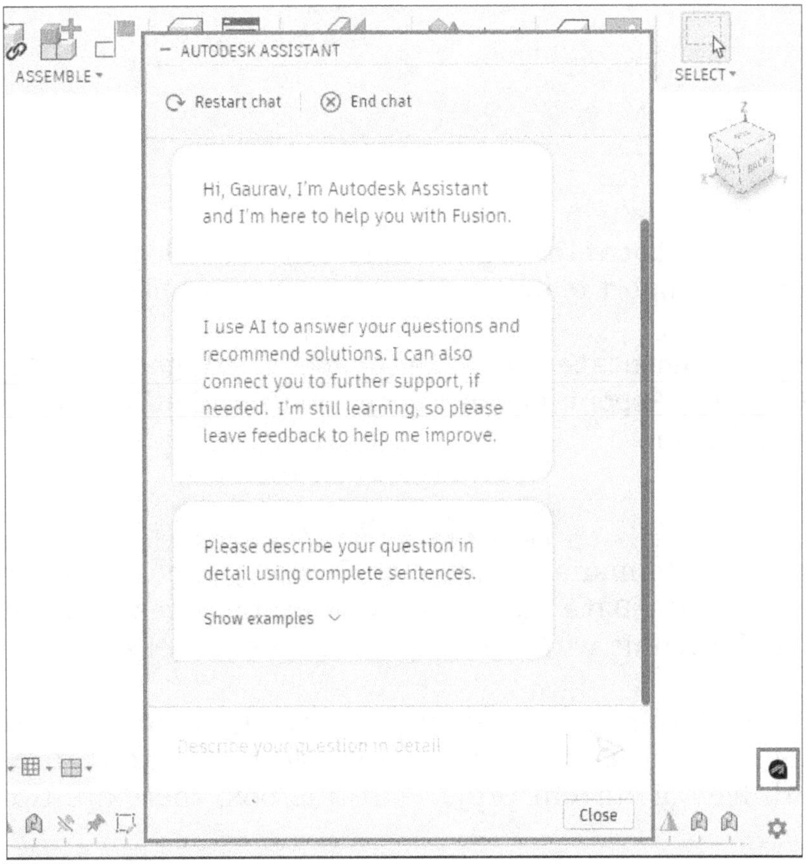

Figure-109. AUTODESK ASSISTANT dialog box

- Ask desired question related to software in the **Describe your question in detail** area and hit **Enter** from the keyboard. You will get the answer from **Generative AI** within seconds.
- After getting the answer, the **Connect with an agent** button will be displayed next to the answer box. Click on that button to ask your question with an agent online.
- Click on the **Restart chat** or **End chat** button to restart or end the ongoing chat, respectively.
- Click on **Close** button to close the dialog box.

Support and Diagnostics

When you are having a problem in Fusion and want **Technical support** team to look at software problem data, then you can create the log files and send it to the support team of Autodesk.

- To create log files, select **Diagnostic Log Files** tool under the **Support and Diagnostics** cascading menu in **Help** drop-down. The **Diagnostic Log Files** dialog box will be displayed; refer to Figure-110.

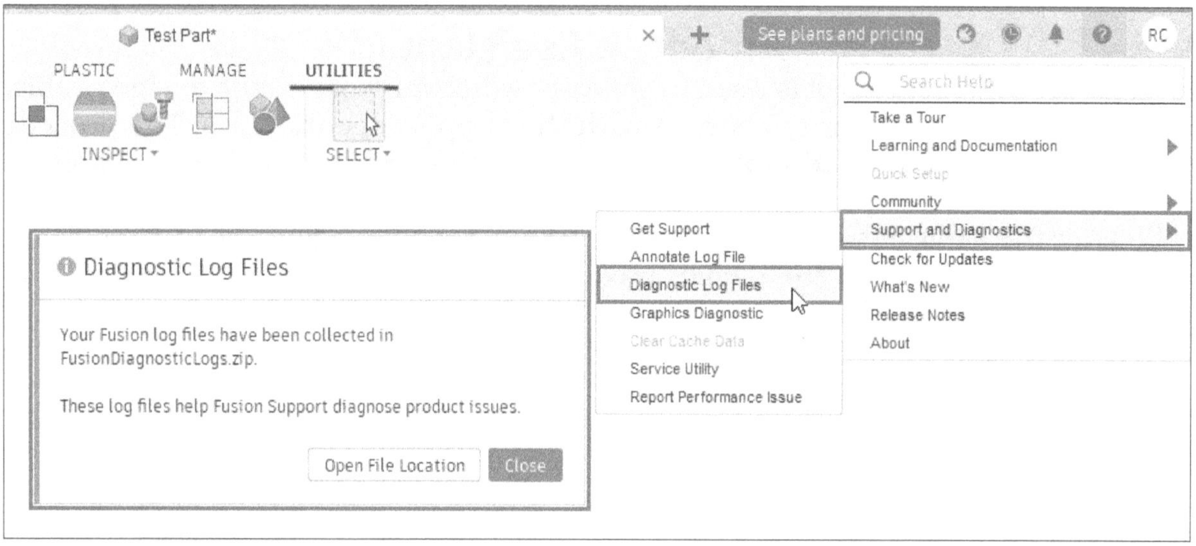

Figure-110. Diagnostic Log Files dialog box

- Click on **Open File Location** button and select the log file which you want to send to technical support team for the solution of problem.

Similarly, you can use **Annotate Log File**, **Graphics Diagnostic**, **Clear user cache data**, **Service Utility**, **Report Performance Issue** and other tools from **Help** drop-down in Autodesk Fusion.

DATA PANEL

The **Data** panel is used to manage Autodesk Fusion projects. The projects you save in cloud are shown in the **Data** panel. You can easily access the saved project files from anywhere and anytime with the help of internet access.

To show or hide the **Data** panel, click on the **Show Data Panel** or **Hide Data Panel** button at upper left corner of the Fusion window; refer to Figure-111. A box will be displayed with files of current project. In this box, there are two sections; **Data** and **People**.

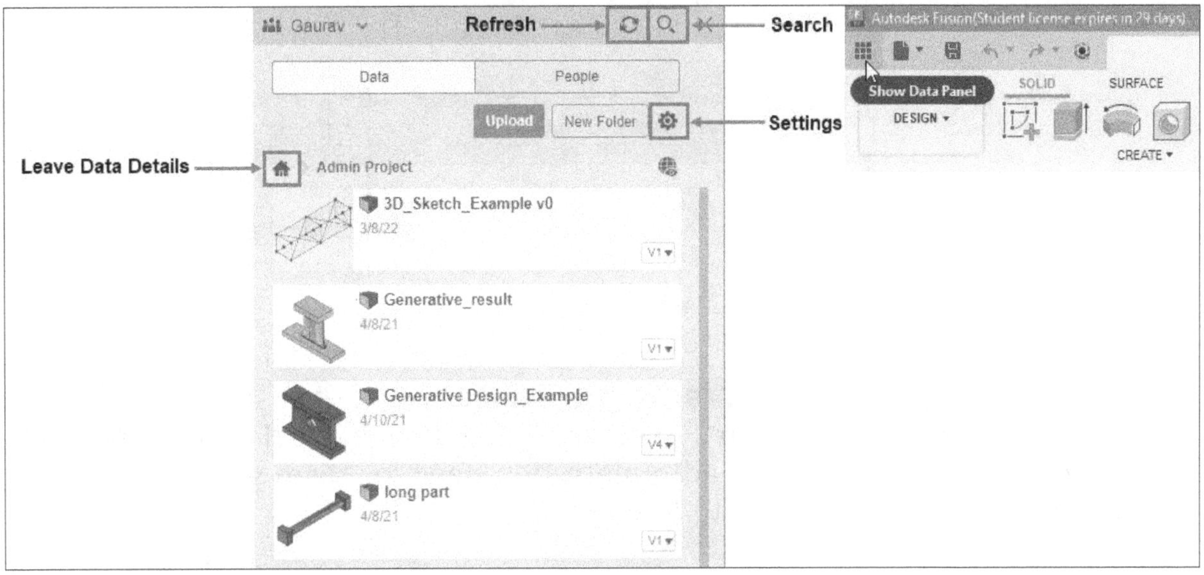

Figure-111. Data Panel

In **Data** section, the files which you have saved earlier in current project will be displayed. You can open any file by double-clicking on it.

In **People** section, the information of users will be displayed who have access the files of current project; refer to Figure-112.

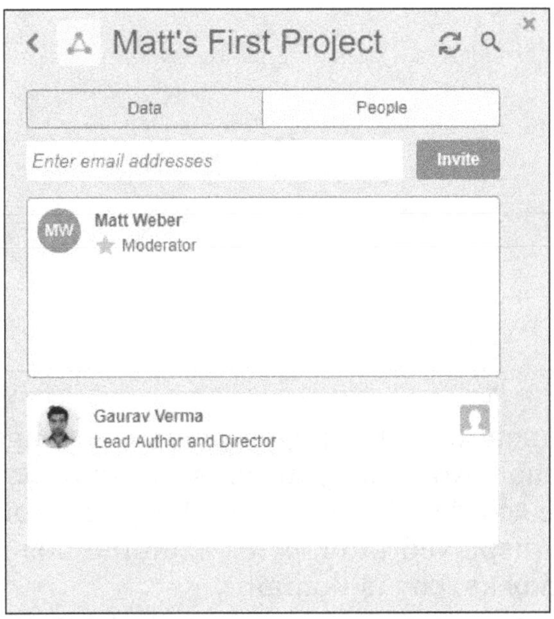

Figure-112. People section in Data panel

Working in a Team

Using the tools in **User** drop-down of **Data Panel**, you can create a new team or work in other's team to create designs in collaboration with others; refer to Figure-113. Various tools of this drop-down are discussed next.

Figure-113. User drop-down

Creating a Team

- Click on the three dots button next to your name and select the **Open Admin Console** option displayed. The administration page for team will be displayed in the default web browser; refer to Figure-114.

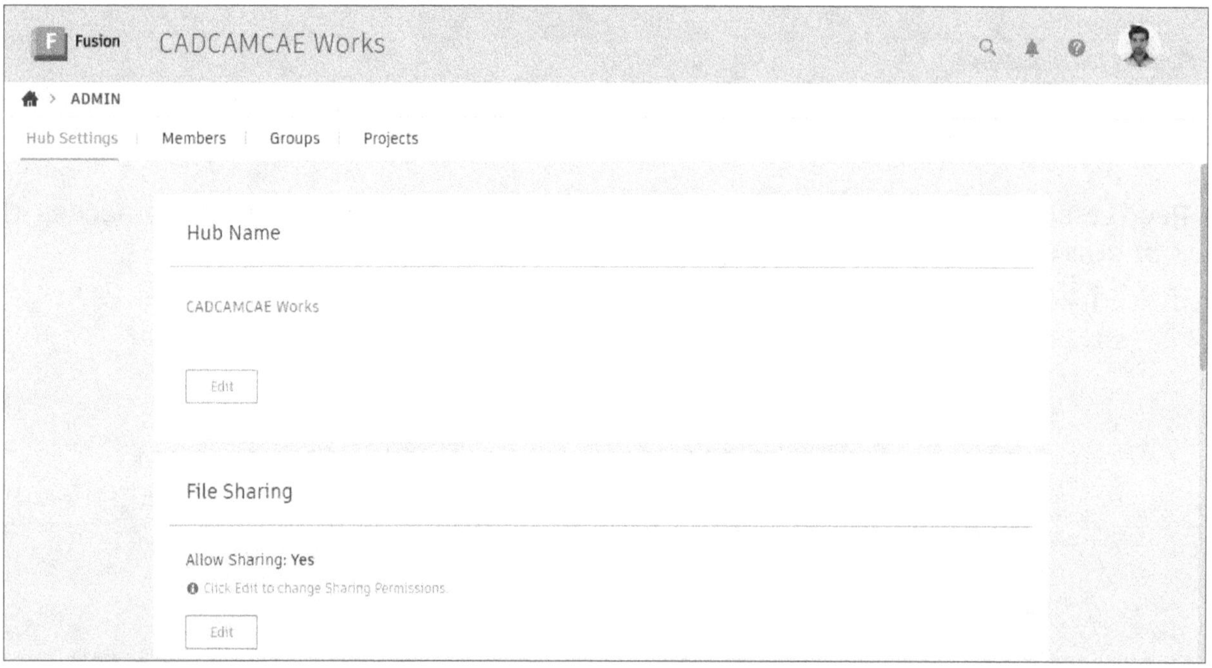

Figure-114. Administration page for hub

- Specify desired parameters in this page to define settings related to file sharing, access, and collaboration. Note that you can set auto-approval settings for specified domains by using the **Add domain** button on this page. You will be asked to specify the text in email ID displayed after @ for example, for matt@cadcamcaeworks.com the **@cadcamcaeworks.com** is domain.
- To add members in your team, click on the **Members** tab in the web page. The options will be displayed as shown in Figure-115.

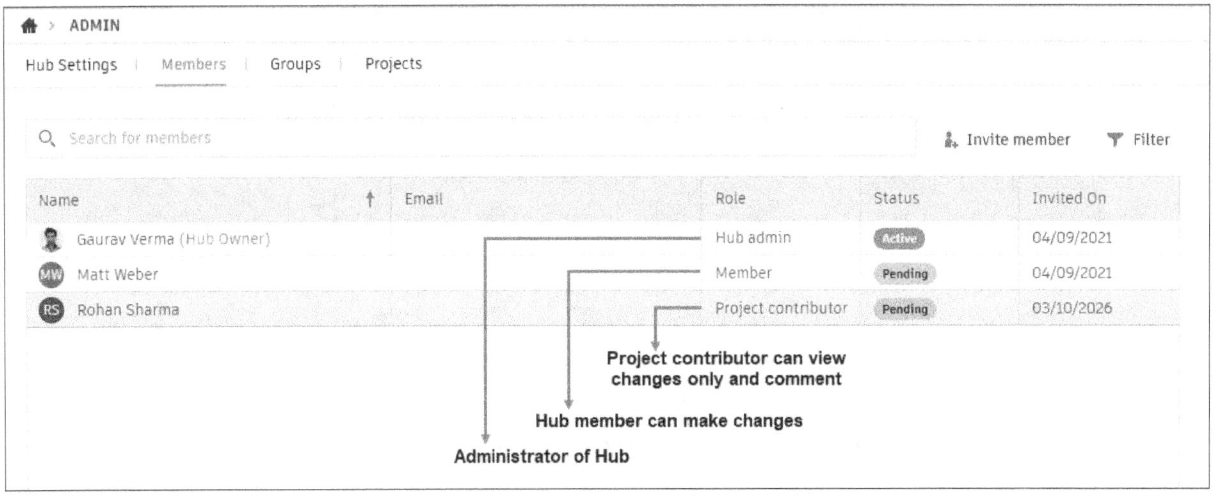

Figure-115. Members page

- To invite a new member, click on the **Invite member** button on this page. The **Invite Members** dialog box will be displayed; refer to Figure-116.

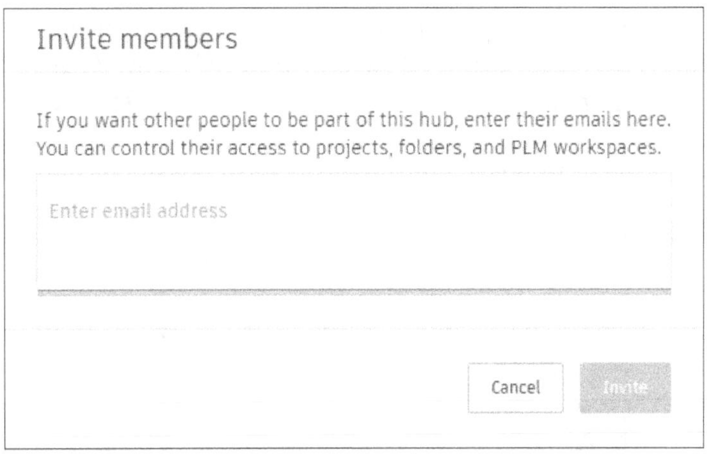

Figure-116. Invite members dialog box

- Specify the email id's of team members separated by comma (,) in the **Enter email address** edit box and click on the **Invite** button. Once they accept invitation on their email ids, they will become members of the team. You can later assign the roles to members as desired using the Administrator page. You can now logout and close the browser to exit the admin panel of Fusion team.

After creating a team, make sure you are log-in by team name in the **Data Panel** and create a new project using **New Project** button in the **Data Panel**. This new project will be shared with all the team members for modifications based on roles assigned to them; refer to Figure-117.

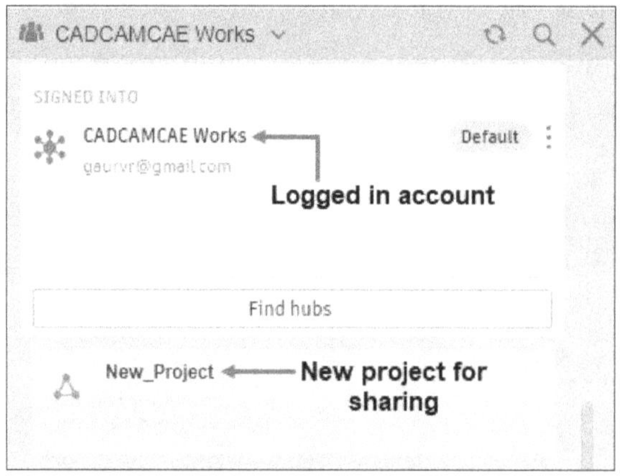

Figure-117. Sharing project with team

Cloud Account of User

To open the cloud account of user, you need to click on the **Open in Web** button from the drop-down displayed on clicking three dot button ⋮ next to the name of user in **Data Panel**; refer to Figure-118. On selecting this button, details of user's cloud storage will be displayed in web browser. You can check and modify the files as desired. Note that you can delete any file available in Cloud account using the tools in web browser which is not possible in **Data Panel**; refer to Figure-119.

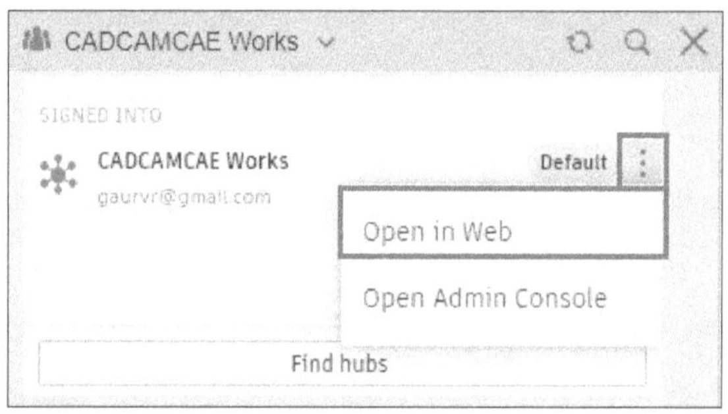

Figure-118. Open in Web button

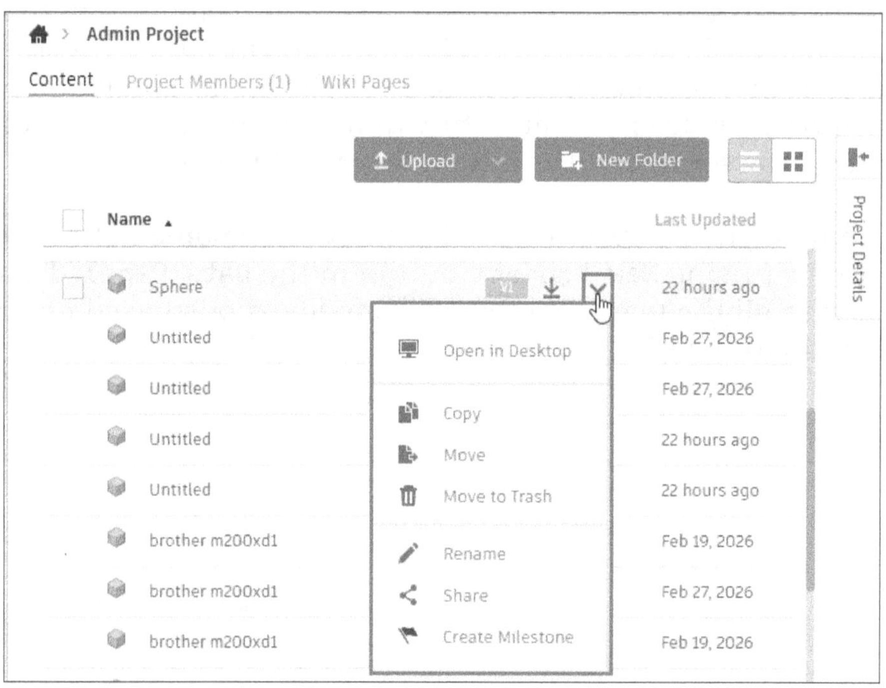

Figure-119. Shortcut menu for modifying files in cloud account using web browser

BROWSER

The **BROWSER** presents an organized view of your design steps in a tree like structure on the left of the Fusion screen; refer to Figure-120. When you select a feature or component in the **BROWSER**, it is also highlighted in the graphics window.

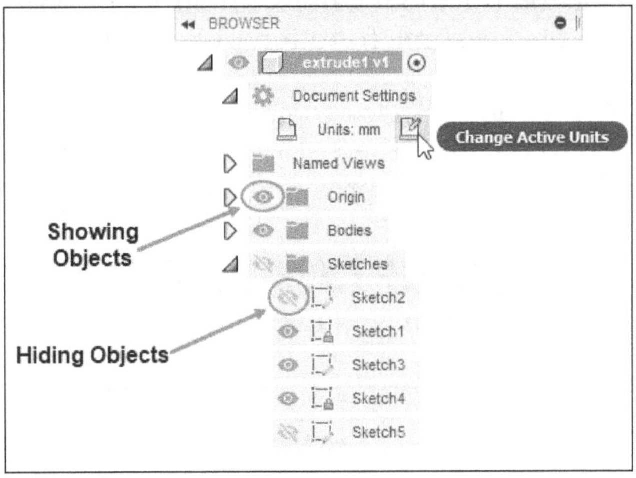

Figure-120. Browser

- Click on the **Eye** button to toggle the visibility of respective object.
- If you select any object in **BROWSER** then it is highlighted in blue color which indicates that the respective object is active for various operations.
- To change the units of the design or sketch, select the **Change Active Units** button as highlighted in the above figure. The **CHANGE ACTIVE UNITS** dialog box will be displayed. Select desired unit and click on the **OK** button.

NAVIGATION BAR

The **Navigation Bar** is available at the bottom of graphics window of Fusion. It provides access of navigation commands for design. To start a navigation command, click on any tool from the **Navigation Bar**; refer to Figure-121. There are various tool in **Navigation Bar** to navigate the model which are discussed next.

- **Orbit**- The **Orbit** tools are used for rotating the current model. There are two types of orbit tools i.e. **Free Orbit** and **Constrained Orbit**. **Free Orbit** is used to rotate the design view freely and **Constrained Orbit** is used to rotate the view in constrained motion relative to current origin point. The **Constrained Orbit** tool is displayed on clicking down arrow next to **Free Orbit** tool. After selecting this tool, click at desired location on model and drag the cursor to rotate model view. You can do the same function by using **SHIFT + Middle Mouse Button** dragging.

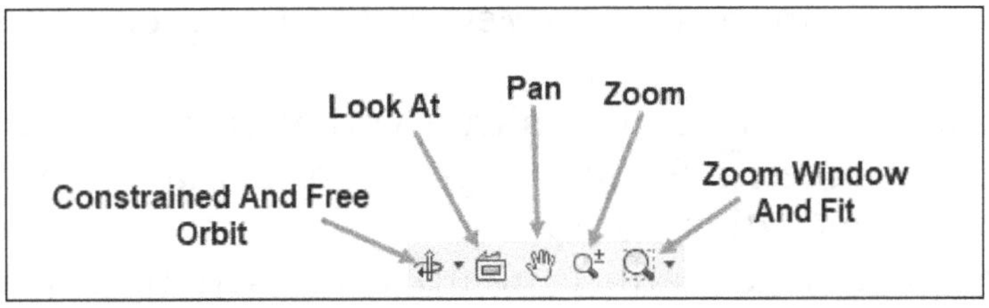

Figure-121. Navigation Bar

- **Look At**- This tool is used to view selected face parallel to screen. To use this tool, select desired face of model, and then click on the **Look At** tool from **Navigation Bar**.

- **Pan**- It is used to move the design parallel to the screen. You can do the same function by middle mouse button drag.

- **Zoom**- It is used to increase or decrease the magnification of the current view. After selecting this tool, click on the model, hold, and drag mouse upward/downward to zoom in/out. You can do the same function by rolling the mouse wheel up/down.

- **Zoom Window** and **Fit** - **Zoom Window** tools are used for magnification of selected area. **Fit** tool is used to position the entire design on the screen. You can do the same function as **Fit** tool does by pressing **F6** from keyboard.

DISPLAY BAR

The tools of **Display Bar** are used to visualize the design in different viewports; refer to Figure-122.

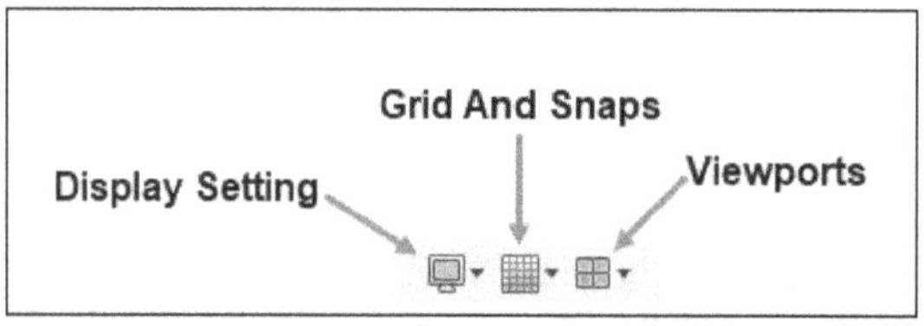

Figure-122. Display Bar

Display Settings

The options in the **Display Settings** flyout are used to enable or disable various commands related to **Visual Style**, **Visibility of objects**, **Camera settings**, and so on; refer to Figure-123.

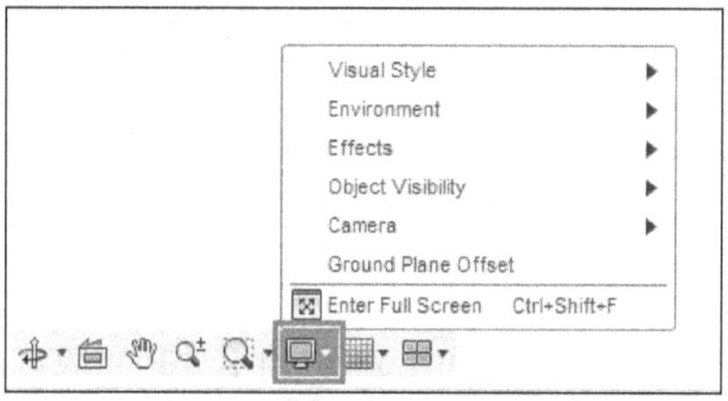

Figure-123. Display Settings flyout

- Select desired visual style of 3D model from the **Visual Style** cascading menu. Various styles available are Shaded, Shaded with Hidden Edges, Shaded with Visible Edges only, Wireframe, Wireframe with Hidden Edges, Wireframe with Visible Edges only. (You can open a sample file of 3D model and check the effects of different visual styles.)
- Select desired option from the **Environment** cascading menu to define color scheme of the canvas.
- Select desired check boxes for effects that you want to add in display style from the **Effects** cascading menu. Similarly, you can display or hide objects from the **Object Visibility** cascading menu.
- The options in **Camera** cascading menu are used to change the display to Orthographic, Perspective, or Perspective with Ortho Faces.

- Click on the **Ground Plane Offset** tool from the **Display Settings** flyout. The **GROUND PLANE OFFSET** dialog box will be displayed; refer to Figure-124. Clear the **Adaptive** check box and set desired offset value if you want to change the location of ground plane. Note that position of ground plane is generally changed for rendering which will be discussed later.

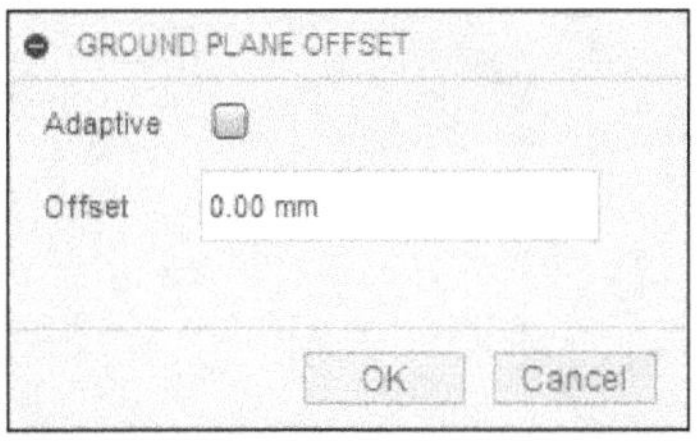

Figure-124. GROUND PLANE OFFSET dialog box

- If you want to run Autodesk Fusion in full screen then press **CTRL+SHIFT+F** from keyboard.

Grids and Snaps

- The **Grid and Snaps** flyout is used to activate or deactivate various options like **Layout Grid**, **Layout Grid Lock**, **Snap to Grid**, and so on. You can also define the size of grid and snapping increments by using **Grid Settings** and **Set Increments** tools in this flyout.

Viewports

- The options in **Viewports** flyout are used to switch between four viewports and single viewport in the Fusion screen. Click on the **Multiple Views** option from the **Viewports** flyout to display the current model in different views in four viewports. You can click in each of the viewport and reorient the model. If you want to set these views to synchronous again then select the **Synchronize Views** check box from **Viewports** flyout. If you want to move back to single viewport then select the **Single View** tool in **Viewports** flyout. By pressing **SHIFT+!** keys, you can toggle between single viewport and multiple viewports modes.

ViewCube

The **ViewCube** tool is used to rotate the view of model to access different faces of model. Click at desired location on model and drag the **ViewCube** to perform a free orbit. There are six faces in **ViewCube**; **Top**, **Bottom**, **Front**, **Back**, **Right**, and **Left** to access different orientations of model. To access the standard orthographic and isometric views, click on the faces and corners of the cube; refer to Figure-125. Right-click on the **ViewCube** to access options related to perspective mode and other view modes.

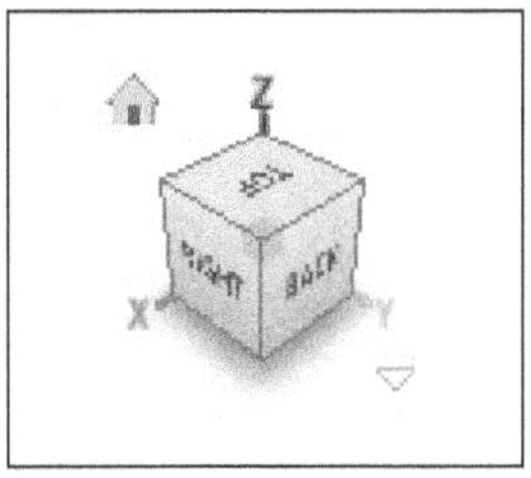

Figure-125. ViewCube

Mouse Functions

You can use the mouse shortcuts to zoom in/out, pan the view, and orbit the view; refer to Figure-126.

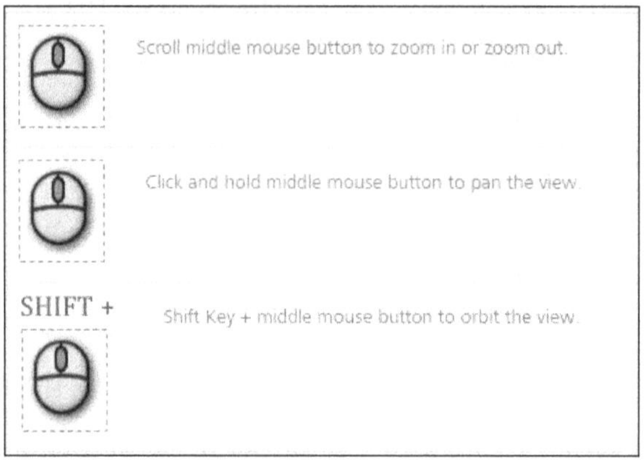

Figure-126. Mouse shourtcut keys

- Scroll the **Middle Mouse Button** downward/upward to zoom in or zoom out, respectively. Note that this function can be reversed by using options in **Preferences** dialog box.
- Click and hold the **Middle Mouse Button** to pan the view.
- Use the **Shift + Middle Mouse Button** to orbit the view.
- Press the left mouse button to select any object or tool.
- Press right mouse button (right-click) to access shortcut menus in the software.

Timeline

The **Timeline** bar is very useful for saving time while editing. It records the design feature in chronological order; refer to Figure-127. Note that the **Capture Design History (Parametric Modeling)** option must be active in the **Design** node of **Preferences** dialog box to access **Timeline** bar.

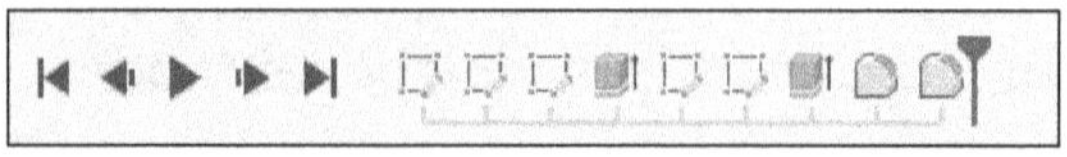

Figure-127. Timeline

If you want to edit any feature of model then double-click on the respective feature from **Timeline** bar. The respective dialog box/interface element will be displayed. Make desired changes and apply the parameters. The final design will be generated automatically with the applied changes; refer to Figure-128.

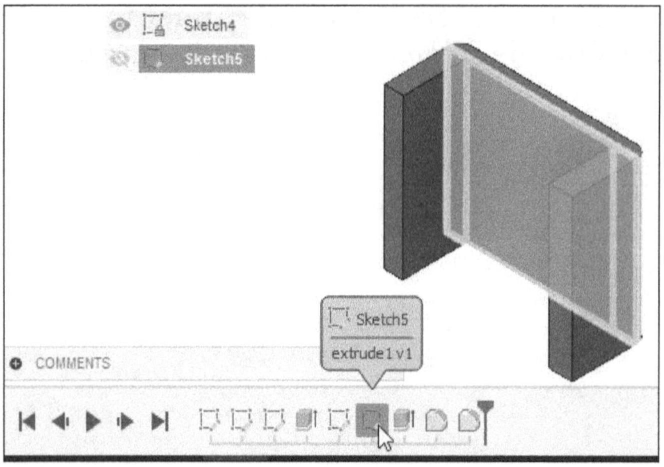

Figure-128. Editing model from timeline

CUSTOMIZING TOOLBAR AND MARKING MENU

In Autodesk Fusion, you can add or remove any tool in the displaying panels of **Toolbar**. You can also add or remove tool from right-click marking menu. These operations are discussed next.

Adding Tools to Panel

- Click on the **Three dot** button next to tool to be added in the panel from the drop-down of **Toolbar**. The shortcut menu to customize toolbar will be displayed; refer to Figure-129.

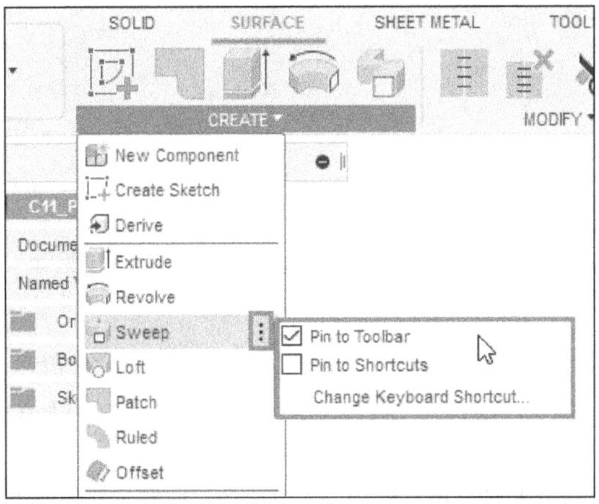

Figure-129. Shortcut menu for tool customization

- Select the **Pin to Toolbar** check box from the shortcut menu. The tool will be added in the panel.

Assigning Shortcut Key

- Click on the **Change Keyboard Shortcut** option from the shortcut menu as shown in Figure-129. The **Change Keyboard Shortcut** dialog box will be displayed; refer to Figure-130.

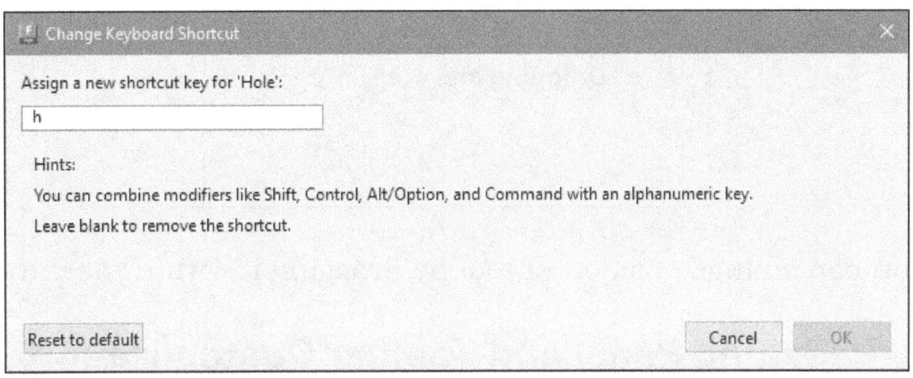

Figure-130. Change Keyboard Shortcut dialog box

- Use desired combine modifier like **SHIFT**, **CTRL**, or **ALT** and then press desired alphanumeric key to create a shortcut button.
- If you want to remove shortcut key then use **Backspace** to delete shortcut key from edit box. Click on the **OK** button from the dialog box to apply the settings.

Adding or Removing tool from Shortcut menu/Marking menu

- Select the **Pin to Shortcuts** check box from the shortcut menu for tool that you want to add in right-click shortcut menu/marking menu; refer to Figure-131.

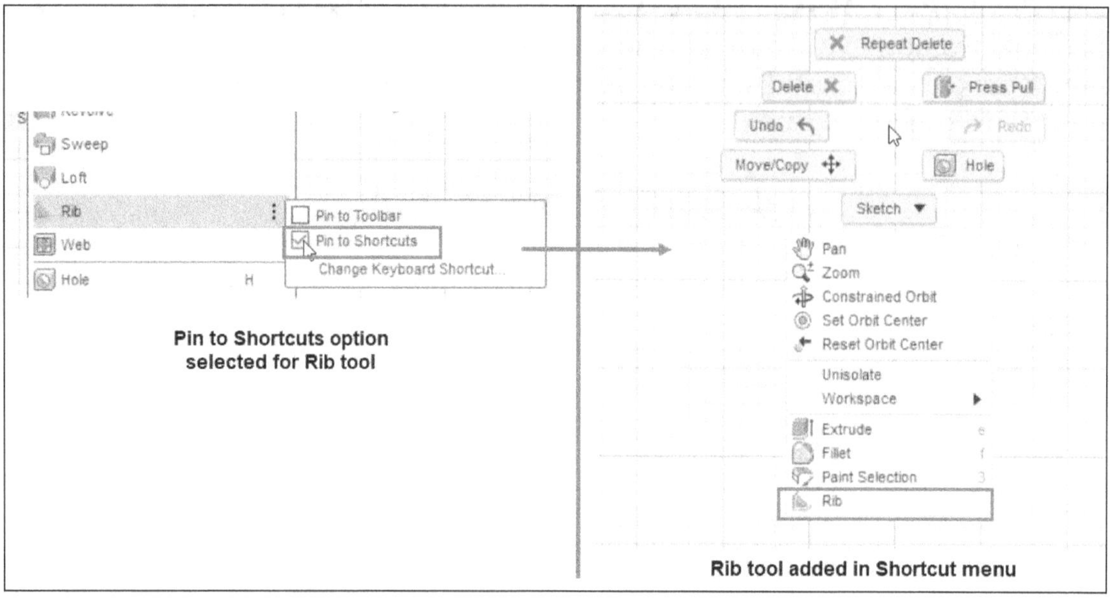

Figure-131. Adding tool to shortcut menu

- Clear the **Pin to Shortcuts** check box from the shortcut menu for tool that you want to remove from right-click shortcut menu/marking menu.

Note that the shortcut menu is workspace specific so what you find in shortcut menu for **DESIGN** workspace will be different from **MANUFACTURE** workspace, and so on.

Removing Tool from Panel in Toolbar

To remove a tool from panel in **Toolbar**, select the tool and drag it to canvas; refer to Figure-132.

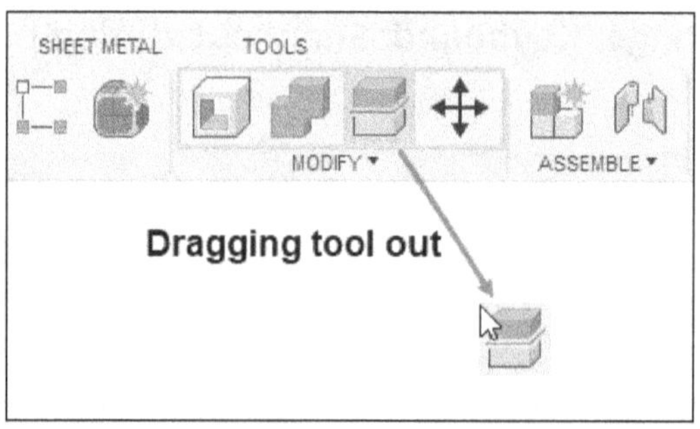

Figure-132. Removing tool from panel

Similarly, you can change position of tool by dragging it within the panel.

Resetting Panel and Toolbar Customization

Right-click on any of the tool in **Toolbar**. A shortcut menu will be displayed as shown in Figure-133.

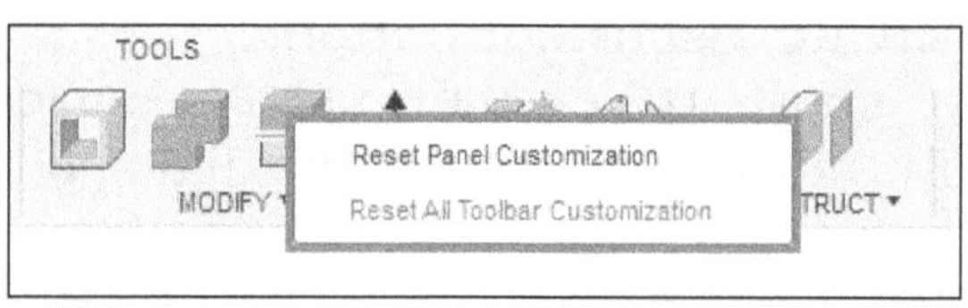

Figure-133. Shortcut menu for resetting toolbar

Click on the **Reset Panel Customization** option to reset current panel to original state. Note that this option will be available only when you have added or removed a tool from the panel.

Click on the **Reset All Toolbar Customization** option from the shortcut menu if you want to reset the complete toolbar including all the panels to its original state.

SELF ASSESSMENT

Q1. .... is used to manage the Fusion project.

Q2. The..............button is used for producing CNC codes.

Q3. Which of the following workspace is not available in Autodesk Fusion application?

a. Patch Workspace
b. Model Workspace
c. Assemble Workspace
d. Drawing Workspace

Q4. Discuss the use of **Save** tool with example.

Q5. Discuss the process of exporting a project in computer with example.

Q6. Discuss the use of **3D Print** tool with example.

Q7. Which tool is used to generate **Toolpaths** for model?

Q8. How to reset the default layout?

Q9. Explain the process of creating **Script** with example.

Q10. Mark the following statements as True or False:

a. Autodesk Fusion software can be used to perform CAD operations.
b. Autodesk Fusion software can be used to perform CAM operations.
c. Autodesk Fusion software can be used to perform CAE operations.
d. Autodesk Fusion software can be used to perform PLM operations.
e. Autodesk Fusion software can be used to perform direct 3D printing on 3D Printer.

Q11. Which of the following tool is used to create a new part model in Autodesk Fusion?

a. New Design
b. New Drawing->From Animation
c. New Drawing->From Design
d. New Drawing->New Drawing Template

Q12. Which of the following workspace is not available in educational version of Autodesk Fusion?

a. Animation
b. Manufacturing
c. Generative Design
d. Simulation

Q13. Which of the following tool is used to save the file in local drive in Autodesk Fusion?

a. Save
b. Save As
c. Export
d. Upload

Q14. STL format is used as standard for 3D printing which abbreviates Standard Triangle Language. (T/F)

Q15. Which parameter of an STL file can decrease the angular distance between two edges of triangle as shown in next figure (from left to right)?

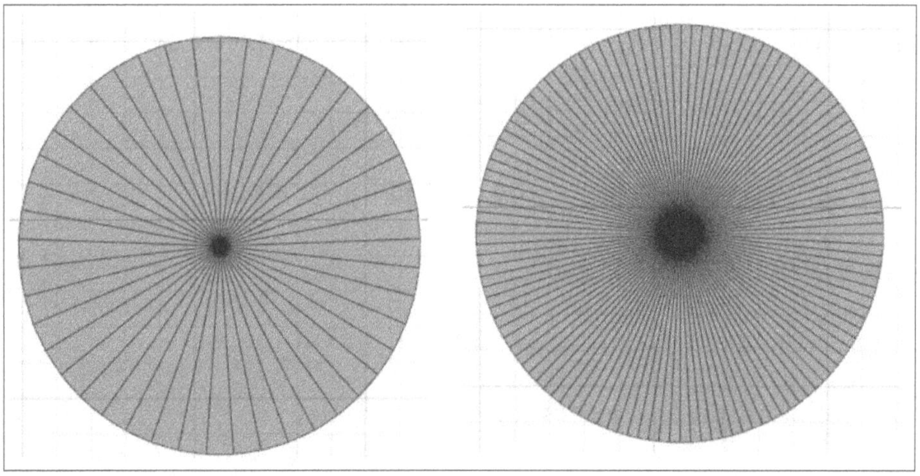

a. Surface Deviation
b. Normal Deviation
c. Aspect Ratio
d. Maximum Edge Length

Q16. What is used on the model itself to rotate or move it for orientation?
A. Grid Tool
B. Bounding Box
C. Manipulator
D. Axis Marker

Q17. What should you drag to rotate the model using Manipulators?
A. Square handle
B. Circle handle
C. Arrow handle
D. Cube handle

Q18. When are Manipulators displayed on the model?
A. When the model is printed
B. When the model is selected
C. When the software starts
D. When zooming

Q19. From which menu can you select the Show Manipulators option?
A. Edit Menu
B. Insert Menu
C. View Menu
D. File Menu

Q20. What is the purpose of the spinners in the ORIENT AXES area?
A. To delete the model
B. To define orientation angles
C. To print the model
D. To export the file

Q21. What is a Bounding Box?
A. A printing tool
B. A support structure
C. An imaginary cuboid defining maximum length, width, and height of the model
D. A slicing tool

Q22. Which button restores the original orientation of the model?
A. Reset Selected
B. Apply
C. Done
D. Home

Q23. What are the two sides of the 3D printing machine bed called?
A. Left and Right
B. Top and Bottom
C. Front and Mixer Side
D. Upper and Lower

Q24. From which side is the 3D printed model extracted?
A. Mixer Side
B. Front Side
C. Bottom Side
D. Back Side

Q25. Where is the material cartridge of the 3D printer located?
A. Front Side
B. Left Side
C. Mixer Side
D. Bottom Side

Q26. Which keys are used for the Home View?
A. CTRL + H
B. CTRL + F
C. F
D. ALT + F

Q27. Which key combination is used for Up View?
A. CTRL + Up Key
B. SHIFT + Up Key
C. ALT + Up Key
D. CTRL + F

Q28. What is the shortcut key for Pan?
A. CTRL + Drag
B. SHIFT + Right-click drag
C. ALT + Drag
D. Left-click drag

Q29. How can you zoom in the view?
A. Press – or scroll down
B. Press + or scroll up
C. Press F
D. Press CTRL

Q30. Which handle is used to scale the model using Manipulators?
A. Rotate Handle
B. Move Handle
C. Size Handle
D. Axis Handle

Q31. What does the Reset button in the Size toolbox do?
A. Deletes the model
B. Reverts to the original scale
C. Changes the printer
D. Exports the file

Q32. Which option displays unsupported areas of a model during print validation?
A. Cups
B. Minima
C. Auto Release
D. Layout

Q33. Which validation option shows areas that can trap air during printing?
A. Minima
B. Cups
C. Layout
D. Reset

Q34. Which tool is used to add supports to a 3D printing object?
A. Supports Tool
B. Layout Tool
C. Texture Tool
D. Label Tool

Q35. Which key can be pressed to open the Supports toolbox?
A. S
B. A
C. C
D. L

Q36. What does the Auto-Generate Selected button do?
A. Prints the model
B. Automatically generates positions of support elements
C. Deletes supports
D. Scales the model

Q37. What does Density represent in support settings?
A. Length of model
B. Thickness of support base
C. Color of supports
D. Speed of printing

Q38. What does Touch Point Size represent?
A. Thickness where support touches the model
B. Model height
C. Printer speed
D. Model color

Q39. Which tool is used to arrange multiple copies of a model on the bed?
A. Supports Tool
B. Layout Tool
C. Texture Tool
D. Label Tool

Q40. Which button arranges model copies to fit maximum number on the bed?
A. Create
B. Layout All
C. Reset
D. Done

Q41. Which tool in the User Account drop-down is used to configure units, material libraries, and display options?
A. Preferences
B. My Profile
C. Extensions
D. Help

Q42. Where can you set the language, graphics settings, and mouse functioning in Preferences?
A. Design node
B. General node
C. Assemblies node
D. API node

Q43. Which option allows you to select the visual appearance of Autodesk Fusion interface?
A. Theme drop-down
B. Visual style
C. Environment
D. Display settings

Q44. The Graphics driver drop-down in Preferences is used to:
A. Change model orientation
B. Select the graphics driver used by Autodesk Fusion
C. Change sketch units
D. Set animation speed

Q45. What is the maximum number of days allowed for Offline cache time period in Autodesk Fusion?
A. 180 days
B. 365 days
C. 360 days
D. 90 days

Q46. What is the minimum number of days allowed for Offline cache time period?
A. 1 day
B. 7 days
C. 10 days
D. 15 days

Q47. Which option automatically saves a newer version of a file when closing Autodesk Fusion?
A. Automatic save on close
B. Automatic recovery backup
C. Save on shutdown
D. Quick save

Q48. In most CAD software, which axis direction is the default modeling orientation?
A. X up
B. Y up
C. Z up
D. X down

Q49. Which option allows repeating the previously used command by pressing the spacebar?
A. Repeat last command
B. Spacebar repeats last command
C. Command repeat option
D. Auto repeat command

Q50. Which two orbit types are available in Autodesk Fusion?
A. Static Orbit and Dynamic Orbit
B. Constrained Orbit and Free Orbit
C. Smart Orbit and Manual Orbit
D. Linear Orbit and Circular Orbit

Q51. In Preferences, the API option is used to define:
A. Graphics settings
B. Model appearance
C. Default location and language of scripts/Add-Ins
D. Default sketch units

Q52. Which modeling mode keeps the history of every operation performed on the model?
A. Direct Modeling
B. Parametric Modeling
C. Free Modeling
D. Static Modeling

Q53. Which modeling mode does NOT save operation details and helps reduce file size?
A. Parametric Modeling
B. Direct Modeling
C. Feature Modeling
D. Constraint Modeling

Q54. Which option automatically projects edges when they are used as references for dimensions or constraints?
A. Auto project edges on reference
B. Auto look at sketch
C. Auto hide sketch
D. Auto dimension

Q55. Which option automatically hides the sketch after it has been used to create a feature?
A. Auto hide sketch on feature creation
B. Hide sketch automatically
C. Sketch visibility option
D. Hide sketch after edit

Q56. Which option enables tools like Arrange, Remove Features, Remove Faces, and Replace with Primitives?
A. Enable Modify tools
B. Enable Arrange and Simplify tools
C. Enable Feature tools
D. Enable Geometry tools

Q57. Which option in Assemblies allows only the currently active component to be visible?
A. Component visibility
B. Active Component Visibility
C. Current Component Mode
D. Component Isolation

Q58. Which option shows a small animation preview of how a joint will work?
A. Animate joint preview
B. Joint simulation
C. Joint motion preview
D. Dynamic joint

Q59. Which option grounds the first component to its parent component automatically?
A. First component grounded to parent
B. Ground parent component
C. Fix first component
D. Lock component

Q60. Which tool allows you to manage project data stored on cloud through a web browser?
A. Autodesk Account
B. My Profile
C. Data Panel
D. Cloud Manager

Q61. Which button toggles between offline and online mode in Autodesk Fusion?
A. Mode switch button
B. Work Offline/Online button
C. Cloud mode button
D. Network toggle

Q62. Which tool displays available extensions to add functionality to Autodesk Fusion?
A. Extensions
B. Plugins
C. Add-Ins
D. Tools Manager

Q63. Which Help menu feature allows users to type keywords to find solutions?
A. Help Finder
B. Search Help Box
C. Help Query
D. Smart Help

Q64. Which Help menu option displays tutorials and documentation in a web browser?
A. Learning and Documentation
B. Help Tutorials
C. Training Center
D. Learning Mode

Q65. Which tool helps beginners understand Autodesk Fusion terminology and basic settings?
A. Beginner Mode
B. Quick Setup
C. Learning Mode
D. Setup Wizard

Q66. Which Autodesk Fusion tool provides AI-powered support and allows connecting with a support agent?
A. Help Assistant
B. Autodesk Assistant
C. Fusion AI Helper
D. Smart Support

Q67. Which section of the Data Panel displays files saved in the current project?
A. Files section
B. Data section
C. Project section
D. Cloud section

Q68. Which section of the Data Panel shows users who have access to the project files?
A. Team section
B. Members section
C. People section
D. Access section

Q69. Which interface element displays design steps in a tree-like structure on the left side of the screen?
A. Timeline
B. Browser
C. Data Panel
D. Toolbar

Q70. Which button in the Browser toggles the visibility of objects?
A. Eye button
B. Visibility toggle
C. View button
D. Object display button

Q71. Which keyboard key performs the same function as the Fit tool?
A. F5
B. F6
C. F7
D. F8

Chapter 2

Sketching

Topics Covered

The major topics covered in this chapter are:

- ***Introduction***
- ***Starting Sketch***
- ***Sketch Creation Tools***
- ***Sketch Editing Tools***
- ***Sketch Palette***
- ***Constraints***
- ***Sketching Practical and Practice***

INTRODUCTION

In Engineering, sketches are based on dimensions of real world objects. These sketches work as building blocks for various 3D operations. In this chapter, we will be working with sketch entities like; line, circle, arc, polygon, ellipse, and so on to create base feature for various 3D operations. Note that the sketching environment is the base of 3D Models so you should be proficient in sketching.

There is no separate workspace for sketching and tools to create sketches are available in **Design** workspace. So, we will be working in **Design** workspace in this chapter. We will learn about various tools of toolbar used in sketching and 3D Sketching.

STARTING SKETCH

- To start a new sketch, click on the **Create Sketch** tool from **CREATE** drop-down in **SOLID** tab of **Toolbar**; refer to Figure-1. The three primary planes will be displayed on canvas screen; refer to Figure-2.

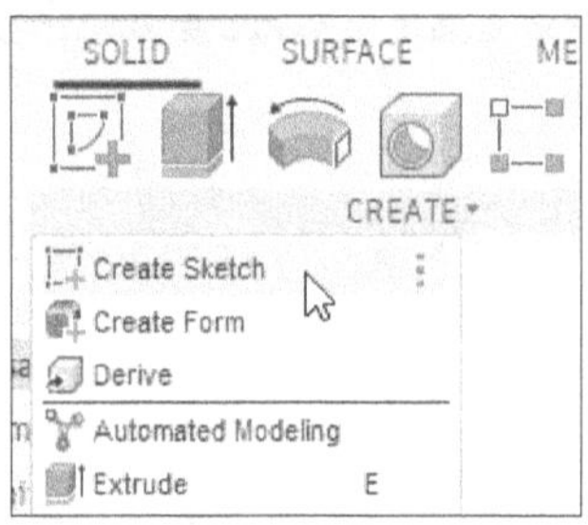

Figure-1. Create Sketch tool

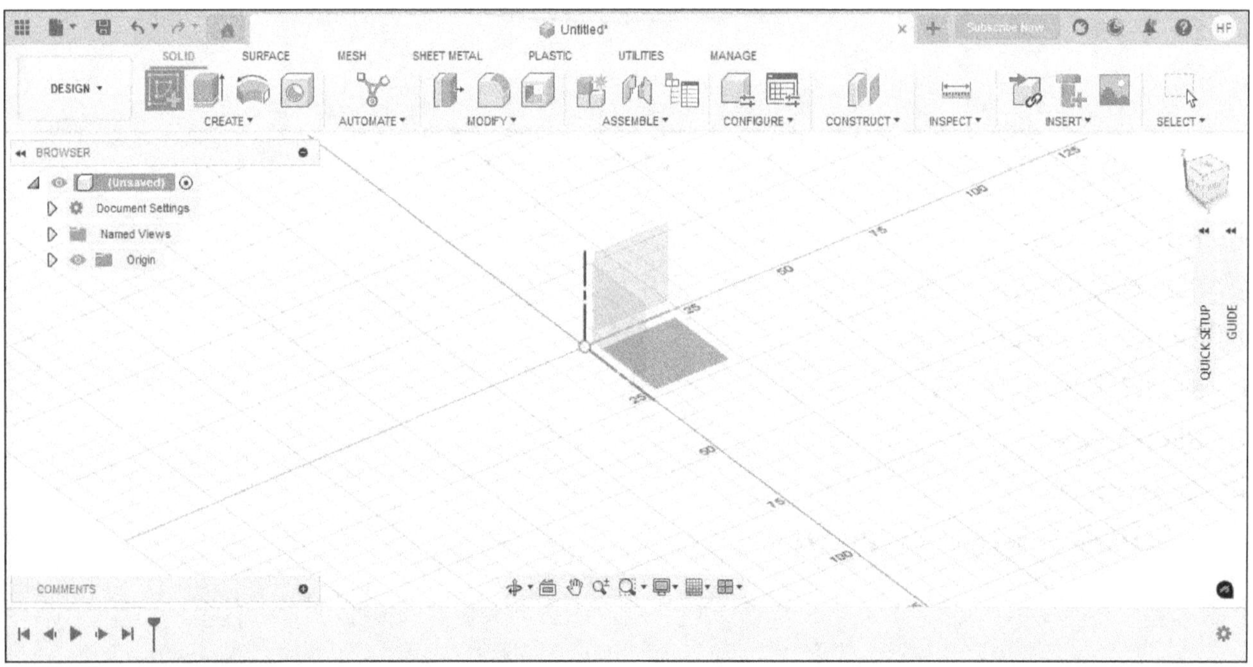

Figure-2. Select sketch plane

- Click on desired plane from the canvas screen. The selected plane will become parallel to the screen and act as current sketching plane. Also, the tools to create sketch will be displayed in **SKETCH** contextual tab in the **Toolbar**; refer to Figure-3. Now, we are ready to draw sketch on the selected plane.

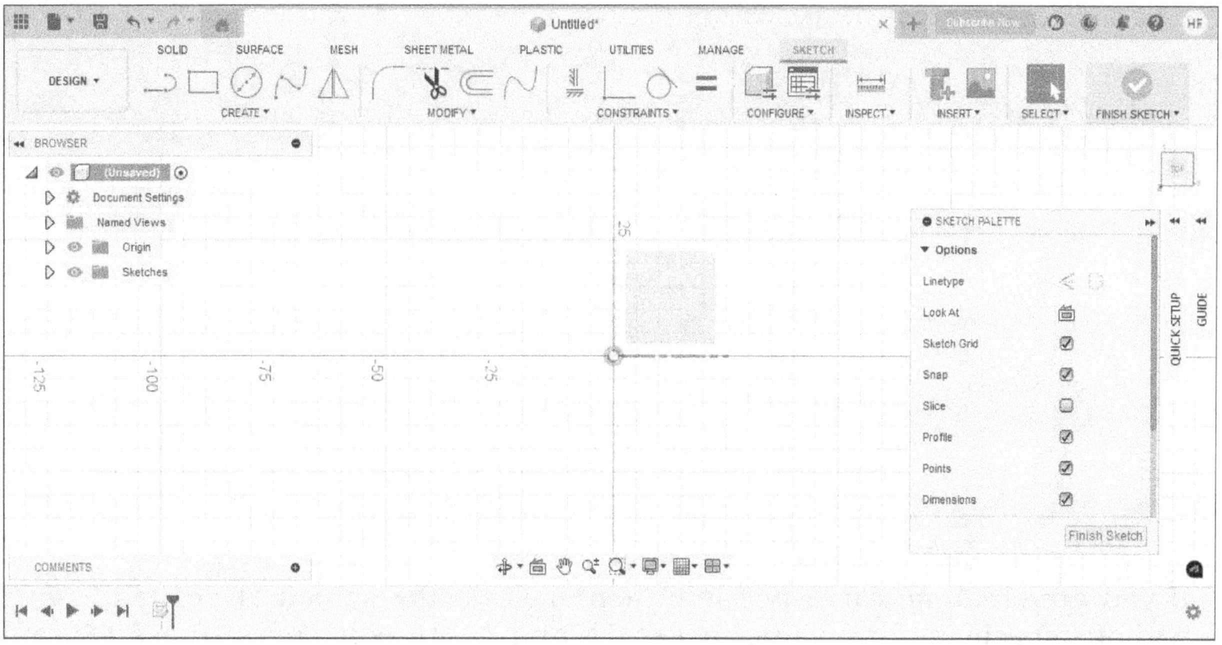

Figure-3. Sketching mode

First, we will start with the sketch creation tools and later, we will discuss the other tools.

SKETCH CREATION TOOLS

There are various tools in **CREATE** drop-down for creating sketch entities. These tools are discussed next.

Line

In Autodesk Fusion, the **Line** tool is used to create a line or arc. The procedure to use this tool is discussed next.

- Click on **Line** tool from **CREATE** drop-down in the **Toolbar**; refer to Figure-4. You can also press **L** key to select the **Line** tool. You will be asked to specify start point of the line.

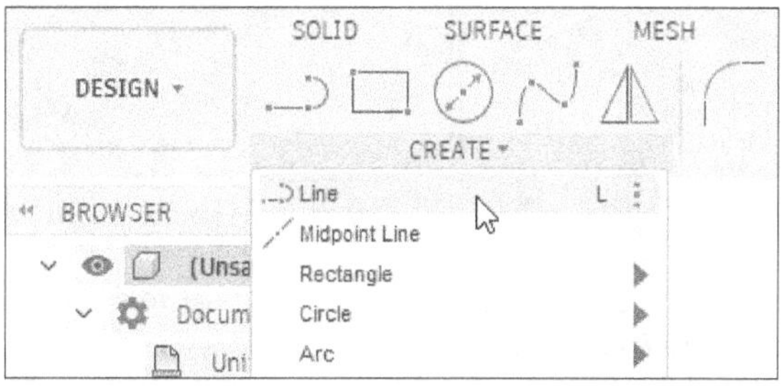

Figure-4. Line tool

- Click at desired location to specify start point and move the cursor away from selected point in desired direction in which you want to create the line. **Angle** and **Length** input boxes will be displayed with the preview of line.
- Specify desired value of length in the **Length** input box. Press **TAB** key to toggle to **Angle** input box; refer to Figure-5.

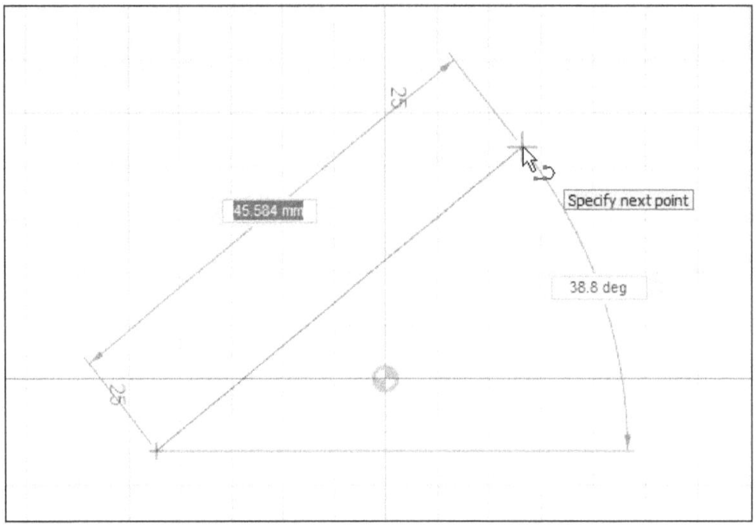

Figure-5. Creating the line

- If you are creating a freestyle line then click on the screen at desired location without specifying any value in **Length** and **Angle** edit boxes. Press **ESC** after specifying end points to exit the tool.
- To create a line for construction purpose, click on the **Construction** button from **SKETCH PALETTE** displayed at the right in the application window after activating **Line** tool; refer to Figure-6. (You will learn more about **SKETCH PALETTE** later in this chapter.) You can also right-click on the line after creating it and then click on **Normal/Construction** button from **Marking menu** to do the same; refer to Figure-7.

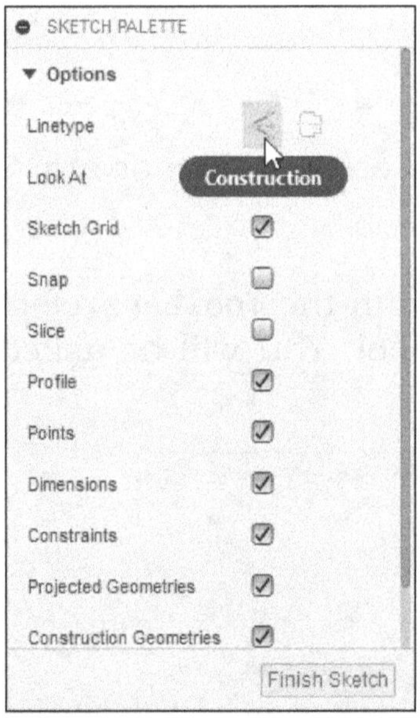

Figure-6. Construction button in SKETCH PALETTE

Figure-7. Marking menu

Marking menu

It is the radical display of most frequently used tool and tools related to selected entities. This menu also provides a quick access to the tools of the toolbar. This menu is the fastest way to activate the tool. To access this menu, right-click anywhere on the screen within the graphics window. To select any tool of this menu, move the cursor towards the tool and the tool will be highlighted. Click on it to activate the tool.

Creating Arc using Line Tool

You can create an arc using the **Line** tool which has one of its end point shared to another entity. In simple words, the starting point of arc created by **Line** tool will lie on end point of another line or arc. The procedure to create arc is given next.

- Click on the end point of a line or curve to define start point of arc, hold the **LMB** (Left - Mouse Button), and drag to the point where you want to specify the end point of arc; refer to Figure-8.

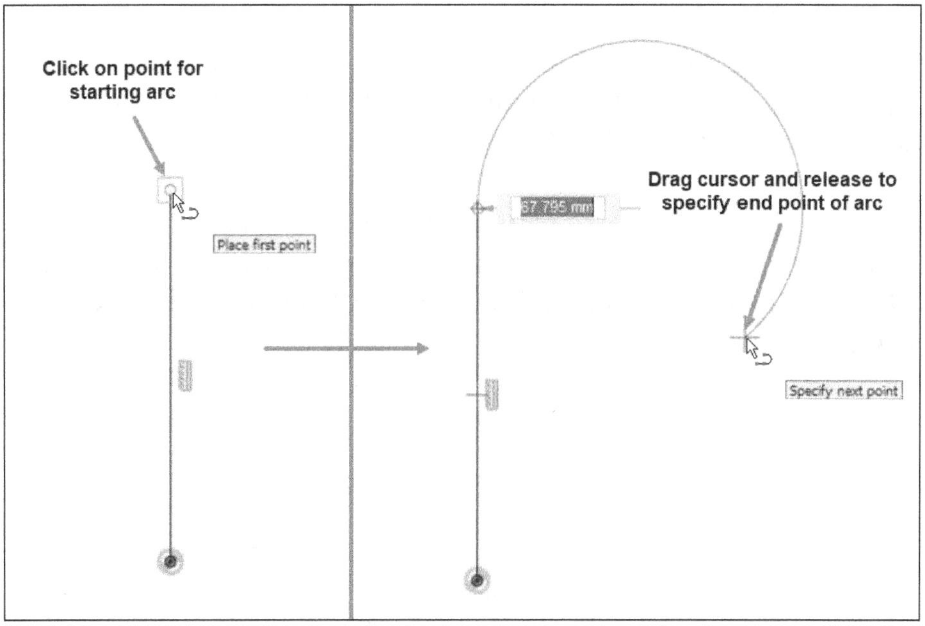

Figure-8. Creating line arc

Midpoint Line

The **Midpoint Line** tool is used to create a line symmetrically about its midpoint. The procedure to use this tool is discussed next.

- Click on the **Midpoint Line** tool from **CREATE** drop-down in the **Toolbar**; refer to Figure-9. You will be asked to specify midpoint of the line.

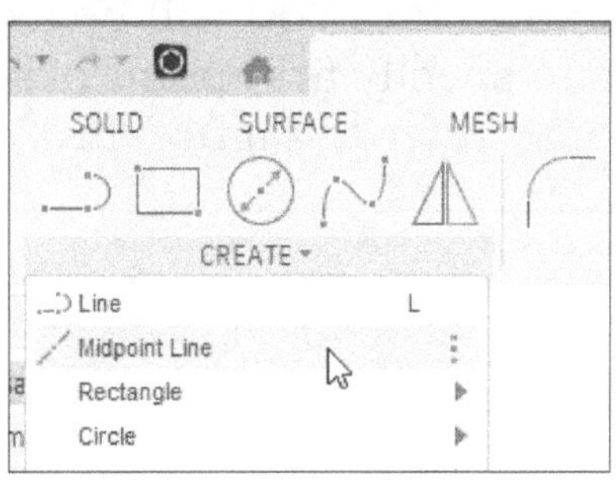

Figure-9. Midpoint Line tool

- Click at desired location to specify the midpoint of line and move the cursor away at desired direction to specify the endpoint of the line. **Angle** and **Length** input boxes will be displayed with the preview of line.
- Specify desired value of length in the **Length** input box. Press **TAB** key to toggle to **Angle** input box; refer to Figure-10.

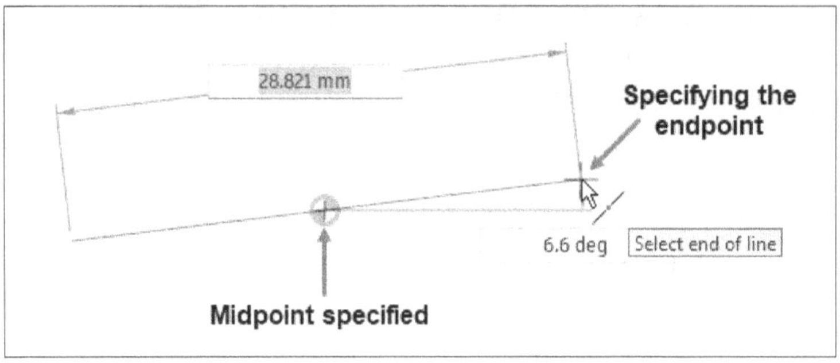

Figure-10. Creating the midpoint line

- If you are creating a freestyle line then click on the screen at desired location without specifying any value in **Length** and **Angle** edit boxes. Press **ESC** after specifying end point to exit the tool.

Rectangle

The tools in **Rectangle** cascading menu are used to create rectangles. There are three tools in **Rectangle** cascading menu; **2-Point Rectangle**, **3-Point Rectangle**, and **Center Rectangle**; refer to Figure-11.

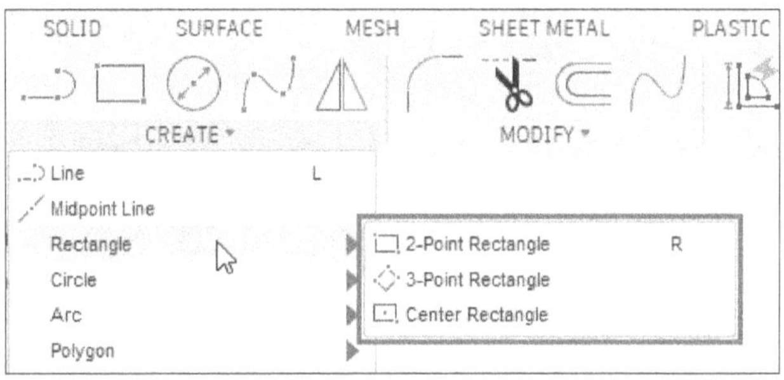

Figure-11. Rectangle cascading menu

You can also activate the **Rectangle** tool by pressing **R** key while in **Sketch** mode. The procedures to use these tools are discussed next.

2-Point Rectangle

- Click on the **2-Point Rectangle** tool of the **Rectangle** cascading menu from **CREATE** drop-down in **SKETCH** contextual tab. You will be asked to specify the first point.
- Click on the sketch canvas to specify first point of rectangle. You will be asked to specify the other corner point; refer to Figure-12.

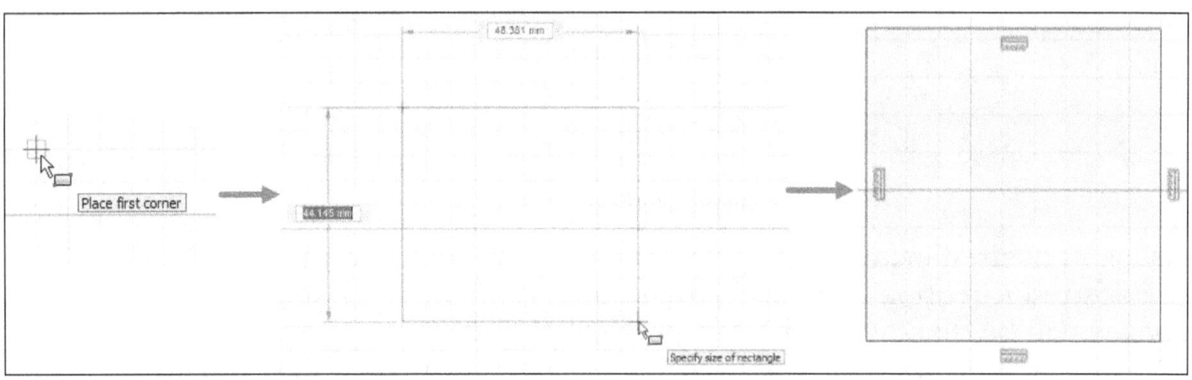

Figure-12. Creation of 2-point rectangle

- Specify the length and width of rectangle in the dynamic input boxes. To switch between the length dynamic input box and width dynamic input box, press **TAB** key.
- After specifying the parameters, press **ENTER** to create the rectangle. To exit the tool, press **ESC** key.
- If you want to create a freestyle rectangle then click on the screen to select the first corner point and other diagonal corner point of the rectangle on the sketch canvas.
- To add dimensions, right-click on the line of rectangle and click on **Sketch Dimension** tool in **Sketch** drop-down from the **Marking menu**. You can also activate the **Dimension** tool by pressing **d** from keyboard after selecting the line. You will learn more about dimensioning later in this chapter.

3-Point Rectangle

- Click on the **3-Point Rectangle** tool of **Rectangle** cascading menu from **CREATE** drop-down. You will be asked to specify location of first corner point of rectangle.
- Click at desired location to specify first corner point of the rectangle on the sketch canvas; refer to Figure-13.

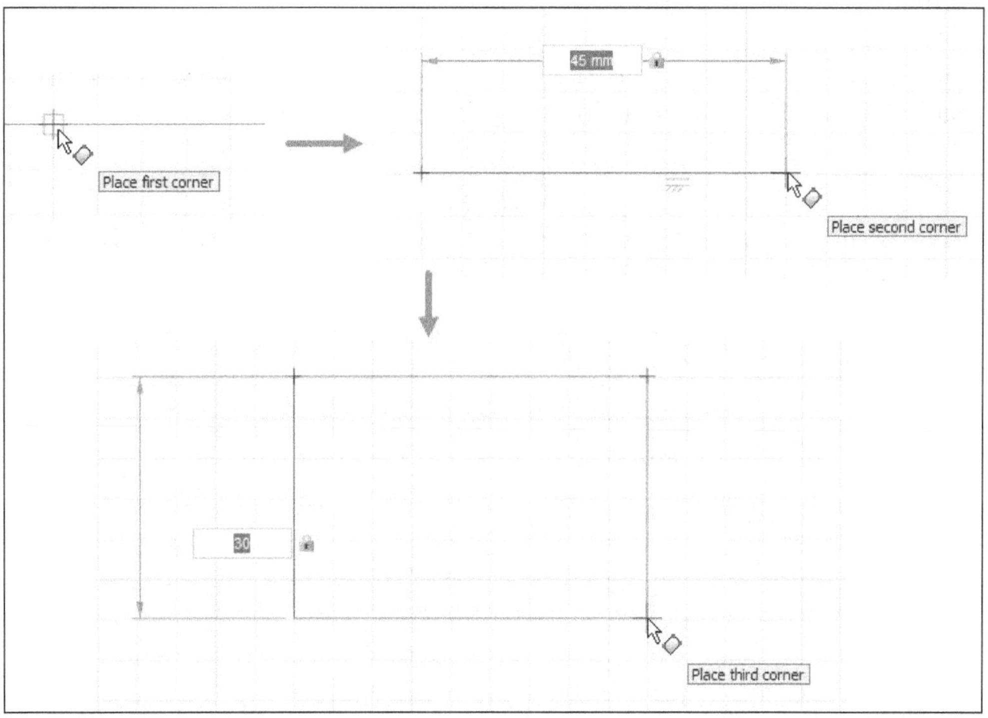

Figure-13. Creation of 3-Point Rectangle

- Next, click to specify the second corner point (end point of base line of rectangle) on the canvas or specify the dimension in dimension box.
- Next, click to specify the third point of the rectangle to define the length of rectangle and complete the rectangle creation.

Center Rectangle

- Click on the **Center Rectangle** tool of the **Rectangle** cascading menu from **CREATE** drop-down. You will be asked to specify center point of the rectangle.
- Click on the canvas to specify the center point of the rectangle; refer to Figure-14. You will be asked to specify corner point of rectangle.

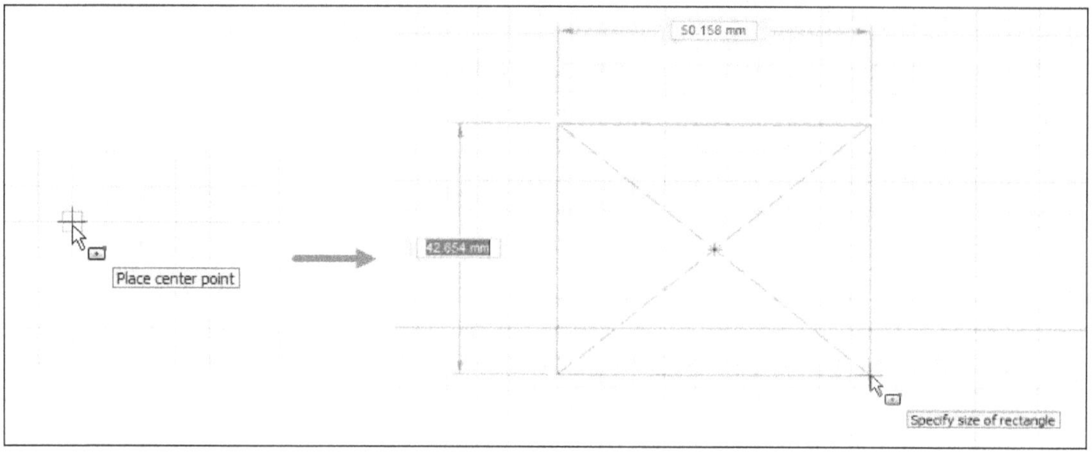

Figure-14. Creation of center rectangle

- Type the dimension for rectangle in the edit boxes and press **ENTER** to create the rectangle.
- If you want to create freestyle rectangle then click on the screen to select the center point and corner point of rectangle.

Note that you can switch between different types of rectangles from the **Rectangle** section of **SKETCH PALETTE** after activating the **Rectangle** tool.

Circle

There are five tools in **Circle** cascading menu to create circles; **Center Diameter Circle**, **2-Point Circle**, **3-Point Circle**, **2-Tangent Circle**, and **3-Tangent Circle**; refer to Figure-15.

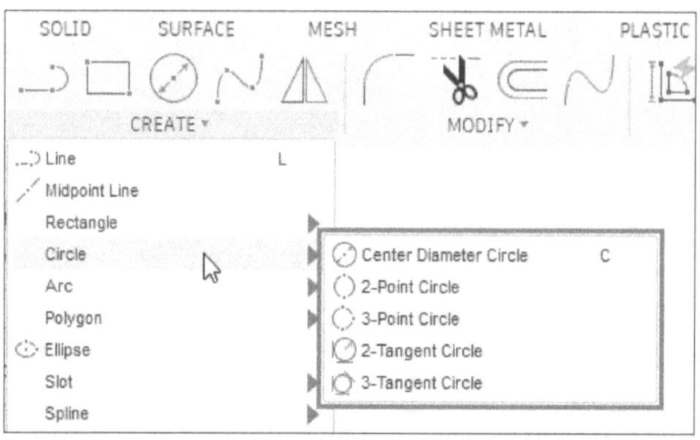

Figure-15. Circle cascading menu

The shortcut key to use the **Center Diameter Circle** tool is by pressing **C** key from keyboard. The tools to create circle are discussed next.

Center Diameter Circle

The **Center Diameter Circle** tool is used to create circle specifying center location and diameter value. The procedure to use this tool is given next.

- Click on the **Center Diameter Circle** tool from **Circle** cascading menu in the **CREATE** drop-down of **SKETCH** contextual tab. You will be asked to specify center point of circle.

- Click to specify the center point for the circle; refer to Figure-16. You will be asked to specify circumferential point of circle to define diameter.

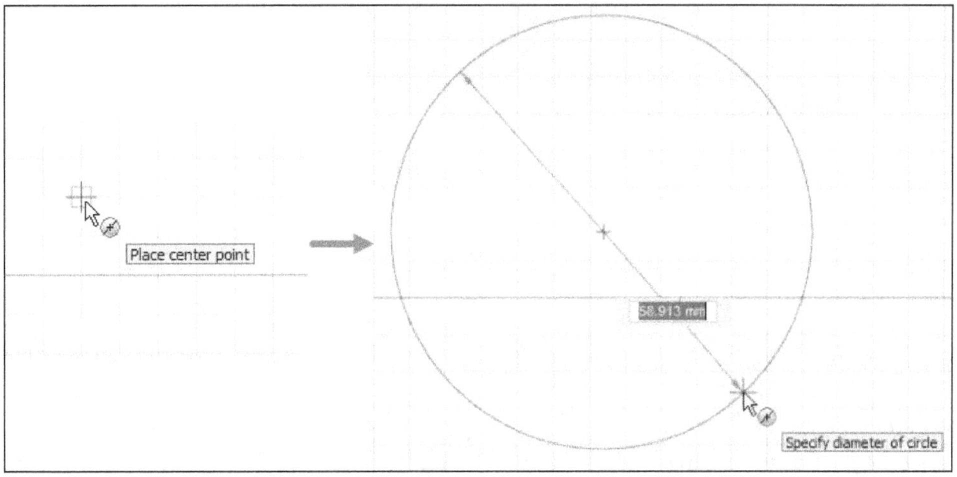

Figure-16. Creation of center diameter circle

- Click to specify the circumferential point or enter desired value of diameter in the dynamic input box.

2-Point Circle

The **2-Point Circle** tool is used to create circle by specifying two circumferential points. The procedure to use this tool is discussed next.

- Click on the **2-Point Circle** tool of **Circle** cascading menu from **CREATE** drop-down and specify the first point for circle; refer to Figure-17.

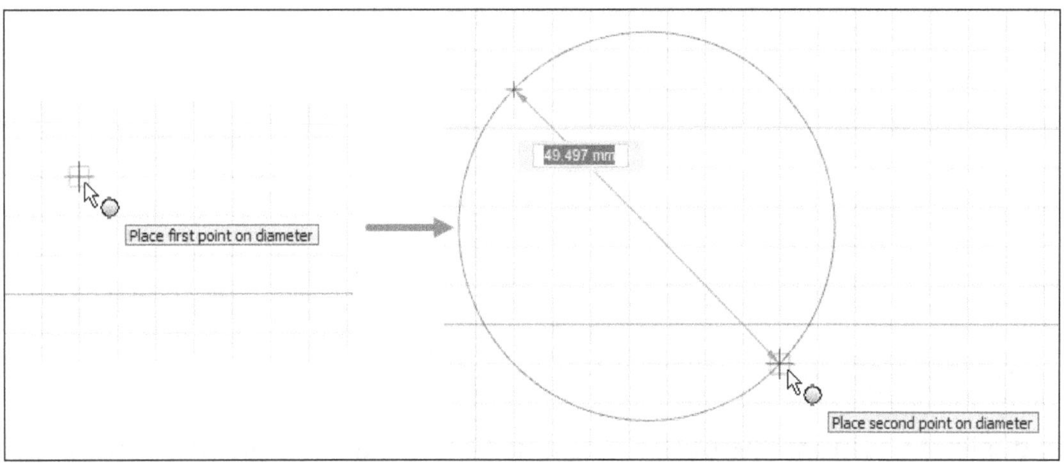

Figure-17. Creation of 2-point circle

- Specify the second point on the canvas screen or type the diameter dimension in the dynamic input box and press **ENTER** key.

3-Point Circle

The **3-Point Circle** tool is used to create circles using 3 circumferential points as references. The procedure to use this tool is discussed next.

- Click on **3-Point Circle** tool of **Circle** cascading menu from **CREATE** drop-down.
- Click on the screen to specify the first point, second point, and third point of circle; refer to Figure-18. Note that you can also select on other entities to define circumferential points for circle.

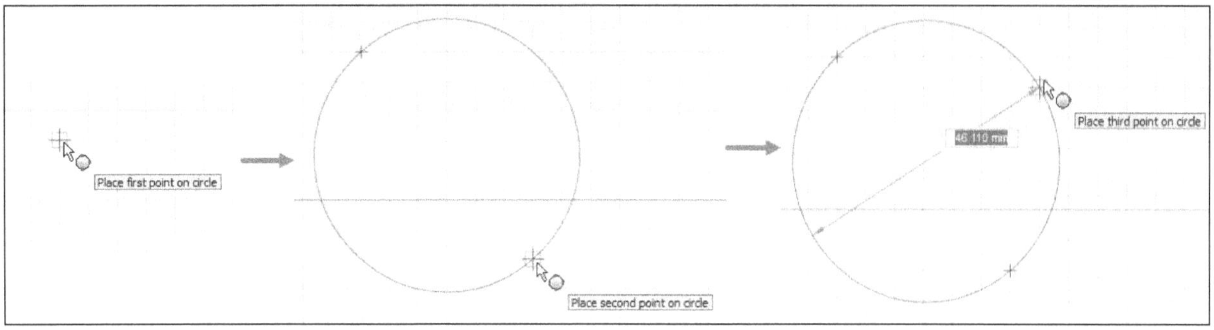

Figure-18. Creation of 3-point circle

- After specifying points, right-click on the screen and click **OK** button from **Marking menu** to complete the process. You can also press **ESC** key to exit the circle tool.
- If you want to add dimensions then right-click on the selected circle and click on the **Sketch Dimension** tool from **Marking menu**. You can also select **Sketch Dimension** tool from **SKETCH** drop-down.

2-Tangent Circle

The **2-Tangent Circle** tool is used to create a circle which is tangent to two selected lines. The procedure to use this tool is discussed next.

- Select **2-Tangent Circle** tool of **Circle** cascading menu from **CREATE** drop-down.
- Click at desired locations on lines that should be tangent to the circle; refer to Figure-19. Preview of circle will be displayed.

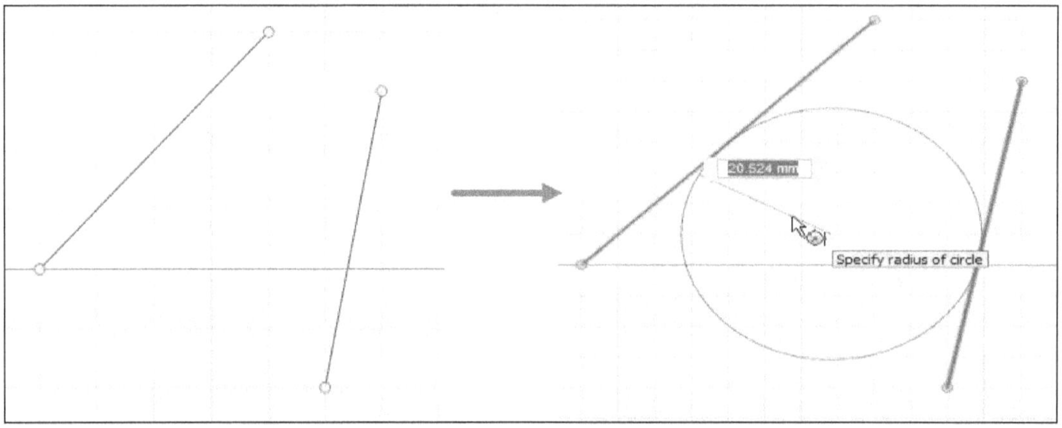

Figure-19. Creation of 2-tangent circle

- Type desired radius value of the circle in the dynamic input box and press **ENTER** to create a circle or click at desired location to define diameter of the circle.
- Press **ESC** to exit the tool.

3-Tangent Circle

The **3-Tangent Circle** tool is used to create a circle using three tangent lines. The procedure to use this tool is discussed next.

- Click on **3-Tangent Circle** tool of **Circle** cascading menu from **CREATE** drop-down.
- Select three lines to be tangent to the circle. You can also use window selection to select the lines; refer to Figure-20. The preview of circle will be displayed.
- Right-click on the screen and click **OK** button from **Marking menu** to create the circle. You can also press **ESC** key to exit the tool.

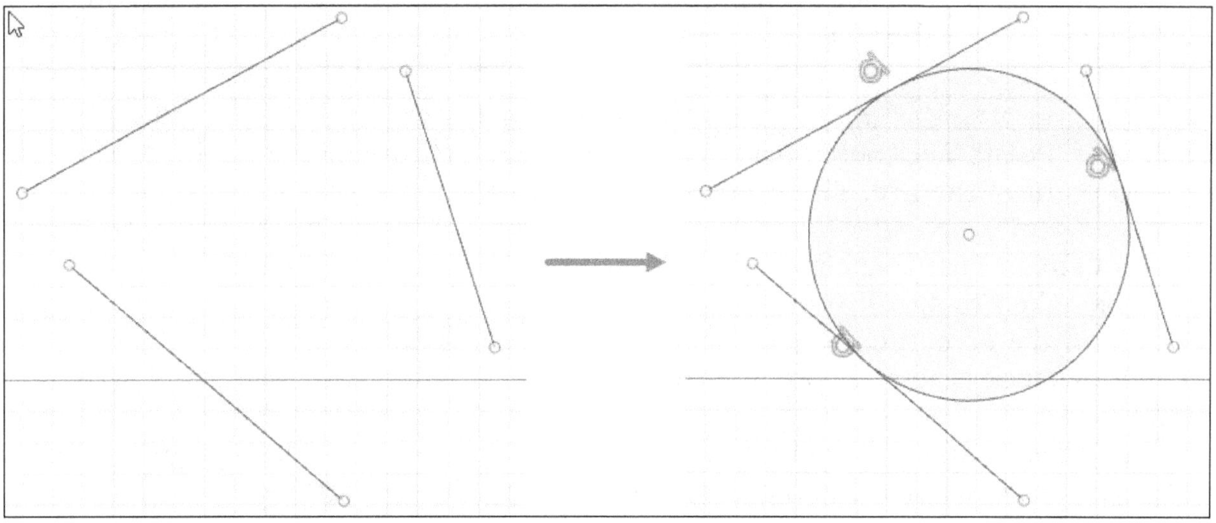

Figure-20. Creation of 3-tangent circle

Arc

The **Arc** tool is used to create arcs. There are three tools in the **Arc** cascading menu; **3-Point Arc**, **Center Point Arc**, and **Tangent Arc**; refer to Figure-21.

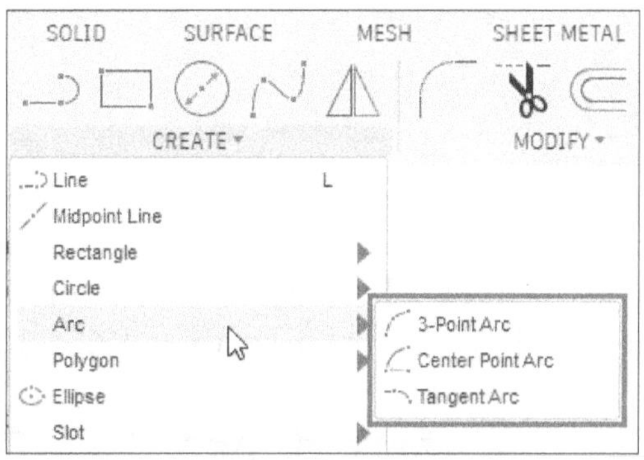

Figure-21. Arc cascading menu

The tools of **Arc** cascading menu are discussed next.

3-Point Arc

The **3-Point Arc** tool is used to create an arc using three points (start point, end point, and circumferential point). To use this tool, you need to specify two end points and one circumferential point of the arc. The procedure to use this tool is discussed next.

- Click on **3-Point Arc** tool of **Arc** cascading menu from **CREATE** drop-down. You will be asked to specify points for arc.
- Click on desired location to specify the start point of the arc; refer to Figure-22.

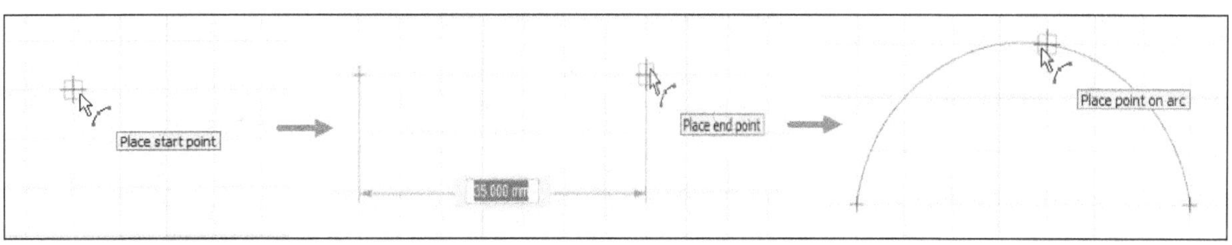

Figure-22. Creation of 3-point arc

- Click on the screen to specify the end point of the arc.

- Click at desired location to define the radius of arc. The arc will be created.
- Press **ESC** to exit the tool.

Center Point Arc

The **Center Point Arc** tool is used to create arc by defining center point, start point, and end point of the arc. The procedure is given next.

- Click **Center Point Arc** tool of **Arc** cascading menu from **CREATE** drop-down. You will be asked to specify center point of the arc.
- Click on the screen canvas to specify the center point of arc.
- Click to specify the start point of the arc or type desired value of radius in dynamic input box.
- Enter desired angle value in dynamic input box to define length of arc or click on the screen to specify the end point of the arc; refer to Figure-23.

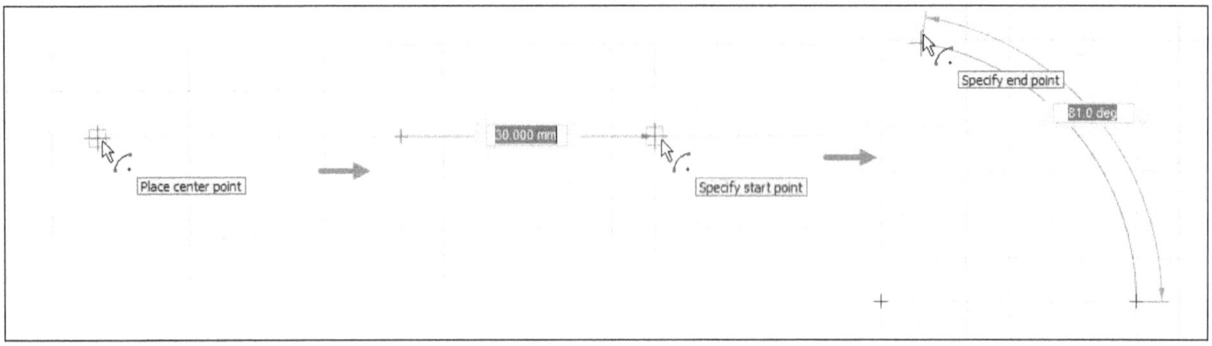

Figure-23. Creation of center point arc

- The arc will be displayed. Right-click on the screen and click **OK** button from **Marking menu** to exit the tool. You can also press **ESC** key to exit the tool.

Tangent Arc

The **Tangent Arc** tool is used to create arc tangent to selected entity.

- Click on the **Tangent Arc** tool of **Arc** cascading menu from **CREATE** drop-down.
- Click near the end point of an entity (line, arc, or curve) from screen to specify the start point of the arc; refer to Figure-24. A rubber-band arc will be attached to cursor starting from selected point.

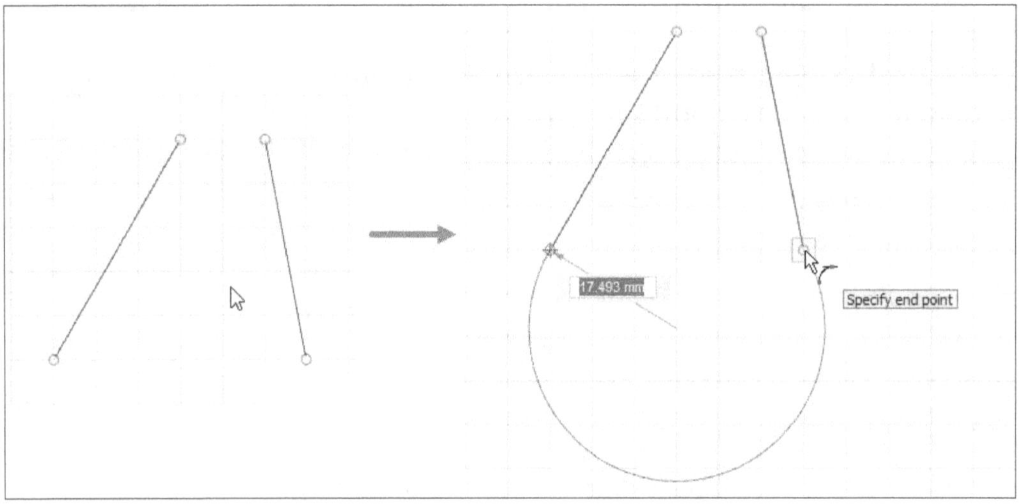

Figure-24. Creation of tangent arc

- Click at desired location to specify the end point of the arc.
- Right-click on the screen and click **OK** button from **Marking menu** to complete the process. You can also press **ESC** key to exit the arc tool.

What happens when you try to create an arc at corner location where two entities meet and selected point is common to both the entities; refer to Figure-25. Will the arc be created tangent to line 1 or line 2? What if the arc is being created tangent to line 1 but we want to create it tangent to line 2. In such conditions, after selecting end point, move the cursor in line with entity to be tangent for few millimeters and then specify the end point at desired location; refer to Figure-26.

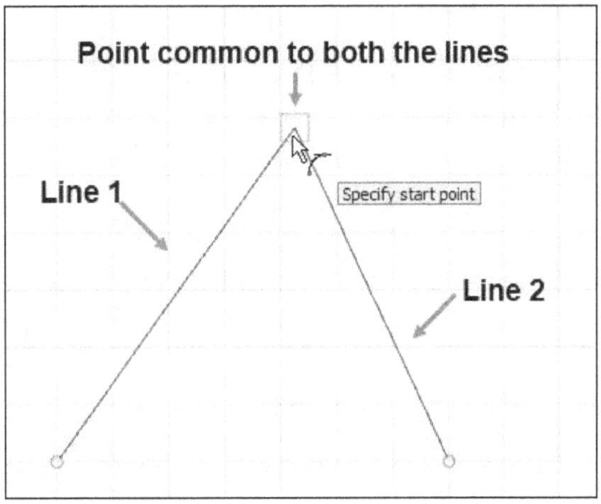

Figure-25. Tangent arc problem at corner point

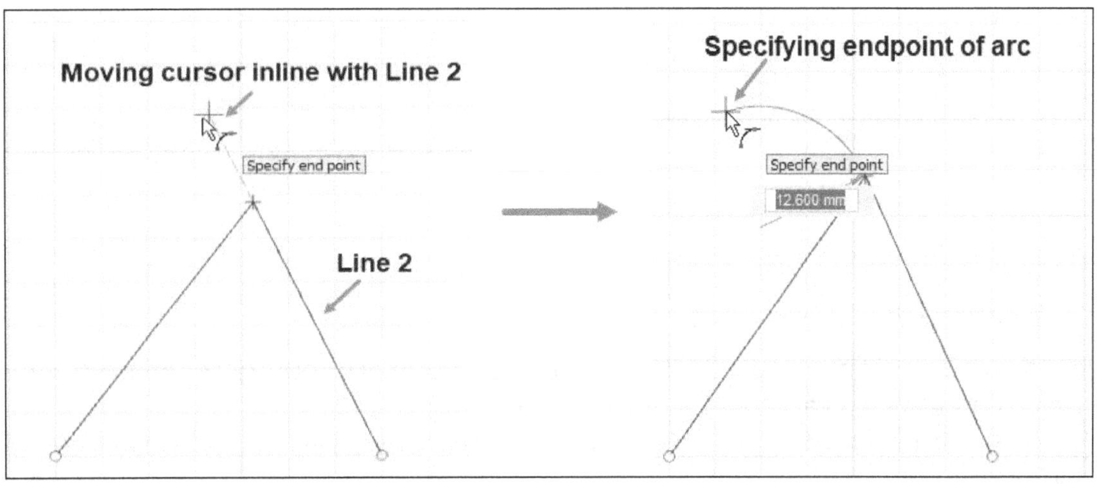

Figure-26. Creating arc tangent to line

Polygon

The **Polygon** tool is used to create polygon of desired number of sides. There are three tools to create polygon in **Polygon** cascading menu; **Circumscribed Polygon**, **Inscribed Polygon**, and **Edge Polygon**; refer to Figure-27. The tools to create the polygons are discussed next.

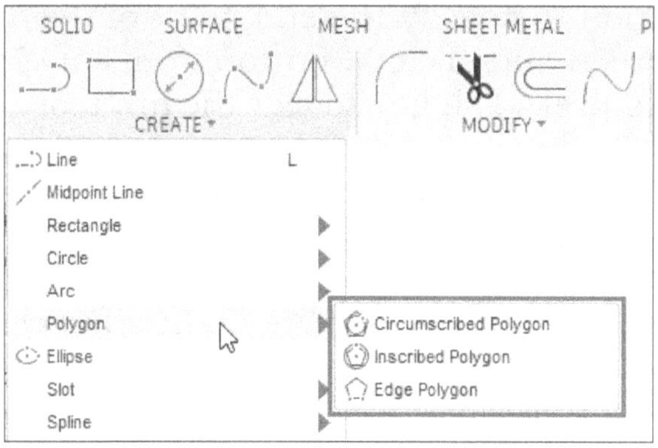

Figure-27. Polygon cascading menu

Circumscribed Polygon

Use the **Circumscribed Polygon** tool to create a polygon formed outside the reference circle. Note that midpoints of polygon lines will lie on the reference circle. The procedure to use this tool is discussed next.

- Click on the **Circumscribed Polygon** tool of **Polygon** cascading menu from **CREATE** drop-down; refer to Figure-28. You will be asked to specify center point of the reference circle.

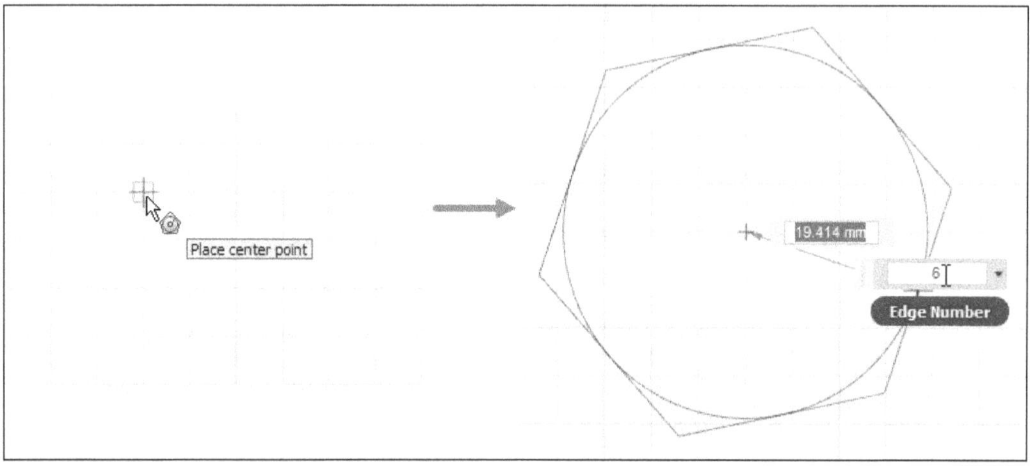

Figure-28. Creation of circumscribed polygon

- Click on the screen to specify the center point of the polygon; refer to . You will be asked to specify radius of reference circle.
- Type the value of radius in the edit box and press **TAB** to activate **Edge Number** edit box.
- Specify desired number of edges of the polygon in **Edge Number** edit box.
- After specifying the parameters, press **ENTER** to create polygon.

Inscribed Polygon

The **Inscribed Polygon** tool is used to create a polygon formed inside the reference circle. The procedure to use this tool is discussed next.

- Click on **Inscribed Polygon** of **Polygon** cascading menu from **CREATE** drop-down. You will be asked to specify center point of reference circle.
- Click on the screen to specify the center point of the circle; refer to Figure-29.

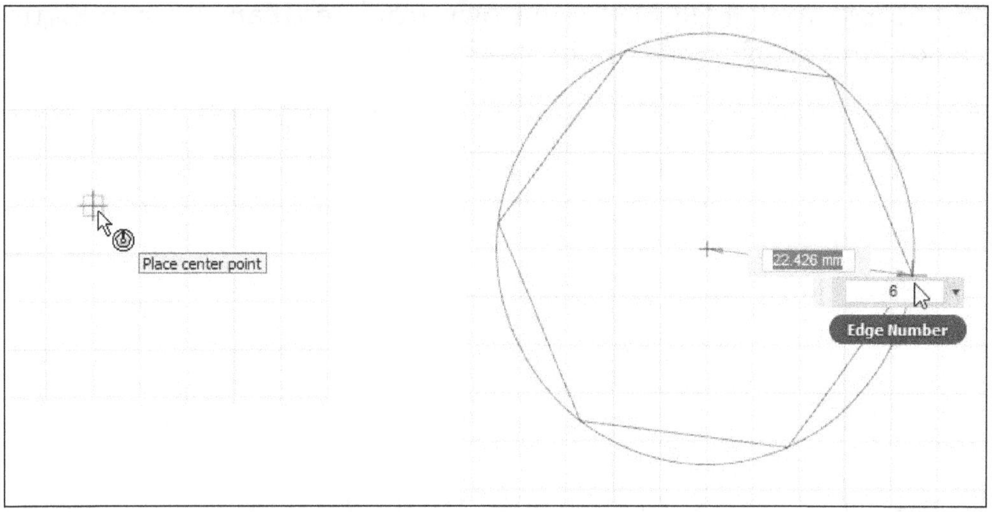

Figure-29. Creation of inscribed polygon

- Specify the distance between center point of polygon and vertex of polygon edge in dynamic input box.
- Press **TAB** and specify the value of number of edges in **Edge Number** dynamic input box.
- Press **ENTER** to create polygon.

Edge Polygon

The **Edge Polygon** tool is used to create a polygon by defining single edge and number of edges of the polygon. The procedure to use this tool is discussed next.

- Click on the **Edge Polygon** tool of **Polygon** cascading menu from **CREATE** drop-down. You will be asked to specify start and end points of the edge line.
- Click on the screen to select the start point and end point of edge. You can also specify the value of angle and length of the edge in dynamic input boxes; refer to Figure-30. After specifying the value in dynamic input boxes, move the cursor to desired side of edge where you want to create the polygon.

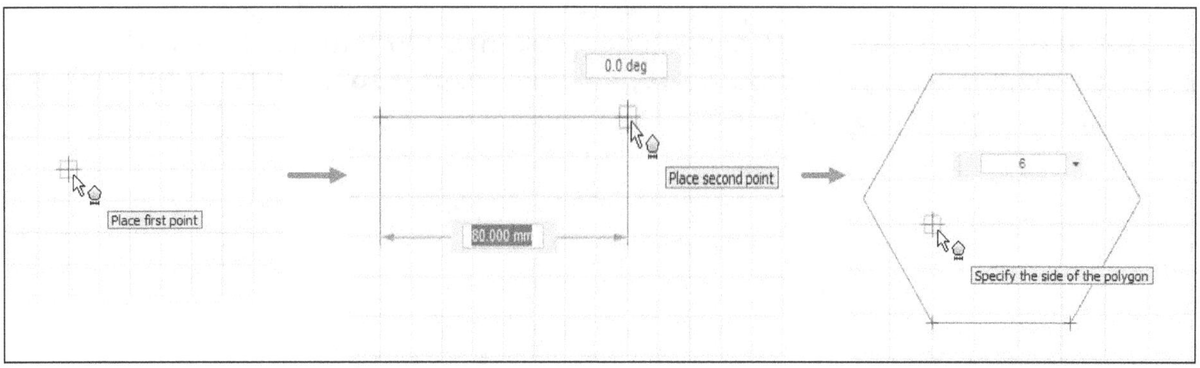

Figure-30. Creation of edge polygon

- Specify the value of number of edges of polygon in **Edge Number** input box.
- Press **ENTER** or click in desired side to create the polygon.

Ellipse

The **Ellipse** tool is used to create ellipses in the sketch. The procedure to create an ellipse is discussed next.

- Click on **Ellipse** tool of **CREATE** drop-down from **Toolbar**; refer to Figure-31. You will be asked to specify center point for ellipse.

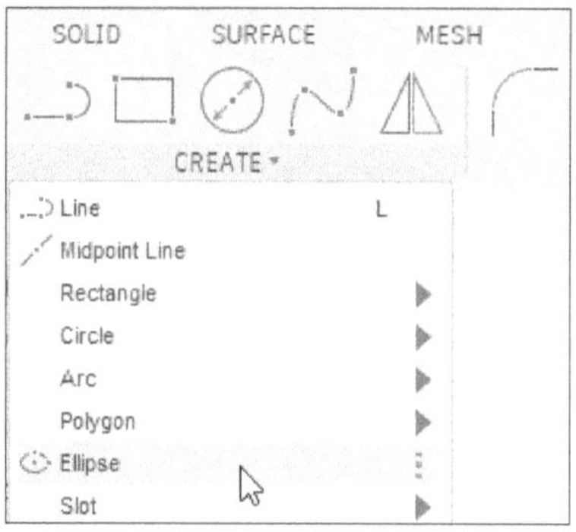

Figure-31. Ellipse tool

- Click on the screen to specify the center point for ellipse.
- Move the cursor in desired direction and specify the value of major diameter in dynamic input box. You can also specify the value of angle in **Angle** dynamic input box if you want major axis to be inclined.
- Click on the screen and move the cursor upward/downward. You will be asked to specify length of minor axis. Enter desired value of minor diameter in the input box; refer to Figure-32. The ellipse will be created.

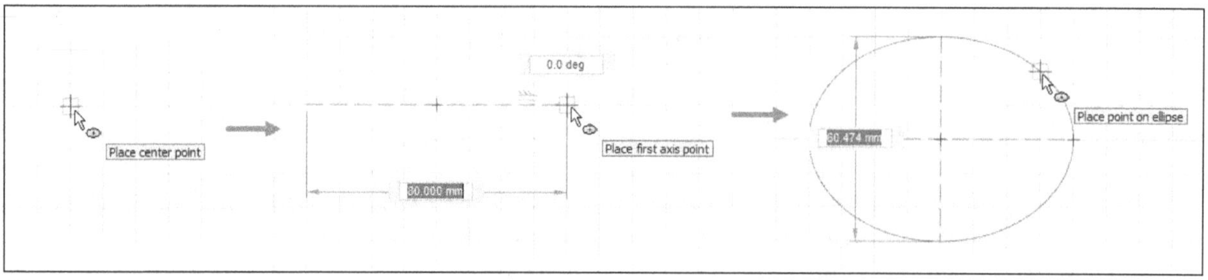

Figure-32. Creation of ellipse

- Right-click on the screen and click **OK** button to exit this tool.

Slot

The **Slot** tool is used to create slots. There are five tools in **Slot** cascading menu; **Center to Center Slot, Overall Slot, Center Point Slot, Three Point Arc Slot,** and **Center Point Arc Slot**; refer to Figure-33.

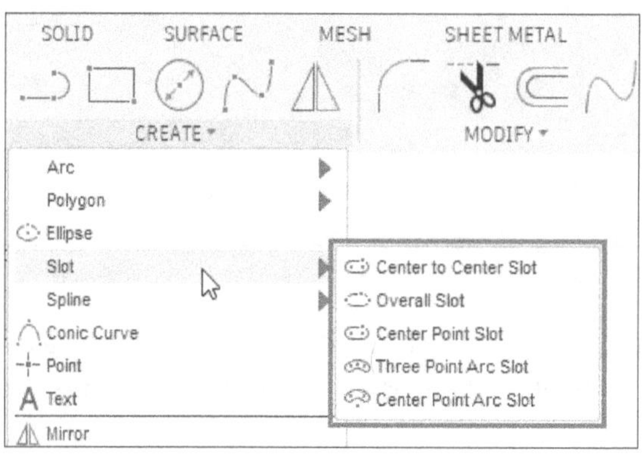

Figure-33. Slot cascading menu

The tools of **Slot** cascading menu are discussed next.

Creating Center To Center Slot

The **Center To Center Slot** tool is used to create the linear slot defined by the distance of slot arc centers and width of slot. The procedure to use this tool is discussed next.

- Click on **Center To Center Slot** tool of **Slot** cascading menu from **CREATE** drop-down.
- Click on the screen to specify the center point of first arc of slot. You will be asked to specify center point of other arc of slot.
- Click to specify the point or specify desired parameters in the input boxes.
- Move the cursor upward/downward. You will be asked to specify width of slot/ diameter of slot arc.
- Enter the value in dynamic input box or click on the screen; refer to Figure-34. The slot will be created.

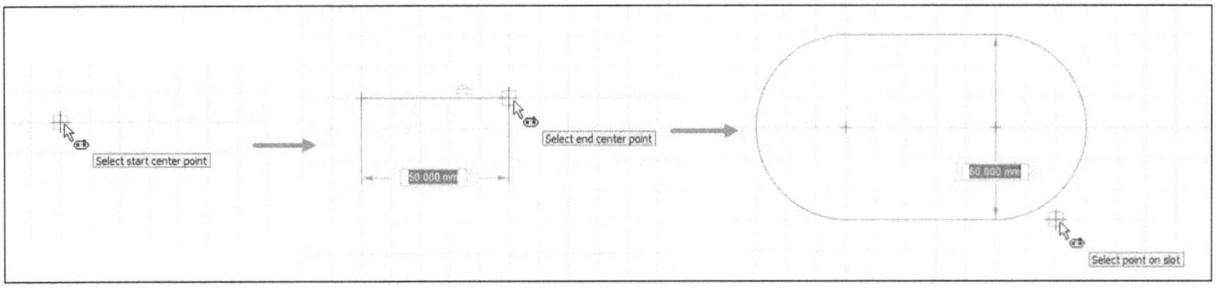

Figure-34. Creation of center to center slot

Creating Overall Slot

The **Overall Slot** tool creates a linear slot defined by total length and total width. The procedure to use this tool is discussed next.

- Click on **Overall Slot** tool of **Slot** cascading menu from **CREATE** drop-down.
- Click on the screen to specify the start point of the slot; refer to Figure-35. You will be asked to specify end point of slot.

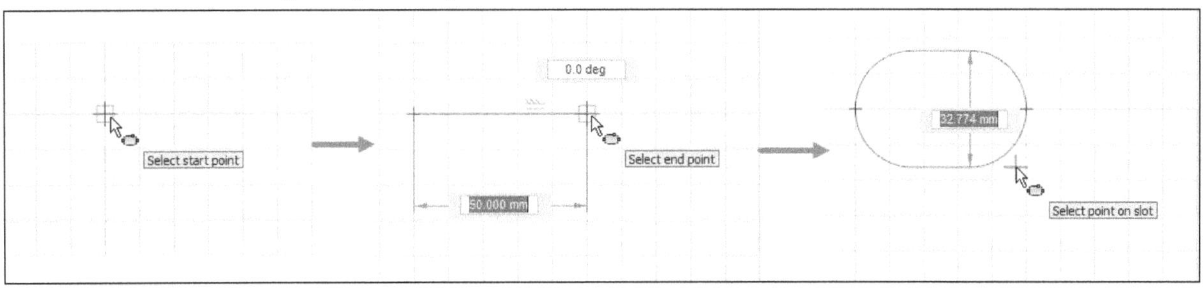

Figure-35. Creation of overall slot

- Click on the screen to specify the end point of the slot or specify the distance between start point and end point in the dynamic input box.
- Move the cursor upward/downward and specify the width of slot in dynamic input box or click at desired location.
- Press **ENTER** to create the slot and exit the tool.

Creating Center Point Slot

The **Center Point Slot** tool is used to create a linear slot which is defined by center point of slot, location of arc center, and width of slot. The procedure to use this tool is discussed next.

- Click on **Center Point Slot** tool of **Slot** cascading menu from **CREATE** drop-down.
- Click on the screen to specify the center of slot; refer to Figure-36.

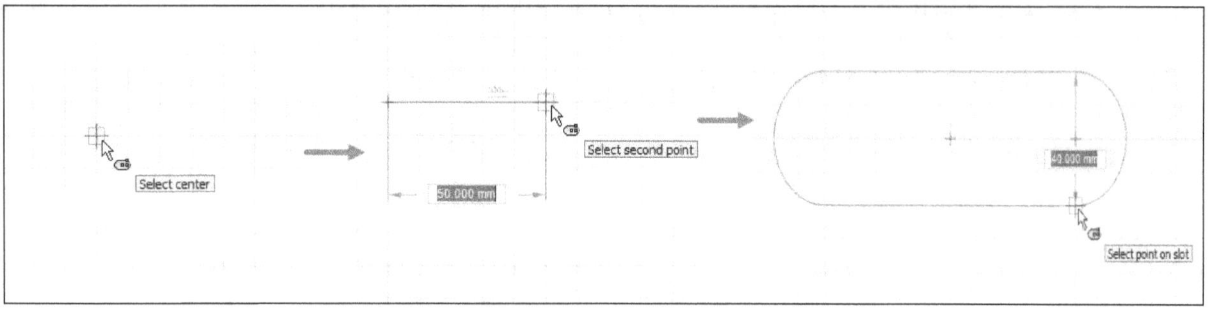

Figure-36. Creation of center point slot

- Click to specify the half length of the center to center distance of the slot.
- Specify the value of width for slot in the dynamic input box and press **ENTER** key. The slot will be created.

Creating Three Point Arc Slot

The **Three Point Arc Slot** tool is used to create a slot along specified arc with defined width. The procedure to use this tool is given next.

- Click on the **Three Point Arc Slot** tool of **Slot** cascading menu from **CREATE** drop-down. You will be asked to specify the start point of center arc.
- Click at desired location. You will be asked to specify end point of center arc.
- Click to specify the end point of arc. You will be asked to specify a circumferential point of the arc.
- Click at desired location and move the cursor upward/downward. Preview of arc will be displayed with dynamic width value.
- Type desired value of slot width in dynamic input box and the press **ENTER** to create the slot; refer to Figure-37.

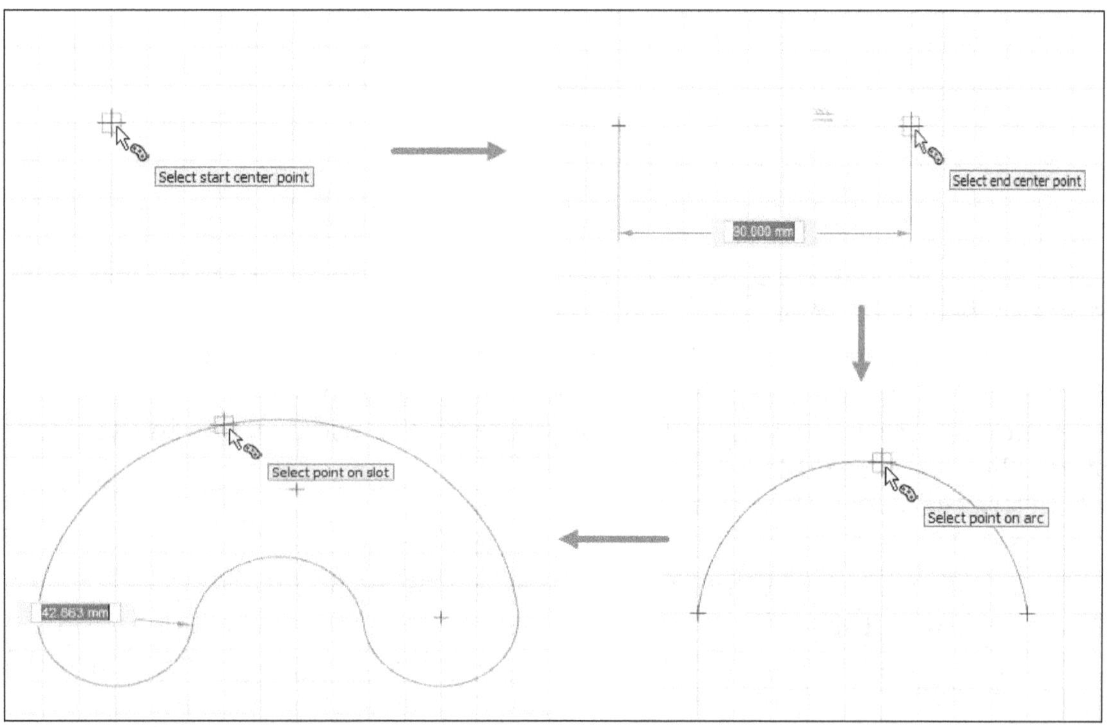

Figure-37. Creation of 3-point arc slot

Creating Center Point Arc Slot

The **Center Point Arc Slot** tool is used to create an arc slot by specifying center point of arc, start & end point of arc, and width of slot. The procedure to use this tool is given next.

- Click on the **Center Point Arc Slot** tool of **Slot** cascading menu from **CREATE** drop-down in the **Toolbar**. You will be asked to specify the center of arc.
- Click at desired location. You will be asked to specify the start point of the arc.
- Click at desired location or type desired value of arc radius in the dynamic input box. You will be asked to specify the end point of arc.
- Click at desired location to specify end point or type desired value of angular span of arc in the dynamic input box. You will be asked to specify the width of slot.
- Click to specify the slot width or enter desired value in dynamic input box to create the slot; refer to Figure-38.

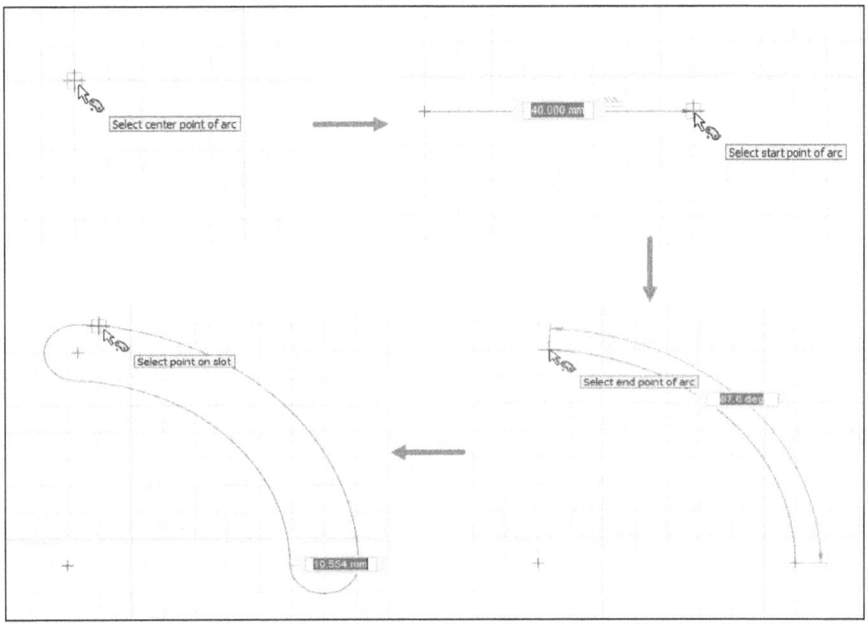

Figure-38. Creation of center point arc slot

Spline

The **Spline** tools are used to create spline curves. There are two tools in **Spline** cascading menu; **Fit Point Spline** and **Control Point Spline**; refer to Figure-39.

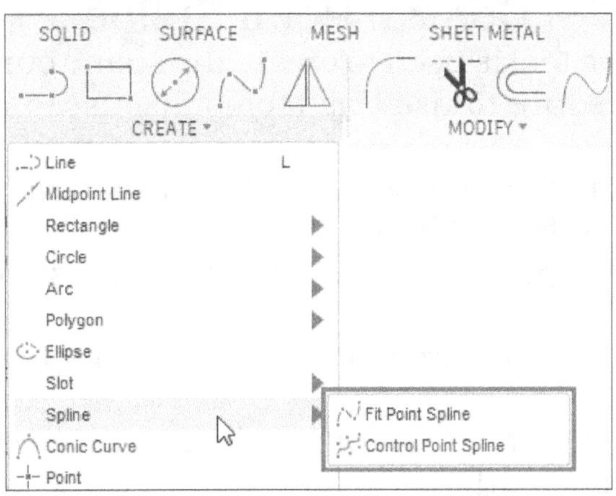

Figure-39. Spline cascading menu

The tools of **Spline** cascading menu are discussed next.

Fit Point Spline

The **Fit Point Spline** tool is used to create spline curve through the selected points. It is a freeform curve creation tool. The procedure to use this tool is discussed next.

- Click on the **Fit Point Spline** tool of **Spline** cascading menu from **CREATE** drop-down in the **Toolbar**; refer to Figure-39.
- Click on the screen to specify the start point for the spline. You will be asked to specify next point of spline.
- Specify other points at desired locations to form spline of desired shape; refer to Figure-40.

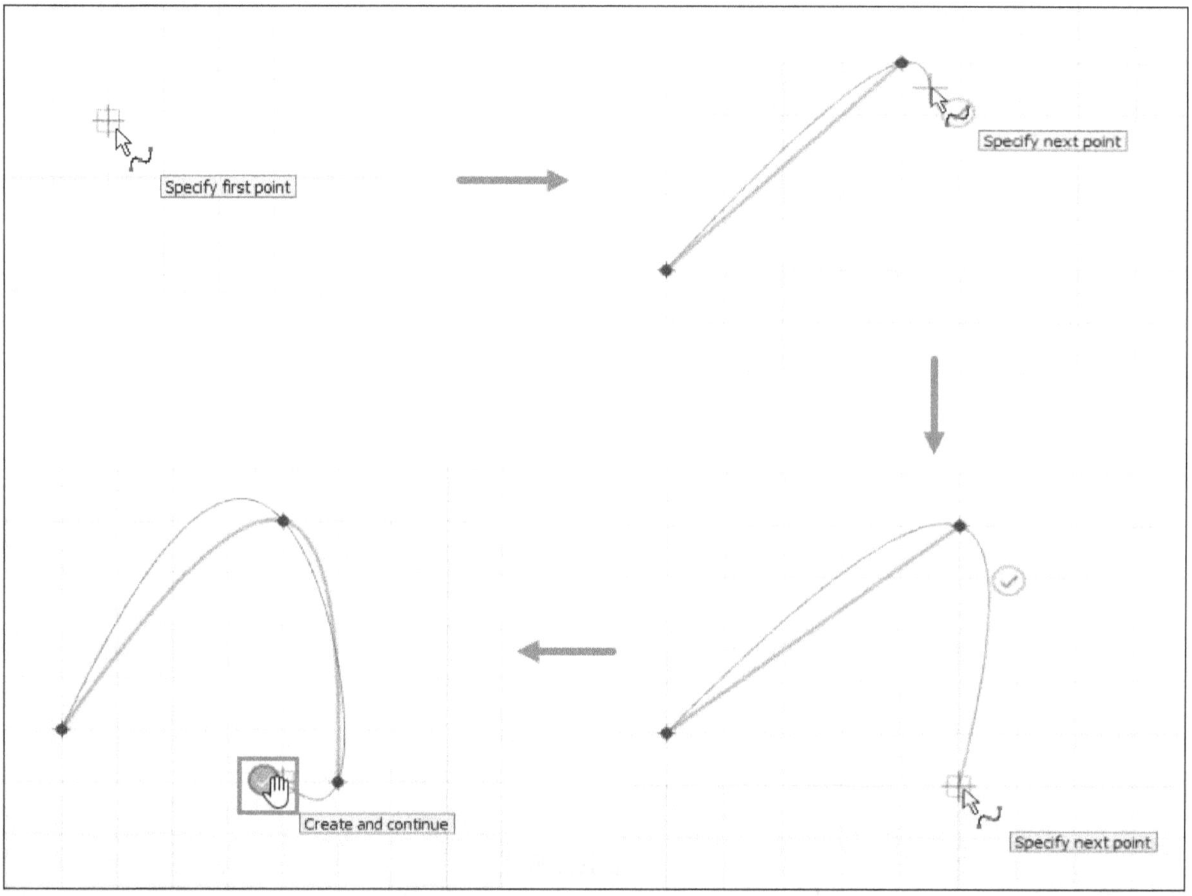

Figure-40. Creation of fit point spline

Control Point Spline

The **Control Point Spline** tool is used to create the spline curve driven by the selected control points. The procedure to use this tool is discussed next.

- Click on **Control Point Spline** tool of **Spline** cascading menu from **CREATE** drop-down in the **Toolbar**; refer to Figure-39.
- Click on the screen to specify the start point for the spline. You will be asked to specify next point of spline.
- Specify the other points at desired locations to form spline of desired shape; refer to Figure-41.
- After specifying desired number of points, click on the **Tick** (**Create and Continue**) button to end the spline path.
- Press **ENTER** or **ESC** to exit the tool.

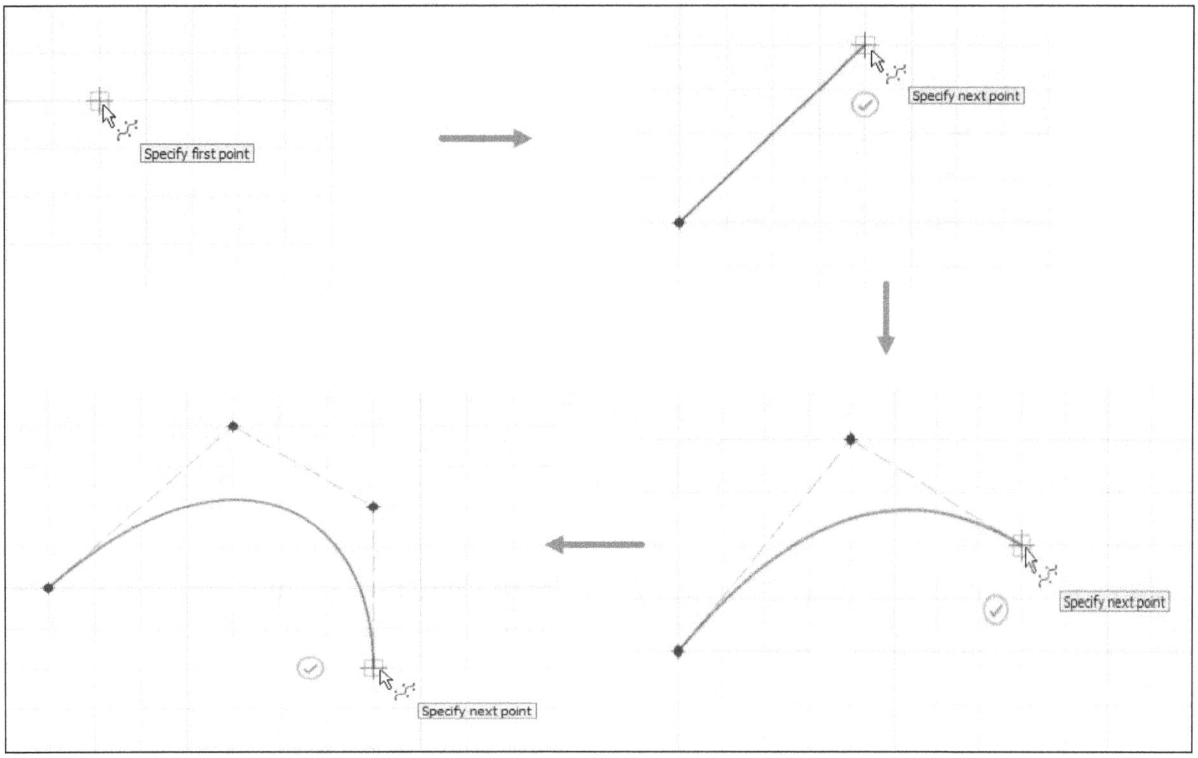

Figure-41. Creation of control point spline

Conic Curve

The **Conic Curve** tool creates a curve driven by points and rho value. The shape of the curve can be elliptical, parabolic, or hyperbolic depending on the value of Rho. The procedure to use this tool is discussed next.

- Click on **Conic Curve** tool of **CREATE** drop-down from **Toolbar**; refer to Figure-42.

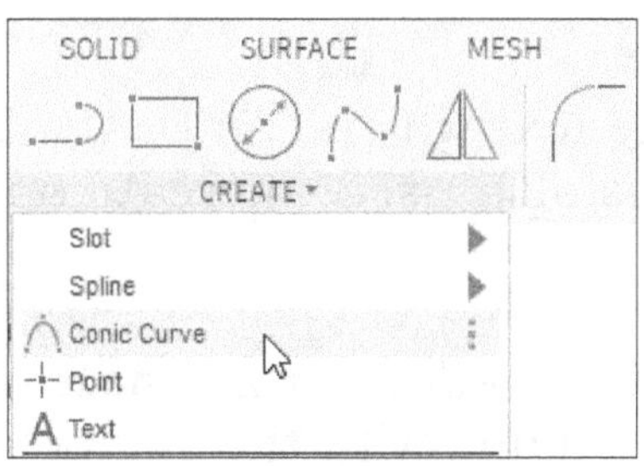

Figure-42. Conic Curve tool

- Click on the screen to specify the start point of the conic curve.
- Click on the screen to specify the end point of the conic curve.
- Click on the screen to specify control point.
- Enter the **Rho** value in **Rho** dynamic input box for the conic curve; refer to Figure-43. The curve will be created. The value of rho lies between **0** to **0.99**.

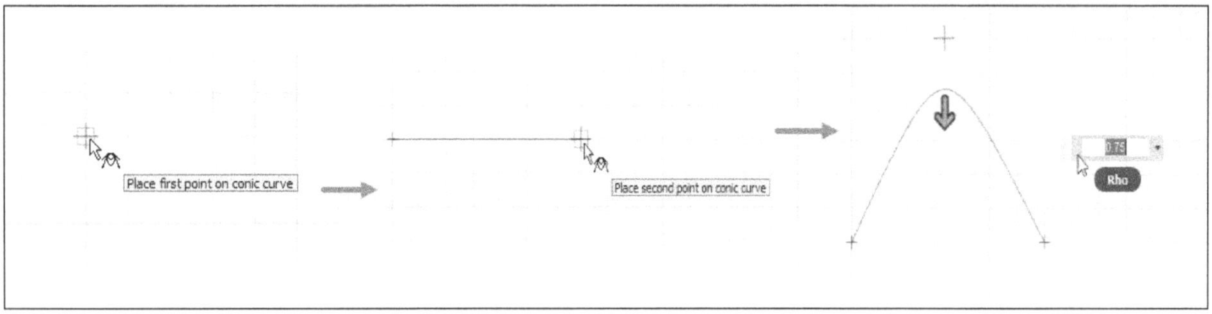

Figure-43. Creation of conic curve

Point

The **Point** tool is used to create sketch points. Sketch points find their major usage when creating surfaces. The point gives the flexibility to parametrically change the surface design.

- Click on **Point** tool of **CREATE** drop-down from **Toolbar**; refer to Figure-44.
- Click at desired locations in the sketch canvas to create points; refer to Figure-45.

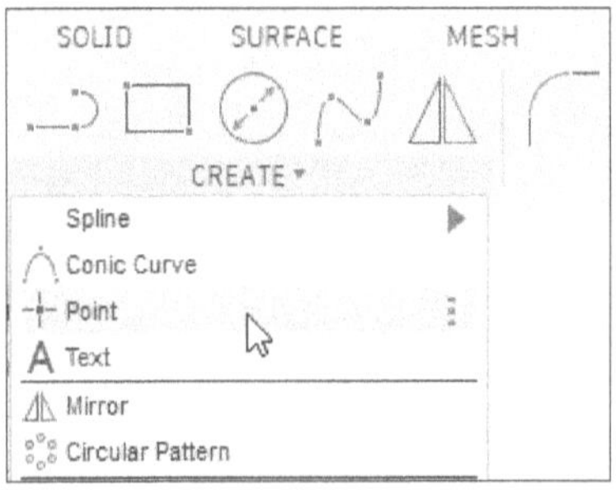

Figure-44. Point tool

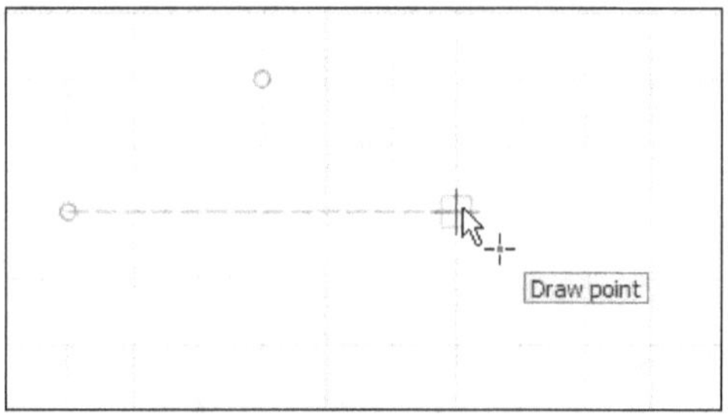

Figure-45. Creation of point

- Press **ESC** key to exit this tool or click **OK** button from **Marking menu**.

Text

The **Text** tool is used to create text which can be used for embossing/engraving on a solid model. The **Text** tool is also used to create notes and other information for the model.

- Click on **Text** tool of **CREATE** drop-down from **Toolbar**; refer to Figure-46. The **TEXT** dialog box will be displayed along with the symbol of text attached to the cursor asking you to specify first corner of the text frame; refer to Figure-46.

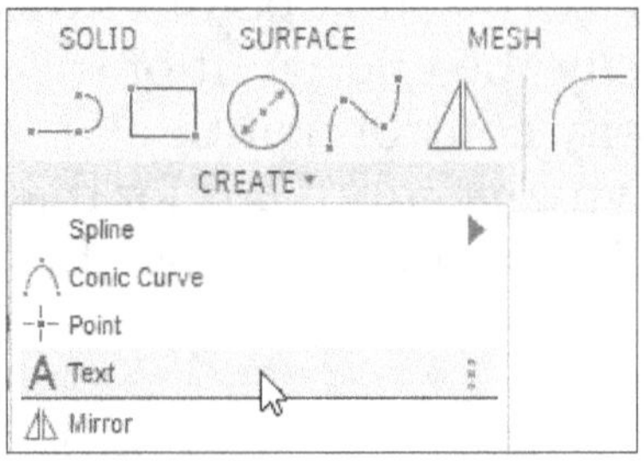

Figure-46. Text tool

Note that **Text** option is selected by default in the **Type** section of the dialog box. Select **Text** option to create the text inside a rectangular frame; refer to Figure-47. and select **Text On Path** option to create the text along selected path; refer to Figure-48.

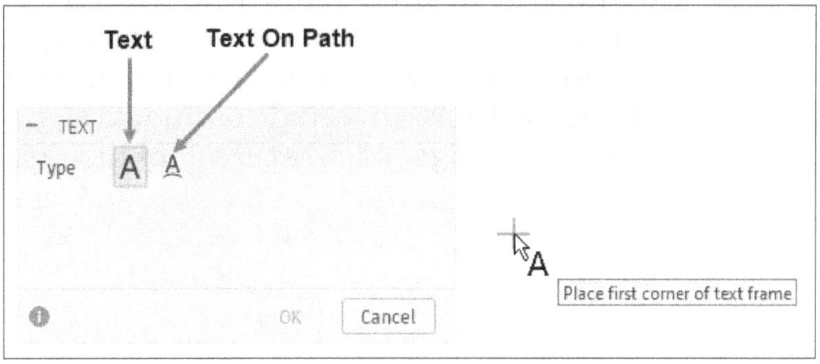

Figure-47. TEXT dialog box with text symbol attached to cursor

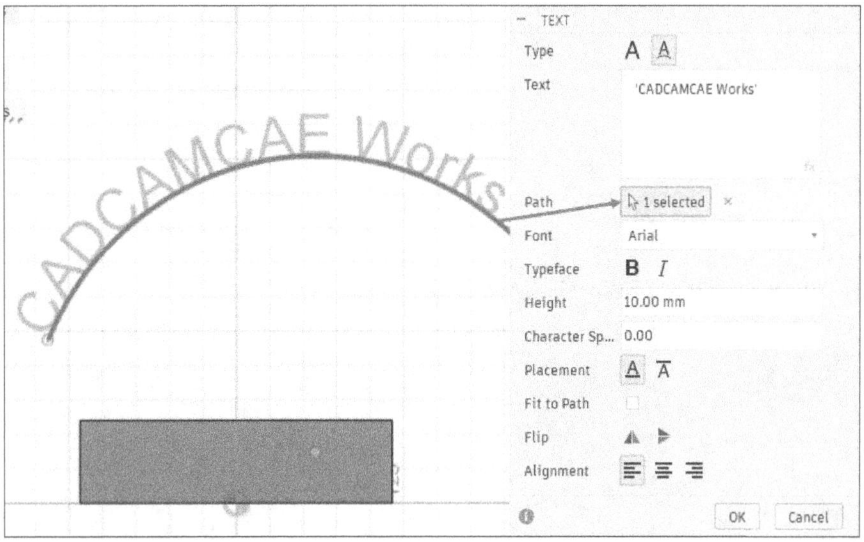

Figure-48. Creating text on path

- Click at desired location to place first corner of text frame. You will be asked to specify second corner of text frame.
- Move the cursor away and click at desired location to place second corner of text frame. The text frame will be created and the **TEXT** dialog box will be updated; refer to Figure-49.

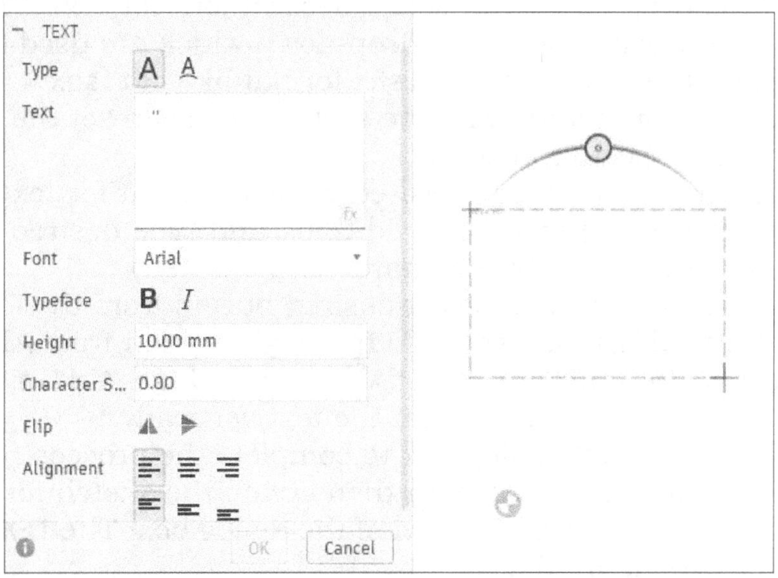

Figure-49. Updated TEXT dialog box with frame created

- Click in the **Text** edit box and type desired text within the single inverted commas present by default in the edit box. Preview of text will be displayed in real-time; refer to Figure-50. You can also place values of various parameters by specifying their name in the **Text** edit box without inverted commas; refer to Figure-51. Note that parameters are created by **Change Parameters** tool discussed in Chapter 6.

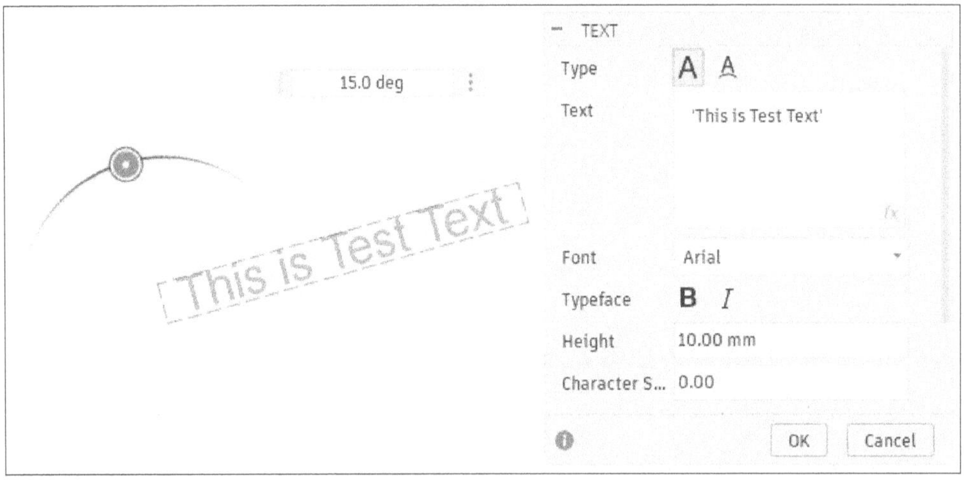

Figure-50. Preview of text created in a rectangular frame

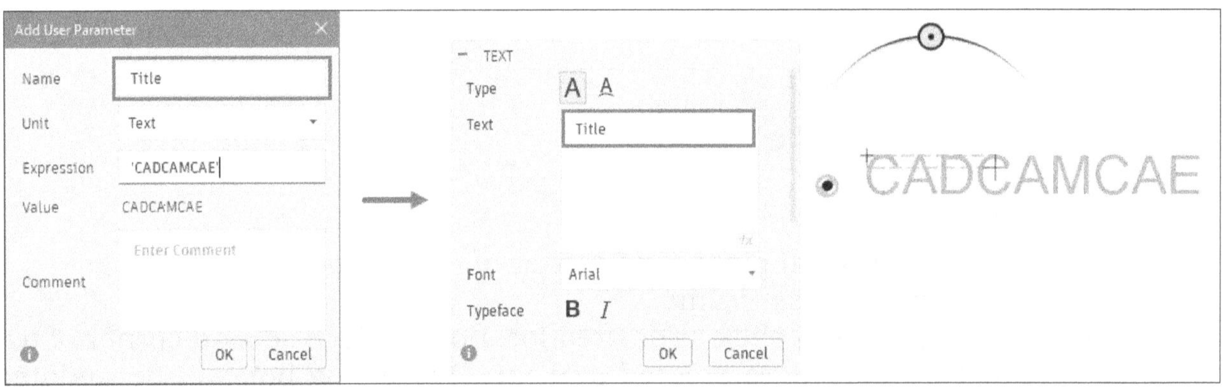

Figure-51. Text created using parameters

- Click on the **Font** drop-down and select desired font for text. There are various single line text fonts available in this drop-down which are used for CAM to name or mark the part. These fonts are of **.shx** format like **cdm.shx**.
- Select desired style for text in **Typeface** section. You can set the text as bold and italic by selecting respective buttons.
- Click in **Height** edit box and type desired value of height for text.
- Click in the **Character Spacing (%)** edit box and type desired value to specify change in default spacing between characters.
- If you want to flip the text then select desired button from the **Flip** section.
- Select **Align Left**, **Align Center**, or **Align Right** option from Alignment section to align the text horizontally and select **Align Top**, **Align Middle**, or **Align Bottom** option from **Alignment** section to align the text vertically.
- Click **OK** button of the **TEXT** dialog box to complete the process.
- If you want to create the text on path then create the sketch for path and select **Text On Path** option from **Type** section of the dialog box. The **TEXT** dialog box will be updated; refer to Figure-52.

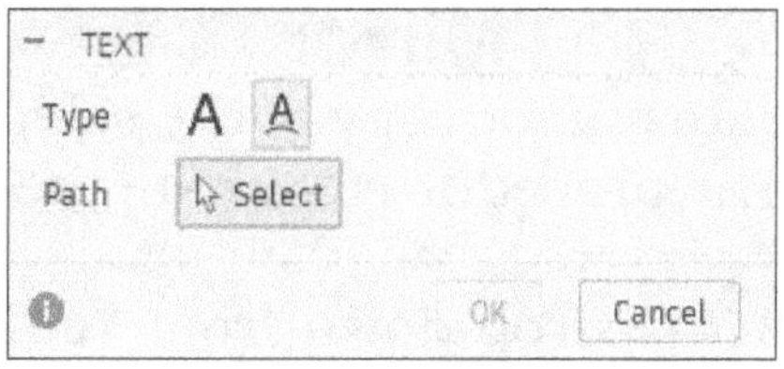

Figure-52. TEXT dialog box with Text On Path options

- The **Path** selection button is active by default and you are asked to select the path.
- Select the path created for the text to follow. The **TEXT** dialog box will be updated and the selected path will be displayed in the **Path** section of the dialog box; refer to Figure-53.

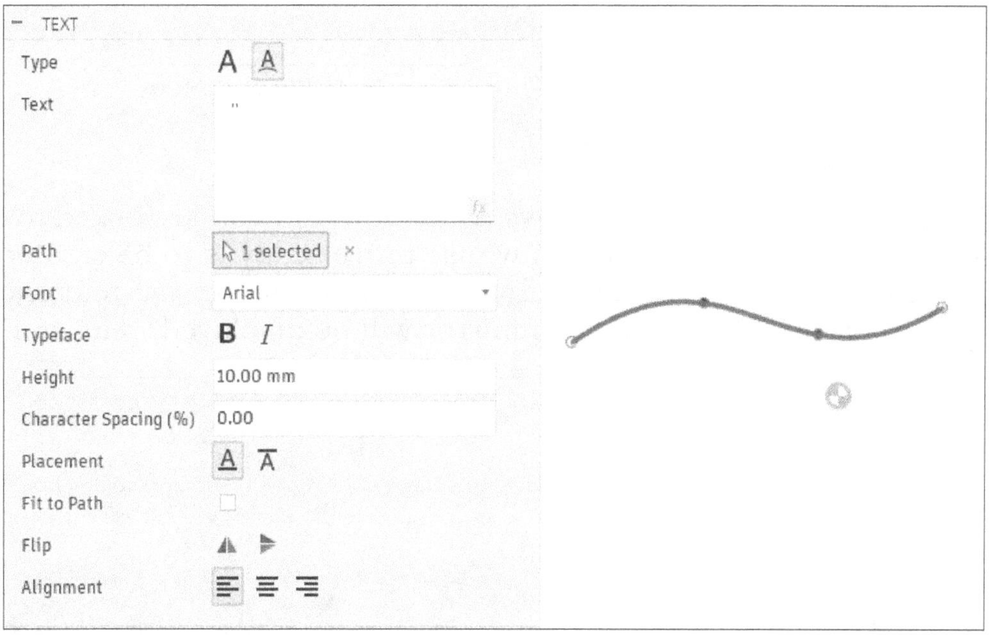

Figure-53. Updated TEXT dialog box with path selected

- Click in the **Text** edit box and type desired text. Preview of text will be displayed in real-time; refer to Figure-54.

Figure-54. Preview of text created on selected path

- Select the placement of the text above or below the path by selecting respective button from **Placement** section of the dialog box.
- Select **Fit to Path** check box to distribute the text evenly along the entire path.
- Specify the other parameters in the dialog box as discussed earlier. Click the **OK** button from the dialog box to complete the process.

After creating the text, you can edit it anytime by double-clicking on it in sketch mode.

Mirror

The **Mirror** tool is used to create mirror copy of the selected entities with respect to a reference called mirror line. The procedure to create the mirror entities is given next.

- Click on **Mirror** tool of **CREATE** drop-down from **Toolbar**; refer to Figure-55. The **MIRROR** dialog box will be displayed; refer to Figure-56.

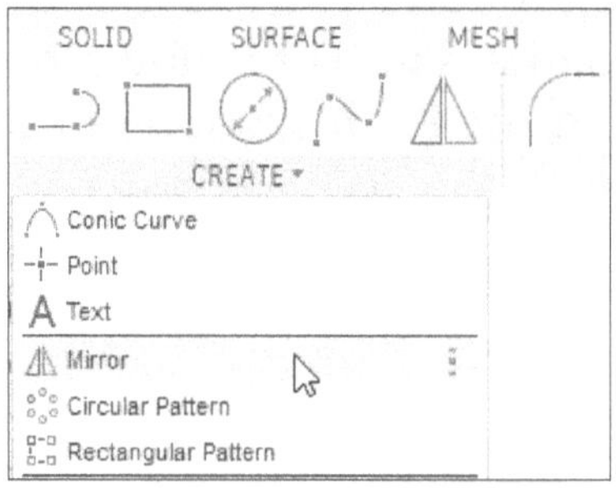

Figure-55. Mirror tool

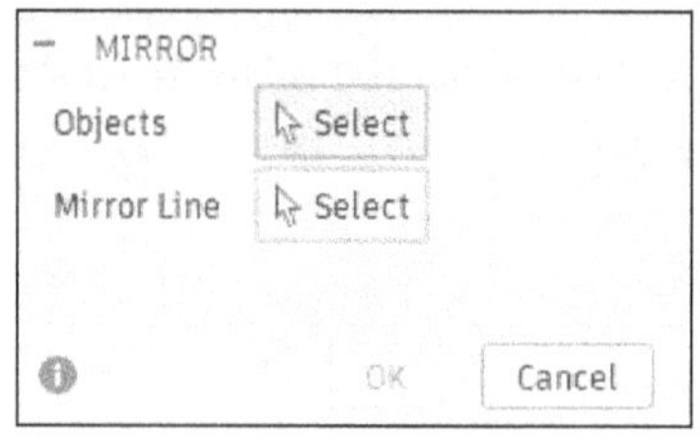

Figure-56. MIRROR dialog box

- The **Objects** selection button is active by default and you are asked to select the objects. Select the entities or sketch whose mirror copy is to be created.
- Click on **Select** button of **Mirror Line** section and select the reference line for creating mirror copy. The preview of mirror will be displayed; refer to Figure-57.

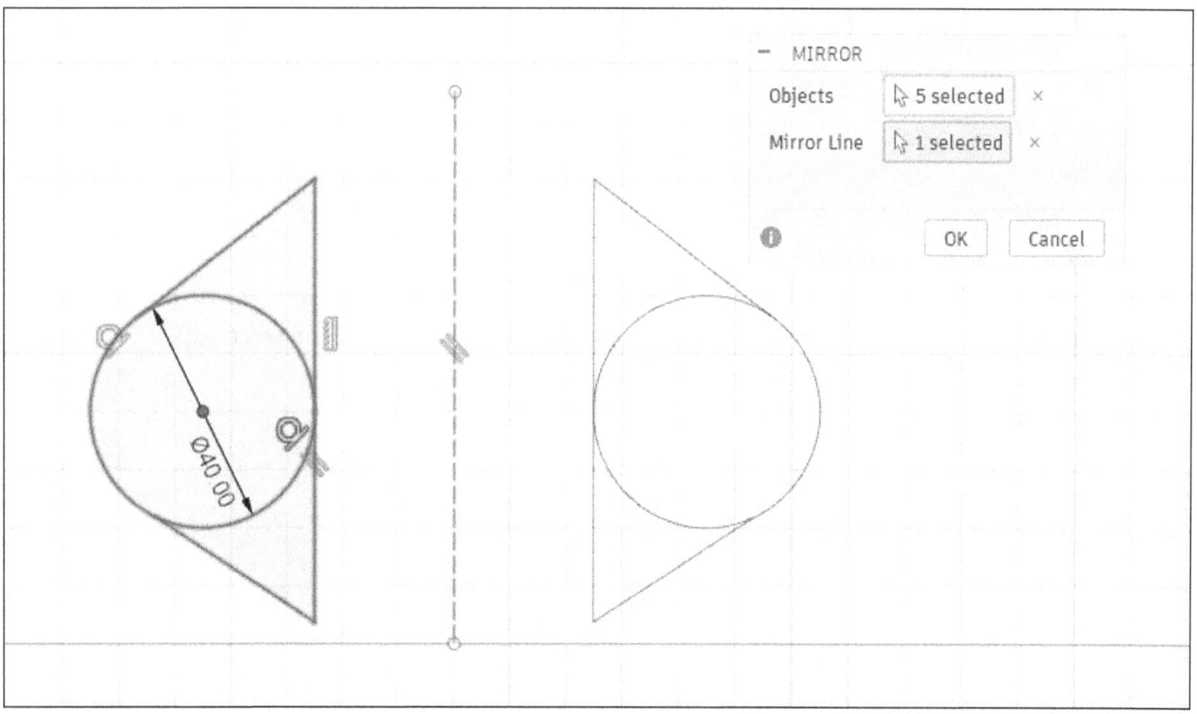

Figure-57. Procedure of mirror

- If preview of mirror is as per your requirement then click on **OK** button from **MIRROR** dialog box to complete the process.

Sometimes, we need to create multiple copies of the sketch entities like in sketch of keyboard or piano. For such cases, Autodesk Fusion provides two tools, **Circular Pattern** and **Rectangular Pattern**. These tools are discussed next.

Circular Pattern

The **Circular pattern** tool is used to create multiple copies of an entity in circular fashion. The procedure to use this tool is discussed next.

- Click on **Circular Pattern** tool of **CREATE** drop-down from **Toolbar**; refer to Figure-58. The **CIRCULAR PATTERN** dialog box will be displayed; refer to Figure-59.

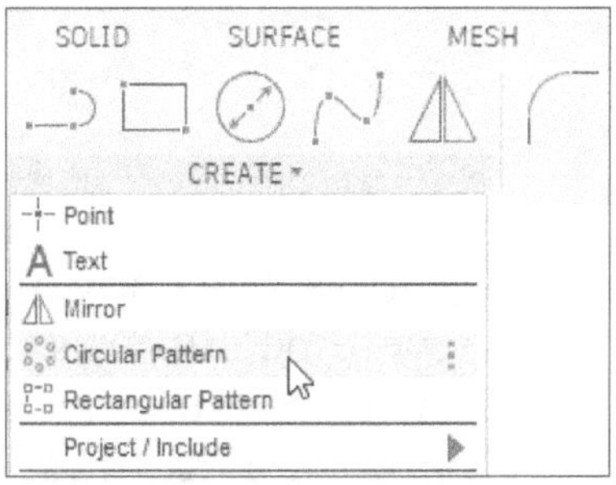

Figure-58. Circular Pattern tool

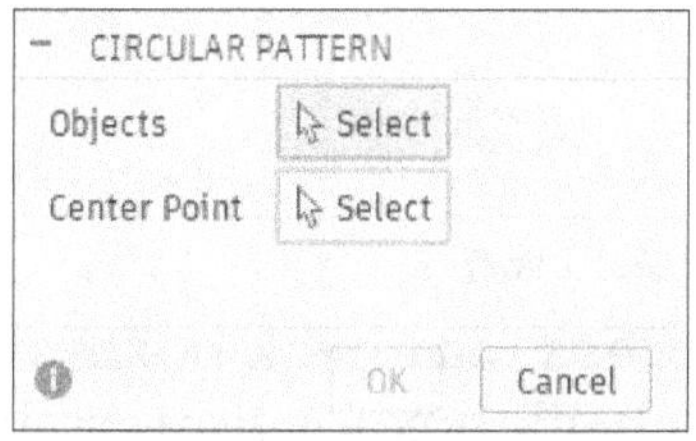

Figure-59. CIRCULAR PATTERN dialog box

- The **Objects** selection button is active by default and you are asked to select the objects. Select the entities or sketch to apply the circular pattern.
- Click on **Select** button for **Center Point** section and select the reference point to be used as center point for circular pattern. The preview of circular pattern will be displayed; refer to Figure-60.

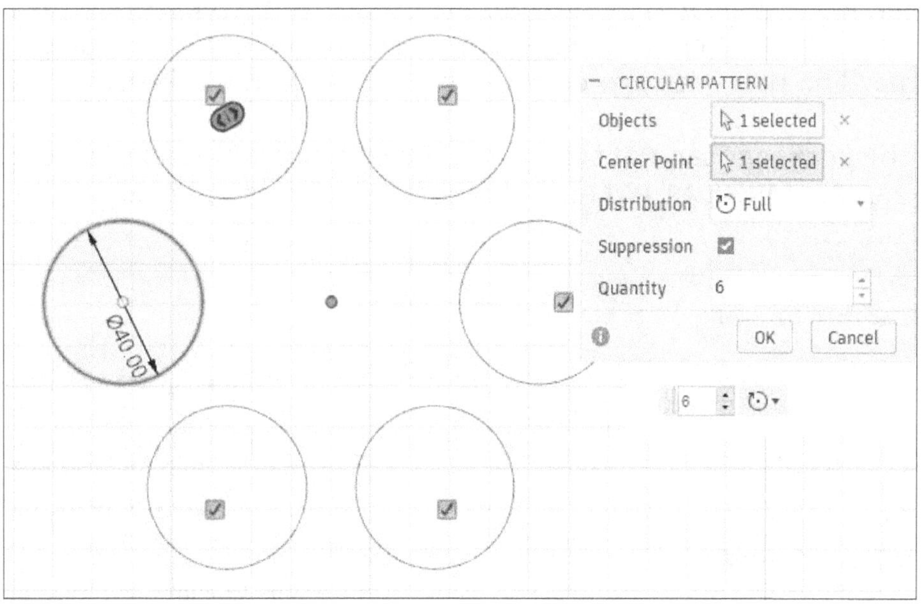

Figure-60. Creation of circular pattern

- Select **Full** option from **Distribution** drop-down if you want to create a pattern over full 360 round. Select the **Partial** option from the drop-down if you want to define the span of pattern in angle value. Select the **Symmetric** option from the drop-down if you want to create a circular pattern symmetric to the center line; refer to Figure-61.

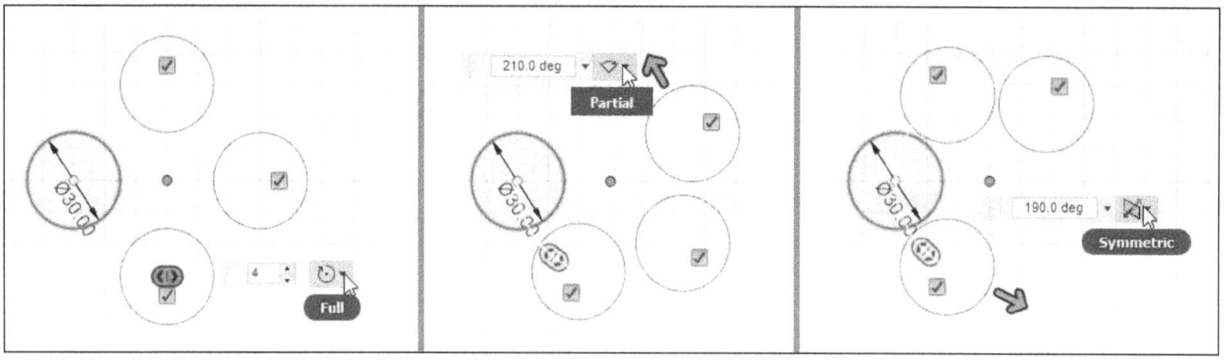

Figure-61. Tools of Type drop down

- Select the **Suppression** check box if you want to suppress any copy in pattern and then clear the check box for that entity in the preview to be suppressed. Clear the **Suppression** check box from the dialog box to generate all instances of pattern.
- Click in the **Quantity** edit box and type desired value for number of copies of object to be created in the circular pattern. You can also set the quantity by moving drag handle.
- After specifying the parameters, click on **OK** button from **CIRCULAR PATTERN** dialog box to complete the process.

Rectangular Pattern

The **Rectangular Pattern** tool is used to create multiple copies of an entity in horizontal and vertical direction. You can create pattern in two linear directions at the same time. The procedure to create rectangular pattern is given next.

- Click on the **Rectangular Pattern** tool of **CREATE** drop-down from **Toolbar**; refer to Figure-62. A **RECTANGULAR PATTERN** dialog box will be displayed; refer to Figure-63.

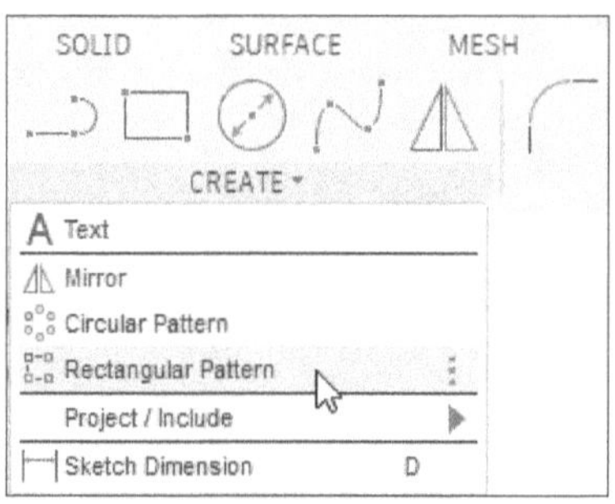

Figure-62. Rectangular Pattern tool

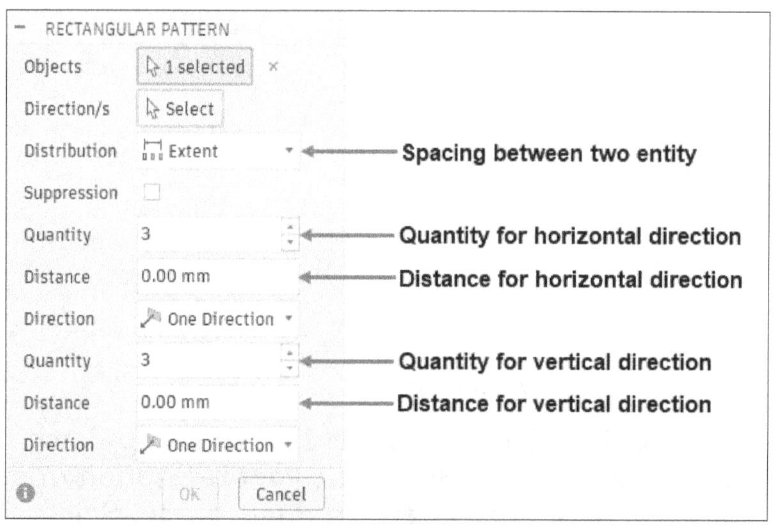

Figure-63. RECTANGULAR PATTERN dialog box

- The **Objects** section button is active by default and you are asked to select the objects. Select the sketch or entities for rectangular pattern.
- Click on **Select** button of **Direction/s** section and select the reference lines for directions of rectangular pattern. If you do not select reference lines then patterns are automatically created along horizontal and vertical axes; refer to Figure-64.

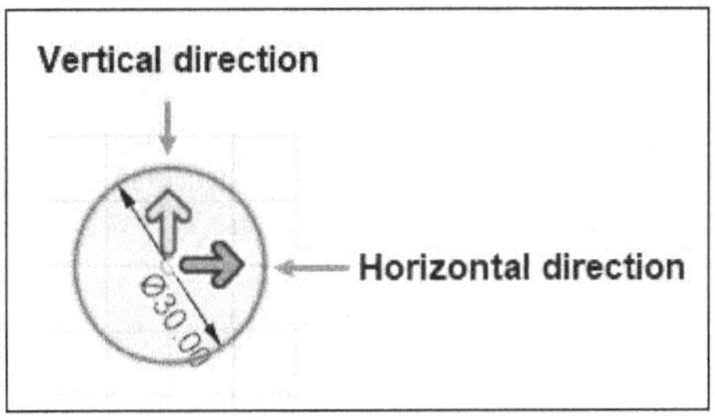

Figure-64. Rectangular pattern direction

- Select **Extent** option from **Distribution** drop-down if you want to specify the total span in which object copies will be created. Select **Spacing** option from the drop-down to set distance between two consecutive copies of object. In our case, we are selecting **Extent** option.
- Select the **Suppression** check box if you want to suppress any entity in the pattern.
- Click in the **Quantity** edit box and type desired value for number of copies.
- Click in the **Distance** edit box and type desired distance within which copies will be created; refer to Figure-65.

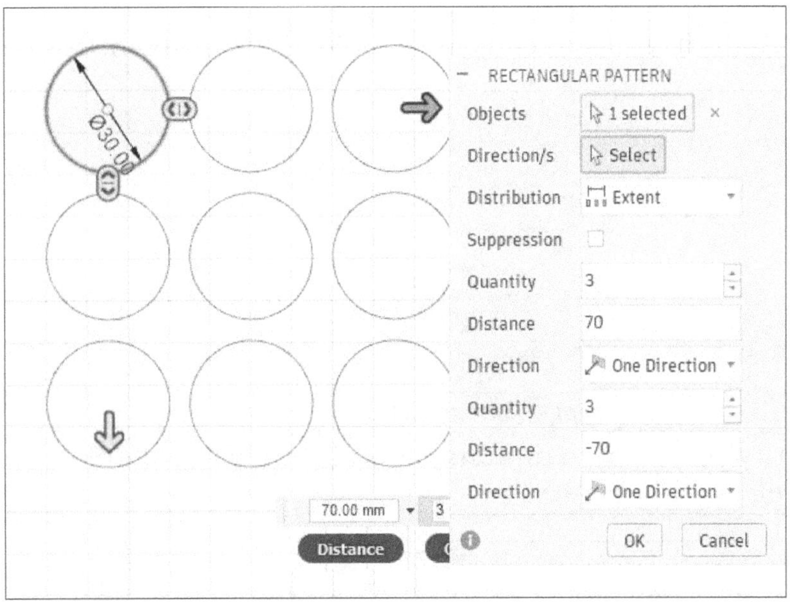

Figure-65. Creation of rectangular pattern

- Select **One Direction** option from **Direction** drop-down if you want to create copies in only one direction. Select **Symmetric** option from the drop-down if you want to create copies in both sides of selected direction.
- Similarly, specify the parameters for other direction.
- After specifying the parameters, click **OK** button from **RECTANGULAR PATTERN** dialog box to complete the process.

Project/Include

The tools in this cascading menu are used to project edges/curves of selected solids or surfaces on the sketch. These tools will be discussed later in this book while working with 3D models. Hover on the **Project/Include** option of **CREATE** drop-down from **Toolbar** to display **Project/Include** cascading menu; refer to Figure-66.

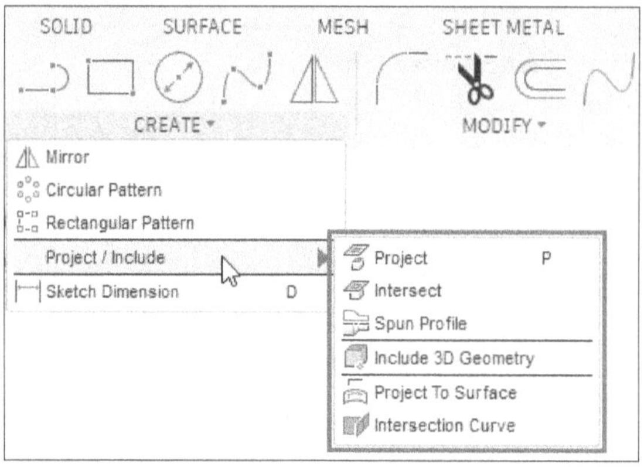

Figure-66. Project or Include cascading menu

Sketch Dimension

The **Sketch Dimension** tool is used to dimension the entities automatically based on selections. This tool can create different type of dimension like horizontal, vertical, diameter, radius, or inclined dimensions. The procedure to use this tool is discussed next.

- Click on the **Sketch Dimension** tool of **CREATE** drop-down from **Toolbar**; refer to Figure-67.

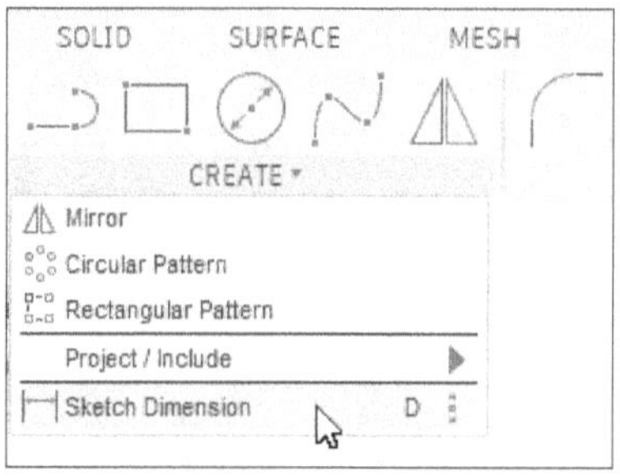

Figure-67. Sketch Dimension tool

- Select the entity you want to dimension and then click at desired distance to place dimension; refer to Figure-68.

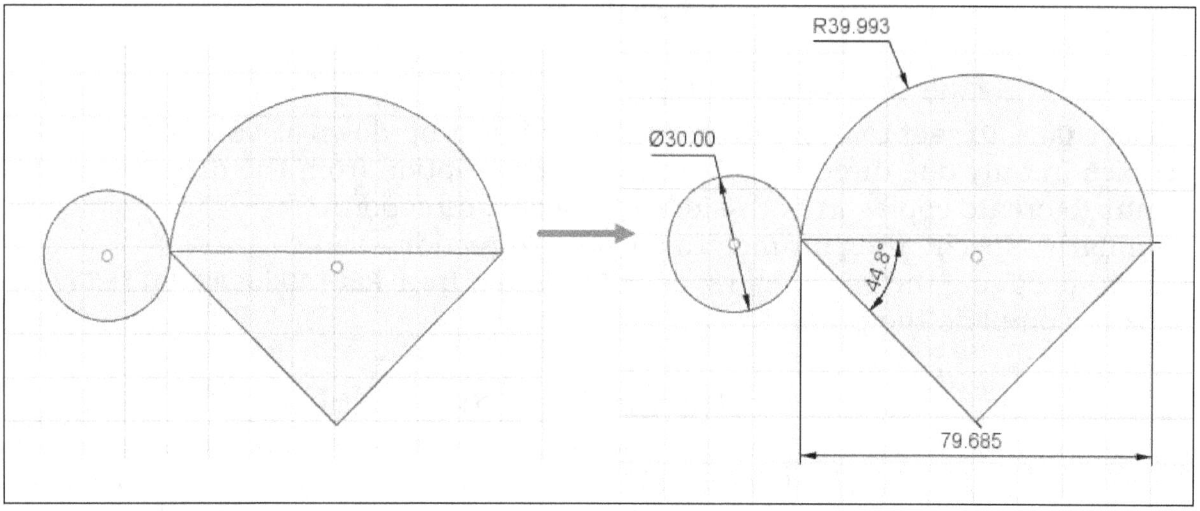

Figure-68. Applying the dimension

Based on how you move the cursor, the dimension will be horizontal, vertical, or inclined. So, after selecting an inclined line, you need to move the cursor in different ways starting from the object to get different type of dimensions. If you want to create inclined dimension for a line then move the cursor perpendicular to the line after selecting it. If you want to create horizontal dimension of an inclined line then move the cursor straight along vertical axis. In the same way, move the cursor straight horizontal to create vertical dimension of an inclined line. This technique can also be applied while dimensioning two points.

SKETCH EDITING TOOL

The standard tools to edit sketch entities are categorized in this section. The tools in this section are discussed next.

Fillet

The **Fillet** tool is used to create fillet at the corners created by intersection of two entities. Fillet is sometimes also referred to as round. The procedure to use this tool is discussed next.

- Click on **Fillet** tool of **MODIFY** drop-down from **Toolbar**; refer to Figure-69. You will be asked to select the entities.

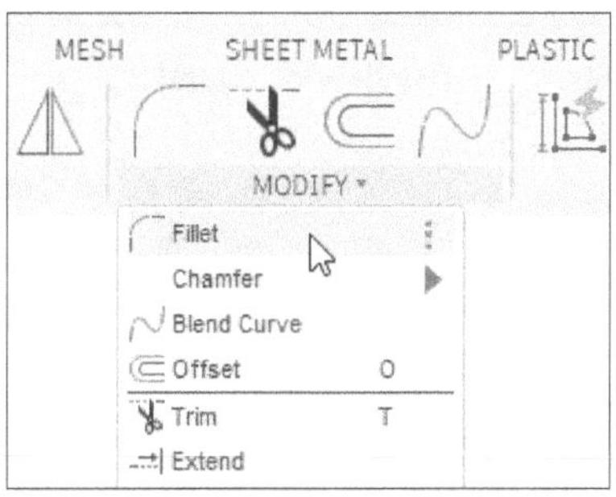

Figure-69. Fillet tool

- Select the first entity and then second entity.
- Enter the value of radius in floating window; refer to Figure-70. The fillet will be created.

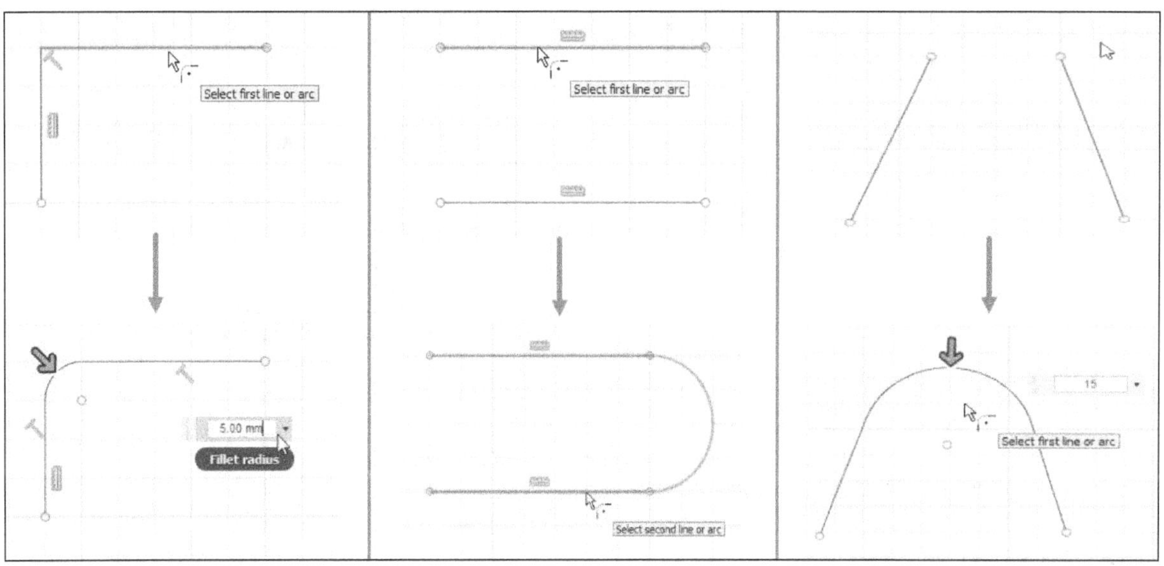

Figure-70. Creation of fillet

Chamfer

The **Chamfer** tool is used to bevel the corners of sketch geometry in an active sketch. There are three tools in **Chamfer** cascading menu of **MODIFY** drop-down in the **Toolbar**; refer to Figure-71. The procedures to use these tools are discussed next.

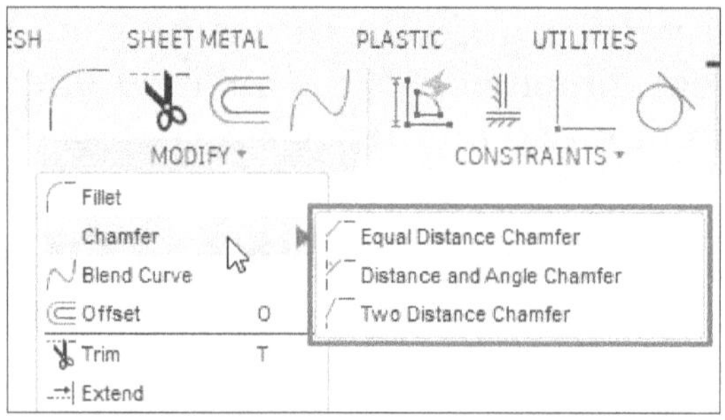

Figure-71. Tools in Chamfer cascading menu

Equal Distance Chamfer

- Click on the **Equal Distance Chamfer** tool from **Chamfer** cascading menu; refer to Figure-71.
- Hover the cursor on the vertex of the sketch or select the first line and hover the cursor on the second line. The preview of chamfer will be displayed; refer to Figure-72.

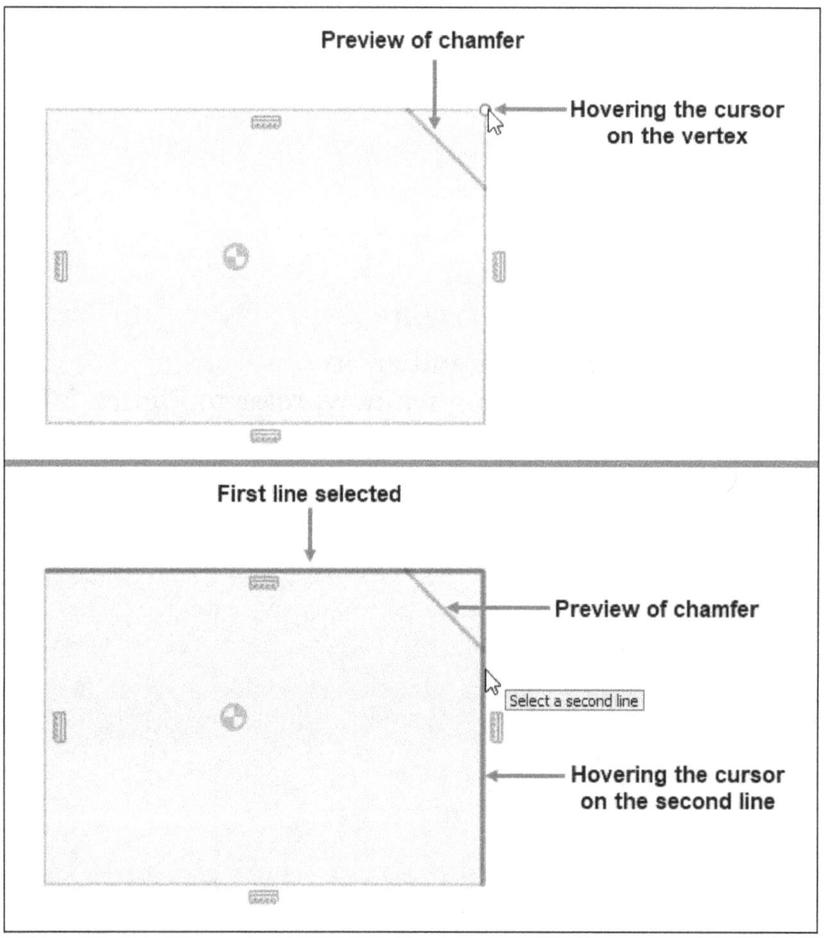

Figure-72. Preview of equal distance chamfer

- Click on the vertex or on the second line of the sketch and type desired distance value in the **Distance** edit box or drag the distance manipulator handle to specify the distance of chamfer; refer to Figure-73.

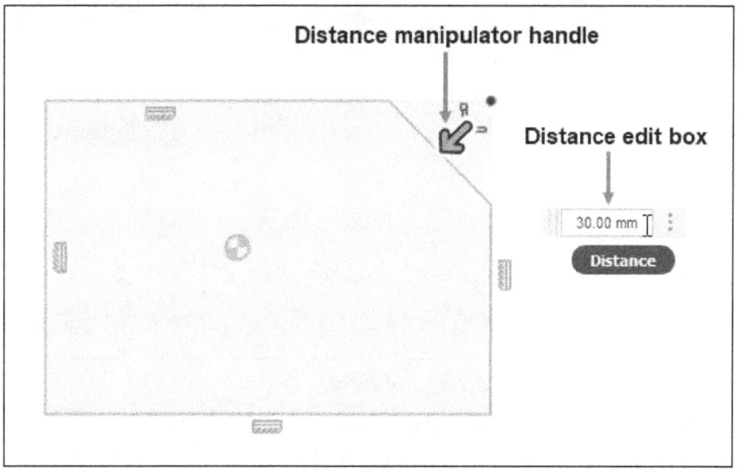

Figure-73. Specifying the distance of chamfer

- After specifying the chamfer distance, press **ENTER**. The equal distance chamfer will be created; refer to Figure-74.

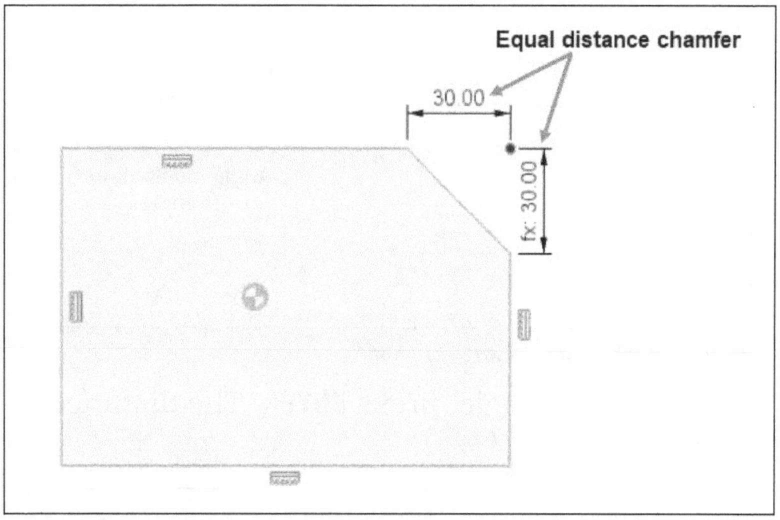

Figure-74. Equal distance chamfer created

Distance and Angle Chamfer

- Click on the **Distance and Angle Chamfer** tool from **Chamfer** cascading menu; refer to Figure-71.
- Hover the cursor on the vertex of the sketch or select the first line and hover the cursor on the second line, the preview of chamfer will be displayed as shown in Figure-75.
- Click on the vertex or on the second line of the sketch and type desired distance value in the **Distance** edit box.
- Or, drag the distance manipulator handle to specify the distance of chamfer; refer to Figure-75.

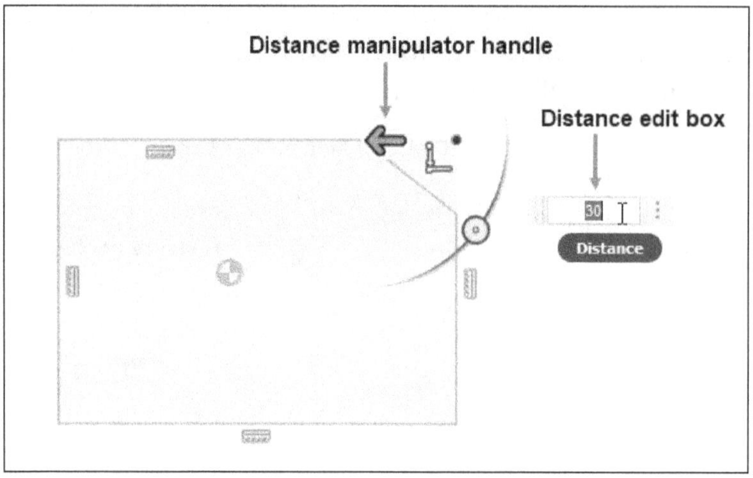

Figure-75. Specifying the distance of chamfer

- After specifying the chamfer distance, press **TAB** key from the keyboard.
- Type desired angle value in the **Angle** edit box or drag the angle manipulator handle to specify the angle of chamfer; refer to Figure-76.

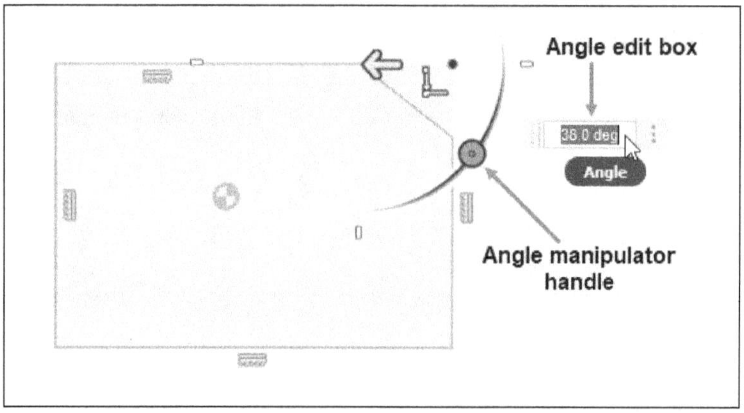

Figure-76. Specifying the angle of chamfer

- After specifying the chamfer angle, press **ENTER**. The distance and angle chamfer will be created; refer to Figure-77.

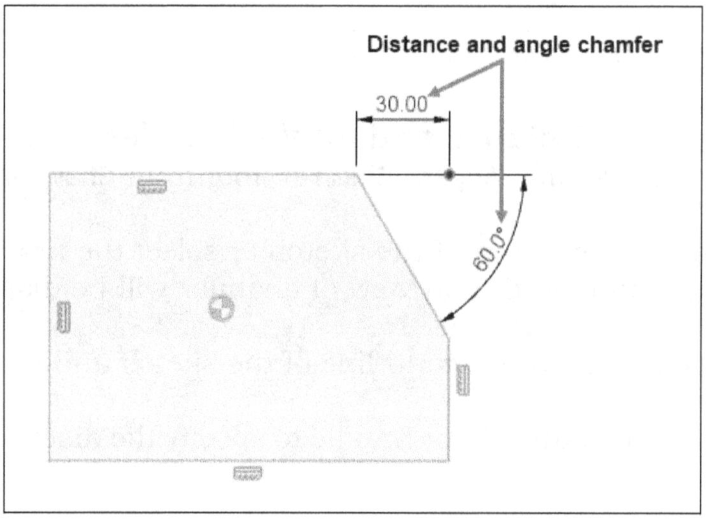

Figure-77. Distance and angle chamfer created

Two Distance Chamfer

- Click on the **Two Distance Chamfer** tool from **Chamfer** cascading menu; refer to Figure-71.
- Hover the cursor on the vertex of the sketch or select the first line and hover the cursor on the second line, the preview of chamfer will be displayed as shown in Figure-78.
- Click on the vertex or on the second line of the sketch and type desired value for the first distance in the **Distance 1** edit box or drag the highlighted distance manipulator handle to specify the first distance of chamfer; refer to Figure-78.

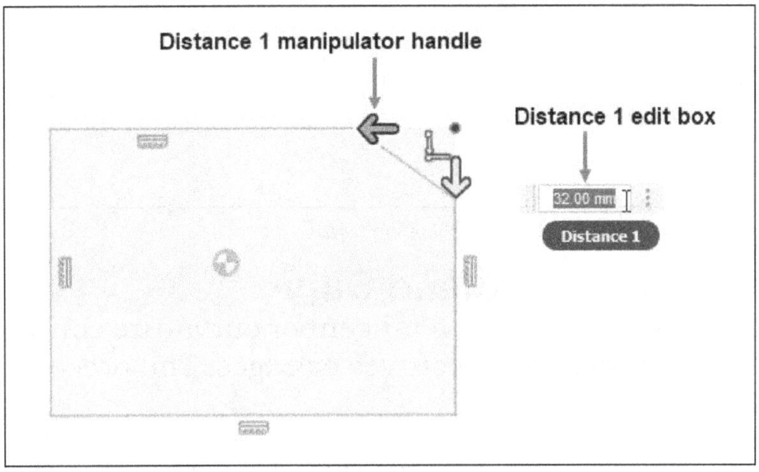

Figure-78. Specifying the first distance of chamfer

- After specifying the first distance, press **TAB** key from the keyboard.
- Type desired value for the second distance in the **Distance 2** edit box or drag the highlighted distance manipulator handle to specify the second distance of chamfer; refer to Figure-79.

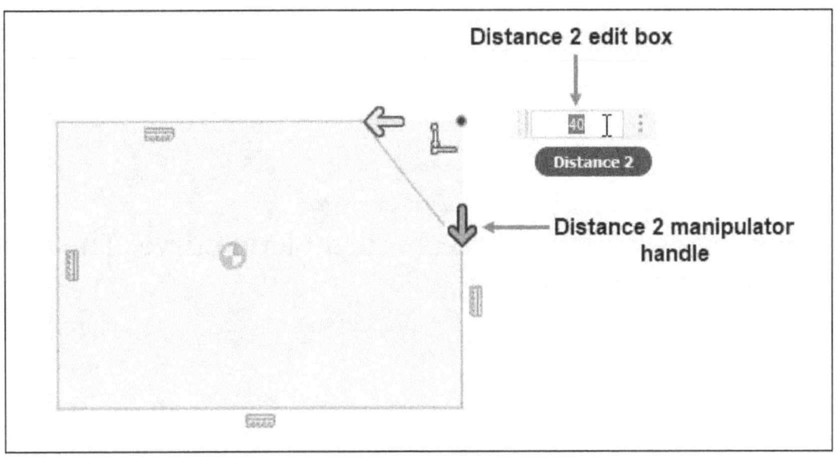

Figure-79. Specifying the second distance of chamfer

- After specifying the second distance of chamfer, press **ENTER**. The two distance chamfer will be created; refer to Figure-80.

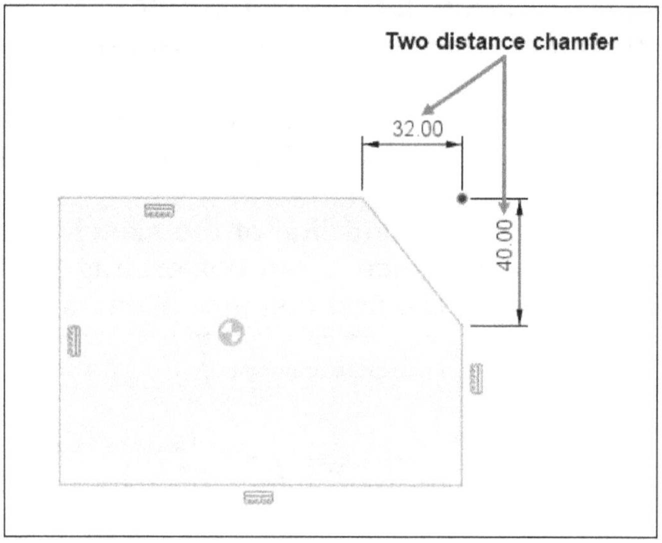

Figure-80. Two distance chamfer created

Blend Curve

The **Blend Curve** tool is used to create a tangent or curvature continuous blend curve between the end points of two sketch curves or edges. The procedure to use this tool is discussed next.

- Click on the **Blend Curve** tool from **Modify** drop-down in the **Toolbar**; refer to Figure-81.

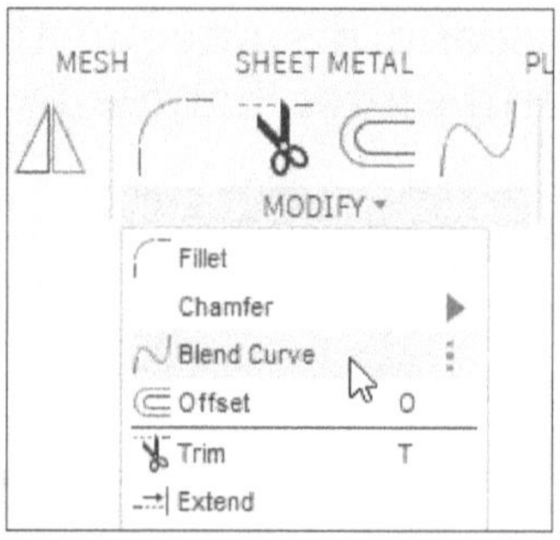

Figure-81. Blend Curve tool

- Select two desired curves or edges to create a blend curve. The continuous blend curve will be created; refer to Figure-82.

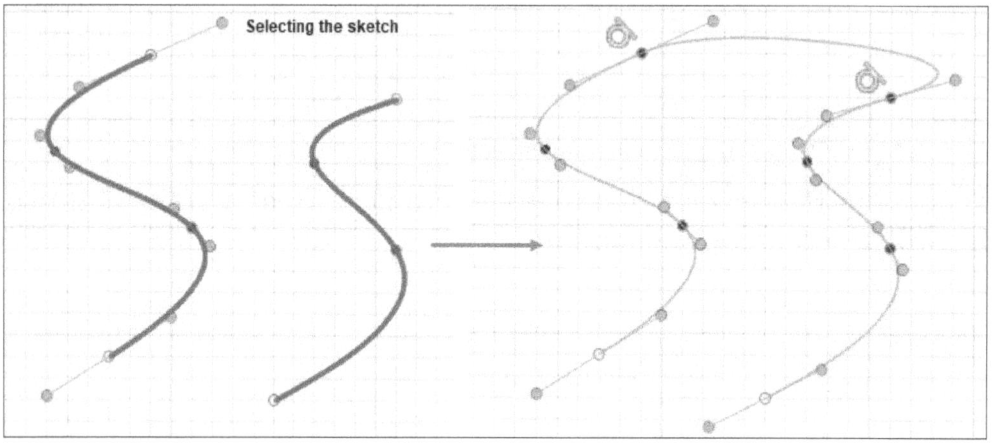

Figure-82. Blend curve created

Offset

The **Offset** tool is used to create copies of the selected entities at a specified distance. If you are the user of **AutoCAD** then this is the most common tool used for creating layouts. The procedure to use this tool is discussed next.

- Click on **Offset** tool of **MODIFY** drop-down from **Toolbar**; refer to Figure-83. The **OFFSET** dialog box will be displayed; refer to Figure-84.

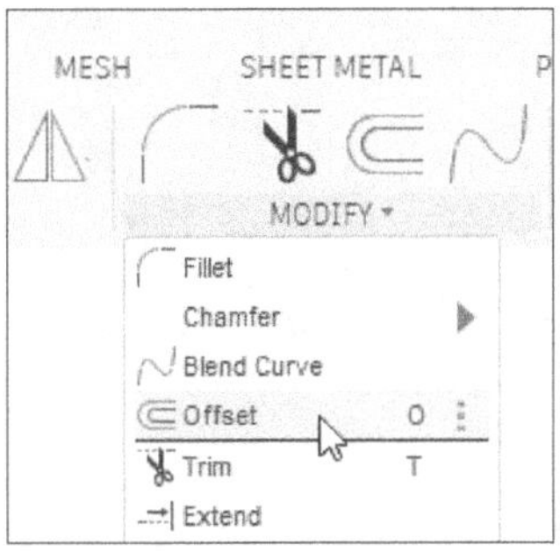

Figure-83. Offset tool

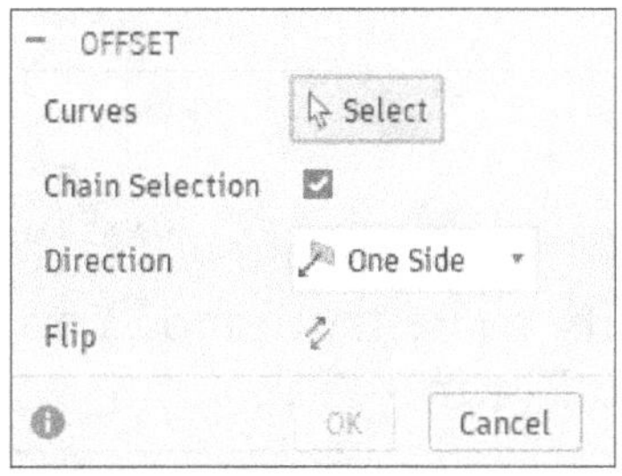

Figure-84. OFFSET dialog box

- The **Curves** selection button is active by default. Select the entities for offset. The updated **OFFSET** dialog box will be displayed.
- Select the **Chain Selection** check box if you want to select all the entities in current chain. Otherwise, clear the check box if you want to select only segments of chain for offset.
- Select **One Side** option from the **Direction** drop-down to create offset copy on one side of the selected curve. Select **Two Sides** option to create offset copies on both sides of the selected curve. Select **Symmetric** option to offset equal distance on both sides of the selected curve.
- Toggle the **Flip** button to flip the side of offset copy with respect to original curve.
- Click in the **Distance** edit box and type desired distance for offset; refer to Figure-85. You can also set the offset distance by moving the drag-handle from screen.

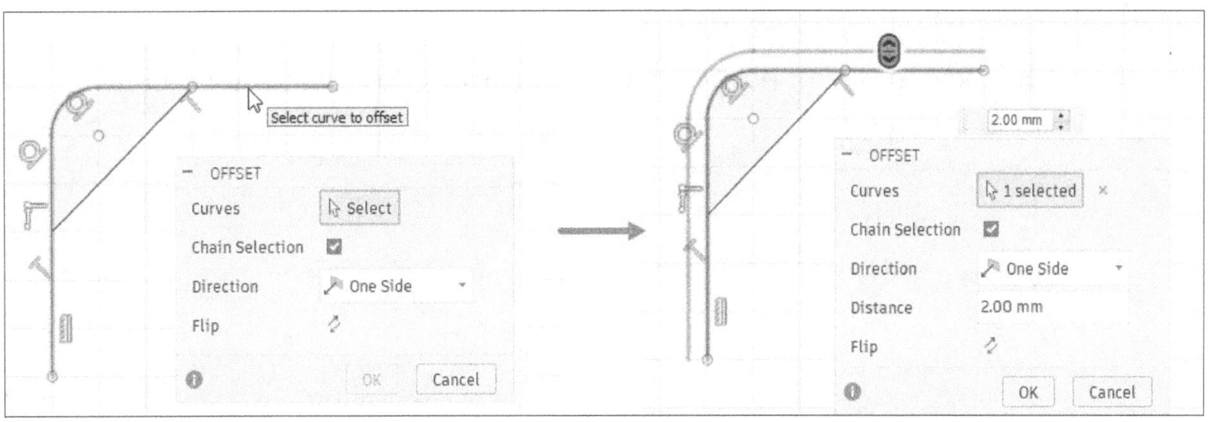

Figure-85. Creating the offset

- Click **OK** button of **OFFSET** dialog box to finish the process.

Trim

The **Trim** tool is used to remove unwanted portion of a sketch entity. While removing the segments, the tool considers intersection point as the reference for trimming. The procedure to use this tool is discussed next.

- Click on **Trim** tool of **MODIFY** drop-down from **Toolbar**; refer to Figure-86.

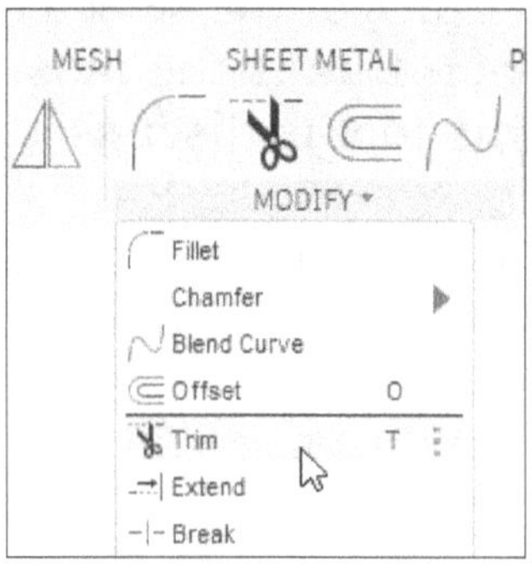

Figure-86. Trim tool

- Click on the entity to be trimmed. You can also trim multiple entities by clicking on them; refer to Figure-87.

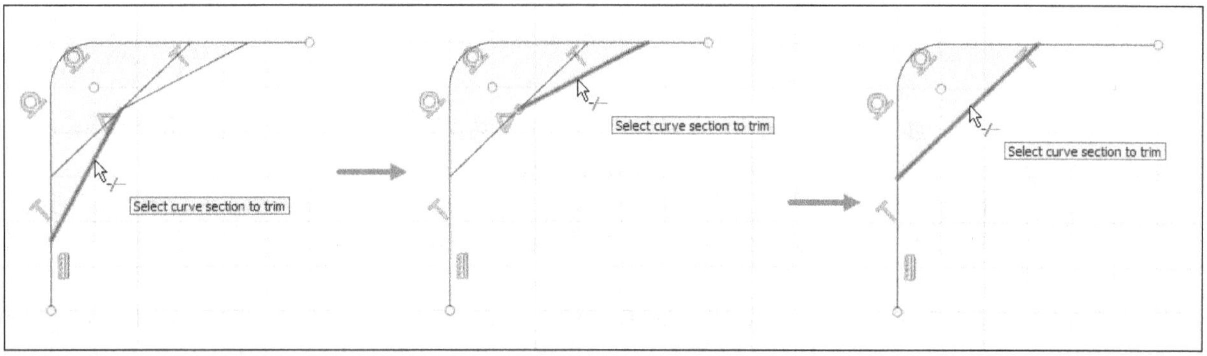

Figure-87. Trimming the multiple entities

- Press **ESC** key to exit this tool.

Extend

The **Extend** tool does the reverse of **Trim** tool. This tool is available below the **Trim** tool. The **Extend** tool extends the sketch entities up to the nearest intersecting entities. The procedure to use this tool is discussed next.

- Click on the **Extend** tool of **MODIFY** drop-down from **Toolbar**; refer to Figure-88.

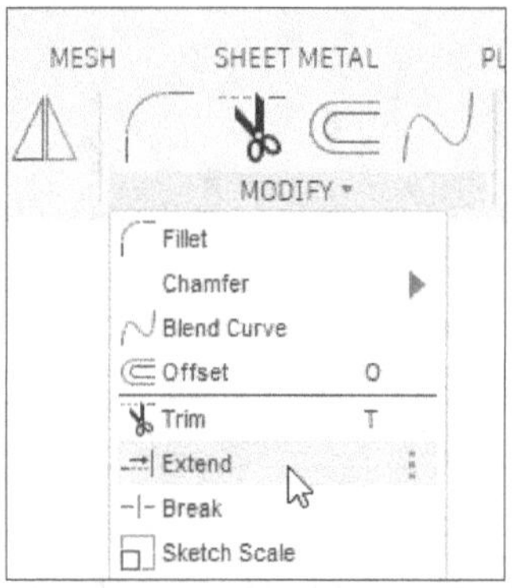

Figure-88. Extend tool

- Hover the cursor on the entity that you want to extend. Preview of extension will display.
- Click on the entity if the preview is as per your requirement. Figure-89 shows the process of extending the entity.

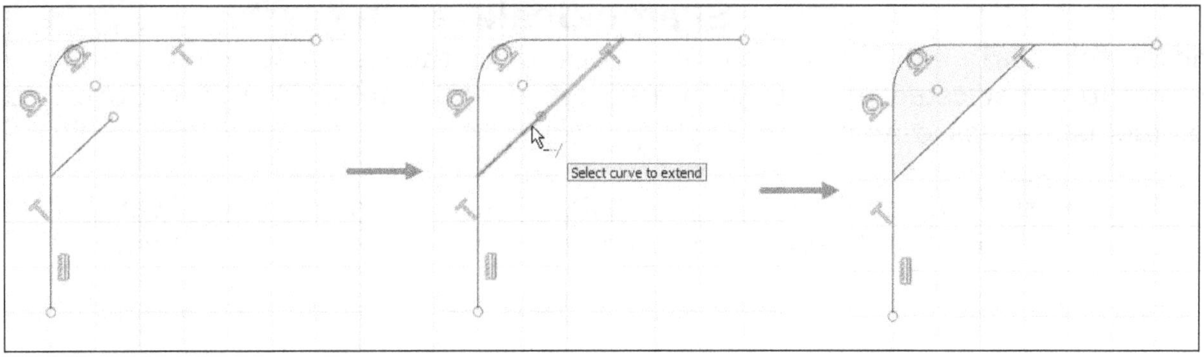

Figure-89. Extending the entity

- Press **ESC** key to exit this tool.

Break

The **Break** tool is used to break the entity at selected reference points. The procedure to use this tool is discussed next.

- Click on **Break** tool of **MODIFY** drop-down from **Toolbar**; refer to Figure-90.

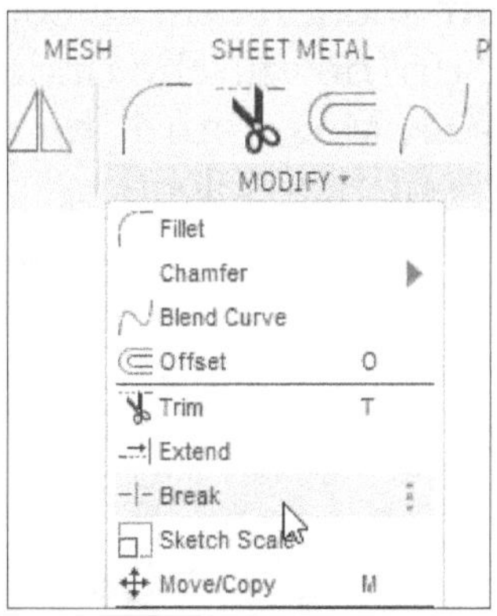

Figure-90. Break tool

- Hover the cursor on the entity. The preview of break will be displayed. Note that there must be an intersecting curve on selected entity to apply break.
- If preview is as per your requirement then click on the entity to break; refer to Figure-91.

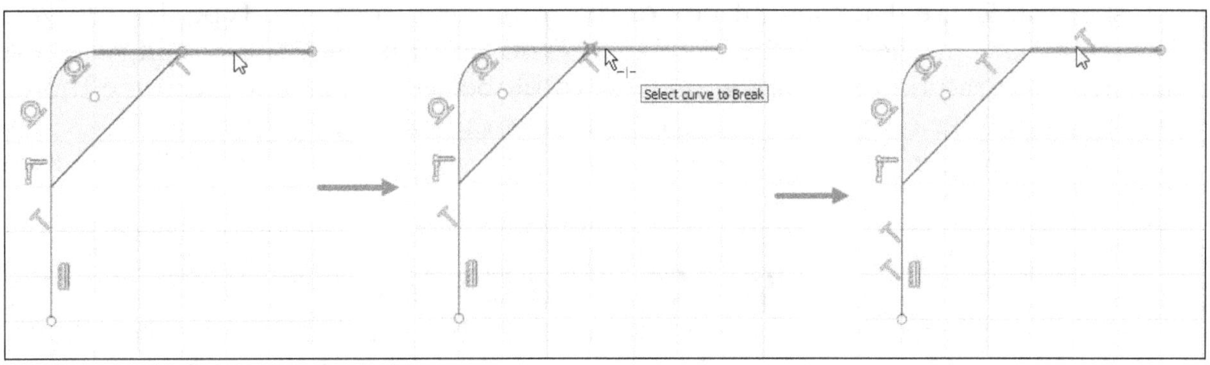

Figure-91. Creation of break

- Press **ESC** key to exit this tool.

Sketch Scale

The **Sketch Scale** tool is used to enlarge or reduce the size of selected entities with respect to the selected point based on specified scale factor. The procedure to use this tool is discussed next.

- Click on the **Sketch Scale** tool of **MODIFY** drop-down from **Toolbar**; refer to Figure-92. The **SKETCH SCALE** dialog box will be displayed; refer to Figure-93.

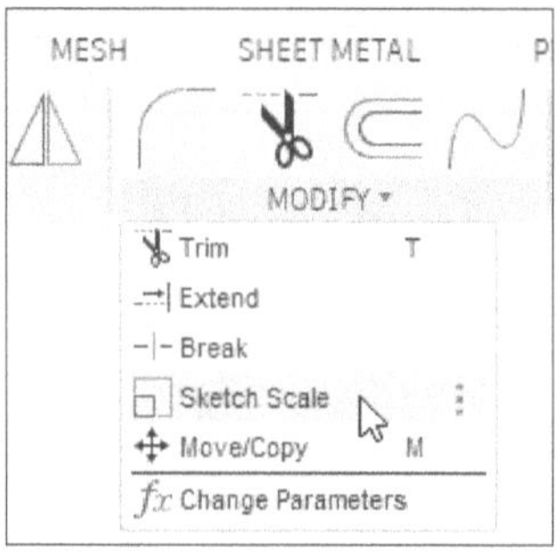

Figure-92. Sketch Scale tool

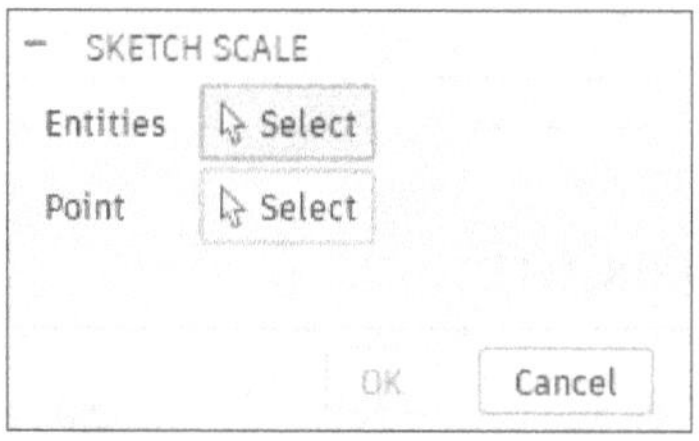

Figure-93. SKETCH SCALE dialog box

- The **Entities** selection box is active by default. Click on the entities to be scaled.
- Click on **Select** button of **Point** section and select the reference point about which selected entities will be scaled up/down. The updated **SKETCH SCALE** dialog box will be displayed; refer to Figure-94. Make sure the point to be selected as reference has not been selected during entities selection.

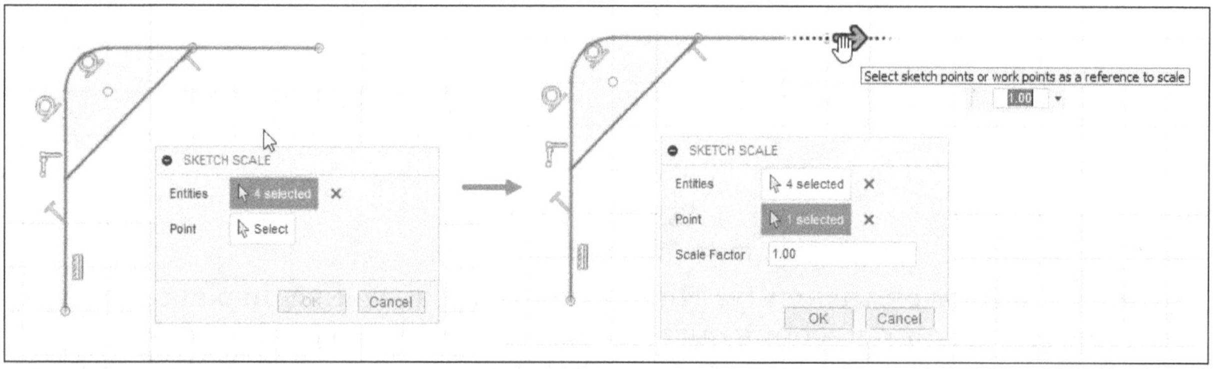

Figure-94. Scaling the sketch

- Click in the **Scale Factor** edit box or dynamic input box and type desired value for scale. The preview will be displayed. You can also set the scaling value by moving the drag handle from screen. A value between **0** to **1** will reduce the size and value higher than **1** will increase the size of selected entities.
- If preview is as per your requirement then click on the **OK** button of **SKETCH SCALE** dialog box to complete the process.

SKETCH PALETTE

When sketch mode is active, the **SKETCH PALETTE** dialog box is displayed at bottom right corner of Fusion screen. This dialog box contain commonly used sketch options and sketch constraints; refer to Figure-95.

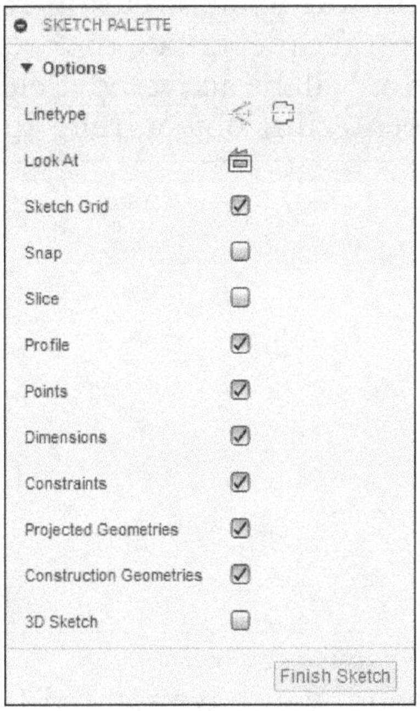

Figure-95. SKETCH PALETTE dialog box

The various tools of Sketch Palette are discussed next.

Options

In **Options** section of **SKETCH PALETTE** dialog box, there are various options to activate or deactivate sketch functions. These options are discussed next.

- **Linetype-** Select **Construction** button from **Linetype** section while creating any sketch object like line, circle, rectangle, etc. The object will be created as construction geometry; refer to Figure-96. Select **Centerline** button from **Linetype** section while creating sketch of only line object to create it as centerline. The object will be created as centerline geometry; refer to Figure-97. Click again on these buttons to return to normal sketching mode.

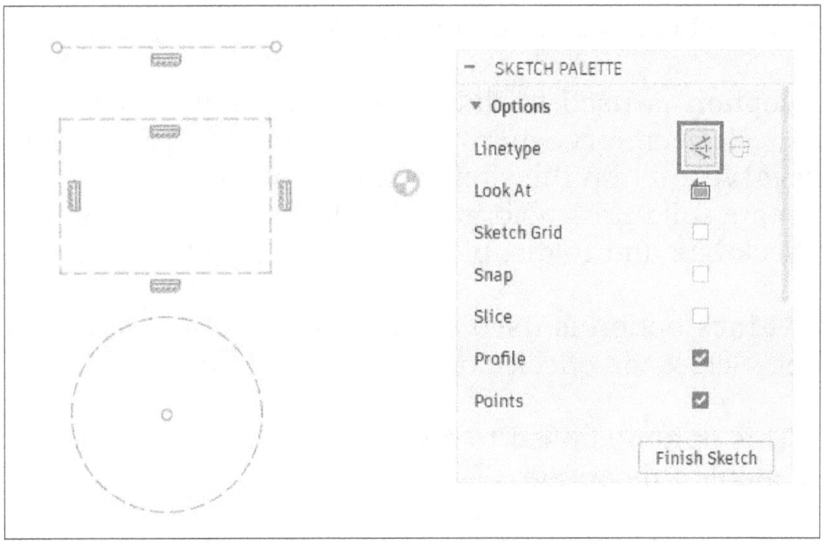

Figure-96. Creating construction geometries

By default, the **Centerline** button while creating rectangle object is disable. To create the rectangle object as centerline, create the rectangle and select it by window selection. The **Centerline** button will be activated. Select the **Centerline** button. The rectangle object will become centerline object; refer to Figure-97.

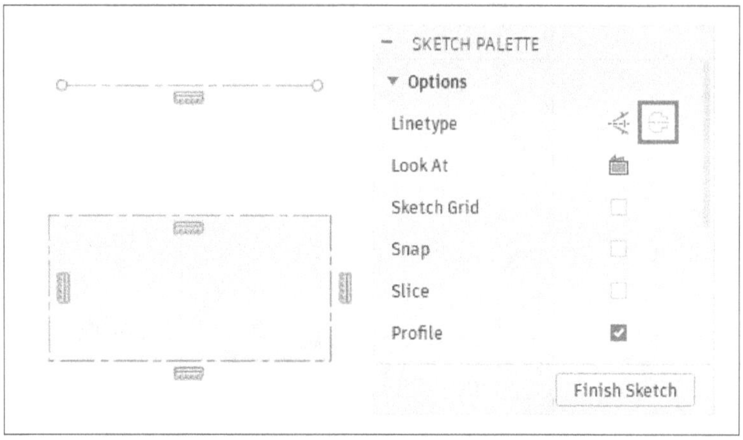

Figure-97. Creating centerline geometries

- **Look At-** If due to any reason, you have rotated the model while sketching and want to make the sketching plane parallel to screen again then click on the **Look At** button once.

- **Sketch Grid-** This option controls the display of sketch grid. To view grid, select the **Grid** check box otherwise clear the check box to hide.

- **Snap-** This option controls the grid Snap. To activate grid snapping, select **Snap** check box and clear the **Snap** check box to disable. Note that the snapping of key points like end point, intersection point, mid point, etc. will still be active even if you clear the **Snap** check box.

- **Slice-** This option cuts the solid/surface part using **Sketch Plane** if it is coming before sketching plane while creating sketch. This tool does not change the geometry because it is only a display option. To enable, select the **Slice** check box and clear the **Slice** check box to disable.

- **Profile-** This option is used to display closed profiles in the sketch. This tool is useful to check geometry when you are going to apply protrusion tools like **Extrude** or **Revolve** later on the sketch. If your sketch is not a closed profile then you cannot create solid protrusions using that sketch. To enable this tool, select the **Profile** check box and to disable it clear the check box.

- **Points-** The **Points** option is used to display points at the end of different open sketch entities. Select the check box to enable this option.

- **Dimensions-** This option is used to display the dimensions of entities. Select the check box to enable this option.

- **Constraints-** This option is used to display or hide the constraints in the sketch. Constrains are used to restrict the movement of object in defined fashion. To display constraints in the sketch, select the **Constraints** check box and clear the check box to hide constraints.

- **Projected Geometries-** This tool is used to display the projected geometries on the sketch. Select the check box to enable and clear the check box to disable this option. Note that projected geometries are generally displayed in dark pink color.

- **Construction Geometries-** This tool is used to display the construction geometries like construction planes, construction axes, construction points, etc.

- **3D Sketch-** This option enables to pull sketch objects out of the sketch plane and create a 3D sketch. To enable this tool, select the **3D Sketch** check box and to disable it clear the check box.

Feature Options

The **Feature Options** section of **SKETCH PALETTE** is displayed when sketch creation tools like rectangle, circle, slot, polygon, and so on are active which have variation in defining their parameters; refer to Figure-98. Select desired option from the **Feature Options** section to switch to different input style for same tool.

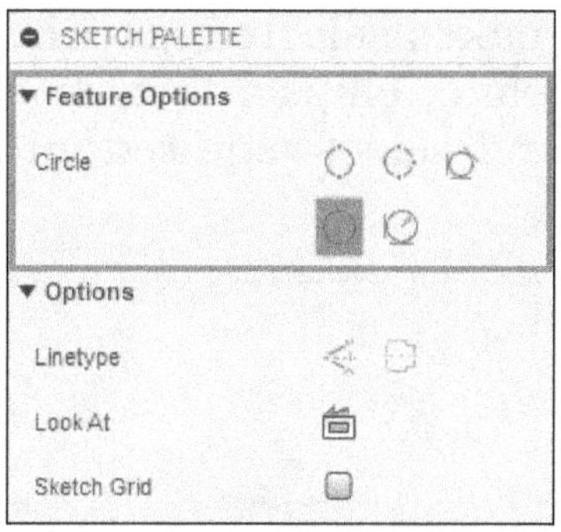

Figure-98. SKETCH PALETTE when Circle tool is active

CONSTRAINTS

The tools in **CONSTRAINTS** panel of **SKETCH** contextual tab are used to apply constraints to the sketch; refer to Figure-99. Constraints are used to restrict the shapes/position of sketch entities with respect to other entities.

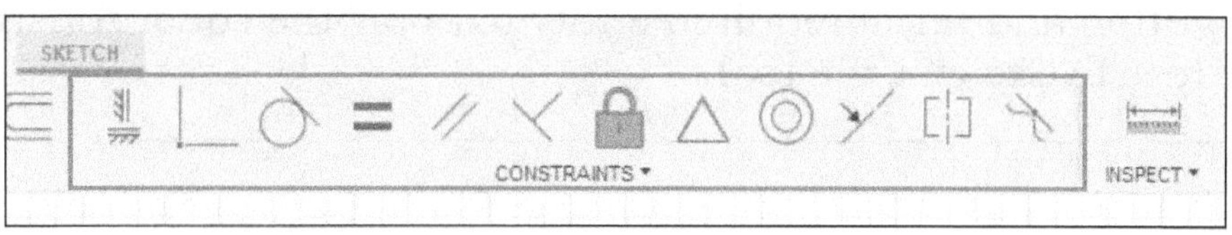

Figure-99. CONSTRAINTS panel

- Make sure the **Constraints** check box is selected from **SKETCH PALETTE** dialog box before working with constraints; refer to Figure-100.

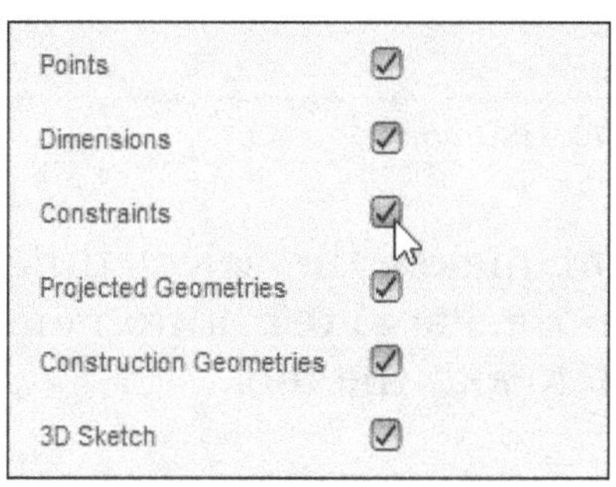

Figure-100. Constraints check box

Various constraints available in Autodesk Fusion are discussed next.

 The **Horizontal/Vertical Constraint** makes one or more selected lines to become horizontal/Vertical. To apply this constraint, click on the **Horizontal/ Vertical** button and select the entities. Press **ESC** to exit the tool. You can also make two points horizontally or vertically in-line by using this constraint.

What if you were trying to make a line vertical constrained but it is becoming horizontal constrained. In such cases, you should drag the end point of line towards vertical orientation and then apply the Horizontal/Vertical constraint.

 The **Coincident Constraint** makes selected point to be coincident with a line, arc, circle, or ellipse. To apply this constraint, select the **Coincident** button from **CONSTRAINTS** panel in **SKETCH** contextual tab and select the entities for coincident. Press **ESC** to exit the tool.

 The **Tangent Constraint** makes selected arc, circle, spline, or ellipse to become tangent to other arc, circle, spline, ellipse, line, or edge. To apply this constraint, click on the **Tangent** button and select required entity. Press **ESC** to exit the tool; refer to Figure-101.

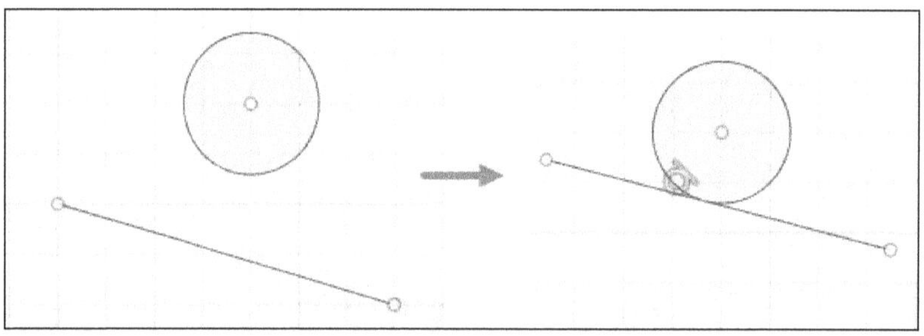

Figure-101. Applying tangent constraint

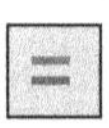 The **Equal Constraint** makes the selected lines to have equal length and the selected arcs or circles to have equal radii/diameter. To apply this constraint, click on the **Equal** button and select required entity to apply the equal constraint; refer to Figure-102. Press **ESC** to exit the tool.

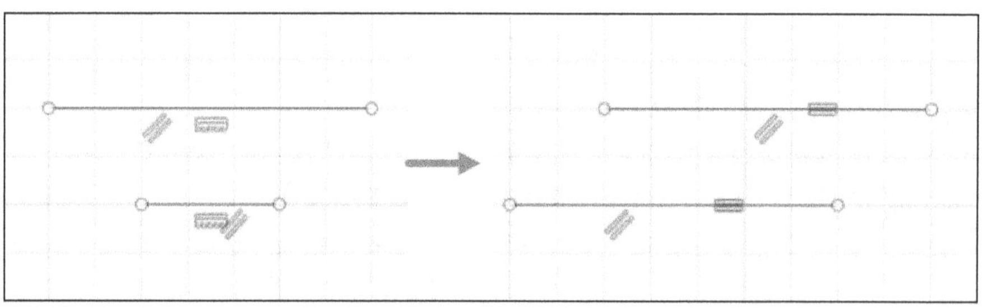

Figure-102. Applying equal constraint

 The **Parallel Constraint** makes the selected lines parallel to each other. To apply this constraint, click on the **Parallel** button and then select desired entities; refer to Figure-103. Press **ESC** to exit the tool.

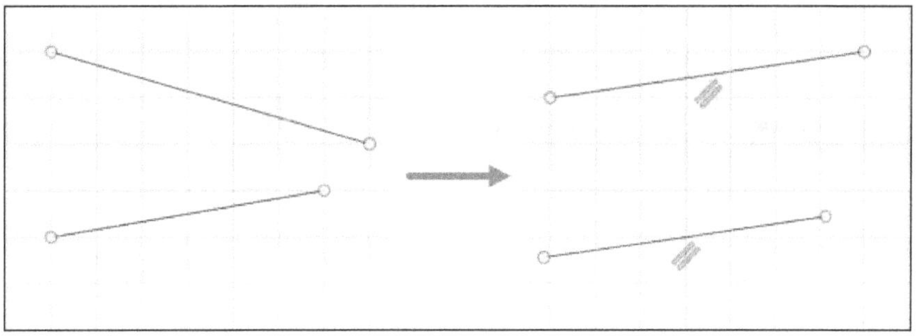

Figure-103. Applying parallel constraint

The **Perpendicular Constraint** makes the selected lines perpendicular to each other. To apply this constraint, click on the **Perpendicular** button and select the entities; refer to Figure-104. Press **ESC** to exit the tool.

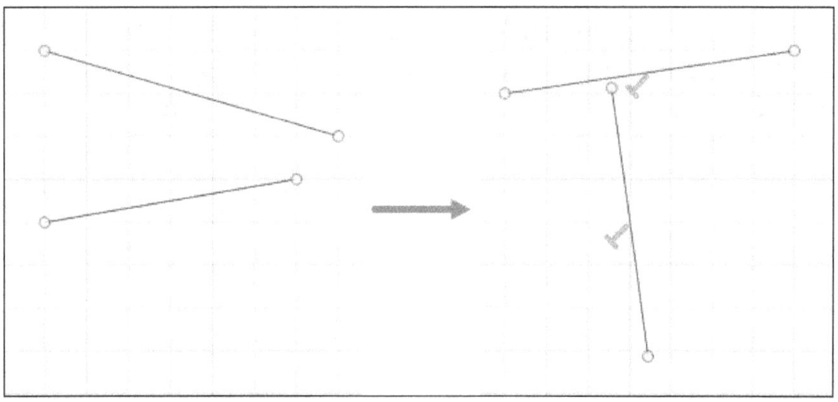

Figure-104. Applying perpendicular constraint

The **Fix/Unfix Constraint** makes the selected entity to be fixed at current position. If you apply this constraint to a line or an arc, its location will be fixed but you can change its size by dragging the endpoints or specifying value. To apply this constraint, click on the **Fix/Unfix** button and select the entities. Press **ESC** to exit the tool.

Fix option is useful when you want to restrict the movement of an entity while applying other constraints. Like, if you want the arc to move in place of line then you can fix the line by applying **Fix** constraint before applying **MidPoint** constraint.

The **MidPoint Constraint** places selected point of an entity as shown in Figure-105 on the midpoint of another sketch entity. To apply this constraint, click on the **MidPoint** button. Select the point and then select the entity whose midpoint is to be used for constraining; refer to Figure-105. Press **ESC** to exit the tool.

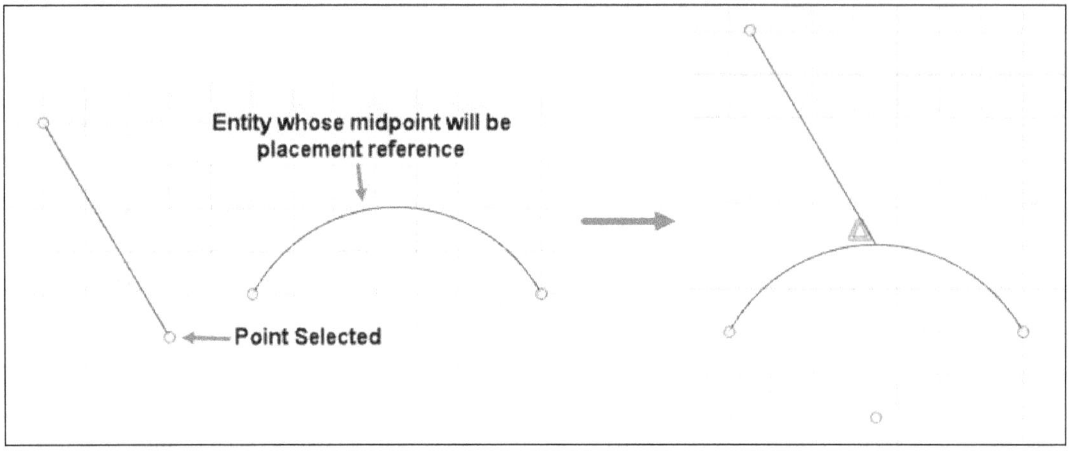

Figure-105. Applying midpoint constraint

The **Concentric Constraint** makes selected arc or circle to share the same center point with other arc, circle, point, vertex, or circular edge. To apply this constraint, click the **Concentric** button and then select the two entities to be made concentric; refer to Figure-106. Press **ESC** to exit the tool.

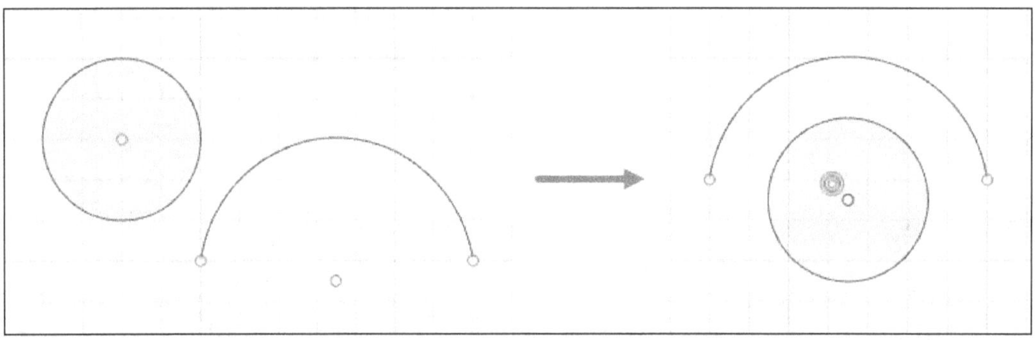

Figure-106. Applying concentric constraint

The **Collinear Constraint** makes the selected lines to lie on the same infinite line; refer to Figure-107. To use this constraint, select the **Collinear constraint** button and select the entities. Press **ESC** to exit the tool.

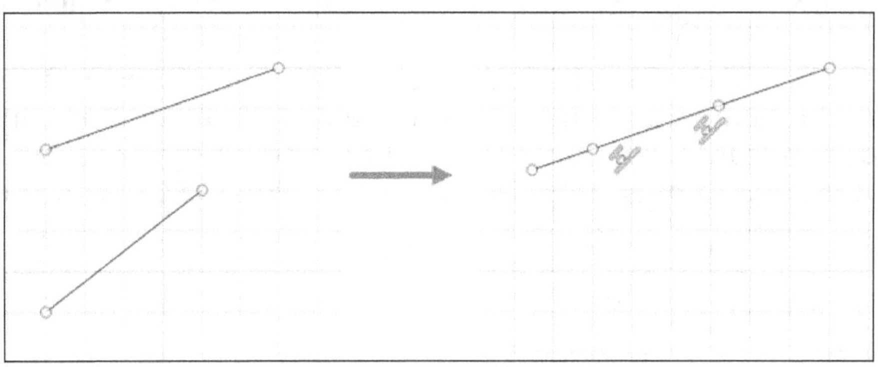

Figure-107. Applying collinear constraint

 The **Symmetry Constraint** makes two selected lines, arcs, points, and ellipses to remain symmetric about a reference line. To apply this constraint, click on the **Symmetric** button and select the two objects to be symmetric about the reference line. You will be asked to select reference object. Select the line to be used as symmetry reference. The constraint will be applied; refer to Figure-108. Press **ESC** to exit the tool.

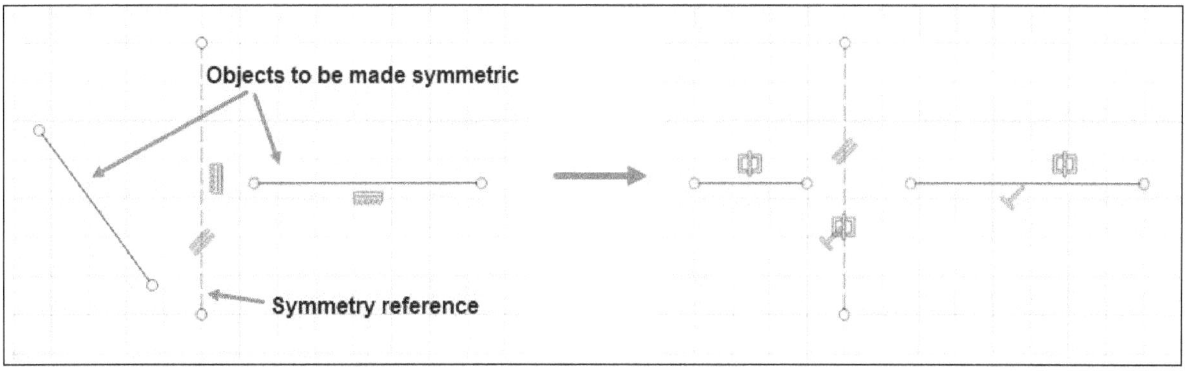

Figure-108. Applying symmetry constraint

 The **Curvature Constraint** is used to create a curvature continuous (G2) condition between selected sketch entities which meet at sharp vertex. To use this tool, click on **Smooth** button and select desired entities near sharp vertex; refer to Figure-109. Press **ESC** to exit the tool.

While applying curvature constraint to splines, make sure you select the splines not the control handles.

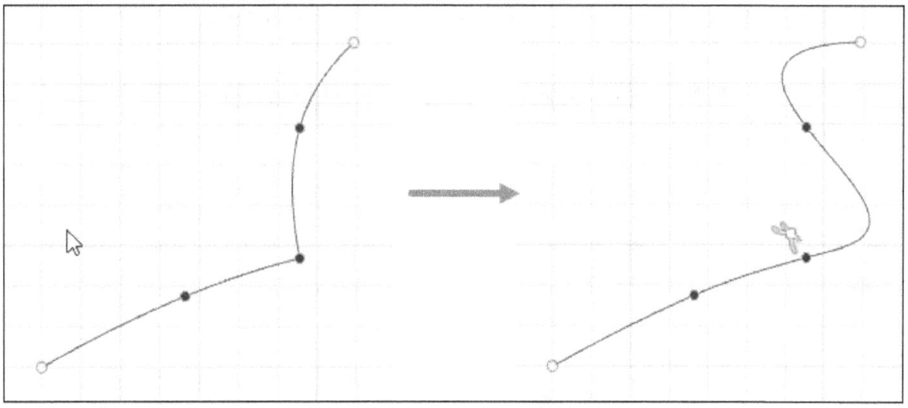

Figure-109. Applying curvature constraint

Except for Horizontal/Vertical and Fix constraint, you can also select an external entity such as an edge, plane, axis, or sketch curve of an external sketch as reference to apply the constraint.

PRACTICAL 1

Create the sketch as shown in Figure-110. Also, dimension the sketch as per the figure.

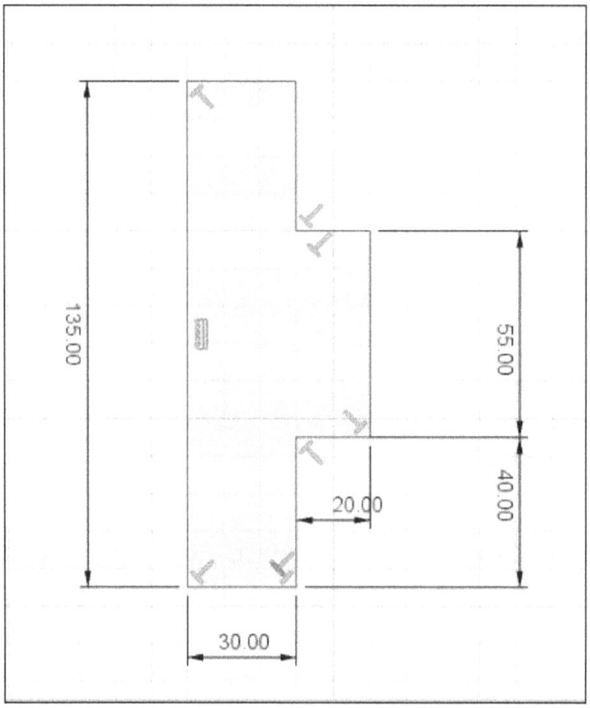

Figure-110. Practical 1

Steps to be Performed:

Below is the step by step procedure of creating the sketch.

Starting Sketching Environment

- Start **Autodesk Fusion** if not started already.
- Select the **New** tool from **File** menu to start a new design; refer to Figure-111.

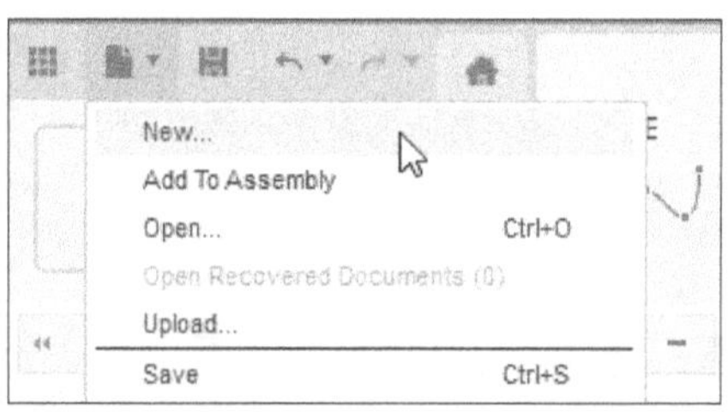

Figure-111. New tool

- Select the **Create Sketch** tool from **CREATE** drop-down; refer to Figure-112. You will be asked to select a sketching plane; refer to Figure-113.

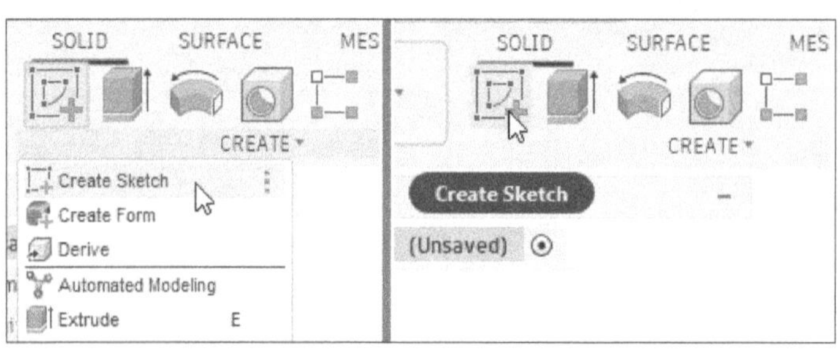

Figure-112. Create Sketch tool

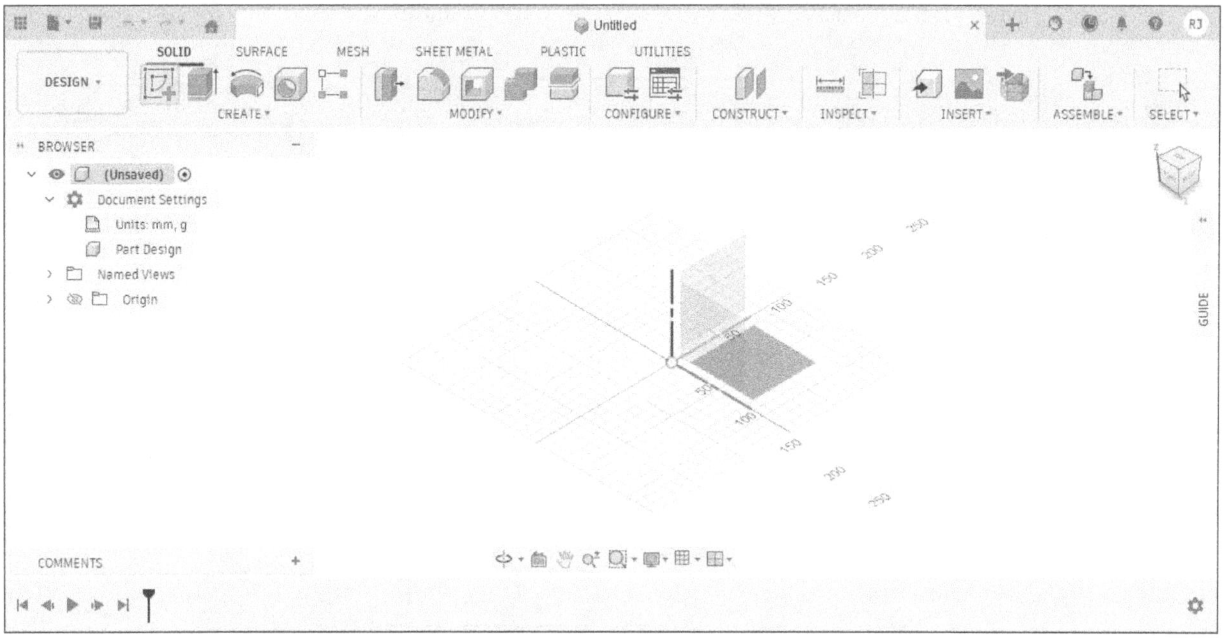

Figure-113. Select plane for sketch

- Select the "**Top**"(XY) plane for sketching.

Creating Lines

- Click on the **Line** button from **CREATE** drop-down or press **L** key from keyboard to select line. The **Line** tool will become active and you will be asked to select the start point.
- Click on the origin and move the cursor towards right; refer to Figure-114.

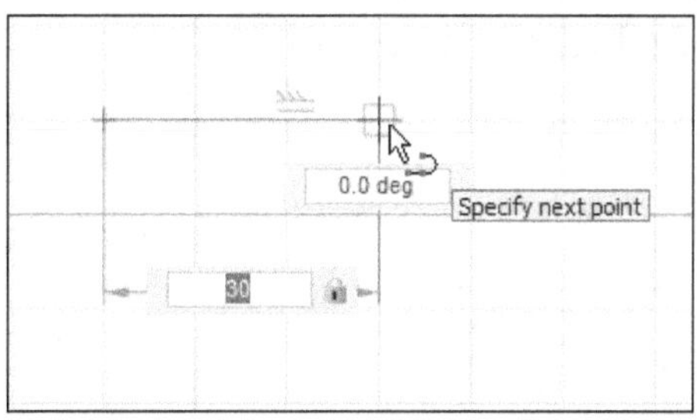

Figure-114. Starting creation of line

- Type the value **30** in the dimension box displayed near line and press **TAB** key to lock the dimension. Click on the screen to create a line.
- Move the cursor vertically upwards and type the value **40** in the dimension box and press **TAB** key to lock the dimension and then click on the screen to complete the line.
- Move the cursor towards right and type the value **20** in the dimension box. Lock the dimension as discussed earlier and click on screen; refer to Figure-115.

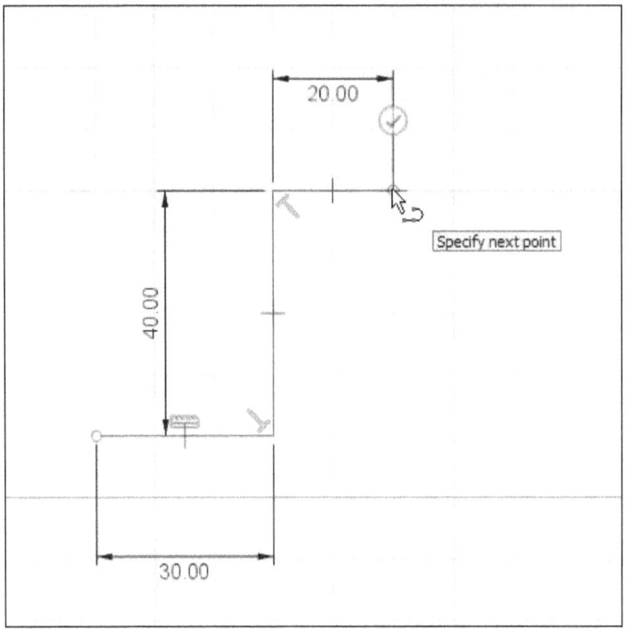

Figure-115. Sketch after specifying 20 value

- Move the cursor upward and type the value **55** in the dimension box. Press **TAB** key to lock the dimension and then click on the screen to complete the line.
- Move the cursor left and type the value **20** in the dimension box. Press **TAB** key to lock the dimension and then click on the screen to complete the line.
- Move the cursor upwards and type the value **40** in the dimension box. Press **TAB** key to lock the dimension and then click on the screen to complete the line.
- Move the cursor towards left and type the value **30** in the dimension box. Press **TAB** key to lock the dimension and then click on the screen to complete the line.
- Move the cursor downward and click on the origin to close the sketch. Press **ESC** to exit the line tool.

The sketch after performing the above steps is displayed as shown in Figure-116.

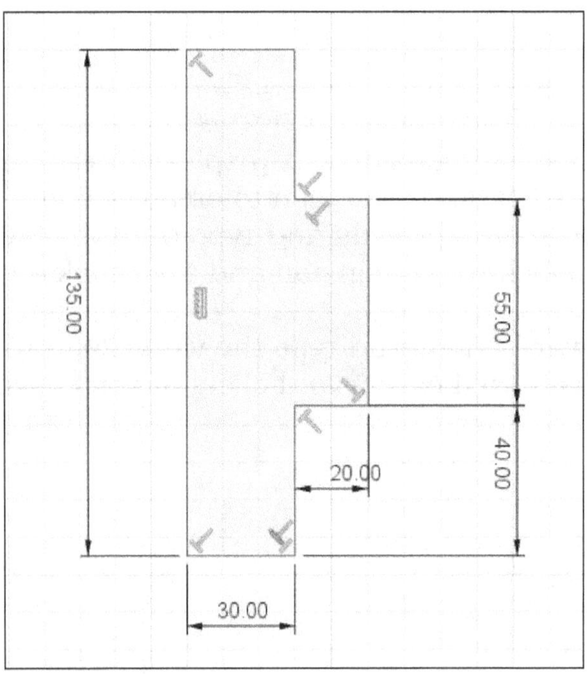

Figure-116. Final Practical 1

PRACTICAL 2

In this practical, you will create the sketch as shown in Figure-117.

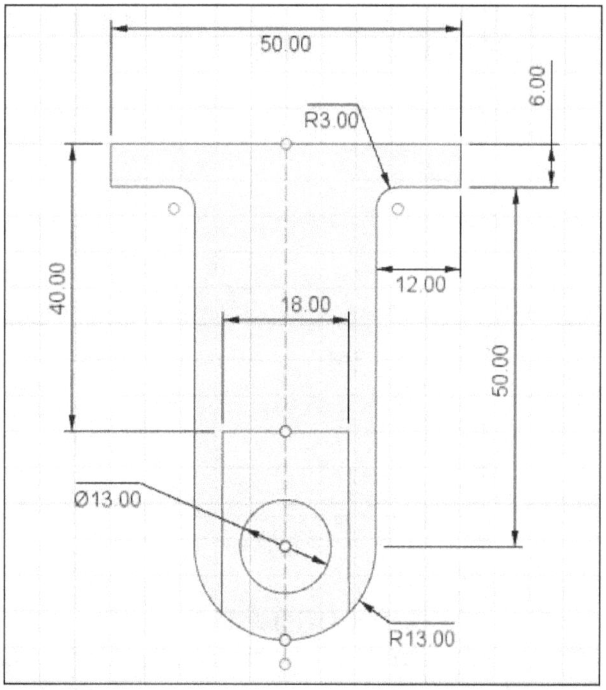

Figure-117. Practical 2

Steps to be performed:

Below is the step by step procedure of creating the sketch shown in the Figure-118.

Starting Sketching Environment

- Start **Autodesk Fusion** if not started already.
- Select the **New Design** tool from **File** menu to start a new design.
- Select the **Create Sketch** tool from **CREATE** drop-down.
- After selecting this tool, you need to select the **plane** for creating sketch.
- Select the **Top Plane** to create the sketch.

Creating Lines

- Click on the **Line** button from **CREATE** drop-down or press **L** key. You are asked to specify the start point of the line.
- Click on the origin and move the cursor towards right. Type the value **25** in the dimension box and press **TAB** key to lock the dimension. Click on the screen to complete the line.
- Move the cursor downward and type the value **6** in the dimension box. Lock the dimension as discussed earlier and click on screen.
- Move the cursor to the left and type the value **12** in the dimension box. Lock the dimension as discussed earlier and click on screen.
- Move the cursor downwards and type the value **50** in the dimension box. Till this point, our sketch should display like Figure-118.

Figure-118. Sketch after creating lines

Creating Arcs

- Select the **Tangent Arc** tool from **Arc** cascading menu in **CREATE** drop-down.
- Click on the end point of the vertical line recently created and move the cursor downwards in such a way that the end point of arc is in-line with the origin.
- Specify the dimension value **13** in the dimension box and press **ENTER** to complete the arc; refer to Figure-119.

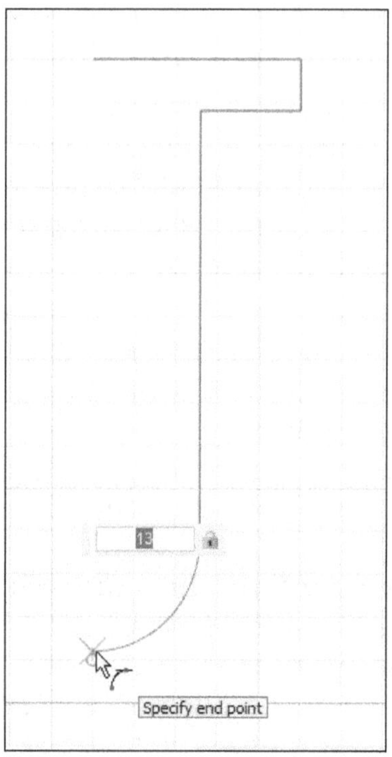

Figure-119. Arc creation

Note that you can also create tangent arc by dragging the cursor while creating line using **Line** tool. To specify dimension of tangent arc, you need to click & hold the **LMB** and then drag the cursor while creating line, specify the radius value for tangent arc, and then release the **LMB**.

Creating Fillet

- Click on the **Fillet** tool from **MODIFY** drop-down/panel in the **SKETCH** contextual tab in the **Toolbar**.
- Select the lines as shown in Figure-120.
- Enter the value as **3** in the radius box.

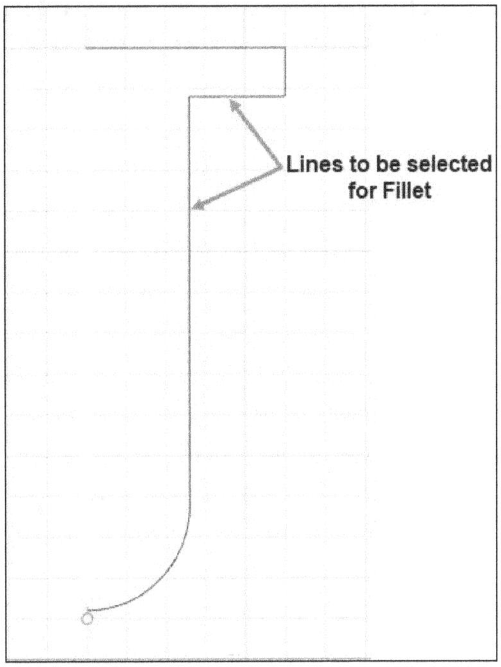

Figure-120. Line selection for fillet

Creating Mirror Copy

- Press **L** key and create a line from origin to end point of the Arc.
- Press **ESC** key from keyboard to exit the tool.
- Now, select the newly created line, right-click on it, and select **Normal Construction** from **Marking menu** or select the newly created line and press **x** from keyboard to convert line into construction geometry. Press **ESC** to exit selection.
- Select the **Mirror** tool from **CREATE** drop-down and select all the entities we have sketched except construction line; refer to Figure-121.

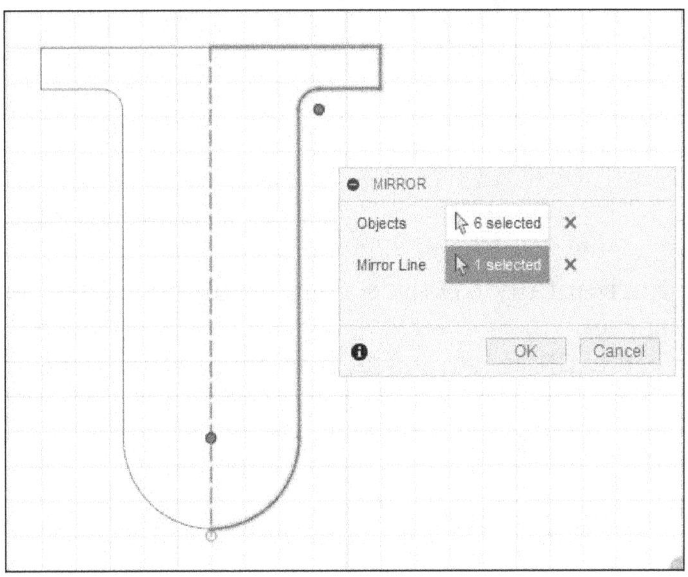

Figure-121. Entities selected for creating mirror

- Click on the **Mirror Line** selection button in the dialog box and select the construction line from sketch. Preview of mirror feature will be displayed.
- Click **OK** button from the **MIRROR** dialog box.

Creating Circle and Lines to complete.

- Click on the **Center Diameter Circle** tool from **Circle** cascading menu.
- Click at the center point of the bottom arc and move the cursor; refer to Figure-122.

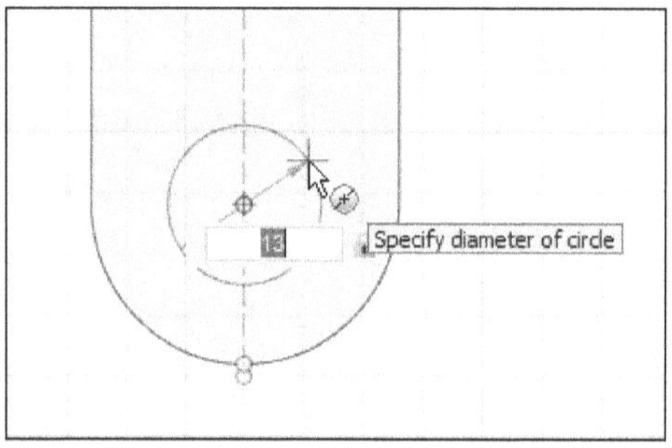

Figure-122. Circle creation

- Enter the dimension as **13** in the input box.
- Click on the **Line** tool from **CREATE** drop-down and click anywhere on the center line (except mid point and end points) to specify the start point of the line; refer to Figure-123.

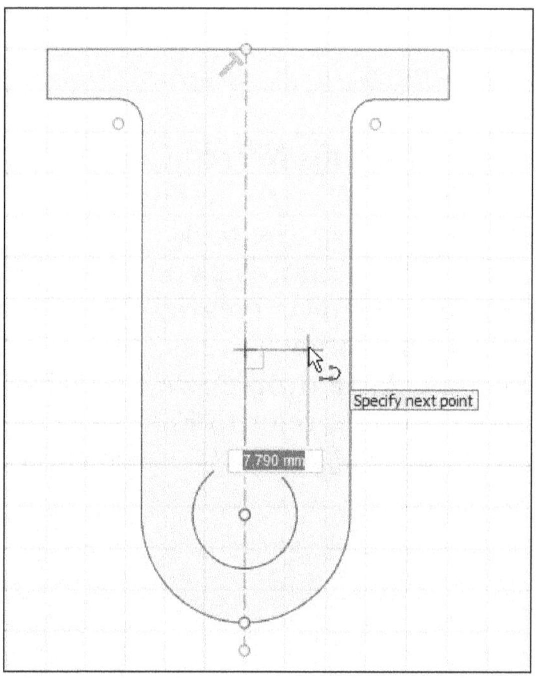

Figure-123. Point selected on centerline

- Move the cursor horizontally towards right and specify the value as **9**. Press **TAB** and click on the screen.
- Move the cursor vertically downwards and click when line passes the arc; refer to Figure-124.

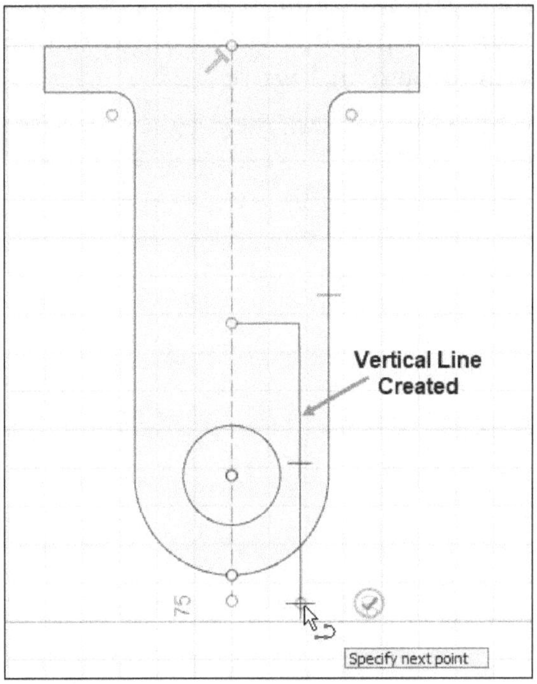

Figure-124. Vertical line created

- Press **ESC** to exit the tool. Click on the **Trim** tool from **MODIFY** drop-down and remove the extra portion outside the arc. Press **ESC** to exit the **Trim** tool.
- Mirror both the lines as we did earlier. The sketch should display as shown in Figure-125.

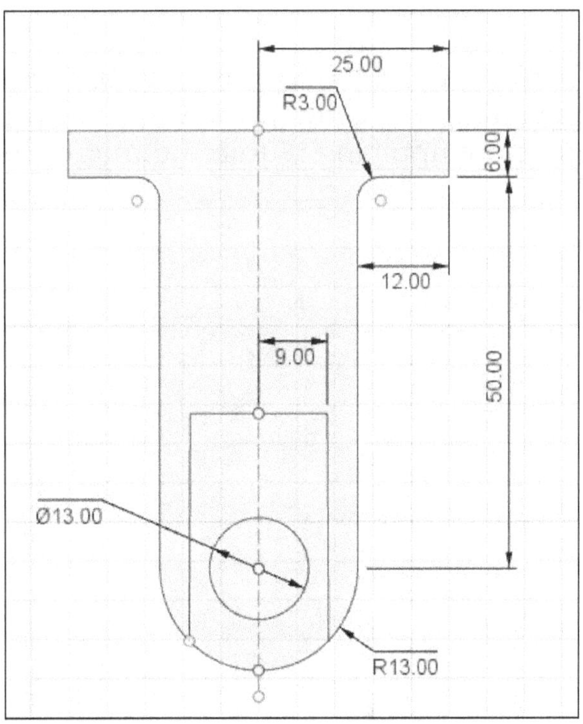

Figure-125. Sketch after all sketching operation

Dimensioning Sketch

Some of the dimensions are applied automatically while creating sketch. To create rest of the dimensions, click on the **Sketch Dimension** tool from **CREATE** panel/drop-down. Dimension symbol will get attached to cursor.

- Click on the arc and place the dimension at proper spacing if not created already. Type the radius in dynamic input box as **13** and press **ENTER.**
- Click on the two lines as shown in Figure-126.

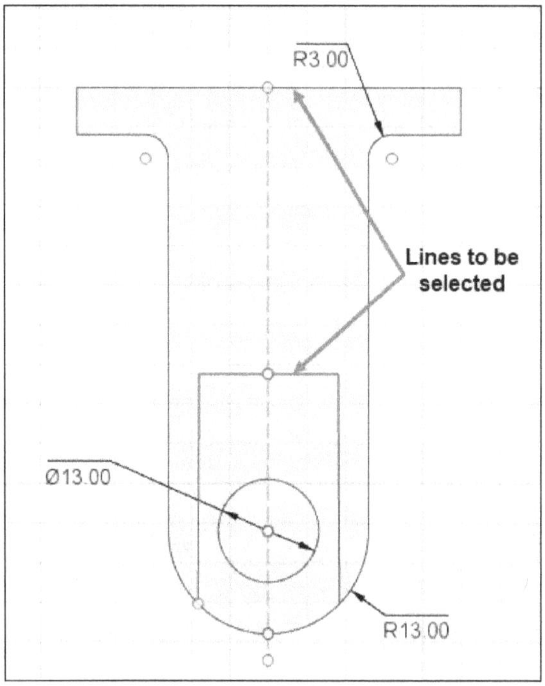

Figure-126. Lines to be selected for dimensioning

- Click to place the dimension at its proper place. In the dynamic input box, enter the value as **40**.

Similarly, dimension all the entity in the sketch until the sketch is fully defined. The final sketch after dimensioning will be displayed as shown in Figure-127. You can delete extra dimensions before applying required dimensions.

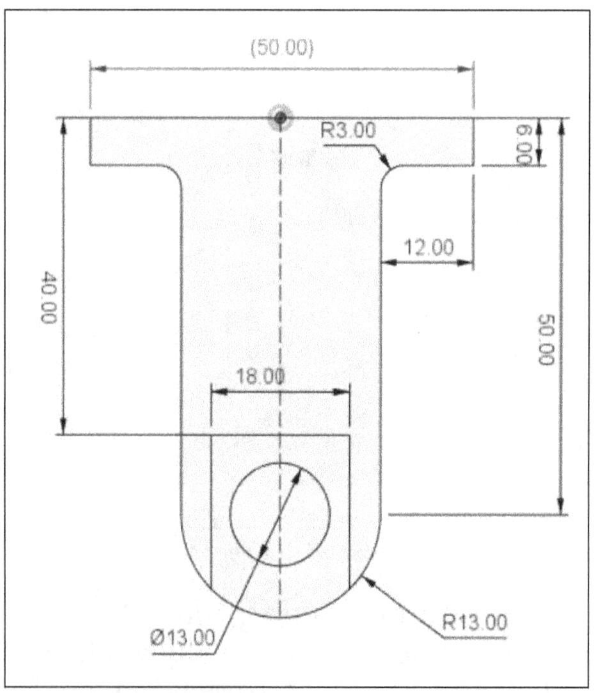

Figure-127. Final sketch

FULLY DEFINED, UNDER-DEFINED, AND OVER-DEFINED SKETCHES

Till this point, you have worked on various sketching tools and you have created sketch for two practical sessions. You might have noticed that some entities are displayed in blue color while some are displayed in bold black color. Also, there are dimensions which are enclosed in bracket. Here, we will discuss why these colors and different dimensions appear.

Fully Defined Sketches

A fully defined sketch is the one whose specifications can not be changed unintentionally. In some complex sketches, when you change the dimension of one entity, the dimension of other entity gets changed automatically. If you have the sketch fully defined then the dimension of the entities will not change unintentionally. In technical terms, a fully defined sketch is the one in which entities have zero degree of freedom. In Autodesk Fusion, the sketch that is fully defined will be displayed in bold black color; refer to Figure-128. In a fully defined sketch, if you try to drag any entity of the sketch then it will not move because its degree of freedom is zero. A fully defined sketch is always recommended for creating features in CAD.

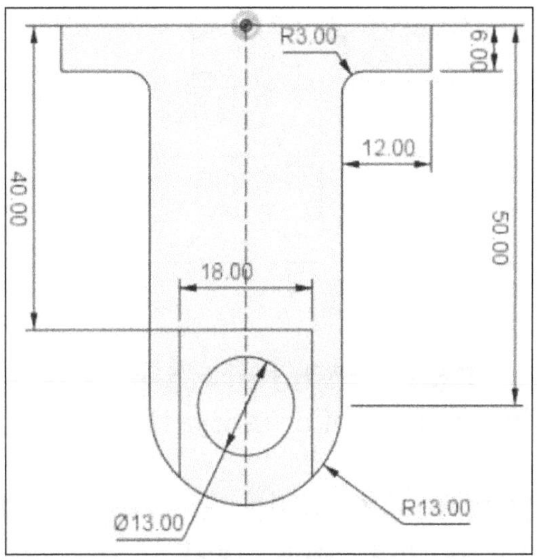

Figure-128. Fully defined sketch

Under Defined Sketches

An under-defined sketch is the one in which all the required dimensions are not applied. An under-defined sketch is displayed in blue color in Autodesk Fusion. When you change the value of a dimension or drag an entity in the under-defined sketch then other entities may change shape/size accordingly. An under-defined sketch is not recommended for CAD modeling.

Over Defined Sketches

An over defined sketch is the one where more dimensions are applied than those required to fully define the sketch. In over-defined sketches, extra dimensions are bound by parenthesis like the **50** dimension; refer to Figure-127.

PRACTICAL 3

Create the sketch as shown in Figure-129. Also, dimension the sketch as per the figure.

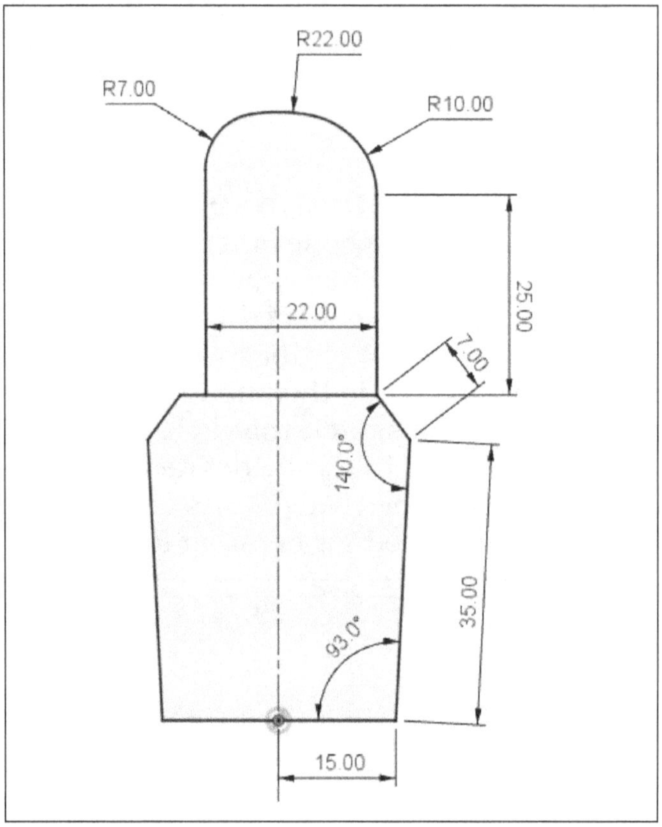

Figure-129. Practical 3

Steps to be performed:

Below is the step by step procedure of creating the sketch.

Starting Sketching Environment

- Start **Autodesk Fusion** if not started already.
- Select the **New Design** tool from **File** menu to start a new design.
- Select the **Create Sketch** tool from **CREATE** drop-down.
- On selecting this tool, you will be asked to select a plane for creating sketch.
- Select the **Top Plane** to create the sketch.

Creating Lines

- Select **Line** tool from **CREATE** drop-down and create a vertical line starting from origin and moving upward. (No need of dimensions, just make it a long one as it is going to be centerline.)
- Select the line and right-click on this line. Marking menu will be displayed. Select **Normal/Construction** tool to make this line as a center line; refer to Figure-130.
- Press **ESC** to exit the tool.

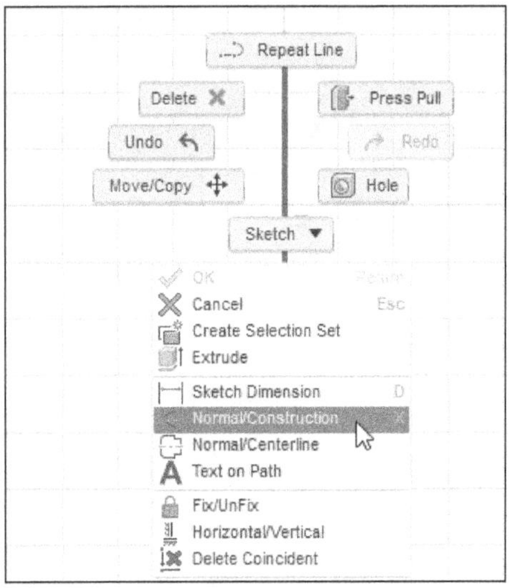

Figure-130. Creating centerline

- Press **L** key to start **Line** tool again and click at the end point of center line to create a line.
- Move the cursor towards right and specify the value as **15** in the dimension box. Press **TAB** key to lock the dimension and click on the screen.
- Move the cursor upward with some outward angle. Specify length as **35** in dimension box. Press **TAB** key to lock the dimension and switch to angle dimension. Specify the angle value as **93** degree and click on the screen.
- Move the cursor to the left, specify the value as **7** in the length input box and **140** degree in angle input box; refer to Figure-131.

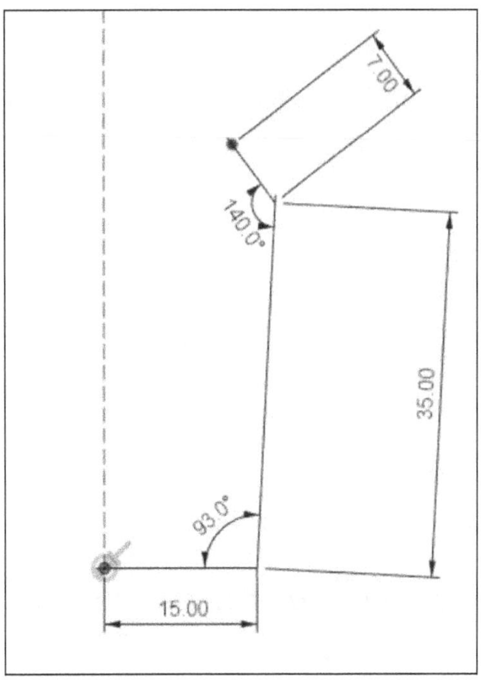

Figure-131. Creating lines with dimensions

Creating Mirror copy

- Select the **Mirror** tool from **CREATE** drop-down and select the entities we have sketched except center line for mirror.
- Click on the **Mirror Line** selection button and select the center line of sketch as mirror line. Preview of mirror will be displayed; refer to Figure-132.

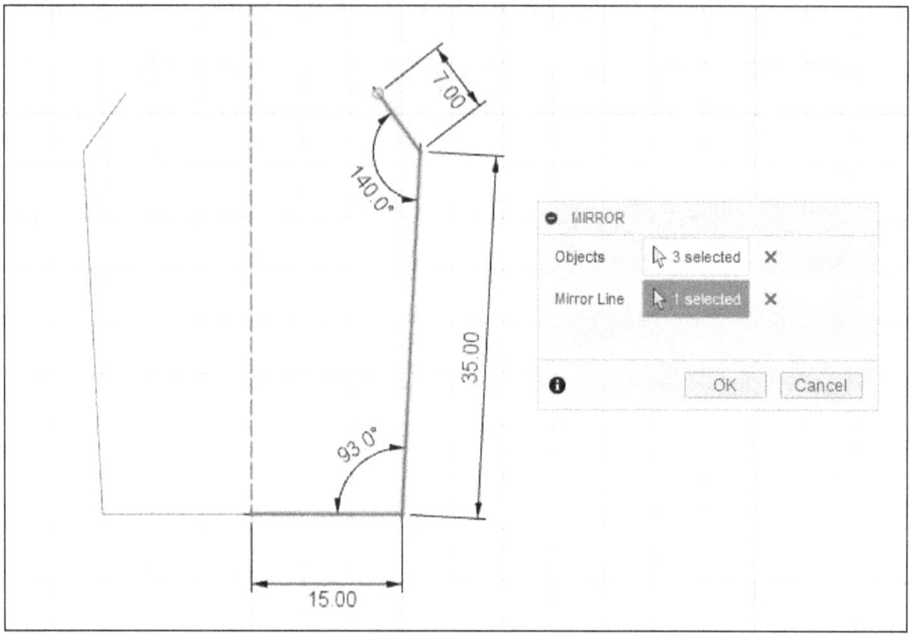

Figure-132. Preview of mirror

- Click **OK** button from **MIRROR** dialog box to complete the mirror copy.
- Now, select **Line** tool and create a line joining the open ends of sketch; refer to Figure-133.

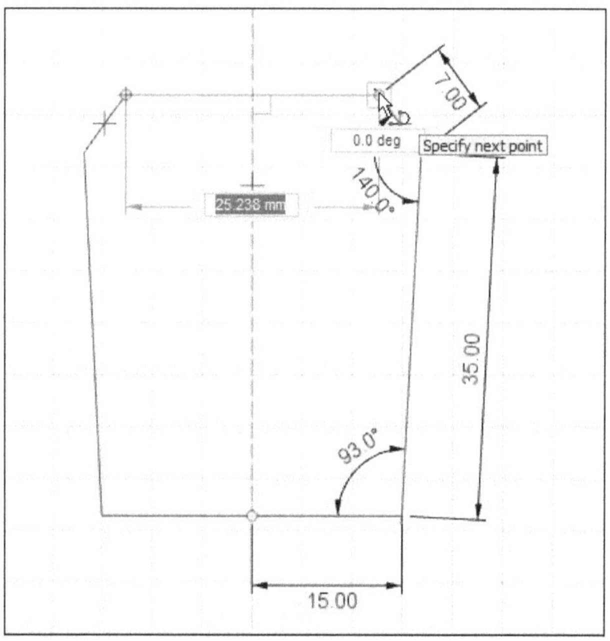

Figure-133. Joining the open ends of sketch

- Create a vertical line from one end of the sketch of length **25** mm as shown in Figure-134.

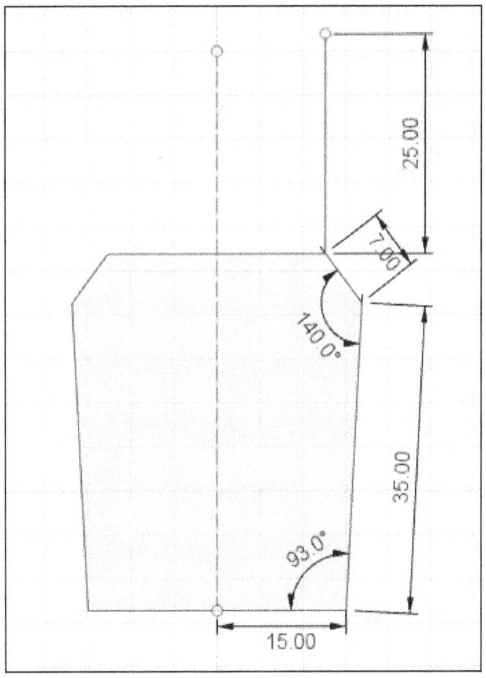

Figure-134. Creating line from right side of sketch

Creating Arcs

- Click **Tangent Arc** tool from **Arc** cascading menu in **CREATE** drop-down.
- Click on the end point of vertical line recently created and move the cursor upwards. Create three consecutive arc joining each other as shown in Figure-135. Press **ESC** to exit the tool.

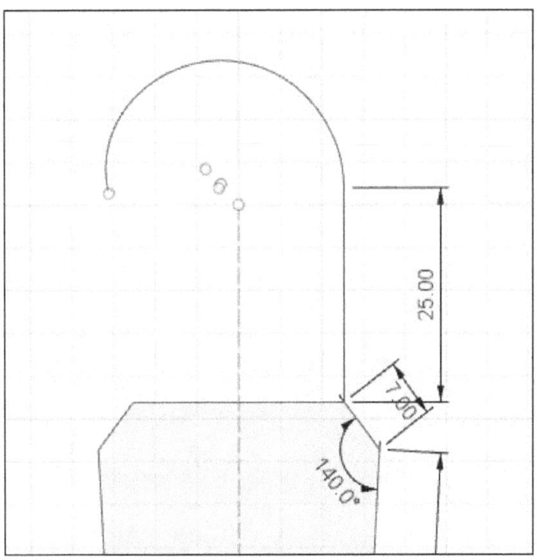

Figure-135. Creating three consecutive arcs

- Select **Sketch Dimension** tool from **CREATE** drop-down or press **D** key to select this tool.
- Apply radius dimensions to three arcs as **10**, **22**, and **7**, respectively; refer to Figure-136. Make sure horizontal and vertical constraints are applied to the straight lines in the sketch.

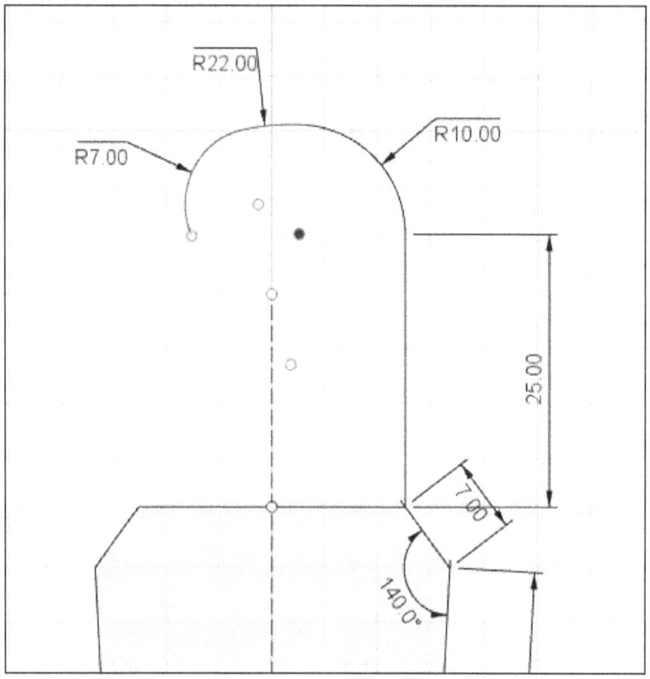

Figure-136. After sketch dimension on arc

- Select the **Line** tool and create a line joining end of recently created arc to horizontal line in the sketch; refer to Figure-137. Press **ESC** tool to exit the command.

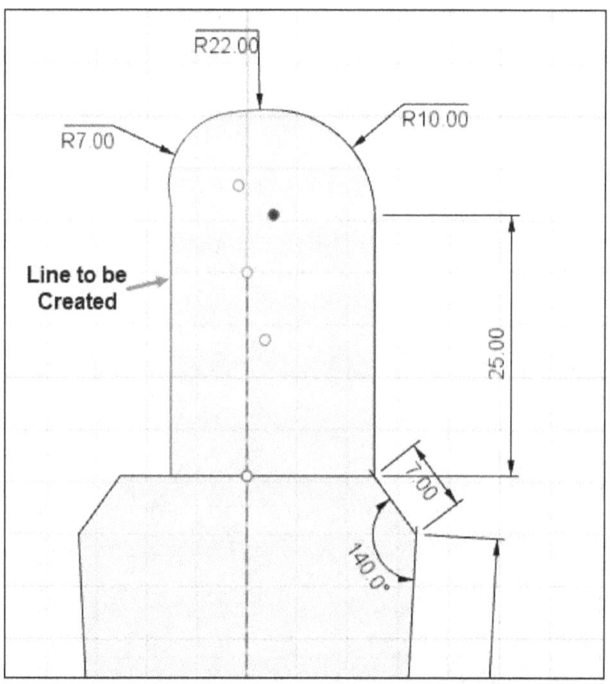

Figure-137. Line to be created

You may find that there is not a smooth transition between newly created line and arc as in our case. In such cases, apply the tangent constraint between line and arc; refer to Figure-138.

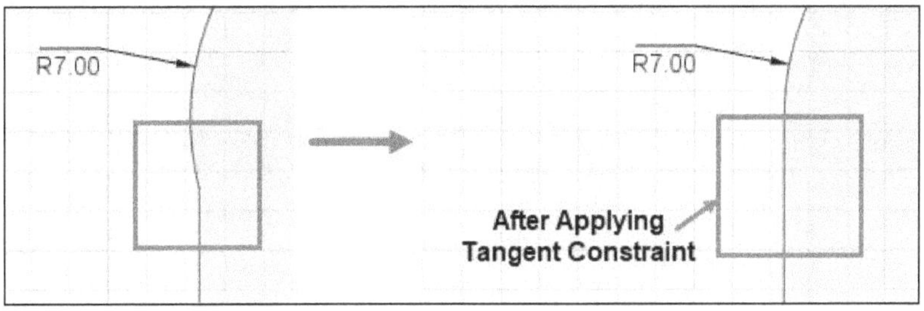

Figure-138. Applying tangent constraint for smooth transition

Dimensioning Sketch

- Select the unwanted dimensions and delete them by pressing **DELETE** key.
- Click on the **Sketch Dimension** tool or press **D** key to select the tool.
- Select the entity and apply the dimension; refer to Figure-139.

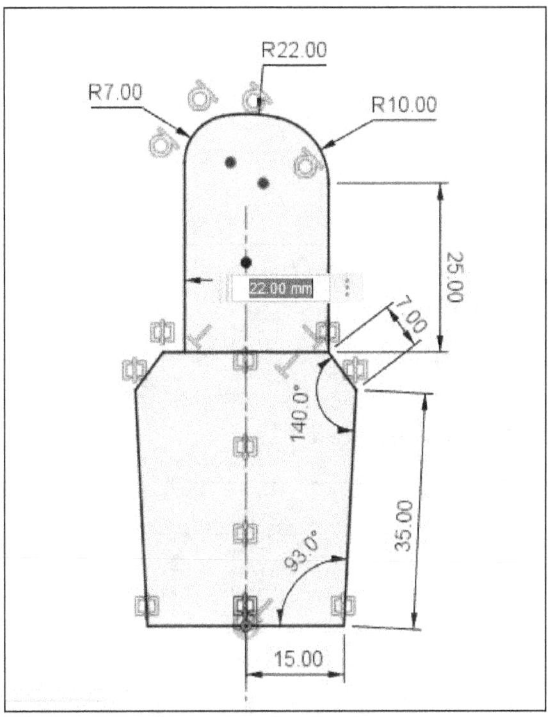

Figure-139. Select entities for dimension

- Drag the dimension to proper place.

Similarly, dimension all the other entities in the sketch until it is fully defined. The final sketch after dimensioning will be displayed as shown in Figure-140.

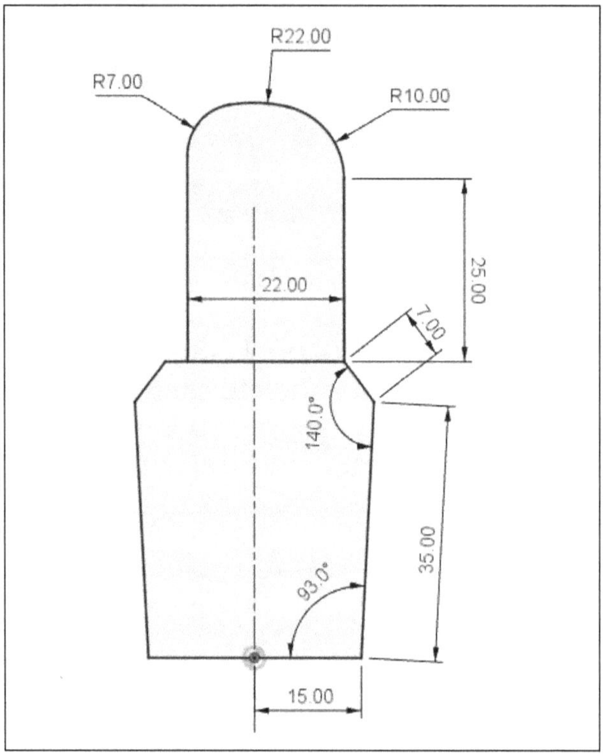

Figure-140. Final sketch of practical 3

Following are some sketches for practice.

PRACTICE 1

Create the sketch as shown in Figure-141.

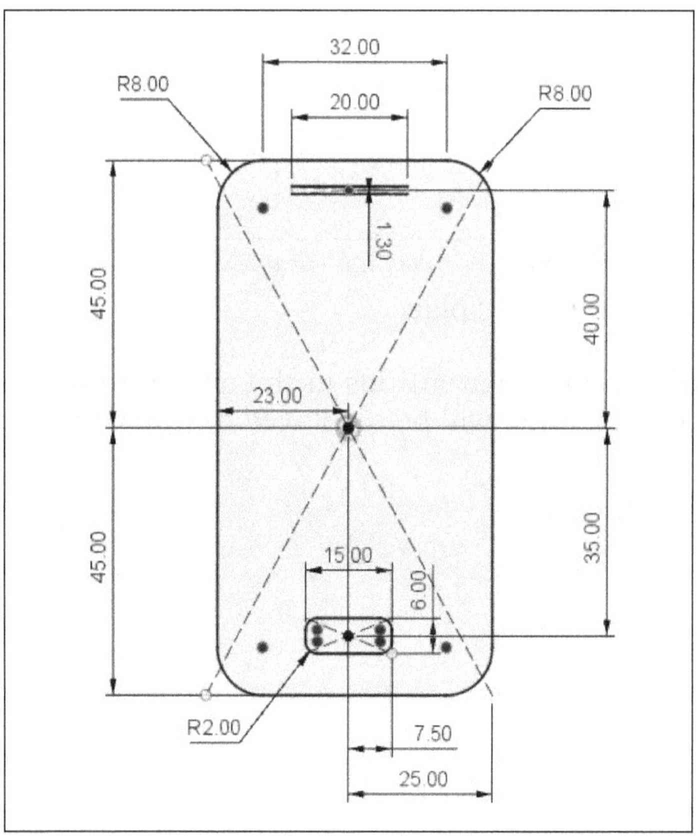

Figure-141. Practice 1

PRACTICE 2

Create the sketch as shown in Figure-142.

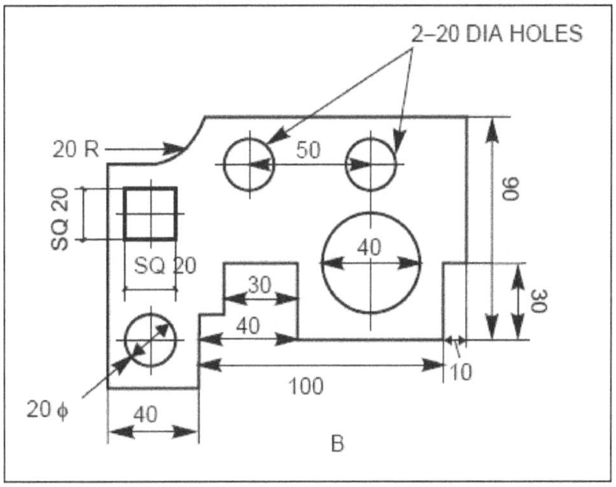

Figure-142. Practice 2

PRACTICE 3

Create the sketch as shown in Figure-143.

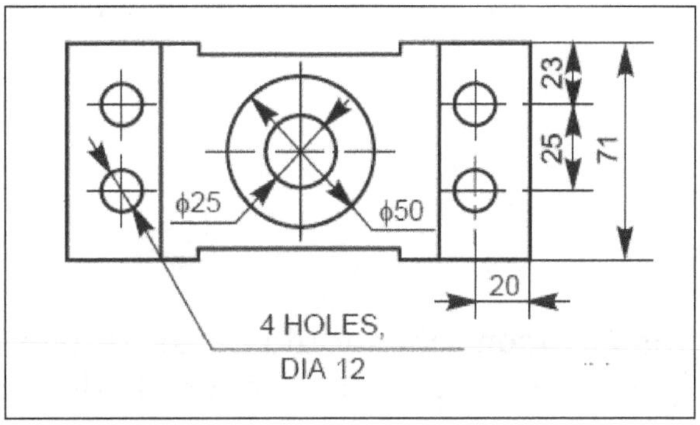

Figure-143. Practice 3

PRACTICE 4

Create the sketch as shown in Figure-144.

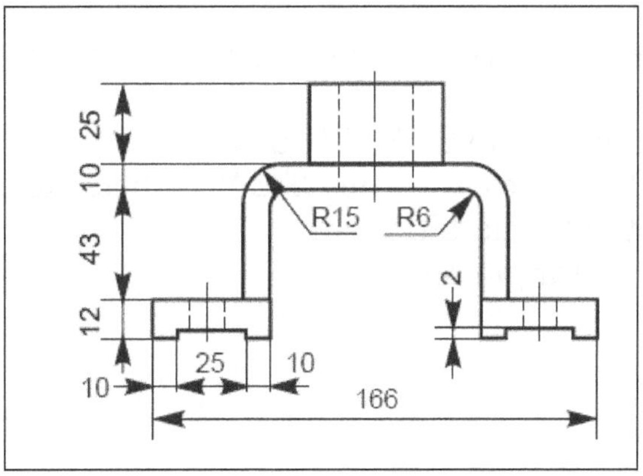

Figure-144. Practice 4

To get more exercise, mail us at cadcamcaeworks@gmail.com

SELF ASSESSMENT

Q1. In Autodesk Fusion, which of the following workspace has tool to start a new sketch?

a. RENDER
b. DESIGN
c. DRAWING
d. SIMULATION

Q2. Which of the following shortcut keys can be used to convert selected line into a construction line?

a. l
b. c
c. y
d. x

Q3. While the **Line** tool is active in sketch, if you drag the cursor then a tangent arc is created. (T/F)

Q4. Which of the following tool is not available in Autodesk Fusion Sketch mode to create an arc?

a. Center Point Arc
b. 3-Point Arc
c. Tangent Arc
d. Elliptical Arc

Q5. Which of the following **Polygon** tool should be used to create polygon if distance between two parallel edges of polygon and number of edges are given?

a. Circumscribed Polygon
b. Inscribed Polygon
c. Edge Polygon
d. All of the above.

Q6: What is the first step to start a new sketch in Autodesk Fusion?

A) Click on the Sketch tool in the SKETCH tab
B) Click on the Create Sketch tool in the CREATE drop-down of the SOLID tab
C) Press the L key to activate the Line tool
D) Click on the Center Rectangle tool

Q7: Which of the following actions displays the three primary planes on the canvas screen?

A) Click on the Create Sketch tool from the CREATE drop-down in the SOLID tab
B) Click on the Line tool from the CREATE drop-down
C) Click on the Rectangle tool from the SKETCH contextual tab
D) Press the ESC key

Q8: Which tool in Autodesk Fusion is used to create a line or arc?

A) Line tool
B) Rectangle tool
C) Circle tool
D) Arc tool

Q9: How can you exit the Line tool after creating a freestyle line?

A) Press the ESC key
B) Right-click and select Exit
C) Press the ENTER key
D) Click on the OK button in the Marking menu

Q10: Which of the following tools is used to create a construction line after drawing a line?

A) Normal/Construction button from the Marking menu
B) Line tool from the CREATE drop-down
C) Rectangle tool from the SKETCH contextual tab
D) Sketch Dimension tool

Q11: To create a rectangle using the 2-Point Rectangle tool, what is the first action you must take?

A) Specify the center point of the rectangle
B) Click to specify the first corner point
C) Enter the radius of the circle
D) Right-click on the screen

Q12: What is the shortcut key for activating the Rectangle tool in Autodesk Fusion?

A) R key
B) L key
C) C key
D) D key

Q13: What is the purpose of the 3-Point Rectangle tool in Autodesk Fusion?

A) To create a rectangle by specifying its center point
B) To create a rectangle by specifying its three corner points
C) To create a rectangle by specifying its length and width
D) To create a rectangle by specifying two corner points

Q14: How can you add dimensions to a rectangle in Autodesk Fusion?

A) Use the Sketch Dimension tool from the SKETCH contextual tab
B) Use the Circle tool
C) Use the Polygon tool
D) Right-click and select Add Dimensions

Q15: What tool in Autodesk Fusion is used to create a circle by specifying the center location and diameter value?

A) Center Diameter Circle tool
B) 3-Point Circle tool
C) 2-Tangent Circle tool
D) Edge Polygon tool

Q16: What is the correct sequence of actions for using the 2-Point Circle tool?

A) Click to specify the center point, then specify two circumferential points
B) Click to specify the first point, then the second point, and finally type the diameter
C) Click to specify the center point and enter the diameter
D) Click on the screen and select three points to define the circle

Q17: How do you create a 3-Tangent Circle in Autodesk Fusion?

A) Select three points to define the circle
B) Select three tangent lines to define the circle
C) Select two circumferential points to define the circle
D) Use the 2-Tangent Circle tool

Q18: What is the function of the Tangent Arc tool?

A) To create an arc that is tangent to a selected entity
B) To create a circle tangent to three selected lines
C) To create a rectangle using the tangent line
D) To draw a line that is tangent to a circle

Q19: When creating a 3-Point Arc, what do you need to specify?

A) Center point, radius, and angle of arc
B) Three points: start, end, and a circumferential point
C) Two circumferential points
D) Diameter and center point of the circle

Q20: Which tool is used to create a polygon inside a reference circle?

A) Circumscribed Polygon tool
B) Edge Polygon tool
C) Inscribed Polygon tool
D) Center Diameter Circle tool

Q21: To create a Circumscribed Polygon, what is the first step?

A) Specify the number of edges of the polygon
B) Specify the center point of the reference circle
C) Specify the length of one edge of the polygon
D) Click on the screen to create a freestyle polygon

Q22: How do you define the radius of a polygon when using the Inscribed Polygon tool?

A) Type the desired radius value in the edit box
B) Click at the center of the polygon
C) Use the dynamic input box to specify the edge length
D) Press the TAB key to switch between edit boxes

Q23: How can you switch between different types of rectangles after selecting the Rectangle tool?

A) Use the SKETCH PALETTE to select the type of rectangle
B) Press the ESC key to cancel the selection
C) Right-click and select a new tool from the Marking menu
D) Use the dynamic input box

Q24: What tool should be used to create a polygon with a single edge and a defined number of edges?

A) Inscribed Polygon tool
B) Circumscribed Polygon tool
C) Edge Polygon tool
D) 3-Point Polygon tool

Q25: When creating a 2-Tangent Circle, how do you specify the size of the circle?

A) Click at the desired location and specify the radius or diameter
B) Enter the angle and length values in the dynamic input box
C) Select the center point of the circle
D) Use the Edge Polygon tool to create the circle

Q26. What is the primary function of the Ellipse tool in the sketching process?

A) To create straight lines
B) To create ellipses
C) To create circles
D) To create arcs

Q27. Which of the following tools is used to create slots in the sketching environment?

A) Ellipse tool
B) Text tool
C) Slot tool
D) Mirror tool

Q28. How do you specify the center point when creating an ellipse?

A) Use the dynamic input box
B) Click on the screen to specify the center point
C) Use the center of the screen
D) Enter the center coordinates manually

Q29. In the Center To Center Slot tool, what defines the slot?

A) Length and width of the arc
B) Distance between arc centers and width of the slot
C) Position of the start and end points
D) Angle of inclination of the arc

Q30. What is required when creating a Center Point Slot?

A) The arc radius
B) The half-length of the center-to-center distance
C) The angle of the arc
D) The start and end points of the arc

Q31. Which tool is used to create a slot defined by the total length and width?

A) Overall Slot
B) Center Point Slot
C) Center To Center Slot
D) Three Point Arc Slot

Q32. What does the Three Point Arc Slot tool require in order to define the slot?

A) A set of concentric circles
B) The start and end points of the arc and a circumferential point
C) A pre-defined arc radius
D) The width of the slot and length of the center-to-center distance

Q33. What determines the shape of the conic curve when using the Conic Curve tool?

A) The number of control points
B) The angle of the curve
C) The Rho value, which defines the curve's type
D) The total length of the curve

Q34. When creating a spline, which tool is used to form a spline curve through selected points?

A) Fit Point Spline
B) Control Point Spline
C) Conic Curve
D) Rectangular Pattern

Q35. How is the Control Point Spline different from the Fit Point Spline?

A) The Control Point Spline uses pre-defined points to form the curve, while the Fit Point Spline is a freeform tool
B) The Fit Point Spline uses control points, while the Control Point Spline does not
C) The Control Point Spline creates more complex curves
D) There is no difference between the two tools

Q36. What does the Text tool allow you to create in the sketch?

A) Notes and information for the model
B) Ellipses and arcs
C) Spline curves
D) Points and vertices

Q37. How can you edit the text after it has been created in the sketch?

A) Right-click on the text and select Edit
B) Double-click on the text in sketch mode
C) Use the Text tool again to modify the text
D) Text cannot be edited after creation

Q38. When using the Mirror tool, what is required to create the mirrored entities?

A) The entities and the reference mirror line
B) Only the entities to be mirrored
C) The mirror line and the angle
D) The entities and the number of copies

Q39. What does the Circular Pattern tool allow you to do?

A) Create multiple copies of an entity along a circle
B) Create a rectangular pattern
C) Create a linear series of copies
D) Reflect an entity about a line

Q40. What happens when you select the Symmetric option in the Angular Spacing drop-down for the Circular Pattern tool?

A) The pattern is distributed evenly across a full circle
B) The pattern is created symmetrically about the center line
C) The number of entities is reduced
D) The entities are mirrored

Q41. What do you need to specify when creating a Rectangular Pattern?

A) The center point of the pattern
B) The distance between each object copy
C) The number of rows and columns
D) The direction and quantity of copies

Q42. What is the purpose of selecting the Extent option from the Distance Type drop-down in the Rectangular Pattern tool?

A) To specify the total span for the pattern
B) To control the spacing between pattern copies
C) To define the distance between the first and last object copy
D) To suppress certain copies from the pattern

Q43. How can you create copies in both directions of the selected line in the Rectangular Pattern tool?

A) Select the Symmetric option from the Direction Type drop-down
B) Enter a negative value for distance
C) Use the Extent option in the dialog box
D) Set the number of copies to 2

Q44. What does the Point tool do in the sketching process?

A) Creates arc points
B) Creates sketch points for surface design
C) Adds notes to the model
D) Creates text frames

Q45. What is the primary function of the Slot tool?

A) To create circles
B) To create straight lines
C) To create slots with various shapes and parameters
D) To add text to the design

Q46. The Fit Point Spline tool is used to create a spline curve through:
A. Selected control points only
B. Selected fit points
C. Selected lines only
D. Selected circles

Q47. Which tool creates a spline curve driven by selected control points?
A. Fit Point Spline
B. Control Point Spline
C. Conic Curve
D. Blend Curve

Q48. Which tool creates a curve driven by points and a rho value?
A. Spline
B. Blend Curve
C. Conic Curve
D. Fillet

Q49. The value of rho for a conic curve lies between:
A. 0 to 10
B. 0 to 0.99
C. 1 to 10
D. 0.5 to 5

Q50. The shape of a conic curve can be elliptical, parabolic, or hyperbolic depending on:
A. Control points
B. Radius
C. Rho value
D. Distance value

Q51. Sketch points are mainly used when creating:
A. Solids
B. Lines
C. Surfaces
D. Patterns

Q52. Which option in the Text tool allows text to follow a selected path?
A. Text Frame
B. Text On Path
C. Text Box
D. Text Follow

Q53. Which file format is commonly used for single line CAM text fonts?
A. .txt
B. .doc
C. .shx
D.

Q54. The reference used to create mirror copies is called:
A. Center line
B. Mirror line
C. Axis line
D. Pattern line

Q55. Which tool creates multiple copies of an entity in a circular arrangement?
A. Rectangular Pattern
B. Circular Pattern
C. Mirror
D. Blend Curve

Q56. Which option in Circular Pattern creates copies over a full 360° rotation?
A. Partial
B. Full
C. Symmetric
D. Circular

Q57. The Rectangular Pattern tool creates copies in which directions?
A. Circular direction only
B. Vertical direction only
C. Horizontal and vertical directions
D. Random directions

Q58. If no reference lines are selected in Rectangular Pattern, patterns are created along:
A. Diagonal axes
B. Horizontal and vertical axes
C. Circular axes
D. Random axes

Q59. Which tool is used to automatically apply dimensions to sketch entities?
A. Text
B. Sketch Dimension
C. Mirror
D. Blend Curve

Q60. The Fillet tool is used to create:
A. Straight edges
B. Rounded corners
C. Sharp corners
D. Text frames

Q61. Fillet is sometimes also referred to as:
A. Bevel
B. Round
C. Pattern
D. Projection

Q62. Which tool is used to bevel the corners of sketch geometry?
A. Chamfer
B. Fillet
C. Mirror
D. Blend Curve

Q63. Which tool creates a tangent or curvature continuous blend between two curves?
A. Blend Curve
B. Fillet
C. Chamfer
D. Pattern

Q64. What is the main purpose of the Offset tool?
A. To delete sketch entities
B. To create copies of selected entities at a specified distance
C. To rotate sketch entities
D. To measure distance between entities

Q65. What happens when the Chain Selection check box is selected in the OFFSET dialog box?
A. Only a single segment is selected
B. All entities in the current chain are selected
C. The chain is deleted
D. Only construction lines are selected

Q66. Which tool is used to remove the unwanted portion of a sketch entity?
A. Break
B. Trim
C. Extend
D. Scale

Q67. While trimming sketch entities, which point is considered as the reference?
A. Start point
B. Midpoint
C. Intersection point
D. Endpoint

Q68. Which tool performs the opposite function of the Trim tool?
A. Break
B. Offset
C. Extend
D. Scale

Q69. What condition must be satisfied to apply the Break tool?
A. The entity must be colored
B. The entity must have an intersecting curve
C. The entity must be a circle
D. The entity must be locked

Q70. What is the function of the Sketch Scale tool?
A. To move entities
B. To enlarge or reduce entities based on a scale factor
C. To rotate entities
D. To trim entities

Q71. A scale factor between 0 and 1 in Sketch Scale will:
A. Increase the size of entities
B. Reduce the size of entities
C. Delete the entities
D. Rotate the entities

Q72. A scale factor greater than 1 will:
A. Reduce the size of entities
B. Increase the size of entities
C. Lock the entities
D. Mirror the entities

Q73. Which option in Sketch Palette is used to create construction geometry while sketching?
A. Snap
B. Linetype Construction
C. Profile
D. Slice

Q74. What is the function of the Look At option in Sketch Palette?
A. Rotates the sketch randomly
B. Makes the sketching plane parallel to the screen
C. Deletes the sketch grid
D. Changes sketch color

Q75. What happens if the Snap check box is cleared?
A. All snapping stops
B. Grid snapping stops but key point snapping remains active
C. Sketch grid disappears
D. Dimensions disappear

Q76. What is the purpose of the Slice option?
A. Permanently cuts the model
B. Deletes solid bodies
C. Temporarily cuts solid/surface for display during sketching
D. Splits sketch entities

Q77. Which option is used to display closed profiles in the sketch?
A. Profile
B. Snap
C. Slice
D. Points

Q78. Why is the Profile option useful?
A. To change sketch color
B. To check if a sketch is closed for operations like Extrude or Revolve
C. To hide constraints
D. To lock the sketch plane

Q79. What is the purpose of the Constraints option in Sketch Palette?
A. To rotate entities
B. To show or hide sketch constraints
C. To change grid spacing
D. To mirror entities

Q80. What does the 3D Sketch option allow?
A. Creating sketches only in 2D plane
B. Pulling sketch objects out of the sketch plane to create 3D sketches
C. Converting sketches to surfaces
D. Deleting sketches

Q81. What is the purpose of constraints in sketching?
A. To decorate sketches
B. To restrict shapes or positions of sketch entities
C. To color the sketch
D. To delete sketch elements

Q82. Which constraint makes a point coincide with a line, arc, circle, or ellipse?
A. Coincident
B. Tangent
C. Parallel
D. Symmetric

Q83. Which constraint ensures that selected lines have equal length or arcs/circles have equal radius or diameter?
A. Parallel
B. Equal
C. Perpendicular
D. Coincident

FOR STUDENT NOTES

Chapter 3

3D Sketch and Solid Modeling

Topics Covered

The major topics covered in this chapter are:

- ***3D Sketches***
- ***Selection Tools***
- ***Solid Modeling***
- ***Create drop-down***
- ***Construction Geometry***
- ***Project/Include Tools***

3D SKETCHES

3D Sketches are those sketches which are not confined to single plane. Assume a line connecting end points of two lines in YZ and ZX planes; refer to Figure-1. Such a sketch can be called 3D Sketch; refer to Figure-2.

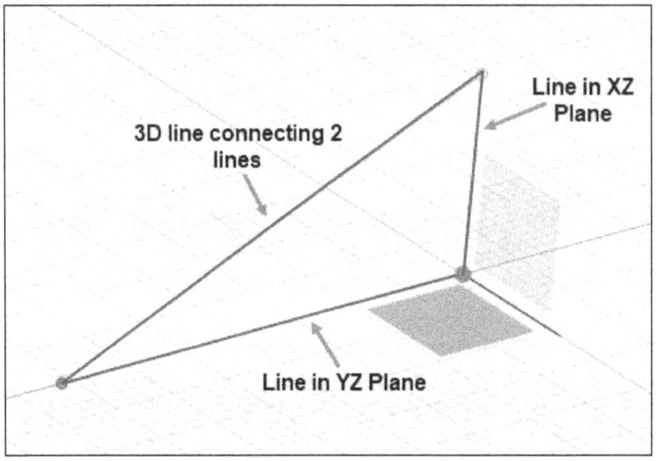

Figure-1. 3D line

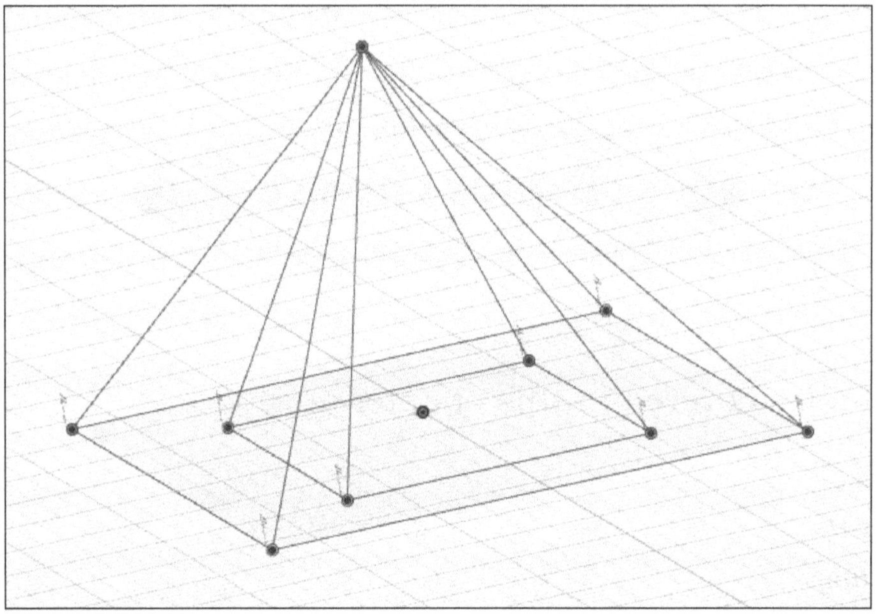

Figure-2. Example of 3D sketch

In Autodesk Fusion, there are no specific tools for creating 3D sketches except a check box to enable or disable 3D sketching in **SKETCH PALETTE**. So, we are back to basics of plane orientations for creating 3D sketches. The process of creating a 3D sketch is explained next with the help of an example.

Creating 3D Sketch

Create the sketch of frame as shown in Figure-3.

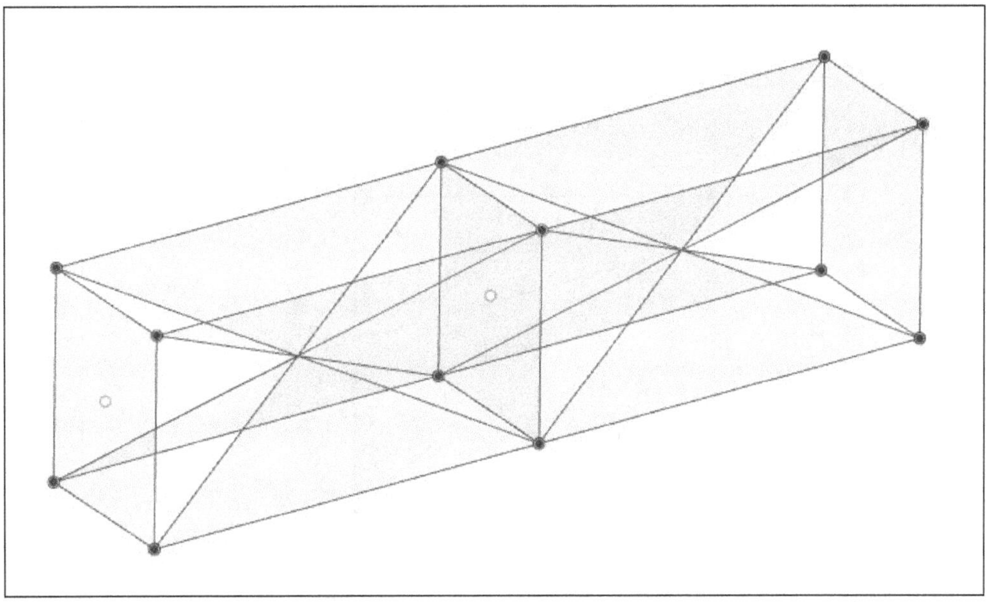

Figure-3. Load bearing frame sketch

Creating Base Sketches and Planes

- After starting a new design file in Autodesk Fusion, click on the **Create Sketch** button from the **CREATE** drop-down. You will be asked to select a sketching plane.
- Select the **XY** plane as sketching plane and create a center point rectangle as shown in Figure-4.

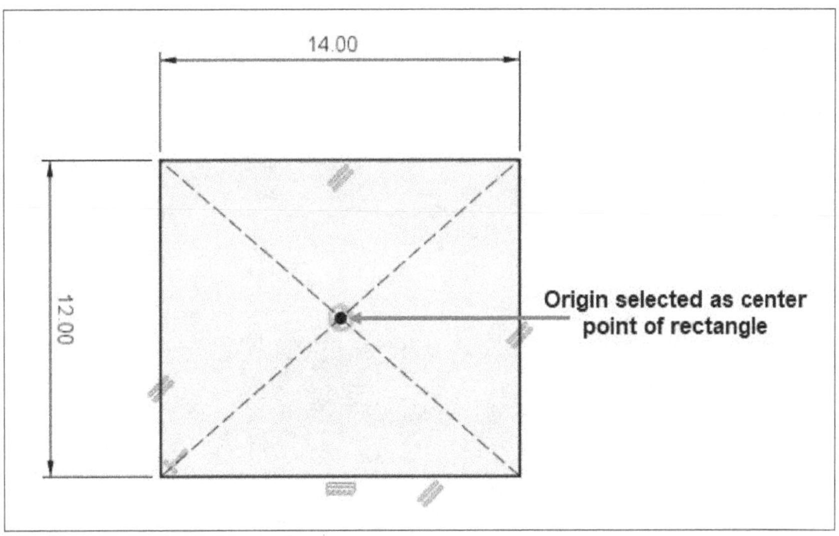

Figure-4. Rectangle created for 3D sketch

- Nope! Don't exit the sketching environment yet!! Select the whole sketch by window selection; refer to Figure-5 and press **CTRL+C** from keyboard. This will keep a copy of current sketch in clipboard memory of software.
- Click on the **Finish Sketch** button from **FINISH SKETCH** panel of the **Toolbar** to exit sketching environment.

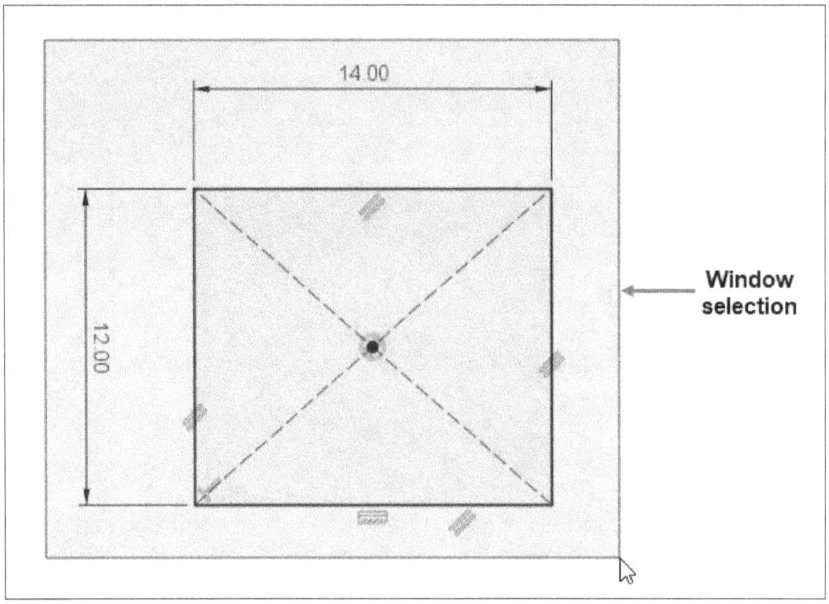

Figure-5. Window selection

- Click on the **Offset Plane** tool from the **CONSTRUCT** drop-down of the **SOLID** tab in the **Toolbar** and select **XY Plane** from **Origin** node of **BROWSER**; refer to Figure-6. (You will learn more about the plane and construction geometries later in this chapter.)

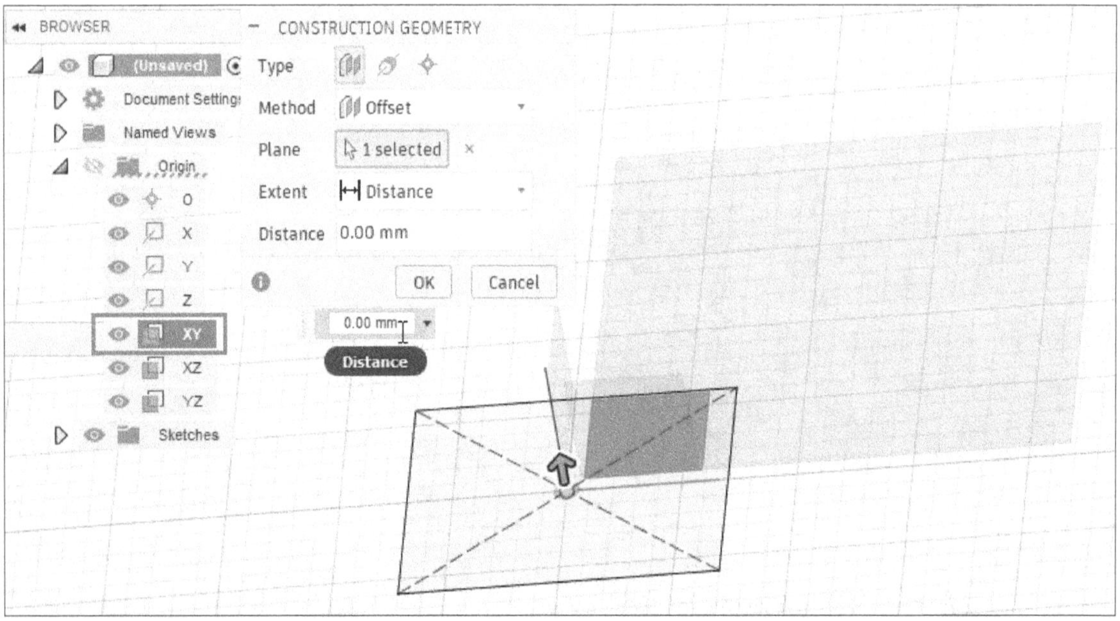

Figure-6. Creating offset plane

- Specify the distance value as **300** in **CONSTRUCTION GEOMETRY** dialog box and click on the **OK** button. A new plane will be created at a distance of **300** from XY plane.
- Click again on the **Offset Plane** tool from the **CONSTRUCT** drop-down in the **Toolbar** and create another plane at an offset distance of **300** from earlier created plane; refer to Figure-7.

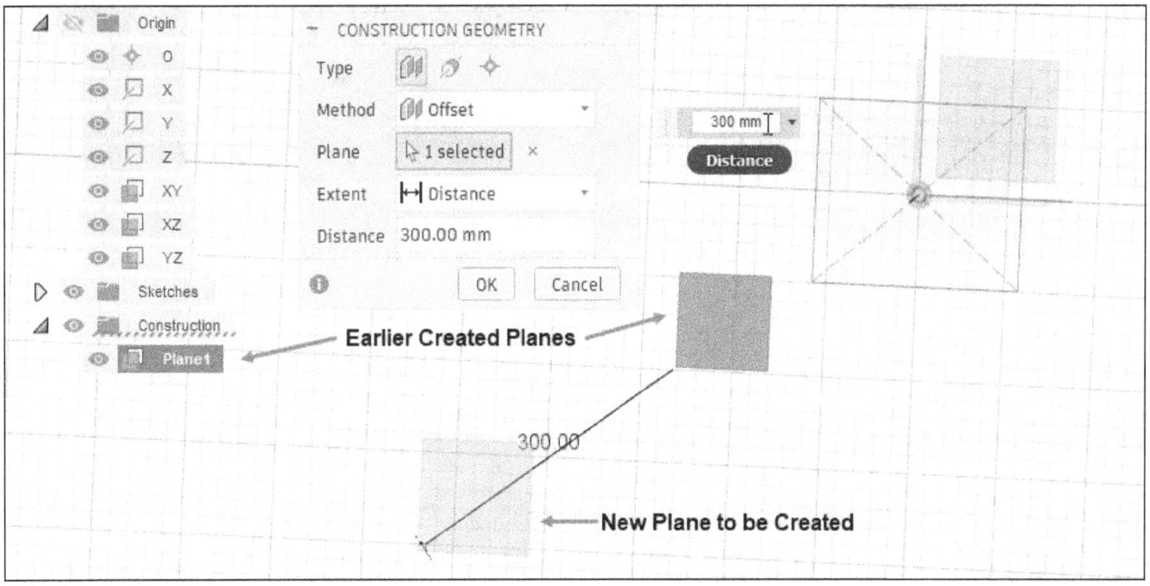

Figure-7. New plane to be created

- Select **Plane1** from the **Construction** node in **BROWSER** and click on the **Create Sketch** button from **CREATE** drop-down in the **Toolbar**. The sketching environment will be activated.
- Press **CTRL+V** from keyboard to paste earlier copied sketch. The **MOVE/COPY** dialog box will be displayed with sketch pasted; refer to Figure-8.

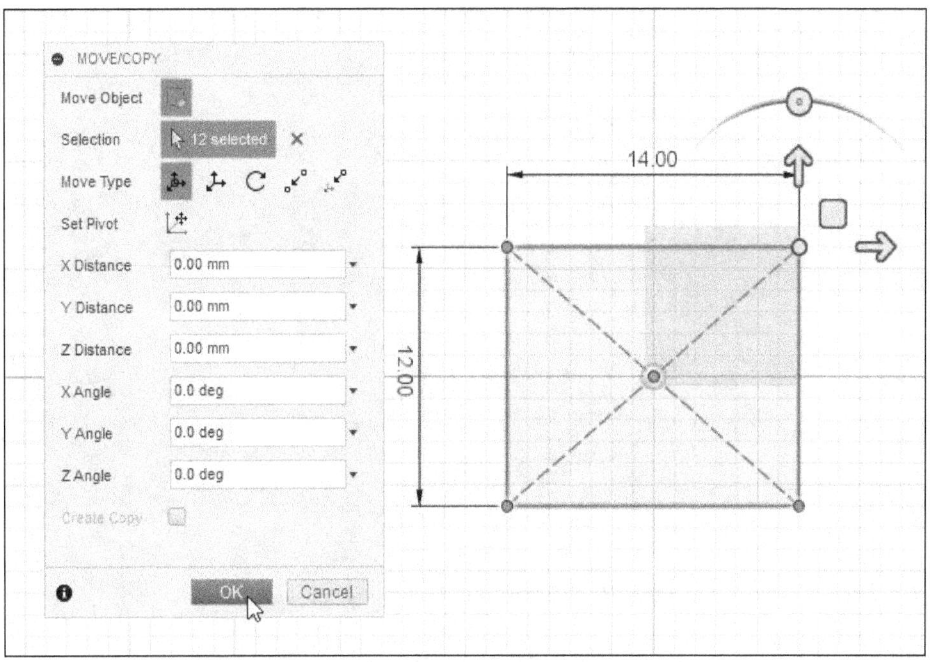

Figure-8. Sketch pasted with MOVE COPY dialog box

- There is no need to change any parameter because our sketch is well constrained and same as we wanted. Click on the **OK** button from the dialog box and exit the sketching environment.
- Create the same sketch on other offset plane. The sketches will be displayed as shown in Figure-9.

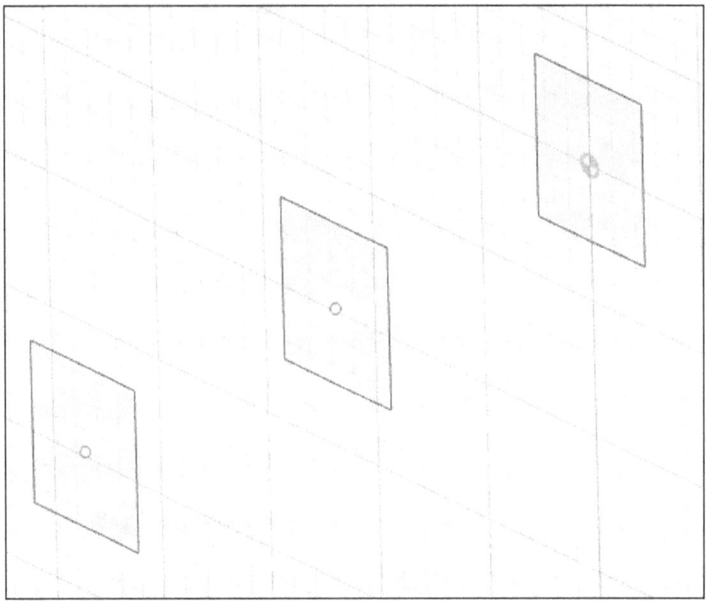

Figure-9. Sketches after copy paste

Creating 3D Lines

- Select the **3D Sketch** check box as highlighted in the **Sketch Palette** drop-down from the sketching environment; refer to Figure-10.

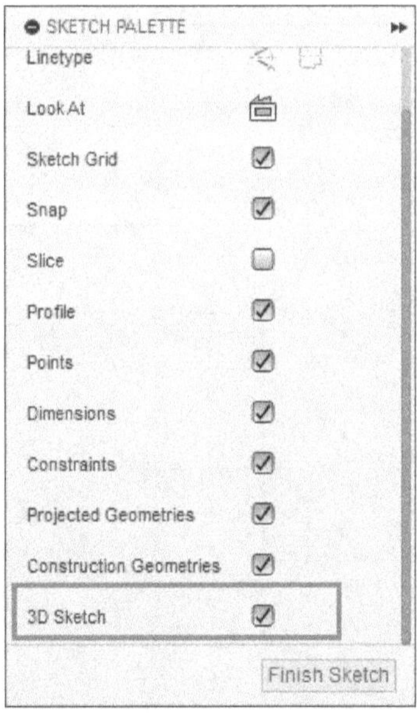

Figure-10. 3D sketch option from sketch palette

Now, we are ready to create 3-dimensional lines.

- Click on the **Create Sketch** tool from the **CREATE** drop-down in the **Toolbar** and select any of the sketching plane. The sketching plane will become parallel to screen.
- Rotate the model by using **SHIFT+Middle Mouse Button (MMB)**.
- Click on the **Line** tool from **CREATE** drop-down and hover the cursor on earlier created sketches. You will find that the snap points of all the sketches get highlighted when you hover the cursor over them.
- Now what left is just clicks and clicks. Join various points of sketches to form frame sketch as shown in Figure-11.

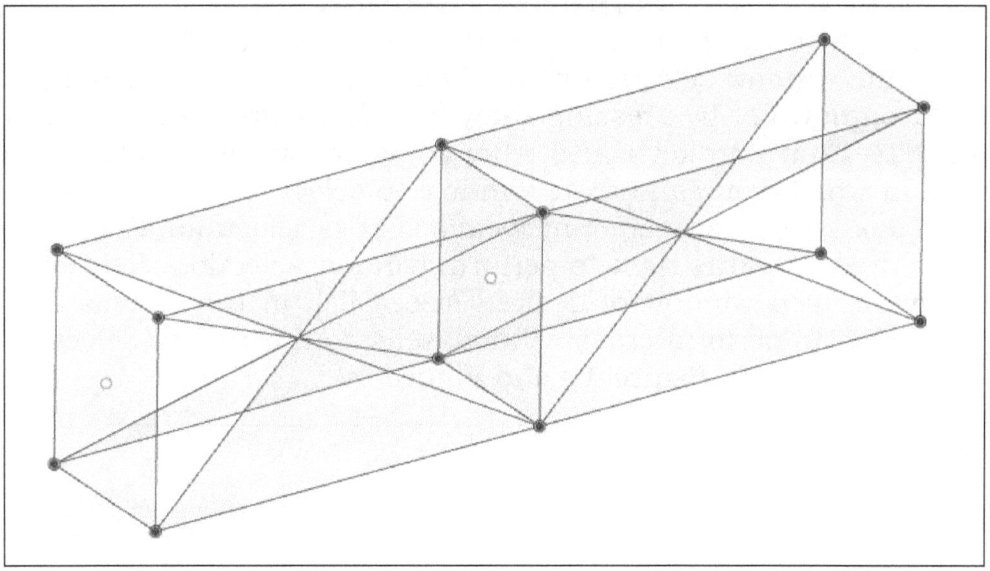

Figure-11. Sketch created for frame

- Click on the **Finish Sketch** tool from the **FINISH SKETCH** panel of the **Toolbar** to exit the sketching environment. So, it is the property of snap points for various elements that allow creating 3D sketch entities.

SELECTION TOOLS

You have earlier selected the objects by clicking on them or by making a window to select them. In Autodesk Fusion, sometimes you will reach in situations where only features are to be selected rather than full body or only faces are to be selected. In such cases, we apply selection filters. You can also define the pattern in which you want to select objects using the options in **SELECT** drop-down of the **Toolbar**; refer to Figure-12. These tools are discussed next.

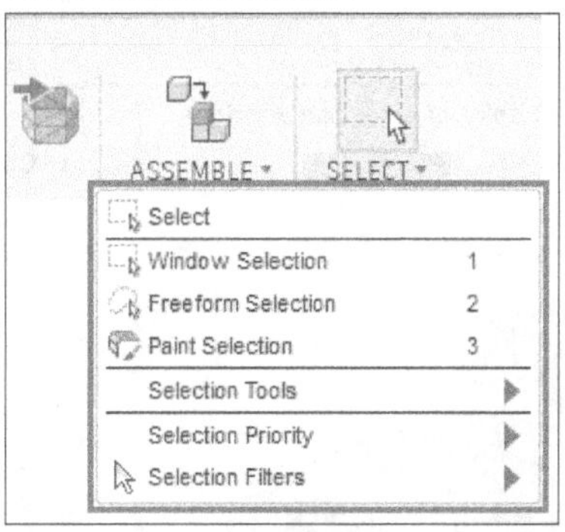

Figure-12. SELECT drop-down

Select Tool

This tool is always active while working in Autodesk Fusion. Because of this tool, you are able to select any tool from toolbar or object from canvas.

Window Selection

This tool is active by default when you start working on Autodesk Fusion. This tool is used to activate window selection mode. You can activate this tool by selecting it from **SELECT** drop-down or by pressing **1** key from keyboard (Note that 1 is not to be pressed from **NUMPAD** on your keyboard). After activating window selection mode, there are two ways in which you can create window to select objects; **Window selection** and **Cross Window selection** (sometimes called Cross selection). Click in the canvas and drag the cursor towards right to perform window selection. Release the button when you have formed window of desired size. Click in the canvas and drag the cursor towards left to perform cross window selection. Both the selection methods and their uses are given in Figure-13 and Figure-14.

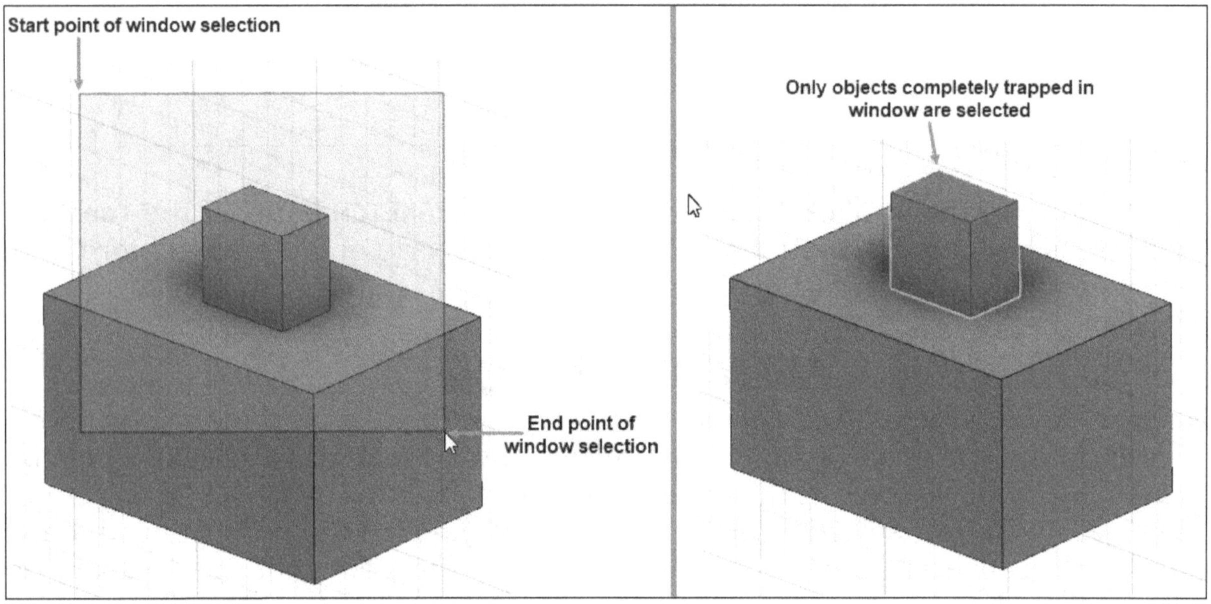

Figure-13. Window selection mode

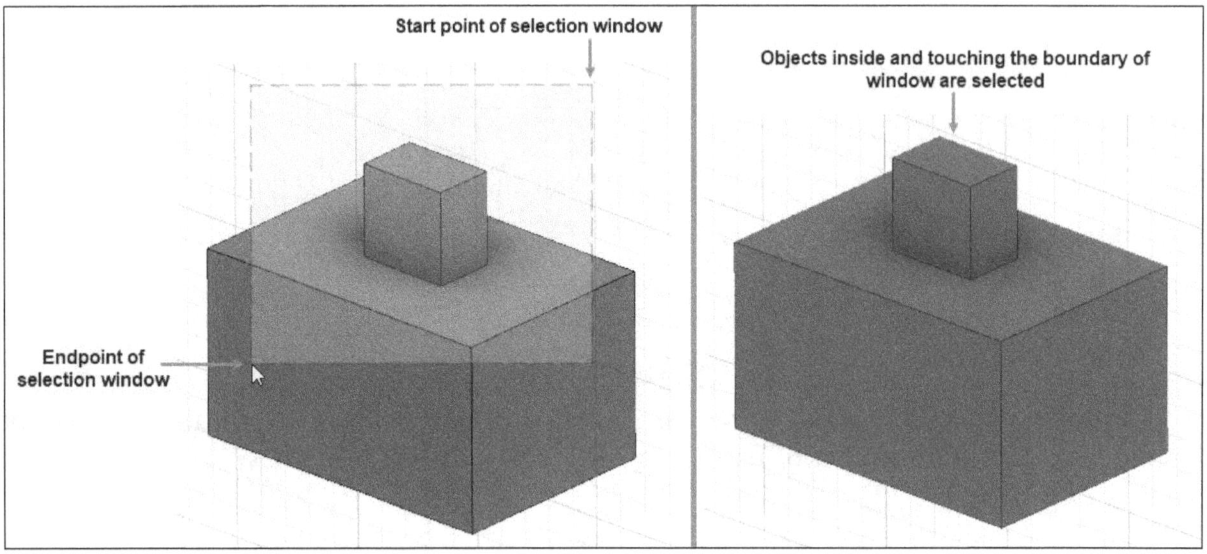

Figure-14. Cross window selection mode

Freeform Selection

Click on the **Freeform Selection** tool from **SELECT** drop-down or press **2** from keyboard to activate this selection mode. Click and drag the cursor to create a freeform boundary for selection. Dragging cursor towards right will make objects completely inside the boundaries selected and dragging cursor towards left will make objects inside or touching the boundaries selected.

Paint Selection

Click on the **Paint Selection** tool from **SELECT** drop-down or press **3** from keyboard to activate this selection mode. In this selection mode, all the objects over which cursor passes while dragging will be selected.

Selection Tools

The selection tools discussed earlier are conventional selection tools. You can also select the objects by their names, types, and sizes. These tools are available in the **Selection Tools** cascading menu of **SELECT** drop-down; refer to Figure-15.

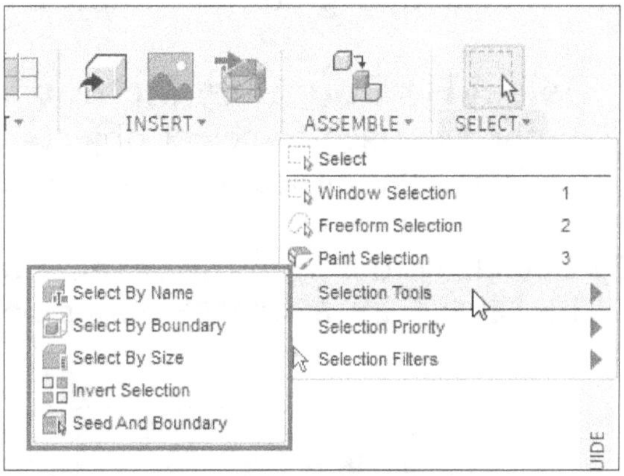

Figure-15. Selection Tools cascading menu

Select By Name Method

- Click on the **Select By Name** tool from the **Selection Tools** cascading menu of **SELECT** drop-down in the **Toolbar**. The **SELECT BY NAME** dialog box will be displayed; refer to Figure-16.

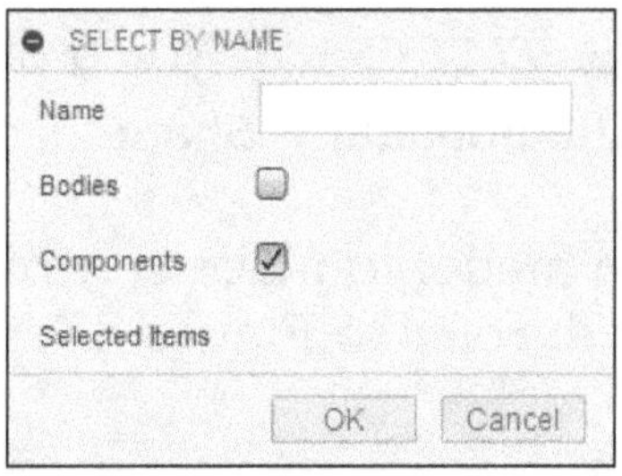

Figure-16. SELECT BY NAME dialog Box

- Type the name of object to be selected in the **Name** edit box of the dialog box.
- Select the **Bodies** check box to allow selection of bodies and select the **Components** check box to allow selection of components.
- Click on the **Find** button in the dialog box. All the components and bodies matching the specified name will be selected; refer to Figure-17.

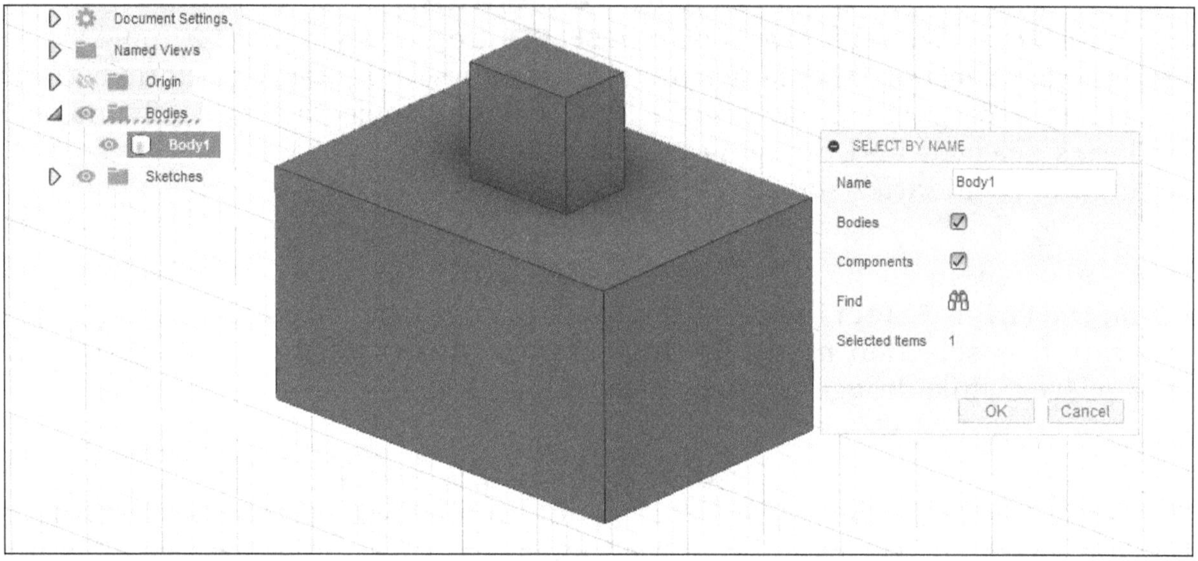

Figure-17. Bodies selected by name

- Click on the **OK** button from the dialog box to complete the process.

Select By Boundary Method

The **Select By Boundary** method is used to select objects which fall under defined shapes of cylinder, box, or sphere. The procedure to use this method is given next.

- Click on the **Select By Boundary** tool from the **Selection Tools** cascading menu of **SELECT** drop-down. The **SELECT BY BOUNDARY** dialog box will be displayed; refer to Figure-18.

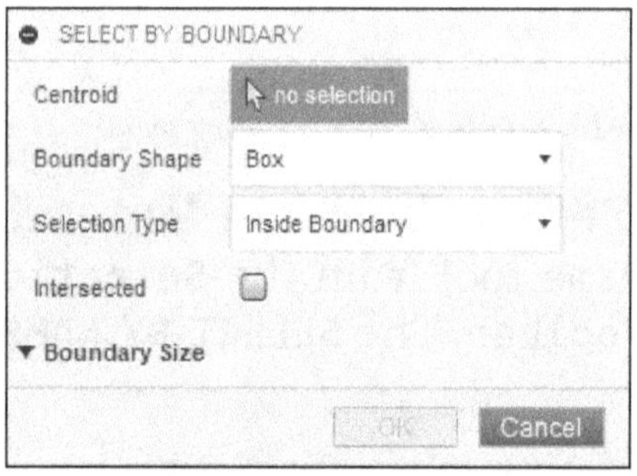

Figure-18. SELECT BY BOUNDARY dialog box

- Select desired option from the **Boundary Shape** drop-down to define the shape of selection boundary.
- Click on desired point in the model to place centroid of boundary shape. Preview of boundary will be displayed; refer to Figure-19.

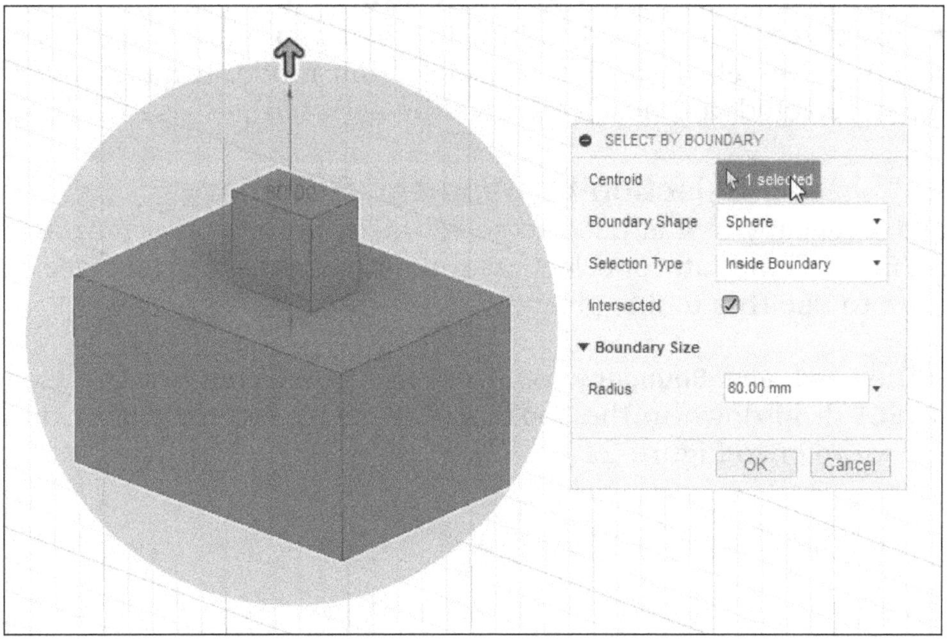

Figure-19. Sphere boundary preview

- Specify desired parameters in the **Boundary Size** section to define size of boundary shape.
- Select the **Inside Boundary** option from the **Selection Type** drop-down if you want to select the objects inside the boundary. Select the **Outside Boundary** option from the **Selection Type** drop-down if you want to select the objects outside the boundary shape.
- Select the **Intersected** check box if you want to select all the objects that are intersecting with created boundary shape.
- Click on the **OK** button from the dialog box to make selection.

Select By Size Method

The **Select By Size** method is used when you want to select the entities based on their sizes. The procedure for using this method is given next.

- Click on the **Select By Size** tool from the **Selection Tools** cascading menu of the **SELECT** drop-down in **Toolbar**. The **SELECT BY SIZE** dialog box will be displayed; refer to Figure-20.

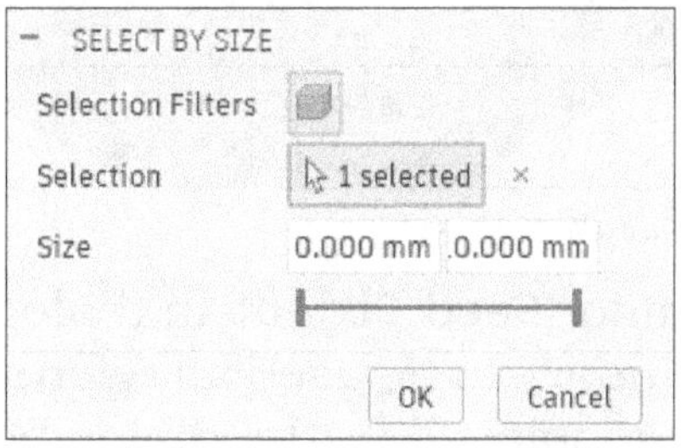

Figure-20. SELECT BY SIZE dialog box

- Specify the range of size within which entities will be selected and then click on the **OK** button.

Invert Selection

The **Invert Selection** tool is used to flip the selection state of all object. Selection is based on the active selection filter and selection mode. It means all the selected object will be deselected and deselected will be selected.

Selection by Seed and Boundary

The **Seed and Boundary** tool is used to select faces on a solid or surface by using a seed surface/face as template for selection and outlines of a face/surface as boundary. The procedure to use this tool is given next.

- Click on the **Seed and Boundary** tool from the **Selection Tools** cascading menu of the **SELECT** drop-down in the **Toolbar**. The **SEED AND BOUNDARY** dialog box will be displayed; refer to Figure-21.

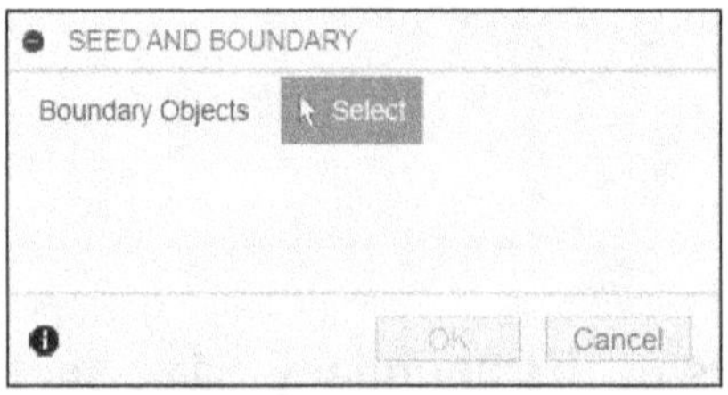

Figure-21. SEED AND BOUNDARY dialog box

- Select the face of model to be used as boundary for selection. (No objects outside this boundary will be selected by the tool). On selecting face for boundary, the **SEED AND BOUNDARY** dialog box will be updated and selection button for seed object will be displayed; refer to Figure-22.

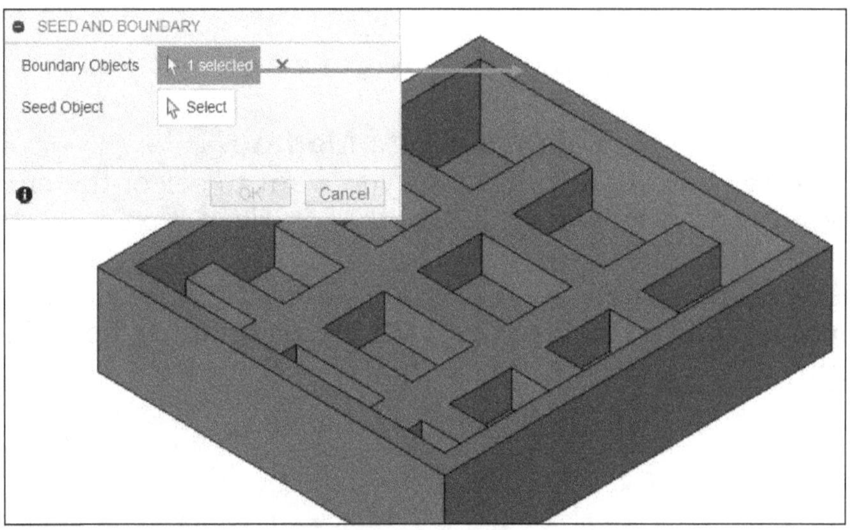

Figure-22. Boundary face selected

- Click on the **Select** button for **Seed Object** in dialog box and then select the face from model within the boundary to be used as reference for selecting nearby faces. The **Update** button will be displayed in the dialog box; refer to Figure-23.

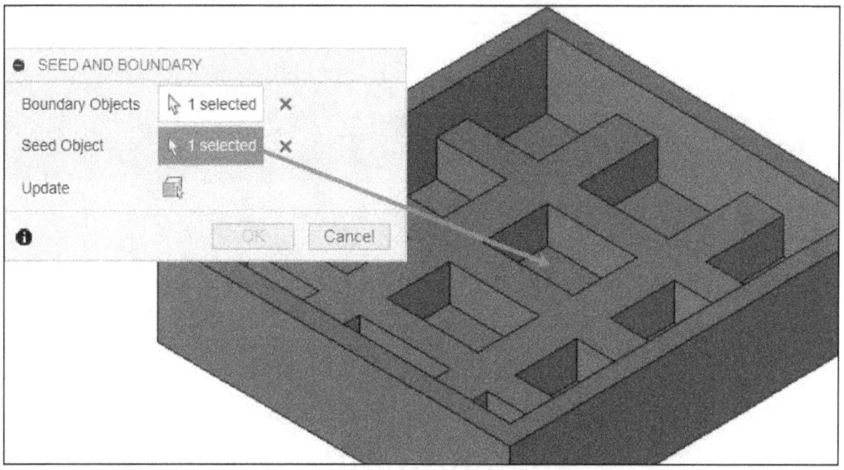

Figure-23. Face selected for seed object

- Click on the **Update** button to update the selection based on seed object. All the nearby faces within boundary will get selected; refer to Figure-24.

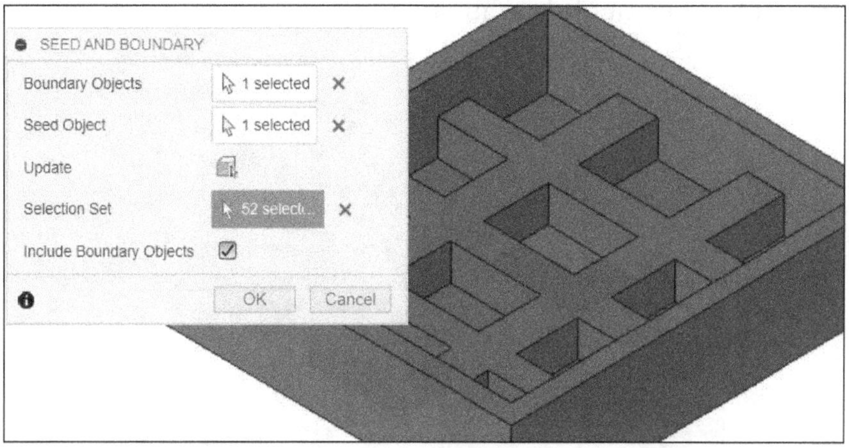

Figure-24. After updating selection

- Clear the **Include Boundary Objects** check box if you do not want to boundary faces in selection.
- Click on the **OK** button to complete selection.

Component Drag

Select the **Component Drag** check box to enable the movement of components by dragging in the canvas. Hold the **Alt** key to move the components by dragging in the canvas.

Selection Priority

The options in **Selection Priority** cascading menu of **SELECT** drop-down in **Toolbar** are used to define which entities will be given preference while selecting objects; refer to Figure-25. Select the **Select Body Priority** option if you want to select bodies in place of faces/edges. Similarly, select other options in the cascading menu to select respective entities.

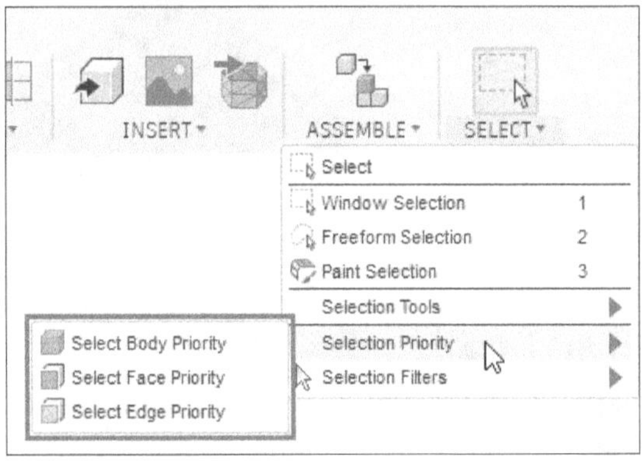

Figure-25. Selection Priority cascading menu

Selection Filters

The check boxes in **Selection Filters** cascading menu are used to define which objects can be selected and which objects cannot be selected; refer to Figure-26. Select desired check boxes to activate selections of respective objects. In default condition, the **Select All** check box is selected.

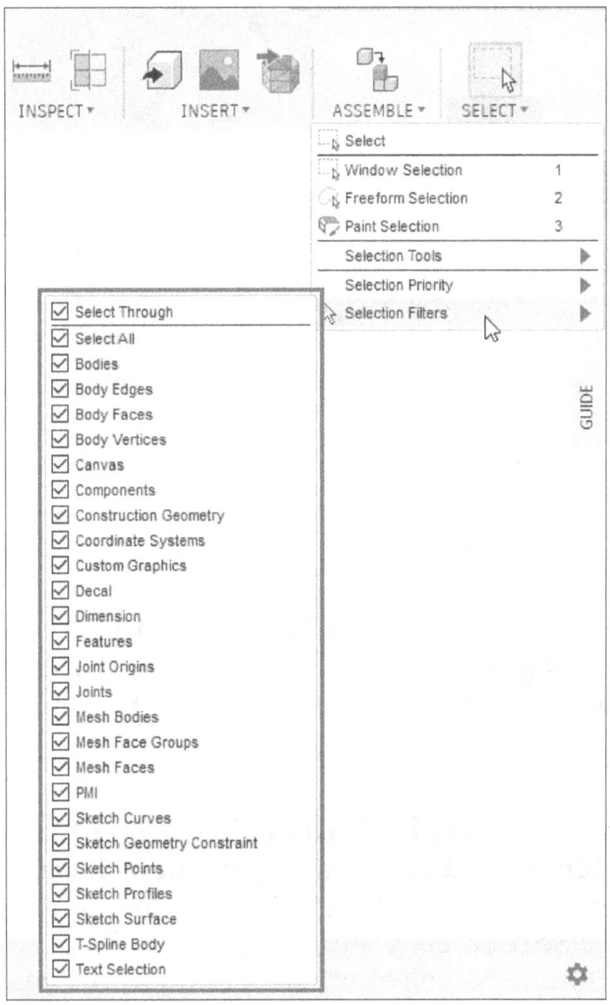

Figure-26. Selection Filters cascading menu

SOLID MODELING

Till this point, we have worked on 2D sketches and have created them on Top or Front plane. We have also created 3D sketches. Now, we will learn the tools for solid modeling. **Solid modeling** is the most advanced method of geometric modeling in three dimensions. Solid modeling is the representation of the solid objects in your computer in digital form. Various tools to perform solid modeling are available in the **SOLID** tab of **Toolbar**. We will learn about various tools and commands used to create solid models in next topic.

CREATE DROP-DOWN

In **Create** drop-down, there are various 3D modeling tools used to create and manage solid objects; refer to Figure-27. These tools are discussed next.

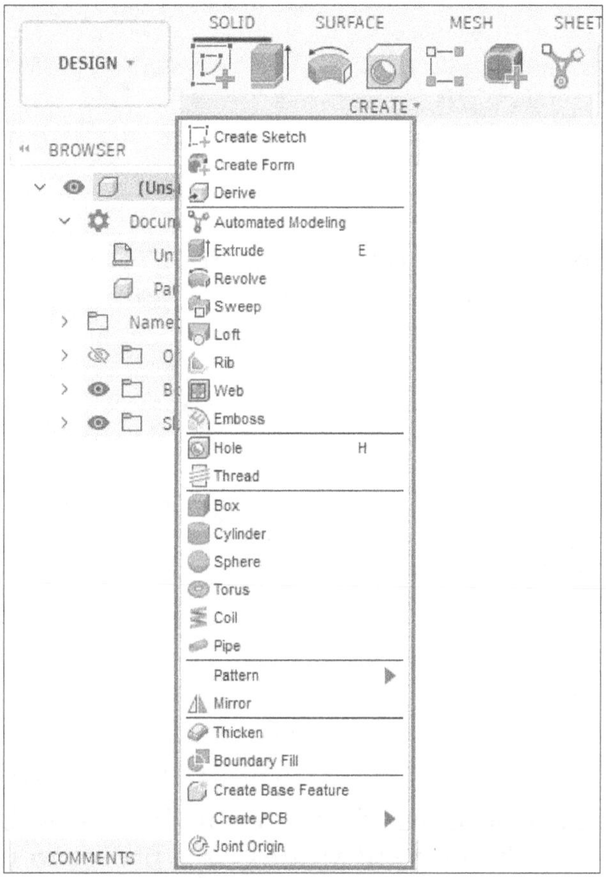

Figure-27. CREATE drop down

Extrude

The **Extrude** tool is used to create a solid volume by adding height to the selected sketch. In other words, this tool adds material in the direction perpendicular to the plane of sketch by using the boundaries of sketch. The procedure to use this tool is discussed next.

- Create a closed profile sketch as discussed in previous chapter.
- After creating sketch, exit the sketch environment by selecting the **Finish Sketch** tool from **Toolbar** or **Right-click** outside the sketch and select **Finish Sketch** button from the **Sketch** drop-down in **Marking menu**; refer to Figure-28.

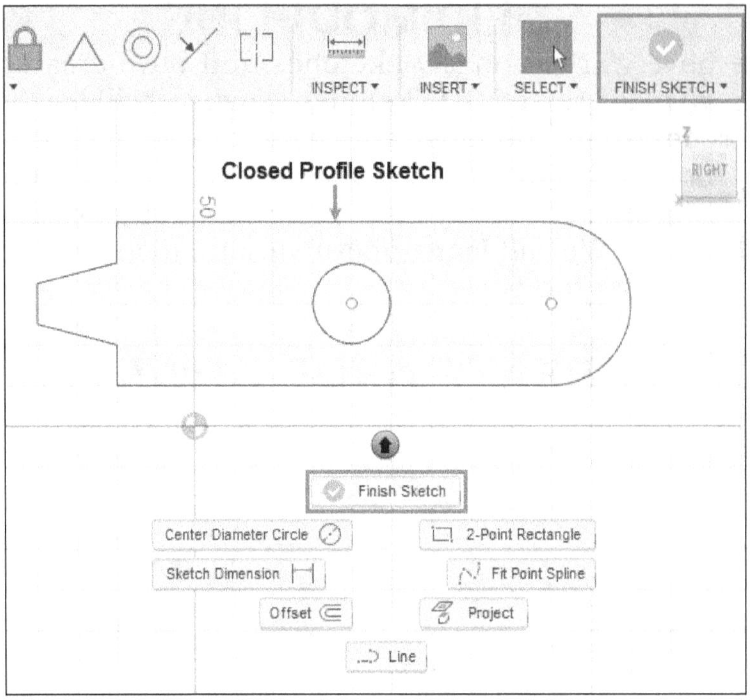

Figure-28. Sketch for extrusion

- Click on **Extrude** tool of **Create** drop-down from **Toolbar**; refer to Figure-29. The **EXTRUDE** dialog box will be displayed; refer to Figure-30.

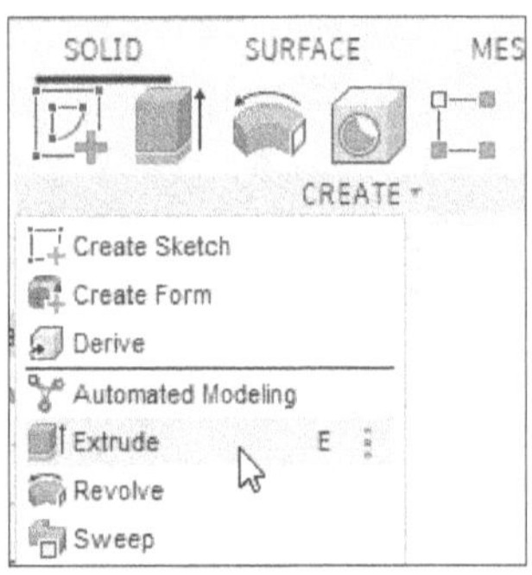

Figure-29. Extrude tool

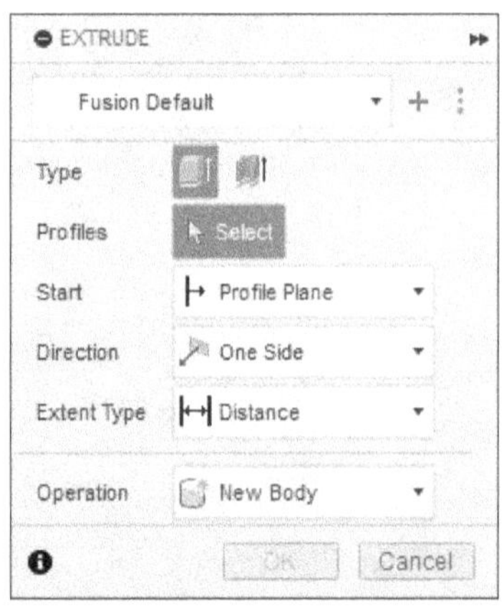

Figure-30. EXTRUDE dialog box

- Click on the **Presets** drop-down from top of the dialog box and select desired preset to apply or save the current values as a preset to use them. Click on the **New Preset** [+] button to create new preset for the dialog box.
- Select the type of extrusion you want to create from **Type** section of the dialog box. Select **Extrude** button to extrude entire area within selected closed profiles as solid. Select **Thin Extrude** button to extrude a thin wall along selected closed profiles.
- The **Extrude** option is selected by default in the **Type** section of the dialog box and the profile selection is active by default. Select the sketch to be extruded by clicking on the shaded area in the sketch. If your sketch has multiple closed profiles then make sure to select correct shaded area. For example, in Figure-28, we can select inside the circle, outside the circle, or both to create extrusion. The extruded body will be of the shape selected here.

Start drop-down

- There are three tools in **Start** drop-down; refer to Figure-31.

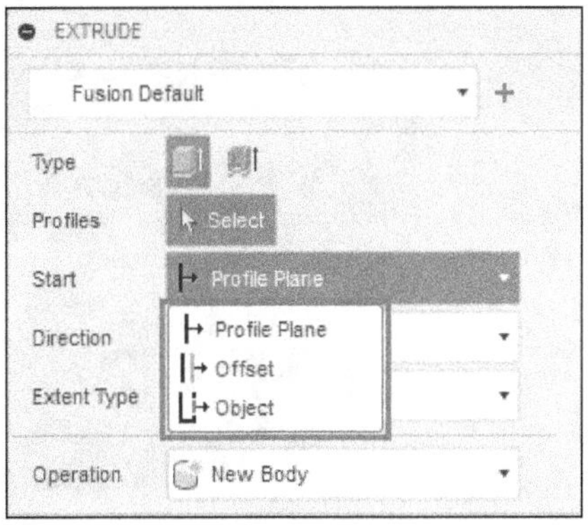

Figure-31. Start drop down

- Select **Profile Plane** option from **Start** drop-down, if you want to extrude the sketch starting from current sketching plane; refer to Figure-32.
- Select **Offset** option if you want to extrude the sketch starting from some offset distance. The updated **EXTRUDE** dialog box will be displayed; refer to Figure-33.
- Click in **Offset** edit box and type desired value of distance between starting of extrusion and sketch plane; refer to Figure-34.

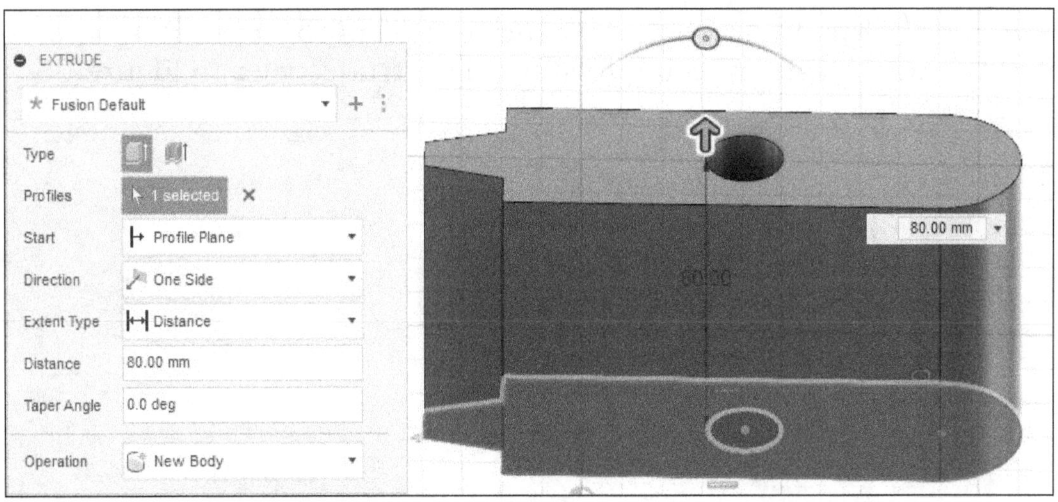

Figure-32. Extrude starting from profile plane

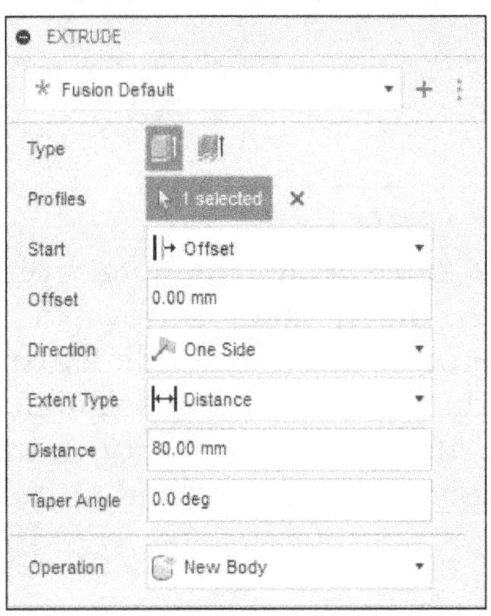

Figure-33. Offset tool in EXTRUDE dialog box

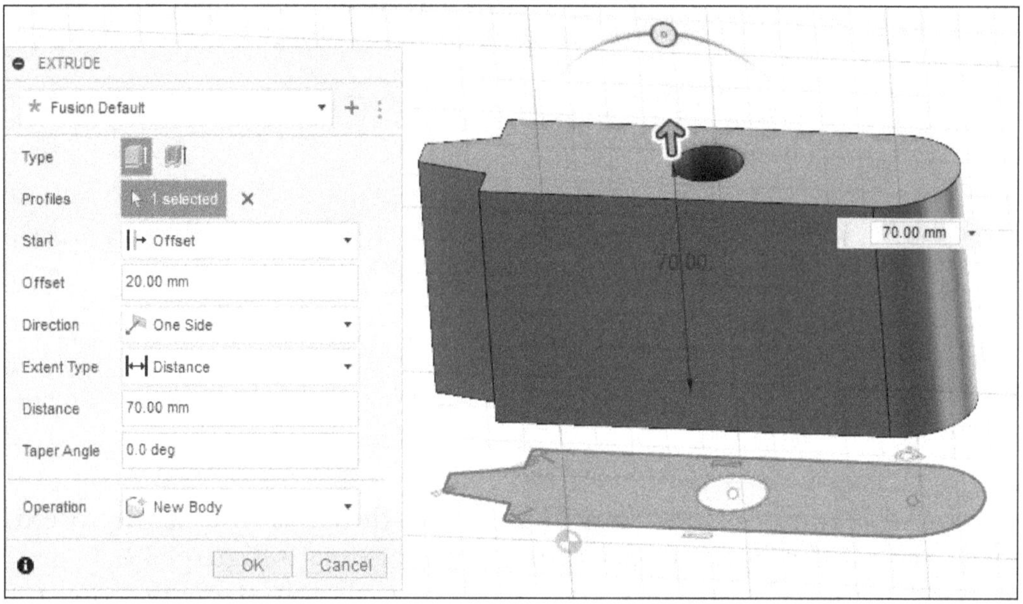

Figure-34. Extruding with offset

- Select the **Object** tool from **Start** drop-down in the dialog box, if you want to extrude the profile starting from selected surface/face (or at a distance from selected face) of another body.
- After selecting **Object** tool, click on **Select** button of **Object** section and select the object from where you are going to start the extrude; refer to Figure-35.

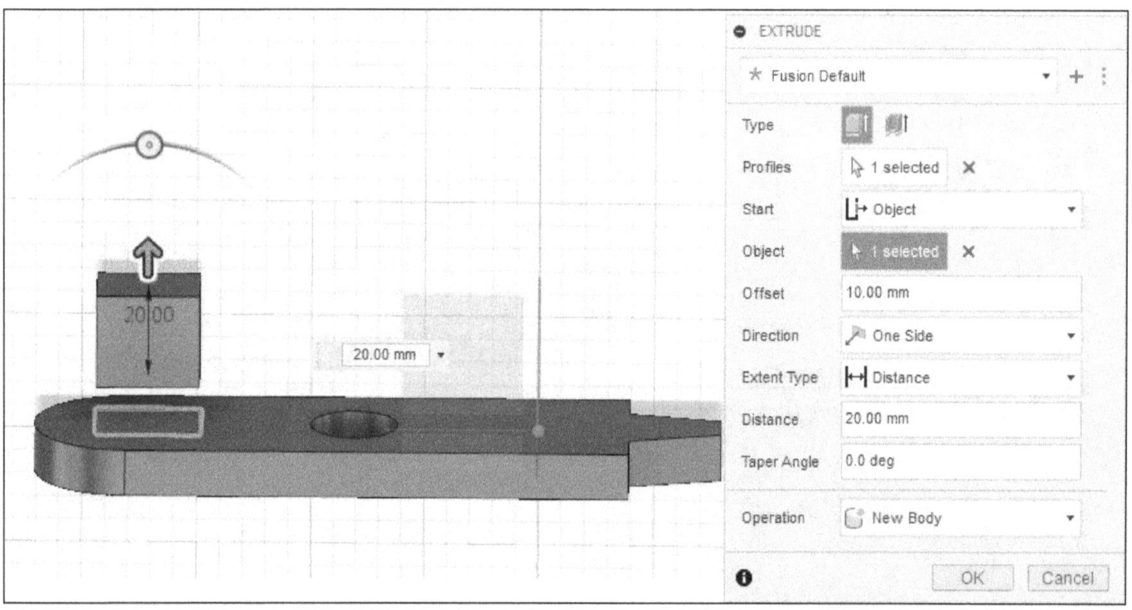

Figure-35. Object tool in EXTRUDE dialog box

- Click in **Distance** edit box and specify the height of extrusion. You can also drag the Arrow handle displayed on the sketch upward to define extrude height.
- If you want to create tapered walls of extrude feature then specify desired angle value in the **Taper Angle** edit box. You can specify both positive and negative values in this edit box. You can also use the rotation handle displayed in the preview to specify taper value. Applying taper angle is also called draft in some software.

Direction drop-down

- There are three tools in **Direction** drop-down of **EXTRUDE** dialog box; refer to Figure-36.

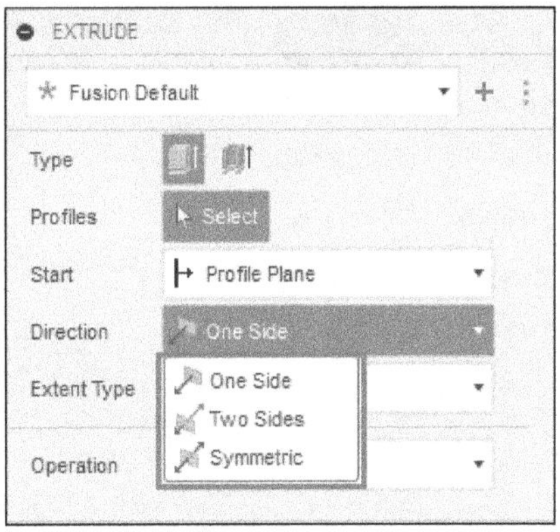

Figure-36. Direction drop down

- Select **One Side** option from **Direction** drop-down if you want to specify the height of extrusion in one direction.
- Select **Two Sides** option from **Direction** drop-down if you want to specify the height of extrusion in both upward and downward directions of sketching plane; refer to Figure-37. The options to specify parameters for side 1 and side 2 will be displayed in the dialog box.

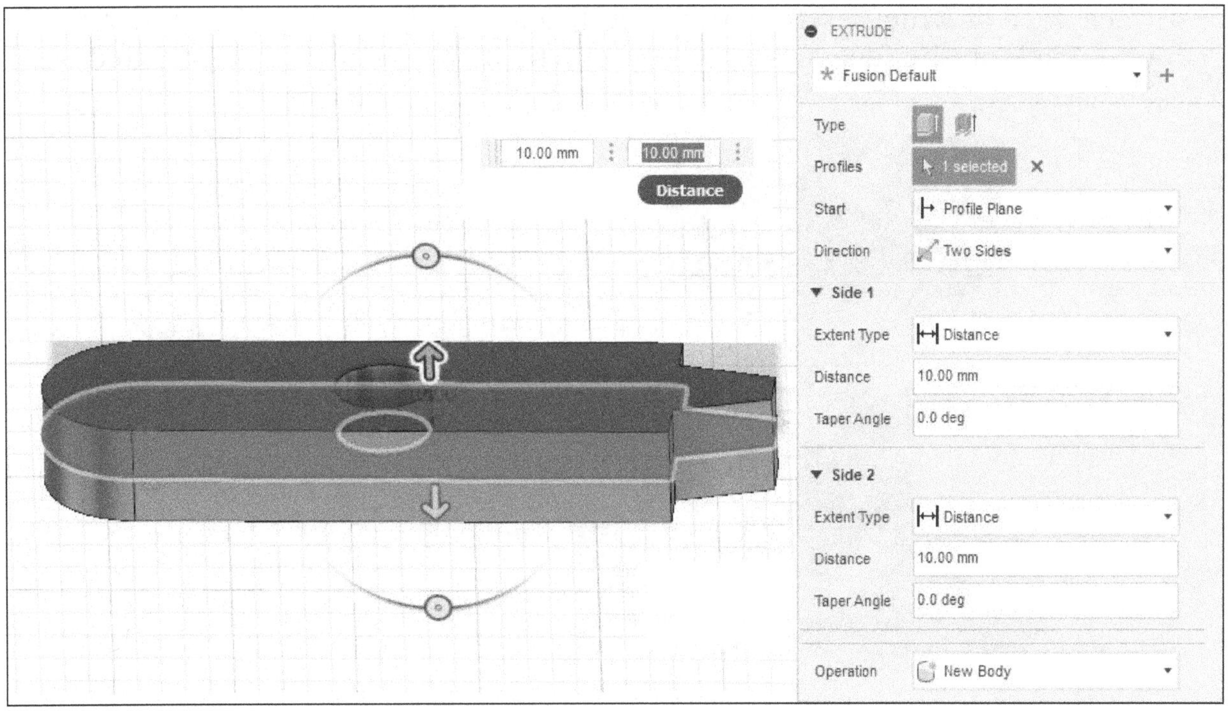

Figure-37. Extrude with two sides

- Select **Symmetric** option from **Direction** drop-down if you want to specify the height of extrusion symmetric in both upward and downward directions of sketching plane. You will be asked to specify height of extrusion for one side and the profile will be extruded symmetrically on the other side with same value. Select the **Half length** or **Whole length** button from **Measurement** section as required; refer to Figure-38.

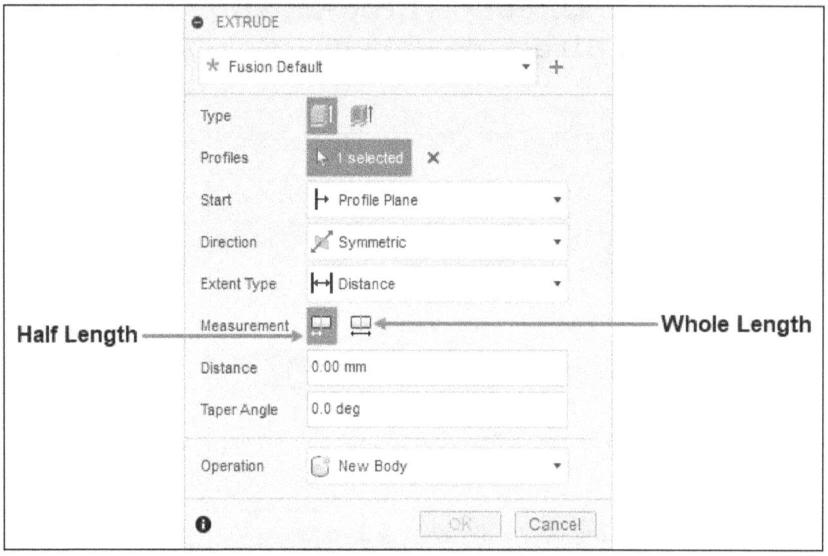

Figure-38. Extrude with symmetric direction

Extent Type drop-down

- Select **Distance** option from **Extent Type** drop-down in the **EXTRUDE** dialog box if you want to set the height of extrusion manually. Click in the **Distance** edit box and specify desired height.
- Select **To Object** option from **Extent Type** drop-down if you want to define a surface/face at which extrusion will end; refer to Figure-39. After selecting this option, click on the face or surface up to which extrusion is to be created.

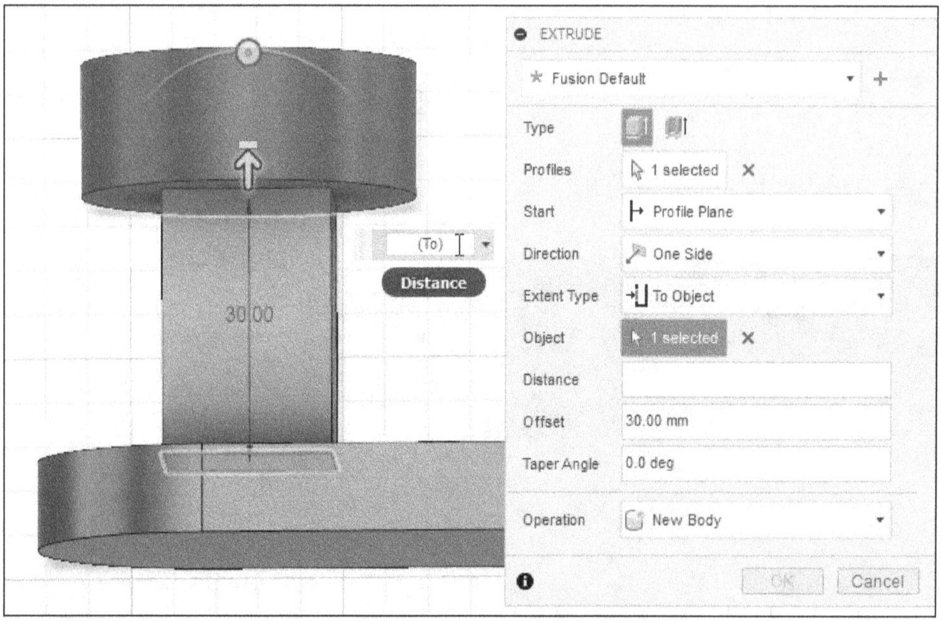

Figure-39. To Object extrude

- Select **All** option from **Extent Type** drop-down, if you want to cut through the model or part from extrusion. The extrusion will goes through from the body of model; refer to Figure-40. If you want to add material in place of removing then select the **Join** option from the **Operation** drop-down in the dialog box.

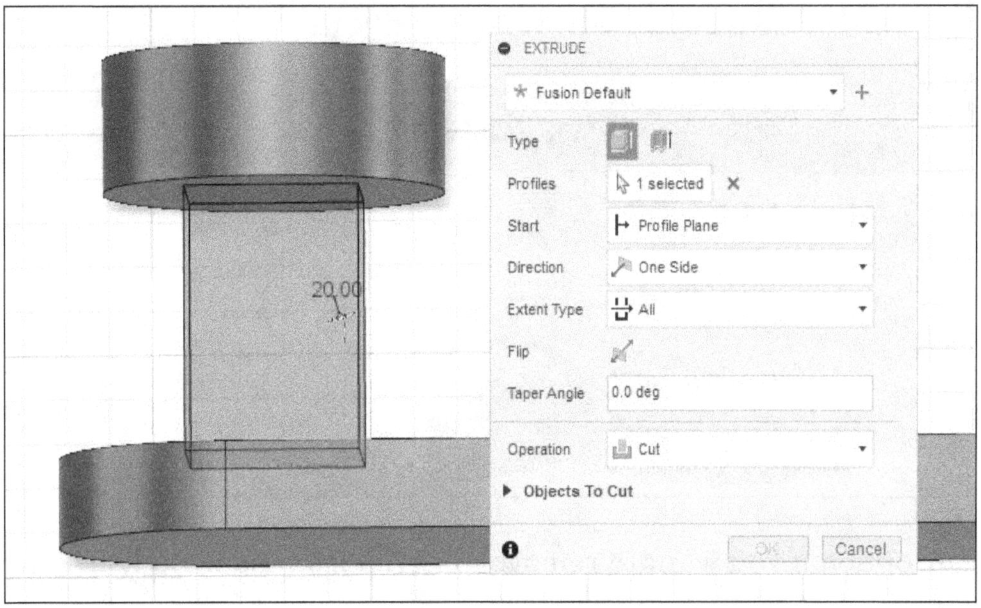

Figure-40. All option in Extent Type drop down

- Click on the **Flip** button to reverse the direction of extrusion.

Operation drop-down

- There are five options in **Operation** drop-down of **EXTRUDE** dialog box; refer to Figure-41. These options are discussed next.

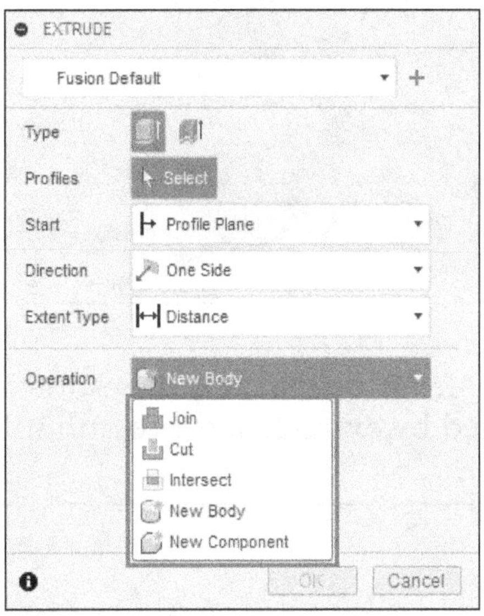

Figure-41. Operation drop down

- Select **Join** option of **Operation** drop-down if you want to combine the extrude feature with intersecting bodies; refer to Figure-42.

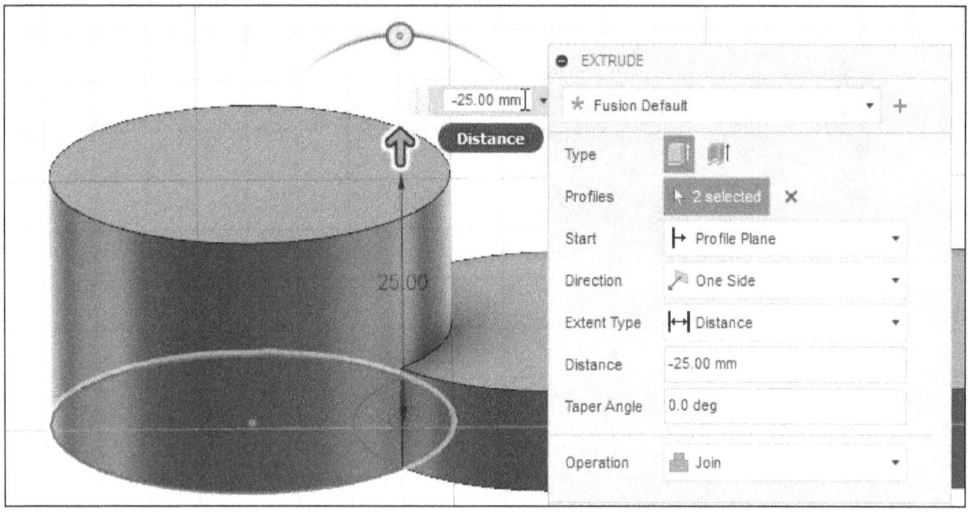

Figure-42. Join tool

- Select **Cut** option if you want to remove material from base body by using current extrude feature; refer to Figure-43.

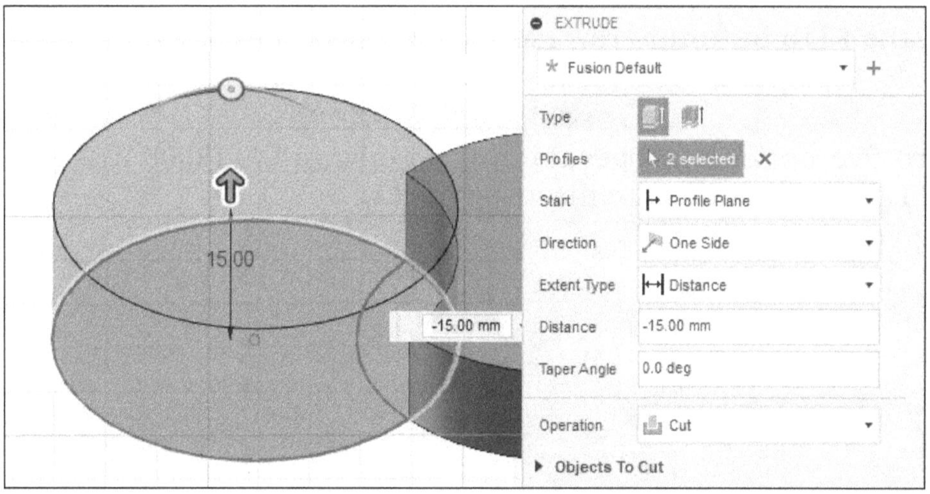

Figure-43. Cut tool

- Select **Intersect** option from **Operation** drop-down if you want to create the region commonly bounded by extrude feature and intersecting solid bodies; refer to Figure-44.

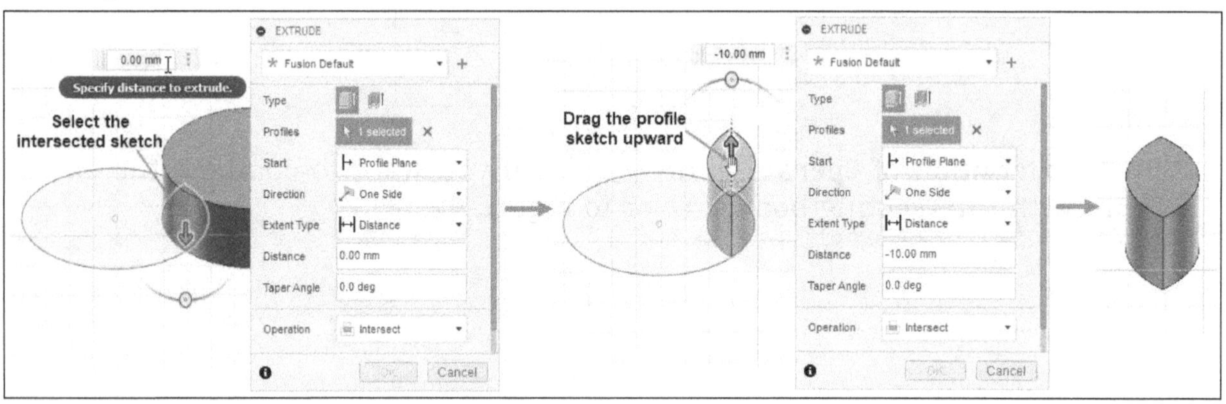

Figure-44. Intersect tool

- Select **New Body** option from **Operation** drop-down if you want to create a new body. A new body creation becomes important when you are creating molds and want all the tool bodies to be individual objects.

- Select the **New Component** option from **Operation** drop-down if you want to create a new component of the current extrude feature. New components are created for assembly. You will learn more about this option later in the book.

Extruding Thin Wall

If you want to extrude a thin wall along selected closed profiles, then select **Thin Extrude** button from **Type** section of the dialog box. The options in the **EXTRUDE** dialog box will be updated; refer to Figure-45.

Wall Location drop-down

There are three options in **Wall Location** drop-down of **EXTRUDE** dialog box; refer to Figure-46. These options are discussed next.

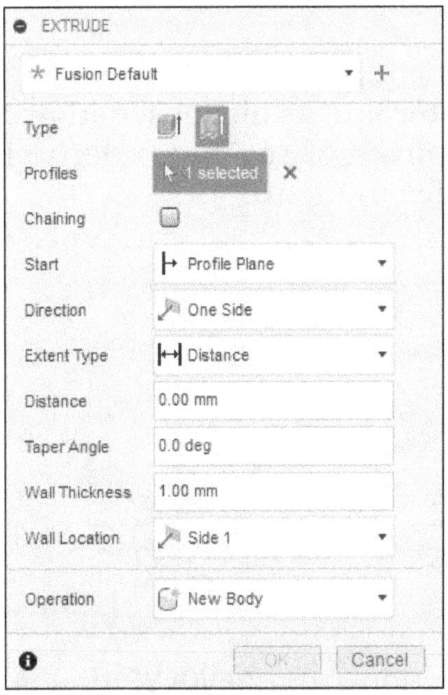

Figure-45. Thin Extrude options in EXTRUDE dialog box

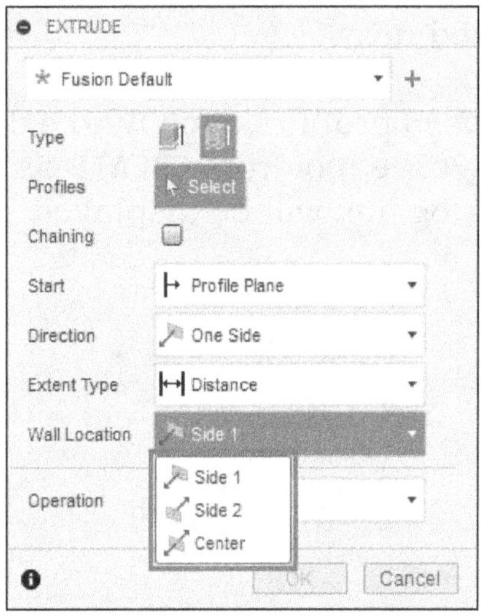

Figure-46. Wall Location drop down

- Select **Side 1** option from the drop-down if you want to offset/move the extrusion to the one side of the profile; refer to Figure-47.

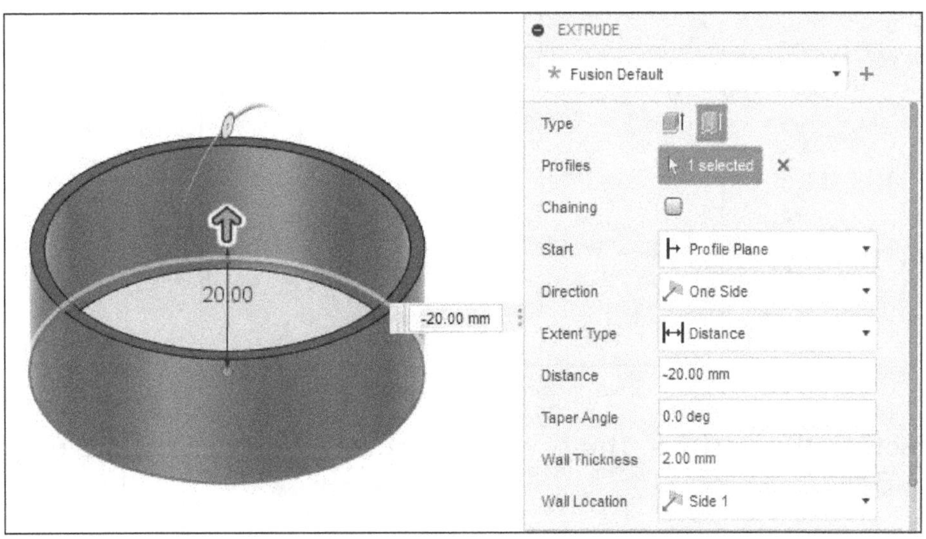

Figure-47. Extrusion inside the profile

- Specify desired thickness of extrusion in the **Wall Thickness** edit box of the dialog box.
- Select the **Chaining** check box to automatically select the connected geometry.
- Specify the parameters in the dialog box as discussed earlier and click on **OK** button. The extrusion inside the profile will be created.
- Similarly, select **Side 2** option from the drop-down to offset/move the extrusion to the other side of the profile and select **Center** option from the drop-down to center the extrusion on the profile.

Revolve

Revolve tool is used to create a solid volume by revolving a sketch about selected axis. In other words, if you revolve a sketch about an axis then the volume covered by revolving sketch boundary is called revolve feature. The procedure to use this tool is discussed next.

- Create a closed profile sketch with a center line as discussed in previous chapter.
- Click on **Revolve** tool from **CREATE** drop-down of **Toolbar**; refer to Figure-48. The **REVOLVE** dialog box will be displayed; refer to Figure-49.

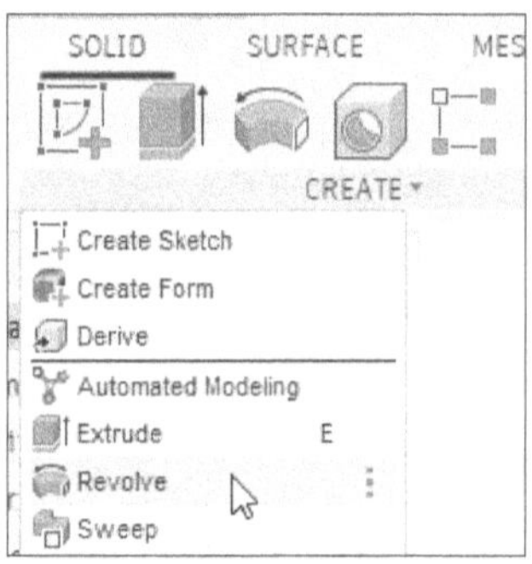

Figure-48. Revolve tool

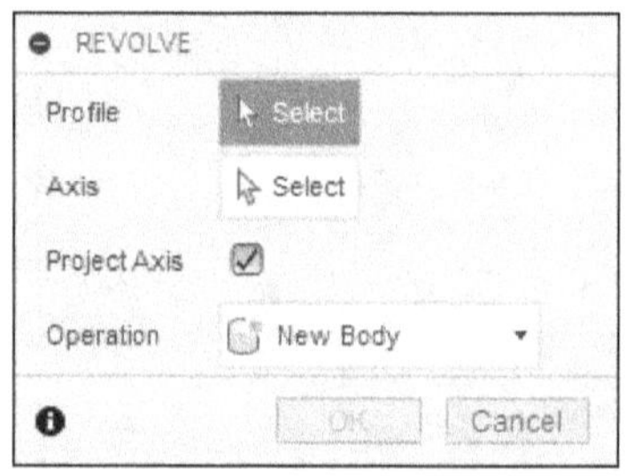

Figure-49. REVOLVE dialog box

- Click on **Select** button for **Profile** selection from **REVOLVE** dialog box and then select the sketch for profile from the screen canvas.
- Click on **Select** button for **Axis** selection from **REVOLVE** dialog box and then select the sketch edge, line, or center line from the screen canvas; refer to Figure-50.

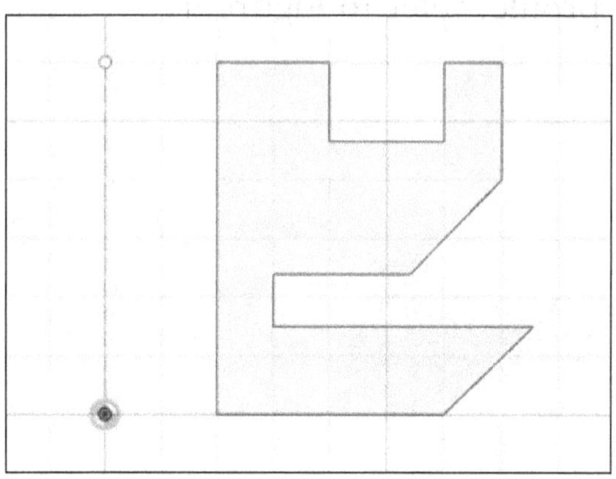

Figure-50. Region selected for revolve

- After selecting the entities, the preview of revolve feature will be displayed; refer to Figure-51.

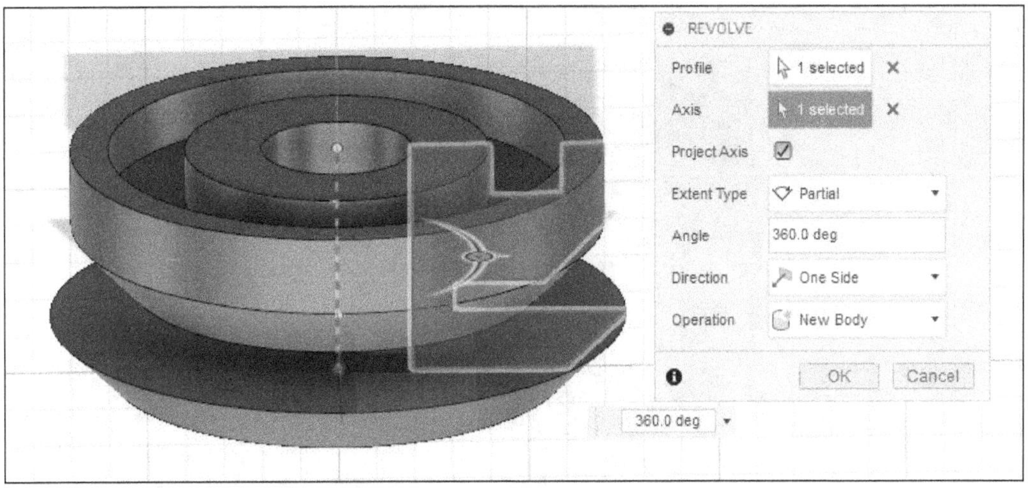

Figure-51. Preview of revolve feature

- Select **Project Axis** check box to project the axis to the same sketch plane as the selected profile.
- Specify desired value of revolve angle in the **Angle** dynamic input box. You can also set the value of angle by moving the drag handle; refer to Figure-52.

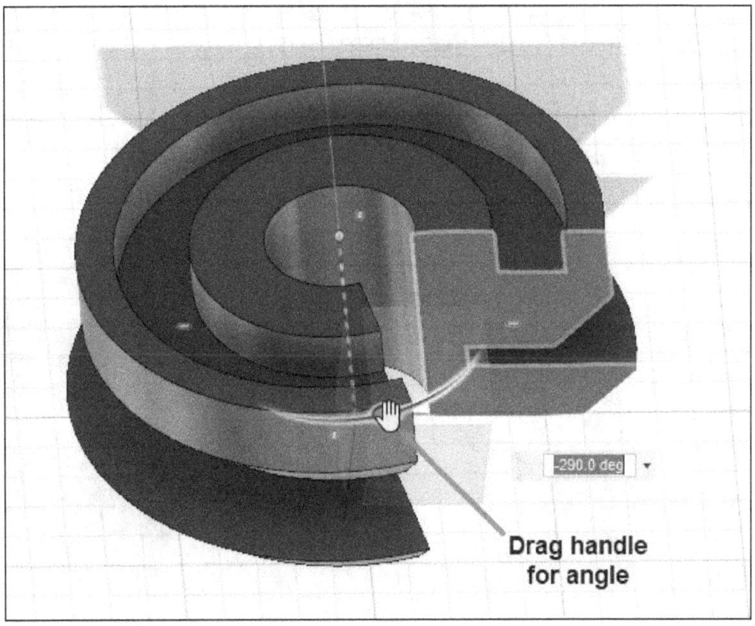

Figure-52. Moving the drag handle

Direction drop-down

The options in **Direction** drop-down are used to define in which direction profile will be revolved.

- Select **One Side** option from **Direction** drop-down to revolve the profile in one direction.
- Select **Two Sides** option from **Direction** drop-down if you want to revolve the profile in both sides with different revolution angles; refer to Figure-53.
- Select the **Symmetric** option from **Direction** drop-down if you want to revolve the model in both direction with same angle i.e. symmetrically.

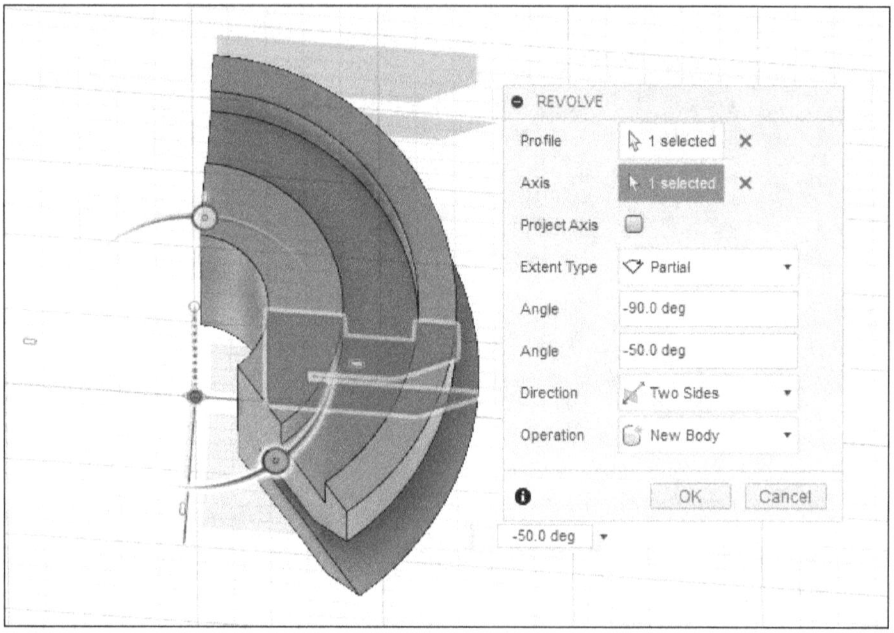

Figure-53. Two Sides option

Extent Type

- Select the **Partial** option from **Type** drop-down if you want to revolve the profile by specified angle.
- Select the **To Object** option from **Type** drop-down if you want to revolve the model up to a plane, face, surface, or vertex; refer to Figure-54.

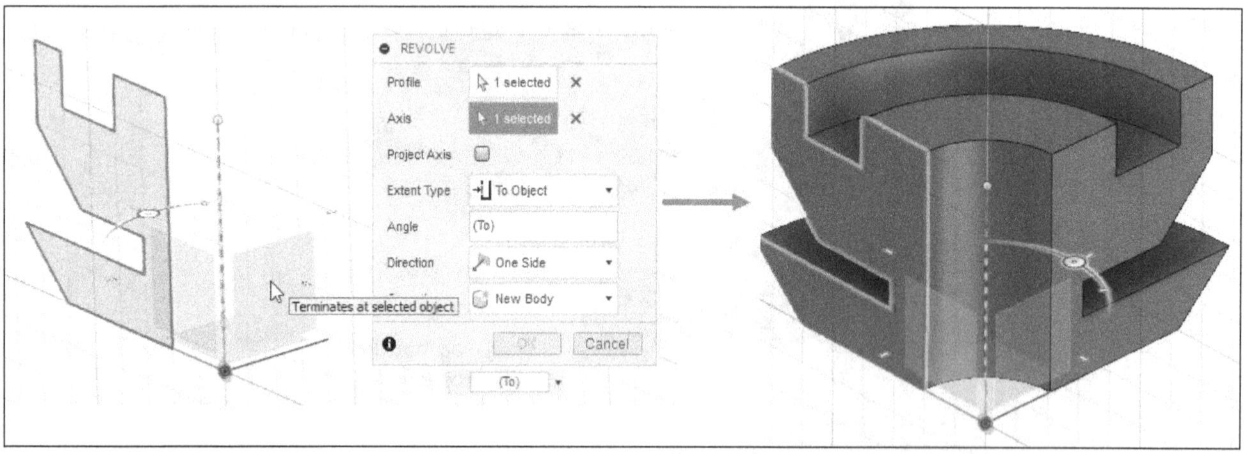

Figure-54. Preview of To Object option

- Select the **Full** option from **Type** drop-down if you want to revolve the profile to 360 degree angle.
- Set the other options as discussed earlier.
- Click **OK** button from **REVOLVE** dialog box to create the feature.

Sweep

The **Sweep** tool is used to create a solid volume by moving a sketch along the selected path. In other words, if you move a sketch along a path then the volume that is covered by moving sketch boundary is called sweep feature. Note that to create a solid sweep feature, you will need two sketches, one for the profile and another for the path already created in the canvas. The steps to use this tool are discussed next.

- Click on **Sweep** tool from **CREATE** drop-down; refer to Figure-55. The **SWEEP** dialog box will be displayed with **Feature** tab opened by default; refer to Figure-56.

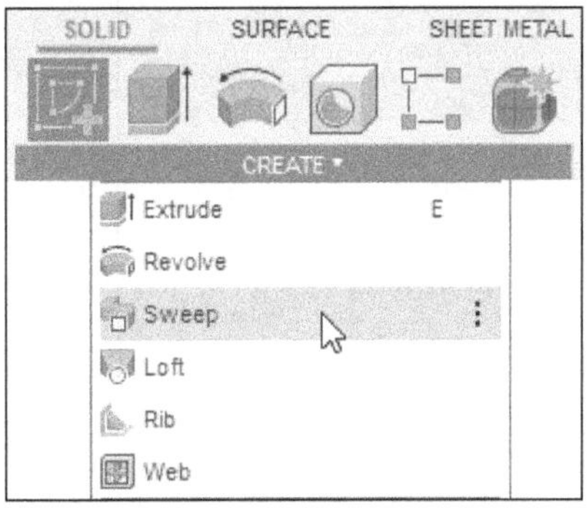

Figure-55. Sweep tool

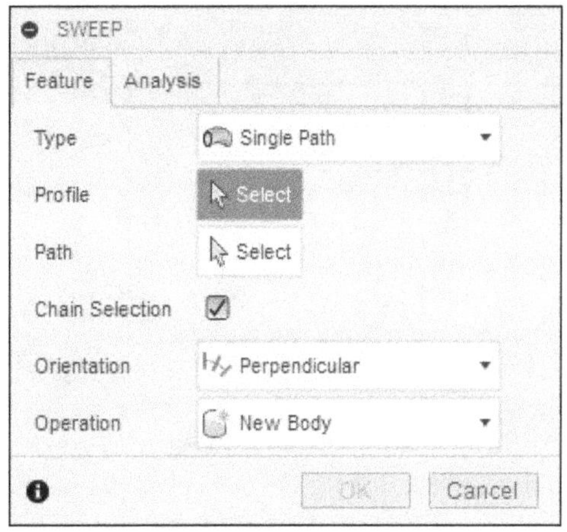

Figure-56. SWEEP dialog box

In this dialog box, there are three options in **Type** drop-down to create sweep feature; **Single Path**, **Path + Guide Rail**, and **Path + Guide Surface**. The procedures to create sweep feature by using these options are discussed next.

Single Path

The **Single Path** tool sweeps the selected profile along a single path.

- Click on the **Select** button of **Profile** section from the **SWEEP** dialog box and select the sketch for profile from the canvas screen.
- Click on the **Select** button of **Path** section from **SWEEP** dialog box and select the path from the canvas screen; refer to Figure-57. Note that few more options are now available in the dialog box.

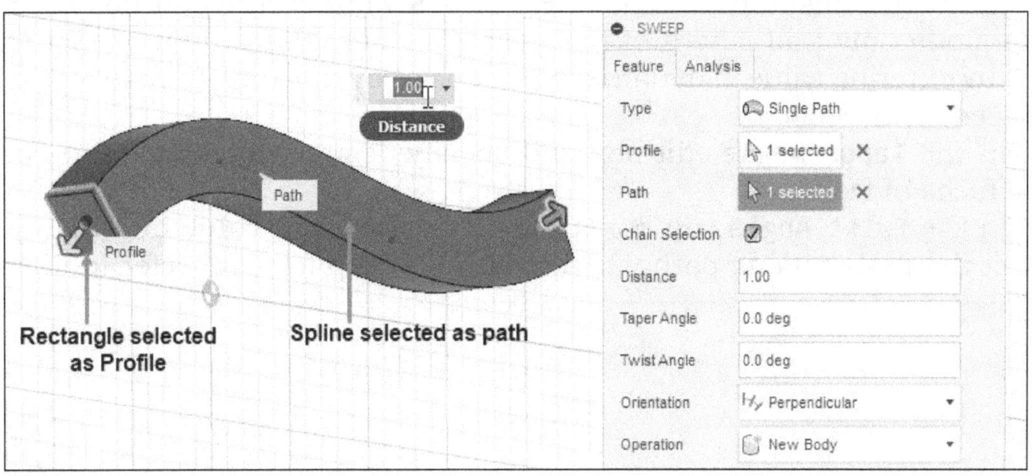

Figure-57. Selection of sketch and path

- Select the **Chain Selection** check box if you want to select chain of entities connected with path curve being selected; refer to Figure-58.

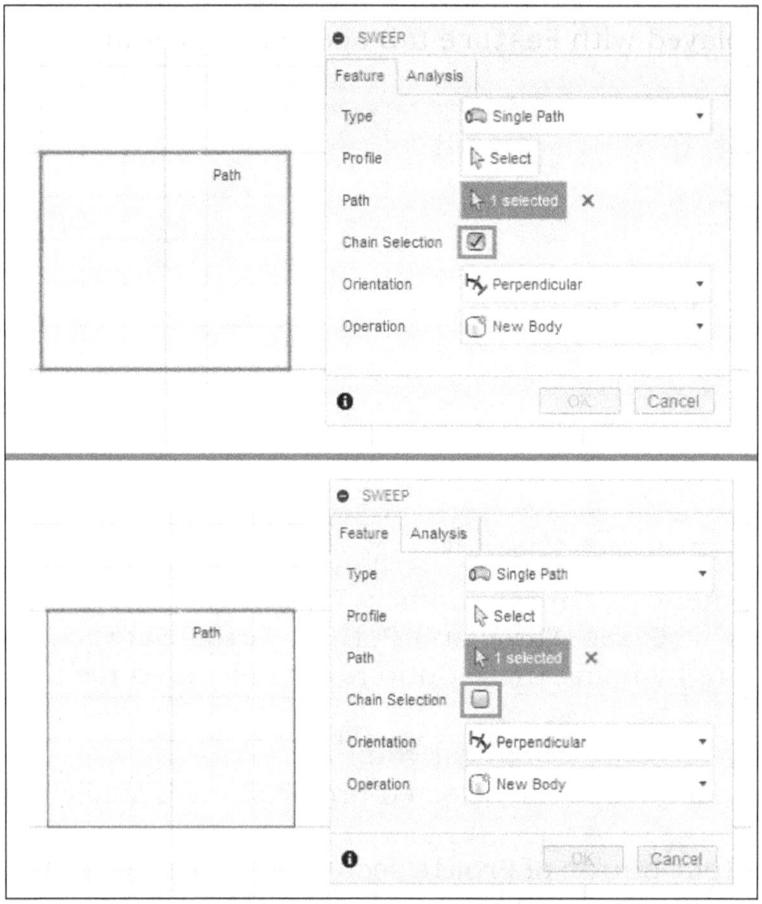

Figure-58. Selecting path with and without chain selection

- The distance in the **Distance** edit box is not the actual distance value rather it is the percentage of total distance along the path. **1** is the maximum value which is the total path distance of sweep. Enter **0.5** value in the edit box to create the sweep along only half length of the path. You can also adjust the length of the sweep by entering value in dynamic input box or by moving the drag arrow handles displayed on the model.
- Click in the **Taper Angle** edit box and specify desired angle value to apply draft to the faces of feature.
- Click in the **Twist Angle** edit box and specify the angle value by which you want to twist the profile along path while creating sweep feature; refer to Figure-59.

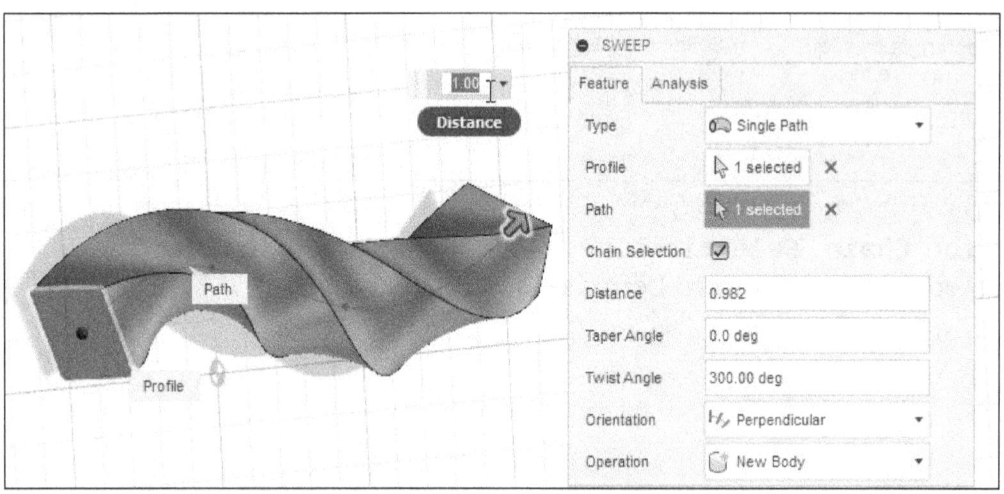

Figure-59. Preview of twisted sweep feature

- The options in the **Orientation** drop-down of **SWEEP** dialog box are used to define how the profile is pulled along the sweep path.
- **Perpendicular** option is the default selection of **Orientation** drop-down. This option creates the sweep feature in such that profile section is always perpendicular to the path. This allow more curvature on the path; refer to Figure-60.

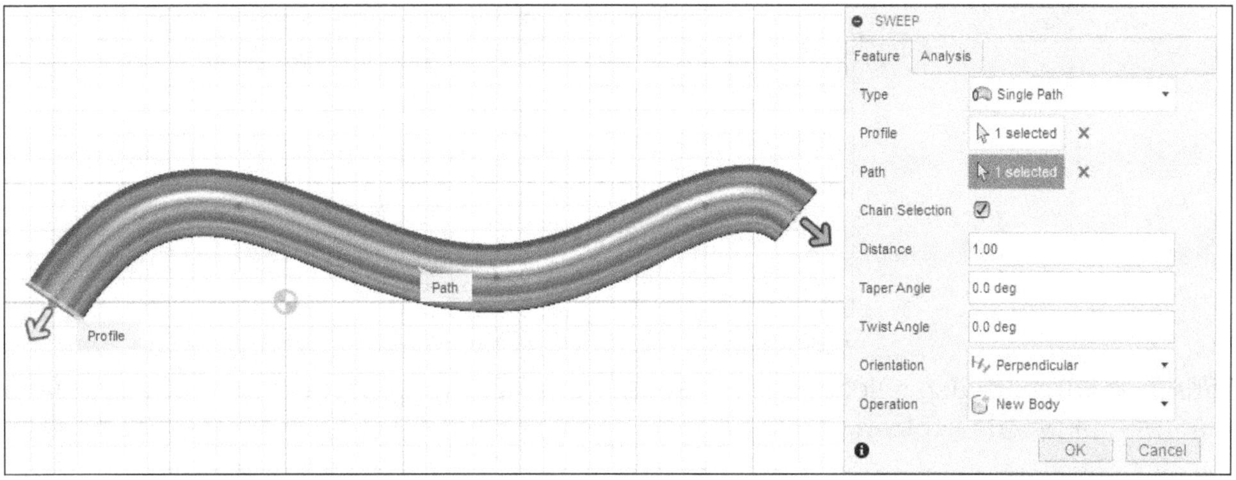

Figure-60. Perpendicular orientation

- **Parallel** option of **Orientation** drop-down creates sweep feature in such a way that the profile section is always parallel to its original orientation; refer to Figure-61.

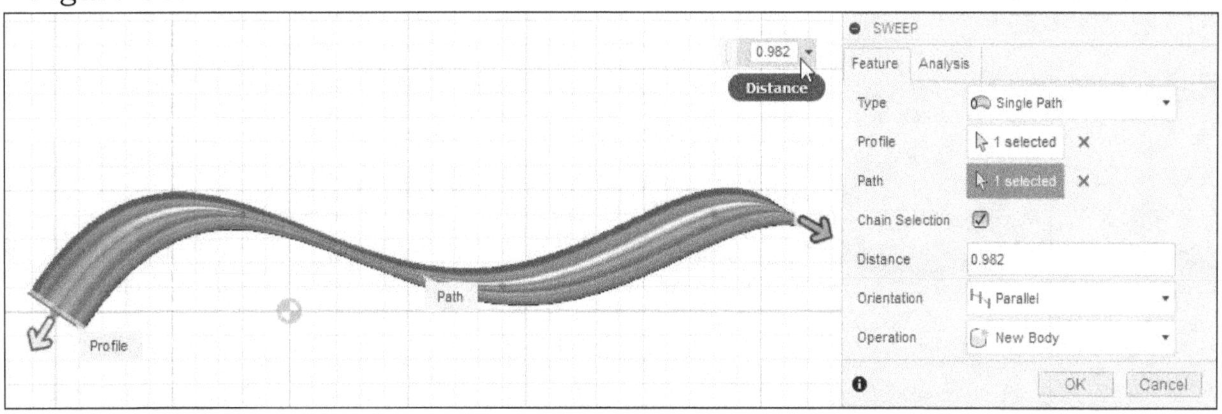

Figure-61. Parallel orientation

- After specifying the parameters, click on **OK** button to create the sweep feature.

Path + Guide Rail

Selecting this option sweeps the selected sketch along the path and uses the guide rail to control the shape. The procedure to use this tool is discussed next.

- Select the **Path + Guide Rail** option from **Type** drop-down of **SWEEP** dialog box. The options in the dialog box will be displayed as shown in Figure-62.
- Click on the **Select** button for **Profile** from the **SWEEP** dialog box and then select the sketch created for profile from the canvas screen.
- Click on the **Select** button for **Path** from **SWEEP** dialog box and then select the sketch/edge for path from the canvas screen.

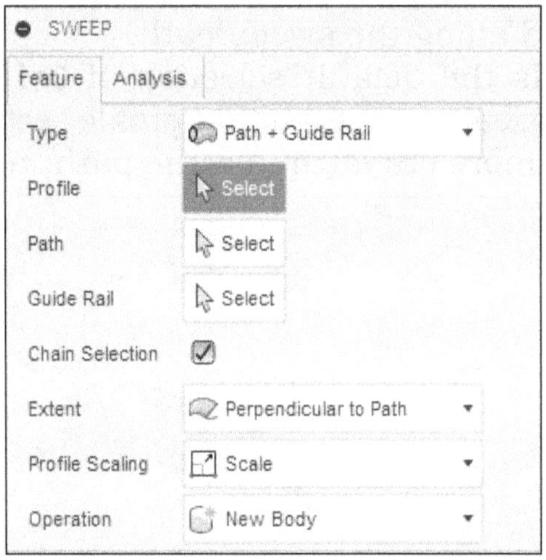

Figure-62. Path + Guide Rail option

Note that you can also select edges of solids/surfaces as path or guide rails and faces of solids as profile section.

- Click on the **Select** button for **Guide Rail** from the **SWEEP** dialog box and then select the sketch for guide from the canvas screen; refer to Figure-63. Preview of sweep feature will be displayed and additional options will be available in the **SWEEP** dialog box.

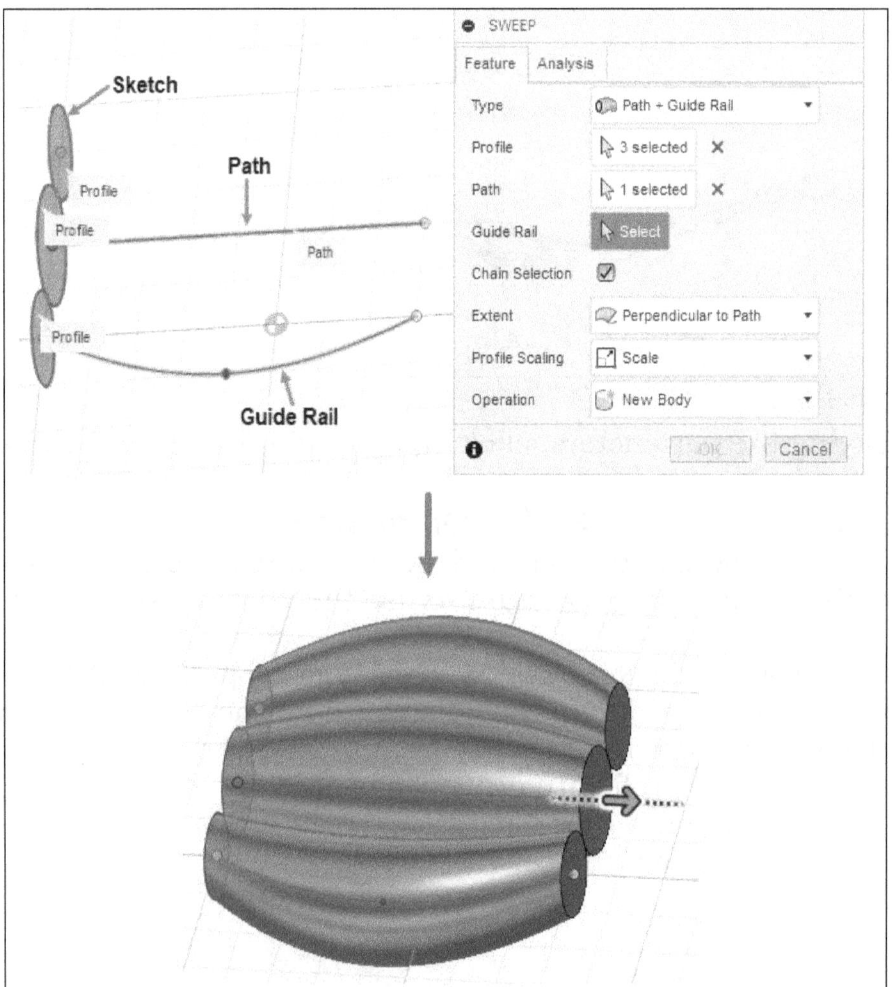

Figure-63. Selection of entities for path + guide rail

- Click in the **Extent** drop-down and select the **Perpendicular to Path** option if you want to create the sweep feature till the profile is perpendicular to path. Select the **Full Extents** option from the drop-down if you want to create sweep till the end point of path.
- Specify desired values for distance in **Path Distance** and **Guide Rail Distance** edit boxes as discussed earlier. Note that the **Guide Rail Distance** edit box will be available only when **Full Extents** option is selected in the **Extents** drop-down.
- Select the **Scale** option from **Profile Scaling** drop-down in **SWEEP** dialog box, if you want to equally scale the profile in both X and Y direction; refer to Figure-64. **The profile will be scaled up depending on the distance between path and guide rail.**
- Select the **Stretch** option from **Profile Scaling** drop-down if you want to scale the profile in X direction only. In this way, profile will keep following guide rail while moving along the path; refer to Figure-64.
- Click on **None** option from **Profile Scaling** drop-down if you don't want to scale the profile along sweep. On selecting this option, guide rail is used as an orientation guide only; refer to Figure-64.

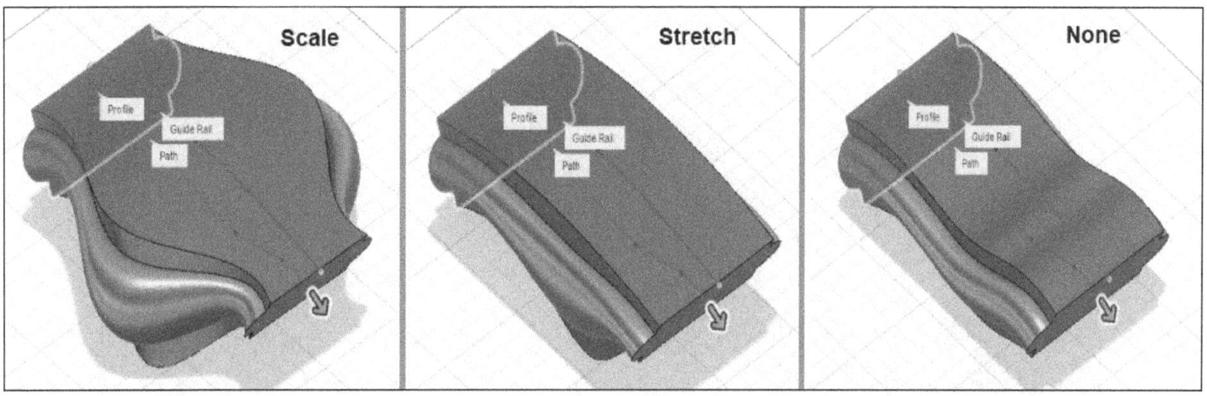

Figure-64. Preview of profile orientation

Note that the profile, path, and guide rail are same in all three cases.

- The tools of **Operation** drop-down are same as discussed earlier in this book. Click on the **OK** button from the dialog box to create the features.

Path + Guide Surface

This option sweeps the selected sketch along the path and uses the guide surface to control the shape. The procedure to use this tool is discussed next.

- Select the **Path + Guide Surface** option of **Type** drop-down from **SWEEP** dialog box. The options in the dialog box will be displayed as shown in Figure-65.

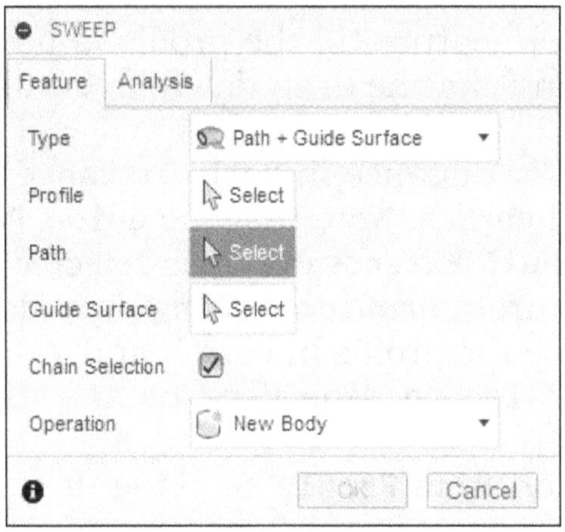

Figure-65. Path + Guide Surface option

- Select the profile for sweep and click on the **Select** button for **Path**.
- Select the curve/edge for path and click on the **Select** button for **Guide Surface**.
- Select the surface by which you want to control the shape of sweep feature; refer to Figure-66. Preview of feature will be displayed.

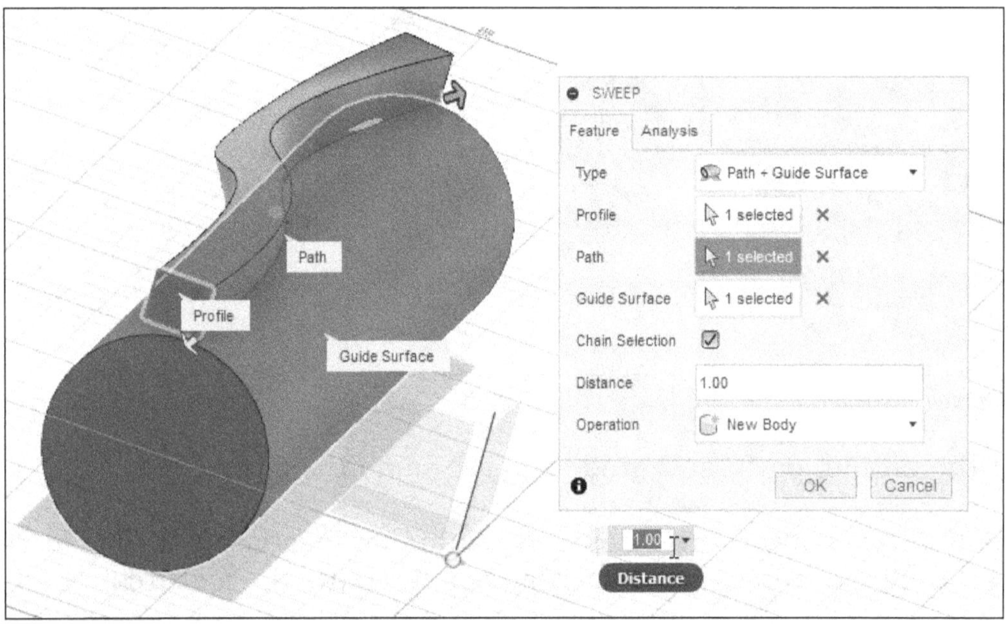

Figure-66. Sweep feature created using guide surface

- Set the parameters as discussed earlier and click on the **OK** button to create the feature.

Part file of this example is available in resources folder of this book. You can try different combinations of sweep for this example.

The **Analysis** tab of **SWEEP** dialog box is used to analyze the previewed result. We will discuss the options of this tab, later in this book.

CONSTRUCTION GEOMETRY

Till now, we have created all the features on default planes but sometimes, we need to create features that cannot be created on default planes. In such cases, we create some construction geometries. Construction geometries are used as references for other features. Some of the well known entities that come under construction geometries are:

- Planes
- Axes
- Points
- Coordinate Systems
- Curves
- Sketches

You have learned about sketches earlier in the book. Now, we will work on other features. All the tools for construction geometry features are available in the **CONSTRUCT** drop-down; refer to Figure-67. These tools are discussed next.

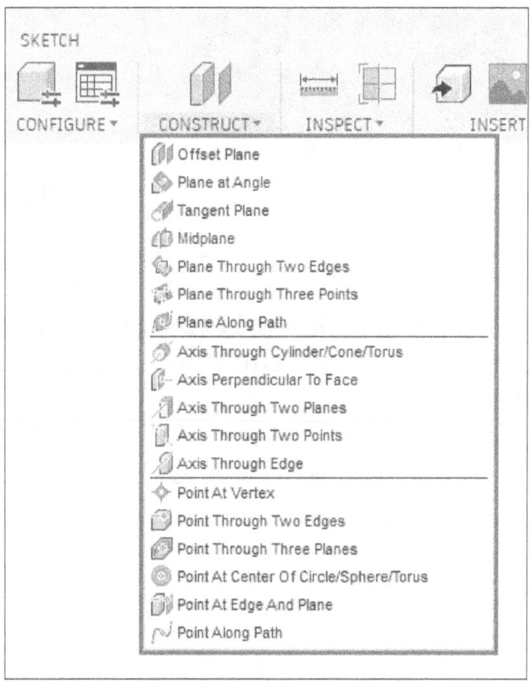

Figure-67. CONSTRUCT panel drop-down

Offset Plane

The **Offset Plane** tool is used to create a plane at specified distance from a face/plane reference. The procedure to use this tool is discussed next.

- Click on the **Offset Plane** tool from **CONSTRUCT** drop-down in the **Toolbar**; refer to Figure-68. The **CONSTRUCTION GEOMETRY** dialog box will be displayed with the **Plane** option selected in the **Type** area and **Offset** option selected in the **Method** drop-down by default; refer to Figure-69.

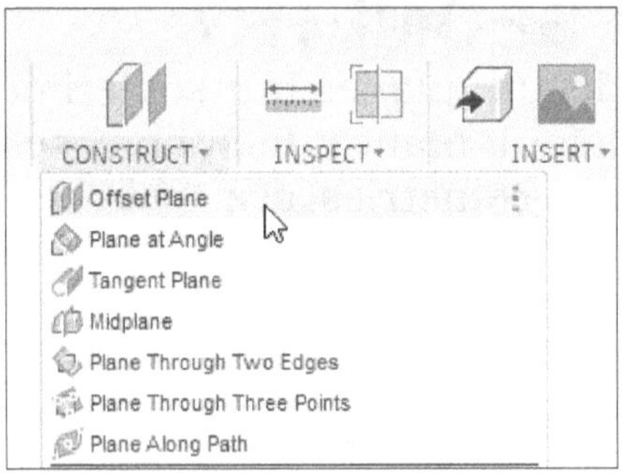

Figure-68. Offset Plane tool

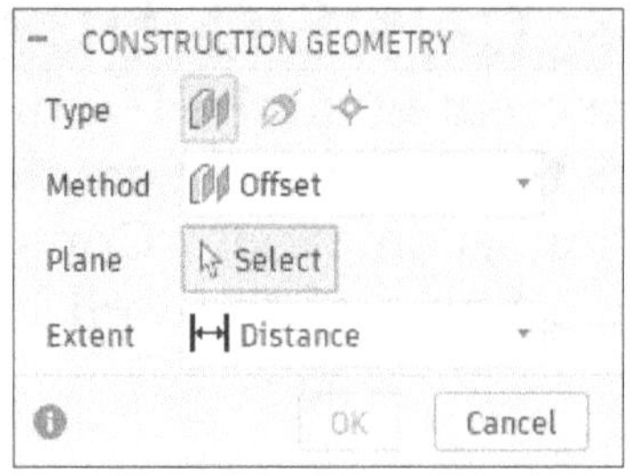

Figure-69. CONSTRUCTION GEOMETRY dialog box with Plane and Offset option

- Plane selection is active by default. Click on the plane/face of model to be used as reference for offset plane; refer to Figure-70. The preview for offset plane will be displayed.

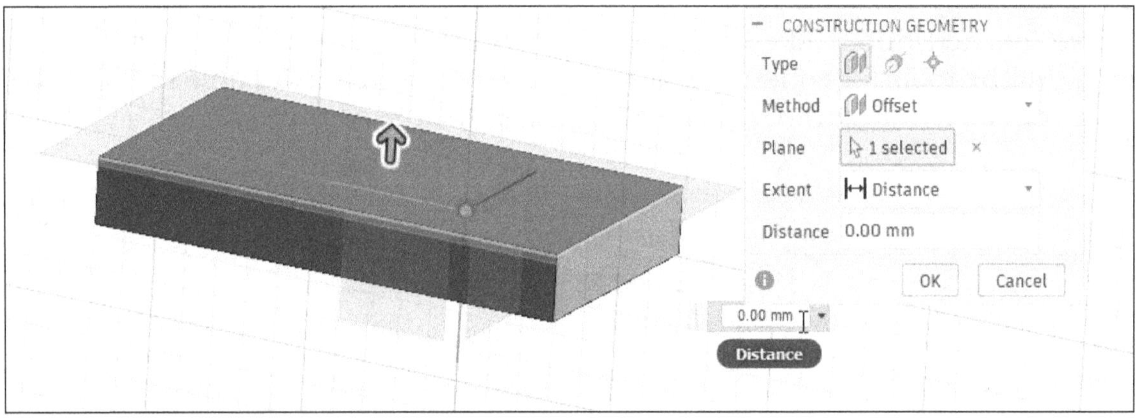

Figure-70. Selection of plane for creating offset plane

- Click in the **Distance** edit box of **CONTRUCTION GEOMETRY** dialog box and enter the distance at which you want to create the plane. You can also set the distance by moving the drag handle.
- After specifying the distance for offset plane, click on the **OK** button from **CONTRUCTION GEOMETRY** dialog box. The plane will be created; refer to Figure-71.

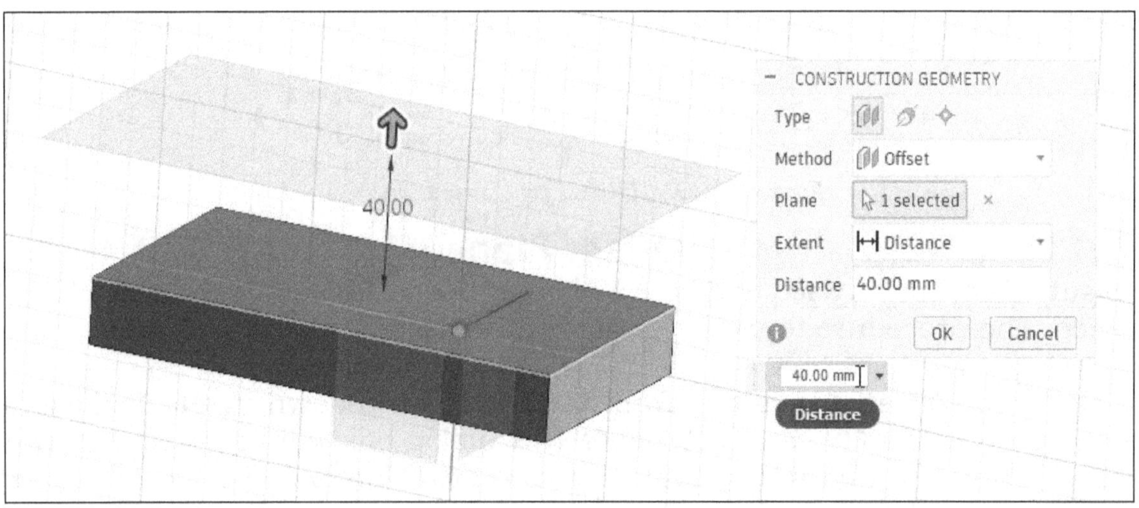

Figure-71. Preview of offset plane

Plane at Angle

The **Plane at Angle** tool is used to create a plane at specified angle. The procedure to use this tool is discussed next.

- Click on the **Plane at Angle** tool from **CONSTRUCT** drop-down in the **Toolbar**; refer to Figure-72. The **CONSTRUCTION GEOMETRY** dialog box will be displayed with the **Plane** option selected in the **Type** area and **At Angle** option selected in the **Method** drop-down by default; refer to Figure-73.

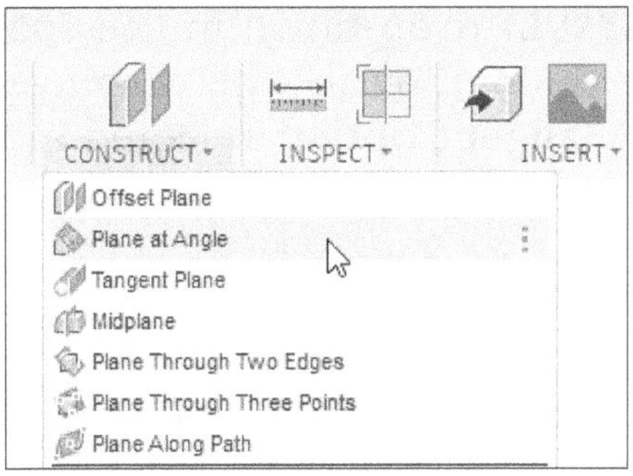

Figure-72. Plane at Angle tool

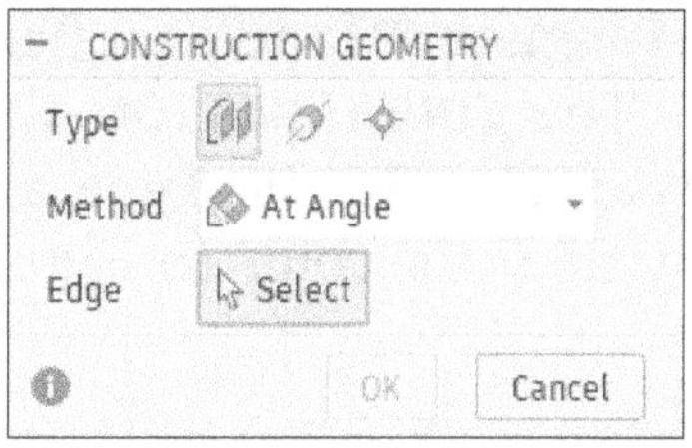

Figure-73. CONSTRUCTION GEOMETRY dialog box with Plane and At Angle option

- **Edge** selection of **CONSTRUCTION GEOMETRY** dialog box is active by default. Click on the line/edge/axis from the model as reference for creating a plane. The updated **CONSTRUCTION GEOMETRY** dialog box will be displayed; refer to Figure-74.

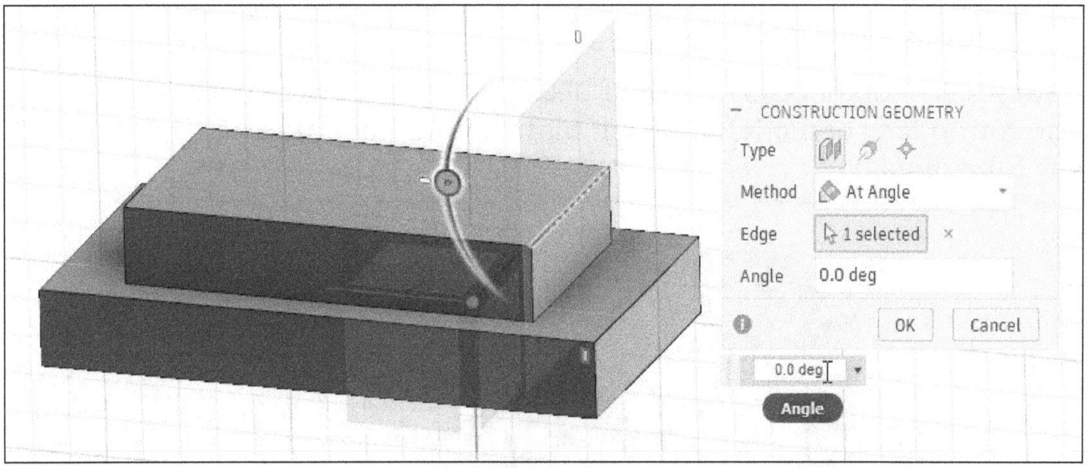

Figure-74. Updated CONSTRUCTION GEOMETRY dialog box

- Specify desired angle value in **Angle** edit box or drag the handle.
- After specifying the angle for plane, click on the **OK** button from **CONSTRUCTION GEOMETRY** dialog box. The plane will be created; refer to Figure-75.

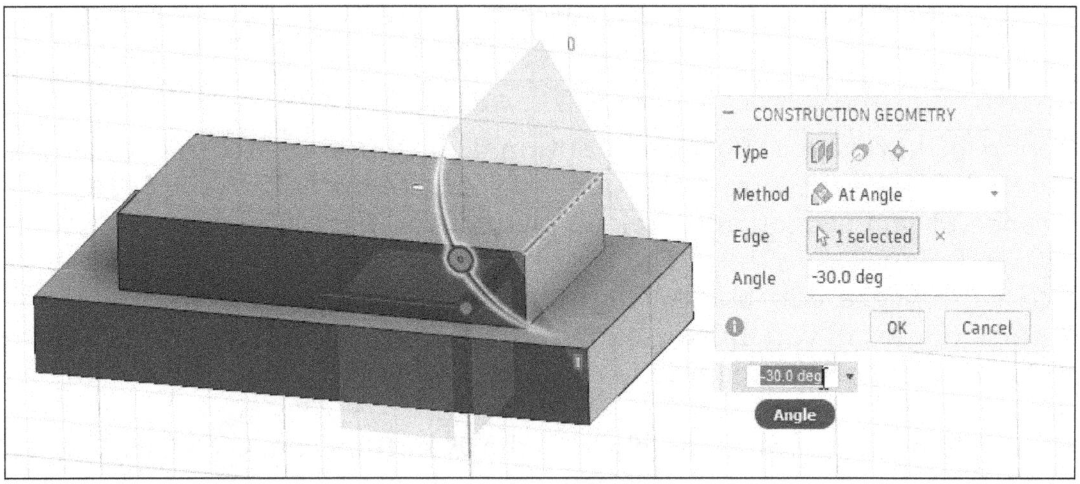

Figure-75. Preview of plane at angle

Tangent Plane

The **Tangent Plane** tool is used to create a plane tangent to the selected face/surface. The procedure to use this tool is discussed next.

- Click on the **Tangent Plane** tool from **CONSTRUCT** drop-down in the **Toolbar**; refer to Figure-76. The **CONSTRUCTION GEOMETRY** dialog box will be displayed with the **Plane** option selected in the **Type** area and **Tangent** option selected in the **Method** drop-down by default; refer to Figure-77.

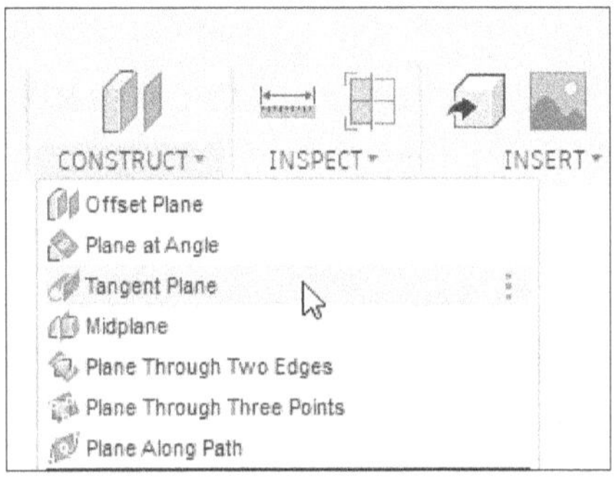

Figure-76. Tangent Plane tool

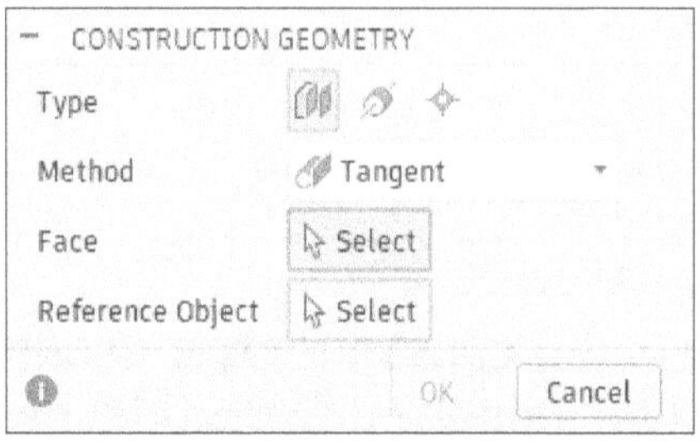

Figure-77. CONSTRUCTION GEOMETRY dialog box with Plane and Tangent option

- The **Face** selection of **CONSTRUCTION GEOMETRY** dialog box is active by default. Click on the round face of model to which plane should be tangent. The updated dialog box will be displayed; refer to Figure-78.

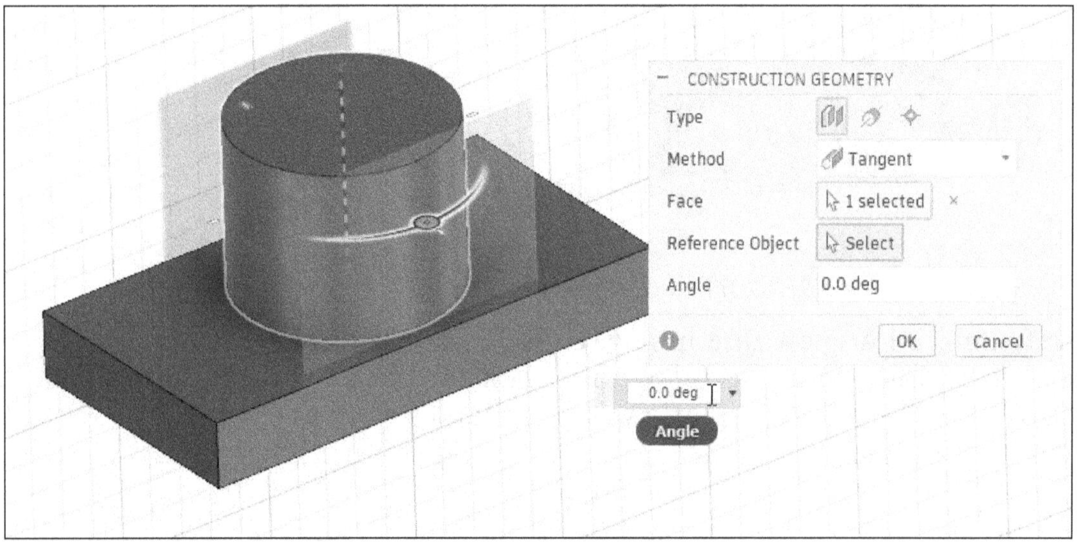

Figure-78. Updated CONSTRUCTION GEOMETRY dialog box

- Selection of **Reference Object** is optional. If you want to select the reference object to define orientation of the tangent plane then click on the **Select** button of **Reference Object** section and click on plane/face. The plane will orient accordingly to selected plane.
- Click in the **Angle** edit box and specify the angle of plane with respect to the reference plane. If you have not specified reference plane then angle will be calculated from original position. You can also set the angle by moving the drag handle.
- After specifying the parameters, click on the **OK** button from **CONSTRUCTION GEOMETRY** dialog box to create a tangent plane; refer to Figure-79.

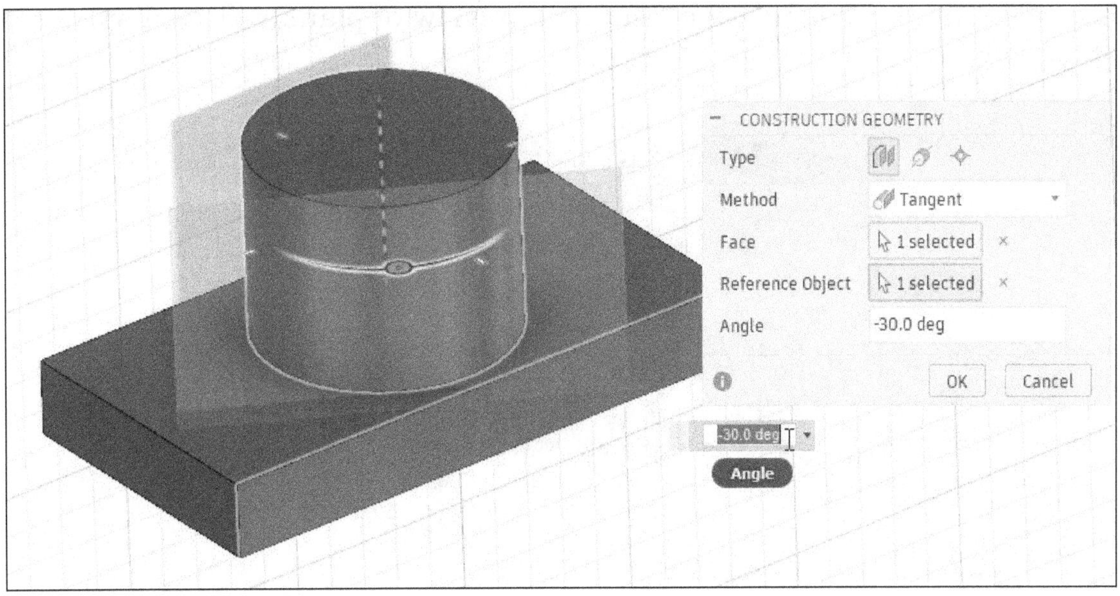

Figure-79. Preview of tangent plane

Midplane

The **Midplane** tool is used to create a plane at the midpoint of two faces/planes. The procedure to use this tool is discussed next.

- Click on the **Midplane** tool from **CONSTRUCT** drop-down in the **Toolbar**; refer to Figure-80. The **CONSTRUCTION GEOMETRY** dialog box will be displayed with the **Plane** option selected in the **Type** area and **Midplane** option selected in the **Method** drop-down by default; refer to Figure-81.

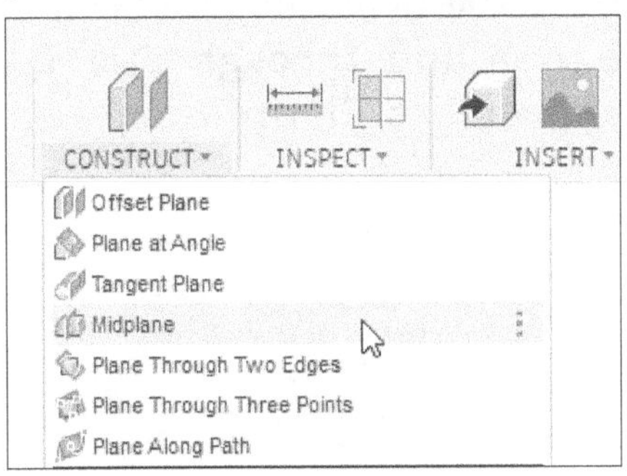

Figure-80. Midplane tool

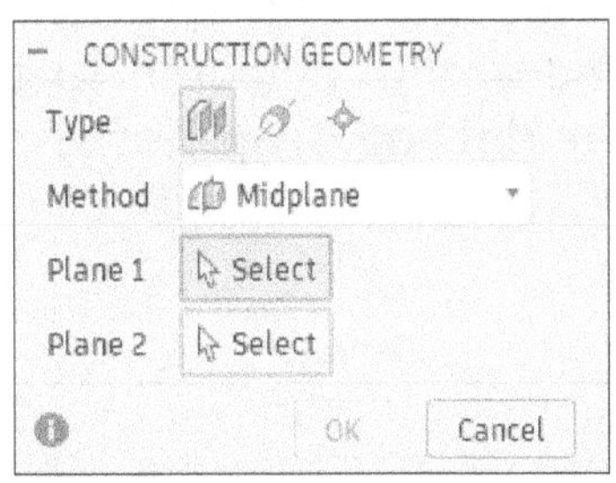

Figure-81. CONSTRUCTION GEOMETRY dialog box with Plane and Midplane option

- Now, you need to select two planes or faces to create a mid plane; refer to Figure-82.

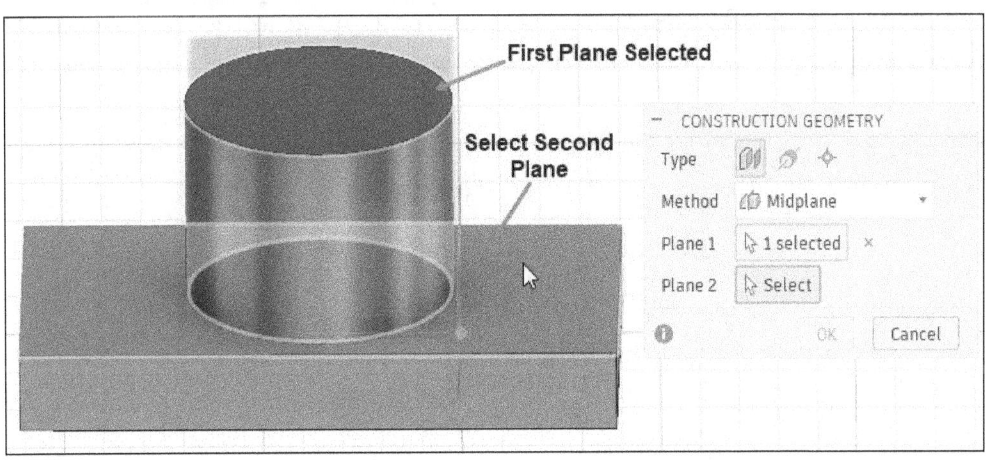

Figure-82. Selection of face to create midplane

- After selecting the second plane or face, preview of plane will be displayed; refer to Figure-83.

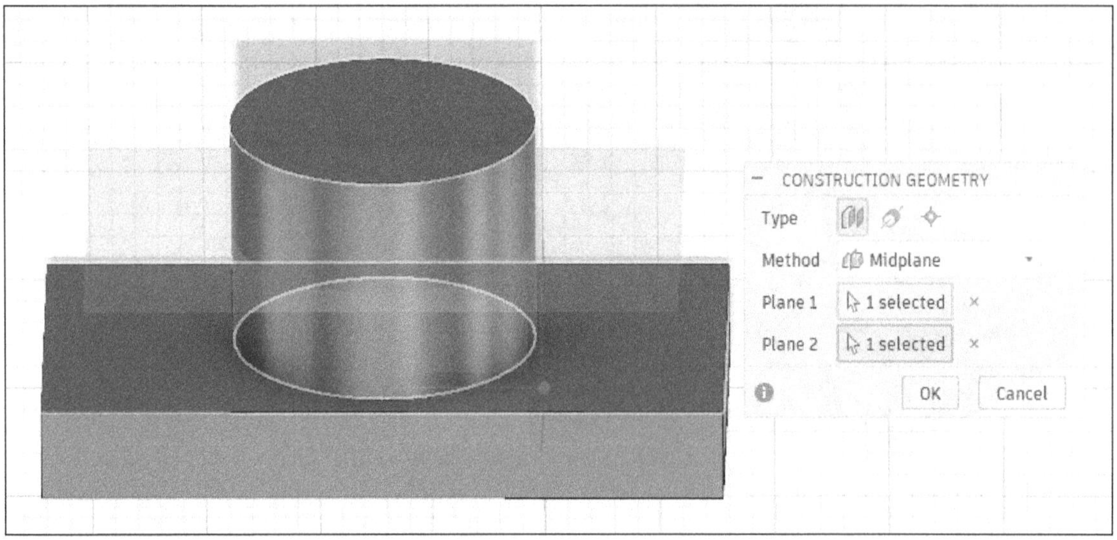

Figure-83. Preview of midplane

- Click on the **OK** button from the dialog box. The plane will be created.

Plane Through Two Edges

The **Plane Through Two Edges** tool is used to create a plane with the reference as two linear edges. The procedure to use this tool is discussed next.

- Click on the **Plane Through Two Edges** tool from **CONSTRUCT** drop-down in the **Toolbar**; refer to Figure-84. The **CONSTRUCTION GEOMETRY** dialog box will be displayed with the **Plane** option selected in the **Type** area and **Through Two Edges** option selected in the **Method** drop-down by default; refer to Figure-85.

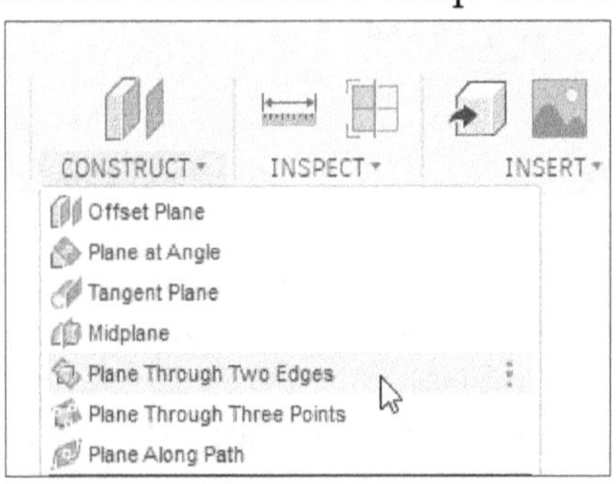

Figure-84. Plane Through Two Edges tool

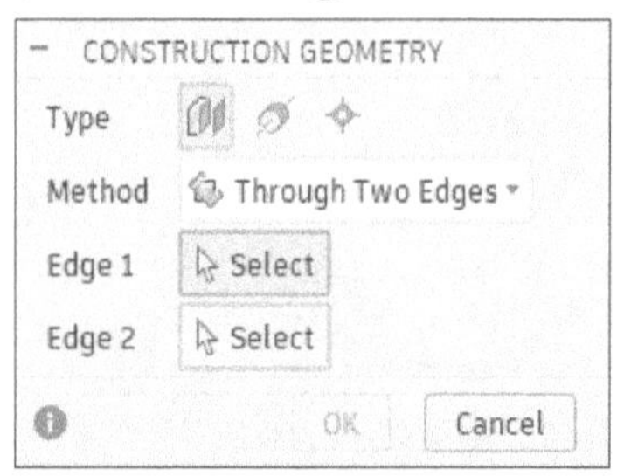

Figure-85. CONSTRUCTION GEOMETRY dialog box with Plane and Through Two Edges option

- Click on two straight edges of model to create plane; refer to Figure-86.

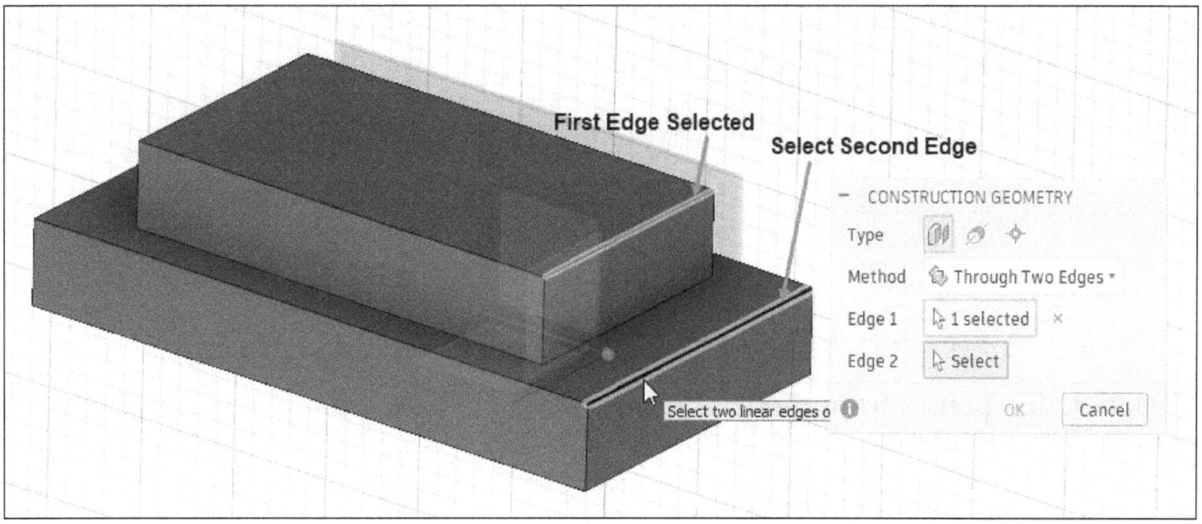

Figure-86. Selection of edges

- On selecting the second edge, the preview of plane will be displayed; refer to Figure-87.

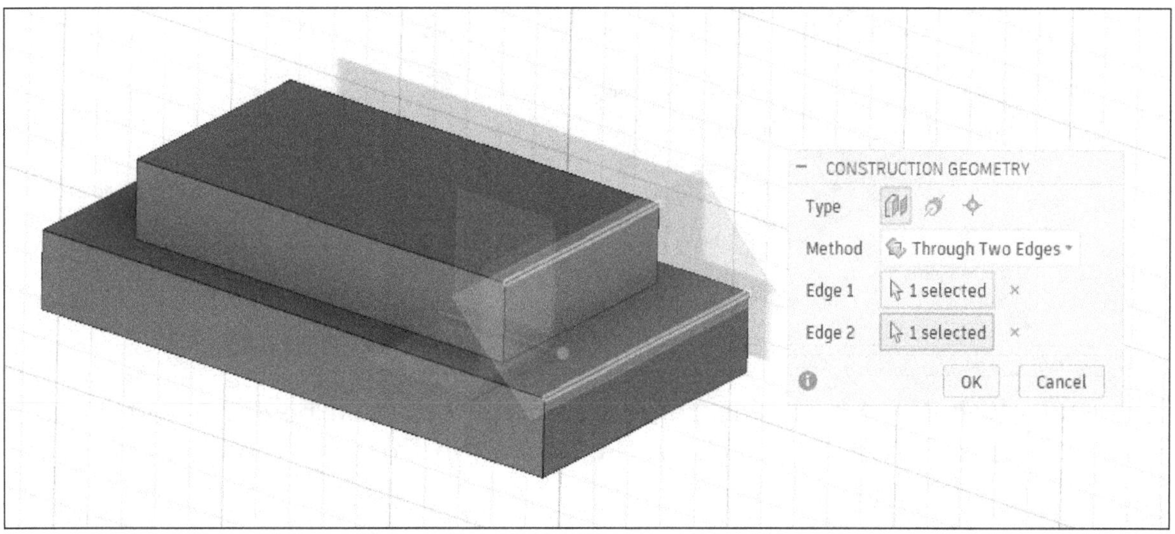

Figure-87. Preview of plane through two edges

- Click on the **OK** button from the dialog box to create the plane.

Plane Through Three Points

The **Plane Through Three Points** tool is used to create a plane with the help of three points as reference. The procedure to use this tool is discussed next.

- Click on the **Plane Through Three Points** tool from **CONSTRUCT** drop-down in the **Toolbar**; refer to Figure-88. The **CONSTRUCTION GEOMETRY** dialog box will be displayed with the **Plane** option selected in the **Type** area and **Through Three Points** option selected in the **Method** drop-down by default; refer to Figure-89.

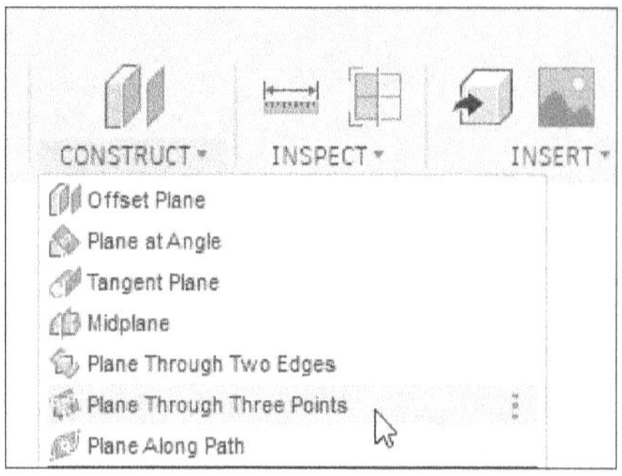

Figure-88. Plane Through Three Points tool

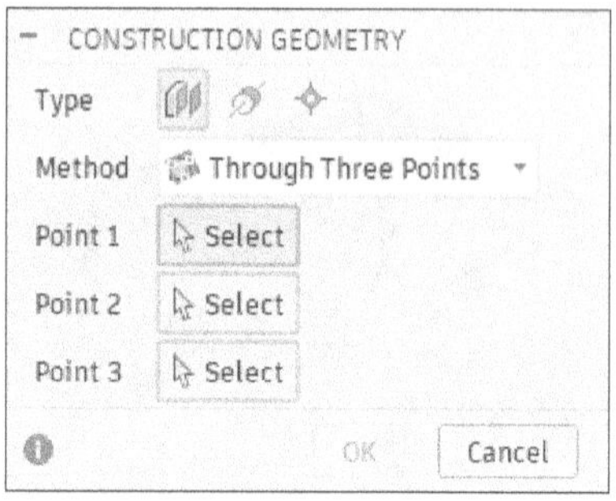

Figure-89. CONSTRUCTION GEOMETRY dialog box with Plane and Through Three Points option

- Select three points from model as reference to create a plane; refer to Figure-90.

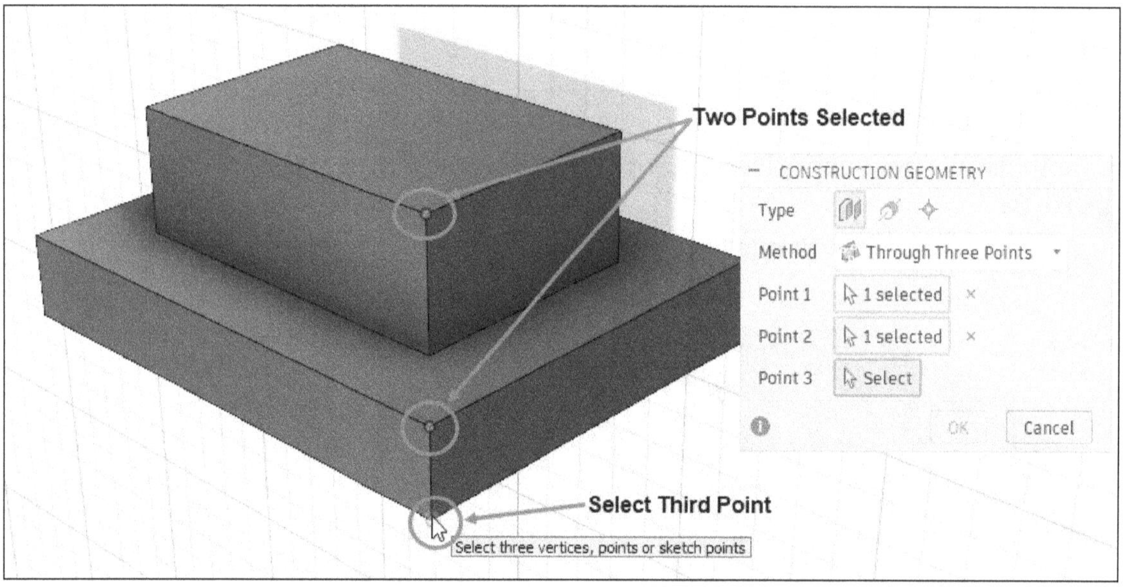

Figure-90. Selection of points for creating plane

- After selecting the third point, the preview of plane will be displayed along with model; refer to Figure-91. Click on the **OK** button from the dialog box.

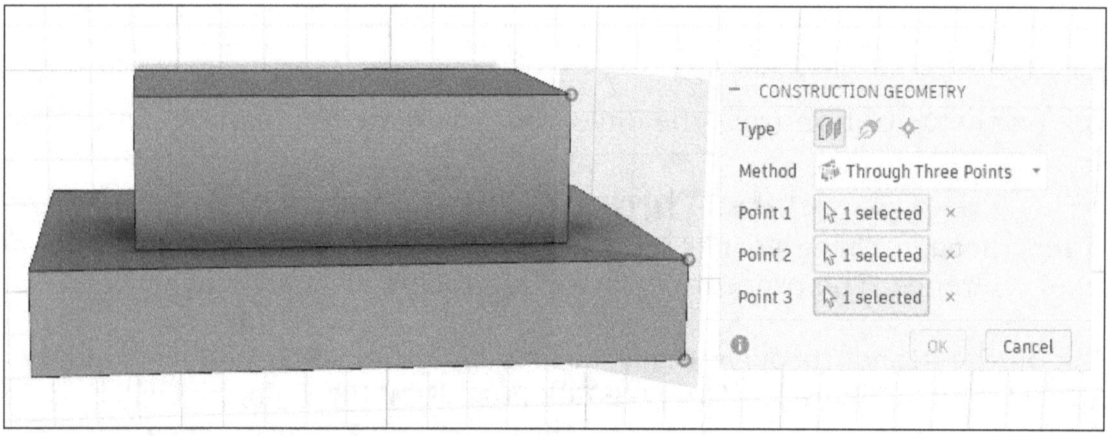

Figure-91. Preview of plane through three points

Plane Along Path

The **Plane Along Path** tool is used to create a plane along selected path. The plane will be perpendicular to the path at selected point. The procedure to use this tool is discussed next.

- Click on the **Plane Along Path** tool from **CONSTRUCT** drop-down in the **Toolbar**; refer to Figure-92. The **CONSTRUCTION GEOMETRY** dialog box will be displayed with the **Plane** option selected in the **Type** area and **Along Path** option selected in the **Method** drop-down by default; refer to Figure-93.

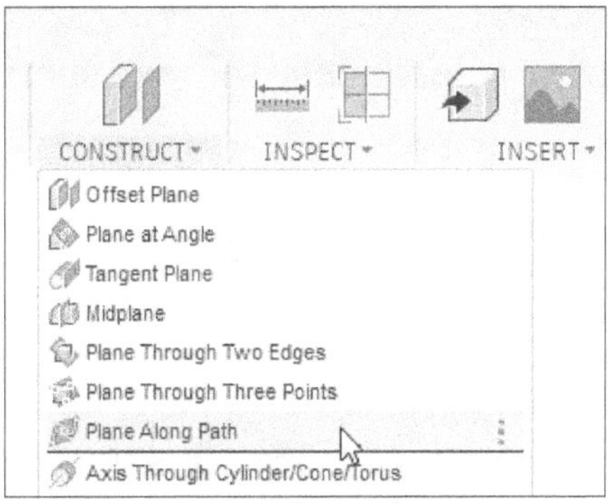

Figure-92. Plane Along Path tool

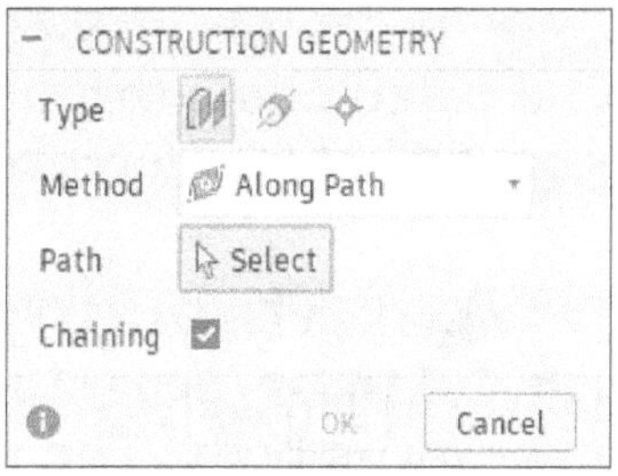

Figure-93. CONSTRUCTION GEOMETRY dialog box with Plane and Along Path option

- **Path** selection of **CONSTRUCTION GEOMETRY** dialog box is active by default. Click on the edge/curve from model as reference for plane; refer to Figure-94.

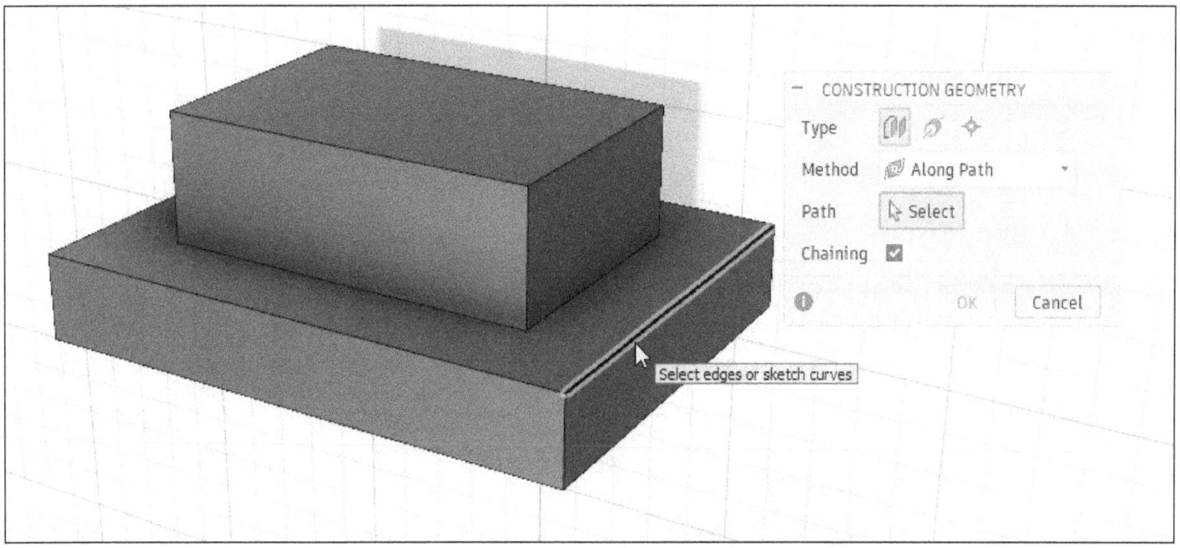

Figure-94. Selection of path

- On selecting the path, the updated **CONSTRUCTION GEOMETRY** dialog box will be displayed along with the preview of plane; refer to Figure-95.

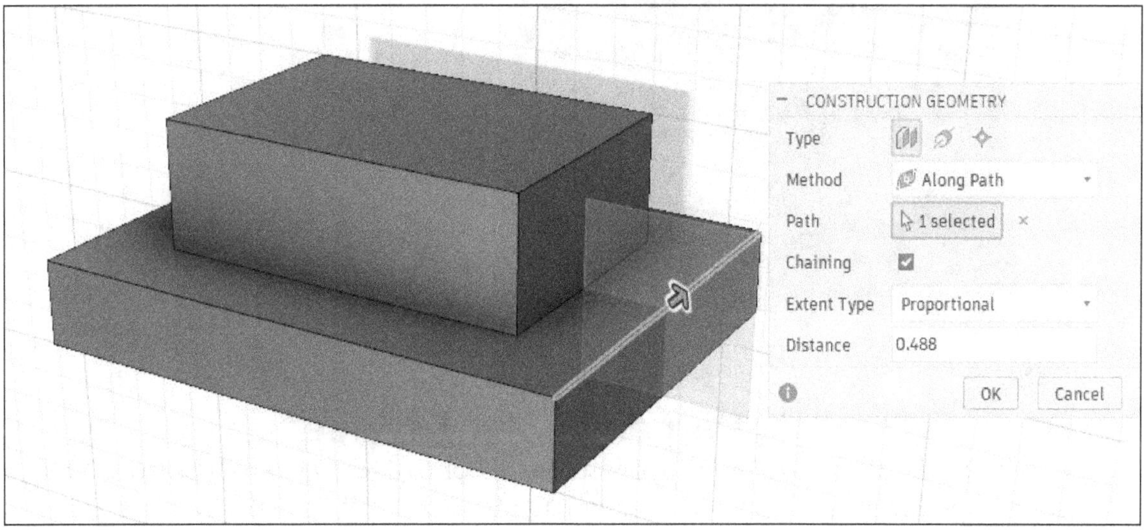

Figure-95. Preview of plane along path

- Click in the **Distance** edit box and specify the distance of plane in percentage between 0 to 1. You can also adjust the distance by moving the drag handle.
- After specifying the parameters, click on the **OK** button from **CONSTRUCTION GEOMETRY** dialog box. The plane will be created.

Till now, we have created plane through different references. In next section, we will create axis through different references.

Axis Through Cylinder/Cone/Torus

The **Axis Through Cylinder/Cone/Torus** tool is used to create axis through center of cylinder, cone, or torus body. The procedure to use this tool is discussed next.

- Click on the **Axis Through Cylinder/Cone/Torus** tool from **CONSTRUCT** drop-down in the **Toolbar**; refer to Figure-96. The **CONSTRUCTION GEOMETRY** dialog box will be displayed with the **Axis** option selected in the **Type** area and **Through Cylinder/ Cone/Torus** option selected in the **Method** drop-down by default; refer to Figure-97.

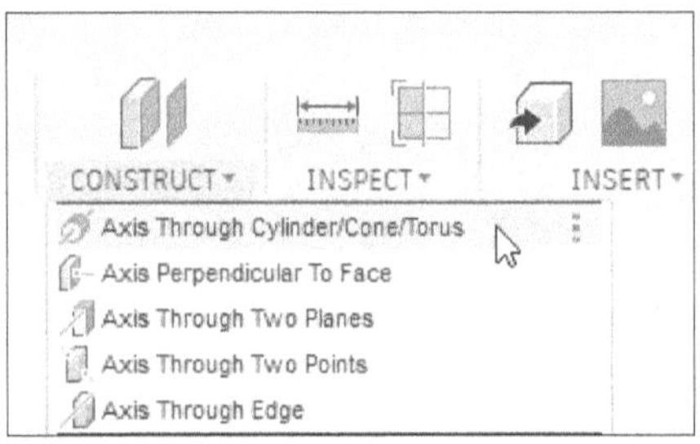

Figure-96. Axis Through Cylinder Cone Torus tool

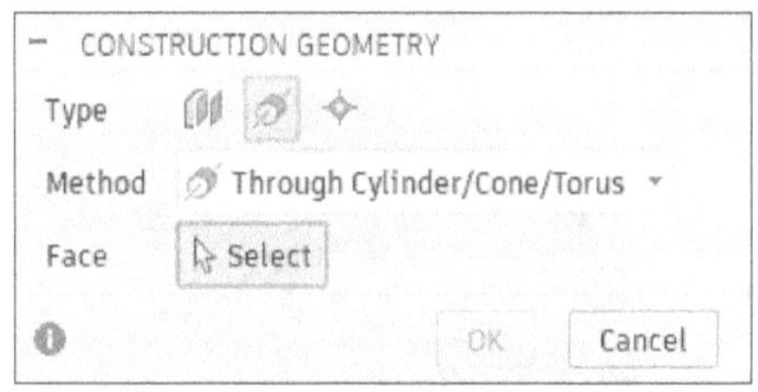

Figure-97. CONSTRUCTION GEOMETRY dialog box with Axis and Through Cylinder Cone Torus option

- Click on the round face of cylinder, cone, or torus from model, preview of the axis will be displayed; refer to Figure-98. Click on the **OK** button from the dialog box to create the axis.

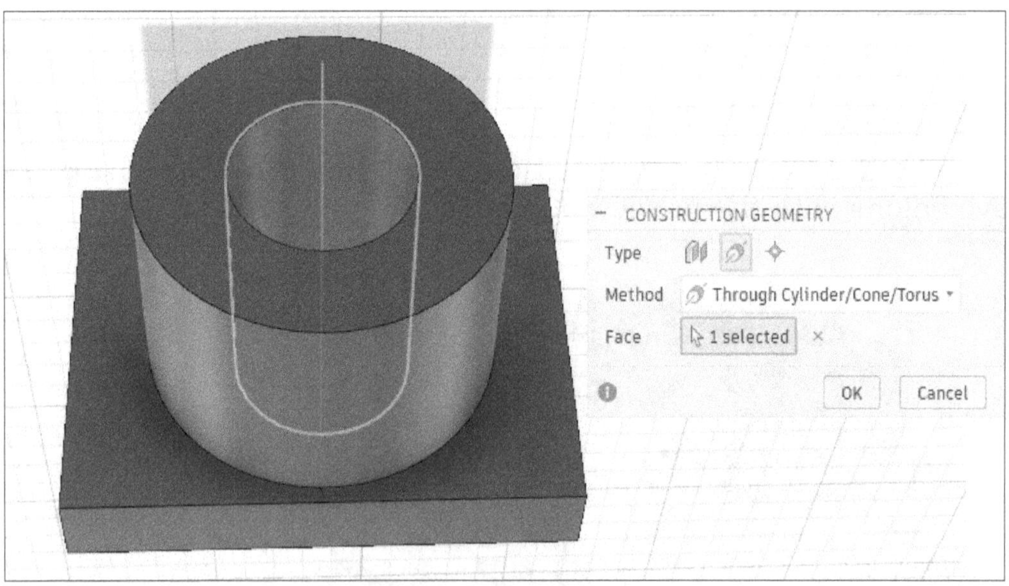

Figure-98. Preview of axis of cylinder

Axis Perpendicular To Face

The **Axis Perpendicular To Face** tool is used to create an axis perpendicular to the selected face at selected point. The procedure to use this tool is discussed next.

- Click on the **Axis Perpendicular To Face** tool from **CONSTRUCT** drop-down in the **Toolbar**; refer to Figure-99. The **CONSTRUCTION GEOMETRY** dialog box will be displayed with the **Axis** option selected in the **Type** area and **Perpendicular To Face** option selected in the **Method** drop-down by default; refer to Figure-100.

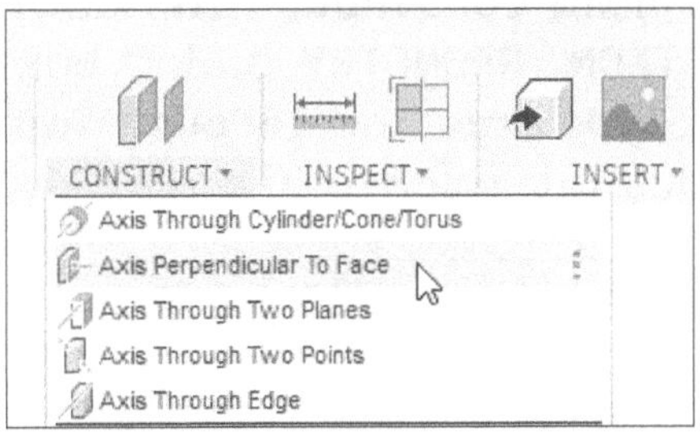

Figure-99. Axis Perpendicular To Face tool

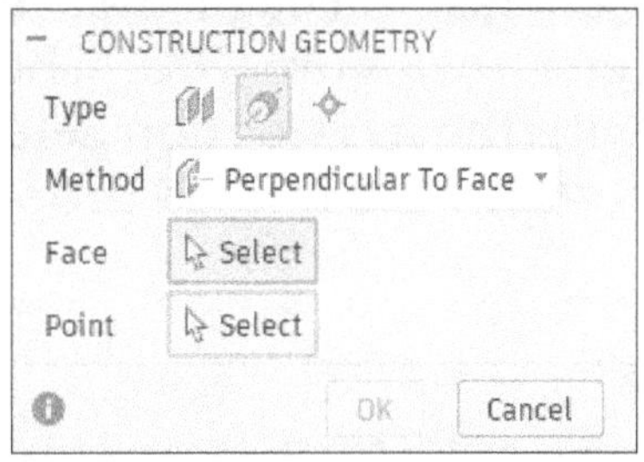

Figure-100. CONSTRUCTION GEOMETRY dialog box with Axis and Perpendicular To Face option

- Click at desired location on the face of model. The preview of axis will be displayed; refer to Figure-101.

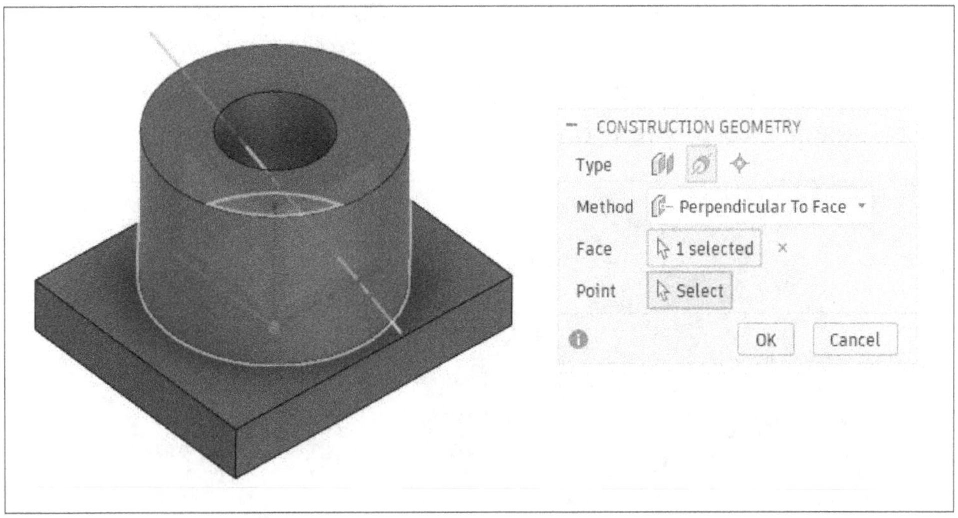

Figure-101. Preview of axis

- After selecting the face, select desired vertex or sketch point from which axis will pass; refer to Figure-102. Click on the **OK** button from the dialog box to create the axis.

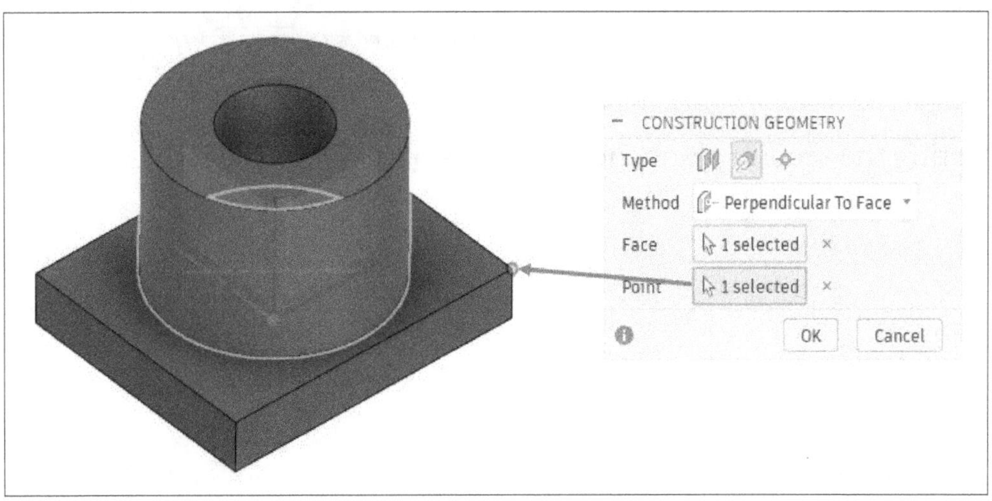

Figure-102. Preview of axis perpendicular to face

Axis Through Two Planes

The **Axis Through Two Planes** tool is used to create an axis at the intersection of two planes or planar faces. The procedure to use this tool is discussed next.

- Click on the **Axis Through Two Planes** tool from **CONSTRUCT** drop-down in the **Toolbar**; refer to Figure-103. The **CONSTRUCTION GEOMETRY** dialog box will be displayed with the **Axis** option selected in the **Type** area and **Through Two Planes** option selected in the **Method** drop-down by default; refer to Figure-104.

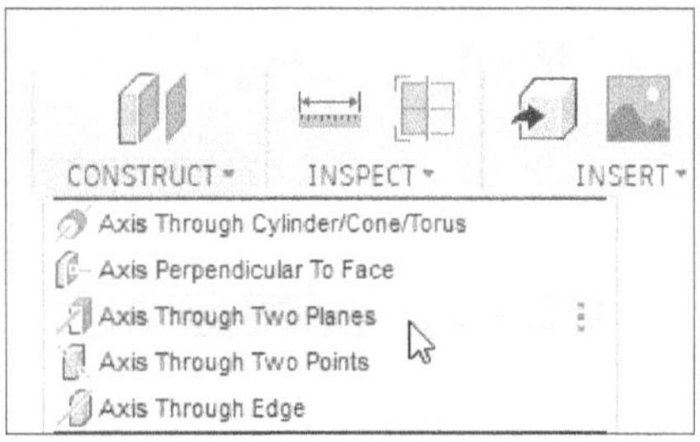

Figure-103. Axis Through Two Planes tool

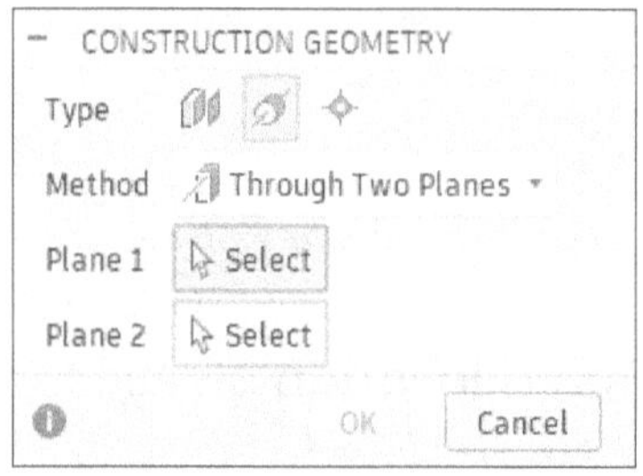

Figure-104. CONSTRUCTION GEOMETRY dialog box with Axis and Through Two Planes option

- **Plane 1** selection button of **CONSTRUCTION GEOMETRY** dialog box is active by default. You need to select two planes to create an axis; refer to Figure-105.

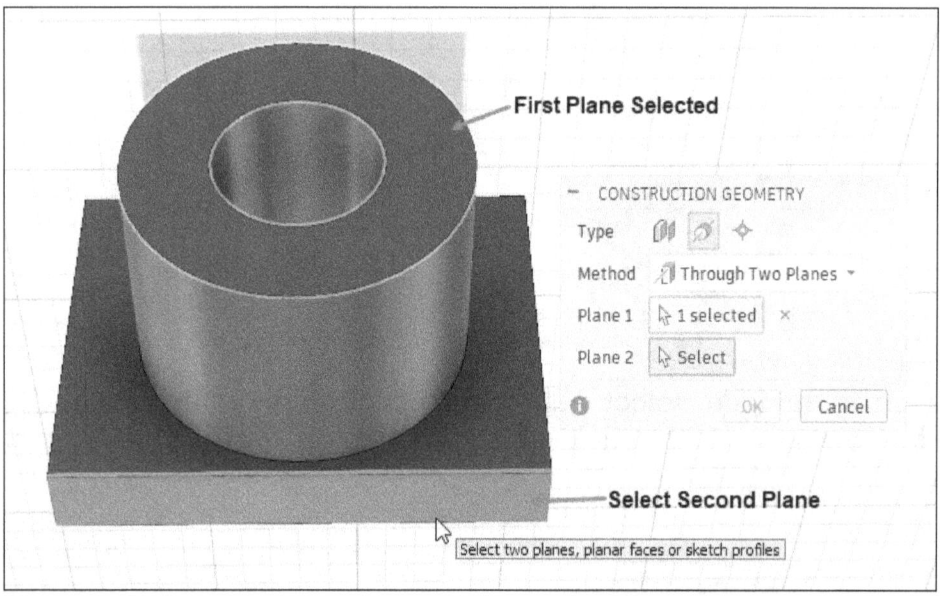

Figure-105. Selection of planes for creating axis

- On selecting the second plane, preview of axis will be displayed; refer to Figure-106.

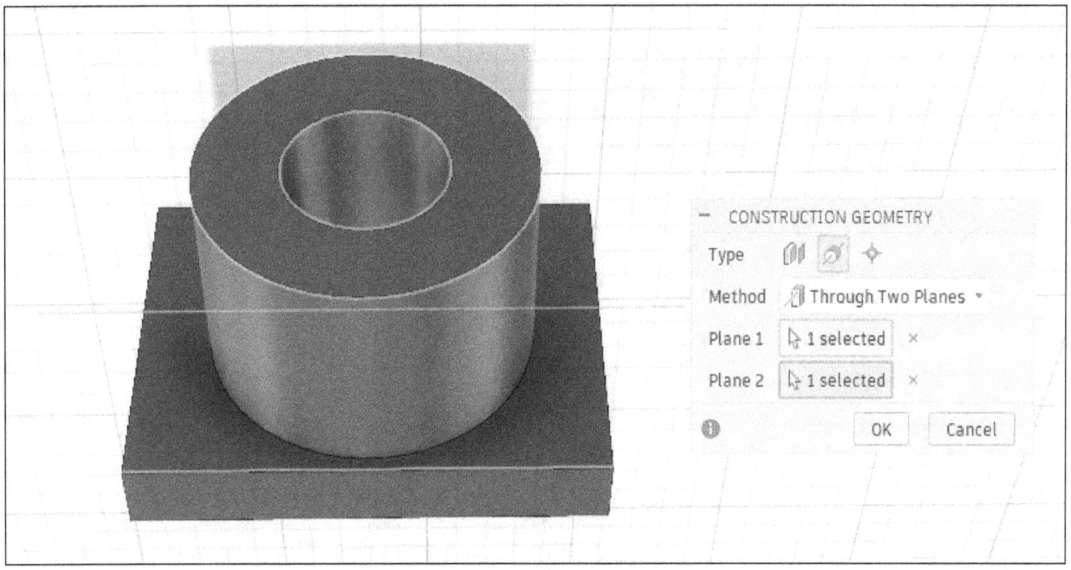

Figure-106. Preview of axis through two planes

- Click on the **OK** button from the dialog box to create the axis.

Axis Through Two Points

The **Axis Through Two Points** tool is used to create an axis passing through two reference points. The procedure to use this tool is discussed next.

- Click on the **Axis Through Two Points** tool from **CONSTRUCT** drop-down in the **Toolbar**; refer to Figure-107. The **CONSTRUCTION GEOMETRY** dialog box will be displayed with the **Axis** option selected in the **Type** area and **Through Two Points** option selected in the **Method** drop-down by default; refer to Figure-108.

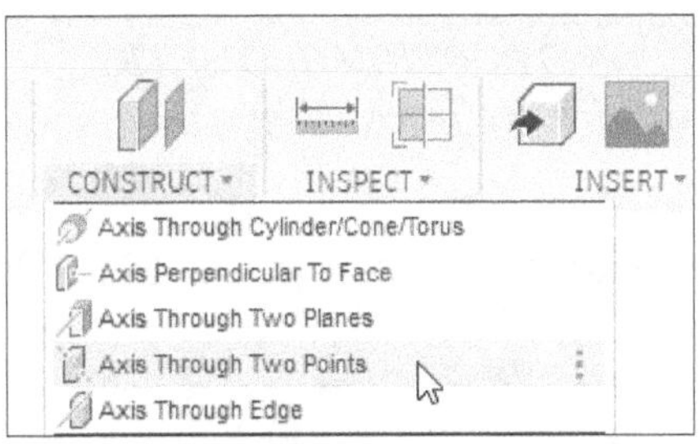

Figure-107. Axis Through Two Points tool

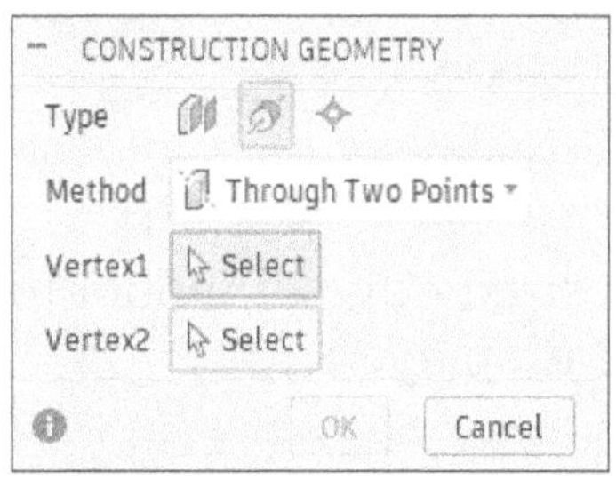

Figure-108. CONSTRUCTION GEOMETRY dialog box with Axis and Through Two Points option

- Select the two points or vertices from the model; refer to Figure-109. Preview of axis will be displayed. Click on the **OK** button from the dialog box to create the axis.

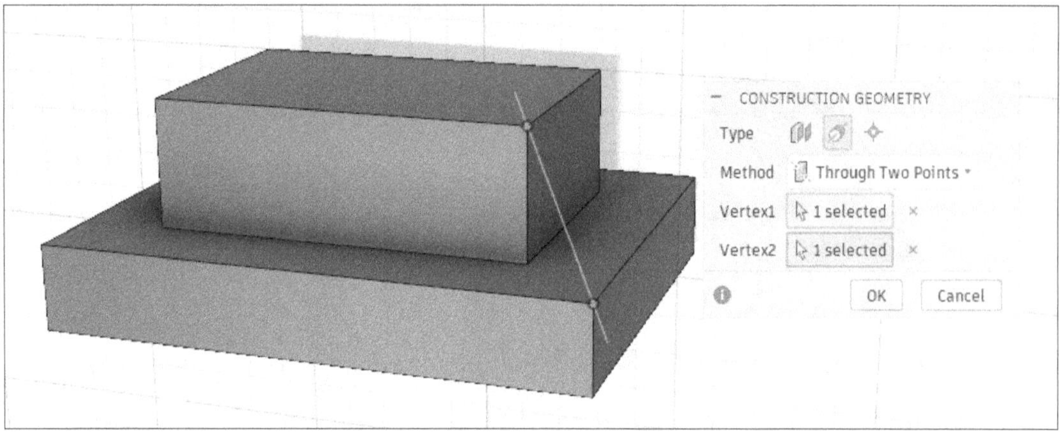

Figure-109. Preview of axis through two points

Axis Through Edge

The **Axis Through Edge** tool is used to create an axis on the selected edge/axis. The procedure to use this tool is discussed next.

- Click on the **Axis Through Edge** tool from **CONSTRUCT** drop-down in the **Toolbar**; refer to Figure-110. The **CONSTRUCTION GEOMETRY** dialog box will be displayed with the **Axis** option selected in the **Type** area and **Through Edge** option selected in the **Method** drop-down by default; refer to Figure-111.

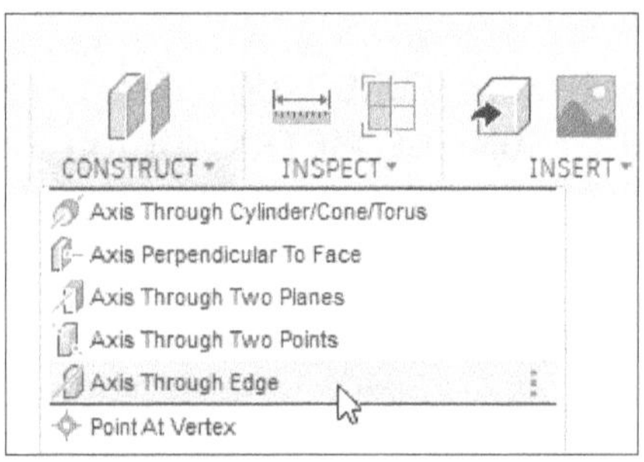

Figure-110. Axis Through Edge tool

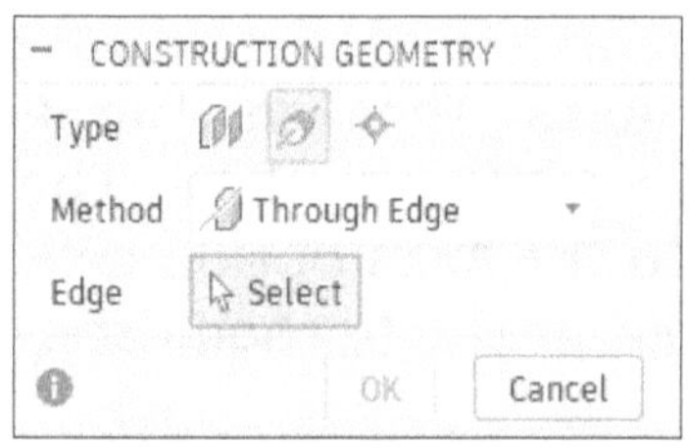

Figure-111. CONSTRUCTION GEOMETRY dialog box with Axis and Through Edge option

- Click on desired edge of model to create the axis; refer to Figure-112. Preview of axis will be displayed.

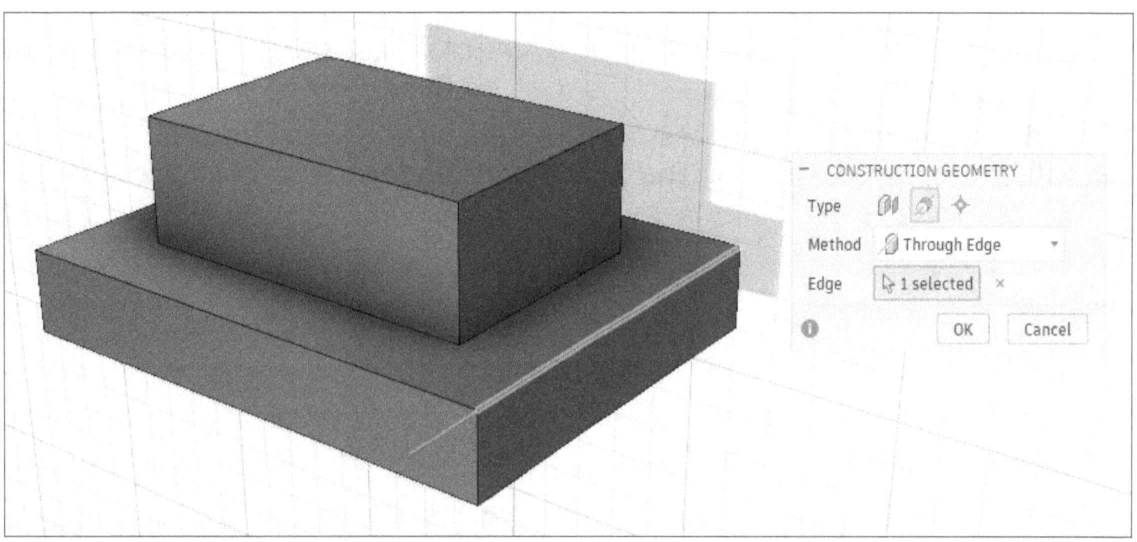

Figure-112. Preview of axis through edge

- Click on the **OK** button from the dialog box to create the axis.

Till now, we have learned to create plane and axis. In next topics, we will learn the procedure to create points. Points can be used as origin, coordinate system location, or reference for other features. The tools to create points are discussed next.

Point At Vertex

The **Point At Vertex** tool is used to create a point by selecting any vertex of the model. The procedure to use this tool is discussed next.

- Click on the **Point At Vertex** tool from **CONSTRUCT** drop-down in the **Toolbar**; refer to Figure-113. The **CONSTRUCTION GEOMETRY** dialog box will be displayed with the **Point** option selected in the **Type** area and **At Vertex** option selected in the **Method** drop-down by default; refer to Figure-114.

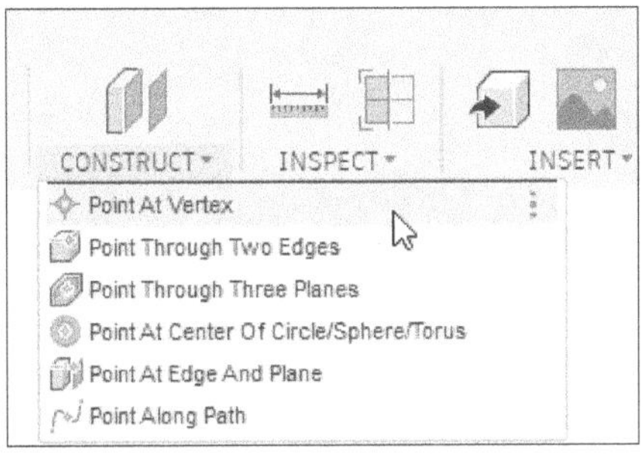

Figure-113. Point At Vertex tool

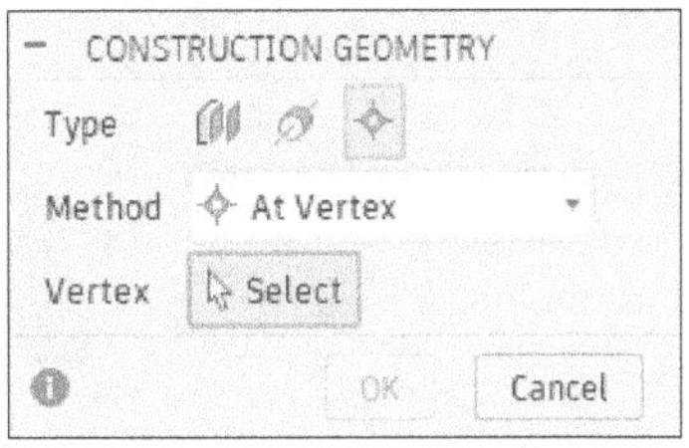

Figure-114. CONSTRUCTION GEOMETRY dialog box with Point and At Vertex option

- Click on the vertex of model to create a constructional point; refer to Figure-115.

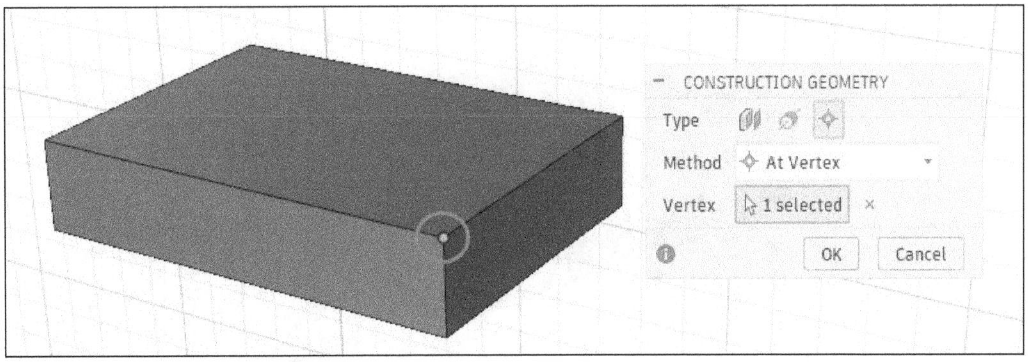

Figure-115. Preview of point at vertex

Note that you can create only one point at a time using this tool.

- Click on the **OK** button from the dialog box to create point.

Point Through Two Edges

The **Point Through Two Edges** tool is used to create a point at intersection of two edges/axes intersecting each other. The procedure to use this tool is discussed next.

- Click on the **Point Through Two Edges** tool from **CONSTRUCT** drop-down in the **Toolbar**; refer to Figure-116. The **CONSTRUCTION GEOMETRY** dialog box will be displayed with the **Point** option selected in the **Type** area and **Through Two Edges** option selected in the **Method** drop-down by default; refer to Figure-117.

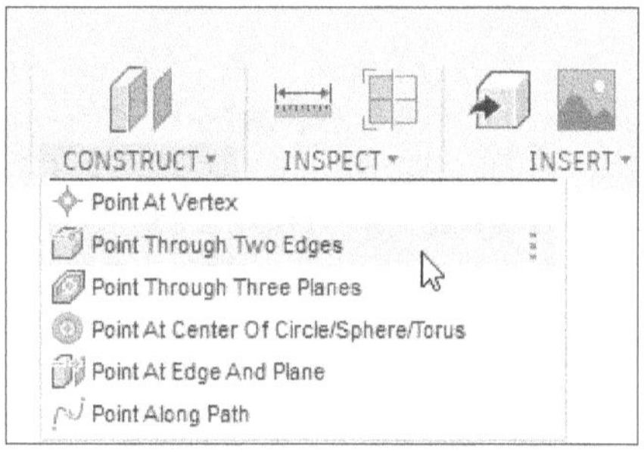

Figure-116. Point Through Two Edges tool

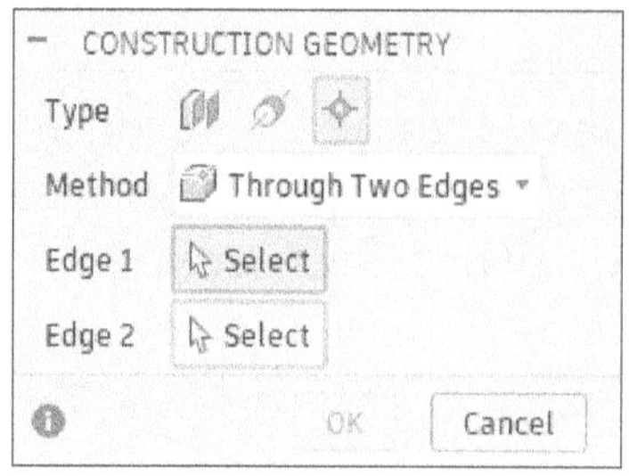

Figure-117. CONSTRUCTION GEOMETRY dialog box with Point and Through Two Edges option

- Select the two intersecting edges on the model to create point; refer to Figure-118.

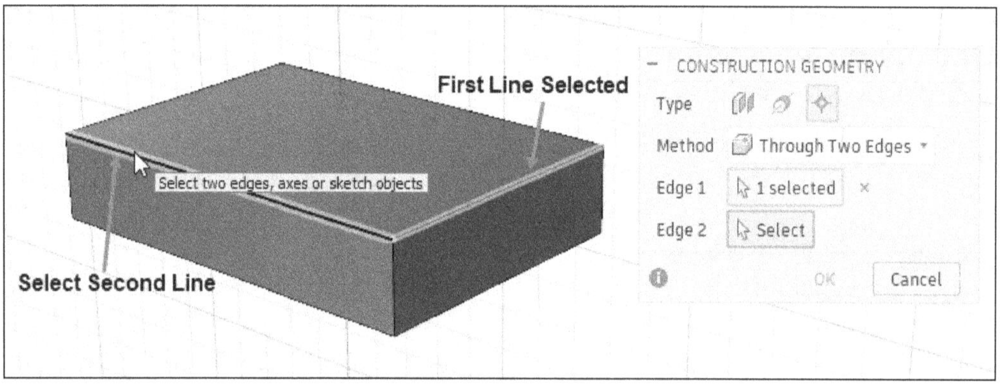

Figure-118. Selection of lines to create point

- On selecting the second edge, preview of point will be displayed. Click on the **OK** button from the dialog box to create the point; refer to Figure-119.

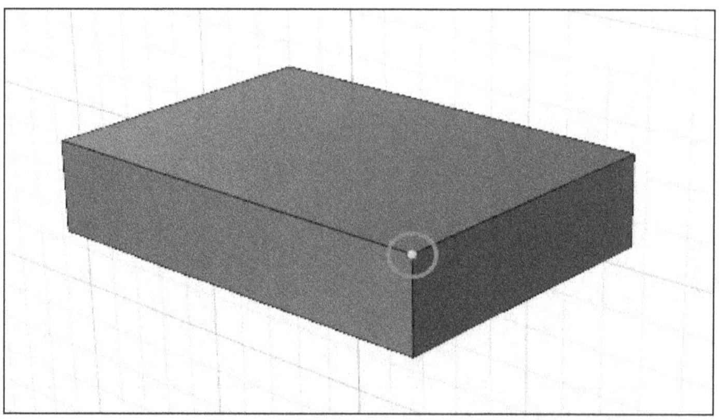

Figure-119. Point created through two edges

Point Through Three Planes

The **Point Through Three Planes** tool is used to create a point at the intersection of three planes/faces. The procedure to use this tool is discussed next.

- Click on the **Point Through Three Planes** tool from **CONSTRUCT** drop-down in the **Toolbar**; refer to Figure-120. The **CONSTRUCTION GEOMETRY** dialog box will be displayed with the **Point** option selected in the **Type** area and **Through Three Planes** option selected in the **Method** drop-down by default; refer to Figure-121.

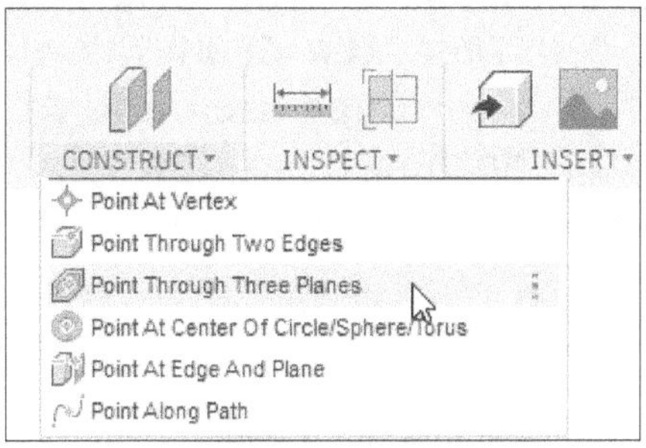

Figure-120. Point Through Three Planes tool

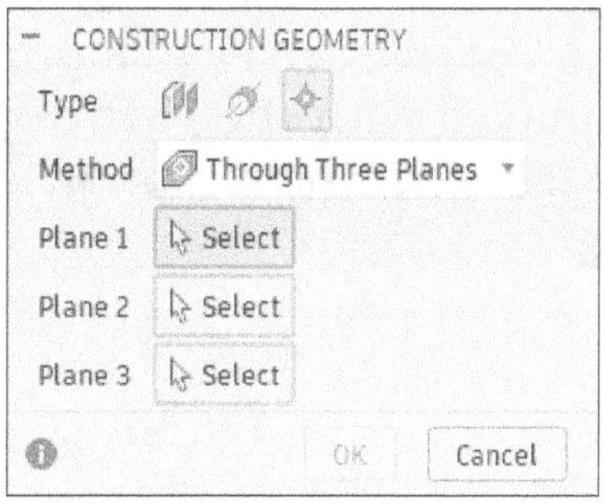

Figure-121. CONSTRUCTION GEOMETRY dialog box with Point and Through Three Planes option

- Select the three intersecting planes/faces from the model; refer to Figure-122.

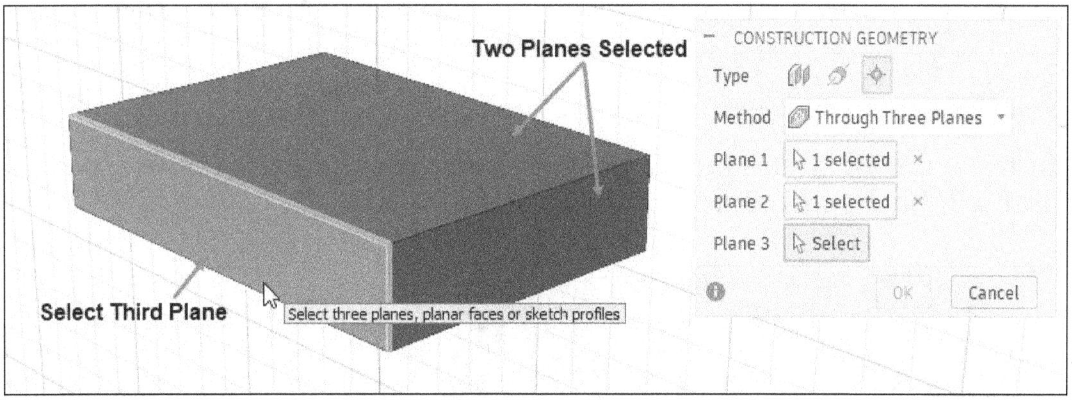

Figure-122. Selection of three planes to create point

- On selecting the third plane, preview of the constructional point will be displayed; refer to Figure-123.

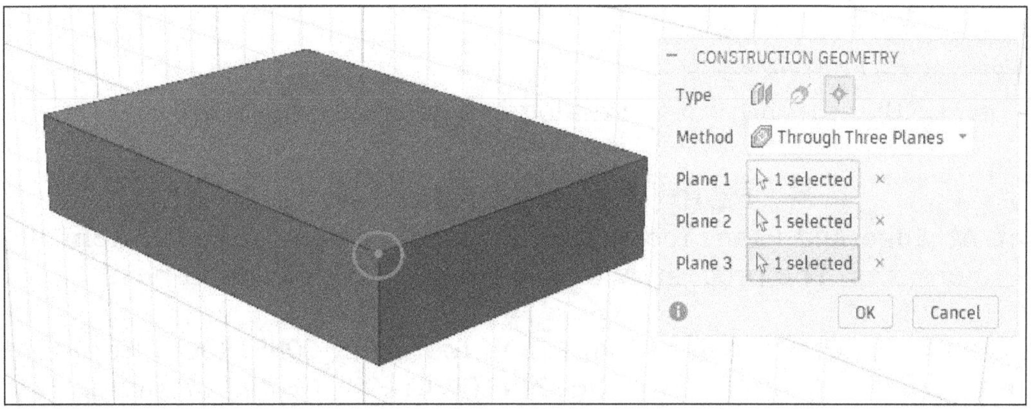

Figure-123. Preview of point through three planes

- Click on the **OK** button from the dialog box to create the point.

Point At Center Of Circle/Sphere/Torus

The **Point At Center Of Circle/Sphere/Torus** tool is used to create a point at the center of selected circle/sphere/torus. The procedure to use this tool is discussed next.

- Click on the **Point At Center Of Circle/Sphere/Torus** tool from **CONSTRUCT** drop-down in the **Toolbar**; refer to Figure-124. The **CONSTRUCTION GEOMETRY** dialog box will be displayed with the **Point** option selected in the **Type** area and **At Center Of Circle/Sphere/Torus** option selected in the **Method** drop-down by default; refer to Figure-125.

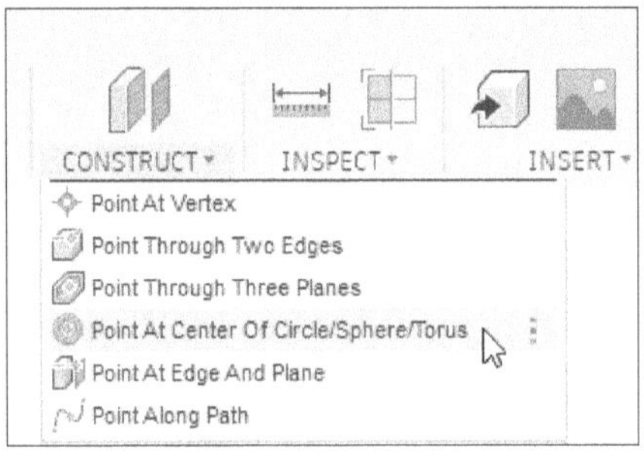

Figure-124. Point At Center Of Circle Sphere Torus tool

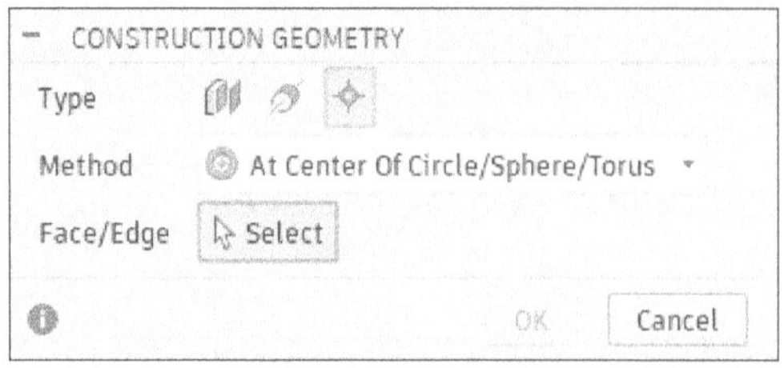

Figure-125. CONSTRUCTION GEOMETRY dialog box with Point and At Center Of Circle Sphere Torus option

- Select the circle or round face of sphere/torus to create the center point. Preview of point will be displayed; refer to Figure-126.

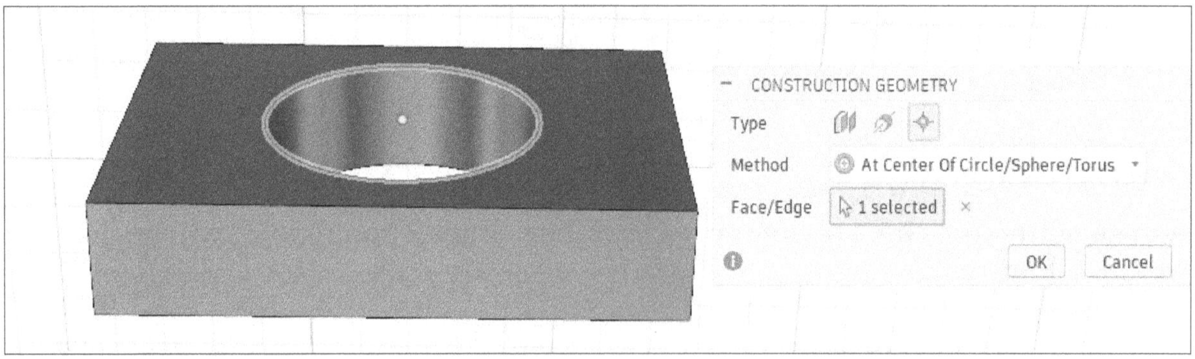

Figure-126. Preview of point at center

- Click on the **OK** button from the dialog box to create the point.

Point At Edge And Plane

The **Point At Edge And Plane** tool is used to create a point with the help of edge and plane as references. The procedure to use this tool is discussed next.

- Click on the **Point At Edge And Plane** tool from **CONSTRUCT** drop-down in the **Toolbar**; refer to Figure-127. The **CONSTRUCTION GEOMETRY** dialog box will be displayed with the **Point** option selected in the **Type** area and **At Edge And Plane** option selected in the **Method** drop-down by default; refer to Figure-128.

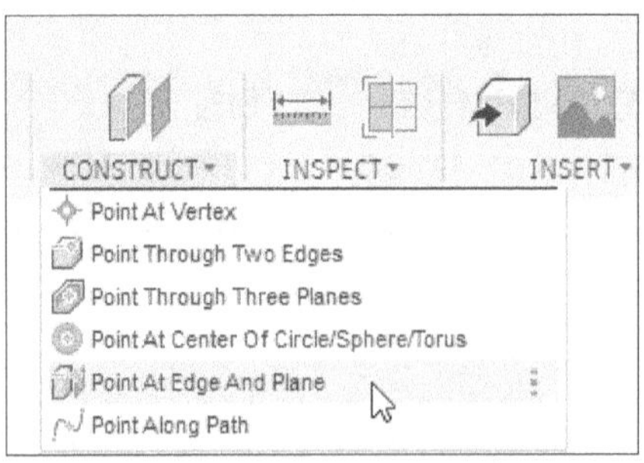

Figure-127. Point At Edge And Plane tool

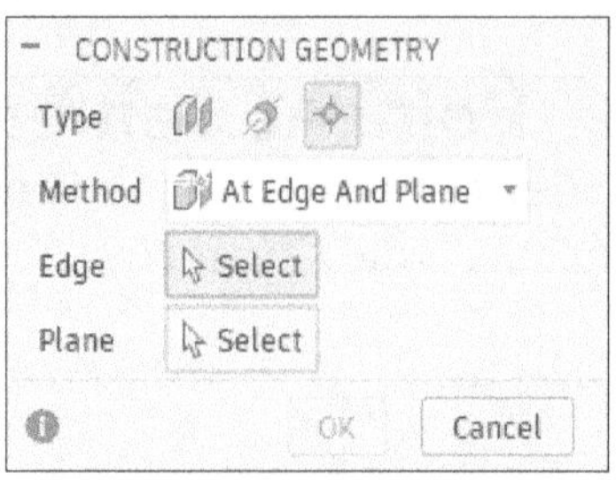

Figure-128. CONSTRUCTION GEOMETRY dialog box with Point and At Edge And Plane option

- Select the edge and plane/face to create a point at the intersection; refer to Figure-129.

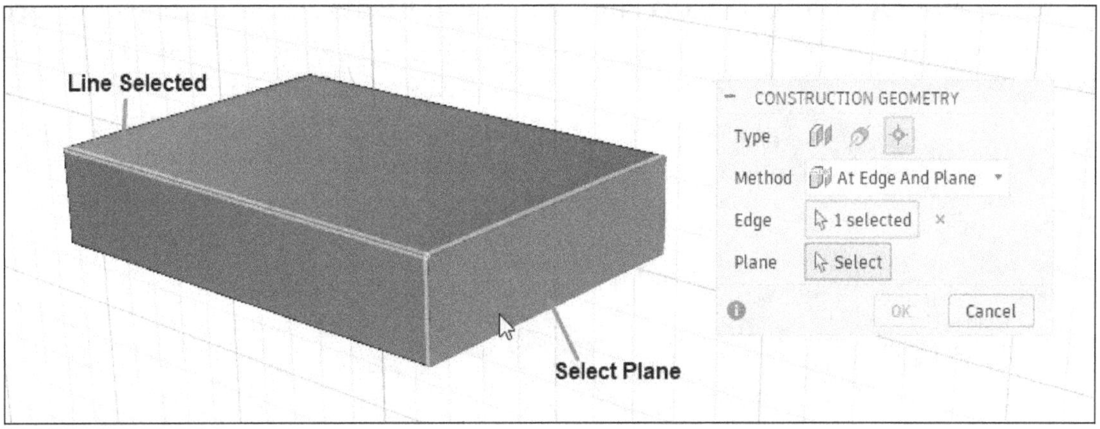

Figure-129. Selection of edge and plane

- On selecting the plane, preview of point will be displayed. Click on the **OK** button from the dialog box to create the point; refer to Figure-130.

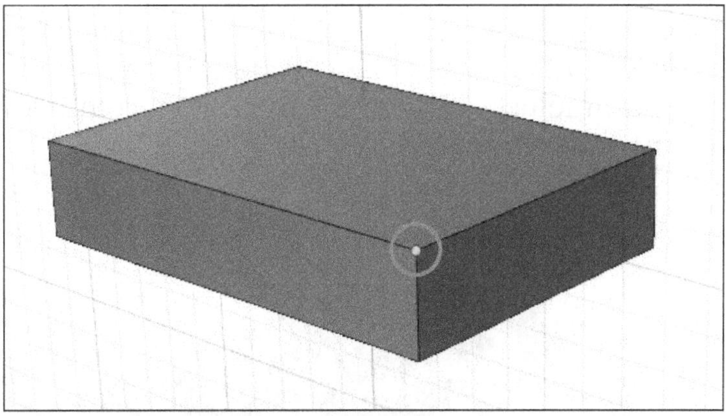

Figure-130. Point at edge and plane created

Point Along Path

The **Point Along Path** tool is used to create a point along selected path. The procedure to use this tool is discussed next.

- Click on the **Point Along Path** tool from **CONSTRUCT** drop-down in the **Toolbar**; refer to Figure-131. The **CONSTRUCTION GEOMETRY** dialog box will be displayed with the **Point** option selected in the **Type** area and **Along Path** option selected in the **Method** drop-down by default; refer to Figure-132.

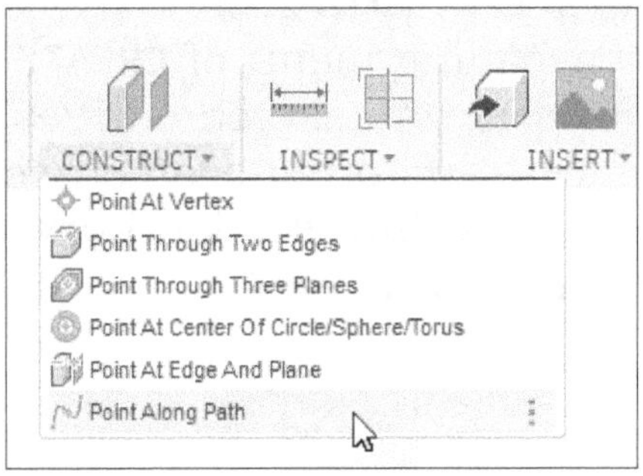

Figure-131. Point Along Path tool

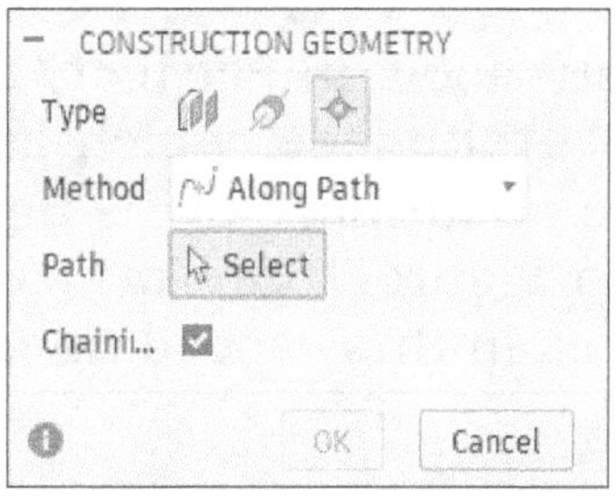

Figure-132. CONSTRUCTION GEOMETRY dialog box with Point and Along Path option

- **Path** selection of **CONSTRUCTION GEOMETRY** dialog box is active by default. Click on the edge/curve from model as reference for point. On selecting the path, the updated **CONSTRUCTION GEOMETRY** dialog box will be displayed; refer to Figure-133.

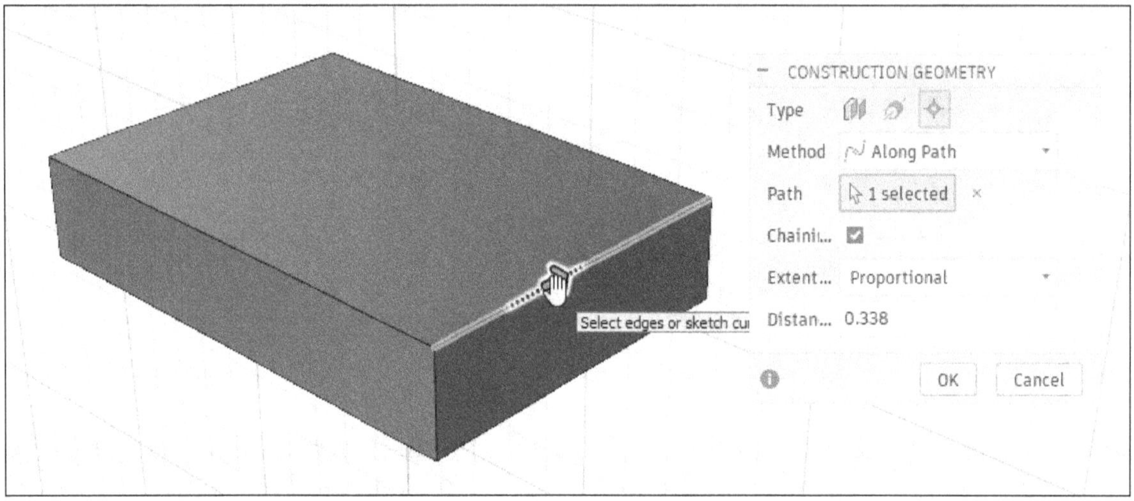

Figure-133. Selection of path to create point

- Click in the **Distance** edit box and specify the distance of point in percentage between 0 to 1. You can also adjust the distance by moving the drag handle.
- After specifying the parameters, click on the **OK** button from **CONSTRUCTION GEOMETRY** dialog box. The point will be created; refer to Figure-134.

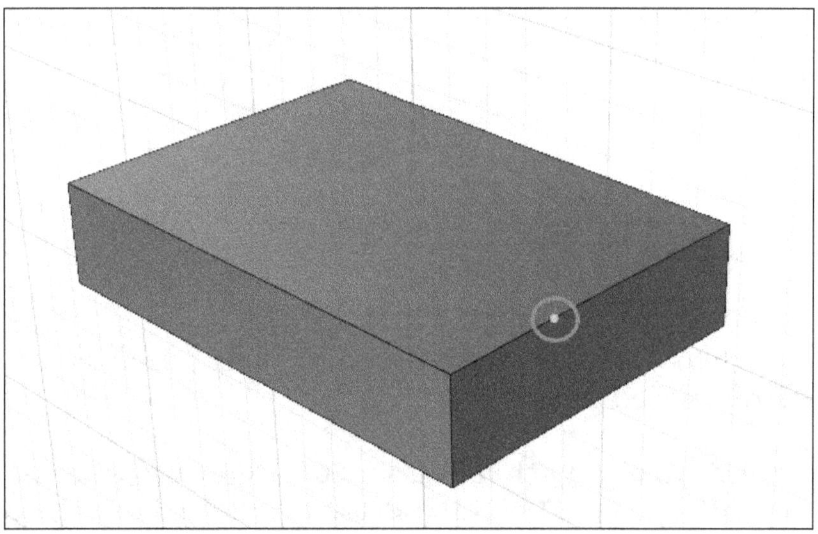

Figure-134. Point along path created

PROJECT/INCLUDE TOOLS

There are various tools in **Project/Include** cascading menu of **CREATE** drop-down in **Toolbar** of **Sketch** mode, which are used to generate sketch entities on current sketching plane or surfaces by using edges, faces, and other geometries of selected objects; refer to Figure-135. You can also generate intersection curves using 3D objects. The tools in this cascading menu are given next.

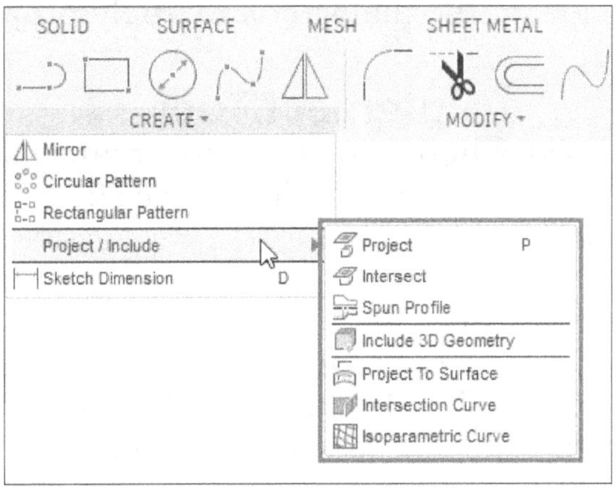

Figure-135. Project / Include cascading menu

Project Tool

The **Project** tool is used to project selected surface/face/edge/point/sketch of other features on selected sketching plane. Like, you can project the boundaries of selected face on the sketching plane. The procedure to use this tool is given next.

- Click on the **Project** tool from **Project/Include** cascading menu of **CREATE** drop-down in the **Toolbar** after activating sketch on desired sketching plane. The **PROJECT** dialog box will be displayed; refer to Figure-136.

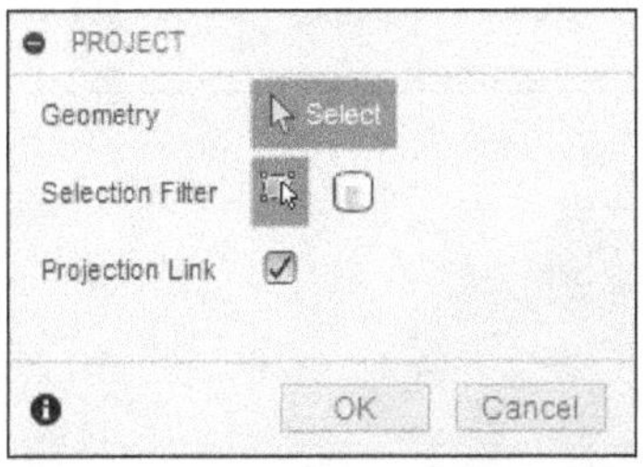

Figure-136. PROJECT dialog box

- Hover the cursor at desired geometry. Preview of project feature will be displayed; refer to Figure-137.

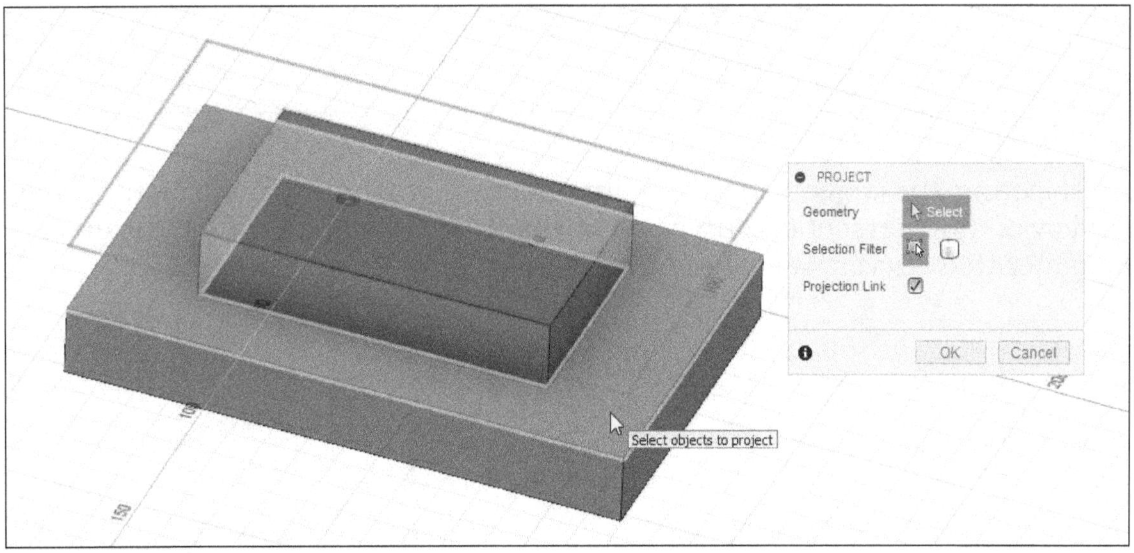

Figure-137. Preview of projected geometry

- Click at desired face/edge/point/curve to project it on sketching plane. You can select multiple objects to project them on sketching plane.

- Click on the **OK** button from the dialog box to apply projection.

Intersect Tool

The **Intersect** tool is used when you want to create sketch geometries at the intersection of selected object and intersecting active sketching plane. The procedure to use this tool is given next.

- Start a sketch on desired plane.
- Click on the **Intersect** tool from **Project/Include** cascading menu of the **CREATE** drop-down in the **Toolbar**. The **INTERSECT** dialog box will be displayed; refer to Figure-138 and you will be asked to select the objects that are intersecting with current sketching plane.

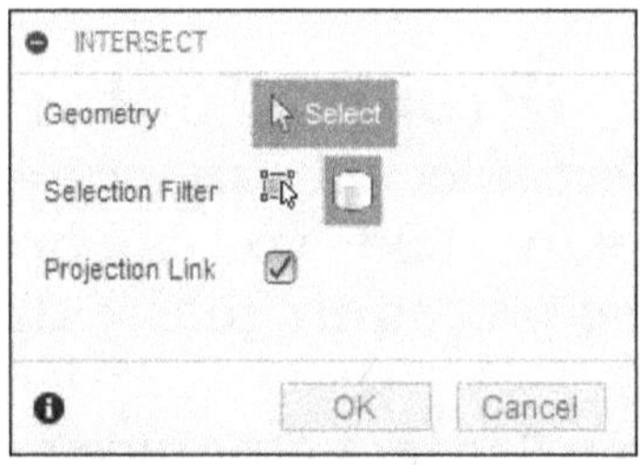

Figure-138. INTERSECT dialog box

- Select the objects that are intersecting with current sketching plane and their intersection curves are to be generated; refer to Figure-139.

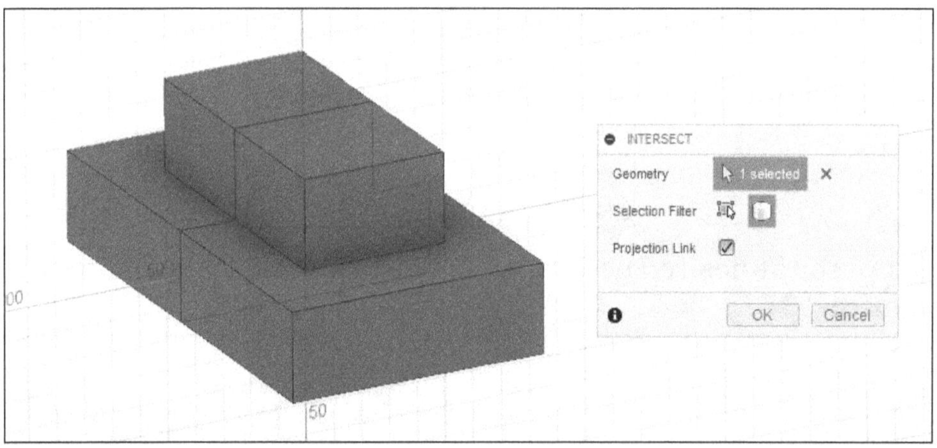

Figure-139. Selection of intersecting objects

- On selecting the objects that are intersecting with current sketching plane, a preview of the intersection curve will be displayed. Click on the **OK** button to create the generated curves; refer to Figure-140.

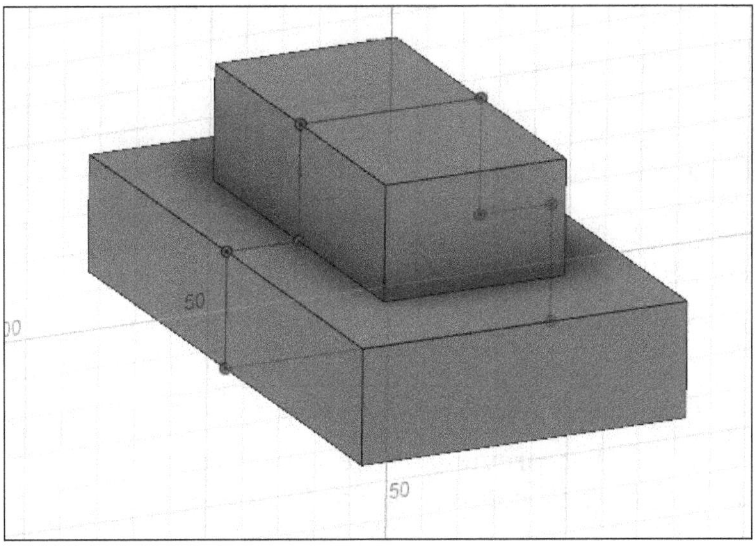

Figure-140. Intersection curves generated

Spun Profile

The **Spun Profile** tool is used to project a 2D spun profile on the active sketch plane and rotate selected geometry around specified axis. The procedure to use this tool is discussed next.

- Click on the **Spun Profile** tool from **Project/Include** cascading menu of **CREATE** drop-down in the **Toolbar**. The **Spun Profile** dialog box will be displayed; refer to Figure-141.

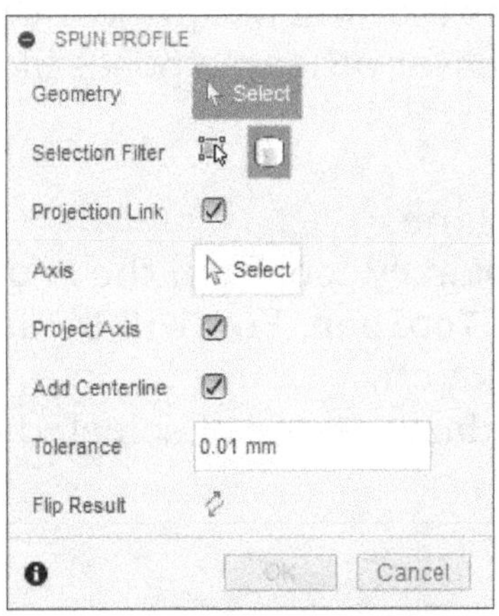

Figure-141. SPUN PROFILE dialog box

- Select the object that you select geometry to spin around the axis.
- Select desired axis to select a linear or circular object to define the axis to spin the profile around sketch; refer to Figure-142.

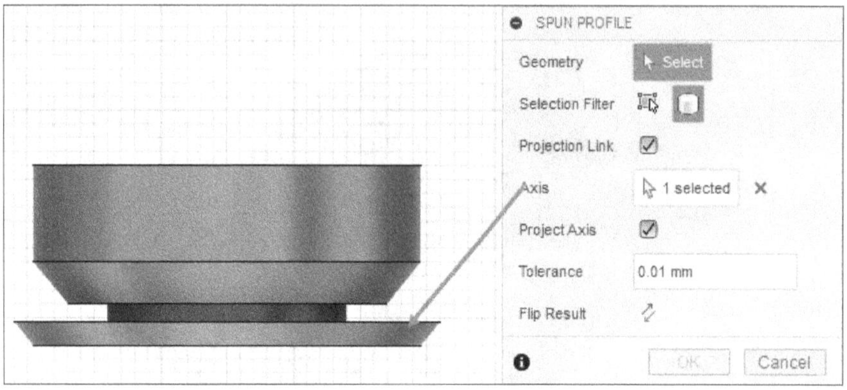

Figure-142. Selecting the geometry and axis of spun profile

- After selecting the object, a preview of the spun profile will be displayed. Click on the **OK** button to create the profile; refer to Figure-143.

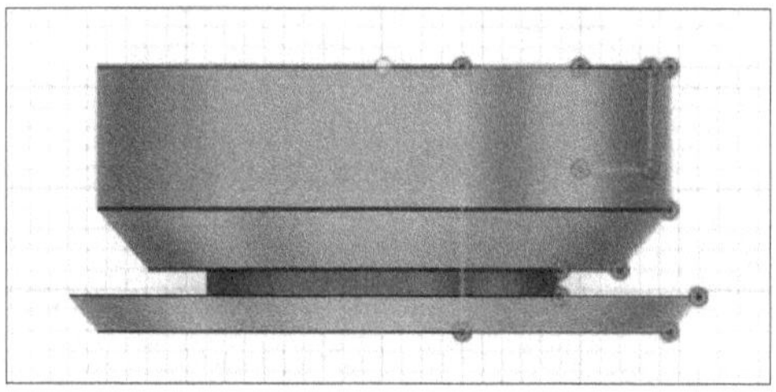

Figure-143. Spun profile created

Include 3D Geometry Tool

The **Include 3D Geometry** tool is used to include the boundaries of selected objects in current sketch. Note that this tool will not project the curves on selected sketching plane but you can use the curves for other purposes like as a reference. The procedure to use this tool is given next.

- Start a sketch on desired plane.
- Click on the **Include 3D Geometry** tool from the **Project/Include** cascading menu of the **CREATE** drop-down in **Toolbar**. You will be asked to select the 3D geometry to be included in current sketch.
- Select desired object. Boundary curves of selected object will be created on itself; refer to Figure-144.

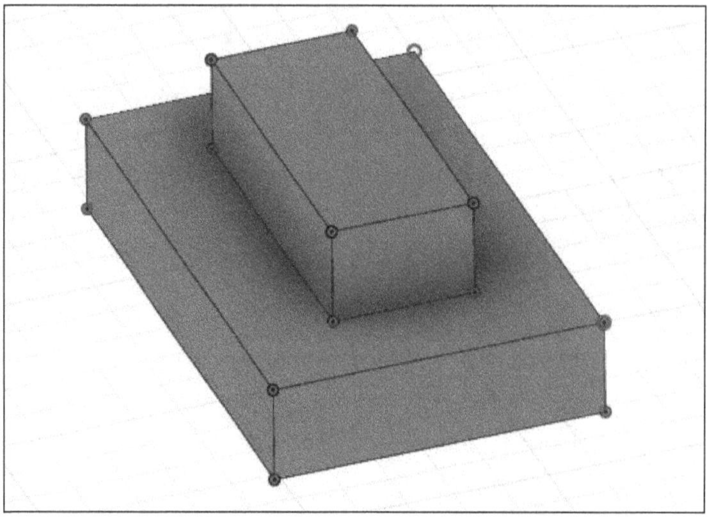

Figure-144. Boundary curves generated

- Press **ESC** to exit the tool.

Project To Surface tool

The **Project To Surface** tool is used to project selected curves on the selected faces/ surfaces. The procedure to use this tool is given next.

- Click on the **Project To Surface** tool from the **Project/Include** cascading menu of the **CREATE** drop-down in the **Toolbar**. The **PROJECT TO SURFACE** dialog box will be displayed; refer to Figure-145. You will be asked to select a sketching plane.

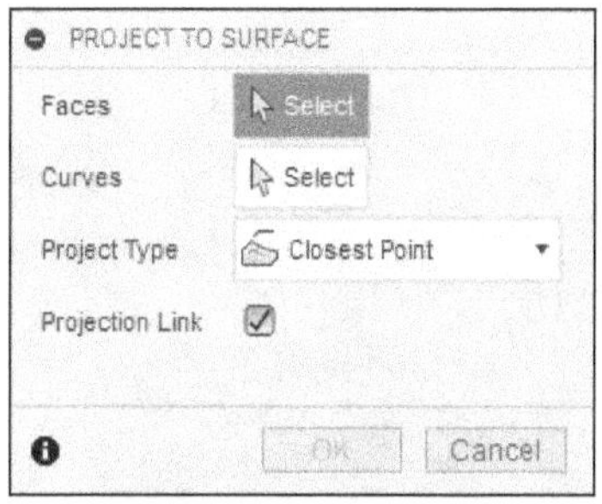

Figure-145. PROJECT TO SURFACE dialog box

- Select the plane which is parallel to face/surface on which sketch is to be projected. The sketching environment will become active. Click on the **Project to Surface** tool, the **PROJECT TO SURFACE** dialog box will be displayed; refer to Figure-146.

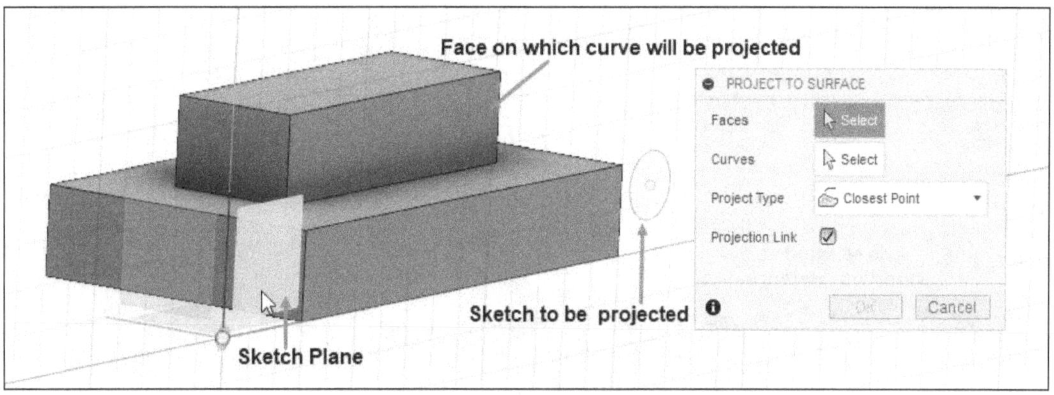

Figure-146. Selection for Project To Surface tool

- Select the face(s) on which you want to project selected curves.
- Click on the **Select** button for Curves from the dialog box and select the curves to be projected. Preview of projection will be displayed; refer to Figure-147.

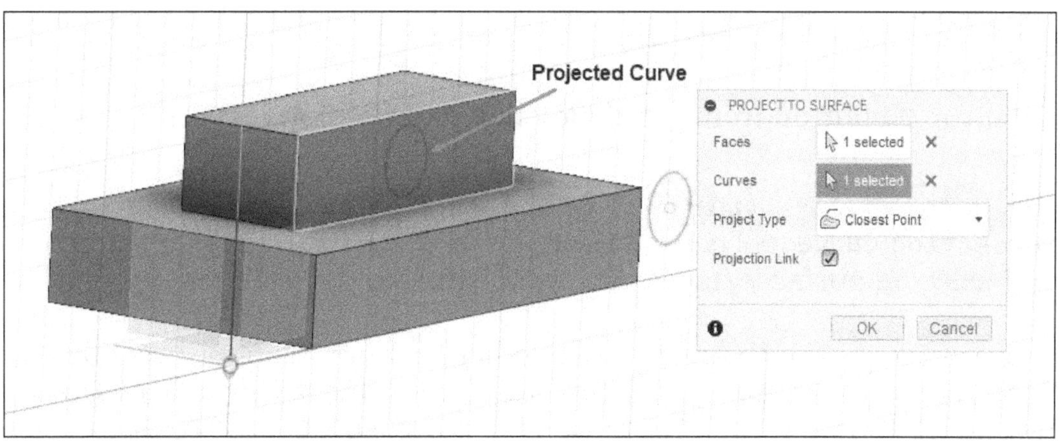

Figure-147. Preview of projected curve

- Select the **Closest Point** option from the **Project Type** drop-down if your object is well within the boundaries of selected face or you want to project along the surface vector to the closest point on the faces; refer to Figure-147. If some of the part of curve is outside the nearest surface then rest of the curve will not be projected; refer to Figure-148. Select the **Along Vector** option from the **Project Type** drop-down if you want to define the direction along which the curve will be projected and select a direction references like edge, axis, face, or plane. Preview of the projection will be displayed; refer to Figure-149.

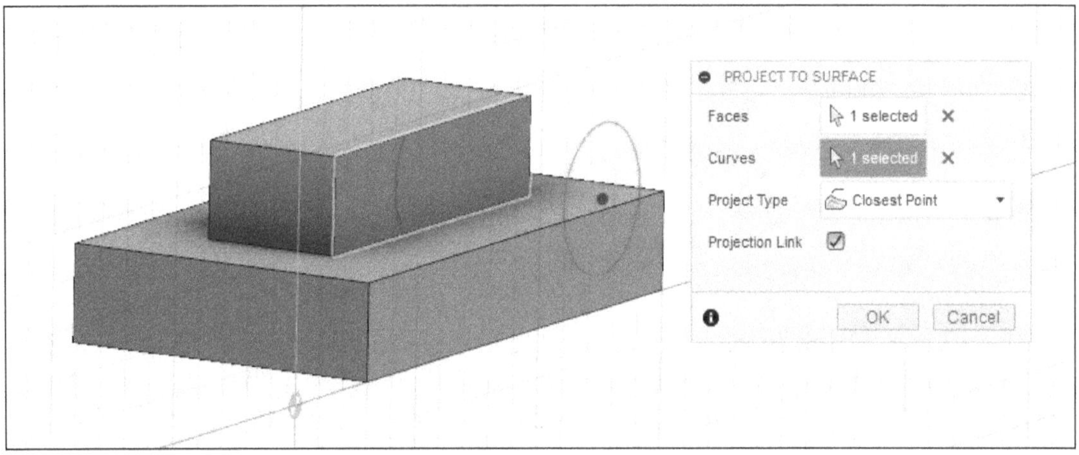

Figure-148. Closest point projection

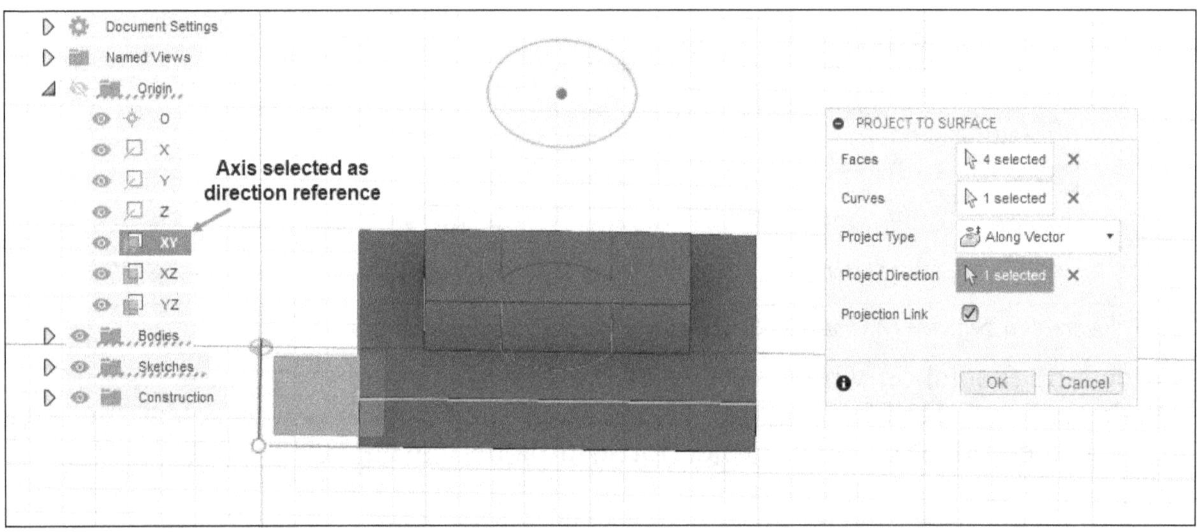

Figure-149. Projection along selected axis

- Click on the **OK** button from the dialog box to create projection.

Intersection Curve tool

The **Intersection Curve** tool is used to create projection curves generated by selected curve and selected surfaces/faces. The procedure to use this tool is given next.

- Start a new sketch on the plane perpendicular to projection direction.
- Click on the **Intersection Curve** tool from the **Project/Include** cascading menu of the **CREATE** drop-down in **Toolbar**. The **INTERSECTION CURVE** dialog box will be displayed; refer to Figure-150.

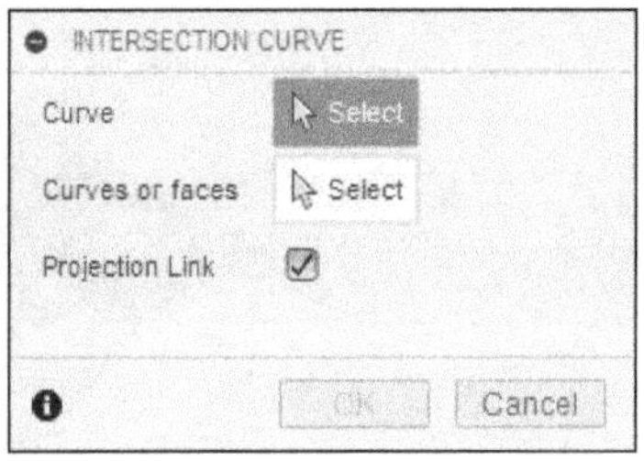

Figure-150. INTERSECTION CURVE dialog box

- Select the curve that you want to be projected and then select the faces/surfaces on which curve is to be projected. Preview of intersection curve will be displayed; refer to Figure-151.

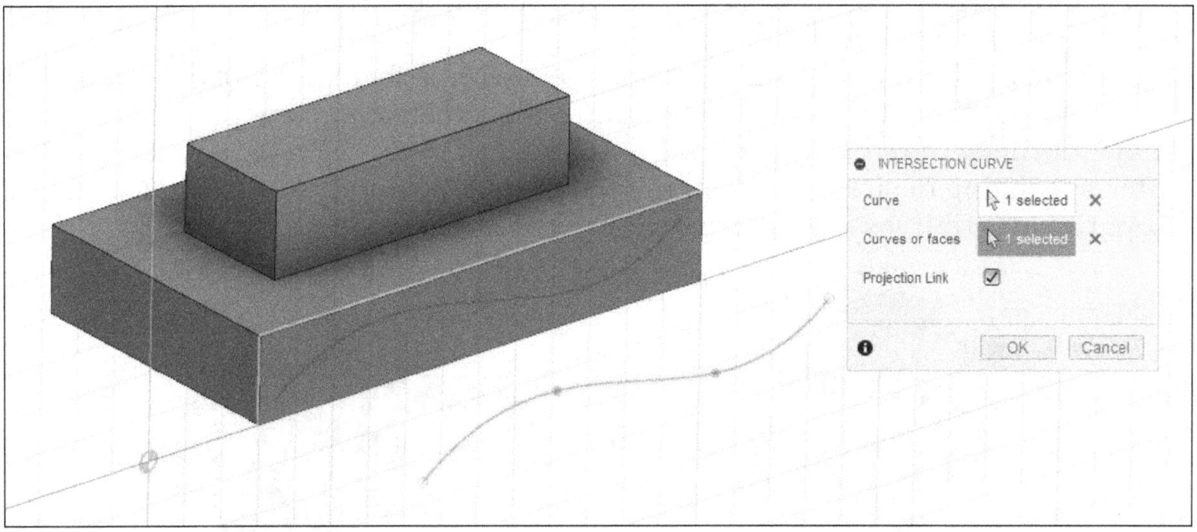

Figure-151. Preview of intersection curve

- Click on the **OK** button from the dialog box to create curves.

Isoparametric Curve tool

The **Isoparametric Curve** tool is used to create smooth curve along a face in the U or V direction. The procedure to use this tool is discussed next.

- Click on the **Isoparametric Curve** tool from the **Project/Include** cascading menu of the **CREATE** drop-down in **Toolbar**. The **ISOPARAMETRIC CURVE** dialog box will be displayed; refer to Figure-152.

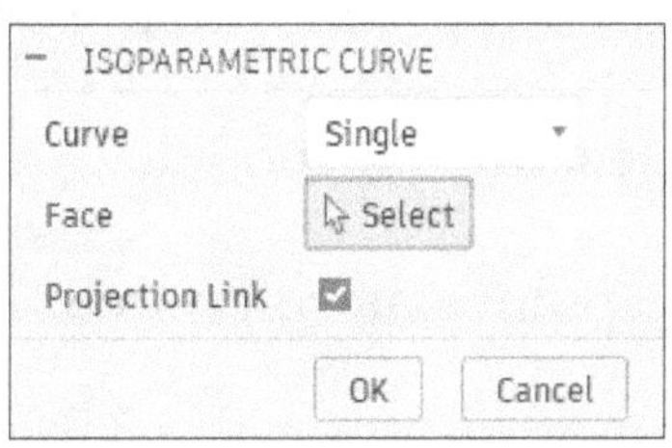

Figure-152. ISOPARAMETRIC CURVE dialog box

- Select **Single** or **Distributed** option from **Curve** drop-down to create single or multiple curves on the selected face, respectively.
- The **Select** button of **Face** section is active by default, select desired face on which the curve(s) is to be created. The preview of isoparametric curve will be displayed; refer to Figure-153.

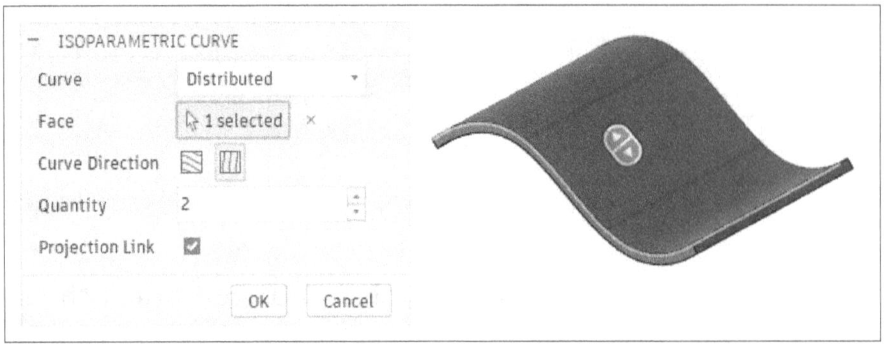

Figure-153. Preview of isoparametric curve

- Select **U** or **V** option from **Curve Direction** section to create the curves along u or v direction, respectively.
- Specify desired number of curves to be created on a face in the **Quantity** edit box.
- Select **Projection Link** check box to link the projected geometry to the size and shape of the selected geometry.
- After specifying desired parameters, click on **OK** button from the dialog box. The isoparametric curves will be created; refer to Figure-154.

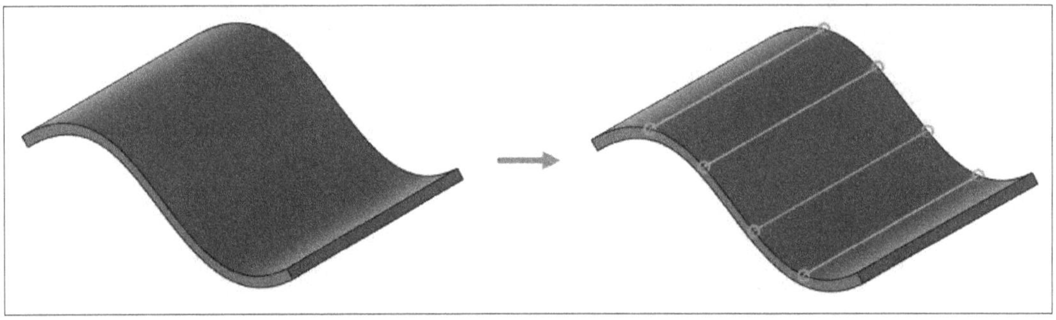

Figure-154. Isoparametric curves created

SELF ASSESSMENT

Q1. Discuss the procedure of cutting material from a body.

Q2. Which tool is used to combine two bodies?

Q3. Discuss the use of **Sweep** tool with example?

Q4. Discuss the procedure of creating plane using **Offset Plane** tool with example.

Q5. Create a plane tangent to the face of model.

Q6. Create a plane using three points as reference.

Q7. Create a plane using edge of a model as reference.

Q8. Create a point at the center of cylinder.

Q9. What are 3D sketches in Autodesk Fusion?

A. Sketches confined to a single plane.
B. Sketches that connect two points in the YZ and ZX planes.
C. Sketches created using only two-dimensional tools.
D. Sketches created only in the XY plane.

Q10. What is required to enable 3D sketching in Autodesk Fusion?

A. Enabling 3D sketching through a checkbox in the SKETCH PALETTE.
B. Activating the 3D sketch option from the Preferences dialog box.
C. Using only specific tools dedicated to 3D sketching.
D. Switching to a 3D drawing mode in the Toolbar.

Q11. What should be done after creating a base sketch on the XY plane in Autodesk Fusion?

A. Exit the sketching environment immediately.
B. Copy the sketch and then finish the sketching process.
C. Change the sketch dimensions before continuing.
D. Add extra sketches to the same plane.

Q12. What is the purpose of the Offset Plane tool in Autodesk Fusion?

A. To create new sketches in a parallel plane to the original sketch.
B. To select bodies within a specific area.
C. To rotate sketches in a new direction.
D. To change the dimensions of an existing sketch.

Q13. What tool allows users to paste a previously copied sketch in Autodesk Fusion?

A. Paste Sketch Tool.
B. Create Sketch Tool.
C. MOVE/COPY dialog box.
D. CTRL+V keyboard shortcut.

Q14. What can be used to create 3D sketches in Autodesk Fusion?

A. Only 3D lines and splines.
B. Only 3D shapes and volumes.
C. Any 3D shape from the tool palette.
D. 3D points and curves.

Q15. Which tool in Autodesk Fusion activates 3D sketching functionality?

A. 3D Sketch check box in the Sketch Palette.
B. 3D Sketch toggle in Preferences.
C. Sketch Type selector in the Toolbar.
D. 3D Selection tool in the Toolbar.

Q16. What does the Line tool in Autodesk Fusion do during 3D sketch creation?

A. Draws a single line between two fixed points.
B. Allows connecting various points from sketches to create frames.
C. Moves the selected points on the plane.
D. Creates predefined 3D shapes.

Q17. What is the purpose of the Select Tool in Autodesk Fusion?

A. To create new objects in the canvas.
B. To select objects or tools from the toolbar or canvas.
C. To set preferences for sketching planes.
D. To create new selections based on size.

Q18. How is the Window Selection mode activated in Autodesk Fusion?

A. By pressing the 2 key on the keyboard.
B. By selecting the Window Selection tool from the Toolbar.
C. By pressing the 1 key on the keyboard.
D. By clicking and dragging in the canvas area.

Q19. What does the Freeform Selection tool allow users to do in Autodesk Fusion?

A. Select objects based on predefined shapes.
B. Select objects using a freeform boundary.
C. Select all objects within the model by clicking.
D. Select objects by crossing a defined window shape.

Q20. What is the function of the Paint Selection tool in Autodesk Fusion?

A. Select objects inside or outside a defined boundary.
B. Select objects as the cursor passes over them while dragging.
C. Select specific faces on a surface.
D. Select objects based on name.

Q21. How can objects be selected based on their names in Autodesk Fusion?

A. By using the Select By Boundary method.
B. By selecting the Select By Name tool from the Selection Tools menu.
C. By pressing the 1 key on the keyboard.
D. By selecting objects manually from the model space.

Q22. What does the Select By Boundary method allow users to do in Autodesk Fusion?

A. Select objects based on their name.
B. Select objects falling within defined shapes like a cylinder or box.
C. Select bodies only inside a specific boundary shape.
D. Select only components or assemblies.

Q23. In the Select By Size method, what does the user define?

A. The range of sizes for selecting bodies.
B. The dimensions of the sketching plane.
C. The shape of the selection boundary.
D. The area where the selection will occur.

Q24. What is the purpose of the Invert Selection tool in Autodesk Fusion?

A. To cancel the selection mode.
B. To switch the selection state of all selected objects.
C. To select only the largest objects in the model.
D. To activate the selection filters.

Q25. How does the Seed and Boundary tool function in Autodesk Fusion?

A. It selects all faces within a defined boundary shape.
B. It selects a reference face to use as a boundary for selecting nearby faces.
C. It allows selecting all objects in the model.
D. It creates a boundary based on user-defined parameters.

Q26. What happens when the Selection Priority menu in Autodesk Fusion is used?

A. It selects objects based on their names.
B. It defines which entities are given selection priority.
C. It adjusts the scale of objects within a boundary.
D. It filters selections based on size.

Q27. What are Selection Filters used for in Autodesk Fusion?

A. To change the orientation of objects.
B. To define which objects can be selected and which cannot.
C. To adjust the size of selected objects.
D. To create new objects in the design.

Q28: What is solid modeling in Autodesk Fusion?

A) Representation of solid objects in two dimensions
B) Representation of solid objects in digital form in three dimensions
C) Creation of 2D sketches only
D) None of the above

Q29: What tool is used to create a new component in Autodesk Fusion?

A) Extrude Tool
B) New Component Tool
C) Revolve Tool
D) Sweep Tool

Q30: What does the Extrude tool do in solid modeling?

A) It adds height to a selected sketch to create a solid volume
B) It removes material from a model
C) It creates revolved shapes from sketches
D) It cuts the model in half

Q31: What is the default type of extrusion in the Extrude tool dialog box?

A) Thin Extrude
B) Surface Extrude
C) Extrude
D) Revolve

Q32: What option in the "Direction" drop-down allows you to extrude a profile in both directions?

A) One Side
B) Two Sides
C) Symmetric
D) Distance

Q33: What does the "Symmetric" option in the Direction drop-down do?

A) Extrudes the model in one direction only
B) Extrudes the model symmetrically in both directions from the sketching plane
C) Allows extrusion of objects inside a boundary
D) None of the above

Q34: What is the "Extent Type" option used for in the Extrude tool?

A) To define the thickness of the extrusion
B) To set the height or limits of the extrusion
C) To rotate the profile
D) To join two bodies

Q35: Which "Operation" option in the Extrude tool allows you to combine the extrude feature with other intersecting bodies?

A) Join
B) Cut
C) Intersect
D) New Body

Q36: What is the purpose of selecting "Thin Extrude" in the Extrude dialog box?

A) To create an extrude with tapered walls
B) To extrude a thin wall along the selected closed profile
C) To cut material from a model
D) To create a new body

Q37: In the Extrude tool, which option under "Wall Location" allows you to offset the extrusion to one side of the profile?

A) Side 1
B) Side 2
C) Center
D) None of the above

Q38: What does the Revolve tool do in Autodesk Fusion?

A) Adds material in one direction
B) Creates a solid volume by revolving a sketch about an axis
C) Cuts material from a model
D) None of the above

Q39: In the Revolve tool, what is required to create a revolve feature?

A) A closed sketch
B) A center line
C) A path for the profile
D) A surface for the object

Q40: What option in the "Direction" drop-down of the Revolve tool allows you to revolve the profile symmetrically in both directions?

A) One Side
B) Two Sides
C) Symmetric
D) Full

Q41: What is the "Extent Type" used for in the Revolve tool?

A) To set the depth of the revolve
B) To specify the angle or plane of revolution
C) To select the extrusion direction
D) To create a new body

Q42: What does the Sweep tool do in solid modeling?

A) Adds a tapered feature to a sketch
B) Creates a solid volume by moving a sketch along a path
C) Revolves a sketch around an axis
D) Cuts material from a body

Q43: What are the types of sweep features that can be created using the Sweep tool?

A) Single Path
B) Path + Guide Rail
C) Path + Guide Surface
D) All of the above

Q44: In the Sweep tool, what does the "Chain Selection" checkbox do?

A) Selects the entire model
B) Allows the selection of connected geometry along the path
C) Defines the length of the sweep
D) Allows twisting the profile

Q45: What is the default "Orientation" for profiles in the Sweep tool?

A) Perpendicular
B) Parallel
C) None
D) Centered

Q46: In the Sweep dialog, what does the "Taper Angle" option control?

A) The height of the extrusion
B) The angle of the profile along the path
C) The symmetry of the sweep
D) The direction of the sweep

Q47: What is the "Twist Angle" used for in the Sweep tool?

A) To control the angle at which the profile twists as it follows the path
B) To set the direction of the extrusion
C) To define the profile's thickness
D) None of the above

Q48. What does the "Path + Guide Rail" option in the Sweep dialog box do?

A. It sweeps the profile along the path using the guide rail to control the shape.
B. It sweeps the profile along the path using the guide surface.
C. It sweeps the profile without using any reference.
D. It scales the profile along the path.

Q49. Which tool should you use in the Sweep dialog box to control the shape of the sweep using a guide rail?

A. Path + Guide Rail
B. Path + Guide Surface
C. Single Path
D. Path + Guide Line

Q50. What happens when you select the "Full Extents" option in the Sweep dialog box?

A. It creates the sweep till the end point of the path.
B. It creates the sweep till the profile is perpendicular to the path.
C. It automatically scales the profile.
D. It stretches the profile along the path.

Q51. What are construction geometries mainly used for?
A. Creating final solid models
B. References for other features
C. Applying colors to models
D. Rendering images

Q52. Which of the following is NOT listed as a construction geometry entity?
A. Planes
B. Axes
C. Materials
D. Points

Q53. The Offset Plane tool is used to create a plane at a specified distance from which reference?
A. Edge only
B. Face or plane
C. Axis only
D. Vertex only

Q54. The Plane at Angle tool creates a plane at a specified angle with reference to what?
A. A vertex
B. A line, edge, or axis
C. A point
D. A sketch dimension

Q55. The Tangent Plane tool is used to create a plane tangent to which element?
A. Selected face or surface
B. Selected sketch
C. Selected dimension
D. Selected vertex

Q56. In the Tangent Plane tool, selecting a Reference Object helps to:
A. Delete the plane
B. Define orientation of the tangent plane
C. Reduce model size
D. Convert plane into sketch

Q57. The Midplane tool creates a plane at the midpoint between:
A. Two points
B. Two edges
C. Two faces or planes
D. Two axes

Q58. The Plane Through Two Edges tool requires selection of:
A. Two curved edges
B. Two straight edges
C. One point and one edge
D. Three points

Q59. The Plane Along Path tool creates a plane that is:
A. Parallel to the path
B. Perpendicular to the path at a selected point
C. Parallel to the sketch plane
D. Tangent to the path

Q60. In the Plane Along Path tool, the distance of the plane along the path is specified between:
A. 0 to 1
B. 0 to 10
C. 1 to 100
D. 10 to 100

Q61. Points in construction geometry can be used for:
A. Coloring surfaces
B. Origin or coordinate system location
C. Rendering models
D. Mesh generation

Q62. Using the Point At Vertex tool, how many points can be created at a time?
A. One
B. Two
C. Three
D. Unlimited

Q63. The Project tool is used to project selected geometry onto:
A. Axis
B. Sketching plane
C. Edge
D. Surface normal

Q64. The Intersect tool creates sketch geometries at the:
A. Center of objects
B. Intersection of objects and sketching plane
C. Edge of sketch
D. Axis midpoint

Q65. The Spun Profile tool is used to:
A. Delete sketches
B. Rotate selected geometry around an axis
C. Create planes automatically
D. Convert surfaces into solids

Q66. The Include 3D Geometry tool:
A. Projects curves onto sketch plane
B. Deletes boundaries
C. Includes boundaries of selected objects without projecting them
D. Creates solid geometry

Q67. The Project To Surface tool projects selected curves onto:
A. Selected faces or surfaces
B. Sketch origin
C. Only axes
D. Only vertices

Q68. In the Project To Surface tool, which option projects curves to the nearest point on the surface?
A. Along Vector
B. Closest Point
C. Tangent Point
D. Direct Projection

Q69. The Intersection Curve tool creates projection curves generated by:
A. Curves and surfaces
B. Points and edges
C. Vertices and axes
D. Planes and points

Q70. The Isoparametric Curve tool creates curves along a face in which directions?
A. X and Y
B. U or V
C. A or B
D. Left or Right

Q71. In the Isoparametric Curve tool, which option allows creation of multiple curves on a face?
A. Single
B. Distributed
C. Parallel
D. Continuous

For Student Notes

Chapter 4

Advanced 3D Modeling

Topics Covered

The major topics covered in this chapter are:

- ***Introduction***
- ***Loft Tool***
- ***Rib Tool***
- ***Web Tool***
- ***Hole Tool***
- ***Thread Tool***
- ***Box Tool***
- ***Cylinder Tool***
- ***Sphere Tool***
- ***Torus Tool***
- ***Coil Tool***
- ***Pipe Tool***
- ***Pattern Tool***
- ***Mirror Tool***
- ***Thicken Tool***
- ***Boundary Fill Tool***
- ***Create Form Tool***
- ***Create Base Feature Tool***
- ***Create Mesh Tool***
- ***Create Mesh Section Sketch Tool***
- ***Create 3D PCB Feature Tool***

INTRODUCTION

In the last chapter, you have learned the procedure to use some 3D modeling tools and creating the constructional geometry. In this chapter, you will use the constructional geometry tools with some advanced 3D modeling tools. The tools are available in the panel of **DESIGN** workspace.

LOFT

The **Loft** tool is used to create a solid volume by joining two or more sketches created on different planes; refer to Figure-1. The procedure to use this tool is given next.

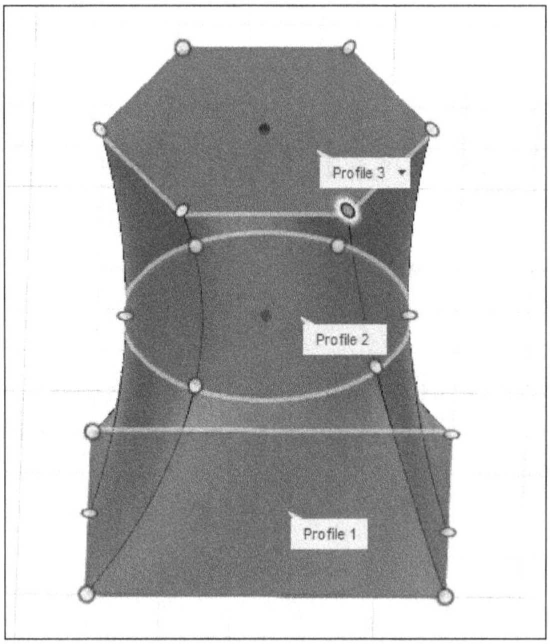

Figure-1. Lofted feature

- Click on the **Loft** tool from **CREATE** drop-down in the **Toolbar**; refer to Figure-2. The **LOFT** dialog box will be displayed as shown in Figure-3.

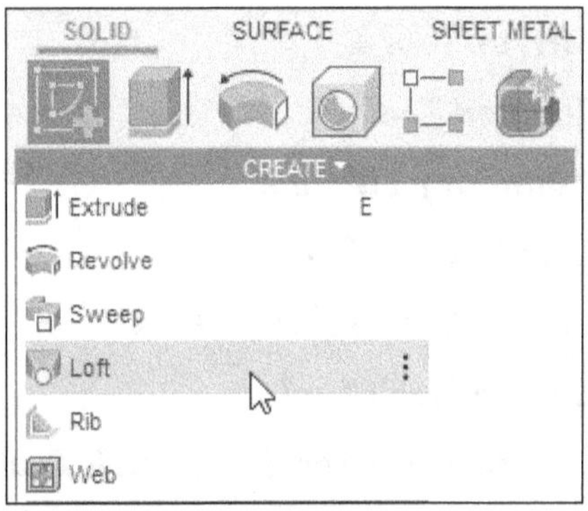

Figure-2. Loft tool

Figure-3. LOFT dialog box

- By default, **Profiles** selection box is active and you are asked to select sketches for loft feature. You can also select faces/surfaces as profile for loft.
- Click one by one on the sketches created at different planes. Note that you need to select the sketches in order by which they can be joined to each other successively. The preview of loft will be displayed; refer to Figure-4.

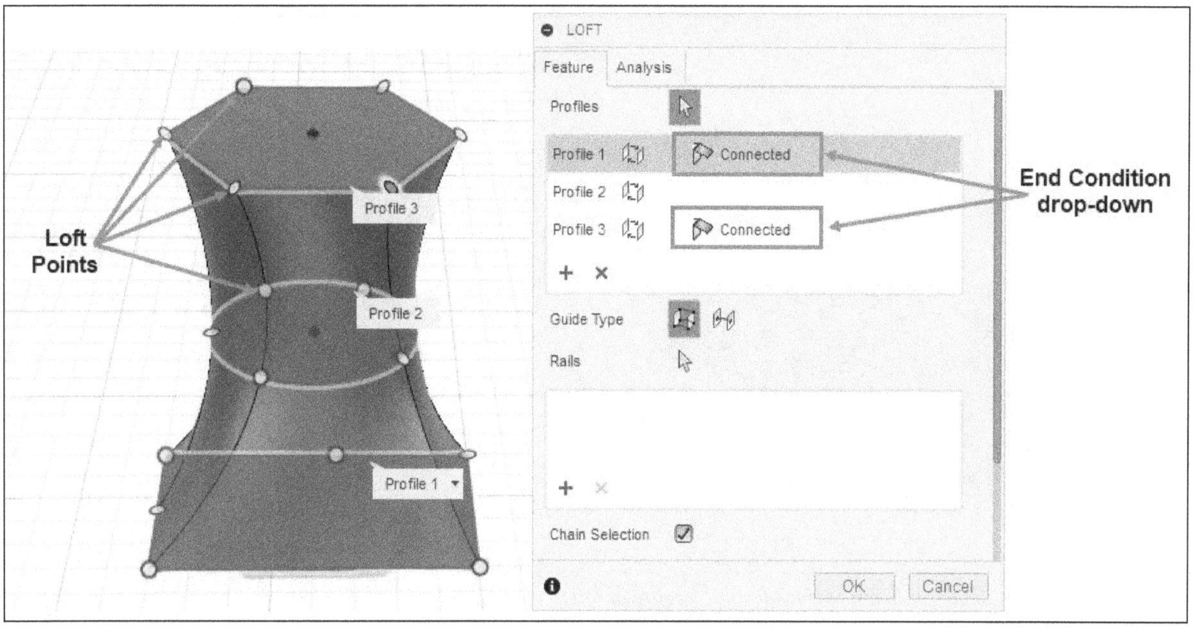

Figure-4. Preview of loft

- To make adjustments to the loft, you can move the loft points along the profile edge.
- Click the **End condition** drop-down of **Profile 1** from **Profiles** selection box. The options will be displayed as per the geometry selected.

If you have selected sketches only as profiles then **Connected** and **Direction** options are available in the drop-down; refer to Figure-5.

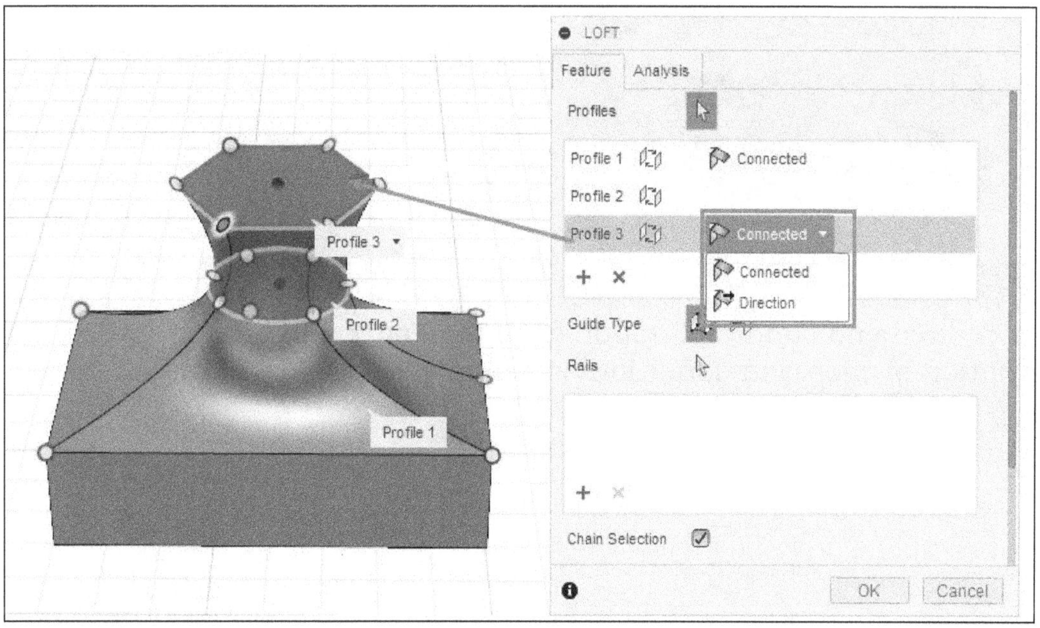

Figure-5. End condition options for sketch profile in loft

If you have selected sketches and faces of model or only faces of the model as profiles then **Connected (G0)**, **Tangent(G1)**, and **Curvature(G2)** options are available in the **End condition** drop-down; refer to Figure-6. If you have selected a point as profile at the end then **Sharp** and **Point Tangent** options will be available in the **End condition** drop-down; refer to Figure-7.

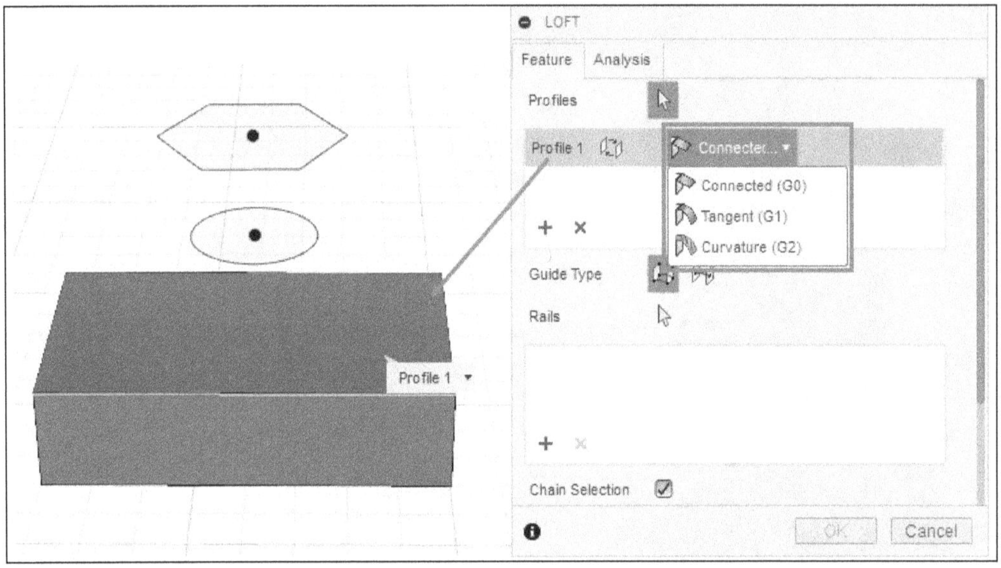

Figure-6. End condition options for face profile in loft

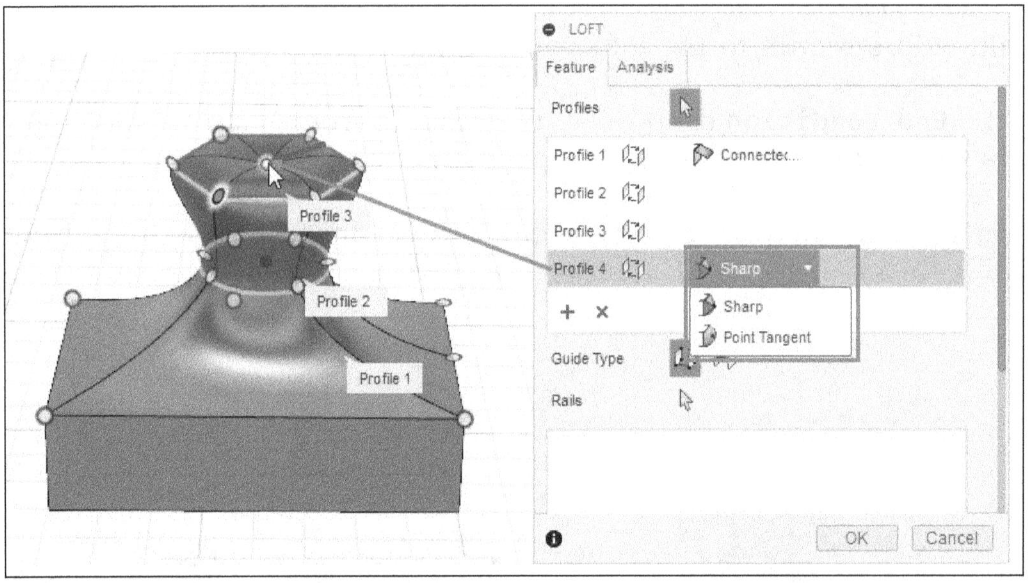

Figure-7. End condition options for point profile in loft

- Select desired end condition option from the **End condition** drop-down. One line explanation of each end condition option is given in Figure-8.

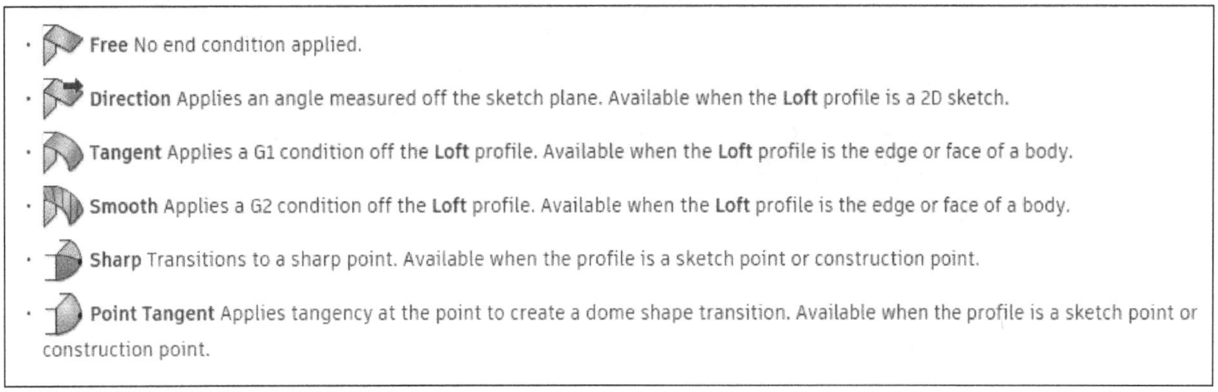

- **Free** No end condition applied.
- **Direction** Applies an angle measured off the sketch plane. Available when the **Loft** profile is a 2D sketch.
- **Tangent** Applies a G1 condition off the **Loft** profile. Available when the **Loft** profile is the edge or face of a body.
- **Smooth** Applies a G2 condition off the **Loft** profile. Available when the **Loft** profile is the edge or face of a body.
- **Sharp** Transitions to a sharp point. Available when the profile is a sketch point or construction point.
- **Point Tangent** Applies tangency at the point to create a dome shape transition. Available when the profile is a sketch point or construction point.

Figure-8. End condition

- Select the **Direction** option from the **End Condition** drop-down. The updated **LOFT** dialog box will be displayed with options to specify **Takeoff Weight** and **Takeoff Angle**; refer to Figure-9. As the name suggests, these options are used to specify scale and angle at which loft will start or end at selected profile.

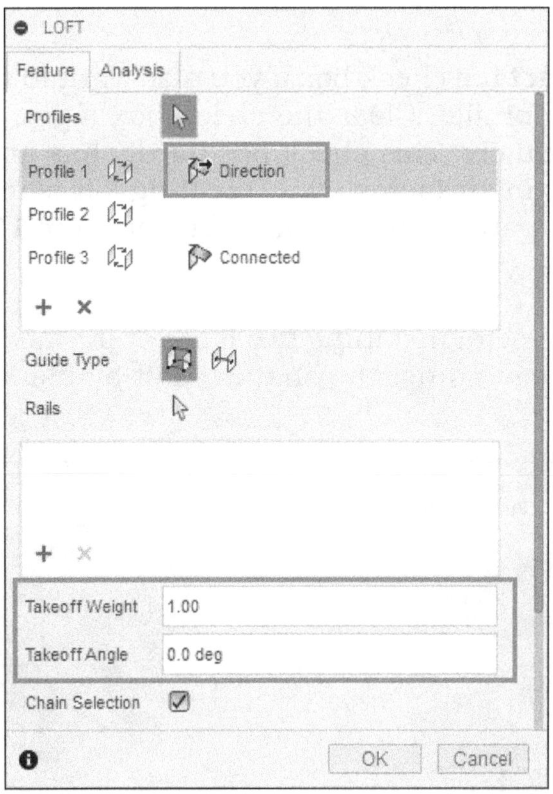

Figure-9. Updated LOFT dialog box

- If you have selected **Tangent**, **Curvature**, or **Point Tangent** option from the **End Condition** drop-down then **Tangency Weight** edit box will be displayed in the dialog box to specify scale factor of tangency.
- Enter the value as **4** in **Takeoff Weight** edit box and specify the outward angle in **Takeoff Angle** edit box by **20** degree. You will find a bulge in the loft feature; refer to Figure-10.

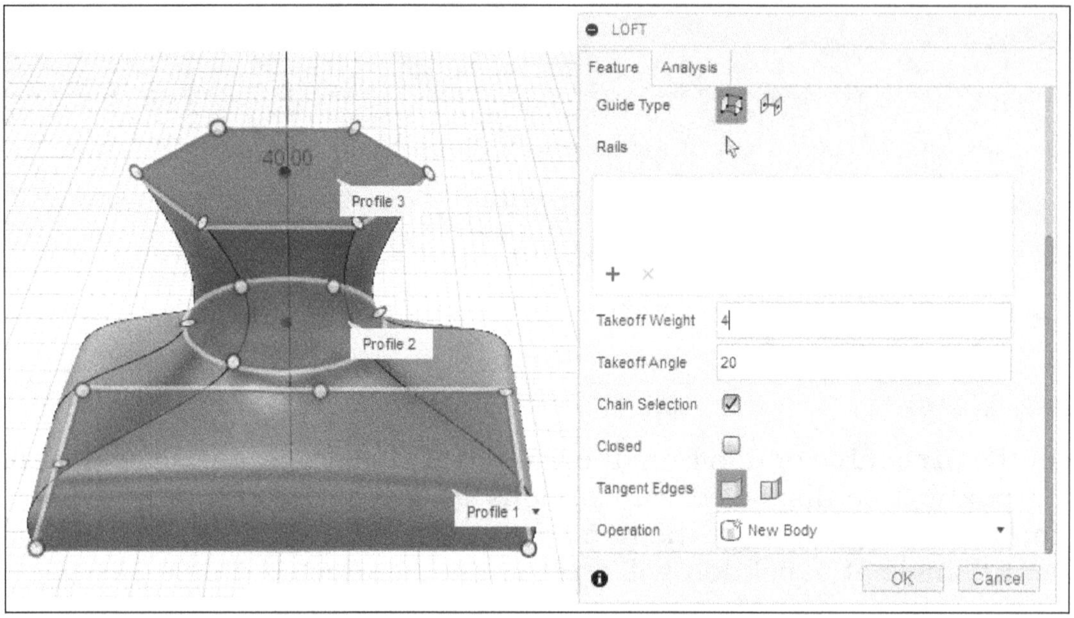

Figure-10. Preview after entering the value

- Select the **Chain Selection** check box if you also want to select the adjacent edges and included as one profile. Clear the check box if you want to select the each edge of profile individually. This check box hardly has any effect in modeling but you will find its uses in surfacing while creating loft feature.
- After setting desired parameters, click **OK** button from **LOFT** dialog box to create the loft feature.

Loft feature can be very useful in joining two faces or surfaces to create solid volume; refer to Figure-11. You can adjust the shape of loft by using the drag points on the edges.

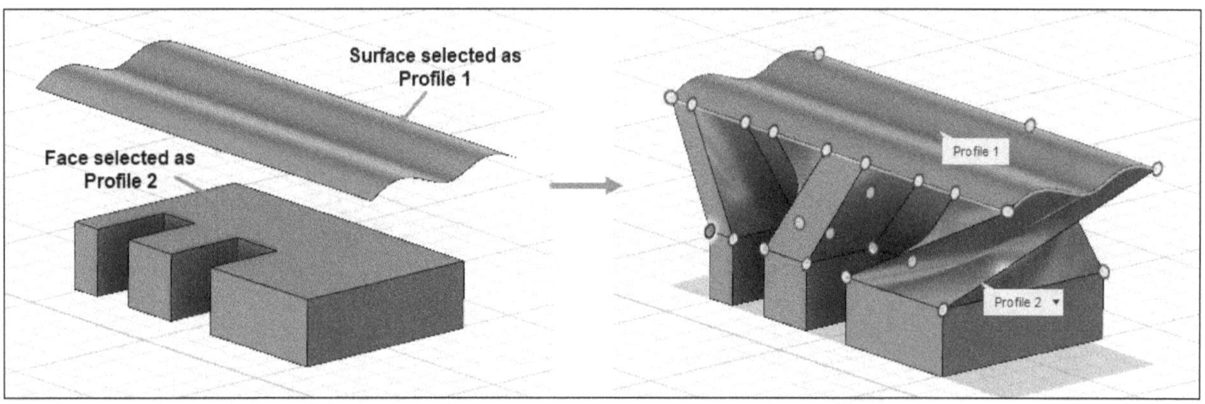

Figure-11. Creating loft using surface and face

Guide Type

There are two ways to control transition between profiles of loft; using **Rails** and using **Centerline**. **Rails** are 2D or 3D curves that affect the loft shape between sections at boundaries. To refine the shape of loft, you need to add number of rails. These rails must intersect each section and terminate on or beyond the first and last sections. **Rails** must be tangentially continuous. A **Centerline** tool is a type of rail to which the loft sections are held normal. It behaves like a sweep path.

Centerline lofts maintain a more consistent transition between the cross-sectional areas of selected loft sections. Center lines follow the same criteria as rails, except they need not intersect the sections and only one centerline can be selected. We have discussed two examples next for tent and ring which use rails and centerline, respectively.

Using Rails

- To select rails for the loft, click the **Rails** button in **Guide Type** section; refer to Figure-12.

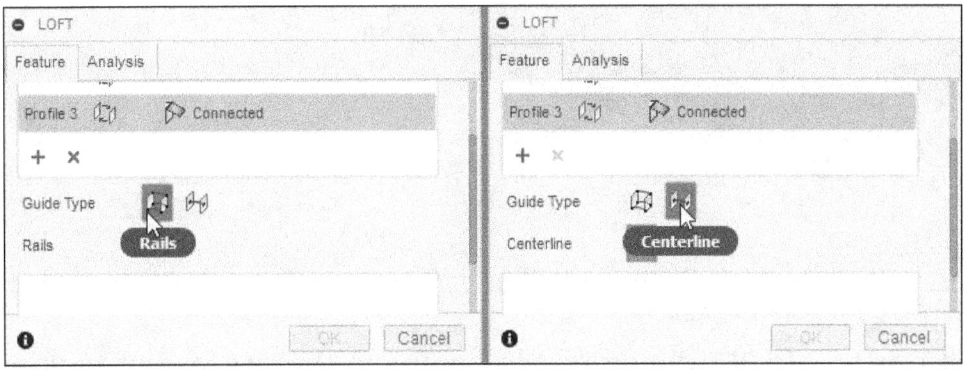

Figure-12. Rails and Centerline tool

- In this case, we have created a sketch of tent like structure using a rectangle and four arcs (to be used as rail) on different planes; refer to Figure-13.

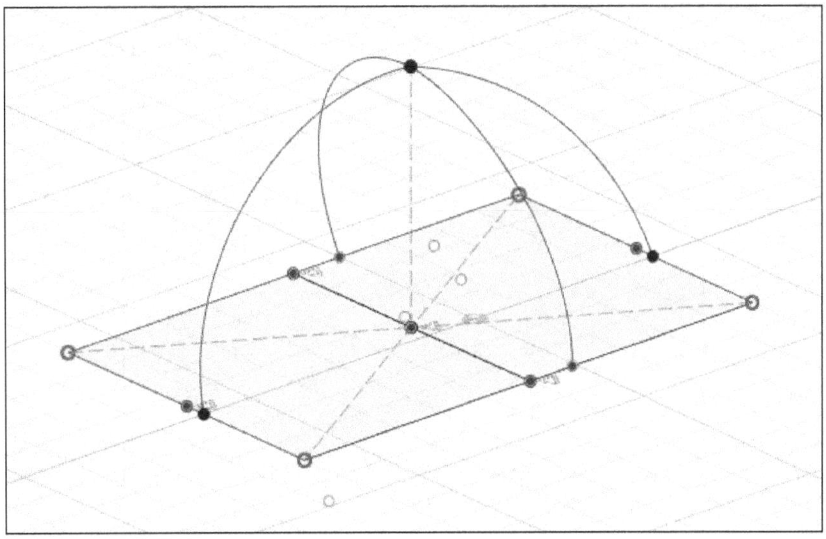

Figure-13. Sketch for using Rails tool

- Select the **Loft** tool from **CREATE** drop-down. The **LOFT** dialog box will be displayed.
- Select the rectangle and point of the sketch in **Profiles** section of **LOFT** dialog box. The preview of model will be shown.
- Click on the **Arrow** selection button of **Rails** from **Guide Type** section box, to select the rails for the loft.
- Select the four arcs of the model; refer to Figure-14.

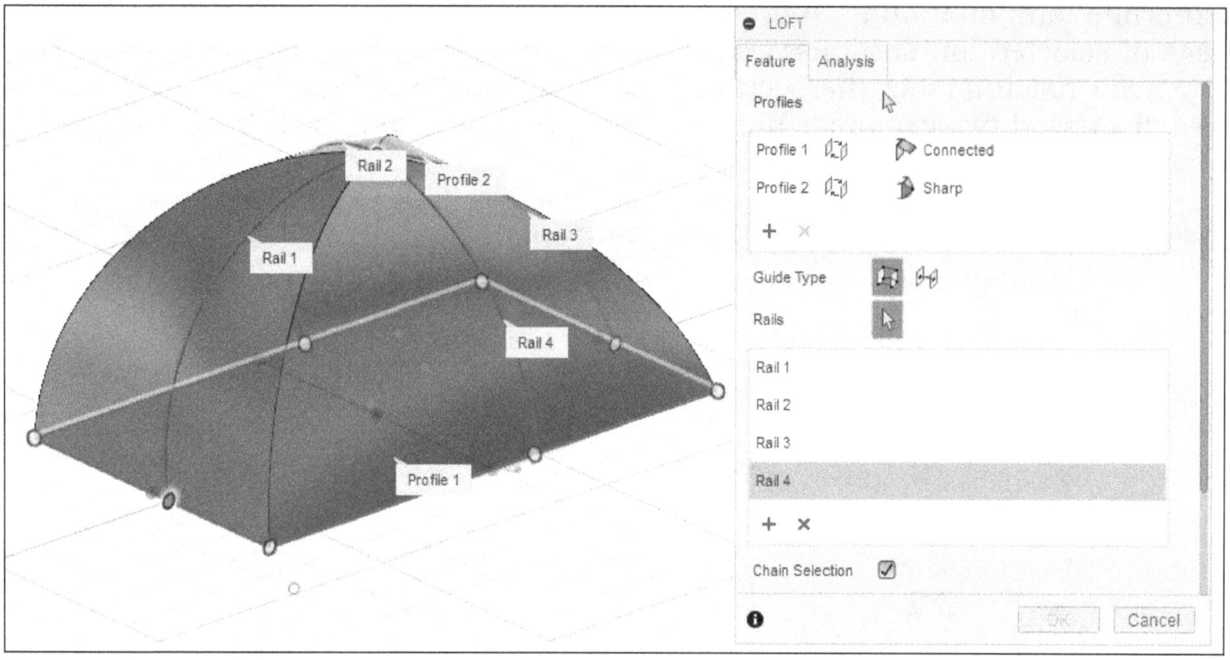

Figure-14. Preview of loft on selecting Rails

- Click **OK** button of **LOFT** dialog box to complete the process of making loft. The shape of loft will be modified according to rails selected.

Using Centerline

- To use the **Centerline** guide type, we have created a sketch of ring like structure with the help of circle and rectangle on different planes; refer to Figure-15.

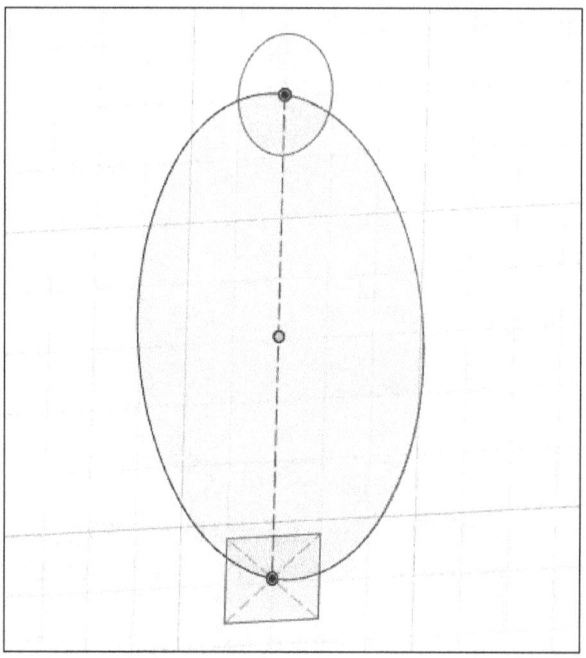

Figure-15. Sketch of ring

- Select the **Loft** tool from **CREATE** drop-down. The **LOFT** dialog box will be displayed.
- Select the circle and rectangle as profile in **Profiles** section of **LOFT** dialog box.
- Since these two profiles are coplanar, you may not get any preview and an error might welcome you.
- Click on **Centerline** button from **Guide Type** section and select the circle to be used as center line. The preview will be displayed; refer to Figure-16.

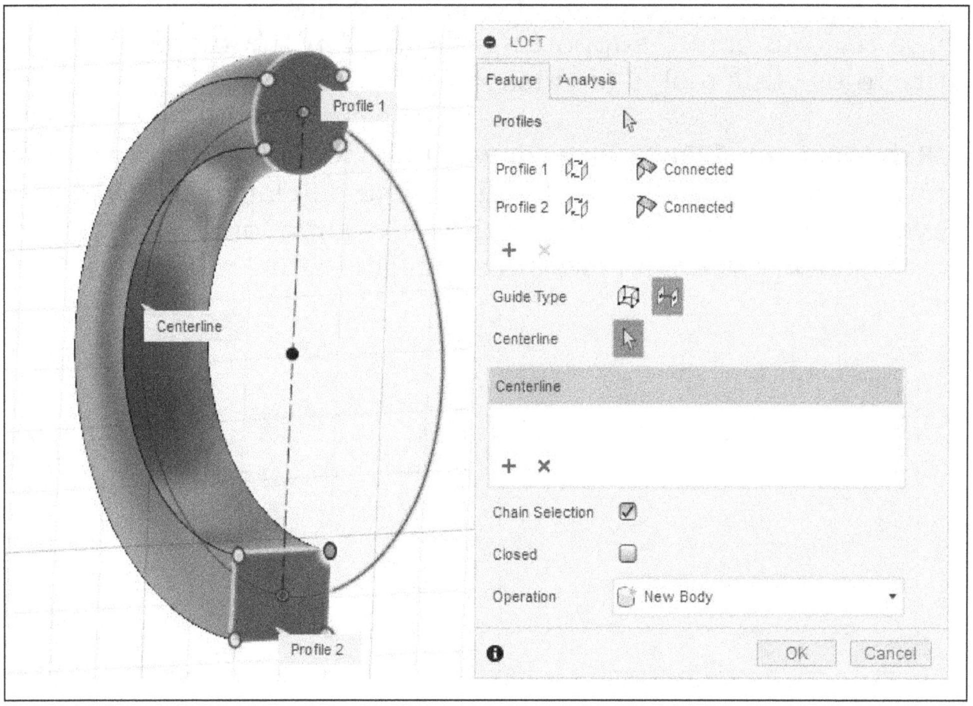

Figure-16. Preview of loft on selecting centerline

- By default, **Closed** check box is clear so you will be getting half of the ring. Select the **Closed** check box to complete the loft. Preview of the loft feature will be modified; refer to Figure-17.

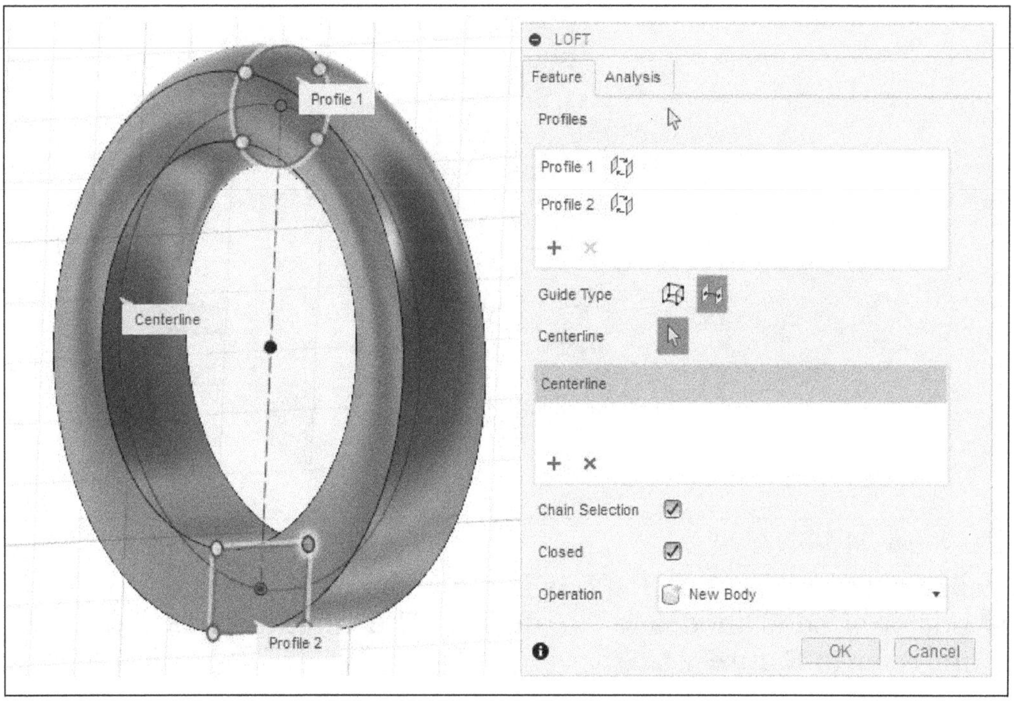

Figure-17. Preview of loft on selecting closed centerline

- Click **OK** button of **LOFT** dialog box to complete the process. The tools of **Operation** drop-down are same as discussed earlier.

RIB

The **Rib** tool is used to create supporting features in the model by using curve(s). The procedure to use this tool is discussed next.

- Click on **Rib** tool from **CREATE** drop-down; refer to Figure-18 or right-click on the screen canvas and select **Rib** from **Marking menu** displayed. The **RIB** dialog box will be displayed; refer to Figure-19. Note that the curve for rib should be created in such a way that its projection is within solid faces of the model; refer to Figure-20.

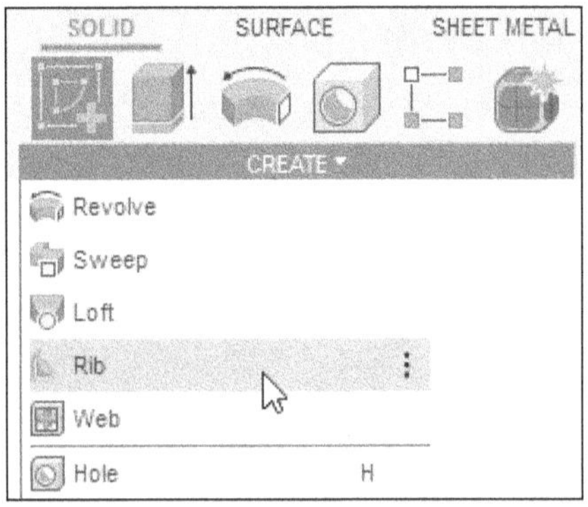

Figure-18. Rib tool

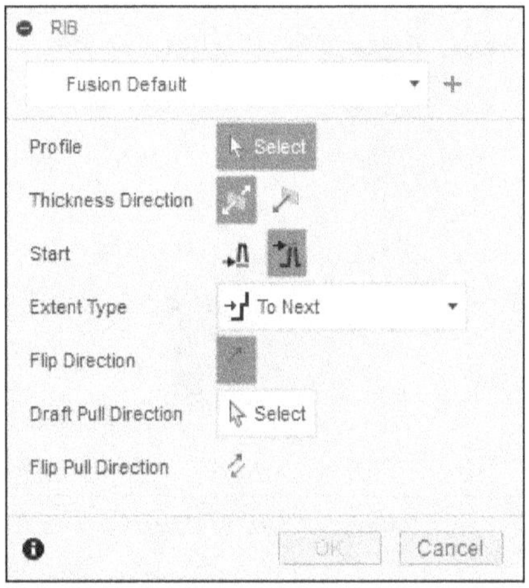

Figure-19. RIB dialog box

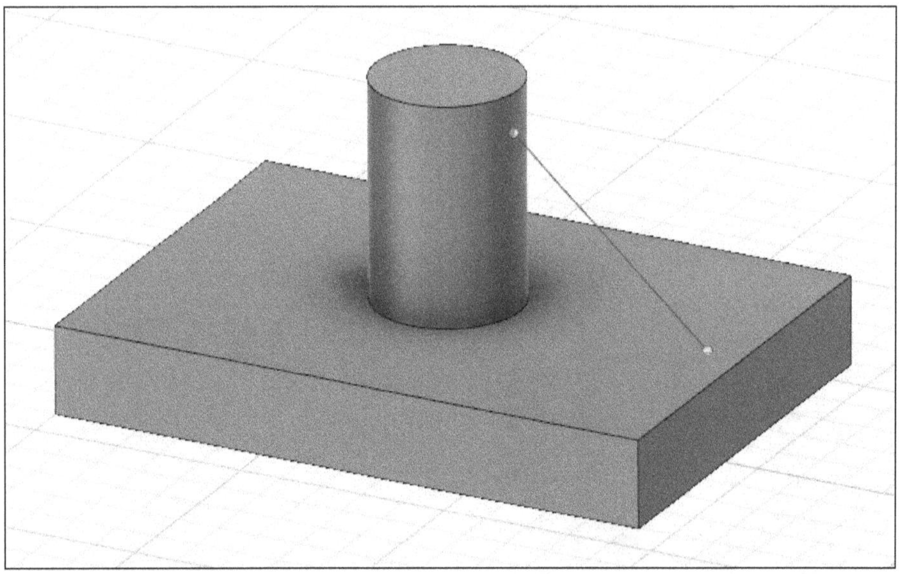

Figure-20. Sketch for rib

- The **Profile** section of **RIB** dialog box is active by default. Select the sketch curve joining edges of solid model to create rib. The updated **RIB** dialog box will be displayed; refer to Figure-21.

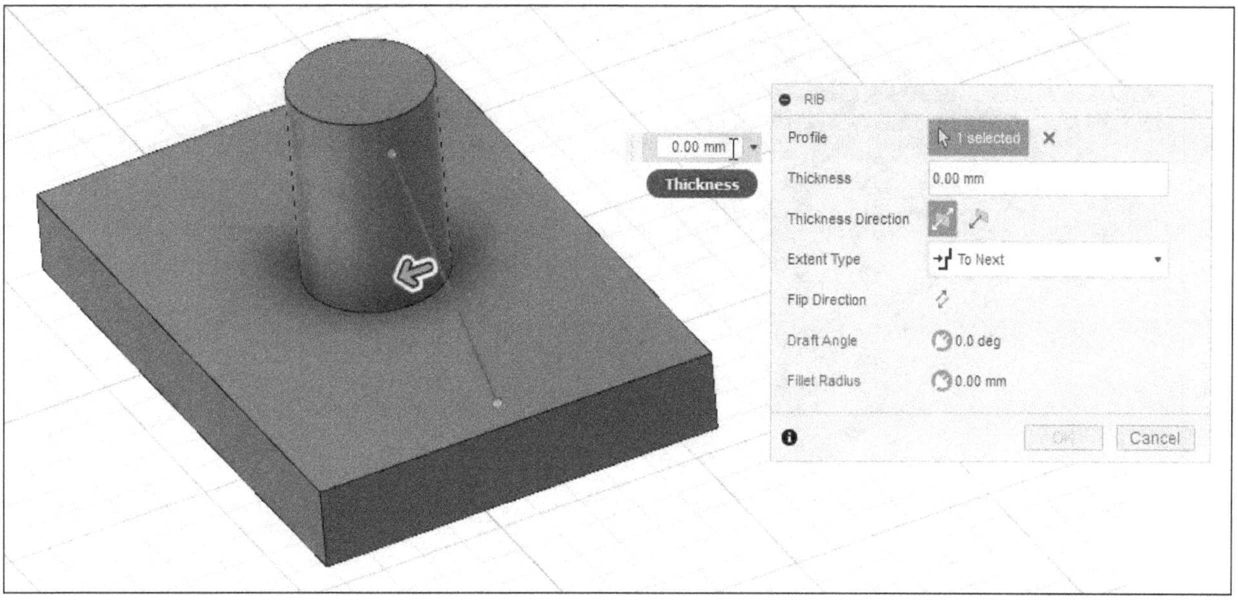

Figure-21. Updated RIB dialog box

- Select the **Symmetric** option from **Thickness Direction** section to set the thickness of rib on both side of curve. Select **One Side** option from **Thickness Direction** section to apply the thickness of rib in one direction or one side.
- Specify desired value of thickness in **Thickness** edit box or floating window.
- Select the **To Next** option from **Extent Type** drop-down from **RIB** dialog box to create the rib up to next surface or model; refer to Figure-22.

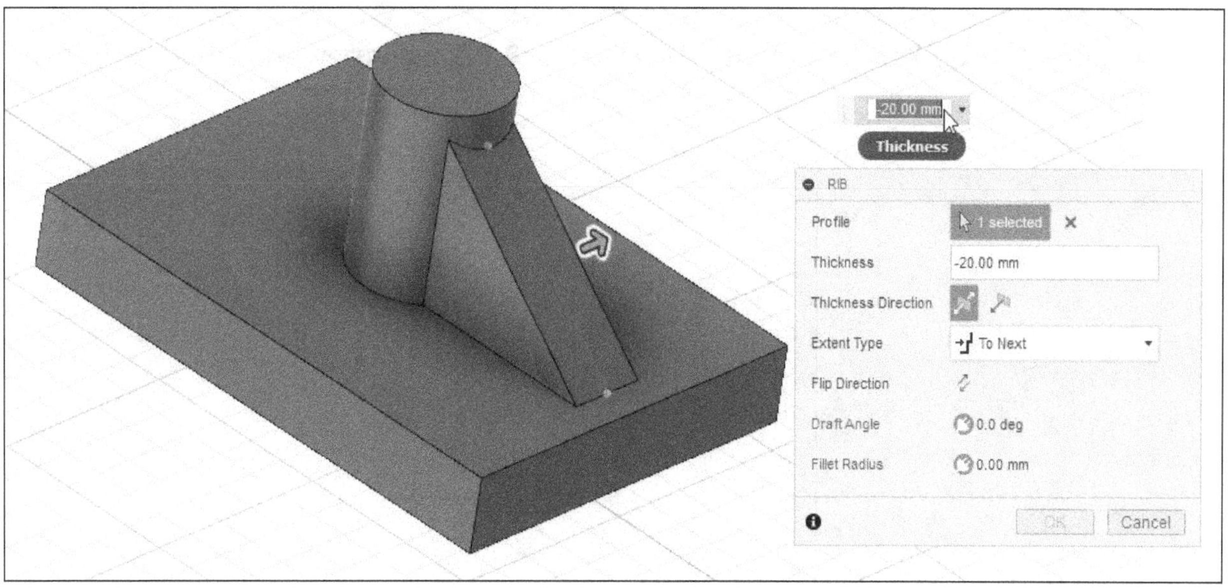

Figure-22. To Next tool in Rib

- Select the **Distance** option from **Extent Type** drop-down to specify the depth of rib. Type the numerical value of depth in **Depth** edit box or adjust the depth by moving the **Drag arrow**.
- You can also enter the value of depth in minus(-) to reverse the direction of depth in **Depth** edit box; refer to Figure-23.

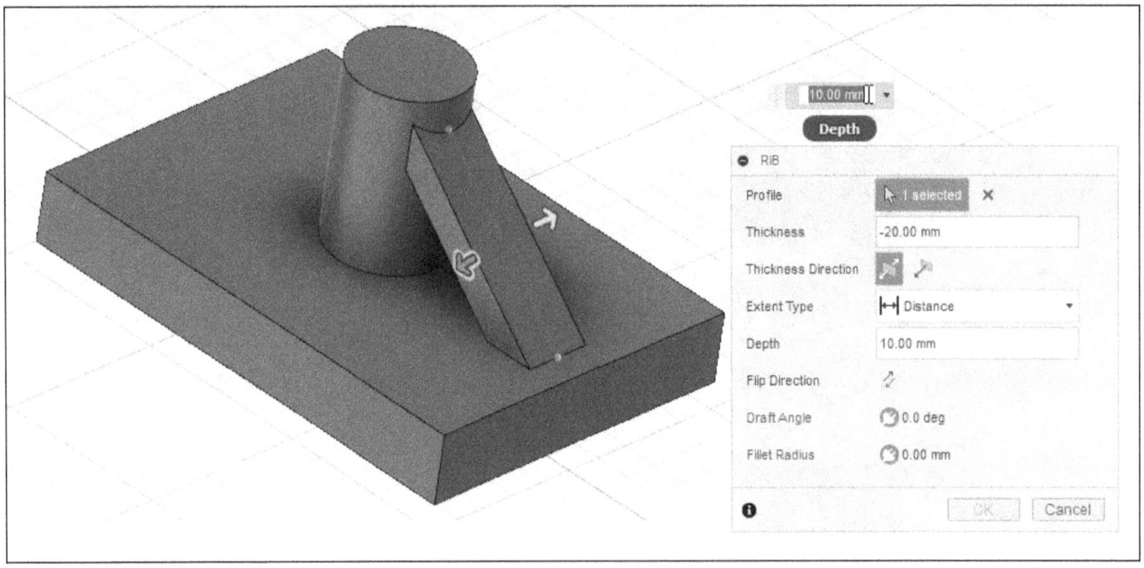

Figure-23. Depth option in Rib

- Click on the **Flip Direction** button to flip the direction of rib.
- After specifying the parameters, click **OK** button of **RIB** dialog box to complete the process.

The **Draft Angle** and **Fillet Radius** section is inactive at this moment. It is a part of the **Design Extension** which is free in student version of this software and the procedure to activate these sections has been discussed earlier in **Chapter 1**.

- Now, click on the **Rib** tool again. The new **RIB** dialog box will be displayed; refer to Figure-24.

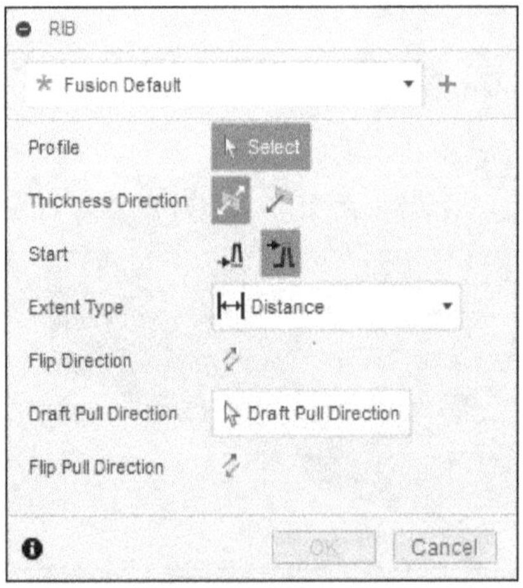

Figure-24. New RIB dialog box

- Select desired preset from **Presets** drop-down to apply or save the current values of the dialog box or create new preset by clicking on the + **New Preset** button.
- Select the sketch curve as profile to create rib. The updated **RIB** dialog box will be displayed; refer to Figure-25.

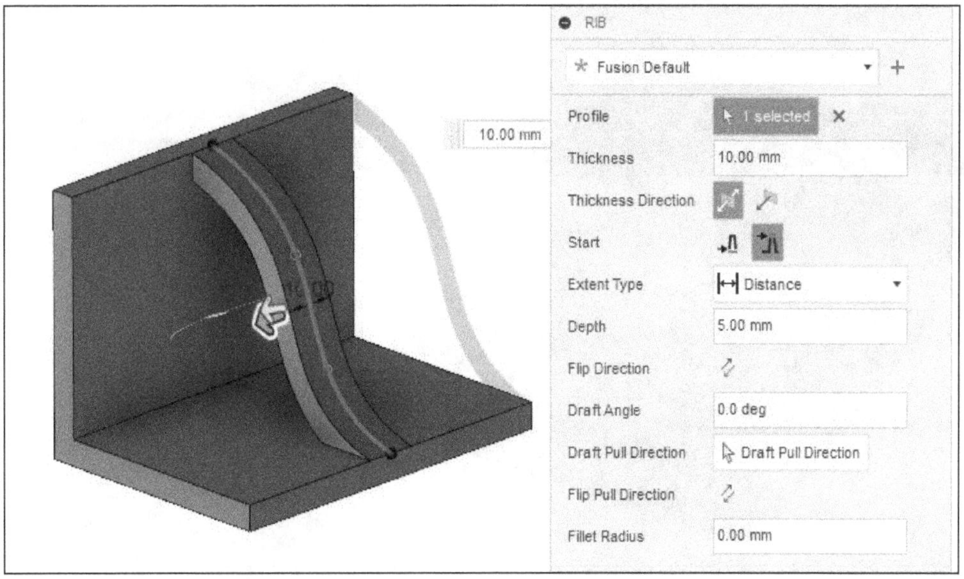

Figure-25. Updated RIB dialog box

- Select **From Bottom** button from **Start** section to measure the thickness starting from the bottom and select **From Top** button to measure the thickness starting from the top.
- Specify desired draft angle and fillet radius value in the **Draft Angle** and **Fillet Radius** edit boxes, respectively.
- Click on the **Draft Pull Direction** button of **Draft Pull Direction** section and select desired plane or face to define the pull direction.
- Select the **Flip Pull Direction** button to flip the pull direction for draft.
- Click on the **OK** button to create the rib feature.

WEB

The **Web** tool works like **Rib** tool which is used to create geometry from sketch curves that intersect with pre-existing bodies. The **Web** tool uses multiple curves to create several merged ribs at once. The procedure to use this tool is discussed next.

- Click on **Web** tool from **CREATE** drop-down of **SOLID** tab in the **Toolbar**; refer to Figure-26. The **WEB** dialog box will be displayed; refer to Figure-27.

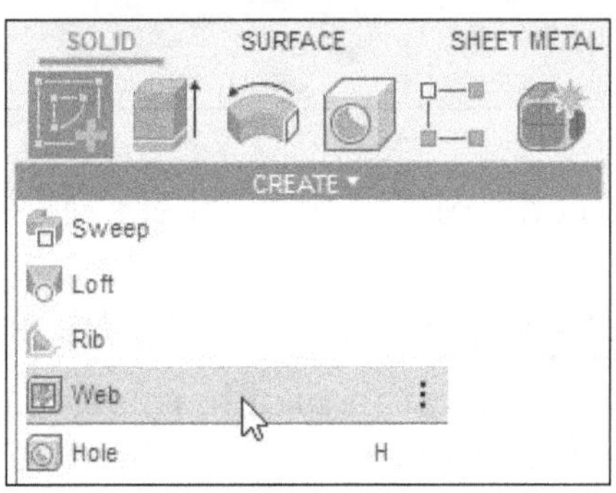

Figure-26. Web tool

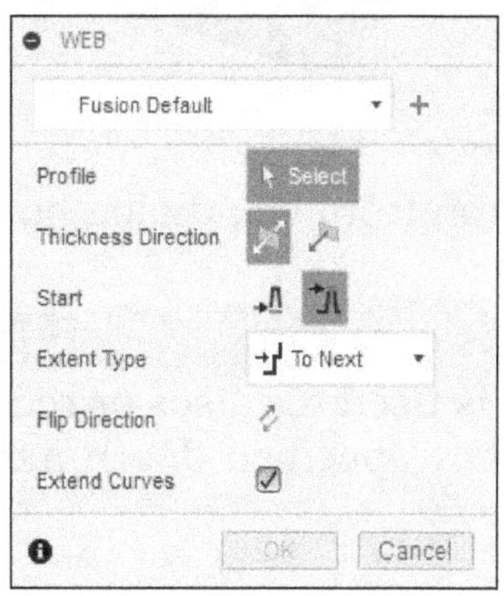

Figure-27. WEB dialog box

- The **Profile** selection is active by default. Select the sketch to create web; refer to Figure-28.

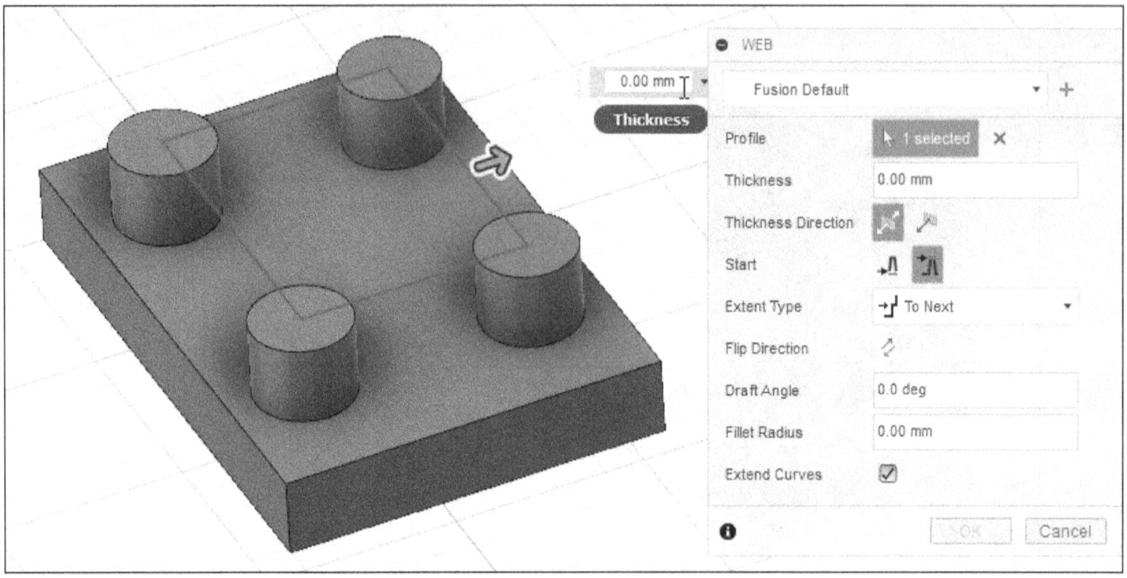

Figure-28. Selecting the sketch

- Enter desired value of thickness in the **Thickness** edit box or floating window. You can also set the thickness by moving the drag handle.
- The other options in the dialog box are same as discussed earlier. Preview of rib will be displayed according to parameters specified; refer to Figure-29.

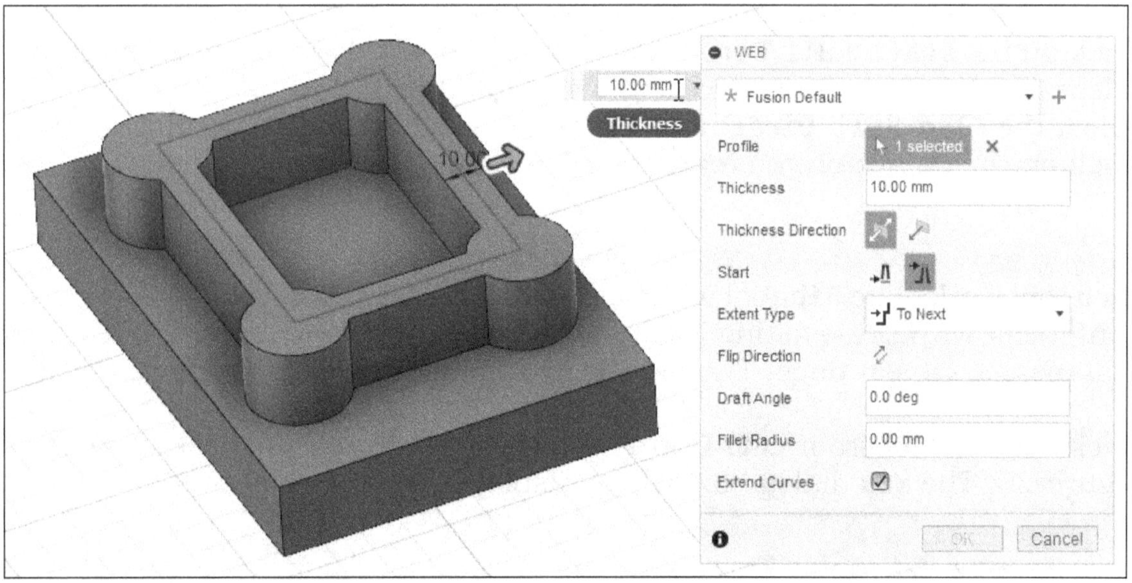

Figure-29. Preview of web

- Click **OK** button from **WEB** dialog box to complete the process.

EMBOSS

The **Emboss** tool is used to raises or recesses a sketch profile relative to selected faces on a solid body by specified depth and direction. The procedure to use this tool is discussed next.

- Click on the **Emboss** tool from **CREATE** drop-down of **SOLID** tab in the **Toolbar**; refer to Figure-30. The **EMBOSS** dialog box will be displayed; refer to Figure-31.

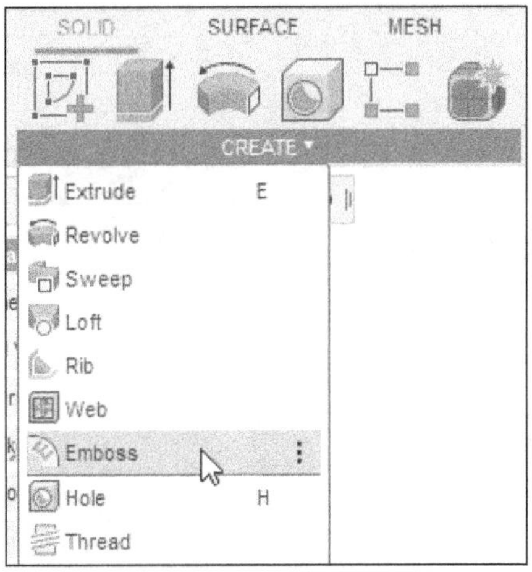

Figure-30. Emboss tool

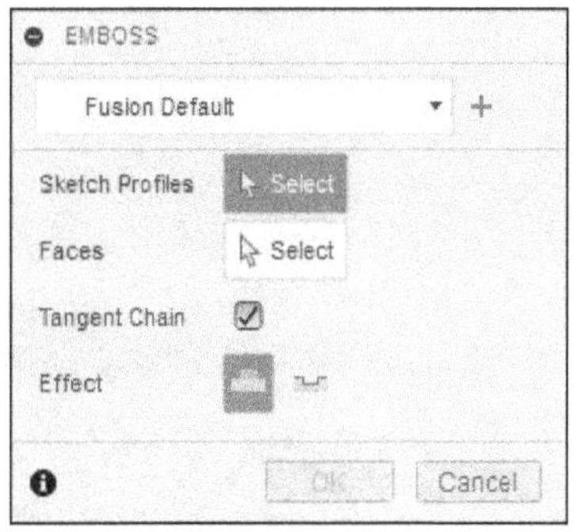

Figure-31. EMBOSS dialog box

- The **Select** button of **Sketch Profiles** section is active by default. Select the sketch profile which you want to emboss on a solid body; refer to Figure-32.

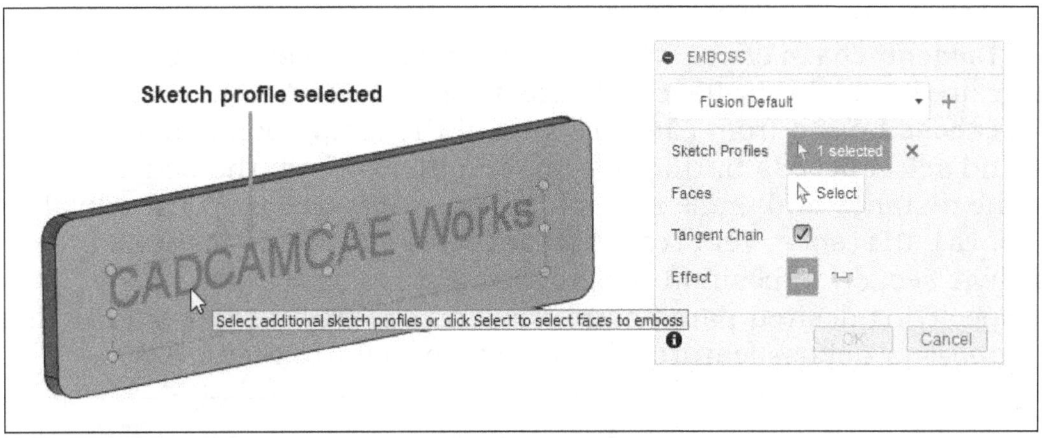

Figure-32. Sketch profile selected

- Click on the **Select** button of **Faces** section and select the face on a solid body on which the sketch profile is to be embossed; refer to Figure-33. The updated **EMBOSS** dialog box along with the preview of emboss will be displayed; refer to Figure-34.

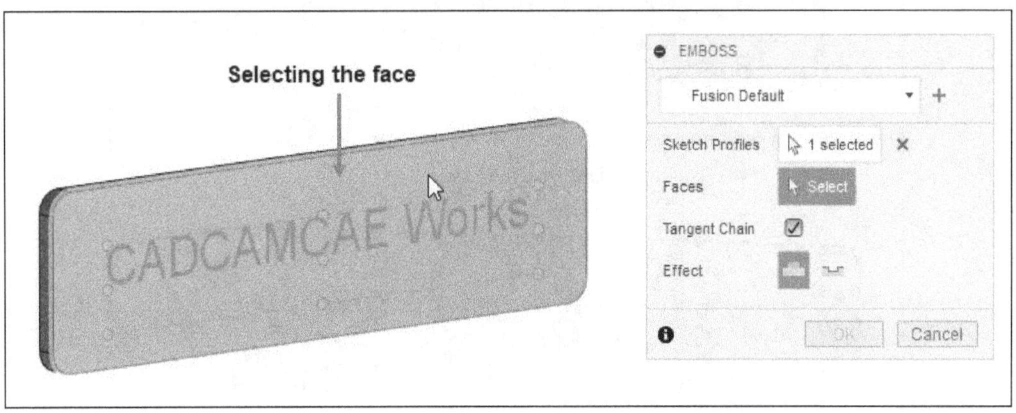

Figure-33. Selecting the face

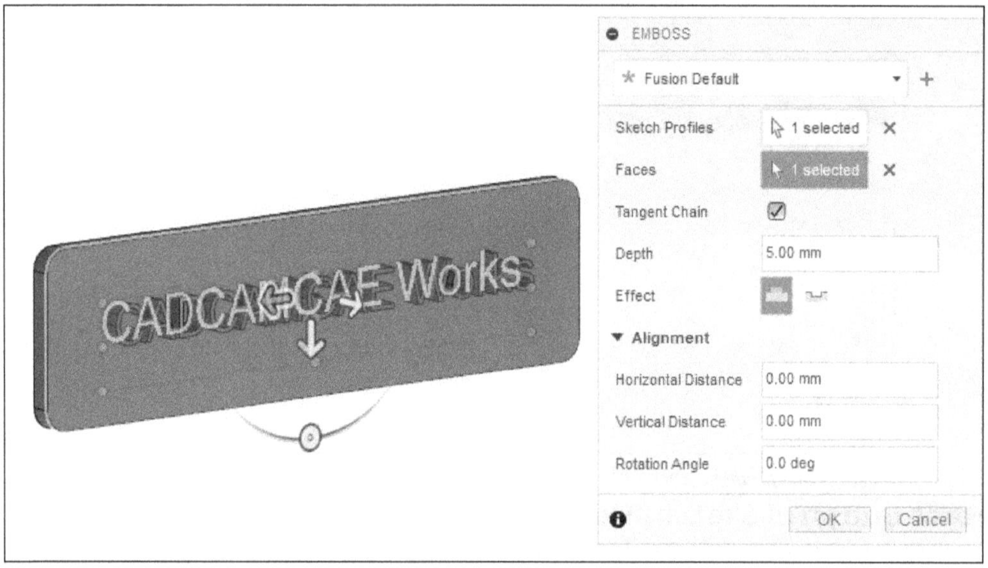

Figure-34. Updated EMBOSS dialog box

- Select **Tangent Chain** check box to automatically select tangent geometry.
- Type desired value in the **Depth** edit box to specify the depth to emboss or deboss.
- Select **Emboss** button from **Effect** section of the dialog box to add material to the body and select **Deboss** button to remove material from the body.
- Drag the distance and angle manipulator handles or enter desired values in the **Horizontal Distance**, **Vertical Distance**, and **Rotation Angle** edit boxes from **Alignment** section to position the emboss feature on the solid body.
- After specifying desired parameters, click on the **OK** button from the dialog box. The emboss or deboss feature will be created; refer to Figure-35.

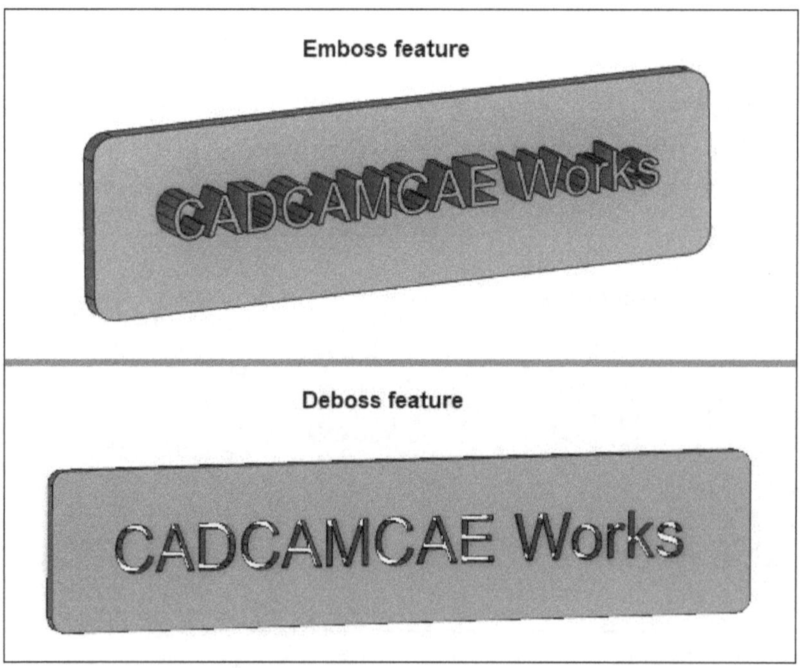

Figure-35. Emboss and Deboss feature created

HOLE

The **Hole** tool is used to create holes that comply with real machining tools. With the help of **Hole** tool, three types of holes are created. The procedure to use this tool is discussed next.

- Click on **Hole** tool from **CREATE** drop-down or right-click on the screen canvas and select **Hole** from **Marking menu** displayed; refer to Figure-36. The **HOLE** dialog box will be displayed; refer to Figure-37.

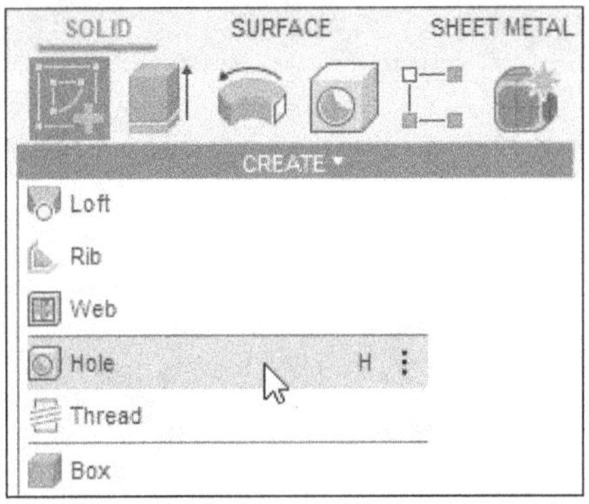

Figure-36. Hole tool

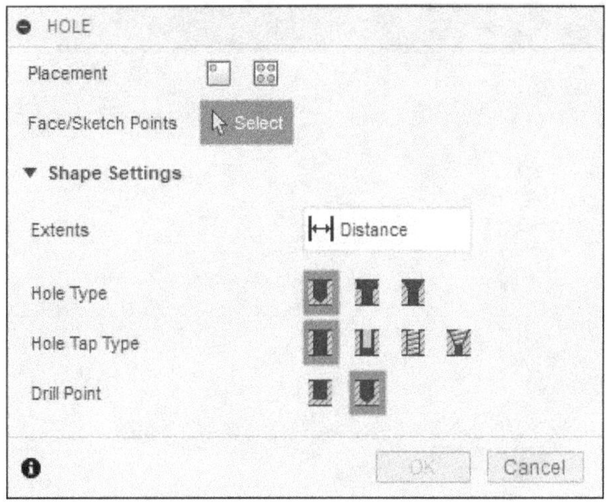

Figure-37. HOLE dialog box

There are two types of tools in **Placement** section which are discussed next.

Single Hole

- Click on **Single Hole** button from **Placement** section to create one hole. The **Select** button for **Face** section will be activated.
- Select the face/plane on which you want to create hole. The updated **HOLE** dialog box will be displayed with preview of hole; refer to Figure-38.

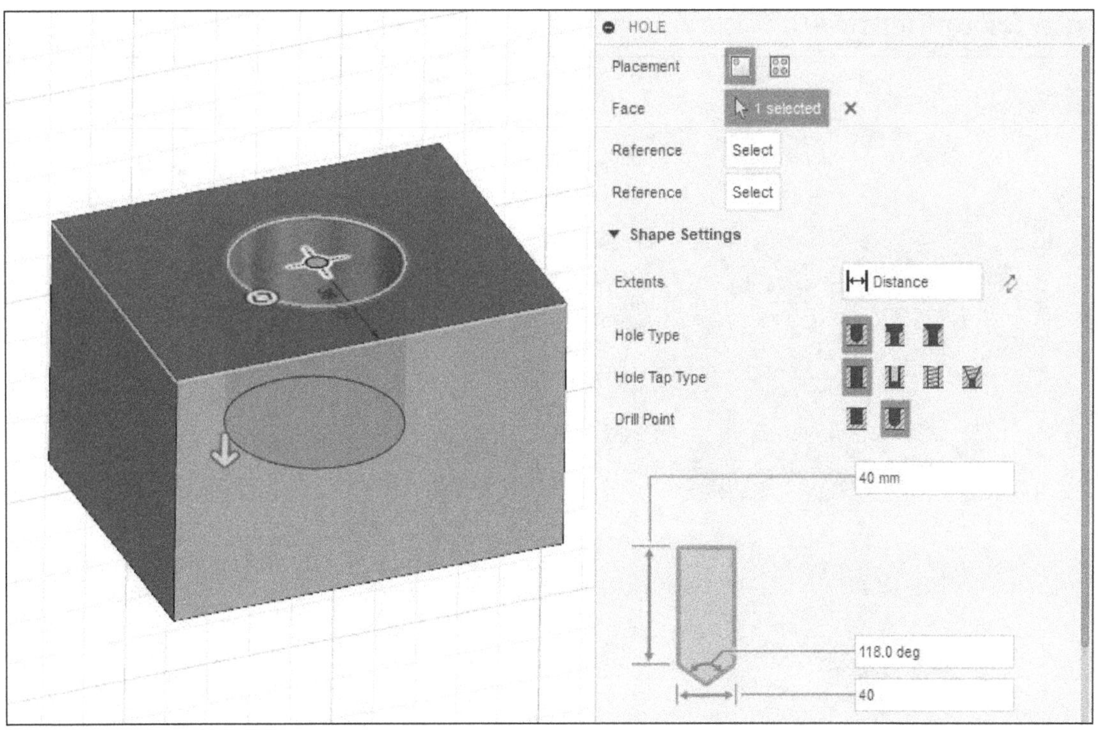

Figure-38. Updated HOLE dialog box

- Click on **Select** button of first **Reference** section from **HOLE** dialog box, click at the center of hole and then click at the edge from where you want to specify the distance of hole; refer to Figure-39.

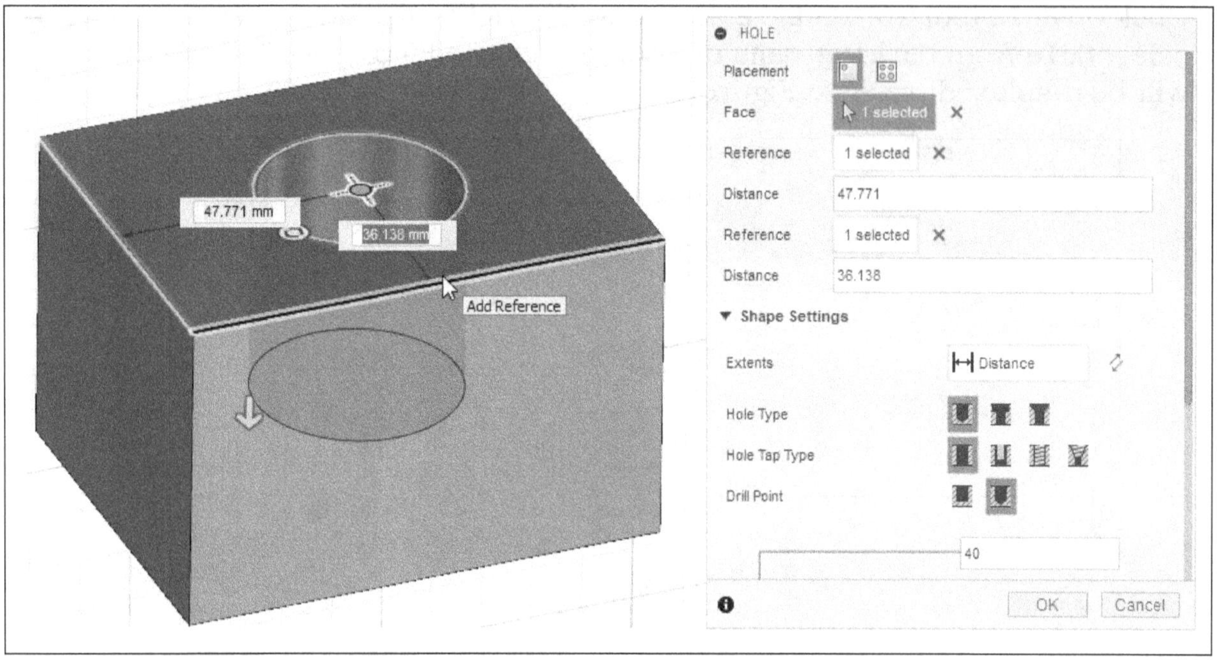

Figure-39. Adding references

- Enter desired value of distance in the dynamic input box or **Distance** edit box in dialog box. Click on another edge to define other reference and set desired distance value.
- Click on **Simple** button in **Hole Type** section to create simple hole of specified dimensions.
- Click on **Counterbore** button in **Hole Type** section to create a counterbore hole and specify the dimension in their respective edit boxes at the bottom in the dialog box; refer to Figure-40.

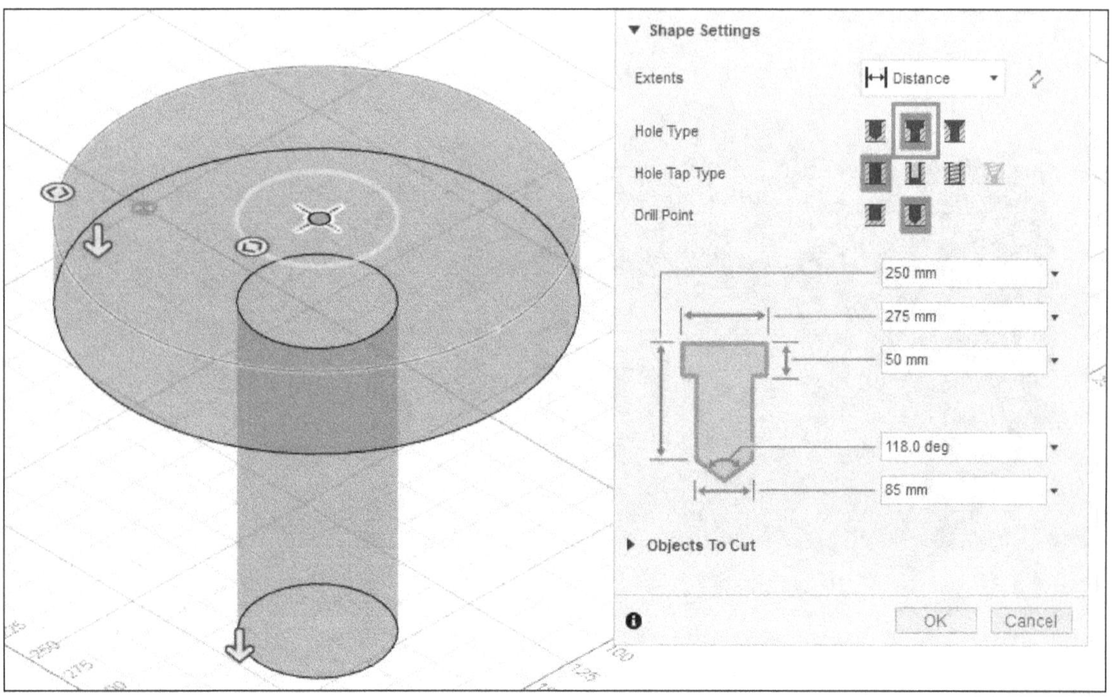

Figure-40. Counterbore hole

- Click on **Countersink** button in **Hole Type** drop-down to create a countersink hole and specify the dimension in their respective edit box at the bottom in the dialog box; refer to Figure-41.

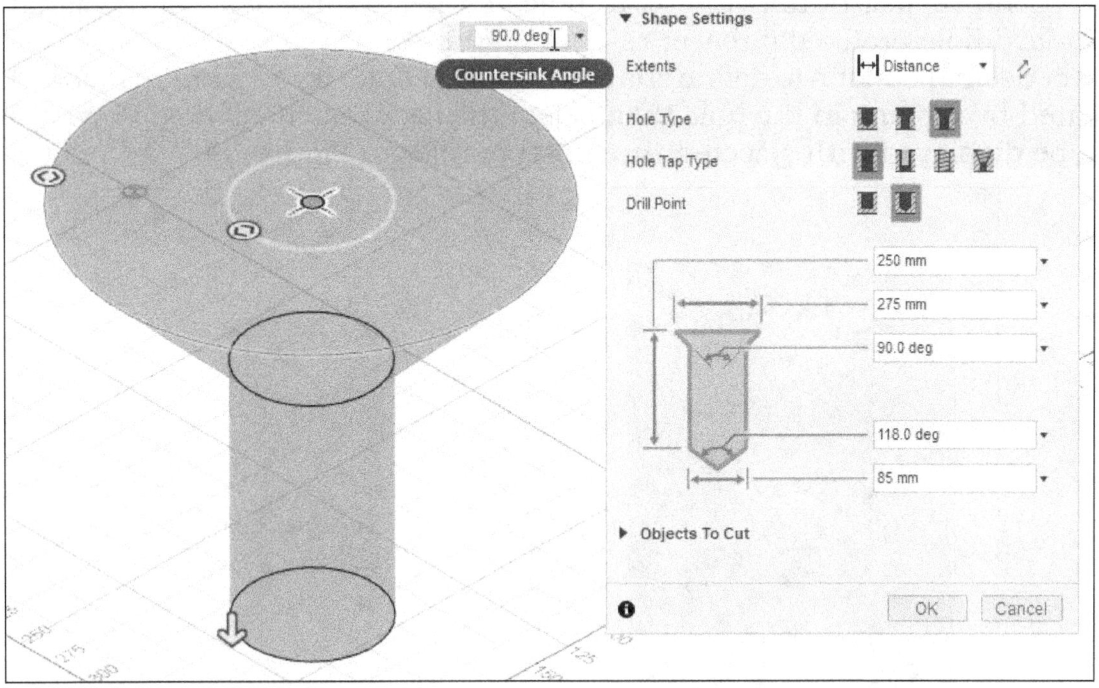

Figure-41. Countersink hole

- Click on desired button in the **Hole Tap Type** section to define tapping inside the hole. Select the **Simple** button to create straight holes without tapping.
- Select the **Clearance** button to create standard holes with defined fit. The options will be displayed accordingly; refer to Figure-42. Select desired options to define size of hole.

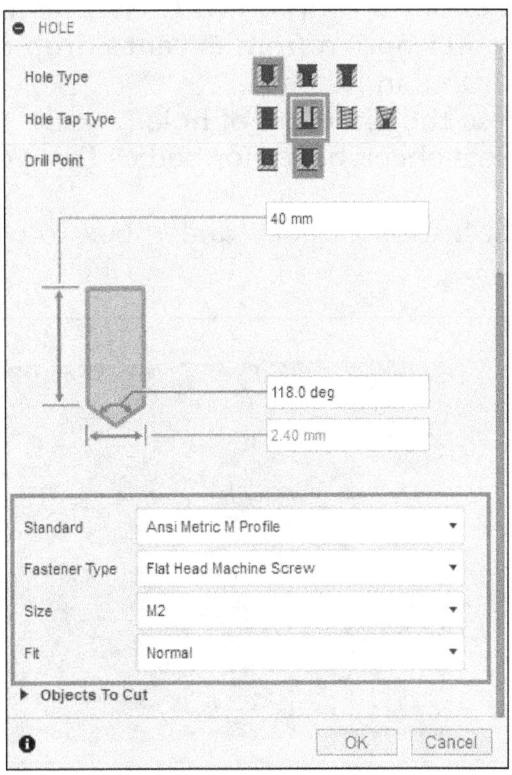

Figure-42. Options for clearance hole tap type

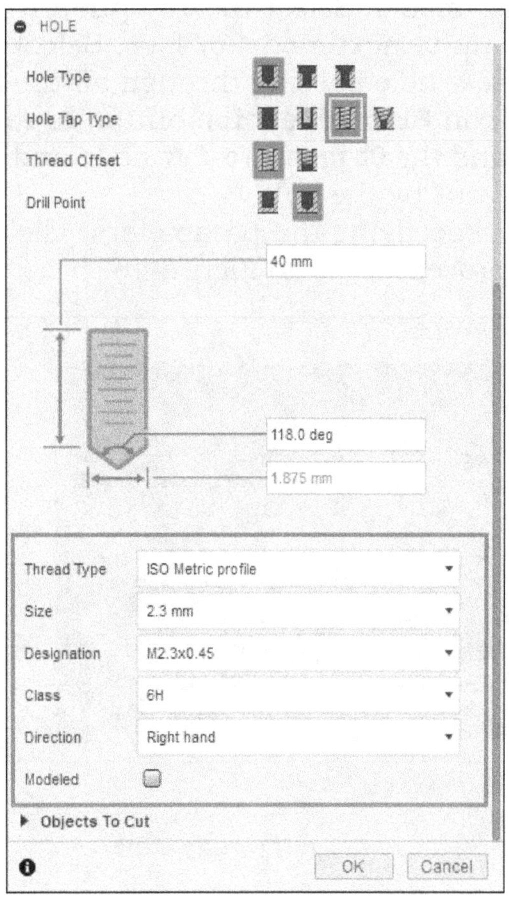

Figure-43. Options for tapped hole tap type

- Select the **Tapped** button to create holes as per their class and designation in standard hole profile database; refer to Figure-43.
- Select desired options to define shape and size of hole. If you want to model threads created by tapping in the hole then select the **Modeled** check box. Preview of hole will be displayed with selected thread type; refer to Figure-44.

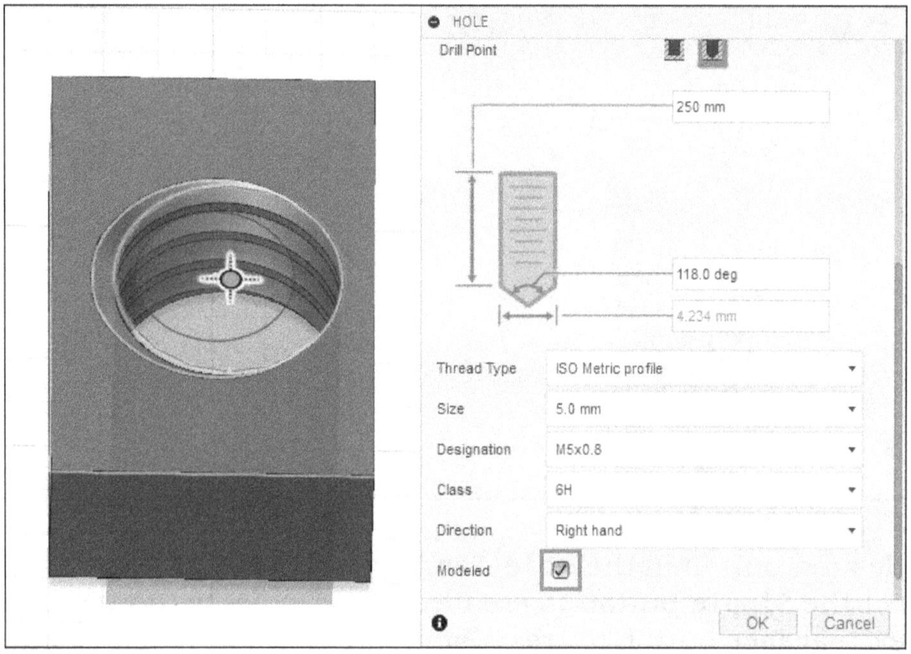

Figure-44. Preview of threads modeled in hole

- Select the **Distance** option from **Extents** drop-down to specify the distance of hole in the model. Select the **To** option from **Extents** drop-down to set the length of hole up to next model or face. Select the **All** option from **Extents** drop-down to create a hole passing through all the features in its path.
- Click on **Flip Direction** button to reverse the direction of hole.
- Expand the **Objects To Cut** node and select check boxes for bodies that you want to be cut by the hole.
- After specifying the parameters, click **OK** button of **HOLE** dialog box to complete the process; refer to Figure-45.

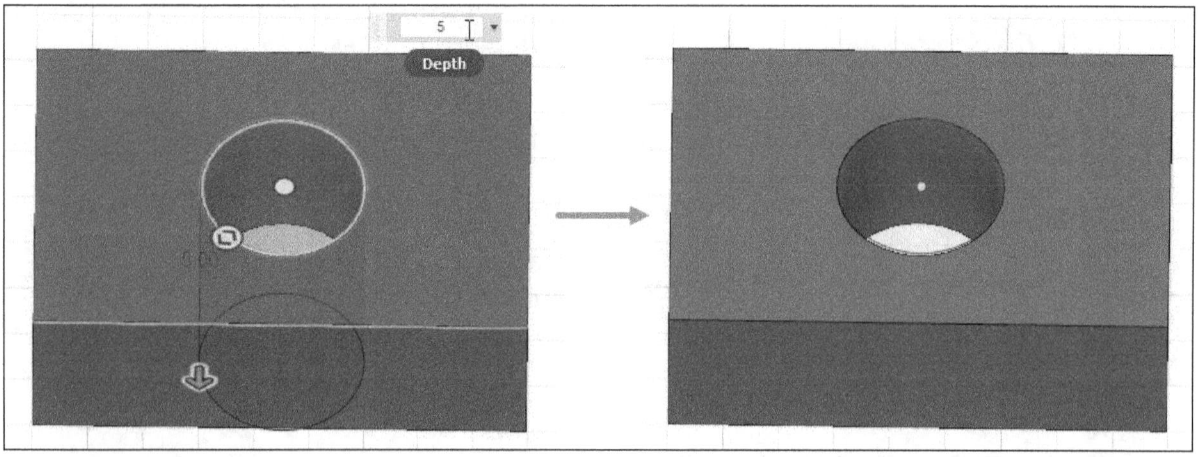

Figure-45. Preview of hole

Multiple Holes

The **Multiple Holes** button in **HOLE** dialog box is used to create multiple similar hole at a time. To use this tool, you must have sketch points already created on the model where you want to cut holes. The procedure to use this tool is discussed next.

- Click on the **Multiple Holes** button in **Placement** section from **HOLE** dialog box. The **Sketch Point** selection tool will be activated. Select the sketch points for defining positions of holes; refer to Figure-46.

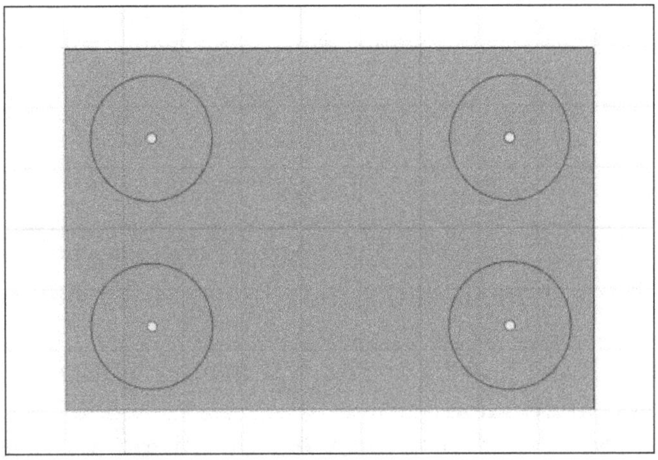

Figure-46. Sketch for multiple holes

- Set the other options as discussed earlier.
- After specifying the parameters, click **OK** button from **HOLE** dialog box to finish the process. The holes will be created; refer to Figure-47.

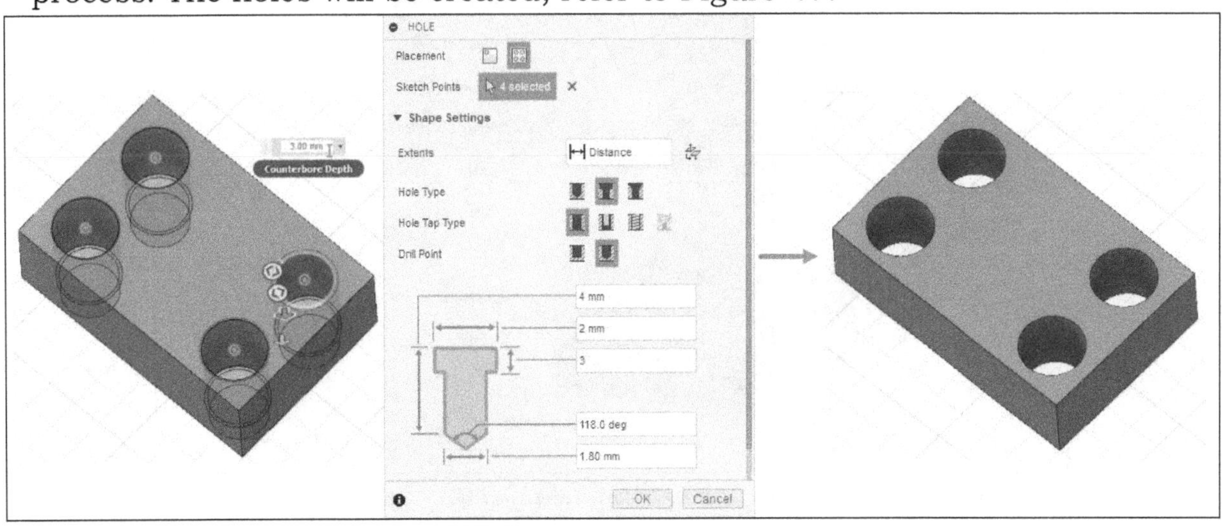

Figure-47. Preview of multiple holes

THREAD

The **Thread** tool is used to cut helical thread on cylindrical faces. Using this tool, you can save the custom threads in library. The procedure to use this tool is discussed next.

- Click on the **Thread** tool from the **CREATE** drop-down in the **Toolbar**; refer to Figure-48. The **THREAD** dialog box will be displayed; refer to Figure-49.

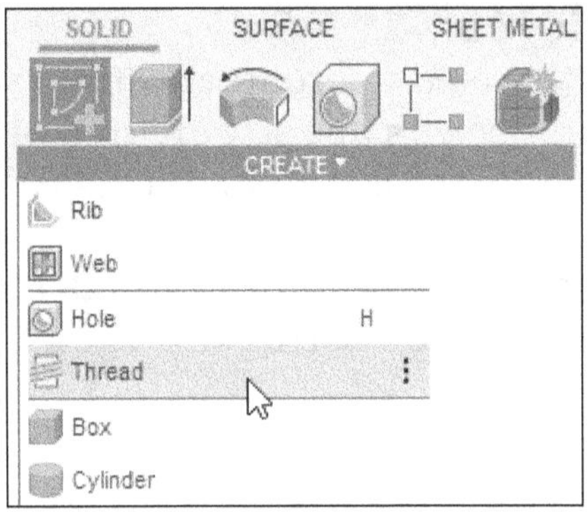

Figure-48. Thread tool

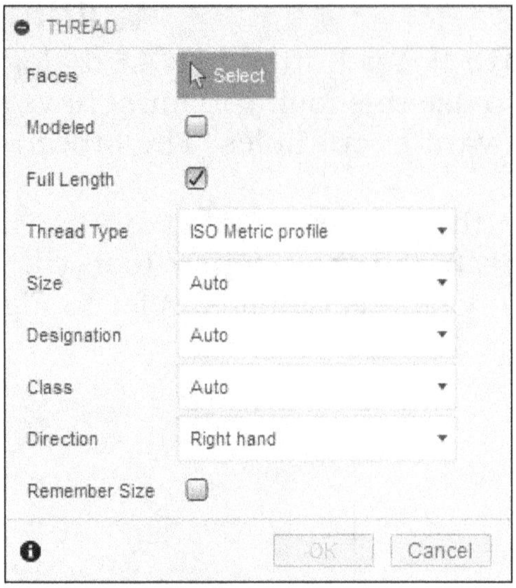

Figure-49. THREAD dialog box

- The **Faces** selection of **THREAD** dialog box is active by default. Select the round faces to which threads are to be applied.
- Select the **Modeled** check box to create the model feature of thread otherwise it will be created as cosmetic feature.
- On selecting **Modeled** check box, preview of thread will be displayed; refer to Figure-50.

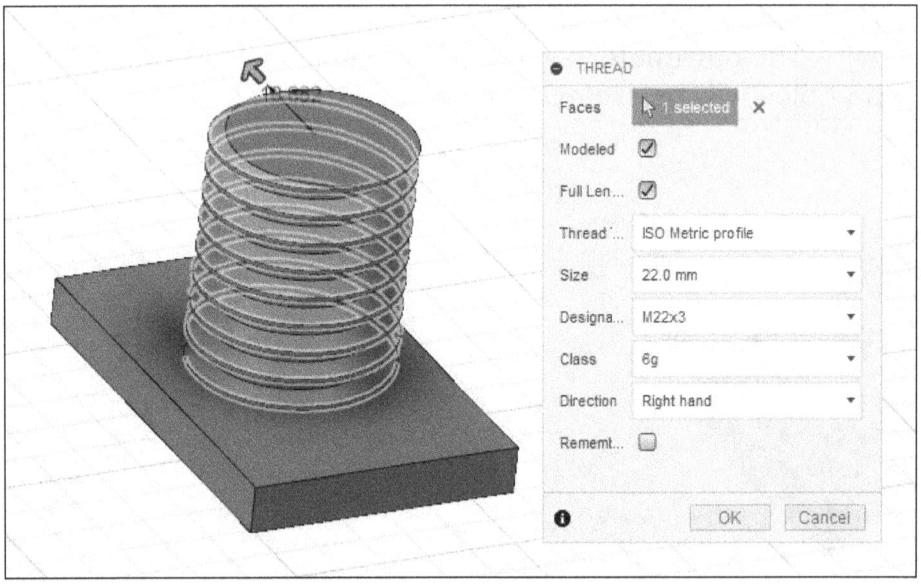

Figure-50. Preview of thread on selecting Modeled check box

- Clear the **Full Length** check box to specify the length of thread on the selected face. Otherwise, thread will be created up to the entire length of selected face.
- Click on the **Thread Type** drop-down to select the type of thread profile; refer to Figure-51. Most of the engineering thread profiles are available in this drop-down.

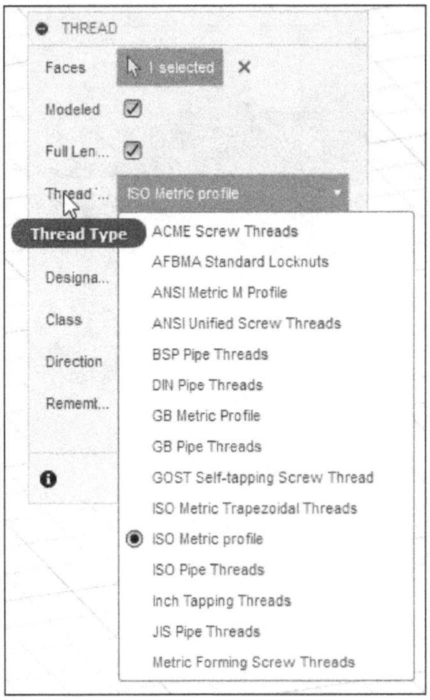

Figure-51. Thread Type drop down

- Click on the **Size** drop-down and select desired size of thread. You can also adjust the size by using the **Drag Handle**.
- Click on the **Designation** drop-down and select the designation of thread; refer to Figure-52.
- Click on the **Class** drop-down and select the class of thread.
- Click on **Direction** drop-down and select the direction for thread; refer to Figure-53.

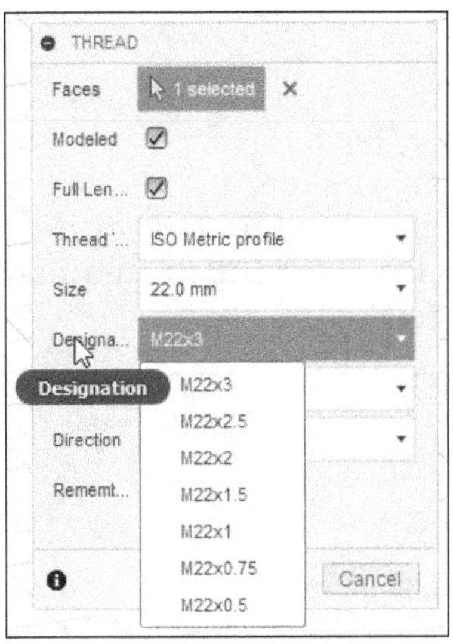

Figure-52. Thread Designation drop down

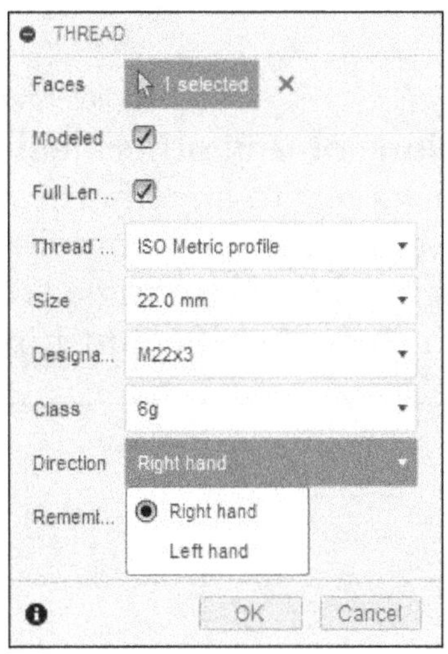

Figure-53. Thread Direction drop down

- Select the **Remember Size** check box to remember these thread setting for the next time, when the **Thread** tool will be invoked.
- Click **OK** button from **THREAD** dialog box to create the thread; refer to Figure-54.

Figure-54. Thread created in solid

BOX

The **Box** tool is used to create a rectangular box on selected work plane. The procedure to use this tool is discussed next.

- Click on **Box** tool from **CREATE** drop-down in the **Toolbar**; refer to Figure-55. You will be asked to select the plane for creating the sketch for box.

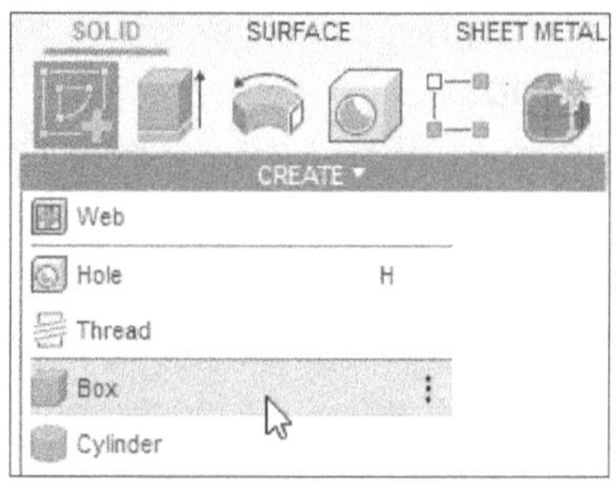

Figure-55. Box tool

- Select **Top** plane or any other desired plane/face.
- Click on the screen to specify the first point of sketch.
- Move the cursor to display preview of rectangle and click at desired location to specify other corner of rectangle. You can also enter the numerical value of **Length** and **Width** in their specific edit box; refer to Figure-56.

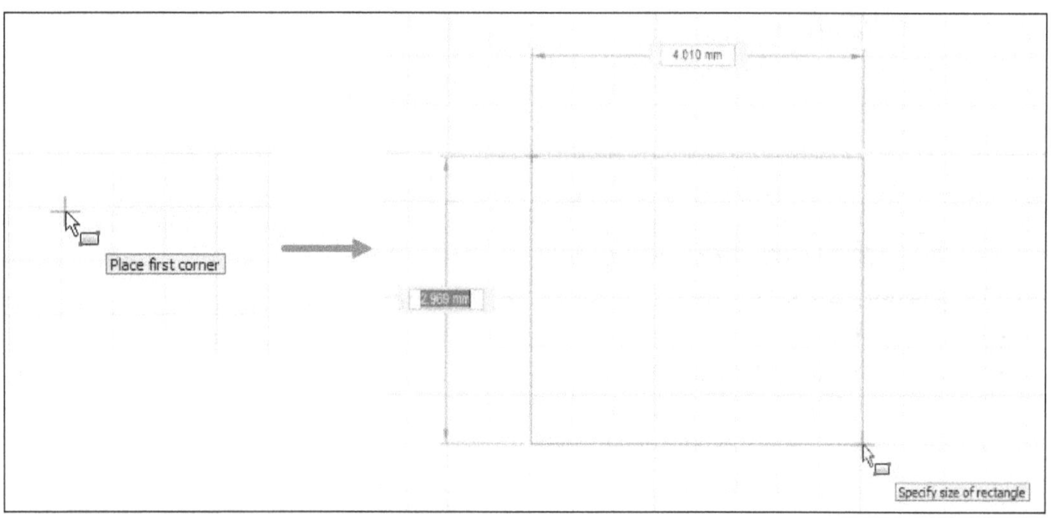

Figure-56. Entering dimension for rectangle

- You can toggle between these two edit boxes by pressing **TAB** key. The **Box** dialog box will be displayed along with the preview of box; refer to Figure-57.

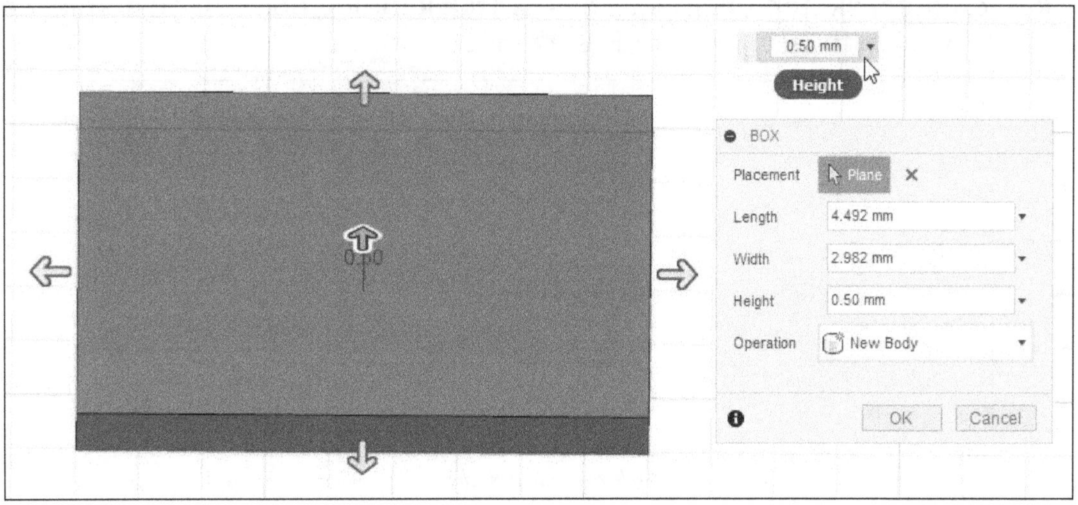

Figure-57. Preview of box with BOX dialog box

- Specify desired value of height in the **Height** edit box of the **BOX** dialog box.
- The options of **Operation** section were discussed earlier.
- Click **OK** button from the **BOX** dialog box to create the box; refer to Figure-58.

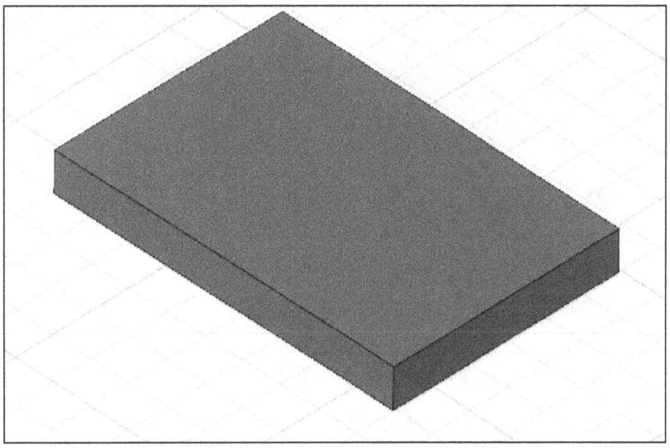

Figure-58. Box created

CYLINDER

This tool is used to create a cylindrical body by adding depth to a circular region. The procedure to use this tool is discussed next.

- Click on **Cylinder** tool from **CREATE** drop-down in the **Toolbar**; refer to Figure-59. You are asked to select plane for creating base sketch. Select desired plane/face.

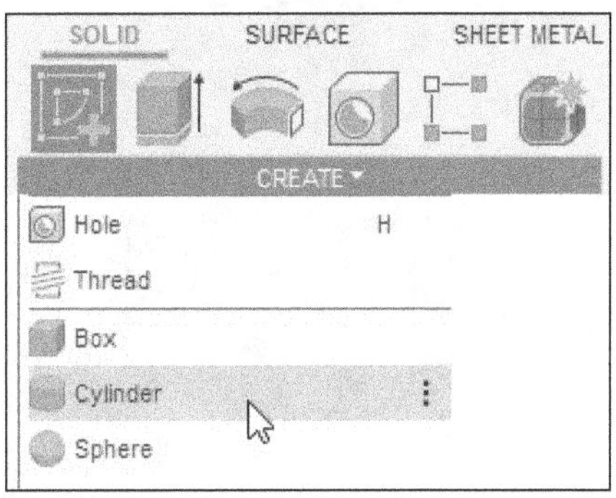

Figure-59. Cylinder tool

- Click on the screen to specify the center point of base circle.
- Type desired value of diameter in the floating window; refer to Figure-60 and press **ENTER** to create a sketch of circle. The **CYLINDER** dialog box will be displayed along with preview of cylinder; refer to Figure-61.

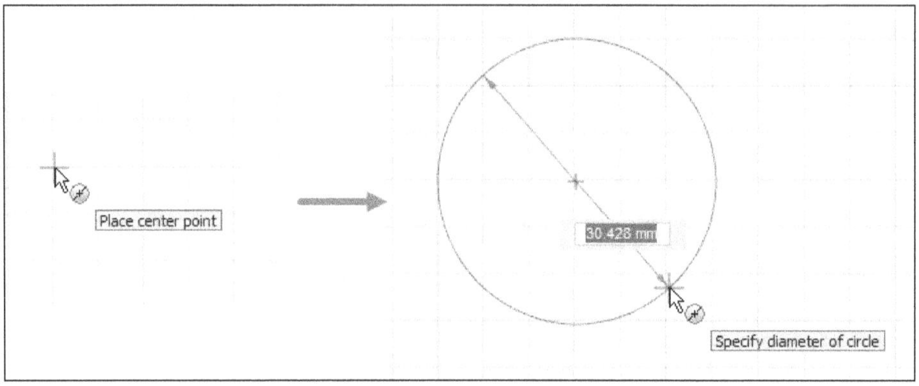

Figure-60. Specifying diameter of circle to create cylinder

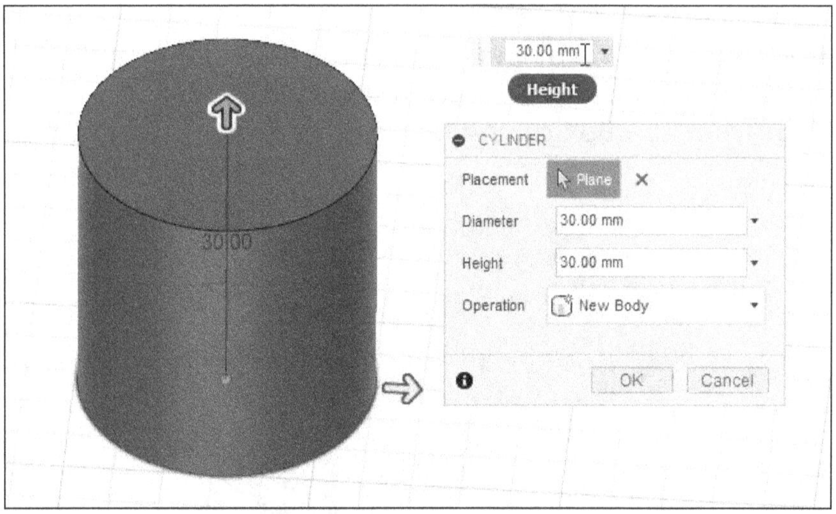

Figure-61. Preview of cylinder with CYLINDER dialog box

- If you want to edit the diameter of cylinder then click in the **Diameter** edit box of **CYLINDER** dialog box and specify desired value.
- Click in the **Height** edit box and specify the height of cylinder.
- Click **OK** button from the **CYLINDER** dialog box to create the cylinder; refer to Figure-62.

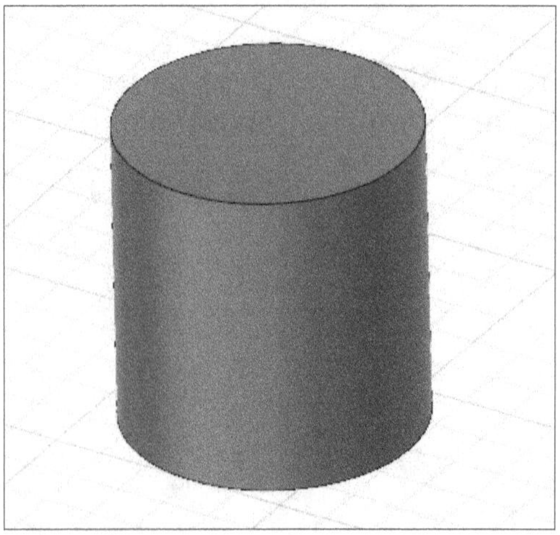

Figure-62. Cylinder created

SPHERE

The **Sphere** tool is used to create a T-spline, solid, or surface sphere on a work plane or face. The procedure to use this tool is discussed next.

- Click on the **Sphere** tool from **CREATE** drop-down in the **Toolbar**; refer to Figure-63. You are asked to select the plane for creating the sketch for circle. Select desired plane/face.

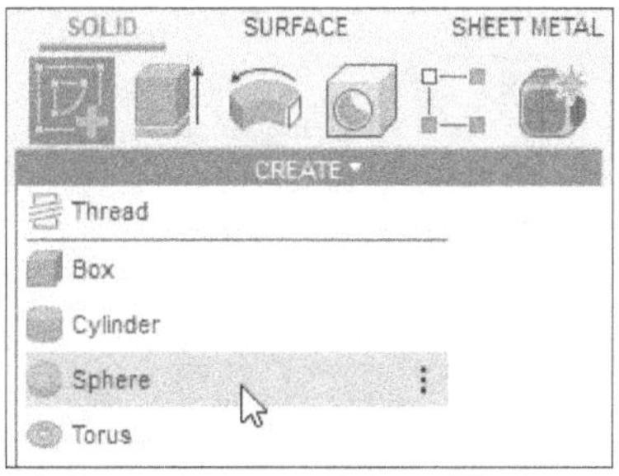

Figure-63. Sphere tool

- Click on the screen at desired location to specify the center point of sphere. The **SPHERE** dialog box will be displayed along with the preview of sphere; refer to Figure-64.

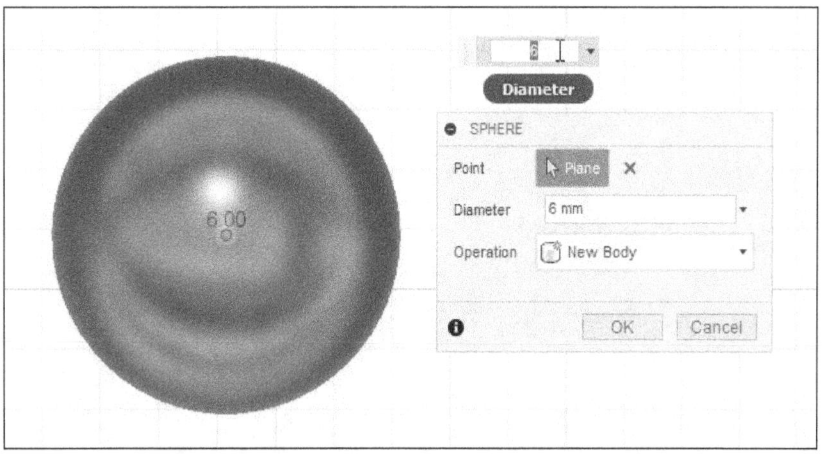

Figure-64. Preview of sphere with SPHERE dialog box

- Click in the **Diameter** edit box and specify desired value of diameter for sphere.
- The options of **Operation** drop-down are same as discussed earlier.
- Click **OK** button of **SPHERE** dialog box to finish the process; refer to Figure-65.

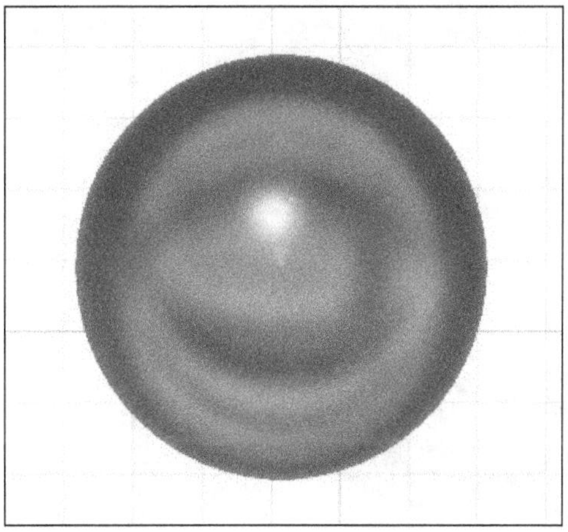

Figure-65. Sphere created

TORUS

The **Torus** tool is used to create T-spline, solid, or surface torus on a work plane or face. The procedure to use this tool is discussed next.

- Click on the **Torus** tool from **CREATE** drop-down in the **Toolbar**; refer to Figure-66. You are asked to select the plane/face for creating the center circle of torus. Select desired face/plane.

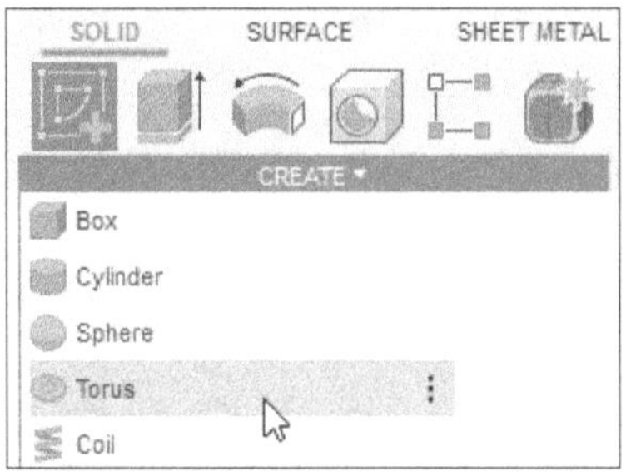

Figure-66. Torus tool

- Click on the screen to specify center point of sketch. Specify the diameter of torus in dynamic input box and press **ENTER**; refer to Figure-67. The **TORUS** dialog box will be displayed along with the preview of torus; refer to Figure-68.

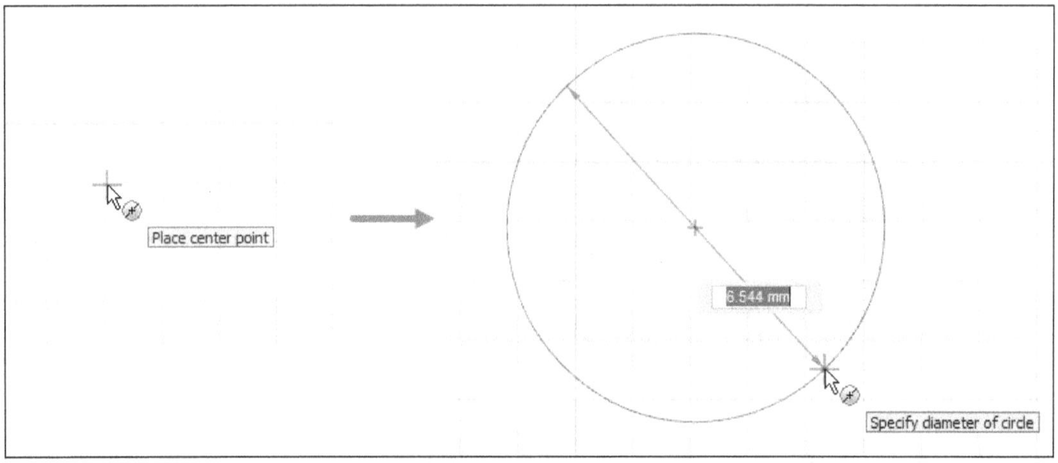

Figure-67. Specifying diameter of circle to create torus

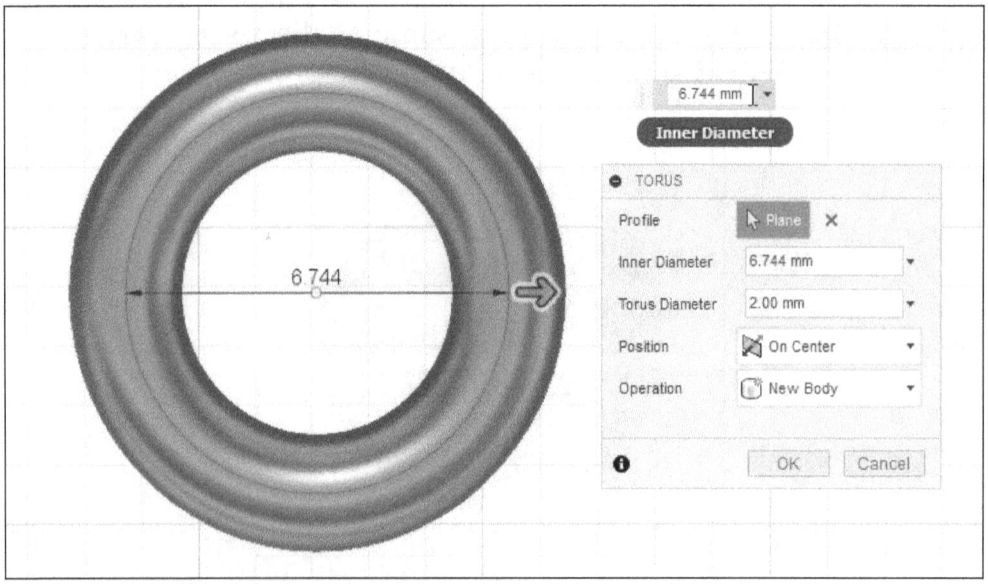

Figure-68. Preview of torus with TORUS dialog box

- If you want to edit the diameter of circle earlier created then click in the **Inner Diameter** edit box and specify desired value.
- Click in the **Torus Diameter** edit box and type the diameter of torus. You can also adjust the diameter of torus by moving the drag handle.
- Select the **On Center** option of **Position** drop-down from **TORUS** dialog box, if you want to use inner circle as center of the torus. Select the **Inside** option of **Position** drop-down if you want to position the torus inside of the inner circle. Select the **Outside** option of **Position** drop-down if you want to position the torus section outside of the inner circle.
- The options of **Operation** drop-down are same as discussed earlier.
- Click **OK** button of **TORUS** dialog box to finish the process; refer to Figure-69.

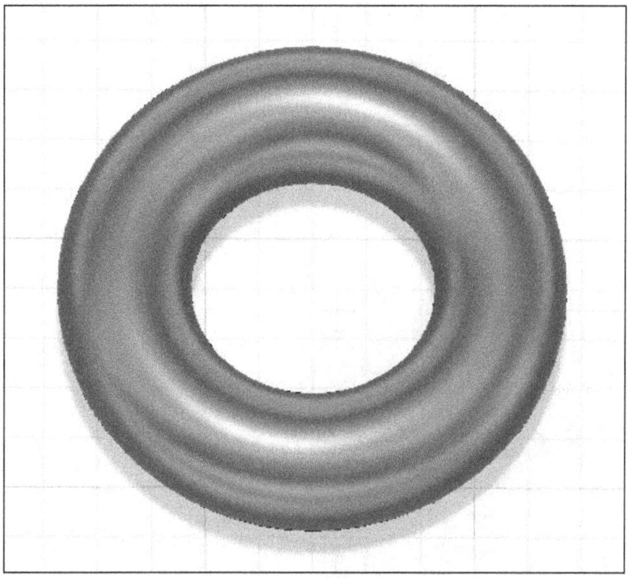

Figure-69. Torus created

COIL

The **Coil** tool is used for creating helix-based features like springs. The procedure to use this tool is discussed next.

- Click on the **Coil** tool from **CREATE** drop-down in the **Toolbar**; refer to Figure-70. You will be asked to select a face/plane to create base sketch.

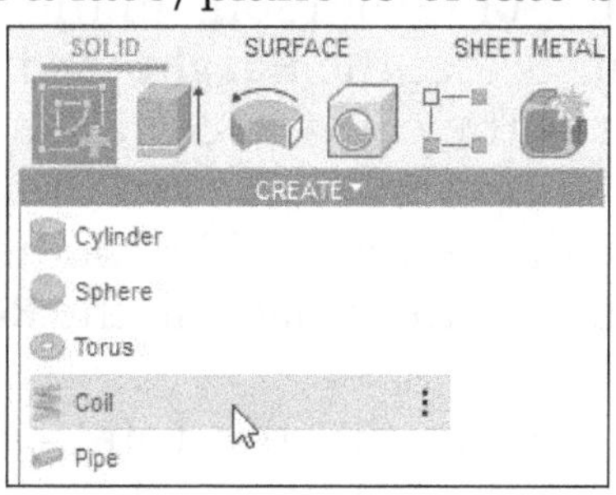

Figure-70. Coil tool

- Click on desired face/plane. You will be asked to specify center of the base circle.
- Click on the screen to specify the center point of sketch. Type desired value of diameter of coil in dynamic input box and press **ENTER**; refer to Figure-71.

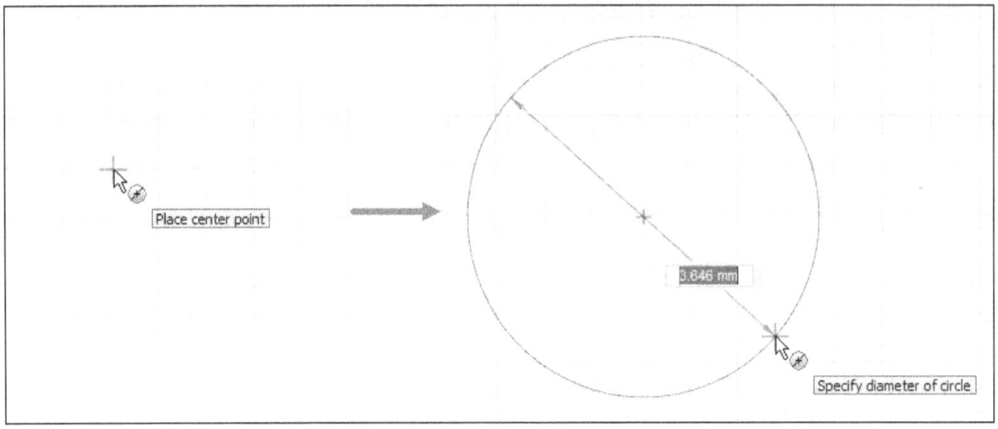

Figure-71. Specifying diameter of circle to create coil

- The **COIL** dialog box will be displayed along with the preview of coil; refer to Figure-72.

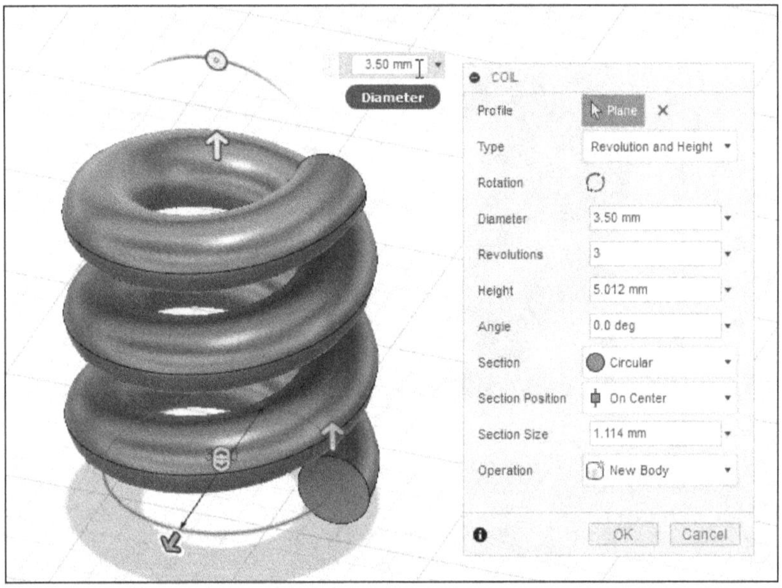

Figure-72. Preview of coil with COIL dialog box

- Select the **Revolution and Height** option from **Type** drop-down if you want to create the coil by specifying number of revolutions in the coil and height of coil. Select the **Revolution and Pitch** option from **Type** drop-down if you want to create the coil by specifying number of revolutions in the coil and distance between two successive turns of the coil. Select the **Height and Pitch** option from **Type** drop-down to specify total height of the coil and distance between two successive turns of the coil. Select the **Spiral** option from **Type** drop-down to create a spiral coil. Note that the options in the dialog box will be modified based on your selection in **Type** drop-down. In our case, we are selecting the **Revolution and Height** option; refer to Figure-73.
- Click on the **Rotation** button to flip the rotation side of coil to clockwise or counterclockwise direction; refer to Figure-74.

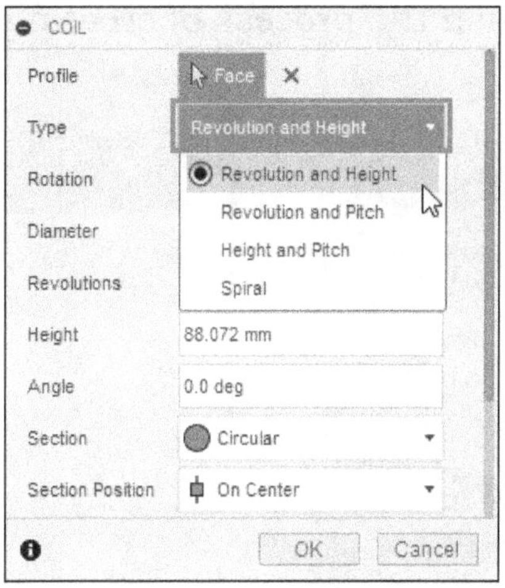

Figure-73. Coil Type drop down

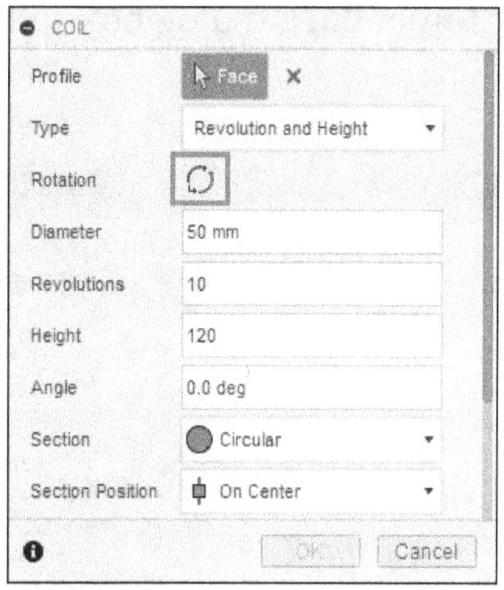

Figure-74. Rotation button

- Click in the **Diameter** edit box and enter desired value to change the diameter of coil.
- Click in the **Revolutions** edit box and enter desired value for number of revolutions of coil.
- Click in the **Height** edit box and specify the total height of coil. You can also set the height of coil by moving the drag handle.
- Click in the **Angle** edit box and specify desired angle value to create taper coil.
- Select **Circular** option from **Section** drop-down of **COIL** dialog box to set the circular profile of coil. Select the **Square** option from **Section** drop-down to set square profile of coil. Select **Triangular(External)** option from **Section** drop-down to set the external triangular profile of coil. Select **Triangular(Internal)** option of **Section** drop-down to set internal triangular profile of coil; refer to Figure-75.

Figure-75. Coil Section drop down

- Select **On Center** option of **Section Position** drop-down from **COIL** dialog box to position the coil in such a way that the base circle is at center of the coil. Click on the **Inside** button of **Section Position** drop-down if you want to position the coil inside the base circle. Click on the **Outside** section of **Section Position** drop-down if you want to position the coil outside the base circle.
- Click in the **Section Size** edit box and specify the size of coil section. If section is circle then this will be diameter and if section is triangle or square then it will be length of one edge of section.
- The options of **Operations** drop-down were discussed earlier.

- Click **OK** button of **COIL** dialog box to finish the process of creating a coil; refer to Figure-76.

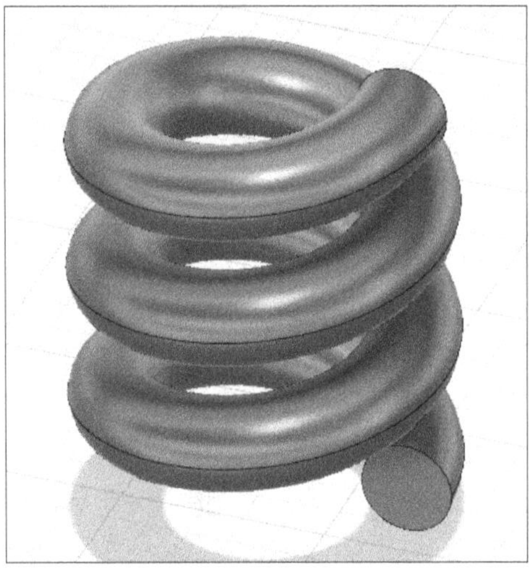

Figure-76. Coil created

PIPE

The **Pipe** tool is used to create pipes of different sections that follow a selected path. The procedure to use this tool is discussed next.

- Click on **Pipe** tool from **CREATE** drop-down in the **Toolbar**; refer to Figure-77. The **PIPE** dialog box will be displayed and you will be asked to select a path for pipe; refer to Figure-78.

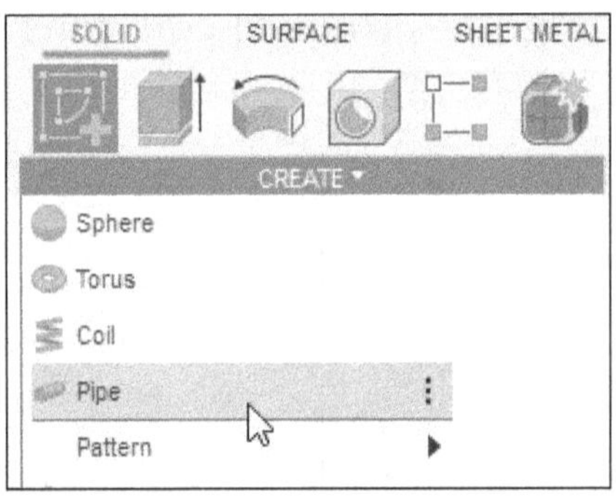

Figure-77. Pipe tool

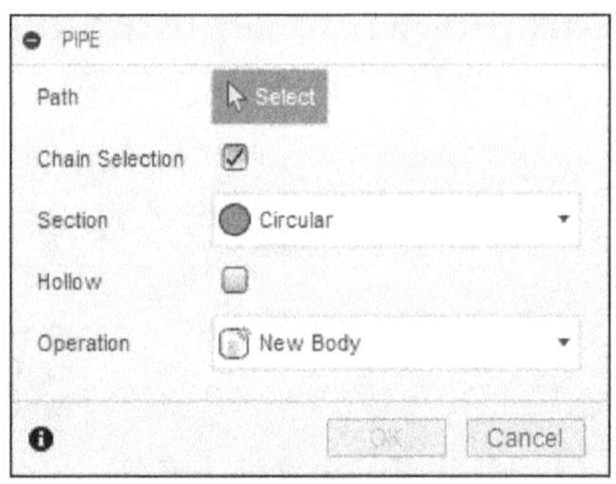

Figure-78. PIPE dialog box

- Select the sketch or edge of a model for path of the pipe; refer to Figure-79.

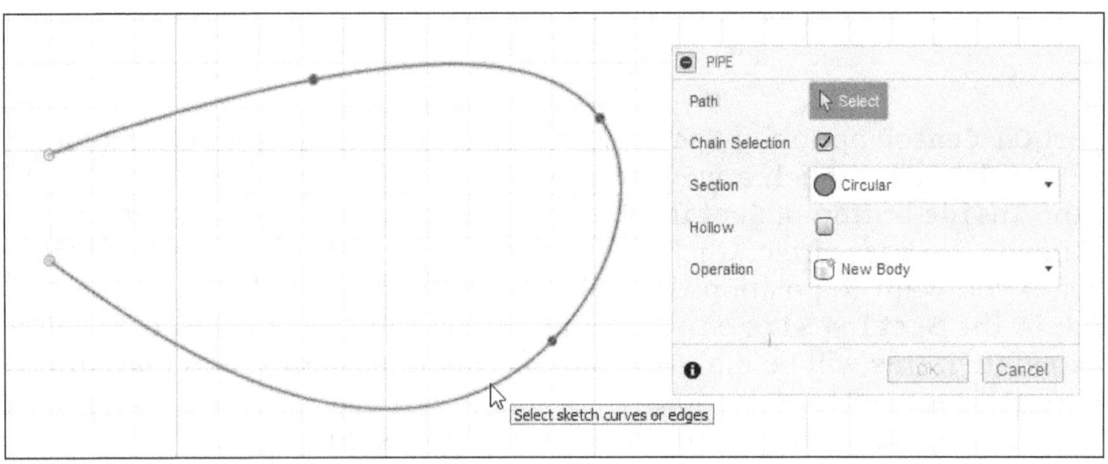

Figure-79. Selection of path to create pipe

- On selecting the path, the updated **PIPE** dialog box will be displayed. Click in the **Distance** edit box and enter desired value. The value of distance lies between 0 to 1. You can also set the distance (length) of pipe on the selected path by moving the drag handle.
- The options of **Section** drop-down were discussed earlier in **Coil** tool.
- Click in the **Section Size** edit box and specify the diameter of pipe.
- Select the **Hollow** check box to create a hollow pipe. The updated **PIPE** dialog box will be displayed along with the preview of pipe; refer to Figure-80.

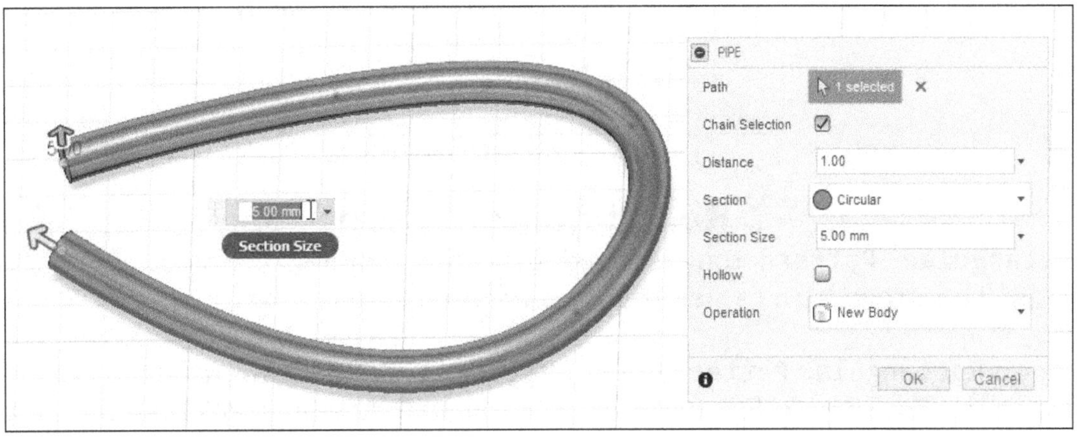

Figure-80. Preview of pipe with PIPE dialog box

- Click in the **Section Thickness** edit box and specify thickness of pipe.
- The options of **Operation** drop-down were discussed earlier in this book.
- Click **OK** button of **PIPE** dialog box to complete the process of creating the pipe; refer to Figure-81.

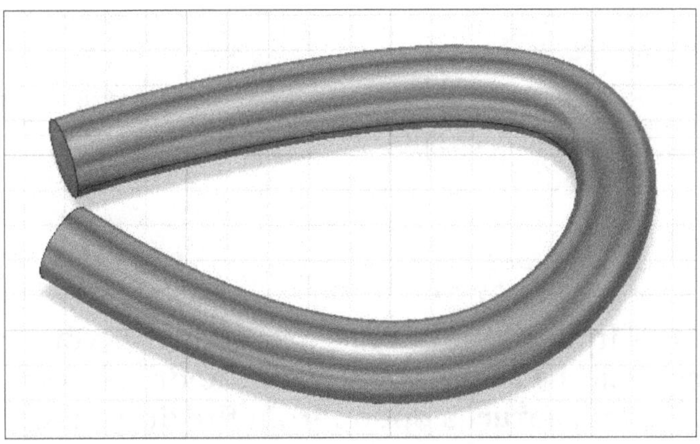

Figure-81. Pipe created

PATTERN

The **Pattern** tool is used to create copies of features or bodies at regular intervals. There are three tools in **Pattern** cascading menu; refer to Figure-82. These tools are discussed next.

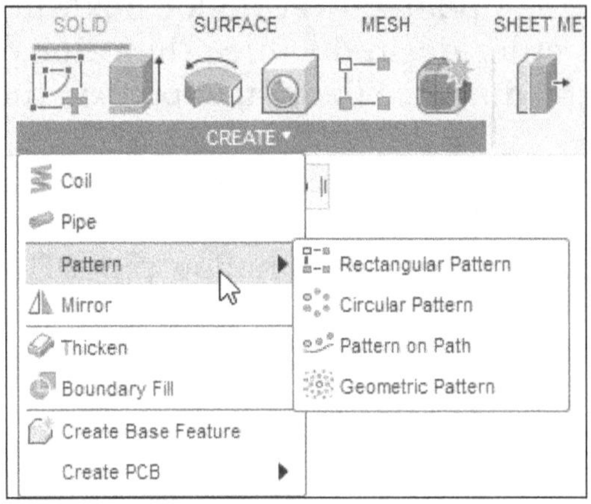

Figure-82. Pattern cascading menu

Rectangular Pattern

The **Rectangular Pattern** tool is used to create copies of objects in one or two directions. The procedure to use this tool are discussed next.

- Click on **Rectangular Pattern** tool of **Pattern** cascading menu from **CREATE** drop-down in the **Toolbar**; refer to Figure-83. The **RECTANGULAR PATTERN** dialog box will be displayed; refer to Figure-84.

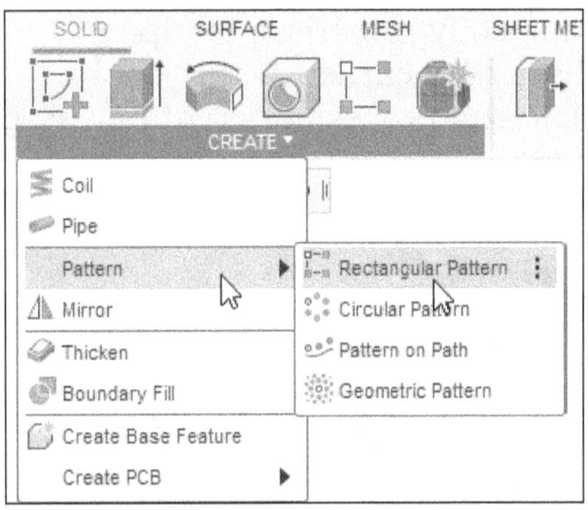

Figure-83. Rectangular Pattern tool in solid

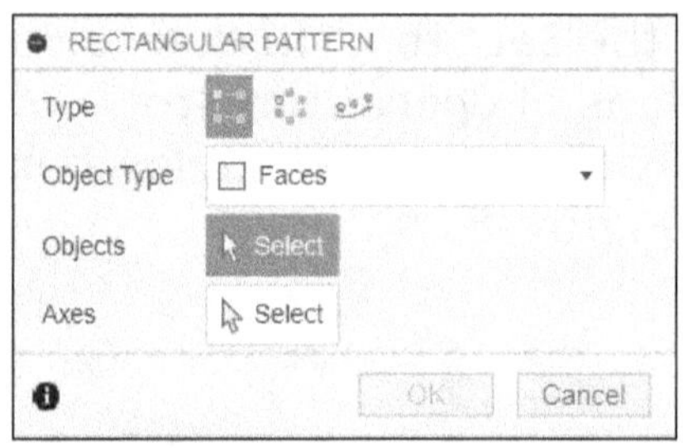

Figure-84. RECTANGULAR PATTERN dialog box in solid

- Select **Bodies** option from **Object Type** drop-down if you want to select bodies for creating copies. Select **Faces** option from the drop-down if you want to select faces for pattern. Select **Features** option from the drop-down if you want to select features for creating copies; refer to Figure-85.

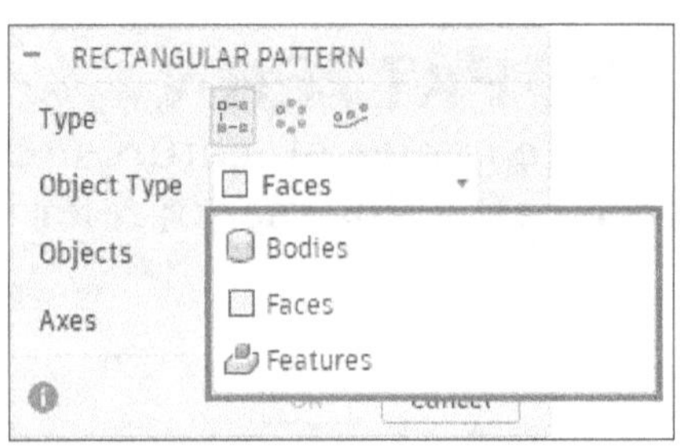

Figure-85. Object Type drop down

- We are using **Bodies** option from **Type** drop-down. Select the body for creating its copies; refer to Figure-86.

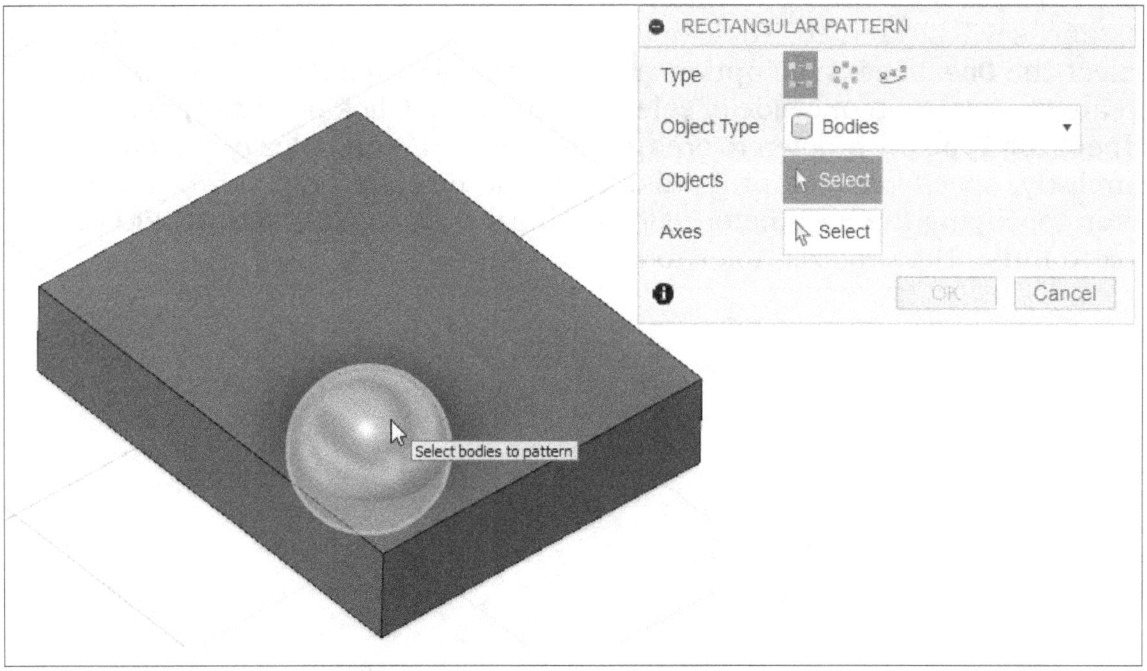

Figure-86. Selection of body for rectangular pattern

- Click on **Select** button of **Axes** option and select the default axes or edges of the model to define direction in which copies will be created; refer to Figure-87.

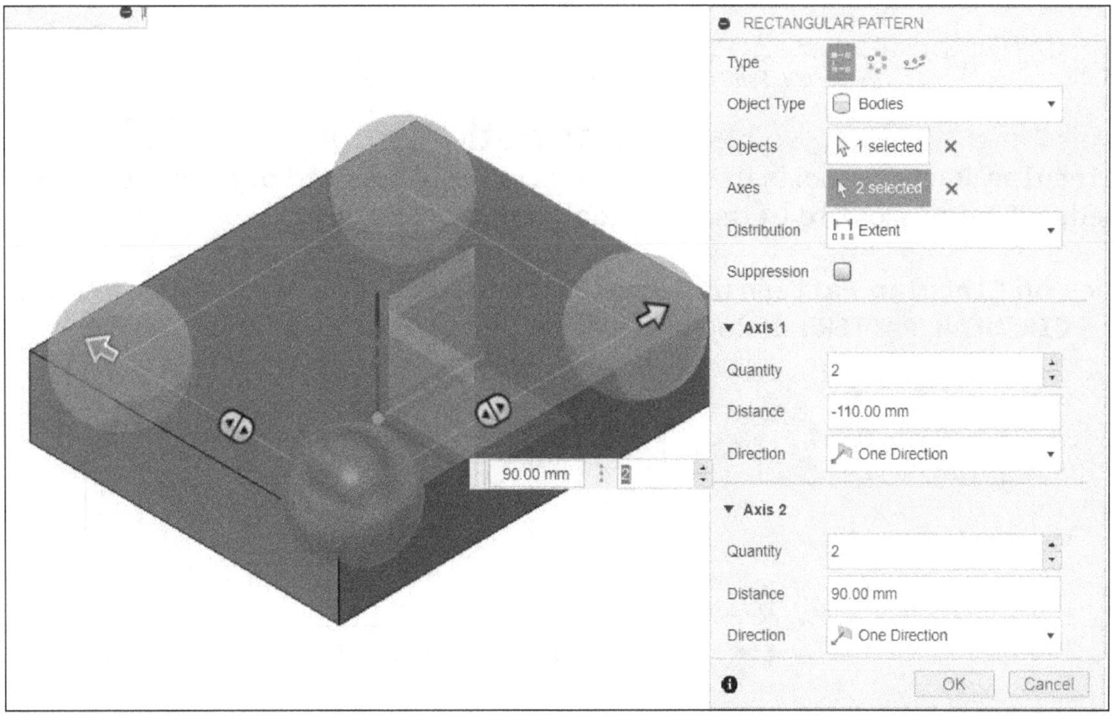

Figure-87. Selection of direction

- Select the **Extent** option from **Distribution** drop-down if you want to specify total length within which copies will be created. Select the **Spacing** option from **Distribution** drop-down to set the distance between two consecutive instances of object. In our case, we have selected **Extent** option.
- Select the **Suppress** check box if you want to suppress any instance of pattern.
- Click in the **Quantity** edit box and specify the number of instances to be created in the pattern along selected direction.

- Click in **Distance** edit box and specify the distance value within which pattern instances will be created. You can also set the distance by moving the drag handle.
- Select the **One Direction** option from **Direction Type** drop-down if you want to create the copies in one side of selected direction. Click on **Symmetric** option from **Direction Type** drop-down to create the copies in both sides of selected direction.
- Similarly, specify the quantity, distance, and direction type for other direction.
- After specifying the parameter, click **OK** button from **RECTANGULAR PATTERN** dialog box to finish the process; refer to Figure-88.

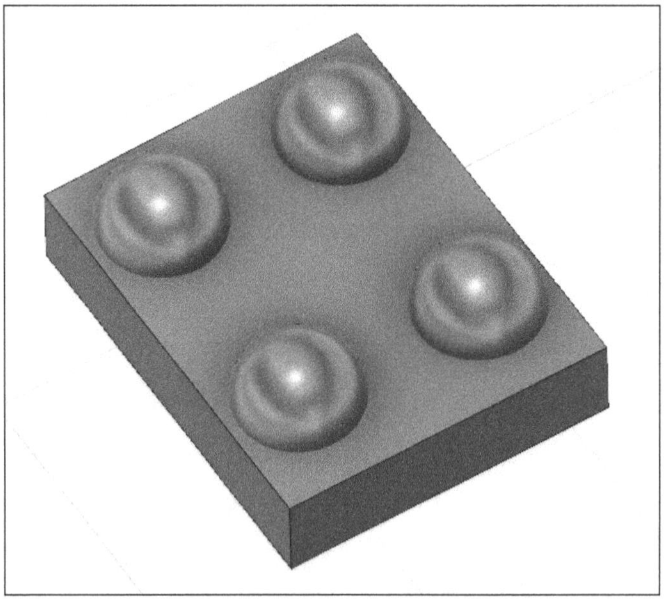

Figure-88. Solid model after applying rectangular pattern tool

Circular Pattern

The **Circular Pattern** tool is used to create copies of selected objects around selected axis/edge. The procedure to use this tool is discussed next.

- Click on **Circular Pattern** tool from **Pattern** cascading menu; refer to Figure-89. The **CIRCULAR PATTERN** dialog box will be displayed; refer to Figure-90.

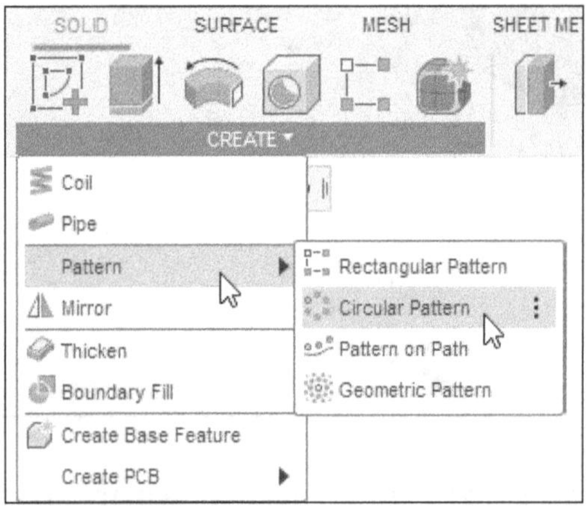

Figure-89. Circular Pattern tool in solid

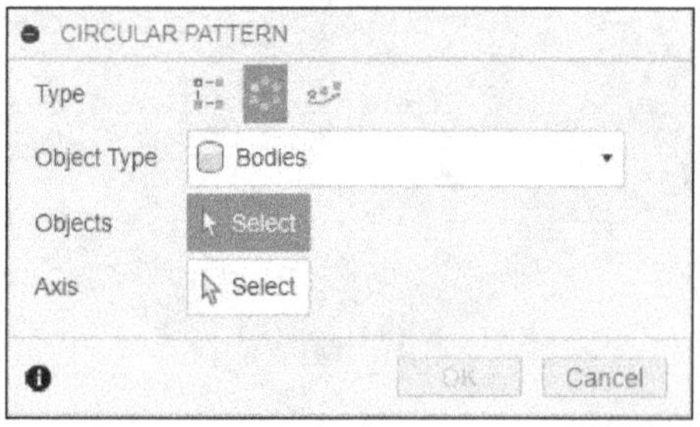

Figure-90. CIRCULAR PATTERN dialog box in solid

- Select desired option from **Type** drop-down. The options of **Type** drop-down are same as discussed in **Rectangular Pattern** tool.
- **Objects** selection is active by default. Select the feature to be patterned; refer to Figure-91.

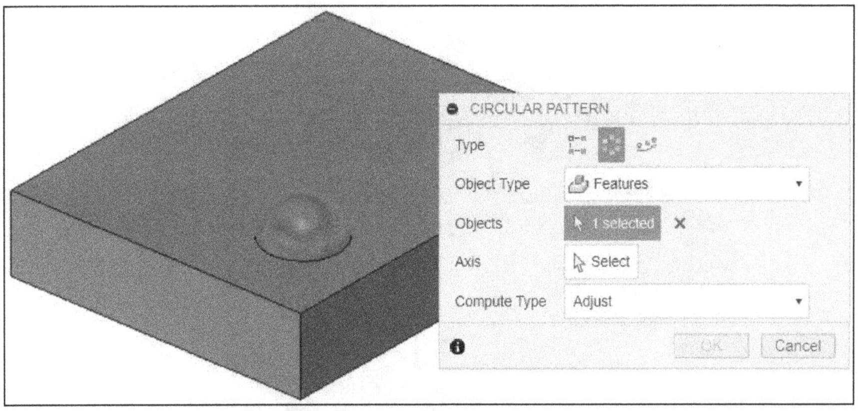

Figure-91. Selection of body for circular pattern

- Click on **Select** button of **Axis** section and select the edge/axis about which the circular pattern will be created; refer to Figure-92.

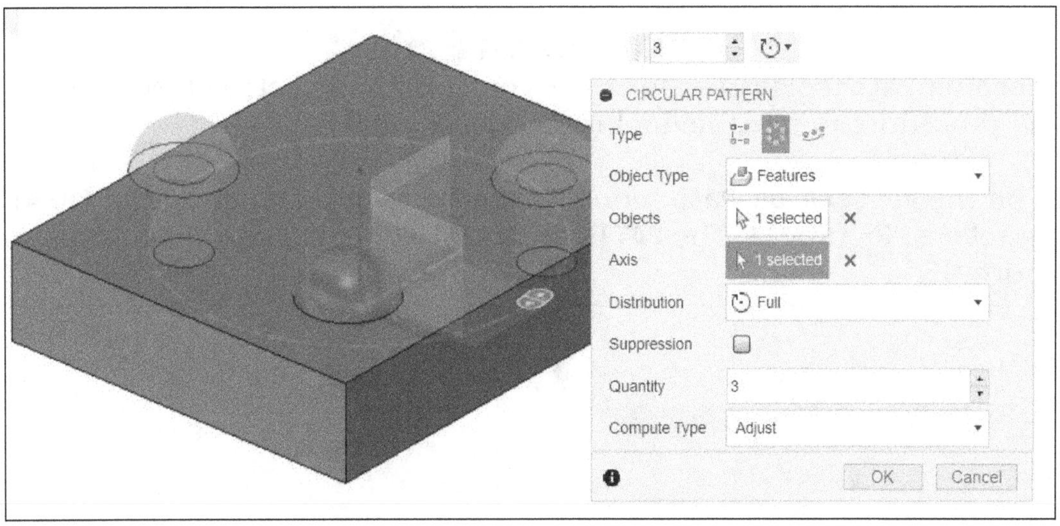

Figure-92. Selection of axis for circular pattern

- Select the **Full** option from **Distribution** drop-down if you want to create the copies of object around 360 degree path. Select **Angle** option from **Distribution** drop-down if you want to create the copies within specified angle range. Click on **Symmetric** option from **Distribution** drop-down if you want to create copies symmetrically in specified angle range.
- Select the **Suppression** check box if you want to suppress the any instance of pattern.
- Click in the **Quantity** edit box and type the number of copies to be created in pattern.
- Select **Optimized** option from **Compute Option** drop-down to create identical copies by patterning feature faces. Select **Identical** option to create identical copies by replicating results of original features. Select **Adjust** option to create potentially different copies by patterning features and calculating extents or terminations of each instance individually.
- After specifying the parameters, click on the **OK** button from **CIRCULAR PATTERN** dialog box to finish the process; refer to Figure-93.

Figure-93. Solid model after applying circular pattern tool

Pattern on Path

The **Pattern on Path** tool is used to create copies of the selected object along selected path. The procedure to use this tool is discussed next.

- Click on the **Pattern on Path** tool of **Pattern** cascading menu from **CREATE** drop-down; refer to Figure-94. The **PATTERN ON PATH** dialog box will be displayed; refer to Figure-95.

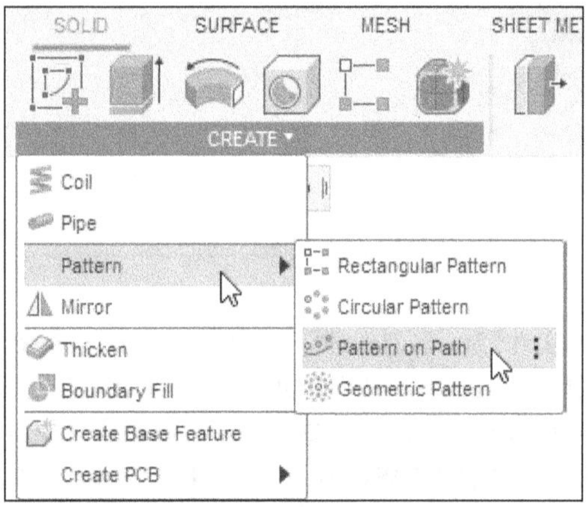

Figure-94. Pattern on Path tool

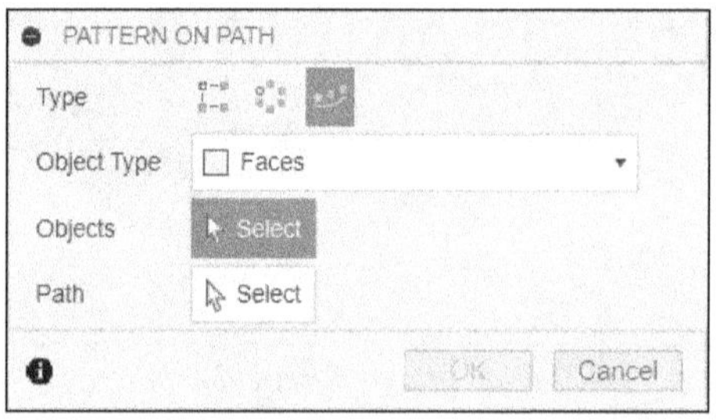

Figure-95. PATTERN ON PATH dialog box

- Click on **Faces** option from **Type** drop-down. Other options of **Type** drop-down are same as discussed earlier.
- **Objects** selection is selected by default. Select the faces for creating the copies; refer to Figure-96.

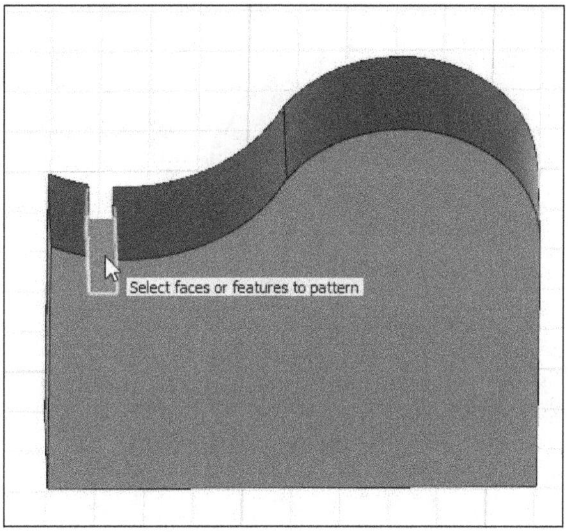

Figure-96. Selection of faces

- Click on **Select** button for **Path** option and select the path for creating copies.
- On selecting path, the updated **PATTERN ON PATH** dialog box will be displayed; refer to Figure-97.

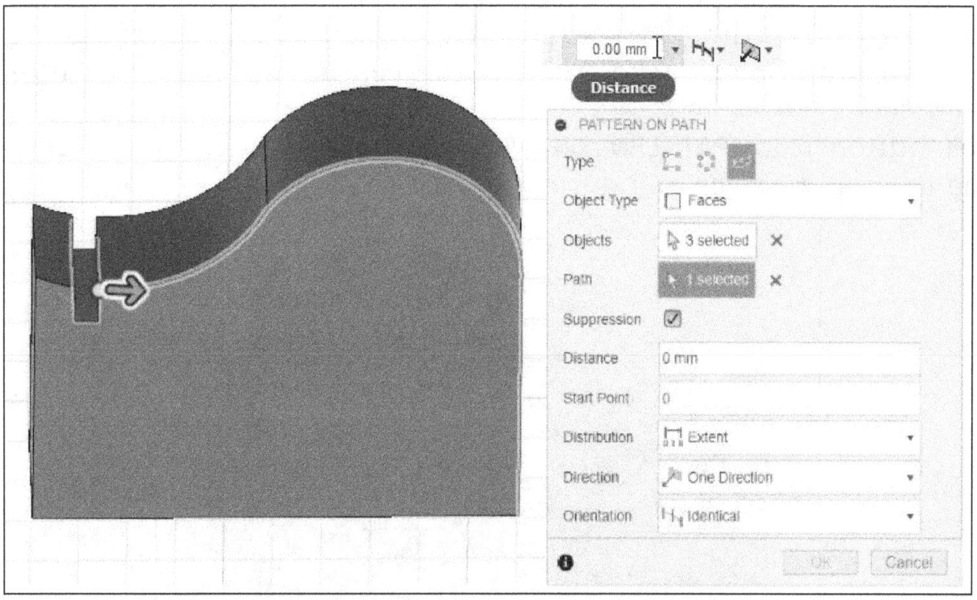

Figure-97. Updated PATTERN ON PATH dialog box on selection of path

- Select the **Suppression** check box if you want to suppress any instance of pattern.
- Click in the **Distance** edit box and specify the distance value along the path.
- Click in the **Quantity** edit box and specify the number of copies to be created.
- The **Start Point** option is used to specify the distance from the start point to place where the first pattern instance will be created. It is shown in the screen canvas as a **white point** and determines the starting point of the selected path. It can be set to any value between zero and one using the **Start Point** edit box, but it is easier to adjust it manually by dragging the start point; refer to Figure-98.

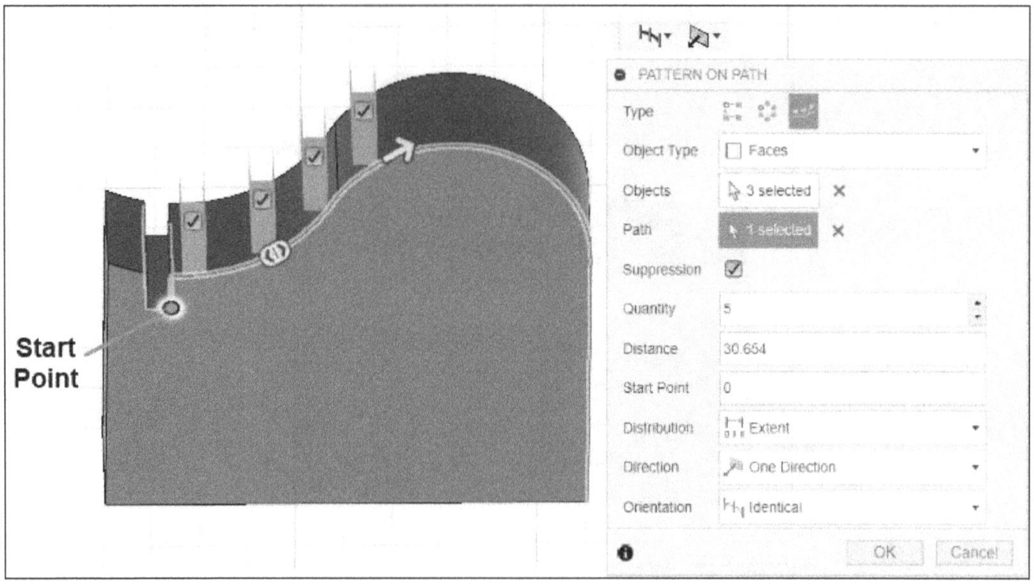

Figure-98. Pattern creation with start point

- The options of **Distance Type** and **Direction** drop-down were discussed earlier in this chapter.
- Select **Path Direction** option from **Orientation** drop-down if you want to rotate each instance according to the pattern path. Select **Identical** option from **Orientation** drop-down to keep the instances in the same orientation as the original object.
- Click **OK** button from **PATTERN ON PATH** dialog box to complete the process of creating the copies; refer to Figure-99.

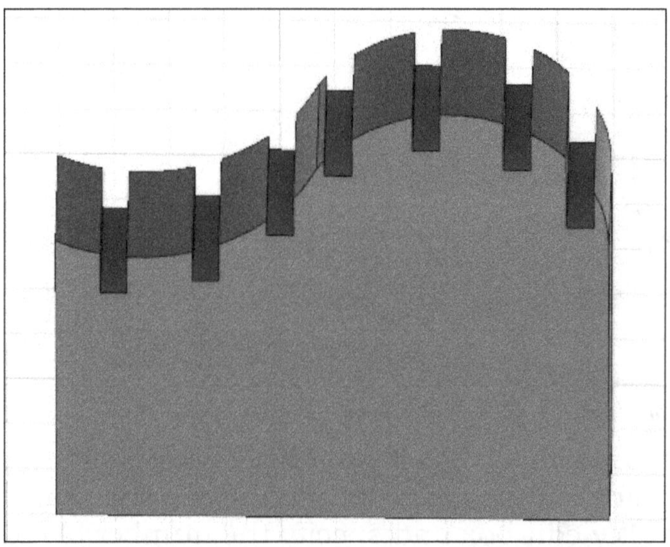

Figure-99. Solid model after applying pattern on path tool

Geometric Pattern

The **Geometric Pattern** tool is used to create a pattern with size and distribution gradients across a face on a solid body. The procedure to use this tool is discussed next.

- Click on the **Geometric Pattern** tool of **Pattern** cascading menu from **CREATE** drop-down; refer to Figure-100. The **GEOMETRIC PATTERN** dialog box will be displayed; refer to Figure-101.

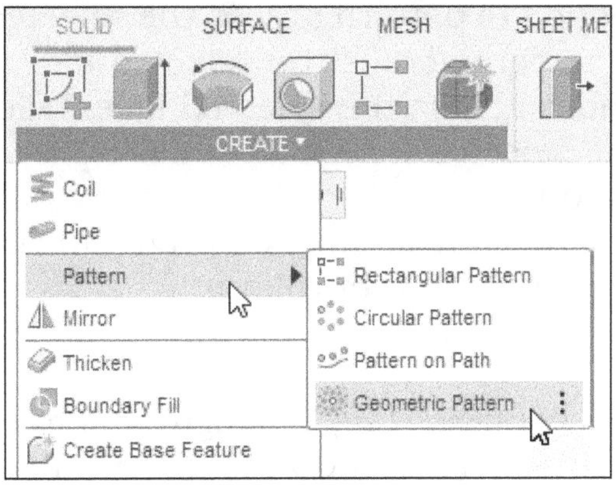

Figure-100. Geometric Pattern tool

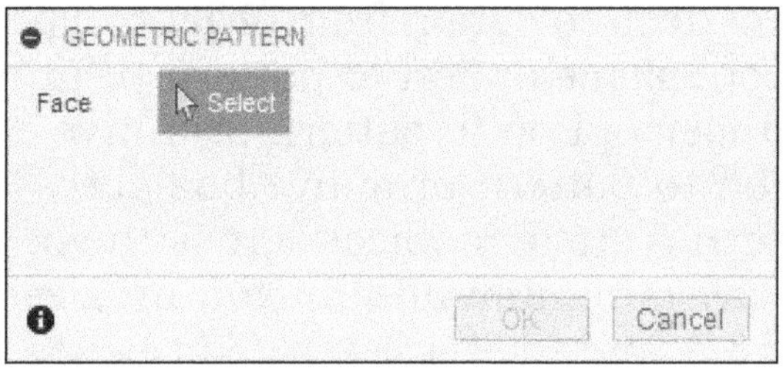

Figure-101. GEOMETRIC PATTERN dialog box

- The **Select** button of **Face** section is active by default. Select desired face on a solid body to create the pattern to it; refer to Figure-102. The updated **Geometric Pattern** dialog box will be displayed; refer to Figure-103.

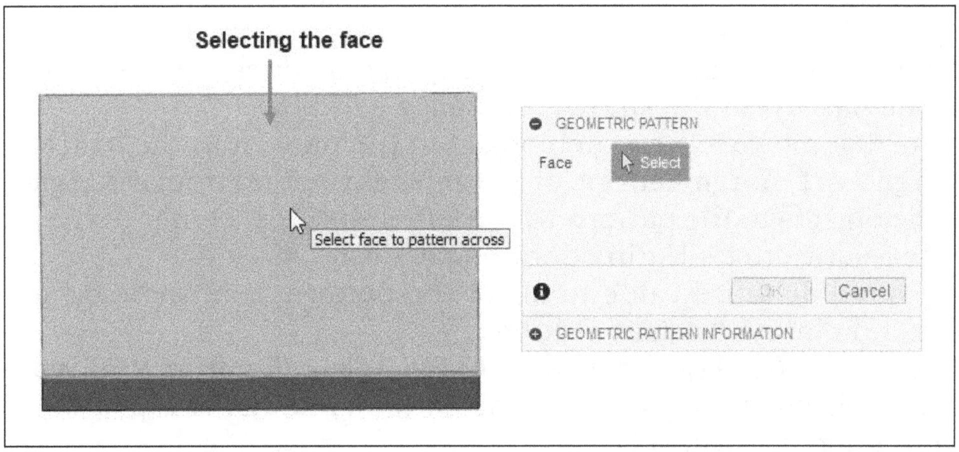

Figure-102. Selecting the face

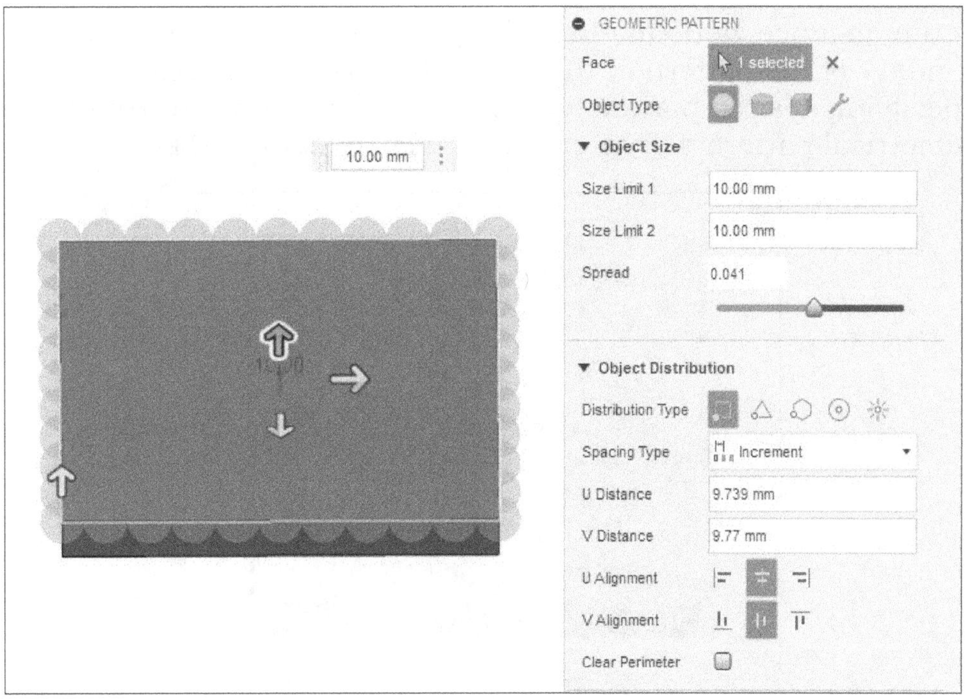

Figure-103. Updated GEOMETRIC PATTERN dialog box

- Select desired option from **Object Type** section to pattern across the selected face. Select **Sphere** option to pattern primitive sphere across the selected face. Select **Cylinder** option to pattern primitive cylinder across the selected face. Select **Box** option to pattern primitive box across the selected face. Select **Custom** option to pattern a custom object across the selected face.
- Specify minimum and maximum sizes for the objects in the pattern in the **Size Limit 1** and **Size Limit 2** edit boxes from **Object Size** rollout.
- Specify the rate of transition from one size limit to the other in the **Spread** edit box or by sliding the **Spread slider**.
- In the **Object Distribution** rollout, select **Rectangular**, **Triangular**, **Hexagonal**, **Circular**, or **Radial** option from **Distribution Type** section to distribute objects across the faces in a repeating rectangular, triangular, hexagonal, circular, or radial pattern, respectively.
- For the rectangular pattern, select desired option from **Spacing Type** drop-down. Select **Increment** option to space objects in the pattern at specified distance relative to each other. Select **Extent** option to space objects in the pattern evenly over the specified distance.
- For the circular and radial pattern, specify the distance between each concentric circle in the pattern in the **Radial Distance** edit box.
- Specify the distance between each object in the pattern in the **Distance** edit box.
- Select **Align Left**, **Align Center**, or **Align Right** option from **U Alignment** section to align the objects in the pattern to the left of the face, center of the face, or right of the face relative to its U direction, respectively.
- Specify desired distance value to offset the pattern from the edge of the face in the U direction in the **U Offset** edit box.
- Select **Align Bottom**, **Align Middle**, or **Align Top** option from **V Alignment** section to align the objects in the pattern to the bottom, middle, or top of the face relative to its V direction, respectively.
- Select **Clear Perimeter** check box to remove incomplete objects from the perimeter of the selected faces.
- Specify the distance value to offset the perimeter of the selected faces to adjust the boundary of the pattern in the **Perimeter Offset** edit box.
- After specifying desired parameters, click on the **OK** button from the dialog box. The geometrical pattern will be created; refer to Figure-104.

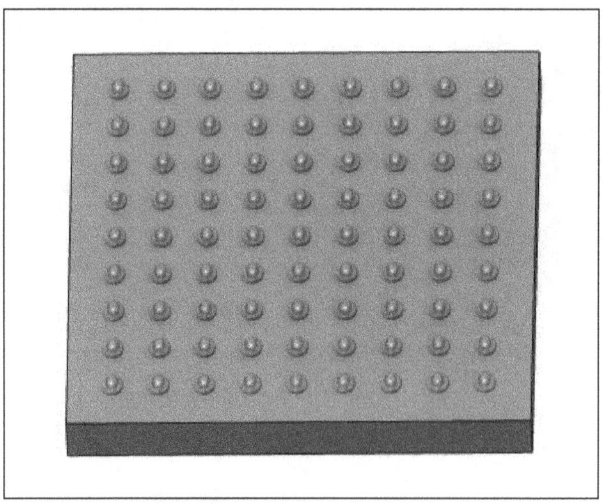

Figure-104. Geometrical pattern created

MIRROR

The **Mirror** tool is used to create mirror copy of selected objects to the opposite side of a selected face or plane. The procedure to use this tool is discussed next.

- Click on **Mirror** tool from **CREATE** drop-down in the **Toolbar**; refer to Figure-105. The **MIRROR** dialog box will be displayed; refer to Figure-106.

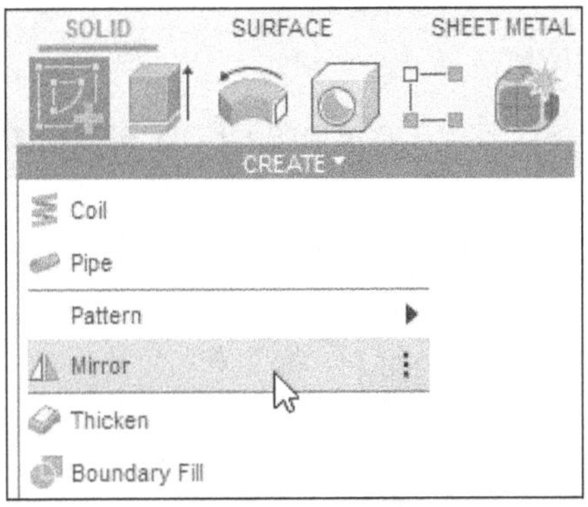

Figure-105. Mirror tool in solid

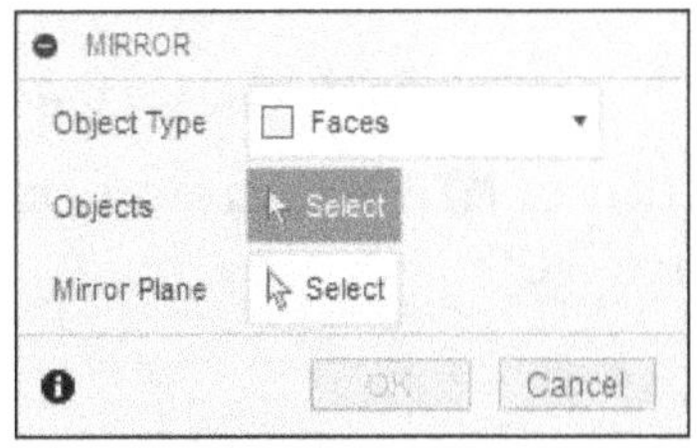

Figure-106. MIRROR dialog box in solid

- Select desired option from **Object Type** drop-down to select respective objects for mirroring. The other options of **Object Type** drop-down have already been discussed earlier.
- Select the bodies to be mirrored.
- Click on **Select** button of **Mirror Plane** section and select the plane/face to be used as mirror plane. Preview of mirror copy will be displayed; refer to Figure-107.

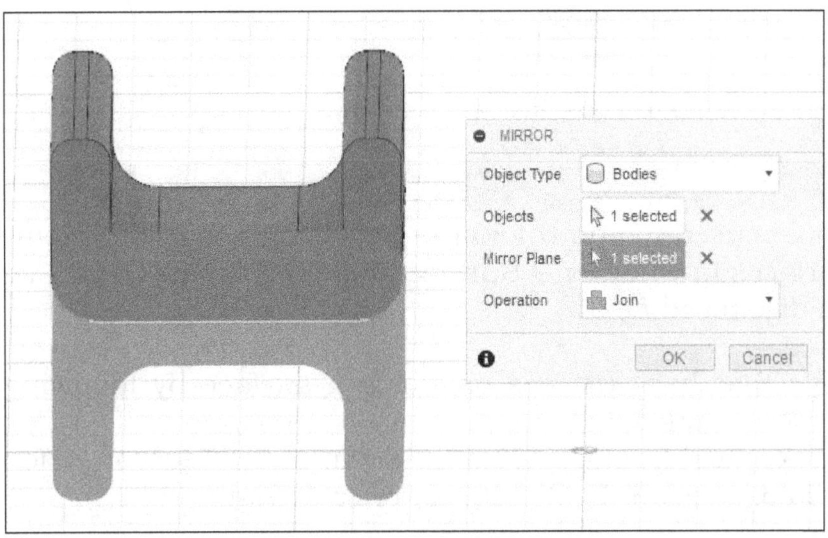

Figure-107. Preview of mirror on selection of plane

- Select desired option from **Operation** drop-down which have been discussed earlier in this chapter.
- If you have selected **Features** in **Object Type** drop-down then **Compute Type** drop-down will also be displayed in the dialog box; refer to Figure-108. Select the **Optimized** option if you want to create copy of feature with minimum processing time and less flexibility to individually change features later. Select **Identical** option if you want to create copy of feature using same background programming which was used while creating the base feature. Select the **Adjust** option if you want to recompute each instance of the feature as a separate feature.

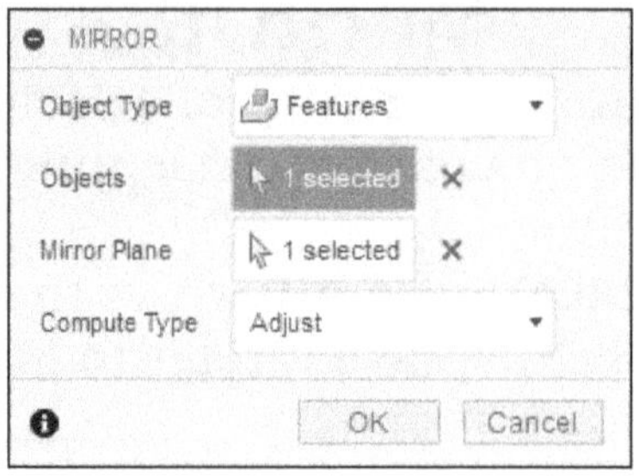

Figure-108. Compute Type in MIRROR dialog box

- Click **OK** button of **MIRROR** dialog box to finish the process of creating mirror copy; refer to Figure-109.

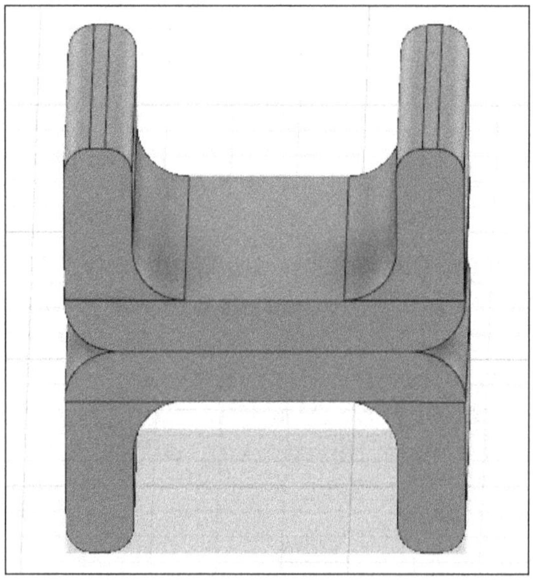

Figure-109. Solid model after applying mirror tool

THICKEN

The **Thicken** tool is used to add thickness to surfaces to make them solid. (You will learn about surfaces in Chapter 9 Surface Modeling of this book.) The procedure to use this tool is discussed next.

- Open any file that has surfaces or create a surface by following basic tools of Chapter 9 of this book.
- Click on **Thicken** tool from **CREATE** drop-down in the **Toolbar**; refer to Figure-110. A **THICKEN** dialog box will be displayed; refer to Figure-111.

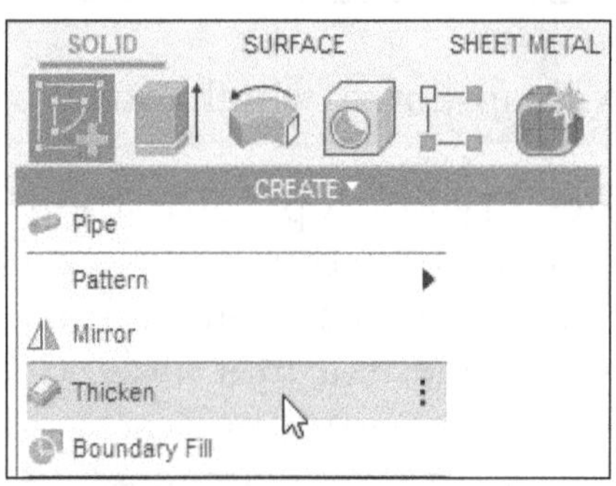

Figure-110. Thicken tool

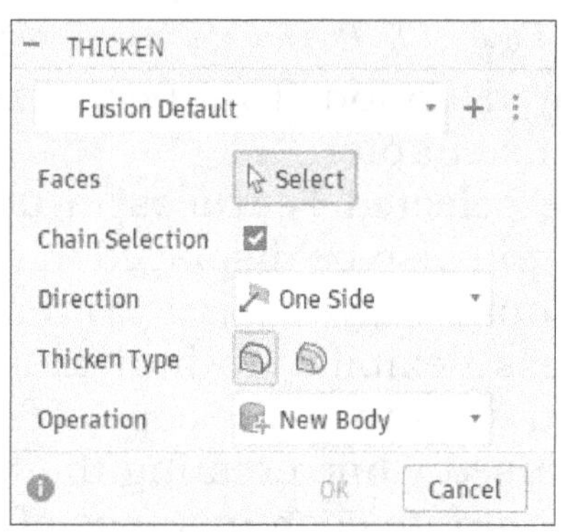

Figure-111. THICKEN dialog box

- **Faces** selection is active by default. Select the surfaces to add thickness; refer to Figure-112.

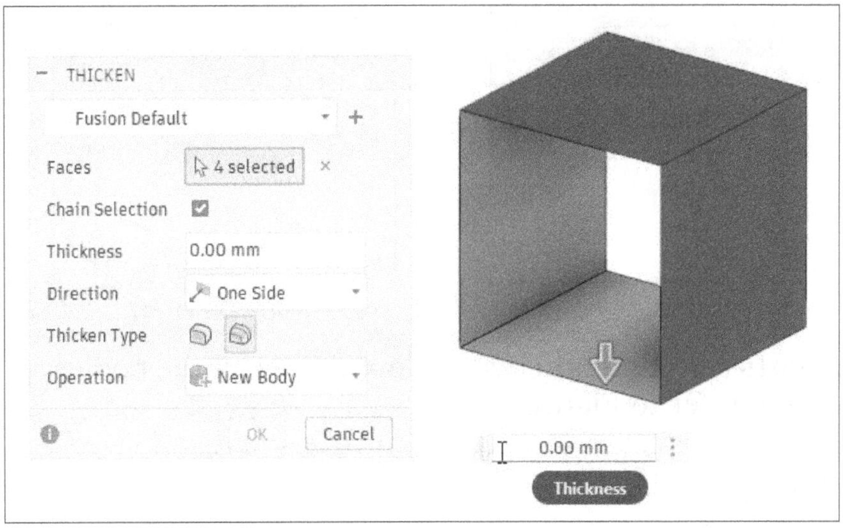

Figure-112. Selection of faces to add thickness

- Click in the **Thickness** edit box of dialog box and specify desired value of thickness.
- Click on **One Side** option from **Direction** drop-down to apply the thickness to one side of surface. Click on **Symmetric** option from **Direction** drop-down to apply the thickness to both sides of surface equally. In our case, we have selected **Symmetric** option.
- Select **Sharp Thicken** option from **Thicken Type** area to create thickness with sharp corners. Select **Rounded Thicken** option to create thickness with rounded corners.
- The options of **Operation** drop-down were discussed earlier in this chapter.
- Click on **OK** button from **THICKEN** dialog box to finish the process; refer to Figure-113.

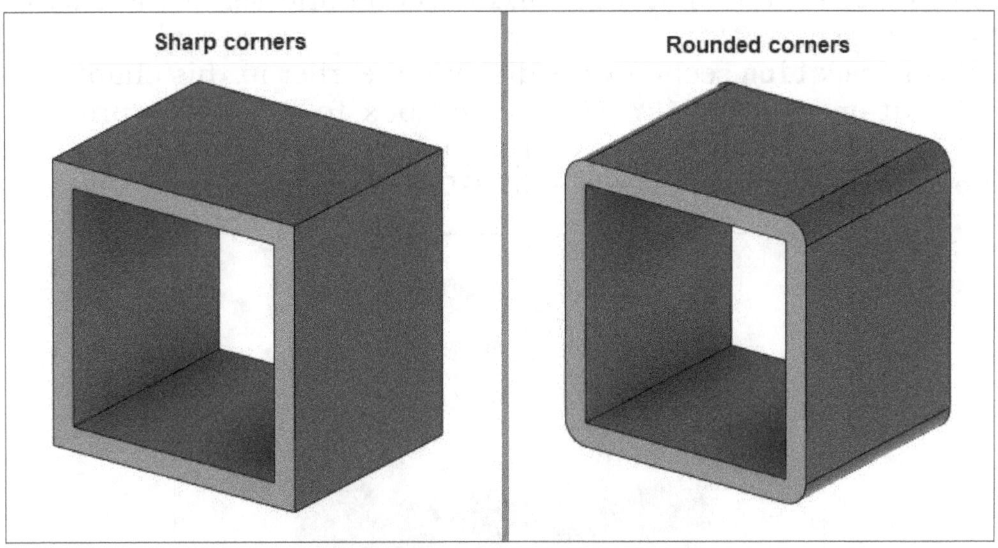

Figure-113. Solid model after applying thicken tool

BOUNDARY FILL

The **Boundary Fill** tool is used to create a volume from bounded by selected planes, bodies, and surfaces. This volume is called cell and can be used to cut, add, or create new body in the model. The procedure to use this tool is discussed next.

- Click on **Boundary Fill** tool from **CREATE** drop-down in the **Toolbar**; refer to Figure-114. The **BOUNDARY FILL** dialog box will be displayed; refer to Figure-115.

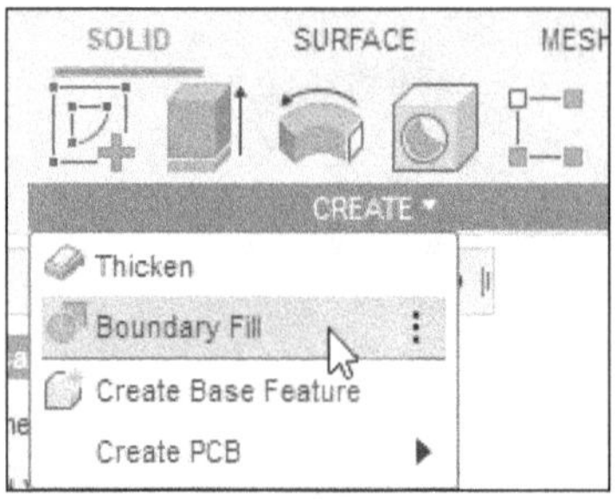

Figure-114. Boundary Fill tool

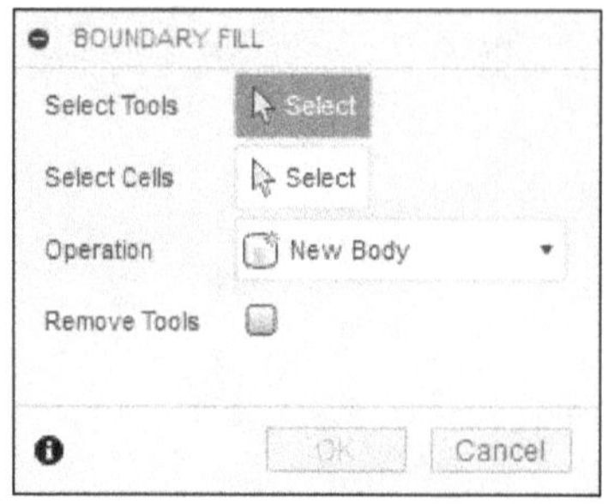

Figure-115. BOUNDARY FILL dialog box

- The **Select Tools** selection is active by default. Select the bodies/planes/surfaces for boundary fill; refer to Figure-116.

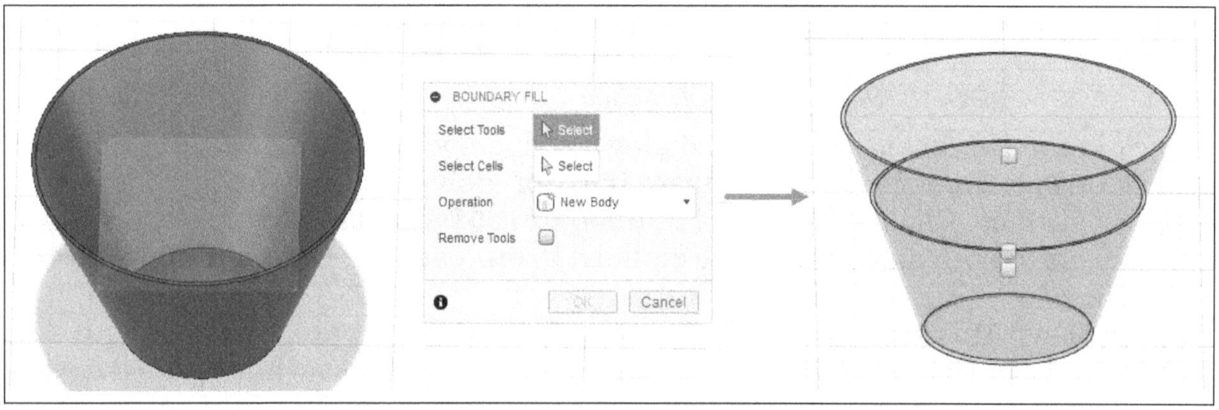

Figure-116. Selection for boundary fill

- Click on **Select** button of **Select Cells** section and select the check boxes for cells to be created.
- The tools of **Operation** section were discussed earlier in this chapter.
- Click **OK** button of **BOUNDARY FILL** dialog box to finish the process; refer to Figure-117. If the parent body is overlapping with new boundary fill bodies then hide the parent body using eye icon in **BROWSER** to check the result.

Figure-117. Result of boundary fill after hiding parent body

CREATE FORM

The **Create Form** tool is used to create or modify the form of model using freestyle editing tools. Clicking this tool takes you to **Form** mode. You will learn more about **Form** mode later in Chapter 12 and 13 of this book. The procedure to use this tool is discussed next.

- Click on **Create Form** tool from **CREATE** drop-down in the **Toolbar**; refer to Figure-118. The **Form mode** will be activated and related toolbar will be displayed; refer to Figure-119.

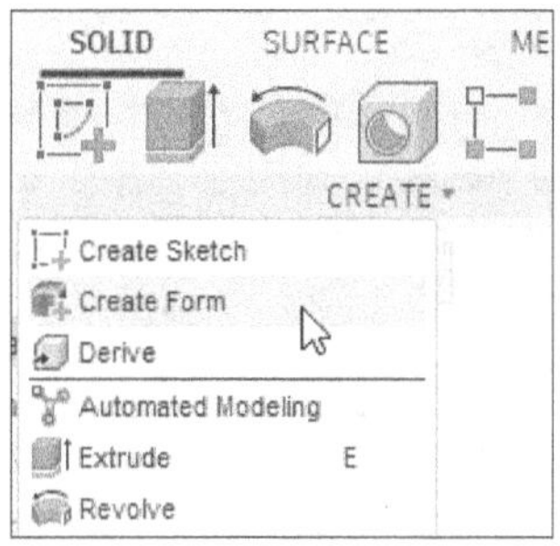

Figure-118. Create Form tool

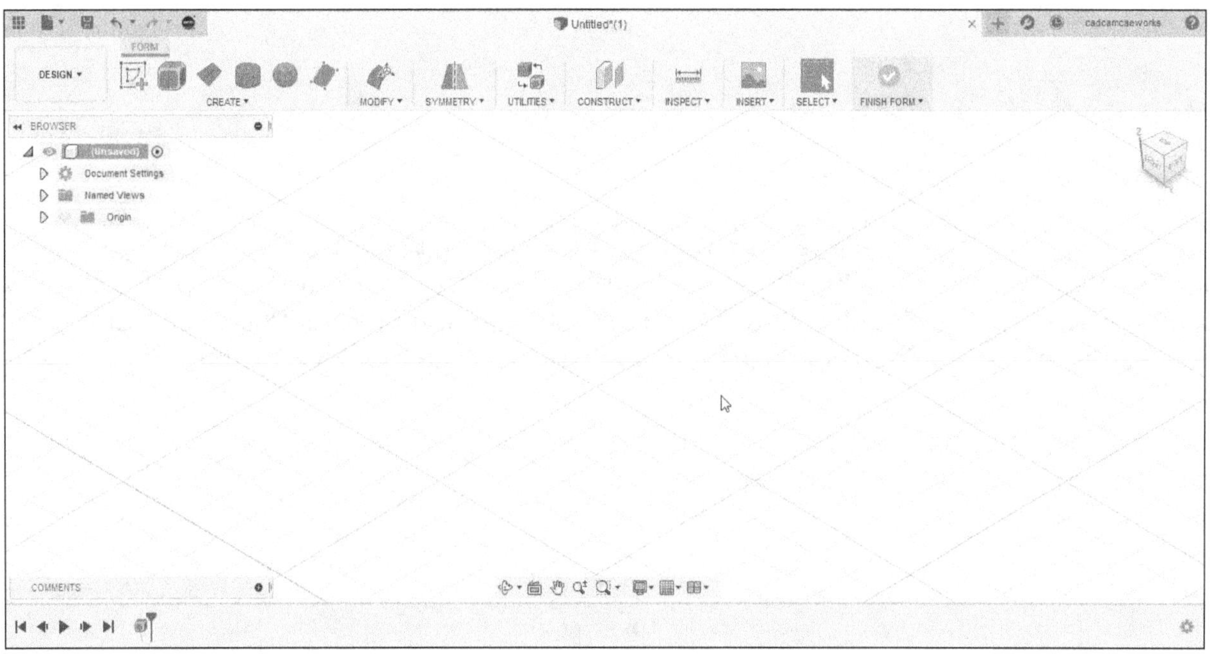

Figure-119. Form mode

- Now, create or modify the model as desired.
- Click **Finish Form** button from **Toolbar** to exit the **Form mode** and return to **Model Workspace**; refer to Figure-120.

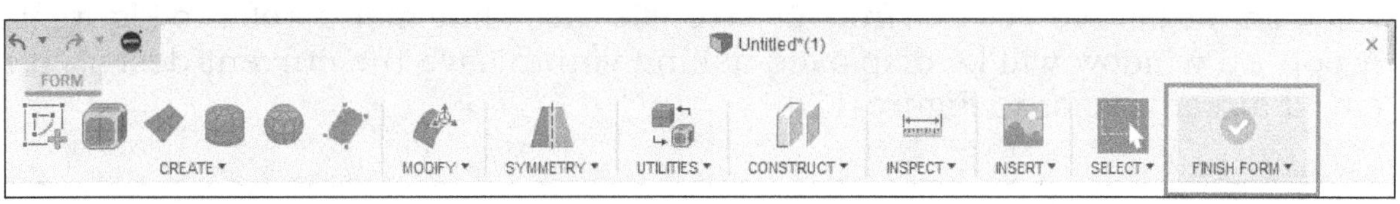

Figure-120. Finish Form button

CREATE BASE FEATURE

The **Create Base Feature** tool inserts a base feature operation in the **Timeline**. Any operations performed on the design while in a base feature are not recorded in the **Timeline**. This tool is used when you want to safeguard some of the operations while sharing the file.

- Click on **Create Base Feature** tool from **CREATE** drop-down in the **Toolbar**; refer to Figure-121. The tools in the **Toolbar** will be same as for **DESIGN** workspace.

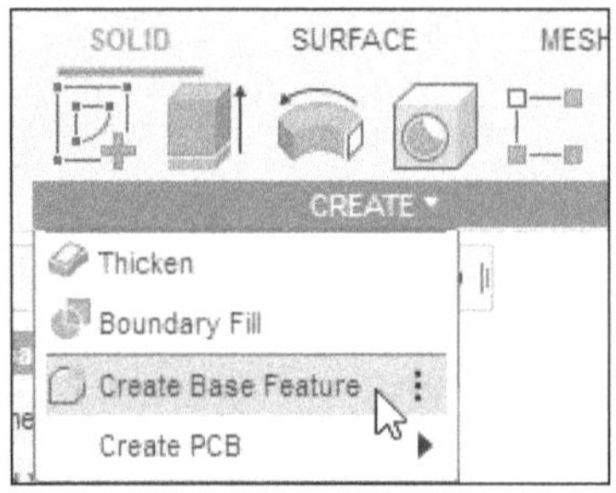

Figure-121. Create Base Feature tool

- Do desired operation that you do not want to record in **Timeline** and then click on **FINISH BASE FEATURE** button from **Toolbar** to exit the mode; refer to Figure-122.

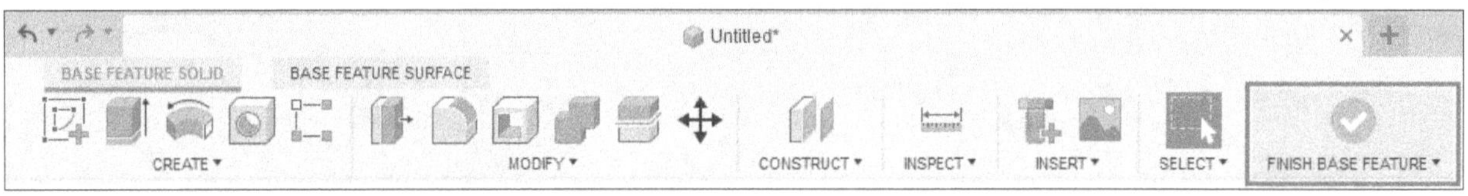

Figure-122. FINISH BASE FEATURE button

CREATE PCB FEATURE

The **Create PCB** tools in **CREATE** drop-down is used to create and modify PCB design in collaboration with **EAGLE** users. There are two tools in **Create PCB** cascading menu; refer to Figure-123. The procedures to use these tools are given next.

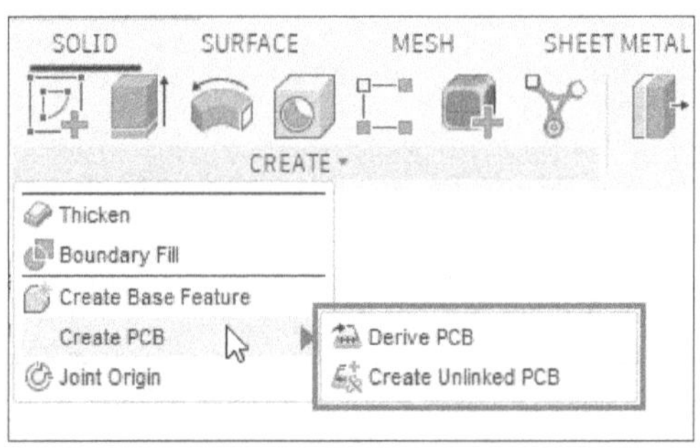

Figure-123. Create PCB cascading menu

Derive PCB

- Click on the **Derive PCB** tool from **Create PCB** cascading menu; refer to Figure-123. A pop-up window will be displayed asking you to save the current design, if not saved already; refer to Figure-124.

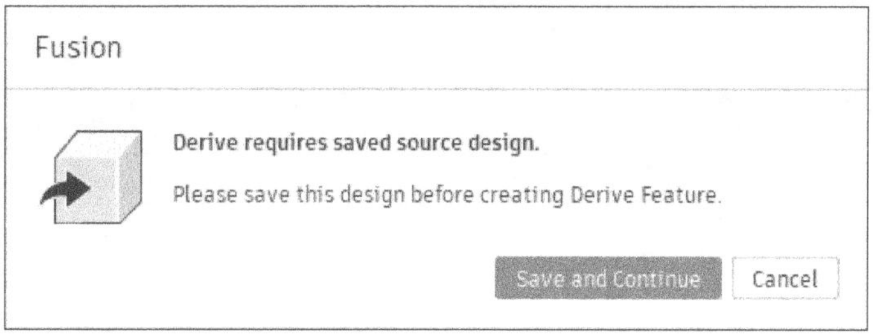

Figure-124. Pop-up window

- Click on the **Save and Continue** button. The **Save** dialog box will be displayed as discussed earlier.
- Specify desired name and location for the file and click on the **Save** button. The **DERIVE PCB** dialog box will be displayed; refer to Figure-125.

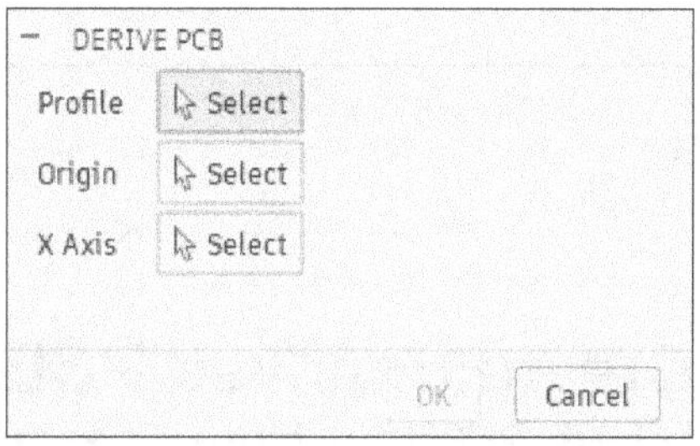

Figure-125. DERIVE PCB dialog box

- Select desired sketch profile from canvas; refer to Figure-126 and specify desired parameters in the dialog box.

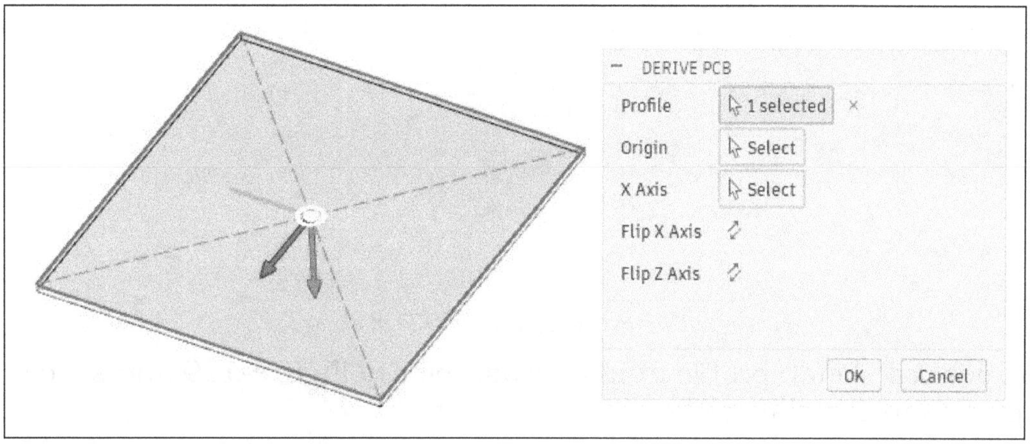

Figure-126. Selecting the profile

- Click on the **OK** button from the dialog box. The **3D PCB Workspace** will be activated and related toolbar will be displayed; refer to Figure-127.

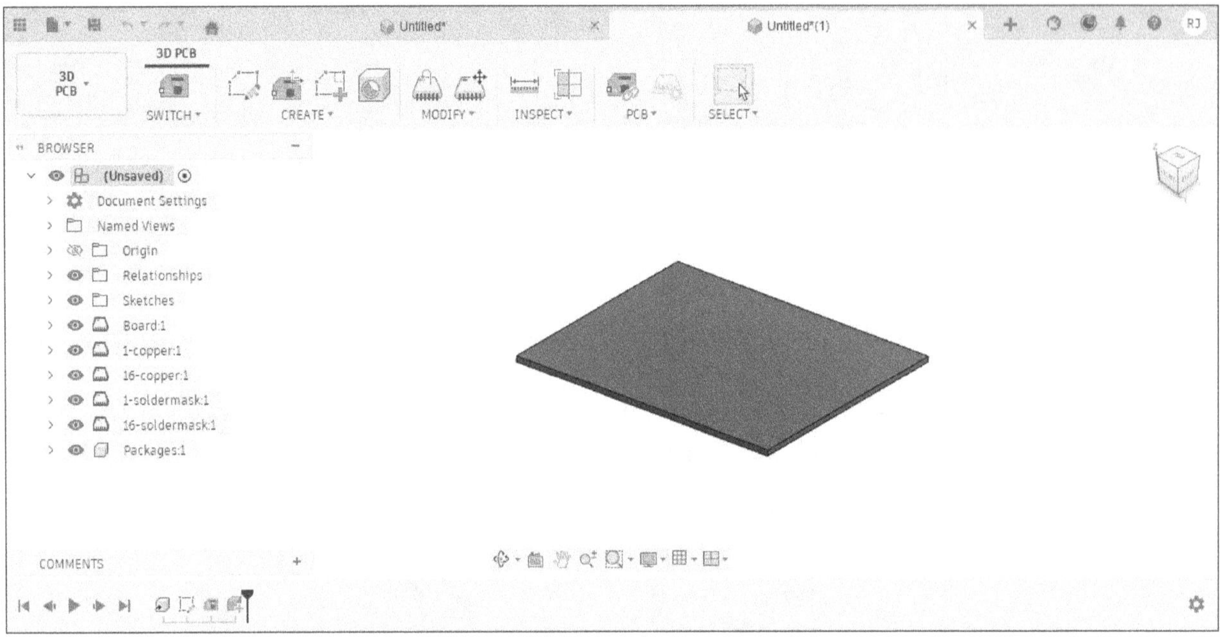

Figure-127. 3D PCB Workspace

Create Unlinked PCB

- Click on the **Create Unlinked PCB** tool from **Create PCB** cascading menu; refer to Figure-123. The **CREATE UNLINKED PCB** dialog box will be displayed; refer to Figure-128.

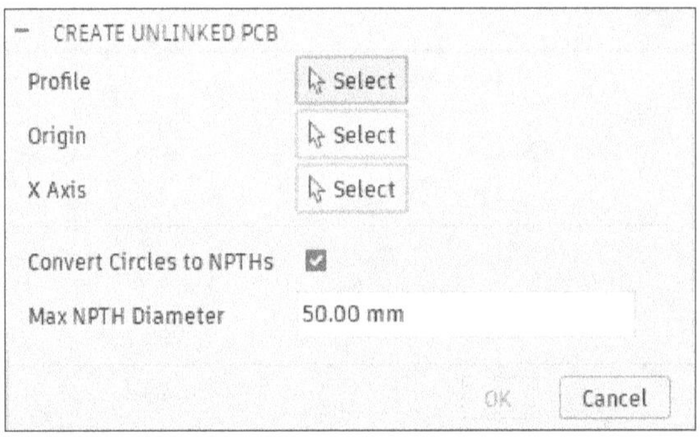

Figure-128. CREATE UNLINKED PCB dialog box

- Select desired sketch profile from canvas; refer to Figure-129 and specify desired parameters in the dialog box.

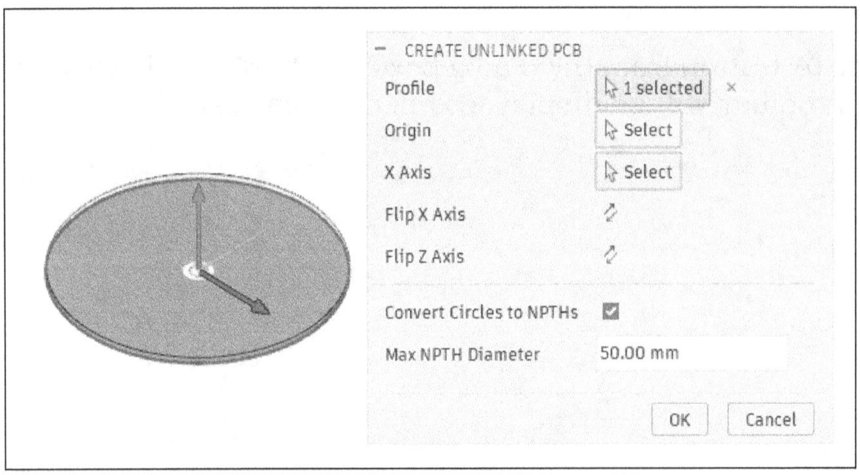

Figure-129. Selecting the profile

- Click on the **OK** button from the dialog box. The **3D PCB Workspace** will be activated and related toolbar will be displayed as discussed earlier.

Adding Holes to PCB

The **PCBHole** tool is used to create holes for adding components to the PCB. The procedure to use this tool is given next.

- Click on the **PCBHole** tool from the **CREATE** drop-down in the **3D PCB** tab of the **Ribbon**. The **PCBHOLE** dialog box will be displayed with **At Point** option selected in the **Placement Type** area, by default.
- Click to place the hole at the specified location on the top or bottom face of the component. Select **From Sketch** option to place the hole at the location defined in the selected sketch.
- Select the face of PCB where you want to place the hole. Preview of hole will be displayed; refer to Figure-130.

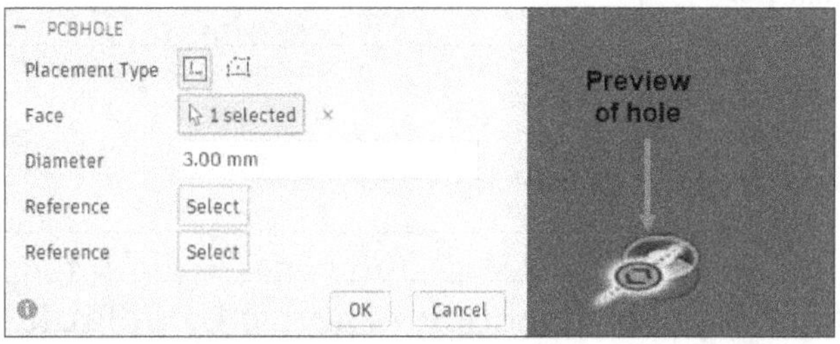

Figure-130. Preview of hole on PCB

- Click at the center of hole and select desired edge of PCB to define first reference. The options to define distance from selected reference will be displayed; refer to Figure-131.

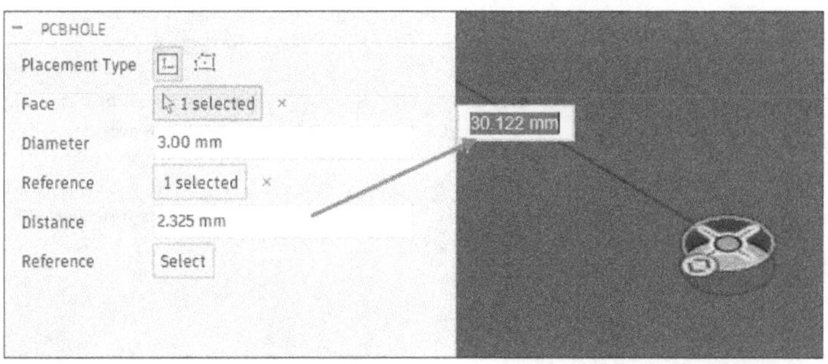

Figure-131. Specifying distance

- Similarly, specify distance for other reference and click on the **OK** button. The hole will be created.

The tools of 3D PCB are beyond the scope of this book. You can learn about PCB and Electronic Design in our another book **Autodesk Fusion PCB Black Book (V2701.1.18)**.

PLASTIC TOOLS

The Plastic tools are used to assign and manage plastic rules applied to the components. These tools are available on activating Design Extension. The tools are discussed next.

Assign Plastic Rule

The **Assign Plastic Rule** tool is used to assign plastic rule to a component to automatically control the properties of plastic features like physical material and thickness. The procedure to use this tool is discussed next.

- Click on the **Assign Plastic Rule** tool from **SETUP** panel in the **PLASTIC** tab of the **Toolbar**; refer to Figure-132. The **ASSIGN PLASTIC RULE** dialog box will be displayed; refer to Figure-133.

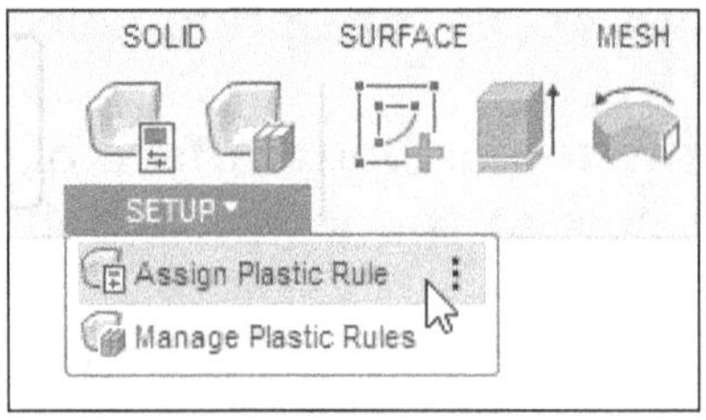

Figure-132. Assign Plastic Rule tool

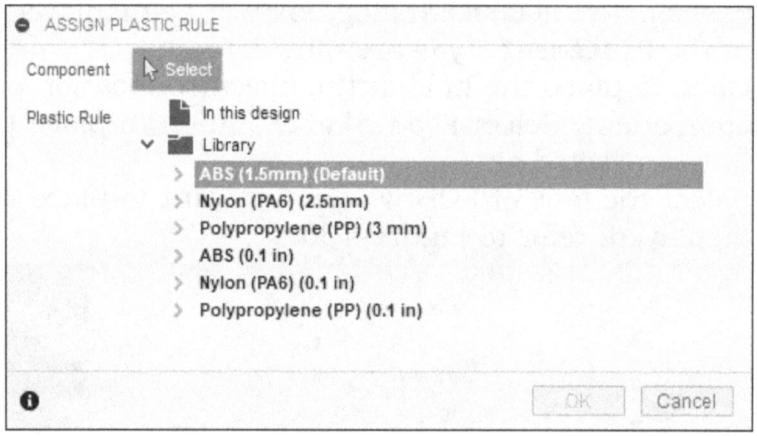

Figure-133. ASSIGN PLASTIC RULE dialog box

- The **Select** button of **Component** section is active by default. Select the component in the Model Space that you want to assign the plastic rule; refer to Figure-134.

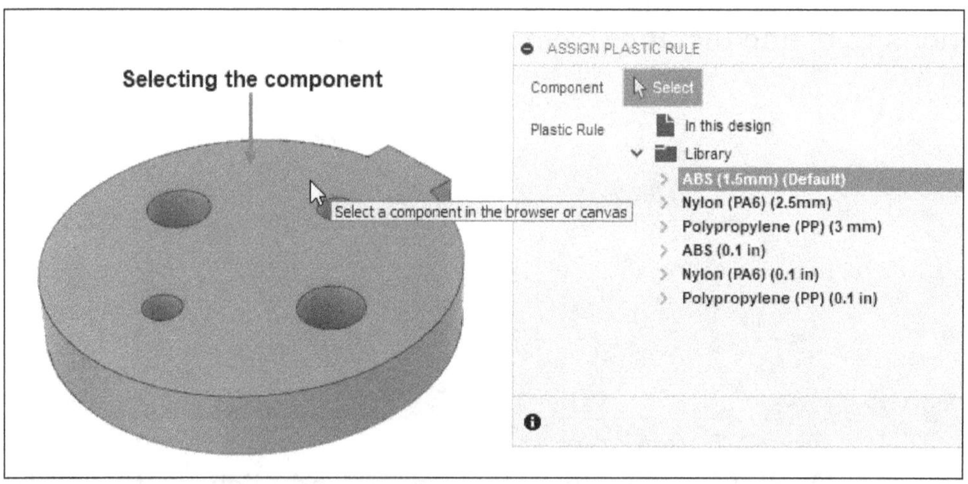

Figure-134. Selecting the component to assign plastic rule

- Select desired plastic rule from the cloud library in the **Library** node of the **Plastic Rule** section in the dialog box.
- After selecting desired plastic rule, click on the **OK** button from the dialog box. The plastic rule will be assigned to the component; refer to Figure-135.

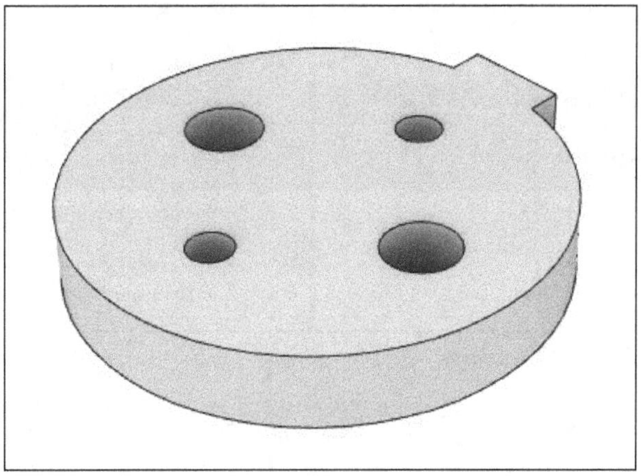

Figure-135. Plastic rule assigned to the component

Manage Plastic Rules

The **Manage Plastic Rules** tool is used to create new rules, edit existing rules, or save rules to a library to use them in multiple designs. The procedure to use this tool is discussed next.

- Click on the **Manage Plastic Rules** tool from **SETUP** panel in the **PLASTIC** tab of the **Toolbar**; refer to Figure-136. The **MANAGE PLASTIC RULES** dialog box will be displayed; refer to Figure-137.

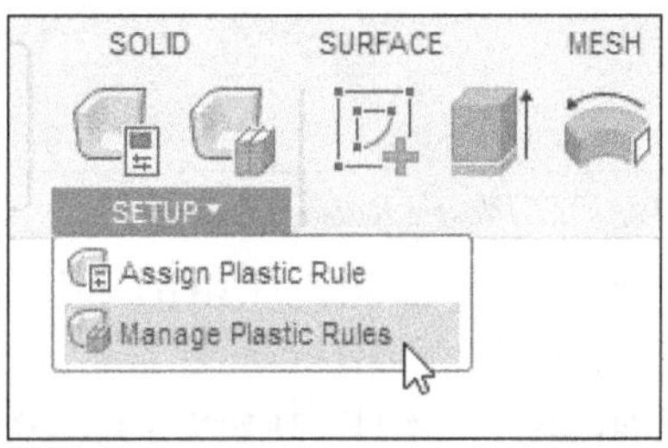

Figure-136. Manage Plastic Rules tool

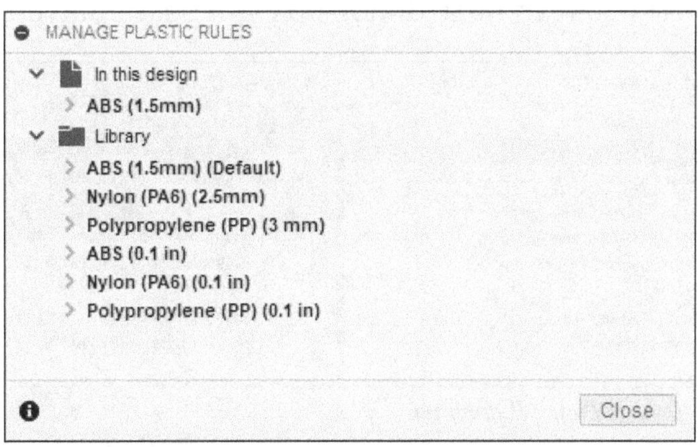

Figure-137. MANAGE PLASTIC RULES dialog box

- If you want to edit the rule, then select the rule you want to edit and click on **Edit Plastic Rule** button or right-click on the rule that you want to edit and select **Edit Plastic Rule** button; refer to Figure-138. The **Edit Plastic Rule** dialog box will be displayed; refer to Figure-139.

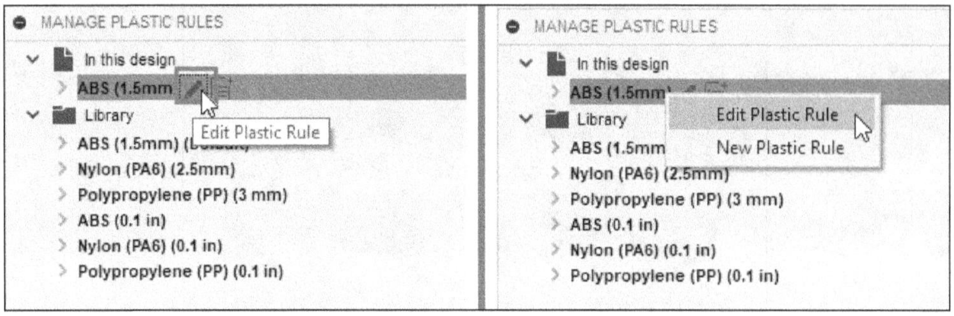

Figure-138. Edit Plastic Rule button

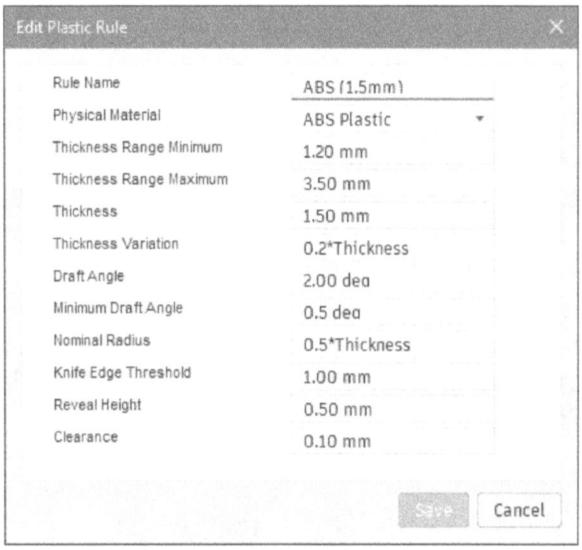

Figure-139. Edit Plastic Rule dialog box

- Edit the parameters of the rule as desired and click on the **Save** button from the dialog box. The plastic rule will be edited.
- If you want to create new plastic rule then select the rule and click on **New Plastic Rule** button or right-click on the rule and select **New Plastic Rule** button; refer to Figure-140. The **New Plastic Rule** dialog box will be displayed; refer to Figure-141.

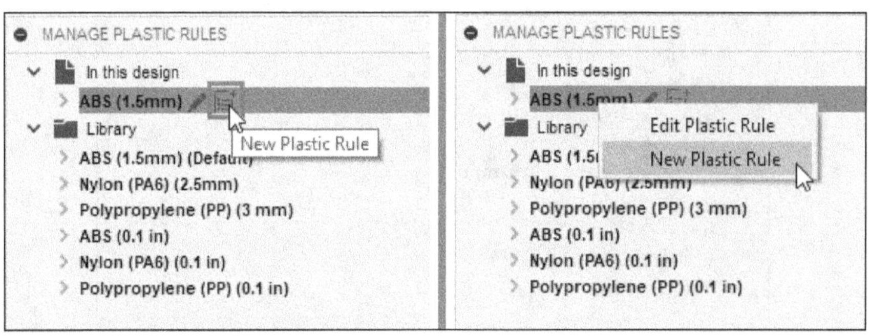

Figure-140. New Plastic Rule button

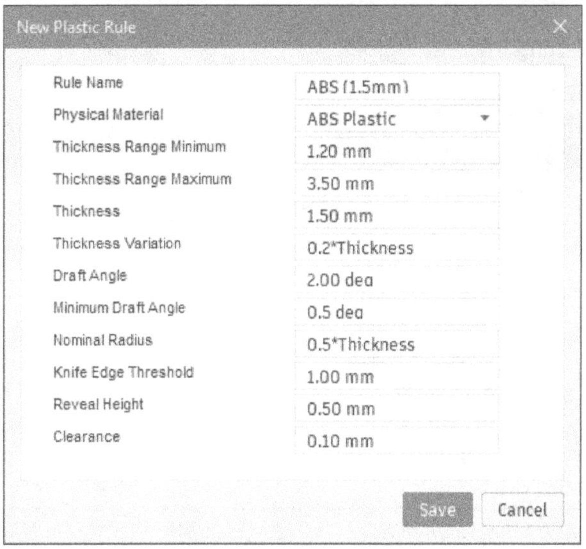

Figure-141. New Plastic Rule dialog box

- Specify desired parameters of the rule in the dialog box and click on the **Save** button. The new plastic rule will be created.

Snap Fit

The **Snap Fit** tool is used to create a cantilever snap fit feature to fasten two solid bodies together in a design. The procedure to use this tool is discussed next.

- Click on the **Snap Fit** tool from **CREATE** panel in the **PLASTIC** tab of the **Toolbar**; refer to Figure-142. The **SNAP FIT** dialog box will be displayed as shown in Figure-143.

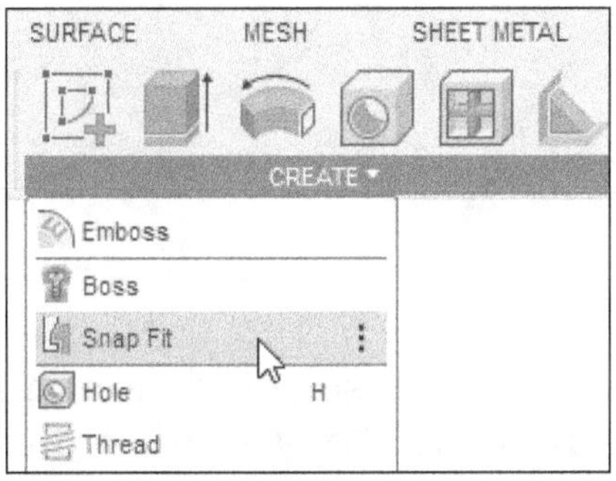

Figure-142. Snap Fit tool

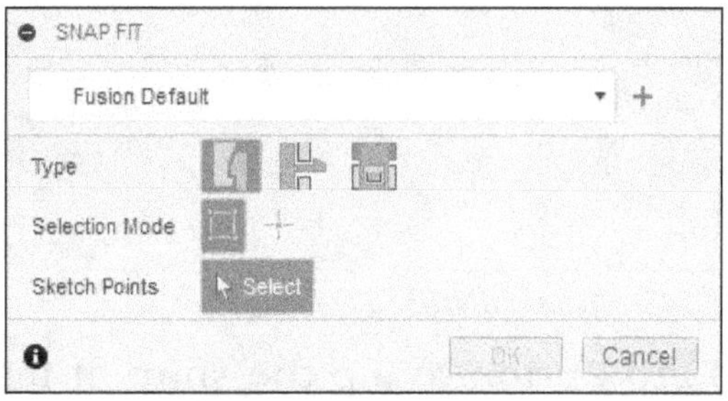

Figure-143. SNAP FIT dialog box

- Select desired option from **Type** section in the dialog box to create the snap fit feature. The **Parallel Hook And Groove** option is selected by default which is used to create a snap fit feature with a hook and groove, parallel to a face on a pair of solid bodies. Select **Perpendicular Hook And Groove** option to create a snap fit feature with a hook and groove, perpendicular to a face on a pair of solid bodies. Select **Hook And Loop** option to create a snap fit feature with a hook and loop on a pair of solid bodies.
- Select the **Automatic** button from the **Selection Mode** section to automatically select all visible sketch points based on reference points. Select the **Manual** button from the section to select each sketch point for snap fit manually.
- The **Select** button of **Sketch Points** section is active by default. Select the sketch point to position the hook side of each snap fit feature; refer to Figure-144. The preview of snap fit along with updated **SNAP FIT** dialog box will be displayed; refer to Figure-145.

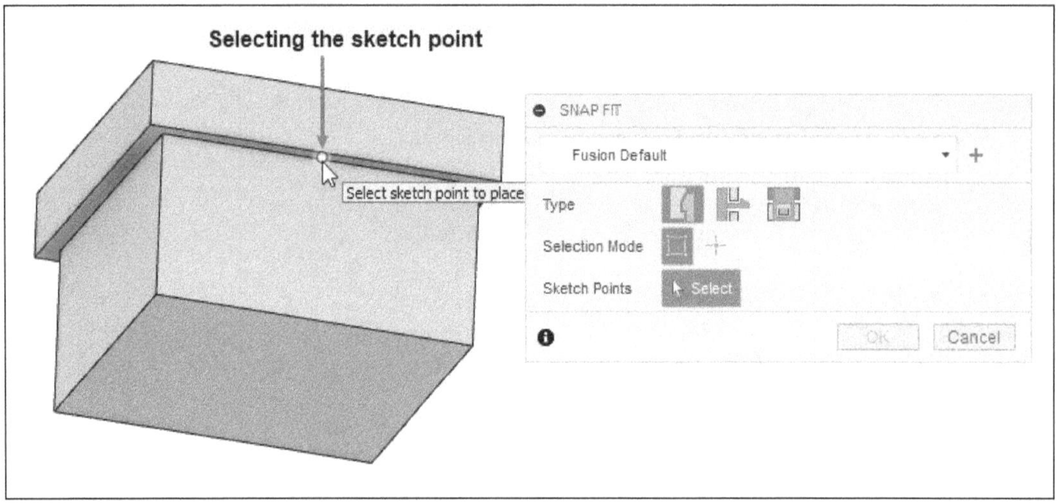

Figure-144. Selecting sketch point for snap fit

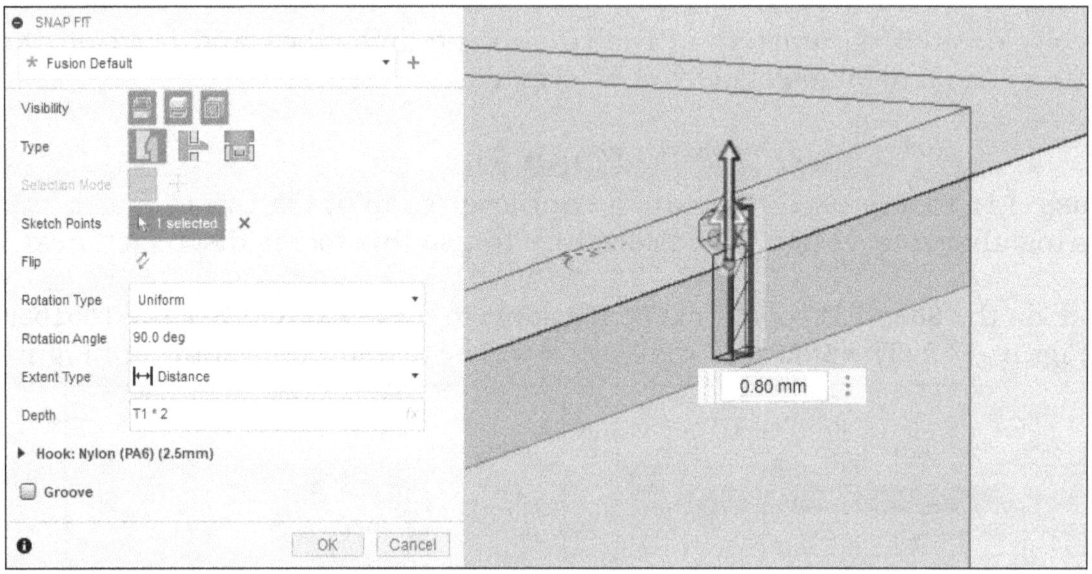

Figure-145. Updated SNAP FIT dialog box

- Select **Flip** button to flip the snap fit feature over the selected sketch point.
- The target body will be selected automatically in the **Body** section on which the snap fit feature will be placed.
- Select desired option from the **Rotation Type** drop-down to define how rotation value will be specified. For example, select the **Aligned** option from drop-down to align the face of snap fit with selected face of the model or select the **Independent** option to specify angle value independent of any model reference.
- Specify desired value in the **Rotation Angle** edit box to rotate the hook around the sketch point or drag the **Rotation manipulator handle**.
- Select **Distance** option from **Extent Type** drop-down to extrude the bottom of the hook from the sketch plane to a specified depth in the **Depth** edit box. Select **To Next** option to extrude the bottom of the hook from the sketch plane to the nearest faces on a solid body.
- Expand the **Hook** node and specify desired values in the edit boxes to adjust the dimensions of the hook side of the snap fit feature.
- Select the **Groove** check box and specify desired values in the edit boxes to create the groove side of the snap fit feature.

- After specifying desired parameters in the dialog box, click on the **OK** button. The snap fit feature will be created; refer to Figure-146.

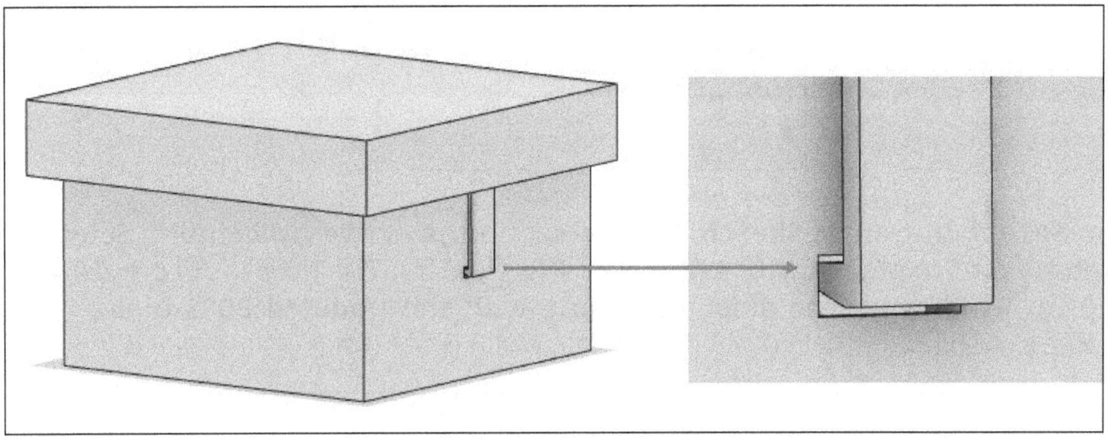

Figure-146. Snap fit feature created

Boss

The **Boss** tool is used to create a boss feature to fasten two solid bodies together and reinforce thin areas of a design. The procedure to use this tool is discussed next.

- Click on the **Boss** tool from **CREATE** panel in the **PLASTIC** tab of the **Toolbar**; refer to Figure-147. If your model is not saved yet then the **Cannot create fastener** pop-up window will be displayed asking you to save the design to create fastener or continue without creating the fastener; refer to Figure-148.

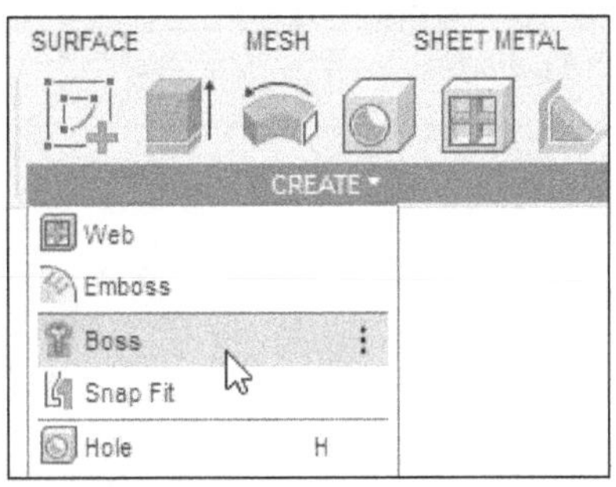

Figure-147. Boss tool

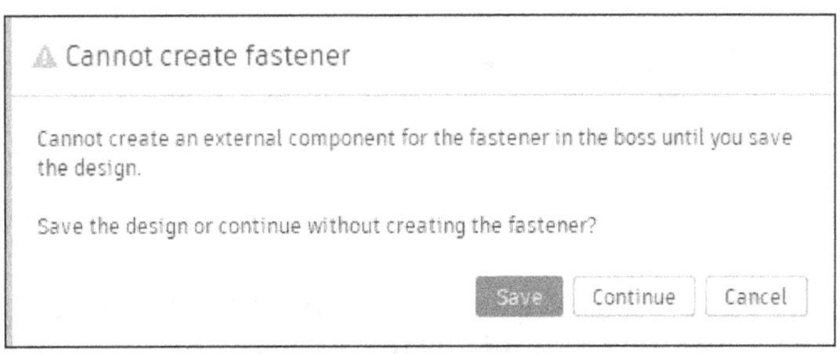

Figure-148. Cannot create fastener pop up window

- Click on the **Save** button to save the design. The **Save As** dialog box will be displayed.
- Specify desired name and location of the design and click on the **Save** button. The design will be saved.
- Click on the **Continue** button to create the boss feature without creating the fastener. The **BOSS** dialog box will be displayed; refer to Figure-149.

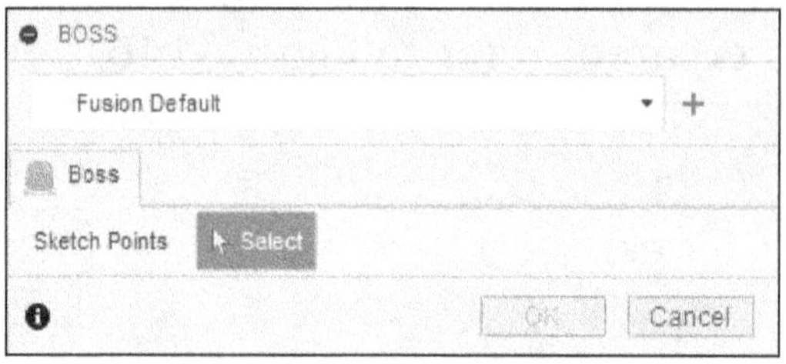

Figure-149. BOSS dialog box

- The **Select** button of **Sketch Points** section is active by default. Select desired sketch point to place the boss; refer to Figure-150. The **No plastic rule assigned** pop-up window will be displayed along with the updated **BOSS** dialog box; refer to Figure-151.

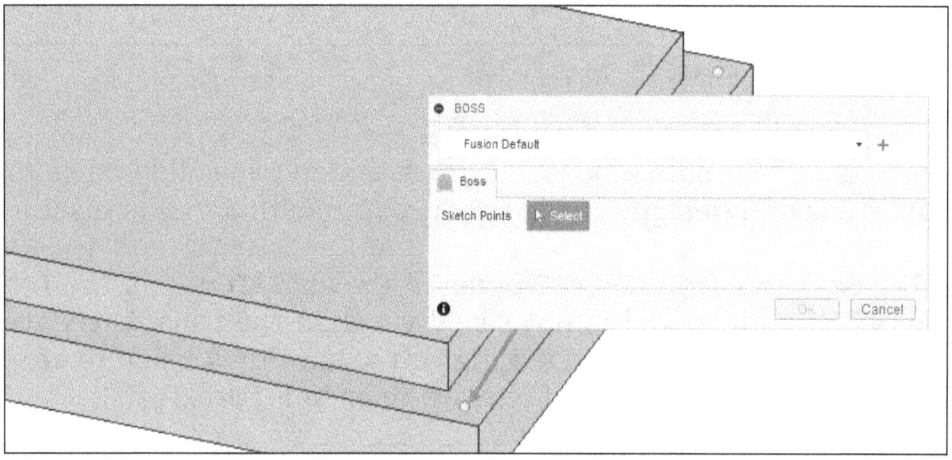

Figure-150. Selecting the sketch point

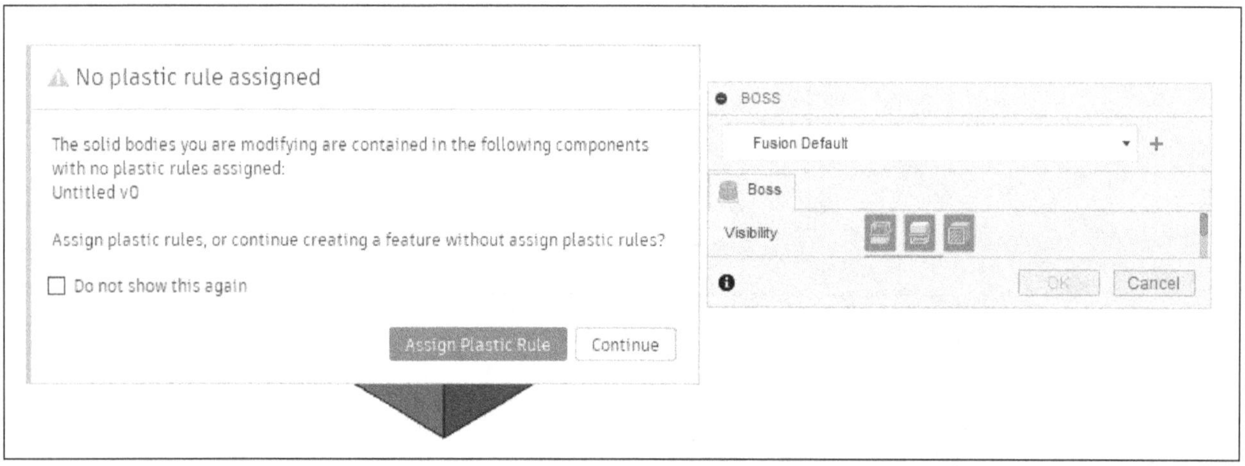

Figure-151. Updated BOSS dialog box

- Click on the **Assign Plastic Rule** button to assign the plastic rule or click on the **Continue** button from the pop-up window to create boss feature without assigning the plastic rule. The preview of boss feature will be displayed; refer to Figure-152. Note that you may need to drag the offset position handle for generating preview of feature.

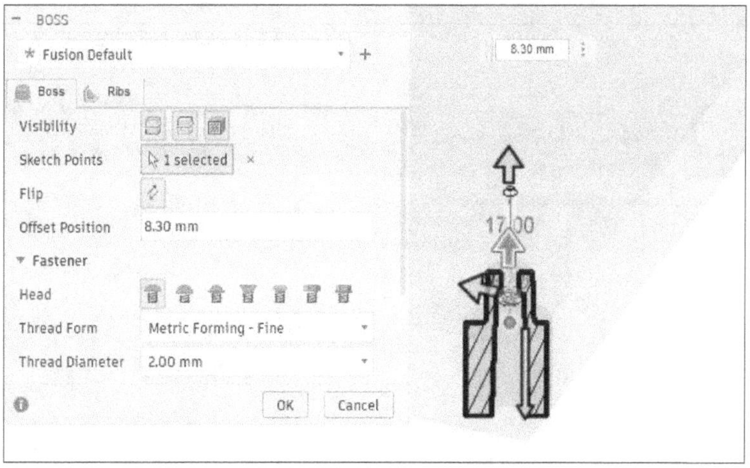

Figure-152. Preview of boss feature

- All buttons are selected by default in the **Visibility** section. The **Side 1 Transparency** button reduces the opacity of the Side 1 body while you edit the boss feature. The **Side 2 Transparency** button reduces the opacity of the Side 2 body while you edit the boss feature. The **Section Analysis** button cuts a section through the center of the boss feature while you edit.
- Select the **Flip** button to flip the boss feature over selected sketch point to switch Side 1 and Side 2 bodies.
- Specify desired distance value in the **Offset Position** edit box to offset the position of the boss feature from the sketch plane.
- Select desired option from **Head** section of the **Fastener** node to create fastener of desired head type.
- Select desired thread form from **Thread Form** drop-down and thread diameter from the **Thread Diameter** drop-down to apply to the fastener.
- Select desired type of hole type and step from **Hole Type** section and **Step Type** section of **Side** node in the dialog box, respectively to create boss feature.
- Expand the **Advanced** node and specify desired values in the edit boxes to adjust the dimensions of the side of the boss feature.
- Click on the **Ribs** tab to create ribs on sides of boss feature. The related options will be displayed.
- Select the **Side 1** check box to activate rib feature on side 1 of boss feature; refer to Figure-153. Set the parameters as discussed earlier for the rib.

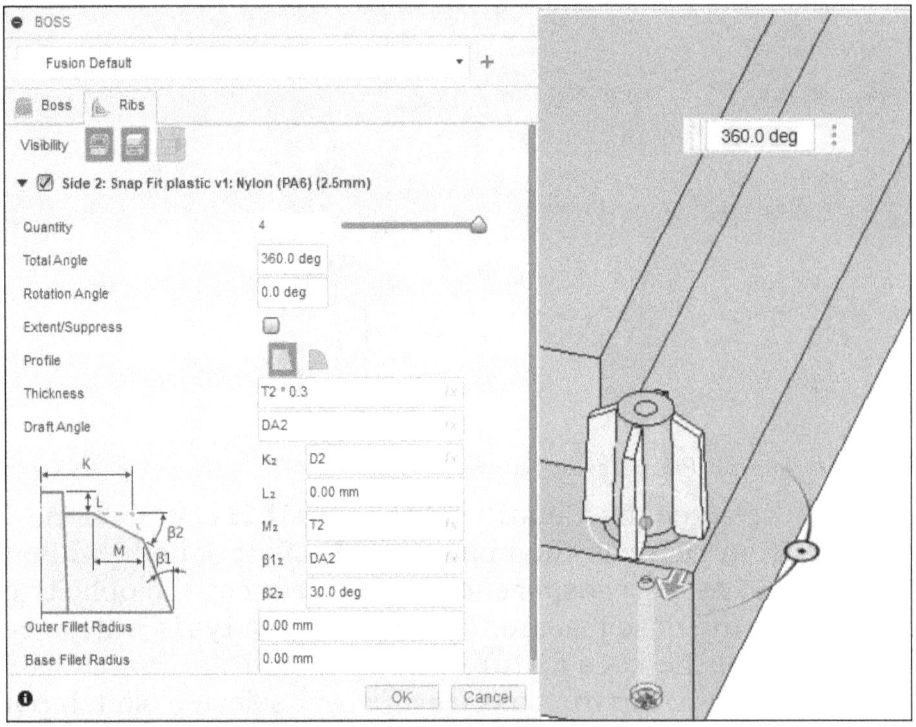

Figure-153. Rib feature for boss

- After specifying desired parameters in the dialog box, click on the **OK** button. The boss feature will be created; refer to Figure-154.

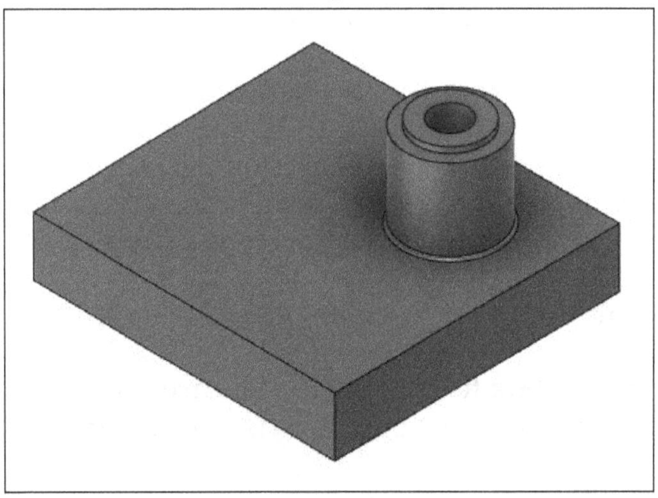

Figure-154. Boss feature created

Creating Lip Feature

The **Lip** tool is used to create a lip, groove, or combined feature on one or two solid bodies. The procedure to use this tool is discussed next.

- Click on the **Lip** tool from **CREATE** drop-down of **PLASTIC** tab in the **Toolbar**. The **LIP** dialog box will be displayed asking you to select the path; refer to Figure-155.

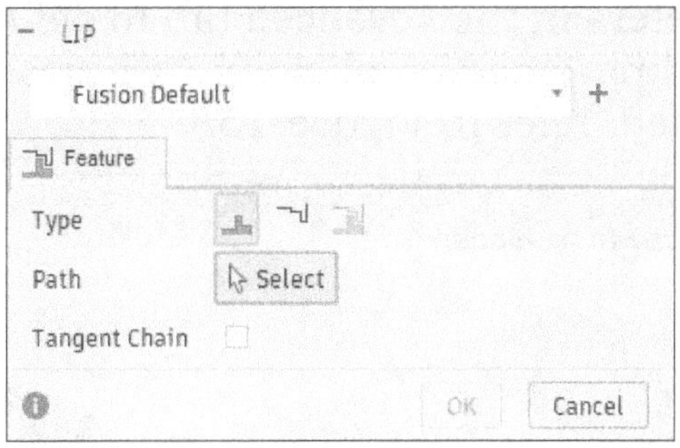

Figure-155. LIP dialog box

- Select **Lip** option from **Type** area to create a raised lip feature on a solid body. Select **Groove** option to create a recessed groove feature on a solid body. Select **Lip** And **Groove** option is used to create a lip and groove features on a pair of solid bodies.
- The **Path** selection button is active by default. Select edge(s) of the component to be used as path. The updated **LIP** dialog box will be displayed; refer to Figure-156.

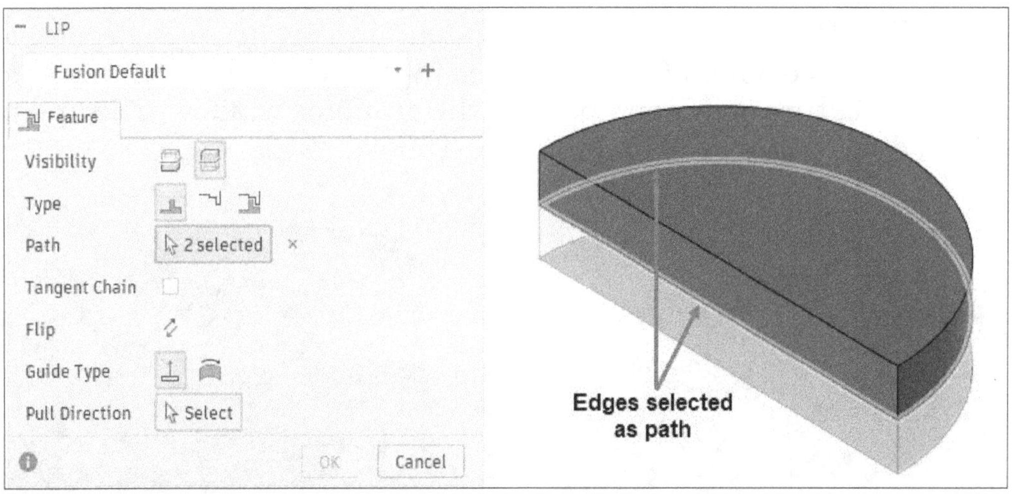

Figure-156. Updated LIP dialog box with edges selected as path

- Select **Tangent Chain** check box to select tangent edges, automatically.
- Select **Pull Direction** option from **Guide Type** area and select desired plane or face to be defined as the pull direction. Selet **Face Guide** option and select desired face to place the lip feature.
- On selecting the pull direction, the preview of lip feature will be displayed with **Advanced** tab in the **LIP** dialog box; refer to Figure-157.

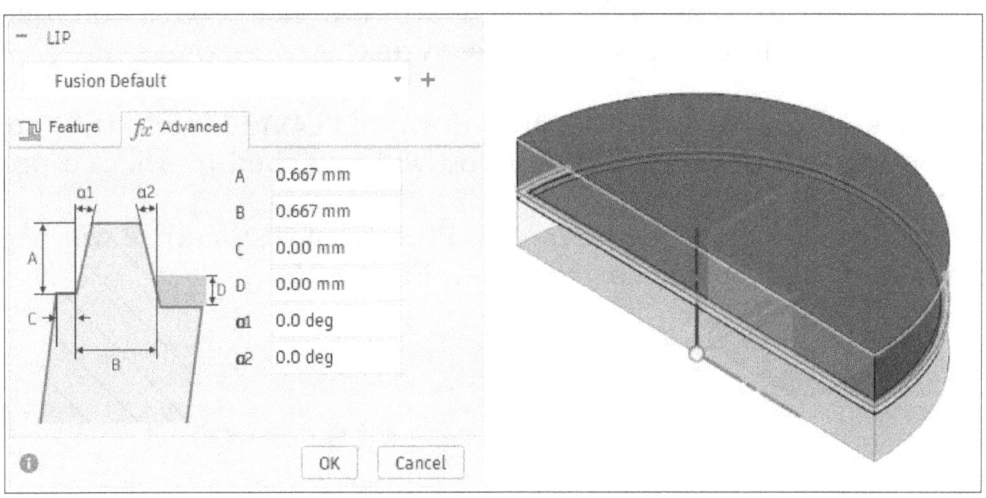

Figure-157. Advanced tab of LIP dialog box

- Specify desired parameters in the **Advanced** tab to define the feature dimensions.
- After specifying desired parameters, click on **OK** button from the dialog box. The lip feature will be created; refer to Figure-158.

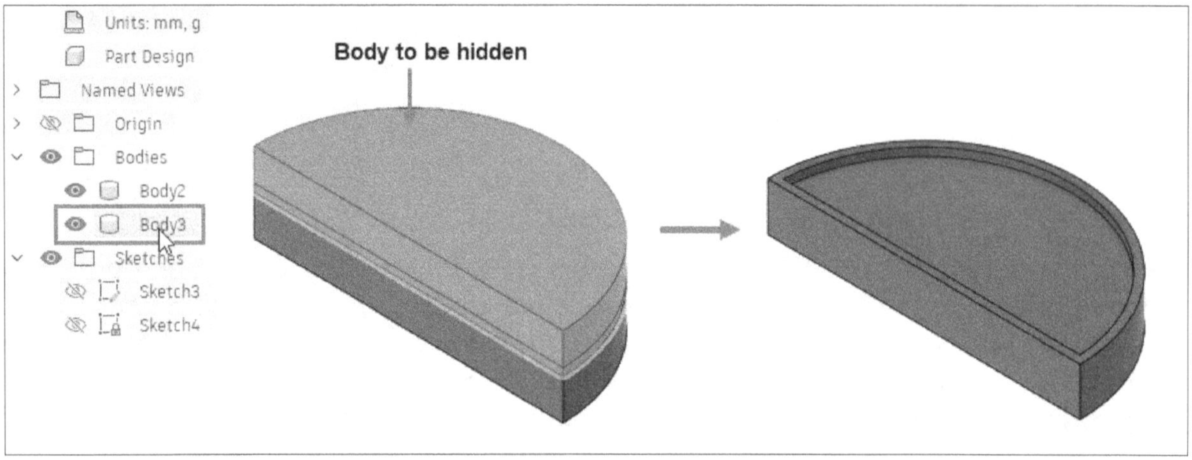

Figure-158. Lip feature created

Similarly, select **Groove** option from **Type** area in the **Feature** tab of the dialog box to create the groove feature on second body in the graphics window. The lip and groove feature will be displayed as shown in Figure-159.

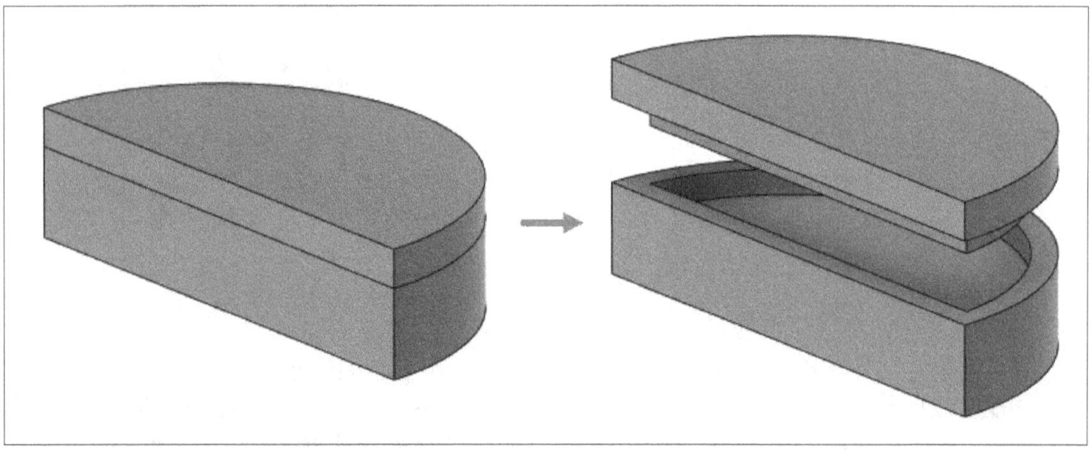

Figure-159. Lip and groove feature created

Creating Rest Feature

The **Rest** tool is used to create a flat rest area in the model based on a closed loop sketch. The procedure to use this tool is given next.

- Click on the **Rest** tool from **CREATE** drop-down of **PLASTIC** tab in the **Toolbar**. The **REST** dialog box will be displayed and you will be asked to select a profile; refer to Figure-160.
- Select the sketch profile from the model. Preview of rest feature will be displayed and options will be displayed as shown in Figure-161.

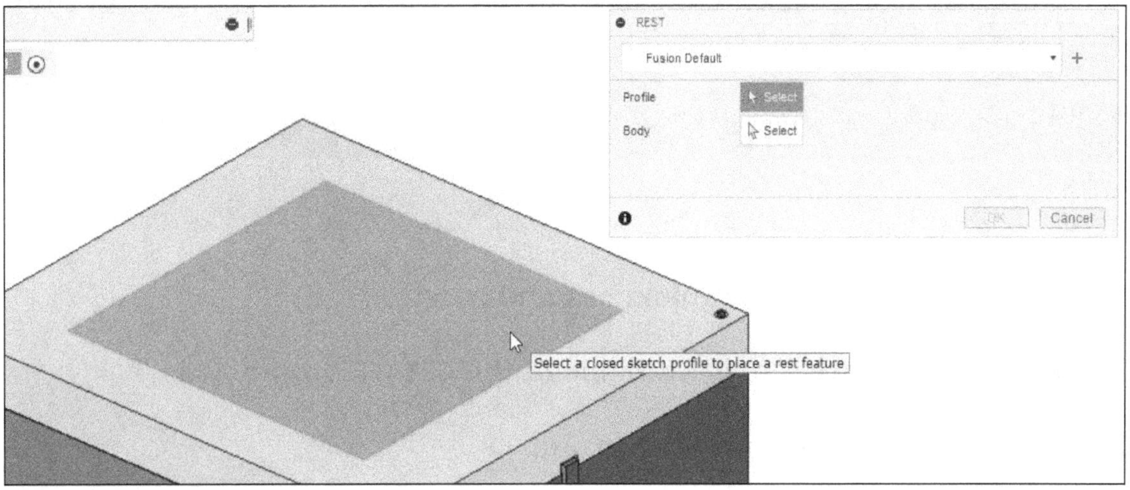

Figure-160. REST dialog box

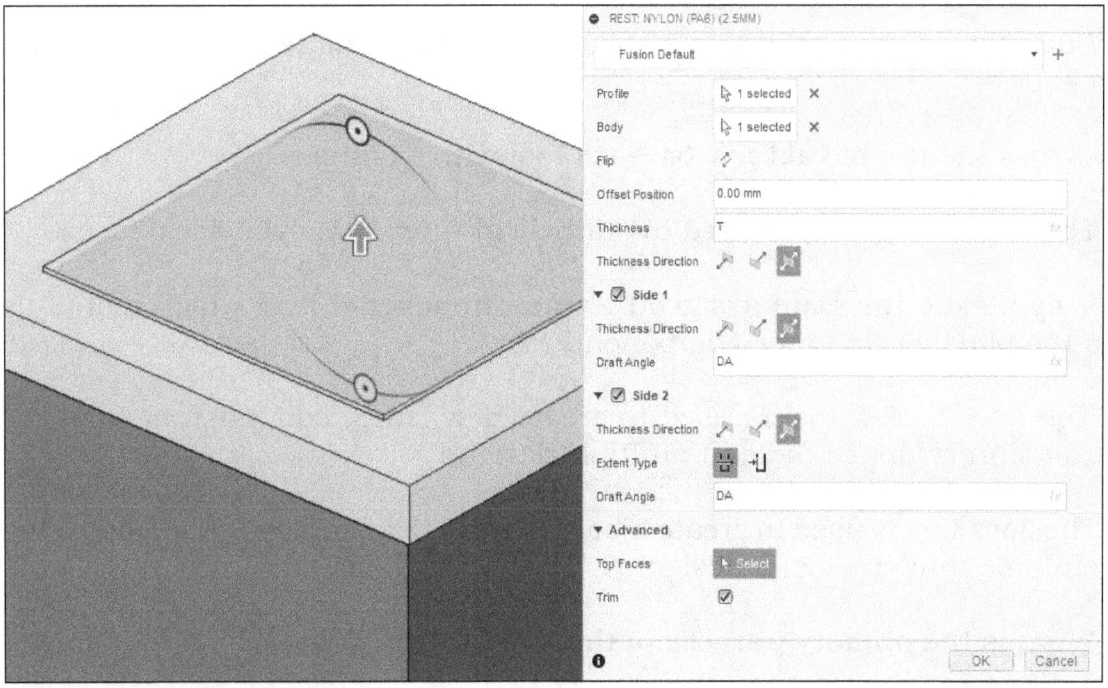

Figure-161. Preview of rest feature

- Set desired parameters in the dialog box and click on the **OK** button.

SELF ASSESSMENT

Q1. Which of the following is not the default plane available in Autodesk Fusion?

a. Front Plane
b. Right Plane
c. Top Plane
d. Left Plane

Q2. Discuss the procedure of creating multiple holes with example.

Q3. Which of the following tool is not available in **CREATE** drop-down of Autodesk Fusion?

a. Thread
b. Box
C. Torus
d. Curve

Q4. **Thicken** tool is used to add thickness and length. (T/F)

Q5. The **Pattern On Path** tool is available in the **CREATE** drop-down. (T/F)

Q6. Discuss the use of **Pipe** tool with examples.

Q7. Discuss the use of **Web** tool with examples.

Q8. Which tool is used to create a solid body connecting two sketch from different planes?

Q9. Discuss the use of **Pattern On Path** tool with examples.

Q10. The .... tool is used to cut helical thread on cylindrical faces.

Q11. Why plastic rules are assigned to the component? And which tool is used to assign the plastic rule to the component?

Q12. The .... tool is used to create new rules, edit existing rules, or save rules to a library to use them in multiple designs.

Q13. The **Boss** tool is used to create a boss feature to fasten two solid bodies together and reinforce thin areas of a design. (T/F)

Q14: What is the primary purpose of the Loft tool in 3D modeling?

A) To create a solid volume by joining two or more sketches
B) To create a 2D shape from a single sketch
C) To create a 3D model by extruding a single sketch
D) To rotate a 3D object along an axis

Q15: Which of the following options are available in the End Condition drop-down when sketches are selected as profiles for loft?

A) Connected and Direction
B) Connected (G0), Tangent (G1), and Curvature (G2)
C) Sharp and Point Tangent
D) Only Direction

Q16: What is the purpose of the "Takeoff Weight" in the Loft dialog box?

A) It determines the scale and angle at which the loft will start or end at the selected profile.
B) It adjusts the shape of the loft by scaling the profiles.
C) It specifies the outward angle of the loft feature.
D) It adjusts the weight of the loft feature in the design.

Q17: Which of the following options is available when you select a point as a profile in the End Condition drop-down?

A) Connected and Direction
B) Sharp and Point Tangent
C) Tangent (G1) and Curvature (G2)
D) Closed and Chain Selection

Q18: What effect does the "Chain Selection" check box have in the Loft dialog box?

A) It allows the selection of the adjacent edges as one profile.
B) It adjusts the angle of the loft shape.
C) It helps in scaling the loft profiles.
D) It affects the visibility of loft previews.

Q19: How can you control the transition between profiles in a loft using rails?

A) By selecting a single centerline as the guide.
B) By selecting multiple rails that intersect each section and are tangentially continuous.
C) By adjusting the loft's outward angle only.
D) By modifying the scale of the profiles individually.

Q20: What is the function of the Centerline tool in lofting?

A) It helps to hold the loft sections normal to each other.
B) It selects multiple intersecting curves for smooth transitions.
C) It adds additional profiles to the loft.
D) It modifies the dimensions of the loft sections.

Q21: When using the Centerline guide type, which of the following is true?

A) You must use multiple intersecting arcs to create a valid loft.
B) A single centerline can be used, and it does not need to intersect the sections.
C) Centerlines cannot be used for lofts in coplanar profiles.
D) The loft will only work if two centerlines are selected.

Q22: What happens if you select the “Closed” check box when using the Centerline guide type?

A) The loft will form a complete ring.
B) The loft will display an error message.
C) The loft will remain open and incomplete.
D) The loft shape will become more complex and irregular.

Q23: What happens when you click the “OK” button in the LOFT dialog box?

A) The loft feature is created according to the settings and profiles selected.
B) The tool resets, and the settings are cleared.
C) The profiles and settings are saved, but no loft is generated.
D) The software automatically selects the best loft profile for you.

Q24: What is the Rib tool used for in 3D modeling?

A) To create supporting features in the model using curves
B) To extrude a solid shape from a sketch
C) To create a hollow volume inside a solid
D) To create a surface from multiple profiles

Q25: What does selecting the “Symmetric” option in the Thickness Direction section of the RIB dialog box do?

A) It sets the thickness of the rib on both sides of the curve.
B) It applies the thickness only on one side of the curve.
C) It adjusts the rib thickness based on the direction of the profile.
D) It makes the rib thickness adjustable from the center.

Q26: How can you specify the depth of a rib using the RIB dialog box?

A) By selecting the “To Next” option from the Extent Type drop-down.
B) By entering the numerical value of depth in the Depth edit box or moving the Drag arrow.
C) By flipping the rib direction using the “Flip Direction” button.
D) By using the “Symmetric” option in the Thickness Direction section.

Q27: What happens when you click on the “Flip Direction” button in the RIB dialog box?

A) The rib direction is reversed.
B) The thickness of the rib is adjusted.
C) The depth of the rib is modified.
D) The profile curve is flipped.

Q28: How can you activate the Draft Angle and Fillet Radius section in the RIB dialog box?

A) By clicking on the Extensions button from the toolbar and starting a trial.
B) By selecting a preset from the Presets drop-down menu.
C) By clicking on the "Flip Direction" button.
D) By entering the desired values in the Thickness edit box.

Q29: What is the Web tool used for?

A) To create multiple merged ribs from several sketch curves
B) To apply a fillet to sharp edges
C) To combine two profiles into a single shape
D) To create a solid volume by lofting curves

Q30: Which of the following options is available in the WEB dialog box when using the Web tool?

A) Select the sketch to create a web and specify thickness
B) Select faces to emboss or deboss
C) Adjust the draft angle of the ribs
D) Flip the direction of the web's profile

Q31: What is the purpose of the Emboss tool in 3D modeling?

A) To raise or recess a sketch profile relative to selected faces on a solid body
B) To apply a surface texture to the model
C) To create a smooth transition between solid faces
D) To extend a sketch profile along an axis

Q32: How can you specify the depth for embossing or debossing in the EMBOSS dialog box?

A) By typing the value in the Depth edit box.
B) By selecting the "Symmetric" option in the dialog box.
C) By adjusting the draft angle using the "Flip Direction" button.
D) By using the Distance and Angle manipulator handles.

Q33: What does selecting the "Emboss" button in the EMBOSS dialog box do?

A) It adds material to the body to create the emboss feature.
B) It removes material from the body to create the deboss feature.
C) It adjusts the draft angle for the emboss.
D) It flips the direction of the embossing effect.

Q34. What is the primary function of the Hole tool?

A) To create a hole for inserting screws
B) To create holes that comply with real machining tools
C) To create decorative holes
D) To create holes for attaching components

Q35. Which option should be selected to create a single hole in the HOLE dialog box?

A) Multiple Holes
B) Single Hole
C) Counterbore
D) Countersink

Q36. What is required to create multiple holes using the Hole tool?

A) Selection of a single reference edge
B) Pre-existing sketch points on the model
C) Selection of the material type
D) Selection of a single hole type

Q37. What does the “Modeled” check box in the Thread tool do?

A) Specifies the direction of the thread
B) Creates a cosmetic feature for the thread
C) Previews the thread with visual representation
D) Creates a modeled feature of the thread

Q38. In the Box tool, how do you specify the dimensions of the box?

A) By selecting the “Length” and “Height” edit boxes
B) By clicking on the screen to create a base rectangle
C) By entering values in the “Width” and “Height” edit boxes
D) By typing the numerical values in the Diameter edit box

Q39. Which of the following is true about the Cylinder tool?

A) It creates a solid or surface sphere
B) It adds depth to a circular region to form a cylinder
C) It creates a hollow cylindrical object
D) It allows the creation of spherical shapes

Q40. What is the purpose of the “Full Length” check box in the Thread tool?

A) To specify the length of the thread on the selected face
B) To create the thread along the entire length of the selected face
C) To adjust the size of the thread
D) To change the thread direction

Q41. When creating a Torus, which option in the Position drop-down lets you place the torus inside the inner circle?

A) On Center
B) Inside
C) Outside
D) Top

Q42. What does the Coil tool primarily create?

A) Solid cylindrical objects
B) Helix-based features like springs
C) Pipe sections
D) Rectangular boxes

Q43. How can the Pipe tool create a hollow pipe?

A) By selecting the "Section Size"
B) By entering a negative value in the Diameter
C) By selecting the "Hollow" check box
D) By adjusting the drag handle

Q44: What is the purpose of the Pattern tool in CAD software?

A) To create random patterns
B) To create copies of features or bodies at regular intervals
C) To create a single copy of a feature or body
D) To modify the features in a model

Q45: Which option is used to select the type of object in the Rectangular Pattern tool?

A) Faces
B) Bodies
C) Features
D) Components

Q46: In the Rectangular Pattern tool, which option allows you to create copies in one direction?

A) Quantity
B) Distance
C) One Direction
D) Symmetric

Q47: What does the Spacing option in the Rectangular Pattern tool do?

A) It sets the number of copies to be created
B) It specifies the total length for the pattern
C) It sets the distance between two consecutive instances
D) It suppresses the pattern instances

Q48: How can you create a circular pattern in CAD software?

A) By selecting Rectangular Pattern tool
B) By selecting Circular Pattern tool from the Pattern cascading menu
C) By using the Pattern on Path tool
D) By using the Mirror tool

Q49: Which option defines the axis around which the Circular Pattern tool will create copies?

A) Select button in the Quantity section
B) Select button in the Axis section
C) Distribution drop-down
D) Symmetric option

Q50: What is the function of the "Suppression" checkbox in both Rectangular and Circular Pattern tools?

A) It suppresses the entire pattern
B) It suppresses individual instances of the pattern
C) It sets the quantity of the pattern
D) It specifies the direction of the pattern

Q51: What does the Pattern on Path tool do?

A) It creates copies along a specified path
B) It creates copies in a circular direction
C) It creates geometric patterns on solid bodies
D) It mirrors objects across a plane

Q52: In the Pattern on Path tool, which option specifies the distance from the start point of the pattern?

A) Start Point
B) Suppression
C) Path Direction
D) Quantity

Q53: Which tool allows you to create a pattern with size and distribution gradients across a face on a solid body?

A) Rectangular Pattern
B) Circular Pattern
C) Geometric Pattern
D) Mirror Tool

Q54: How do you align objects in a geometric pattern to the left of the selected face?

A) Select Align Right
B) Select Align Center
C) Select Align Left
D) Select Clear Perimeter

Q55: What is the purpose of the Mirror tool in CAD software?

A) To create multiple copies of objects in a grid pattern
B) To create a mirror copy of selected objects across a plane or face
C) To add thickness to a surface
D) To create a 3D shape from surfaces

Q56: Which option in the Mirror tool allows you to specify how the mirrored objects are created?

A) Select button in Mirror Plane
B) Object Type
C) Operation drop-down
D) Compute Type drop-down

Q57: What does the Thicken tool do in CAD modeling?

A) It adds color to the model
B) It adds thickness to surfaces to make them solid
C) It creates a mirror image of an object
D) It creates a circular pattern of objects

Q58: In the Thicken tool, which option applies thickness to both sides of the surface equally?

A) One Side
B) Symmetric
C) Identical
D) Direction

Q59: What is the Boundary Fill tool used for in CAD modeling?

A) To mirror objects across a plane
B) To create volumes from selected planes, bodies, and surfaces
C) To create a geometric pattern
D) To thicken surfaces

Q60: How do you create a new body using the Boundary Fill tool?

A) By selecting the bodies/planes/surfaces for boundary fill
B) By adjusting the quantity in the dialog box
C) By selecting the Mirror option
D) By clicking the Thicken button

For Student Notes

Chapter 5

Practical and Practice

Topics Covered

The major topics covered in this chapter are:

- ***Practical***
- ***Practice***

PRACTICAL 1

Create the model as shown in Figure-1. The views of the model with dimension are given in Figure-2.

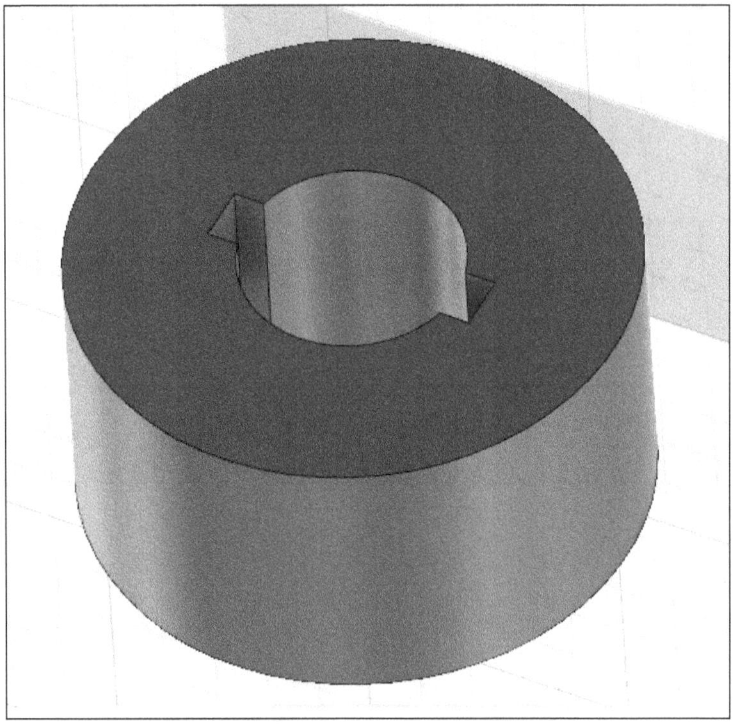

Figure-1. Model for Practical 1

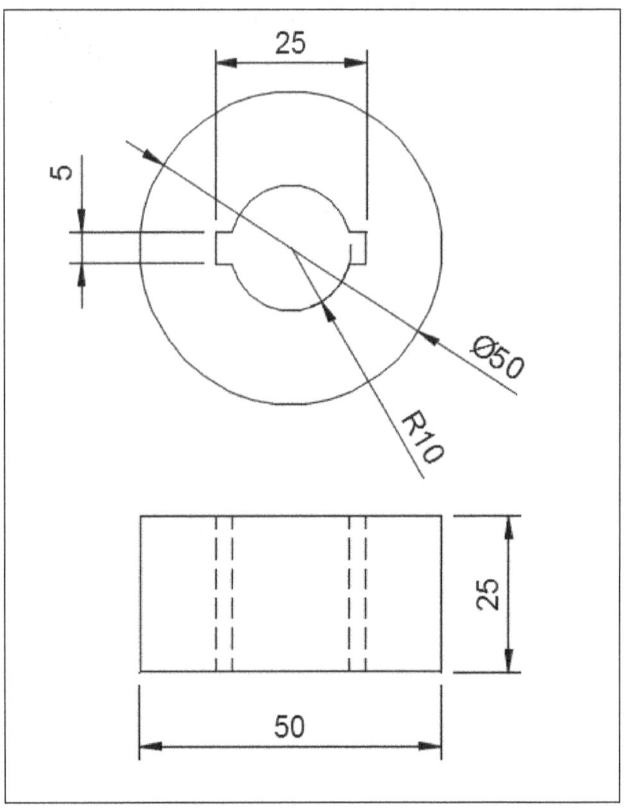

Figure-2. Views of Practical 1

Before we start working on Practical 1, it is important to understand two terms; first angle projection and third angle projection. These are the standards of placing views in the engineering drawings. The views placed in the above figure are using third angle projection. In first angle projection, the top view of model is placed below the front view and right side view is placed at the left of the front view. You will learn more about projection in chapter related to drafting.

Creating the Sketch

- Click on **Create Sketch** tool from **CREATE** drop-down in the **Toolbar**. You will be asked to select a plane for creating sketch.
- Select **Top Plane** from the canvas screen.
- Click on **Center Diameter Circle** tool from **Circle** cascading menu of **CREATE** drop-down in the **Toolbar**. You will be asked to place the center point of circle.
- Click at the **Origin** to place the center point of circle. Enter **50** in floating window as diameter of circle and press **ENTER** key.
- Sketch another circle of radius **10** (diameter **20**) taking center point as origin.

How to show radius in place of diameter of circle? Create the circle with diameter value. Right-click on diameter dimension and select **Toggle Radius** button from Marking menu; refer to Figure-3.

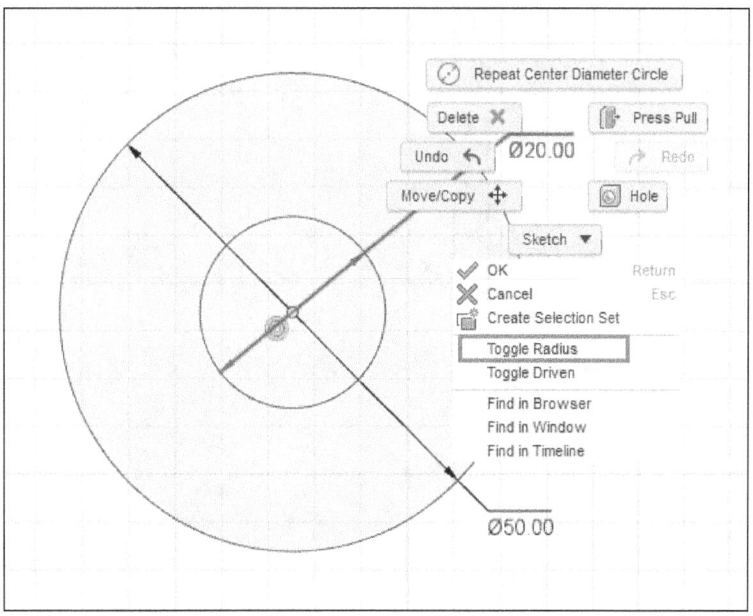

Figure-3. Toggle Radius option

- Select **Center Rectangle** tool from **Rectangle** cascading menu of **CREATE** drop-down in the **Toolbar**.
- Click at **Origin** as center point for rectangle and enter **5** as width & **25** as length in floating window to create a rectangle; refer to Figure-4.

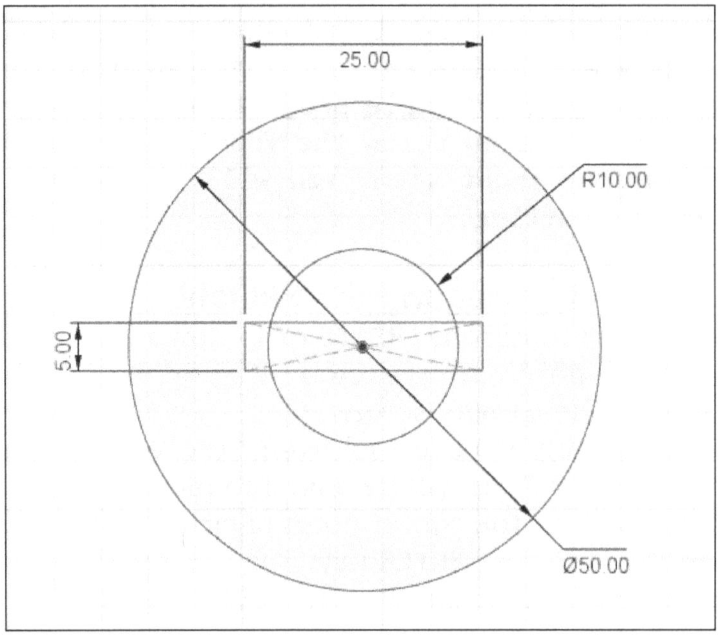

Figure-4. Sketch after creating circle and rectangle

- Select **Trim** tool from **MODIFY** drop-down in the **Toolbar** and trim the entities in such a way that the sketch is displayed as shown in Figure-5.

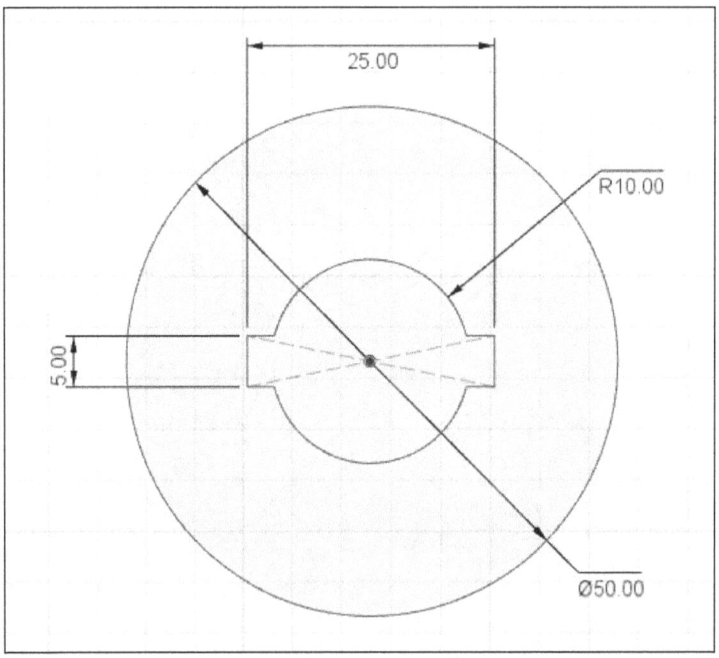

Figure-5. Sketch after trimming

- Click on **Finish Sketch** button from **Toolbar** to exit the sketch mode.

Creating Extrude Feature

- Click on the **Extrude** tool from **CREATE** drop-down in the **Toolbar** or press **E** key from keyboard to select **Extrude** tool. The **EXTRUDE** dialog box will be displayed.
- Profile selection is active by default. Select the recently created sketch profile. The updated **EXTRUDE** dialog box will be displayed.
- Specify the height of extrusion as **25** in **Distance** edit box or floating window. The preview of extrusion will be displayed; refer to Figure-6. (You need to rotate the model by using **SHIFT+Middle Mouse Button** to check the preview.)

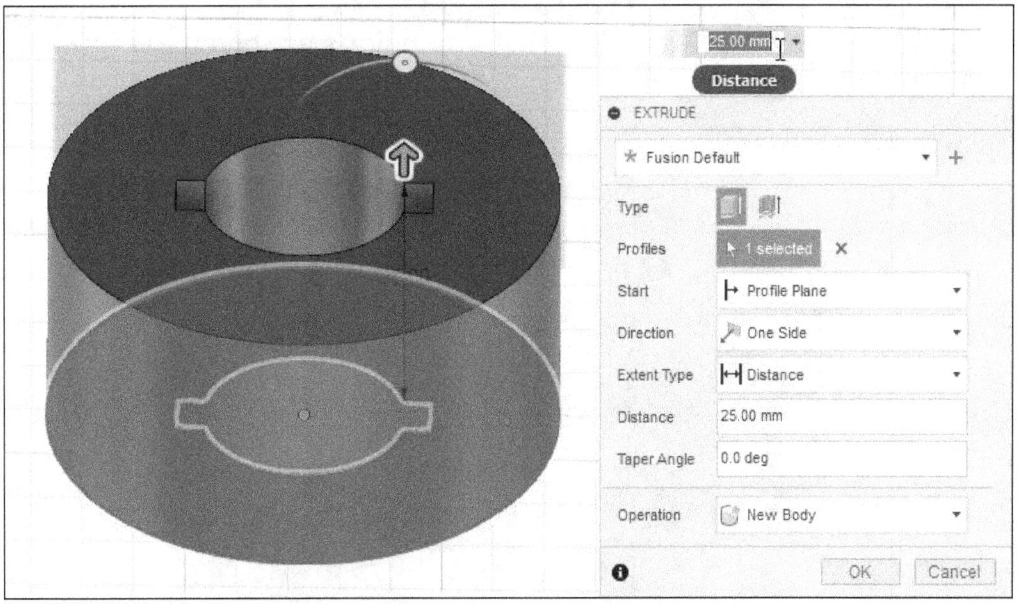

Figure-6. Preview of extrusion

- Click **OK** button from **EXTRUDE** dialog box to complete the process of extrusion. The model will be displayed as shown in Figure-7.
- Save the file and close it.

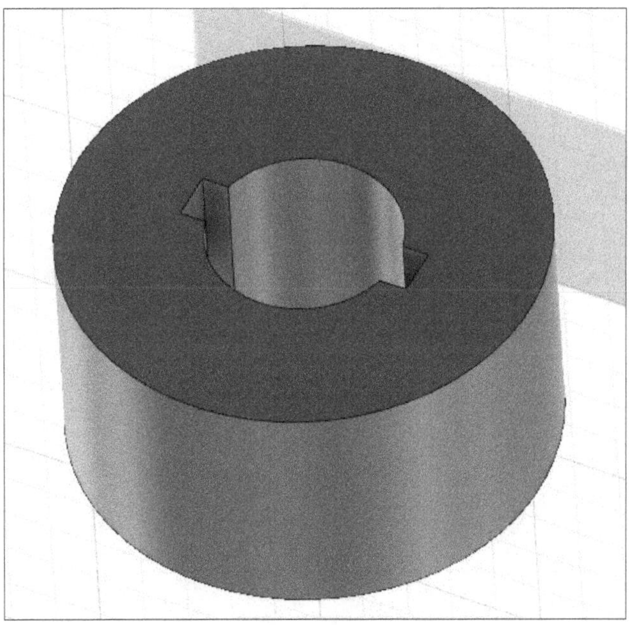

Figure-7. Final model of Practical 1

PRACTICAL 2

Create the model as shown in Figure-8. The dimensions are given in Figure-9. Assume the missing dimensions.

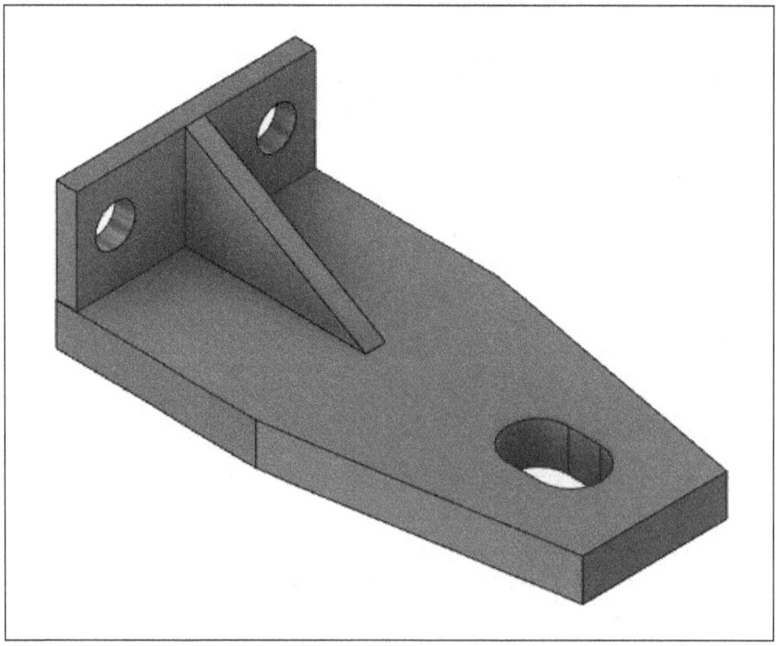

Figure-8. Model for Practical 2

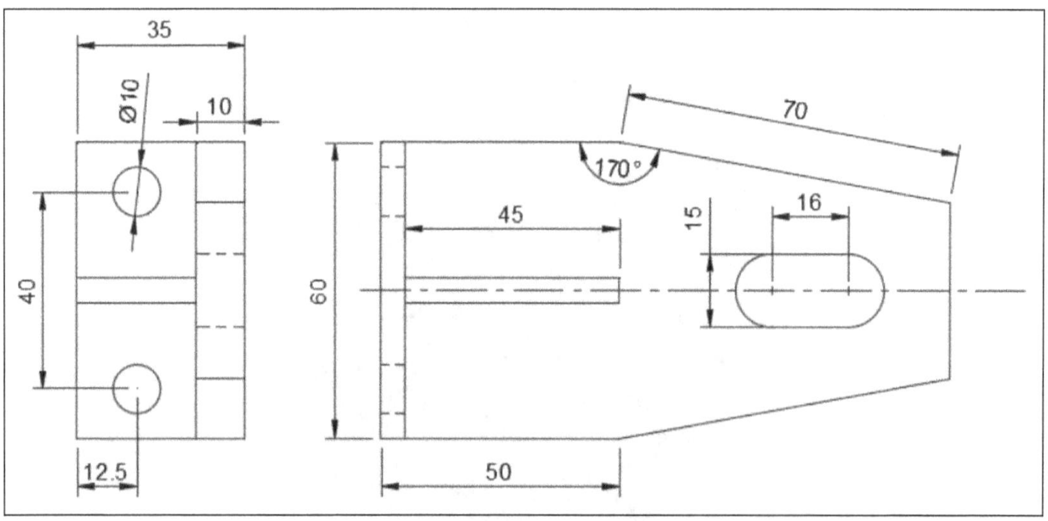

Figure-9. Practical 2 drawing

Creating sketch for model

- Start a new sketch using **Top Plane**.
- Select **Centre Rectangle** tool from **Rectangle** cascading menu of **CREATE** drop-down.
- Click on the origin to specify the centre point of rectangle and specify **60** and **50** in floating window as dimensions of rectangle; refer to Figure-10. Press **TAB** to toggle between edit boxes.

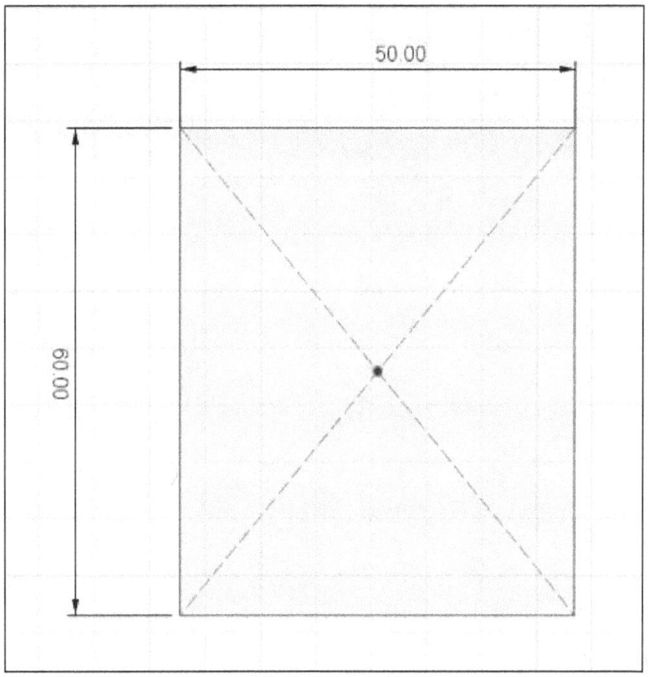

Figure-10. Sketch After Creating Rectangle

- Select **Line** tool from **CREATE** drop-down. Create a line of length as **70** and angle of **80** degree as shown in Figure-11.

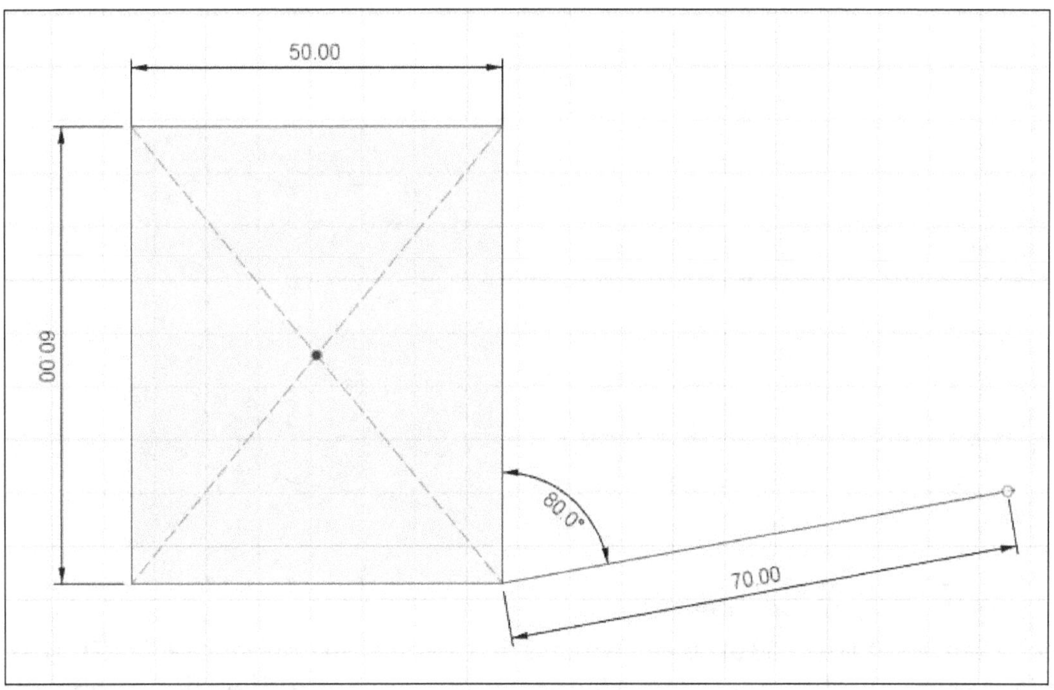

Figure-11. Creating Angular Line

- Select **Mirror** tool from **CREATE** drop-down in the **Toolbar** and create a mirror copy of recently created line about centerline as shown in Figure-12.

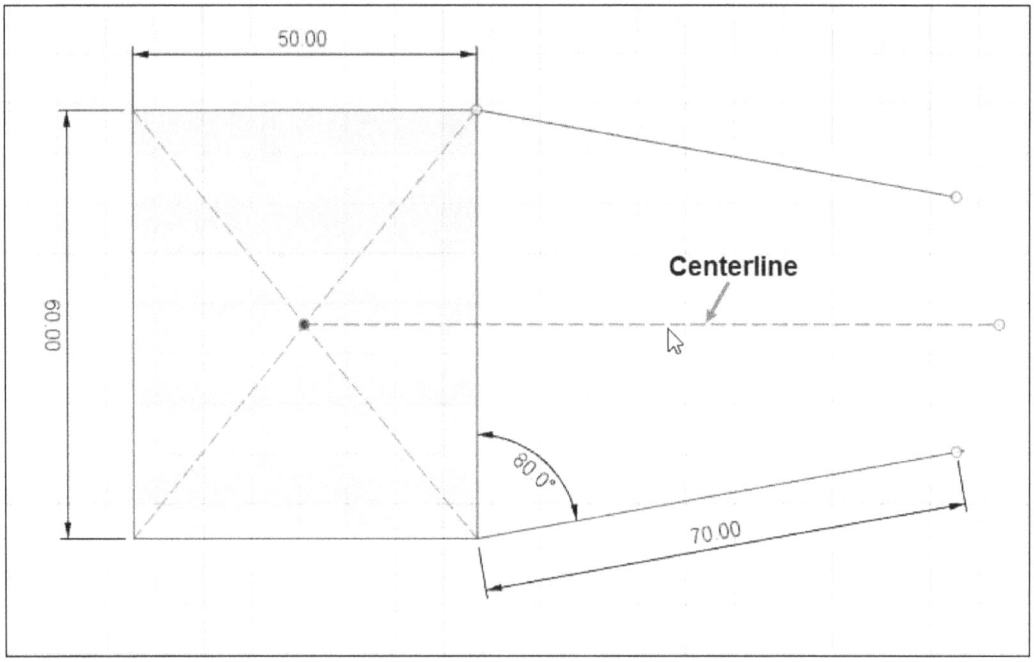

Figure-12. Creating mirror copy

- Create a line joining end points of two earlier created lines as shown in Figure-13.

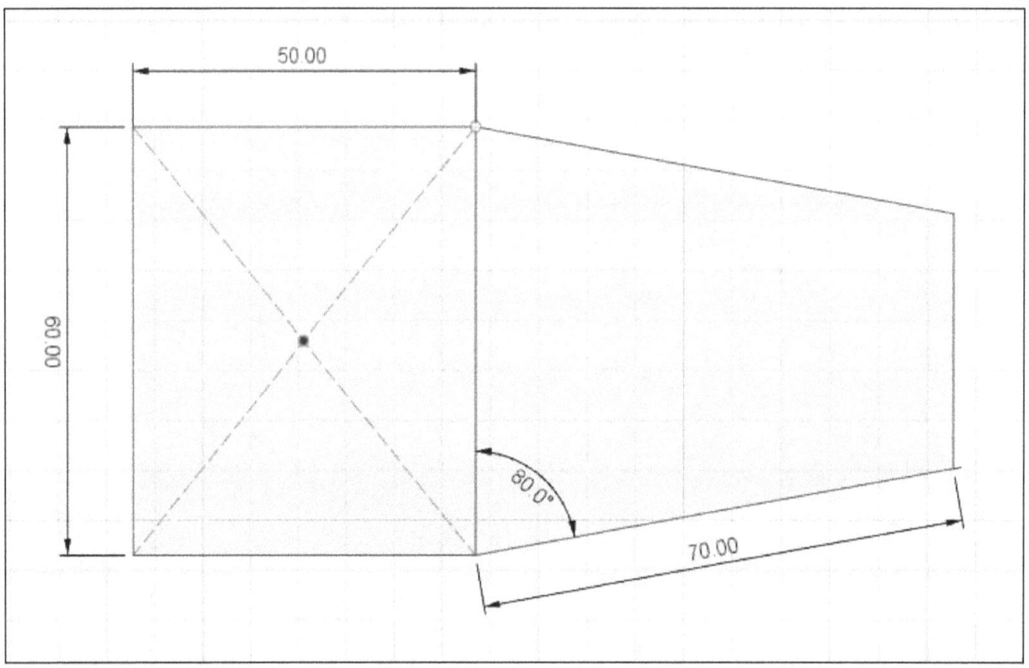

Figure-13. Joining end points of lines

- Select **Center Point Slot** tool from **Slot** cascading menu of **CREATE** drop-down and create a slot of diameter as **15** and length as **8** at a distance of **65** from origin on the centerline; refer to Figure-14.

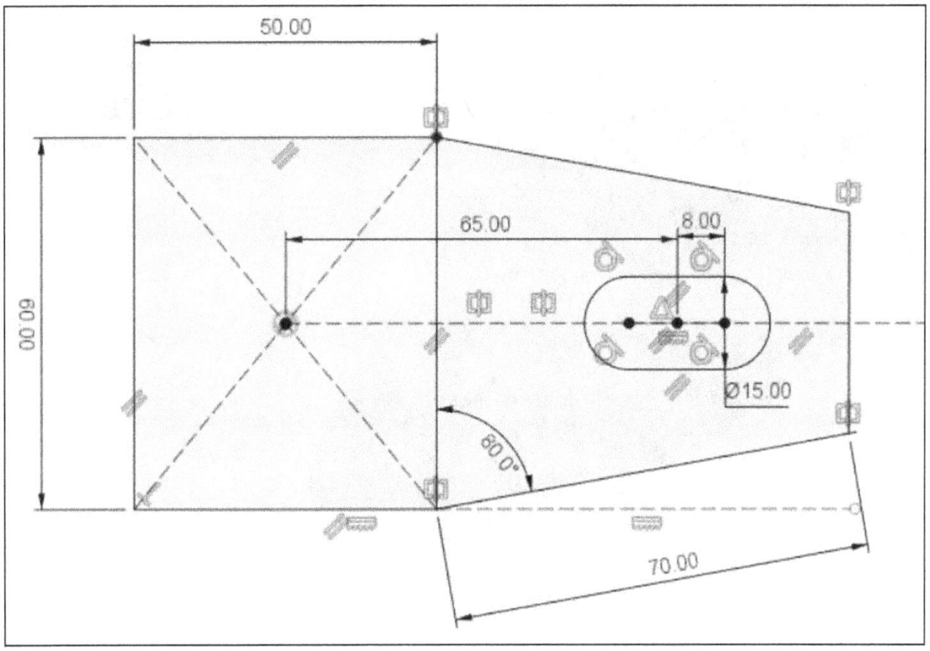

Figure-14. Creating slot

- Press **T** from keyboard or click on the **Trim** tool from **MODIFY** drop-down in the **Toolbar** to activate trimming tool. Select the inner lines of rectangle to remove them; refer to Figure-15.

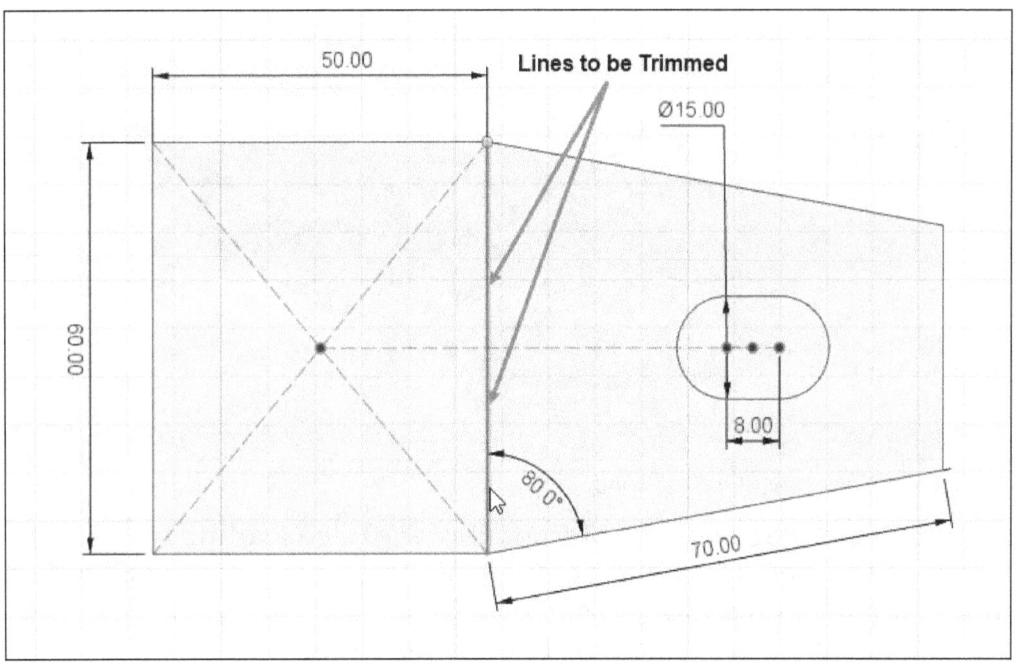

Figure-15. Lines to be trimmed

- Click on the **Finish Sketch** button to exit sketch.

Creating Extrude Feature

- Select **Extrude** tool from **CREATE** drop-down or press **E** key. The **EXTRUDE** dialog box will be displayed.
- Profile selection is active by default. Click in the sketch outside the slot.
- Specify **10** as height of extrusion in **Distance** edit box of **EXTRUDE** dialog box; refer to Figure-16. (Rotate the model to get clear view.)

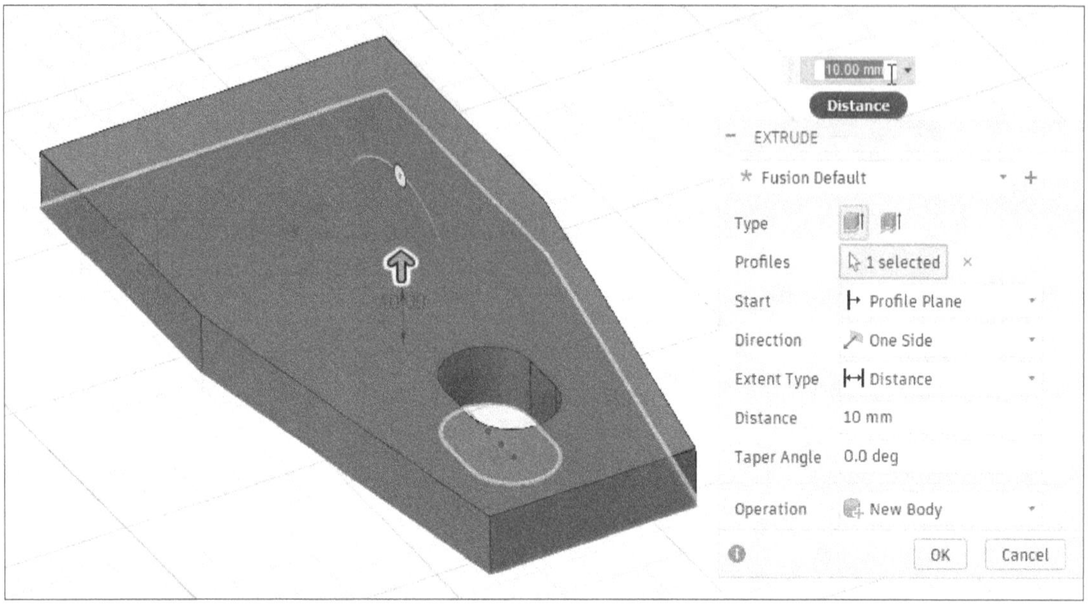

Figure-16. Preview of extrusion

- Click **OK** button from **EXTRUDE** dialog box to complete the process of extrusion.
- Click on the **Create Sketch** tool from **CREATE** drop-down. You are asked to select the plane to create sketch. Select the side face of model as shown in Figure-17.

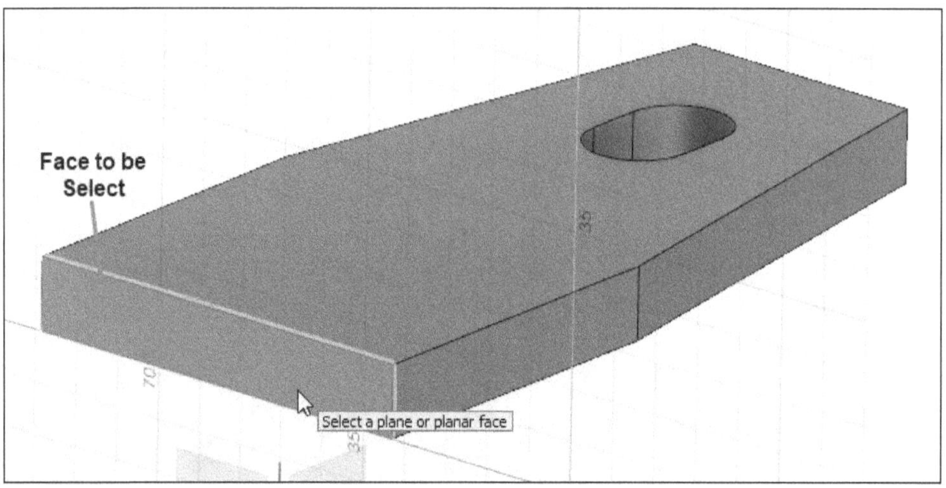

Figure-17. Face to be select for sketching

- Select the **2-Point Rectangle** tool from **Rectangle** cascading menu in the **CREATE** drop-down of **Toolbar**. Create a rectangle of dimensions **25** and **60** with two holes of diameter **10** as shown in Figure-18.
- Click on the **Finish Sketch** button to exit sketching.

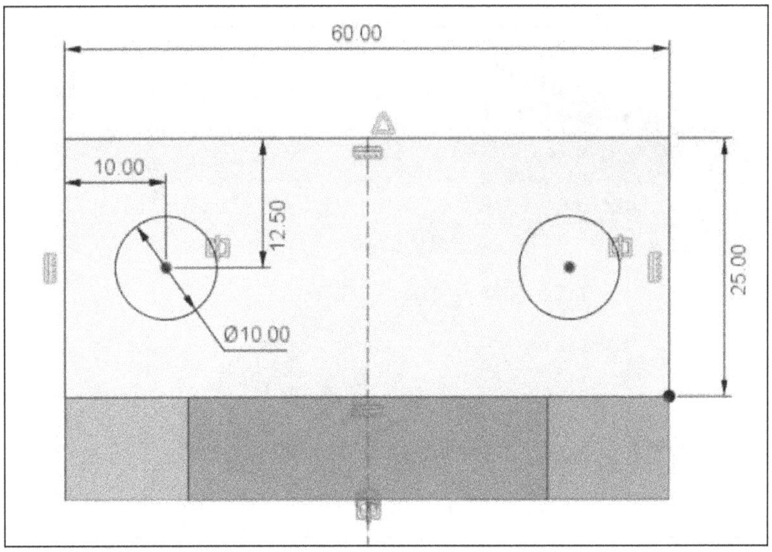

Figure-18. Creating the rectangle with holes

- Select **Extrude** tool from **CREATE** drop-down. The **EXTRUDE** dialog box will be displayed.
- Select the upper portion of recently created sketch in **Profiles** selection and specify **-5** as height of extrusion.
- Select **Join** from **Operation** drop-down of **EXTRUDE** dialog box to join the two extrusions.
- Click **OK** button from **EXTRUDE** dialog box to finish this process; refer to Figure-19.

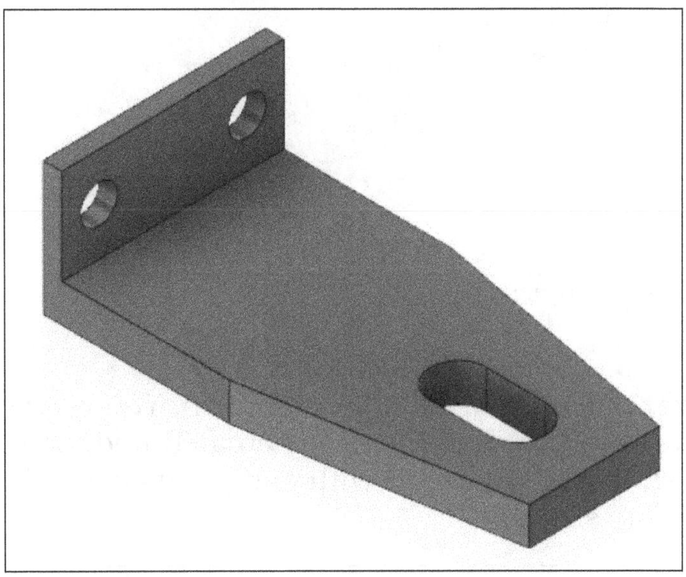

Figure-19. Extrude feature created

Creating Midplane

- Select **Midplane** tool from **CONSTRUCT** drop-down in the **Toolbar**. The **CONSTRUCTION GEOMETRY** dialog box will be displayed. You are asked to select the faces between which you want to create a midplane.
- Select both the faces as shown in Figure-20.
- The preview of midplane will be displayed. Click **OK** button from the **CONSTRUCTION GEOMETRY** dialog box to complete the process; refer to Figure-21.

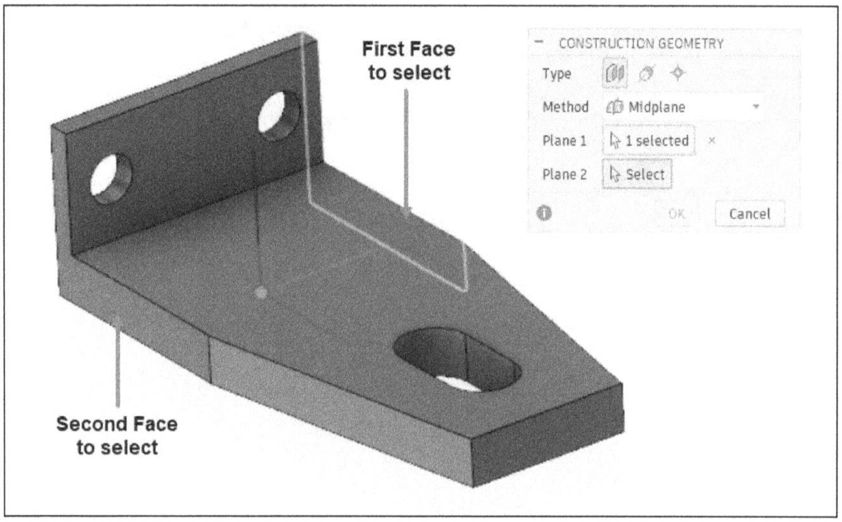

Figure-20. Face selection

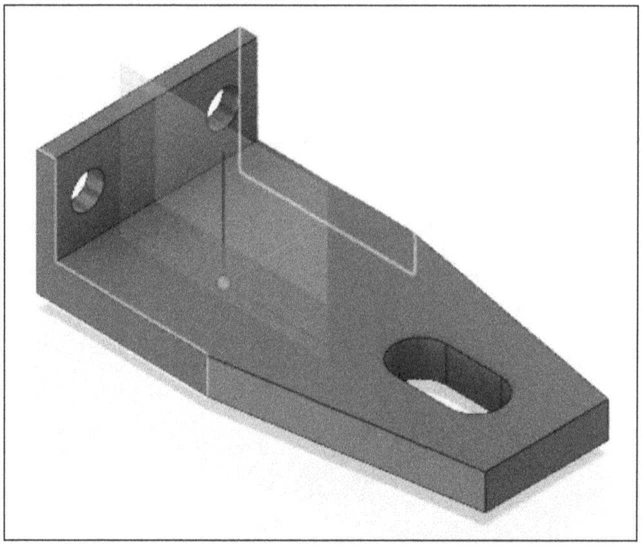

Figure-21. Midplane created

Creating Rib

- Select **Create Sketch** tool from **CREATE** drop-down. You will be asked to select the plane for creating sketch. Select the newly created midplane from **BROWSER**.
- Create a line as shown in Figure-22 with end points coincident to the vertices of model and finish the sketch.

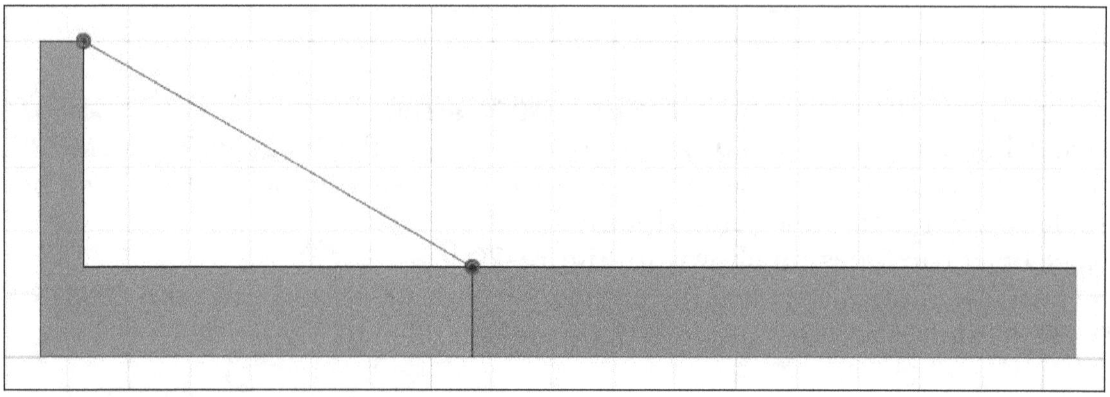

Figure-22. Creating sketch for rib

- Select **Rib** tool from **CREATE** drop-down. The **RIB** dialog box will be displayed.
- Select the recently created line for **Profile** section.
- Select **Symmetric** option from **Thickness Direction** section.
- Select **To Next** option from **Extent Type** drop-down.
- Click in **Thickness** edit box and enter **5** as thickness of rib; refer to Figure-23. (You might need to click on the **Flip Direction** button from the dialog box to get desired preview.)

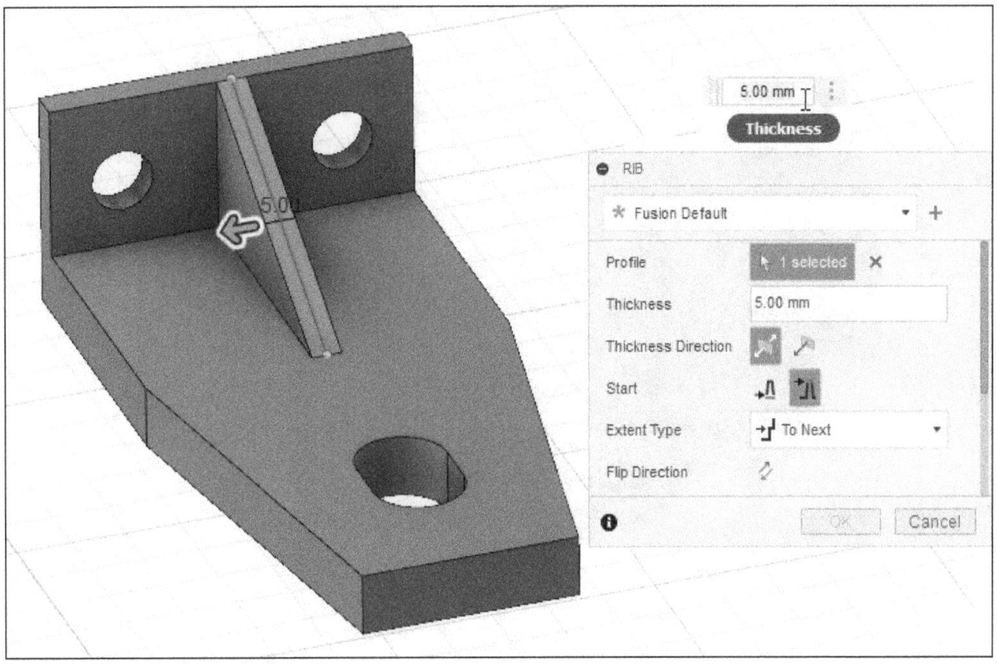

Figure-23. Preview of rib

- Click **OK** button of **RIB** dialog box to finish the process. The model will be displayed as shown in Figure-24.

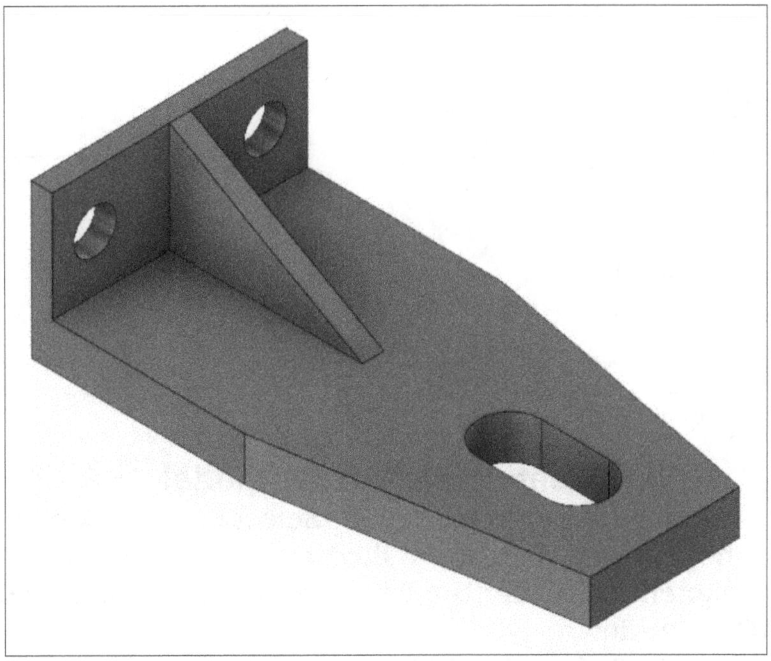

Figure-24. Final model of Practical 2

PRACTICAL 3

Create the model as shown in Figure-25. The dimensions of the model are given in Figure-26.

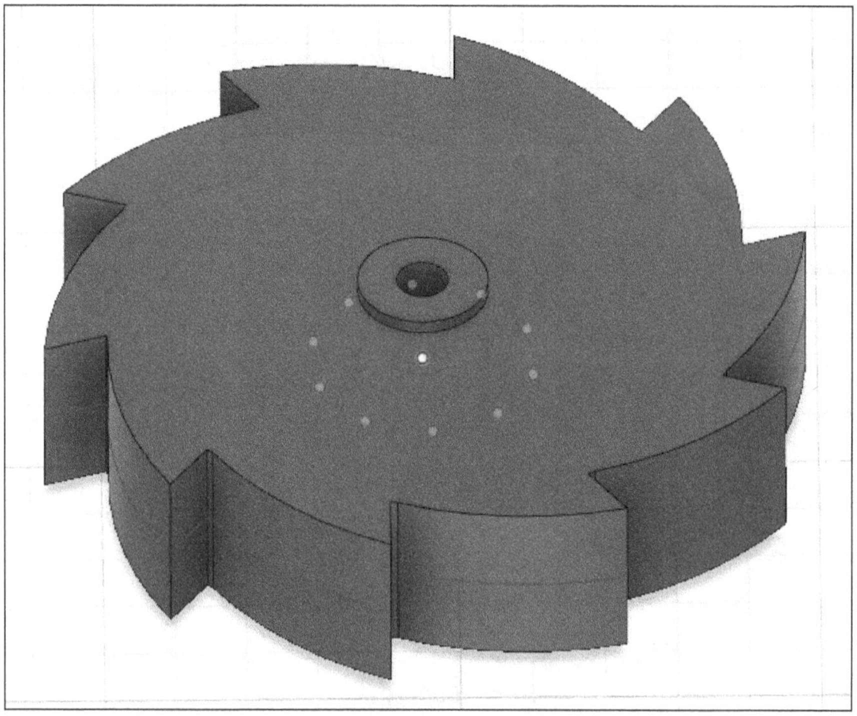

Figure-25. Model for Practical 3

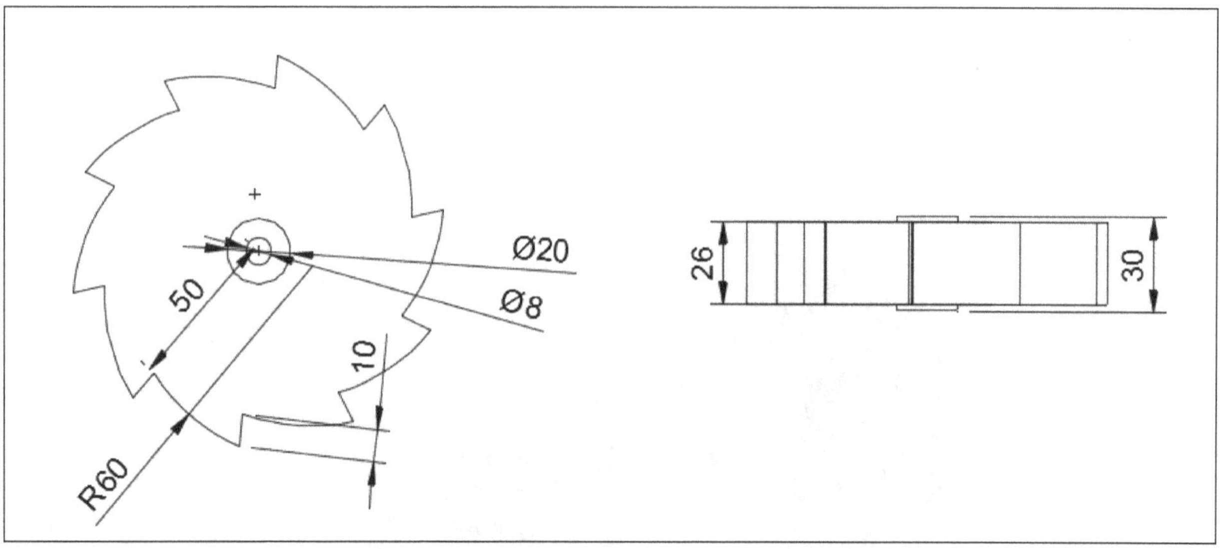

Figure-26. Practical 3 drawing views

Creating sketch for model

- Start a new design file in Autodesk Fusion. Select **Create Sketch** tool from **CREATE** drop-down in the **Toolbar**. You are asked to select sketching plane. Select **Top Plane** to create sketch. Select **Center Diameter Circle** tool from **Circle** cascading menu of **CREATE** drop-down.
- Create three circle of **8**, **20**, and **100** as diameter dimension of circles; refer to Figure-27.

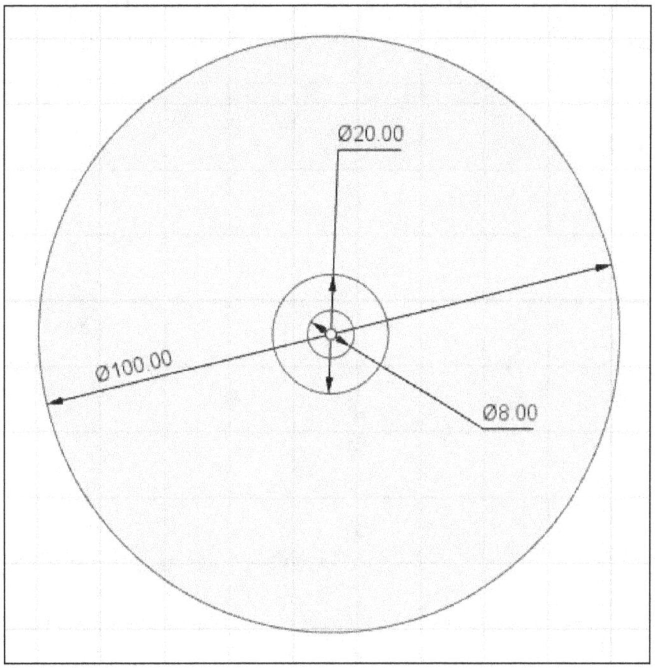

Figure-27. Creating circles

- Press **L** key to select **Line** tool and create a line of length **10**.
- Select **3-Point Arc** tool from **Arc** cascading menu and create an arc of **60** radius and **35** length as shown in Figure-28.

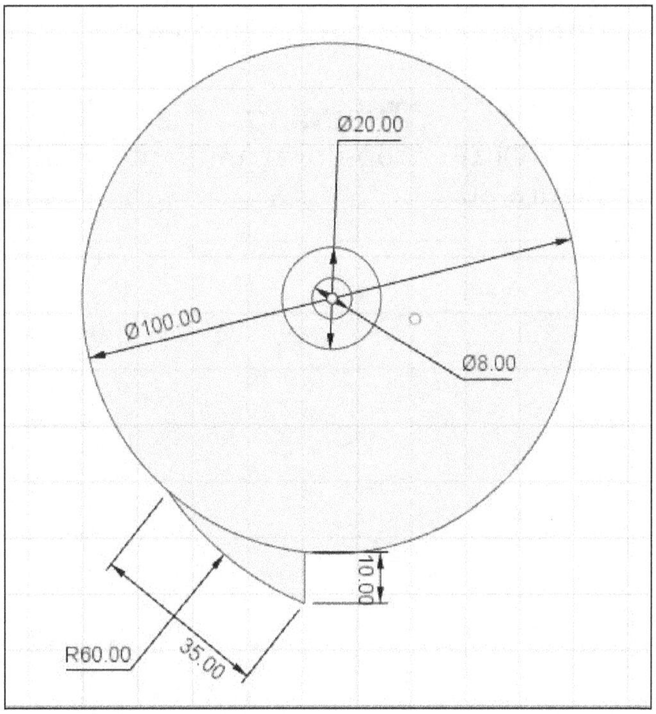

Figure-28. Creating line and arc

Creating Circular Pattern

- Select **Circular Pattern** tool from **CREATE** drop-down. The **CIRCULAR PATTERN** dialog box will be displayed.
- Objects selection is active by default. Select the recently created line and arc for circular pattern.

- Click on **Select** button of **Center Point** section and select the major circle to define its center as center point for pattern; refer to Figure-29.

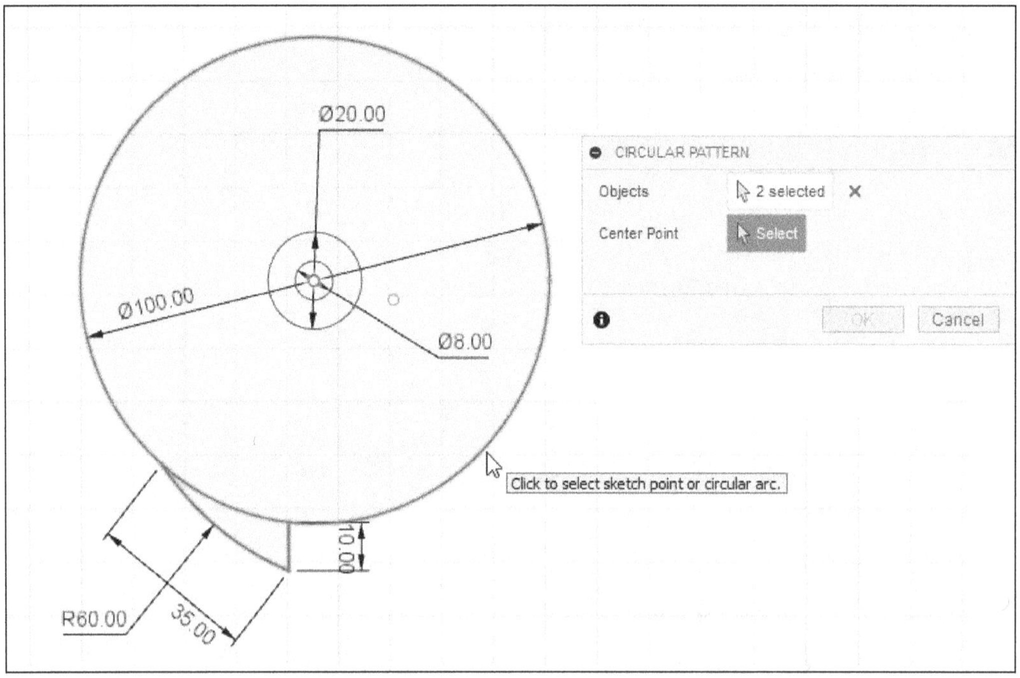

Figure-29. Creating circular pattern

- The updated **CIRCULAR PATTERN** dialog box will be displayed. Click in **Quantity** edit box and specify **10** as quantity of circular pattern.
- Click **OK** button from **CIRCULAR PATTERN** dialog box to complete the process.

Trimming

- Select the **Trim** tool from **MODIFY** drop-down and remove all the extra entities from sketch as shown in Figure-30.

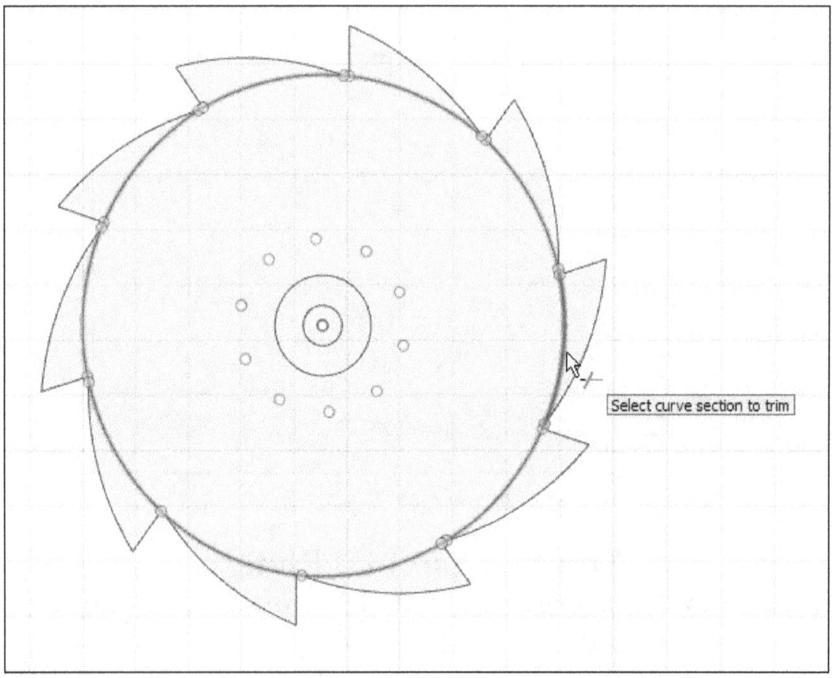

Figure-30. Trimming the extra entities

- After removing extra entities from sketch, the sketch will be displayed as shown in Figure-31.

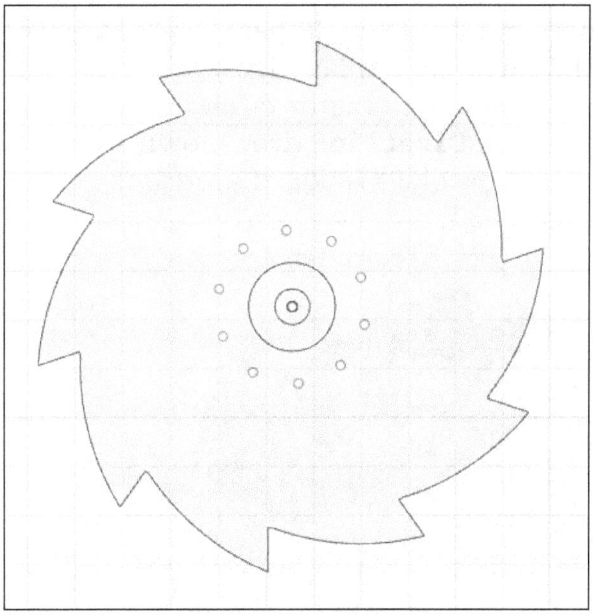

Figure-31. After removing extra entities

Creating Extrude

- Select **Extrude** tool from **CREATE** drop-down or press **E** key. The **EXTRUDE** dialog box will be displayed.
- Profile selection is active by default. Click between **20** diameter and **8** diameter circle to extrude the middle section.
- Select **Symmetric** option of **Direction** drop-down from **EXTRUDE** dialog box.
- Click in **Distance** edit box of **EXTRUDE** dialog box and specify **15** as height of extrusion. Rotate the model to check preview; refer to Figure-32.

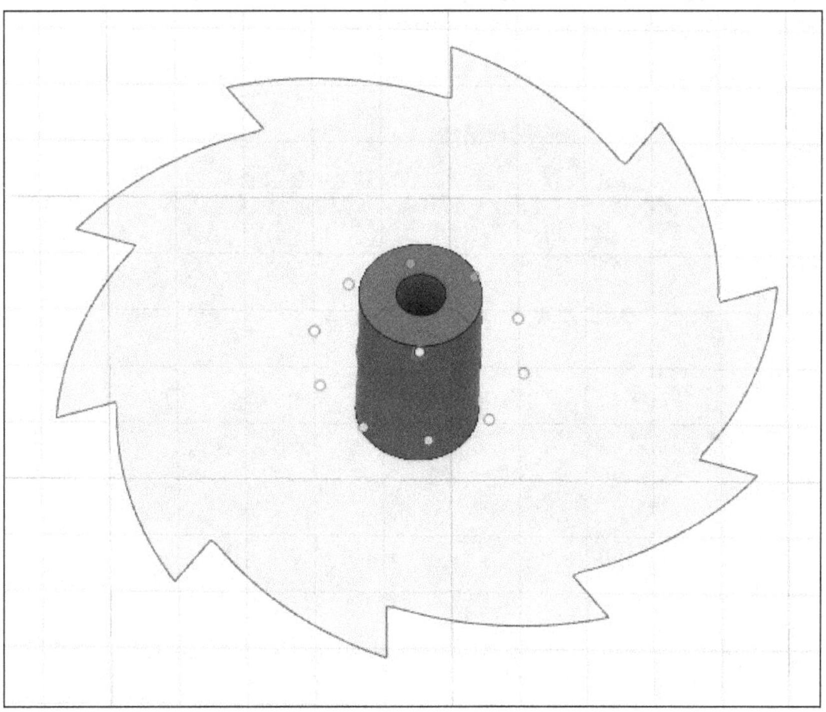

Figure-32. Preview of first extrusion

- Click **OK** button of **EXTRUDE** dialog box to finish this extrusion. The sketch of extrude feature will hide automatically. Click on the crossed eye icon before **Sketch 1** in the **Sketches** node of **BROWSER** to display the sketch again.
- Right-click on the screen and select **Repeat Extrude** button from **Marking Menu**. The **EXTRUDE** dialog box will be displayed.
- Select the area outside the **20** diameter circle earlier created.
- Select **Symmetric** button of **Direction** drop-down from **EXTRUDE** dialog box.
- Click in **Distance** edit box of **EXTRUDE** dialog box and specify **13** as height of extrusion; refer to Figure-33.

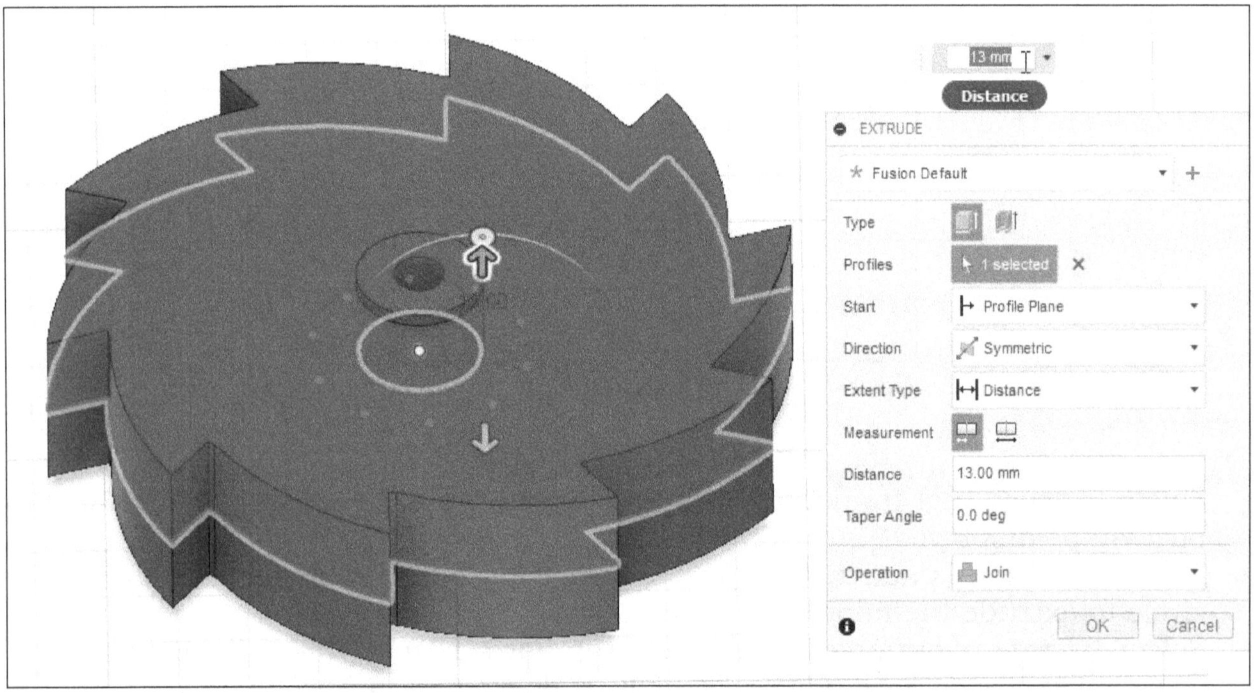

Figure-33. Preview of second extrusion

- Click **OK** button from **EXTRUDE** dialog box to complete the process of extrusion. The model will be displayed as shown in Figure-34.

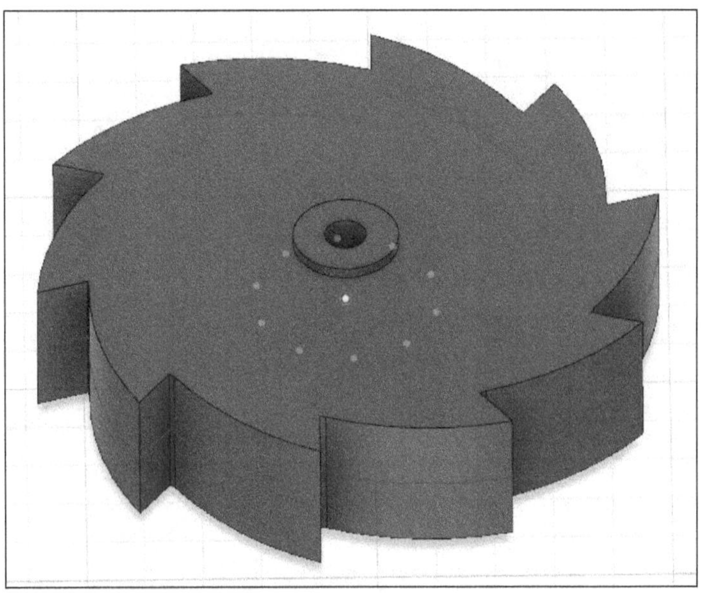

Figure-34. Final model of Practical 3

You can now hide the sketch and save the file.

PRACTICAL 4

Create the model as shown in Figure-35. The dimensions of the model are given in Figure-36.

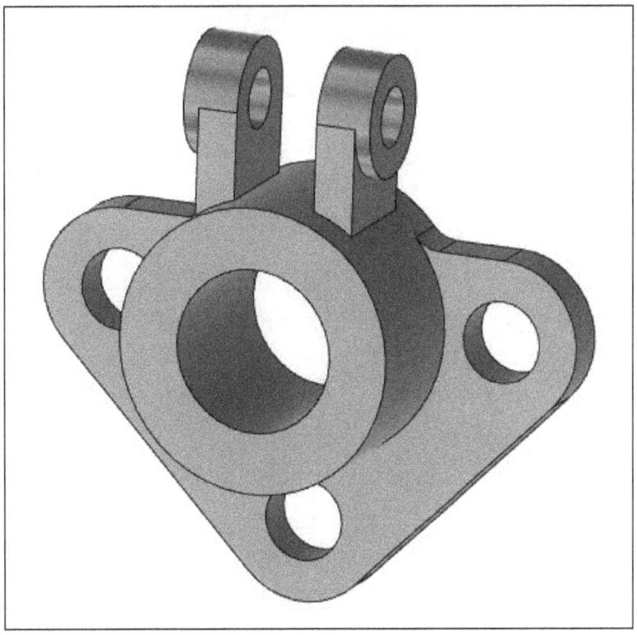

Figure-35. Model for Practical 4

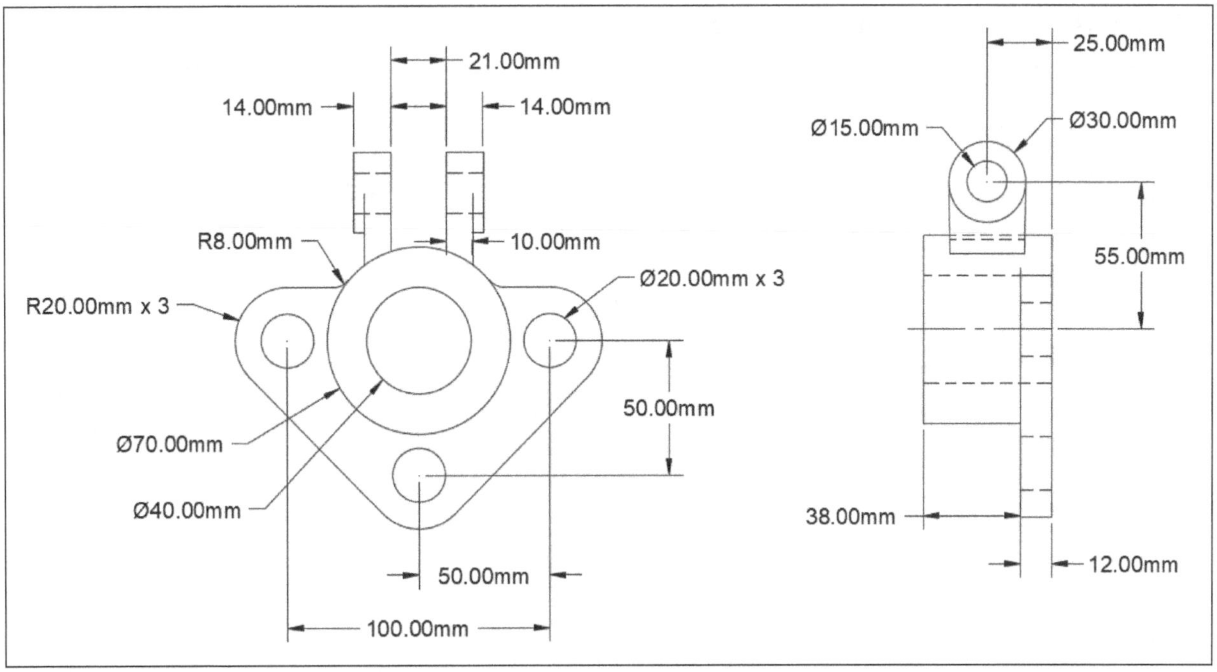

Figure-36. Practical 4 drawing views

Creating sketch for model

- Start a new design file in Autodesk Fusion. Click on the **Create Sketch** tool from **CREATE** drop-down in the **Toolbar**. You are asked to select sketching plane.
- Select **Top Plane** to create sketch. Select **Center Diameter Circle** tool from **Circle** cascading menu of **CREATE** drop-down.

- Create two circles of diameter **70** mm and **40** mm and create three circles of diameter **20** mm each; refer to Figure-37. After creating the circles, apply **Horizontal/Vertical** constraint to the circles.

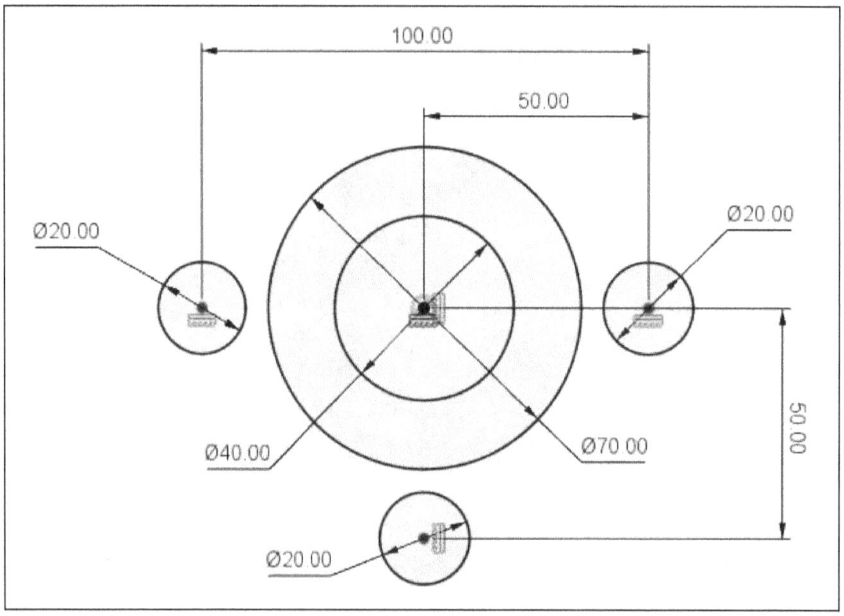

Figure-37. Creating circles

- Select **3-Point Arc** tool from **Arc** cascading menu of **CREATE** drop-down and create three arcs of radius **20** mm each; refer to Figure-38. After creating the arcs, apply **Concentric** constraint to all the arcs.

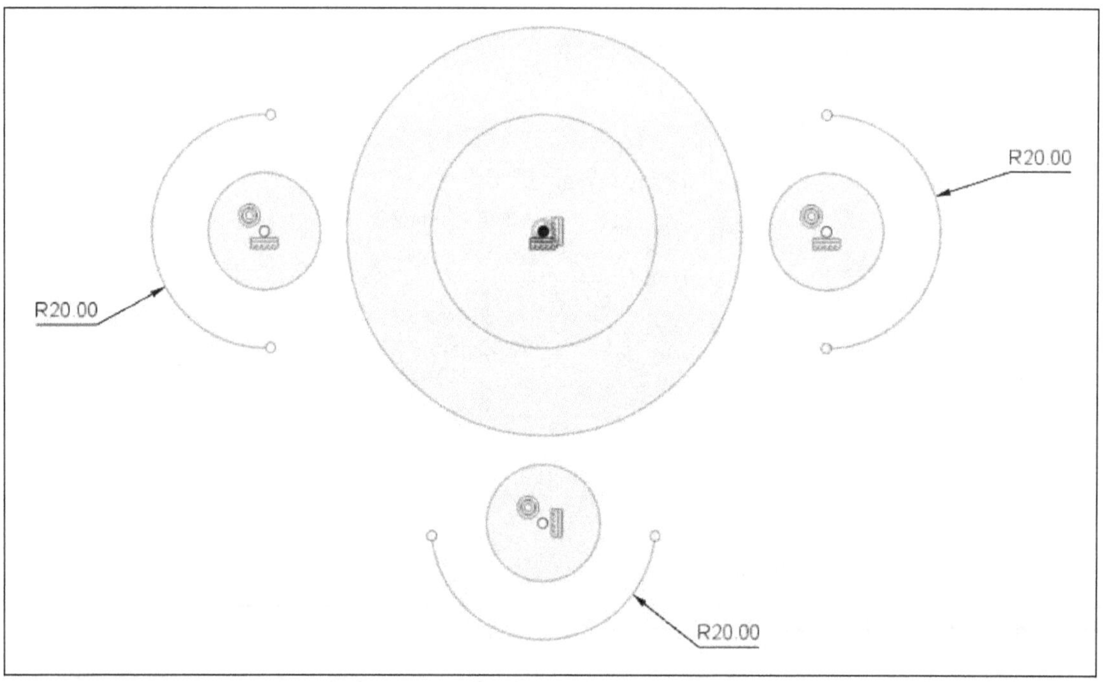

Figure-38. Creating arcs

- Select **Line** tool from **CREATE** drop-down and create three lines joining the arcs; refer to Figure-39. After creating the lines, apply **Tangent** constraint to all the lines.

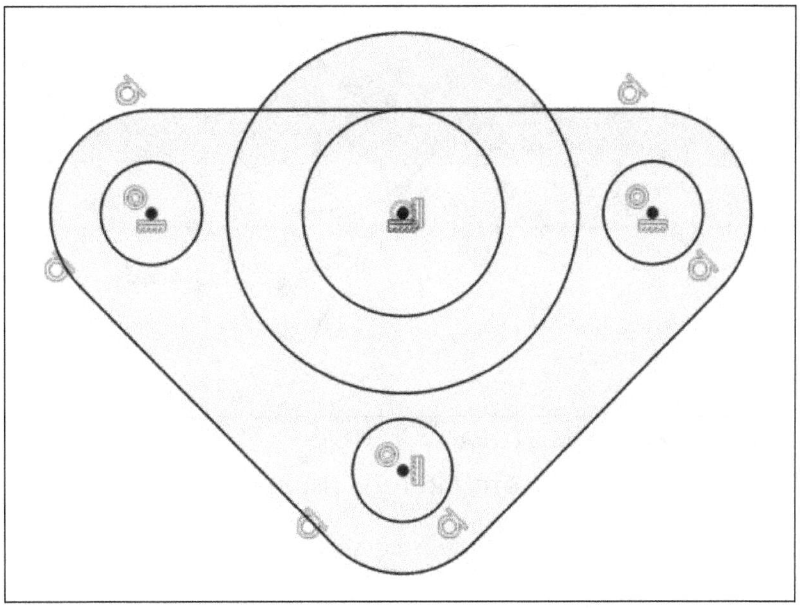

Figure-39. Creating lines joining the arcs

- Select **3-Point Arc** tool from **Arc** cascading menu and create two arcs of radius **8** mm each; refer to Figure-40. After creating the arcs, apply **Tangent** constraint to the arcs.

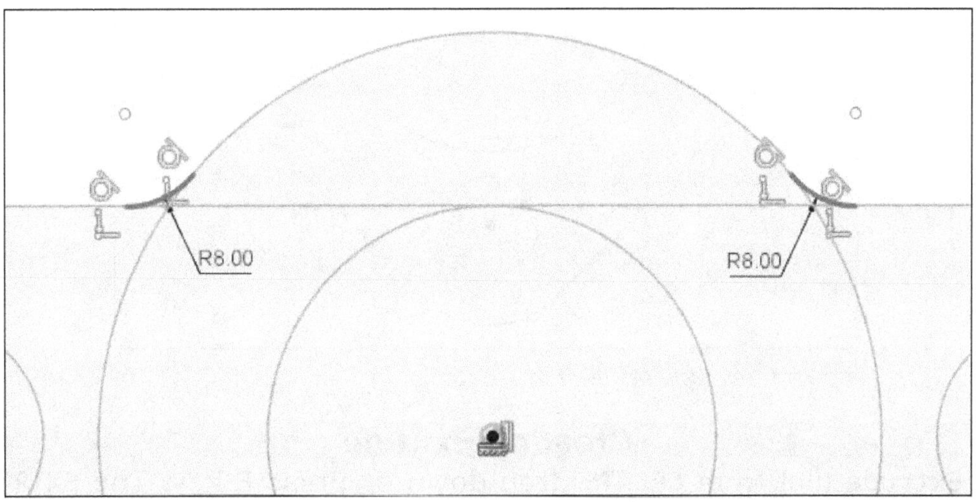

Figure-40. Creating arcs

Trimming

- Select the **Trim** tool from **MODIFY** drop-down and remove extra entities from sketch as shown in Figure-41.

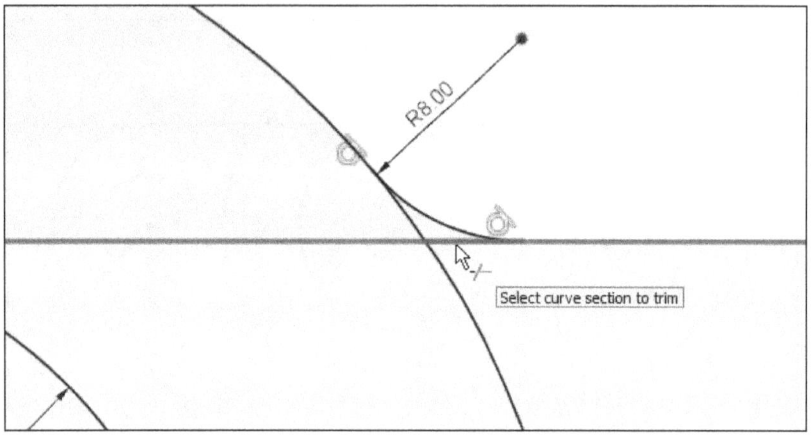

Figure-41. Removing extra entities

- After removing extra entities from sketch, the sketch will be displayed as shown in Figure-42.

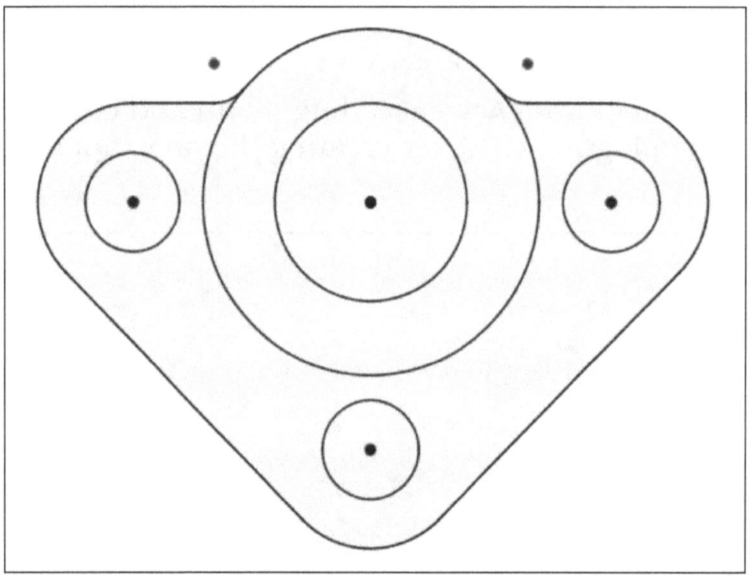

Figure-42. Sketch after trimming

Creating Extrude

- Select **Extrude** tool from **CREATE** drop-down or press **E** key. The **EXTRUDE** dialog box will be displayed.
- Profile selection is active by default. Select the profile from the sketch as shown in Figure-43.

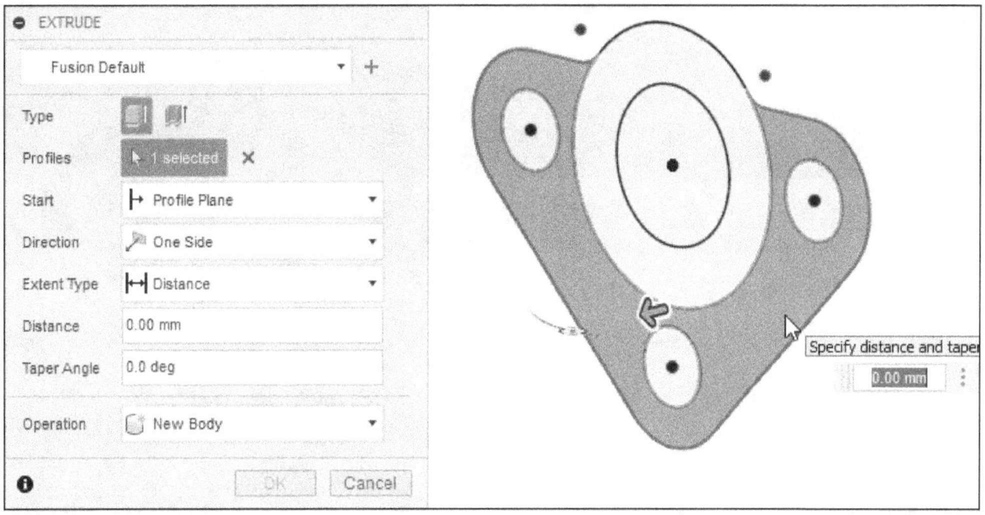

Figure-43. Extruding the sketch

- Select **One Side** option of **Direction** drop-down from **EXTRUDE** dialog box.
- Click in **Distance** edit box of **EXTRUDE** dialog box and specify **12** as distance of extrusion.
- Click **OK** button of **EXTRUDE** dialog box to finish this extrusion. The first sketch will be extruded and another sketch to be extruded will hide automatically; refer to Figure-44.

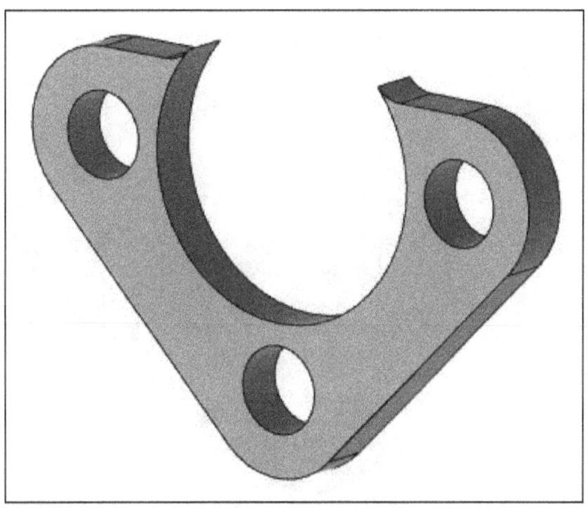

Figure-44. First sketch extruded

- Click on the crossed eye icon before **Sketch 1** in the **Sketches** node of **BROWSER** to display the sketch again.
- Right-click on the screen and select **Repeat Extrude** button from **Marking Menu**. The **EXTRUDE** dialog box will be displayed.
- Select the profile to extrude as shown in Figure-45.

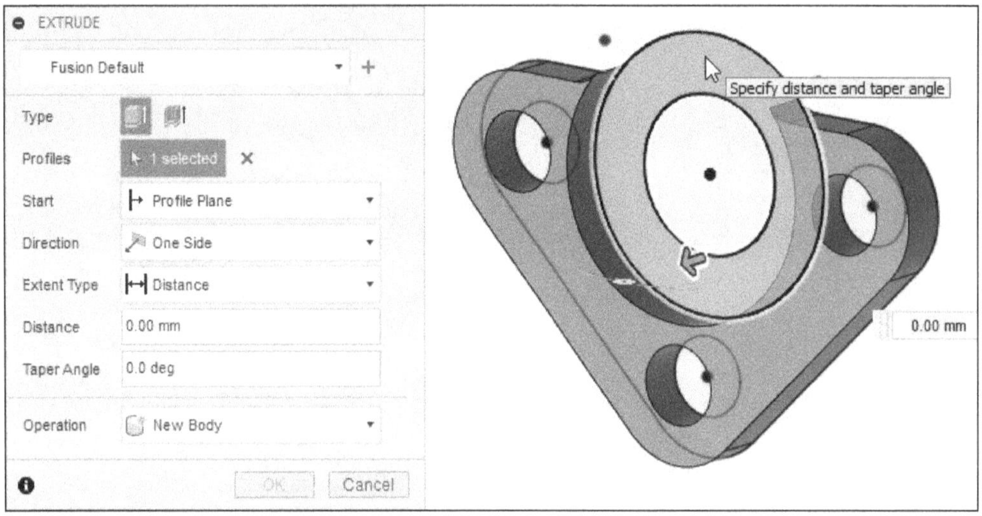

Figure-45. Extruding the second sketch

- Select **One Side** option of **Direction** drop-down from **EXTRUDE** dialog box.
- Click in **Distance** edit box of **EXTRUDE** dialog box and specify **50** as distance of extrusion.
- Click on the **OK** button from **Extrude** dialog box to finish the extrusion. The second sketch will be extruded; refer to Figure-46.

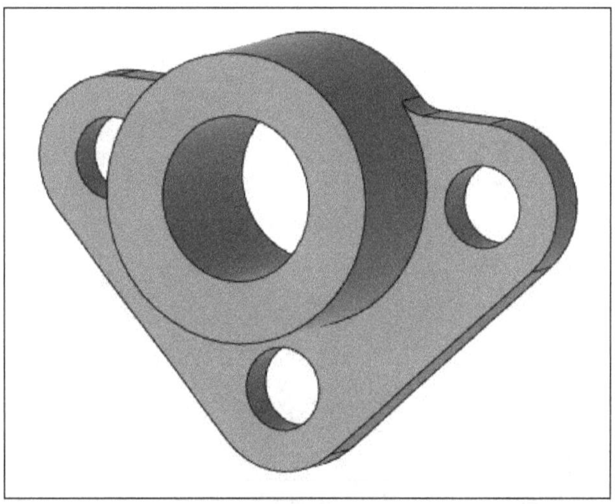

Figure-46. Second sketch extruded

Creating Offset Plane

- Select **Offset Plane** tool from **CONSTRUCT** drop-down. The **CONSTRUCTION GEOMETRY** dialog box will be displayed and you are asked to select the plane.
- The **Select** button of **Plane** section is active by default. Select **YZ** plane from **BROWSER**.
- Click in the **Distance** edit box of the dialog box and enter **24.5** as distance value; refer to Figure-47.
- Click on **OK** button from the dialog box to complete the process.

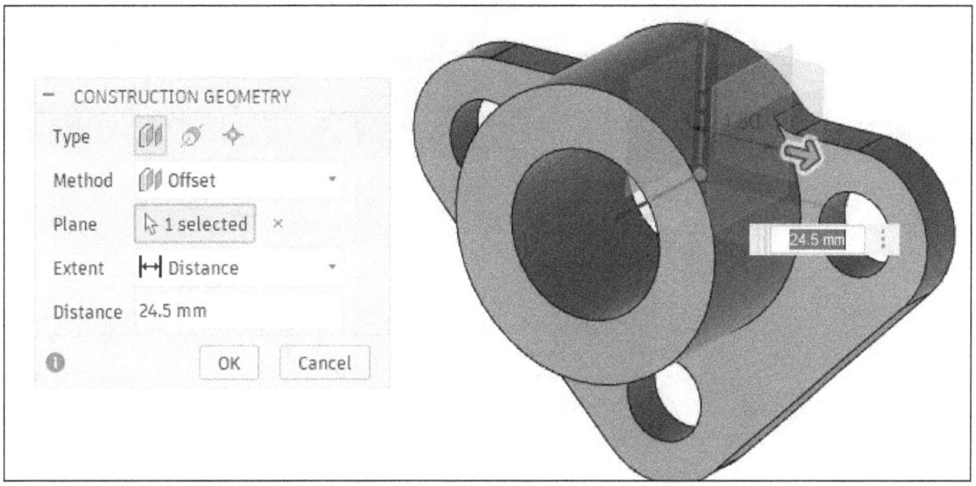

Figure-47. Creating the offset plane

Creating the Sketch

- Select **Create Sketch** tool from **CREATE** drop-down. You are asked to select the plane.
- Select newly created offset plane from **BROWSER** as sketching plane. The sketching environment will be displayed.
- Select **Center Diameter Circle** tool from **Circle** cascading menu of **CREATE** drop-down and create two circles of diameter **15** mm and **30** mm; refer to Figure-48.

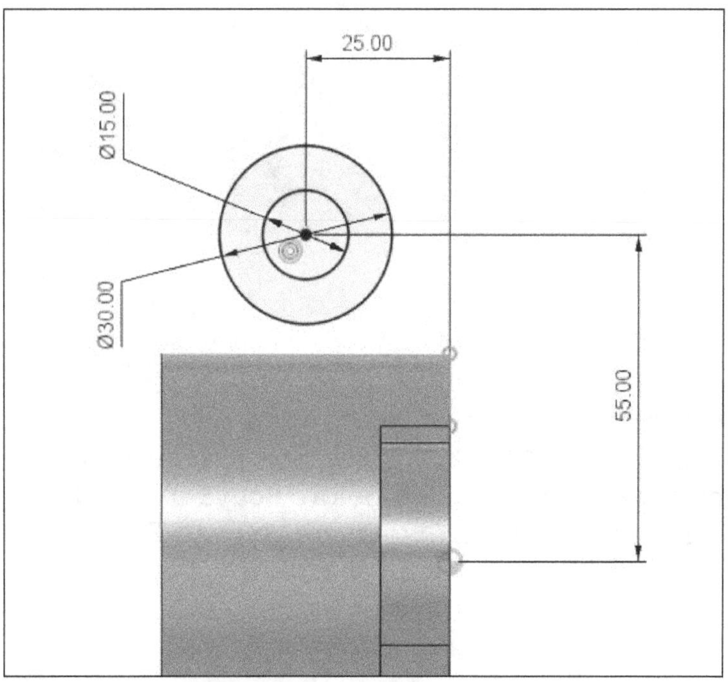

Figure-48. Creating the sketch

Intersecting the Sketch

- Select **Slice** check box from **SKETCH PALETTE** dialog box. The slice of the model will be created; refer to Figure-49.

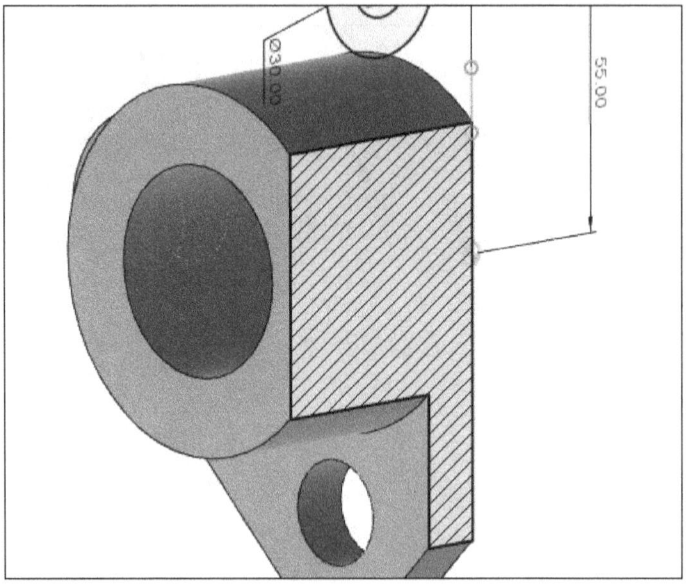

Figure-49. Slice created

- Select **Intersect** tool of **Project/Include** cascading menu from **CREATE** drop-down. The **INTERSECT** dialog box will be displayed. You are asked to select the geometries.
- The **Select** button of **Geometry** section is active by default. Select sliced part of the model as geometry to be intersect; refer to Figure-50.

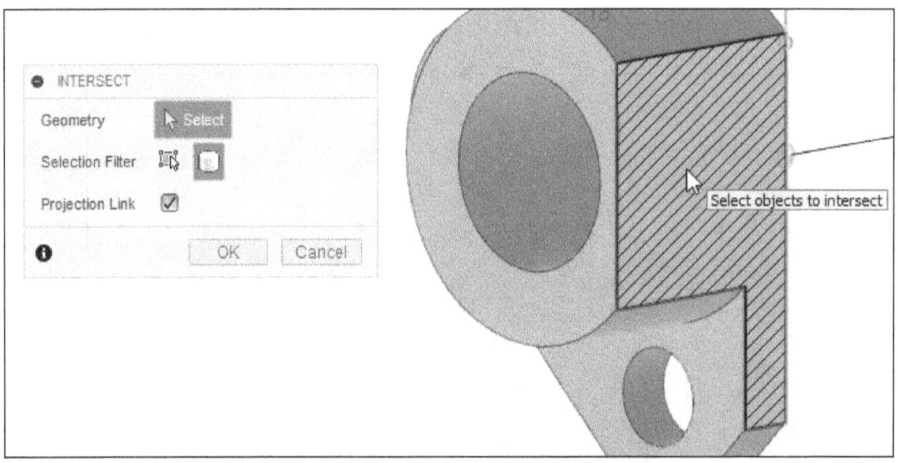

Figure-50. Geometry selected

- Click on **OK** button from **INTERSECT** dialog box to complete the process.
- Hide the body by clicking on eye icon before **Body1** in the **Bodies** node of **BROWSER**. The intersected geometry will be displayed; refer to Figure-51.

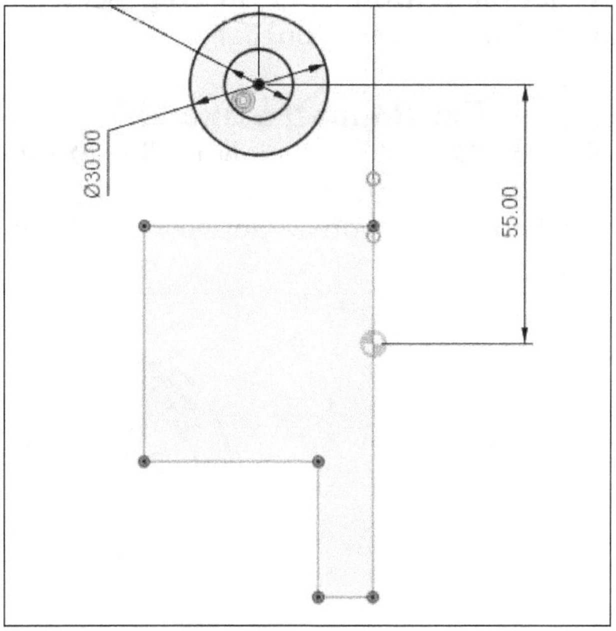

Figure-51. Intersected geometry

- Select **Line** tool from **CREATE** drop-down and create the lines as shown in Figure-52.

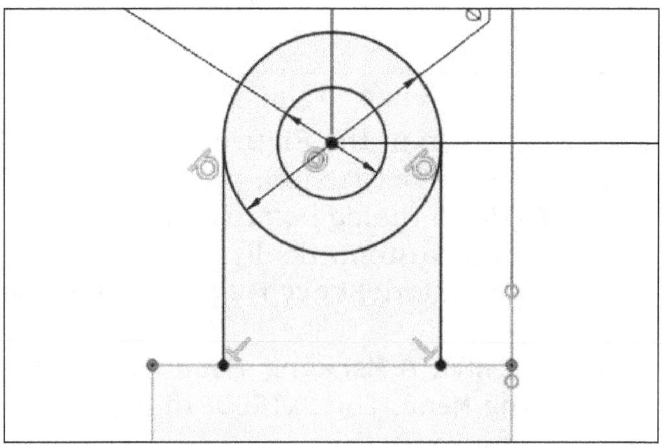

Figure-52. Lines created

- Select the intersected geometry by pressing **CTRL** key and right-click; refer to Figure-53. A **Marking Menu** will be displayed.

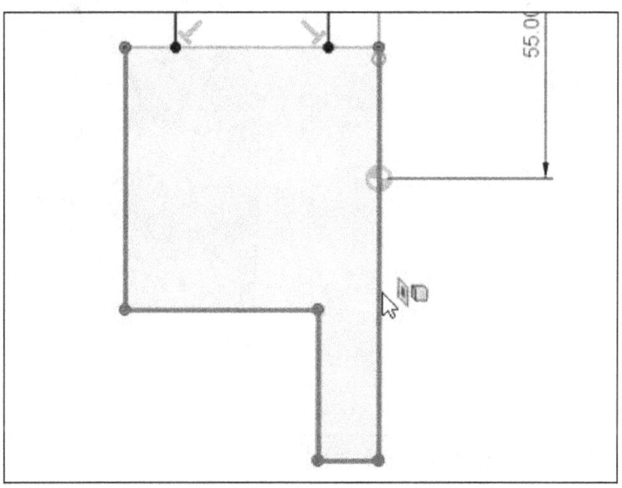

Figure-53. Selecting intersected geometry

- Select **Normal/Construction** button from **Marking Menu**.
- Click on **Finish Sketch** button from **Toolbar**.

Extruding the sketch

- Select **Extrude** tool from **CREATE** drop-down. The **EXTRUDE** dialog box will be displayed. You are asked to select the profile.
- The **Select** button of **Profile** section is active by default. Select the sketch to extrude as shown in Figure-54.

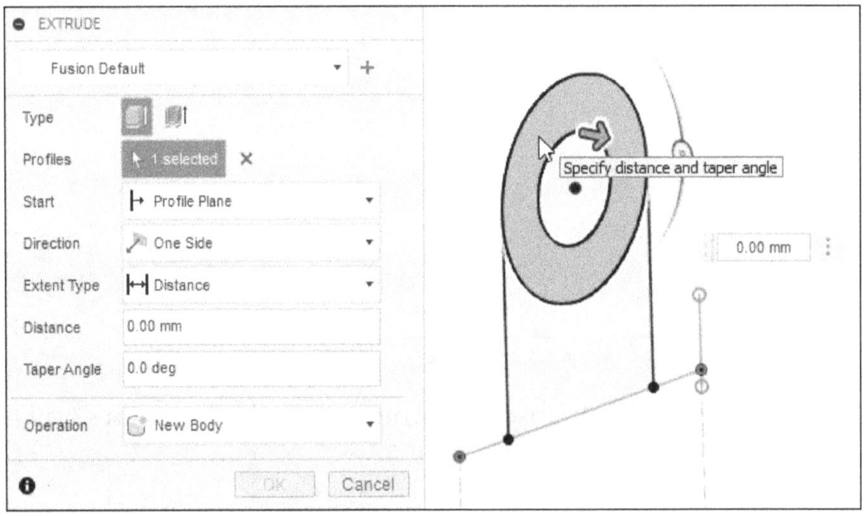

Figure-54. Selecting the sketch to extrude

- Specify the parameters as shown in the Figure-54. Click in the **Distance** edit box and enter **-14** mm as distance of extrusion.
- Click on **OK** button from **EXTRUDE** dialog box to complete the process. The another sketch to be extruded will hide automatically.
- Click on the crossed eye icon before **Sketch 2** in the **Sketches** node of **BROWSER** to display the sketch again.
- Select the sketch and click **RMB**. A **Marking Menu** will be displayed. Click **Repeat Extrude** button from **Marking Menu**. The **EXTRUDE** dialog box will be displayed again along with profile selected for extrusion.
- Specify the parameters as specified for previous extrusion; refer to Figure-55.

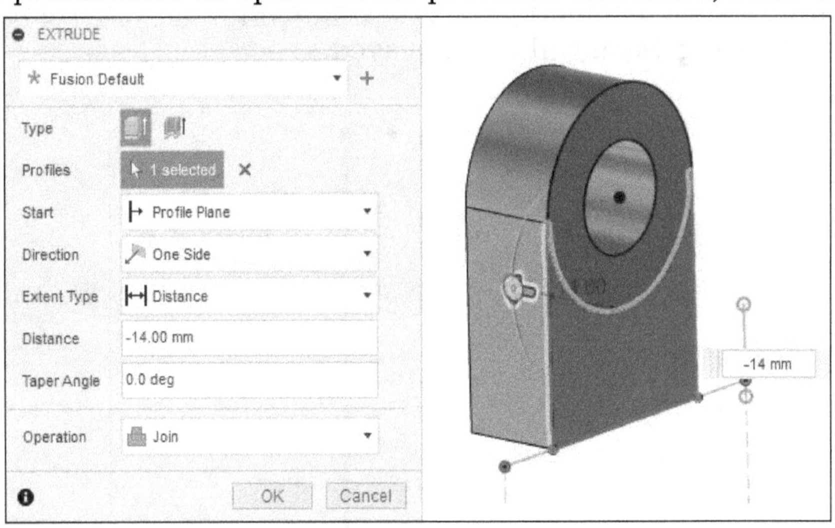

Figure-55. Extruding another sketch

- Click on **OK** button from the dialog box to complete the extrusion.

- Select recently extruded sketch and click **RMB**. A **Marking Menu** will be displayed; refer to Figure-56.

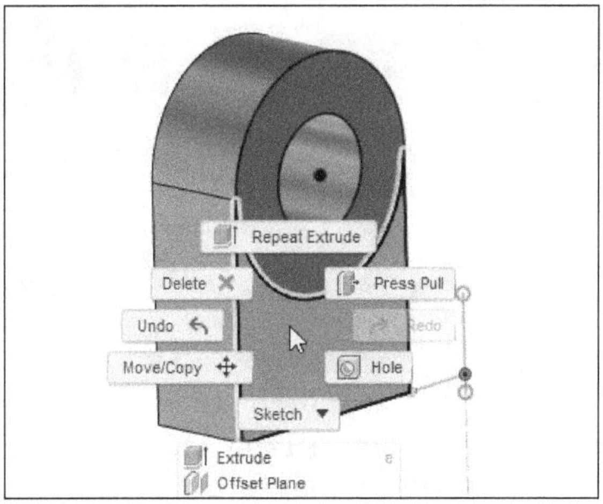

Figure-56. Selecting recently extruded sketch

- Click **Repeat Extrude** button from **Marking Menu**. The **EXTRUDE** dialog box will be displayed along with profile selected for extrusion.
- Click in the **Distance** edit box and enter **-4** as the distance for extrusion.
- Select **Cut** option from **Operation** drop-down. The preview of extrusion will be displayed; refer to Figure-57.

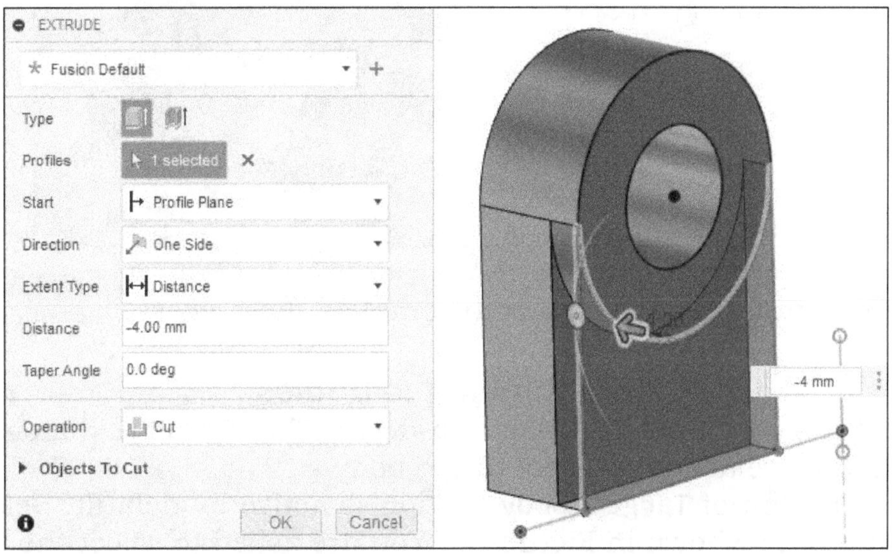

Figure-57. Preview of extrusion

- Click on **OK** button from **EXTRUDE** dialog box to complete the process.

Mirroring the body

- Click on the crossed eye icon before **Body1** in the **Bodies** node of **BROWSER** to display the body.
- Select **Mirror** tool from **CREATE** drop-down. The **MIRROR** dialog box will be displayed. You are asked to select the object.
- Select **Bodies** option from **Object Type** drop-down of dialog box.
- The **Select** button of **Objects** section is active by default. Select recently created body to be mirror; refer to Figure-58. You are asked to select the mirror plane.

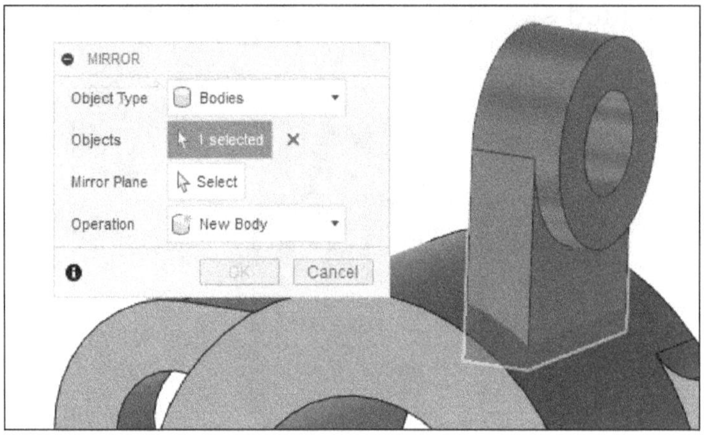

Figure-58. Body selected to be mirror

- Click on the **Select** button of **Mirror Plane** section and select **YZ** plane as mirror plane. The preview of mirror will be displayed; refer to Figure-59.

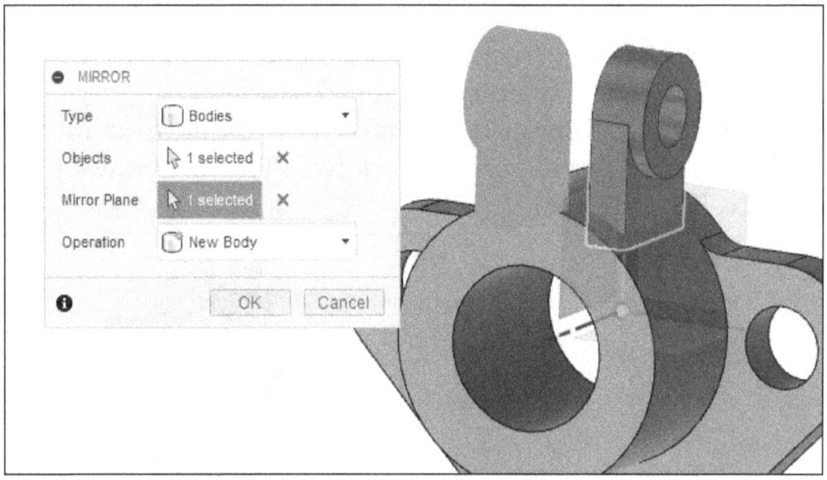

Figure-59. Preview of mirror

- Click on **OK** button from dialog box to complete the process.

Combining the bodies

- Select **Combine** tool from **MODIFY** drop-down. The **COMBINE** dialog box will be displayed. You are asked to select target body.
- The **Select** button of **Target Body** section is active by default. Select the body from the model as shown in Figure-60. You are asked to select the tool body.

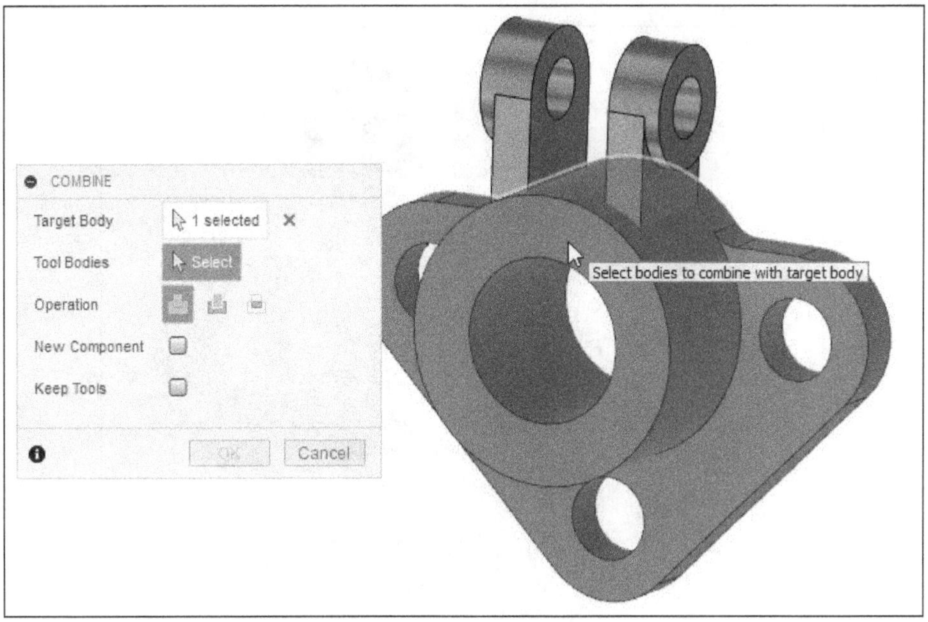

Figure-60. Selecting the target body

- The **Select** button of **Tool Bodies** section is active by default. Select the bodies to combine with target bodies as shown in Figure-61.

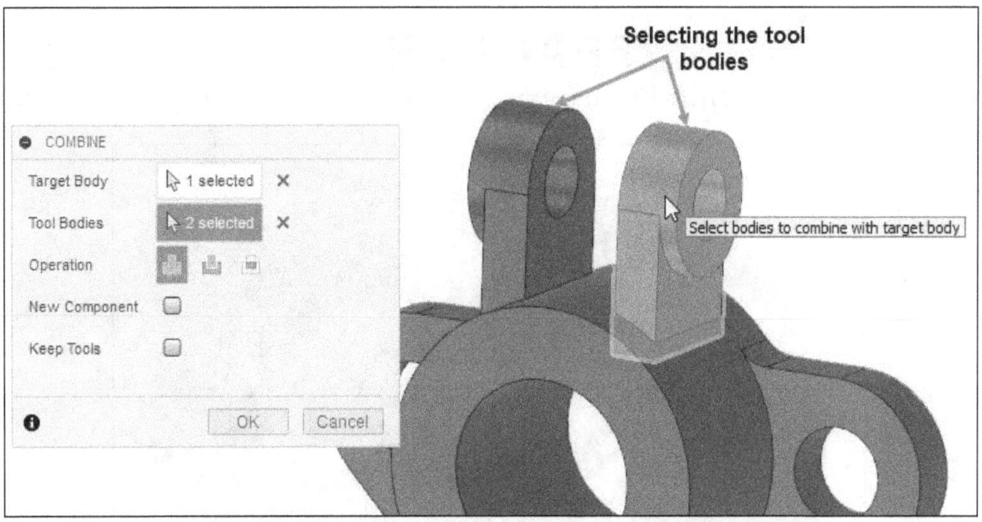

Figure-61. Selecting the tool bodies

- Click on **OK** button from the dialog box to complete the process of combining the bodies. The model will be displayed as shown in Figure-62.

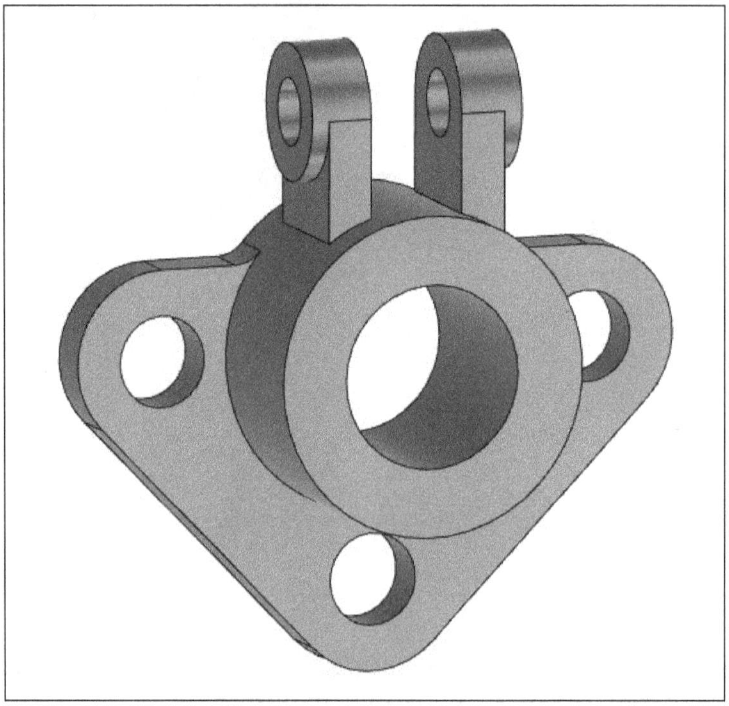

Figure-62. Final model of Practical 4

PRACTICE 1

Create the model as shown in Figure-63. The dimensions are given in Figure-64.

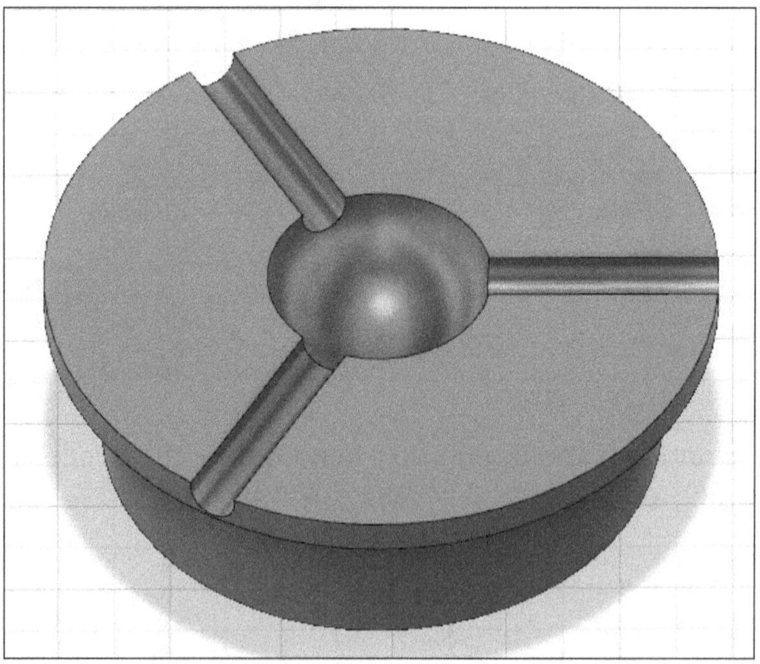

Figure-63. Model for Practice 1

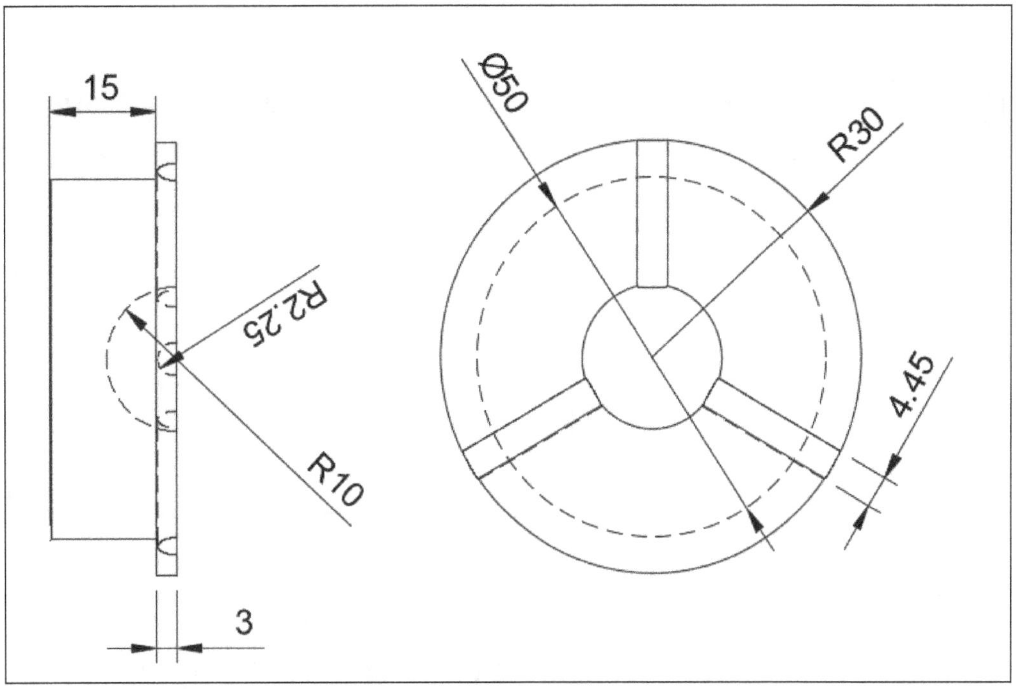

Figure-64. Dimensions for Practice 1

PRACTICE 2

Create the model as shown in Figure-65. The dimensions are given in Figure-66.

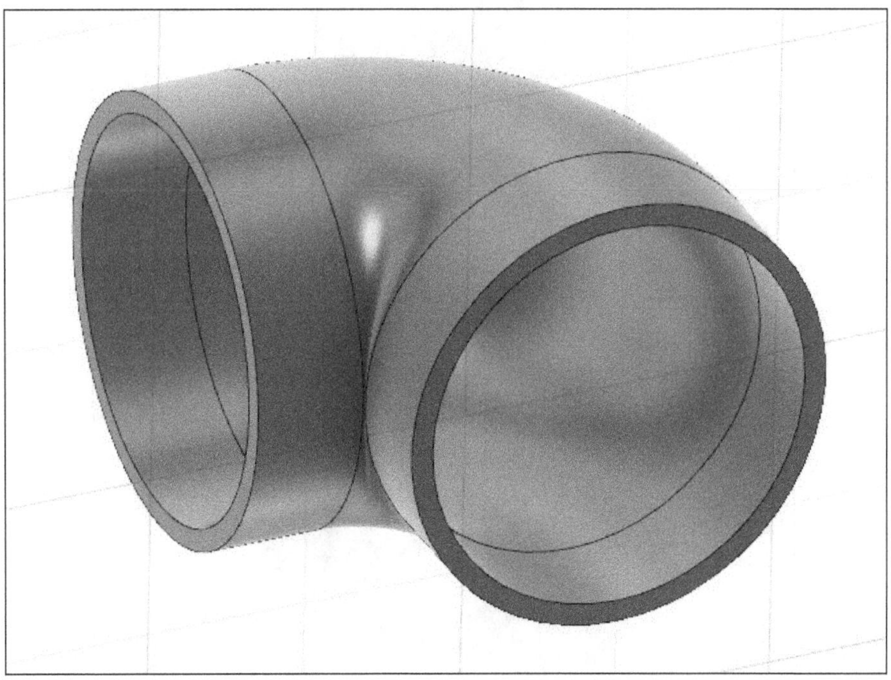

Figure-65. Model for Practice 2

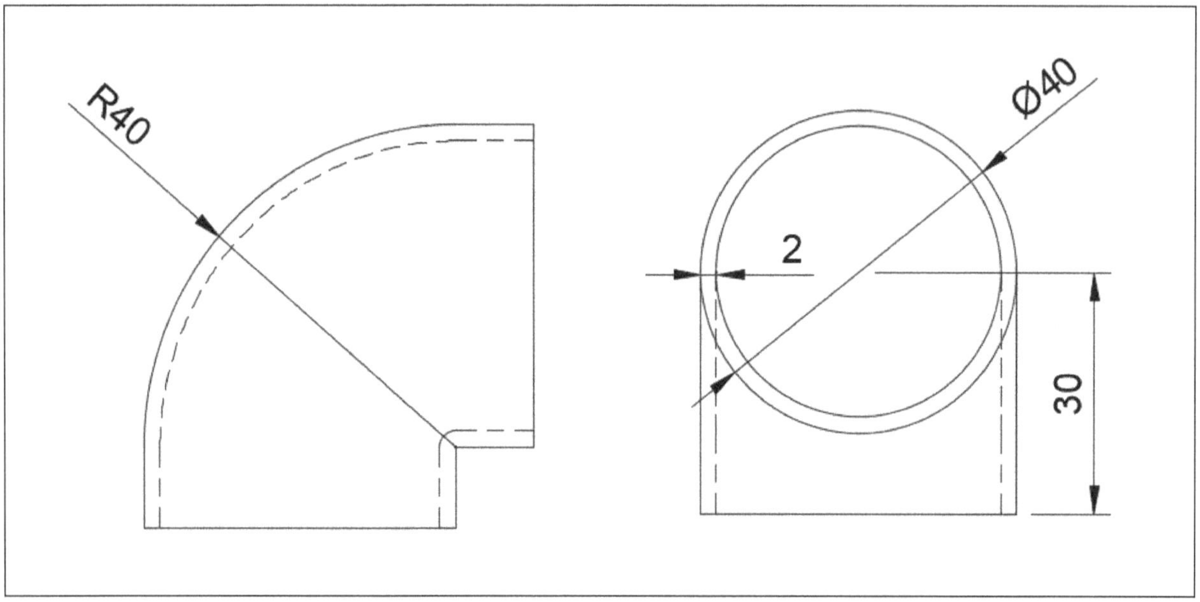

Figure-66. Dimensions for Practice 2

PRACTICE 3

Create the model as shown in Figure-67. The dimensions are given in Figure-68.

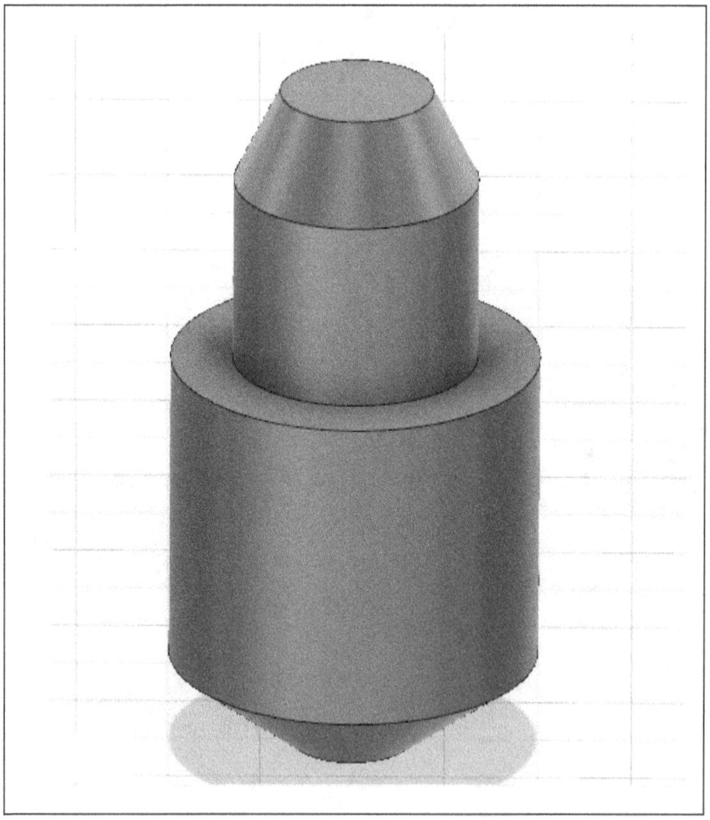

Figure-67. Model for Practice 3

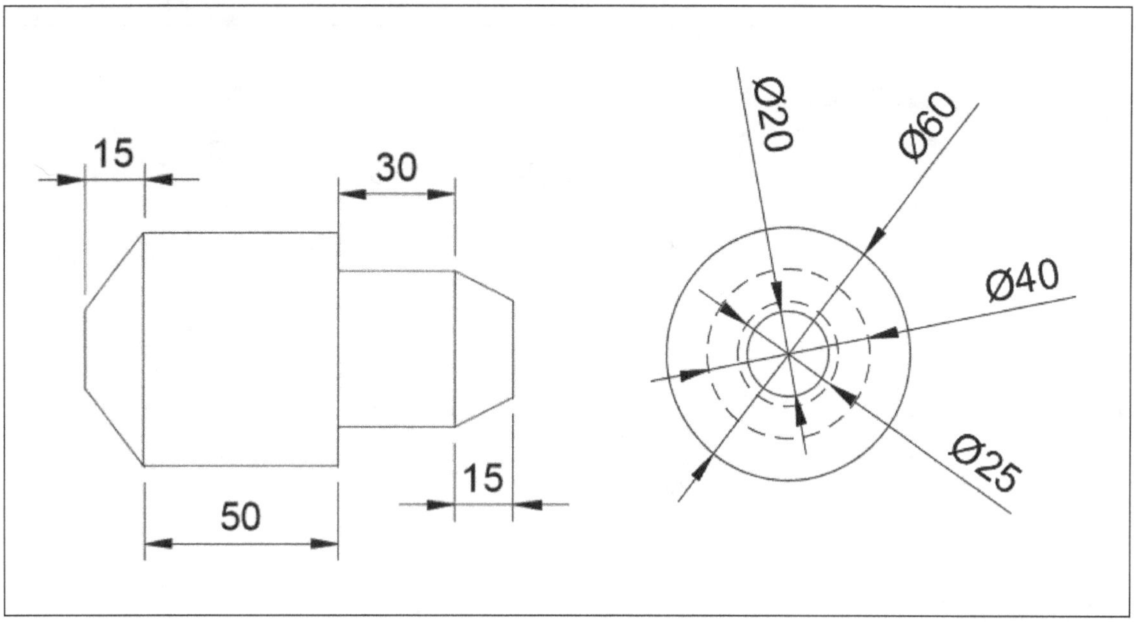

Figure-68. Dimensions for Practice 3

PRACTICE 4

Create the model as shown in Figure-69. The dimensions are given in Figure-70

Figure-69. Model for Practice 4

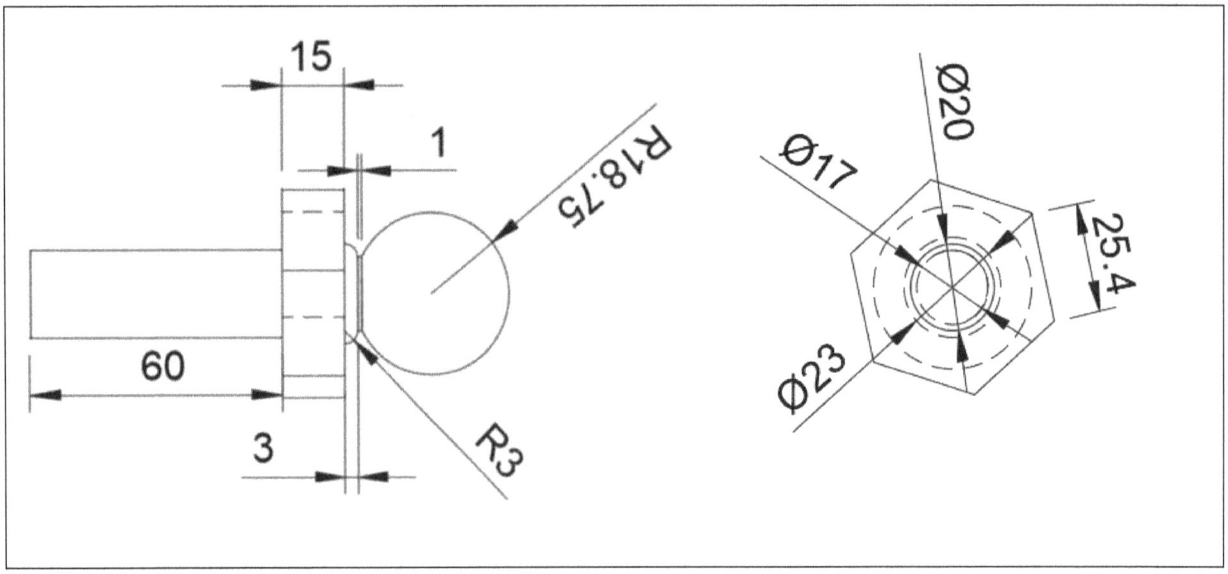

Figure-70. Dimensions for Practice 4

PRACTICE 5

Create the model as shown in Figure-71. The dimensions are given in Figure-72. (Hint: You will need **Rectangular Pattern** tool and **Move/Copy** tool in this model.)

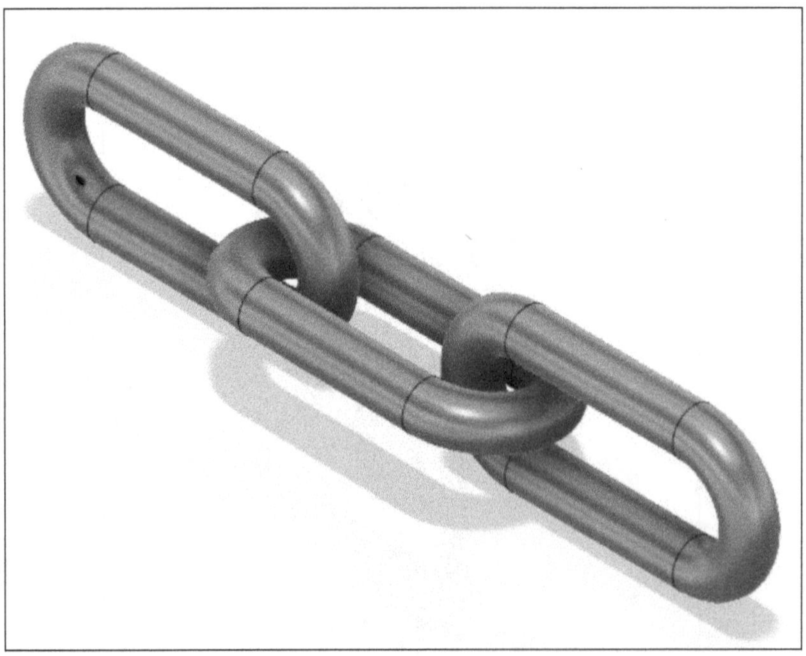

Figure-71. Model for Practice 5

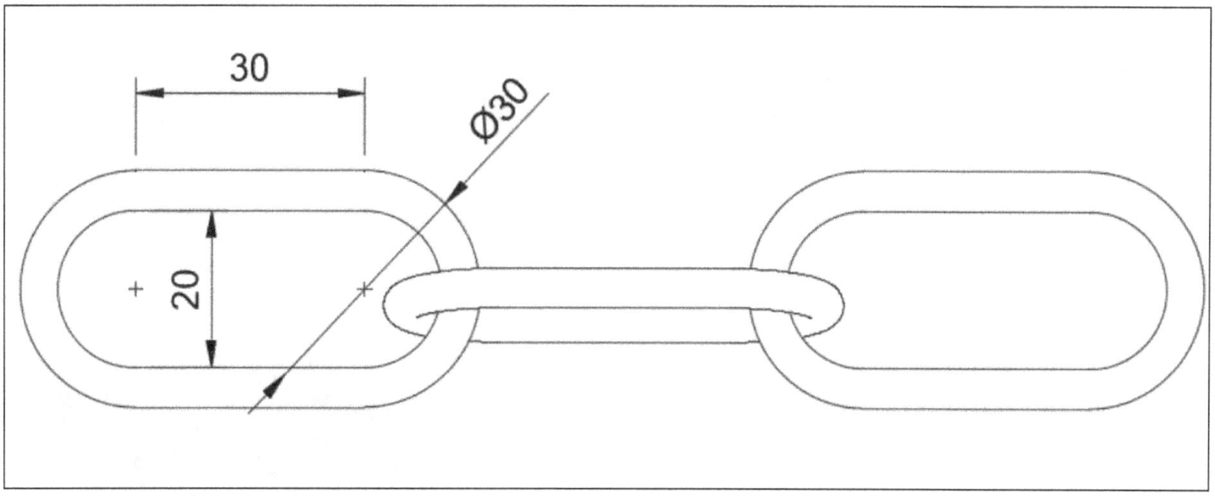

Figure-72. Dimensions for Practice 5

PRACTICE 6

Create the model as shown in Figure-73. The dimensions are given in Figure-74.

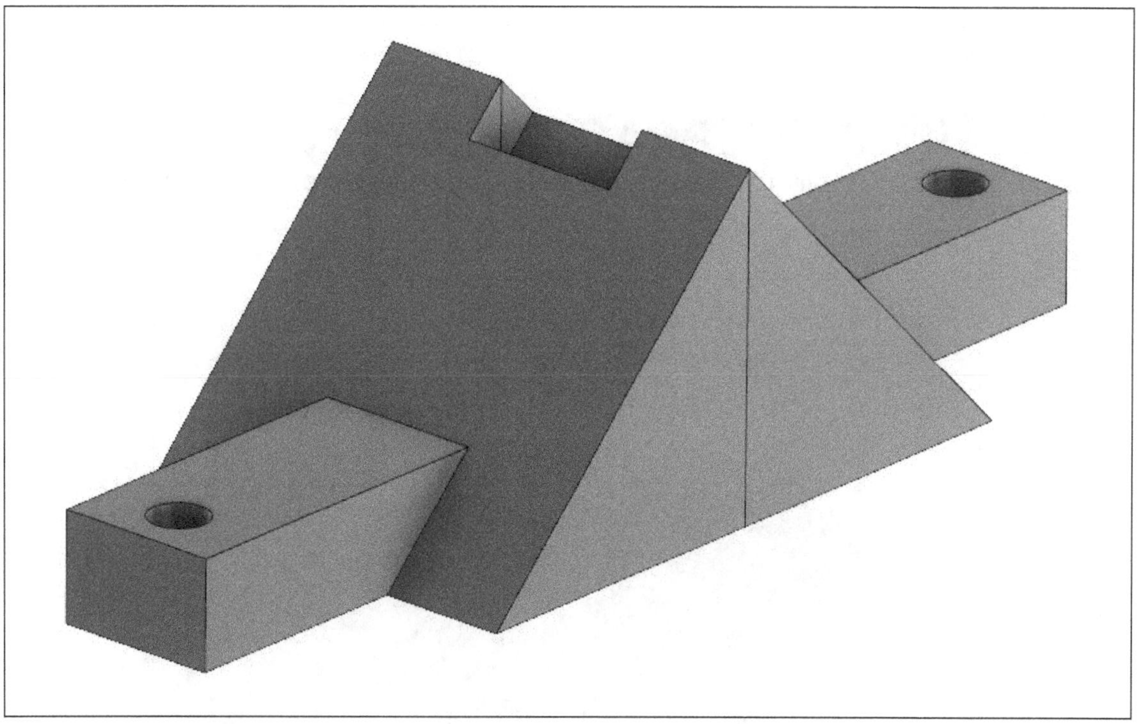

Figure-73. Model for Practice 6

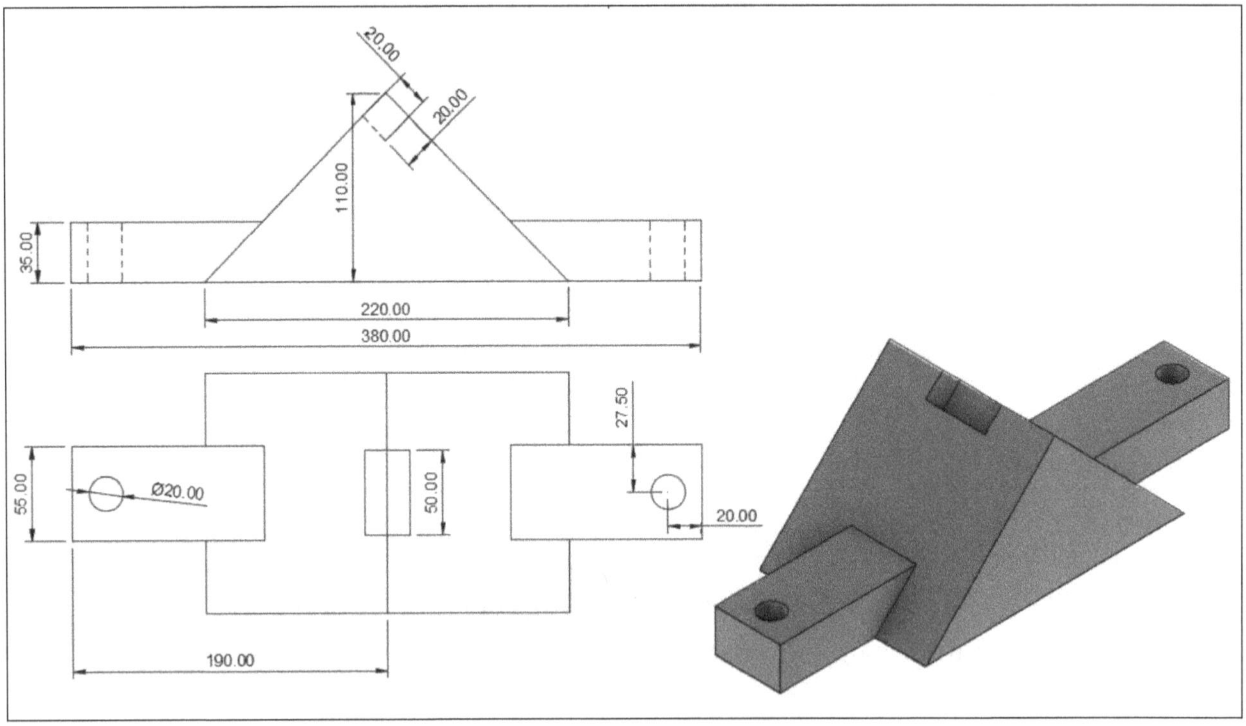

Figure-74. Dimensions for Practice 6

PRACTICE 7

Create the model as shown in Figure-75. The dimensions are given in Figure-76.

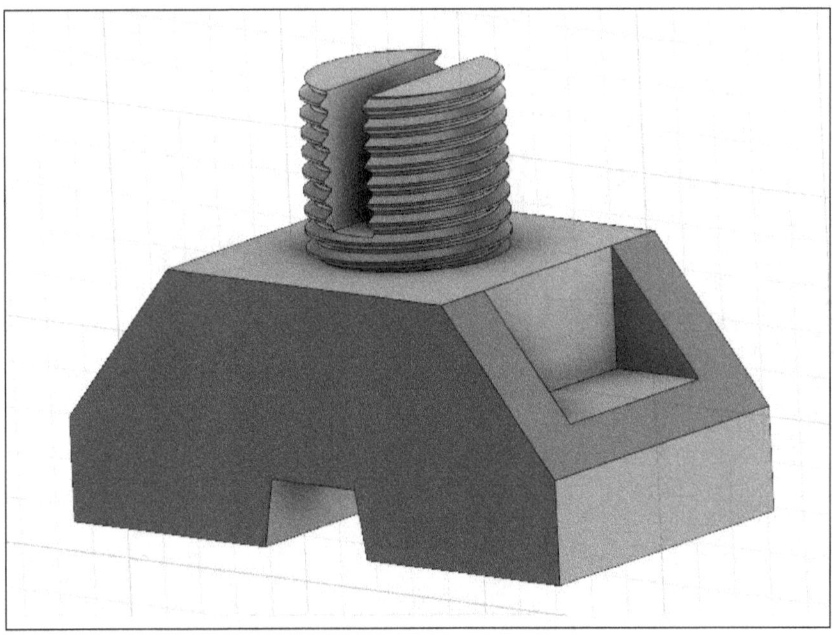

Figure-75. Model for Practice 7

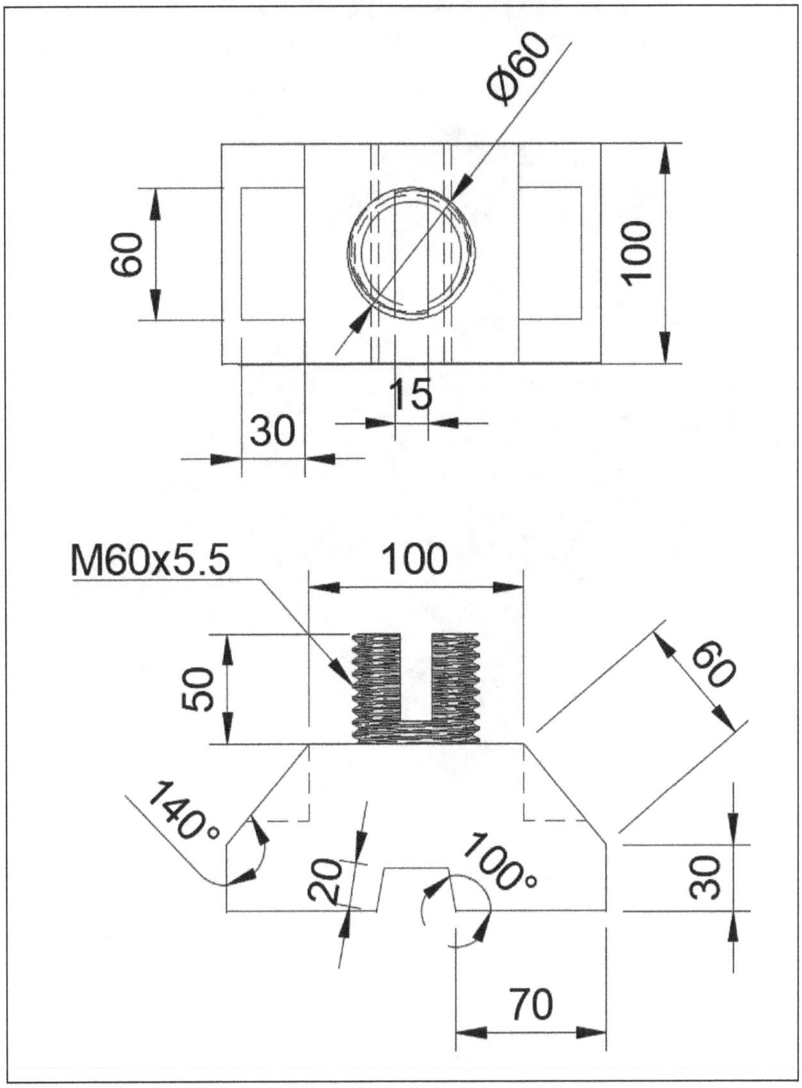

Figure-76. Dimensions for Practice 7

PRACTICE 8

Create the model as shown in Figure-77. The dimensions are given in Figure-78.

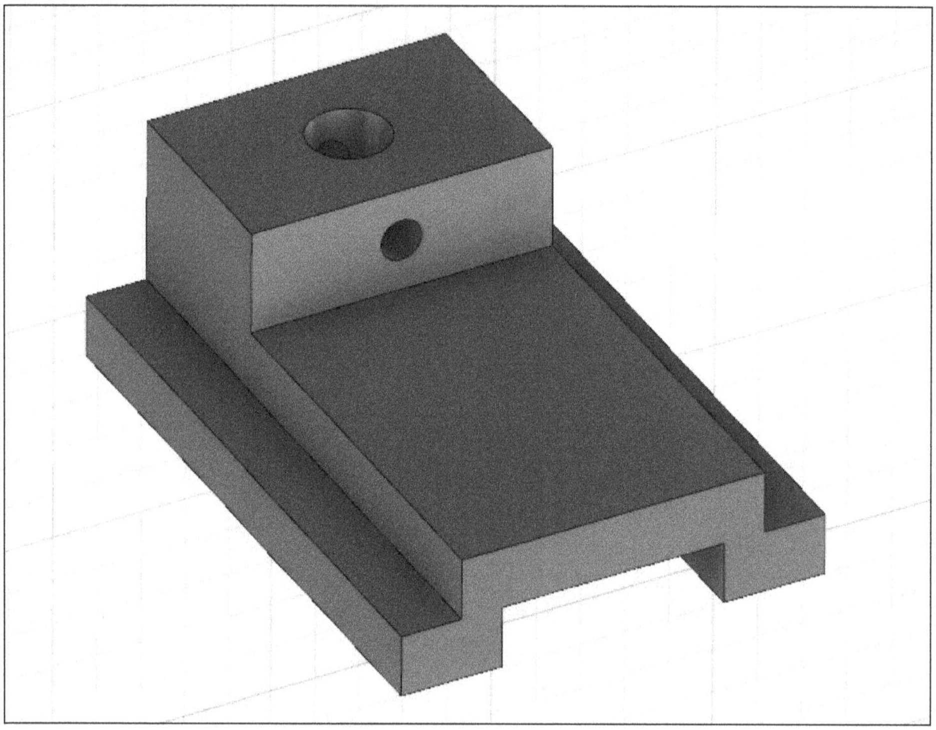

Figure-77. Model for Practice 8

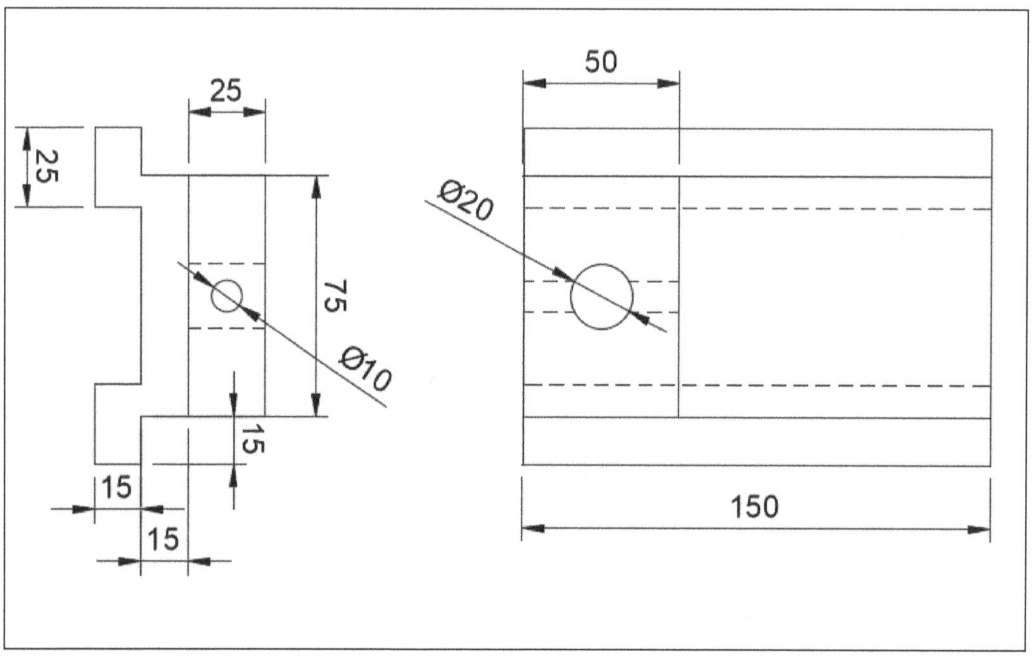

Figure-78. Dimensions for Practice 8

PRACTICE 9

Create the model as shown in Figure-79. The dimensions are given in Figure-80.

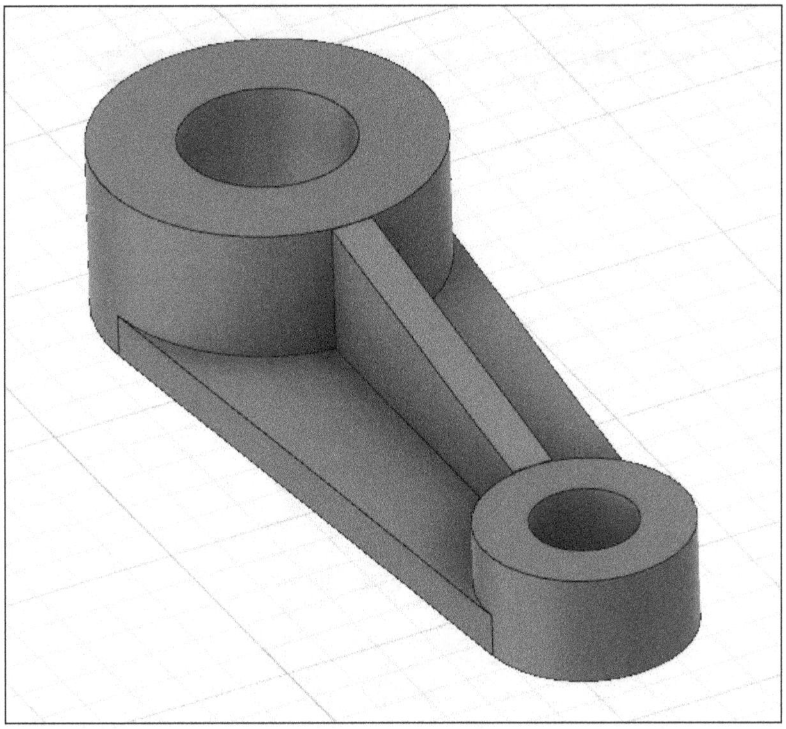

Figure-79. Model for Practice 9

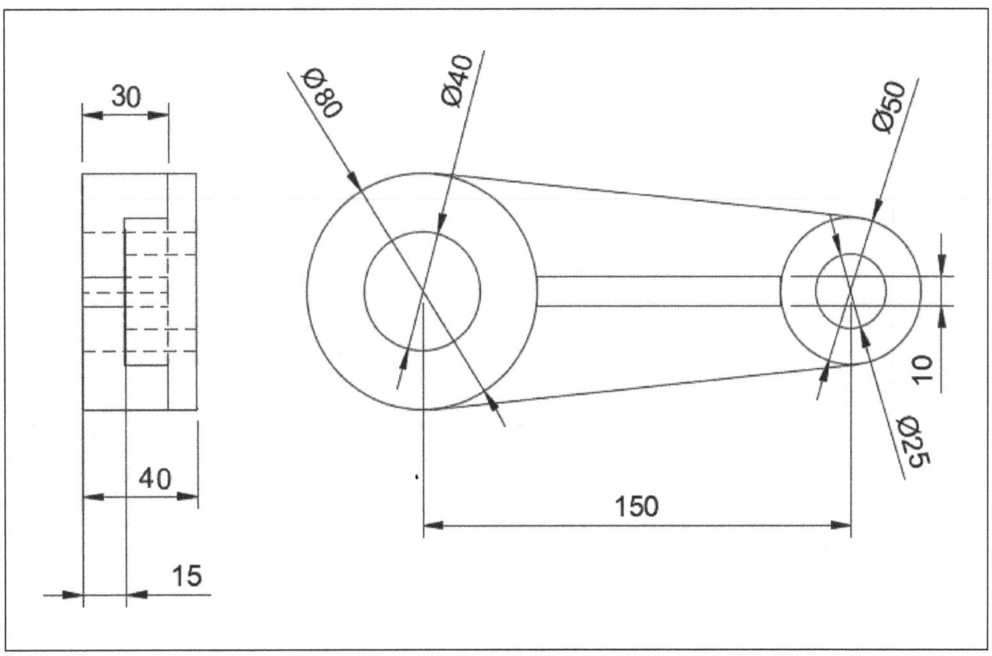

Figure-80. Dimensions for Practice 9

PRACTICE 10

Create the model as shown in Figure-81. The dimensions are given in Figure-82.

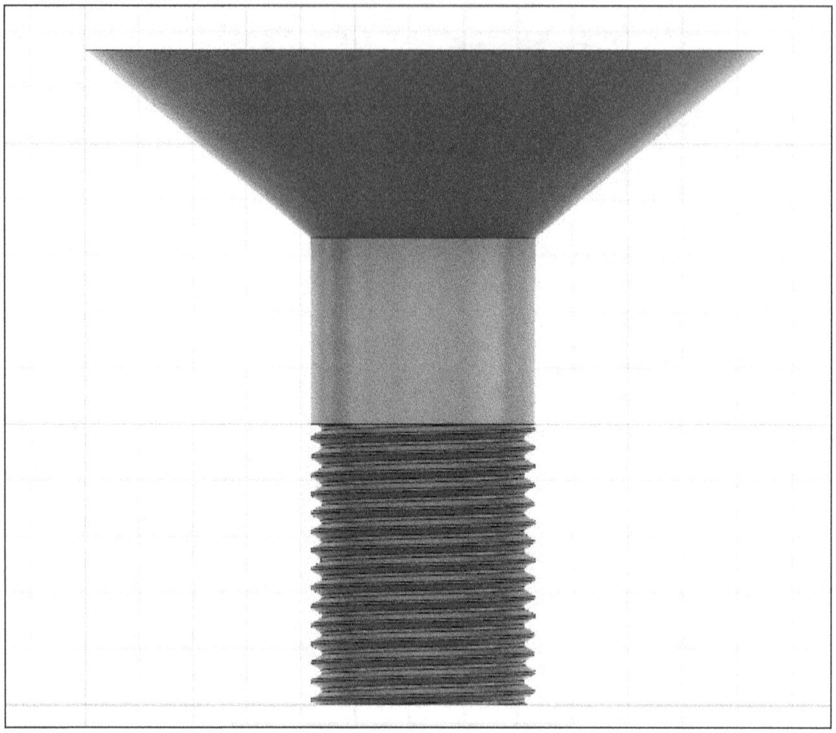

Figure-81. Model for Practice 10

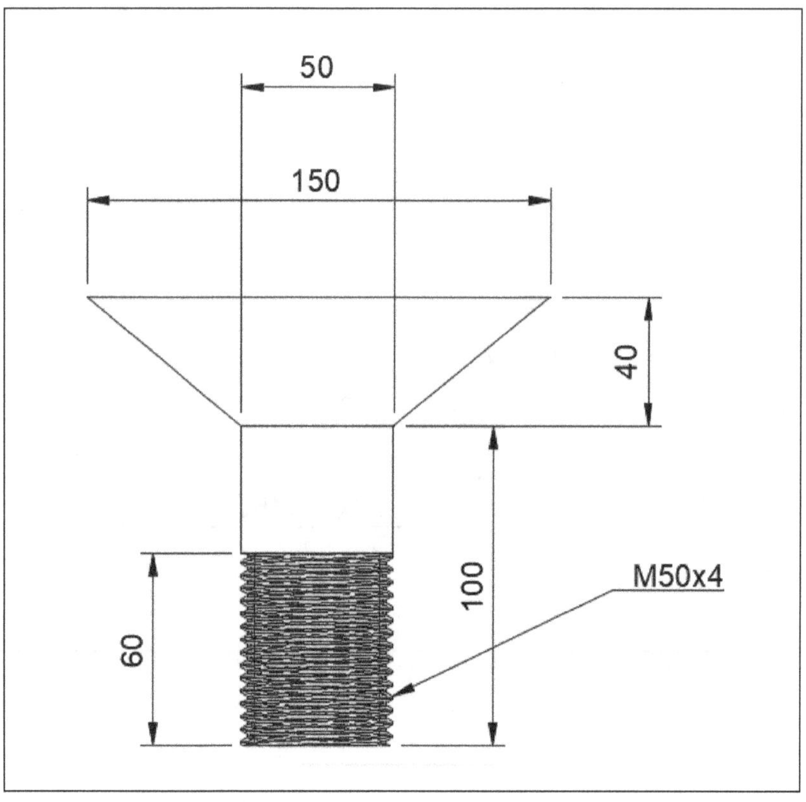

Figure-82. Dimensions for Practice 10

Chapter 6

Solid Editing

Topics Covered

The major topics covered in this chapter are:

- ***Solid Editing Tools***
- ***Press Pull Tool***
- ***Fillet Tool***
- ***Chamfer Tool***
- ***Shell Tool***
- ***Draft Tool***
- ***Scale Tool***
- ***Combine Tool***
- ***Replace Face Tool***
- ***Split Face Tool***
- ***Split Body Tool***
- ***Silhouette Split Tool***
- ***Move/Copy Tool***
- ***Align Tool***
- ***Delete Tool***
- ***Physical Material Tool***
- ***Appearance Tool***
- ***Manage Materials Tool***
- ***Change Parameters Tool***
- ***Volumetric Lattice Tool***

SOLID EDITING TOOLS

In the previous chapters, we have learned to create solid models and remove materials from them. In this chapter, we will learn to edit the models. Like the other tools, Autodesk Fusion has packed all the editing tools into one drop-down. These tools are available in **MODIFY** drop-down from **Toolbar**; refer to Figure-1. The tools in this drop-down are discussed next.

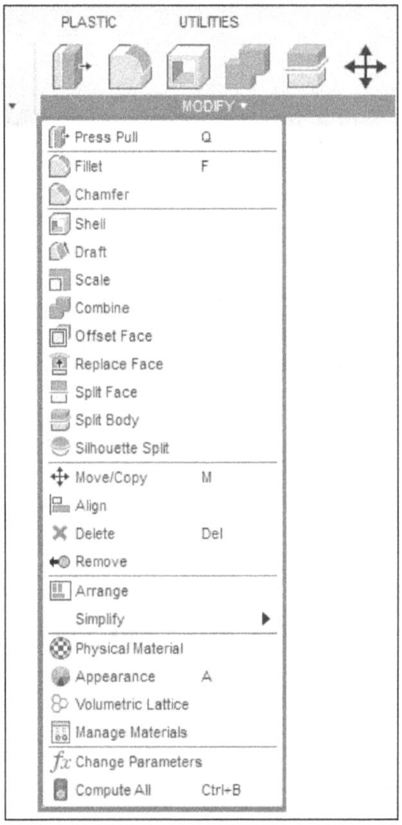

Figure-1. Modify drop down

PRESS PULL

The **Press Pull** tool is used to modify the body by drag and drop methods. The options displayed to perform press pull operations depends on the selected geometry. The procedure to use this tool is discussed next.

- Select **Press Pull** tool from **MODIFY** drop-down in the **Toolbar**; refer to Figure-2. The **PRESS PULL** dialog box will be displayed; refer to Figure-3. You can also select **Press Pull** tool by pressing **Q** key.

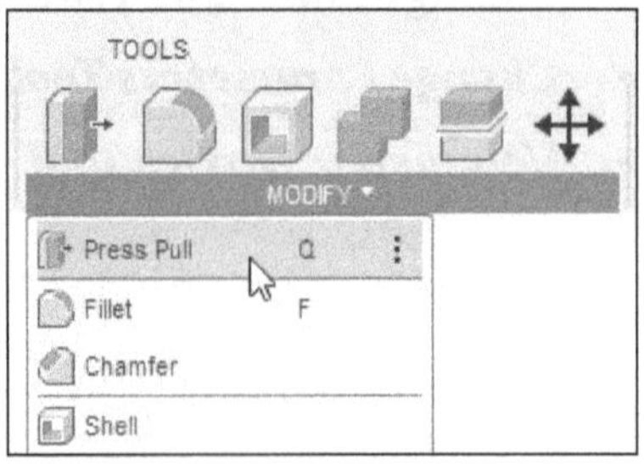

Figure-2. Press Pull tool

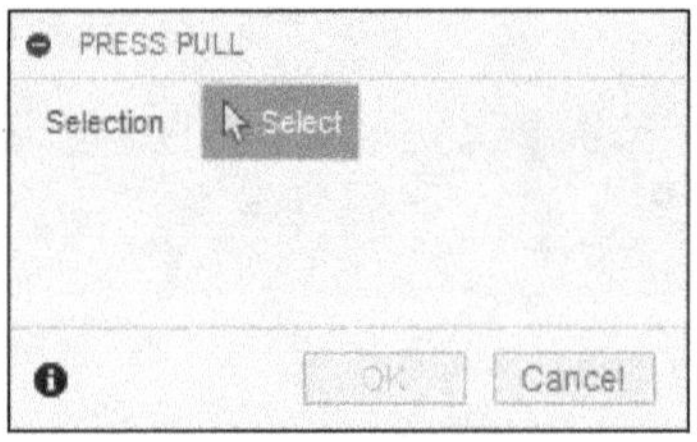

Figure-3. PRESS PULL dialog box

- Select a face, if you want to offset or move the face. The **OFFSET FACE** dialog box will be displayed. The **Offset Face** tool will be discussed later.

- Select an edge, if you want to fillet the edge. The **FILLET** dialog box will be displayed. The **Fillet** tool will be discussed later in this unit.
- Select a sketch, if you want to extrude the profile. The **EXTRUDE** dialog box will be displayed. This tool was discussed earlier in this book.

Offset Face

The **Offset Face** tool is used to offset or move the face. The procedure to use this tool is discussed next.

- Select **Press Pull** tool from **MODIFY** drop-down. The **PRESS PULL** dialog box will be displayed.
- Click on the face of the model to offset. The **OFFSET FACE** dialog box will be displayed; refer to Figure-4.

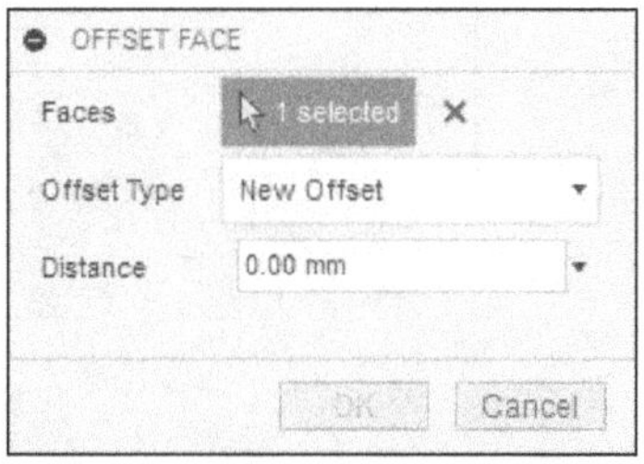

Figure-4. OFFSET FACE dialog box

- Select **Automatic** option from **Offset Type** drop-down if you do not want to update the sketch or base feature on applying the offset. This action is not added to time line.
- Select **Modify Existing Feature** option from **Offset Type** drop-down if you want to update the sketch or base feature on applying offset. This action is not added to time line.
- Select **New Offset** option from **Offset Type** drop-down if you want to create a new face. This action is added to time line.
- Click in **Distance** edit box of **OFFSET FACE** dialog box or floating window from screen and enter desired value as the distance for offset. You can also move drag handle to set the distance. The preview of offset face will be displayed; refer to Figure-5.

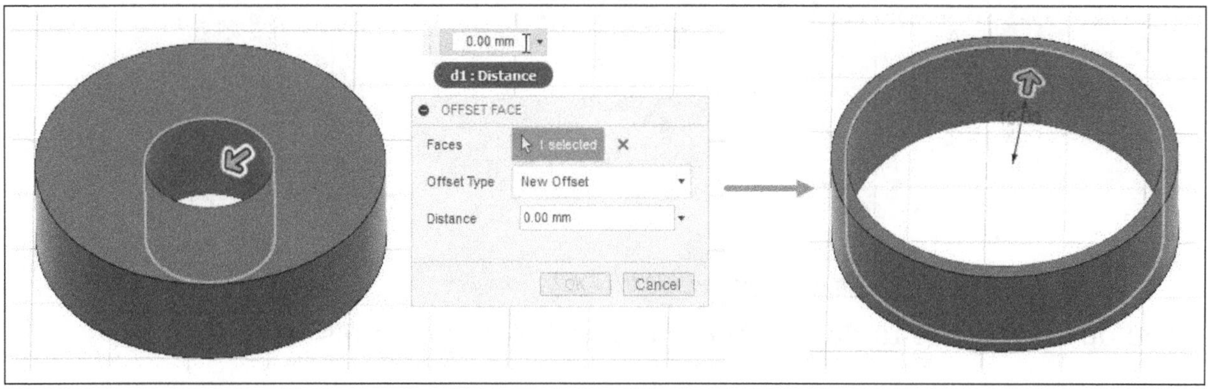

Figure-5. Preview on applying offset face

- Click **OK** button from **OFFSET FACE** dialog box to complete the process.

FILLET

The **Fillet** tool is used to apply round at the edges. This tool works in the same way as the **Sketch Fillet** do. It is recommended that, apply the fillets after creating all the features required in the model because fillets can increase the processing time during modifications. The procedure to use this tool is given next.

- Select **Fillet** tool from **MODIFY** drop-down in the **Toolbar**; refer to Figure-6 or press **Q** and select an edge. The **FILLET** dialog box will be displayed; refer to Figure-7.

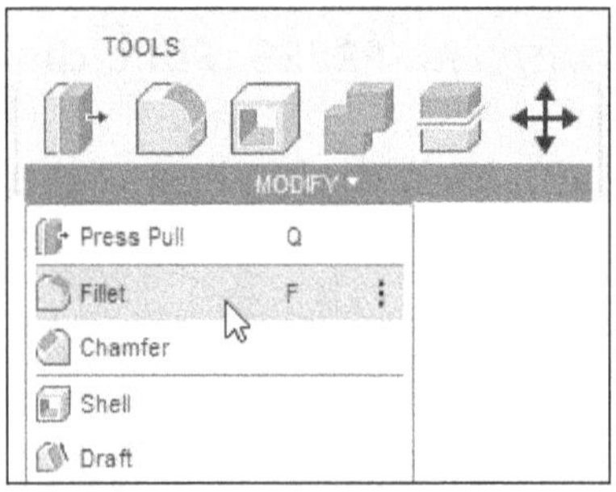

Figure-6. 3D Fillet tool

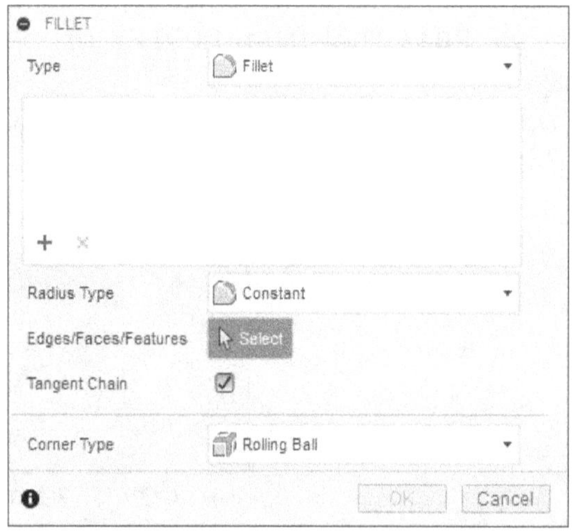

Figure-7. FILLET dialog box

- **Edges** selection is active by default. Click on the edge(s) from the model to apply fillet. You can select multiple edges also without holding the **CTRL** key. The updated **FILLET** dialog box will be displayed; refer to Figure-8.

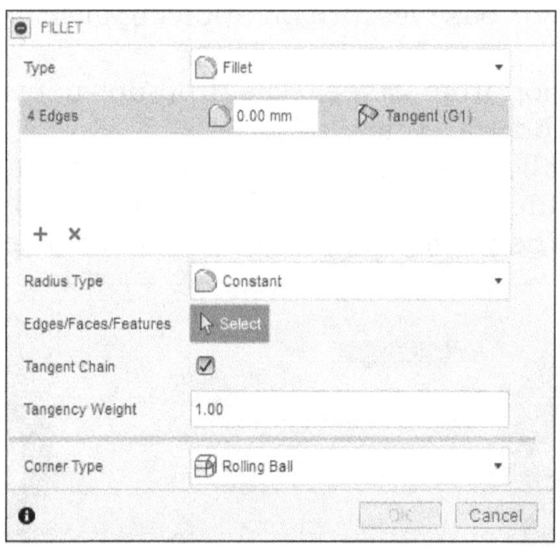

Figure-8. Updated 3D FILLET dialog box

- The options of the updated **FILLET** dialog box are discussed next.

Radius Type Drop-Down

There are three options in **Radius Type** drop-down; refer to Figure-9. These options are used to specify the type of round to be created. These options are discussed next.

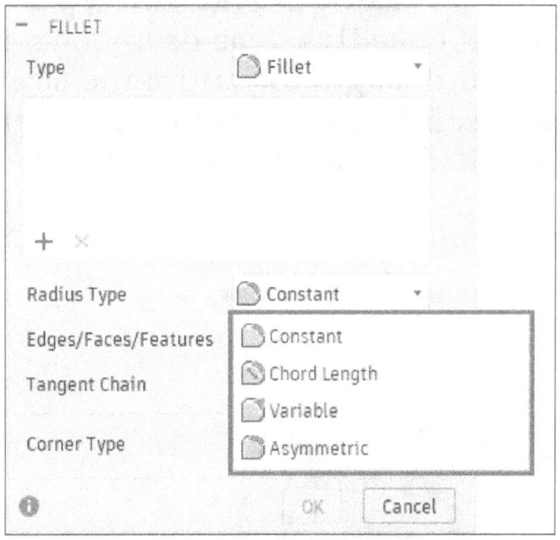

Figure-9. Fillet Radius Type drop down

Constant Radius Type

- Select **Constant** option from **Radius Type** drop-down to apply the fillet of fix size on the selected edge.
- Click in the **Radius** edit box of **FILLET** dialog box and enter **10** as the radius of fillet. You can also move the drag-handle from canvas screen to set the radius of fillet; refer to Figure-10.

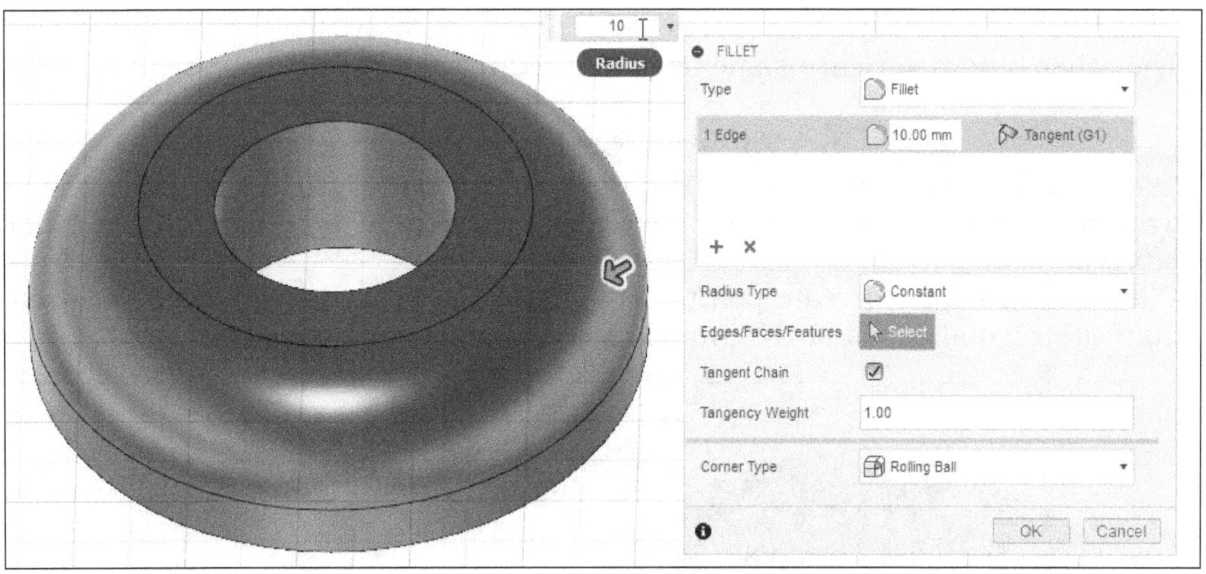

Figure-10. Preview of constant radius type

- Select the **Tangent Chain** check box to include tangentially connected edges in fillet.
- Specify desired value in **Tangency Weight** edit box to increase or decrease the scale of tangency weight.
- Select the **Curvature (G2)** option from **Continuity** drop-down if you want to apply the curvature continuity to the selected fillet.
- Select desired option from **Corner Type** section to define fillet shape at vertex formed by three edges meeting at single point.
- Click **OK** button from **FILLET** dialog box to apply the fillet.

Chord Length Radius Type

- Select **Chord Length** option of **Radius Type** drop-down from **FILLET** dialog box if you want to specify the chord length to control the size for the fillet.
- Click in the **Chord Length** edit box and enter desired value for fillet. You can also set the value by moving the drag handle. The preview will be displayed; refer to Figure-11.

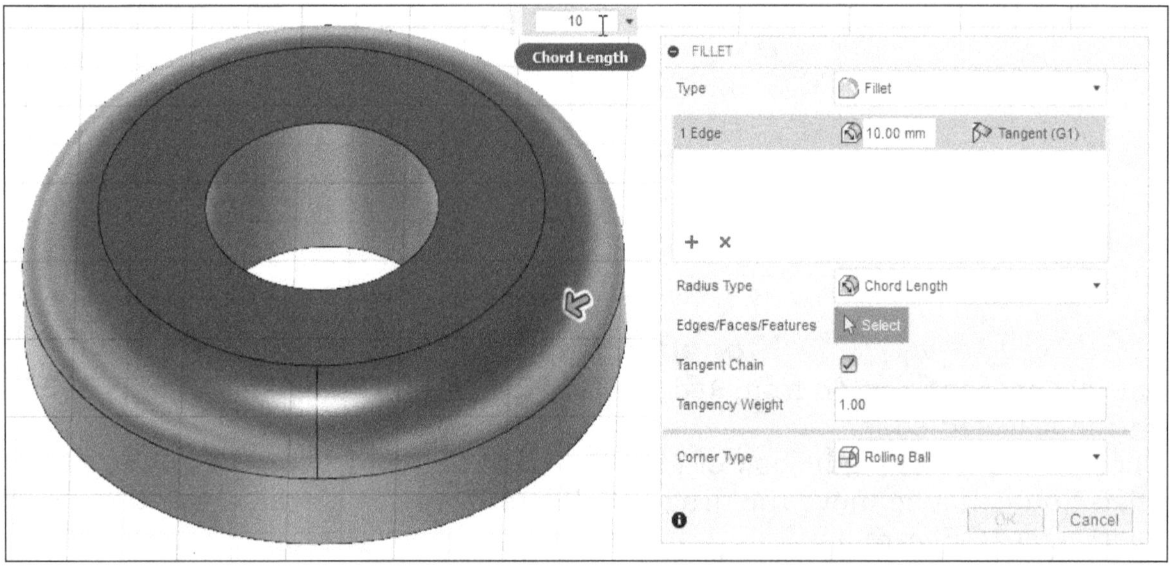

Figure-11. Preview of chord length fillet

- The other parameters are same as discussed in last topic.

Variable Radius Type

- Select **Variable** option from **Radius Type** drop-down of **FILLET** dialog box if you want to specify radii at selected points along the edge. The updated **FILLET** dialog box will be displayed.
- Click on the edge to create points for applying fillet and specify radius for each point in the dialog box or dynamic input box; refer to Figure-12.

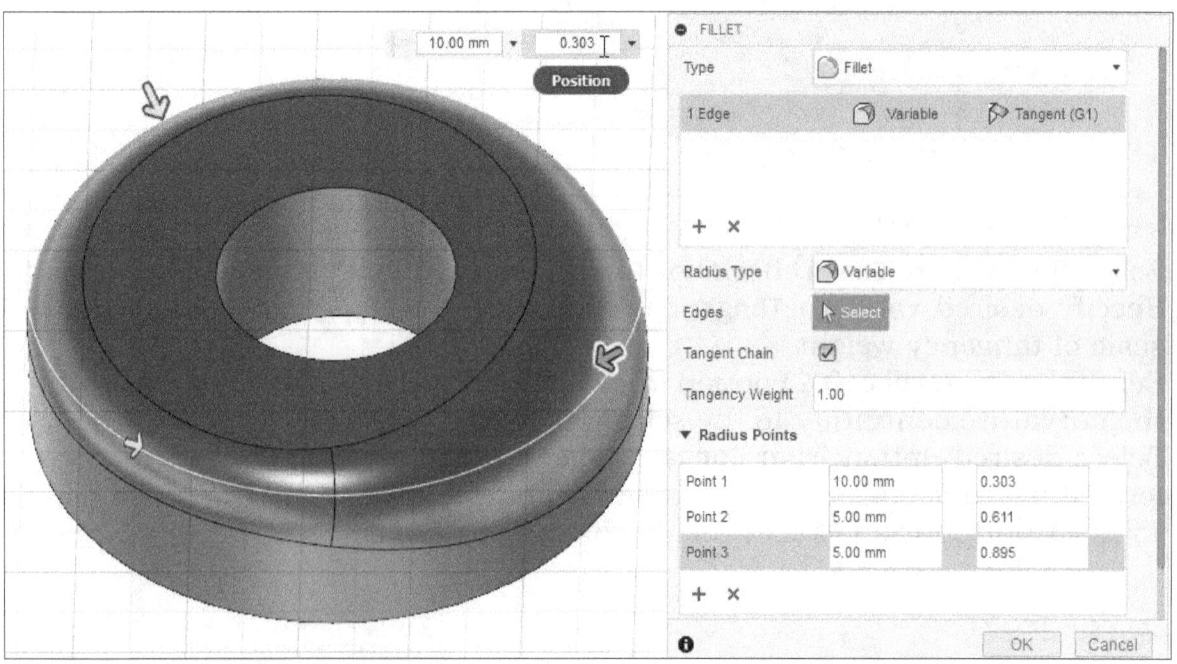

Figure-12. Preview of variable radius type

- To delete the created point, select the specific point from the edge and click on the **Remove selection set** button from the **FILLET** dialog box. Point earlier created to apply fillet will be displayed with arrows.
- The other parameters of this dialog box were discussed earlier.
- After specifying the parameters, click on the **OK** button from **FILLET** dialog box to create the fillet.

Asymmetric Radius Type

- Select **Asymmetric** option from **Radius Type** drop-down to apply different radius to each side of the fillet along its entire length.
- Other parameters of this radius type are same as discussed earlier for other radius types.

RULE FILLET

The **Rule Fillet** option is used to add fillets or rounds to a design based on specified rules. The edges are determined by specified rules rather than selection in the canvas. The procedure to use this tool is discussed next.

- Select **Rule Fillet** option from **Type** drop down in **FILLET** dialog box; refer to Figure-13. The **FILLET** dialog box with rule fillet options will be displayed; refer to Figure-14.

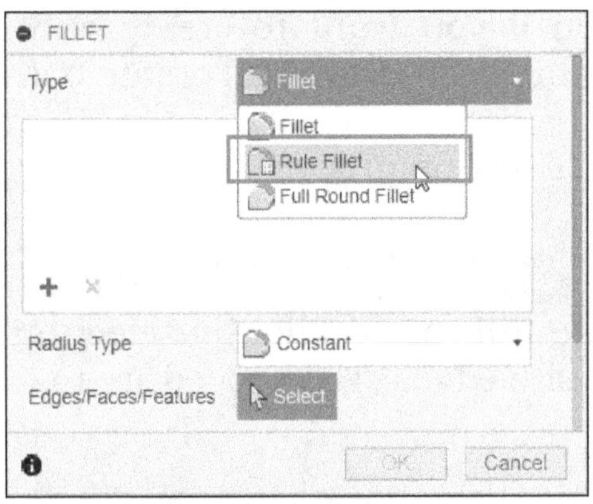

Figure-13. Rule Fillet tool in FILLET dialog box

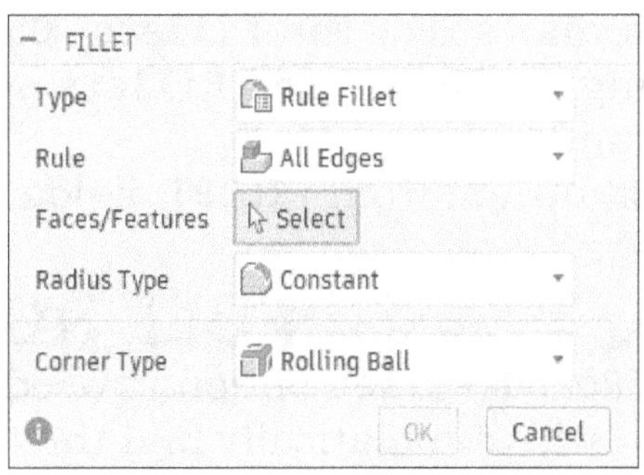

Figure-14. FILLET dialog box with rule fillet options

- The **Faces/Features** selection is active by default. Select desired faces/features from model to apply rule fillet.
- Click in the **Radius** edit box and specify desired value of radius for fillet. The preview of fillet will be displayed; refer to Figure-15. You can also set the radius by moving the drag handle.

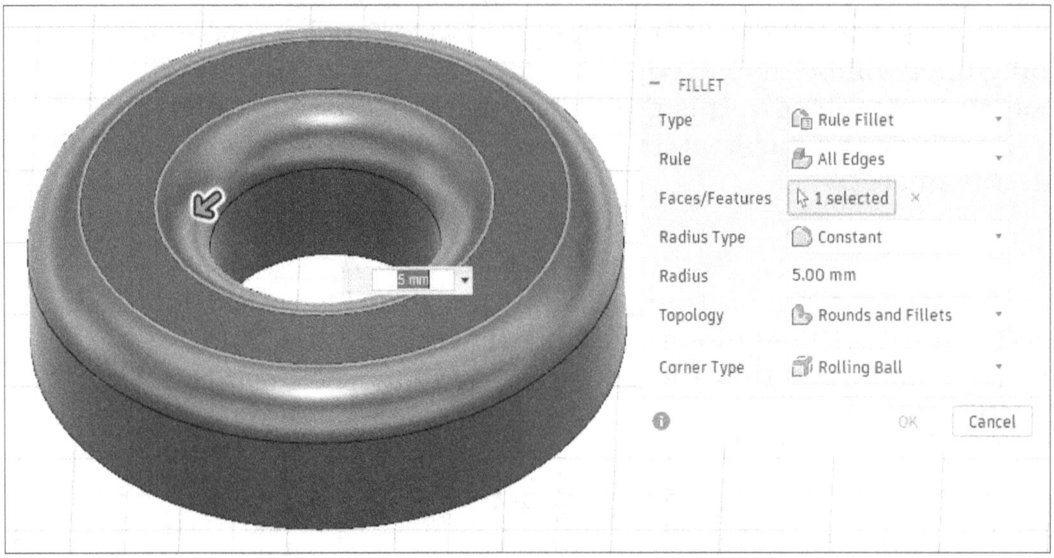

Figure-15. Preview of rule fillet

- Select **All Edges** option from **Rule** drop-down if you want to add the fillets to all edges of the input faces/features and select **Between Faces/Features** option if you want to add the fillets at the intersection of the input faces/features. Note that you can also select features from Time line.
- Select **Rounds Only** option from **Topology** drop-down if you want to create only rounds and select the **Fillets Only** option if you want to create only fillets. Selecting the **Rounds And Fillets** option in this drop-down will create both fillets and rounds.
- Click **OK** button from **FILLET** dialog box to finish this process.

FULL ROUND FILLET

The **Full Round Fillet** option is used to create full round fillet by selecting a face only and it will automatically find the two opposite edges. The procedure to use this tool is discussed next.

- Select **Full Round Fillet** option from **Type** drop-down in **Fillet** dialog box; refer to Figure-16. The **FILLET** dialog box with full round fillet options will be displayed; refer to Figure-17.

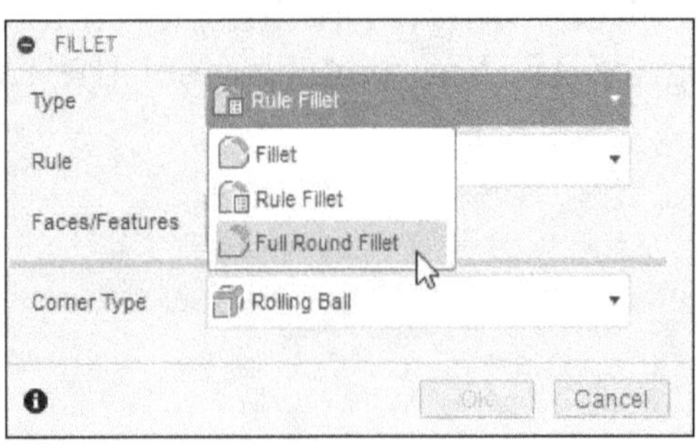

Figure-16. Full Round Fillet tool in FILLET dialog box

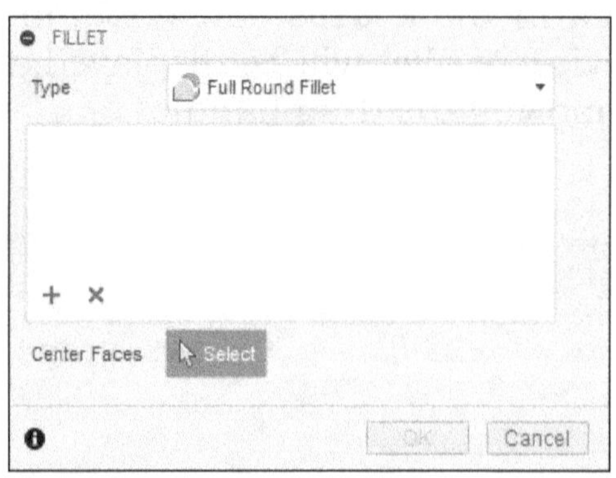

Figure-17. FILLET dialog box with full round fillet options

- The **Select** button of the **Center Faces** section is active by default. Select desired center face of the model to create full round fillet; refer to Figure-18.

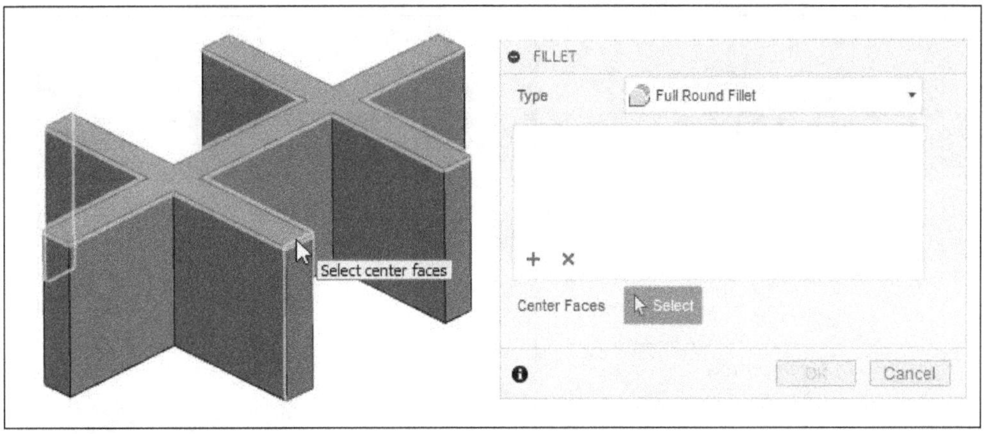

Figure-18. Selecting center face of the model

- On selecting center face of the model, full round fillet of the model will be created and the updated **FILLET** dialog box will be displayed; refer to Figure-19.

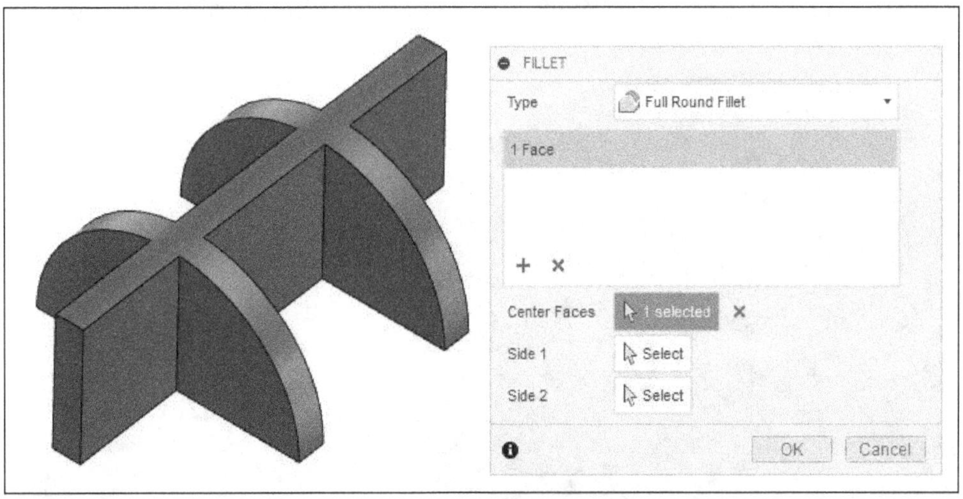

Figure-19. Full round fillet of model created with updated FILLET dialog box

- Click on **Select** button of **Side 1** section and press & hold **CTRL** key to select faces on first side of the full round fillet and click on **Select** button of **Side 2** section and press & hold **CTRL** key to select faces on second side of the full round fillet to modify the fillet.
- After specifying the parameters, click on **OK** button from the dialog box to finish the process.

CHAMFER

The **Chamfer** tool is used to bevel the sharp edges of the model. The procedure to create chamfer by using this tool is given next.

- Click on the **Chamfer** tool from **MODIFY** drop-down in the **Toolbar**; refer to Figure-20. The **CHAMFER** dialog box will be displayed; refer to Figure-21.

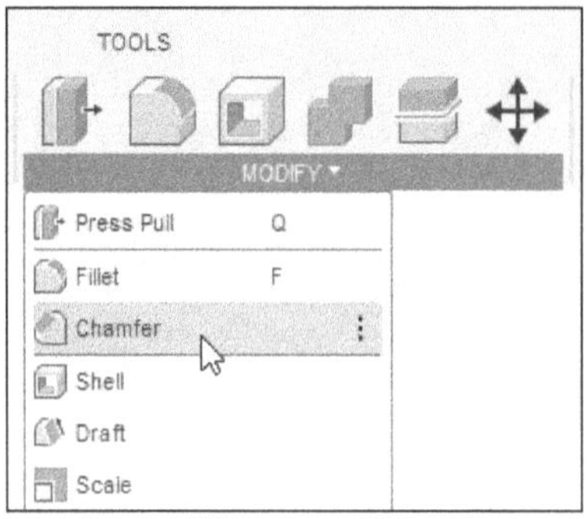

Figure-20. Chamfer tool

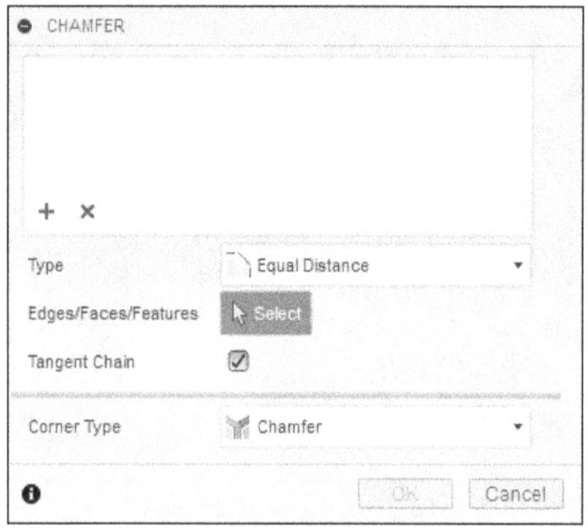

Figure-21. CHAMFER dialog box

- **Edges/Faces/Features** selection is active by default. Click on the edge of model to apply chamfer. The updated **CHAMFER** dialog box will be displayed; refer to Figure-22.

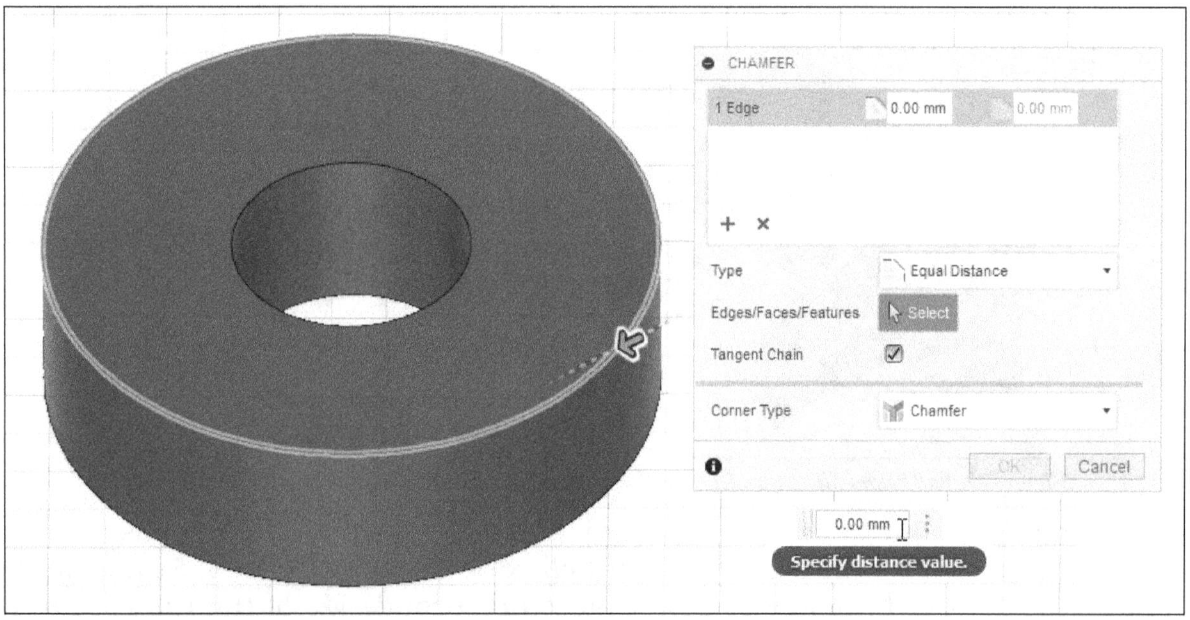

Figure-22. Updated CHAMFER dialog box

- Select the **Tangent Chain** check box to include tangentially connected edges in selection.
- Select **Equal Distance** option from **Type** drop-down of **CHAMFER** dialog box if you want to specify equal distance for both sides of the chamfer.
- Select **Two Distance** option from **Type** drop-down of **CHAMFER** dialog box if you want to specify distance for each side of the chamfer.
- Enter the value of distance for each side in the respective edit box. You can also set the distance by moving the drag handle from canvas screen.
- Select **Distance and Angle** option from **Type** drop-down if you want to specify distance and angle values to create the chamfer.
- Click in the **Specify distance value** edit box and enter desired value for distance for chamfer. The preview of chamfer will be displayed; refer to Figure-23.

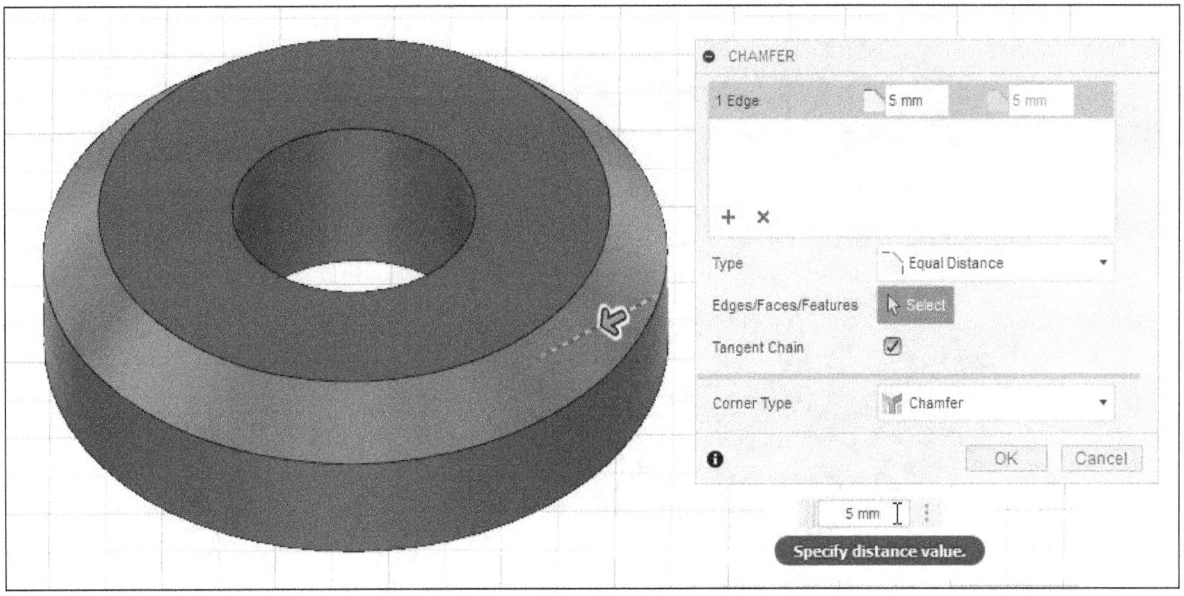

Figure-23. Preview of chamfer

- Select **Chamfer** option from **Corner Type** drop-down to create a chamfer to join beveled edges at the corner.
- Select **Miter** option from **Corner Type** drop-down to merge beveled edges into a mitered corner point.
- Select **Blend** option from **Corner Type** drop-down to blend beveled edges into adjacent faces.
- Click **OK** button of **CHAMFER** dialog box to finish the process.

SHELL

The **Shell** tool is used to make a solid part hollow and remove one or more selected faces. The procedure to use this tool is given next.

- Select **Shell** tool from **MODIFY** drop-down in the **Toolbar**; refer to Figure-24. The **SHELL** dialog box will be displayed; refer to Figure-25.

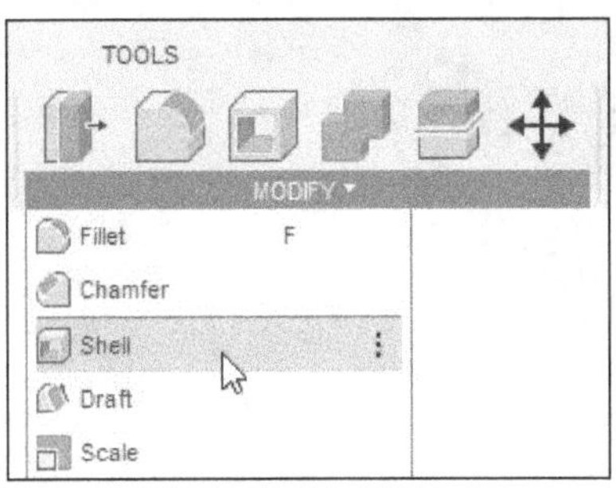

Figure-24. Shell tool

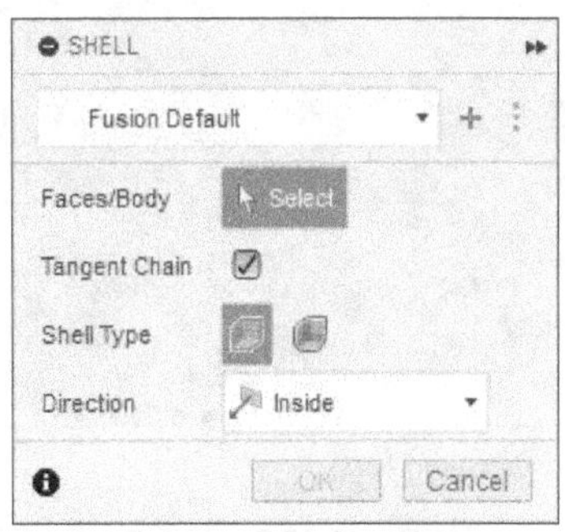

Figure-25. SHELL dialog box

- The **Faces/Body** selection button is active by default. Click on the face/body of the solid to apply shell. The updated **SHELL** dialog box will be displayed; refer to Figure-26.

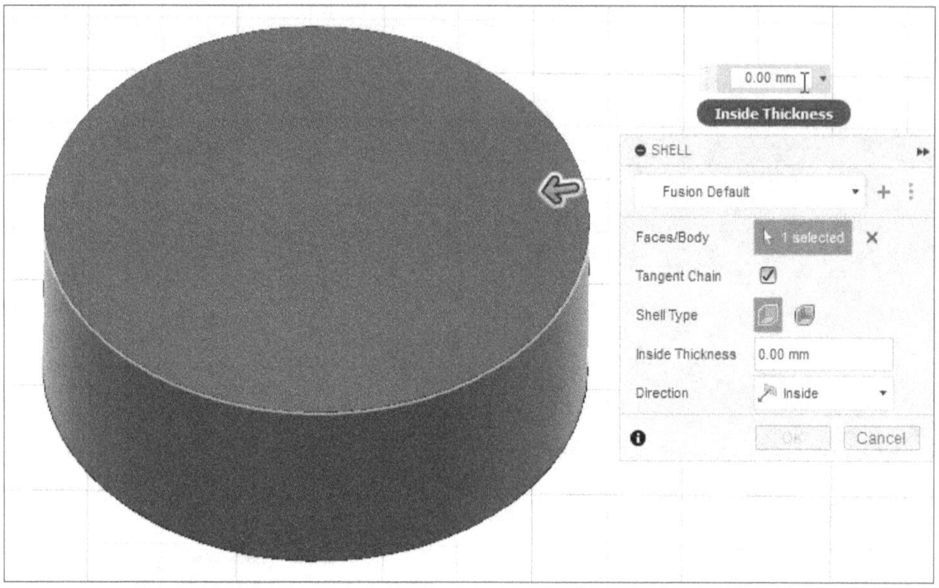

Figure-26. Updated SHELL dialog box

- Select the **Tangent Chain** check box to include tangentially connected edges in selection.
- Select **Sharp Shell** option from the **Shell Type** area to create sharp offset corners. Select **Rounded Shell** option to create rounded offset corners.
- Click in the **Inside Thickness** edit box and specify desired value of shell thickness. The preview of shell will be displayed; refer to Figure-27.

Figure-27. Preview of shell

- Select **Inside** option from **Direction** drop-down if you want to shell the faces towards the interior of the part.
- Select **Outside** option from **Direction** drop-down if you want to shell the faces towards the exterior of the part.
- Select **Both** option from **Direction** drop-down if you want to shell the faces towards the interior and the exterior of the part by equal amount. Click in the **Inside Thickness** and **Outside Thickness** edit boxes and specify desired value to specify thickness for shell.
- Click **OK** button from **SHELL** dialog box to complete the process.

DRAFT

The **Draft** tool is used to apply taper to the faces of a solid model. This tool is mainly useful when you are designing components for moulding or casting. **Draft** tool applies taper on the face and this taper allows easy & safe ejection of parts from dies. The procedure to use this tool is discussed next.

- Select **Draft** tool from **MODIFY** drop-down in the **Toolbar**; refer to Figure-28. The **DRAFT** dialog box will be displayed; refer to Figure-29.

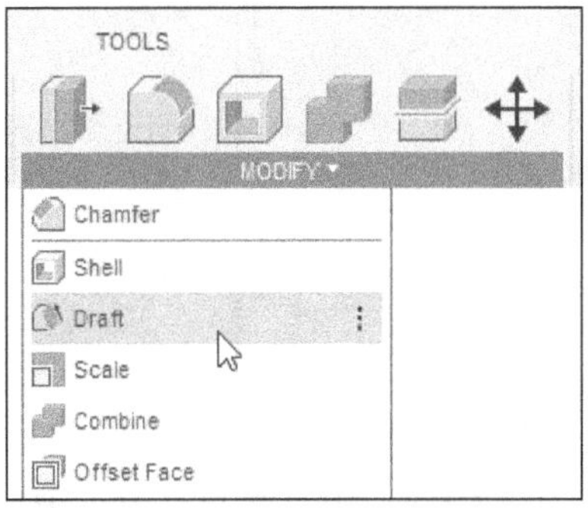

Figure-28. Draft tool

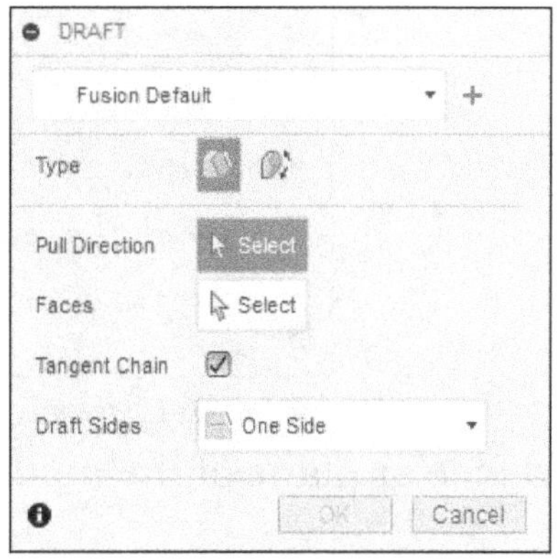

Figure-29. DRAFT dialog box

- The **Fixed Plane** draft type is selected by default in the **Type** section of the dialog box. **Fixed Plane** draft type creates tapered face using angle specified from selected fixed plane.
- The **Pull Direction** selection button is active by default. Click on the face or plane of the model which you want to use as fixed reference.
- Click on **Select** button of **Faces** section and select the faces to be tapered.
- Click on the **Flip Pull Direction** button from **DRAFT** dialog box to flip the direction of draft.
- Click in the **Angle** edit box and specify desired value of angle for draft. The preview of draft will be displayed; refer to Figure-30. You can also set the angle of draft by moving the drag handle.

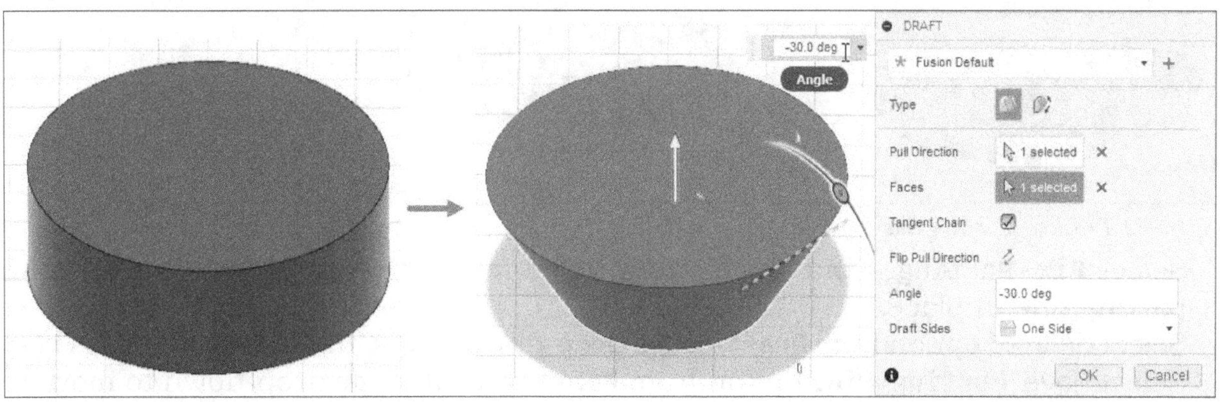

Figure-30. Preview of draft

- The options of **Draft Sides** drop-down were discussed earlier in this book.
- Click **OK** button from **DRAFT** dialog box to finish the process.
- Select **Parting Line** draft type from **Type** section of the dialog box to create draft along a parting line. The updated **DRAFT** dialog box will be displayed; refer to Figure-31.

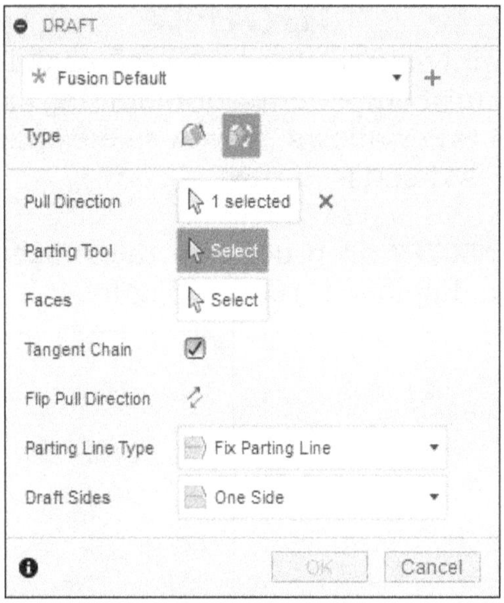

Figure-31. Updated DRAFT dialog box

- Select desired face or plane of the model to define pull direction in **Pull Direction** section.
- Select desired plane, face, edge, or sketch curve on the model to use as parting tool in **Parting Tool** section.
- Select desired faces on the model which you want to draft in the **Faces** section of the dialog box.
- Specify desired value of angle for draft in the **Angle** edit box. The preview of parting line draft type will be displayed; refer to Figure-32.

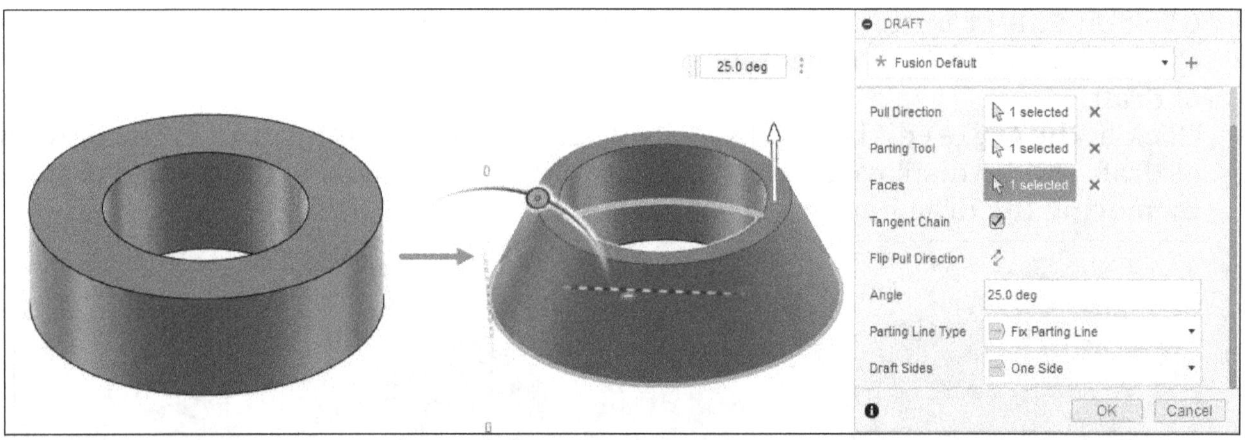

Figure-32. Preview of parting line draft type

- Select **Fix Parting Line** option from **Parting Line Type** drop-down to fix the parting line in place.
- Select desired option from **Draft Sides** drop-down as discussed earlier in this book.
- Select **Move Parting Line** option from **Parting Line Type** drop-down to move the parting line to apply draft.
- Select **Angle Above** option from **Direction** drop-down to maintain angle above parting line.
- Select **Angle Below** option from **Direction** drop-down to maintain angle below parting line.
- Select **Both** option from **Direction** drop-down to maintain angle on both sides of parting line.

- Click on the **Select** button from **Fixed Edges** section of the dialog box and select edges of the model to prevent deformation when parting line moves.
- The other options in the dialog box have been discussed earlier.
- Click **OK** button from **DRAFT** dialog box to finish the process.

SCALE

The **Scale** tool is used to enlarge or reduce selected bodies, sketches, or components based on specified scale factor. The procedure to use this tool is discussed next.

- Select **Scale** tool from **MODIFY** drop-down in the **Toolbar**; refer to Figure-33. The **SCALE** dialog box will be displayed; refer to Figure-34.

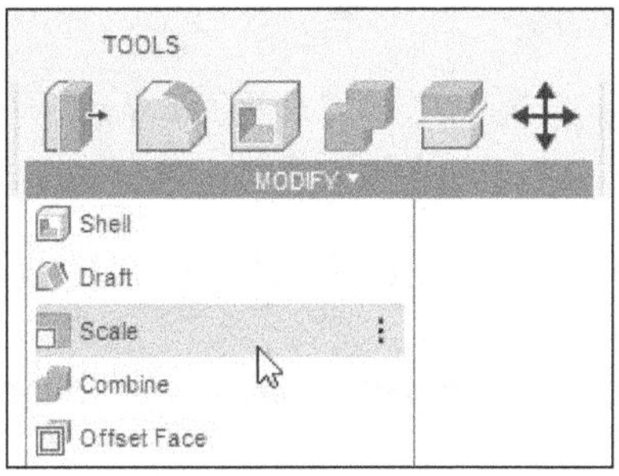

Figure-33. Scale tool

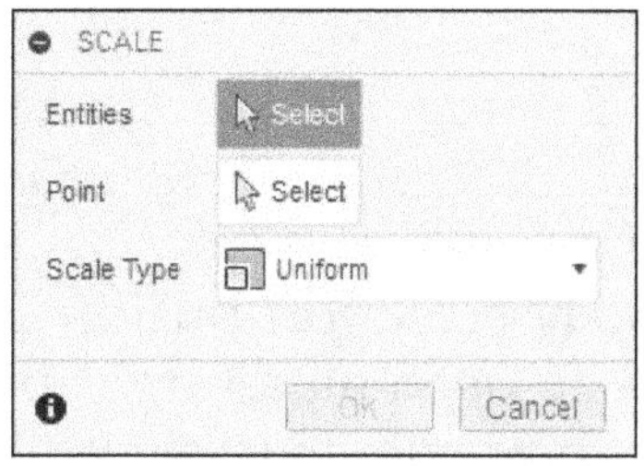

Figure-34. SCALE dialog box

- The **Entities** selection is active by default. Click on the entities to be scaled up or down.
- On selecting the entity for scale, point is automatically selected in **Point** section. If you want to use a different point as scale reference then click on the **Select** button for **Point** option in the dialog box and select desired point.
- Select **Uniform** option from **Scale Type** drop-down if you want to scale the selected entities uniformly in all the directions.
- Select **Non-Uniform** option from **Scale Type** drop-down if you want to scale the entity non-uniformly in x, y, and z direction.
- Click in the **Scale Factor** edit box and specify desired value for scale. The preview will be displayed; refer to Figure-35.
- Click on **OK** button of **SCALE** dialog box to complete the process.

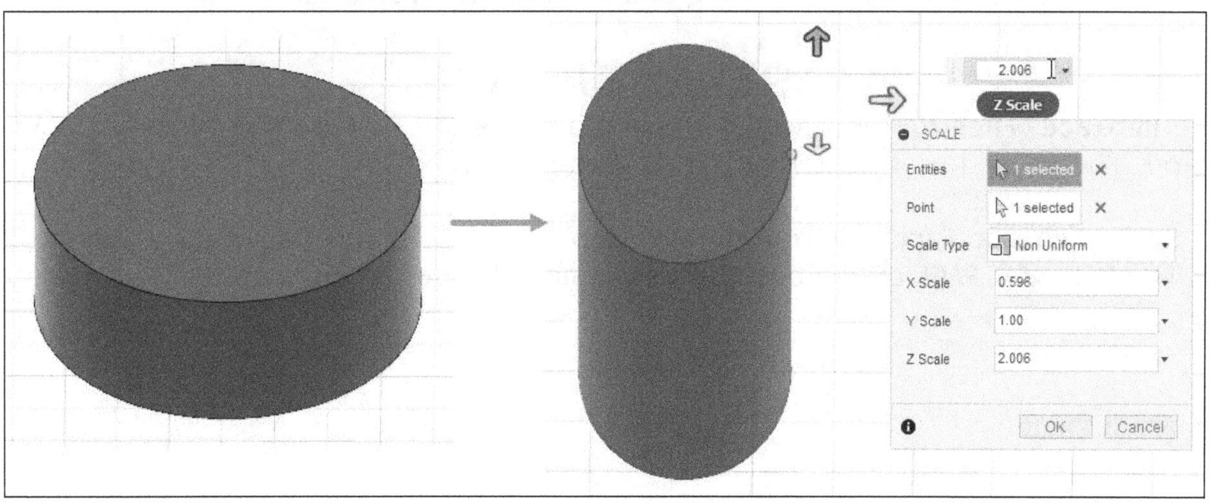

Figure-35. Preview of scale

COMBINE

The **Combine** tool is used to cut, join, and intersect the selected bodies. The procedure to use this tool is discussed next.

- Select **Combine** tool from **MODIFY** drop-down in the **Toolbar**; refer to Figure-36. The **COMBINE** dialog box will be displayed; refer to Figure-37.

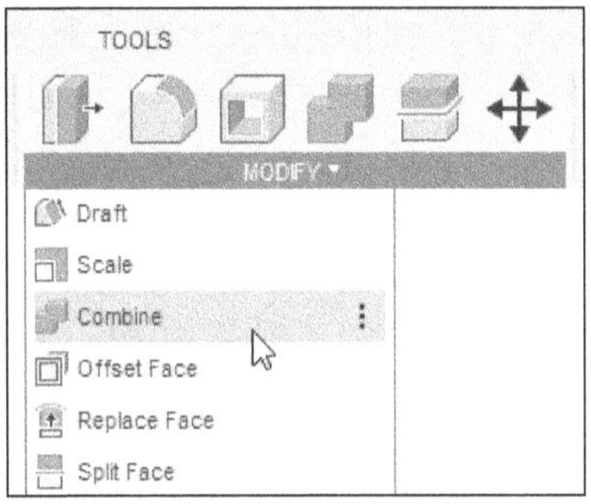

Figure-36. Combine tool

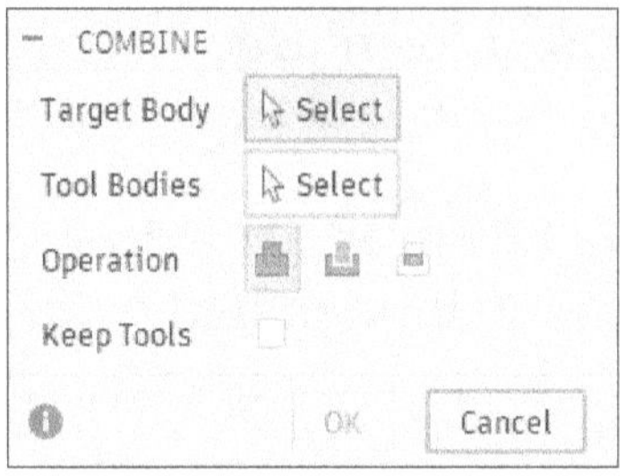

Figure-37. COMBINE dialog box

- The **Target Body** selection button is active by default. Click on the component from model to be used as a target body.
- Click on other components to select in **Tool Bodies** section. The preview of combine will be displayed; refer to Figure-38.

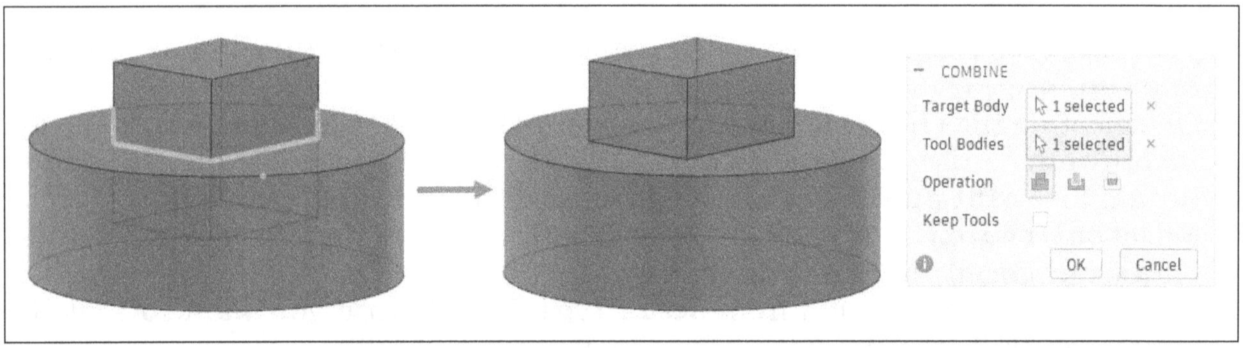

Figure-38. Preview of combine

- The options of **Operations** drop-down have been discussed earlier in this book.
- Select the **Keep Tools** check box to retain the tool bodies after the combine result.
- Click **OK** button of **COMBINE** dialog box to finish the process.

REPLACE FACE

The **Replace Face** tool is used to replace an existing face with a surface or work plane. The procedure to use this tool is discussed next.

- Select **Replace Face** tool from **MODIFY** drop-down in the **Toolbar**; refer to Figure-39. The **REPLACE FACE** dialog box will be displayed; refer to Figure-40.

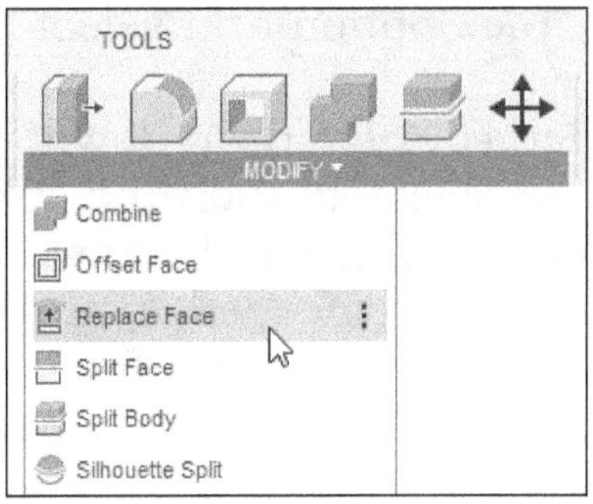

Figure-39. Replace Face tool

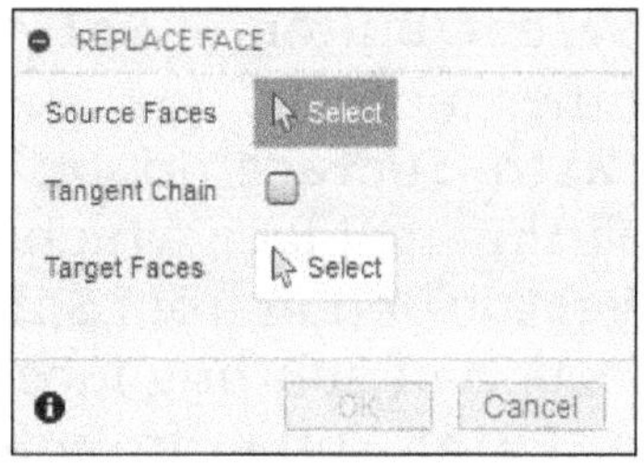

Figure-40. REPLACE FACE dialog box

- **Source Faces** selection is active by default. Click on the component face to select the face.
- Select the **Tangent Chain** check box to include tangentially connected faces in selection.
- Click **Select** button of **Target Faces** section and click on the face or plane to apply this tool. The preview will be displayed; refer to Figure-41.

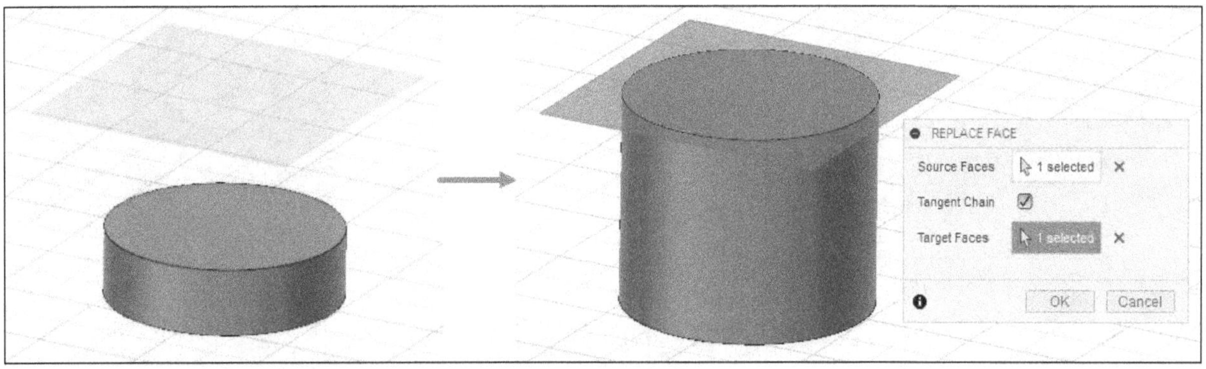

Figure-41. Preview of replace face

- Click **OK** button of **REPLACE FACE** dialog box to finish the process.

SPLIT FACE

The **Split Face** tool is used to divide faces of a surface or solid to add draft, delete an area, or create features. The procedure to use this tool is discussed next.

- Select **Split Face** tool from **MODIFY** drop-down in the **Toolbar**; refer to Figure-42. The **SPLIT FACE** dialog box will be displayed; refer to Figure-43.

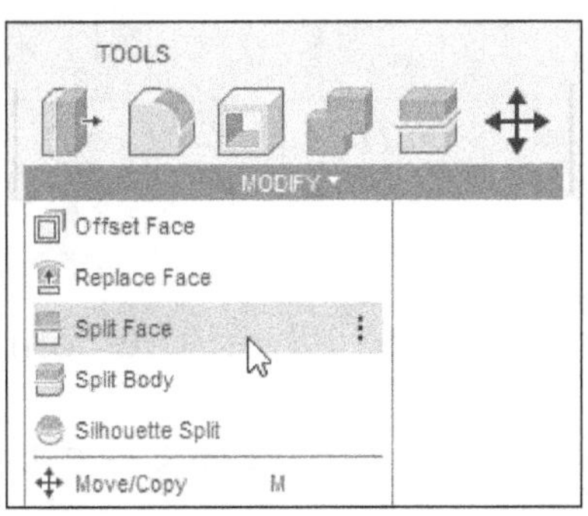

Figure-42. Split Face tool

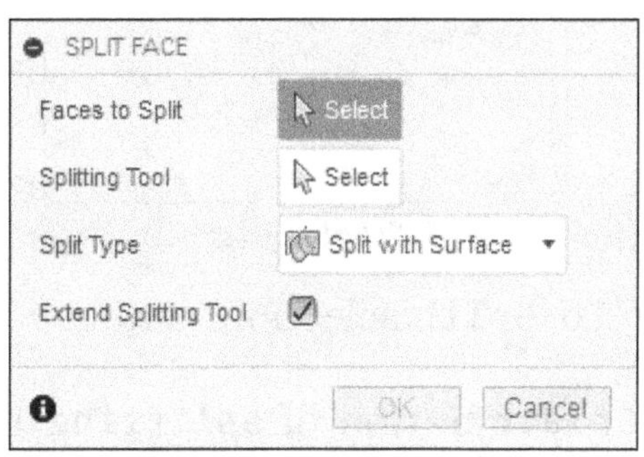

Figure-43. SPLIT FACE dialog box

- The **Faces To Split** option is active by default. Click on the model face to be split. You can select multiple faces by holding the **CTRL** key.

- Click on the **Select** button of **Splitting Tool** option and select the face which will split the other faces.
- Select **Split With Surface** option from **Split Type** drop-down, if you want to project the splitting tool face which you had selected upon the splitting face.
- Select **Along Vector** option from **Split Type** drop-down, if you want to define the projection direction of splitting face by selecting a face, edge, or axis.
- Select **Closest Point** option from **Split Type** drop-down, if you want to define the direction of projection as the closest distance between the splitting body and target faces.
- Select the **Extend Splitting Tool** check box to extend the tool to completely intersect the target faces.
- After specifying the parameters, click on **OK** button from **SPLIT FACE** dialog box to finish the process; refer to Figure-44.

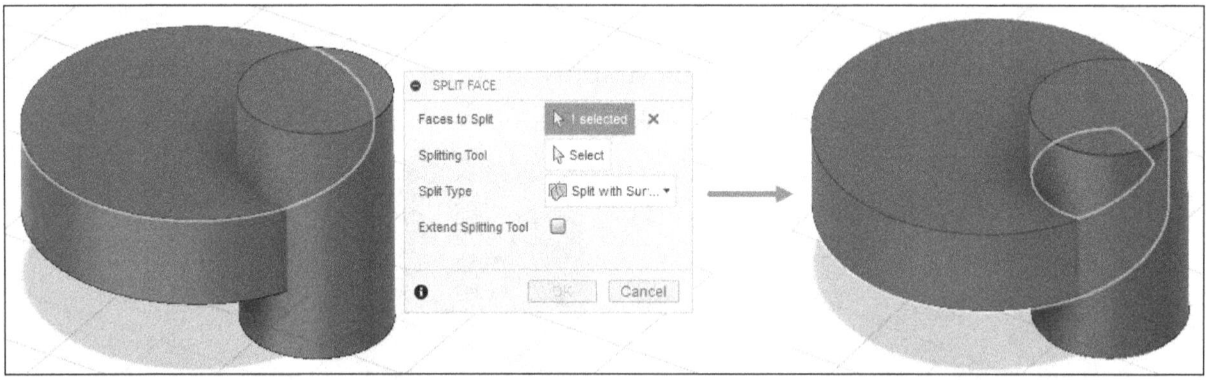

Figure-44. Preview of split face

SPLIT BODY

The **Split Body** tool works similar to **Split Face** tool but in this tool, component or part is selected in place of faces. The procedure to use this tool is discussed next.

- Select **Split Body** tool from **MODIFY** drop-down in the **Toolbar**; refer to Figure-45. The **SPLIT BODY** dialog box will be displayed; refer to Figure-46.

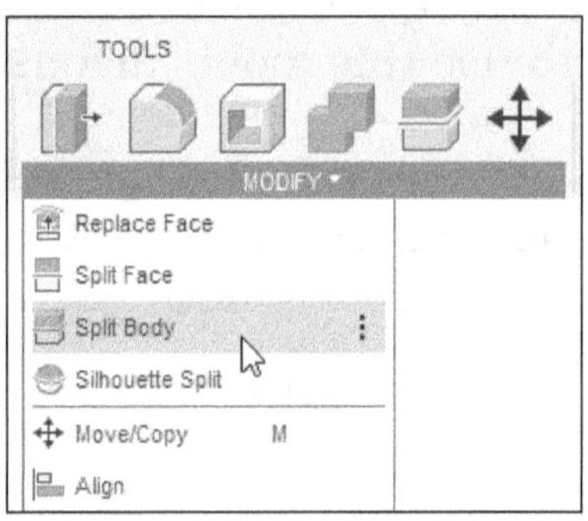

Figure-45. Split Body tool

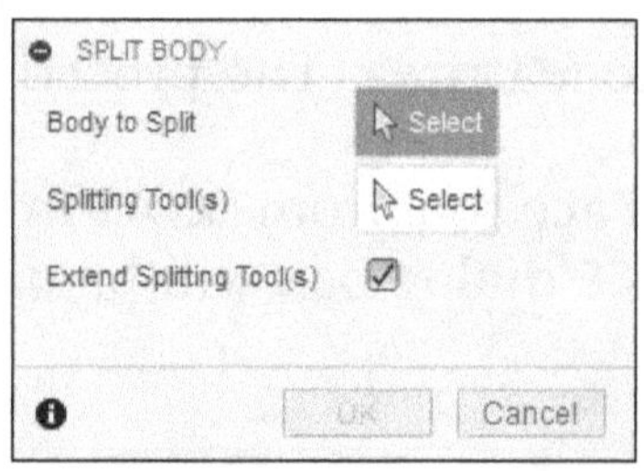

Figure-46. SPLIT BODY dialog box

- The **Body To Split** selection is active by default. Click on the component to be split.
- Click on **Select** button of **Splitting Tool** option and select the body of which splitting will be done.
- Select the **Extend Splitting Tool(s)** check box to extend the tool to completely intersect the target faces.
- After specifying various parameters, click **OK** button of **SPLIT BODY** dialog box to complete the process; refer to Figure-47.

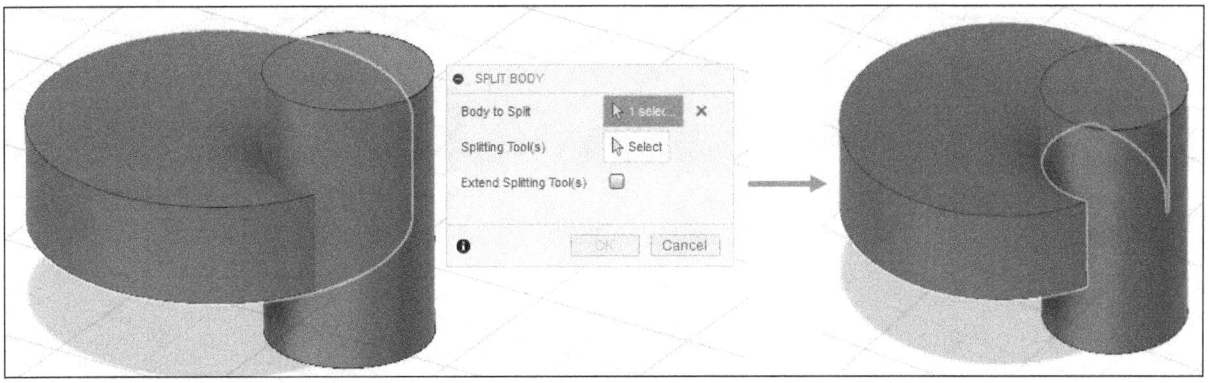

Figure-47. Preview of split body

SILHOUETTE SPLIT

The **Silhouette Split** tool is used to split selected body at the silhouette outline visible from the view direction. The procedure to use this tool is discussed next.

- Select **Silhouette Split** tool from **MODIFY** drop-down in the **Toolbar**; refer to Figure-48. The **SILHOUETTE SPLIT** dialog box will be displayed; refer to Figure-49.

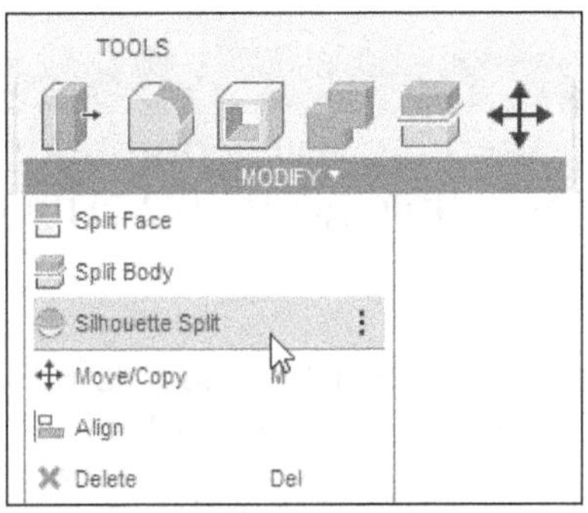

Figure-48. Silhouette Split tool

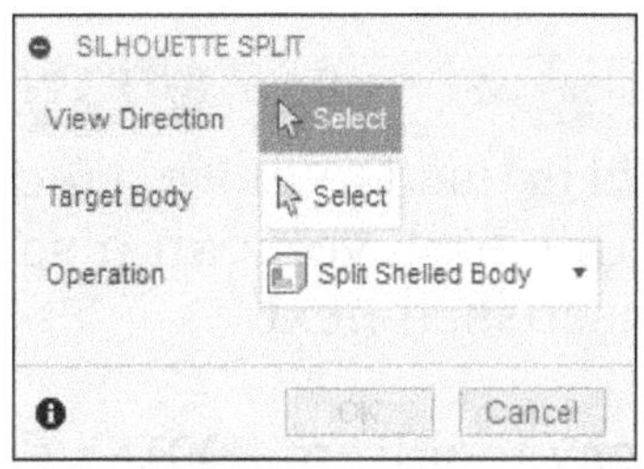

Figure-49. SILHOUETTE SPLIT dialog box

- The **View Direction** selection option is active by default. Click on the plane or face to select the direction to split.
- Click on **Select** button of **Target Body** and select the body which you want to split.
- Select **Split Faces Only** option from **Operation** drop-down, if you want to split the faces of the selected body but keeps it as a single body.
- Select **Split Shelled Body** option from **Operation** drop-down, if you want to split the selected body into two bodies. To use this option , the selected body must be shelled first.
- Select **Split Solid Body** option from **Operation** drop-down, if you want to split the selected body at the parting line. The parting line of the selected body must be planar.
- After specifying the parameters, click **OK** button of **SILHOUETTE SPLIT** dialog box to finish the process; refer to Figure-50.

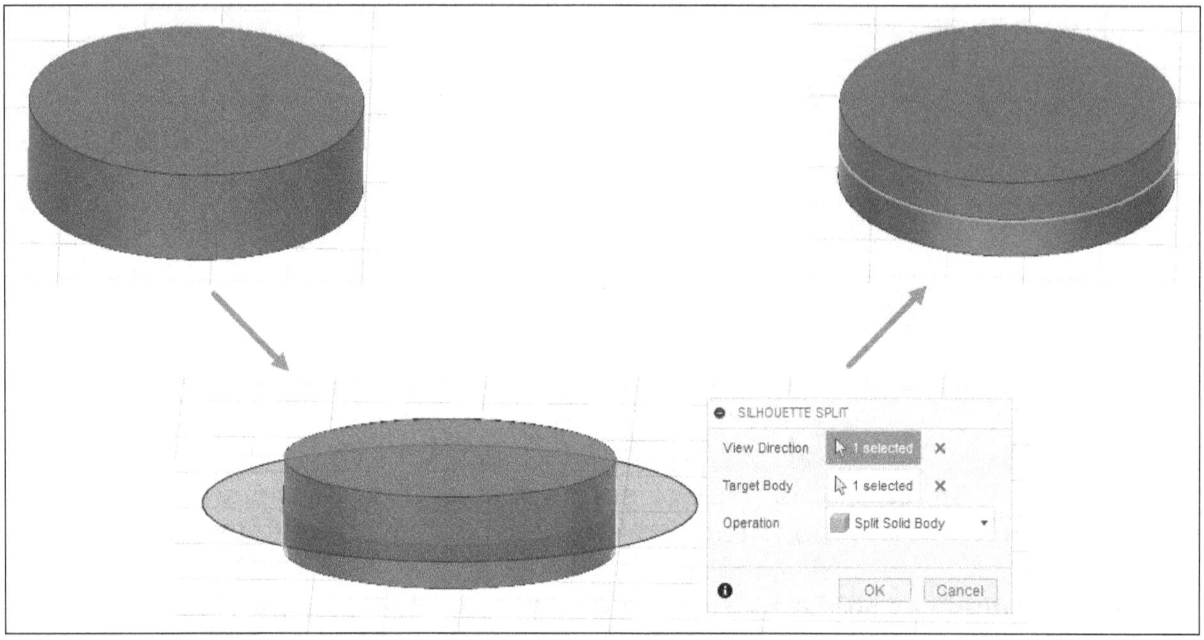

Figure-50. Preview of silhouette split

MOVE/COPY

The **Move/Copy** tool is used to move a face, body, sketch curve, components, or sketch geometry. Using this tool, you can also move the whole geometry. The procedure to use this tool is discussed next.

- Select **Move/Copy** tool from **MODIFY** drop-down in the **Toolbar**; refer to Figure-51. The **MOVE/COPY** dialog box will be displayed; refer to Figure-52.

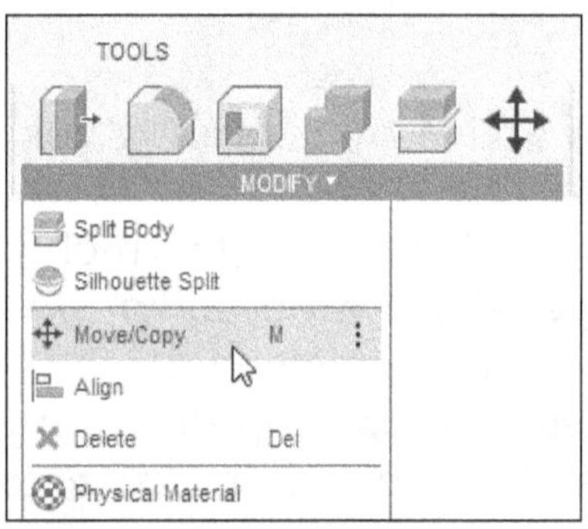

Figure-51. Move Copy tool

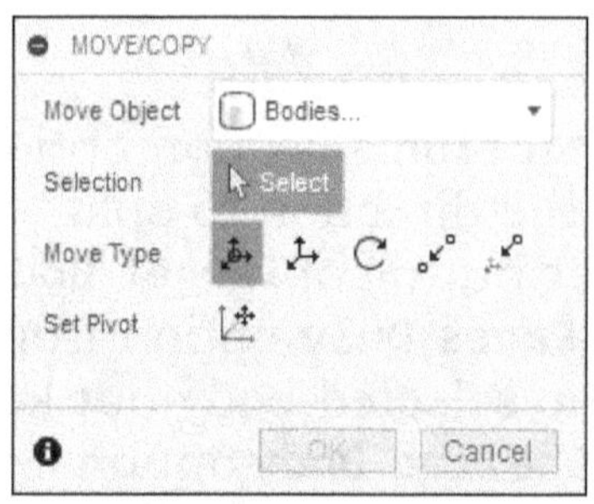

Figure-52. MOVE COPY dialog box

- Select **Component** option from **Move Object** drop-down, if you want to move a component.
- Select **Bodies** option from **Move Object** drop-down, if you want to move a body.
- Select **Faces** option from **Move Object** drop-down, if you want to move a face.
- Select **Sketch Objects** option from **Move Object** drop-down, if you want to move the selected sketch.
- In our case, we are selecting the **Bodies** option from **Move Object** drop-down.
- **Selection** section is active by default. Click on the body to be moved. The updated **MOVE/COPY** dialog box will be displayed.
- Select **Free Move** button from **Move Type** section, if you want to move selected body freely.

- On selecting the **Free Move** button, a Manipulator will be displayed on the selected body. Use the Manipulator to move the body or enter the value in respective field of **MOVE/COPY** dialog box; refer to Figure-53.

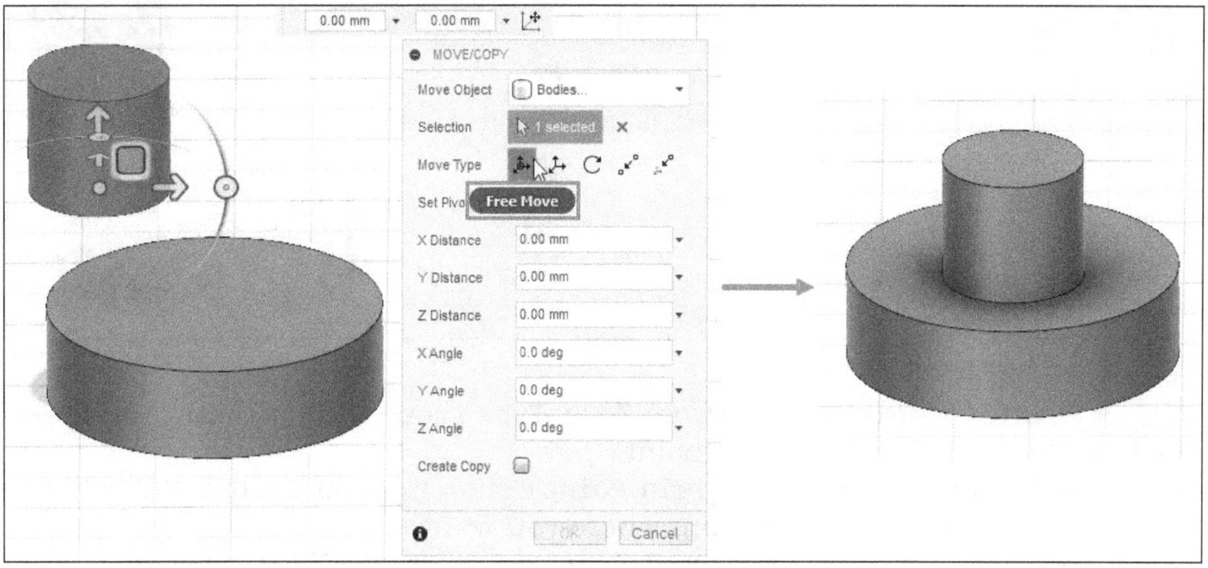

Figure-53. Free Move tool in Move Type section

- Select **Translate** button from **Move Type** section, if you want to move the body along X, Y, and Z directions.
- On selecting the **Translate** button, three arrows will be displayed on the entity. Drag desired arrow to move the body in respective direction. You can also enter the specific value of direction in the respective edit box from **MOVE/COPY** dialog box; refer to Figure-54.

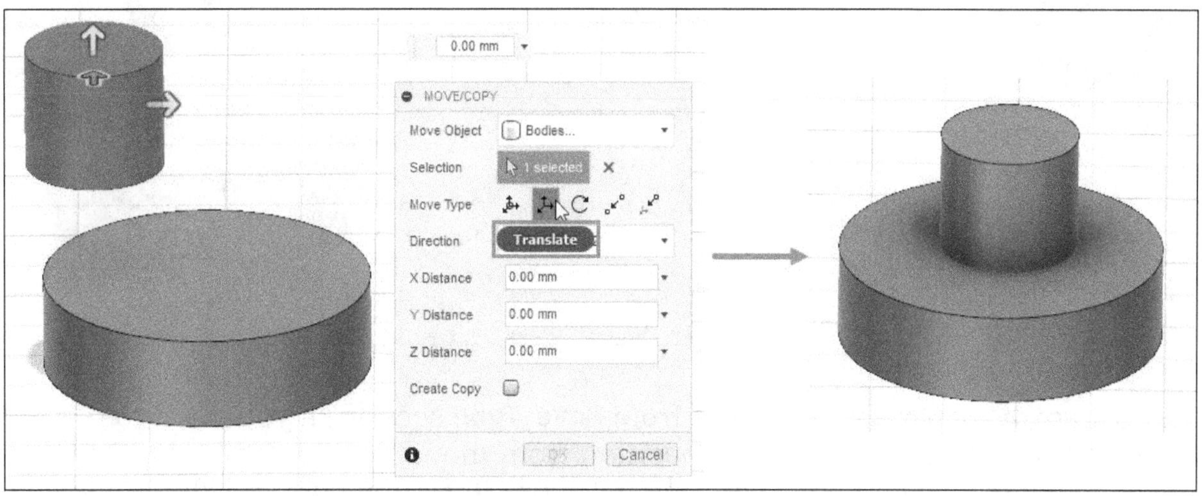

Figure-54. Translate tool in Move Type section

- Select **Rotate** button from **Move Type** section, if you want to rotate the entity.
- On selecting the **Rotate** option, the **Axis** option will be displayed in the **MOVE/COPY** dialog box.
- Click on the **Select** button from **Axis** section of **MOVE/COPY** dialog box and select the axis/edge for rotation of entity. The drag handle will be displayed on the selected face.
- Move the drag handle as required or specify the value in the **Angle** edit box of **MOVE/COPY** dialog box; refer to Figure-55.

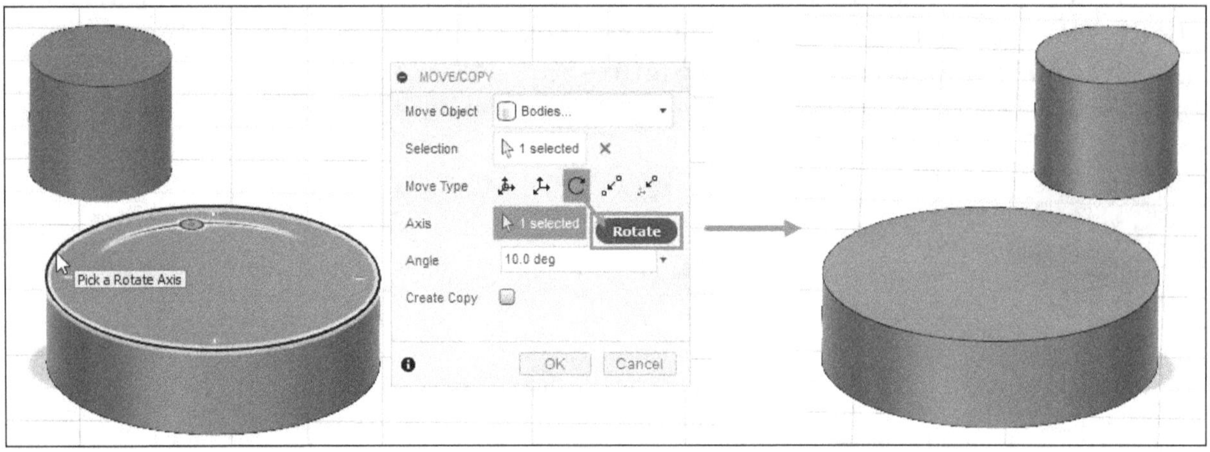

Figure-55. Rotate tool in Move Type section

- Select **Point to Point** button from **Move Type** section, if you want to move the body from one point to another point.
- Click on the **Select** button of **Origin Point** option from **MOVE/COPY** dialog box and select the start point of body from where you want to move the body.
- Click on the **Select** button of **Target Point** option from **MOVE/COPY** dialog box and select the finish point from model.
- After selecting the points, the preview will be displayed.
- If the preview is as required then click on **OK** button from **MOVE/COPY** dialog box to complete the process; refer to Figure-56.

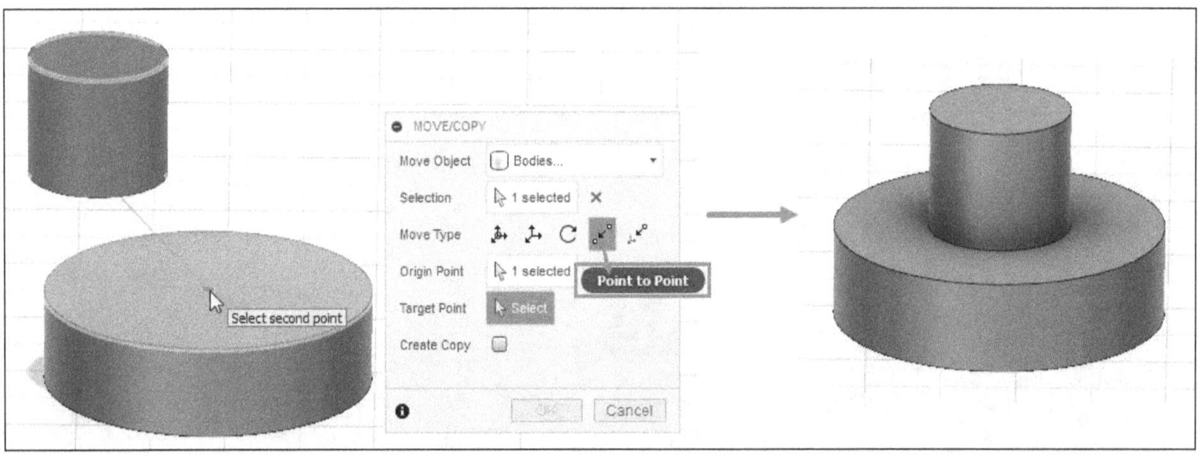

Figure-56. Point to Point tool in Move Type section

- Select **Point to Position** button from **Move Type** section, if you want to move the body by selecting a point and a position from model.
- Select a point of the body. The updated **MOVE/COPY** dialog box will be displayed; refer to Figure-57.

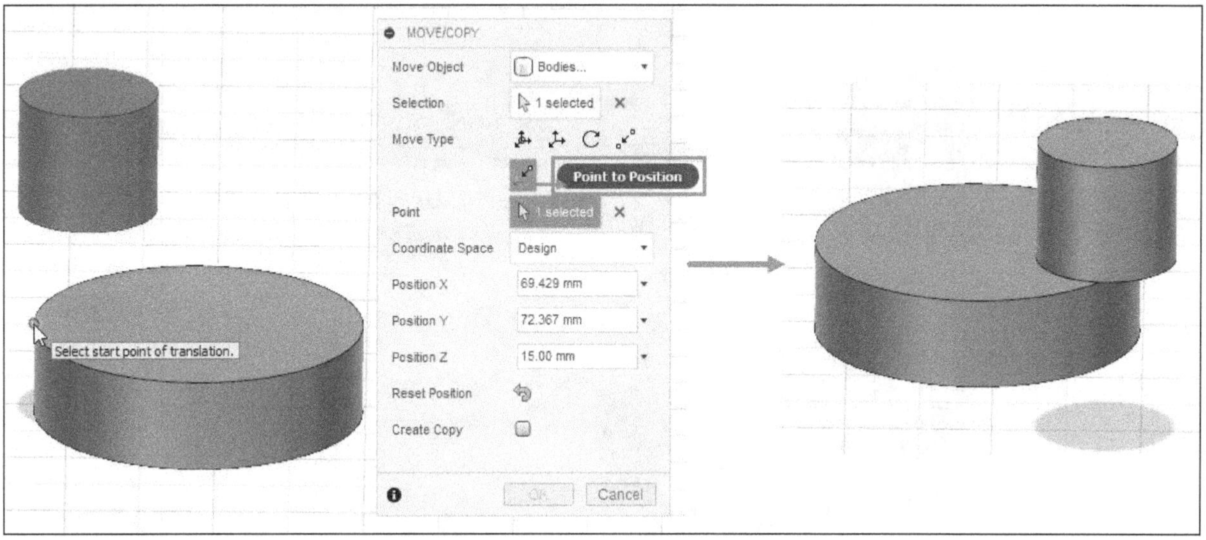

Figure-57. Point to Position tool in Move Type section

- Click in the **Position X** edit box and specify the value. Similarly, specify the value in **Position Y** and **Position Z** edit boxes as required.
- After specifying the parameters, click on the **OK** button from **MOVE/COPY** dialog box to complete the process.

ALIGN

The **Align** tool is used to align selected object to another object. The procedure to use this tool is discussed next.

- Click on the **Align** tool from **MODIFY** drop-down in the **Toolbar**; refer to Figure-58. The **ALIGN** dialog box will be displayed; refer to Figure-59.

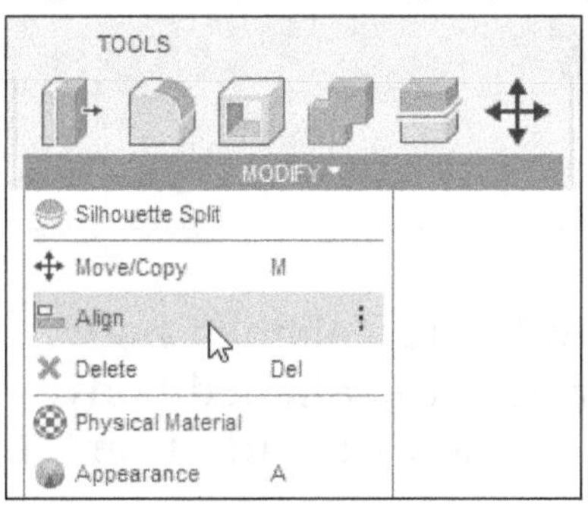

Figure-58. Align tool

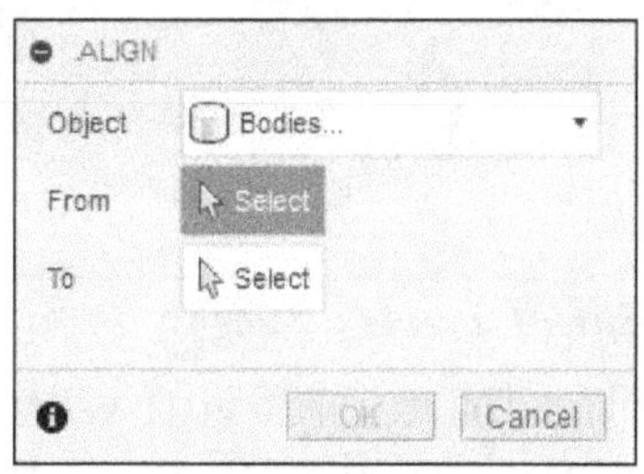

Figure-59. ALIGN dialog box

- Select **Bodies** option from **Object** drop-down of **ALIGN** dialog box if you want to select bodies to align.
- Select **Components** option from **Object** drop-down of **ALIGN** dialog box if you want to select components to align.
- In our case, we are selecting **Bodies** option from **Object** drop-down.
- Click on **Select** button of **From** section of **ALIGN** dialog box and select point on the first body from which you want to align that body.
- Click on **Select** button of **To** section of **ALIGN** dialog box and select point on the second body to which the body to be aligned; refer to Figure-60.

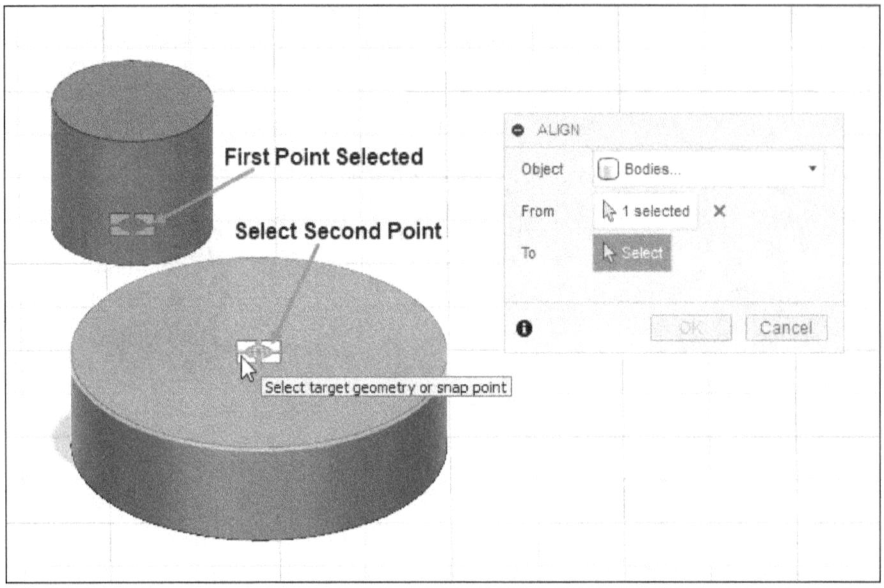

Figure-60. Selection of points to align body

- On selecting the point on second body, the two selected body will align to each other at selected location; refer to Figure-61.

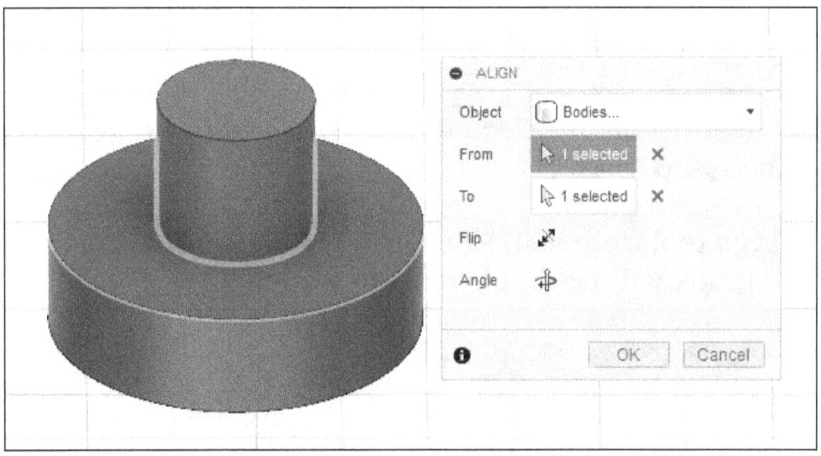

Figure-61. Preview of align

- Click on the **Flip** button, if you want to flip the aligned body.
- Click on **Angle** button, if you want to rotate the aligned body.
- After specifying the parameters, click on the **OK** button from **ALIGN** dialog box to finish the process.

DELETE

The **Delete** tool is used to delete the selected object or component. You can also press **DELETE** from keyboard to do the same. The procedure to use this tool is discussed next.

- Click on the **Delete** tool from **MODIFY** drop-down in the **Toolbar**; refer to Figure-62. The **DELETE** dialog box will be displayed; refer to Figure-63.

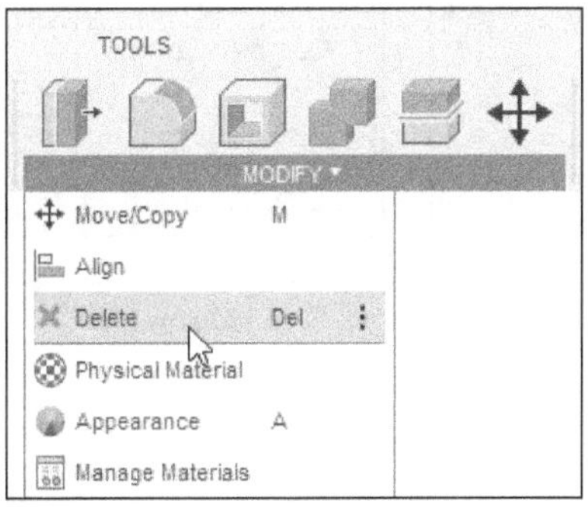

Figure-62. Delete tool

Figure-63. DELETE dialog box

- The **Objects** selection is active by default. Select the object to be deleted from the existing model.
- After selecting desired object, click on the **OK** button from **DELETE** dialog box to delete the selected object; refer to Figure-64.

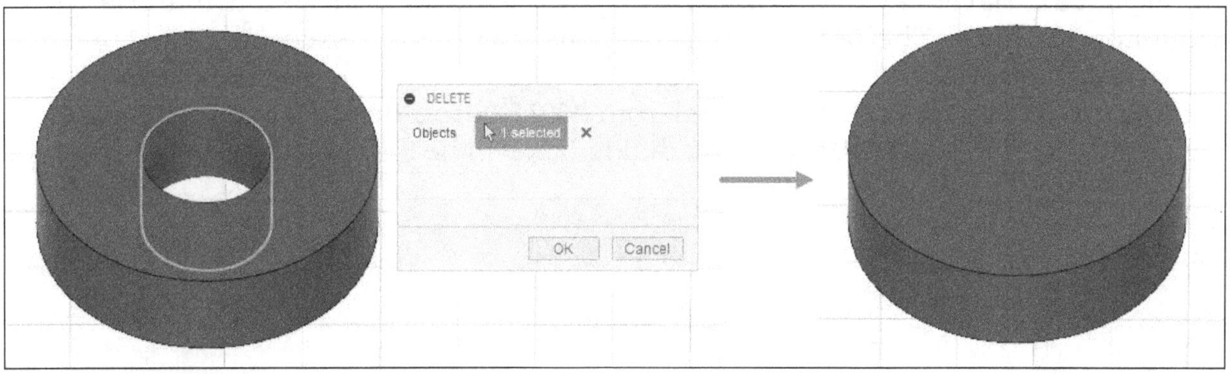

Figure-64. Object deleted

REMOVE TOOL

The **Remove** tool is used to delete selected components and bodies from the design while preserving the operations in the timeline. The procedure to use this tool is given next.

- Click on the **Remove** tool from the **MODIFY** drop-down in the **SOLID** tab of **Ribbon**. The **REMOVE** dialog box will be displayed; refer to Figure-65.

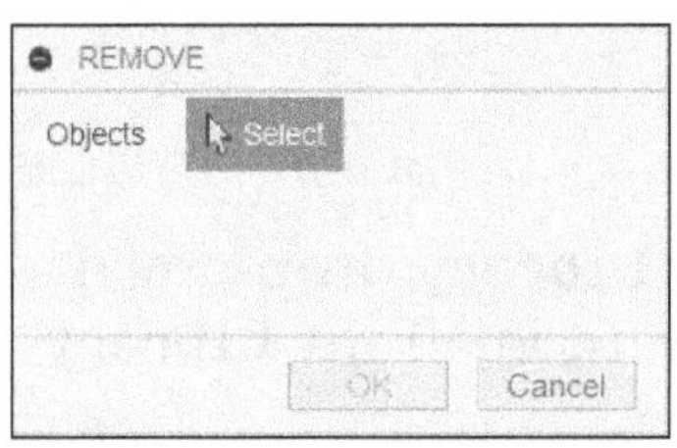

Figure-65. REMOVE dialog box

- Select the body to be removed from the graphics area; refer to Figure-66 and click on the **OK** button. Selected body will be removed from graphics area but still will be available in the timeline bar; refer to Figure-67.

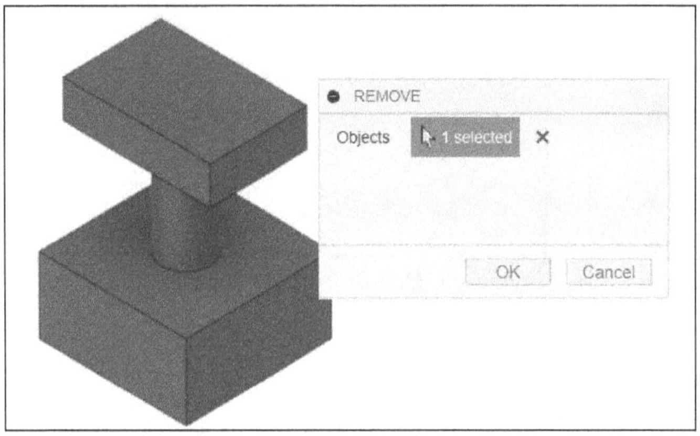

Figure-66. Body selected for removing

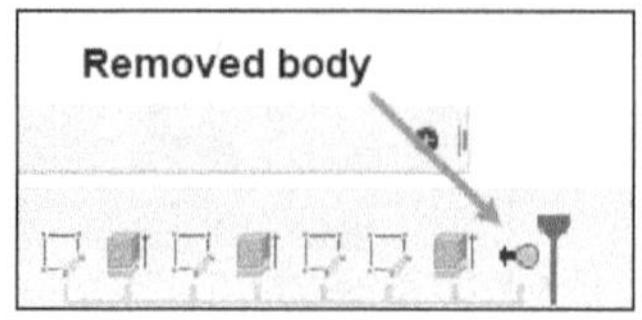

Figure-67. Removed body mark in timeline

PHYSICAL MATERIAL

The **Physical Material** tool is used to apply physical and visual material to the component or body. The procedure to use this tool is discussed next.

- Click on the **Physical Material** tool from **MODIFY** drop-down in the **Toolbar**; refer to Figure-68. The **PHYSICAL MATERIAL** dialog box will be displayed; refer to Figure-69.

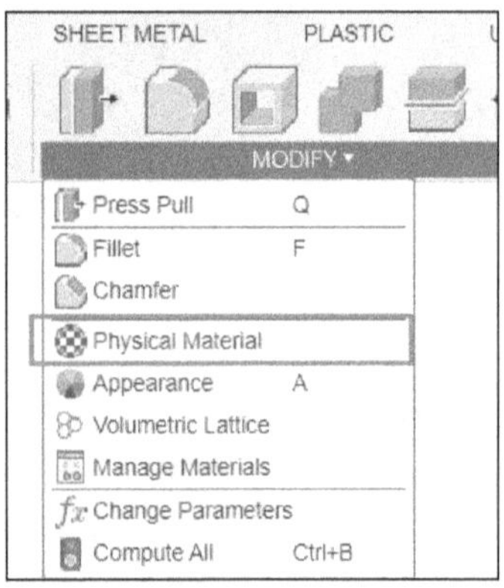

Figure-68. Physical Material tool

Figure-69. PHYSICAL MATERIAL dialog box

- Select required option from **Library** drop-down.
- Select required physical material from **Library** section of **PHYSICAL MATERIAL** dialog box.
- Now, drag the specific material from the **Library** section and drop it to the body or component. The physical material of body/component will be changed; refer to Figure-70.

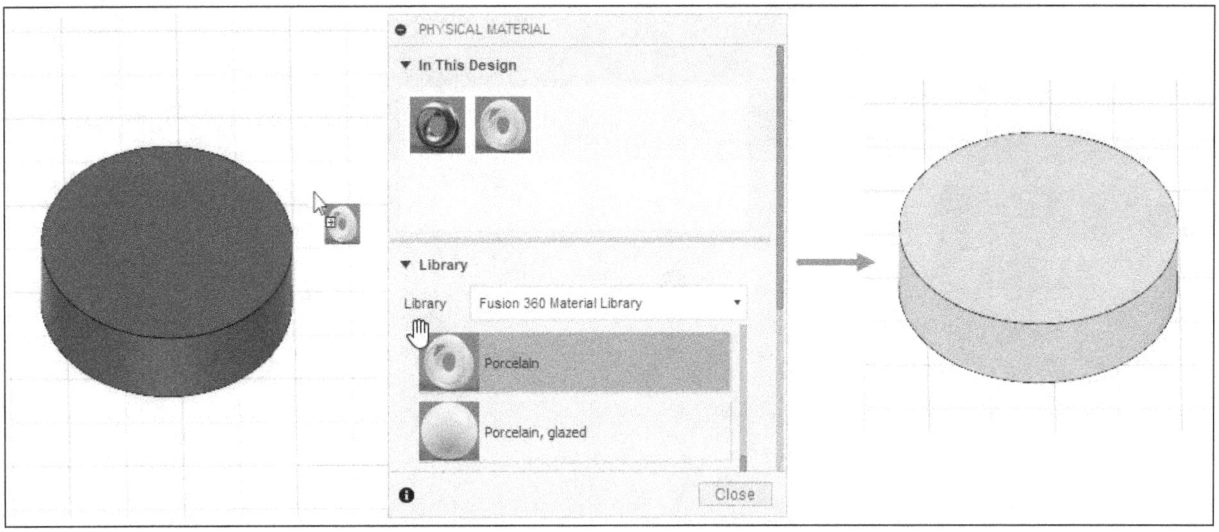

Figure-70. Applying physical material on the body

- After applying material, click on the **Close** button of **PHYSICAL MATERIAL** dialog box to apply changes.

APPEARANCE

The **Appearance** tool is used to change the appearance of body. This tool is generally used to change the color of the body. The procedure to use this tool is discussed next.

- Click on the **Appearance** tool from **MODIFY** drop-down in the **Toolbar**; refer to Figure-71. The **APPEARANCE** dialog box will be displayed; refer to Figure-72.

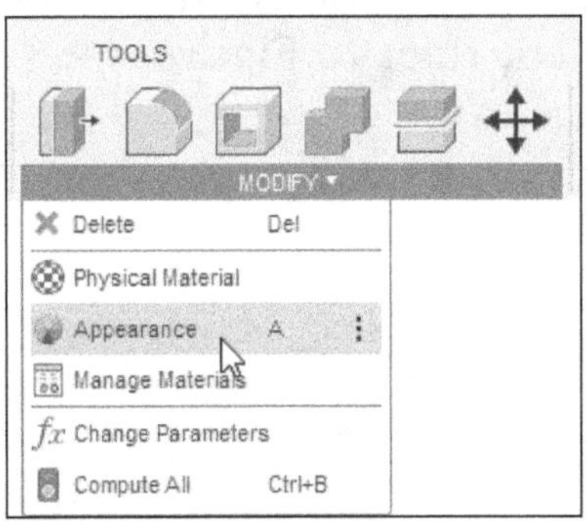

Figure-71. Appearance tool

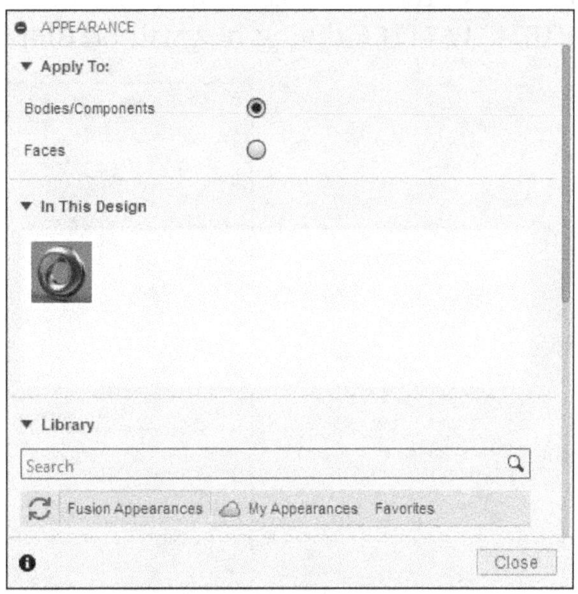

Figure-72. APPEARANCE dialog box

- Select required radio button of **Apply To** section from **APPEARANCE** dialog box to select bodies/components or faces.
- Drag an appearance and drop it to the body or face; refer to Figure-73.

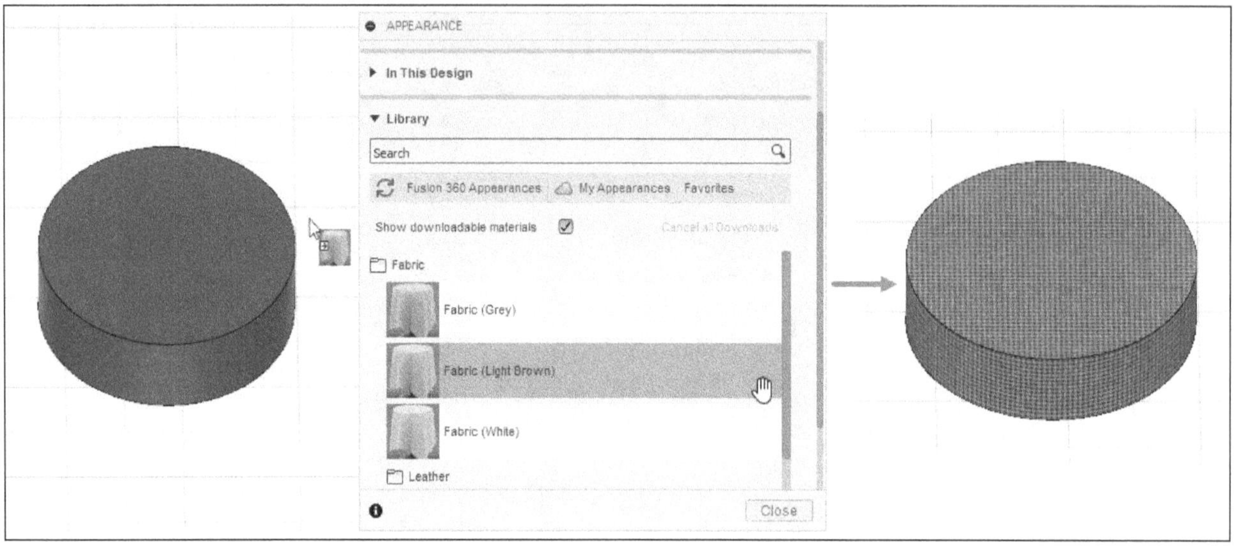

Figure-73. Applying appearance on the body

- After applying the appearance, click on the **Close** button from **APPEARANCE** dialog box to finish the process.

CREATING VOLUMETRIC LATTICE

The **Volumetric Lattice** tool is used to create internal lattice structure within the boundary of selected body. This tool is useful for converting solid body into a 3D printable lattice which can reduce total material consumption. The procedure to use this tool is given next.

- Click on the **Volumetric Lattice** tool from **MODIFY** drop-down in the **Toolbar**. The **VOLUMETRIC LATTICE** dialog box will be displayed; refer to Figure-74.

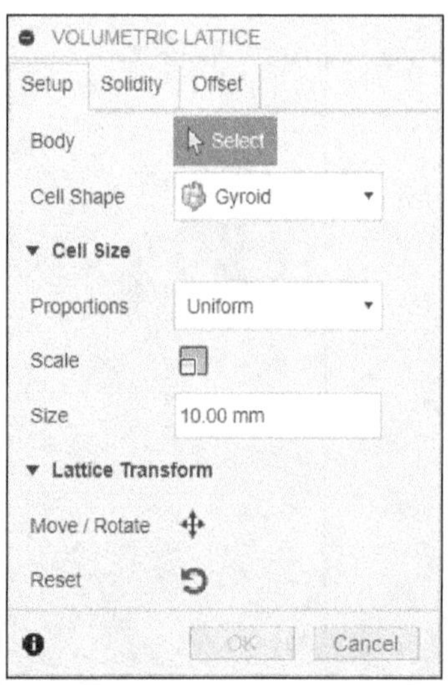

Figure-74. VOLUMETRIC LATTICE dialog box

- Select the body which you want to convert to volumetric lattice. Preview of lattice will be displayed; refer to Figure-75.

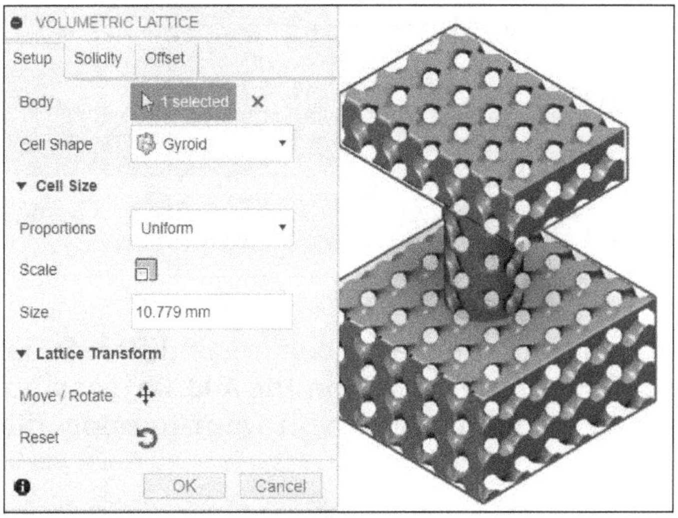

Figure-75. Preview of volumetric lattice

- Select desired shape of lattice element from the **Cell Shape** drop-down; refer to Figure-76.

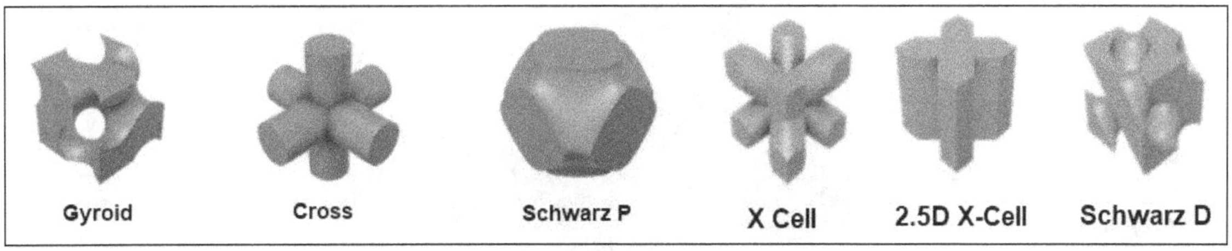

Figure-76. Cell shapes

- Select the **Uniform** option from the **Proportions** drop-down to set the size of cell length, width, and height equal. Specify the size value in the **Size** edit box. You can also set the size of cell using the scale handle displayed on model on selecting the **Scale** toggle button from dialog box; refer to Figure-77.

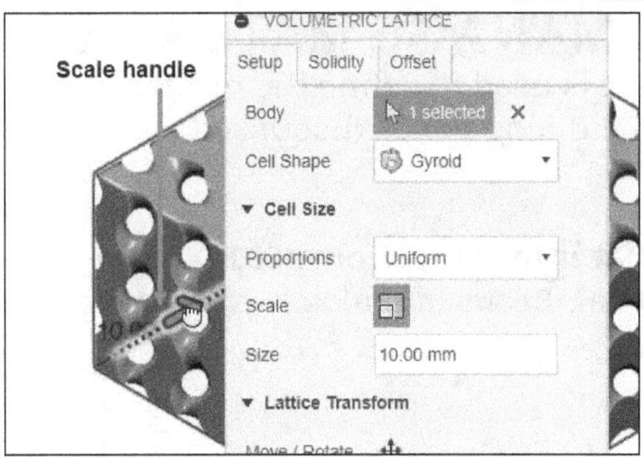

Figure-77. Scale handle

- Select the **Nonuniform** option from the **Proportions** drop-down to specify different sizes of cell shapes in each direction.
- Click on the **Move/Rotate** button from the **Lattice Transform** section of the dialog box and set desired parameters to reorient the lattice cells.
- Click on the **Solidity** tab to define the percentage of model which will be solid after applying lattice; refer to Figure-78.

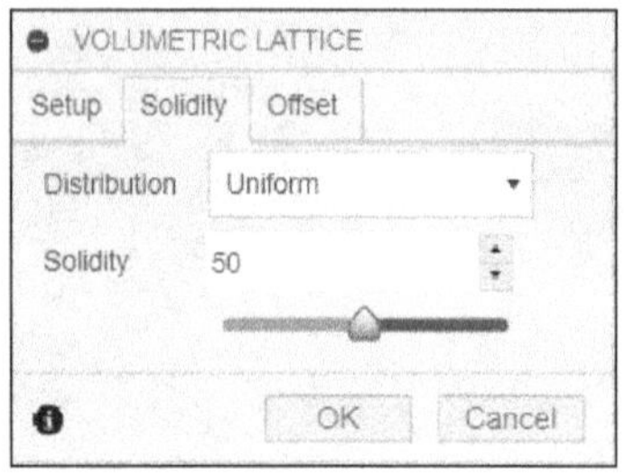

Figure-78. Solidity tab

- Click on the **Offset** tab from the dialog box to set different solidity percentage for selected face; refer to Figure-79. Click on the **Add Objects** button from the dialog box and select face of model to which you want to apply different solidity; refer to Figure-80.

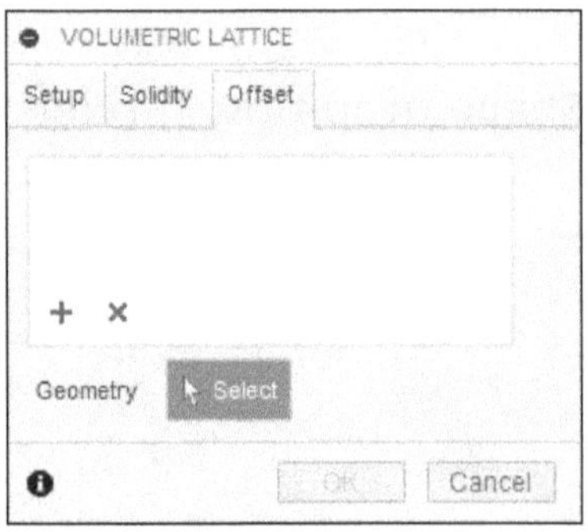

Figure-79. Offset tab

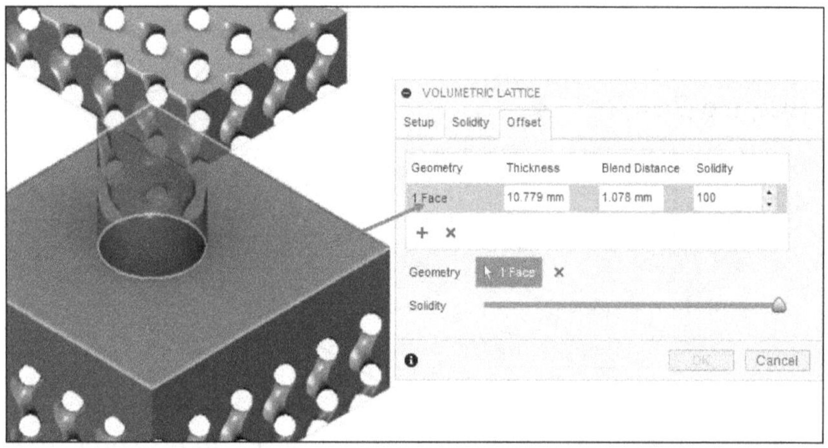

Figure-80. Face selected for offset solidity

- Set the parameters as discussed earlier and click on the **OK** button to create lattice.

MANAGE MATERIALS

The **Manage Materials** tool is used to define the material properties shown in **PHYSICAL MATERIAL** and **APPEARANCE** dialog boxes discussed earlier. The procedure to use this tool is discussed next.

- Click on the **Manage Materials** tool from **MODIFY** drop-down in the **Toolbar**; refer to Figure-81. The **Material Browser** dialog box will be displayed; refer to Figure-82.

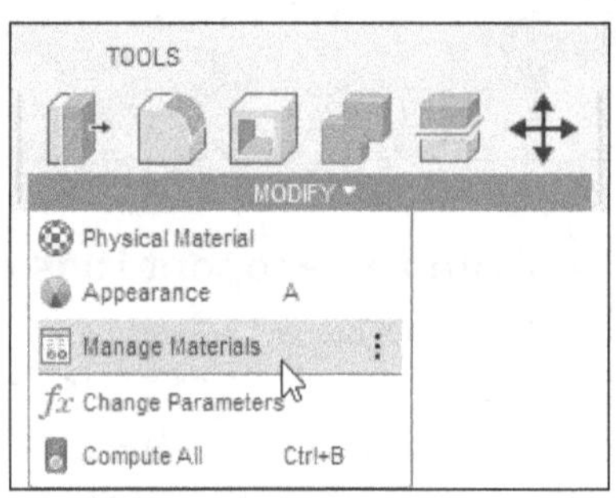

Figure-81. Manage Materials tool

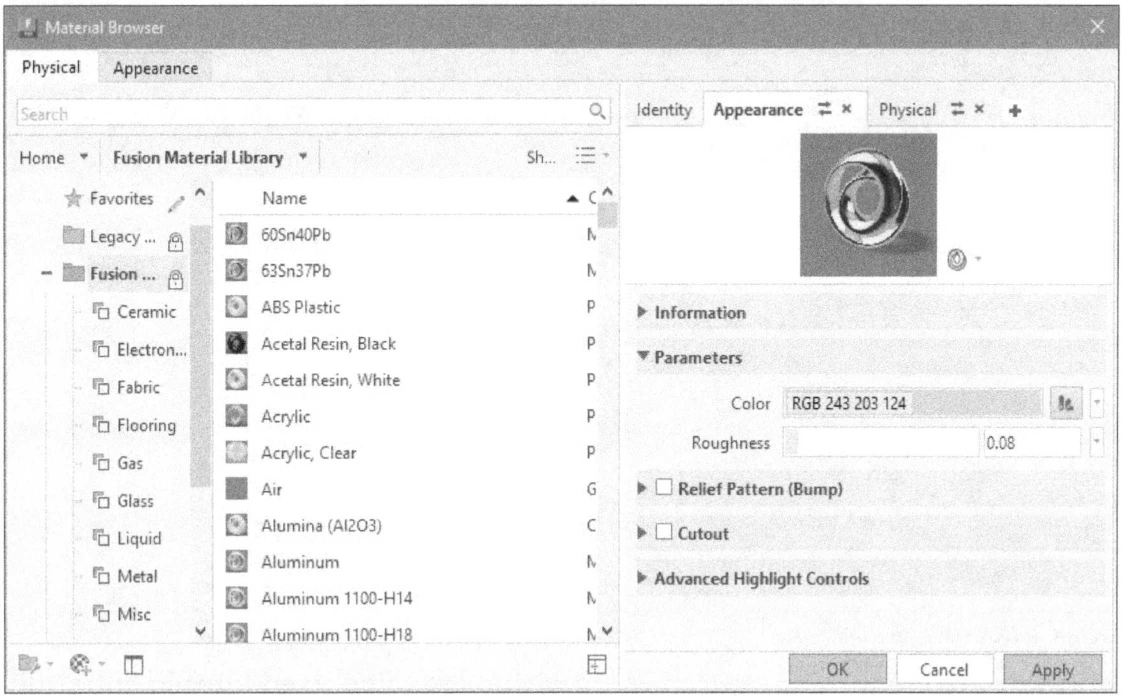

Figure-82. Material Browser dialog box

- Click on any material or appearance from list section to check or modify the property of selected material or appearance.
- To edit properties of any material, select it from the list and then click on the **Add to Favorites & Edit** button at the bottom-right in the dialog box.
- Change the properties as required using the options displayed in the right area of **Material Browser** dialog box and click on the **OK** button to apply changes.
- Close the dialog box once changes have been applied. Next time, when you will be applying material, make sure to select them from favorites list. You will learn more about modifying material properties in Chapter 20.

CHANGE PARAMETERS

The **Change Parameters** tool is used to change the parameters and apply equations to the model. The procedure to use this tool is discussed next.

- Click on the **Change Parameters** tool of **MODIFY** drop-down from **Toolbar**; refer to Figure-83. The **PARAMETERS** dialog box will be displayed; refer to Figure-84.

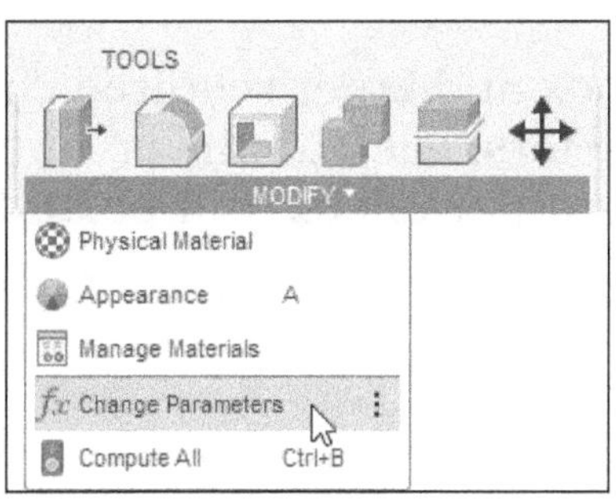

Figure-83. Change Parameters tool

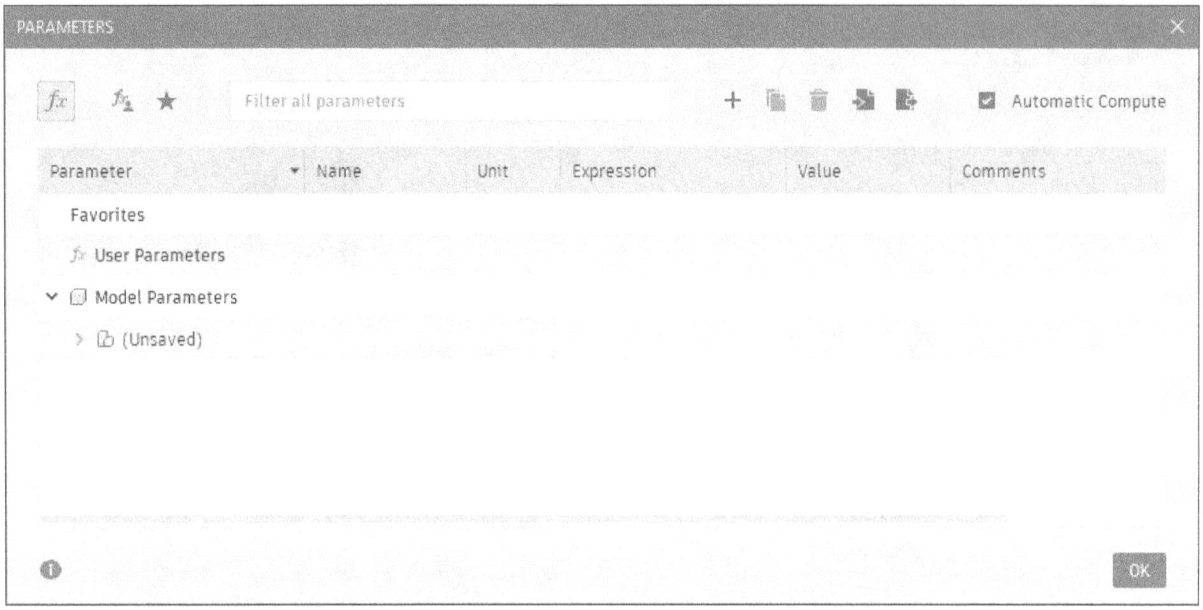

Figure-84. PARAMETERS dialog box

- If you want to create some parameters which are to be used later in equation then click on the **+ Add User Parameter** button from the **PARAMETERS** dialog box. The **Add User Parameter** dialog box will be displayed; refer to Figure-85.

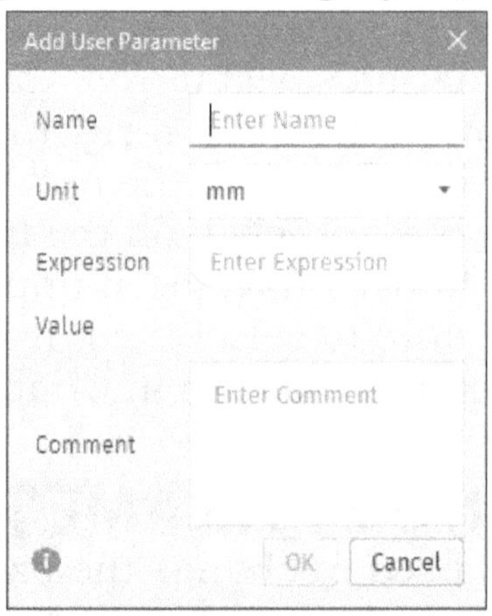

Figure-85. Add User Parameter dialog box

- Click in the **Name** edit box and specify the name of parameter.
- Click on the **Unit** drop-down and select desired unit of the parameter.
- Click on the **Expression** edit box and enter desired expression like d1/4. The **Value** will be displayed.
- Click in the **Comment** edit box and enter required comment.
- After specifying the parameters, click on the **OK** button from **Add User Parameter** dialog box. The user defined parameter will be added in **Parameters** dialog box; refer to Figure-86.

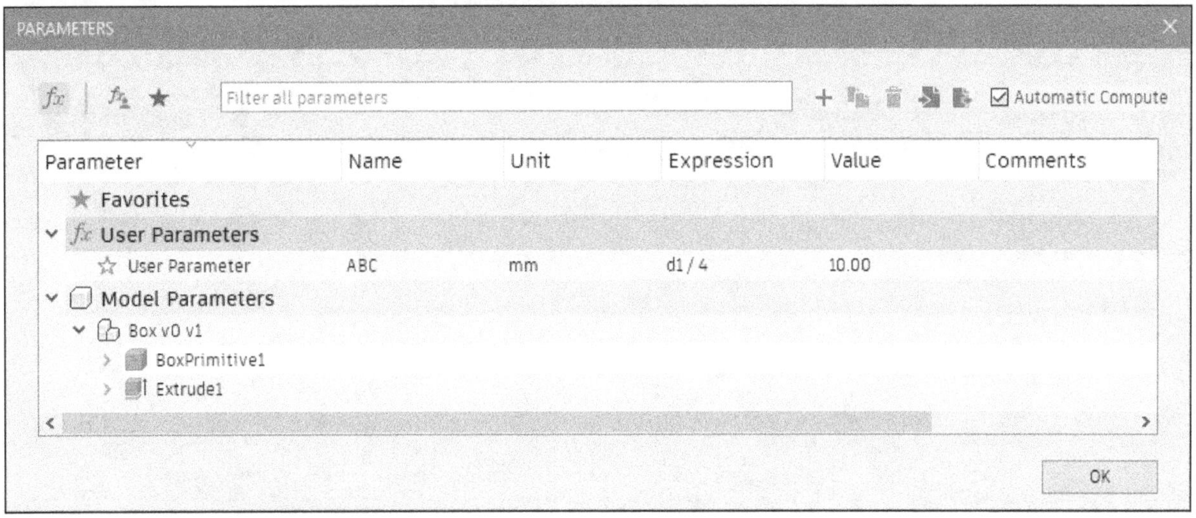

Figure-86. User Parameter added

- Click on the **Model Parameters** node from **PARAMETERS** dialog box, all the model features will be displayed.
- Click on desired model feature node to check its parameters, the parameters applied in that feature will be displayed; refer to Figure-87.

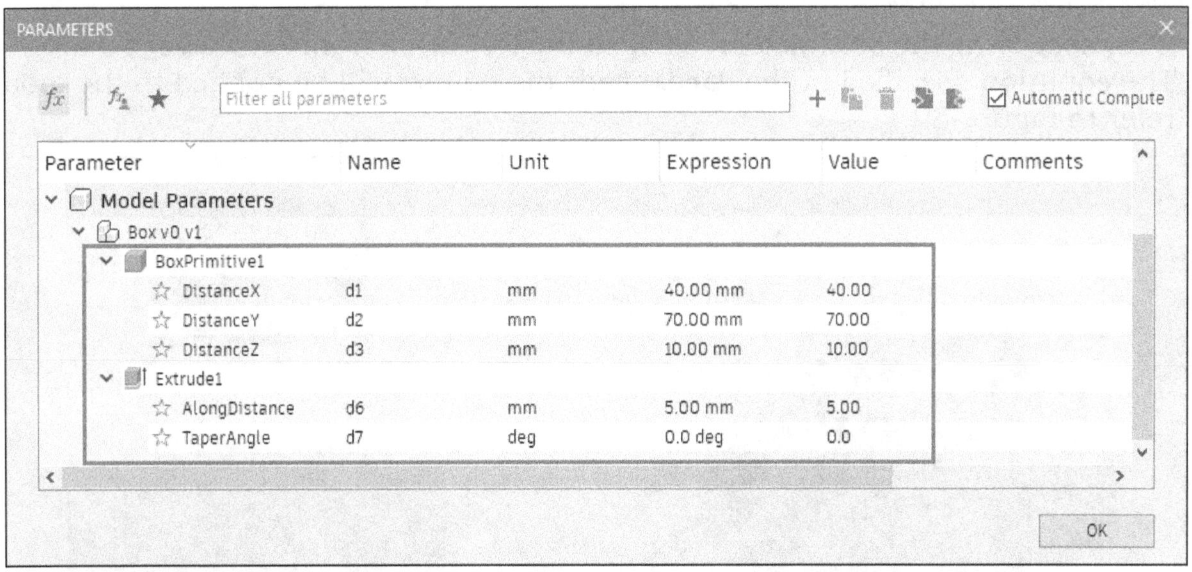

Figure-87. Parameters Applied In The Model

- If you want to apply equation in parameters then click on the dimension parameter and enter desired equation like d1*2; refer to Figure-88. Note that here d1 is dimension number applied automatically to the sketch dimension.

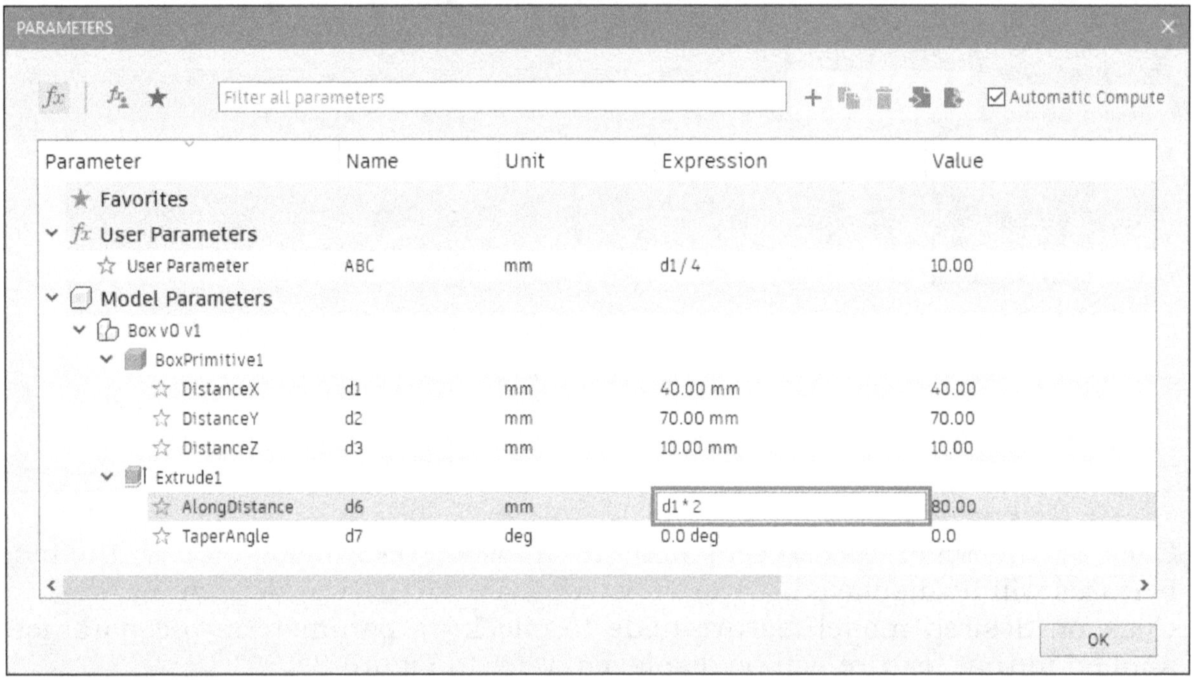

Figure-88. Entering Equation

- After specifying the parameters, click on the **OK** button from **Parameters** dialog box
- The equation specified in the **Parameters** dialog box will be applied to the model; refer to Figure-89.

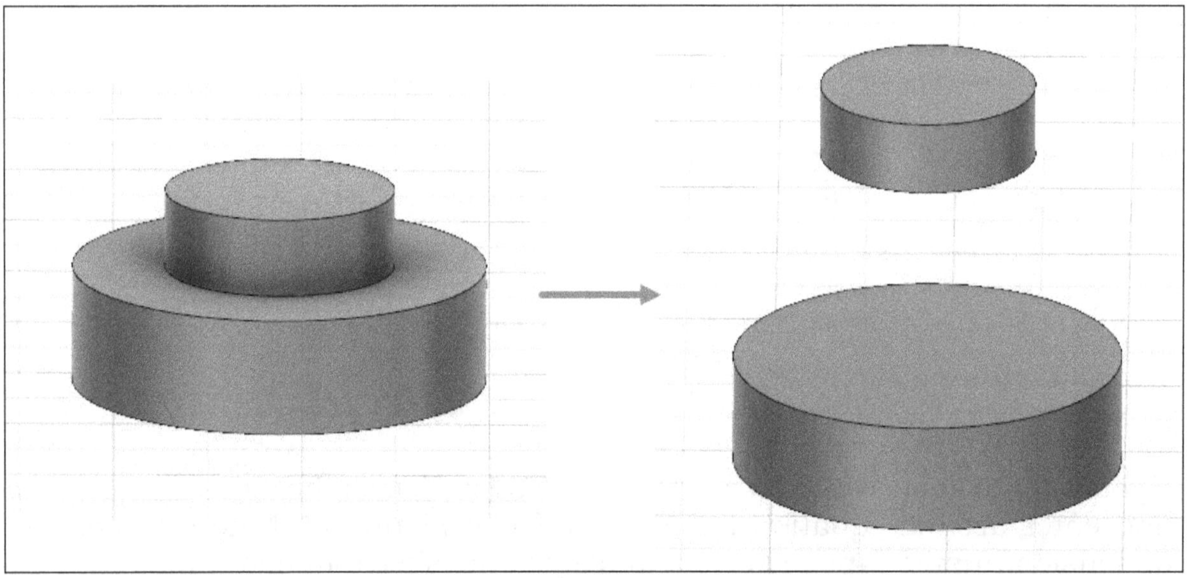

Figure-89. Parameter changed

Click on the **Compute All** tool from the **MODIFY** drop-down to re-calculate all the parameters.

PRACTICAL 1

In this practical, you will create a model of hook as shown in Figure-90. The dimensions of the hook are given in Figure-91.

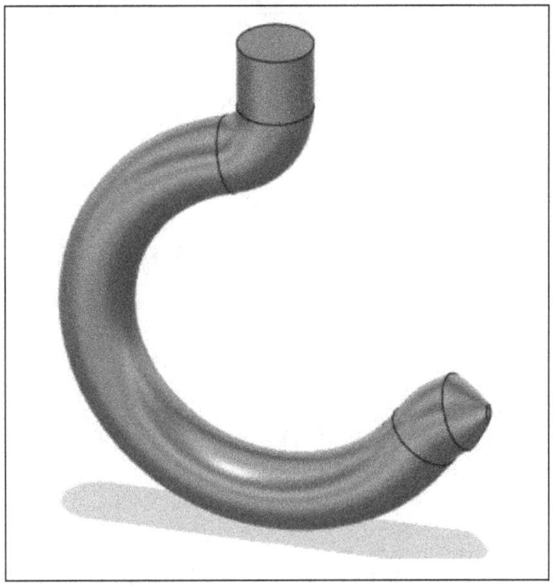

Figure-90. Hook model

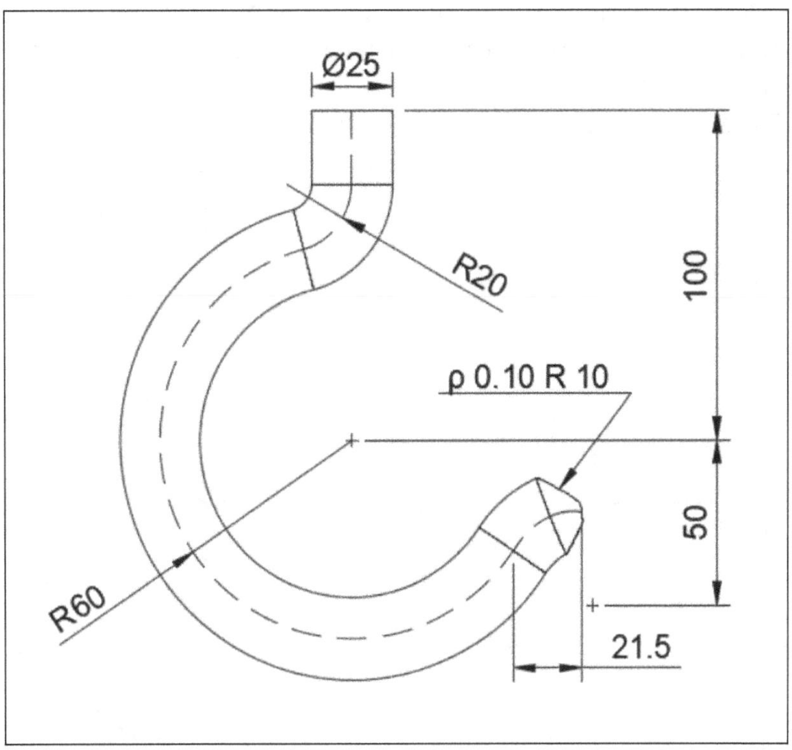

Figure-91. Practical 1 Hook drawing

Creating sketch for model

- Start a new sketch using **Top Plane**.
- Click on the **Circle** tool and create the circle of diameter **120** taking coordinate system as center.
- Draw a straight line starting from top quadrant point and having length of approximately **40**.

- Draw a three point arc in the bottom area of the circle; refer to Figure-92. (It should look like the one given in figure. Accuracy is no required.)
- Click on the **Trim Entities** tool and trim the portion between the straight line and the arc; refer to Figure-93.

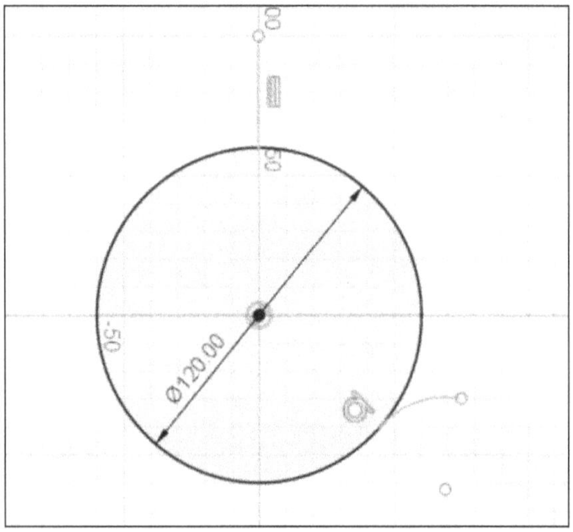

Figure-92. Circle arc and line created

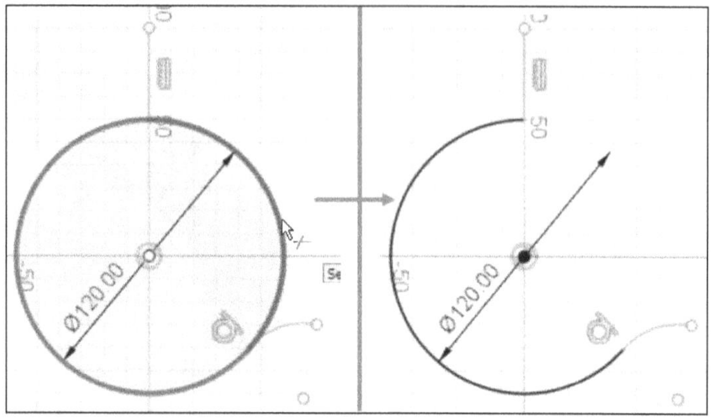

Figure-93. Trimming circle

- Click on the **Fillet** tool from **MODIFY** drop-down in the **Ribbon** and apply a fillet of **20** radius at the intersection of line and circle; refer to Figure-94.
- Click on the **Sketch Dimension** tool from **Ribbon** and apply the dimensions as shown in Figure-95. Note that you can toggle the diameter dimension to radius dimension using shortcut menu.
- Click on the **Finish Sketch** button to exit the sketching environment.

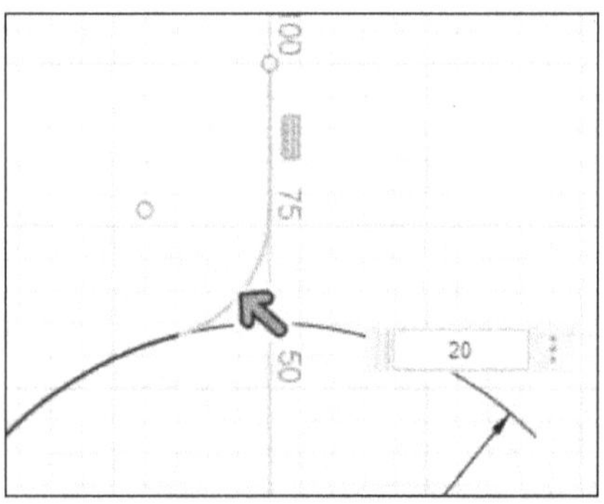

Figure-94. Applying fillet

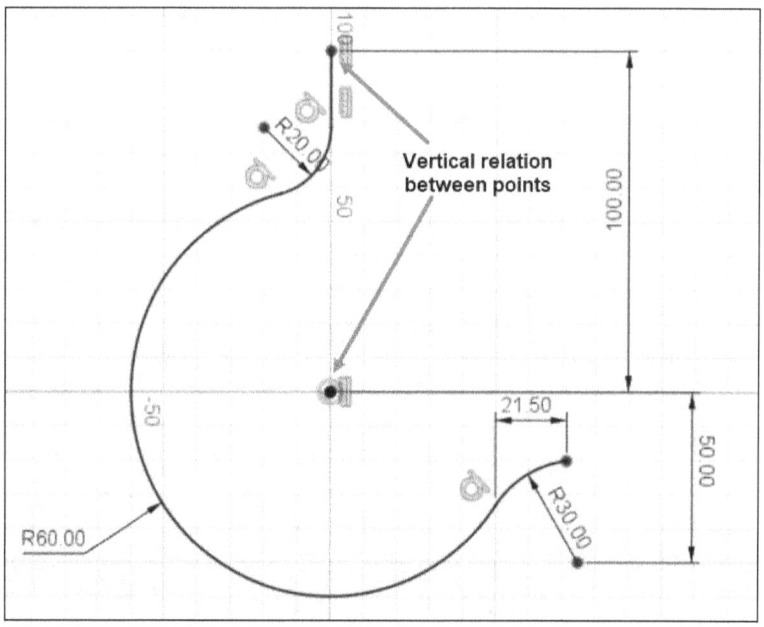

Figure-95. Dimensioning sketch

Creating Plane and Second Sketch

Earlier, the sketch was created for path of sweep feature and now we will create sketch for section.

- Toggle to Isometric view of model using **ViewCube** and click on the **Offset Plane** tool from **CONSTRUCT** drop-down in the **Ribbon**. The **CONSTRUCTION GEOMETRY** dialog box will be displayed.
- Create a plane offset of XZ plane and distance up to top point of sketch; refer to Figure-96.
- After setting parameters as shown in Figure-96, click on the **OK** button from the dialog box.

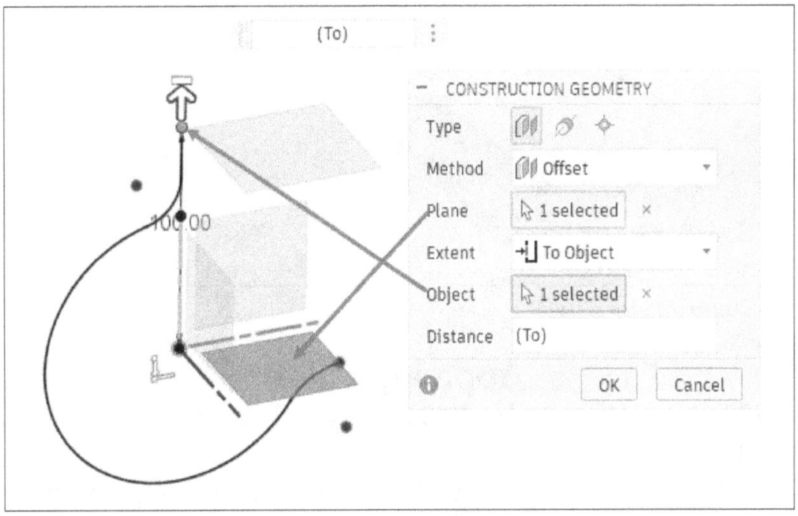

Figure-96. Creating offset plane for section sketch

- Select the new plane and click on the **Create Sketch** tool from **Ribbon**. The sketching environment will be activated.
- Create a circle of diameter **25** at the origin; refer to Figure-97 and click on the **Finish Sketch** tool from the **Ribbon** to exit sketching environment.

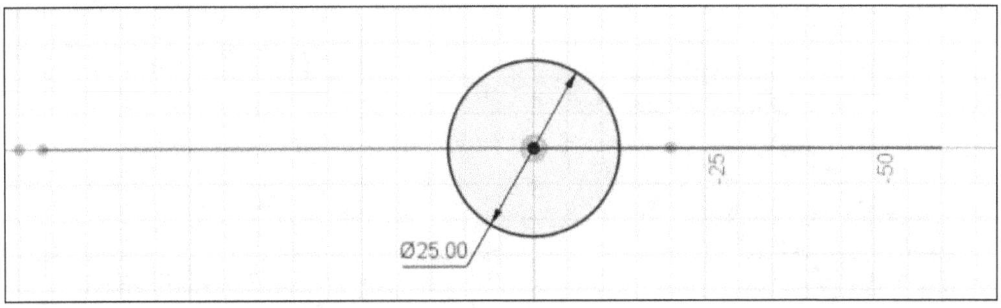

Figure-97. Section sketch circle

Creating Sweep Feature

- Switch to Isometric view using **ViewCube** and click on the **Sweep** tool from **CREATE** drop-down in the **Ribbon**. The **SWEEP** dialog box will be displayed.
- Select profile, path, and other parameters as shown in Figure-98. Click on the **OK** button from the dialog box to create the feature.

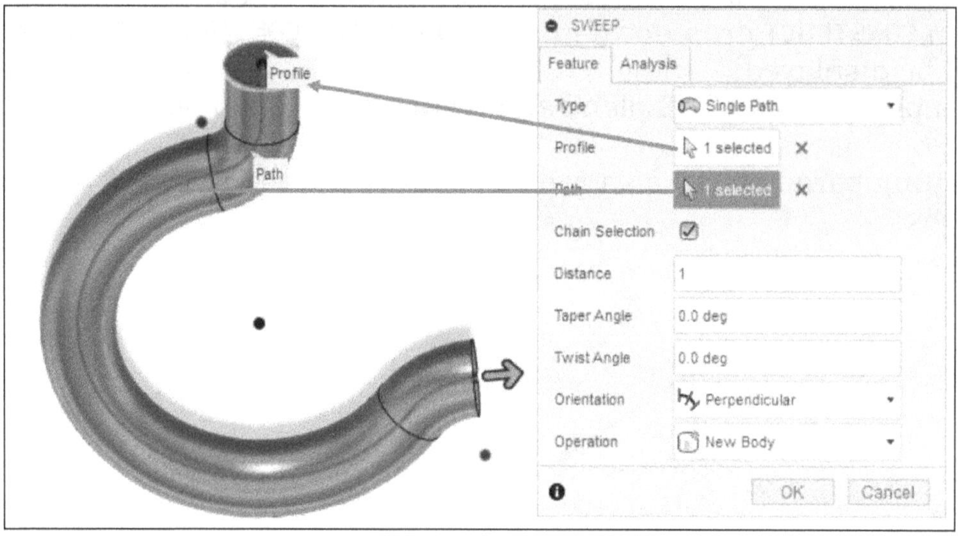

Figure-98. Creating sweep feature

Applying Fillet

- Click on the **Fillet** tool from the **MODIFY** panel in the **Ribbon**. The **FILLET** dialog box will be displayed.
- Select the bottom edge of model and specify the fillet parameters as shown in Figure-99. Click on the **OK** button to create the feature. The final model will be displayed; refer to Figure-100.

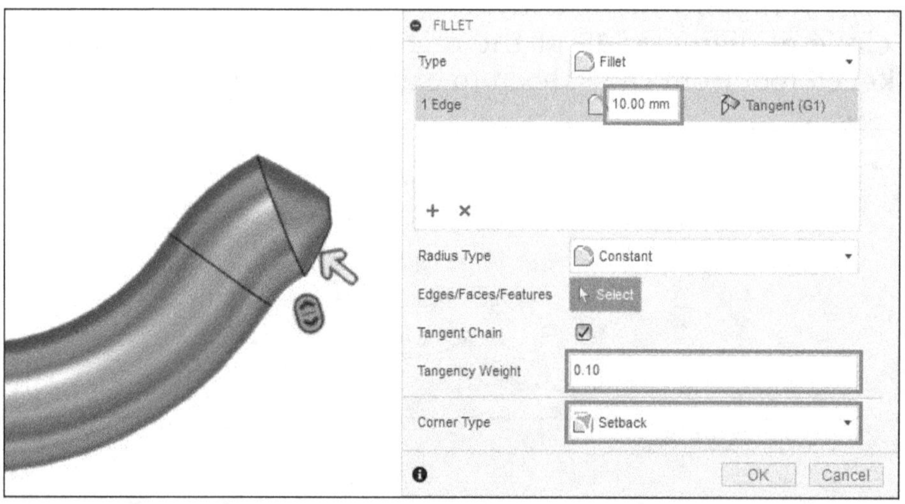

Figure-99. Applying setback corner fillet

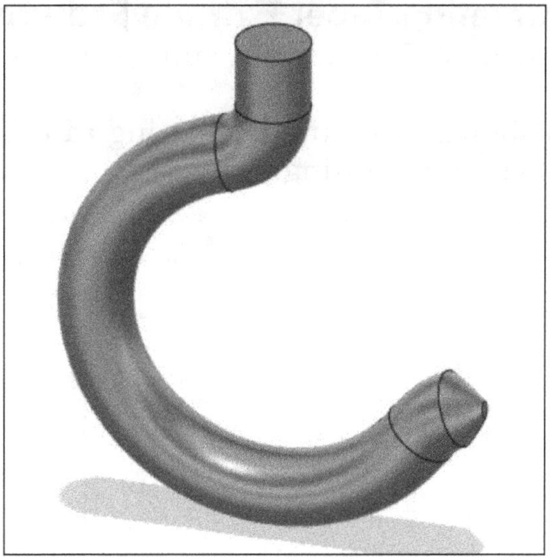

Figure-100. Hook model

Note that we have used fillet and round interchangeably because software provides same tool for both features but the difference between two can be seen in Figure-101.

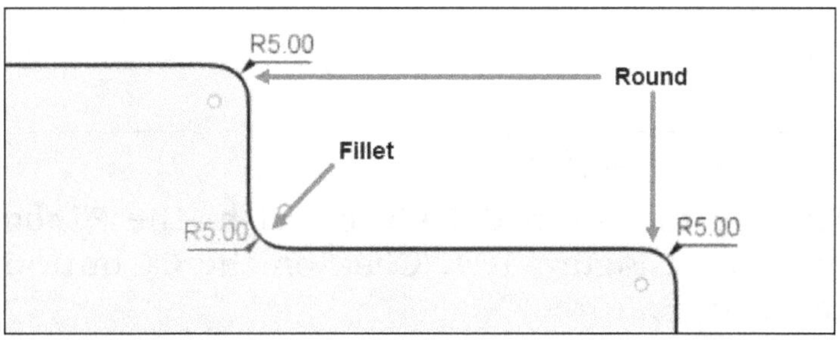

Figure-101. Round vs fillet

PRACTICAL 2

Create the model of wing nut using drawing shown in Figure-102. Use the diameter value **D** as 8, 10, 12, and 14.

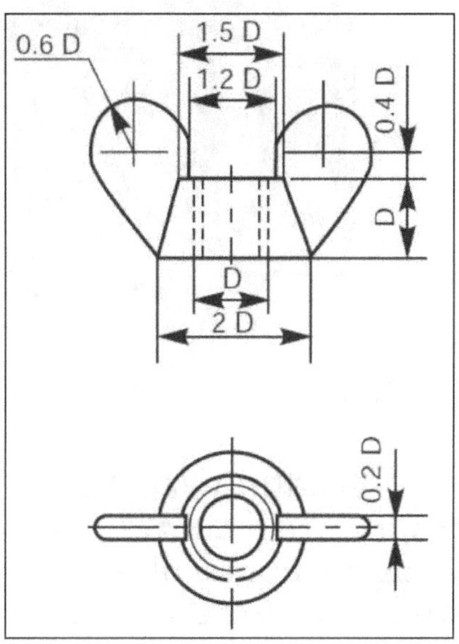

Figure-102. Wing Nut

Creating Taper Extrude Feature

- Start a new file in Autodesk Fusion and start a new sketch using Front plane (XY plane).
- Create the sketch as shown in Figure-103 using **Line** tool. Click on the **Finish Sketch** tool from **Ribbon** after creating sketch.

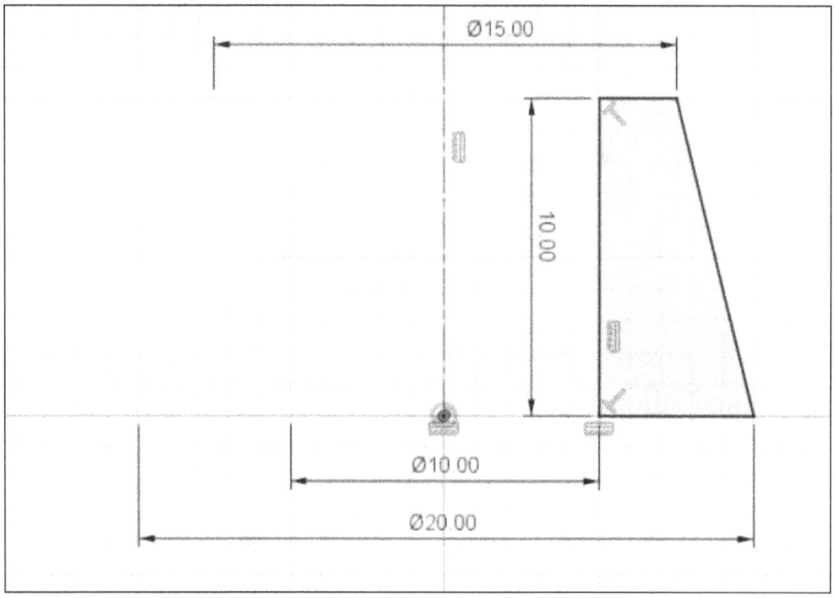

Figure-103. Sketch for wing base

- Click on the **Revolve** tool from **CREATE** panel in the **Ribbon** and specify the parameters as shown in Figure-104. Click on the **OK** button from the **REVOLVE** dialog box to create the feature.

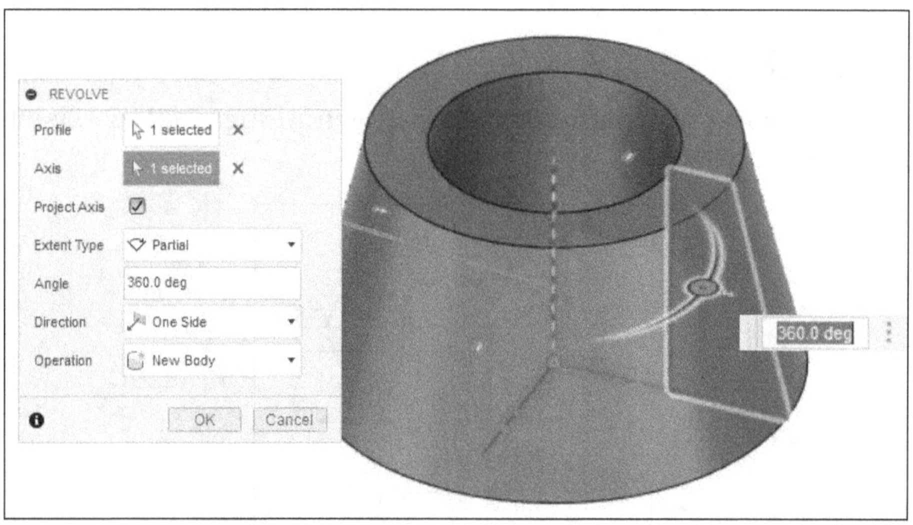

Figure-104. Creating revolve feature

Creating Wings

- Click on the **Create Sketch** tool from **CREATE** panel in the **Ribbon** and select the Top (XY) plane. The sketching environment will be activated.
- Create the sketch as shown in Figure-105. Click on the **Finish Sketch** tool from the **Ribbon** to exit sketching environment.

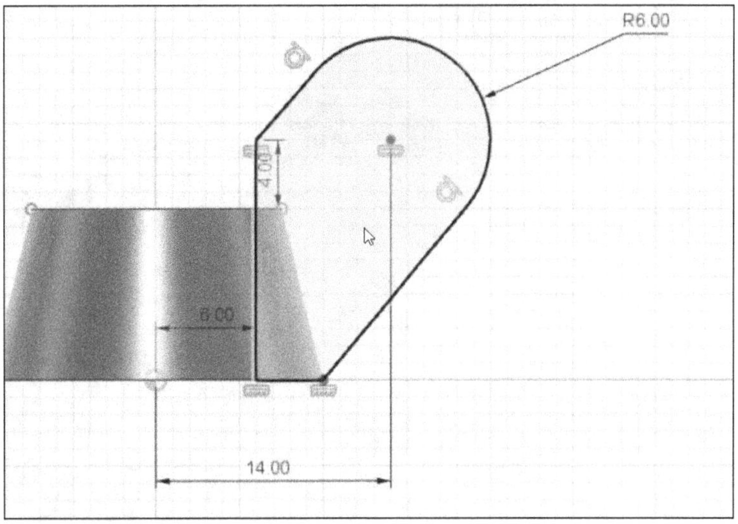

Figure-105. Sketch for nut wing

- Extrude this new sketch to both sides symmetrically by total thickness of **2**; refer to Figure-106.

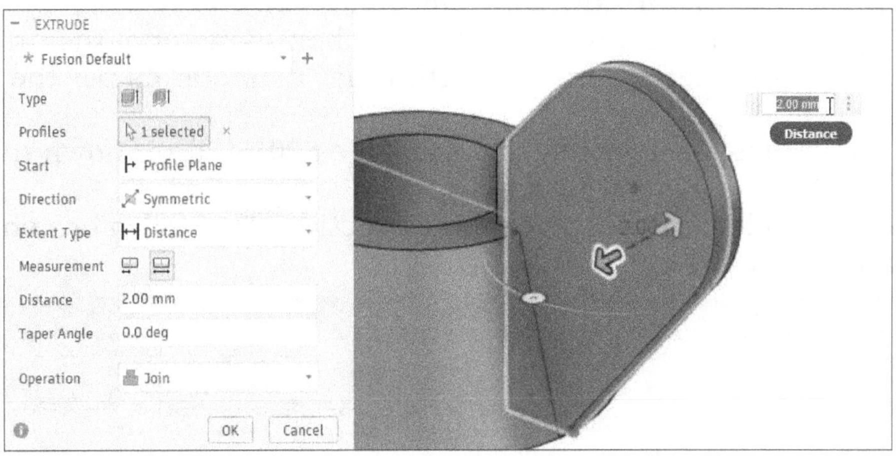

Figure-106. Creating wing for nut

- After creating wing of one side, create its mirror copy on other side of YZ plane; refer to Figure-107.

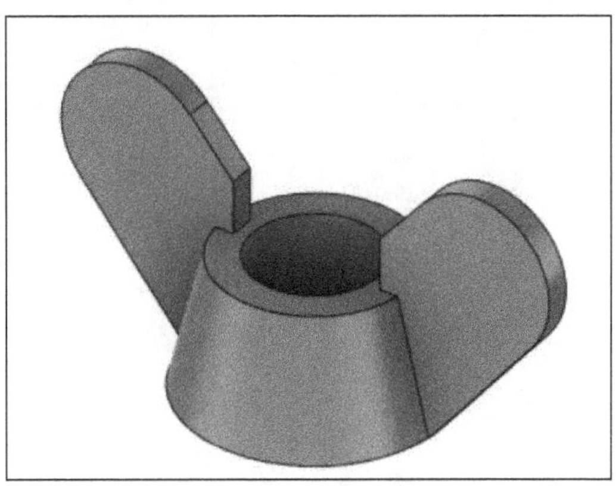

Figure-107. Wing after mirror copy

- Click on the **Thread** tool from **CREATE** drop-down in the **Ribbon** and select internal face of nut to generate threads. Specify the parameters as shown in Figure-108 and click on the **OK** button create the model.

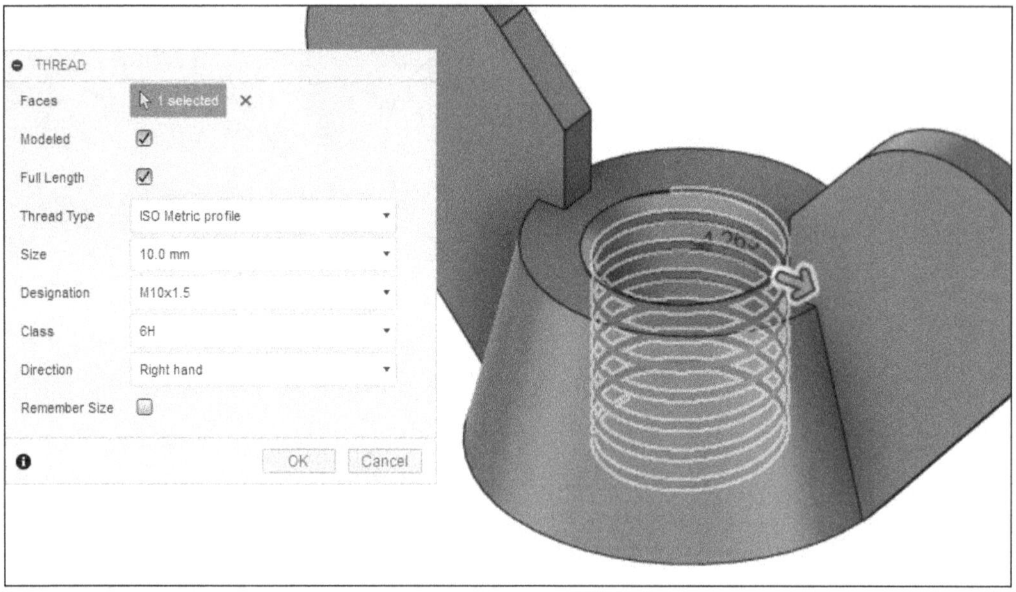

Figure-108. Creating threads

Defining Dimension Relations

Every parameter given in drawing is related to inner diameter of the nut. So, we will not apply relations to other parameters with inner diameter as per the drawing.

- Click on the **Change Parameters** tool from the **MODIFY** drop-down in the **Ribbon**. The **PARAMETERS** dialog box will be displayed.
- Expand all the nodes in **Model Parameters** section. The dialog box should display as shown in Figure-109.

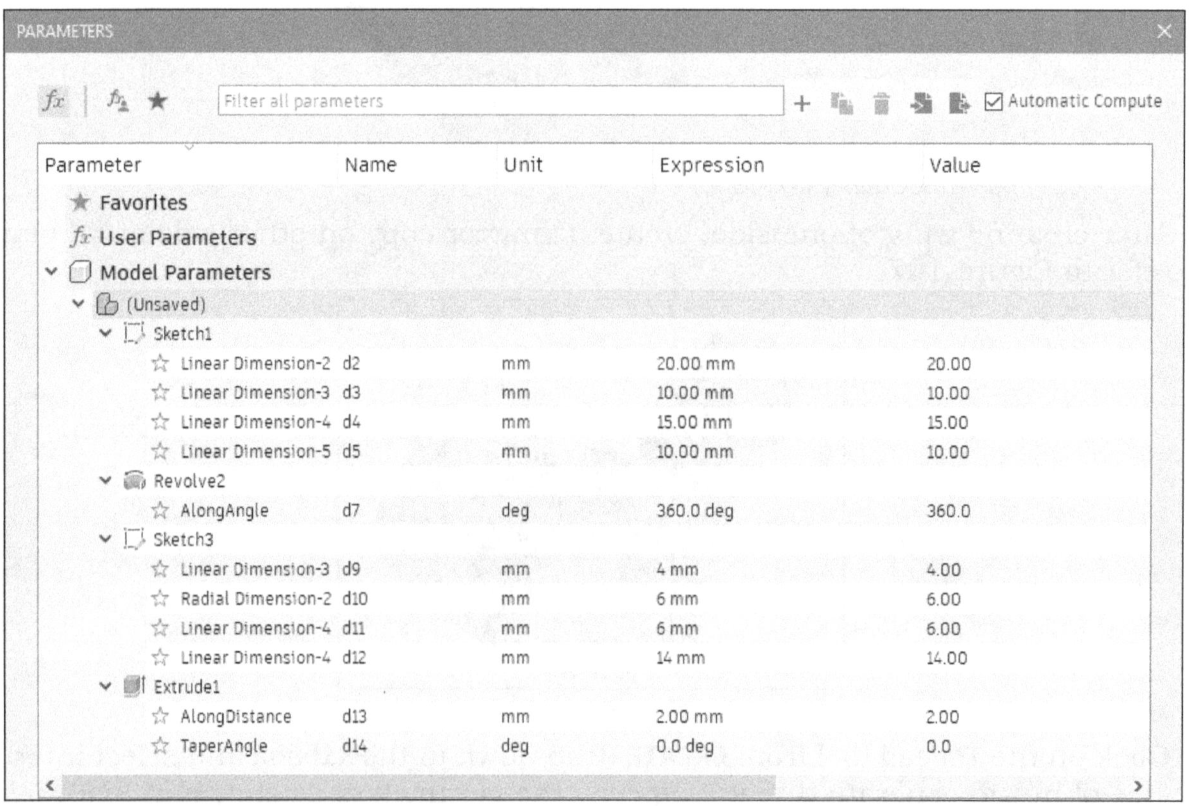

Figure-109. Parameters dialog box for wing

- Note that in Sketch1, **d3** is used to specify inner diameter of wing nut which drives all the other equations. If you are wondering how we know that, then this is hit and trial method until Autodesk updates the software to display dimension variables as well in sketch along with values. To find the diameter, we tried changing **d5** and that caused increase in length of nut so there is only one **10 mm** value dimension left which is diameter of nut. So, change the name of **d3** variable to **D** and set the relations as shown in Figure-110.

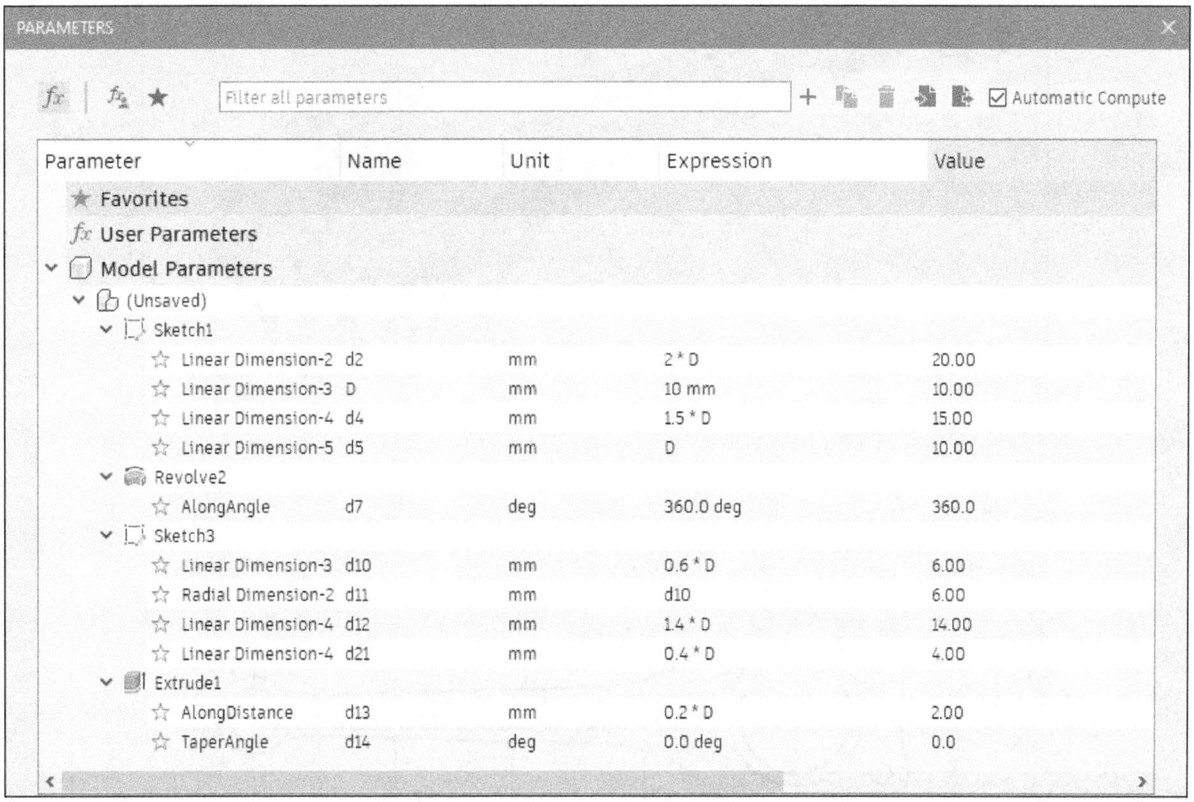

Figure-110. Table after specifying relations

- Now, change the value of **D** in table to get desired size of nut. All the other dimensions will be modified as per relation and model will change accordingly in graphics area. Check what happens when you modify the diameter value in sketch and then exit the Sketching environment!!

PRACTICE 1

Create the model of connecting rod as shown in Figure-111. The dimensions are given in Figure-112.

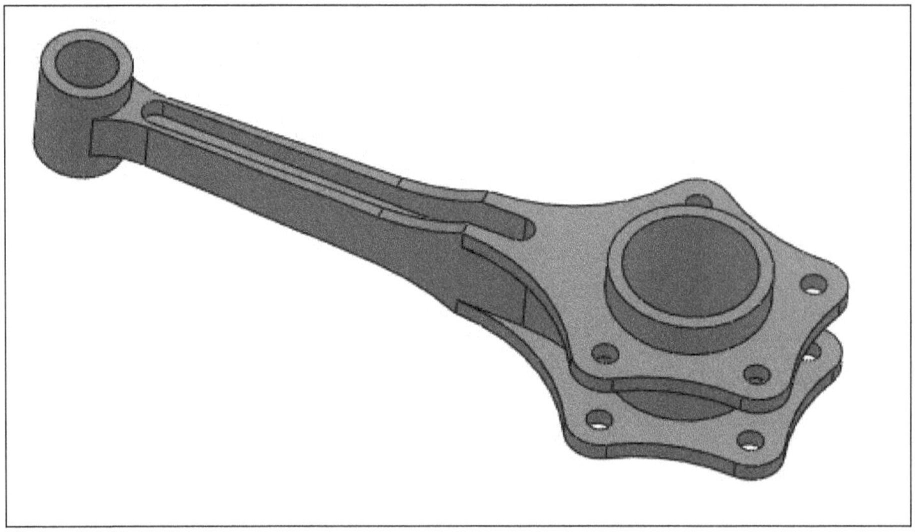

Figure-111. Practice 1

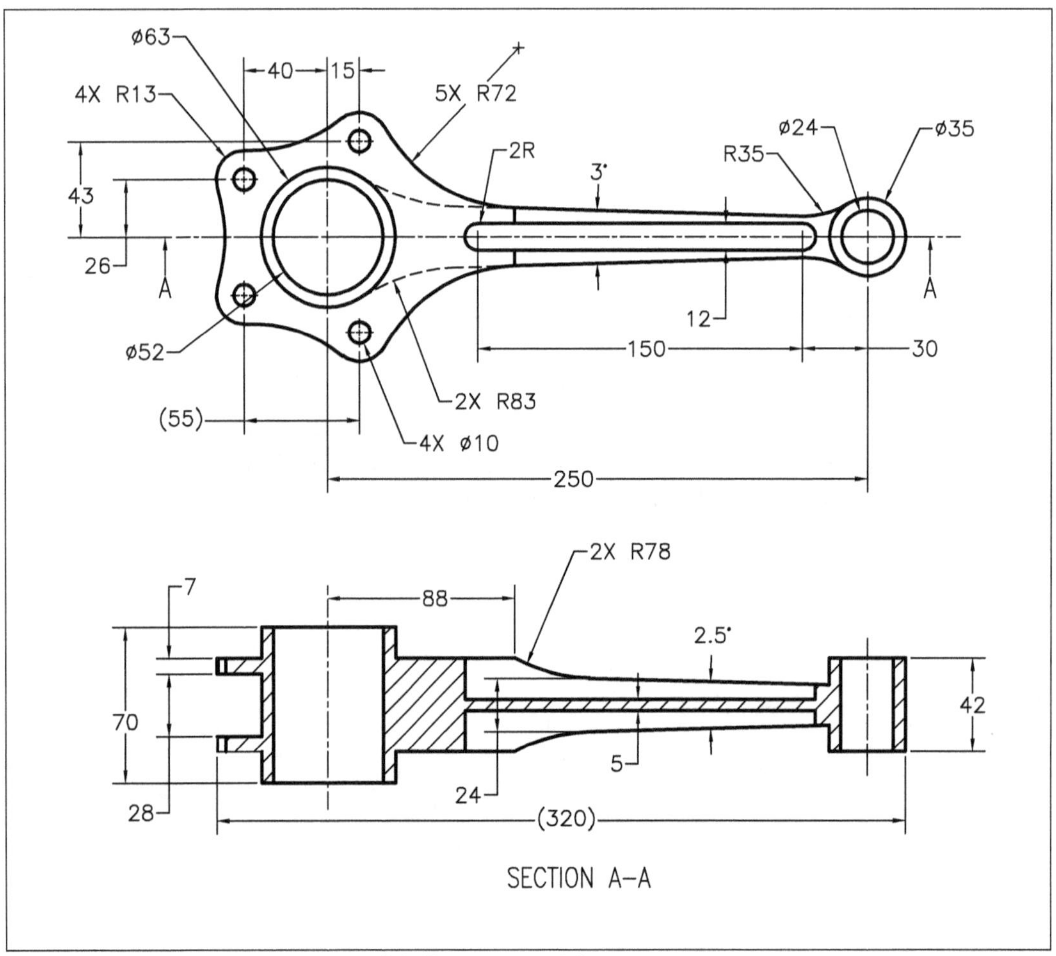

Figure-112. Dimensions of the Practice 1 model

PRACTICE 2

Create a ring nut with value of **D** as **5**,**6**,**8**, and **10** using equation and design table. Dimensions are given in Figure-113.

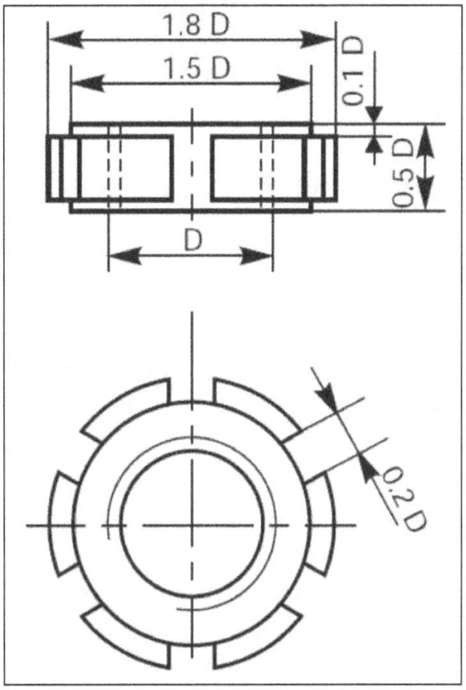

Figure-113. Ring Nut

SELF-ASSESSMENT

Q1. Which of the following tools can be used to dynamically use offset face or fillet function depending on the selection?

a. Fillet b. Offset Face
c. Press Pull d. Combine

Q2. Which of the following tool is used to apply round at the edges?

a. Fillet b. Chamfer
c. Draft d. Shell

Q3. Which of the following tool is used by casting mold designer to allow easy extraction of part from the die?

a. Fillet b. Draft
c. Shell d. Chamfer

Q4. Which of the following tool is used to create a body using intersection of two bodies?

a. Combine b. Shell
c. Split Body d. Split Face

Q5. The **Move/Copy** tool in Autodesk Fusion **Design** workspace can also be used to rotate the objects. (T/F)

Q6. What is the difference between applications of **Physical Material** tool and **Appearance** tool in **Modify** drop-down of **Design** workspace?

Q7. In Autodesk Fusion, you can create a fillet with changing radius at specified points. (T/F)

Q8. Which of the following tools is used to remove material from a solid body and convert it into a thin body of specified thickness?

a. Combine b. Shell
c. Split Body d. Split Face

Q9: What is the main purpose of the Press Pull tool in Autodesk Fusion?

A) To modify the body using drag and drop methods
B) To add fillets to edges
C) To create sketches
D) To bevel the sharp edges of a model

Q10: What happens when you select an edge in the Press Pull tool?

A) The OFFSET FACE dialog box will be displayed
B) The FILLET dialog box will be displayed
C) The EXTRUDE dialog box will be displayed
D) The model will be extruded

Q11: What does the Offset Face tool allow you to do?

A) Create new sketches
B) Offset or move the face of the model
C) Apply fillets to edges
D) Apply taper to the model

Q12: Which option in the Offset Face tool allows you to create a new face?

A) Automatic
B) Modify Existing Feature
C) New Offset
D) Distance

Q13: When applying fillets in Autodesk Fusion, what is the recommended order?

A) Apply fillets before creating features
B) Apply fillets after creating all features
C) Apply fillets during the creation of features
D) Apply fillets before using the shell tool

Q14: What does the Constant Radius option in the Radius Type drop-down of the Fillet tool apply?

A) A fillet with varying radius
B) A fixed size fillet
C) A fillet based on curvature
D) A fillet with a predefined tangent chain

Q15: How can you delete a point created in the Variable Radius Fillet option?

A) Click on the Remove selection set button
B) Click on the Remove Point button
C) Select the point and press delete
D) Right-click and select Delete

Q16: What does the Rule Fillet tool use to determine the edges for the fillet?

A) User selection from the canvas
B) Specified rules
C) The time line
D) Tangent edges

Q17: In the Full Round Fillet option, how do you modify the fillet after selecting the center face?

A) Select Side 1 and Side 2 faces while holding CTRL
B) Select Tangent Chain
C) Select Radius Type drop-down
D) Select the Sharp Shell option

Q18: What is the purpose of the Chamfer tool in Autodesk Fusion?

A) To create rounds and fillets automatically
B) To bevel sharp edges of the model
C) To make the model hollow
D) To apply taper to faces of a model

Q19: In the Shell tool, what does the Inside option in the Direction drop-down do?

A) Shell the faces towards the interior of the part
B) Shell the faces towards the exterior of the part
C) Shell both the interior and exterior of the part
D) Create rounded offset corners

Q20: What is the Draft tool mainly used for?

A) To bevel sharp edges
B) To create hollow models
C) To apply taper to faces for molding or casting
D) To apply fillets to edges

Q21: Which draft type creates a tapered face using an angle specified from a selected fixed plane?

A) Fixed Plane
B) Parting Line
C) Tangent Chain
D) Variable Angle

Q22: What can the Parting Line draft type be used to do?

A) Apply taper to multiple faces at once
B) Create drafts along a specified parting line
C) Apply curvature continuity to fillets
D) Bevel sharp edges

Q23: What happens when you select the "Fix Parting Line" option in the Parting Line draft type?

A) It fixes the parting line in place
B) It moves the parting line
C) It creates a fixed angle above the parting line
D) It removes any draft from the model

Q24: What is the primary function of the Scale tool?

A. To rotate bodies, sketches, or components
B. To enlarge or reduce selected bodies, sketches, or components
C. To combine multiple components into one
D. To move components or sketches

Q25: What is the default selection when using the Scale tool?

A. Non-Uniform scale
B. Entities selection
C. Point of reference selection
D. Uniform scale

Q26: In the Scale tool dialog box, how do you specify a different point as a scale reference?

A. By clicking on the OK button
B. By selecting the Uniform option
C. By clicking on the Select button for the Point option
D. By selecting the Scale Factor edit box

Q27: What is the result when the "Non-Uniform" option is selected in the Scale tool?

A. The entity is scaled uniformly in all directions
B. The entity is scaled differently in the x, y, and z directions
C. The entity is only rotated
D. The entity is split into multiple components

Q28: What action is performed by the Combine tool?

A. It scales selected bodies
B. It cuts, joins, and intersects selected bodies
C. It replaces faces on a model
D. It deletes selected components

Q29: What happens when the "New Component" checkbox is selected in the Combine tool dialog box?

A. The tool bodies are deleted
B. A new component is created with the result of the combine
C. The target body is deleted
D. The operation is not applied

Q30: When using the Replace Face tool, what happens if the Tangent Chain option is selected?

A. It replaces only one face
B. It includes tangentially connected faces in the selection
C. It only applies the tool to solid bodies
D. It replaces multiple components

Q31: Which option from the Split Face tool's Split Type drop-down is used to project a splitting tool face upon the target face?

A. Closest Point
B. Split With Surface
C. Along Vector
D. Extend Splitting Tool

Q32: What does the Split Body tool do?

A. It splits faces on a model
B. It splits components or parts, not just faces
C. It deletes selected bodies
D. It combines bodies

Q33: What is the purpose of the Silhouette Split tool?

A. To split a body at the silhouette outline visible from the view direction
B. To split a body into multiple components
C. To combine two bodies into one
D. To delete selected components

Q34: Which operation will split a shelled body into two bodies in the Silhouette Split tool?

A. Split Faces Only
B. Split Shelled Body
C. Split Solid Body
D. View Direction

Q35: In the Move/Copy tool, what happens when the “Translate” button is selected?

A. The body is moved freely
B. The body is rotated
C. The body is moved along X, Y, and Z directions using arrows
D. The body is duplicated

Q36: What is the function of the “Rotate” button in the Move/Copy tool?

A. To move the body to a specific point
B. To rotate the body around a selected axis
C. To scale the body
D. To delete the body

Q37: When using the Align tool, what does the “Flip” button do?

A. It moves the body to another location
B. It flips the aligned body
C. It rotates the body
D. It deletes the selected body

Q38: What is the purpose of the Delete tool?

A. To delete a selected object or component from the model
B. To move a body
C. To create a new component
D. To apply materials to the body

Q39: What does the Remove tool do?

A. It deletes selected bodies and components permanently
B. It removes selected bodies while preserving operations in the timeline
C. It moves selected bodies
D. It scales the bodies

Q40: How do you apply physical material using the Physical Material tool?

A. By selecting a component and clicking the “Delete” button
B. By selecting a material from the Library drop-down and dragging it to the body
C. By selecting the body and clicking the “OK” button
D. By entering a specific value in the Size edit box

FOR STUDENT NOTES

Chapter 7

Assembly Design

Topics Covered

The major topics covered in this chapter are:

- ***Introduction***
- ***New Component Tool***
- ***Joint Tool***
- ***As-Built Joint Tool***
- ***Joint Origin Tool***
- ***Rigid Group Tool***
- ***Drive Joints Tool***
- ***Motion Link Tool***
- ***Enable Contact Sets Tool***
- ***Motion Study Tool***

INTRODUCTION

Most of the things you find around you in real-world are assembly of various components; the computer you are working on is an assembly, the automotive you may be driving or sitting in for travelling is an assembly, there are lots of examples. Till this point, we have learned to create solid parts. But most of the time, we need to assemble the parts to get some use of them. In this chapter, we will work on the assembly design of Autodesk Fusion in which we will be assembling two or more components using some assembly constraints.

STARTING ASSEMBLY ENVIRONMENT

If you are starting Autodesk Fusion then a dialog box is displayed on starting the software which allows you to select the type of design you want to work with; refer to Figure-1. You can also display this dialog box on selecting the **New** button from **File** menu in application. Select the **Assembly Design** option from the dialog box and click on the **Create New** button to start a new assembly design file. Similarly, select the **Hybrid Design** option from the dialog box and click on the **Create New** button to start a hybrid design file. Note that tools of Assembly environment are also available in Hybrid Design. The Hybrid Design environment combines tools of Modeling environment and Assembly environment, giving you greater flexibility of designing objects. If you are working on small assemblies and want flexibility of using design and assembly tools together then you should use Hybrid Design. If you are working on large assemblies then you should use Assembly Design.

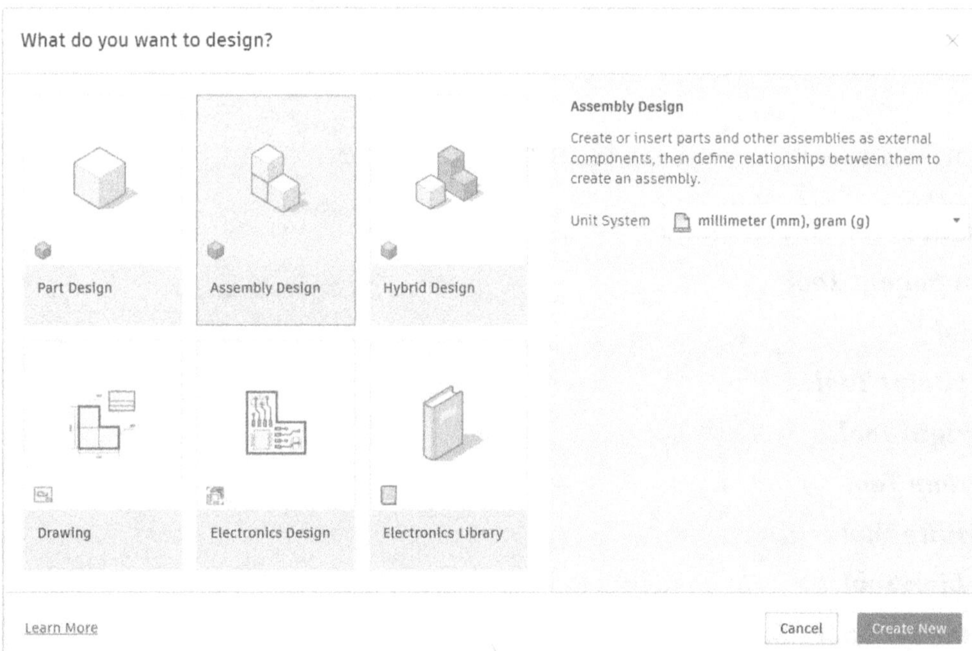

Figure-1. Dialog_box_for_starting_new_design.png

ADD TO ASSEMBLY

The **Add To Assembly** tool is used to add current model to assembly design model. This tool is available in both Part Design and Assembly Design environment. The tool is available in **ASSEMBLE** drop-down of **SOLID** tab in the **Ribbon** of Part Design environment and **INSERT** drop-down of **ASSEMBLY** tab in the **Ribbon** of Assembly Design environment. On clicking this tool, a dialog box will be displayed asking you whether to add model to new assembly or an existing assembly. The procedure to use this tool has been discussed earlier in **Chapter 1**.

We will now discuss the tools of Hybrid Design environment and you can use these tools in Assembly Design environment as well.

INSERT COMPONENT

The **Insert Component** tool is used to insert desired component in the current active document. The procedure to use this tool is discussed in Chapter 8.

NEW COMPONENT

The **New Component** tool is used to create an empty component or components from the selected bodies. Note that we need to convert all parts to components before performing their assembly. The procedure to use this tool is discussed next.

- Click on the **New Component** tool from **ASSEMBLE** drop-down in the **Toolbar**; refer to Figure-2. The **NEW COMPONENT** dialog box will be displayed; refer to Figure-3.

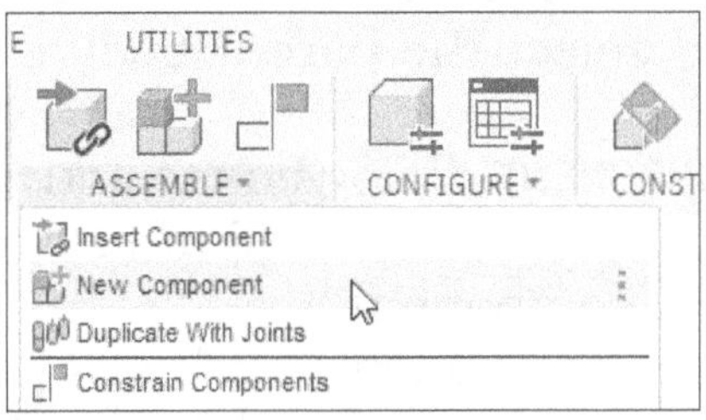

Figure-2. New Component tool

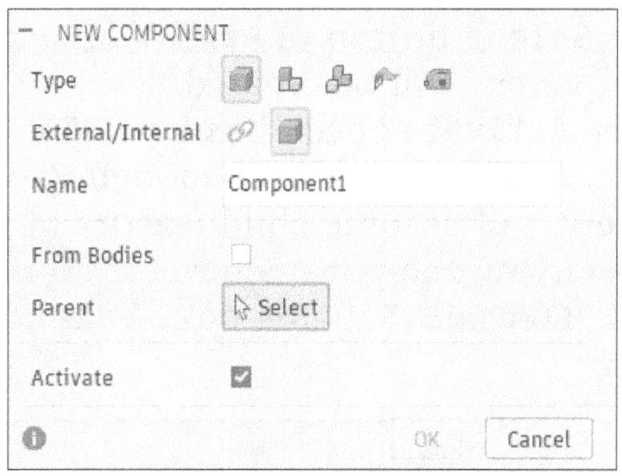

Figure-3. NEW COMPONENT dialog box

- Select **Standard** option from **Type** area in the dialog box if you want to create a standard component using 3D model design in the assembly structure.
- Select **Assembly** option from **Type** area if you want to create an assembly design component in the assembly structure.
- Select **Hybrid** option from **Type** area if you want to create a hybrid design component in the assembly structure. Hybrid Design is a flexible design method where you create internal components, add external components, and define relationships between them.
- Select **Sheet Metal** option from **Type** area if you want to create a sheet metal component in the assembly structure.
- Select **Linked PCB** option from **Type** area if you want to create a linked electronic PCB component in the assembly structure.

Standard Component

In this topic, we will discuss the procedure of creating standard component.

- Select **Standard** option from **Type** area of **NEW COMPONENT** dialog box if not selected by default.
- Select **External** option from **External/Internal** area of the dialog box to create an external component and referenced into the assembly in the current design. The options related to **External** option will be displayed in the **NEW COMPONENT** dialog box; refer to Figure-4.

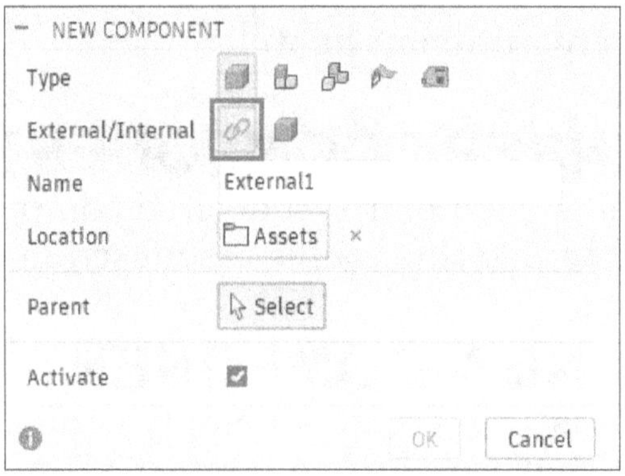

Figure-4. Options on selecting External option

- Click in the **Name** edit box of **NEW COMPONENT** dialog box and enter the name of component.
- Specify desired location where you want to save the new design that will contain the new component by clicking on the button from **Location** area of the dialog box.
- Click on **Select** button of **Parent** area and select the parent body under which new component will be created.
- Select the **Activate** check box from **NEW COMPONENT** dialog box to activate the new component. Note that all the modeling operations performed after activating the component will become child feature of that component.
- After specifying the parameters for standard component, click on the **OK** button from **NEW COMPONENT** dialog box. A standard component will be created; refer to Figure-5.

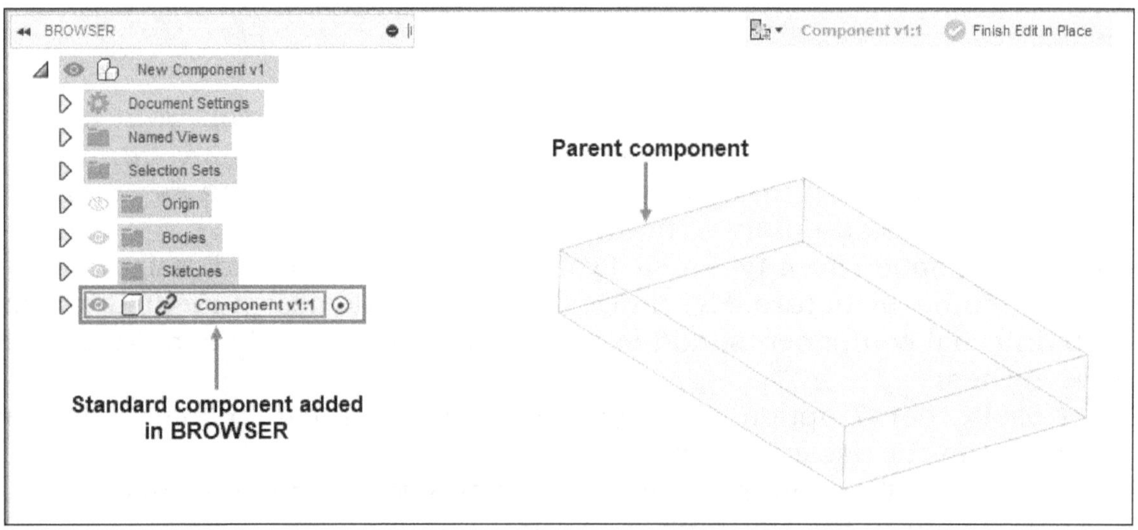

Figure-5. Standard component created

- If you want to create an internal component directly in the current design then select **Internal** option from **External/Internal** area in the dialog box. This will increase the file size of model but it will reduce efforts in managing multiple design files. The options related to **Internal** option will be displayed in the **NEW COMPONENT** dialog box; refer to Figure-6.

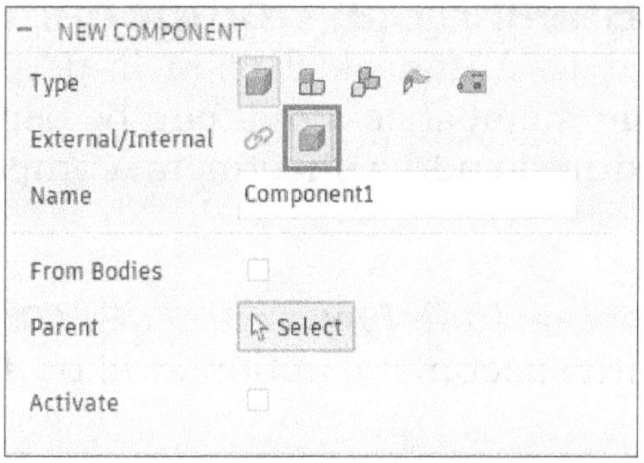

Figure-6. Options on selecting Internal option

- Select **From Bodies** check box from **NEW COMPONENT** dialog box to convert existing bodies into individual components. The updated **NEW COMPONENT** dialog box will be displayed; refer to Figure-7.

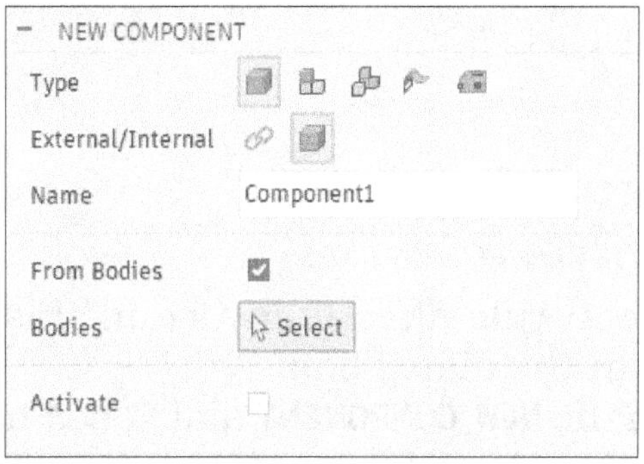

Figure-7. Updated NEW COMPONENT dialog box

- The **Select** button of **Bodies** section is active by default. Click on the parts/bodies from model to create a new component; refer to Figure-8. You can select multiple bodies by holding the **CTRL** key.

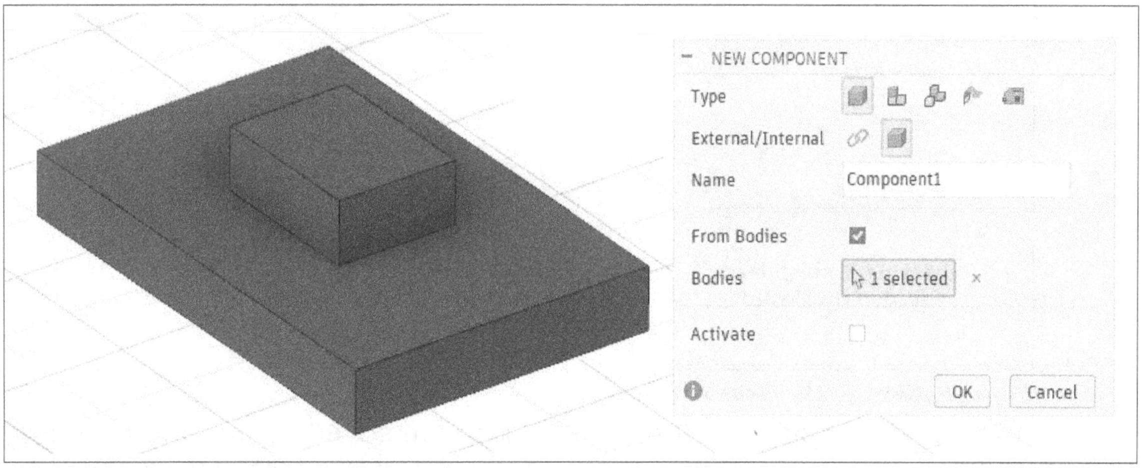

Figure-8. Bodies selected for new component

- After selecting the body, click on the **OK** button from **NEW COMPONENT** dialog box. The new component will be created and action will be displayed in **BROWSER**.

Sheet Metal Component

A **Sheet Metal** component in Autodesk Fusion is a type of component used to design parts made from thin metal sheets that can be bent, folded, and flattened for manufacturing. The procedure to add a sheetmetal component in assembly is given next.

- Select the **Sheet Metal** option from **Type** area of **NEW COMPONENT** dialog box. The **NEW COMPONENT** dialog box with sheet metal options will be displayed; refer to Figure-9.

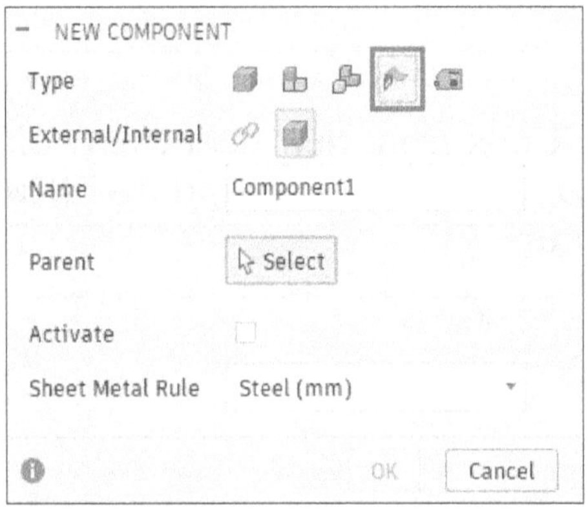

Figure-9. NEW COMPONENT dialog box with sheet metal options

- Select desired sheet metal rule already in use in this design or from the **Sheet Metal Rule** drop-down in the dialog box.
- The other parameters in the **NEW COMPONENT** dialog box have been discussed earlier.
- After specifying parameters for sheet metal component, click on the **OK** button from **NEW COMPONENT** dialog box. A sheet metal component will be created; refer to Figure-10.

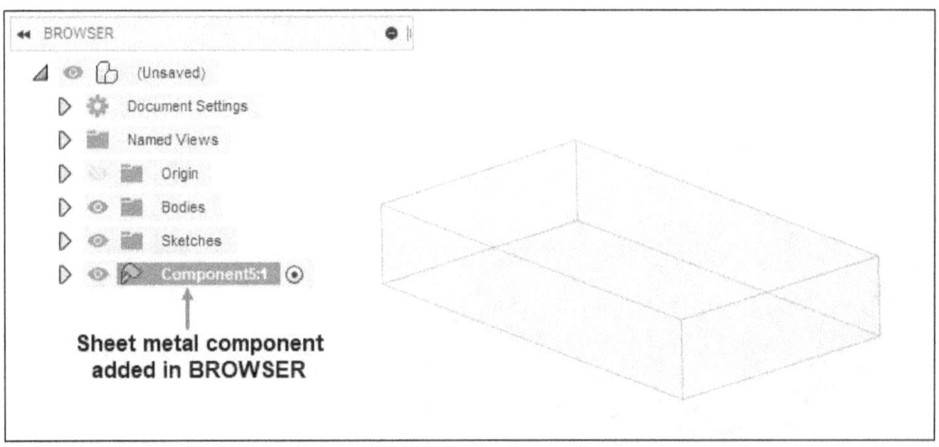

Figure-10. Sheet metal component created

Similarly, you can create **Assembly**, **Hybrid**, and **Linked PCB** components using **NEW COMPONENT** dialog box. After adding component, you can model them as needed while they are selected as active document in the **BROWSER**.

JOINT

The **Joint** tool is used to define joints between components to allow movement of components relative to each other. To apply **Joint** tool, you need to create the component of bodies. The procedure to use this tool is discussed next.

- Click on the **Joint** tool from **ASSEMBLE** drop-down in the **Toolbar**; refer to Figure-11. The **JOINT** dialog box will be displayed; refer to Figure-12.

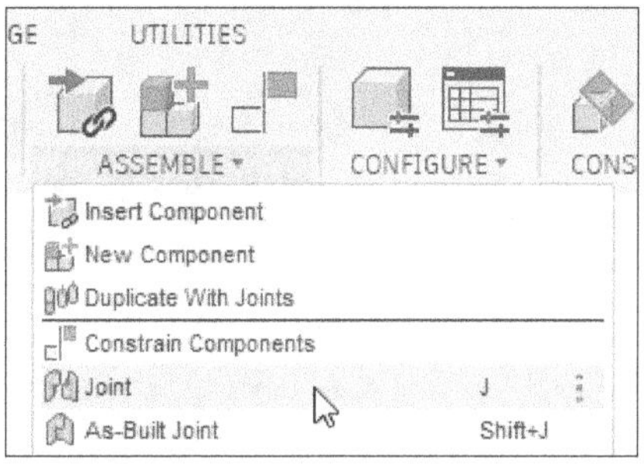

Figure-11. Joint tool

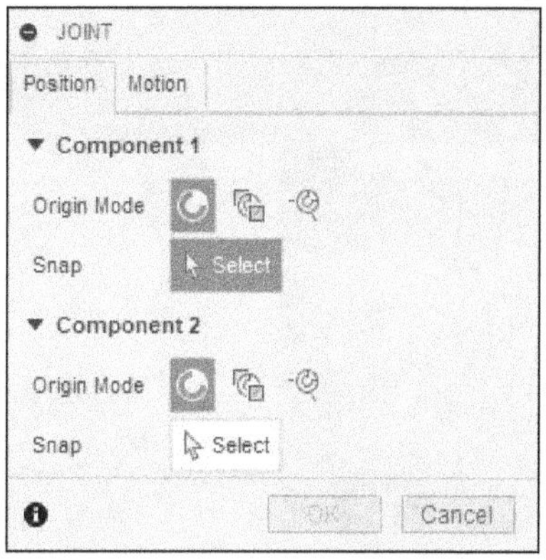

Figure-12. JOINT dialog box

- Select desired option from **Origin Mode** section of **Component 1** area in the **Position** tab of the dialog box. Select **Simple** option from **Origin Mode** section to select a **Snap** point to place the joint origin. Select **Between Two Faces** option from **Origin Mode** section to select **Plane 1** and **Plane 2** to center the joint origin between them then select a **Snap** point. Select **Two Edge Intersection** option from **Origin Mode** section to select **Edge 1** and a non-parallel **Edge 2** to locate the joint origin at the extended intersection.
- **Select** button of **Snap** section from **Component 1** area is active by default. Click on the first component at desired location to assemble; refer to Figure-13. You will be asked to select a location on second component.

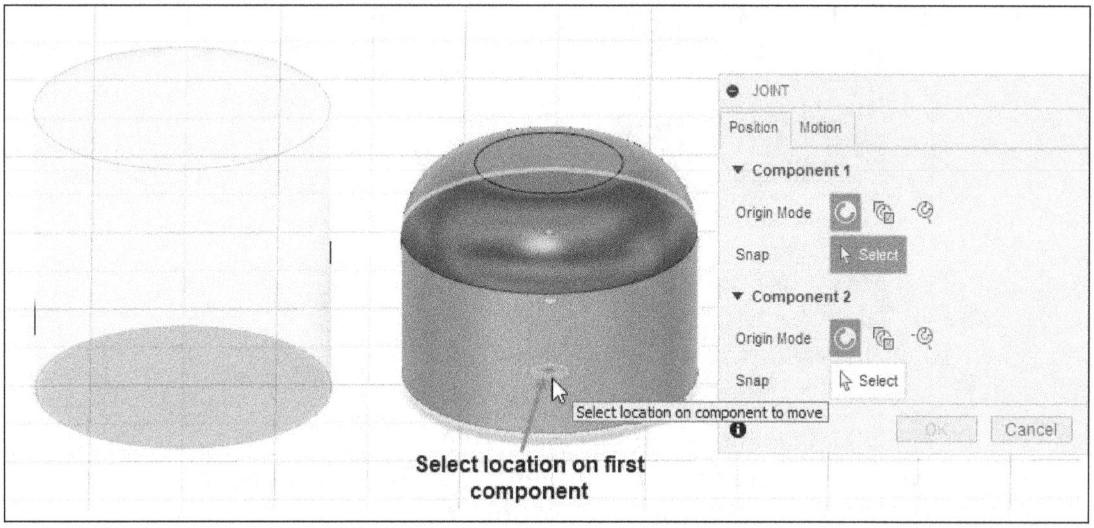

Figure-13. Selection of component 1 location

- Select desired option from **Origin Mode** section of **Component 2** area in the **Position** tab of the dialog box. The options of **Origin Mode** section have been discussed earlier.
- Click on the second component on mating location to select; refer to Figure-14.

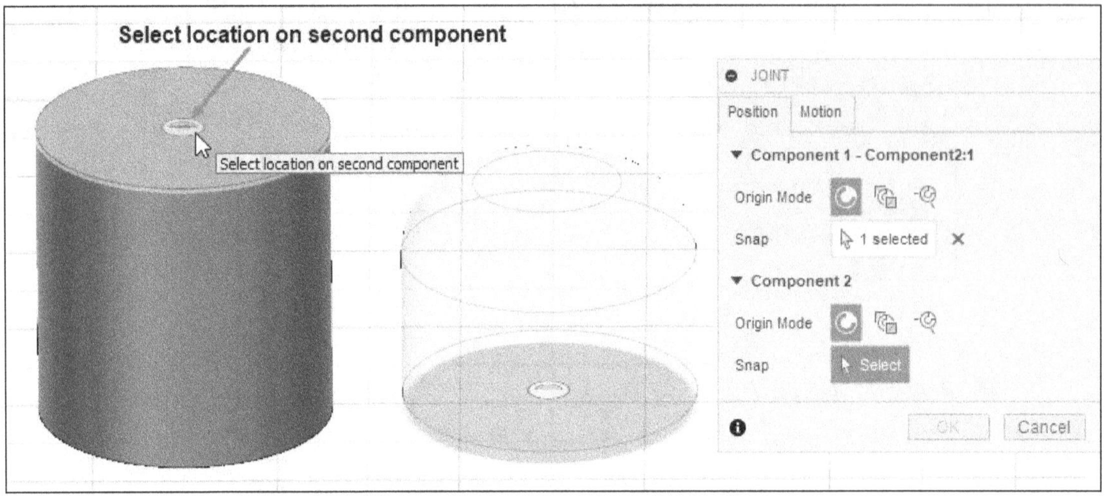

Figure-14. Selection of component 2 location

- On selecting the second component, the selected two component will be joined to each other at the locations selected on them and the updated **JOINT** dialog box will be displayed; refer to Figure-15.

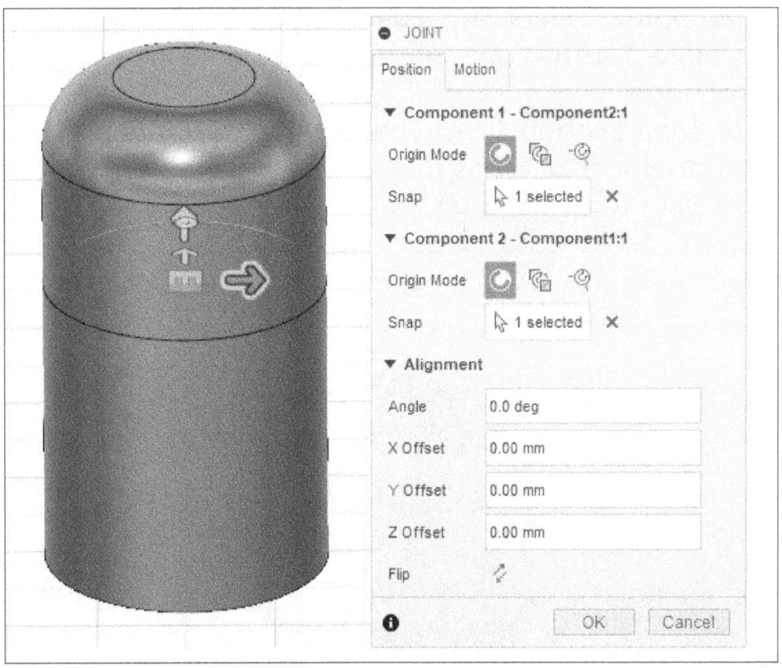

Figure-15. Components joined with updated JOINT dialog box

- Click in the **Angle** edit box from **Alignment** area in **Position** tab of the dialog box and specify the angle of rotation of component.
- If you want to specify offset distance between components then click in the **Offset X**, **Offset Y**, and **Offset Z** edit boxes as required and enter the value. You can also set the offset distance by moving the drag handles.
- Click on the **Flip** button from **Alignment** area of the dialog box, if you want to flip the direction of second component.

Motion

There are seven motion types in **Motion** tab of **JOINT** dialog box which we can apply to the component as required; refer to Figure-16. These motion types are described next.

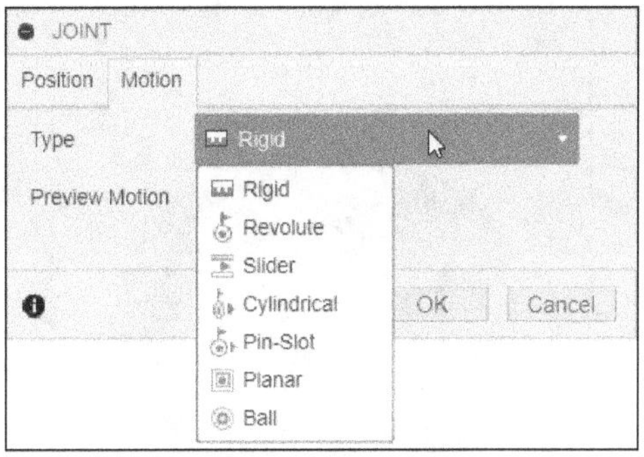

Figure-16. Types of motion in JOINT dialog box

Rigid Motion

- Select the **Rigid** option from **Type** drop-down in the **Motion** tab of the **JOINT** dialog box, if you want the joint of two component to be rigid to each other and there should be no motion between the two joined component.

Revolute Motion

- Select the **Revolute** option from **Type** drop-down in the **Motion** tab of the **JOINT** dialog box, if you want to revolve the component about other at the joint location. On selecting the **Revolute** option, a revolve drag handle will be displayed. You can revolve the component by moving the drag handle; refer to Figure-17.

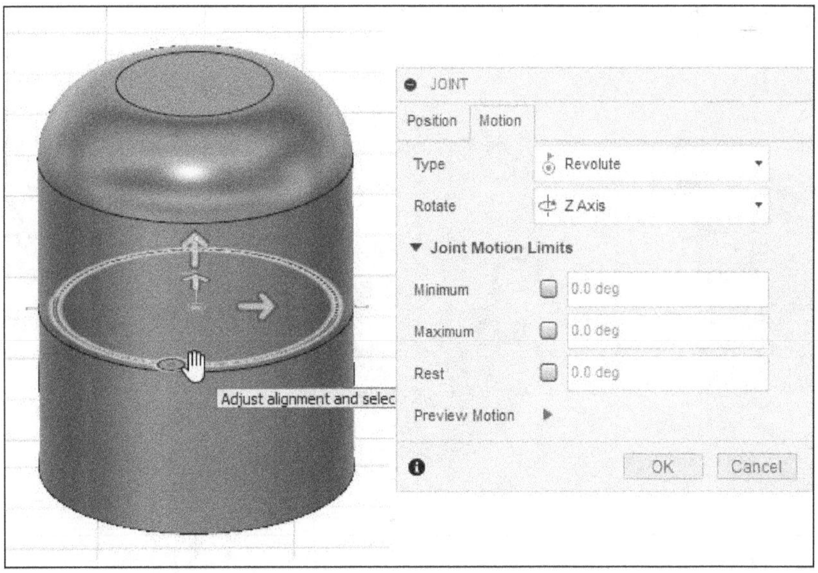

Figure-17. Revolute motion

- Select **Minimum** and **Maximum** check box from **Joint Motion Limits** rollout to specify the minimum and maximum motion limit for the joint in the respective edit boxes. Select the **Rest** check box to specify the default position of the joint at rest in the respective edit box.

Slider Motion

- Click on the **Slider** option from **Type** drop-down in the **Motion** tab of the **JOINT** dialog box, if you want to assemble the component in such a way that selected component can slide over the other; refer to Figure-18.

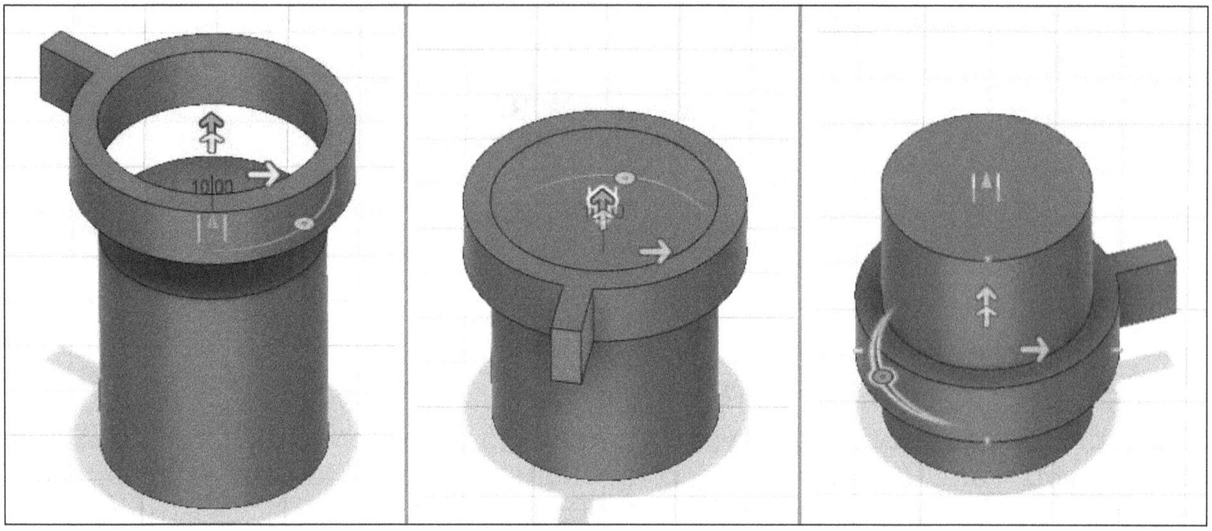

Figure-18. Slider motion

Cylindrical Motion

- Click on the **Cylindrical** option from **Type** drop-down in the **Motion** tab of the **JOINT** dialog box, if you want to assemble the component in such a way that it is free to move along the selected axis and free to rotate about the same selected axis; refer to Figure-19.

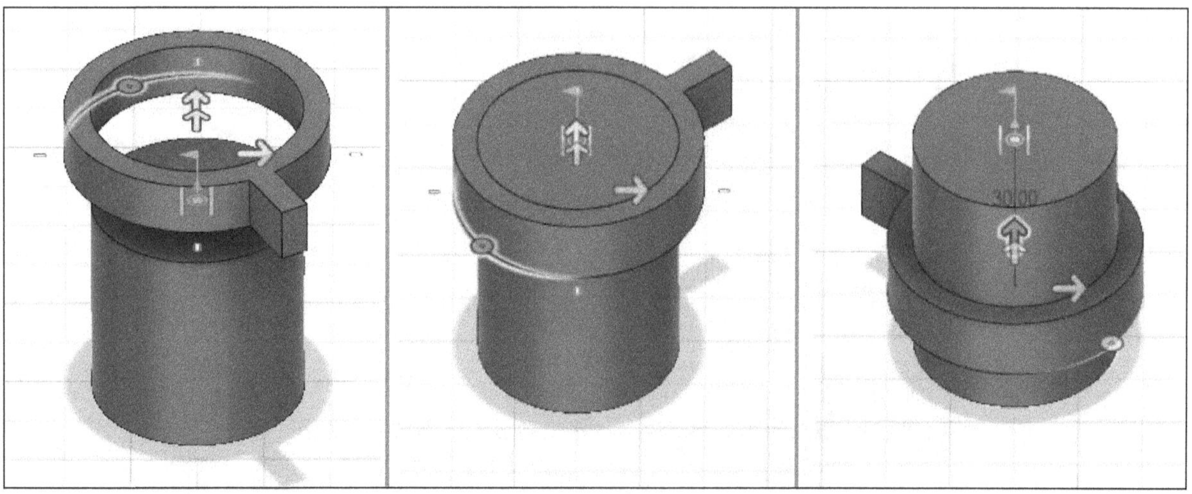

Figure-19. Cylindrical motion

Pin-Slot Motion

- Click on the **Pin-Slot** option from **Type** drop-down in the **Motion** tab of **JOINT** dialog box, if you want to revolve and slide the component together like in nut & bolt locking-unlocking.

Planar Motion

- Click on the **Planar** option from **Type** drop-down in the **Motion** tab of **JOINT** dialog box, if you want to assemble the component in such a way that the component can move over the selected plane only in defined boundary.

Ball Motion

- Click on the **Ball** option from **Type** drop-down in the **Motion** tab of **JOINT** dialog box, if you want to assemble the component in such a way that the component is free to move 360 degree in 3D space pivoted to a point; refer to Figure-20.

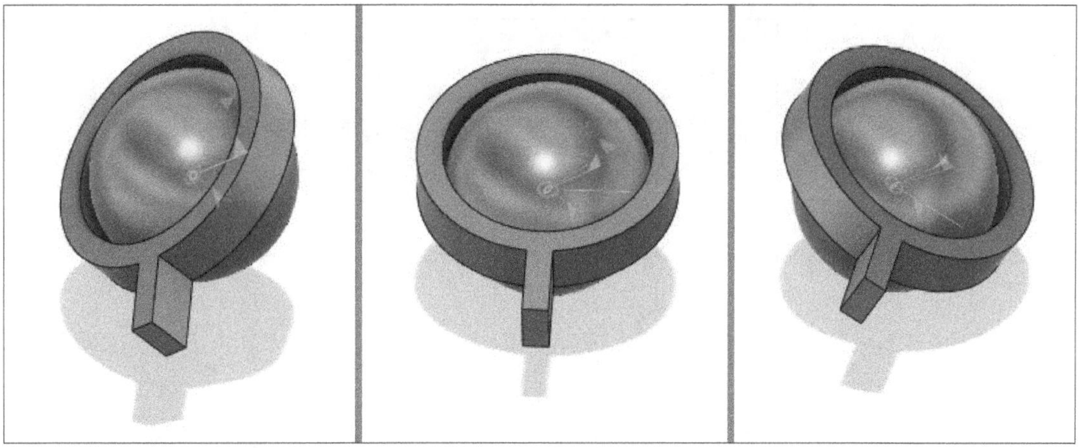

Figure-20. Ball motion

- Click on the **Animate** button from **Motion** tab of **JOINT** dialog box to watch the applied motion by animating **Component 1**. Click the button again to stop the animation.

After specifying the parameters for joint, click on the **OK** button from **JOINT** dialog box to complete the process.

DUPLICATE WITH JOINTS

The **Duplicate With Joints** tool duplicates components in an assembly and the joints attached to them in Fusion. The procedure to use this tool is discussed next.

- Click on the **Duplicate With Joints** from **ASSEMBLE** drop-down in the **Toolbar**; refer to Figure-21. The **DUPLICATE WITH JOINTS** dialog box will be displayed; refer to Figure-22.

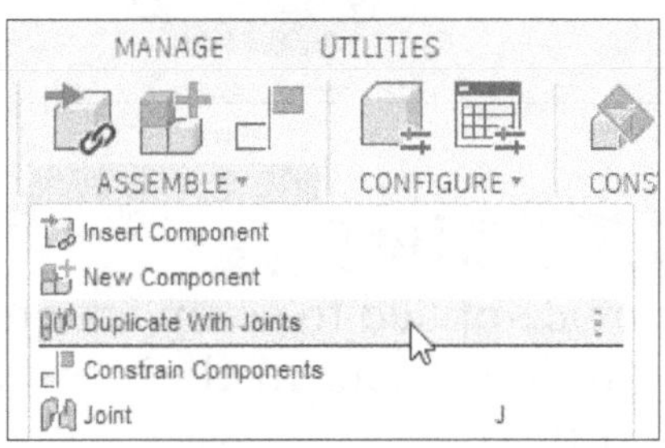

Figure-21. Duplicate With Joints tool

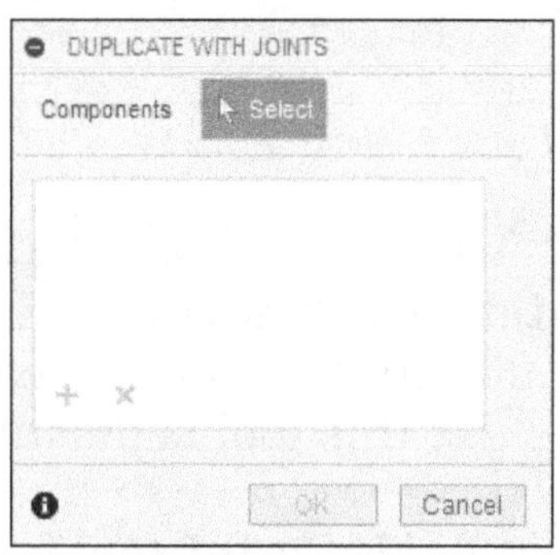

Figure-22. DUPLICATE WITH JOINTS dialog box

- Select desired component from the canvas, browser, or timeline to duplicate. The updated **DUPLICATE WITH JOINTS** dialog box will be displayed; refer to Figure-23.

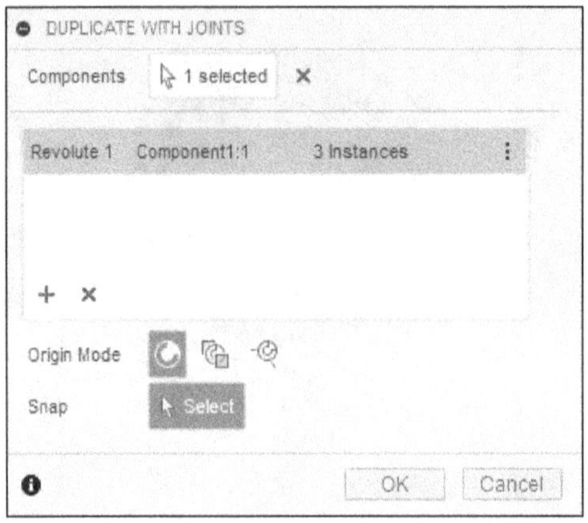

Figure-23. Updated DUPLICATE WITH JOINTS dialog box

- Select desired option from **Origin Mode** section of the dialog box which have been discussed earlier.
- Select desired snap point in the component to place the joint origin.
- After specifying desired parameters, click on **OK** button from the dialog box. The joint will be duplicated; refer to Figure-24.

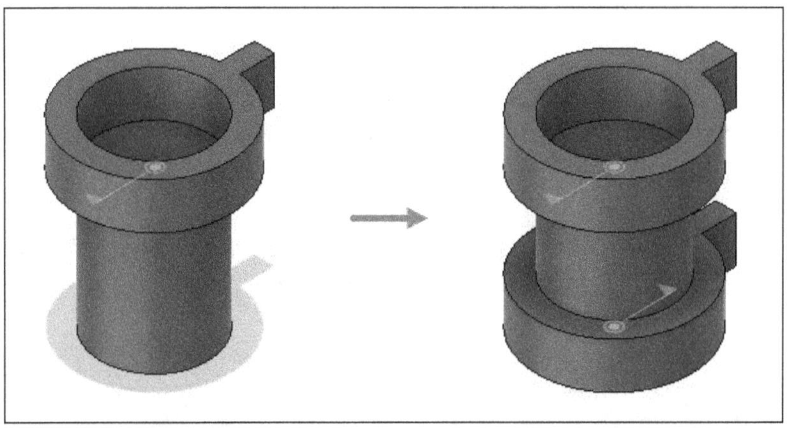

Figure-24. Joint duplicated

AS-BUILT JOINT

The **As-Built Joint** tool allows the joints to be applied to components in their current position as they are built, making it easy to join them in their original orientation. The procedure to use this tool is discussed next.

- Click on the **As-Built Joint** tool from **ASSEMBLE** drop-down in the **Toolbar**; refer to Figure-25. The **AS-BUILT JOINT** dialog box will be displayed; refer to Figure-26.

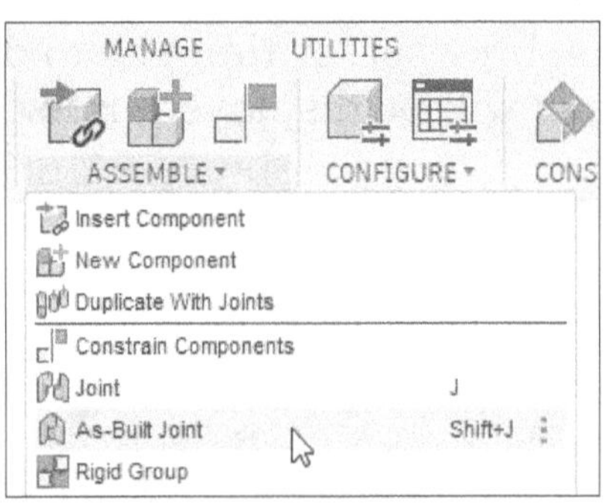

Figure-25. As Built Joint tool

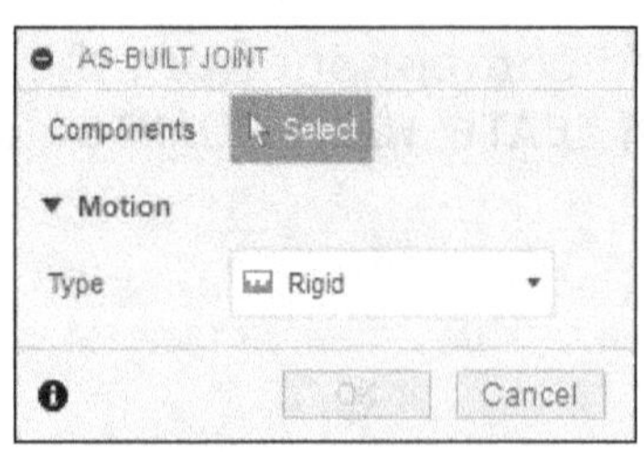

Figure-26. AS BUILT JOINT dialog box

- Select the components from the canvas.
- Select required motion from **Type** drop-down in **Motion** area of the dialog box. The updated **AS-BUILT JOINT** dialog box will be displayed; refer to Figure-27.

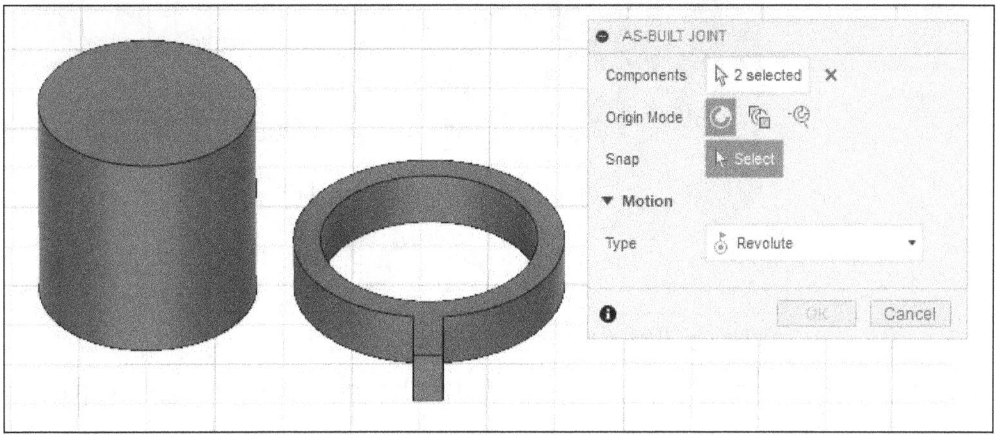

Figure-27. Updated AS BUILT JOINT dialog box

- Select desired option from **Origin Mode** section of the dialog box which have been discussed earlier.
- Select desired references on the components based on the option selected in **Type** drop-down; refer to Figure-28.

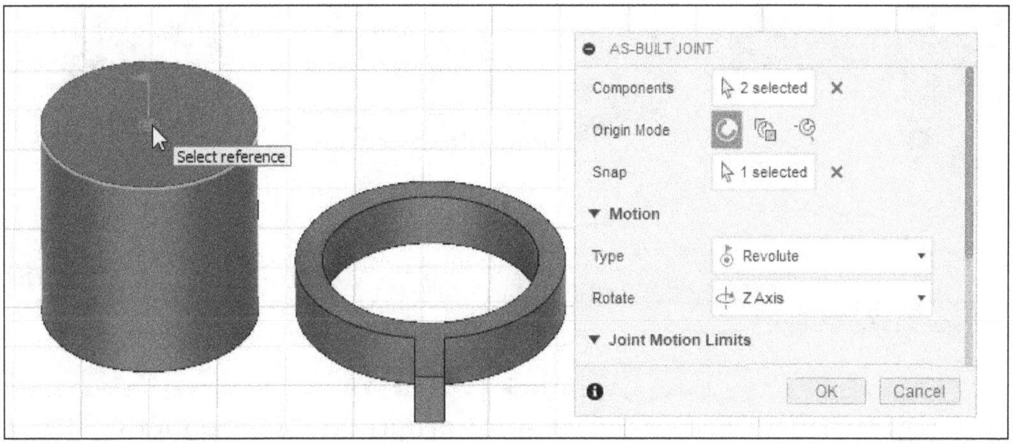

Figure-28. Selecting reference for motion

- Select desired option from **Rotate** drop-down to specify the axis for rotation of the component.
- Click on the **Preview Motion** button from **Joint Motion Limits** area of the dialog box to watch the applied motion by animating the component. Click the button again to stop the animation.
- After specifying the parameters, click on the **OK** button from **AS-BUILT JOINT** dialog box to complete the process.
- If you want to rotate the component after creating joint then double-click on the flag displayed; refer to Figure-29.

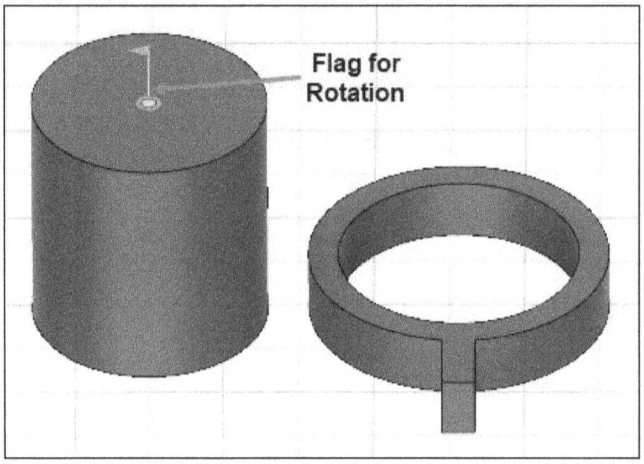

Figure-29. Flag for rotation

- The drag handle will be displayed. Rotate the component as required; refer to Figure-30.

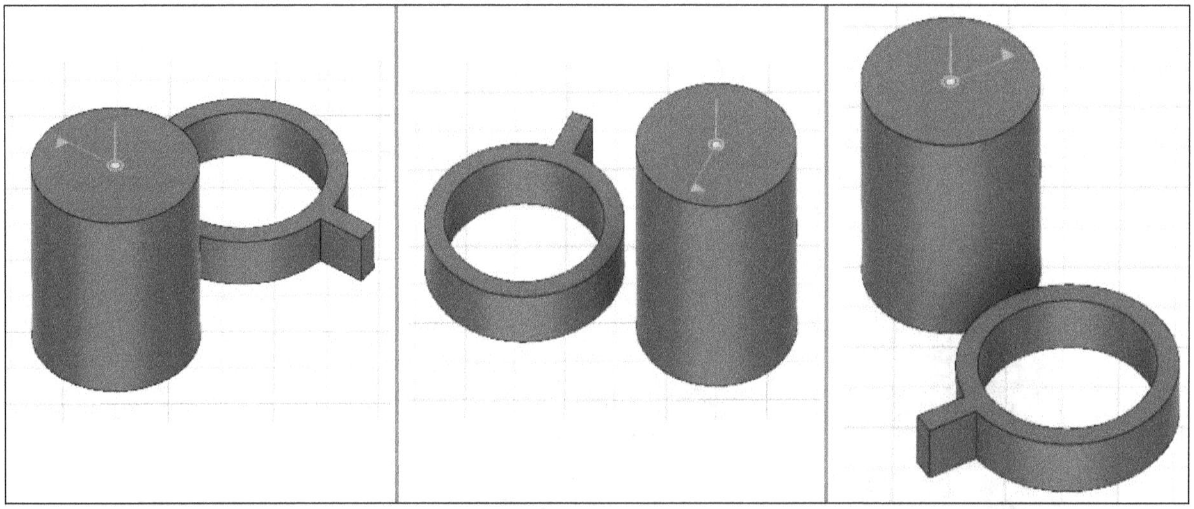

Figure-30. Rotation of component

JOINT ORIGIN

The **Joint Origin** tool is used to define joint origin on a component. The procedure to use this tool is discussed next.

- Click on the **Joint Origin** tool from **ASSEMBLE** drop-down in the **Toolbar**; refer to Figure-31. The **JOINT ORIGIN** dialog box will be displayed; refer to Figure-32.

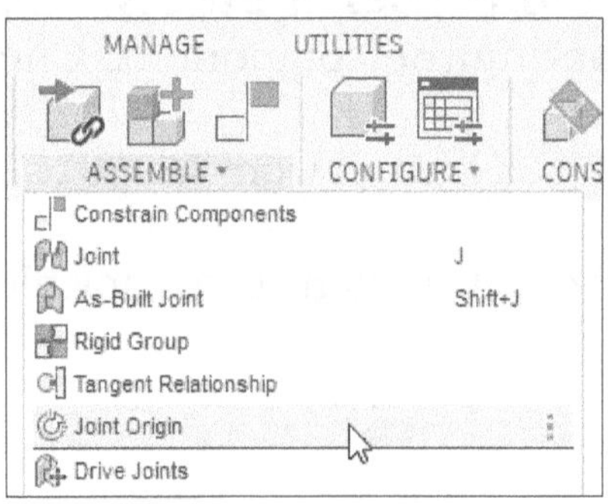

Figure-31. Joint Origin tool

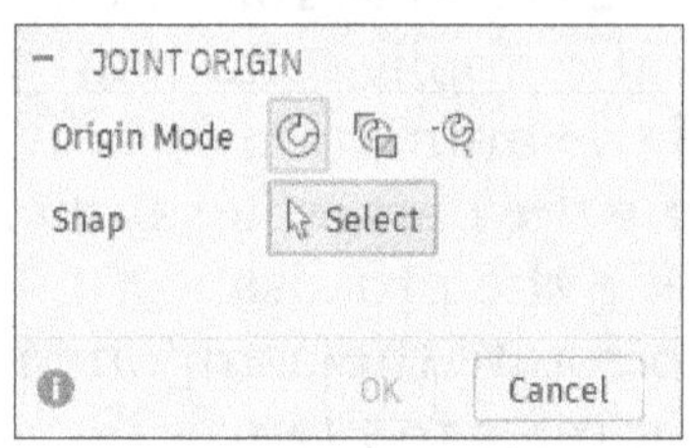

Figure-32. JOINT ORIGIN dialog box

- Select **Simple** option from **Origin Mode** section of **JOINT ORIGIN** dialog box, if you want to place the joint origin on a face.

- Select **Between Two Faces** option from **Origin Mode** section of **JOINT ORIGIN** dialog box if you want to place the joint origin midway between the faces.
- In our case, we are selecting the **Between Two Faces** option from **Origin Mode** section. The updated **JOINT ORIGIN** dialog box will be displayed as shown in Figure-33.

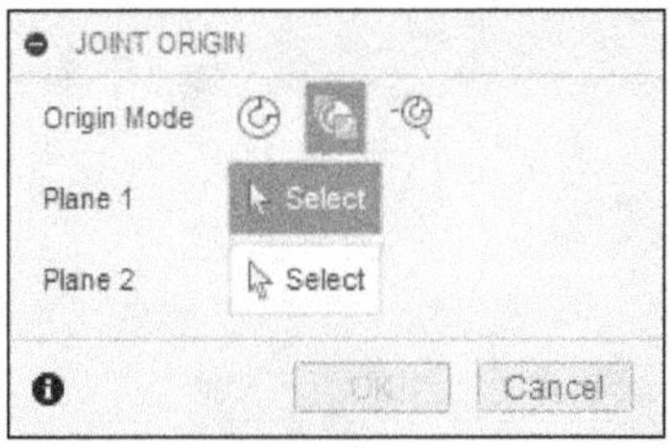

Figure-33. Updated JOINT ORIGIN dialog box

- The **Select** button of **Plane 1** section is active by default. Click on the first face from model to select; refer to Figure-34.

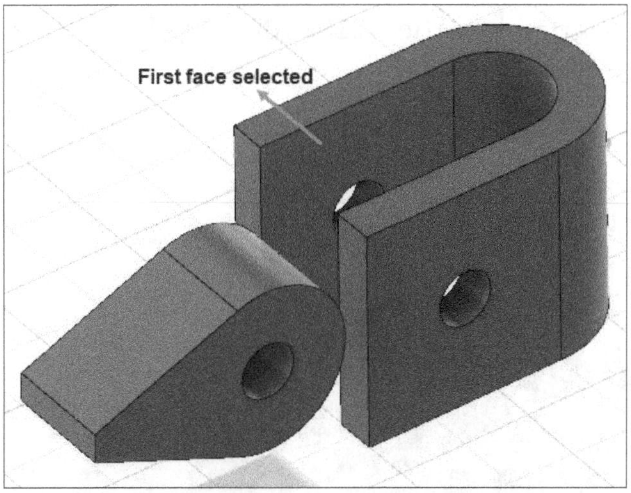

Figure-34. Selection of first face

- On selecting the first face, the **Select** button of **Plane 2** section will be activated. Similarly, select the second face of the model; refer to Figure-35. The updated **JOINT ORIGIN** dialog box will be displayed.

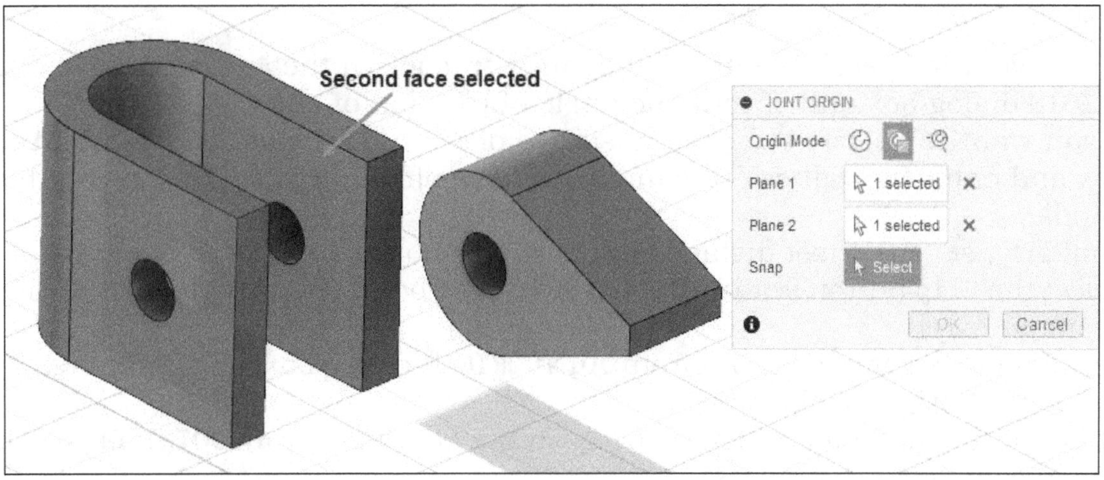

Figure-35. Selection of second face

- The **Select** button of **Snap** option is active by default. Click at desired location to define the snap point; refer to Figure-36.

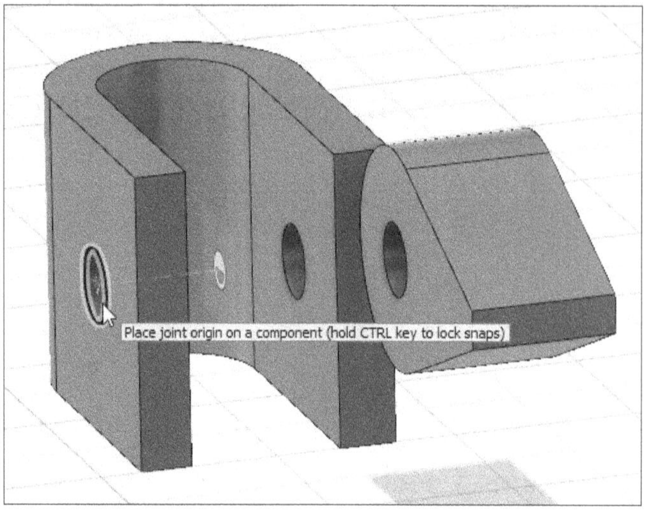

Figure-36. Selection of snap point

- On selecting the snap point, the **JOINT ORIGIN** dialog box will be updated; refer to Figure-37.

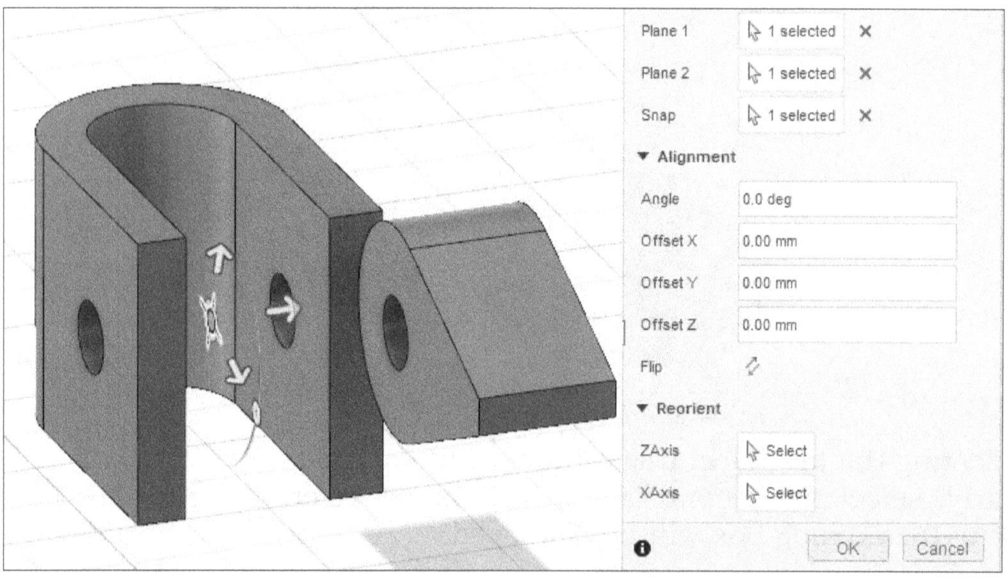

Figure-37. Specifying the location of snap

- If you want to specify the angle of snap then click in the **Angle** edit box of **JOINT ORIGIN** dialog box and specify the angle of rotation of snap.
- If you want to specify the offset distance of snap then click on the **Offset X** edit box and enter the value. You can also set the offset distance by moving the drag handle.
- Similarly, set the offset distance in other edit boxes.
- Select the **Flip** button from **JOINT ORIGIN** dialog box if you want to flip the direction of snap.
- Select the **Reorient** check box from **JOINT ORIGIN** dialog box, if you want to position the axes of origin of geometry.
- After specifying the parameters, click on the **OK** button from **JOINT ORIGIN** dialog box to complete the process.
- Now, you will be able to join the two component with the help of **Joint** tool using newly created joint origin; refer to Figure-38 and Figure-39.

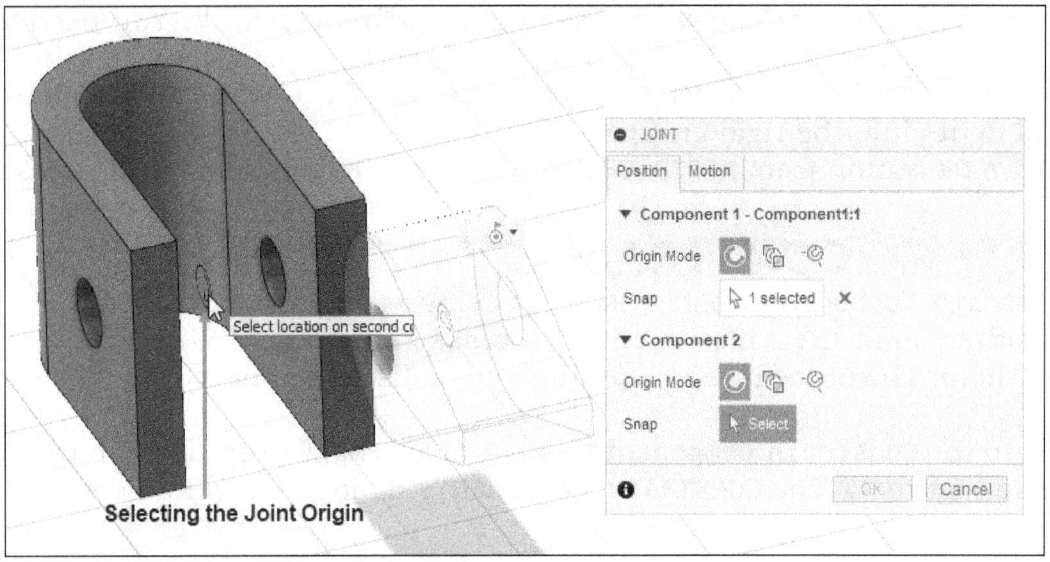

Figure-38. Selection of newly created joint origin

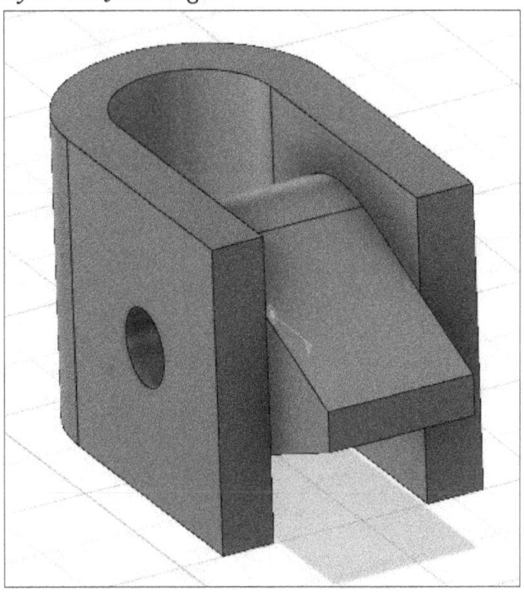

Figure-39. Joint created

RIGID GROUP

The **Rigid Group** tool is used to combine selected components into one group so that the created group act as one object. The procedure to use this tool is discussed next.

- Click on the **Rigid Group** tool from **ASSEMBLE** drop-down in the **Toolbar**; refer to Figure-40. The **RIGID GROUP** dialog box will be displayed; refer to Figure-41.

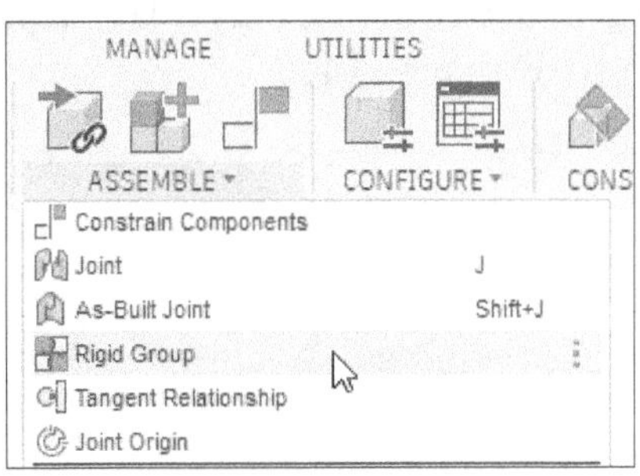

Figure-40. Rigid Group tool

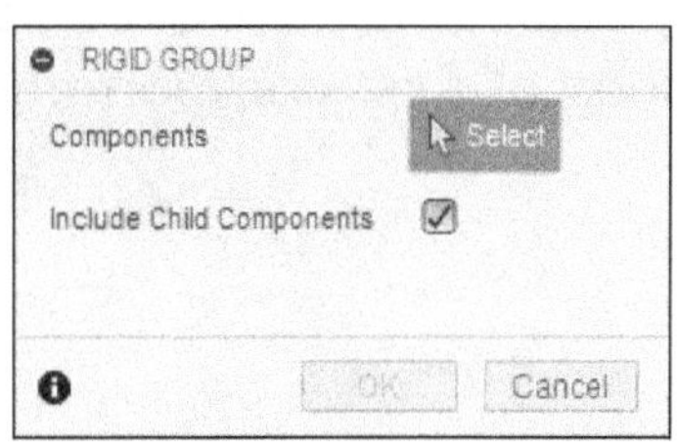

Figure-41. RIGID GROUP dialog box

- The **Select** button of **Components** section is active by default. You need to select the components from the model to create a rigid group.
- Select the **Include Child Components** check box if you want to include the child components into the rigid group.
- Click on **OK** button from **RIGID GROUP** dialog box to complete the process.

CONSTRAIN COMPONENTS

The **Constrain Components** tool is used to position two or more components relative to each other, limit their movement in the assembly, and define the relationship between them. The procedure to use this tool is discussed next.

- Click on the **Constrain Components** tool from **ASSEMBLE** drop-down in the **Toolbar**; refer to Figure-42.The **CONSTRAIN COMPONENTS** dialog box will be displayed; refer to Figure-43.

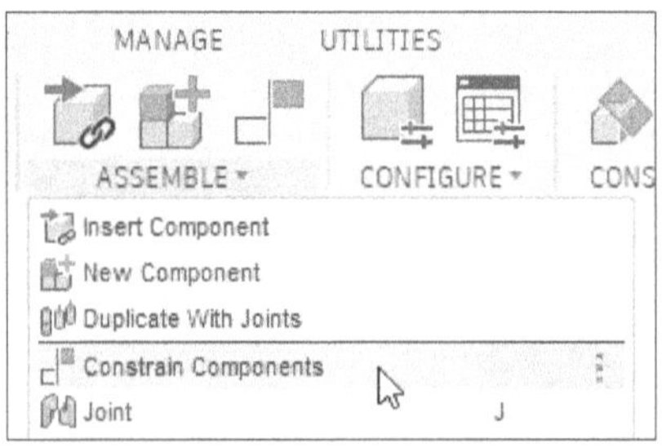

Figure-42. Constrain Components tool

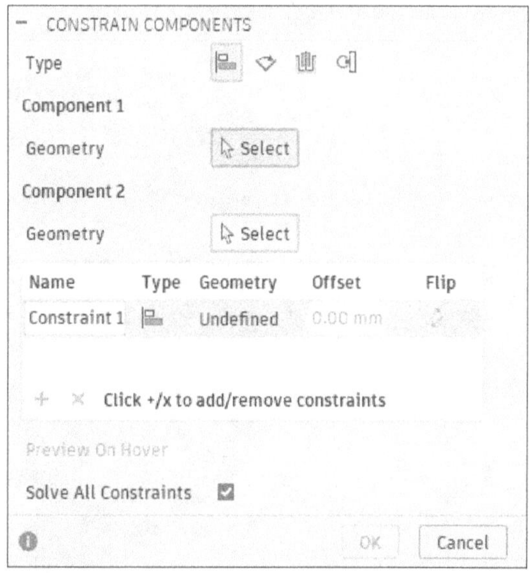

Figure-43. CONSTRAIN COMPONENTS dialog box

Align Constraint Type

The **Align** option is used to place the components so that their selected geometries are coincident or concentric with each other. The procedure to use this option is discussed next.

- Select **Align** option from **Type** area of **CONSTRAIN COMPONENTS** dialog box, if not selected by default. The options will be displayed as shown in Figure-43.
- The **Geometry** selection button of **Component 1** area is active by default. Select a face on the body of first component; refer to Figure-44.

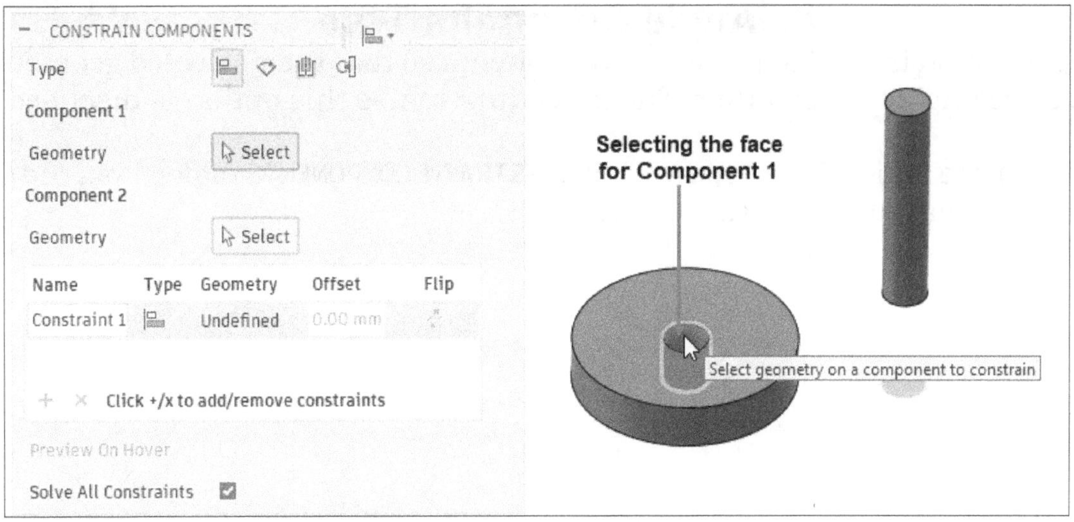

Figure-44. Selecting the face for Component 1

- After selecting face on a body in the first component, select the face on a body in the second component as shown in Figure-45.

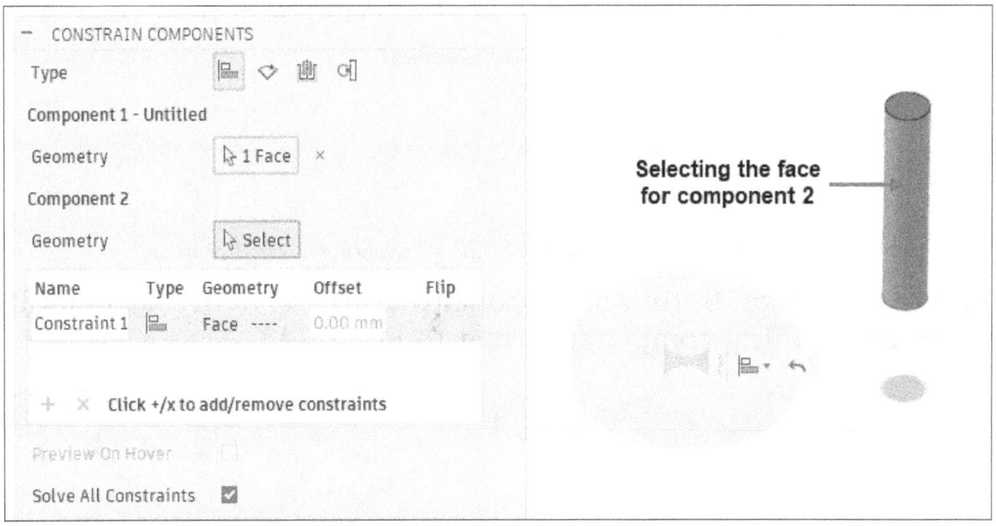

Figure-45. Selecting the face for Component 2

- After selecting face on a body in the second component, click on the **OK** button from the dialog box. The align constraint will be applied between the components; refer to Figure-46.

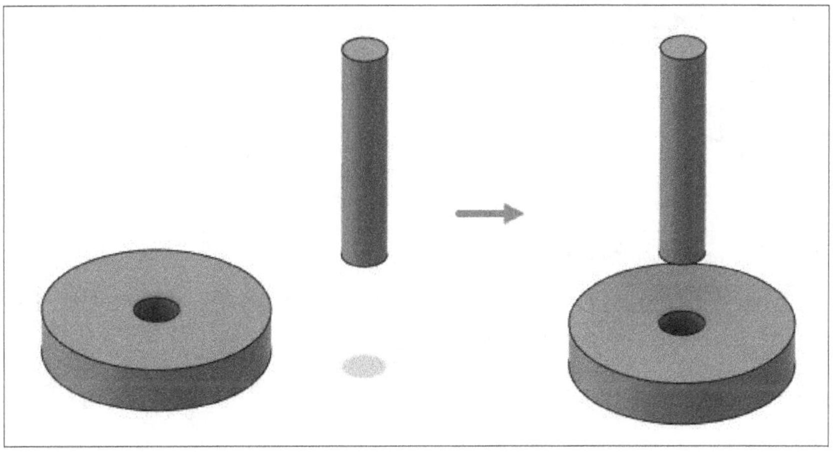

Figure-46. Align constraint applied

Angle Constraint Type

The **Angle** option is used to place the components so that their selected geometries are at a relative angle to each other. The procedure to use this option is discussed next.

- Select **Angle** option from **Type** area of **CONSTRAIN COMPONENTS** dialog box, the options will be displayed as shown in Figure-47.

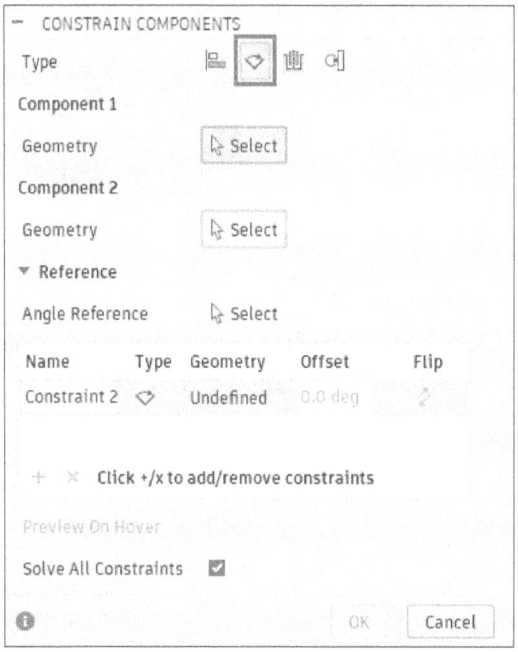

Figure-47. CONSTRAIN COMPONENTS dialog box with Angle constraint options

- The **Geometry** selection button of **Component 1** area is active by default. Select a face on the body of first component; refer to Figure-48.

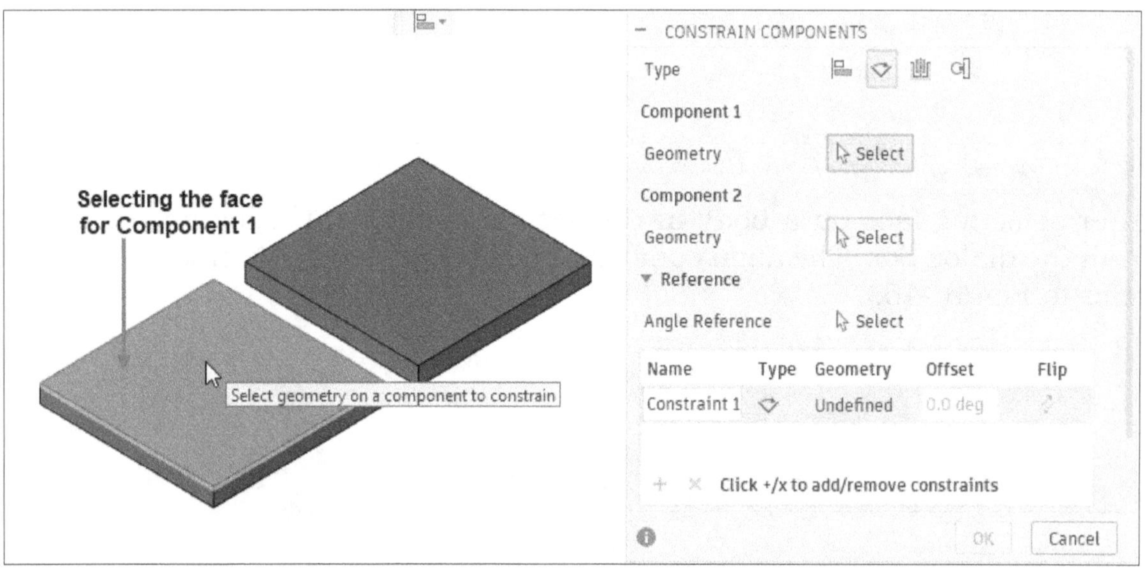

Figure-48. Selecting the face for Component 1

- After selecting face on a body in the first component, select the face on a body in the second component as shown in Figure-49.

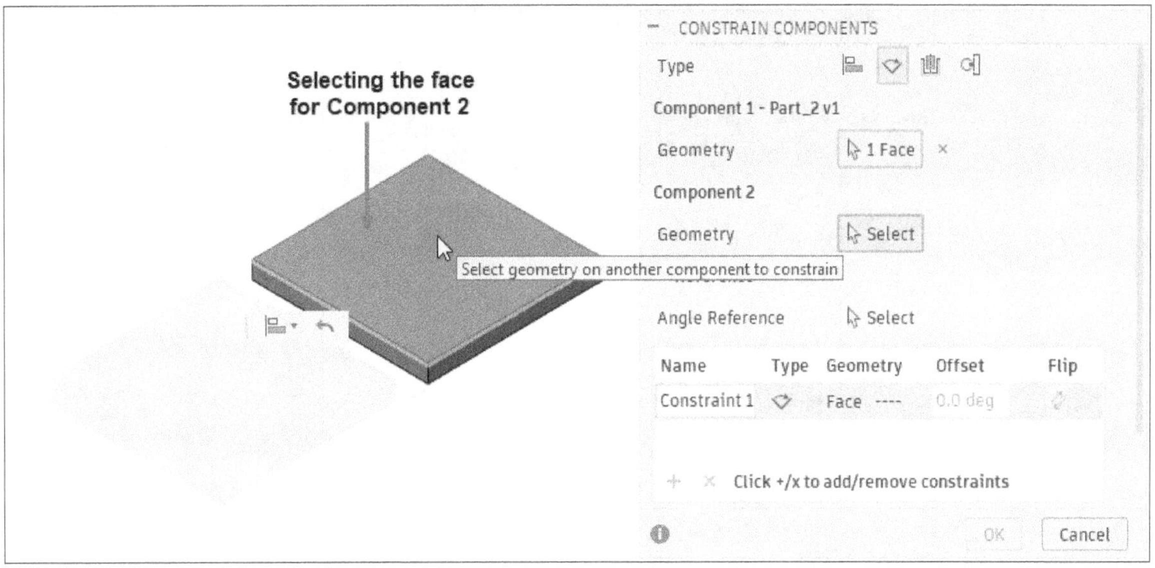

Figure-49. Selecting the face for Component 2

- After selecting face on a body in the second component, optionally select desired face or an edge for the angle reference and specify desired offset angle value in the **Offset** edit box.
- After specifying desired parameters, click on the **OK** button from the dialog box. The angle constraint will be applied between the components; refer to Figure-50.

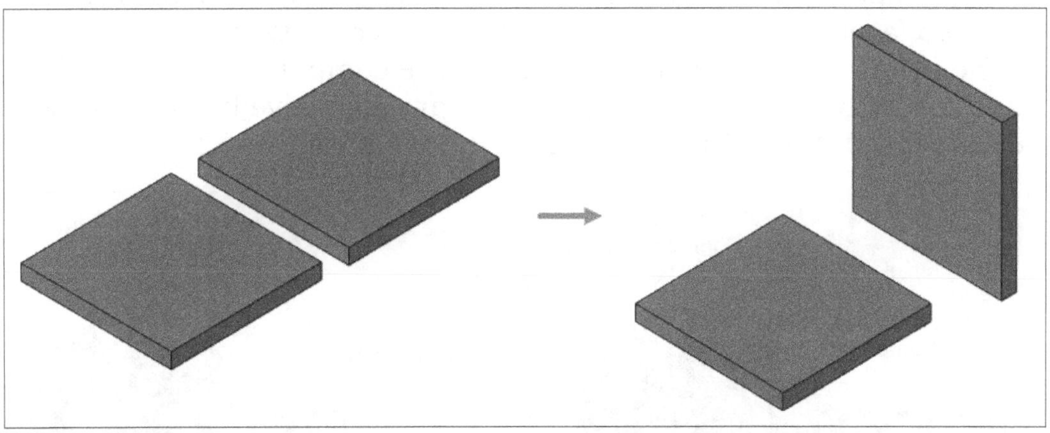

Figure-50. Angle constraint applied

Center Constraint Type

The **Center** is used to place a component centered between two faces of another component. The procedure to use this option is discussed next.

- Select **Center** option from **Type** area of **CONSTRAIN COMPONENTS** dialog box, the options will be displayed as shown in Figure-51.

Figure-51. CONSTRAIN COMPONENTS dialog box with Center constraint options

- Select **Simple** option from **Position Mode** area to center a face of the first component between two faces of the second component. Select **Between Two Faces** option to center the constraint between two faces on the component.
- The **Face 1** selection button of **Component 1** area is active by default. Select faces on the **Component 1** and **Component 2** as shown in Figure-52.

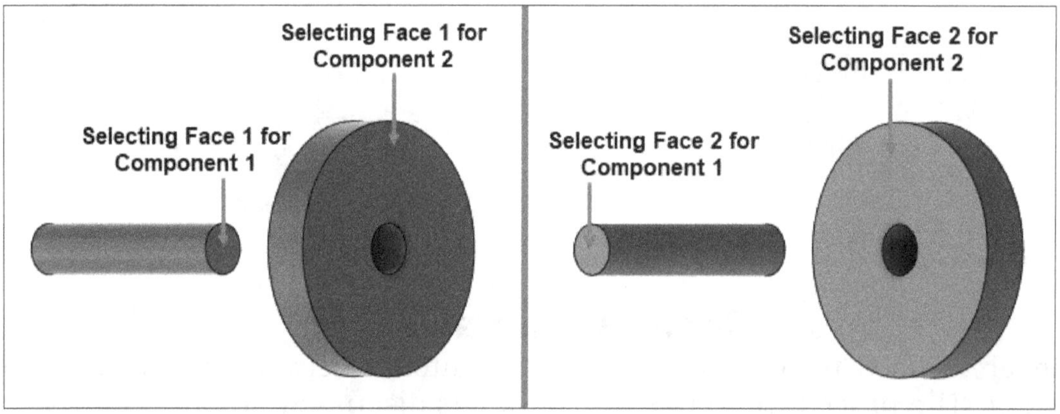

Figure-52. Selecting the faces for center constraint

- On selecting the second face for **Component 2**, the preview of center constraint will be displayed.
- After specifying desired parameters, click on **OK** button from the dialog box. The center constraint will be applied between the components; refer to Figure-53.

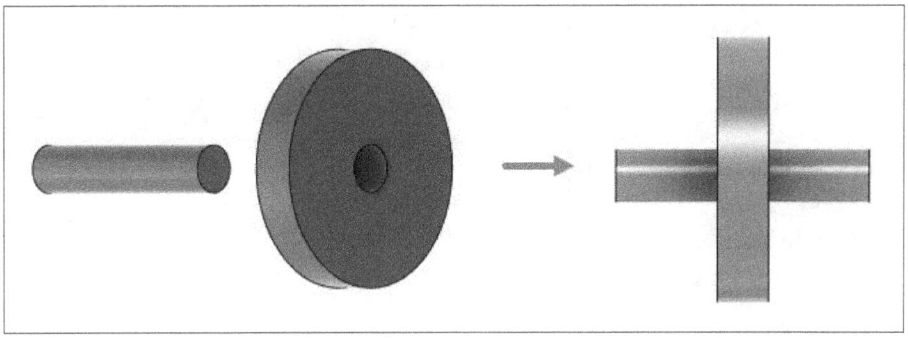

Figure-53. Center constraint applied

Tangent Constraint Type

The **Tangent** option is used to create tangent relationship between face on a body in one component and a set of connected faces on a body in another component within an assembly in Fusion. The procedure to use this option is discussed next.

- Select **Tangent** option from **Type** area of **CONSTRAIN COMPONENTS** dialog box, the options will be displayed as shown in Figure-54.

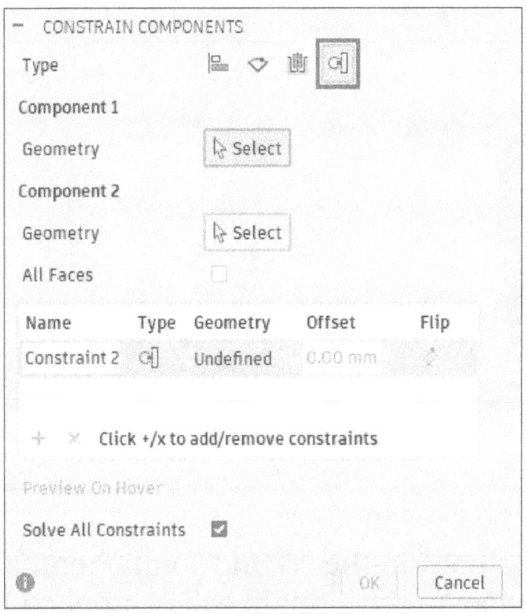

Figure-54. CONSTRAIN COMPONENTS dialog box with Tangent constraint options

- The **Geometry** selection button of **Component 1** area is active by default. Select a face on the body of first component; refer to Figure-55.

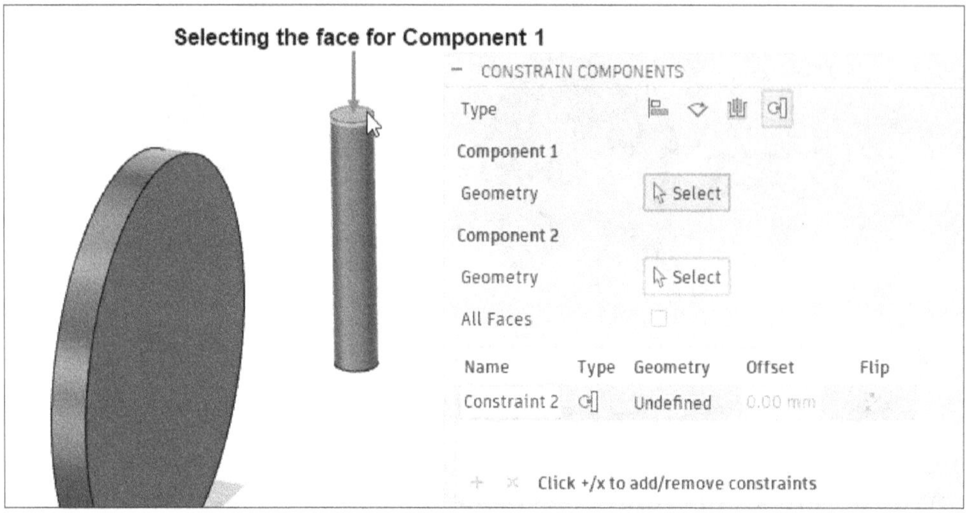

Figure-55. Selecting the face of first component

- After selecting face on a body in the first component, select the face on a body in the second component as shown in Figure-56.

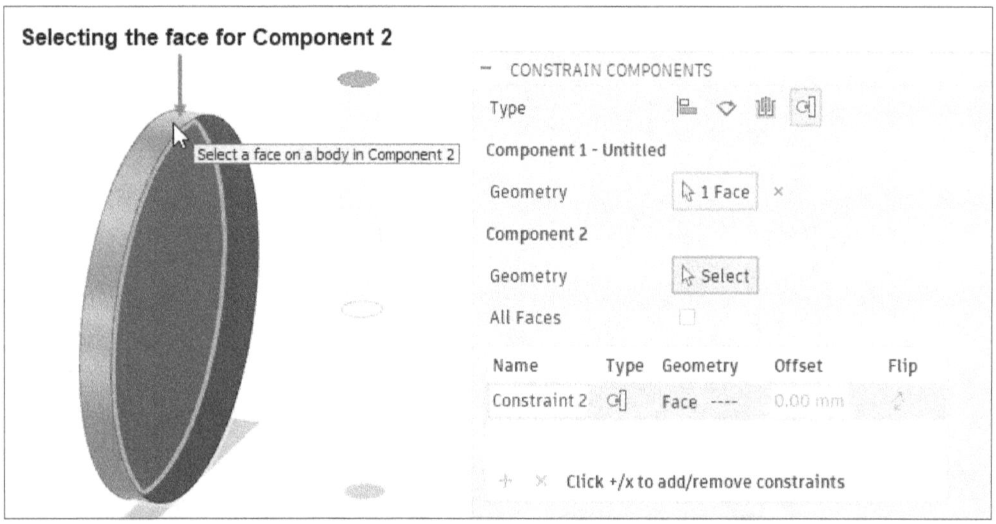

Figure-56. Selecting the face of second component

- After selecting face on a body in the second component, click on the **OK** button from the dialog box. The tangent relationship will be applied between the components; refer to Figure-57.

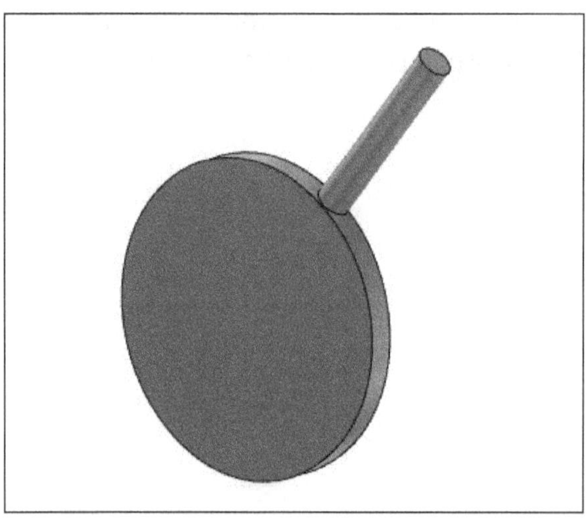

Figure-57. Tangent relationship applied between the components

DRIVE JOINTS

The **Drive Joints** tool is used to specify the rotation angle or distance value based on joint's degrees of freedom. The procedure to use this tool is discussed next.

- Click on the **Drive Joints** tool from **ASSEMBLE** drop-down in the **Toolbar**; refer to Figure-58. The **DRIVE JOINTS** dialog box will be displayed; refer to Figure-59.

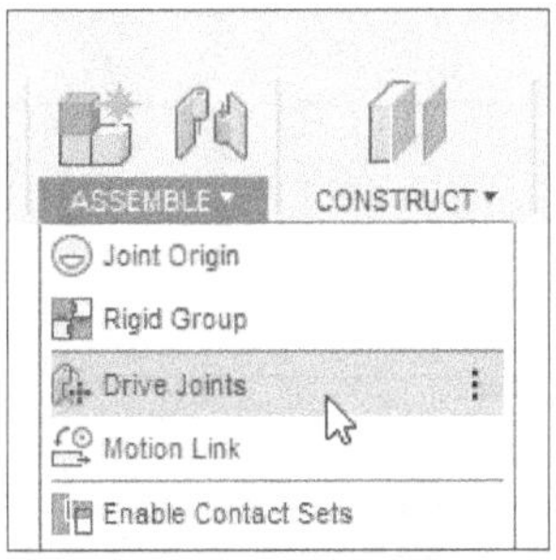

Figure-58. Drive Joints tool

Figure-59. DRIVE JOINTS dialog box

- The **Joint Input** selection is active by default. Click on the joint from model. The updated **DRIVE JOINTS** dialog box will be displayed; refer to Figure-60.

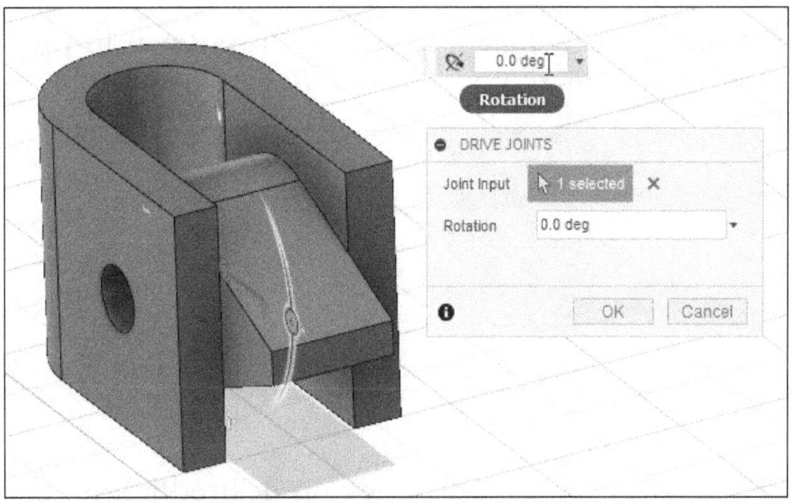

Figure-60. Updated DRIVE JOINTS dialog box

- Click in the **Rotation** edit box and specify the angle of rotation. You can also specify rotation limits by moving the drag handle; refer to Figure-61.

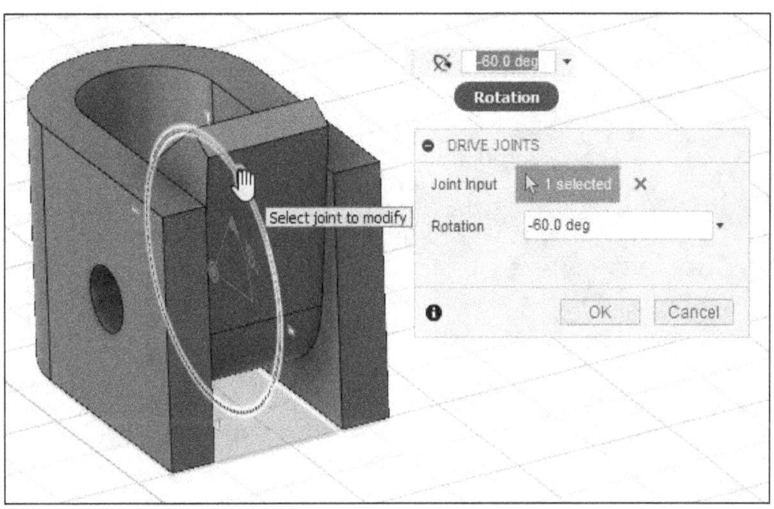

Figure-61. Specifying the rotation limits

- After specifying the parameters, click on the **OK** button from **DRIVE JOINTS** dialog box.

Note that on changing position of joint after driving, the **POSITION** panel is displayed in the **SOLID** tab of **Toolbar**; refer to Figure-62. Select the **Capture Position** tool from the panel if you want to make current position of joint as new start position. Select the **Revert Position** option from the panel if you want to revert the joint to original position.

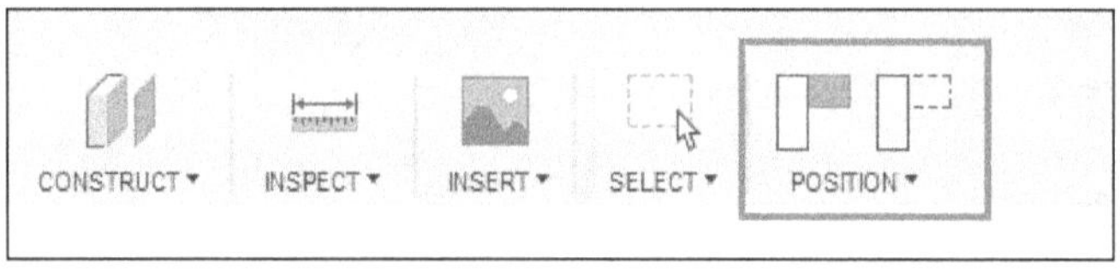

Figure-62. POSITION panel

MOTION LINK

The **Motion Link** tool is used to specify the relationship between motion of two selected joints like relation between two gear rotation or relation between bolt rotation and translation while fastening. The procedure to use this tool is discussed next.

- Click on the **Motion Link** tool from **ASSEMBLE** drop-down in the **Toolbar**; refer to Figure-63. The **MOTION LINK** dialog box will be displayed; refer to Figure-64.

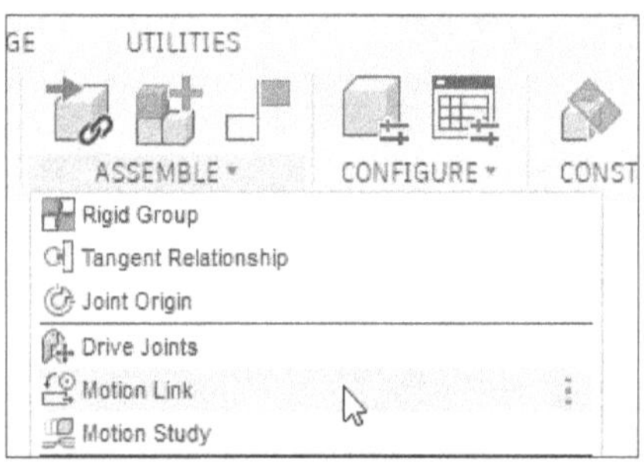

Figure-63. Motion Link tool

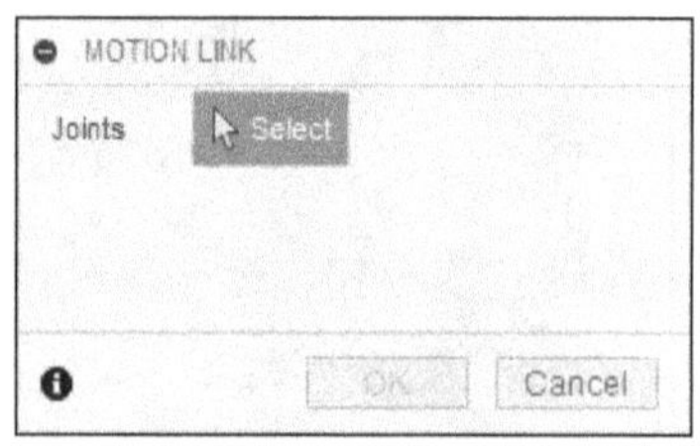

Figure-64. MOTION LINK dialog box

- **Joints** selection is active by default. Click on desired joints. In our case, we are selecting the slider and revolve joints to create a motion of vice.
- On selecting the two joints, the animation of vice will start and the dialog box will be updated; refer to Figure-65.

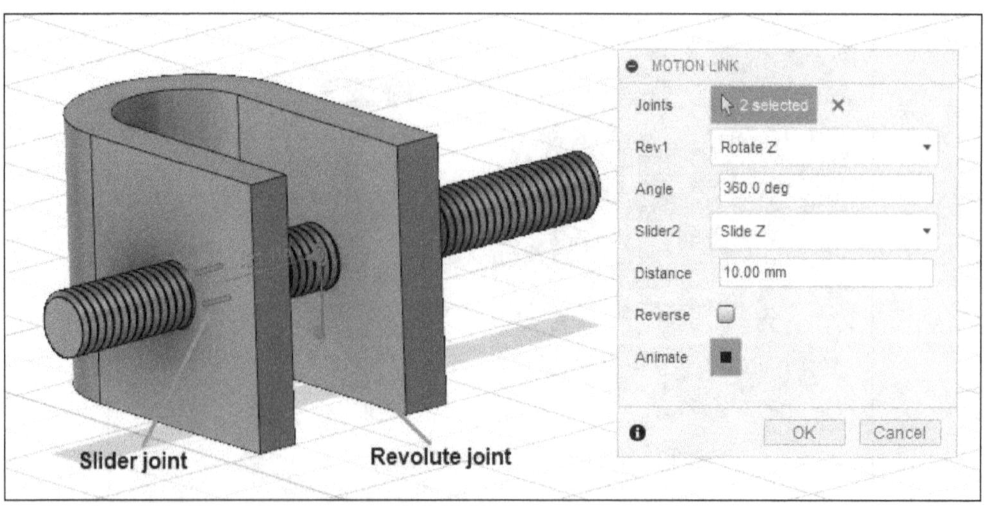

Figure-65. Selection of joints for Motion Link

- Click in the **Distance** edit box of **MOTION LINK** dialog box and specify the value of distance per revolution.
- Click in the **Angle** edit box of **MOTION LINK** dialog box and specify the value of angle of revolution. The combination of distance and angle value define the range of motion like in our case, for one full rotation of **360** degree by handle, the jaw will move **10 mm** of distance.
- Select the **Reverse** check box of **MOTION LINK** dialog box, if you want to reverse the direction of revolution.
- Click on the **Animate** button to watch the animation of joints.
- After specifying the parameters, click on **OK** button of **MOTION LINK** dialog box to complete the process; refer to Figure-66.

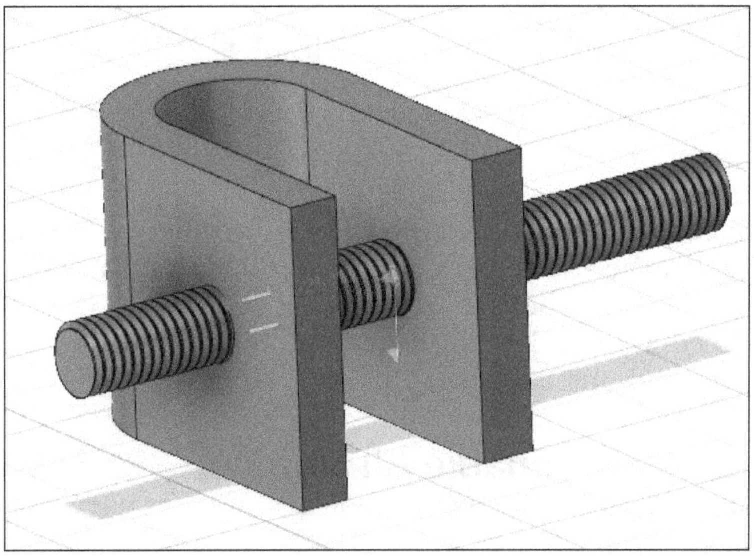

Figure-66. Motion Link created between joints

ENABLE CONTACT SETS

The **Enable Contact Sets** tool is used to enable the physical contact conditions. The procedure to use this tool is discussed next.

- Click on the **Enable Contact Sets** tool from **ASSEMBLE** drop-down in the **Toolbar**; refer to Figure-67. The tool will be displayed in **BROWSER**; refer to Figure-68.

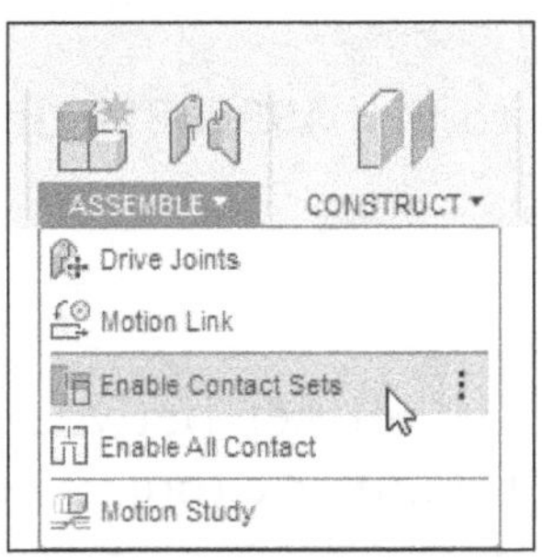

Figure-67. Enable Contact Sets tool

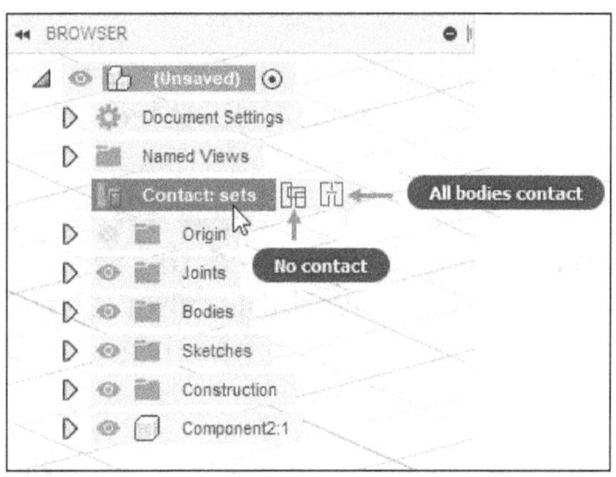

Figure-68. Contact sets

- Click on **All Bodies Contact** button to activate the contact analysis between sets; refer to Figure-69.

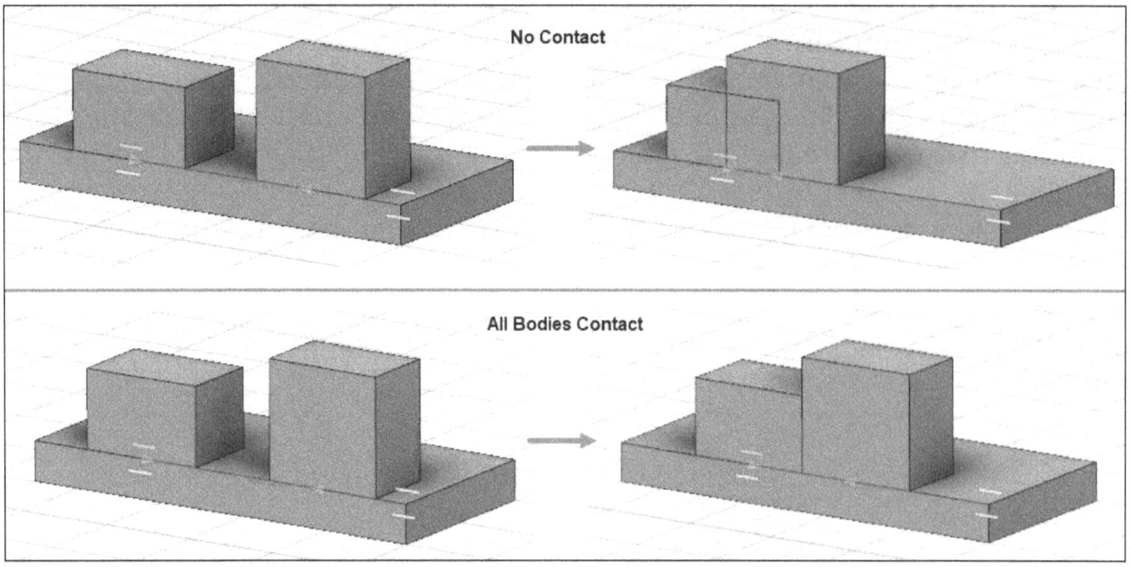

Figure-69. Applying contact sets tool

- Click on **No Contact** button to disable the contact between sets.
- In the above figure, the first case is with contact sets not active and the second case is with contact sets active. So, when contact set is active then physical properties of objects are taken into account like one solid object cannot pass through another solid object.

Enable All Contact

The **Enable All Contact** tool is used to enable all contacts which were applied earlier in the part or model.

- To enable contact, click on the **Enable All Contact** tool from **ASSEMBLE** drop-down in the **Toolbar**. All contacts will be enabled and the **ASSEMBLE** drop-down will be updated with two new tools which are discussed next.

Disable Contact

The **Disable Contact** tool is used to disable all contacts which were made earlier in the part or model.

- To disable contact, click on the **Disable Contact** tool of **ASSEMBLE** drop-down from **Toolbar**. All contacts will be disabled.

New Contact Set

The **New Contact Set** tool is used to create new contact set between two selected components. This tool is available when **Enable All Contact** tool is selected. These contact sets prevent parts from passing through one another. The procedure to use this tool is discussed next.

- Click on the **New Contact Set** tool from **ASSEMBLE** drop-down in the **Toolbar**; refer to Figure-70. The **NEW CONTACT SET** dialog box will be displayed; refer to Figure-71.

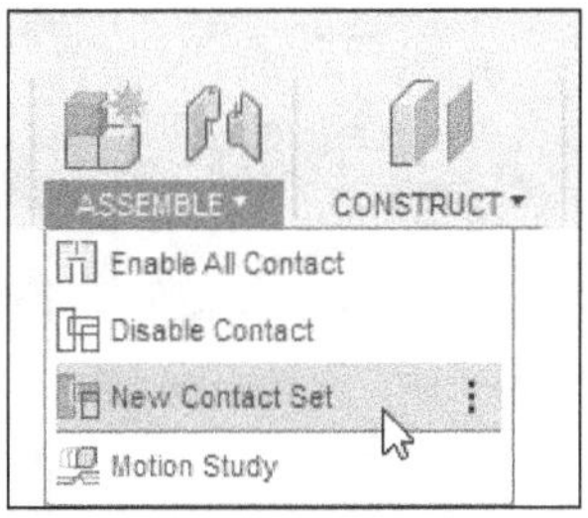

Figure-70. New Contact Set tool

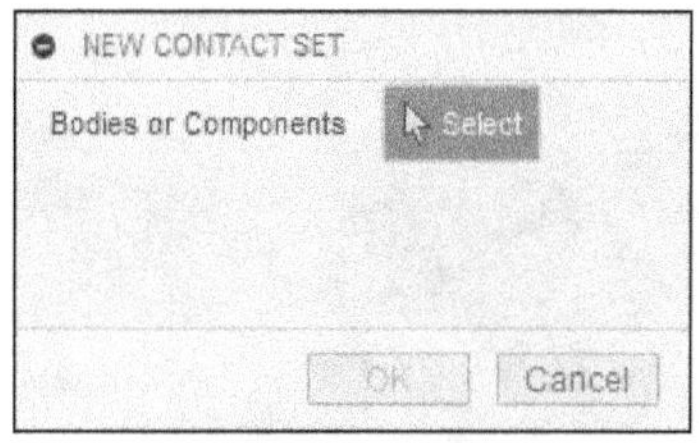

Figure-71. NEW CONTACT SET dialog box

- The **Select** button of **Bodies or Components** section is active by default. Select the two component or bodies to create sets and click on **OK** button from **NEW CONTACT SET** dialog box to complete the process.

MOTION STUDY

The **Motion Study** tool is used to perform kinematic motion analysis based on joints. The procedure to use this tool is discussed next.

- Click on the **Motion Study** tool from **ASSEMBLE** drop-down in the **Toolbar**; refer to Figure-72. The **Motion Study** dialog box will be displayed; refer to Figure-73.

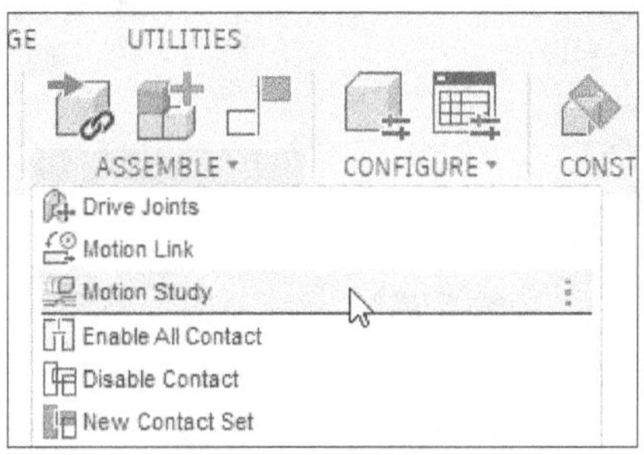

Figure-72. Motion Study tool

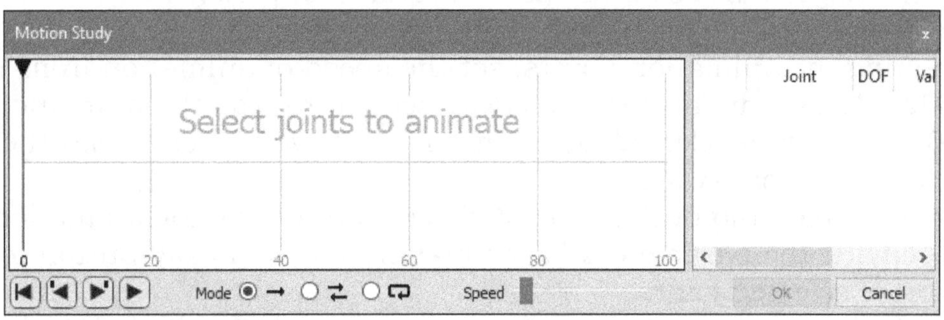

Figure-73. Motion Study dialog box

- You need to select the joint from part or model. Click to select the joint; refer to Figure-74.

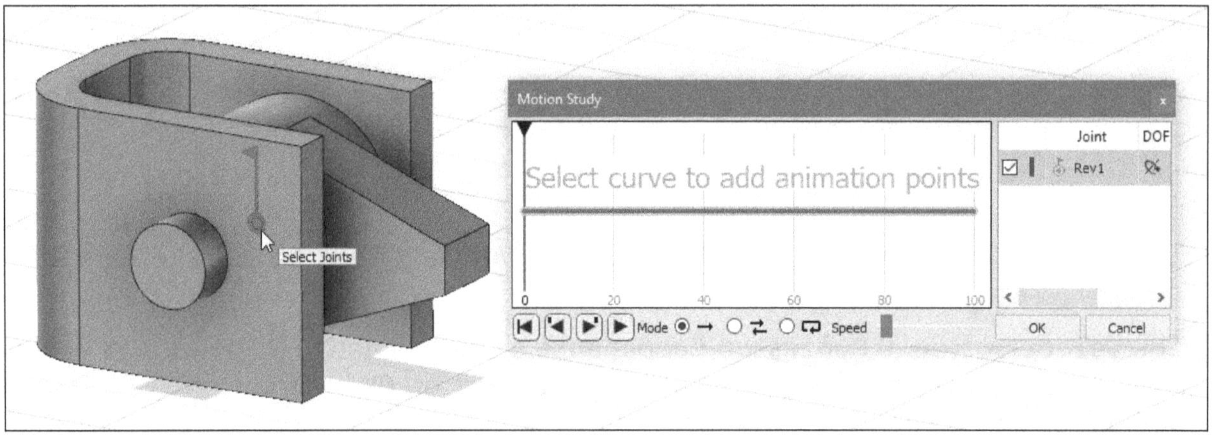

Figure-74. Selecting joint for animation

- After selecting joint, create the points of motion curve as required by clicking in the graph line of motion; refer to Figure-75.

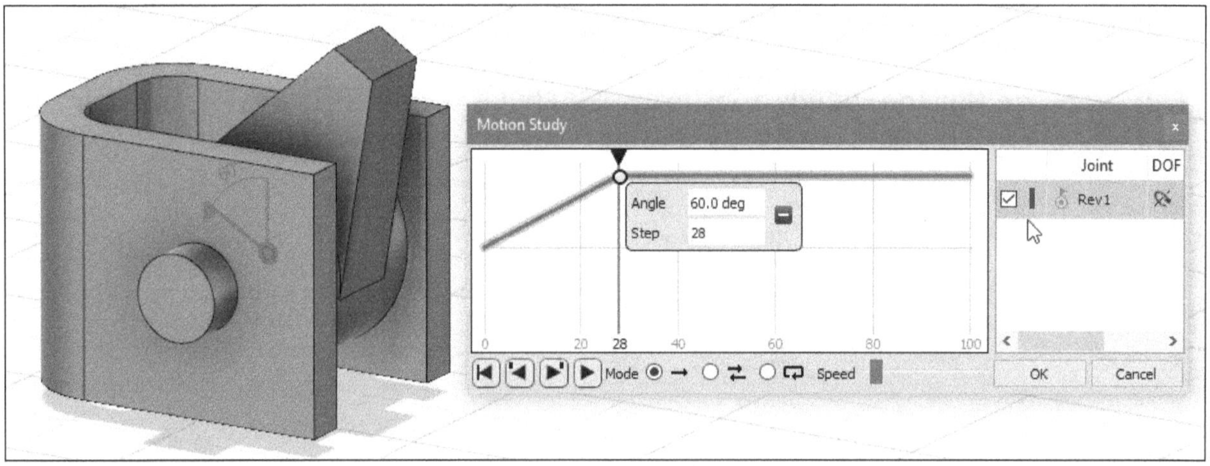

Figure-75. Adjusting points for animation

- Click in the **Angle** edit box and specify required angle for animation point. Note that the options will be displayed based on selected joint.
- After creating the animation points, set the speed of animation from **Speed** bar.
- Select **Play Once** radio button from **Mode** section to play the animation once.
- Select **Play Forward/Backward** radio button from **Mode** section to play the animation forward and then backward.
- Select **Play Loop** radio button from **Mode** section to play the animation in cycle.
- After specifying the parameters for animation, click on **Play** button to check the animation of selected joint.
- Click on **OK** button from **Motion Study** dialog box to exit the motion study of components.

BILL OF MATERIALS

The **Bill of Materials** tool is used to display the bill of materials (list of components with purchase related details) for the current design. The procedure to use this tool is discussed next.

- Click on the **Bill of Materials** tool from the **MANAGE** tab in the **Toolbar**. The **BILL OF MATERIALS** dialog box will be displayed; refer to Figure-76.

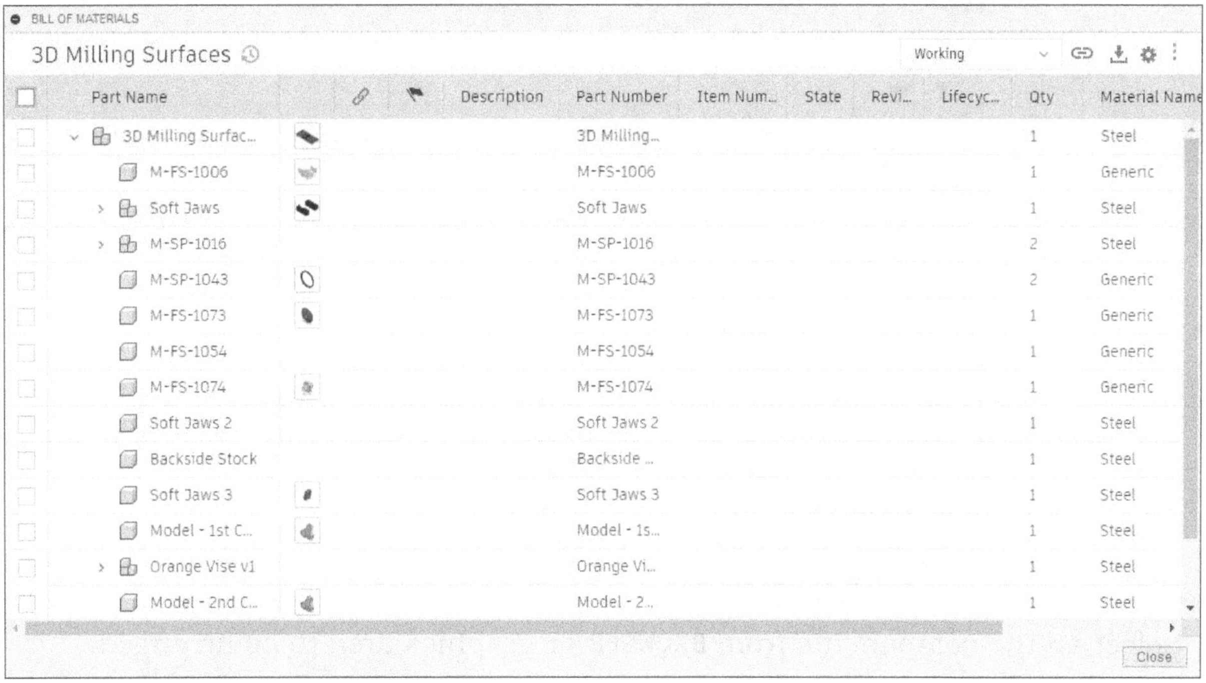

Figure-76. BILL OF MATERIALS dialog box

- Click on the **Refresh** button to update the bill of materials with the changes made to the referenced components.
- Select **Working** option from **BOM Switcher** drop-down to create BOM for the design currently working on and select **Released** option from the drop-down to create BOM for the recently released version of the current design.
- Click on the **Copy Link** button to share a link of the current bill of materials with the other members of the community.
- Click on the **Export BOM** button to download the bill of materials to the current device as an Excel or CSV file.
- Click on the **Manage Extension** button to access the manage extension functions on subscription basis. These options are not active in educational version.

ARRANGING COMPONENTS IN ENCLOSURES

The **Arrange** tool is used to arrange assembly components in a specified 2D or 3D enclosure utilizing the space optimally. The procedure to use this tool is given next.

- Click on the **Arrange** tool from the **MODIFY** drop-down in the **SOLID** tab of **Toolbar**. The **ARRANGE** dialog box will be displayed; refer to Figure-77 and you will be asked to select components for arranging.

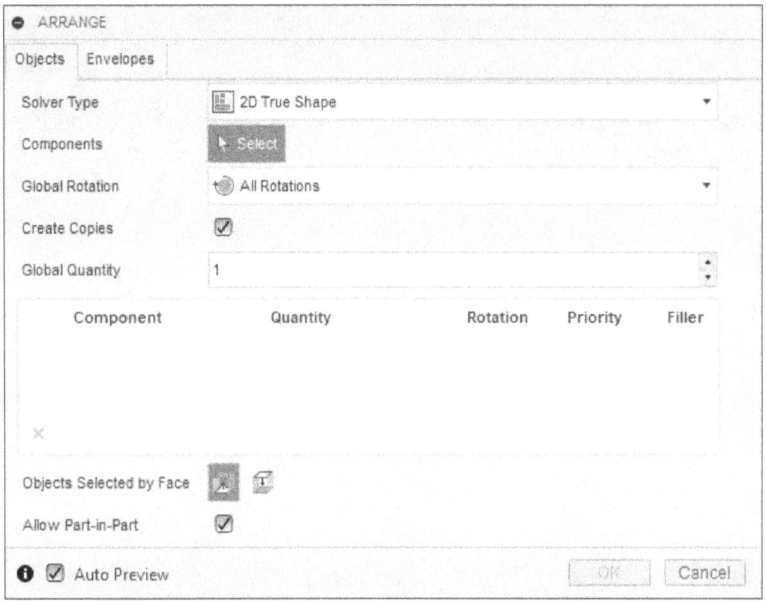

Figure-77. ARRANGE dialog box

- Select all the components from **BROWSER** or graphics area to be arranged.

Arranging in 2 Dimensions

- Select the **2D True Shape**, **2D Rectangular**, or **3D Arrange** option from the **Solver Type** drop-down to arrange components in 2D plane. Select the **2D True Shape** option if your components are of irregular shape and can be densely packed. Select the **2D Rectangular** option from the drop-down if your components are rectangular in shape. Select the **3D Arrange** option to arrange components in 3D space within a given volume.
- Select desired option from **Global Rotation** drop-down to specify the rotation type in which the components can be rotated within the arrangement.
- Select the **Create Copies** check box to create copies of the components to use for the arrangement.
- Specify desired quantity for all the components in the **Global Quantity** edit box.
- Select the **Face Up** button from **Objects Selected by Face** section if you want the selected faces of object to point upward when arranging them. Similarly, select the **Face Down** button if you want the faces of selected objects to be pointing downward when arranging them.
- Click on the **Envelopes** tab to define the boundaries for arranging components. The options will be displayed as shown in Figure-78 and you will be asked to select a plane/face/sketch for defining boundary of envelope.
- If you have selected a sketch then components will be automatically arranged within sketch boundary and options will be displayed as shown in Figure-79.
- Select **Allow Partial Arrange** check box if you want to arrange as many components as possible when there is not sufficient space in envelope. Clear this check box if you want to generate an error when there is no sufficient space for all the components in envelope.

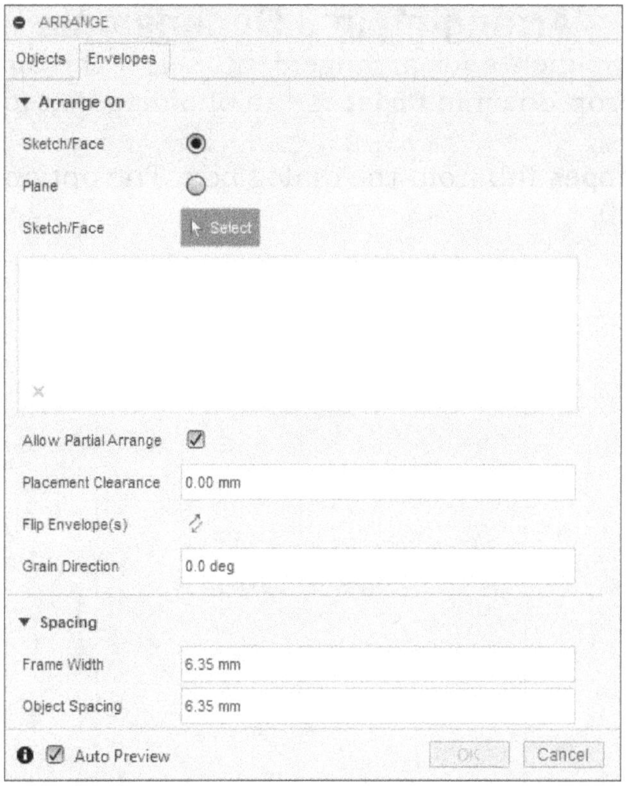

Figure-78. Envelopes tab

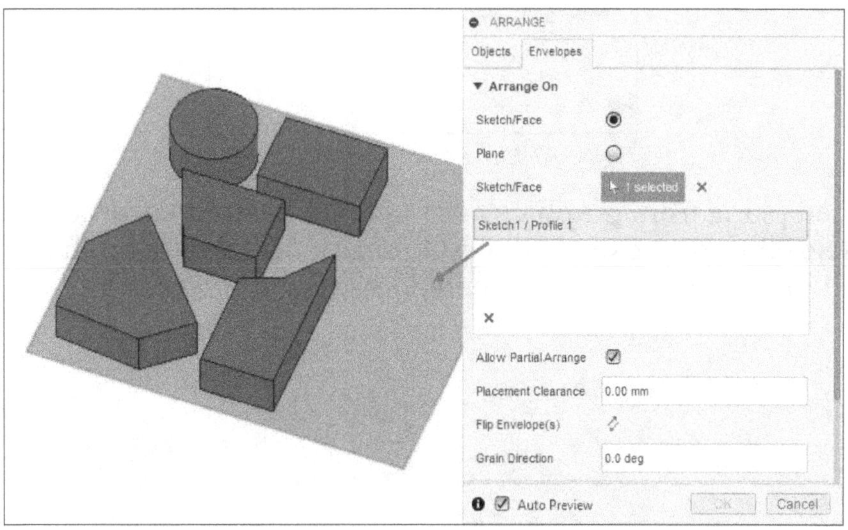

Figure-79. Arranging in 2D sketch

- Specify desired value in **Placement Clearance** edit box to raise the components from sketch plane at respective height.
- Click on the **Flip Envelope(s)** button to reverse the arrangement between above and below plane.
- Set desired value in the **Grain Direction** edit box to define angle for orienting components.
- Set desired values in the **Frame Width** edit box to define distance from border at which objects will be placed after arrangement.
- Specify desired value in the **Object Spacing** edit box to define the distance between current object and nearby objects in the arrangement.

Arranging in 3 Dimensions

- After selecting components for arrangement, select the **3D Arrange** option from the **Solver Type** drop-down in **Objects** tab of dialog box to arrange components in 3 dimensions.
- Click on the **Envelopes** tab from the dialog box. The options will be displayed as shown in Figure-80.

Figure-80. Envelopes tab for 3D

- Select desired plane from graphics area and set desired parameters in the **Length**, **Width**, and **Height** edit boxes to define limits of 3D envelope. The components will be arranged automatically in 3 dimension; refer to Figure-81.

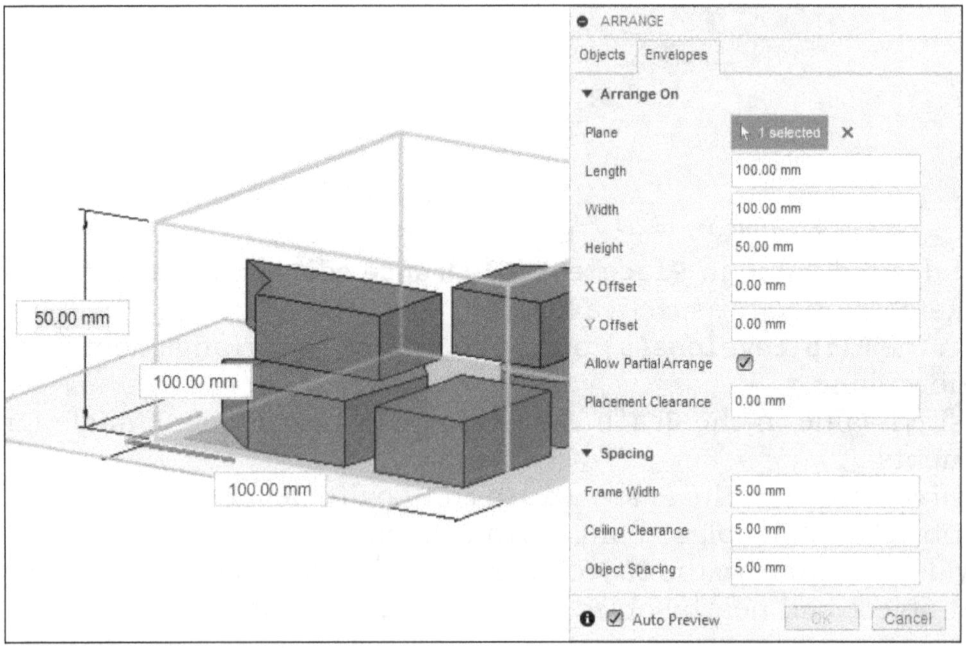

Figure-81. 3D envelope arrangement

- Enter desired value in the **X Offset** and **Y Offset** edit boxes to specify the distance between the envelope origin and the main origin along the x-axis and y-axis, respectively.
- In the **Spacing** section of dialog box, set desired parameters in edit boxes to define spacing of components with respect to frame, ceiling, and consecutive objects.
- After setting parameters, click on the **OK** button to generate the arrangement.

AUTOMATED MODELING

The **Automated Modeling** tool is used to automatically generate designs for an assembly part based on specified connecting faces and avoiding bodies. The tool generates freeform shapes that can be used as base reference for further designing the components. The procedure to use this tool is given next.

- Click on the **Automated Modeling** tool from the **CREATE** drop-down in the **Toolbar**. The **AUTOMATED MODELING** dialog box will be displayed; refer to Figure-82 and you will be asked to select faces to be connected.

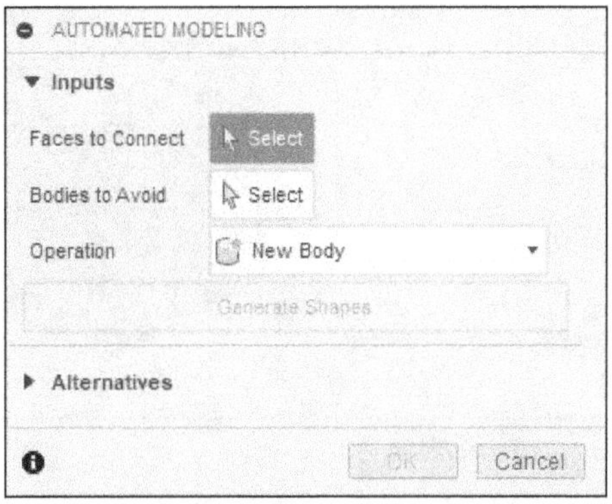

Figure-82. AUTOMATED MODELING dialog box

- Select the faces to be connected by automated modeling and click on the **Select** button for **Bodies to Avoid** section. You will be asked to select the bodies to be avoided.
- Select desired bodies/components to be avoided; refer to Figure-83.

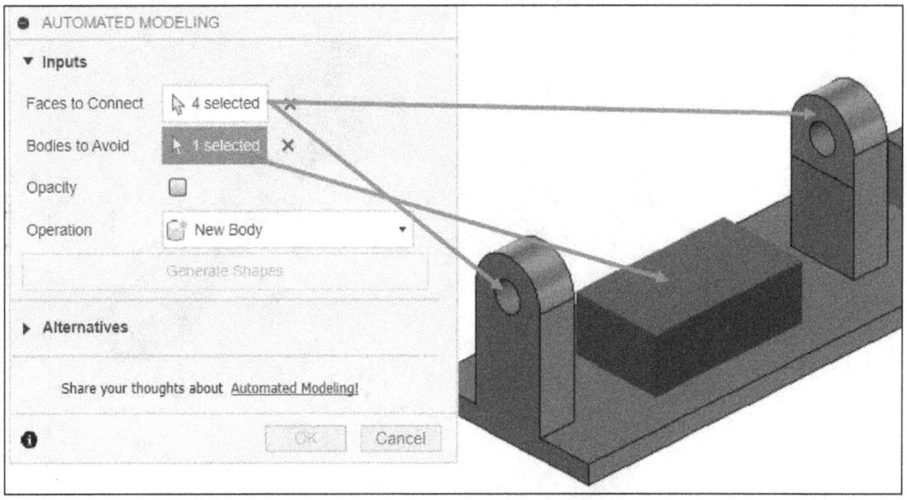

Figure-83. Selection for automated modeling

- Select the **Opacity** check box to make the avoidance bodies transparent.
- Select the **New Body** option from the **Operation** drop-down if you want to create a new body by automated modeling. Select the **New Component** option from the drop-down if you want to create a new component using automated modeling.
- Click on the **Generate Shapes** button from the dialog box to generate the shapes. After calculation, preview of alternatives will be displayed; refer to Figure-84.

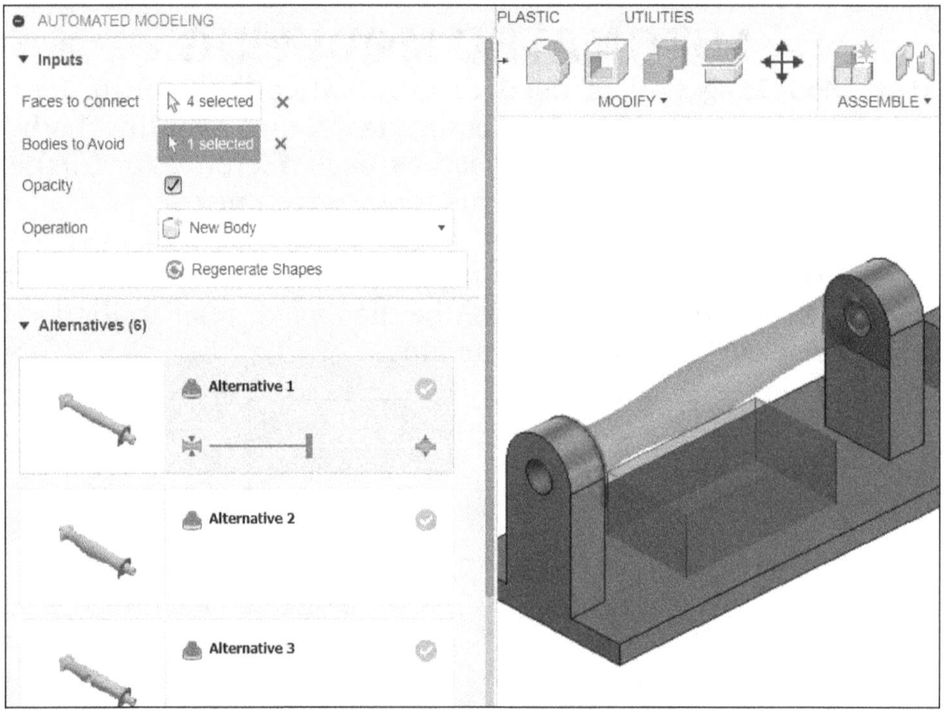

Figure-84. Preview of model alternatives

- Select desired alternative and click on the **OK** button to create the model.

PRACTICAL 1

Assemble the parts of handle as shown in Figure-85. The exploded view of assembly is displayed as shown in Figure-86.

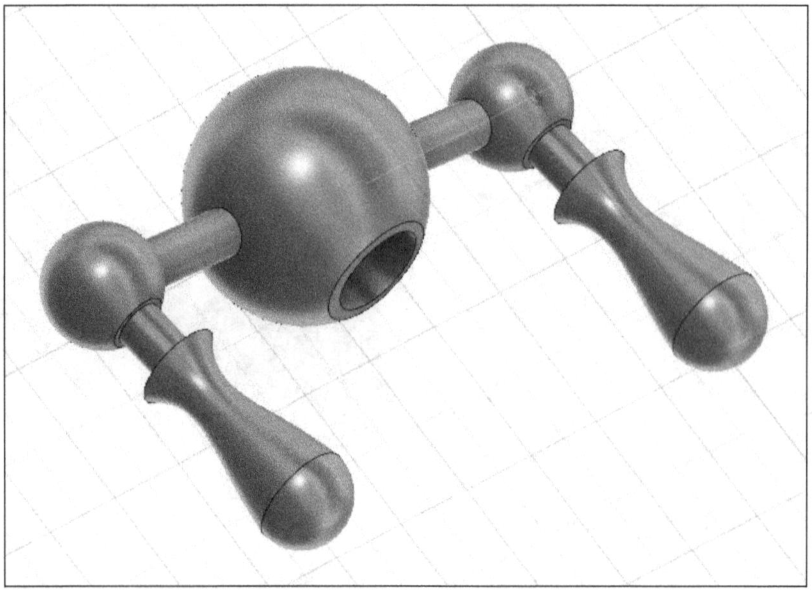

Figure-85. Assembled handle

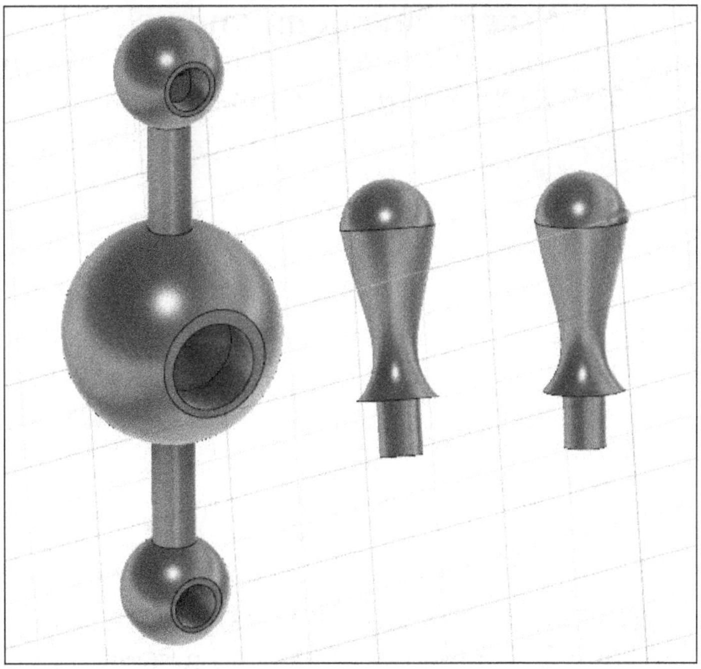

Figure-86. Exploded view of handle

All the part files can be downloaded from resource kit of Fusion software, which is available at **WWW.CADCAMCAEWORKS.COM**.

The steps to assemble these parts are given next.

Adding file into Fusion

- After downloading the resource kit from **CADCAMCAEWORKS.COM**, open the **Chapter 7** folder.
- Double-click on **Handle v0.f3d** file. The file will open in **Autodesk Fusion** software; refer to Figure-87.

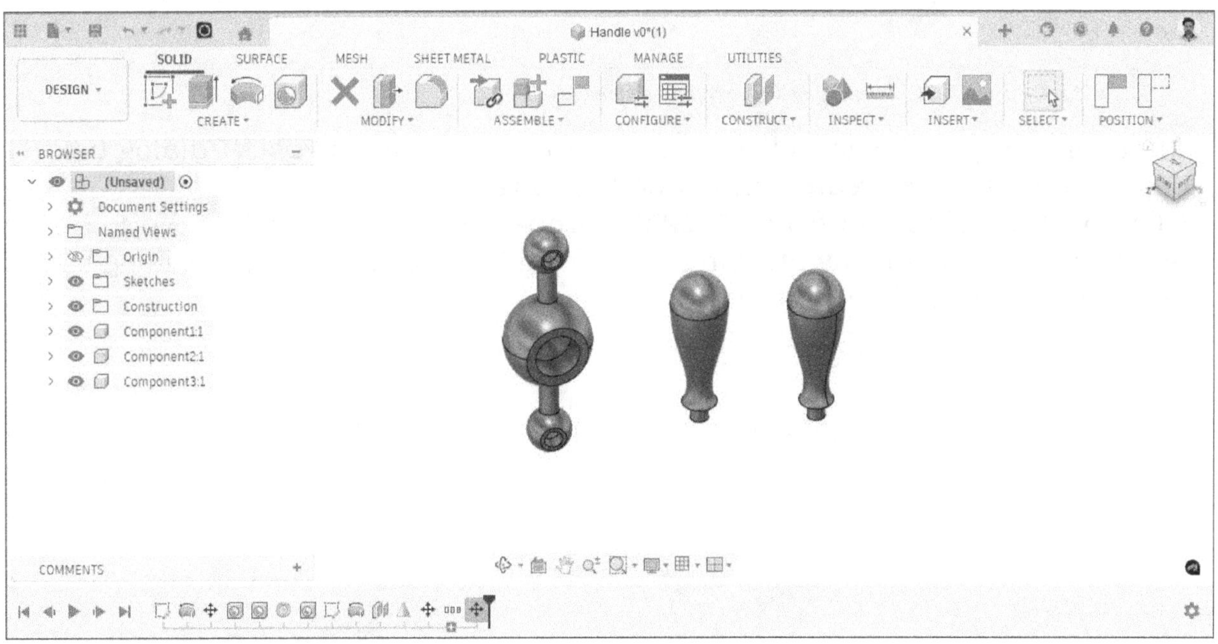

Figure-87. Fusion startup window

Assembling components

- Click on **New Component** tool from **ASSEMBLE** drop-down in the **Toolbar**; refer to Figure-88. The **NEW COMPONENT** dialog box will be displayed; refer to Figure-89.

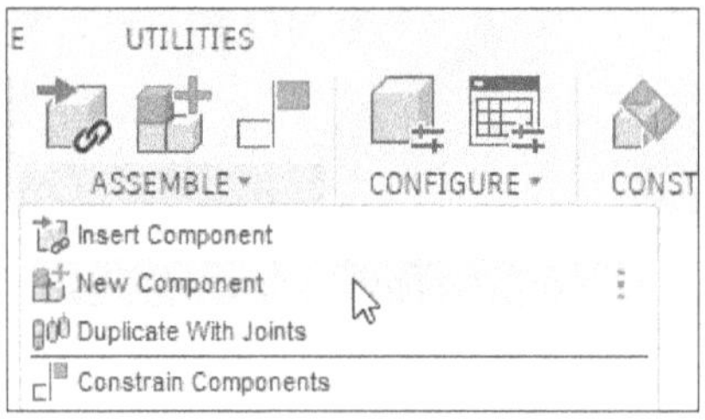

Figure-88. New Component tool

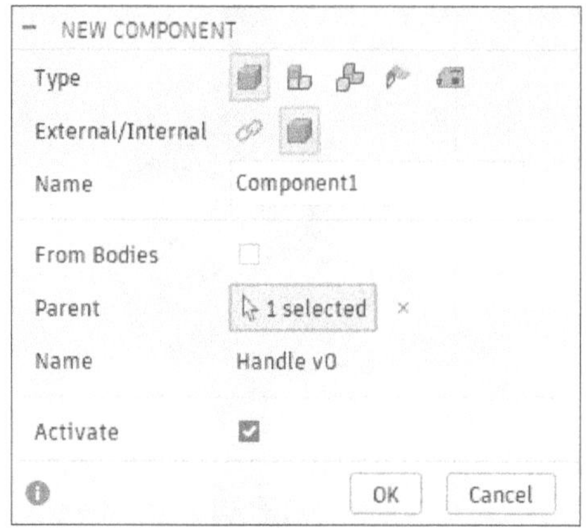

Figure-89. NEW COMPONENT dialog box

- Select the **From Bodies** check box from **NEW COMPONENT** dialog box and select all the bodies to make them component; refer to Figure-90.

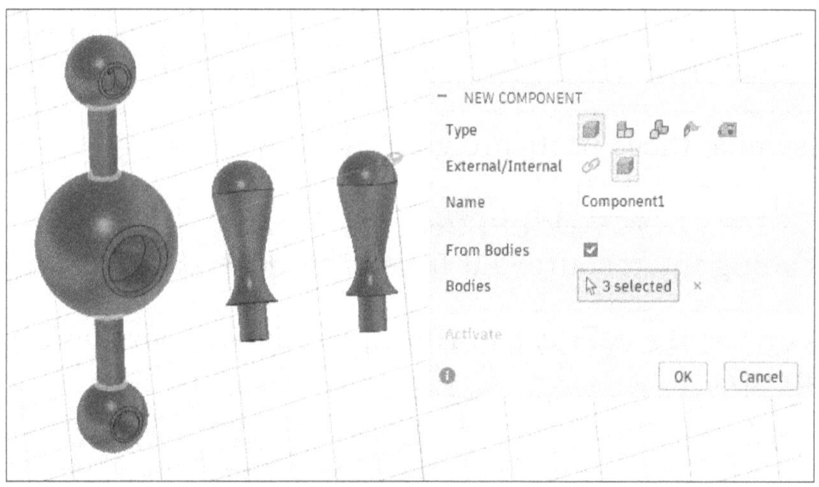

Figure-90. Selecting bodies to create components

- After selecting the bodies, click on **OK** button from **NEW COMPONENT** dialog box. The components will be created and added in **Timeline**.
- Click on the **Joint** tool from **ASSEMBLE** drop-down in the **Toolbar**. You can also activate the **Joint** tool by pressing **J** key from keyboard. The **JOINT** dialog box will be displayed; refer to Figure-91.

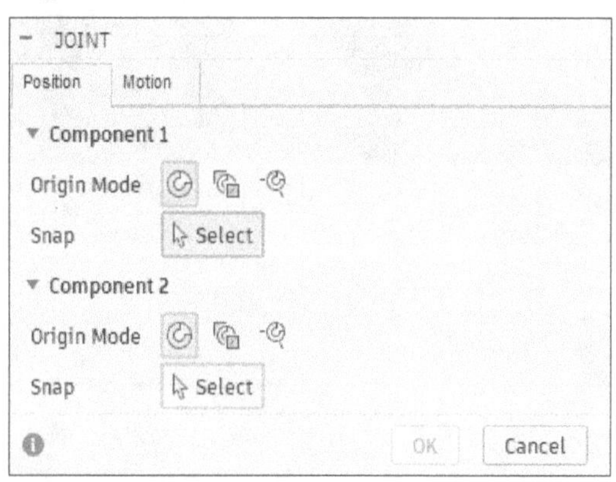

Figure-91. JOINT dialog box

- The **Select** button of **Snap** section from **Component 1** area in **Position** tab is selected by default. Click on the component to join; refer to Figure-92.

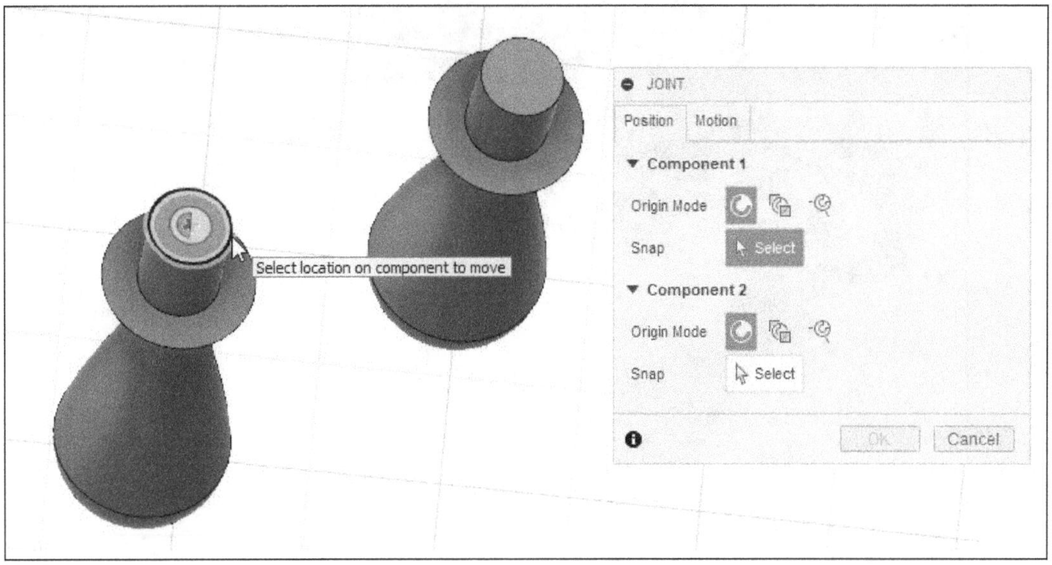

Figure-92. Selection of location on Component 1

- After selection of first component, select the second component; refer to Figure-93.

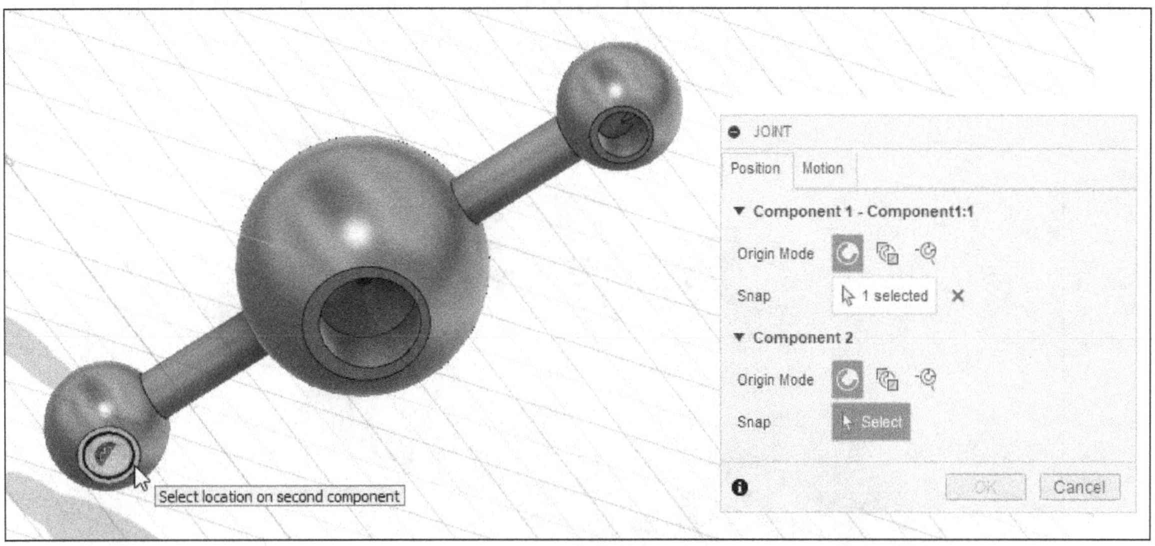

Figure-93. Selection of location on Component 2

- Select **Rigid** option from **Type** drop-down in **Motion** tab of the dialog box to create a rigid joint between two component.
- After specifying the parameters, click on **OK** button from **JOINT** dialog box to create a rigid joint.
- Similarly, create another rigid joint between other component.
- After joining these components, the assembly will be displayed as shown in Figure-94.

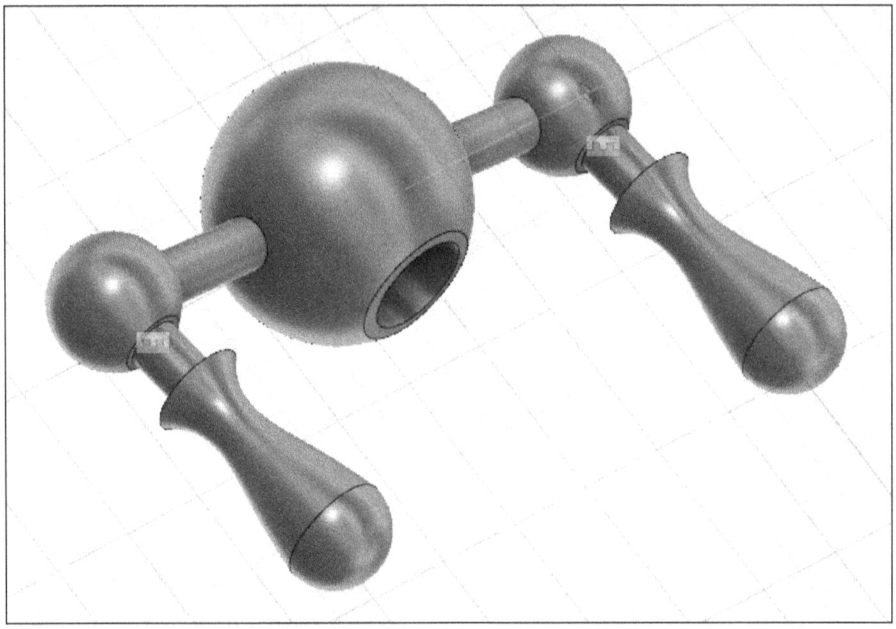

Figure-94. Final assembly of component

PRACTICAL 2

Assemble the parts of **F1 brake balance shifting mechanism** as shown in Figure-95. The exploded view of assembly is displayed as shown in Figure-96.

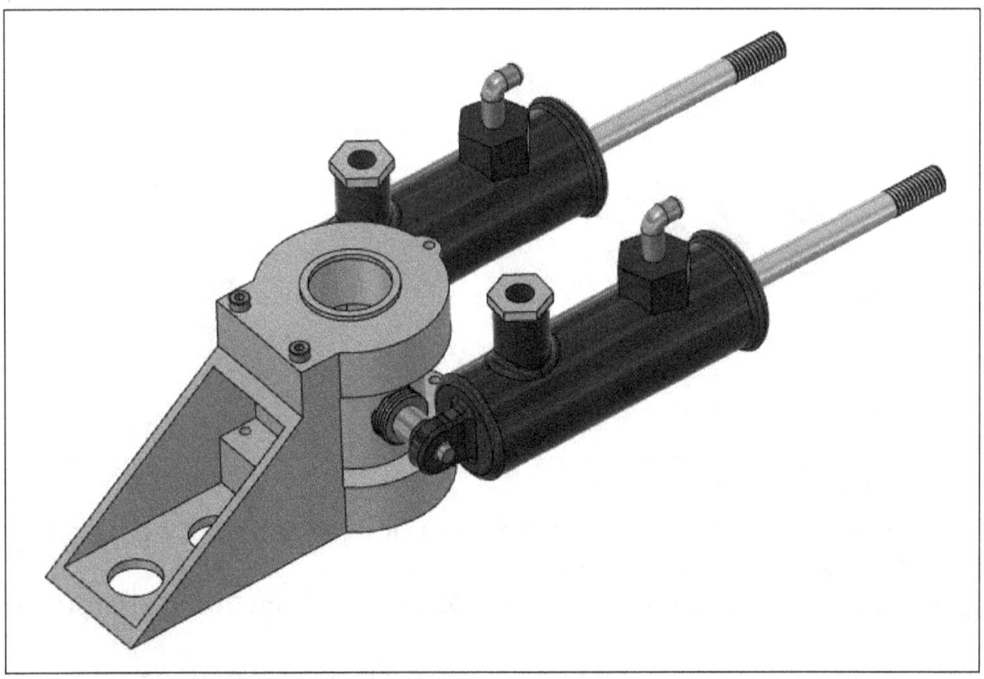

Figure-95. Brake balance shifting mechanism assembly

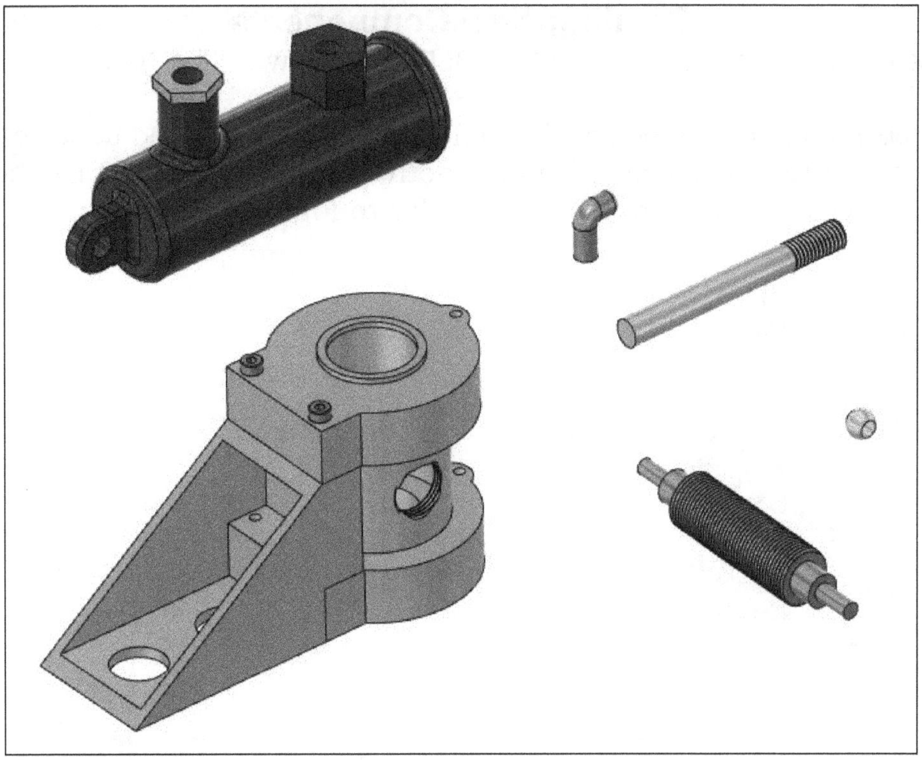

Figure-96. Exploded view of assembly

The steps to assemble these parts are given next.

Adding file into Fusion

- After downloading the resource kit from **CADCAMCAEWORKS.COM**, open the **Chapter 7** folder.
- Double-click on **F1 brake balance shifting mechanism.f3d** file. The file will open in **Autodesk Fusion** software; refer to Figure-97.

Figure-97. Fusion startup window

Creating New Components

- Select **New Component** tool from **ASSEMBLE** drop-down. The **NEW COMPONENT** dialog box will be displayed.
- Select **From Bodies** check box in the dialog box. You are asked to select the bodies.
- The **Select** button of **Bodies** section is active by default. Select the bodies which you want to convert into components; refer to Figure-98.

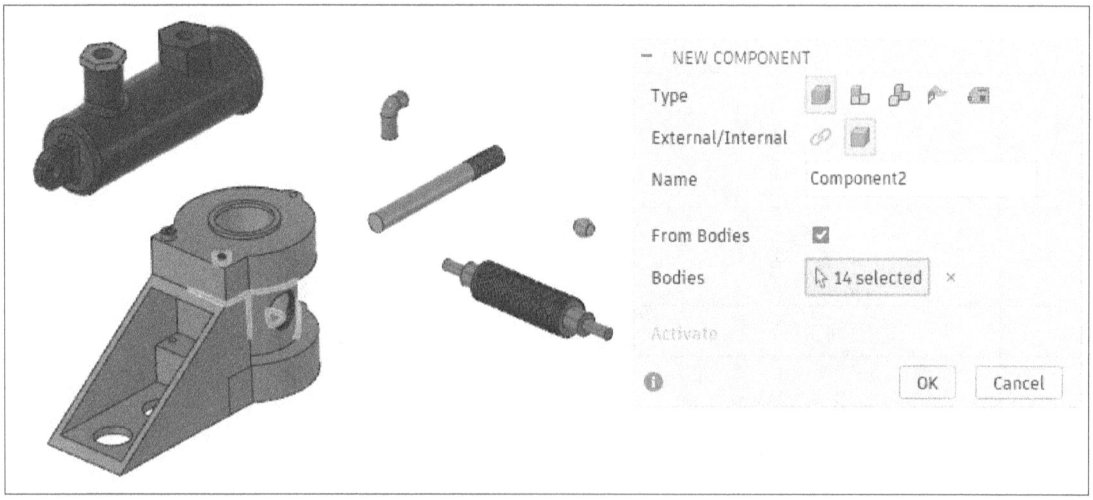

Figure-98. Selecting the bodies to create component

- Click on **OK** button from the dialog box to complete the process.

Assembling the Components

- Select **Joint** tool from **ASSEMBLE** drop-down. The **JOINT** dialog box will be displayed.
- Select **Between Two Faces** option from **Origin Mode** section of **Component 1** area in **Position** tab of the dialog box. You are asked to select the first face.
- The **Select** button of **Plane 1** section is active by default. Select first face of the component as shown in Figure-99. You are asked to select the second face.

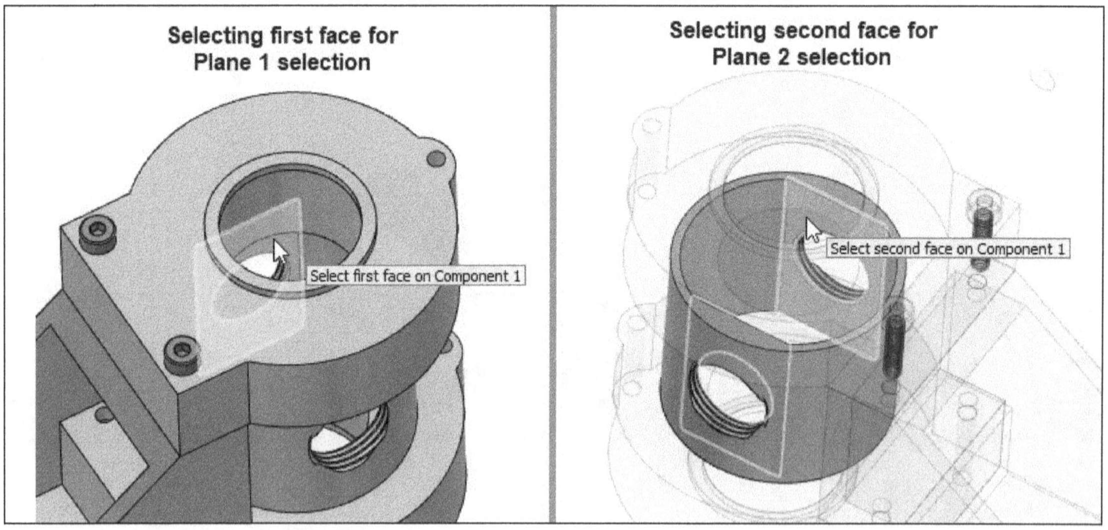

Figure-99. Selecting faces for Component 1

- The **Select** button of **Plane 2** section will become active. Select second face of component as shown in Figure-99. You are asked to select a snap point.
- The **Select** button of **Snap** section will become active. Select the snap point on the component as shown in Figure-100.

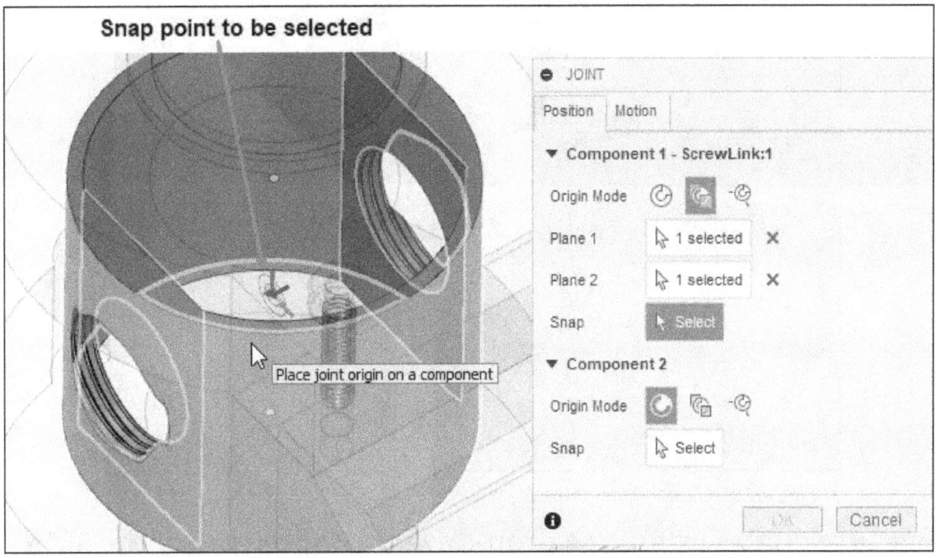

Figure-100. Selecting snap point for Component

- Similarly, select **Between Two Faces** option from **Origin Mode** section of **Component 2** area. You are asked to select first and second face of the component.
- Select first face of the component for **Plane 1** selection and select second face of the component for **Plane 2** selection as shown in the Figure-101. You are asked to select the snap point on the component.

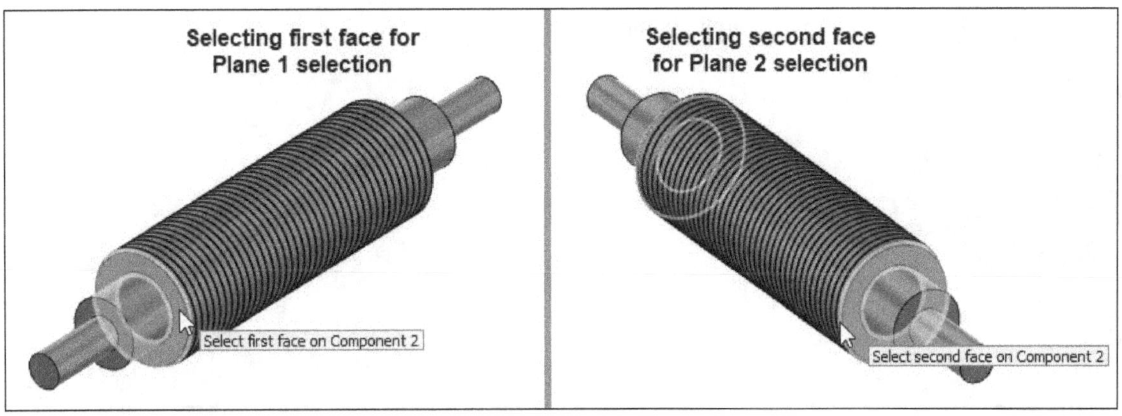

Figure-101. Selecting faces for Component 2

- The **Select** button of **Snap** section will become active. Select the snap point on the component as shown in Figure-102. The components will be joined together; refer to Figure-103.

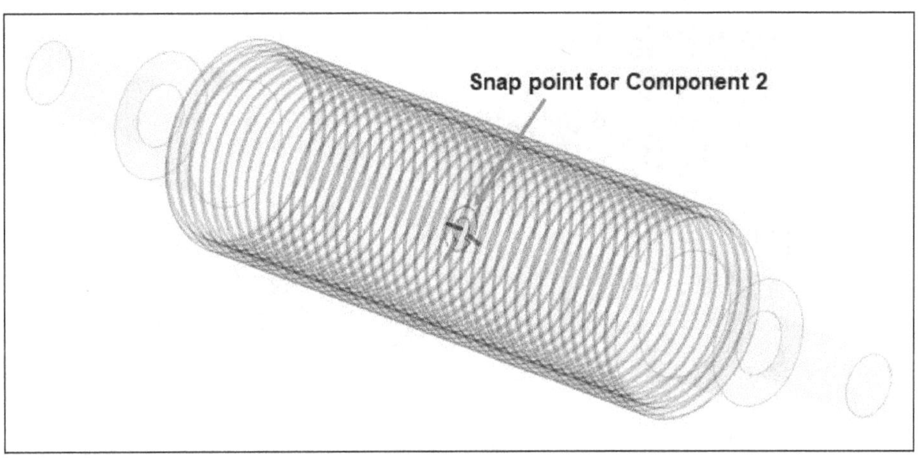

Figure-102. Selecting snap point for Component 2

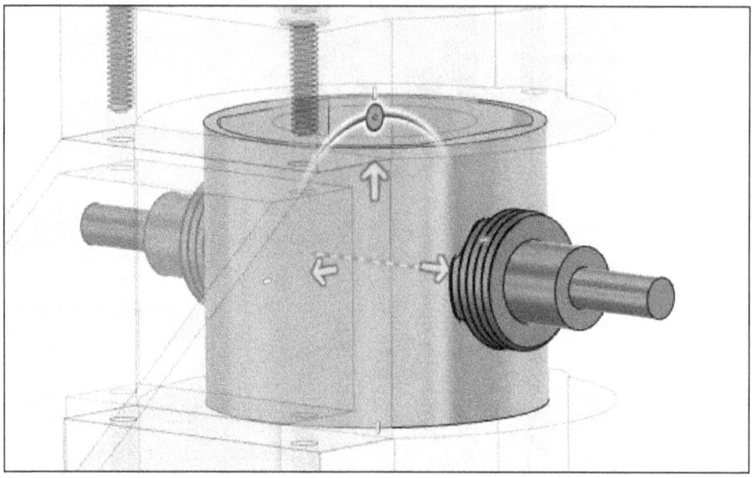

Figure-103. Components joined

- Select **Revolute** option from **Type** drop-down in **Motion** tab of the **JOINT** dialog box.
- After specifying parameters, click on the **OK** button from the dialog box to complete the process.
- Now, select **Joint** tool from **ASSEMBLE** drop-down. The **JOINT** dialog box will be displayed. You are asked to select the snap point on the components.
- Select snap point on both Component 1 and Component 2 as shown in Figure-104.

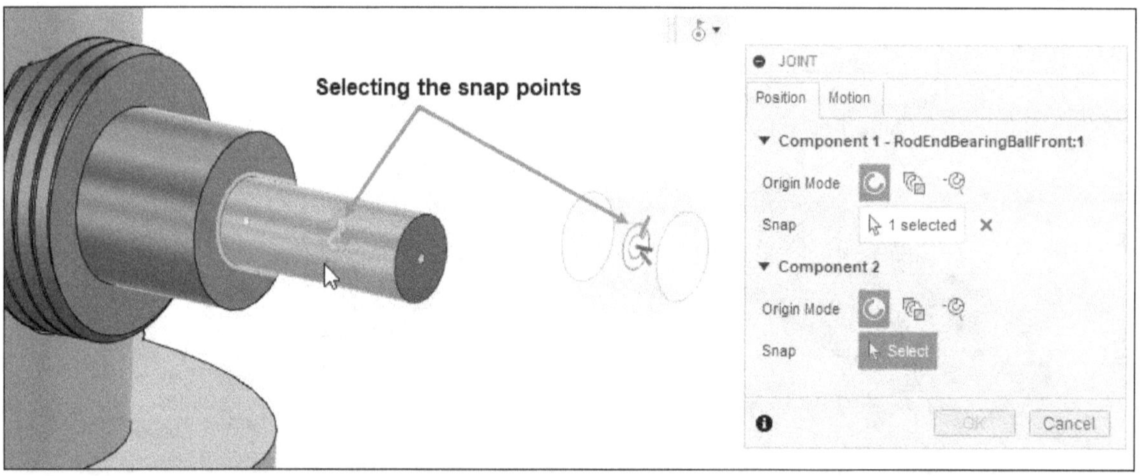

Figure-104. Selecting the snap points

- On selecting the snap point on second component, both the components will be joined; refer to Figure-105.

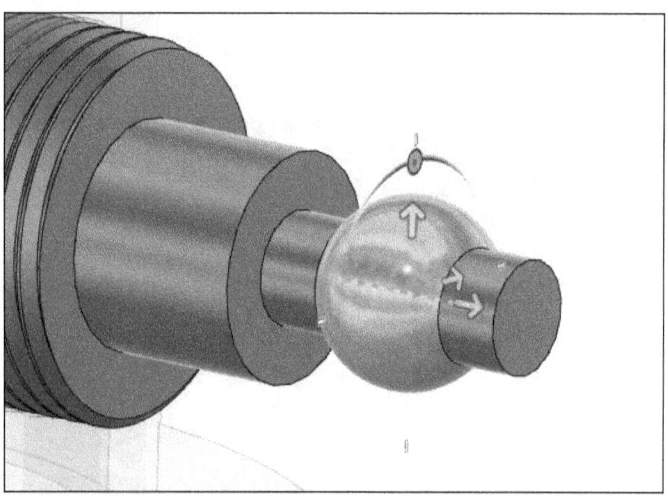

Figure-105. Components joined

- Select **Rigid** option from **Type** drop-down in **Motion** tab of the dialog box.
- After specifying parameters, click on the **OK** button from the dialog box to complete the process.
- Now, select **Joint** tool again from **ASSEMBLE** drop-down. The **Joint** dialog box will be displayed. You are asked to select the snap points on the components.
- Select snap point on both Component 1 and Component 2 as shown in Figure-106.

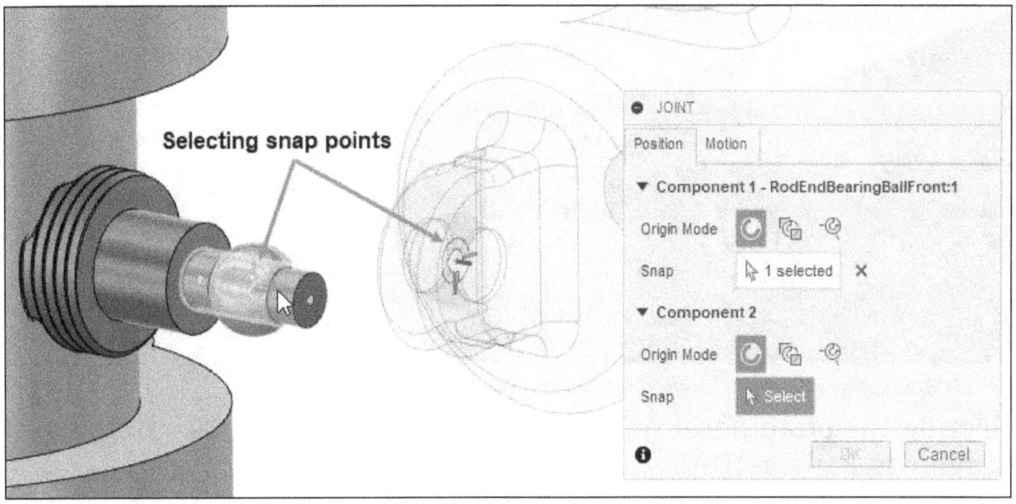

Figure-106. Selecting snap point on the components

- On selecting the snap point on second component, both the components will be joined; refer to Figure-107.

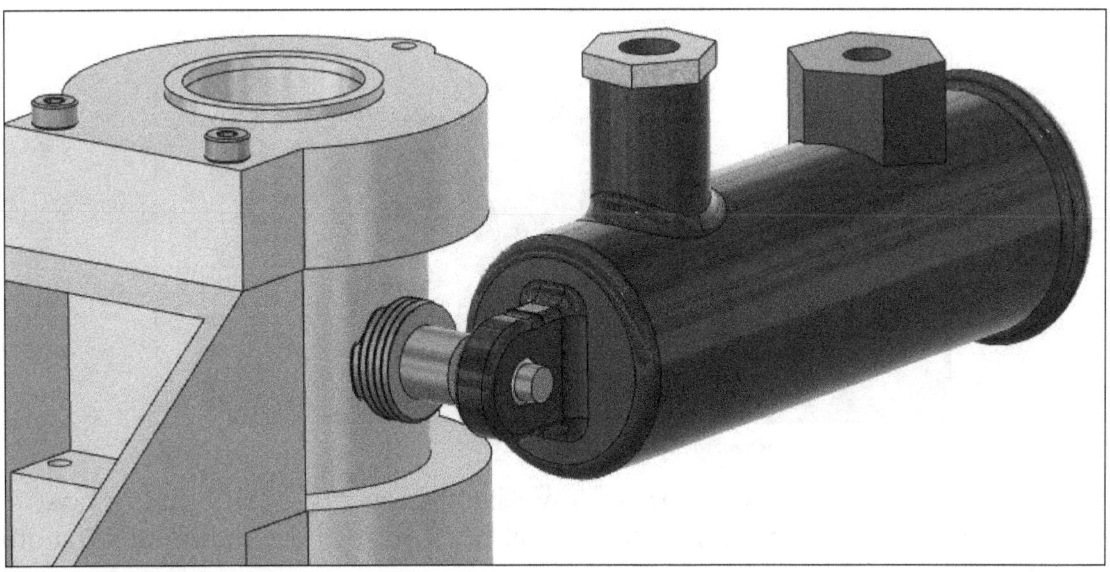

Figure-107. Components joined

- Select **Revolute** option from **Type** drop-down in **Motion** tab of the dialog box.
- After specifying the parameters, click on **OK** button from the dialog box to complete the process.
- Now, select the **Joint** tool from **ASSEMBLE** drop-down. The **JOINT** dialog box will be displayed. You are asked to select the snap point on the components.
- Select snap point on both Component 1 and Component 2 as shown in Figure-108.

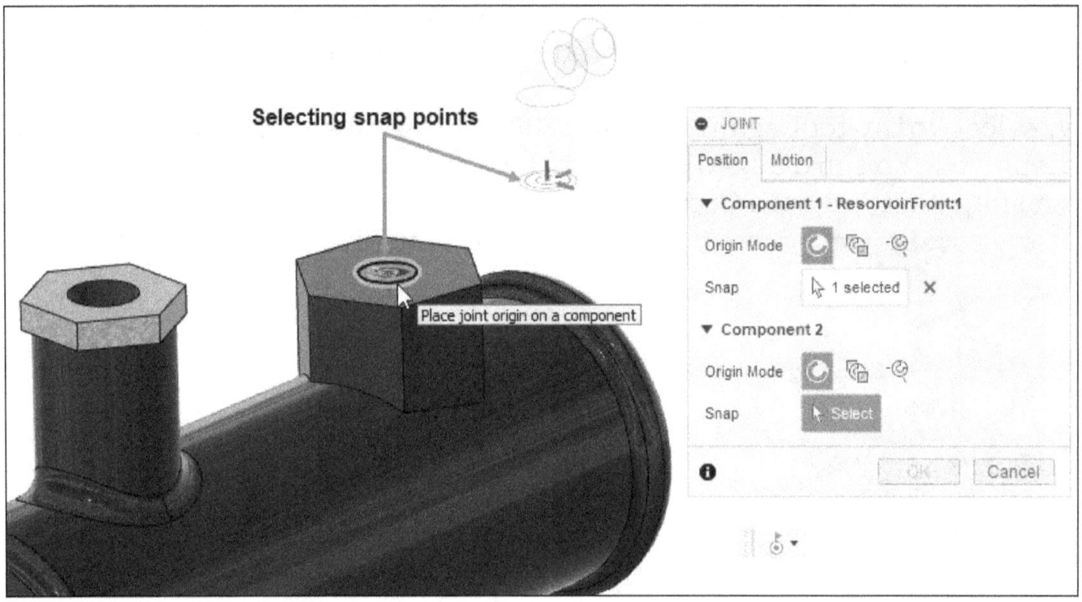

Figure-108. Selecting snap point on the components

- On selecting the snap point on second component, both the components will be joined; refer to Figure-109.

Figure-109. Components joined

- Select **Rigid** option from **Type** drop-down in **Motion** tab of the dialog box.
- After specifying the parameters, click on **OK** button from the dialog box to complete the process.
- Click on **Joint** tool again from **ASSEMBLE** drop-down. The **JOINT** dialog box will be displayed. You are asked to select the snap point on the components.
- Select snap point on both Component 1 and Component 2 as shown in Figure-110.

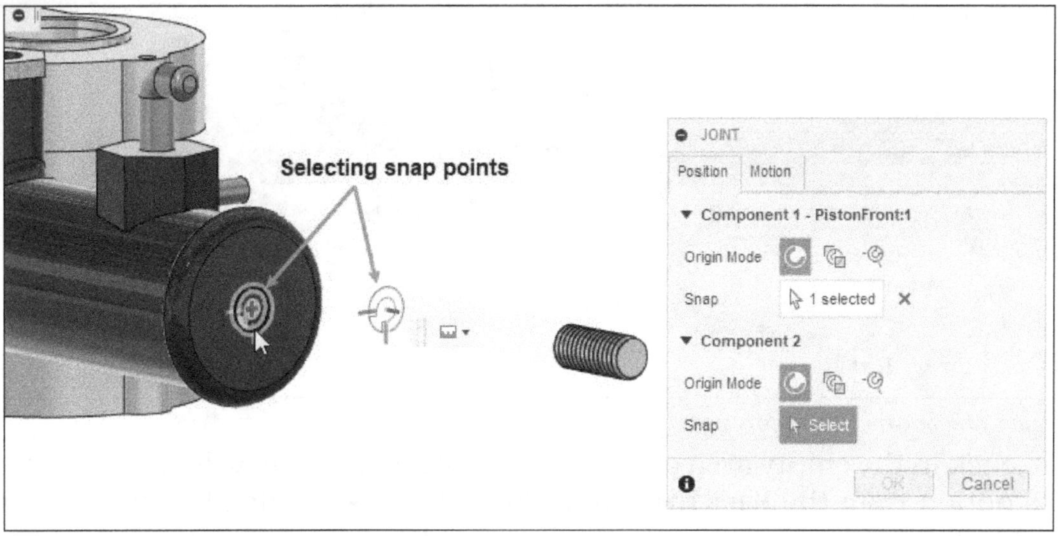

Figure-110. Selecting snap point on components

- On selecting snap point on second component, both the components will be joined; refer to Figure-111.

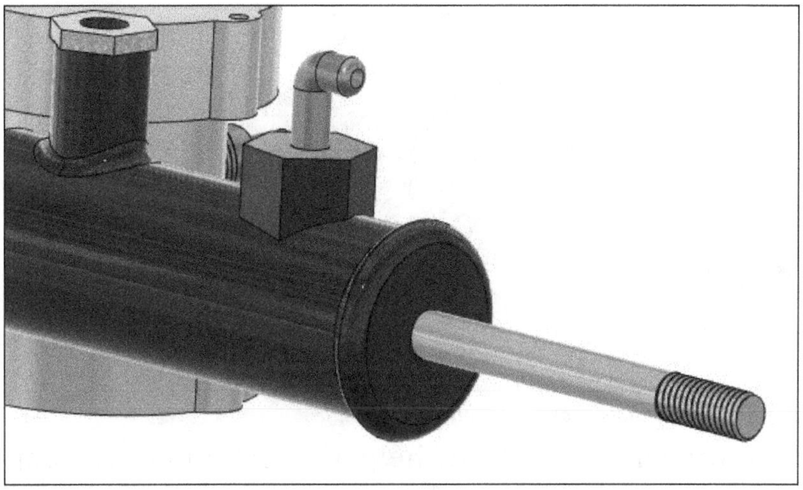

Figure-111. Components joined

- Select **Slider** option from **Type** section in **Motion** tab of the dialog box.
- After specifying the parameters, click on **OK** button from the dialog box to complete the process.

Copying the Components

- Select the components to be copied while holding the **CTRL** key from **BROWSER** as shown in Figure-112. Right-click on any of the selected components, a shortcut menu will be displayed. Select **Copy** option from the shortcut menu.

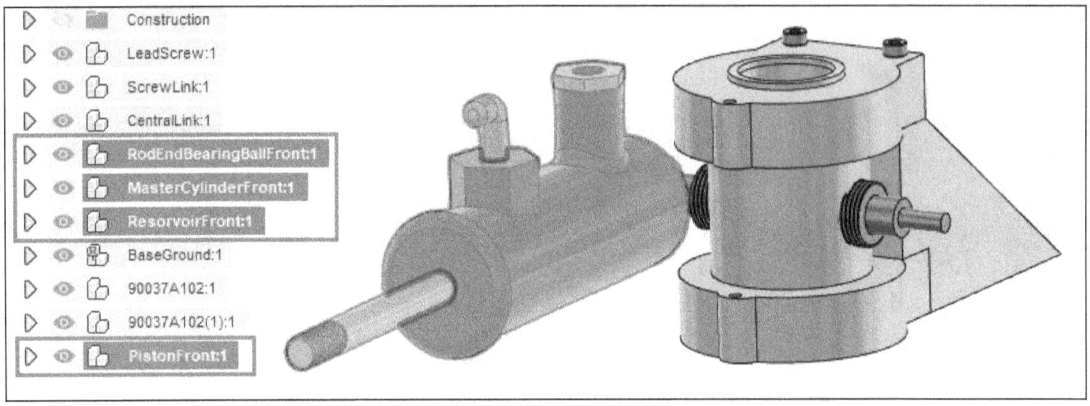

Figure-112. Selecting the components to copy

- Right-click in the empty area of the screen, a **Marking Menu** will be displayed. Select **Paste** option from the **Marking Menu**. The **MOVE/COPY** dialog box will be displayed along with the drag handle; refer to Figure-113.

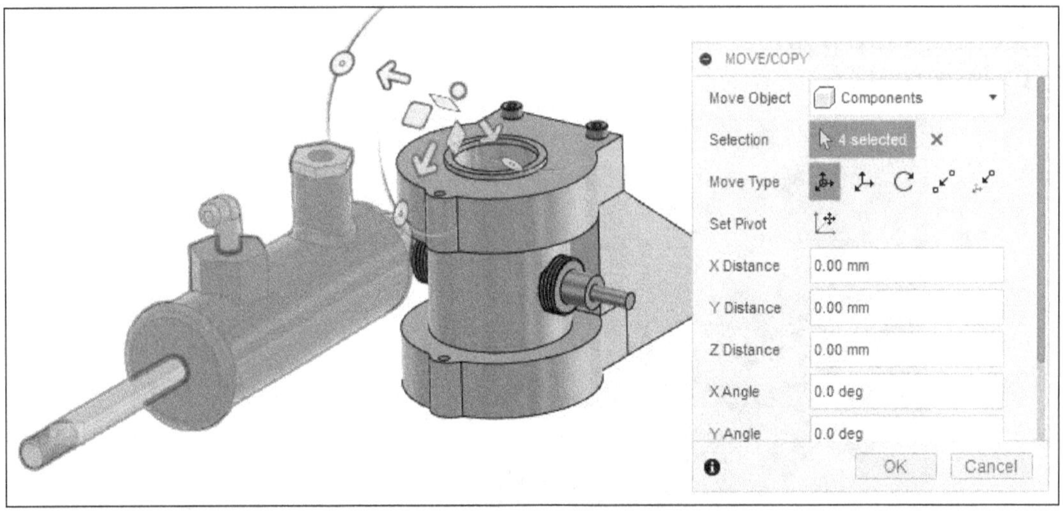

Figure-113. MOVE COPY dialog box along with drag handle

- Drag the copied components with the help of drag handle. The copied components will be displayed; refer to Figure-114.

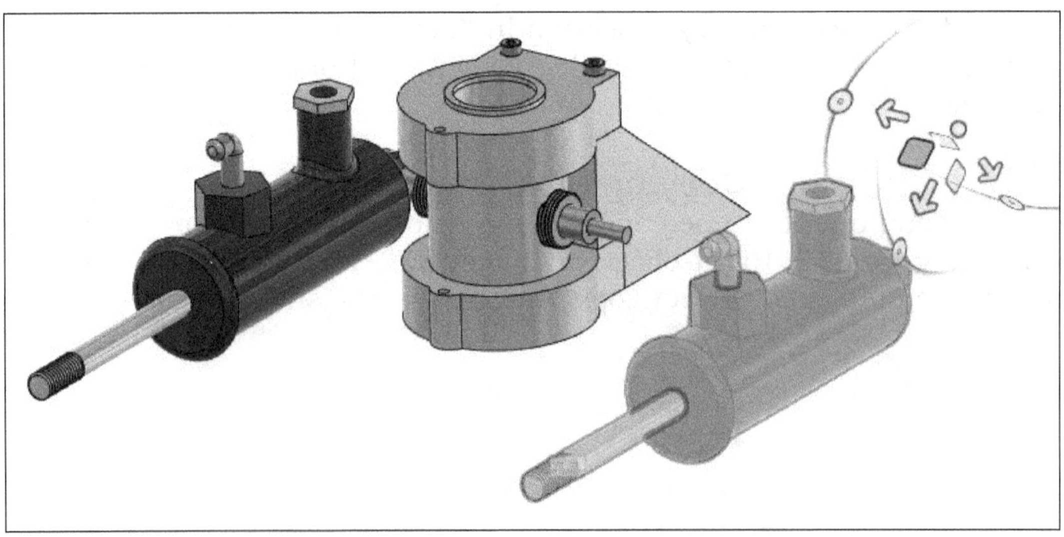

Figure-114. Components copied

- Click on **OK** button from **MOVE/COPY** dialog box to complete the process.

Assembling the Copied Components

- Select **Joint** tool from **ASSEMBLE** drop-down. The **JOINT** dialog box will be displayed and you will be asked to select snap point on components.
- Select snap point on both the Component 1 and Component 2 as shown in Figure-115.

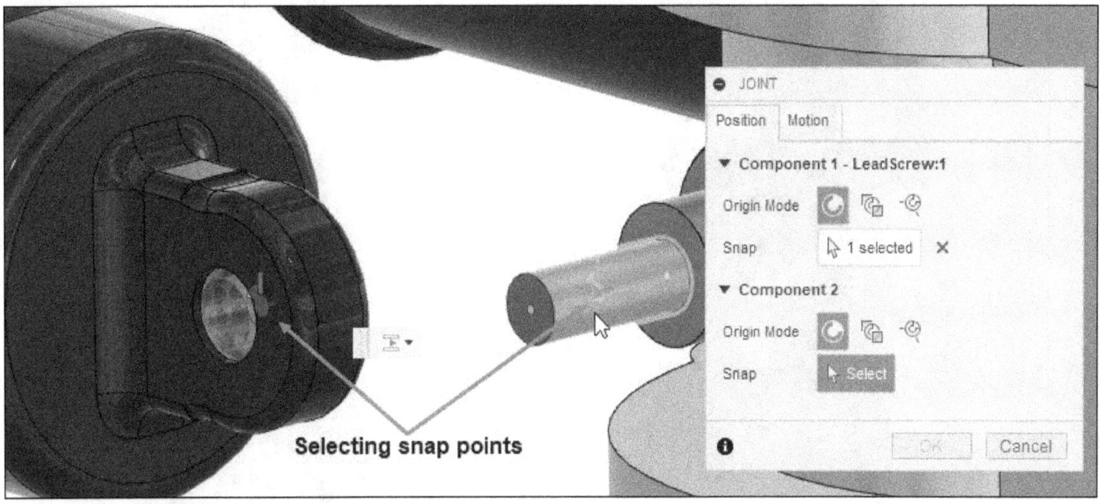

Figure-115. Selecting snap point on components

- On selecting snap point of second component, both the components will be joined.
- Select **Revolute** option from **Type** section in **Motion** tab of the dialog box.
- After specifying the parameters, click on **OK** button from the dialog box to complete the process. The final assembly of components will be displayed; refer to Figure-116.

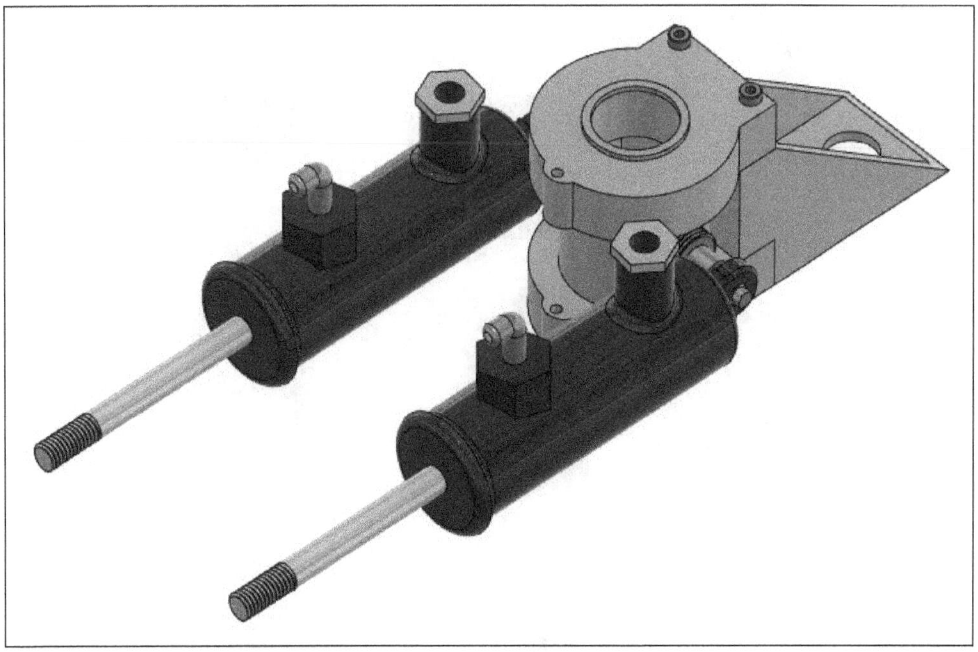

Figure-116. Final assembly of components

PRACTICE 1

Assemble the parts of motor assembly as shown in Figure-117 and Figure-118. The exploded view of assembly is shown in Figure-119. Note that you can open this practice file from the resource kit downloaded for this book.

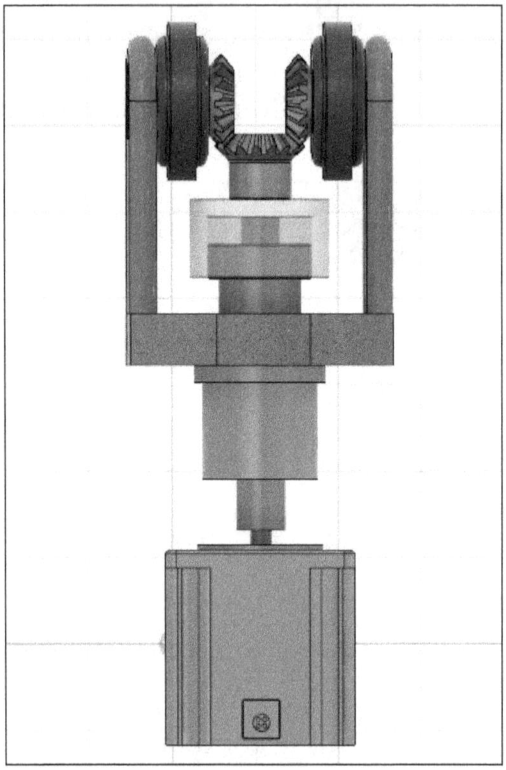

Figure-117. Assembly view 1

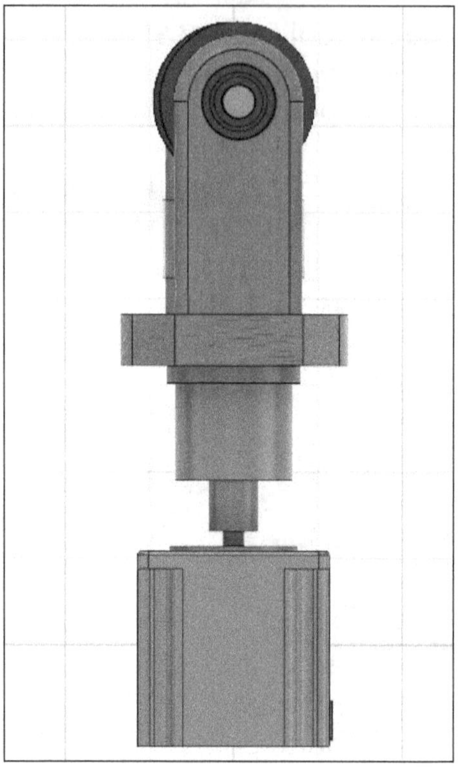

Figure-118. Assembly view 2

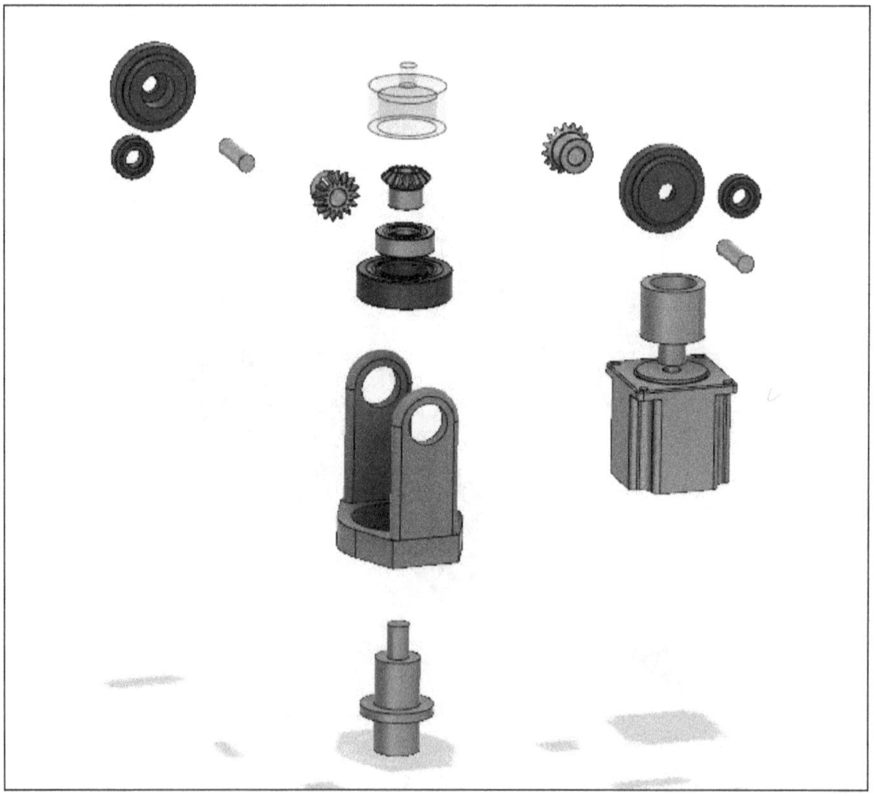

Figure-119. Exploded view of assembly

PRACTICE 2

Assemble the parts of crank assembly as shown in Figure-120. The exploded view in which you will get the model is shown in Figure-121.

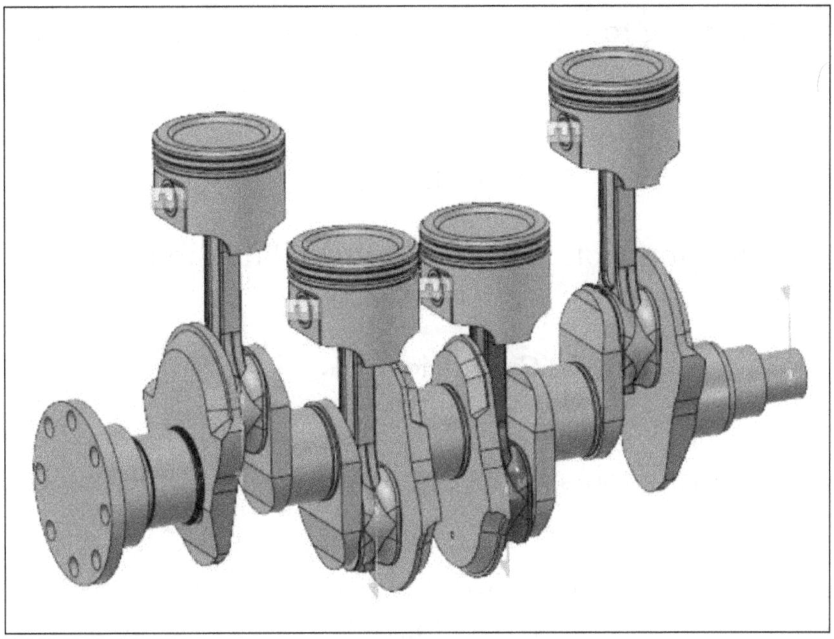

Figure-120. Assembled crank piston model

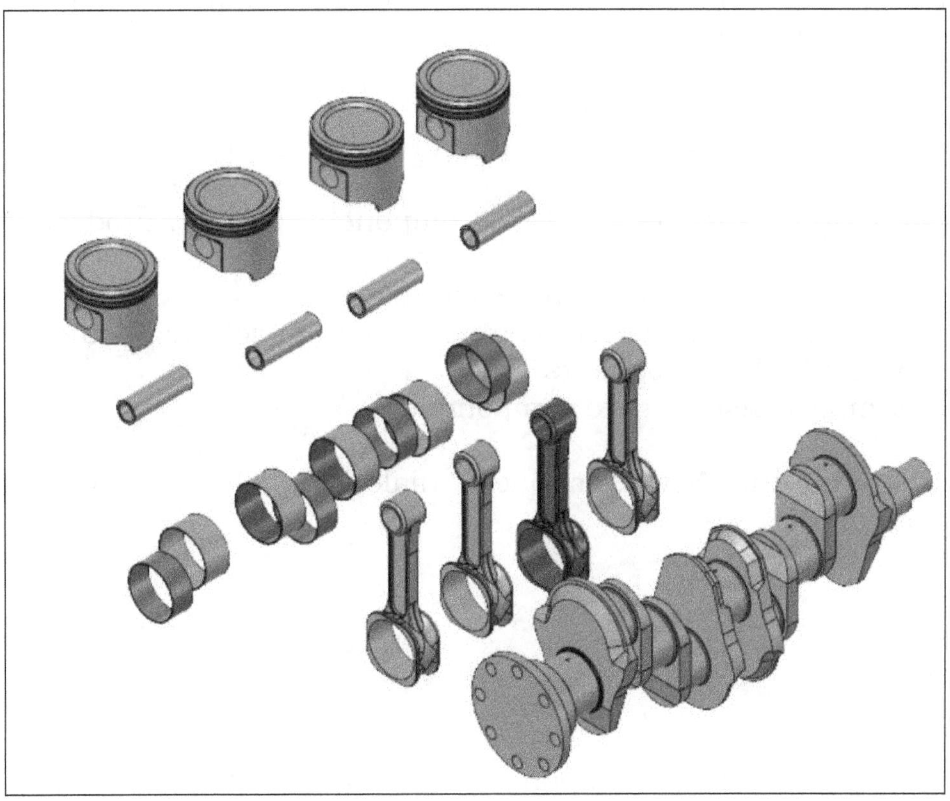

Figure-121. Exploded view of crank assembly

SELF-ASSESSMENT

Q1. The .... tool is used to create a standard component or sheet metal component from the selected bodies.

Q2. Which of the following tool is used to define motion type of a component in an assembly?

a. New Component
b. Joint
c. Rigid Group
d. Drive Joints

Q3. Which of the following motion type is not available to apply joints in assembly of Autodesk Fusion?

a. Slider
b. Cylindrical
c. Pin-slot
d. Symmetry

Q4. Which of the following tools is used to combine multiple components to act as a single component?

a. New Component
b. Joint
c. Rigid Group
d. Drive Joints

Q5. Which of the following tools is used to define relation between motion of two components of assembly?

a. Motion Link
b. Joint
c. Rigid Group
d. Drive Joints

Q6. What is the primary use of the "New Component" tool in Autodesk Fusion?

A) To convert existing components into solid parts
B) To create an empty component or components from selected bodies
C) To assemble multiple components
D) To add assembly constraints to components

Q7. Which option in the "New Component" dialog box allows you to create a sheet metal component?

A) External
B) Internal
C) Sheet Metal
D) Standard

Q8. When creating a standard component, what does the "Activate" check box do in the "New Component" dialog box?

A) It activates the parent component
B) It activates the new component so all modeling operations become part of it
C) It activates the offset feature
D) It activates the motion feature

Q9. To create an internal component directly in the current design, which option should you select in the "New Component" dialog box?

A) External
B) From Bodies
C) Internal
D) Sheet Metal

Q10. What is the function of the "Joint" tool in Autodesk Fusion?

A) To define and apply assembly constraints between components
B) To create new components from bodies
C) To add color to components
D) To simulate the motion of a single component

Q11. When using the "Joint" tool, which option is selected to allow a component to revolve about the joint location?

A) Revolute Motion
B) Rigid Motion
C) Slider Motion
D) Planar Motion

Q12. What does the "Slider" motion type in the "Joint" tool allow for?

A) Rotation of components about a joint
B) Translation of one component over another
C) 360-degree free movement in 3D space
D) Movement along a specific plane

Q13. In the "Joint" dialog box, which motion type would be suitable for a joint that allows free rotation and sliding?

A) Planar Motion
B) Cylindrical Motion
C) Ball Motion
D) Pin-Slot Motion

Q14. What is the purpose of the "Duplicate With Joints" tool in Autodesk Fusion?

A) To create multiple copies of a component without joints
B) To duplicate components along with their attached joints
C) To modify the position of joints
D) To remove joints from a component

Q15. What does the "As-built Joint" tool allow you to do?

A) Define joint origins on existing components
B) Apply joints to components based on their current position and orientation
C) Duplicate joints between different components
D) Flip the direction of a joint

Q16. In the "Joint Origin" dialog box, what does the "Between Two Faces" option do?

A) Places the joint origin on a face
B) Places the joint origin midway between two selected faces
C) Defines the direction of the joint
D) Rotates the joint origin

Q17. What action can be performed after creating a joint using the "As-built Joint" tool?

A) The component can be rotated by double-clicking on the flag
B) The joint can be deleted immediately
C) The component can only be moved along one axis
D) The motion is fixed and cannot be changed

Q18. What is the primary purpose of the Rigid Group tool in Fusion?

A. To create new components
B. To combine selected components into one group
C. To apply constraints between components
D. To perform motion analysis

Q19. What happens when the "Include Child Components" check box is selected in the Rigid Group dialog box?

A. Only parent components are included in the rigid group
B. Child components are excluded from the rigid group
C. Child components are included in the rigid group
D. The rigid group becomes inactive

Q20. Which tool is used to create a tangent relationship between two faces in Fusion?

A. Tangent Relationship tool
B. Motion Link tool
C. Rigid Group tool
D. Drive Joints tool

Q21. When creating a tangent relationship, which component's face is selected first?

A. The second component's face
B. The first component's face
C. Both components' faces simultaneously
D. No specific order is required

Q22. What is the purpose of the Drive Joints tool in Fusion?

A. To create tangent relationships
B. To specify the rotation angle or distance of a joint
C. To create new components
D. To animate the assembly

Q23. What option is available after driving a joint in Fusion to make the joint's current position the new start position?

A. Revert Position
B. Capture Position
C. Disable Joint
D. Enable Joint

Q24. What does the Motion Link tool specify in Fusion?

A. The rotation angle of a joint
B. The relationship between the motion of two joints
C. The new component creation
D. The arrangement of components in a 3D space

Q25. When using the Motion Link tool, which checkbox would reverse the direction of revolution?

A. Reverse checkbox
B. Enable checkbox
C. Animate checkbox
D. Play Loop checkbox

Q26. What does the Enable Contact Sets tool do in Fusion?

A. Creates new joints
B. Enables physical contact conditions between parts
C. Creates a new contact set
D. Animates the assembly

Q27. What action does the Enable All Contact tool perform?

A. Disables contact between components
B. Enables all contacts applied earlier in the model
C. Creates a new contact set
D. Selects the bodies for contact

Q28. What happens when the Disable Contact tool is used?

A. All contacts applied earlier are enabled
B. New contact sets are created
C. All contacts applied earlier are disabled
D. The assembly is animated

Q29. What is the purpose of the New Contact Set tool in Fusion?

A. To create new components
B. To create a new contact set between two components
C. To animate the joint movement
D. To create a tangent relationship

Q30. Which tool is used for kinematic motion analysis based on joints?

A. Drive Joints tool
B. Tangent Relationship tool
C. Motion Study tool
D. Enable Contact Sets tool

Q31. What does the Motion Study tool allow you to do in Fusion?

A. Select components for a rigid group
B. Create motion analysis based on joints
C. Specify joint rotation angle
D. Animate the entire assembly

Q32. What happens when the Arrange tool is used in Fusion?

A. It creates new contacts between components
B. It arranges assembly components in a 2D or 3D enclosure
C. It performs motion analysis
D. It generates automated designs for an assembly

Q33. In the Arrange tool, which option is used to arrange components in a 2D plane?

A. 2D True Shape
B. 3D Rectangular
C. 2D Rectangular
D. 2D Circular

Q34. What happens if the "Allow Partial Arrange" check box is selected in the Arrange tool?

A. Components will be arranged in a perfect fit within the envelope
B. Components will be arranged even if there is not enough space
C. An error will occur if the space is insufficient
D. Components will be excluded from the arrangement

Q35. What does the Automated Modeling tool do in Fusion?

A. Generates designs for an assembly part automatically
B. Creates motion analysis for joints
C. Arranges components in a 2D or 3D space
D. Creates a rigid group between components

Q36. Which option allows you to make bodies transparent in Automated Modeling?

A. New Component
B. Opacity
C. Allow Partial Arrange
D. Flip Envelope

Chapter 8

Importing Files and Inspection

Topics Covered

The major topics covered in this chapter are:

- ***Introduction***
- ***Insert Derive***
- ***Decal tool***
- ***Attached Canvas***
- ***Insert Mesh***
- ***Insert SVG***
- ***Insert DXF***
- ***Insert McMaster-Carr Component***
- ***Inserting a Manufacturing Part***
- ***Insert TraceParts Supplier Components***
- ***Measure Tool***
- ***Interference Tool***
- ***Curvature Comb Analysis***
- ***Zebra Analysis***
- ***Draft Analysis***
- ***Curvature Map Analysis***
- ***Accessibility Analysis***
- ***Minimum Radius Analysis***
- ***Section Analysis***
- ***Center of Mass Tool***

INTRODUCTION

In the previous chapter, we have learned about the procedure of creating and assembling component. Till now, we have worked on the components that are/have been created in Autodesk Fusion. Now, you will learn to insert external model objects like canvas, decal, dxf, and manufacturer parts. In this chapter, you will learn the procedures of inspecting the part and importing files in **Autodesk Fusion** software.

INSERTING FILE

In this section, you will learn the procedure to insert various types of files in **Autodesk Fusion**.

Insert Component

The **Insert Component** tool is used to insert desired component in the current active document. The procedure to use this tool is discussed next.

- Click on the **Insert Component** tool from **INSERT** drop-down in the **Toolbar**; refer to Figure-1. The **Insert Component** dialog box will be displayed; refer to Figure-2.

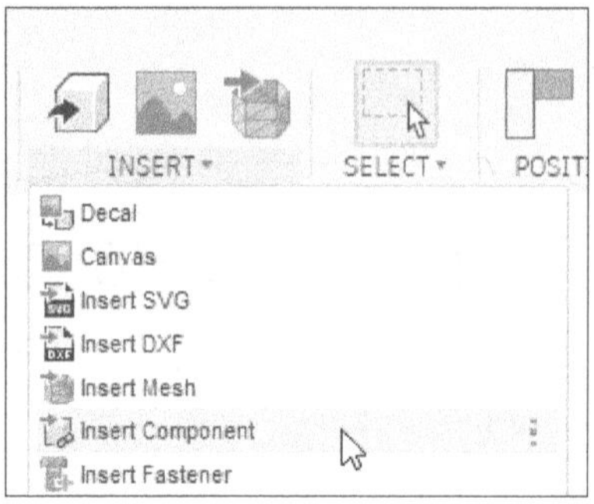

Figure-1. Insert Component tool

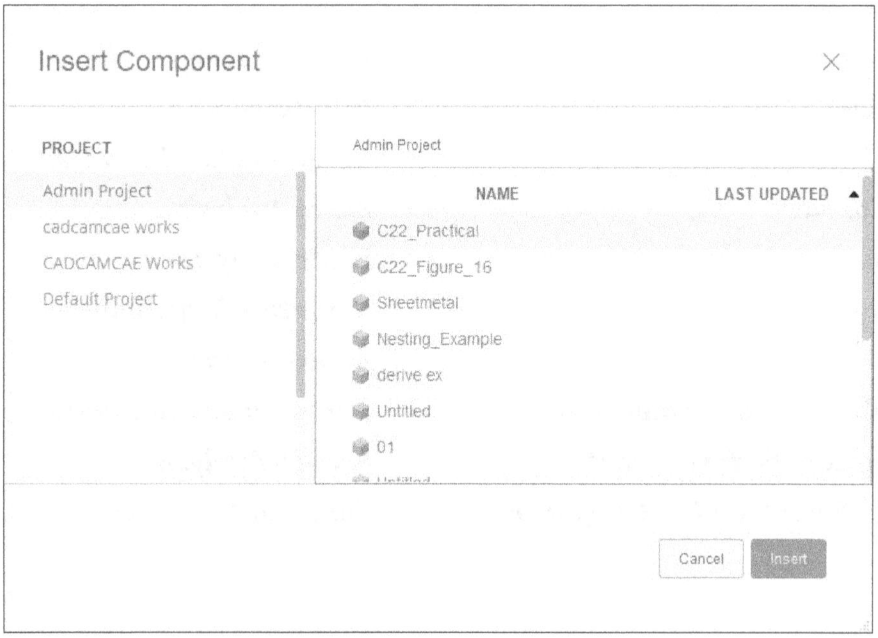

Figure-2. Insert Component dialog box

- Select desired component from the dialog box to be inserted and click on the **Insert** button. The selected component will be inserted in the design canvas and the **INITIAL POSITION** dialog box will be displayed; refer to Figure-3.

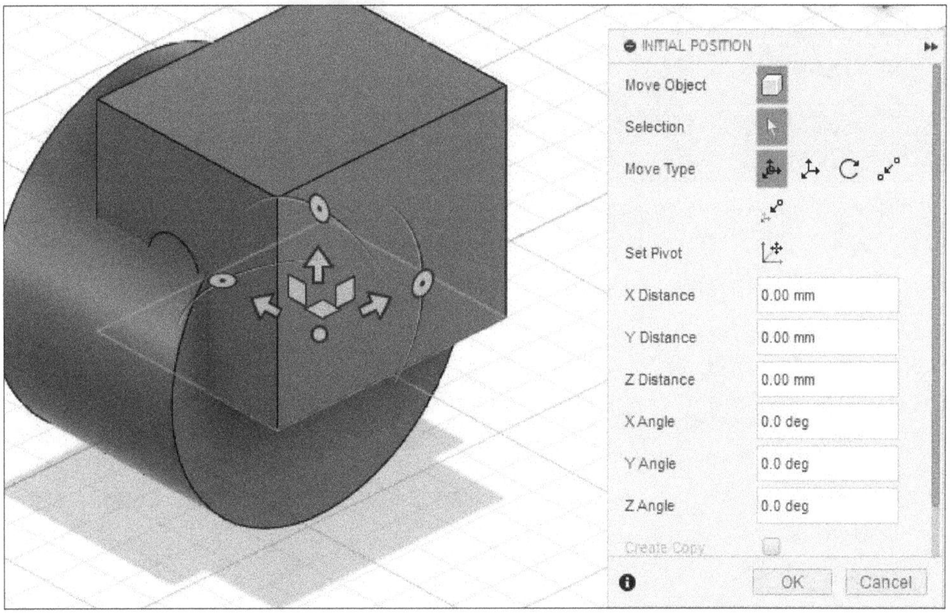

Figure-3. Component inserted along with INITIAL POSITION dialog box

- The parameters in the **INITIAL POSITION** dialog box have been discussed earlier.

Insert Fastener

The **Insert Fastener** tool is used to insert a fastener in the current active document. The procedure to use this tool is discussed next.

- Click on the **Insert Fastener** tool from **INSERT** drop-down in the **Toolbar**; refer to Figure-4. The **INSERT FASTENER** dialog box will be displayed; refer to Figure-5.

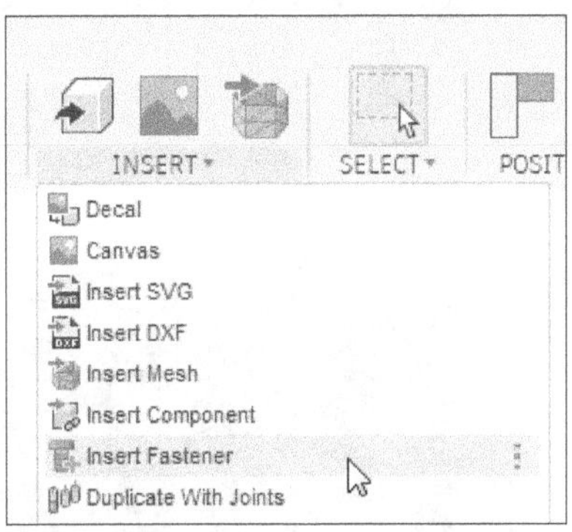

Figure-4. Insert Fastener tool

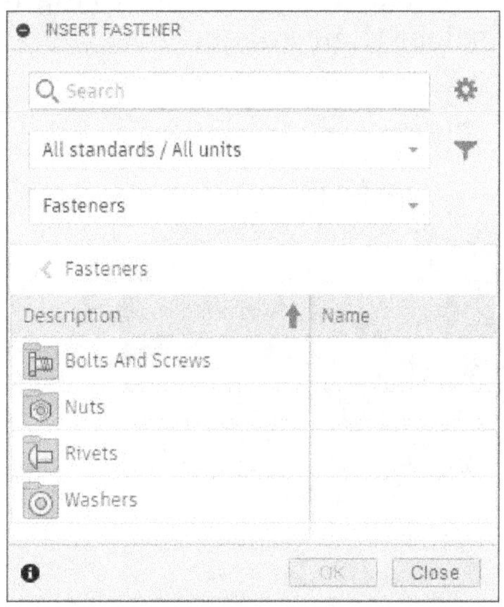

Figure-5. INSERT FASTENER dialog box

- Specify desired name of fastener in the **Search** edit box to be find.
- Select desired fastener from the fastener categories listed in the **Fasteners** area. The updated **INSERT FASTENER** dialog box will be displayed with the **Feature** tab opened and the fastener attached to the cursor; refer to Figure-6. You will be asked to select a circular edge, a cylindrical face, or a sketch point.

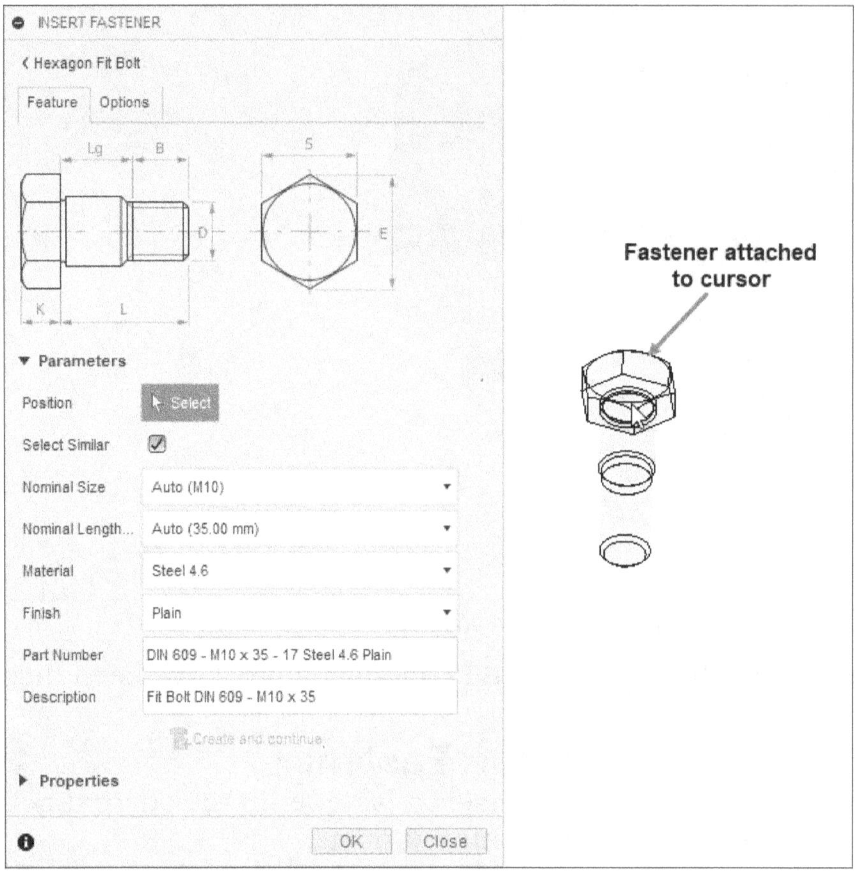

Figure-6. Updated INSERT FASTENER dialog box with the Feature tab

- Select desired circular edge of the component in the canvas to insert the fastener. The fastener will be inserted; refer to Figure-7. Note that you must have components created to select their edges.

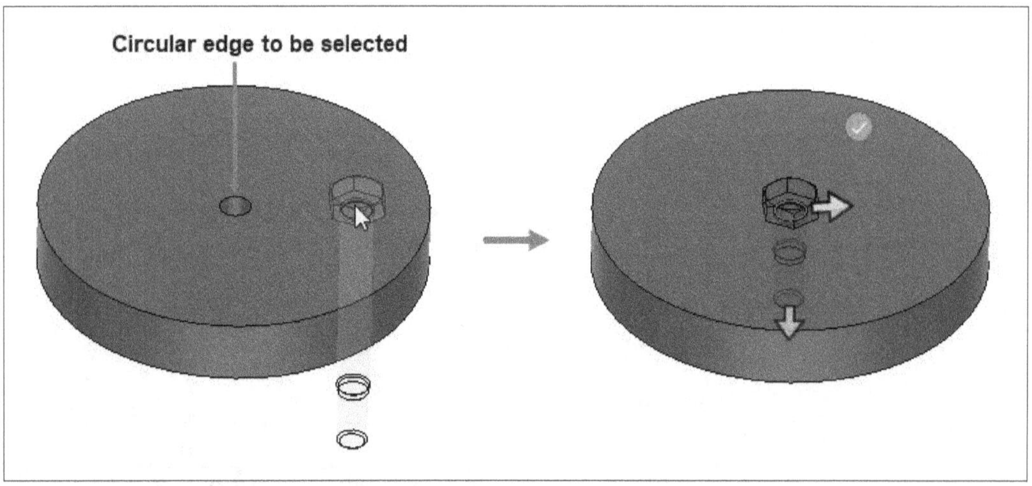

Figure-7. Fastener inserted

- Select the **Select Similar** check box from **Parameters** node to insert fasteners to the same holes or to the same fasteners on the same plane.
- Select desired size and length of fastener to be inserted from **Nominal Size** and **Nominal Length** drop-downs, respectively.
- Select desired material and surface finish to apply to the fastener from **Material** and **Finish** drop-downs, respectively.

- Specify desired part number and description for the fastener in the **Part Number** and **Description** edit boxes, respectively.
- The **Properties** node of the **Feature** tab displays the properties of selected fastener.
- Click on the **Create and continue** button to continue placing desired number of fasteners.
- After specifying desired parameters in the **Feature** tab of the dialog box, click on the **Options** tab, the parameters will be displayed as shown in Figure-8.

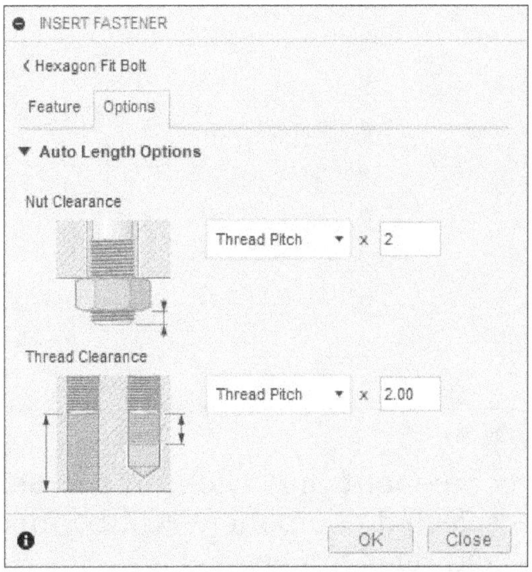

Figure-8. Options tab of INSERT FASTENER dialog box

- Specify desired thread pitch or diameter for **Nut Clearance** of fastener in their respective edit boxes. Similarly, specify thread pitch or diameter for **Thread Clearance** of fastener in their respective edit boxes of **Auto Length Options** node of the **Options** tab.
- After specifying desired parameters, click on **OK** button from the dialog box. The fastener will be placed.

Insert Derive

The **Insert Derive** tool is used to insert components, sketches, parameters, or bodies from another design file into the current model file. Note that before using this tool, you need to save the current model file. The procedure to use this tool is discussed next.

- Click on the **Insert Derive** tool from **INSERT** drop-down in the **Toolbar**; refer to Figure-9. The **Select Source** dialog box will be displayed; refer to Figure-10.

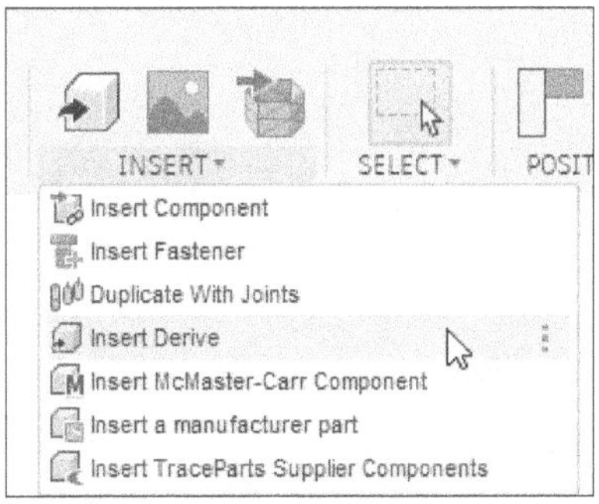

Figure-9. Insert Derive tool

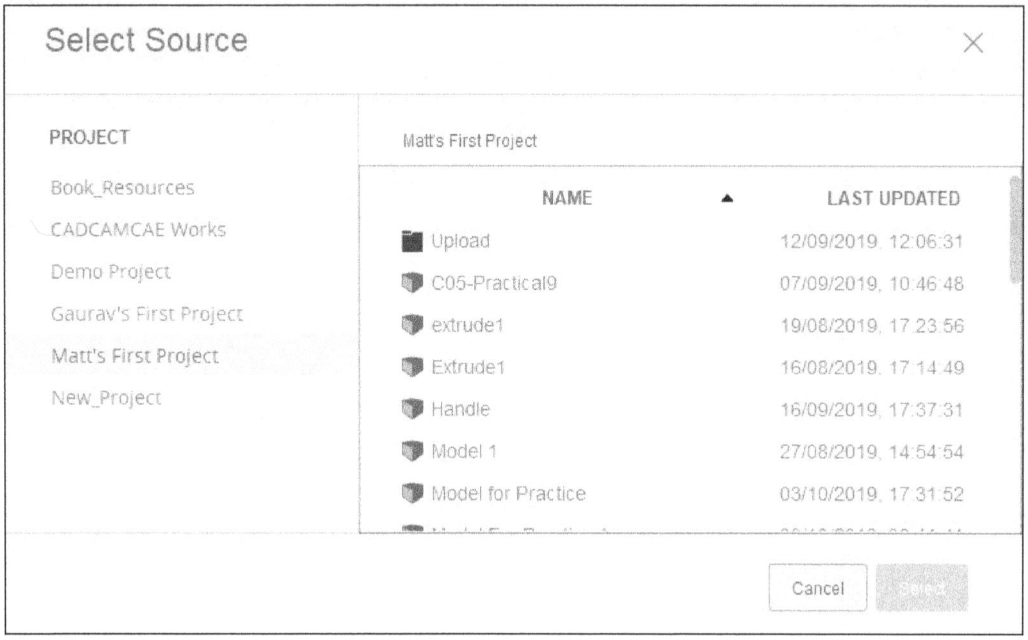

Figure-10. Select Source dialog box

- Select desired source component and click on the **Select** button from **Select Source** dialog box. The selected component will be inserted in the canvas along with the **DERIVE** dialog box; refer to Figure-11.

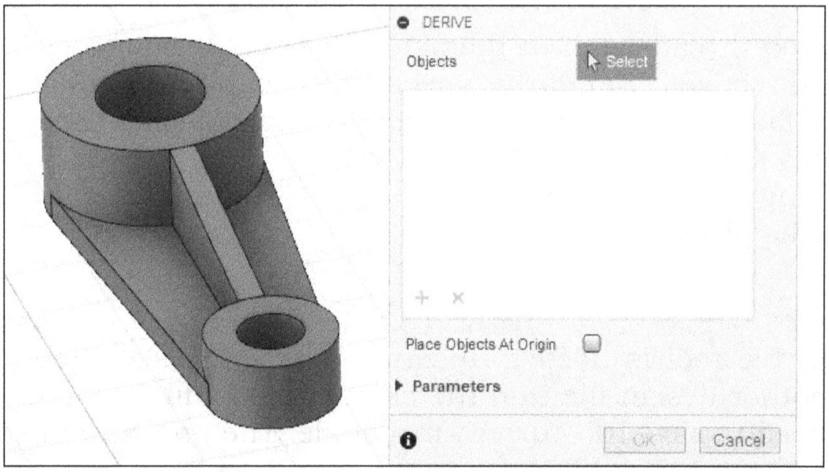

Figure-11. DERIVE dialog box

- The **Select** button of **Model Objects** section is active by default. Click on the inserted component to select the model. The updated **DERIVE** dialog box will be displayed; refer to Figure-12. You can select the sketch and other objects from **BROWSER**.

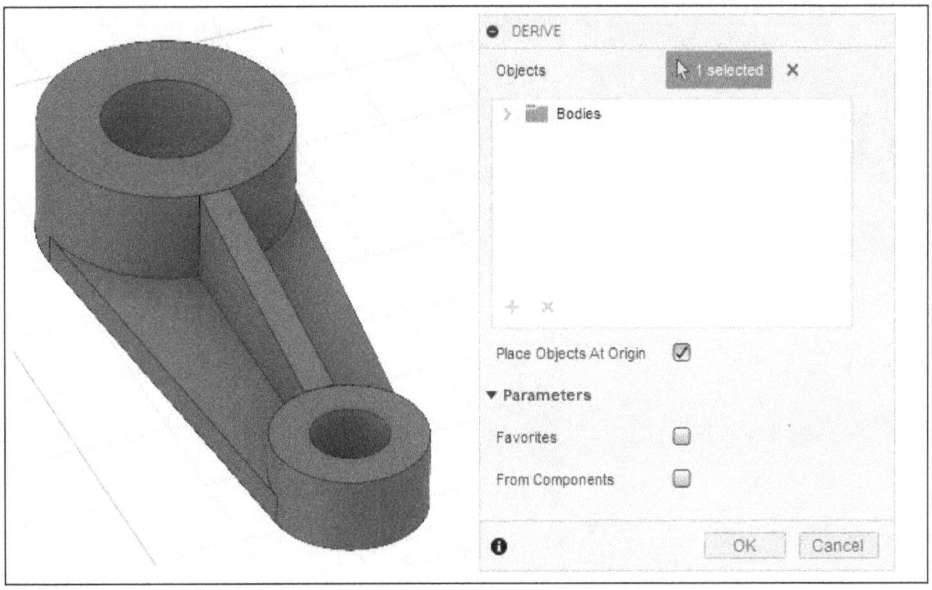

Figure-12. Updated DERIVE dialog box

- Select the **Place Objects At Origin** check box to place the component origin aligned to model origin.
- Expand the **Parameters** node and select desired check boxes to include parameters in desired part.
- After specifying all the parameters, click on **OK** button from the **DERIVE** dialog box to complete the process.

Decal

The **Decal** tool is used to place an image on the selected face/plane. The procedure to use this tool is discussed next.

- Click on the **Decal** tool from **INSERT** drop-down in the **Toolbar**; refer to Figure-13. The **Insert** dialog box will be displayed; refer to Figure-14.

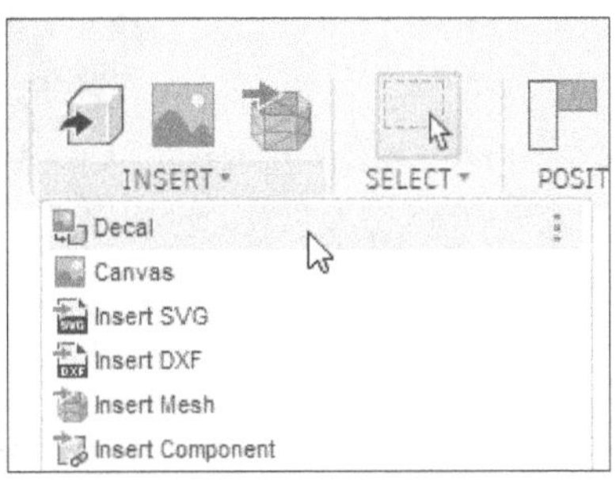

Figure-13. Decal tool

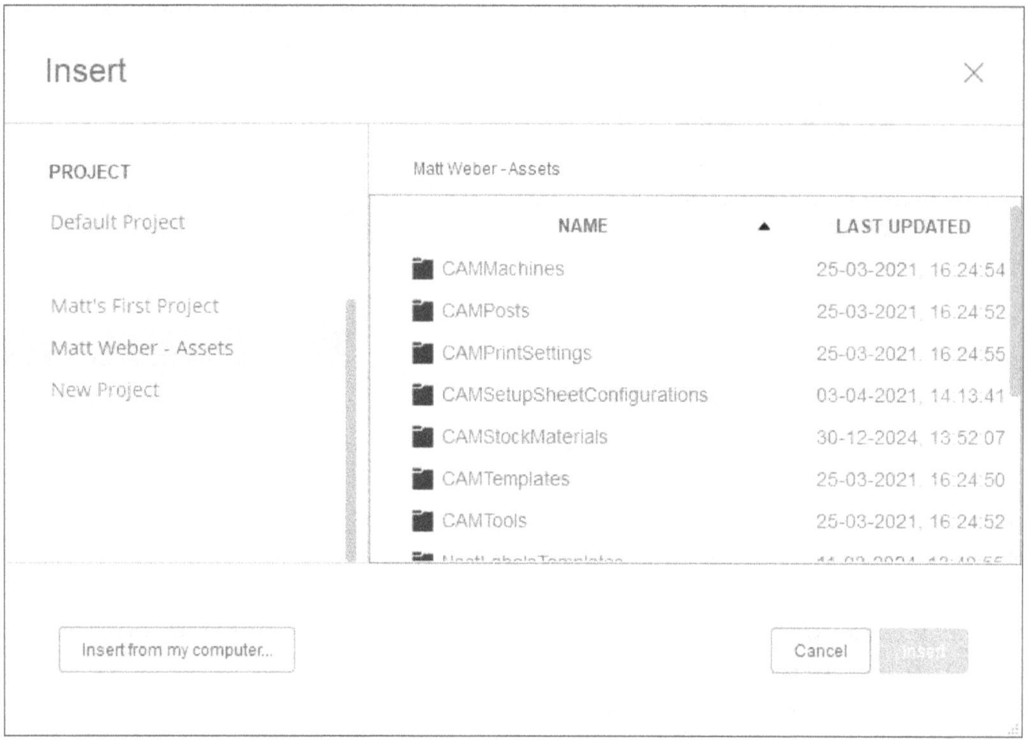

Figure-14. Insert dialog box

- Select required image from **Insert** dialog box and click on **Insert** button from the dialog box. The image will be inserted or click on **Insert from my computer** button from **Insert** dialog box. The **Open** dialog box will be displayed; refer to Figure-15.

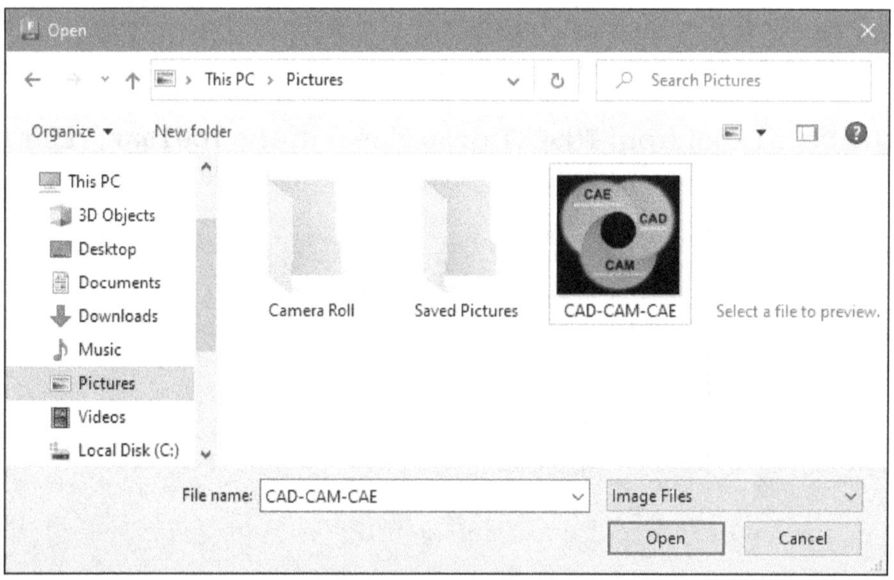

Figure-15. Open dialog box for importing file

- Select desired image which you want to import and click on **Open** button from **Open** dialog box. The **DECAL** dialog box will be displayed with the image inserted; refer to Figure-16.
- The **Select** button of **Face** section is active by default. Click on the face of model to which decal is to be applied. The updated **DECAL** dialog box will be displayed; refer to Figure-17.

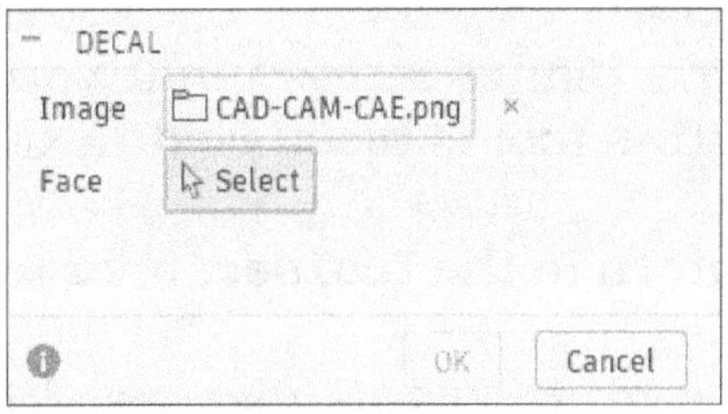

Figure-16. DECAL dialog box

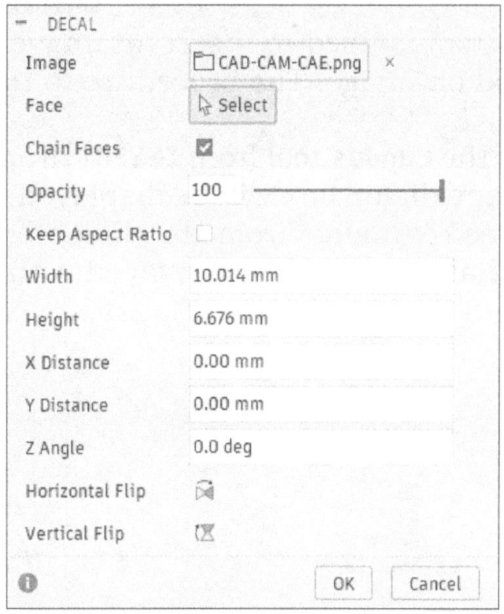

Figure-17. Updated DECAL dialog box

- Set the image on the selected face with the help of drag handle displayed on image. You can also set the image by specifying the values in respective edit boxes in the dialog box.
- Select the **Chain Faces** check box to include tangent faces in selection.
- Click on the **Horizontal Flip** button to flip the image horizontally.
- Click on the **Vertical Flip** button to flip the image vertically.
- After specifying the parameters, the preview of model along with image will be displayed; refer to Figure-18.

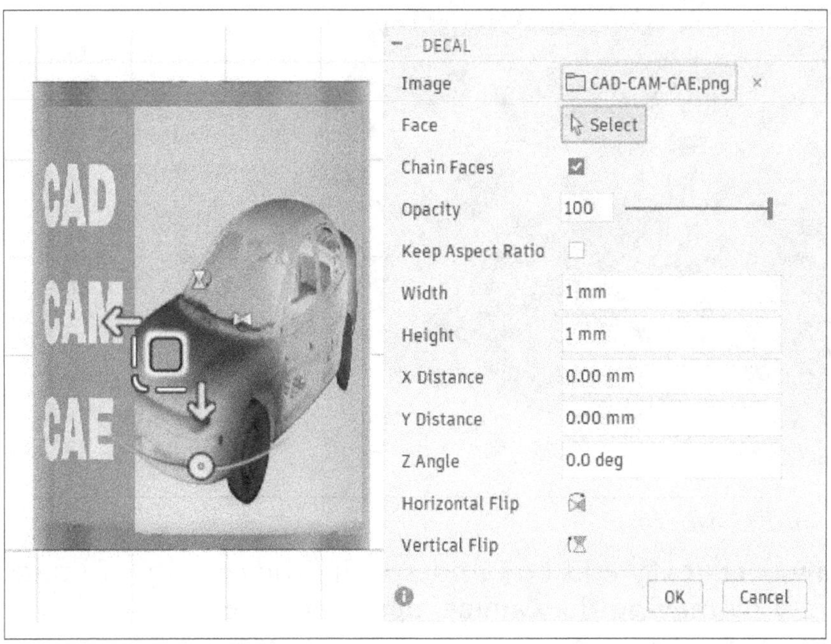

Figure-18. Preview of image on model

If the preview is as desired then click on the **OK** button from the **DECAL** dialog box to complete the process.

Canvas

The **Canvas** tool is used to insert an image on a planer face so that you can create model based on image. The procedure to use this tool is discussed next.

- Click on the **Canvas** tool from **INSERT** drop-down in the **Toolbar**; refer to Figure-19. The **Insert** dialog box will be displayed.
- Select desired image from the dialog box and import as discussed earlier. The **CANVAS** dialog box will be displayed with the image inserted; refer to Figure-20.

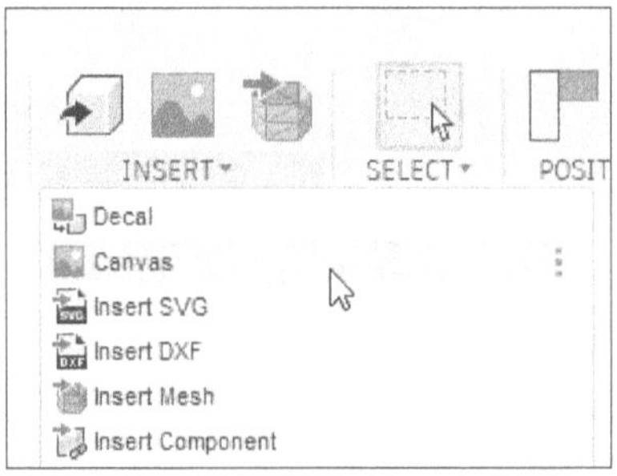

Figure-19. Canvas tool

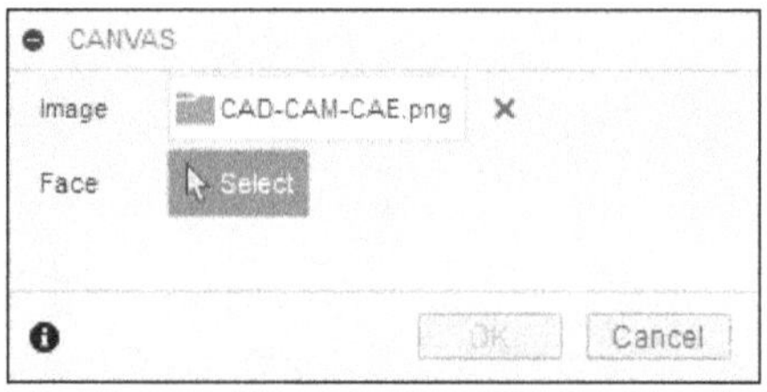

Figure-20. CANVAS dialog box

- The **Select** button of **Face** section is active by default. Click on the face of model/ plane where you want to place the canvas image. The updated **CANVAS** dialog box will be displayed; refer to Figure-21.

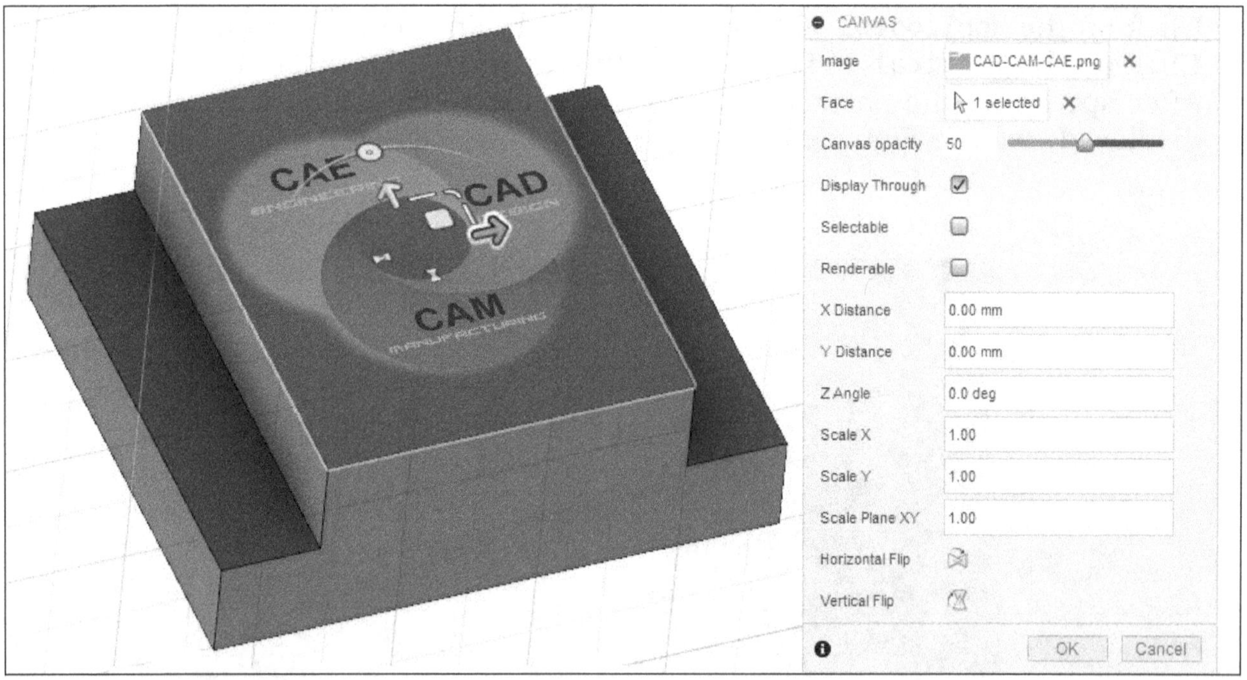

Figure-21. Updated CANVAS dialog box

- Click on **Canvas opacity** edit box and specify the opacity of image. You can also set the opacity by moving the **Canvas opacity** slider.
- Select the **Display Through** check box if you want to make the image visible through the component.
- Select the **Selectable** check box if you want the image to be selectable.
- Select the **Renderable** check box if you want to include the image in renderings of model.
- Click in the **X Distance** edit box and specify a value of distance to move in X direction.

- Click in the **Y Distance** edit box and specify a value of distance to move in Y direction
- Click in the **Z Angle** edit box and specify a value to rotation around z axis.
- Click in the **Scale X** edit box and specify a scale value in X direction.
- Click in the **Scale Y** edit box and specify a scale value in Y direction.
- Click in the **Scale Plane XY** edit box and specify the value of scale in the XY plane.
- Click on the **Horizontal Flip** button to mirror the image horizontally.
- Click on the **Vertical Flip** button to mirror the image vertically.
- After specifying the parameters, click on the **OK** button from **CANVAS** dialog box to complete the process.

Insert SVG

The **Insert SVG** tool is used to insert an SVG image file into sketch. The procedure to use this tool is discussed next.

- Click on the **Insert SVG** tool from **INSERT** drop-down in the **Toolbar**; refer to Figure-22. The **Insert** dialog box will be displayed.
- Select desired file from the dialog box and insert the file as discussed earlier. The **INSERT SVG** dialog box will be displayed with the file selected; refer to Figure-23.

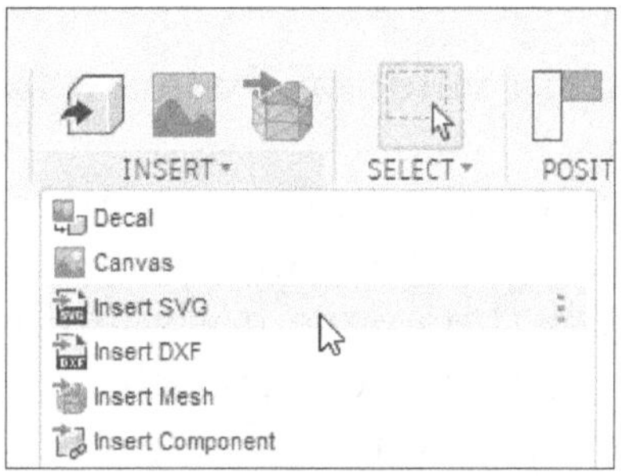

Figure-22. Insert SVG tool

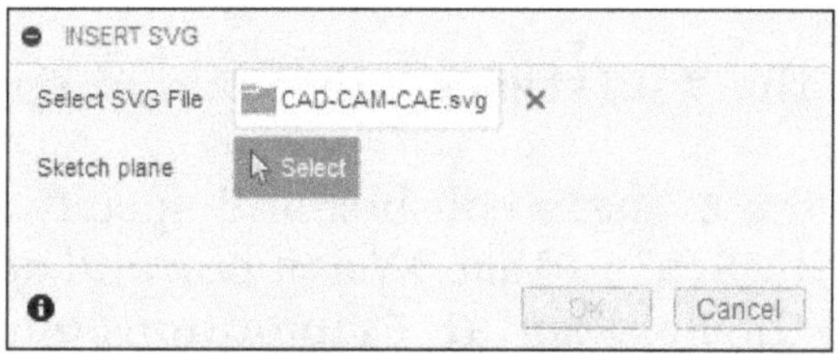

Figure-23. INSERT SVG dialog box

- The **Select** button of **Sketch plane** section is active by default. You need to select the plane for adding SVG file. Click on the plane to select; refer to Figure-24.

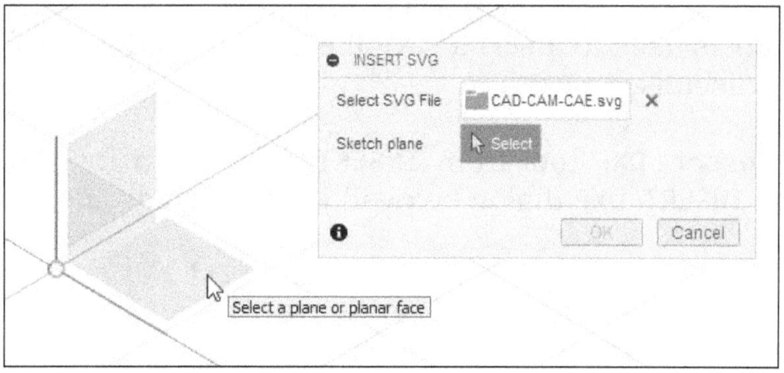

Figure-24. Selecting face or plane

- On selecting the face or plane, the sketching environment will be enabled with updated **INSERT SVG** dialog box; refer to Figure-25.

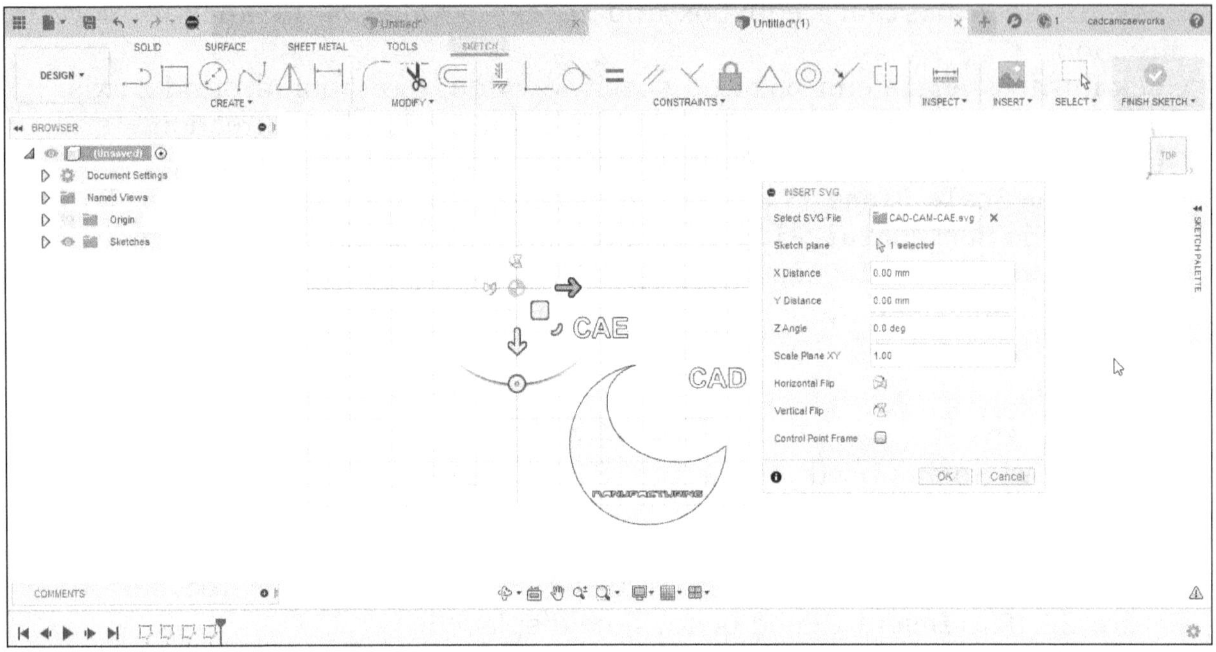

Figure-25. File along with updated INSERT SVG dialog box

- Click in the **X Distance** edit box and specify a value of distance to move in X direction.
- Click in the **Y Distance** edit box and specify a value of distance to move in Y direction.
- Click in the **Z Angle** edit box and specify a value to rotation around z axis.
- Click in the **Scale Plane XY** edit box and specify the value of scale in the XY plane.
- Click on the **Horizontal Flip** button to mirror the image horizontally.
- Click on the **Vertical Flip** button to mirror the image vertically.
- You can also use the drag handle to move or flip the model.
- After specifying the parameters, click on the **OK** button from **INSERT SVG** dialog box to complete the process.

Insert DXF

The **Insert DXF** tool is used to insert a DXF file into the active design. The procedure to use this tool is discussed next.

- Click on the **Insert DXF** tool from **INSERT** drop-down in the **Toolbar**; refer to Figure-26. The **INSERT DXF** dialog box will be displayed; refer to Figure-27.

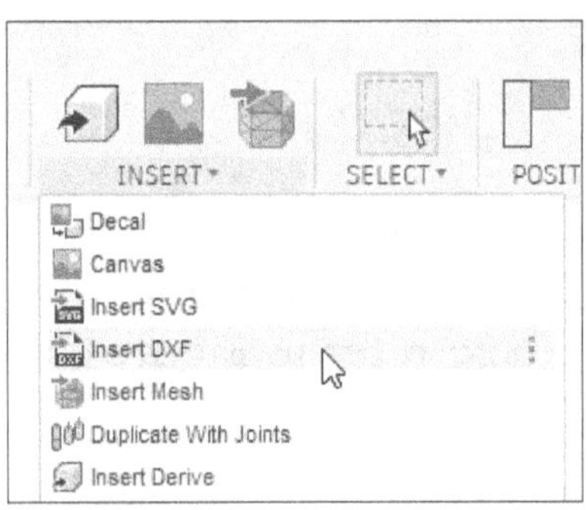

Figure-26. Insert DXF tool

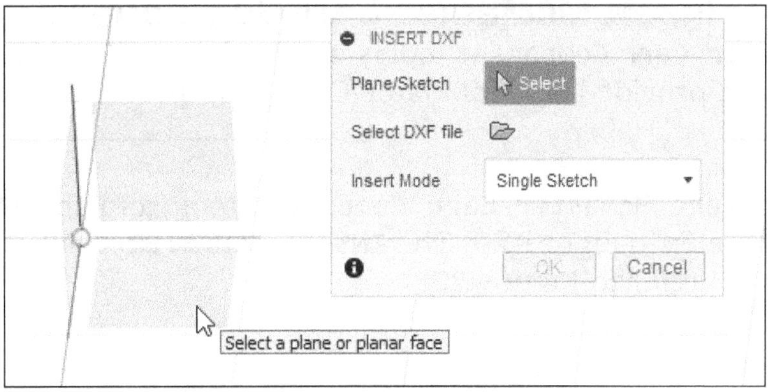

Figure-27. INSERT DXF dialog box

- The **Select** button of **Plane/Sketch** section is active by default. Click on the plane to select.
- Click on **Select DXF file** button from **INSERT DXF** dialog box. The **Open** dialog box will be displayed.
- You need to select the file of **.dxf** format and click on **Open** button. The preview of DXF file will be displayed along with updated **INSERT DXF** dialog box; refer to Figure-28.

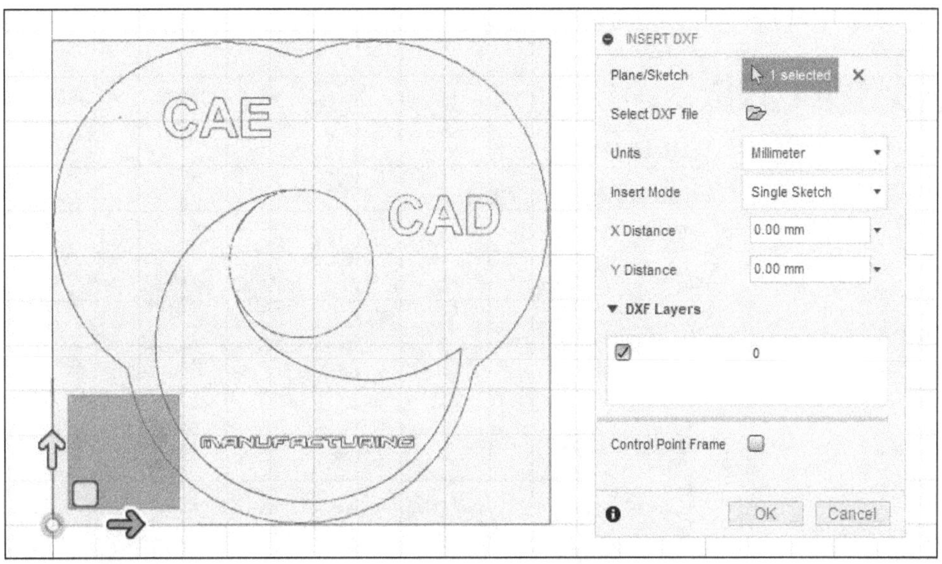

Figure-28. Updated INSERT DXF dialog box

- Click on the **Units** drop-down and select required unit.
- Select **Single Sketch** option from **Insert Mode** drop-down to insert the layers of selected .DXF file into one sketch.
- Select **One Sketch per Layer** option from **Insert Mode** drop-down to insert each sketch of DXF file on different layer.
- Click in the **X Distance** edit box and specify a value of distance to move in X direction.
- Click in the **Y Distance** edit box and specify a value of distance to move in Y direction.
- Select the **DXF Layers** check box to list the layers available in the selected DXF file. Select the layers to import.
- After specifying the parameters, click on the **OK** button from **INSERT DXF** dialog box to complete the process.

Insert McMaster-Carr Component

The **Insert McMaster-Carr Component** tool is used to insert 2D or 3D model of various library components provided by McMaster-Carr. The procedure to use this tool is given next.

- Click on the **Insert McMaster-Carr Component** tool from the **INSERT** drop-down in the **Toolbar**; refer to Figure-29. The **INSERT MCMASTER-CARR COMPONENT** window will be displayed; refer to Figure-30.

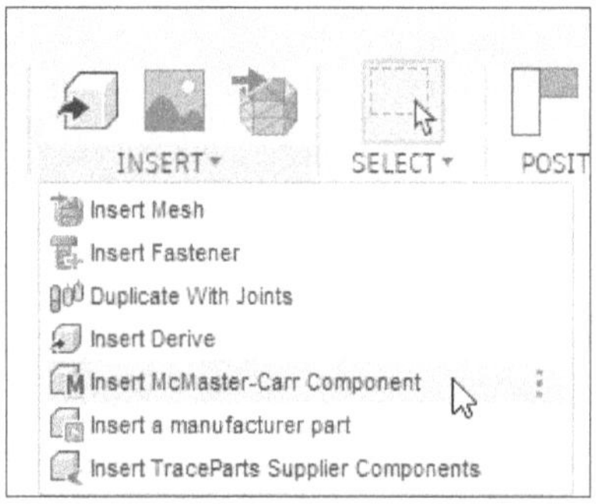

Figure-29. Insert McMaster Carr Component tool

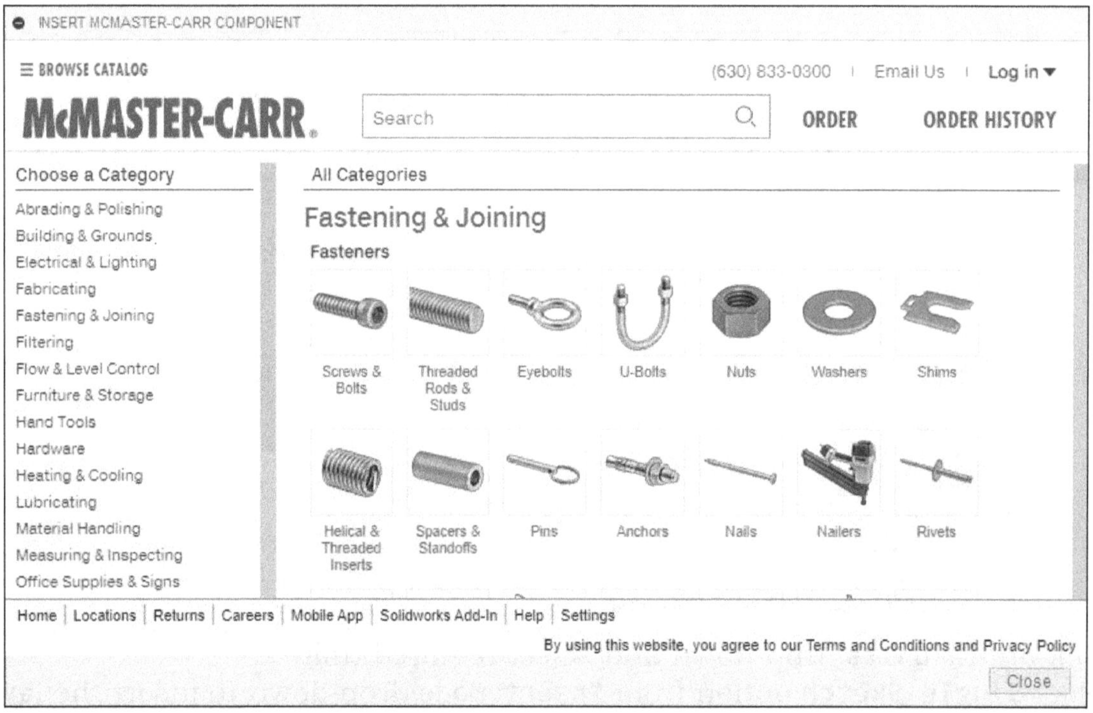

Figure-30. INSERT MCMASTER CARR COMPONENT window

- Select desired component and its model number from the window. The page in window will be displayed as shown in Figure-31.

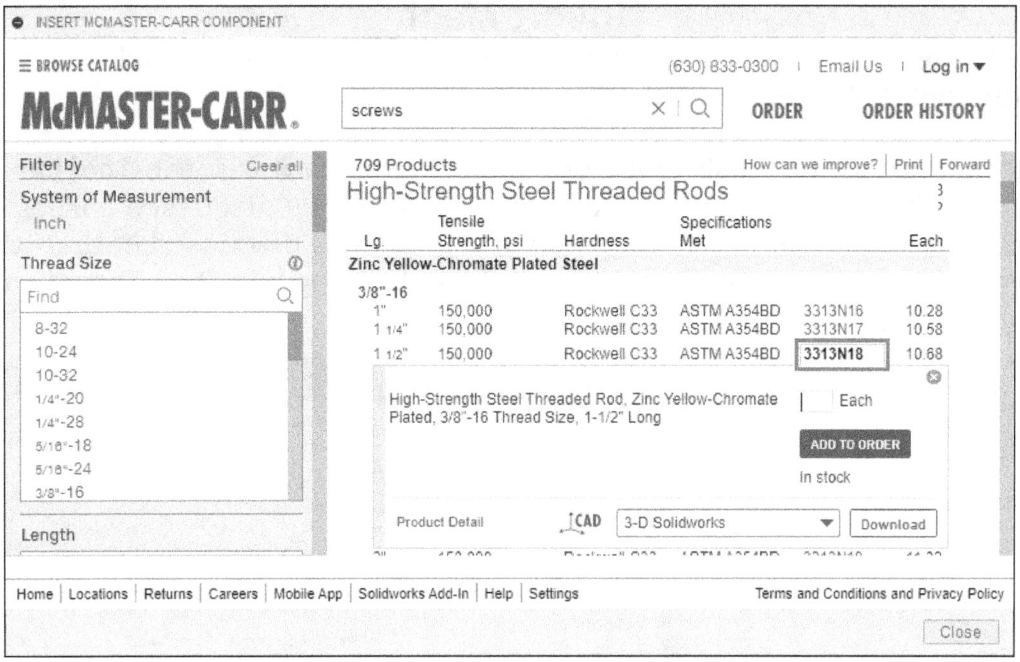

Figure-31. Component selected

- Click on the **Product Detail** link button for selected component. The drawing and model of selected component will be displayed at the bottom in the window; refer to Figure-32.

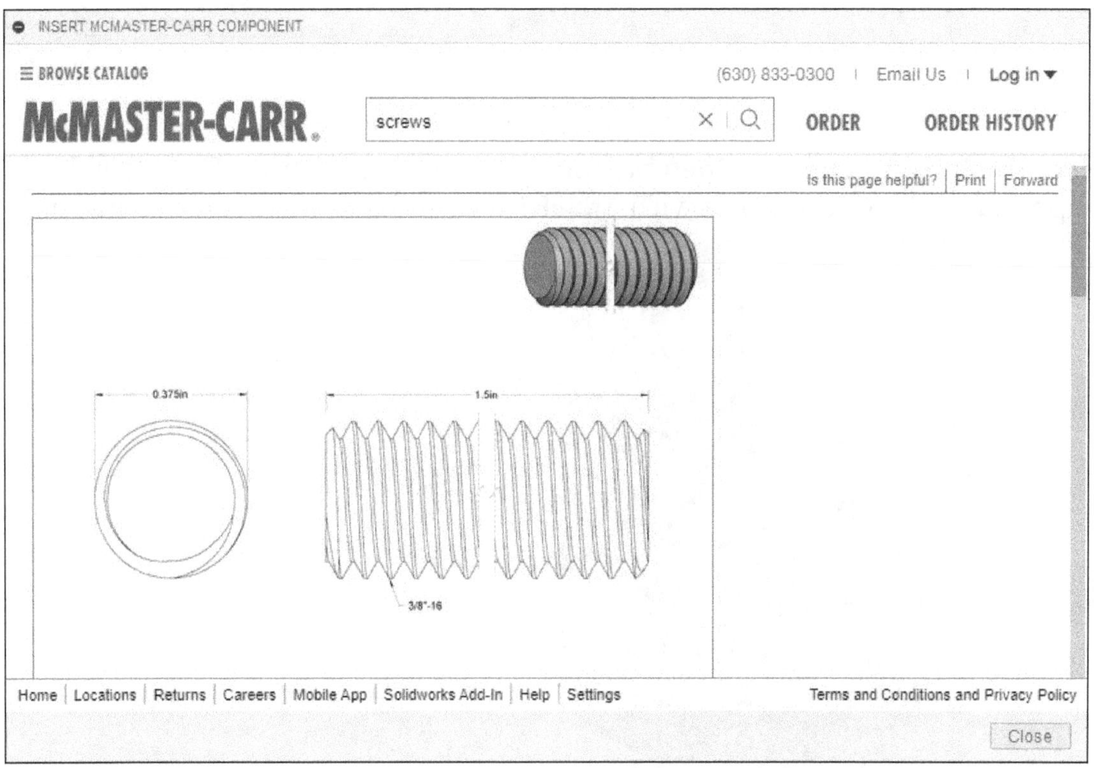

Figure-32. Model for selected component

- Select desired format from drop-down above the drawing and click on the **Save** button to save the model in local drive.
- Close the window by selecting **Close** button.

Insert Mesh

The **Insert Mesh** tool is used to insert a mesh file in current model. The procedure to use this tool is discussed next.

- Click on the **Insert Mesh** tool from **INSERT** drop-down in the **Toolbar**; refer to Figure-33. The **Insert** dialog box will be displayed as discussed earlier.
- Select desired file from the dialog box and import as discussed earlier or click on **Insert from my computer** button from **Insert** dialog box. The **Insert** dialog box will be displayed; refer to Figure-34.

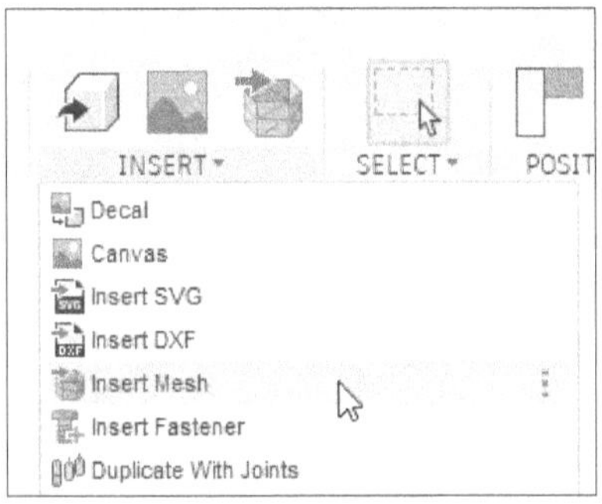

Figure-33. Insert Mesh tool

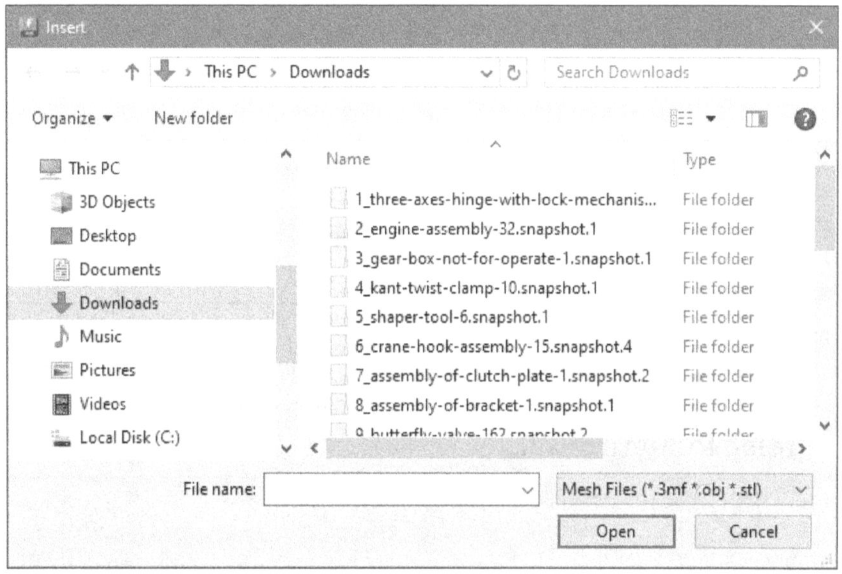

Figure-34. Insert dialog box for inserting file

- Select the file and click on **Open** button of **Insert** dialog box. The file will be added in application window along with **INSERT MESH** dialog box; refer to Figure-35.

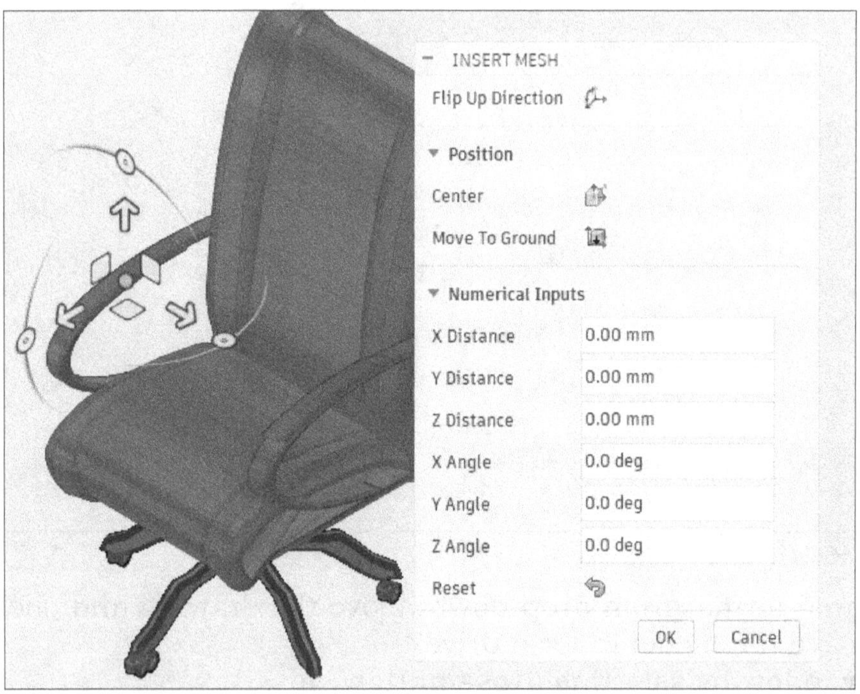

Figure-35. INSERT MESH dialog box

- Click on the **Flip Up Direction** button to flip the direction of model.

- Click on the **Center** button from **Position** section to drag the model to center or coordinate system.
- Click on **Move To Ground** button from **Position** section to move the model to ground plane.
- If you want to enter the numerical value to move the model then click on the **Numerical Inputs** section and enter desired value. You can also move and rotate the model by using drag handles.
- Click on **Reset** button from **Numerical Inputs** section to reset the model position to the original state.
- After specifying the parameters, click on the **OK** button from **INSERT MESH** dialog box to complete the process.

Insert a manufacturer part

The **Insert a manufacturer part** tool is used for inserting a part of manufacturer or supplier in model through parts4cad. The procedure to use this tool is discussed next.

- Click on the **Insert a manufacturer part** tool from **INSERT** drop-down in the **Toolbar**; refer to Figure-36. The Part Community web page will be displayed in default web browser; refer to Figure-37.

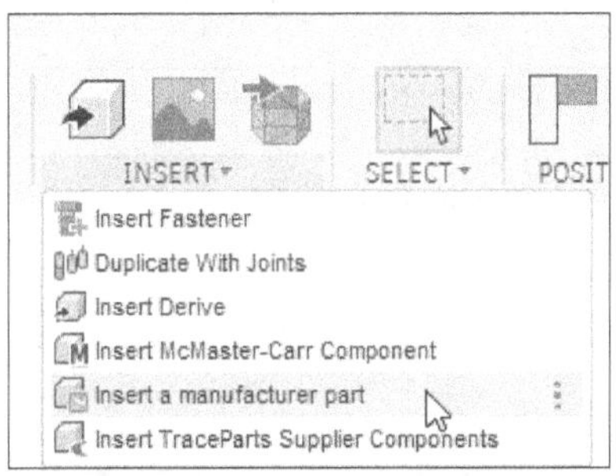

Figure-36. Insert a manufacturer part tool

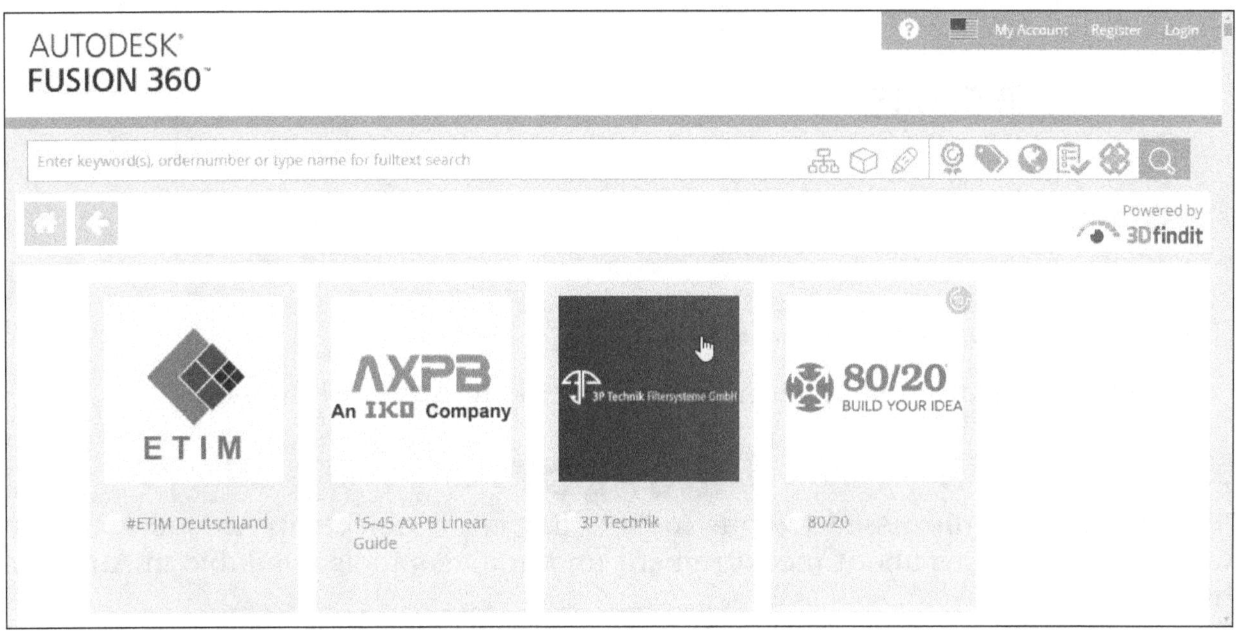

Figure-37. AUTODESK Fusion part community window

- Select the part from manufacturer or supplier and open the file in Autodesk Fusion.

Insert TraceParts Supplier Components

The **Insert TraceParts Supplier Components** tool gives you access to millions of supplier components, 3D models, CAD files, and 2D drawings. Simply navigate to what you are looking for, sign-in with your TraceParts account, download, and insert a supplier component directly into Fusion canvas. The procedure to use this tool is discussed next.

- Click on the **Insert TraceParts Supplier Components** tool from **INSERT** drop-down in the **Toolbar**; refer to Figure-38. The **AUTODESK Fusion DESIGN LIBRARY** window will be displayed; refer to Figure-39.

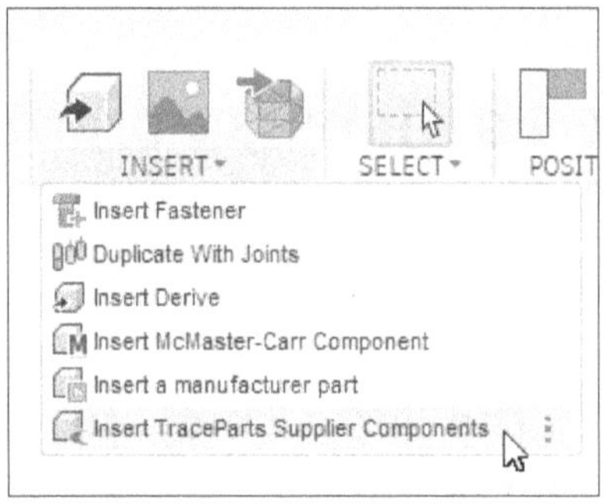

Figure-38. Insert TraceParts Supplier Components tool

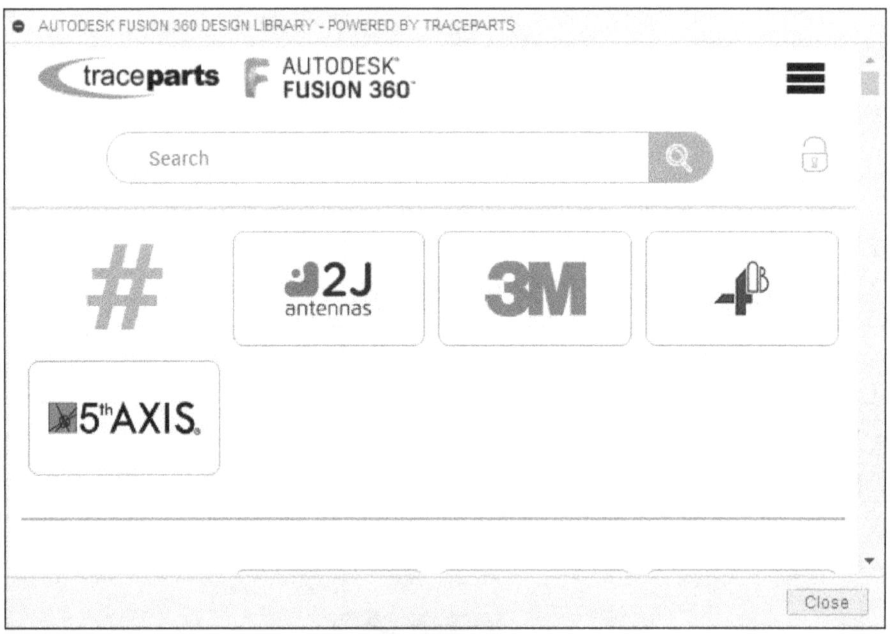

Figure-39. AUTODESK Fusion DESIGN LIBRARY window

- Select the part from supplier and open the file in Autodesk Fusion.

INSPECT

Till now, we have discussed various tools to insert the objects in Autodesk Fusion. Now, we will discuss about measurement and analysis tools available in Autodesk Fusion.

Measure

The **Measure** tool is used to measure selected geometry. The procedure to use this tool is discussed next.

- Click on the **Measure** tool from **INSPECT** drop-down in the **Toolbar**; refer to Figure-40. The **MEASURE** dialog box will be displayed; refer to Figure-41.

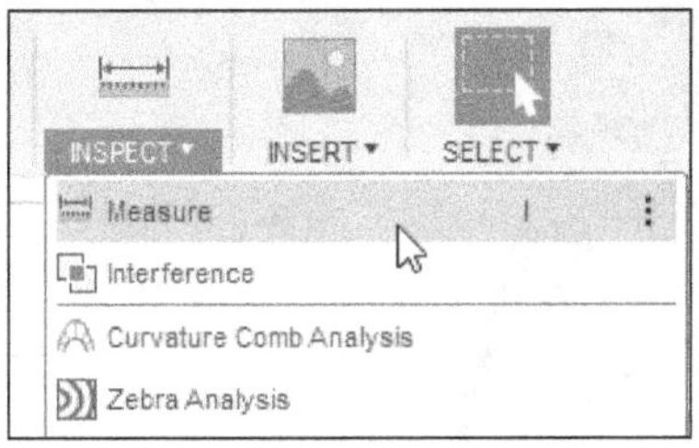

Figure-40. Measure tool

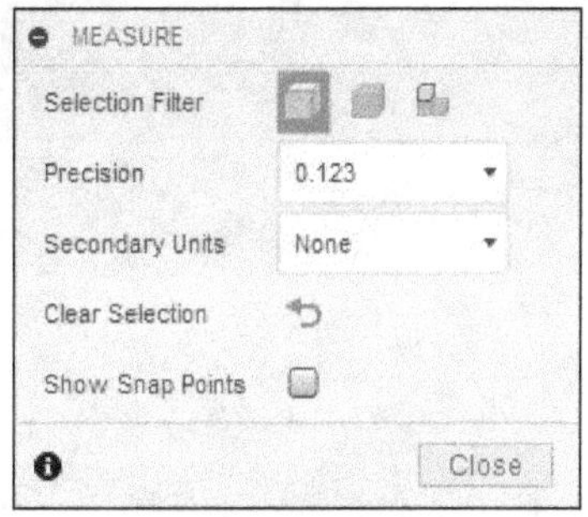

Figure-41. MEASURE dialog box

- Select the **Select Face/Edge/Vertex** button from **Selection Filter** section if you want to select face/edge/vertex for measurement.
- Select the **Select Body** button from **Selection Filter** section if you want to select body for measurement.
- Select the **Select Component** button from **Selection Filter** section if you want to select component for measurement.
- Click on the **Precision** drop-down and select desired precision option for displaying the required number of decimal places in results.
- Select desired secondary unit for the measurement from **Secondary Units** drop-down if you want to display secondary unit as well.
- Click on the **Clear Selection** button to restart the selection process once you have performed measurement.
- In our case, we are selecting **Select Face/Edge/Vertex** button from **Selection Filter** section. Click on the face to measure; refer Figure-42.

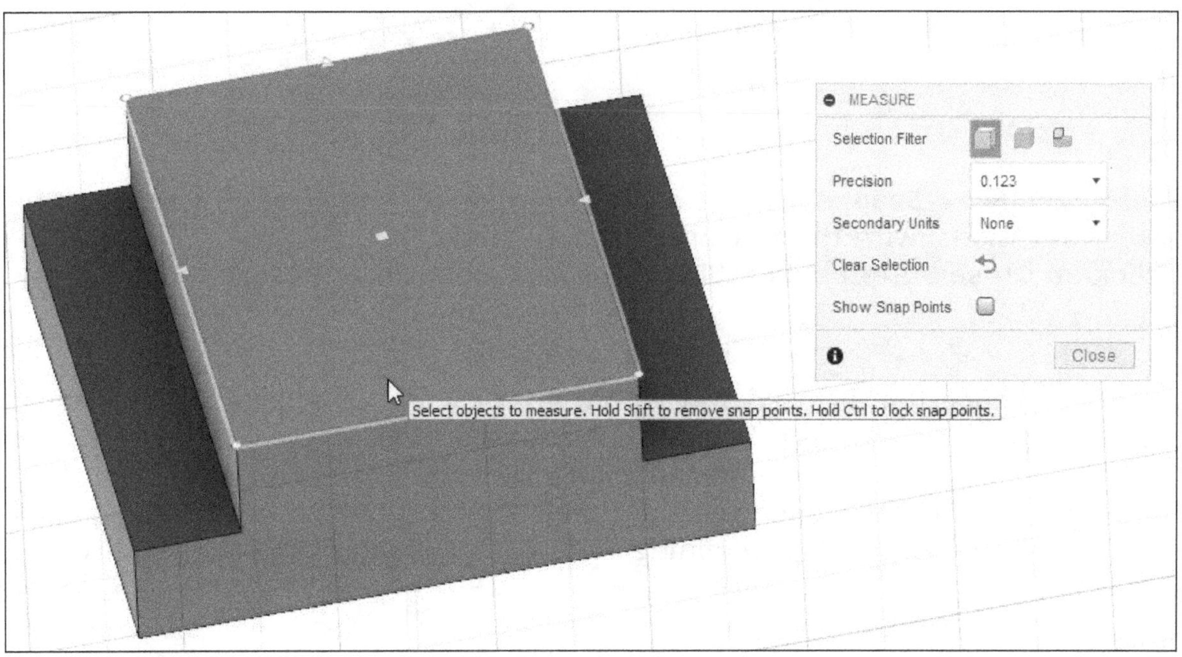

Figure-42. Selection of face for measurement

- On selecting the face, the updated **MEASURE** dialog box will be displayed with the measurement of selected face; refer to Figure-43.

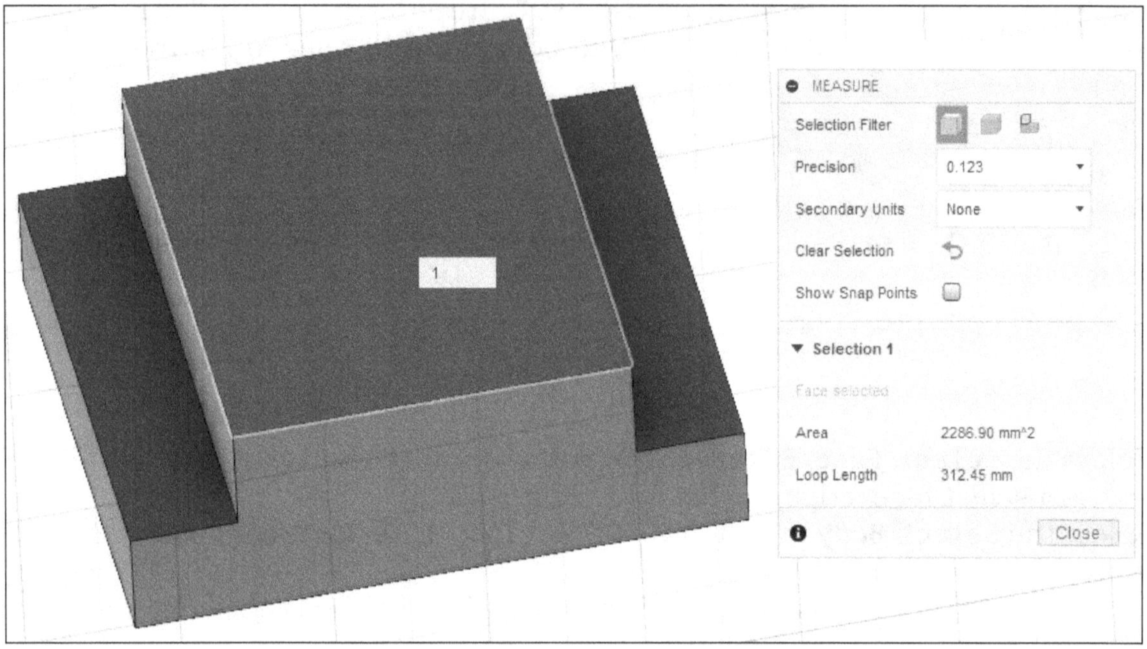

Figure-43. Updated MEASURE dialog box

- If you want to measure the distance between two faces then select the other face.
- Hover the cursor on the respective measurement to copy the value to clipboard; refer to Figure-44.

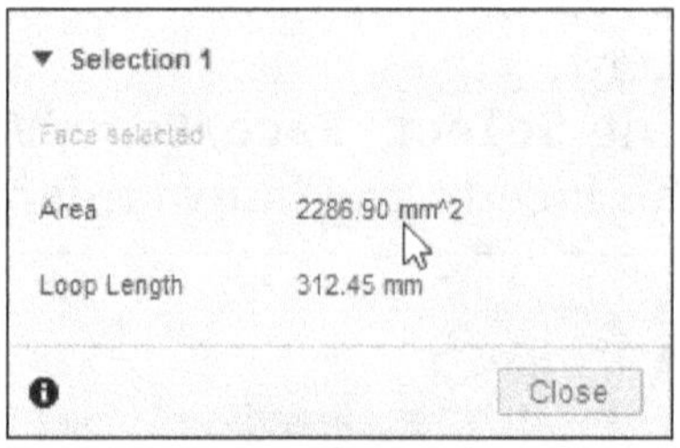

Figure-44. Copying measurement

- Select the **Show Snap Points** check box to display snap points when you hover over your model with the **Measure** tool activated.
- Click on **Close** button of **MEASURE** dialog box to exit the **Measure** tool.

Interference

The **Interference** tool is used to display interference of selected components or bodies. The procedure to use this tool is discussed next.

- Click on the **Interference** tool of **INSPECT** drop-down from **Toolbar**; refer to Figure-45. The **INTERFERENCE** dialog box will be displayed; refer to Figure-46.

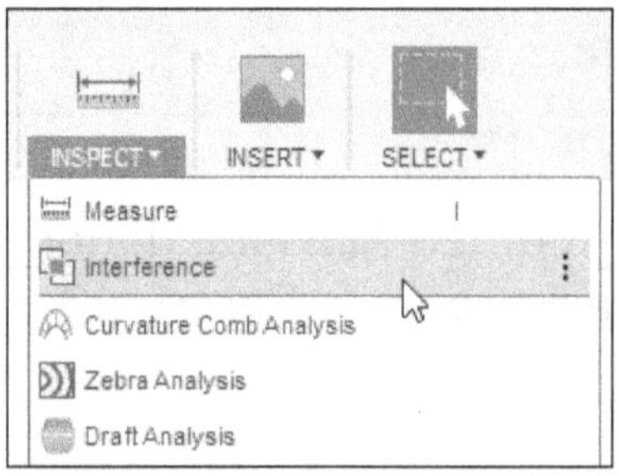

Figure-45. Interference tool

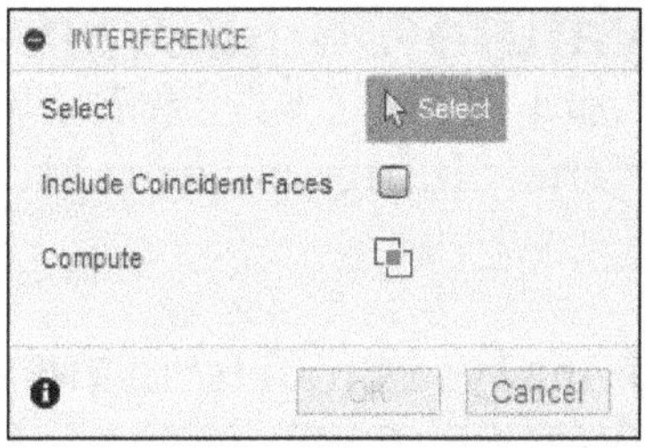

Figure-46. INTERFERENCE dialog box

- The **Select** button of **Select** section is active by default. Click on the model to check interference. You can also use window selection.
- Select the **Include Coincident Faces** check box if you want to include the faces in selection which are touching with each other.
- In our case, we are using window selection to select the component; refer to Figure-47.

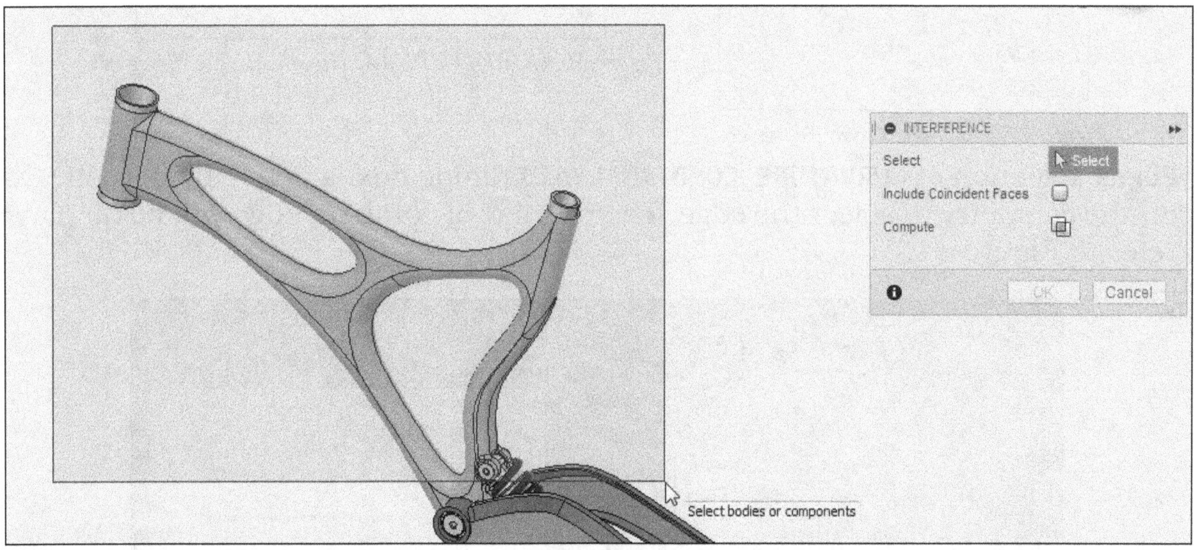

Figure-47. Selection of component for interference

- After selecting the components, click on **Compute** button to calculate the interference. The **Interference Results** dialog box will be displayed; refer to Figure-48.

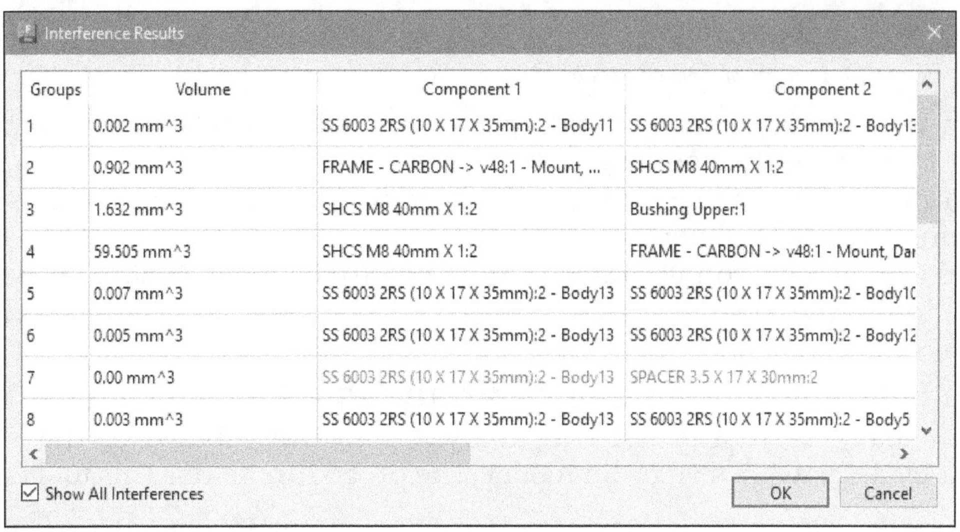
Interference Results

Groups	Volume	Component 1	Component 2
1	0.002 mm^3	SS 6003 2RS (10 X 17 X 35mm):2 - Body11	SS 6003 2RS (10 X 17 X 35mm):2 - Body13
2	0.902 mm^3	FRAME - CARBON -> v48:1 - Mount, ...	SHCS M8 40mm X 1:2
3	1.632 mm^3	SHCS M8 40mm X 1:2	Bushing Upper:1
4	59.505 mm^3	SHCS M8 40mm X 1:2	FRAME - CARBON -> v48:1 - Mount, Dai
5	0.007 mm^3	SS 6003 2RS (10 X 17 X 35mm):2 - Body13	SS 6003 2RS (10 X 17 X 35mm):2 - Body10
6	0.005 mm^3	SS 6003 2RS (10 X 17 X 35mm):2 - Body13	SS 6003 2RS (10 X 17 X 35mm):2 - Body12
7	0.00 mm^3	SS 6003 2RS (10 X 17 X 35mm):2 - Body13	SPACER 3.5 X 17 X 30mm:2
8	0.003 mm^3	SS 6003 2RS (10 X 17 X 35mm):2 - Body13	SS 6003 2RS (10 X 17 X 35mm):2 - Body5

☑ Show All Interferences   OK   Cancel

Figure-48. Interference Results dialog box

- Click on the **OK** button from **Interference Results** dialog box to exit the **Interference** tool.

Curvature Comb Analysis

The **Curvature Comb Analysis** tool is used to display a curvature comb on the spline or circular edges to determine the change in curvature. The procedure to use this tool is discussed next.

- Click on the **Curvature Comb Analysis** tool from **INSPECT** drop-down in the **Toolbar**; refer to Figure-49. The **CURVATURE COMB ANALYSIS** dialog box will be displayed; refer to Figure-50.

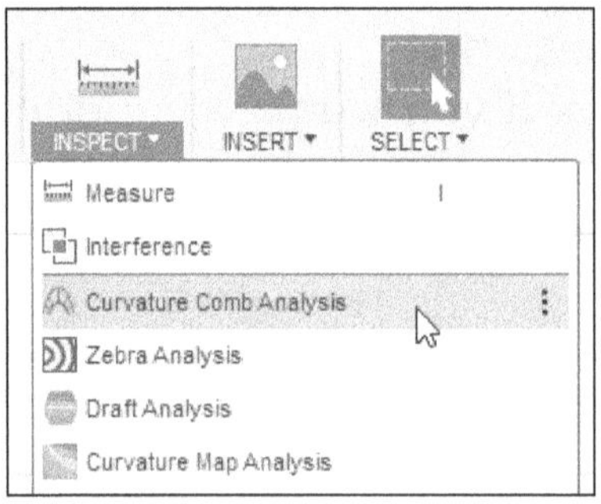

Figure-49. Curvature Comb Analysis tool

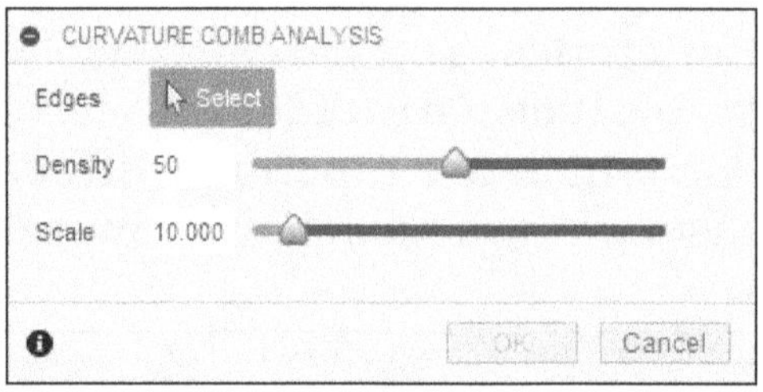

Figure-50. CURVATURE COMB ANALYSIS dialog box

- **Edges** selection of **CURVATURE COMB ANALYSIS** dialog box is active by default. Click on the geometry to select the edge. The preview of comb on edge will be displayed; refer to Figure-51.

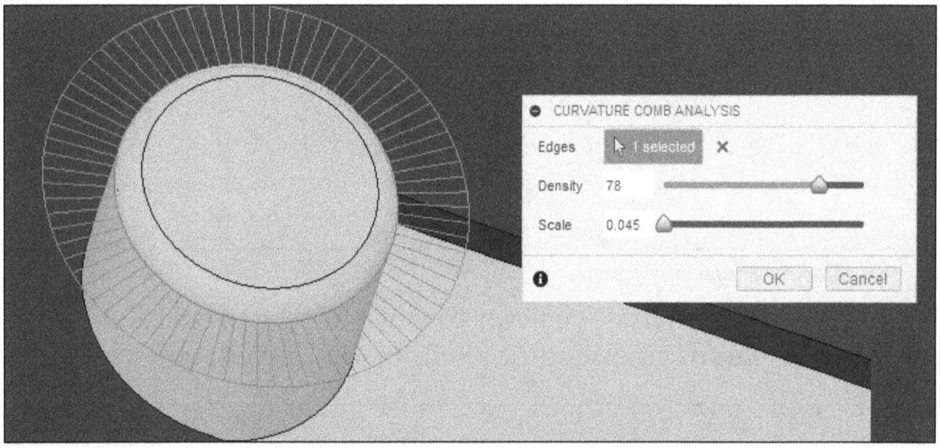

Figure-51. Preview of comb on circular edge

- Click in the **Density** edit box and specify the value. You can also set the comb density by moving the **Density** slider.
- Click in the **Scale** edit box and specify the value. You can also set the comb scale by moving the **Scale** slider.
- After analyzing, click on **OK** button from **CURVATURE COMB ANALYSIS** dialog box to exit the tool.

Zebra Analysis

The **Zebra Analysis** tool is used to analyze continuity between the surfaces of component by displaying stripes on model. The procedure to use this tool is discussed next.

- Click on the **Zebra Analysis** tool from **INSPECT** drop-down in the **Toolbar**; refer to Figure-52. The **ZEBRA ANALYSIS** dialog box will be displayed; refer to Figure-53.

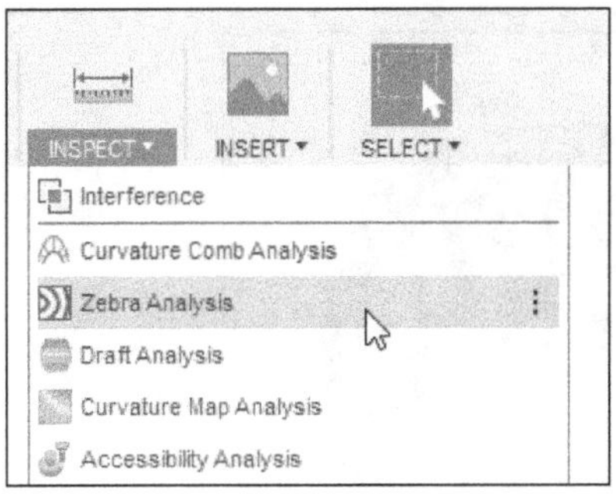

Figure-52. Zebra Analysis tool

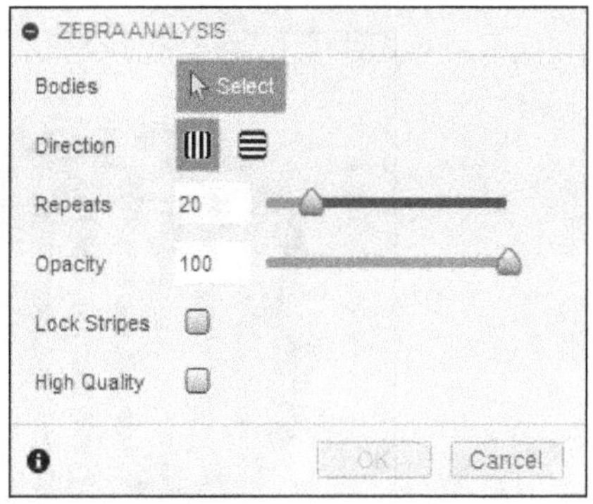

Figure-53. ZEBRA ANALYSIS dialog box

- The **Select** button of **Bodies** section is active by default. Click to select the body for analysis.
- On selecting the body, preview of zebra stripes will be displayed; refer to Figure-54.

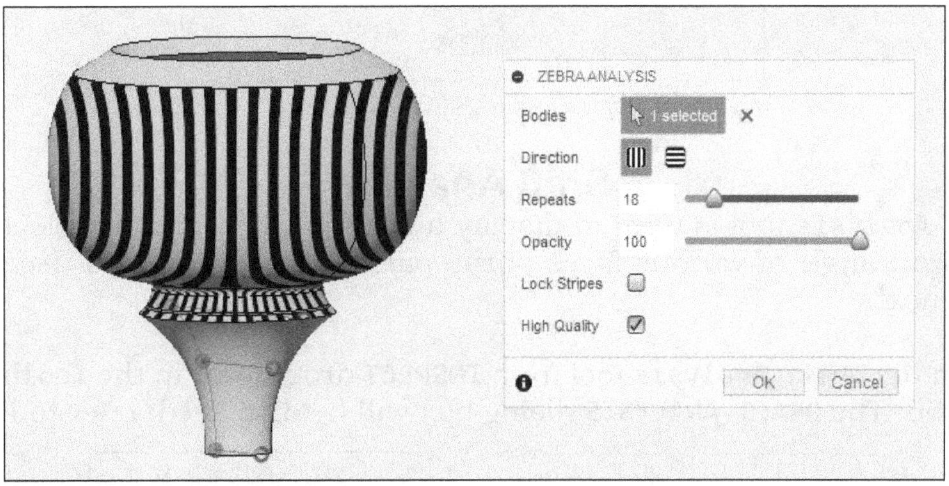

Figure-54. Selection of body for zebra analysis

- Select **Vertical** option from **Direction** section for display of vertical lines on model.
- Select **Horizontal** option from **Direction** section for display of horizontal lines on model.
- Set the number of stripes for model from **Repeats** slider.
- Click on the **Opacity** edit box and enter the value for opacity. You can also set the value of opacity by moving the **Opacity** slider.
- Select the **Lock Stripes** check box of **ZEBRA ANALYSIS** dialog box to freeze the stripes on body.
- Select the **High Quality** check box of **ZEBRA ANALYSIS** dialog box to increase the display quality of stripes.
- After specifying the parameters, click on **OK** button from **ZEBRA ANALYSIS** dialog box. The stripes will be displayed on model; refer to Figure-55.

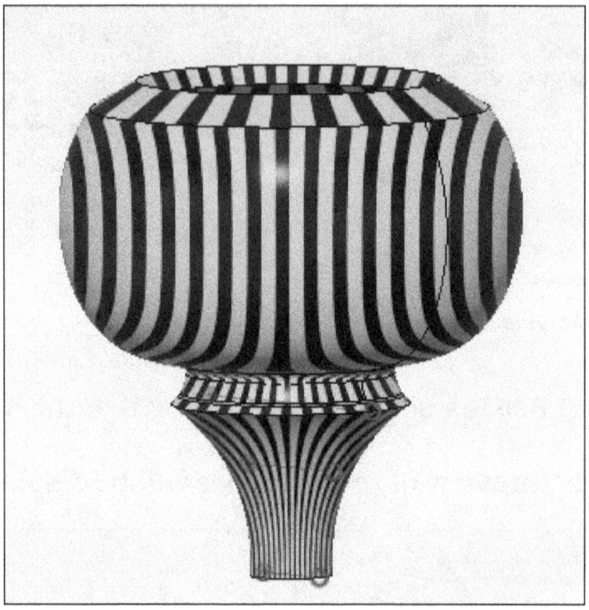

Figure-55. Strips on model

Draft Analysis

The **Draft Analysis** tool is used to display a color gradient on the selected body to evaluate draft angle of various faces of the part. The procedure to use this tool is discussed next.

- Click on the **Draft Analysis** tool from **INSPECT** drop-down in the **Toolbar**; refer to Figure-56. The **DRAFT ANALYSIS** dialog box will be displayed; refer to Figure-57.

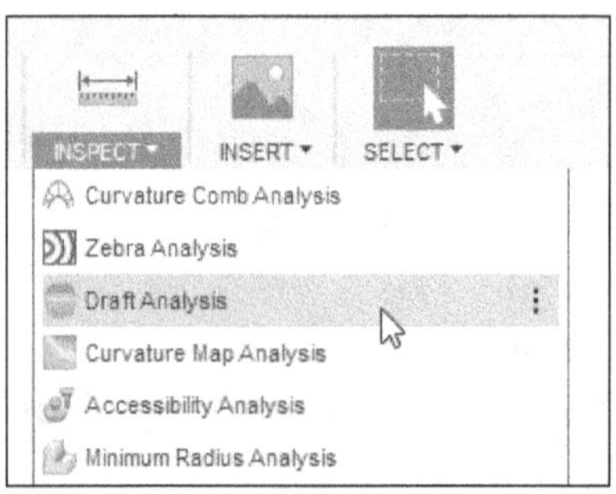

Figure-56. Draft Analysis tool

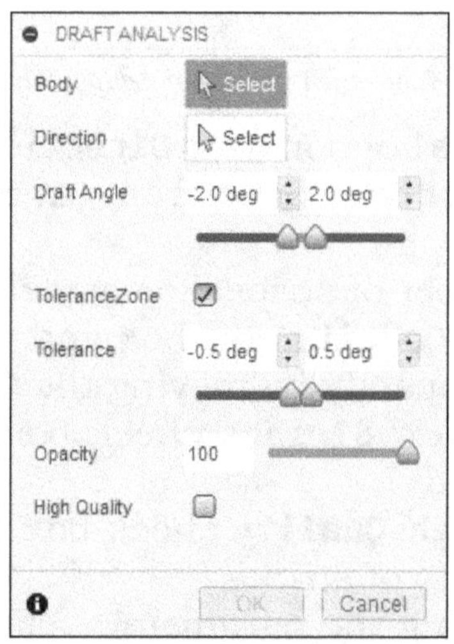

Figure-57. DRAFT ANALYSIS dialog box

- The **Select** button of **Body** section is active by default. Click on the body to perform analysis.
- Click on **Select** button of **Direction** section and select the direction for analysis. On selection, the preview will be displayed; refer to Figure-58.

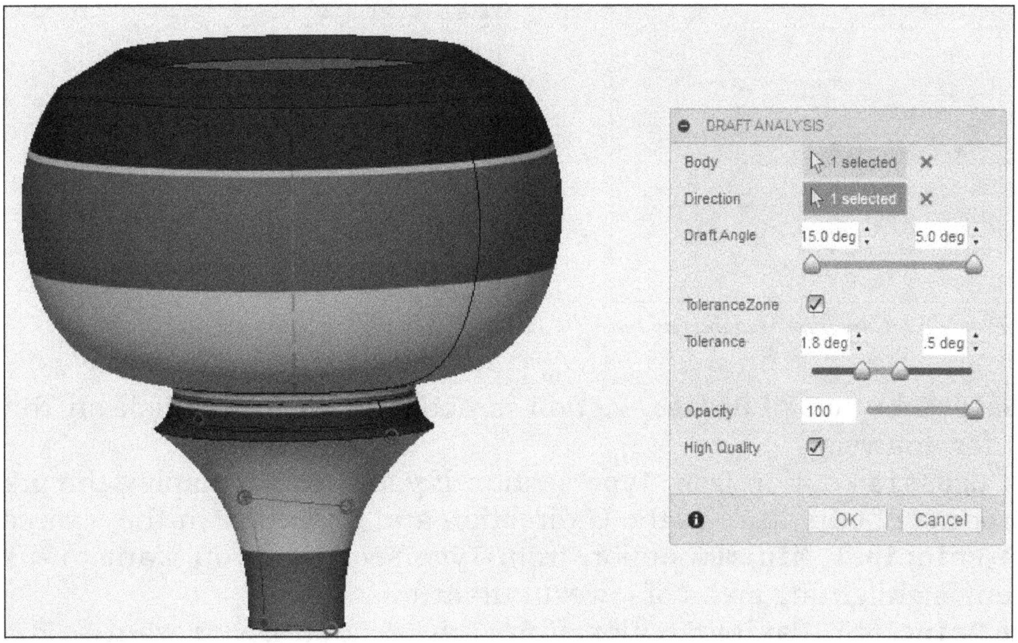

Figure-58. Preview of draft analysis

- Click in **Draft Angle** edit boxes and specify the range of draft angle for which you want to perform analysis. You can also set the draft angle limits by moving the **Draft angle** slider.
- Select the **ToleranceZone** check box if you want to display a tolerance gradient on the results.
- Click on the **Tolerance** edit box and specify the start and stop angles tolerance. You can also set the tolerance angle by moving the slider.
- Click on the **Opacity** edit box and enter the value for opacity for draft colors. You can also set the value of opacity by moving the **Opacity** slider.
- Select the **High Quality** check box of **DRAFT ANALYSIS** dialog box to increase the display quality of gradient.
- After specifying the parameters for analysis, click on **OK** button from **DRAFT ANALYSIS** dialog box to complete the analysis.

Curvature Map Analysis

The **Curvature Map Analysis** tool is used to displays a color gradient on the faces of selected bodies to evaluate the amount of curvature. The procedure to use this tool is discussed next.

- Click on the **Curvature Map Analysis** tool from **INSPECT** drop-down in the **Toolbar**; refer to Figure-59. The **CURVATURE MAP ANALYSIS** dialog box will be displayed; refer to Figure-60.

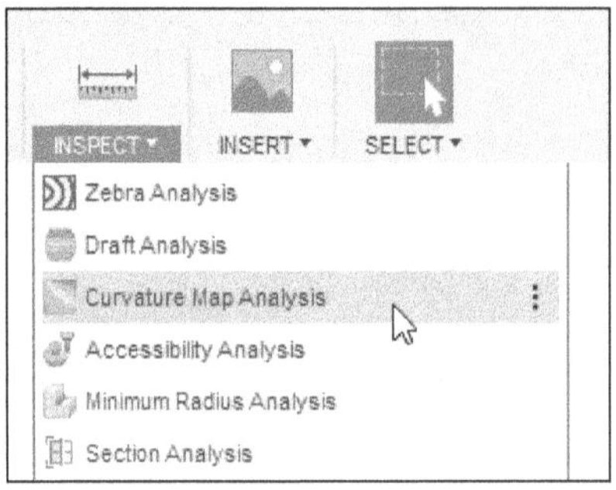

Figure-59. Curvature Map Analysis tool

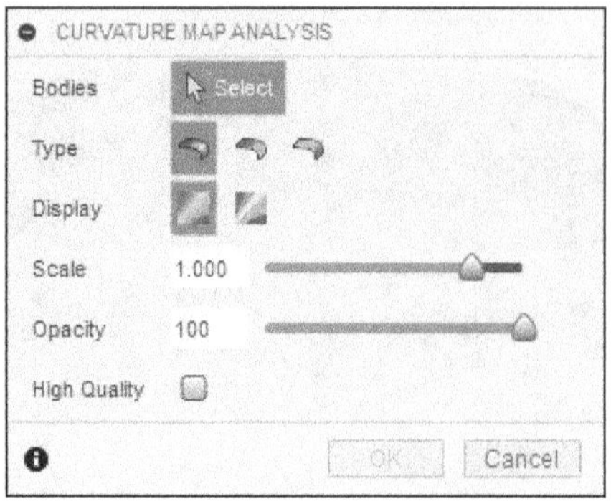

Figure-60. CURVATURE MAP ANALYSIS dialog box

- The **Select** button of **Bodies** section is active by default. Click on the body to select for analysis.
- Select **Gaussian** option from **Type** section if you want to display the gradient as the product of curvature in the U direction and curvature in the V direction.
- Select **Principal Minimum** option from **Type** section if you want to display the gradient highlighting areas of lowest curvature.
- Select **Principal Maximum** option from **Type** section if you want to display the gradient highlighting areas with the highest curvature.
- Select **Smooth** option from **Display** section if you want to display a blend of two colors.
- Select **Bands** option from **Display** section if you want to display no transition between colors.
- Click in the **Scale** edit box of **CURVATURE MAP ANALYSIS** dialog box and enter the value. You can also set the value of scale by moving the **Scale** slider.
- Click on the **Opacity** edit box and enter the value for opacity. You can also set the value of opacity by moving the **Opacity** slider.
- Select the **High Quality** check box of **CURVATURE MAP ANALYSIS** dialog box to increase the display quality of gradient.
- After specifying the parameters for analysis, click on **OK** button from **CURVATURE MAP ANALYSIS** dialog box to exit this analysis; refer to Figure-61.

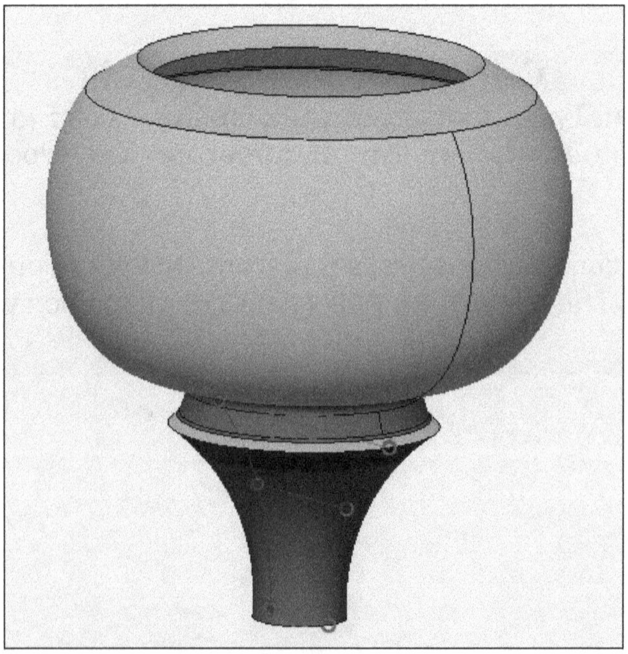

Figure-61. Curvature map analysis of model

Isocurve Analysis

The **Isocurve Analysis** tool is used to analyze the quality of the curvature of a surface by applying UV mapping and curvature combs in Fusion. The procedure to use this tool is discussed next.

- Click on the **Isocurve Analysis** tool from **INSPECT** drop-down in the **Toolbar**; refer to Figure-62. The **ISOCURVE ANALYSIS** dialog box will be displayed; refer to Figure-63.

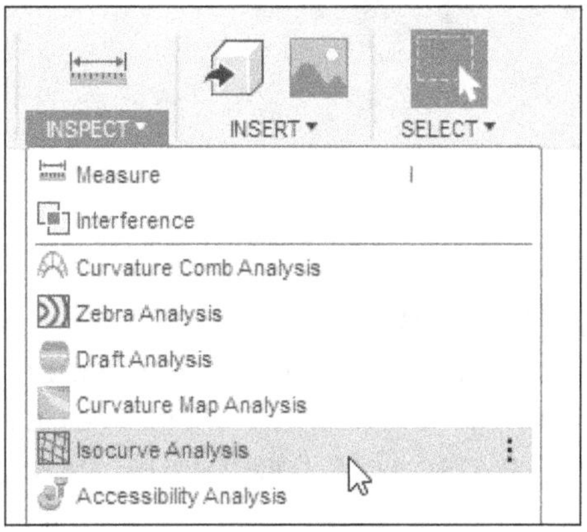

Figure-62. Isocurve Analysis tool

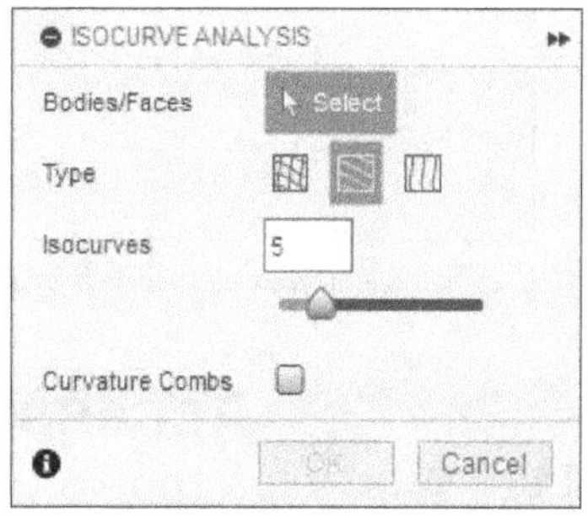

Figure-63. ISOCURVE ANALYSIS dialog box

- The **Bodies/Faces** selection button is active by default. Select the body or face which you want to analyze; refer to Figure-64.

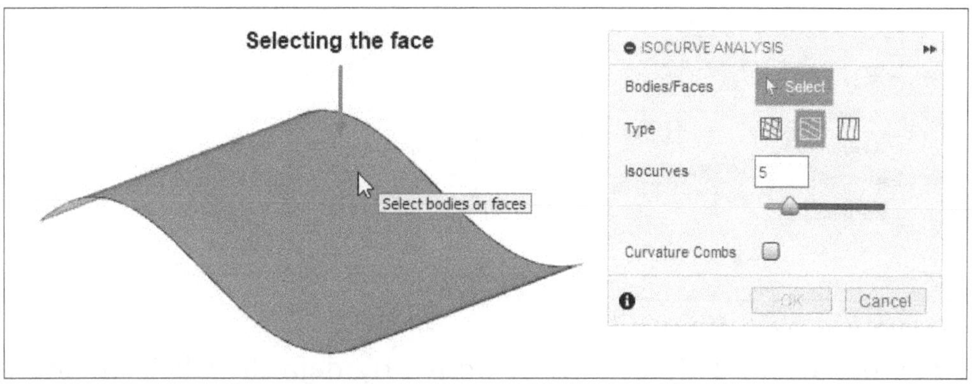

Figure-64. Selecting the face to analyze

- Select desired isocurve type from **Type** section of the dialog box. Select the **U and V** option to display isocurves in U and V directions. Select the **U** option to display isocurves in the U direction. Select the **V** option to display isocurves in the V direction.
- Specify number of isocurves to display on selected bodies or faces in the **Isocurves** edit box. You can also set the number of isocurves by moving the **Isocurves** slider.
- Select **Curvature Combs** check box to display curvature combs on isocurves.
- Specify number of teeth to display on curvature combs in the **Density** edit box. You can also set the number of teeth by moving the **Density** slider.
- Specify scale of curvature combs in the **Scale** edit box. You can also set the value of scale by moving the **Scale** slider.
- After specifying desired parameters for analysis, click on the **OK** button from the dialog box to exit the analysis; refer to Figure-65.

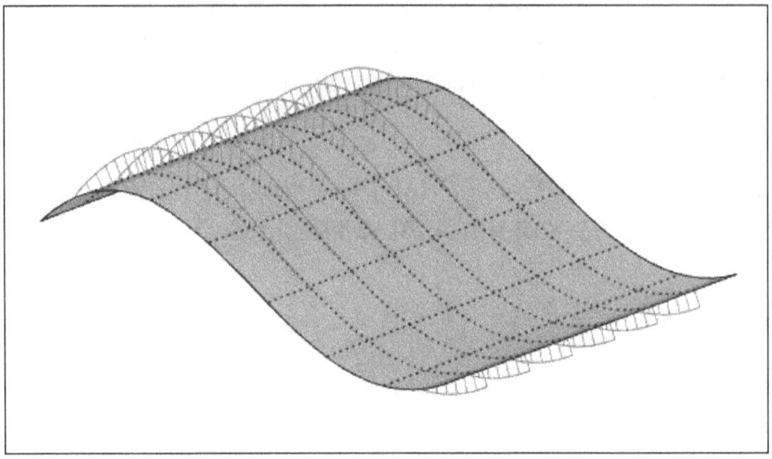

Figure-65. Isocurve analysis of the body

Accessibility Analysis

The **Accessibility Analysis** tool is used to determine whether the area of the model is accessible or inaccessible through selected view of the plane. This analysis is used to perform undercut analysis. The procedure to use this tool is discussed next.

- Click on the **Accessibility Analysis** tool from **INSPECT** drop-down in the **Toolbar**; refer to Figure-66. The **ACCESSIBILITY ANALYSIS** dialog box will be displayed; refer to Figure-67.

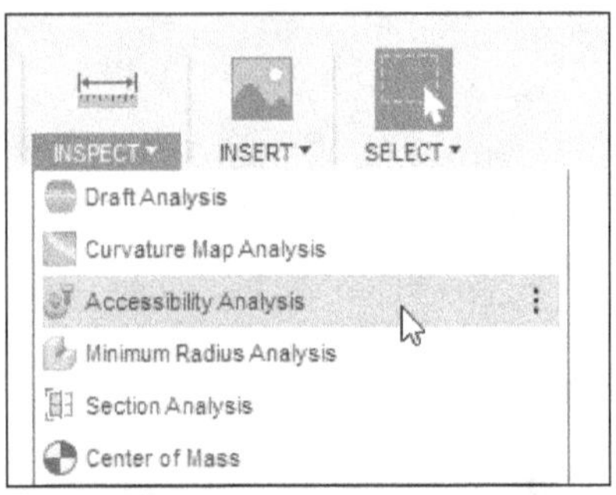

Figure-66. Accessibility Analysis tool

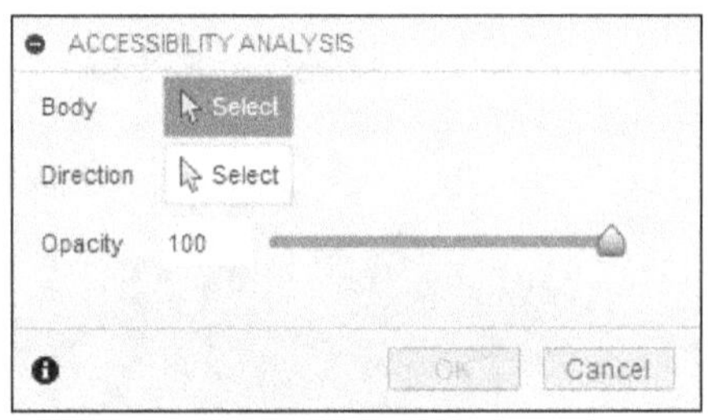

Figure-67. ACCESSIBILITY ANALYSIS dialog box

- The **Select** button of **Body** section is active by default. Click on the face of the body to select; refer to Figure-68. You will be asked to select a direction.

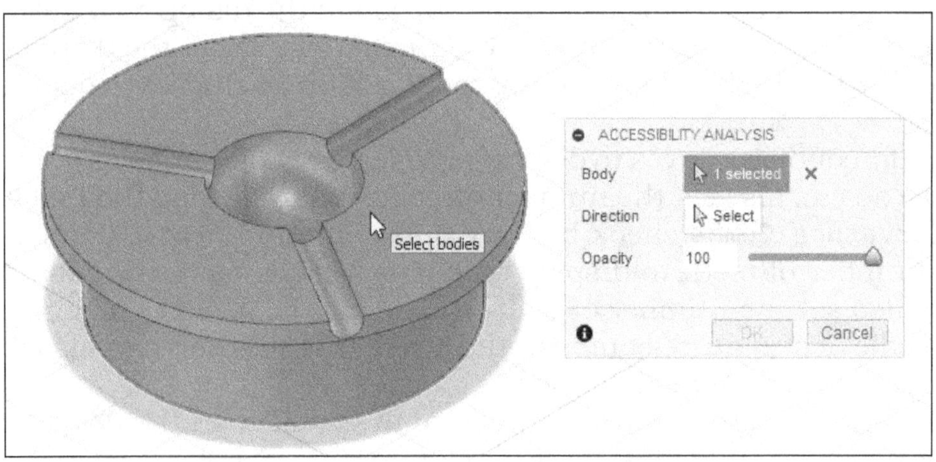

Figure-68. Selecting the body

- Click on the **Select** button of **Direction** section and select the edge, plane, or axis of the model to indicate the direction of analysis. The preview of the accessible areas will be displayed along with updated **ACCESSIBILITY ANALYSIS** dialog box; refer to Figure-69.

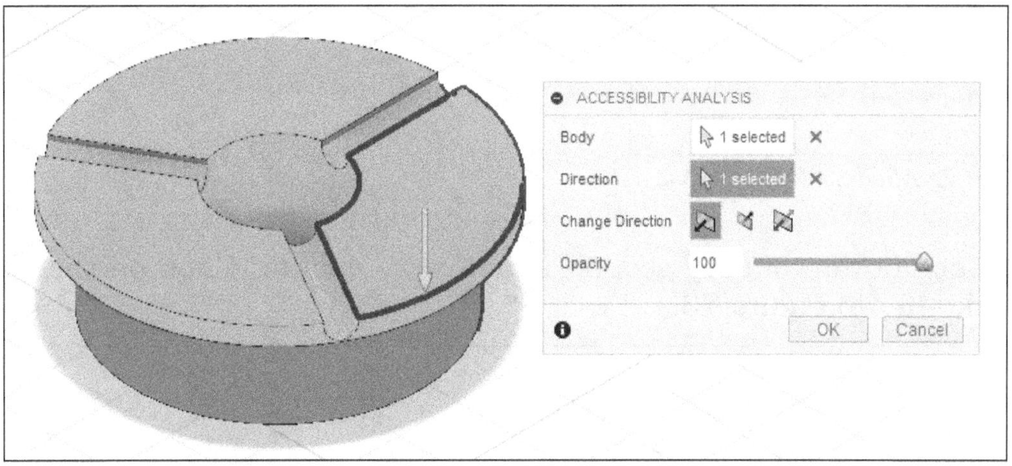

Figure-69. Updated ACCESSIBILITY ANALYSIS dialog box

- On selecting the direction, the areas that are accessible from selected direction are shaded in green and the areas that are inaccessible are shaded in red.
- Select desired option from **Change Direction** section to change the direction of analysis.
- You can also set the opacity by sliding the slider button or edit the opacity in edit box of **Opacity** section.
- The visibility of this analysis can be controlled by expanding the **Analysis** folder in the **BROWSER** and clicking on the eye button to view or hide the analysis; refer to Figure-70.

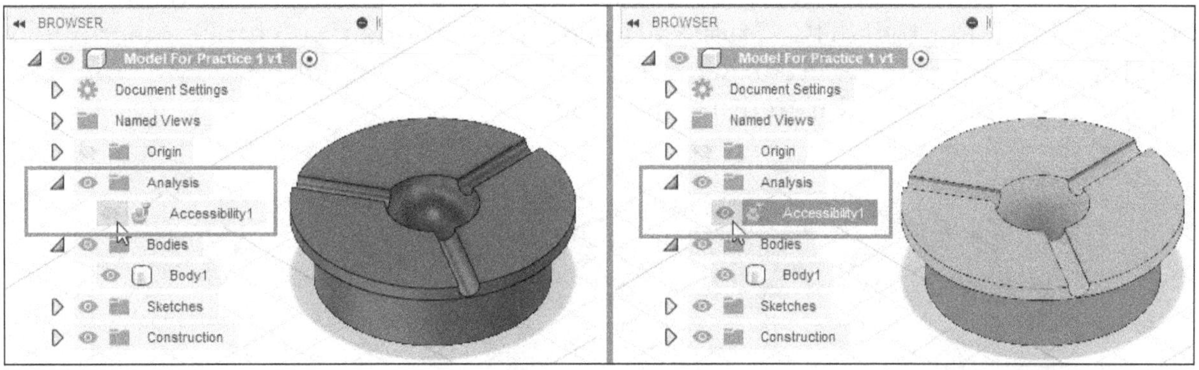

Figure-70. Visibility of analysis

- After specifying the parameters for analysis, click on **OK** button from **ACCESSIBILITY ANALYSIS** dialog box to exit this analysis.

Minimum Radius Analysis

The **Minimum Radius Analysis** tool is used to highlight the areas of the model which are at or below the minimum radius. It also detects the minimum fit for fillets and holes. The procedure to use this tool is discussed next.

- Click on the **Minimum Radius Analysis** tool from **INSPECT** drop-down in the **Toolbar**; refer to Figure-71. The **MINIMUM RADIUS ANALYSIS** dialog box will be displayed; refer to Figure-72.

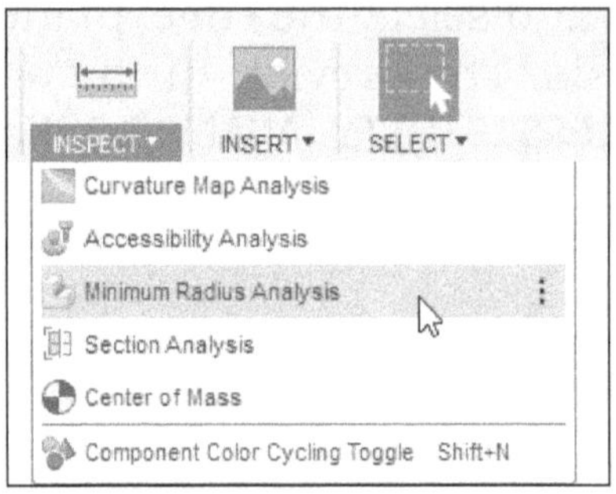

Figure-71. Minimum Radius Analysis tool

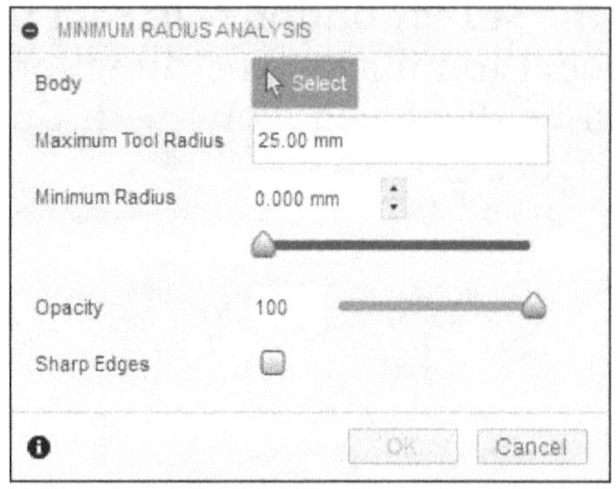

Figure-72. MINIMUM RADIUS ANALYSIS dialog box

- The **Select** button of **Body** section is active by default. Click on the body to be selected; refer to Figure-73.

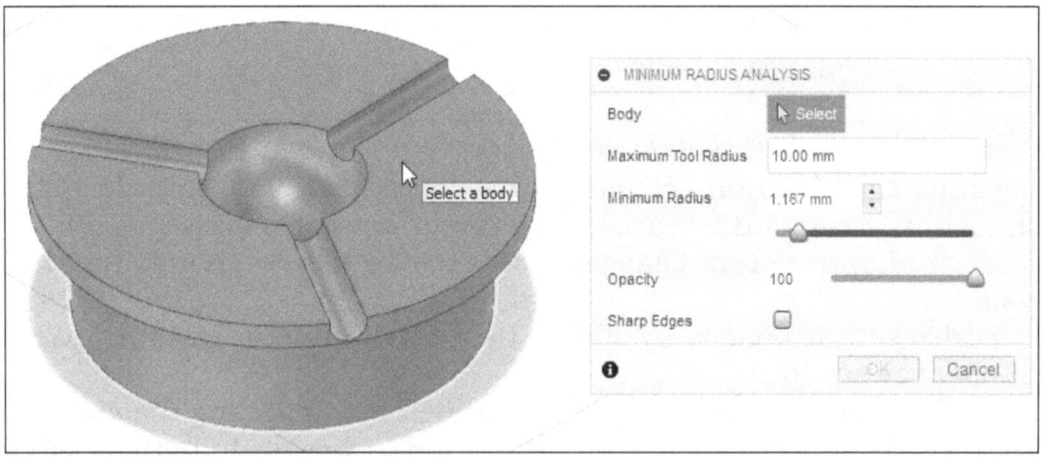

Figure-73. Selection of face of the body

- After selecting the body, set the **Maximum Tool Radius** in the edit box for analysis of the model. For tool of **Minimum Radius** 8, the sections that can be machined are highlighted in green whereas sections with cannot be machined by 8 mm radius tool will be highlighted in red; refer to Figure-74.

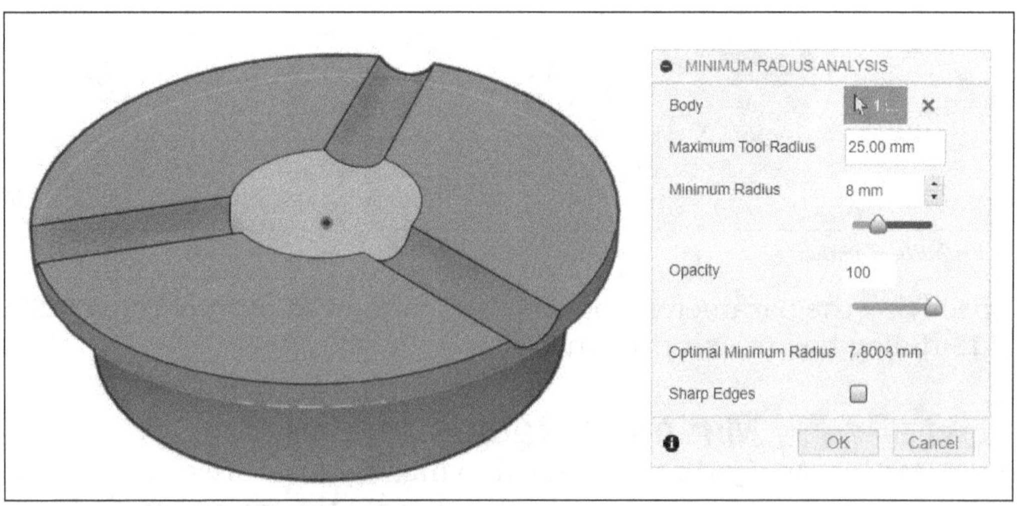

Figure-74. Minimum radius color

- Note that software automatically calculates the optimum minimum radius of tool which can machine most of the sections of model in **Optimal Minimum Radius** field of the dialog box which is 7.8003 mm in our case; refer to Figure-74.
- Set the opacity of the analysis as you did in the **Accessibility Analysis** tool.

- Select the **Sharp Edges** check box to display sharp edges of the model.
- After specifying all the parameters, click on the **OK** button of **MINIMUM RADIUS ANALYSIS** dialog box to exit this analysis.
- The visibility of this analysis can be control by expanding the **Analysis** folder in the **BROWSER** and clicking on the eye button to view or hide the analysis; refer to Figure-75.

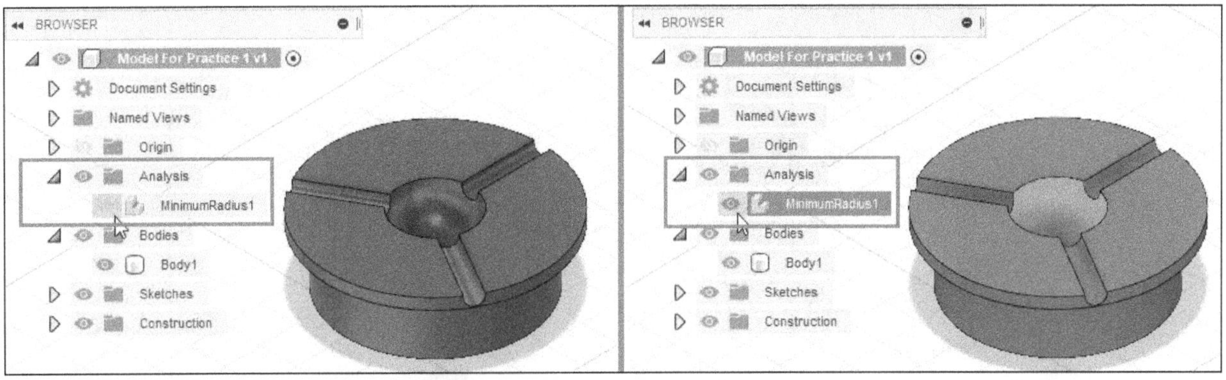

Figure-75. Visibility of minimum radius analysis

Section Analysis

The **Section Analysis** tool is used to cut the model at selected plane reference and check the temporary view. The procedure to use this tool is discussed next.

- Click on the **Section Analysis** tool from **INSPECT** drop-down in the **Toolbar**; refer to Figure-76. The **SECTION ANALYSIS** dialog box will be displayed; refer to Figure-77.

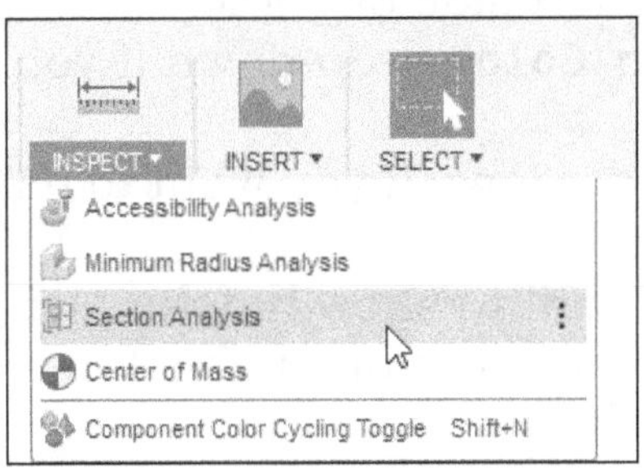

Figure-76. Section Analysis tool

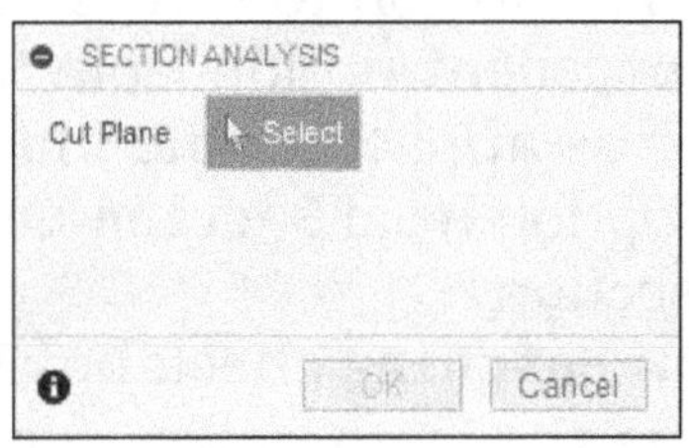

Figure-77. SECTION ANALYSIS dialog box

- The **Select** button of **Cut Plane** section is active by default. Click on the face to select.
- On selection of face, the dialog box will be updated along with the preview of model; refer to Figure-78.

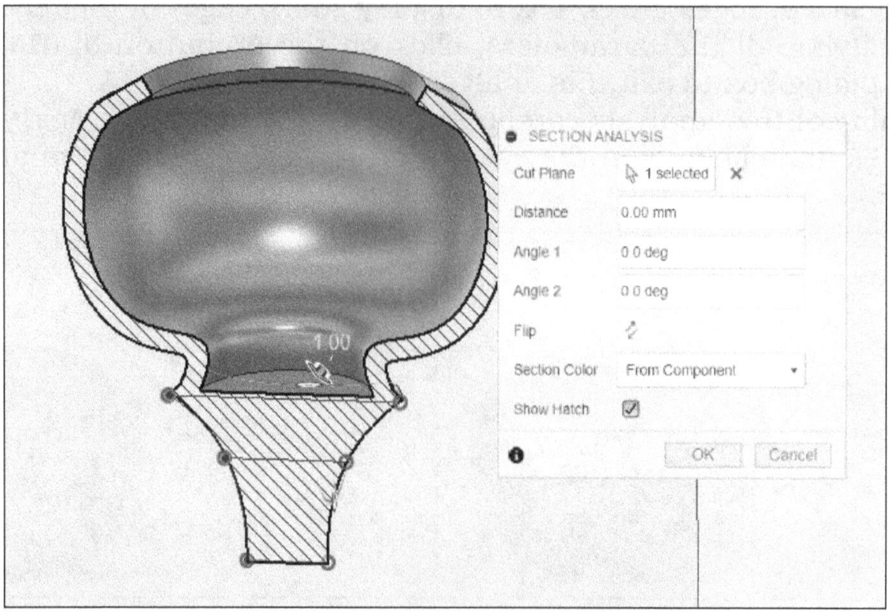

Figure-78. Updated SECTION ANALYSIS dialog box

- Click in the **Distance** edit box and specify the location of the section plane along y direction. You can also set the value by moving the drag handle.
- Click in the **Angle 1** edit box and specify the angle of plane about x direction. You can also set the value by moving the drag handle.
- Click in the **Angle 2** edit box and specify the angle of plane about y direction. You can also set the value by moving the drag handle.
- Click on the **Flip** button to reverse the section side of plane.
- Select **From Component** option from **Section Color** drop-down if you want to use the same color as applied to the model.
- Select **Custom** option from **Section Color** drop-down if you want to use the custom color for the section.
- Select the **Show Hatching** check box if you want to show hatching on the section.
- After specifying the parameters for analysis, click on **OK** button from **SECTION ANALYSIS** dialog box to complete the analysis.

Center of Mass

The **Center of Mass** tool is a center point of body used for representing the mean position of matter in a body. The procedure to use this tool is discussed next.

- Click on the **Center of Mass** tool of **INSPECT** drop-down from **Toolbar**; refer to Figure-79. The **CENTER OF MASS** dialog box will be displayed; refer to Figure-80.

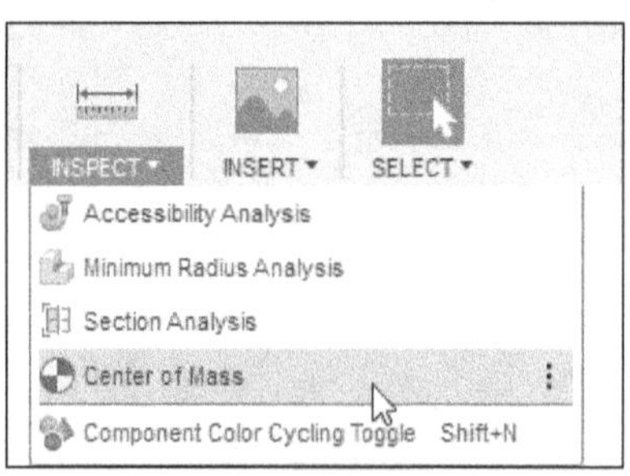

Figure-79. Center of Mass tool

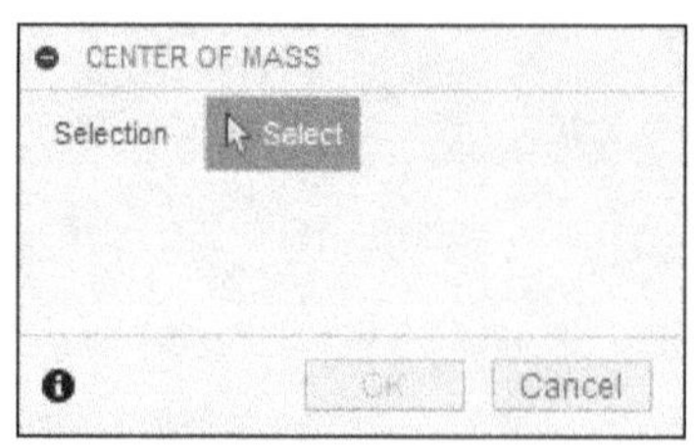

Figure-80. CENTER OF MASS dialog box

- You need to select the body and click on **OK** button from **CENTER OF MASS** dialog box. The center of mass of the body will be displayed; refer to Figure-81.

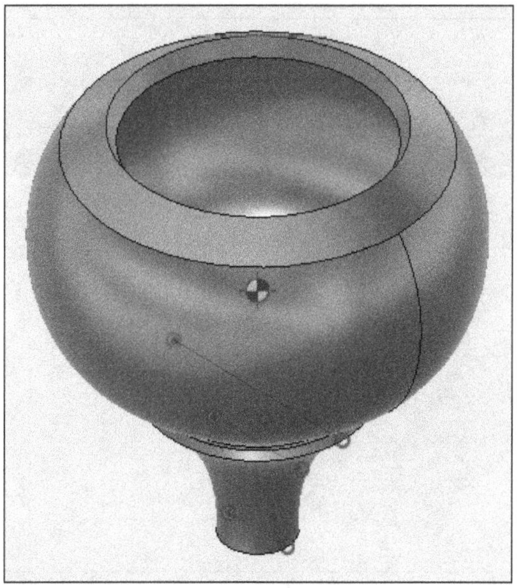

Figure-81. Center of mass of the body

Plastic Injection Molding Design Advice

The **Design Advice** tool is used to analyze the part and check its manufacturability using plastic injection modeling process. The procedure to use this tool is given next.

- Open part for which you want to check plastic injection molding recommendations and click on the **Design Advice** tool from the **INSPECT** drop-down of **PLASTIC** tab in the **Toolbar**. The **DESIGN ADVICE** dialog box will be displayed; refer to Figure-82.

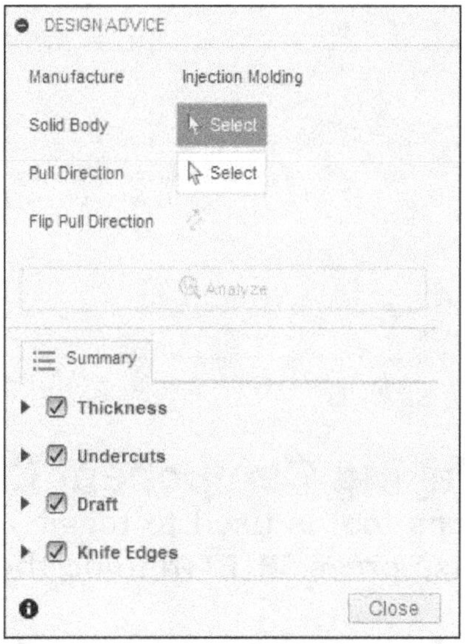

Figure-82. DESIGN ADVICE dialog box

- Select the solid body to be manufactured by injection molding. You will be asked to assign plastic rules if not applied earlier. Assign the rules as discussed earlier.
- Click on the **Select** button for **Pull Direction** and select reference to be used for defining direction of core/cavity pull.
- Click on the **Flip Pull Direction** button to reverse direction of pulling mold plate.
- Select check boxes from the **Summary** section of dialog box and define properties of model to be analyzed for molding; refer to Figure-83.

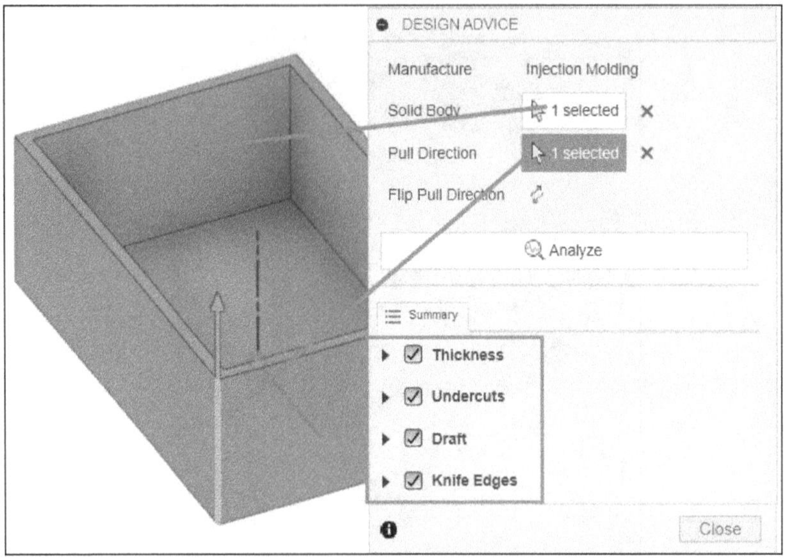

Figure-83. Parameters specified for design advice

- After setting desired parameters, click on the **Analyze** button. The results of analysis will be displayed; refer to Figure-84. Modify the part as per the analysis results and if there are green tick marks for all the parameters then your part is good to go for manufacturing.

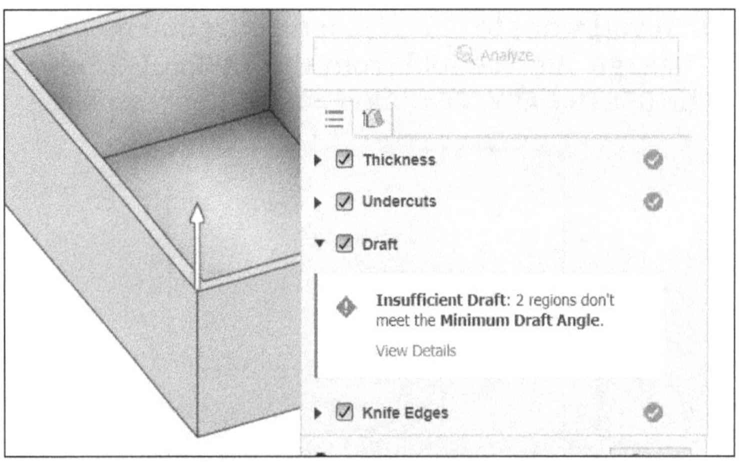

Figure-84. Design advice results

Displaying Component Colors

The **Display Component Colors** tool is used to toggle coloring of various objects in Autodesk Fusion. You can also press **SHIFT+N** to do the same thing.

Similarly, the **Display Mesh Face Groups** tool is used to display mesh face groups with different colors.

SELF ASSESSMENT

Q1. Which of the following tools is used for inserting image on the face of a model?

a) Insert Mesh
b) Insert Derive
c) Decal
d) Insert SVG

Q2. What is the use of **Reset Transformation** button in **INSERT MESH** dialog box?

Q3. What is the use of **Insert Mc-Master Carr Component** tool and what is Mc-Master Carr?

Q4. Write the procedure of inserting manufacturer or supplier part in the model.

Q5. Write the procedure to measure the distance between two faces.

Q6. Write the procedure to find interference between two components.

Q7. The **Curvature Comb Analysis** tool is used to display a curvature comb on the spline or circular edges to determine the ....

Q8. The **Zebra Analysis** tool is used to analyze continuity between the surfaces of component by ....on model.

Q9. Write the procedure to display zebra stripes on body.

10. The **Draft Analysis** tool is used to display a color gradient on the selected body to .... of various faces of the part.

11. The .... tool is used to displays a color gradient on the faces of selected bodies to evaluate the amount of curvature.

12. What is the use of **Gaussian** option in **Curvature Map Analysis**?

13. The **Section Analysis** tool is used to define the view of component from .... side.

14. Which of the following analyses uses **ToleranceZone** option to display a tolerance gradient on the results?

a) Section Analysis
b) Zebra Analysis
c) Curvature Comb Analysis
d) Draft Analysis

Q15. The .... tool is used to analyze the quality of the curvature of a surface by applying UV mapping and curvature combs in Fusion.

Q16. What is the main purpose of the Insert Derive tool in Autodesk Fusion?

A. To insert components, sketches, parameters, or bodies from another design
B. To insert a mesh file into the current model
C. To add decals and images to the design
D. To import a DXF file into the design

Q17. What should you do before using the Insert Derive tool in Autodesk Fusion?

A. Save the current model file
B. Delete the existing components
C. Import the components manually
D. Open the new design file

Q18. Which dialog box is displayed after selecting the Insert Derive tool from the Toolbar?

A. Select Source dialog box
B. Insert Component dialog box
C. Open dialog box
D. Insert DXF dialog box

Q19. What option in the DERIVE dialog box aligns the component origin to the model origin?

A. Place Objects At Origin
B. Select Face
C. Include Parameters
D. Adjust Scale

Q20. What tool is used to insert a component into the current design in Autodesk Fusion?

A. Insert Derive tool
B. Insert Component tool
C. Insert Mesh tool
D. Insert DXF tool

Q21. Which tool is used to place an image on a selected face or plane in Fusion?

A. Insert Component tool
B. Insert Derive tool
C. Decal tool
D. Canvas tool

Q22. What does the Horizontal Flip button do in the Decal dialog box?

A. Flips the image vertically
B. Flips the image horizontally
C. Resizes the image
D. Rotates the image

Q23. What is the purpose of the Canvas tool in Autodesk Fusion?

A. To import SVG files
B. To insert an image on a planar face for creating models based on the image
C. To insert a mesh file
D. To create new components

Q24. In the Canvas dialog box, which option controls the visibility of the image through the component?

A. Selectable checkbox
B. Display Through checkbox
C. Renderable checkbox
D. Opacity slider

Q25. What does the Insert SVG tool do in Autodesk Fusion?

A. Inserts an SVG image file into the sketch
B. Inserts a DXF file into the design
C. Inserts a 2D or 3D model from McMaster-Carr
D. Imports a mesh file into the design

Q26. What is the default action after selecting the desired plane in the Insert SVG dialog box?

A. It inserts the SVG image directly onto the design
B. It enables the sketching environment for SVG insertion
C. It scales the image to fit the model
D. It rotates the SVG image automatically

Q27. What tool allows you to insert a DXF file into the active design?

A. Insert Derive tool
B. Insert DXF tool
C. Insert Component tool
D. Insert McMaster-Carr Component tool

Q28. In the Insert DXF dialog box, which option allows you to import each layer of a DXF file on a different layer in Fusion?

A. Single Sketch
B. One Sketch per Layer
C. DXF Layers
D. Display Through

Q29. What is the purpose of the Insert McMaster-Carr Component tool?

A. To insert 2D or 3D models from McMaster-Carr's library into the design
B. To insert a mesh file from McMaster-Carr
C. To create a new component from a library
D. To import SVG files from McMaster-Carr

Q30. How do you move the model to the center or coordinate system in the Insert Mesh tool?

A. Use the Flip Up Direction button
B. Select the Center button from the Position section
C. Use the Reset button
D. Select the Select button from the Model Objects section

Q31. What action does the Flip Up Direction button perform in the Insert Mesh dialog box?

A. It moves the model to the center
B. It flips the direction of the model
C. It changes the scale of the model
D. It adjusts the opacity of the model

Q32. What does the Insert Mesh tool allow you to do after importing a mesh file?

A. Scale the mesh file in one direction
B. Change the unit type and move the mesh to a specific position
C. Convert the mesh into a component
D. Import multiple mesh files simultaneously

Q33. Which option in the Insert Mesh dialog box allows you to reset the model position to its original state?

A. Flip Up Direction
B. Move To Ground
C. Reset button
D. Numerical Inputs section

Q34. What must be done after selecting the desired component and clicking the Insert button in the Insert Component dialog box?

A. The component will automatically be added to the project
B. You must specify the initial position of the component
C. The model will be rendered
D. The component will be saved to the local drive

Q35. What tool is used to import files from McMaster-Carr in Autodesk Fusion?

A. Insert DXF tool
B. Insert McMaster-Carr Component tool
C. Insert SVG tool
D. Insert Mesh tool

Q36. What is the purpose of the "Insert a Manufacturer Part" tool in Autodesk Fusion?

A) To insert a part from a manufacturer or supplier into the model through Parts4CAD.
B) To insert an image onto a plane.
C) To measure the dimensions of a part.
D) To inspect the curvature of a model.

Q37. How can you access the "Insert TraceParts Supplier Components" tool in Autodesk Fusion?

A) By clicking on the Insert button in the Tool section.
B) By navigating to the INSERT drop-down from the Toolbar.
C) By clicking on the Measure tool in the Inspect section.
D) By opening the Design Library window directly.

Q38. Which section of Autodesk Fusion's toolbar allows you to access the "Measure" tool?

A) Model
B) Insert
C) Inspect
D) View

Q39. What action does the "Interference" tool in Autodesk Fusion perform?

A) It displays interference between selected components or bodies.
B) It measures the distance between two faces.
C) It analyzes the curvature of spline edges.
D) It inspects the minimum radius of a tool for machining.

Q40. What does the “Curvature Comb Analysis” tool in Autodesk Fusion display?

A) It displays a curvature comb on spline or circular edges to determine curvature change.
B) It shows the draft angle of a selected model.
C) It performs an undercut analysis on the model.
D) It calculates interference between components.

Q41. How does the “Zebra Analysis” tool help in analyzing a model in Autodesk Fusion?

A) It displays stripes on the model to analyze continuity between surfaces.
B) It displays the color gradient to evaluate curvature.
C) It checks the accessibility of the model through a plane.
D) It shows the draft angles of various faces of the model.

Q42. What is the purpose of the “Draft Analysis” tool in Autodesk Fusion?

A) To analyze the continuity of surfaces.
B) To evaluate the draft angle of various faces of the model.
C) To measure the curvature of spline edges.
D) To display snap points while measuring the model.

Q43. In which section can you find the “Curvature Map Analysis” tool in Autodesk Fusion?

A) Insert
B) Inspect
C) View
D) Model

Q44. What does the “Isocurve Analysis” tool in Autodesk Fusion help to analyze?

A) The draft angles on the model’s faces.
B) The quality of the curvature of a surface using UV mapping and curvature combs.
C) The accessibility of the model through different planes.
D) The interference between selected components.

Q45. What does the “Minimum Radius Analysis” tool help you identify in Autodesk Fusion?

A) The accessibility of a model from different directions.
B) Areas of the model that are at or below the minimum radius for tooling.
C) The optimal pull direction for injection molding.
D) The center of mass of the body.

Chapter 9

Surface Modeling

Topics Covered

The major topics covered in this chapter are:

- ***Introduction to Surface Designing***
- ***Extrude Tool***
- ***Patch Tool***
- ***Surface Trim and Untrim Tool***
- ***Extend Tool***
- ***Stitch and Unstitch Tool***
- ***Reverse Normal Tool***
- ***Practical***
- ***Practice***

INTRODUCTION

Surface Designing or surfacing is a technique used to create complex shapes. The most general application of surfacing can be seen in the object that are made with good aerodynamics like car body, aeroplanes, ships, and so on. Sometimes, surface modeling is also used to add complex geometry to the models. The models created by surfacing are called surface models and they do not exist in real world because they have zero thickness. After converting these surfaces to solids, we make real objects.

In Autodesk Fusion, there is no separate workspace for creating surface designs. We have all the surfacing tools available in the **SURFACE** tab of **DESIGN** workspace; refer to Figure-1.

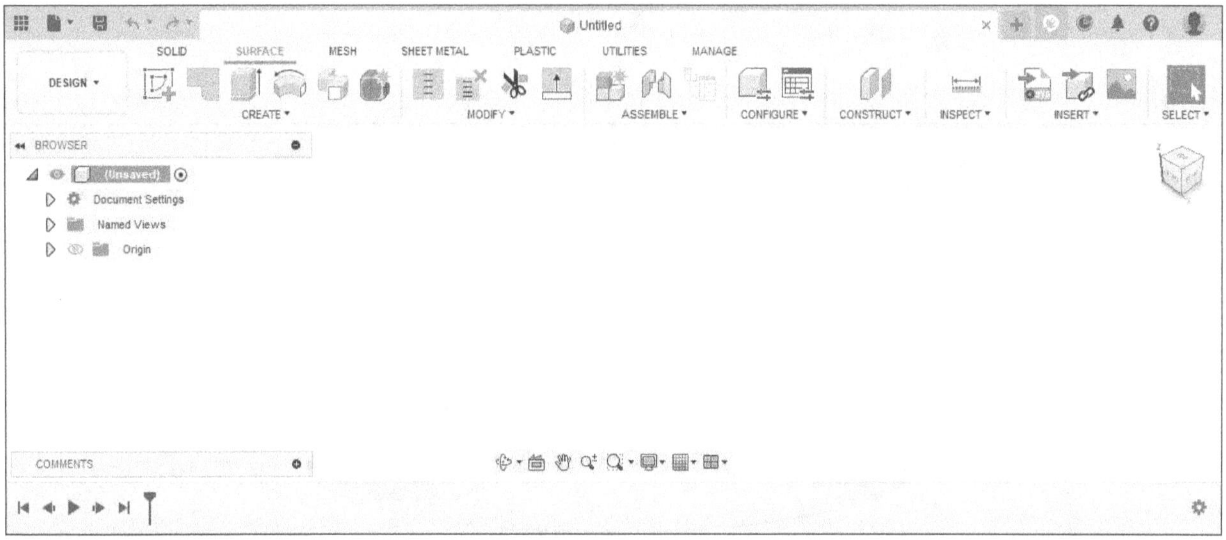

Figure-1. SURFACE modeling tools

Note that we have already used many tools of surface design earlier while creating solid models. Various surface modeling tools are discussed next.

Extrude

The **Extrude** tool can also be used to create the extruded surfaces. The procedure to use this tool is discussed next.

- Click on the **Extrude** tool from **CREATE** drop-down in the **Toolbar** of **SURFACE** tab; refer to Figure-2. The **EXTRUDE** dialog box will be displayed; refer to Figure-3.

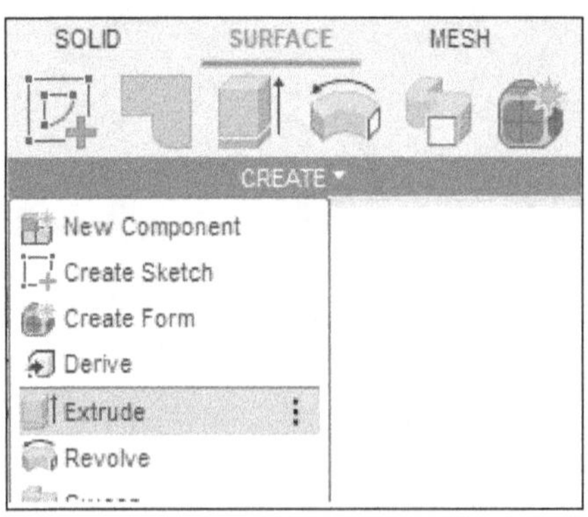

Figure-2. Extrude tool

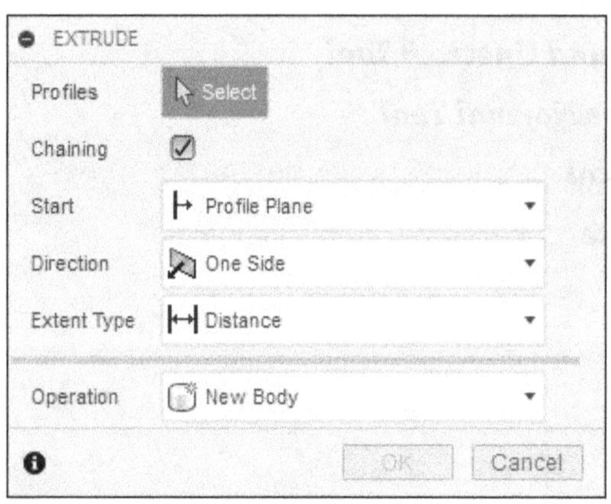

Figure-3. EXTRUDE dialog box

- The **Select** button of **Profiles** section is active by default. Click on the profile to select. The updated **EXTRUDE** dialog box will be displayed; refer to Figure-4.

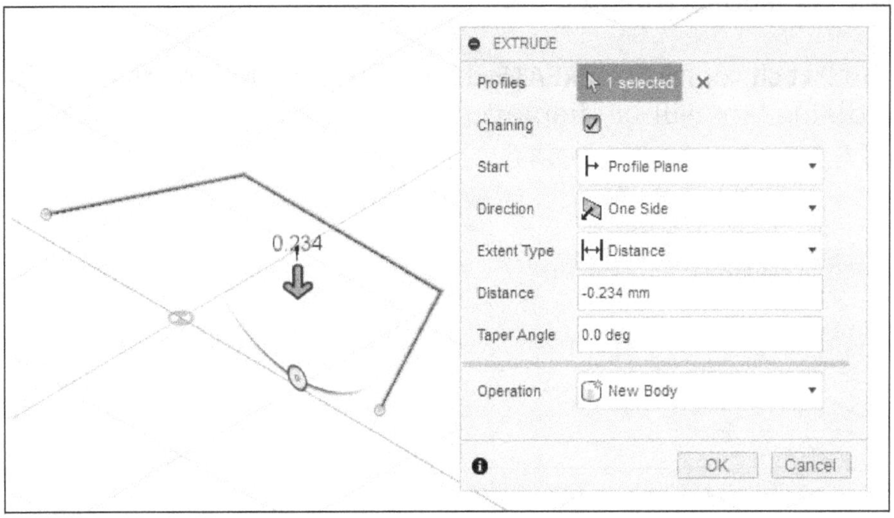

Figure-4. Updated EXTRUDE dialog box

Note that you can select open as well as closed sketch for profile selection to extrude.

- Select the **Chaining** check box if you want to select all the sketch entities in chain.
- The other options of **EXTRUDE** dialog box are same as discussed earlier for solid modeling.
- After specifying the parameters, preview of extrude will be displayed; refer to Figure-5.

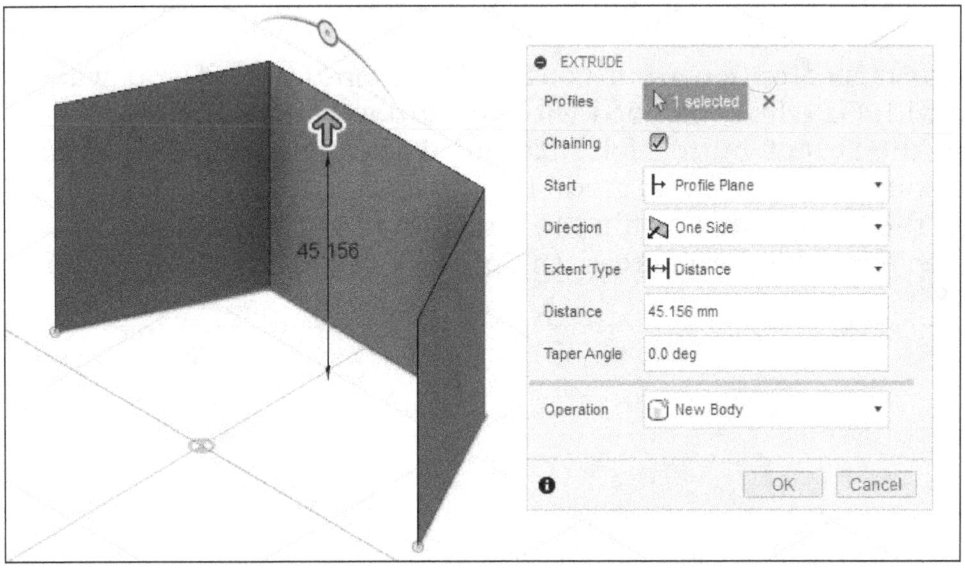

Figure-5. Preview of extrude

- If the preview of extrude is as required then click on **OK** button from **EXTRUDE** dialog box. The extruded surface will be created.

You can use the **Revolve**, **Sweep**, and **Loft** tools in the same way as discussed in previous chapters.

Patch

The **Patch** tool is used to create a surface by connecting edges/curves. The procedure to use this tool is discussed next.

- Click on the **Patch** tool from **CREATE** drop-down in the **Toolbar**; refer to Figure-6. The **PATCH** dialog box will be displayed; refer to Figure-7.

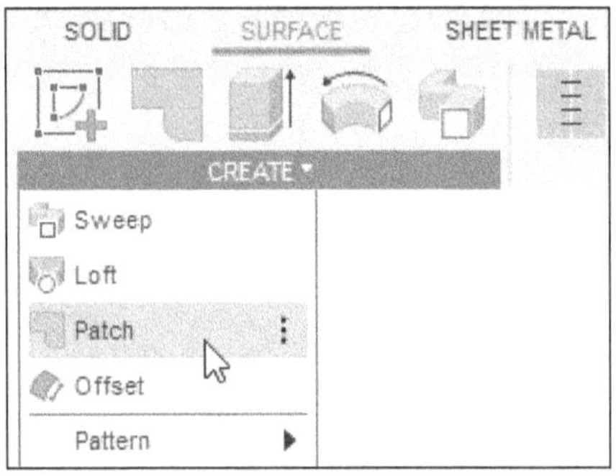

Figure-6. Patch tool

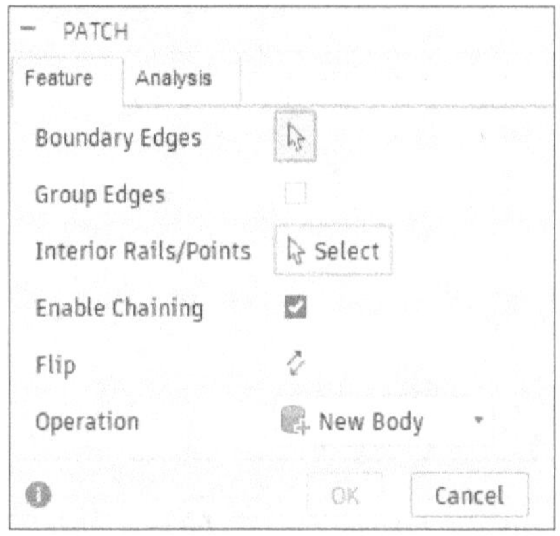

Figure-7. PATCH dialog box

- The **Select** button of **Boundary Edges** section is active by default. Click on the edges/curves forming close loop.
- Select the **Group Edges** check box if you want to select all the edges in a group.
- Select the **Enable Chaining** check box if you want to select all the adjacent edges when clicking on one edge.
- Select **Connected** option from **Continuity** drop-down if you want to create a surface with G0 edges (connected at an angle).
- Select **Tangent** option from **Continuity** drop-down if you want to create a surface with G1 edges (tangential).
- Select **Curvature** option from **Continuity** drop-down, if you want to create a surface with G2 edges (blended with continuous curvature).
- Click on the **Select** button for **Interior Rails/Points** selection and select the curves/points to be used as guide rails/points.
- Click on the **Flip** button to flip the direction of surface normal.
- After specifying the parameters, the preview of patch will be displayed; refer to Figure-8.

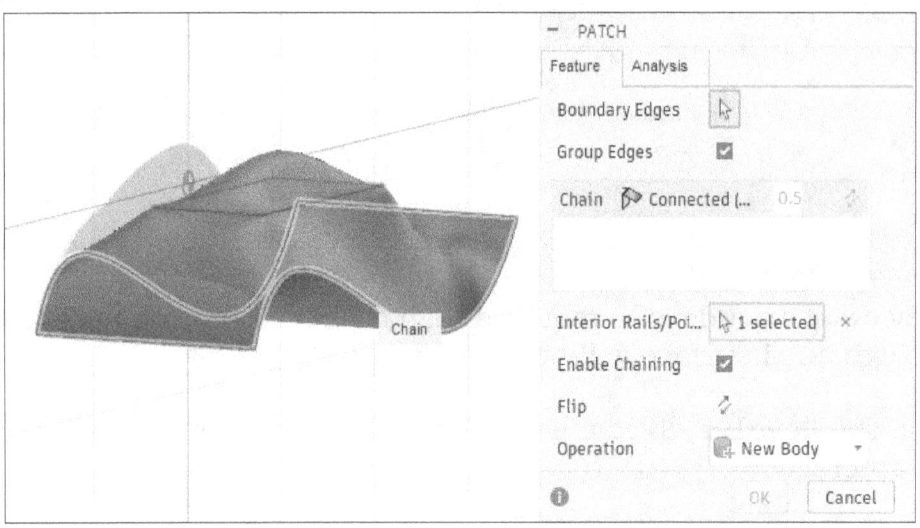

Figure-8. Preview of patch

- Click on **OK** button from **PATCH** dialog box to complete the process.

Ruled

The **Ruled** tool is used to create a ruled surface at a specified distance and angle from selected edges. The procedure to use this tool is discussed next.

- Click on the **Ruled** tool from **CREATE** drop-down in the **Toolbar**; refer to Figure-9. The **RULED** dialog box will be displayed; refer to Figure-10.

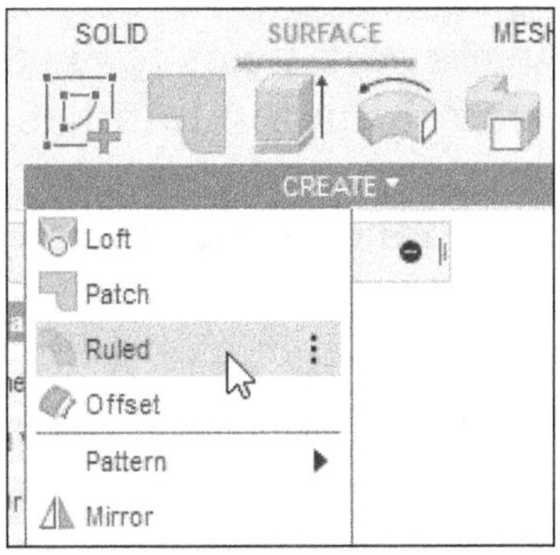

Figure-9. Ruled tool

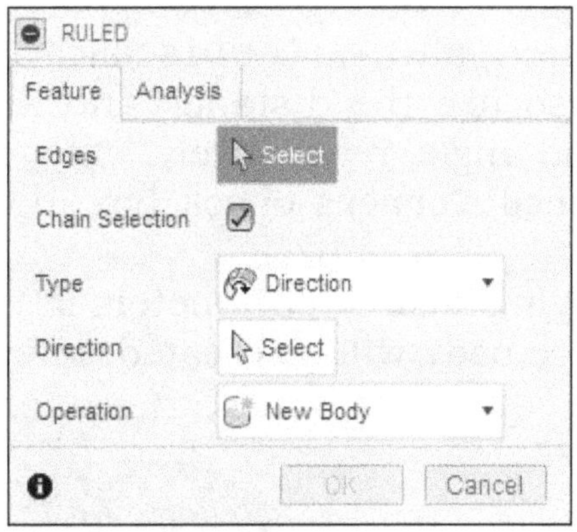

Figure-10. RULED dialog box

- The **Edges** selection button of **Feature** tab is active by default. Select edges on a solid body, surface body, or sketch to extend the ruled surface from; refer to Figure-11. The updated **RULED** dialog box will be displayed; refer to Figure-12.

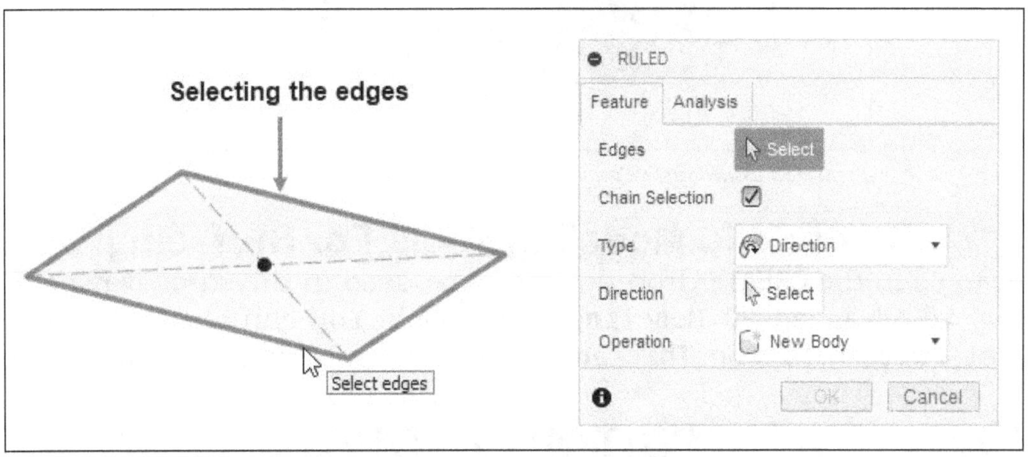

Figure-11. Selecting the edges

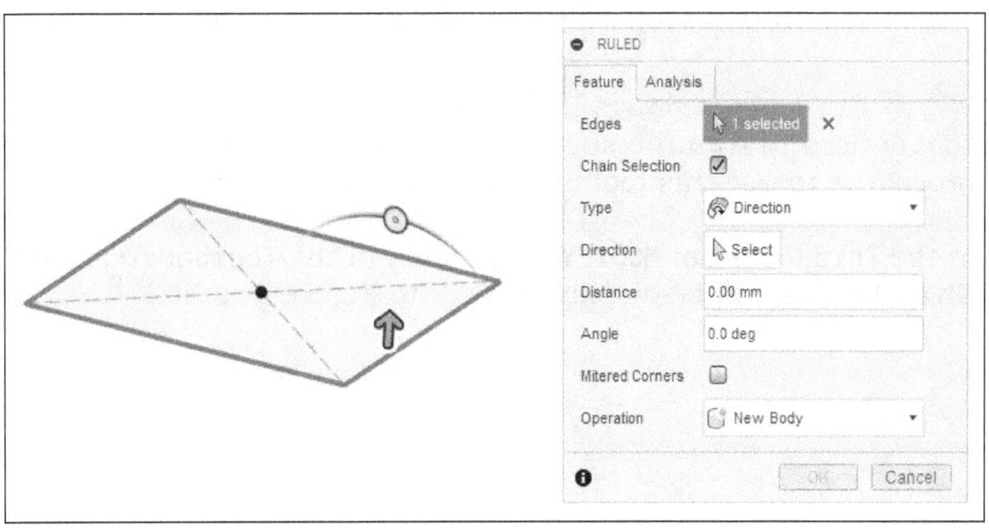

Figure-12. Updated RULED dialog box

- Select **Chain Selection** check box to automatically select the connected geometry.
- Select desired ruled surface type from **Type** drop-down. Select **Normal** option to create a ruled surface normal to the face of the selected edges. Select **Tangent** option to create a ruled surface tangent to the face of the selected edges. Select **Direction** option to create a ruled surface in a direction that you select.
- Click on the **Select** button of **Direction** section and select a linear edge, plane, or axis.
- Specify desired values in the **Distance** and **Angle** edit boxes to extend the surface. You can also use the distance and angle manipulator handles to specify the distance and angle, respectively.
- Select **Mitered Corners** check box to create sharp corners instead of rounded corners.
- After specifying desired parameters in the dialog box, click on the **OK** button. The ruled surface body will be created; refer to Figure-13.

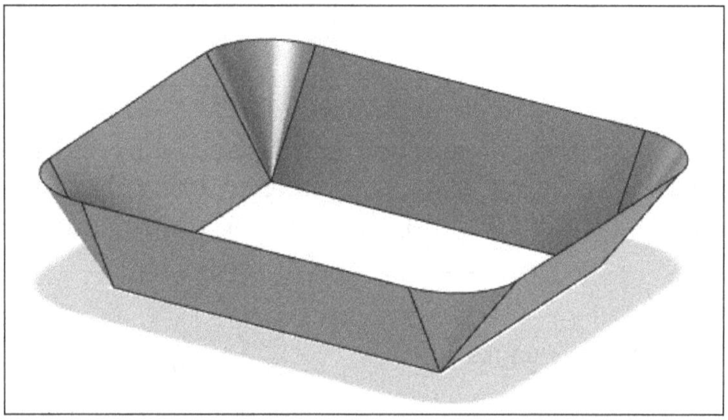

Figure-13. Ruled surface body created

Other Solid Modeling Tools For Surfacing

The other tools in the **CREATE** drop-down can be used in the same way as discussed in **Chapter 4: Advanced 3D Modeling** of the book. You can also create surfaces by using **Offset**, **Pattern**, **Mirror**, **Thicken**, and **Boundary Fill** tools as discussed earlier.

EDITING TOOLS

In the previous section, we have learned about different surface creation tools used in surface modeling. In this section, we will discuss the surface editing tools.

Trim

The **Trim** tool is used to trim the surface using selected trimming object as cutting tool. The procedure to use this tool is discussed next.

- Click on the **Trim** tool from **MODIFY** drop-down in the **Toolbar**; refer to Figure-14. The **TRIM** dialog box will be displayed; refer to Figure-15.

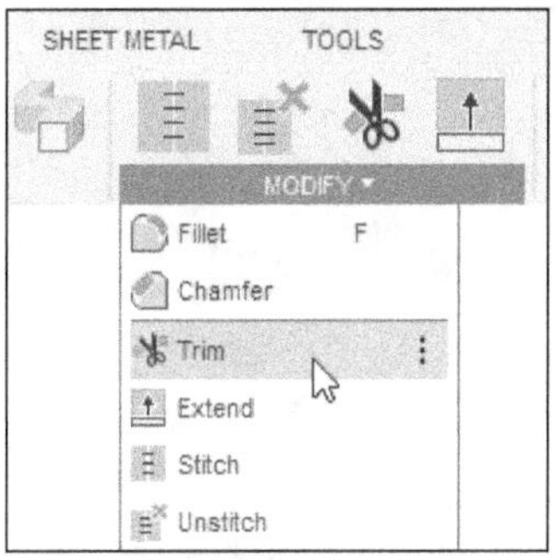

Figure-14. Trim tool

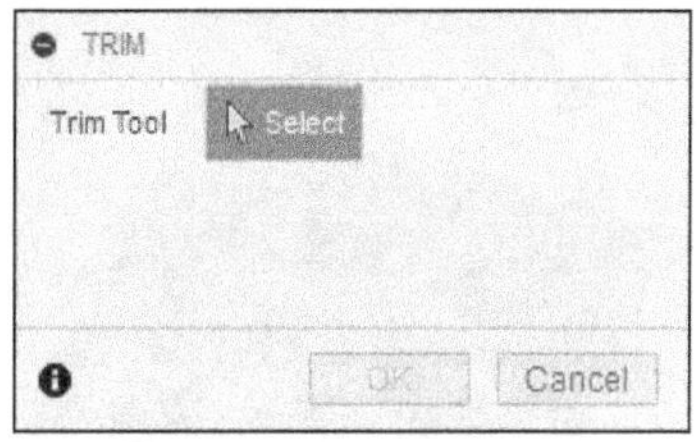

Figure-15. TRIM dialog box

- The **Select** button of **Trim Tool** section is active by default. You need to select an existing sketch to trim the surface. You can also select a plane/face intersecting with the surface as trim tool; refer to Figure-16.

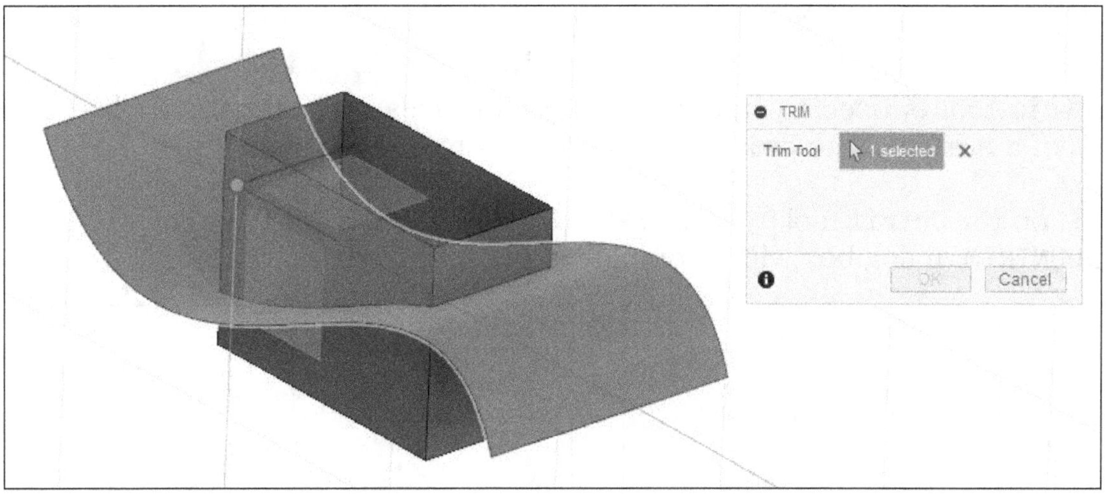

Figure-16. Selection of face as trim tool

- Now, you need to select the area to be removed. Click on desired area of sketch to trim; refer to Figure-17.

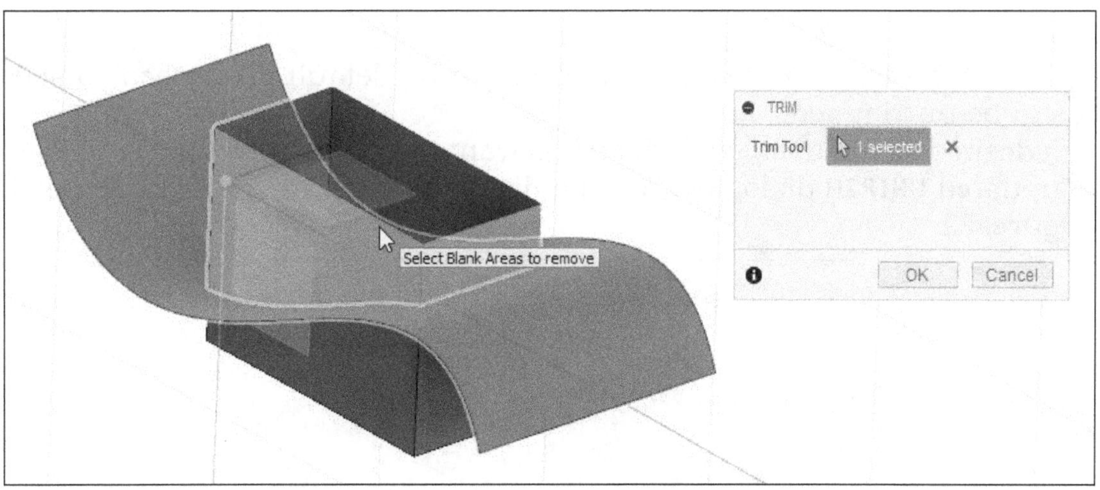

Figure-17. Selection of area to trim

- Click on the **OK** button from **TRIM** dialog box to trim the selected area; refer to Figure-18.

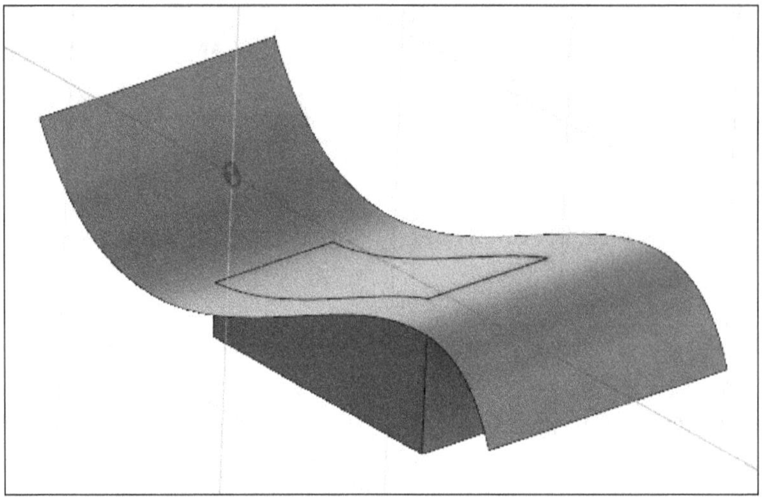

Figure-18. Selected area trimmed

Untrim

The **Untrim** tool is used to extend trimmed surfaces and fill gaps, holes, or empty regions of a surface. The procedure to use this tool is discussed next.

- Click on the **Untrim** tool from **MODIFY** drop-down in the **Toolbar**; refer to Figure-19. The **UNTRIM** dialog box will be displayed; refer to Figure-20.

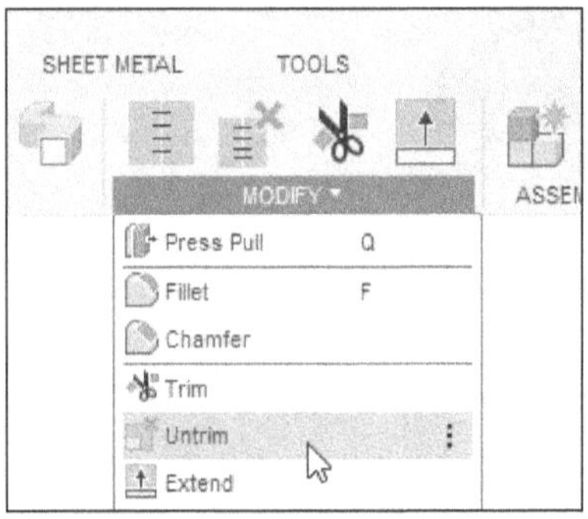

Figure-19. Untrim tool

Figure-20. UNTRIM dialog box

- The **Select** button of **Faces** section is active by default. You need to select the faces to be untrimmed.
- Select desired face of the model which you want to be untrimmed; refer to Figure-21. The updated **UNTRIM** dialog box will be displayed with the face untrimmed; refer to Figure-22.

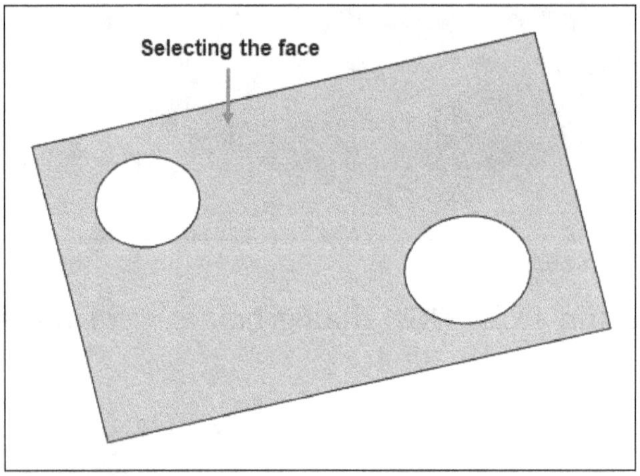

Figure-21. Selecting the face to be untrimmed

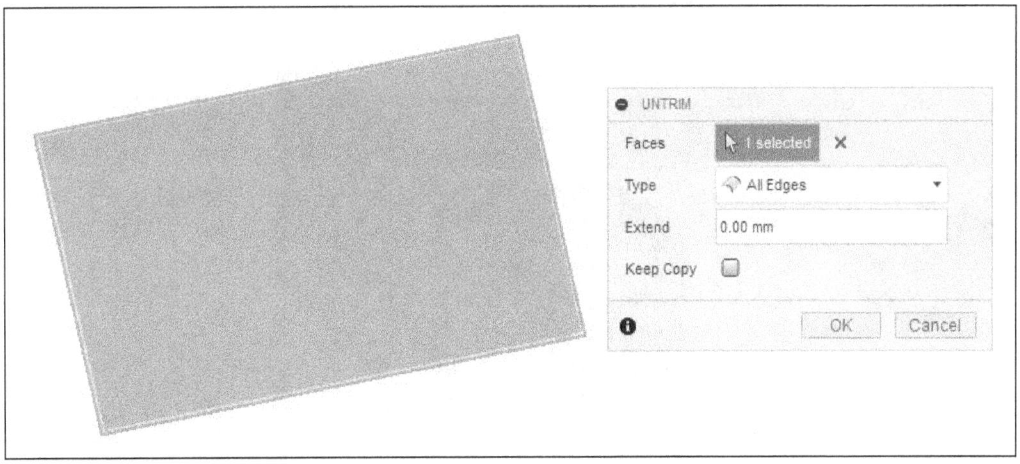

Figure-22. Updated UNTRIM dialog box

- Select **All Edges** option from **Type** drop-down to untrim all internal and external edges of a surface.
- Select **Internal Edges** option from **Type** drop-down to untrim internal edges only.
- Select **External Edges** option from **Type** drop-down to untrim external edges only.
- Select **Manual** option from **Type** drop-down to untrim manually selected edges of a face. Hold **CTRL** button to suppress command preview after selecting first edge and then select multiple edges.
- Specify desired value in **Extend** edit box to extend untrimmed surface.
- Select **Keep Copy** check box to create a copy of original trimmed surface.
- After specifying parameters, click on **OK** button from **UNTRIM** dialog box.

Extend

The **Extend** tool is used to extend the surface edge. The procedure to use this tool is discussed next.

- Click on the **Extend** tool from **MODIFY** drop-down in the **Toolbar**; refer to Figure-23. The **EXTEND** dialog box will be displayed; refer to Figure-24.

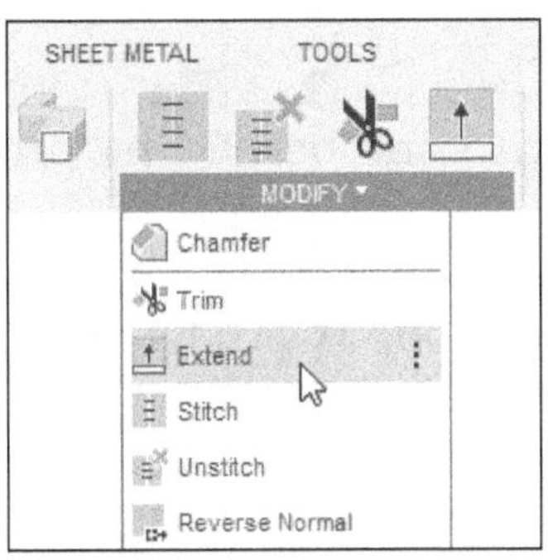

Figure-23. Extend tool

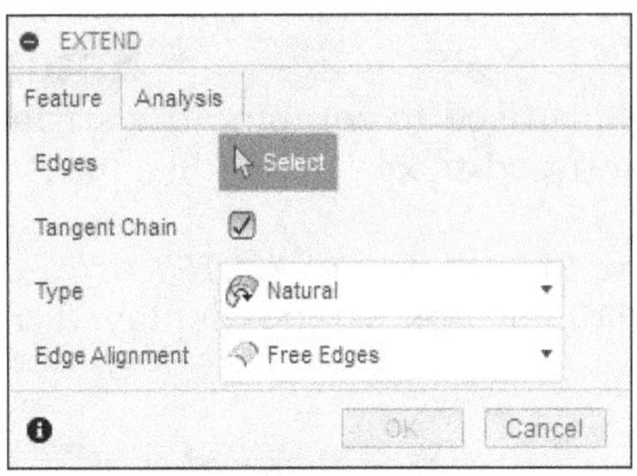

Figure-24. EXTEND dialog box

- The **Select** button of **Edges** section is active by default. You need to select the edge to extend. The updated **EXTEND** dialog box will be displayed; refer to Figure-25.

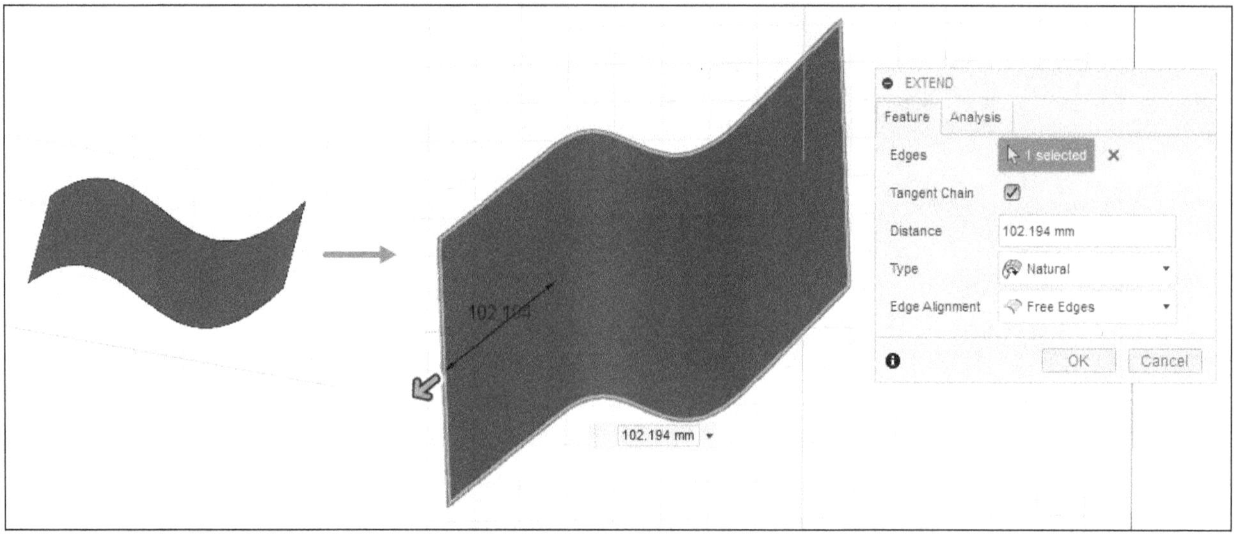

Figure-25. Preview of extend

- Select the **Target Chain** check box if you want to select all tangent or adjacent faces on selection of single face.
- Click in the **Distance** edit box and specify the distance for extend. You can also set the distance by moving the manipulator.
- Select **Natural** option from **Type** drop-down if you want to extend the surface naturally.
- Select **Perpendicular** option from **Type** drop-down if you want to extend the selected edge perpendicularly.
- Select **Tangent** option from **Type** drop-down if you want to extend the selected edge tangentially.
- Select **Free Edges** option from **Edge Alignment** drop-down to apply G0 point continuity to align edges of extended surface.
- Select **Align Edges** option from **Edge Alignment** drop-down to apply G1 tangent continuity to align edges of extended surface.
- After specifying the parameters, click on **OK** button from **EXTEND** dialog box.

Stitch

The **Stitch** tool is used to combine the surface into one body. The procedure to use this tool is discussed next.

- Click on the **Stitch** tool of **MODIFY** drop-down from **Toolbar**; refer to Figure-26. The **STITCH** dialog box will be displayed; refer to Figure-27.

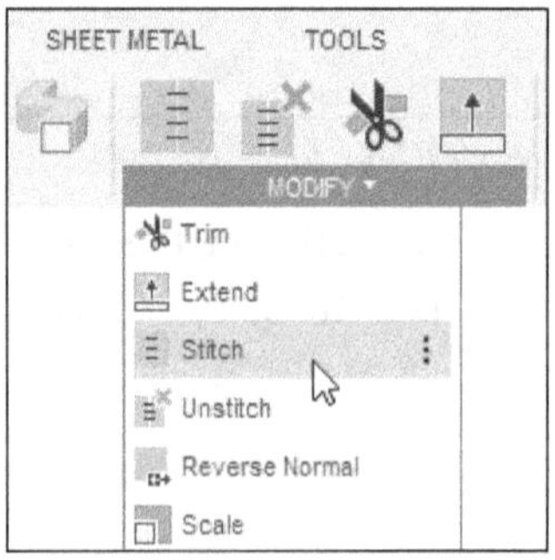

Figure-26. Stitch tool

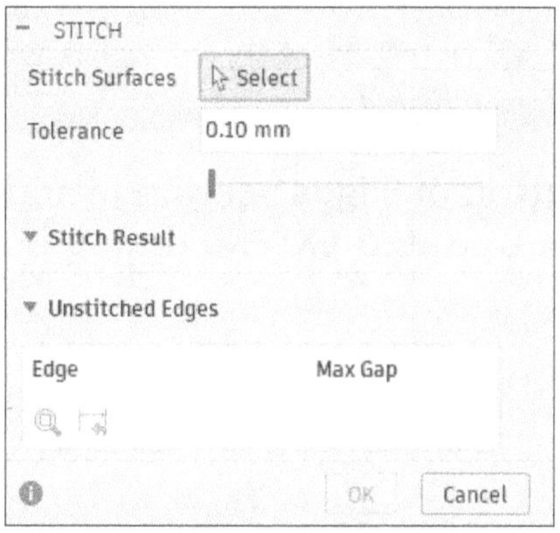

Figure-27. STITCH dialog box

- The **Select** button of **Stitch Surfaces** section is active by default. You need to select the surfaces of model to be stitched; refer to Figure-28.

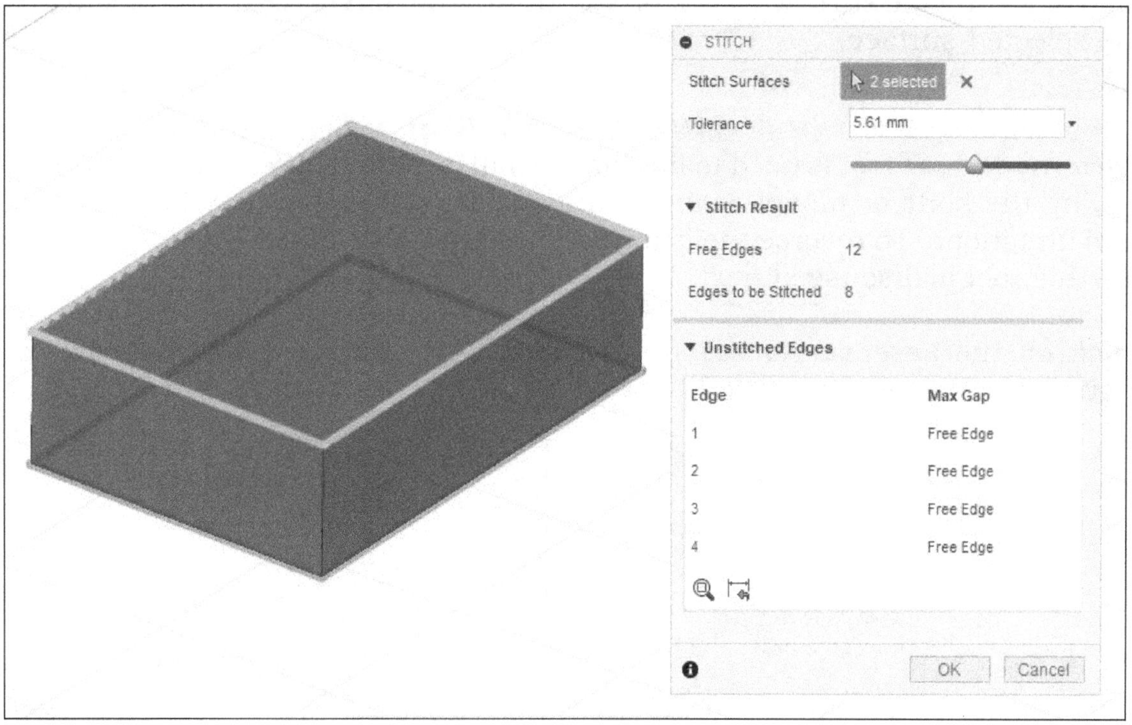

Figure-28. Selection of face to stitch

- The green line on the model shows the stitched surface and red line shows the loose surface connection.
- You need to increase the tolerance from **Tolerance** edit box or **Tolerance** slider to stitch the remaining surfaces which have higher gap between consecutive edges.
- You can also check the result of stitched and unstitched edges from **Stitch Result** section.
- After specifying the parameters, click on the **OK** button from **STITCH** dialog box to complete the process.

Unstitch

The **Unstitch** tool is used to unstitch the earlier stitched surface from model. The procedure to use this tool is discussed next.

- Click on the **Unstitch** tool of **MODIFY** drop-down from **Toolbar**; refer to Figure-29. The **UNSTITCH** dialog box will be displayed; refer to Figure-30.

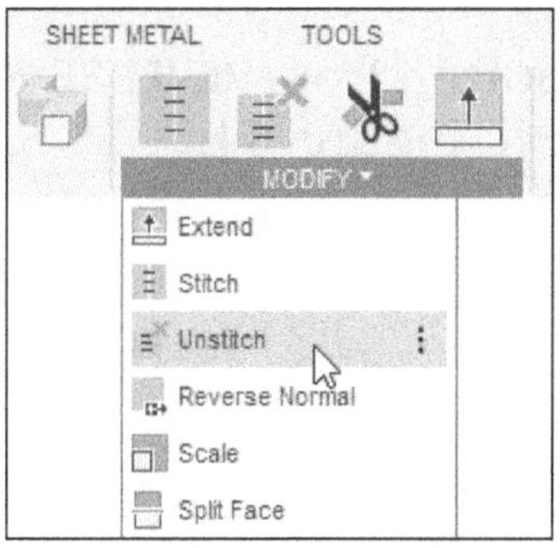

Figure-29. Unstitch tool

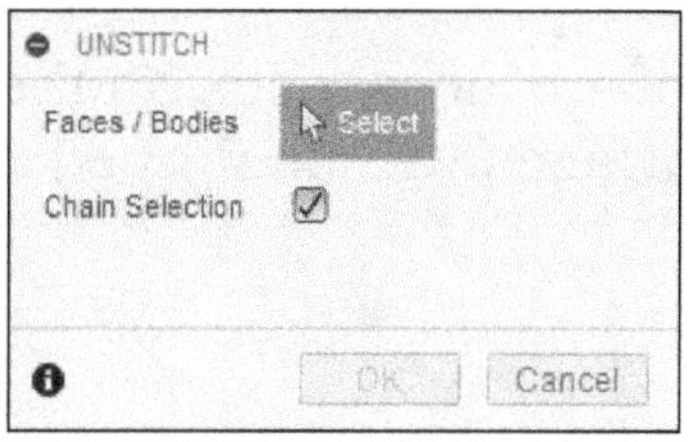

Figure-30. UNSTITCH dialog box

- The **Select** button of **Faces/Bodies** section is active by default. You need to select the surface or body to be unstitched.

- Select the **Chain Selection** check box to select the adjacent surface of the selected surface.
- After selecting the surfaces, click on **OK** button from **UNSTITCH** dialog box to unstitch the selected surface.

Reverse Normal

The **Reverse Normal** tool is used to flip the normal direction of selected surfaces. When modifying the body or model, some of the surfaces of model may have unexpected normal directions. To reverse their normal direction, this tool is used. The procedure to use this tool is discussed next.

- Click on the **Reverse Normal** tool of **Modify** drop-down from **Toolbar**; refer to Figure-31. The **REVERSE NORMAL** dialog box will be displayed; refer to Figure-32.

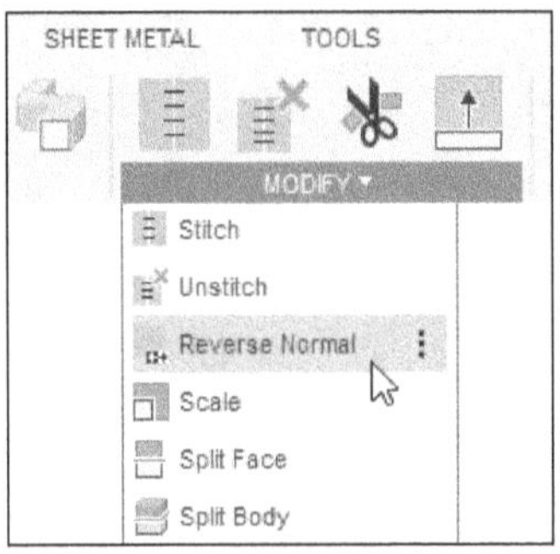

Figure-31. Reverse Normal tool

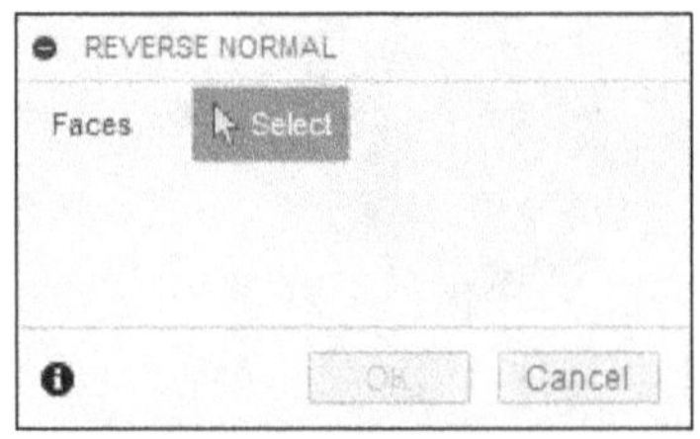

Figure-32. REVERSE NORMAL dialog box

- The **Select** button of **Faces** section is active by default. You need to select the face to flip; refer to Figure-33.

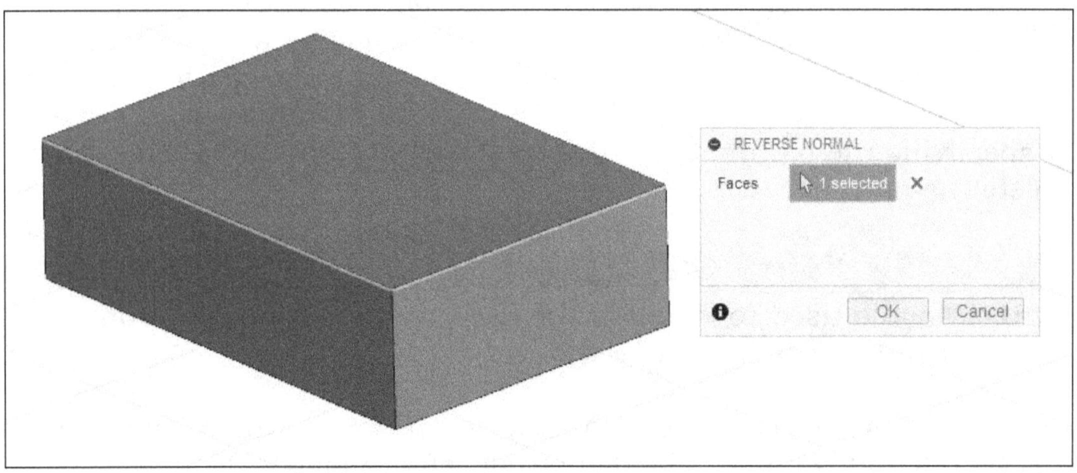

Figure-33. Selection of surface to flip

- After selection of surfaces, click on the **OK** button from **REVERSE NORMAL** dialog box. The selected surfaces will be flipped; refer to Figure-34.

Figure-34. Flipped surface

The other tools of **SURFACE** tab have been discussed earlier in this book.

PRACTICAL 1

Create the model of aircraft toy as shown in Figure-35. (This is an open dimension problem, you need to get the shape of an aircraft using surfaces.)

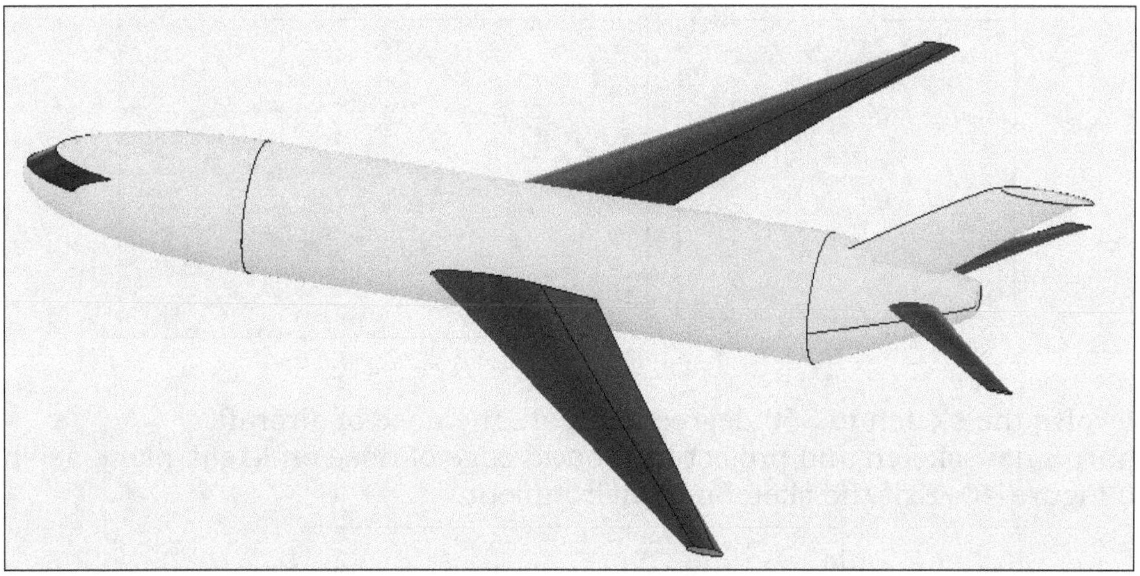

Figure-35. Practical 1 model

Creating first sketch

- Click on the **SURFACE** tab from **Toolbar**; refer to Figure-36. The tools to create surface will be activated.

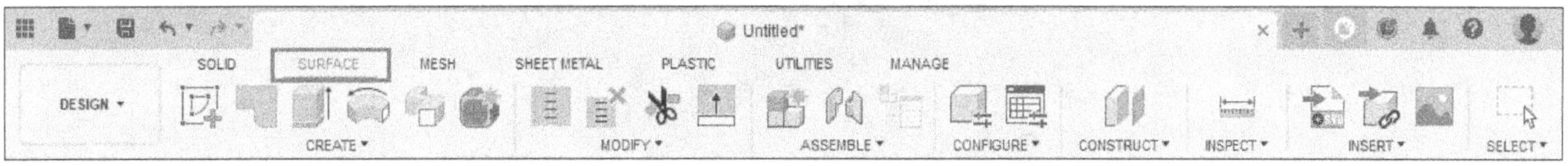

Figure-36. Tools to create surface

- Create the sketch on **Top** plane using **Ellipse**, **Line**, and **Trim** tools; refer to Figure-37.

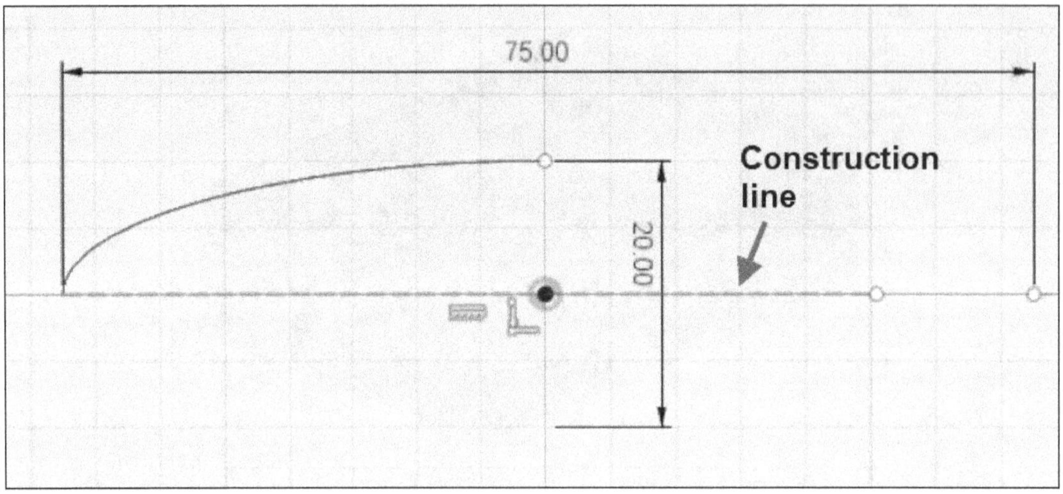

Figure-37. First sketch

Creating Surface

- Click on **Revolve** tool from **CREATE** drop-down in the **Toolbar**. The **REVOLVE** dialog box will be displayed; refer to Figure-38.
- You need to select the sketch and axis of sketch to apply the revolve feature; refer to Figure-39.

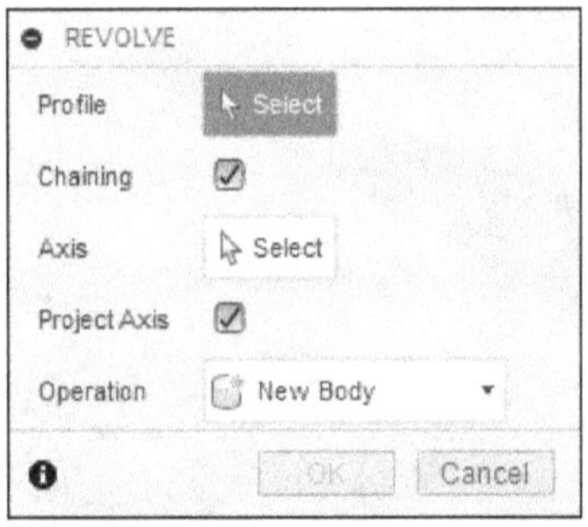

Figure-38. Revolve dialog box

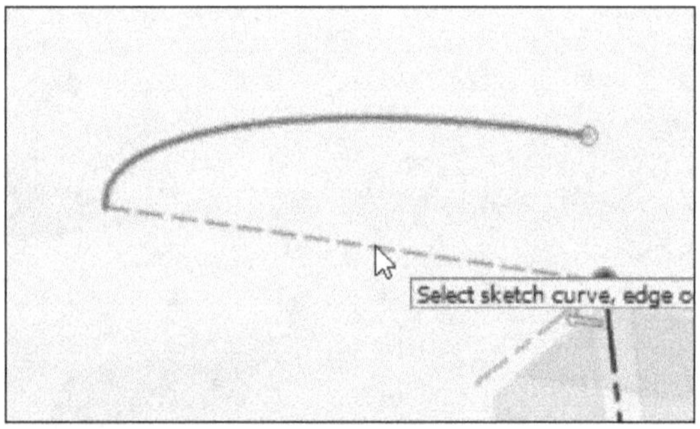

Figure-39. Selecting sketch and axis

- Revolve the sketch to 360 degree to create the nose of aircraft.
- Start a new sketch and project the round edge of nose on **Right** plane as shown in Figure-40. Exit the sketching environment.

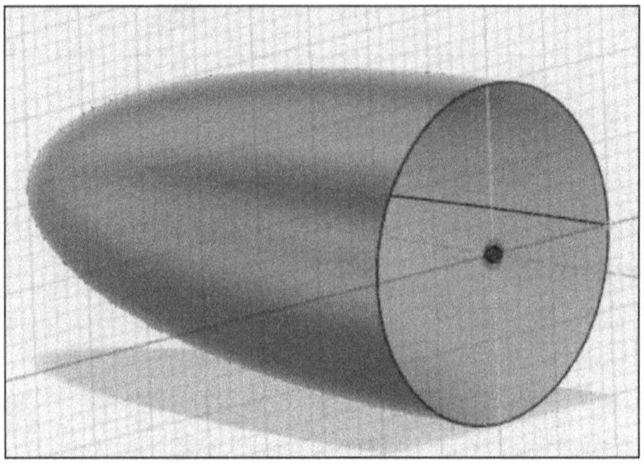

Figure-40. Edge projected on plane

- Click on **Extrude** tool from **CREATE** drop-down in the **Toolbar**. The **EXTRUDE** dialog box will be displayed.
- Select the sketch as displayed to extrude; refer to Figure-41.

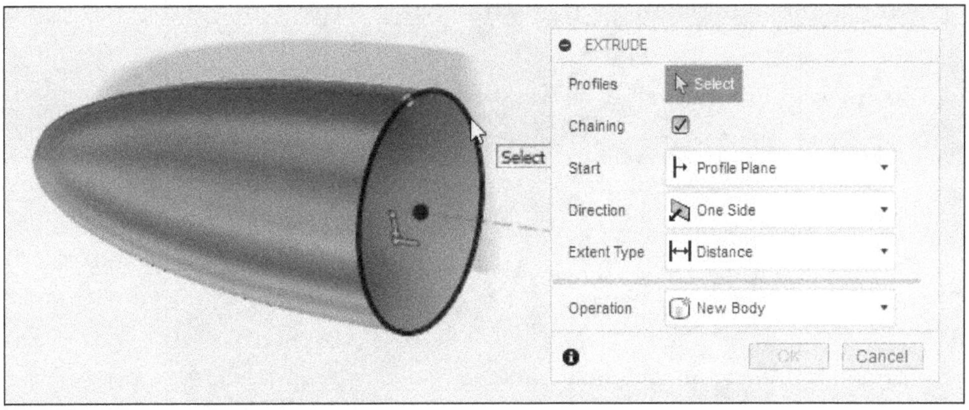

Figure-41. Selecting sketch to extrude

- Click in the **Distance** edit box and enter the value as **90**.
- After specifying the parameters, click on **OK** button from **EXTRUDE** dialog box to complete the extrusion process.
- Click on **Offset Plane** tool from **CONSTRUCT** drop-down in the **Toolbar**. The **OFFSET PLANE** dialog box will be displayed.
- Select the **YZ** plane as shown in Figure-42.

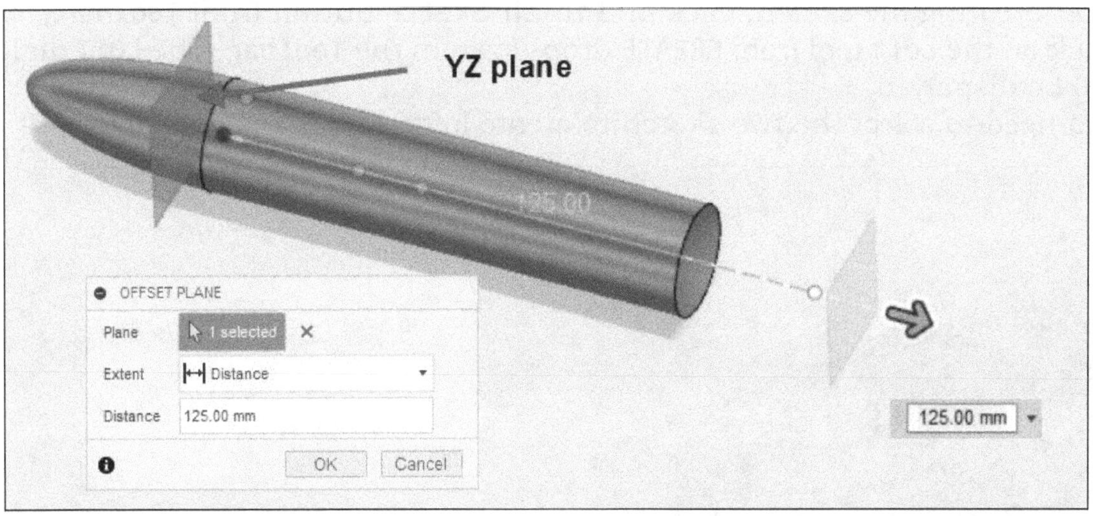

Figure-42. Creating offset plane

- Click in the **Distance** edit box of **OFFSET PLANE** dialog box and specify the value as **125**.
- After specifying the parameters, click on **OK** button from **OFFSET PLANE** dialog box to create the plane.
- Start a new sketch using newly created plane and click on the **Center Diameter Circle** tool from **CREATE** drop-down.
- Create the circle as shown in Figure-43.

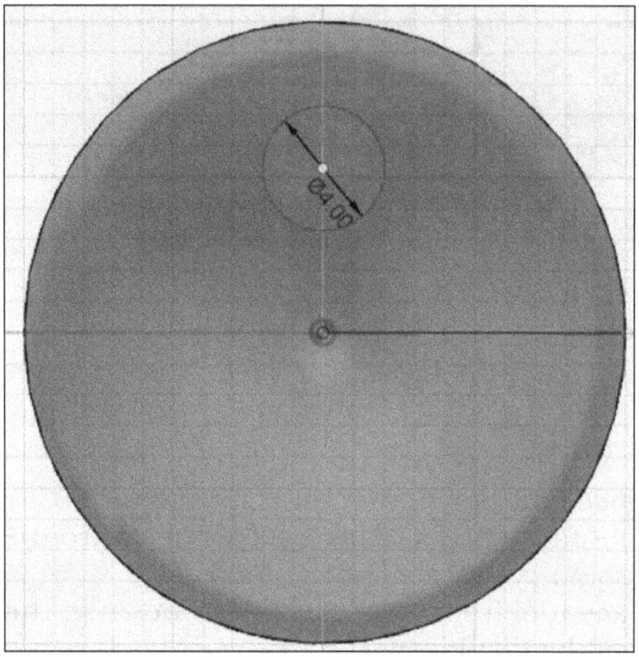

Figure-43. Creating circle

- After creating the sketch, click on **Finish Sketch** button from **Toolbar**.
- Click on the **Loft** tool from **CREATE** drop-down in the **Toolbar**. The **LOFT** dialog box will be displayed.
- You need to select the two sketch to create loft feature; refer to Figure-44.

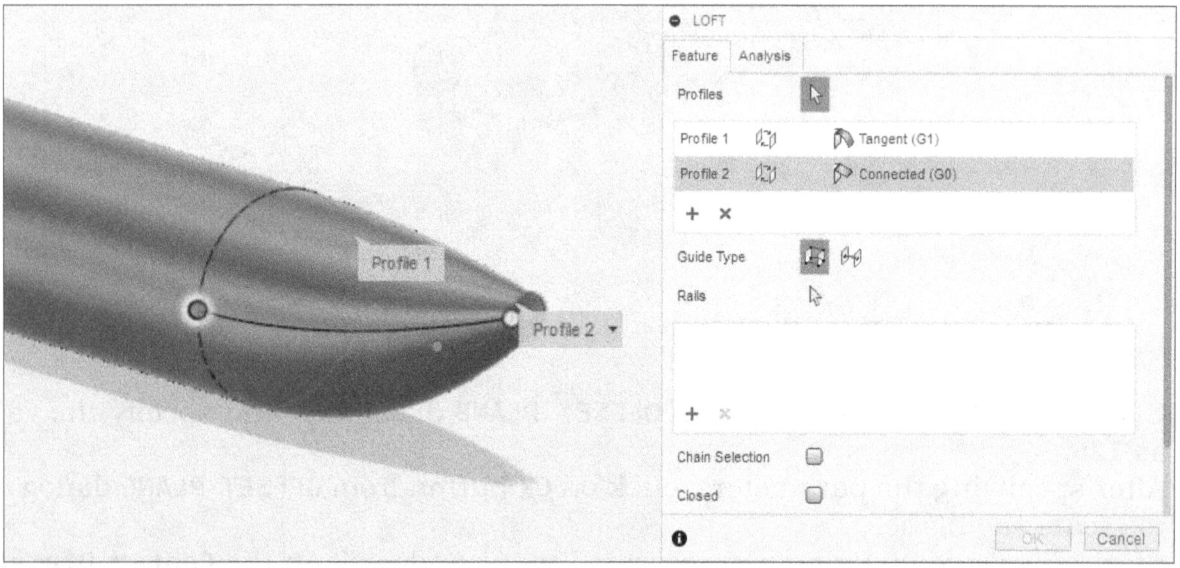

Figure-44. Selecting sketch for loft feature

- Specify the parameters as desired and click on **OK** button from **LOFT** dialog box to complete the process.
- Click on the **Create Sketch** tool and select the **XZ** plane as sketching plane. Create the sketch with the help of **Ellipse** and **Line** tool as shown in Figure-45.

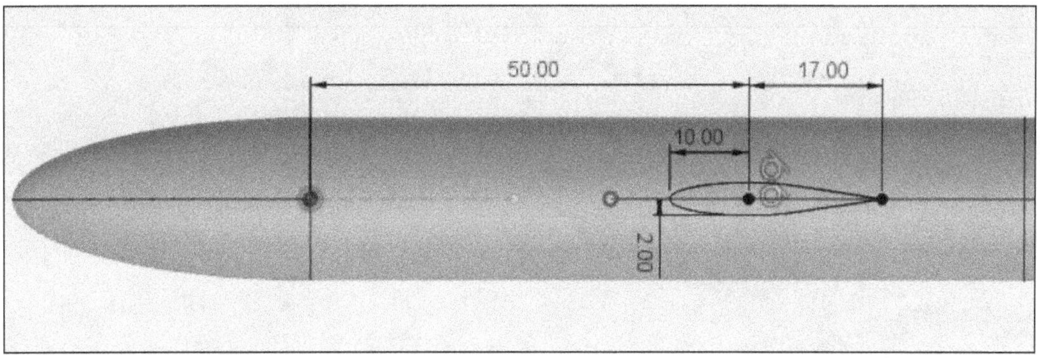

Figure-45. Sketch for wing

- After creating the sketch, click on **Finish Sketch** button from **Toolbar**.
- Now, create the offset plane at a distance of **75** from the **XZ** plane; refer to Figure-46.

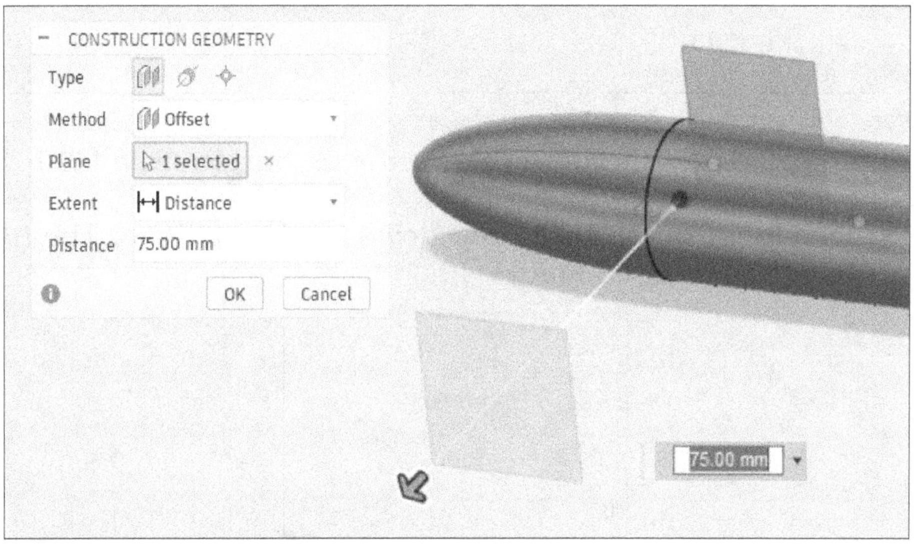

Figure-46. Creating third offset plane

- Click on the **Ellipse** tool from **CREATE** drop-down and select the recently created plane.
- Create the ellipse on current plane as shown in Figure-47.

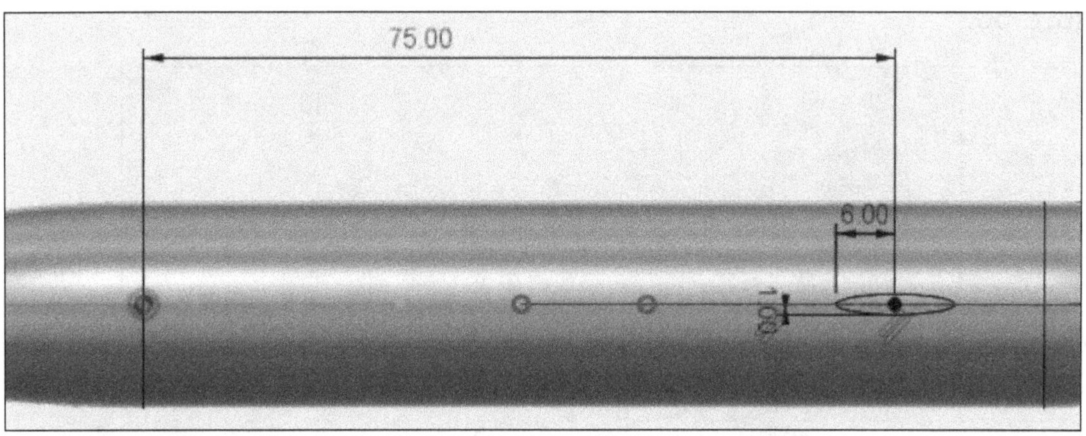

Figure-47. Creating ellipse

- Click on the **Finish Sketch** tool from **Toolbar**.
- Click on the **Loft** tool from **CREATE** drop-down. The **LOFT** dialog box will be displayed.
- Select the recently created sketches (ellipse forms) and create the loft; refer to Figure-48. Make sure the **Chain Selection** check box is selected.

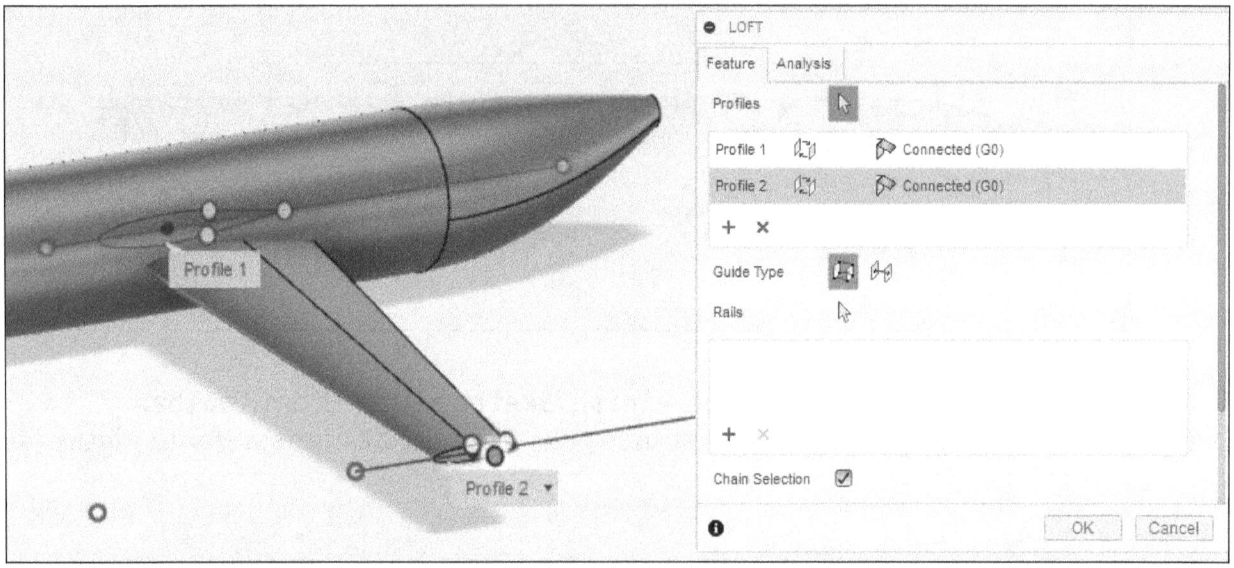

Figure-48. Creating wing

- After selection of profiles for loft, click on the **OK** button from **LOFT** dialog box to complete the loft process.
- Click on **Mirror** tool from **CREATE** drop-down in the **Toolbar**. The **MIRROR** dialog box will be displayed; refer to Figure-49.

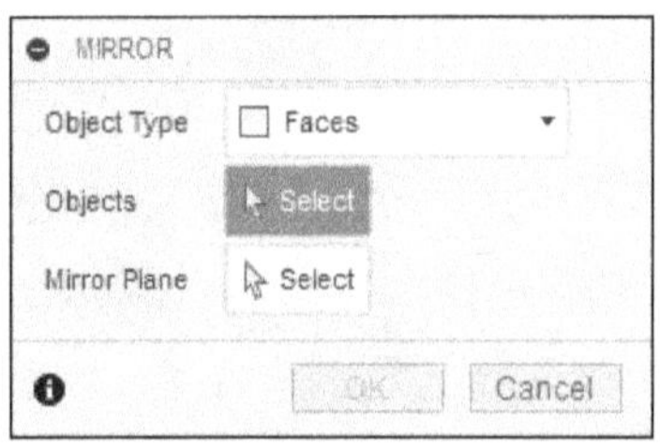

Figure-49. MIRROR dialog box

- Click on **Type** drop-down from **MIRROR** dialog box and select **Bodies** option.
- Click on **Select** button of **Objects** section and select the recently created wing.
- Click on **Select** button of **Mirror Plane** section and select the **XZ** plane; refer to Figure-50.

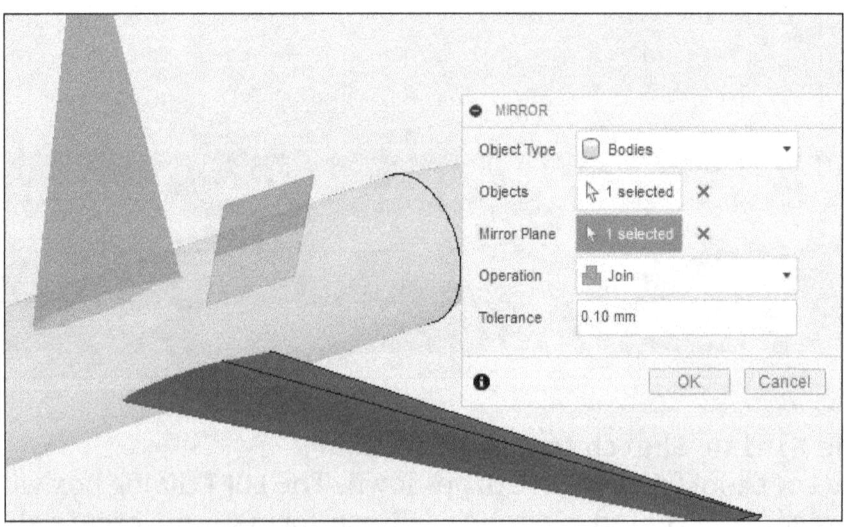

Figure-50. Creating Mirror copy of wing

- Click on **OK** button from **MIRROR** dialog box to complete the process.
- Click on the **Offset Plane** tool from **CONSTRUCT** drop-down in the **Toolbar**. The **CONSTRUCTION GEOMETRY** dialog box will be displayed.
- Create an offset plane at distance of **23** mm from **XZ** plane as shown in Figure-51.

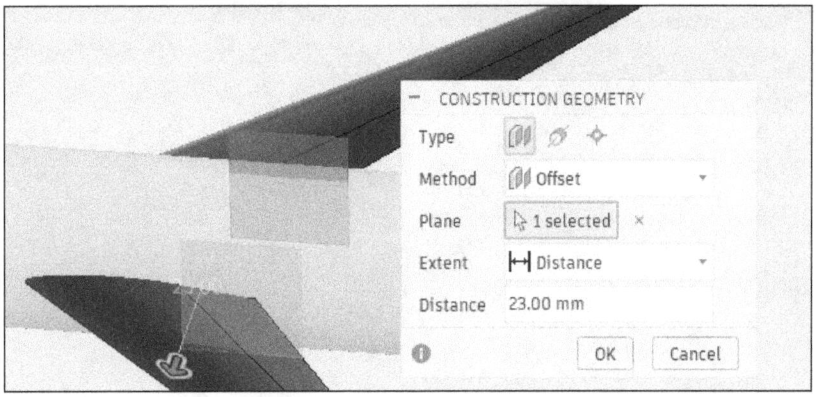

Figure-51. Creating fourth offset plane

- Create an ellipse on the **XZ** plane using **Ellipse** tool as shown in Figure-52.

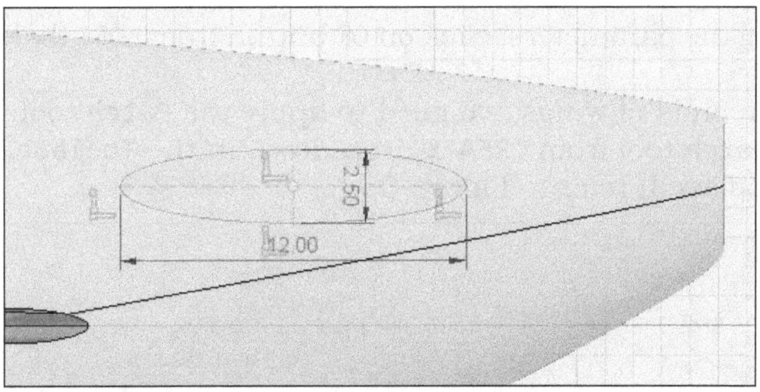

Figure-52. Creating sketch for rear wing

- After creating sketch, click on **Finish Sketch** button from **Toolbar**.
- Create another ellipse on the newly created offset plane as shown in Figure-53.

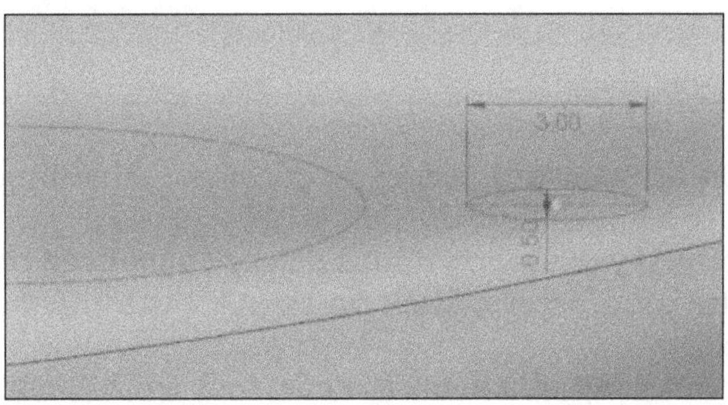

Figure-53. Sketch for rear wing

- Click on **Finish Sketch** button from **Toolbar** to exit the sketch.
- Click on **Loft** tool from **CREATE** drop-down in the **Toolbar**. The **LOFT** dialog box will be displayed.
- You need to select two recently created sketch in **Profiles** section of **LOFT** dialog box; refer to Figure-54.

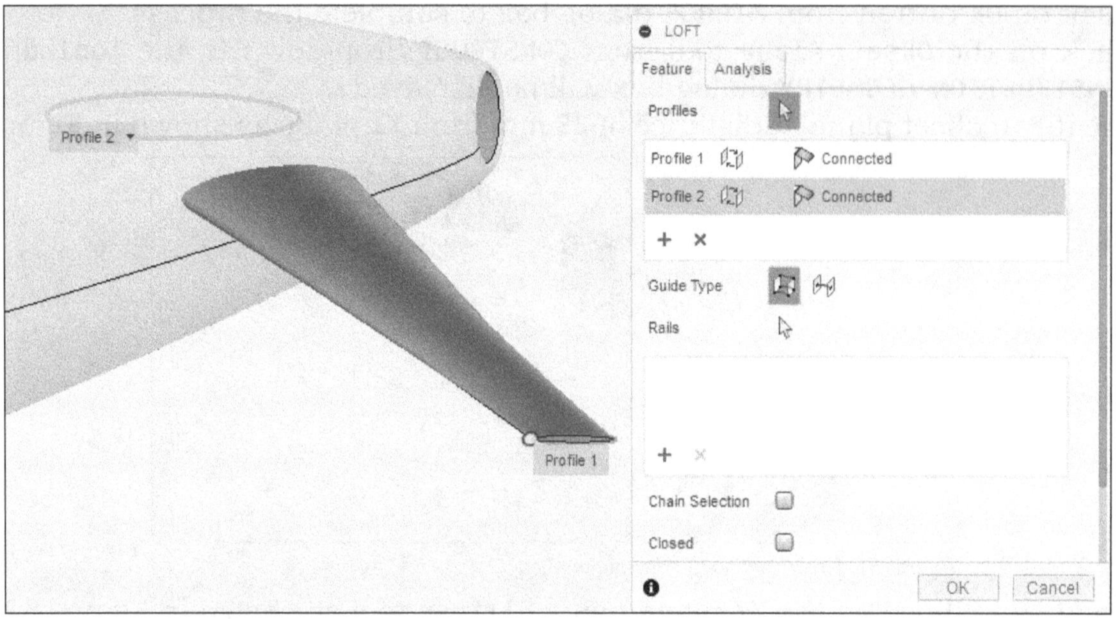

Figure-54. Applying loft tool for rear wing

- After specifying the parameters, click on **OK** button from **LOFT** dialog box to complete the process.
- To fill the open ends of wings, we need to apply the **Patch** tool.
- Click on the **Patch** tool from **CREATE** drop-down in the **Toolbar**. The **PATCH** dialog box will be displayed; refer to Figure-55.

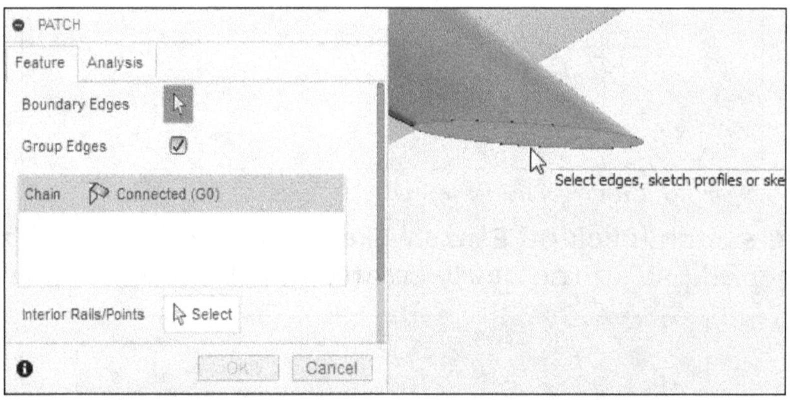

Figure-55. Applying Patch tool

- The **Select** button of **Boundary Edges** section is active by default. Click on the area displayed in the above figure.
- Click on the **Continuity** drop-down and select **Connected** option.
- After specifying the parameters, click on the **OK** button from **PATCH** dialog box to complete the process.
- To create other rear wing, click on **Mirror** tool from **CREATE** drop-down in the **Toolbar**. The **MIRROR** dialog box will be displayed.
- Select the recently created wing in **Objects** section of **MIRROR** dialog box.
- Click on **Select** button of **Mirror Plane** section of **MIRROR** dialog box and select the **XY** plane as reference; refer to Figure-56.

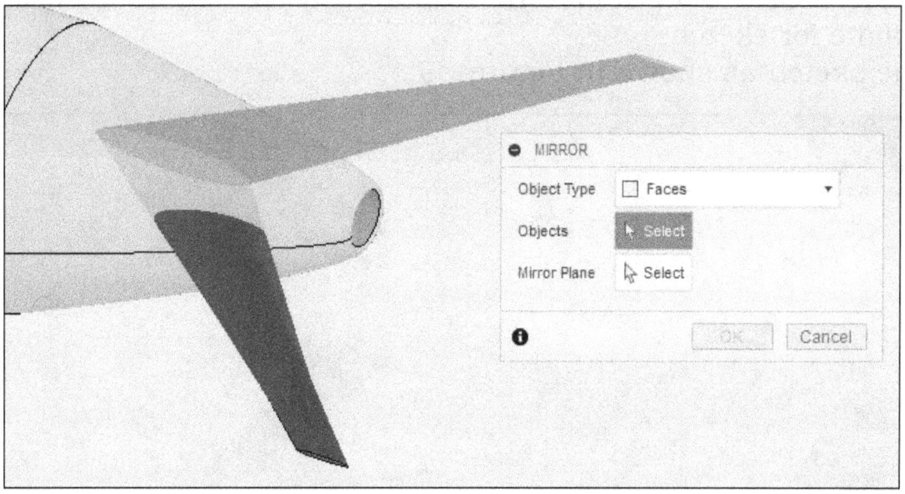

Figure-56. Creating other rear wing

- Click on **OK** button from **MIRROR** dialog box to create the copy.
- Click on **Create Sketch** tool from **CREATE** drop-down and select the **XY** plane for creation of sketch. Create the ellipse as shown in Figure-57.

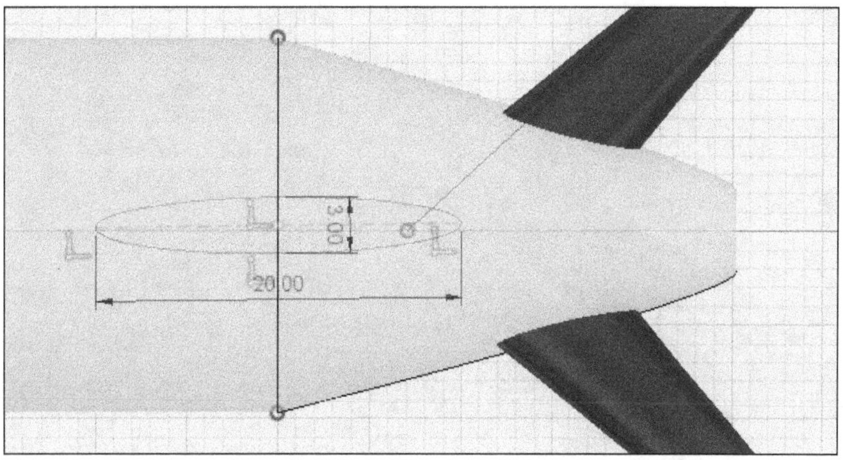

Figure-57. Creating sketch for third wing

- After creating the sketch, click on **Finish Sketch** button from **Toolbar**.
- Click on **Offset Plane** tool from **CONSTRUCT** drop-down and create a plane with **XY** plane as reference; refer to Figure-58.

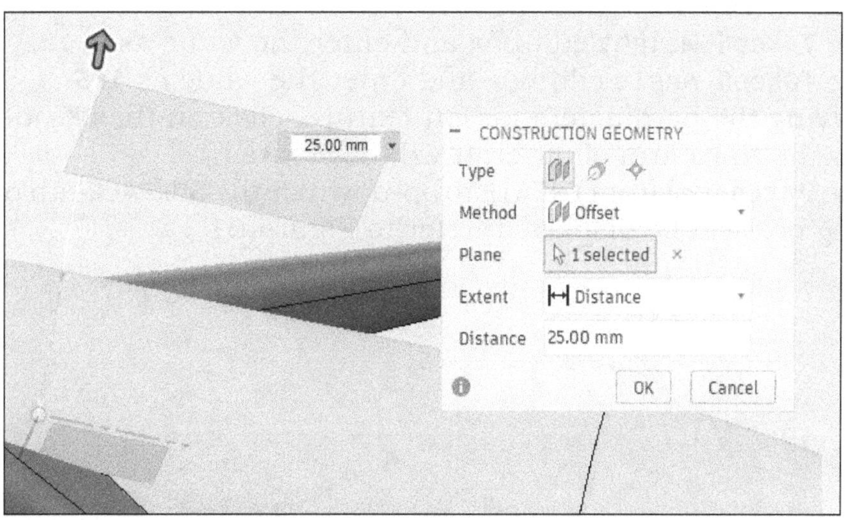

Figure-58. Creating offset plane for third rear wing

- Click on the **Create Sketch** tool from **CREATE** drop-down and select the recently created plane for sketch.
- Create the sketch as shown in Figure-59.

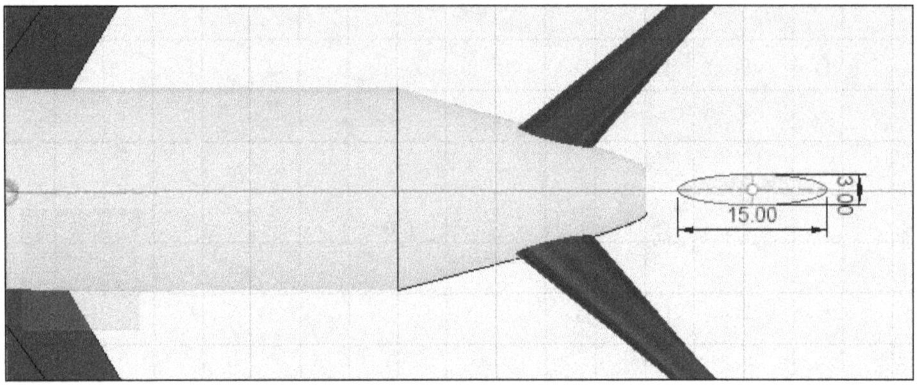

Figure-59. Creating another sketch for rear wing

- Click on **Finish Sketch** button from **Toolbar** to exit the sketch.
- Click on **Loft** tool from **CREATE** drop-down and select the recently created sketch under **Profiles** section; refer to Figure-60.

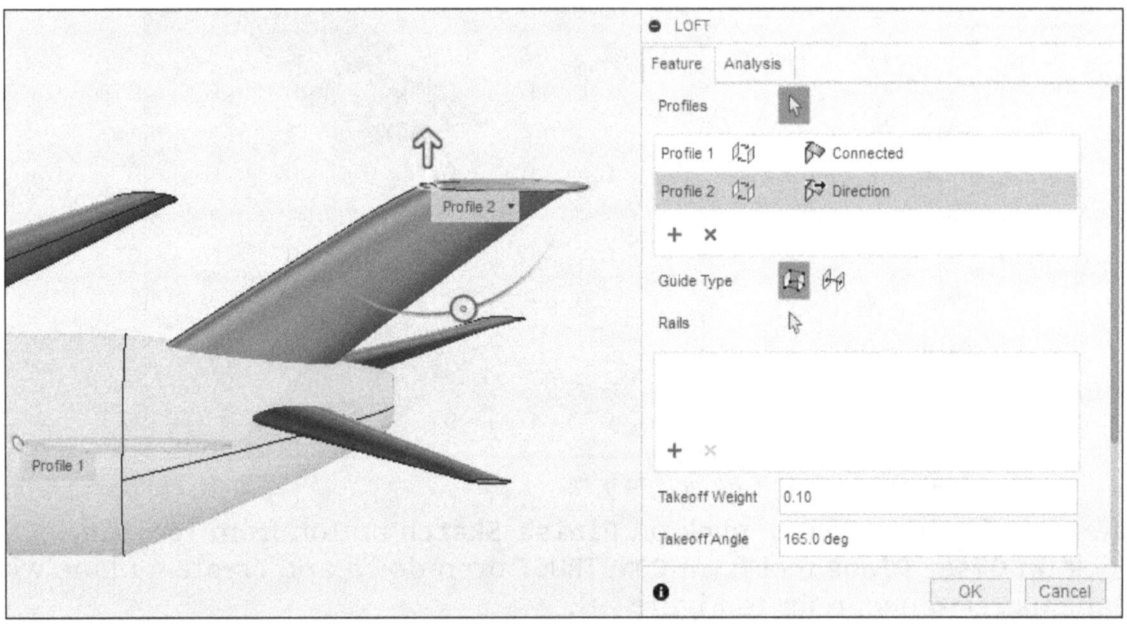

Figure-60. Applying Loft feature

- Click in the **Takeoff Weight** edit box and enter the value as **0.10**.
- Click in the **Takeoff Angle** edit box and enter the value as **165**.
- After specifying the parameters for loft feature, click on the **OK** button from **LOFT** dialog box. The third arm of air craft will be created.
- Click on the **Patch** tool from **CREATE** drop-down in the **SURFACE** tab of **Toolbar**. The **PATCH** dialog box will be displayed; refer to Figure-61.

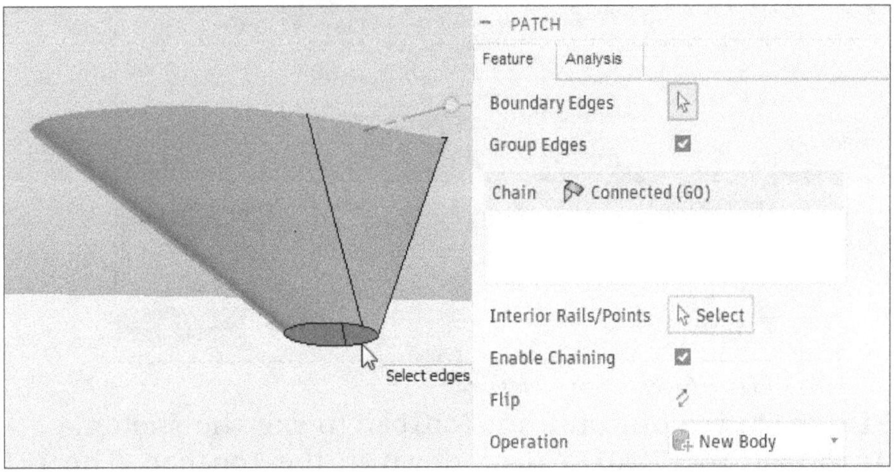

Figure-61. Applying patch on wing

- Select the open edge and click on **OK** button from **PATCH** dialog box to complete the process.
- Similarly, apply the patch tool to all wings and back of aircraft body.
- Click on **Reverse Normal** tool from **MODIFY** drop-down in the **Toolbar**. The **REVERSE NORMAL** dialog box will be displayed.
- The **Select** button of **Faces** section is active by default. Click on the faces with wrong normal; refer to Figure-62.

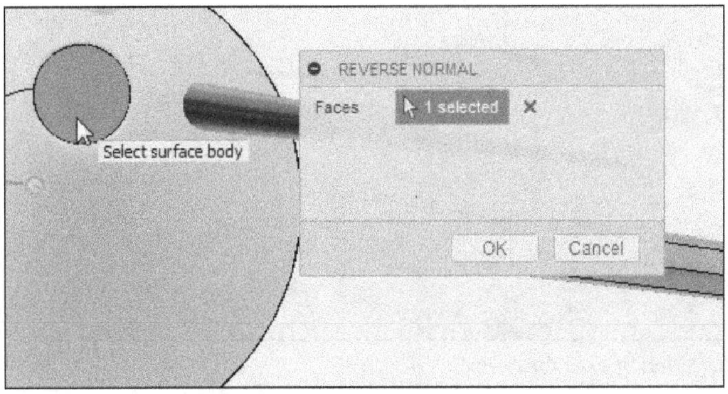

Figure-62. Applying Reverse Normal tool

- Click on the **OK** button from **Reverse Normal** dialog box to complete the process.
- Click on **Center Rectangle** tool from **CREATE** drop-down and select the **YZ** plane for sketch; refer to Figure-63.

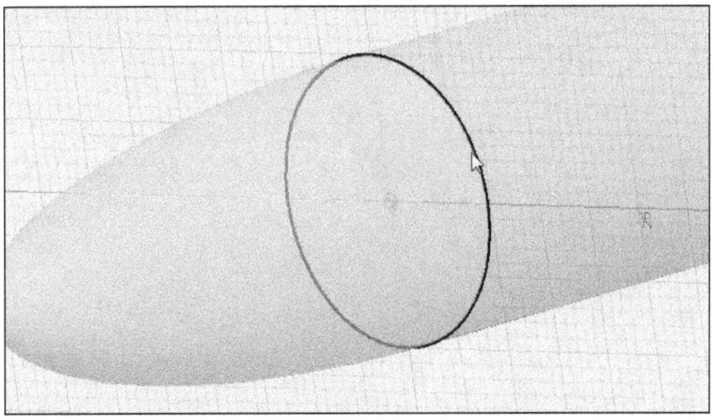

Figure-63. Selecting plane for sketch

- Create a rectangle on the selected plane as shown in Figure-64.

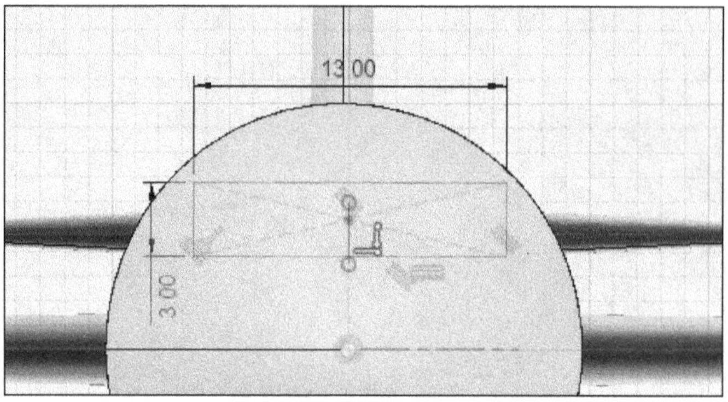

Figure-64. Sketch for windshield

- Click on **Finish Sketch** button from **Toolbar** to exit the sketch.
- Click on **Trim** tool from **MODIFY** drop-down in the **Toolbar**. The **TRIM** dialog box will be displayed.
- The **Select** button of **Trim Tool** section is active by default. Select the recently created rectangular sketch and click on the inner area of trim preview; refer to Figure-65.

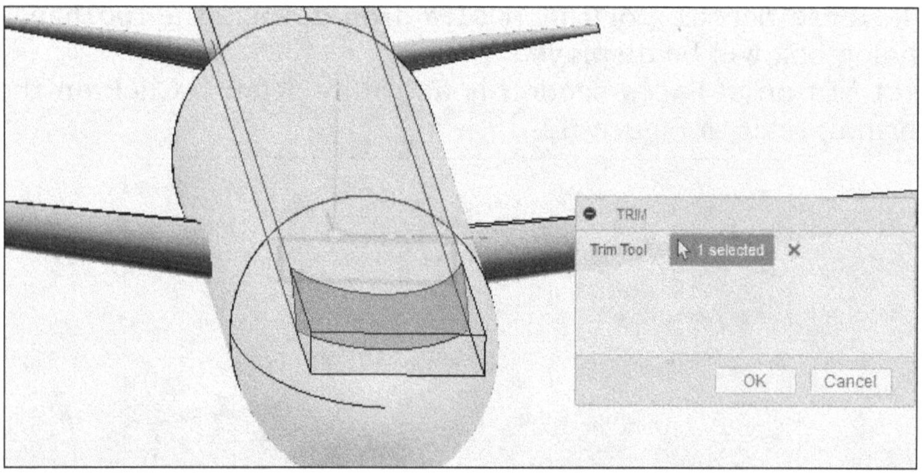

Figure-65. Selection of area for trim

- After selecting, click on the **OK** button of **TRIM** dialog box to exit the **Trim** tool.
- Click on **Loft** tool from **CREATE** drop-down. The **LOFT** dialog box will be displayed.
- Select the area in **Profiles** section as displayed in Figure-66.

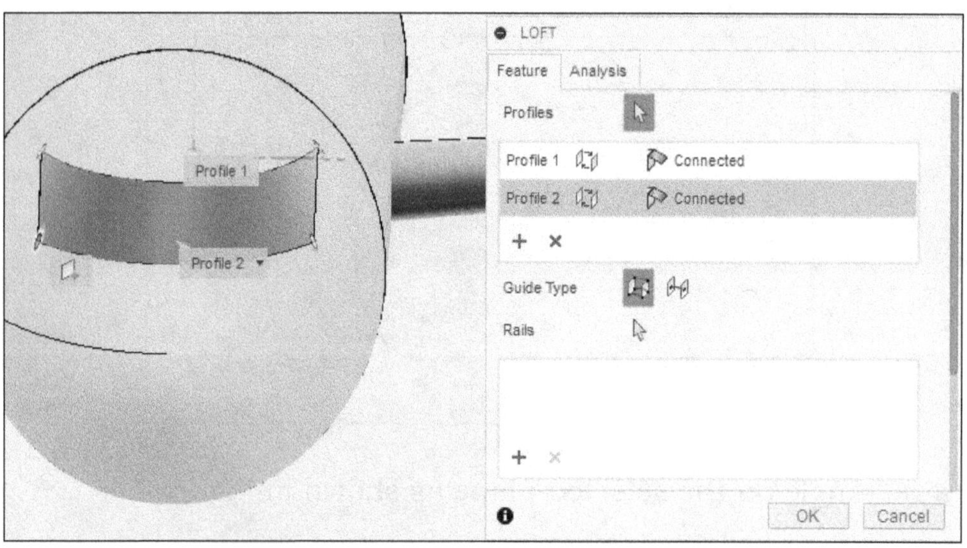

Figure-66. Creating windshield

- Click on the **OK** button from **LOFT** dialog box to complete the process.

Removing extra material

- Click on the **Trim** tool from **MODIFY** drop-down. The **TRIM** dialog box will be displayed; refer to Figure-67.

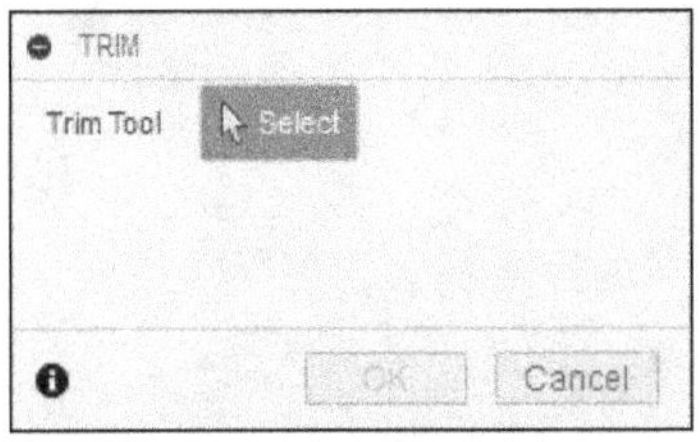

Figure-67. TRIM dialog box

- The **Select** button of **Trim Tool** section is active by default. Click on the extra material to remove; refer to Figure-68.

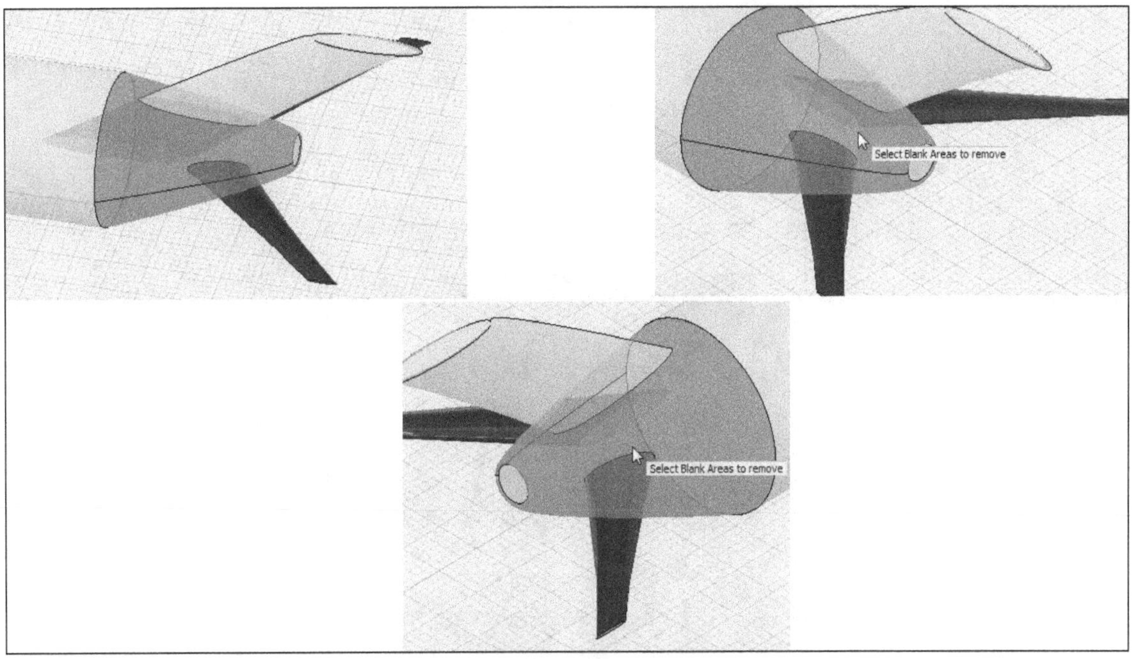

Figure-68. Removing extra material

- After selection of material to remove, click on the **OK** button from **TRIM** dialog box.
- After applying all the tools from above section. The aircraft will be created completely; refer to Figure-69.

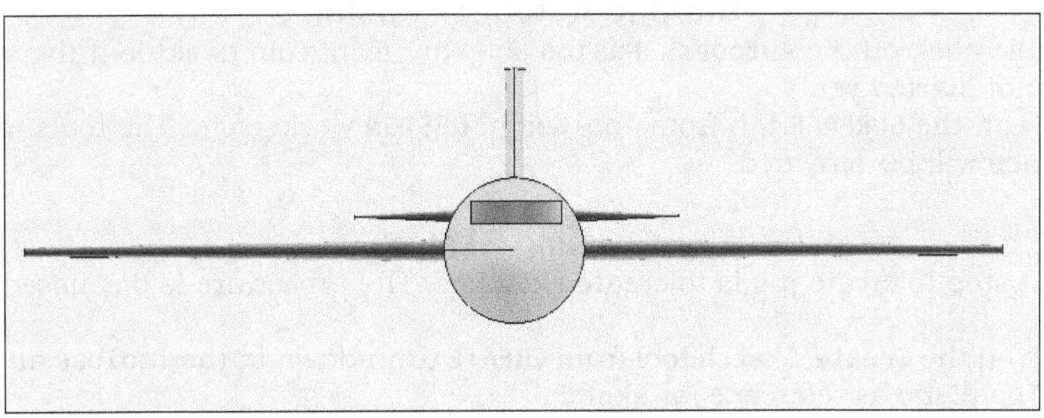

Figure-69. Front view of aircraft

PRACTICAL 2

Create the model of Jug as shown in Figure-70 and Figure-71.

Figure-70. Model of Jug

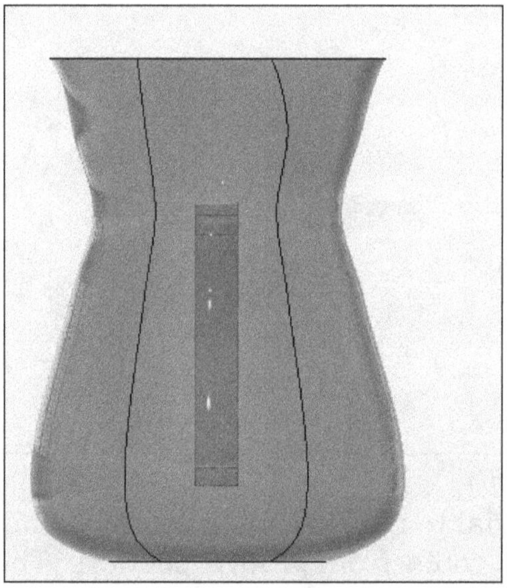

Figure-71. Another view of Jug

Starting Autodesk Fusion

- Double-click on the **Autodesk Fusion** software icon from desktop if the software has not started yet.
- Click on the **SURFACE** tab from **Toolbar** in **DESIGN** workspace. The tools to create surface will be activated.

Creating Sketch

The first step to create jug is to create sketches. The procedure is discussed next.

- Click on the **Create Sketch** tool from **CREATE** drop-down in the **Toolbar** and select the **Top** plane as reference for sketch.
- Create the sketch as shown in Figure-72. Click on the **Finish Sketch** tool to exit.

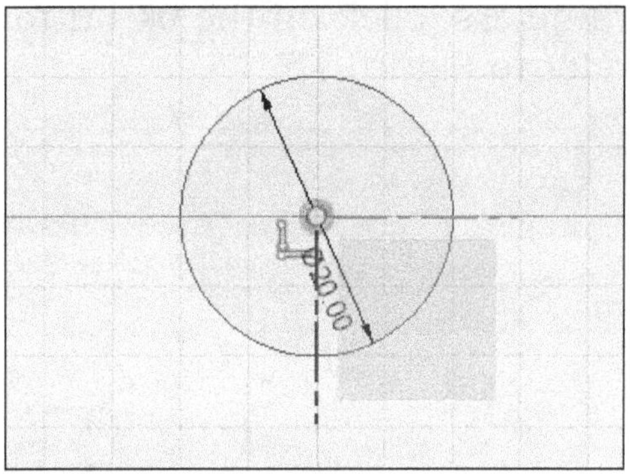

Figure-72. Creating base sketch

- Click on the **Offset Plane** tool from **CONSTRUCT** drop-down in the **Toolbar**. The **CONSTRUCTION GEOMETRY** dialog box will be displayed.
- The **Select** button of **Plane** section is active by default. Select the **Top** plane as reference.
- Click in the **Distance** edit box and enter the value as **2**; refer to Figure-73.

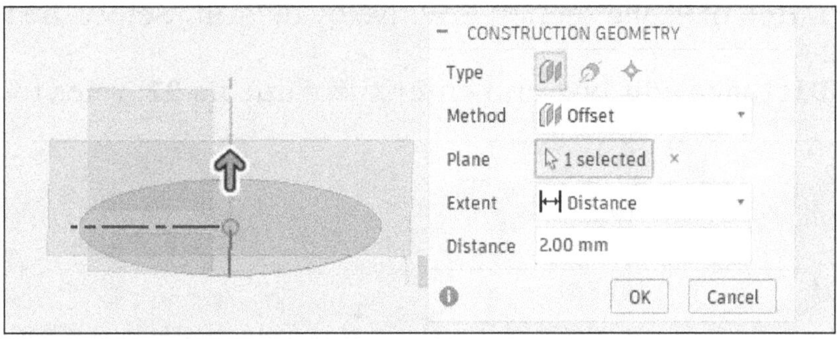

Figure-73. Creating first offset plane

- After specifying the parameters, click on the **OK** button from **CONSTRUCTION GEOMETRY** dialog box to complete the process of creating plane.
- Create a center diameter circle on recently created offset plane; refer to Figure-74.

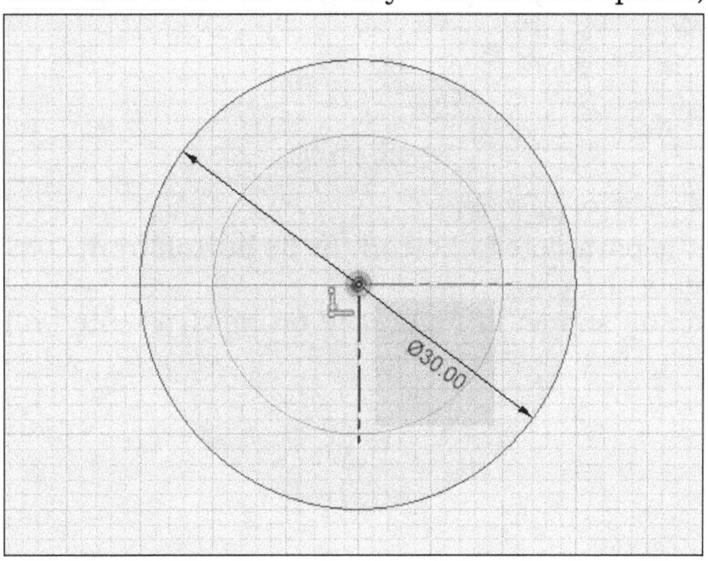

Figure-74. Creating second sketch

- Click on the **Patch** tool from **CREATE** drop-down. The **PATCH** dialog box will be displayed.
- The **Select** button of **Boundary Edges** section from **PATCH** dialog box is active by default. You need to select the first sketch to patch.

- After specifying the parameters, click on the **OK** button from **PATCH** dialog box to complete the process; refer to Figure-75.

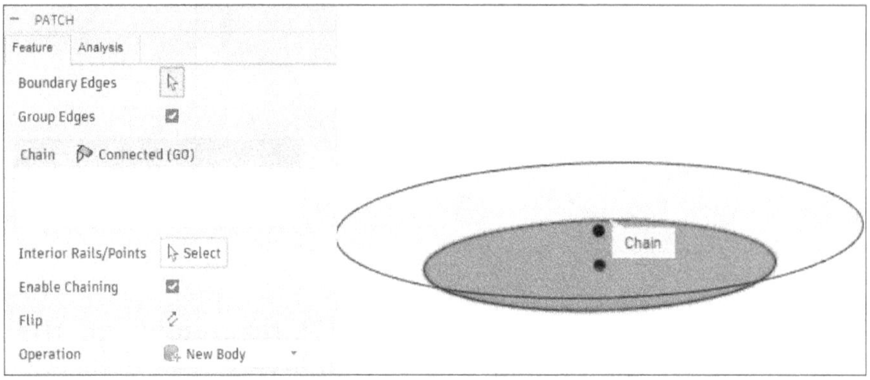

Figure-75. Creating Patch of first sketch

- Click on the **Offset Plane** tool from **CONSTRUCT** drop-down in the **Toolbar**. The **CONSTRUCTION GEOMETRY** dialog box will be displayed.
- The **Select** button of **Plane** section is active by default. Select the first offset plane as reference.
- Click in the **Distance** edit box and enter the value as **22**; refer to Figure-76.

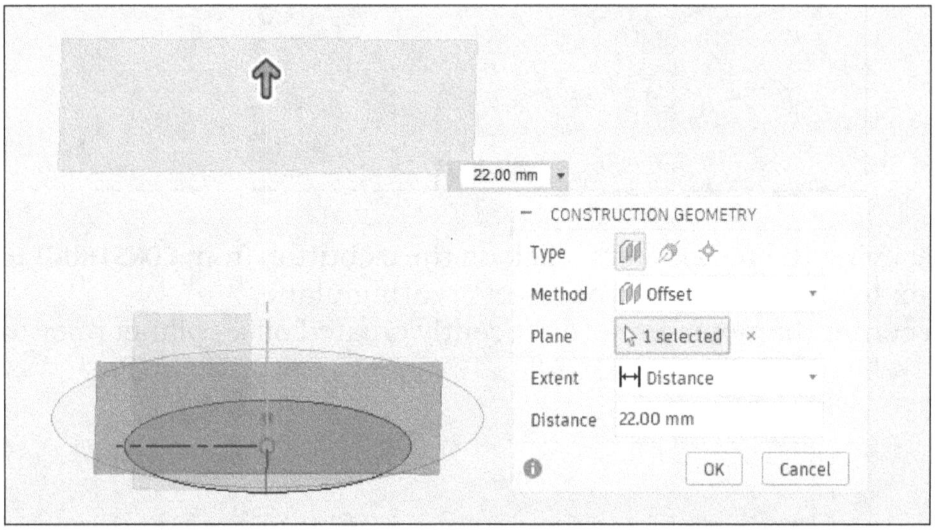

Figure-76. Creating third offset plane

- After specifying the parameter, click on the **OK** button from **CONSTRUCTION GEOMETRY** dialog box to create the plane.
- Create the sketch as shown in Figure-77 on newly created offset plane.

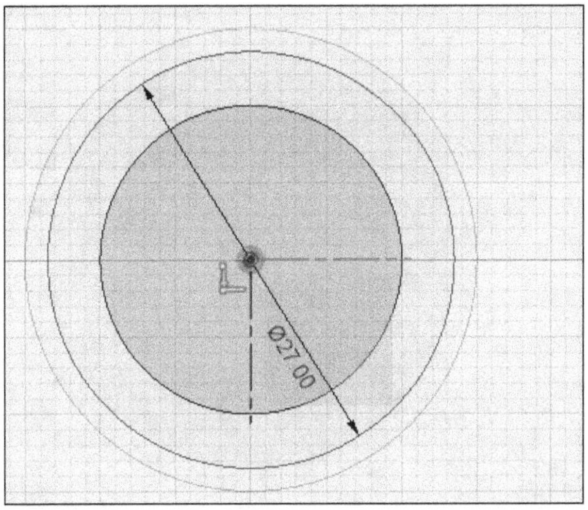

Figure-77. Creating third sketch

- Click on the **Finish Sketch** button from **Toolbar** to exit the sketch.
- Click on the **Offset Plane** tool from **CONSTRUCT** drop-down in the **Toolbar**. The **CONSTRUCTION GEOMETRY** dialog box will be displayed.
- The **Select** button of **Plane** section is active by default. Select the second offset plane as reference.
- Click in the **Distance** edit box and enter the value as **7**; refer to Figure-78. You can also set the distance by moving the drag handle.

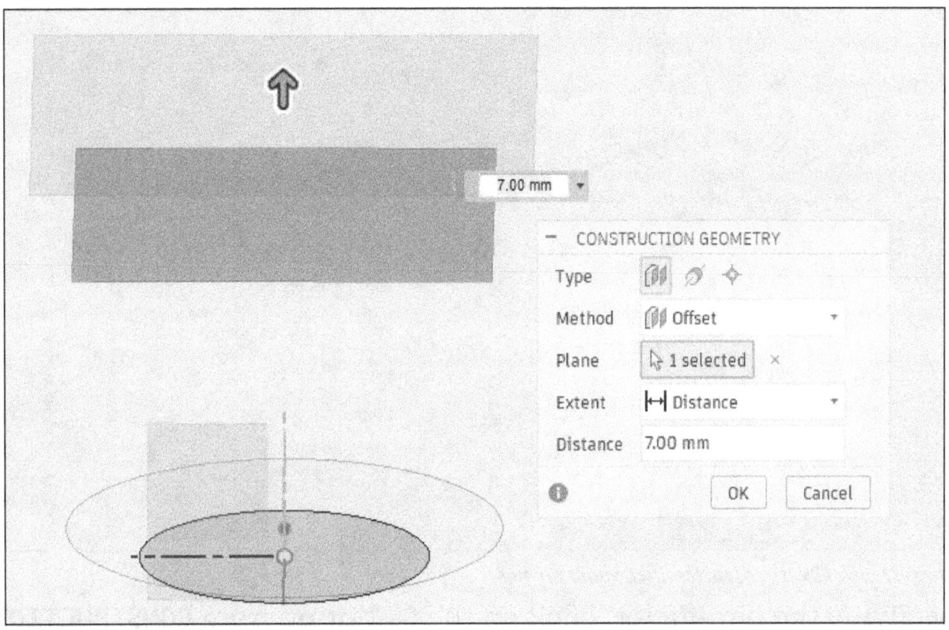

Figure-78. Creation of third offset plane

- After specifying the parameter, click on the **OK** button from **CONSTRUCTION GEOMETRY** dialog box to create the plane.
- Create the sketch as shown in Figure-79 on newly created offset plane.

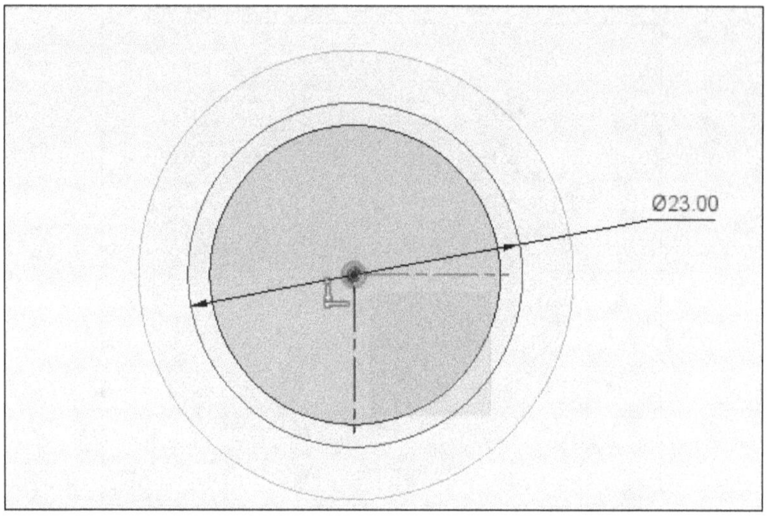

Figure-79. Creating third sketch of jug

- Click on the **Offset Plane** tool from **CONSTRUCT** drop-down in the **Toolbar**. The **CONSTRUCTION GEOMETRY** dialog box will be displayed.
- The **Select** button of **Plane** section is active by default. Select the third offset plane as reference.
- Click in the **Distance** edit box and specify the value as **8**; refer to Figure-80. You can also set the distance by moving the drag handle.

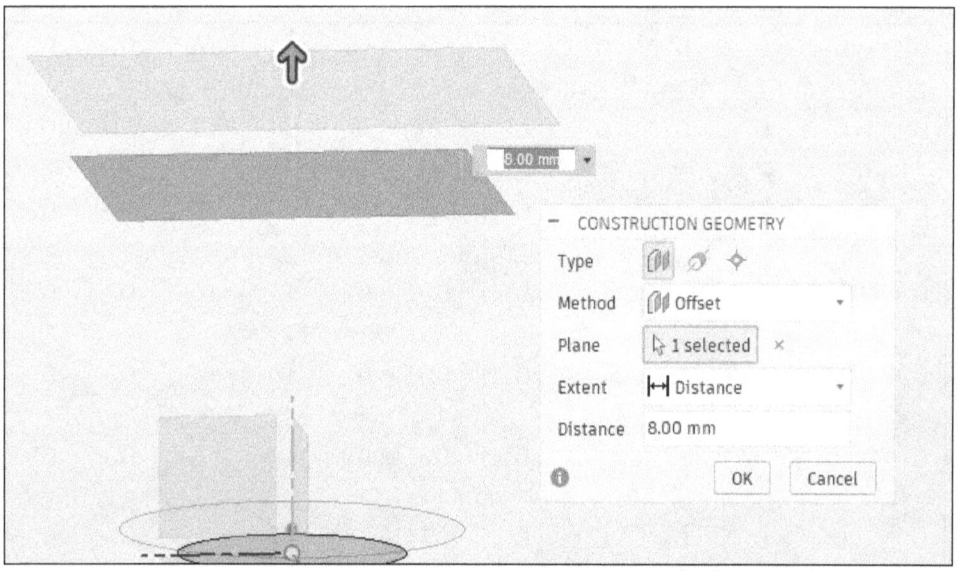

Figure-80. Creating fourth offset plane for jug

- After specifying the parameter, click on the **OK** button from **CONSTRUCTION GEOMETRY** dialog box to create the plane.
- Create the sketch as shown in Figure-81 on newly created offset plane.

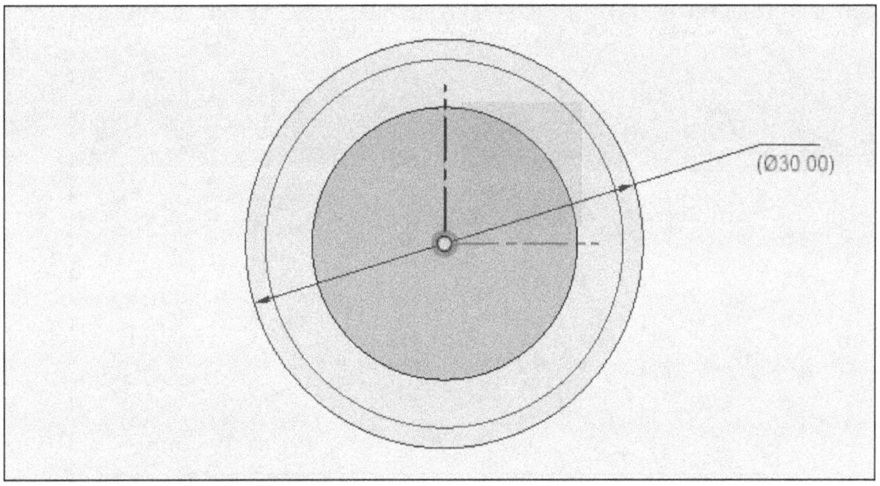

Figure-81. Creating fifth sketch for Jug

- Click on the **Offset Plane** tool from **CONSTRUCT** drop-down in the **Toolbar**. The **CONSTRUCTION GEOMETRY** dialog box will be displayed.
- The **Select** button of **Plane** option is active by default. Select the third offset plane as reference.
- Click in the **Distance** edit box and enter the value as **6**; refer to Figure-82. You can also set the distance by moving the drag handle.

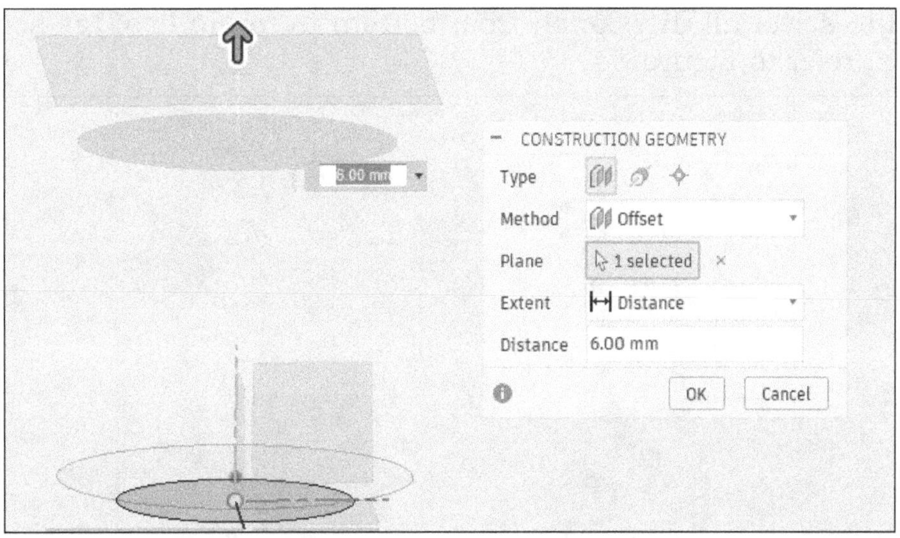

Figure-82. Creating fifth offset plane

- After specifying the parameter, click on the **OK** button from **CONSTRUCTION GEOMETRY** dialog box to create the plane.
- Click on the **Circle** tool from **CREATE** drop-down in the **Toolbar** and select the recently created plane as reference.
- Create the sketch as shown in Figure-83 with the help of **Circle**, **Trim**, and **Arc** tool.

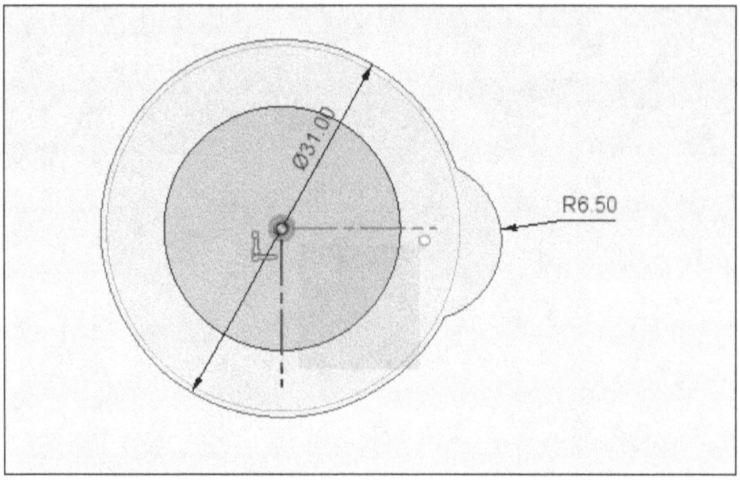

Figure-83. Creating sixth sketch

Creating Loft feature

Till now, we have created the sketch for jug. Now, we will apply the loft feature to join all the sketches. The procedure is discussed next.

- Click on the **Loft** tool from **CREATE** drop-down in the **Toolbar**. The **LOFT** dialog box will be displayed.
- You need to select all the sketch from bottom to top in **Profiles** section of **LOFT** dialog box; refer to Figure-84.

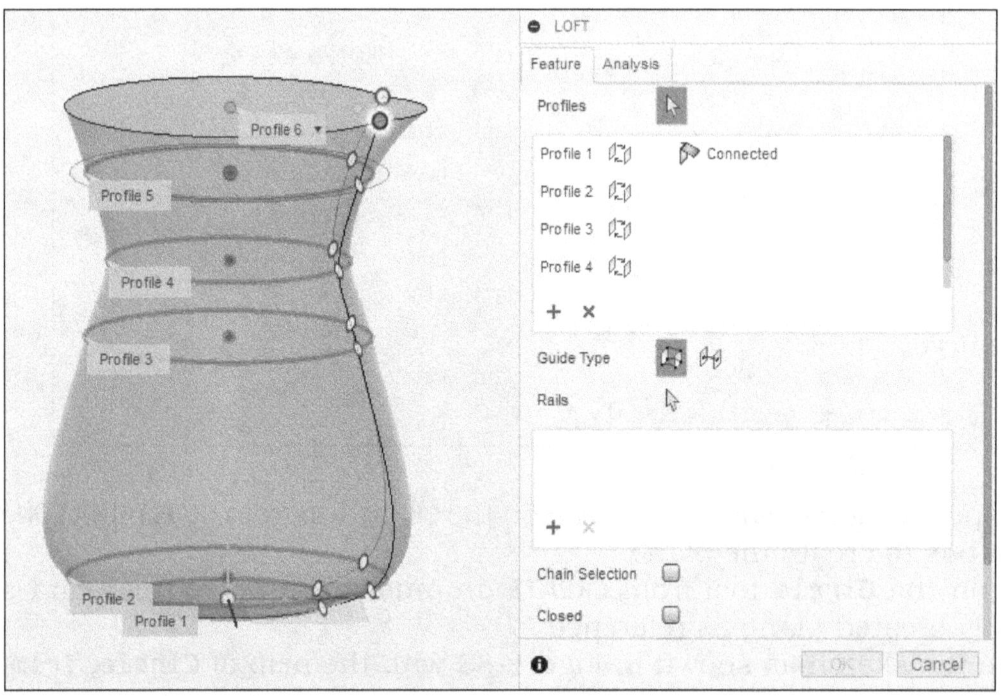

Figure-84. Creating loft feature of jug

- After selecting the profiles, click on the **OK** button from **LOFT** dialog box to complete the loft feature.

Here loft feature is completed. Now, we will create the handle of jug.

- Click on the **Offset Plane** tool of **CONSTRUCT** drop-down from **Toolbar**. The **CONSTRUCTION GEOMETRY** dialog box will be displayed.
- The **Select** button of **Plane** section is active by default. Select the **YZ** plane as reference.
- Click in the **Distance** edit box and specify the value as **-10**; refer to Figure-85.

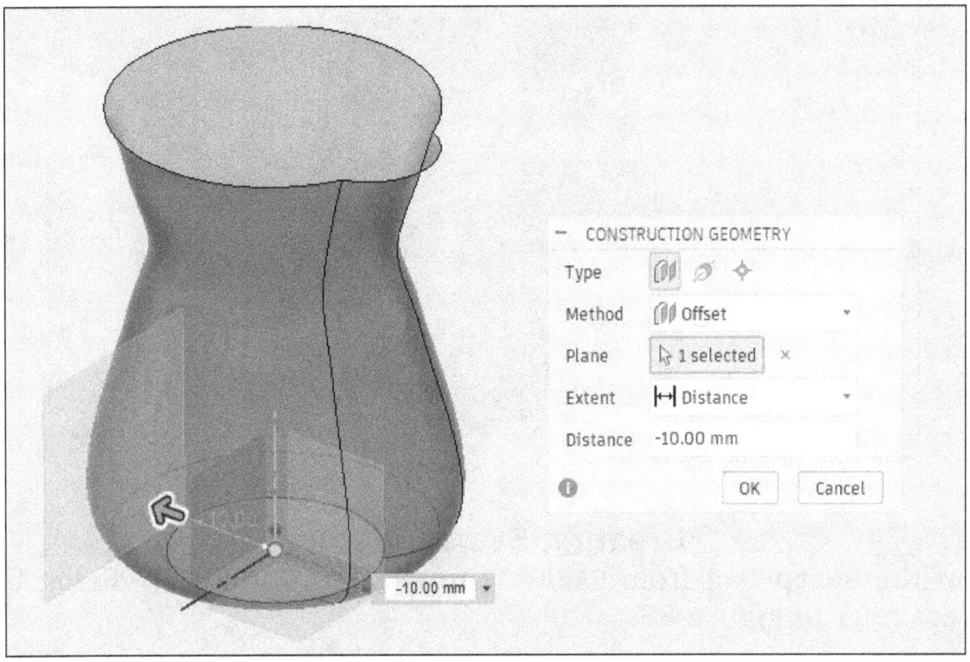

Figure-85. Creating sixth offset plane

- After specifying the parameter, click on the **OK** button from **CONSTRUCTION GEOMETRY** dialog box to create the plane.
- Create the sketch as shown in Figure-86 on newly offset plane.

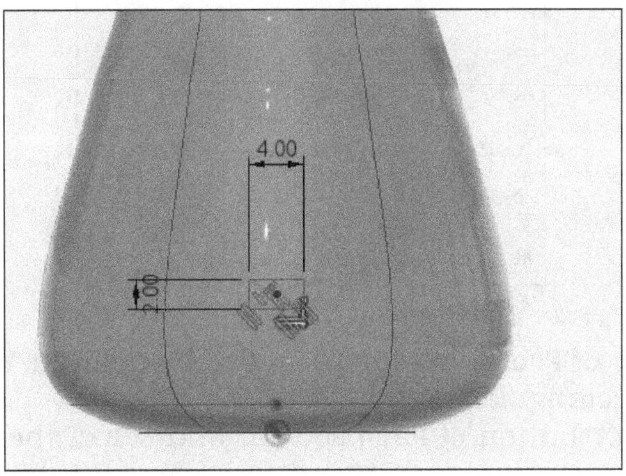

Figure-86. Creating seventh sketch

- Click on the **Create Sketch** tool from **CREATE** drop-down and select the **XZ** plane.
- Create the sketch as shown in Figure-87.

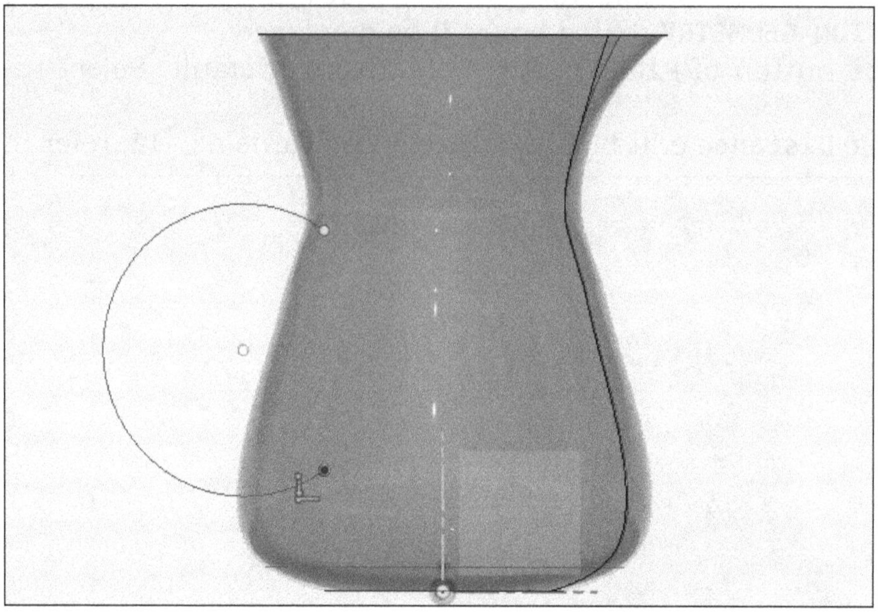

Figure-87. Creating eighth sketch

Creating Sweep feature

- Click on the **Sweep** tool from **CREATE** drop-down. The **SWEEP** dialog box will be displayed; refer to Figure-88.

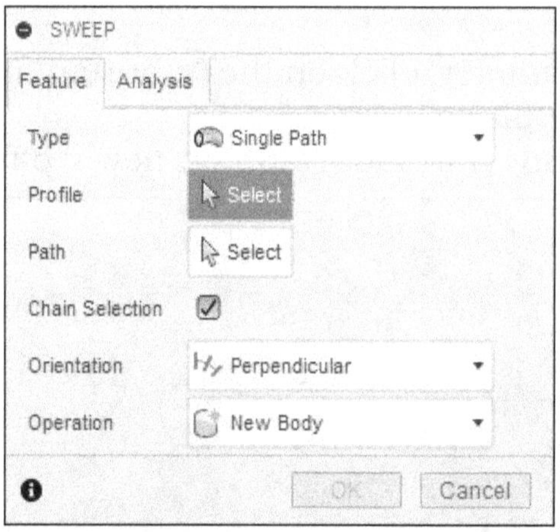

Figure-88. SWEEP dialog box

- The **Select** button of **Profile** section is active by default. You need to select the recently created rectangular sketch.
- Click on the **Select** button of **Path** section and select the recently created arc; refer to Figure-89.

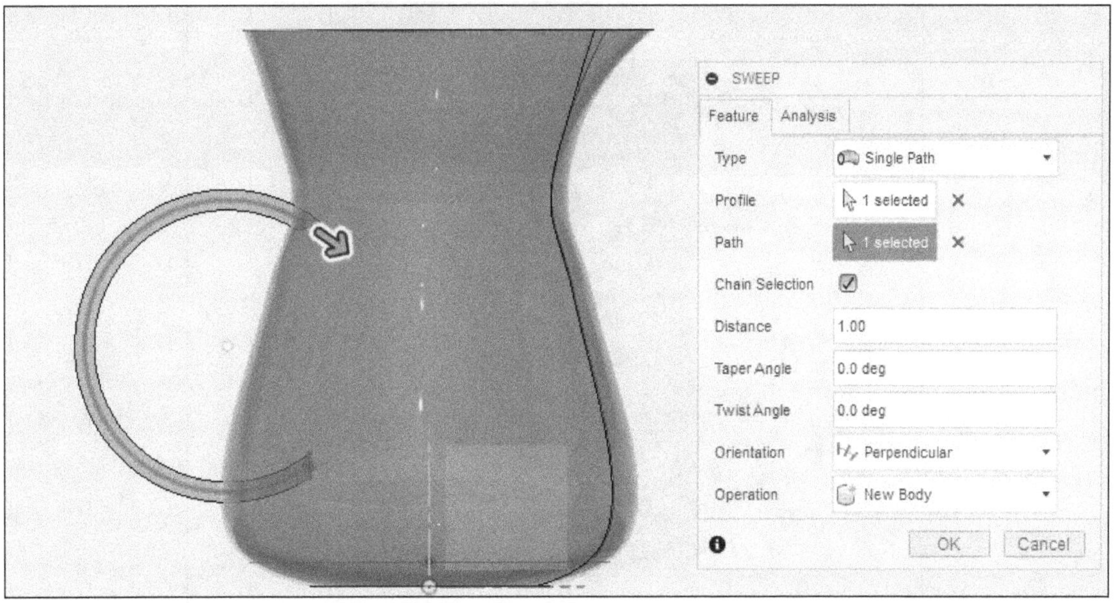

Figure-89. Creating sweep feature for jug

- Click on the **Orientation** drop-down of **SWEEP** dialog box and select the **Perpendicular** option.
- After specifying the parameters, click on the **OK** button from **SWEEP** dialog box to complete the feature.

Till this point, we have created the model of jug but we need to apply the trim tool on the jug to remove the unwanted parts.

Trimming Extra Entities

- Click on the **Trim** tool from **MODIFY** drop-down in the **Toolbar**. The **TRIM** dialog box will be displayed.
- The **Select** button of **Trim Tool** section is active by default. Click on the interior of jug and select the unwanted parts; refer to Figure-90.

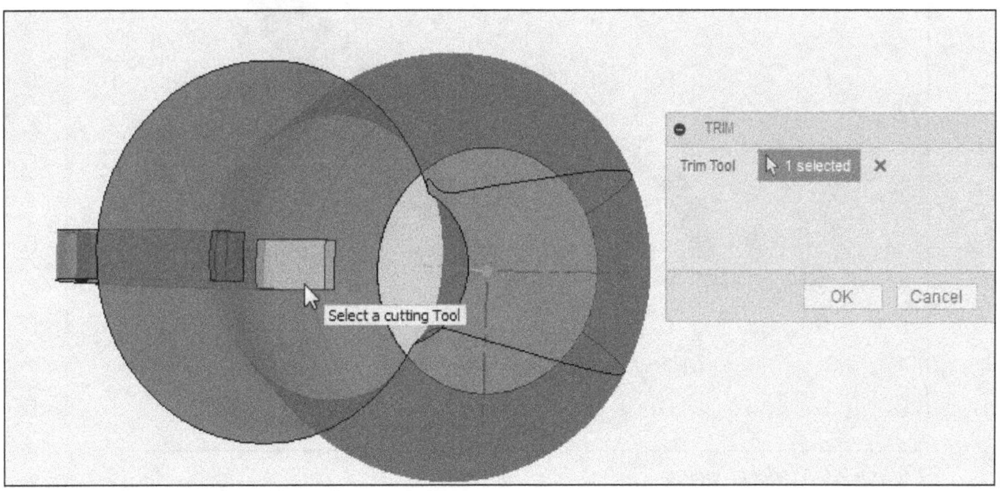

Figure-90. Applying the Trim tool

- After selecting, click on the **OK** button from **Trim** dialog box to trim the material. The model of jug will be created successfully; refer to Figure-91.

Figure-91. Model of Jug created

- You can apply the physical material or appearance as required to the jug.
- You can also create the model of jug with the help of **Revolve** tool in place of **Loft** tool.

PRACTICE 1

Create the model of mouse as shown in Figure-92 and Figure-93. Assume appropriate dimensions. If you are working on your system using a computer mouse then you can use that as reference for creating model.

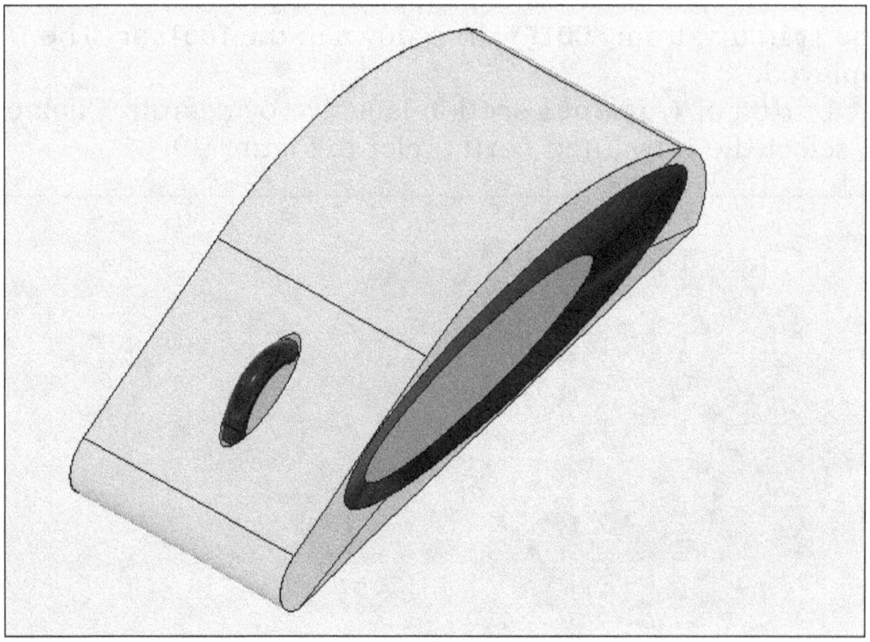

Figure-92. Model of mouse

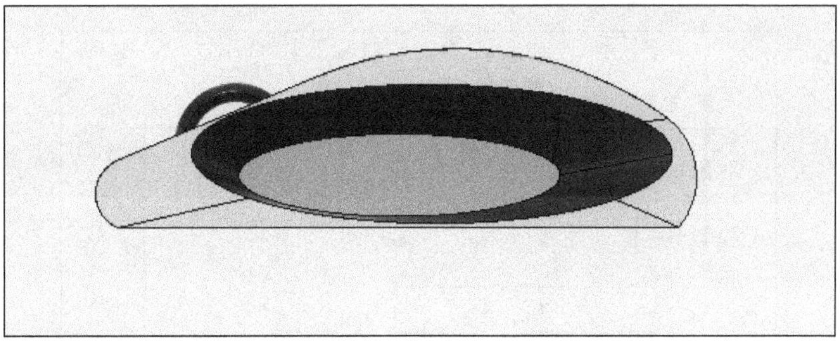

Figure-93. Right view of mouse

PRACTICE 2

Create the model of water bottle as shown in Figure-94 and Figure-95. The drawing view of water bottle is shown in Figure-96. (You are free to apply your artistic mind for improving design of bottle and when at it, why not start a competition in your class for designing bottle.)

Figure-94. Model of Water Bottle

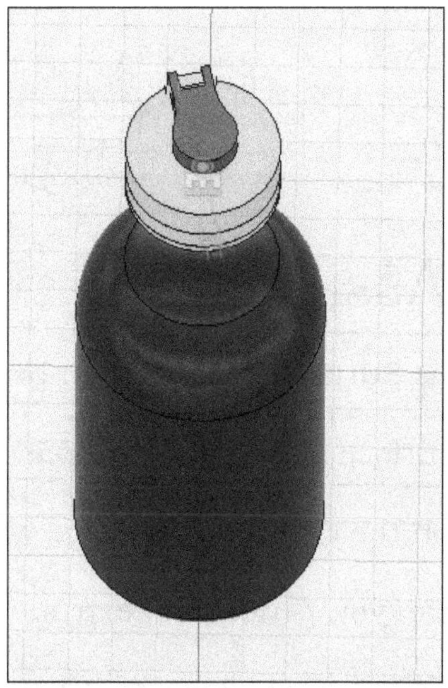

Figure-95. Top view of water bottle

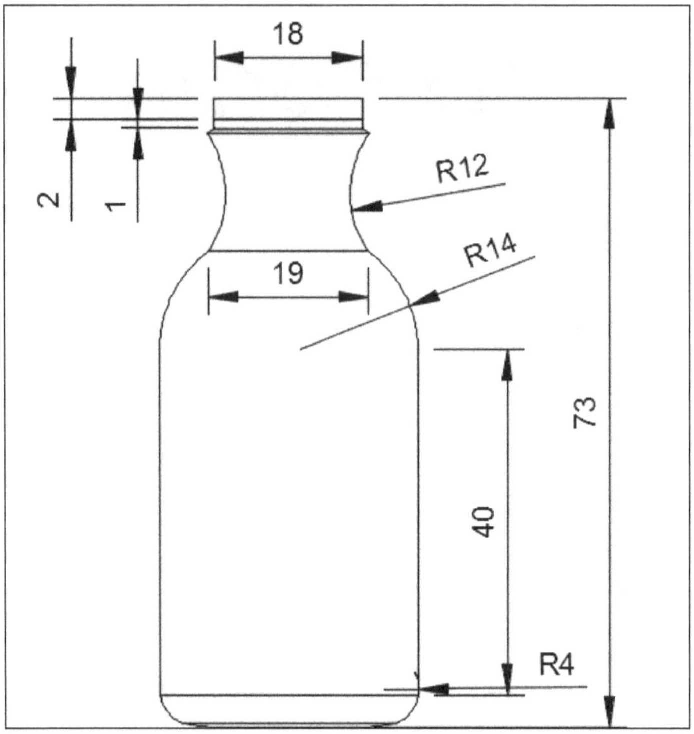

Figure-96. Dimensions of Water Bottle

SELF ASSESSMENT

Q1. What is Surfacing? Explain in brief.

Q2. Why surface models can not exist in real world and how they can be made real?

Q3. Explain the creation of surface with G0 edges, G1 edges, and G2 edges.

Q4. How can you perform an extrude protrusion of an open sketch?

Q5. What is the use of **Reverse Normal** tool?

Q6. The .... tool is used to combine the surfaces into one body.

Q7: What is the primary use of surfacing in Autodesk Fusion?

A) To create solid models
B) To create complex shapes for aerodynamic objects
C) To add colors to solid models
D) To perform solid modeling calculations

Q8: Where can you find the surfacing tools in Autodesk Fusion?

A) In the SOLID tab
B) In the CREATE drop-down menu
C) In the SURFACE tab of the DESIGN workspace
D) In the ASSEMBLY tab

Q9: Which tool in Autodesk Fusion is used to create extruded surfaces?

A) Revolve tool
B) Extrude tool
C) Loft tool
D) Sweep tool

Q10: When using the Extrude tool, what can you select for extrusion?

A) Only closed sketches
B) Only open sketches
C) Both open and closed sketches
D) Only solid bodies

Q11: What does the Patch tool in Autodesk Fusion create?

A) Solid bodies
B) Surfaces by connecting edges/curves
C) Sketches for extrusions
D) Mesh bodies

Q12: What options can you select from the Continuity drop-down in the Patch tool?

A) Flat, Tangent, Curvature
B) Connected, Tangent, Curvature
C) Rough, Smooth, Curvature
D) Linear, Connected, Curvature

Q13: In the Ruled tool, which option creates a ruled surface normal to the selected edges?

A) Tangent
B) Direction
C) Normal
D) Perpendicular

Q14: What is the main use of the Trim tool in Autodesk Fusion?

A) To cut the surface at an angle
B) To trim the surface using selected trimming objects
C) To extend the surface
D) To merge multiple surfaces

Q15: Which option is available in the Untrim tool?

A) Select all edges
B) Reverse the direction of edges
C) Untrim internal edges only
D) Untrim external edges only

Q16: What does the Extend tool do in Autodesk Fusion?

A) Flips the surface
B) Connects surfaces together
C) Extends the edge of a surface
D) Deletes edges from a surface

Q17: What happens when you use the Extrude tool with an open sketch?

A) The sketch is automatically closed
B) It creates a solid body
C) It creates an extruded surface
D) It generates a boundary fill

Q18: Which option in the Patch tool is used to create a surface with blended continuous curvature?

A) G0
B) G1
C) G2
D) Tangent

Q19: Which tool in Autodesk Fusion allows the creation of a ruled surface at a specified distance and angle?

A) Sweep tool
B) Ruled tool
C) Extrude tool
D) Revolve tool

Q20: In the Ruled tool, what is the purpose of the Mitered Corners check box?

A) To create rounded corners
B) To create sharp corners
C) To add curves to corners
D) To smooth the edges of the surface

Q21: What does the Stitch tool in Autodesk Fusion do?

A) Combines multiple surfaces into one body
B) Reverses the surface normal
C) Extends the edge of a surface
D) Trims a surface using a cutting tool

Q22: Which of the following is true about the Unstitch tool in Autodesk Fusion?

A) It is used to combine multiple bodies into a single body
B) It is used to unstitch a surface that was previously stitched
C) It stitches surfaces together at a specified distance
D) It trims the edges of a surface

Q23: What happens when you use the Reverse Normal tool in Autodesk Fusion?

A) It flips the selected surfaces' normal direction
B) It trims the surfaces
C) It merges the surfaces into one body
D) It untrims the surface

Q24: Which option in the Extend tool allows you to extend the edge perpendicularly?

A) Natural
B) Perpendicular
C) Tangent
D) Free Edges

Q25: Which feature in the Untrim tool allows you to untrim all edges of a surface?

A) Manual
B) All Edges
C) Internal Edges
D) External Edges

Q26: What is the purpose of the 'Chain Selection' check box in the Ruled tool?

A) To select all the edges of the model
B) To automatically select all connected geometry
C) To allow freeform surface creation
D) To select the shape for extrusion

FOR STUDENTS NOTES

Chapter 10

Rendering and Animation

Topics Covered

The major topics covered in this chapter are:

- ***Introduction to Rendering***
- ***Appearance Tool***
- ***Scene Settings Tool***
- ***Environment Library Tab***
- ***Texture Map Control***
- ***In-Canvas Render Setting***
- ***Capture Image Tool***
- ***Render***
- ***Introduction to Animation Workspace***
- ***New Storyboard***
- ***Transform Components***
- ***Restore Home Tool***
- ***Auto Explode : One Level***
- ***Auto Explode : All Levels***
- ***Manual Explode***
- ***Show/Hide Tool***
- ***Create Callout Tool***
- ***View Tool***
- ***Publish Video Tool***

INTRODUCTION

When a designer is working on a 3D Model, the model he/she creates is generally a mathematical representation of points and surfaces in three-dimensions. Sometimes, a realistic 2D image of 3D model is required for presentation to the client. The conversion of 3D model with specified environmental scenario through mathematical approximation to a finalized 2D image is known as Rendering. During this process, the entire scene's textural and lighting information are combined to determine the color value of each pixel in the finalized image. To perform rendering, select the **RENDER** option from the **Change Workspace** drop-down in the **Ribbon**.

INTRODUCTION TO RENDER WORKSPACE

The tools in **Render Workspace** are used to create photo-realistic image from a scene of model. There are various tools used for rendering process which are discussed next.

Appearance Tool

The **Appearance** tool is used to apply different materials to selected bodies/ components/faces. The procedure to use this tool has been discussed earlier in the book. So, we are not repeating the tool here.

Scene Settings

The **Scene Settings** tool is used to control the lighting, background color, ground effects, and camera rendering. The procedure to use this tool is discussed next.

- Click on the **Scene Settings** tool from **SETUP** panel in the **Toolbar**; refer to Figure-1. The **SCENE SETTINGS** dialog box will be displayed; refer to Figure-2.

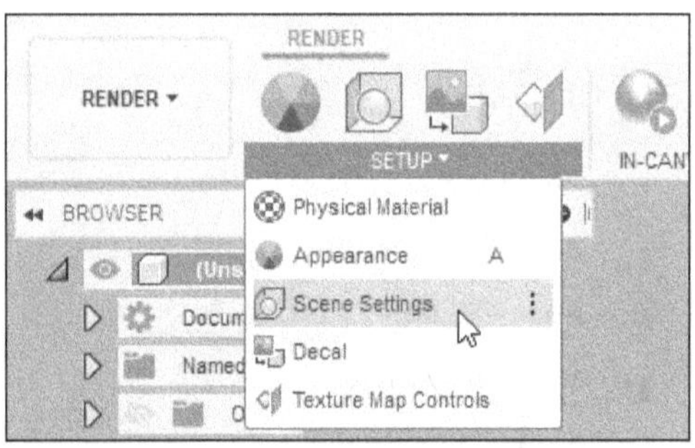

Figure-1. Scene Settings tool

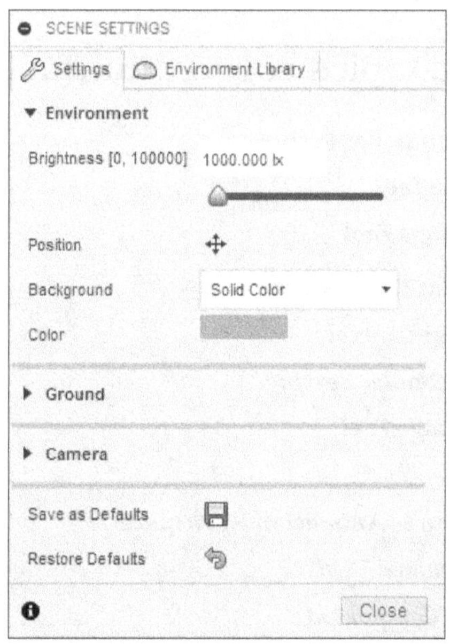

Figure-2. SCENE SETTINGS dialog box

Environment section

- Click on the **Brightness** edit box and specify the value of brightness for model. You can also move the **Brightness** slider to adjust the brightness for the model.

- If you want to control the position and rotation of lights then click on the **Position** button of **Environment** section from **Settings** tab. The drag handle along with some tools will be displayed on the canvas screen; refer to Figure-3.

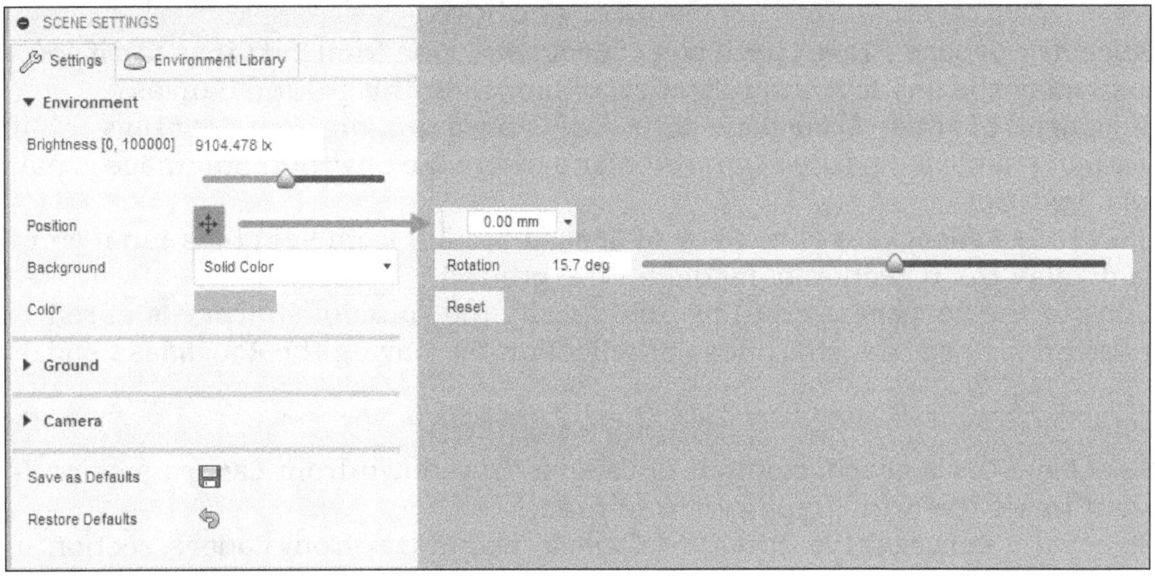

Figure-3. Tools of Position button

- Click in the floating window and specify the position of lights. You can also set the position by moving the drag handle from model.
- Click in the **Rotation** edit box and specify the value of rotation of lights. You can also adjust the value by moving the **Rotation** slider.
- If you want to reset all the changed settings, then click on the **Reset** button from rotation tools.
- Select **Environment** option from **Background** drop-down if you want to use environment image. The environments are available in **Environment Library** tab of this dialog box.
- Select **Solid Color** option from **Background** drop-down if you want to set a particular color to the background.
- To select a solid color, click on the **Color** button. A color box will be displayed; refer to Figure-4.

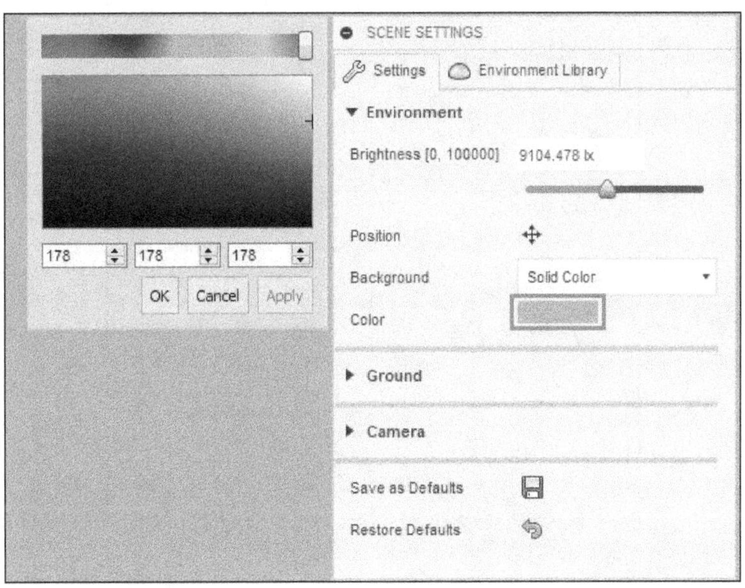

Figure-4. Color box

- Select required color from color box and click on the **Apply** button to set the selected color as background color.

Ground section

- Select the **Ground Plane** check box of **Ground** section from **Settings** tab if you want to display the shadow and reflection of model on the ground canvas.
- Select the **Flatten Ground** check box of **Ground** section from **Settings** tab if you want to enable a "textured" ground plane where the environment image is mapped as a texture.
- Select the **Reflections** check box of **Ground** section from **Settings** tab if you want to display the reflection of model on the ground.
- Click in the **Roughness** edit box and specify the value of sharpness of reflection. You can also set the sharpness of reflection by moving the **Roughness** slider.

Camera section

- Select the **Orthographic** option of **Camera** drop-down from **Camera** section if you want to set the orthographic view of model.
- Select the **Perspective** option of **Camera** drop-down from **Camera** section if you want to set the perspective view of model.
- Select the **Perspective with Ortho Faces** option from **Camera** drop-down if you want to set the perspective view of model with ortho faces.
- Click in the **Exposure** edit box of **Camera** section from **Settings** tab and enter the value of camera exposure. You can also set the camera exposure by moving the **Exposure** slider.
- Select the **Depth of Field** check box if you want to apply depth of field effect. Depth of field is used to focus on specific area of the model. This effect is only enabled when **Ray Tracing** is enabled. On selecting the **Depth of Field** check box, the dialog box will be updated; refer to Figure-5.

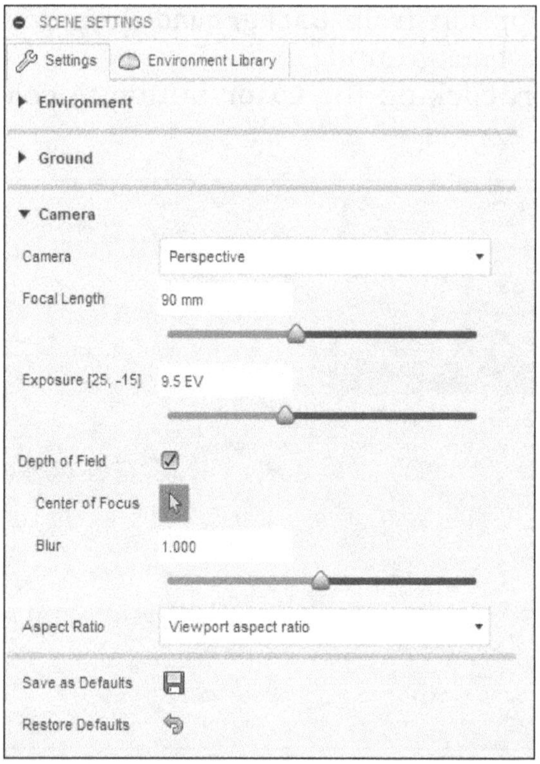

Figure-5. Updated dialog box on selecting Depth of Field check box

- The **Center of Focus** selection button is active by default. You need to select a location on model for focusing.
- Click in the **Blur** edit box and enter the value of blur the model except the selected center of focus. You can also set the value of blur by moving the **Blur** slider.
- Click on the **Aspect Ratio** drop-down and select required aspect ratio of canvas screen.
- Click on **Save as Defaults** button to save the setting as default setting.
- Click on the **Restore Defaults** button to restore the changed settings to default.

Environment Library tab

- Click on the **Environment Library** tab from the **SCENE SETTINGS** dialog box. The tab will be displayed; refer to Figure-6.

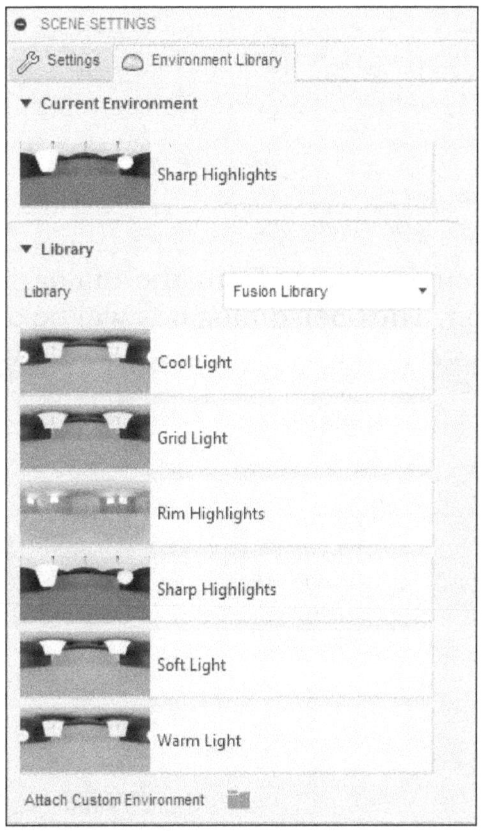

Figure-6. Environment Library tab

- The **Current Environment** section shows the applied environment on the current model.
- If you want to change the environment of the model then drag a specific environment from **Library** section and drop it to the current model or in the **Current Environment** section. You can download the environments in library by using the **Download** button next to them in the list.
- If you want to apply custom environment for model then click on the **Attach Custom Environment** button of **Environment Library** tab from **SCENE SETTINGS** dialog box. The **Attach Custom Environment** dialog box will be displayed; refer to Figure-7.

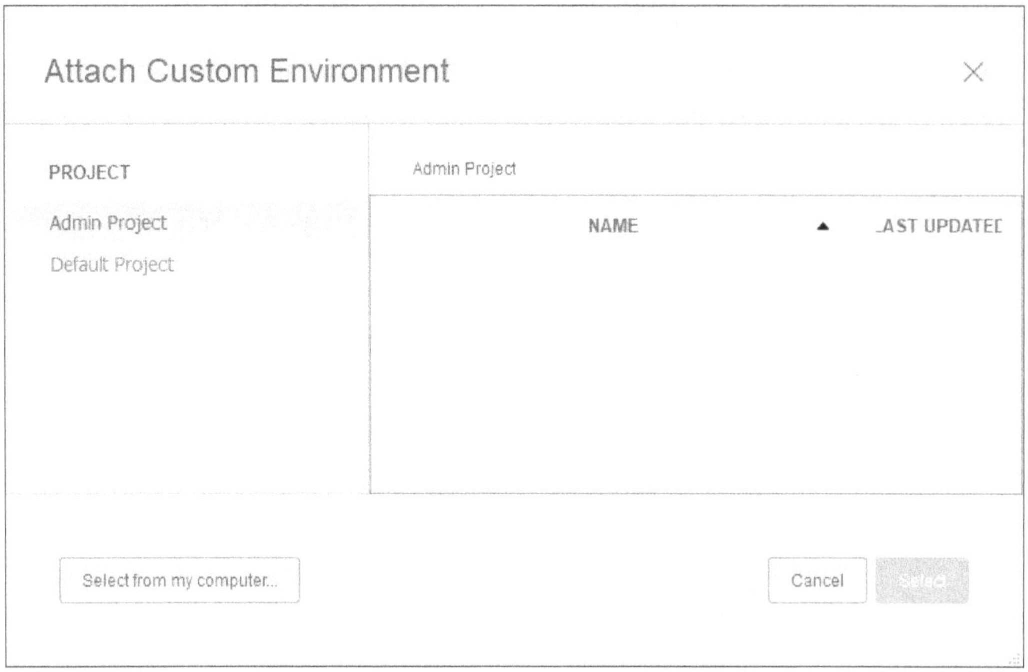

Figure-7. Attach Custom Environment dialog box

- Select desired custom environment from the dialog box or click on the **Select from my computer** button. The **Open** dialog box will be displayed; refer to Figure-8.

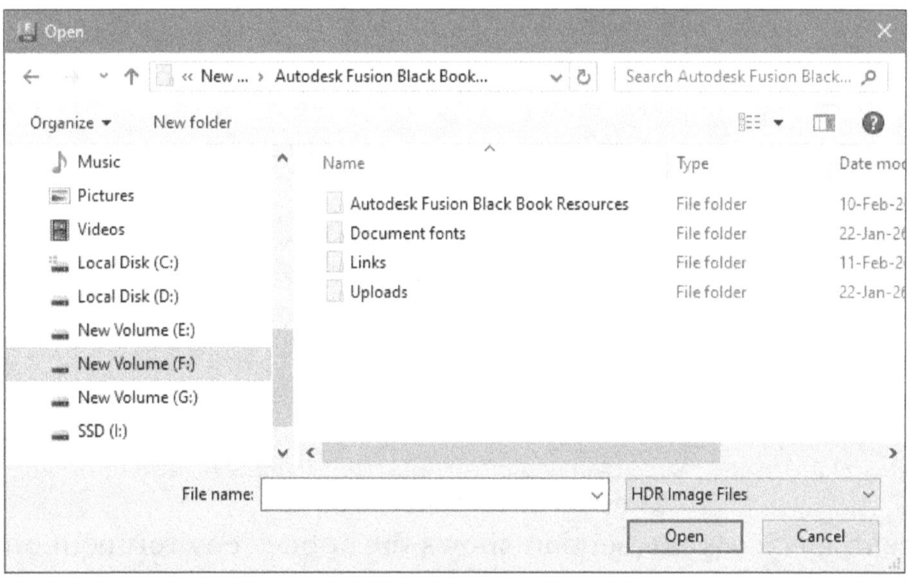

Figure-8. Open dialog box for attaching custom environment

- Select required file and click on **Open** button. The environment will be applied to model.
- After selecting required environment from **Environment Library** tab, click on **Close** button to exit the **Scene Settings** tool.

Note- There is no **Timeline** in the **Render** workspace. The tools applied in the **RENDER** workspace will not be recorded.

Decal tool has been discussed earlier in the book.

Texture Map Controls

The **Texture Map Controls** tool is used to set the orientation of the texture applied to the face or model. The procedure to use this tool is discussed next.

- Click on the **Texture Map Controls** tool of **SETUP** panel from **Toolbar**; refer to Figure-9. The **TEXTURE MAP CONTROLS** dialog box will be displayed; refer to Figure-10.

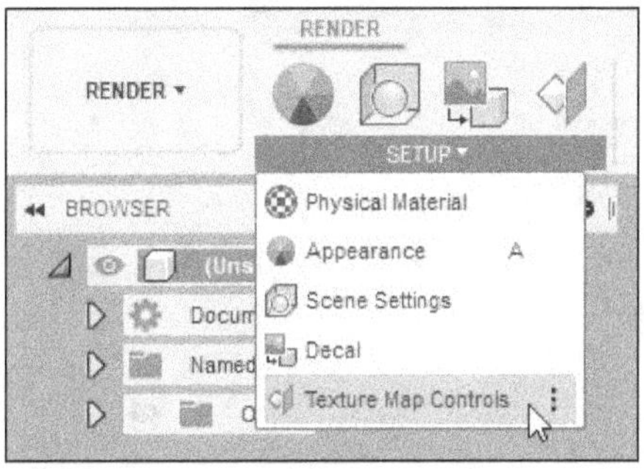

Figure-9. Texture Map Controls tool

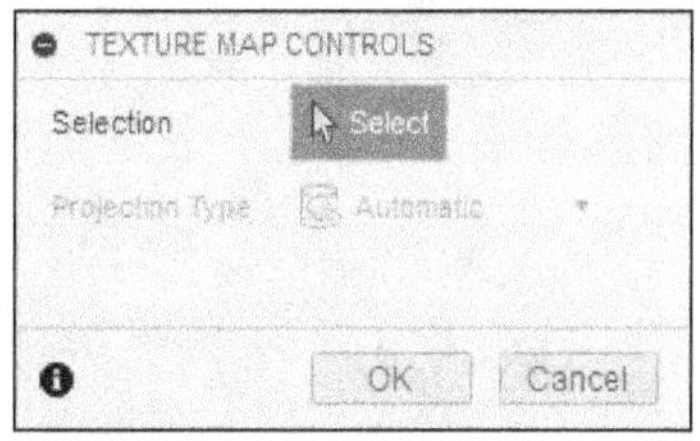

Figure-10. TEXTURE MAP CONTROLS dialog box

- The **Select** button of **Selection** option is selected by default. You need to select the texture of model. The updated **TEXTURE MAP CONTROLS** dialog box will be displayed; refer to Figure-11.

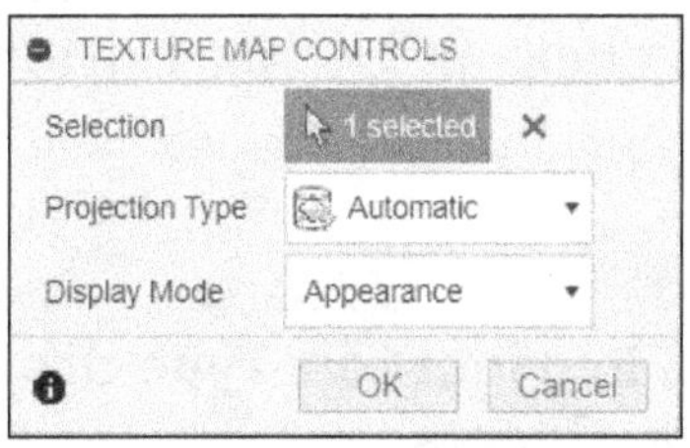

Figure-11. Updated TEXTURE MAP CONTROLS dialog box

Automatic

- Select the **Automatic** option from **Projection Type** drop-down if you want to adjust the texture on the model using model topology.

Planar

- Select the **Planar** option from **Projection Type** drop-down if you want to map the image or texture on the model as projection.
- On selecting the **Planar** option, you need to select the axis for adjusting the texture. On selecting the texture, the dialog box will be updated; refer to Figure-12.

Figure-12. Updated dialog box after selecting axis

- Adjust the image or texture by using the manipulator or by specifying the values in related edit boxes in **TEXTURE MAP CONTROLS** dialog box.
- After adjusting the texture, click on the **OK** button from **TEXTURE MAP CONTROLS** dialog box.

Box

- Click on the **Box** option from **Projection Type** drop-down if you want to map the image on model into box like objects.
- On selecting the **Box** option, the manipulator and updated dialog box will be displayed; refer to Figure-13.

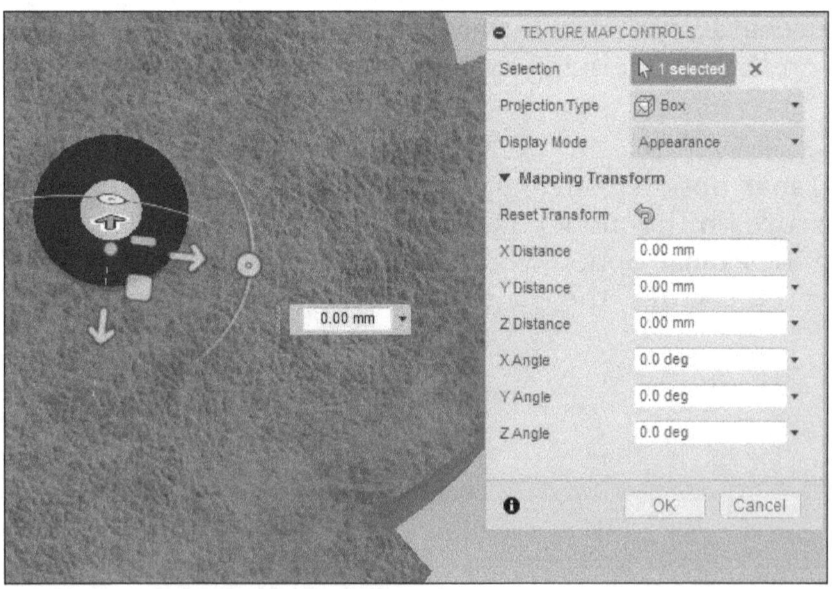

Figure-13. Dialog box on selecting Box-option

- Click in the specific edit box and enter desired value. You can also set the value by moving the arrow of manipulator.
- If you want to reset the values of **Mapping Transform** or manipulator then click on the **Reset Transform** button.

Spherical

- Select the **Spherical** option from **Projection Type** drop-down if you want to map texture into a spherical object.
- On selecting the **Spherical** option, the manipulator along with updated dialog box will be displayed.
- The options were discussed in last topic.

Cylindrical

- Select the **Cylindrical** option from **Projection Type** drop-down if you want to map texture into a cylindrical object.
- On selecting the **Cylindrical** option, the manipulator along with updated dialog box will be displayed.
- The options were discussed in last topic. After specifying the parameters, click on the **OK** button from **TEXTURE MAP CONTROLS** dialog box to exit the tool.

In-canvas Render

The **In-canvas Render** button is used to start and stop the In-canvas rendering process. The procedure to use this tool is discussed next.

- Click on the **In-canvas Render** button from **IN-CANVAS RENDER** drop-down; refer to Figure-14. The render quality slider will be displayed to display at the bottom right area of canvas screen; refer to Figure-15.

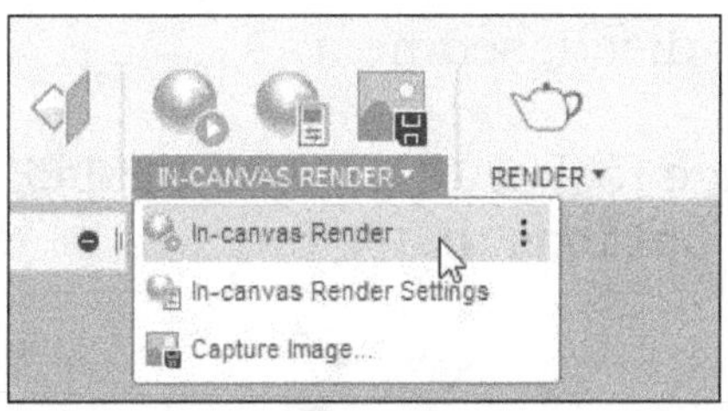

Figure-14. In-canvas Render tool

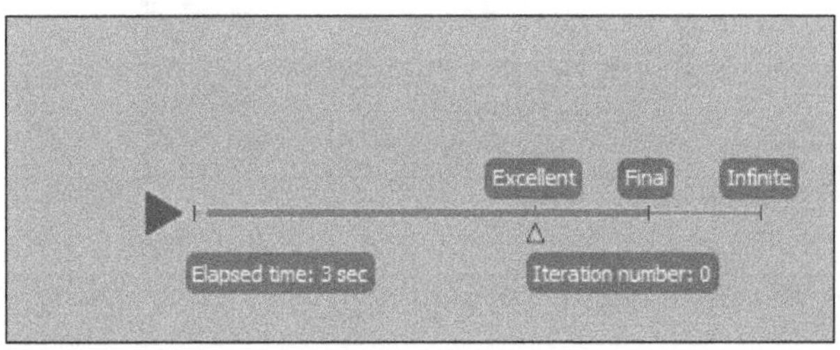

Figure-15. Render quality slider

- The current scene of the model will be changed into the photo-realistic 2D image.
- Clicking again on the **In-canvas Render Stop** button will stops the rendering process.

In-Canvas Render Setting

The **In-canvas Render Setting** tool is used to change the setting of rendering process. The procedure to use this tool is discussed next.

- Click on the **In-Canvas Render Settings** tool from **IN-CANVAS RENDER** drop-down; refer to Figure-16. The **IN-CANVAS RENDER SETTINGS** dialog box will be displayed; refer to Figure-17.

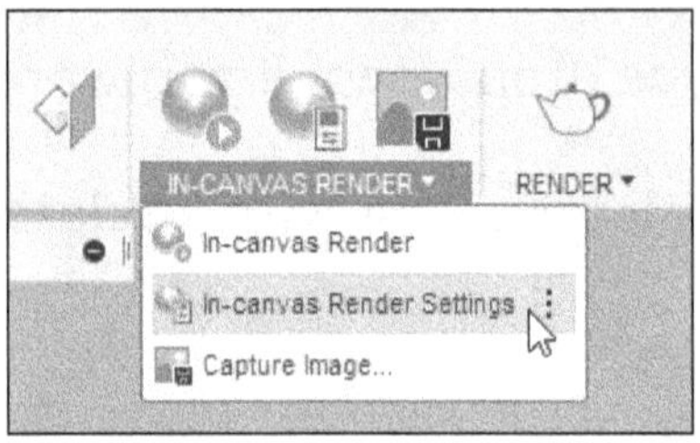

Figure-16. In-canvas Render Settings tool

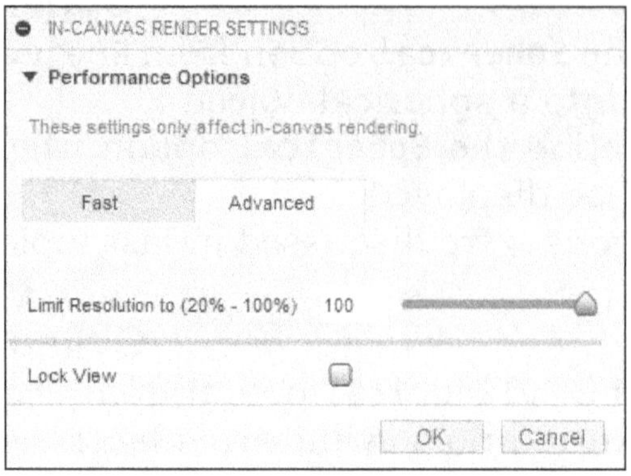

Figure-17. IN-CANVAS RENDER SETTINGS dialog box

- Set the quality of rendering by adjusting the **Limit Resolution to** slider. The higher quality rendering takes more time to calculate rendering process and lower quality rendering takes less time to calculate the rendering process.
- Select the **Lock View** check box to lock the current view of model for rendering. If this check box is selected then you can not reorient the model during rendering process.
- After specifying the parameters, click on the **OK** button from **IN-CANVAS RENDER SETTINGS** dialog box.

Capture Image

The **Capture Image** tool is used to capture the current canvas as an image. The procedure to use this tool is discussed next.

- Click on the **Capture Image** tool of **IN-CANVAS RENDER** drop-down in **Toolbar**; refer to Figure-18. The **Image Options** dialog box will be displayed; refer to Figure-19.

Figure-18. Capture Image tool

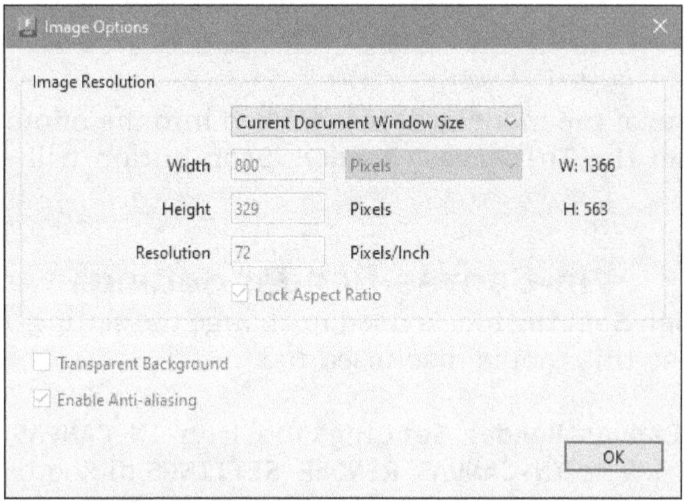

Figure-19. Image Options dialog box

- Click on the **Image Resolution** drop-down and select required resolution of image.
- Select the **Transparent Background** check box if you want to set the transparent background of model.
- Select the **Enable Anti-aliasing** check box if you want to activate the anti-aliasing property.
- After specifying the parameters, click on the **OK** button from **Image Options** dialog box. The **Save As** dialog box will be displayed; refer to Figure-20.

Figure-20. Save As dialog box

- Click in the **Name** edit box of **Save As** dialog box and enter the specific name for image.
- Click on the **Type** drop-down and select required format of image file.
- Click on the **Location** drop-down button and select the location of saving image.
- Select the **Save to my computer** check box if you want to save the file to computer.
- Select the **Save to a project in the cloud** check box to save the image file on cloud.
- After specifying the parameters for image, click on the **Save** button from **Save As** dialog box. The image will be saved to the specified location.

Render

The **Render** tool is used to create a high quality rendered image of the current scene. The procedure to use this tool is discussed next.

- Click on the **Render** tool from **Toolbar**; refer to Figure-21. The **RENDER SETTINGS** dialog box will be displayed; refer to Figure-22.

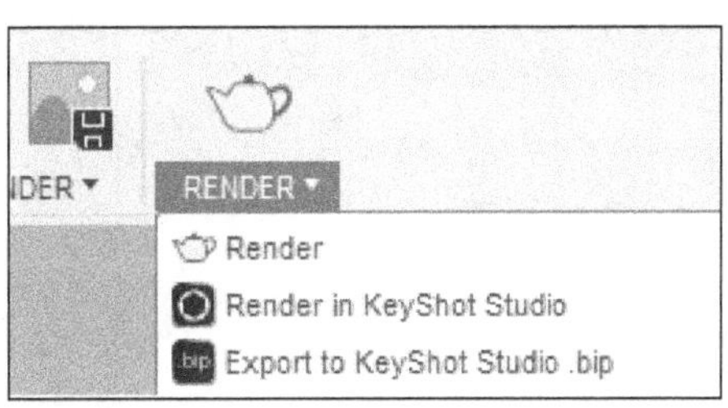

Figure-21. Render tool

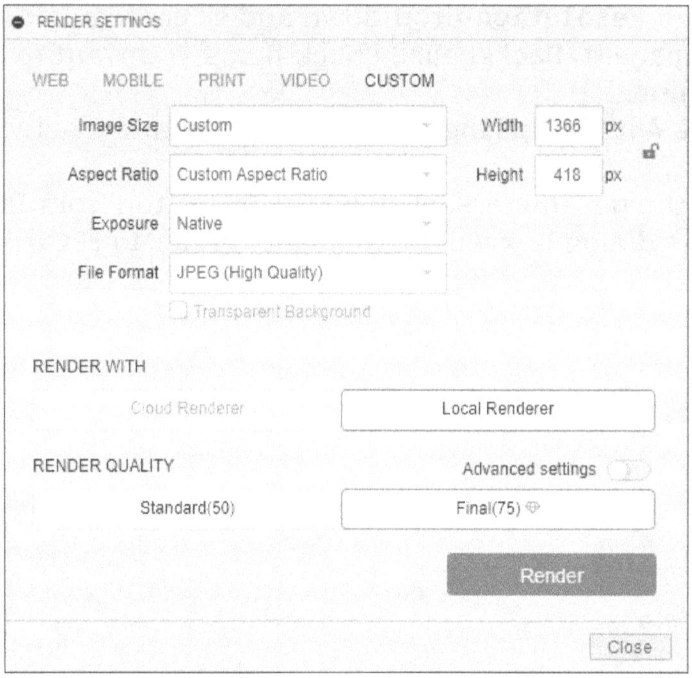

Figure-22. RENDER SETTINGS dialog box

WEB

- Click on the **WEB** tab of **RENDER SETTINGS** dialog box. Various options under **WEB** tab will be displayed; refer to Figure-23.

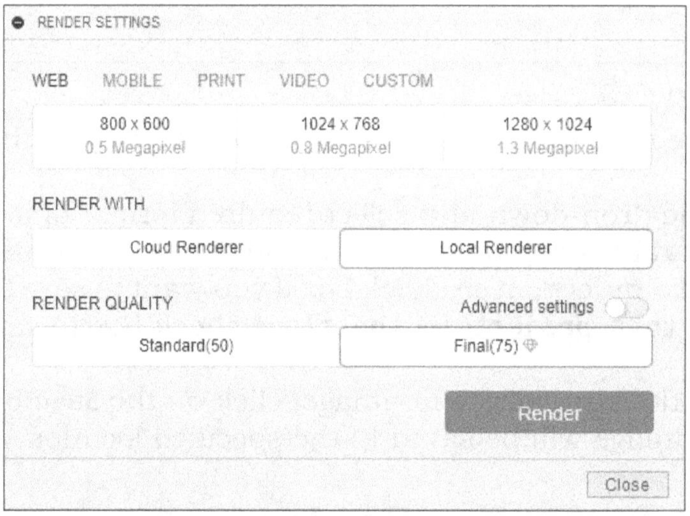

Figure-23. WEB tab

- Three highlighted options are the size of image in which your rendered file will be saved. Click on required size.
- Click on the **Cloud Renderer** option from **RENDER WITH** section, if you want to render the file from Autodesk cloud. On selecting the **Cloud Renderer** button, the dialog box will be updated; refer to Figure-24.

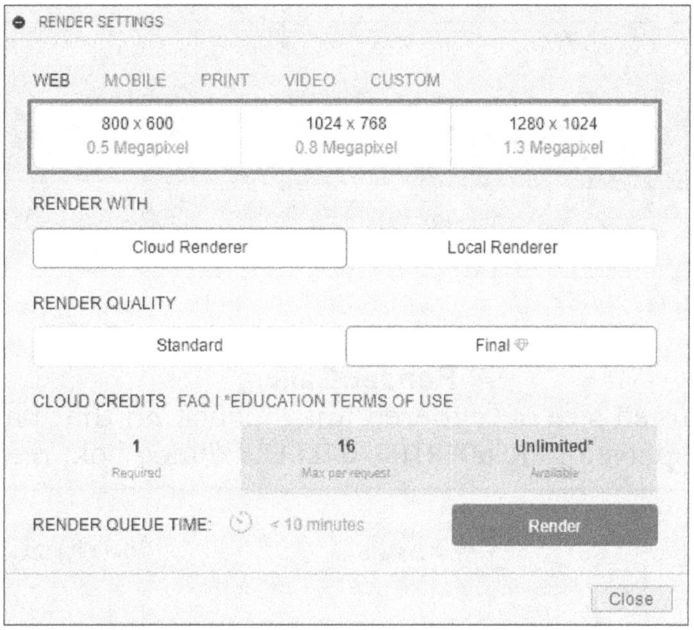

Figure-24. Updated WEB tab

- With **Local Renderer** option selected, click on the **Advanced settings** toggle button from **WEB** tab to manually set the render quality value. The **RENDER QUALITY** slider will be displayed; refer to Figure-25.

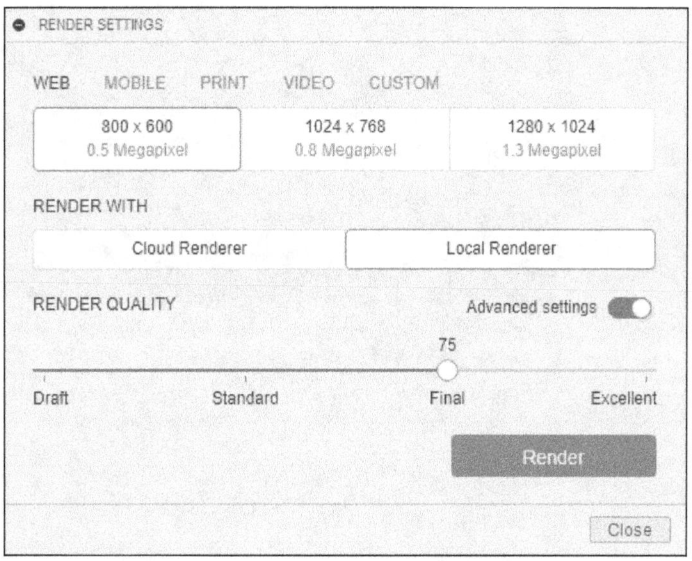

Figure-25. RENDER QUALITY slider in WEB tab

- Set the value of quality from slider as required. If you want to automatically set the quality of render then again click on the **Advanced settings** toggle button. The **Standard(50)** and **Final(75)** option will be displayed.
- Click on required option from **RENDER QUALITY** section and click on the **Render** button from **WEB** tab. The rendering process will start.
- The completed rendered file will be saved in **RENDERING GALLERY**; refer to Figure-26.

Figure-26. RENDERING GALLERY

Render Gallery

- To view the enlarged size of rendered image, click on that particular image. The image will be displayed in **RENDERING GALLERY** dialog box; refer to Figure-27.

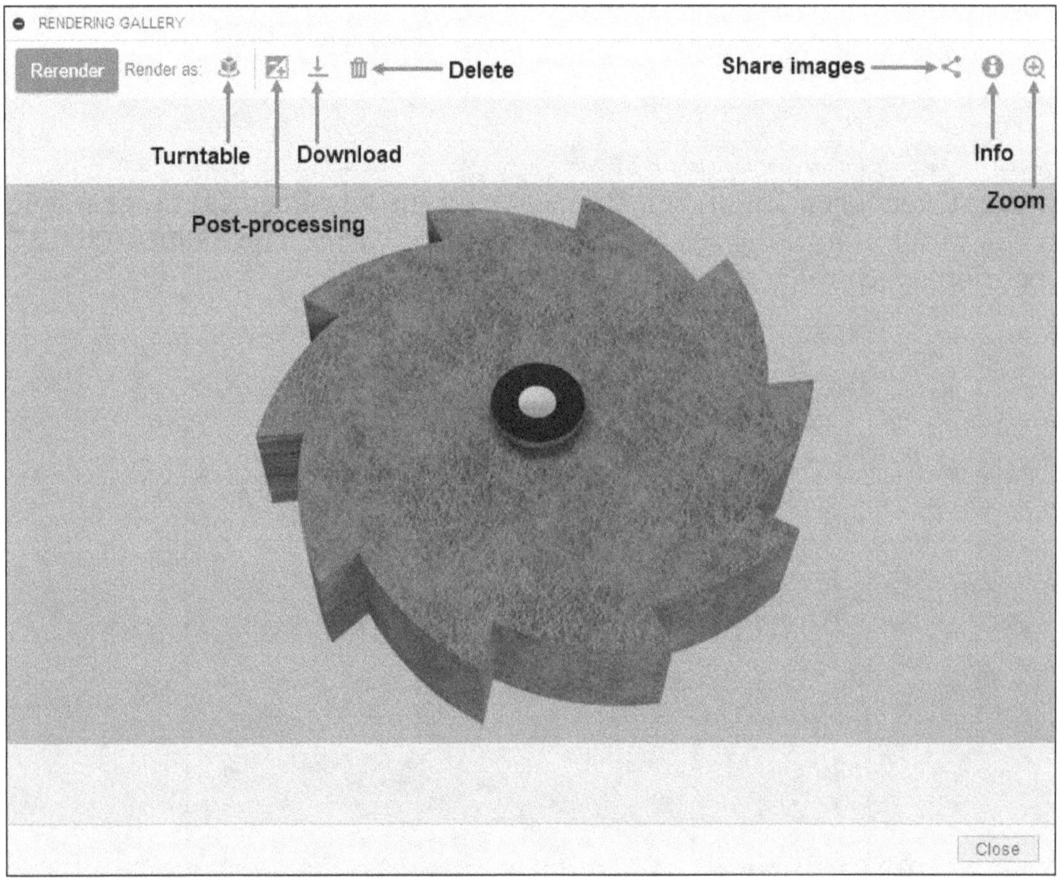

Figure-27. RENDERING GALLERY dialog box

- If you want to create a video of the rotating model then click on the **Turntable** button from **RENDERING GALLERY** dialog box. The **Render Settings - Turntable** dialog box will be displayed; refer to Figure-28.

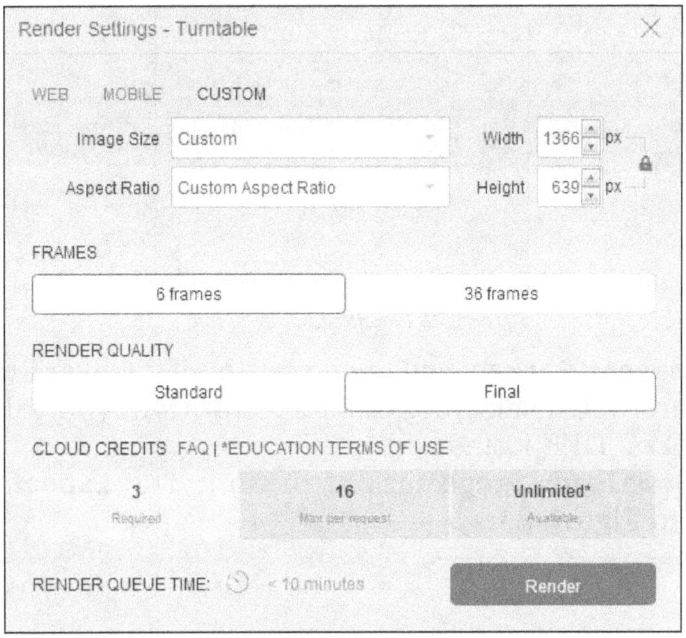

Figure-28. Render Settings-Turntable dialog box

- Specify desired parameters and click on the **Render** button. The file will be re-created and displayed in **RENDERING GALLERY**.

Post Processing

- If you want to adjust the exposure of model then click on the **Post-processing** button. The **Post-processing** dialog box will be displayed; refer to Figure-29.

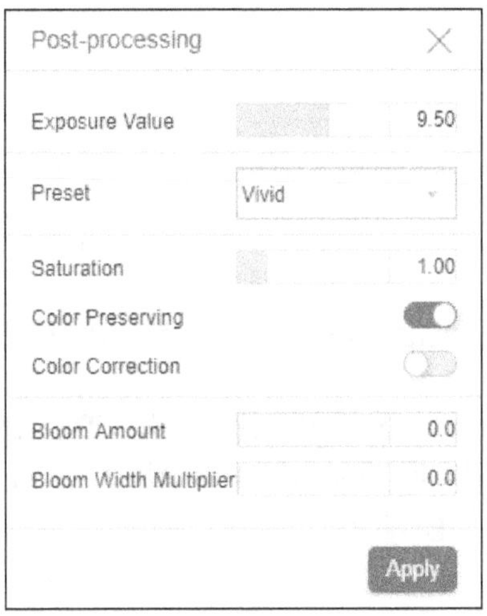

Figure-29. Post processing dialog box

- The value of exposure can be adjusted by using the slider for **Exposure Value**.
- Select desired option from the **Preset** drop-down. The options in the dialog box will be automatically adjusted presentation settings for rendering.
- Similarly, you can set the other parameters in the dialog box. After setting the parameters, click on the **Apply** button.

Downloading Render Image File

- If you want to download the current file then click on the **Download** button from **RENDERING GALLERY** dialog box. The drop-down will be displayed as shown in Figure-30.

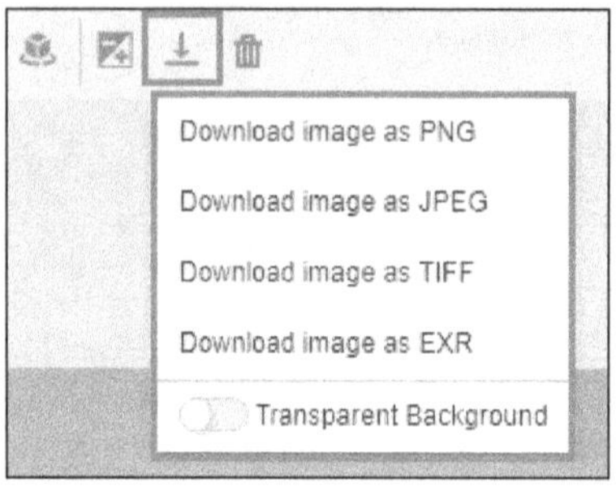

Figure-30. Download drop-down

- Select the **Transparent Background** toggle button if you want to make background of model transparent. On selecting this toggle button, you will be able to save the image file in PNG or TIFF format only.
- Select desired **Download image as...** button. The **Export** dialog box will be displayed; refer to Figure-31.

Figure-31. Export dialog box

- Specify the location for saving file and click on the **Save** button from the dialog box to save the file.
- If you want to delete the current file from **RENDERING GALLERY** then click on the **Delete** button from **RENDERING GALLERY** dialog box. The **Delete Image** dialog box will be displayed; refer to Figure-32.

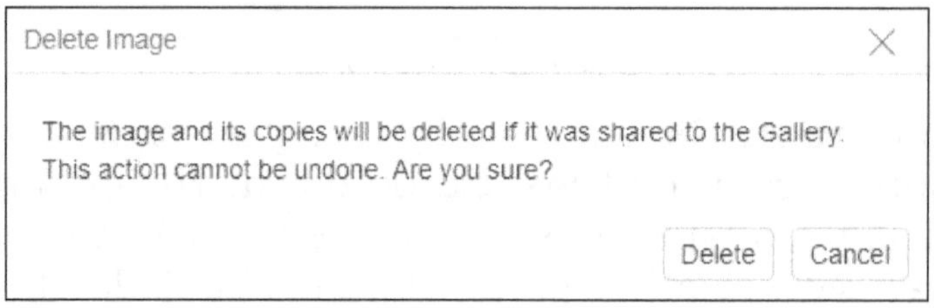

Figure-32. Delete Image dialog box

- If you are sure about deleting the particular file then click on the **Delete** button from **Delete Image** dialog box otherwise click on **Cancel** button.
- If you want to share the image to Fusion Gallery or A360 then click on the **Share images** button at the top right in **RENDERING GALLERY** dialog box and select the respective option.

- If you want to see the information of the current file then click on the **Info** button from **RENDERING GALLERY** dialog box.
- If you want to zoom-in/zoom-out the rendered image then click on the **Zoom** button from the dialog box.
- After rendering the file, click on the **Close** button from **RENDERING GALLERY** dialog box to exit the rendering process.

ANIMATION

The **Animation** workspace is used to animate the joints of assembly. This workspace is also used to create exploded view of assembly. You can create the exploded view automatically as well as manually in this workspace. To activate the workspace, click on the **ANIMATION** option from the **Workspace** drop-down. The tools to perform animation will be displayed.

New Storyboard

A storyboard is automatically generated for each model when you switch to **ANIMATION** workspace. In the process of creating animation, additional storyboard can be added at any time as well. Each new storyboard has a default name "Storyboardx" where x is a number. You can edit this name by double-clicking on it at the bottom in application window. Storyboard acts as base for animation. To create different animations of same assembly, you can create different storyboards. The procedure to create new storyboard is discussed next.

- Click on the **New Storyboard** tool from **STORYBOARD** drop-down of **Toolbar** in **ANIMATION** workspace; refer to Figure-33. The **NEW STORYBOARD** dialog box will be displayed; refer to Figure-34.

Figure-33. New Storyboard tool

Figure-34. NEW STORYBOARD dialog box

- Select the **Clean** option from **Storyboard Type** drop-down if you want to delete all previous actions of animation and want to create a new storyboard.
- Select the **Start from end of previous** option from **Storyboard Type** drop-down if you want to use position of components at the end of previous animation as the starting position for the new animation.
- After setting desired options, click on the **OK** button from the dialog box. The created storyboard will be added at the bottom of **ANIMATION TIMELINE**; refer to Figure-35.

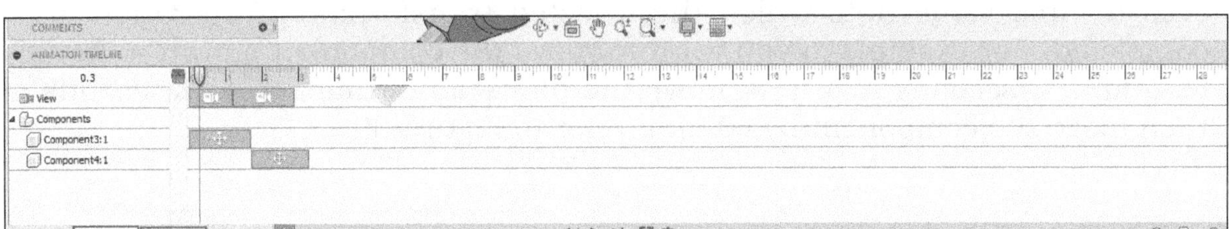

Figure-35. ANIMATION TIMELINE

Transform Components

The **Transform Components** tool is used to move and rotate the component. Note that the movement and rotation performed in this workspace will be recorded in animation. The procedure to use this tool is discussed next.

- Click on the **Transform Components** tool of **TRANSFORM** drop-down; refer to Figure-36. The **TRANSFORM COMPONENTS** dialog box will be displayed; refer to Figure-37.

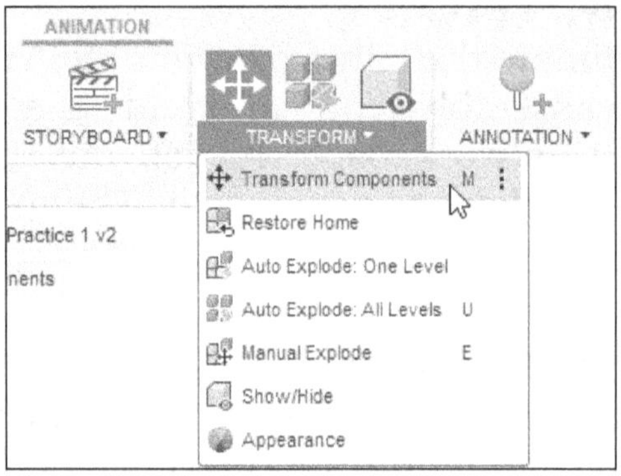

Figure-36. Transform Components tool

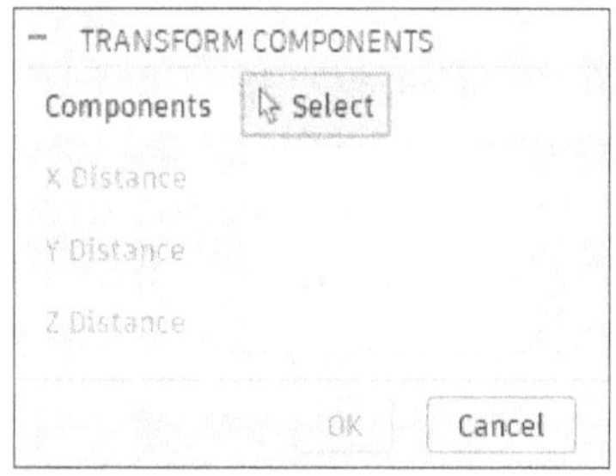

Figure-37. TRANSFORM COMPONENTS dialog box

- The **Select** button of **Components** section is active by default. Click on the component that you want to move or rotate. On selection of component, a manipulator will be displayed on the selected component along with updated **TRANSFORM COMPONENTS** dialog box; refer to Figure-38.

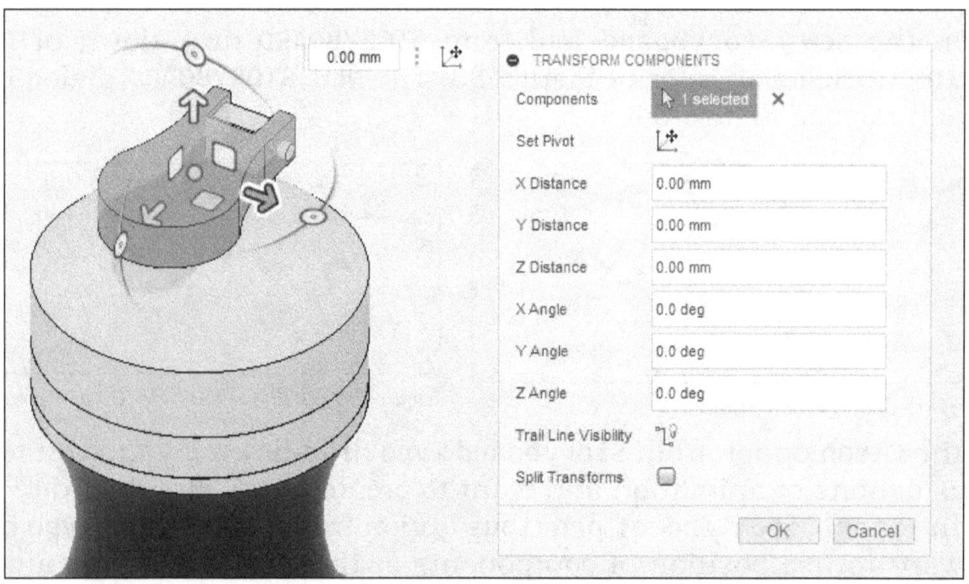

Figure-38. Manipulator on selected component

- The actions like moving or rotating the components are registered as animation in storyboard. To register the movement, drag the playhead in **ANIMATION TIMELINE** area to time value upto which the selected transformation operation will be completed. For example, if you want to move the component shown in figure by **60** mm in **2** seconds then first move the playhead of timeline to **2** seconds and then move the component by **60** mm; refer to Figure-39.

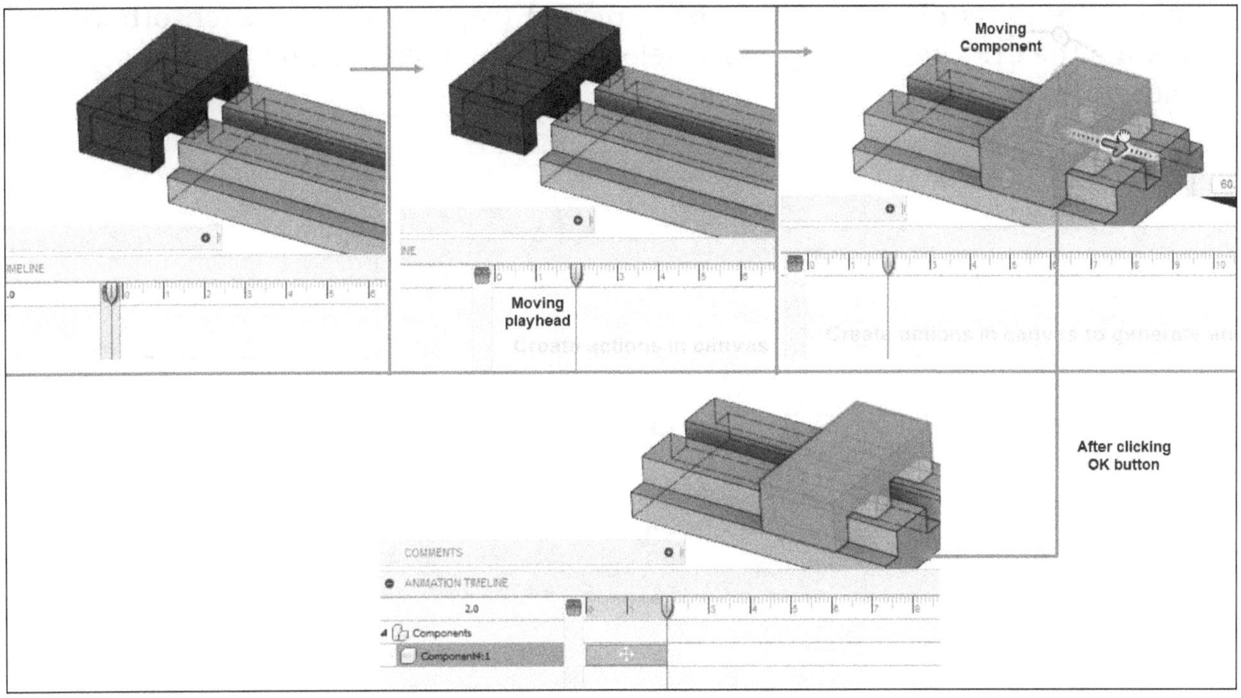

Figure-39. Registering movement of component in timeline

- You can specify desired values for movement in the **TRANSFORM COMPONENTS** dialog box or you can set the parameters by moving the manipulator.
- After specifying the parameters, click on the **OK** button from **TRANSFORM COMPONENTS** dialog box to add the action in animation timeline.
- To play the animation, you need to click on the **Play** button from **ANIMATION TIMELINE.**

Restore Home

The **Restore Home** tool is used to restore the model position as it is at the end of animation.

- Click on the **Restore Home** tool from **TRANSFORM** drop-down; refer to Figure-40. The position of model will be restored.

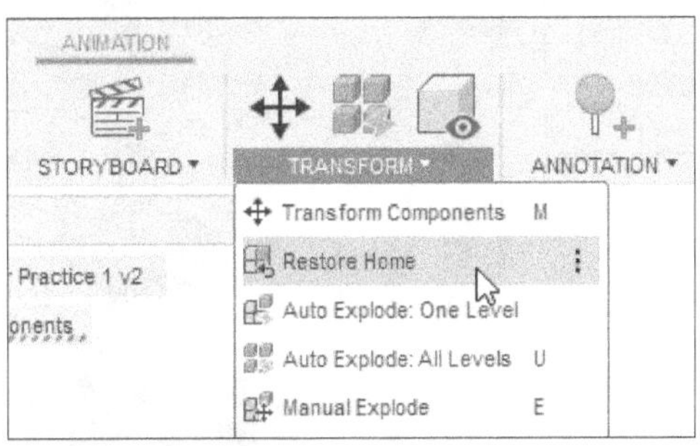

Figure-40. Restore Home tool

Auto Explode: One Level

The **Auto Explode: One Level** tool is used to automatically separate all selected components down to one level in hierarchy. The procedure to use this tool is discussed next.

- Select the parts of assembly to be exploded (separated from each other) while holding the **CTRL** key. You can also select all components using window selection; refer to Figure-41.

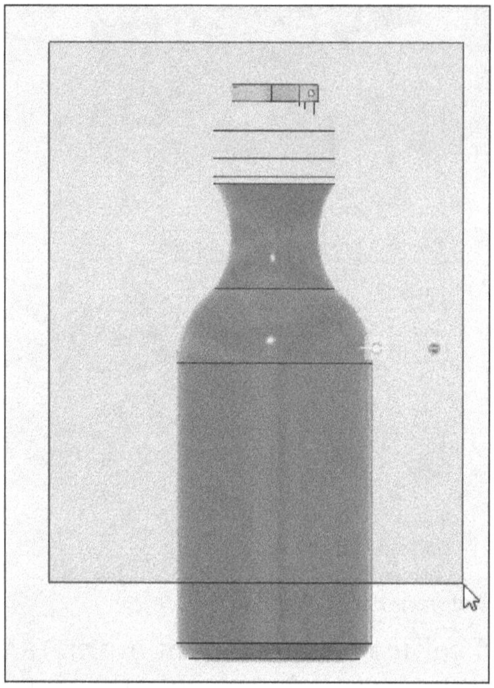

Figure-41. Window selection of component

- Click on the **Auto Explode: One Level** tool from **TRANSFORM** drop-down; refer to Figure-42. The components will be separated on the canvas screen; refer to Figure-43.

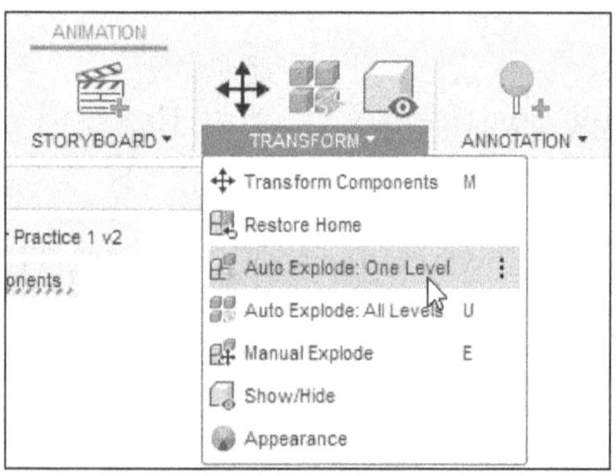

Figure-42. Auto Explode One Level tool

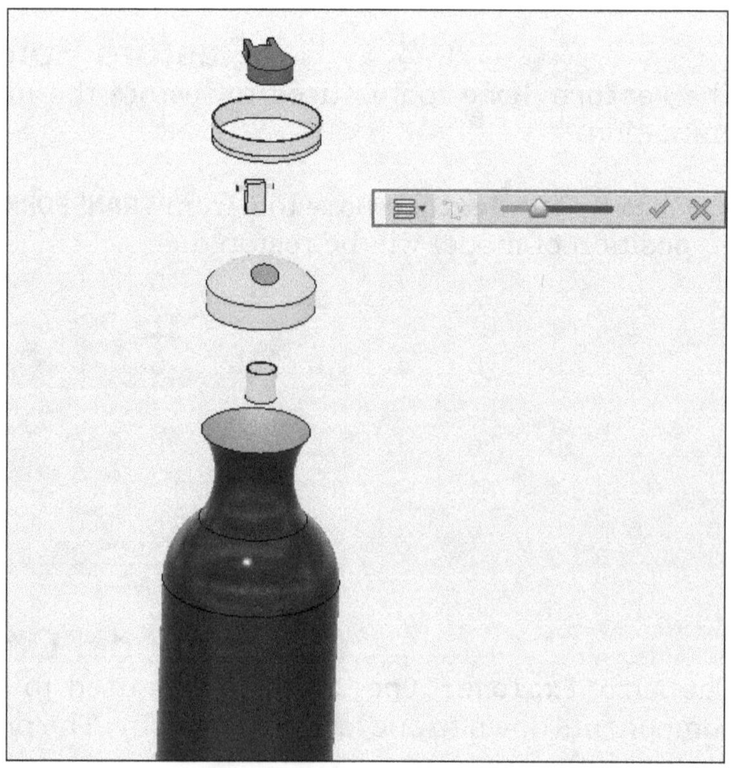

Figure-43. Preview of Auto Explode One Level

- By moving the highlighted slider (**Explosion Scale**), you can set the distance between component.

- After adjusting the space between components, click on the **OK** button from slider.

Auto Explode: All Levels

The **Auto Explode: All Levels** tool is used to automatically separate all selected components down to all levels in component hierarchy (including sub-assemblies). The procedure to use this tool is discussed next.

- Select the parts of components to separate by holding the **CTRL** key. You can also select the components using window selection.
- Click on the **Auto Explode: All Levels** tool from **TRANSFORM** drop-down; refer to Figure-44. The components of selected model will be separated.
- Click on the screen to view the separated component properly; refer to Figure-45.

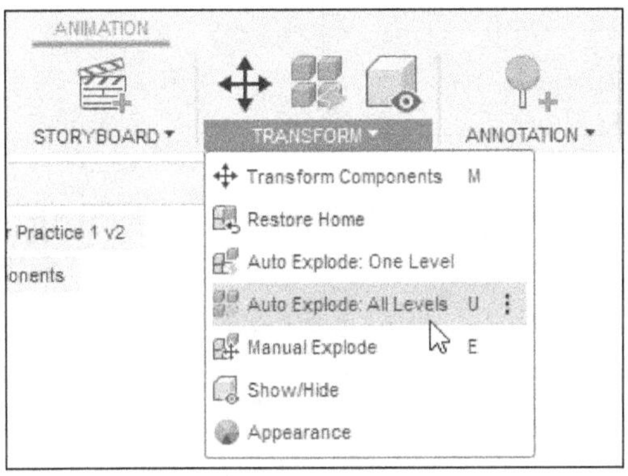

Figure-44. Auto Explode All Levels tool

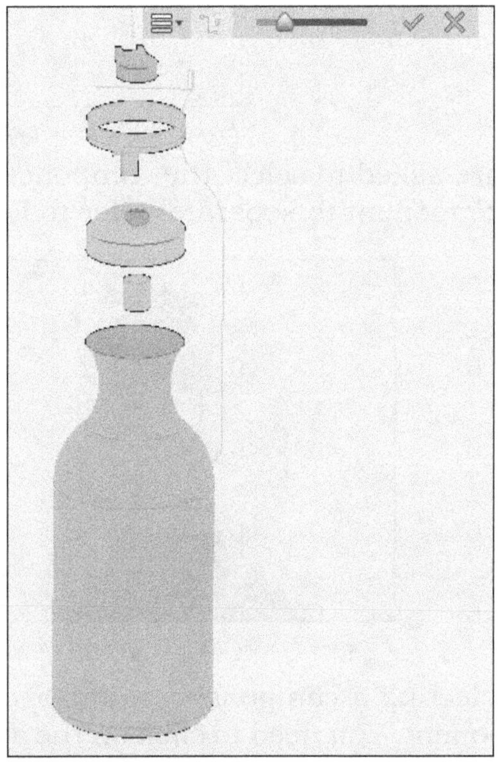

Figure-45. Preview of Explode

- Move the slider to adjust the distance between separated components of model.
- After adjusting the components, click on the **OK** button. The exploded view of assembly will be displayed; refer to Figure-46.

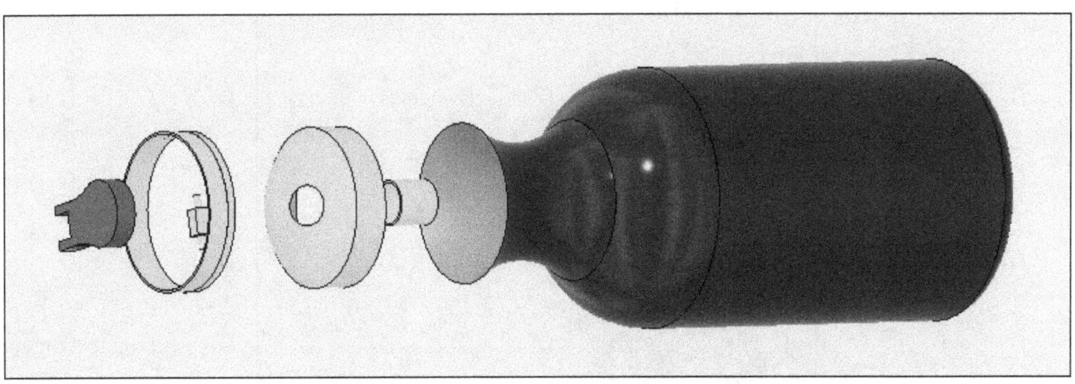

Figure-46. Exploded view of water bottle assembly

Manual Explode

The **Manual Explode** tool is used to manually separate the selected component. The procedure to use this tool is discussed next.

- Click on the **Manual Explode** tool of **TRANSFORM** drop-down from **Toolbar**; refer to Figure-47.

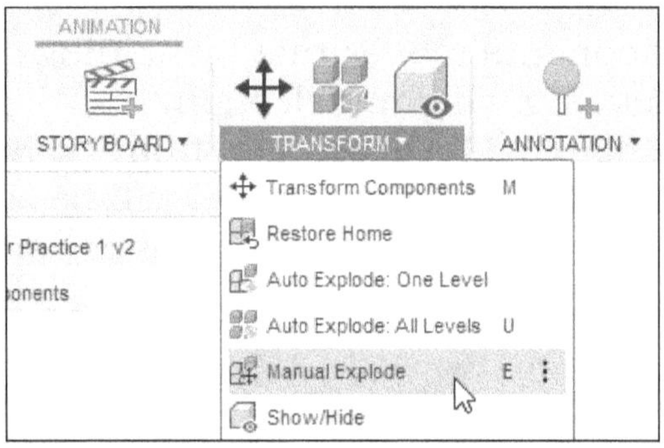

Figure-47. Manual Explode tool

- You are asked to select the components to be moved during exploding. Click on the component to separate; refer to Figure-48.

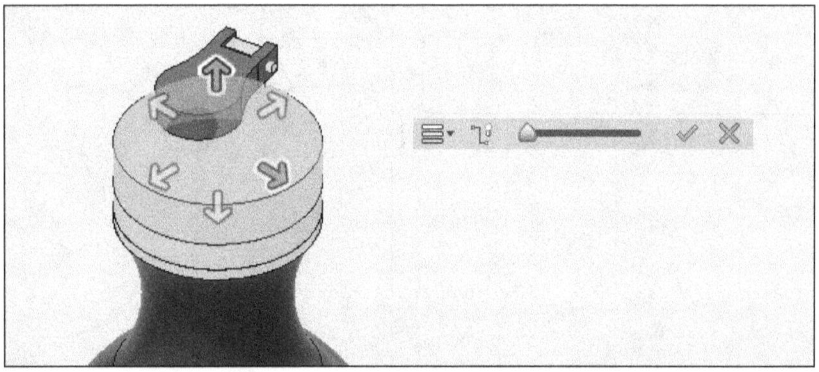

Figure-48. Separating component manually

- On selecting a component, number of arrows will be displayed on the selected component. You need to click on the arrow of direction in which you want to move the selected component.
- Move the **Explosion Scale** slider to separate the selected component from remaining model; refer to Figure-49.

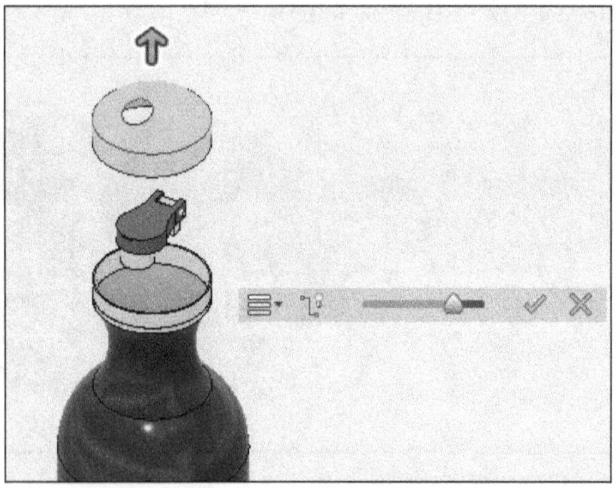

Figure-49. Separating the selected component

Show/Hide

The **Show/Hide** tool is used to show or hide the selected component. The procedure to use this tool is discussed next.

- Click on desired component from model to show or hide.
- Now, click on the **Show/Hide** tool from **TRANSFORM** drop-down; refer to Figure-50. The selected component will be shown or hidden based on its condition.
- To display the hidden component, click on the crossed eye button from **Browser**; refer to Figure-51.

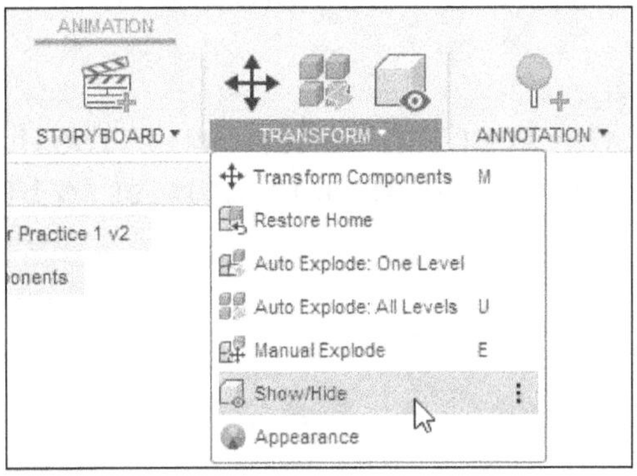

Figure-50. Show/Hide tool

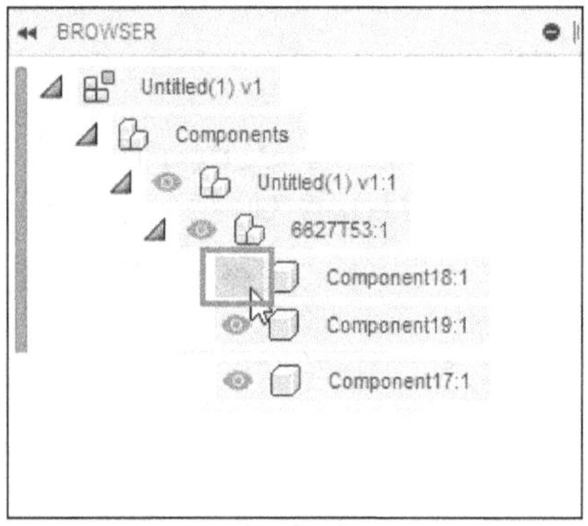

Figure-51. Viewing the hidden component

Create Callout

The **Create Callout** tool is used to add annotation to the animation. The procedure to use this tool is discussed next.

- Click on the **Create Callout** tool from **ANNOTATION** panel; refer to Figure-52. The callout symbol will be attached to the cursor.
- Click on the component to add the callout. A text box will be displayed; refer to Figure-53.

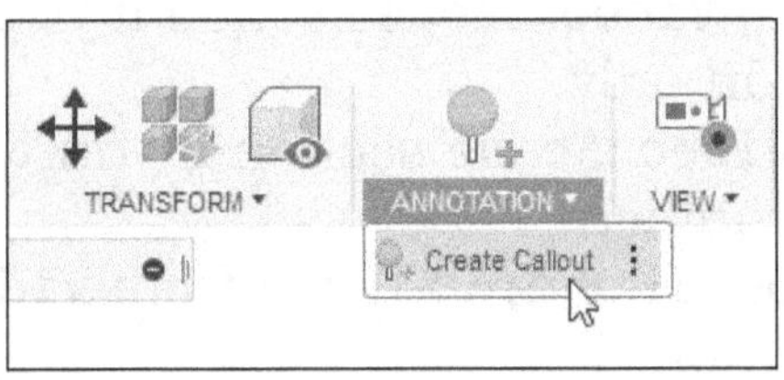

Figure-52. Create Callout tool

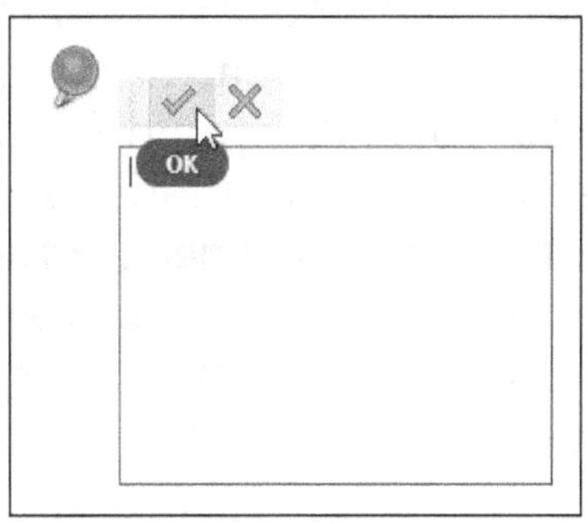

Figure-53. Callout text box

- Type desired text in the text box and click on **OK** button. The annotation callout will be added to the selected component.

View

The **View** tool is used to start and stop the recording of the actions or commands occurring on the model or component. When **View** tool is activated then it captures the actions like move for animation and when the **View** tool is deactivated it does not record the process; refer to Figure-54.

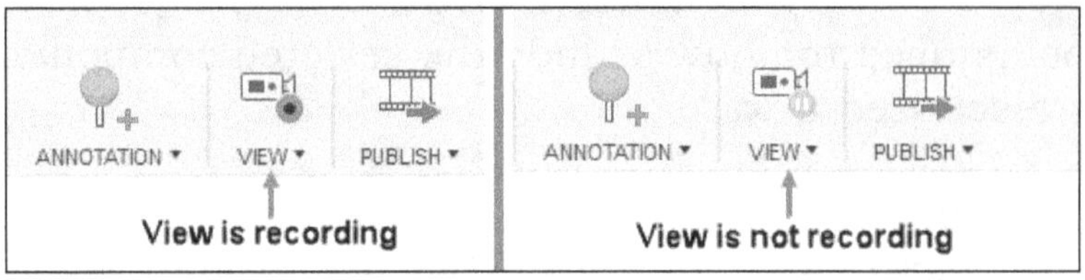

Figure-54. View tool

Publish Video

The **Publish Video** tool is used to publish the video. The procedure to use this tool is discussed next.

- Click on the **Publish Video** tool from the **PUBLISH** panel in the **Toolbar**; refer to Figure-55. The **Video Options** dialog box will be displayed; refer to Figure-56.

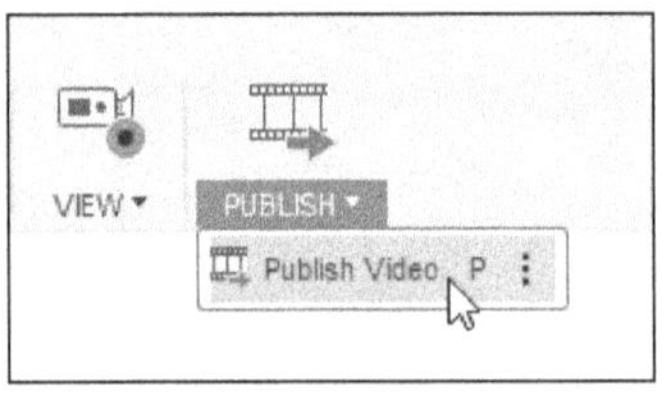

Figure-55. Publish Video tool

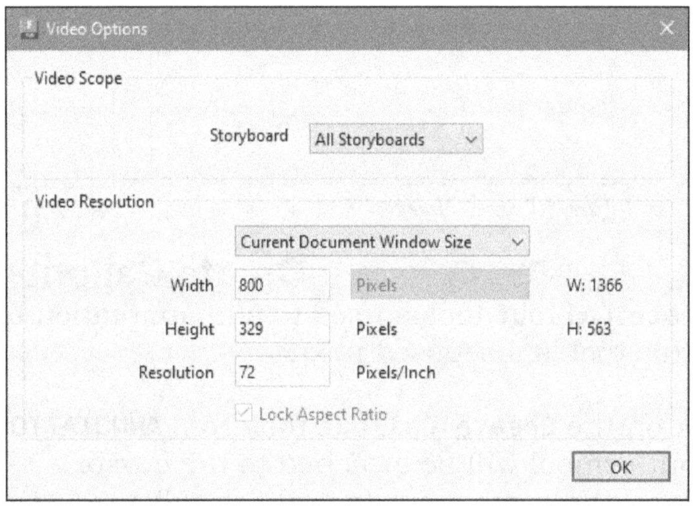

Figure-56. Video Options dialog box

- Select **Current Storyboard** option from **Video Scope** section if you want to create a video of current storyboard animation only.
- Select **All Storyboards** option from **Video Scope** section if you want to create a video of all storyboard animations combined.
- Click on the **Current Document Window Size** drop-down from **Video Resolution** section or select required video resolution.
- After specifying the parameters, click on the **OK** button from **Video Options** dialog box. The **Save As** dialog box will be displayed; refer to Figure-57.

Figure-57. Save As dialog box for Publish Video tool

- Click in the **Name** edit box and specify the name of file.
- Select the **Save to a project in the cloud** check box if you want to save the file online or in your Autodesk account.
- Select the **Save to my computer** check box if you want to save the file in your computer.
- After specifying the parameters, click on the **Save** button from **Save As** dialog box. The **Publish Video** progress dialog box will be displayed which tells about the progress of publishing video; refer to Figure-58.

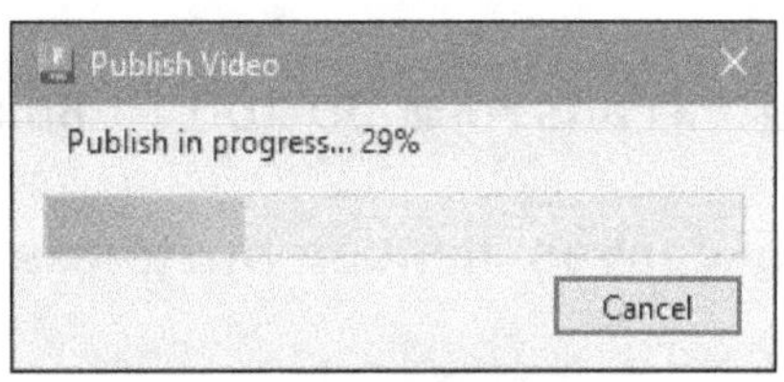

Figure-58. Publish Video dialog box

The video will be published online and saved to the computer at preferred location.

Self Assessment

Q1. What is Rendering?

Q2. The .... is used to create the photo-realistic image from a scene of model.

Q3. The .... tool is used to control the lighting, background color, ground effects, and camera rendering.

Q4. From where can you get the environments for background as well as for model?

Q5. How can you display the shadow and reflections of model on ground canvas?

Q6. A textured ground plane where the environment image is mapped as a texture can be enabled by selecting **Ground Plane** check box. (T/F)

Q7. The reflection of model on the ground can be displayed by selecting the **Reflections** check box. (T/F)

Q8. What is Depth of Field and how it can be enabled?

Q9. If you want to change the environment of the model then drag a specific environment from .... section and drop it to the current model or in the **Current Environment** section.

Q10. The **Appearance** tool is used to set the orientation of the texture applied to the face or model. (T/F)

Q11. What is the use of **Reset Transform** button in **Box** dialog box?

Q12. What happens when **In-canvas Render** button is selected?

Q13. What is the use of Animation Workspace?

Q14. Which tool is used to add annotation to the animation?

Q15. What is the process of converting a 3D model into a finalized 2D image with specified environmental scenarios called?

A. Modeling
B. Rendering
C. Texturing
D. Sculpting

Q16. Which tool in the Render Workspace is used to apply different materials to selected bodies or faces?

A. Scene Settings
B. Appearance
C. Camera
D. Texture Map Controls

Q17. What happens when you click the "Position" button in the Environment section of Scene Settings?

A. You can adjust the brightness of the model.
B. You can specify the position and rotation of lights.
C. You can apply a texture map.
D. You can change the background color to solid.

Q18. What is the purpose of the "Ground Plane" checkbox in the Ground section?

A. To apply texture to the ground.
B. To display the shadow and reflection of the model on the ground.
C. To enable depth of field effects.
D. To adjust the camera exposure.

Q19. Which option is selected to map a texture into a spherical object?

A. Box
B. Planar
C. Spherical
D. Cylindrical

Q20. What is the effect of selecting the "Depth of Field" checkbox in Camera settings?

A. It focuses on a specific area of the model.
B. It adjusts the brightness of the model.
C. It changes the background to solid color.
D. It maps a texture to the model.

Q21. How can you save the customized settings in the Scene Settings tool as default?

A. Click on the Reset button.
B. Click on the Save as Defaults button.
C. Click on the Restore Defaults button.
D. Click on the Apply button.

Q22. What tool is used to adjust the orientation of a texture applied to a model?

A. In-Canvas Render
B. Scene Settings
C. Texture Map Controls
D. Capture Image

Q23. Which checkbox in the Capture Image tool should be selected to activate anti-aliasing?

A. Enable Anti-aliasing
B. Transparent Background
C. Lock View
D. Flatten Ground

Q24. Where are completed rendered files saved after the rendering process is finished?

A. Scene Settings
B. Rendering Gallery
C. Local Renderer
D. Environment Library

Q25. Which dialog box is displayed when you click on a rendered image to enlarge it?

A. RENDERING SETTINGS
B. RENDERING GALLERY
C. POST-PROCESSING
D. IMAGE INFO

Q26. What is the purpose of the Turntable button in the Rendering Gallery?

A. To create an exploded view
B. To adjust exposure
C. To create a video of the rotating model
D. To share the image

Q27. How can you adjust the exposure of a model in the Post-Processing dialog box?

A. By clicking the Turntable button
B. By using the slider for Exposure Value
C. By selecting the Zoom button
D. By using the Transform Components tool

Q28. Which format is available when you select the Transparent Background toggle button while downloading a rendered image?

A. JPEG or BMP
B. PNG or TIFF
C. GIF or MP4
D. DWG or DXF

Q30. How is the animation created for moving or rotating a component recorded?

A. By using the Post-Processing dialog box
B. By dragging the playhead in the Animation Timeline
C. By selecting Auto Explode
D. By clicking the Delete button

Q31. What does the Auto Explode: One Level tool do?

A. Separates selected components down to all hierarchy levels
B. Separates selected components down to one hierarchy level
C. Manually moves components for explosion
D. Restores the model position

Q32. Which tool is used to add annotation to an animation?

A. Transform Components
B. Restore Home
C. Create Callout
D. Show/Hide

Q33. What is the purpose of the Publish Video tool?

A. To add callouts to components
B. To publish a video of the animation
C. To adjust video resolution
D. To transform components

Q34. Which option in the Video Scope section allows creating a video of the current storyboard animation only?

A. All Storyboards
B. Current Storyboard
C. Save to a project
D. Video Resolution

FOR STUDENT NOTES

Chapter 11

Drawing

Topics Covered

The major topics covered in this chapter are:

- ***Introduction to Drawing Workspace***
- ***Specifying Drawing Preferences***
- ***Drawing View***
- ***Projected view***
- ***Section View***
- ***Detail View***
- ***Break View***
- ***Moving and Rotating Views***
- ***Center line***
- ***Center Mark and Center Mark Pattern***
- ***Edge Extension***
- ***Creating Sketch***
- ***Dimensioning***
- ***Annotation Settings***
- ***Editing Dimensions***
- ***Creating Text and Note***
- ***Applying Surface Texture***
- ***Feature Control Frame***
- ***Datum Identifier***
- ***Generating Tables and Balloon***
- ***Bend Identifier and Table***
- ***Renumbering and Aligning Balloons***
- ***Output DWG, CSV, DXF, and PDF***

INTRODUCTION

Drawing is the engineering representation of a model on the paper. For manufacturing a model in the real world, we need some means by which we can tell the manufacturer what to manufacture. For this purpose, we create drawings from the models. These drawings have information like dimensions, material, tolerances, objective, precautions, and so on.

STARTING DRAWING WORKSPACE

In Autodesk Fusion, we create drawings in the **DRAWING** workspace. The procedure to open a file in **DRAWING** workspace is discussed next.

- Open desired model from **Data Panel** or saved directory.
- Click on **From Design** option from **DRAWING** cascading menu in **Change Workspace** drop-down. The **CREATE DRAWING** dialog box will be displayed along with the model; refer to Figure-1.

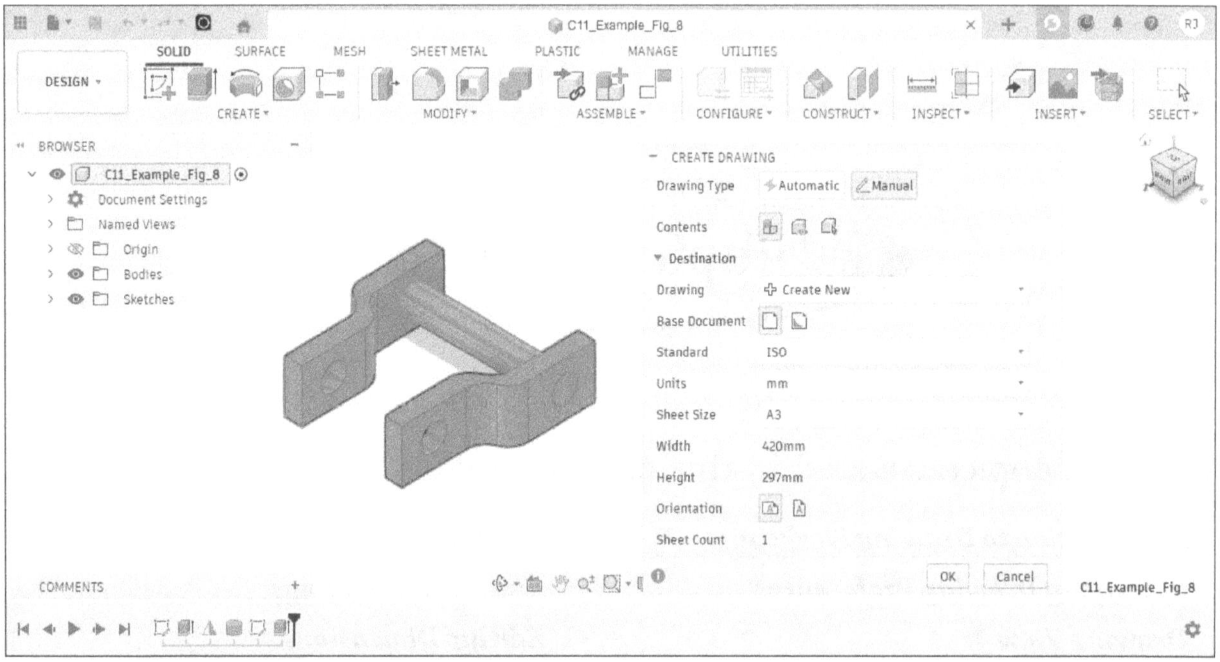

Figure-1. CREATE DRAWING dialog box

- Select **Automatic** option from **Drawing Type** area to set automatic mode of creating drawing from design. Selecting this option will automatically generate standard views and design dimensions. Note that you can still modify the drawing later.
- Select **Manual** option from **Drawing Type** area to manually insert views and dimension in the drawing based on design.
- Select the **Full Assembly** option from **Contents** area in the dialog box if you want to create drawing using whole assembly. Select the **Visible Only** option to automatically select only visible components of assembly. Select the **Select** option to manually select components in the canvas or browser.
- Click on the **Standard** drop-down from **CREATE DRAWING** dialog box and select the standard for the drawing. **ASME** option can use the third angle projection as well as first angle projection but **ISO** option uses first angle projection for placing views. There are also many other differences between two standards which you can find better in relevant books. Note that these projections are default settings but you can override them using **Preferences** dialog box.

- Click on the **Units** drop-down from **CREATE DRAWING** dialog box and select the unit for drawing.
- Click on the **Sheet Size** drop-down from **CREATE DRAWING** dialog box and select the size of sheet for drawing. Note that there is difference between A (8.5x11) and A (11x8.5) sheet size. The size A (8.5x11) will generate Portrait sheet whereas size A(11x8.5) will generate Landscape sheet.
- If **Automatic** radio button is selected, select desired sheet creation settings from **Structure** drop-down.
- After specifying the parameters, click on the **OK** button from **CREATE DRAWING** dialog box. The **DRAWING** workspace will be activated along with **DRAWING VIEW** dialog box in a new drawing file; refer to Figure-2.

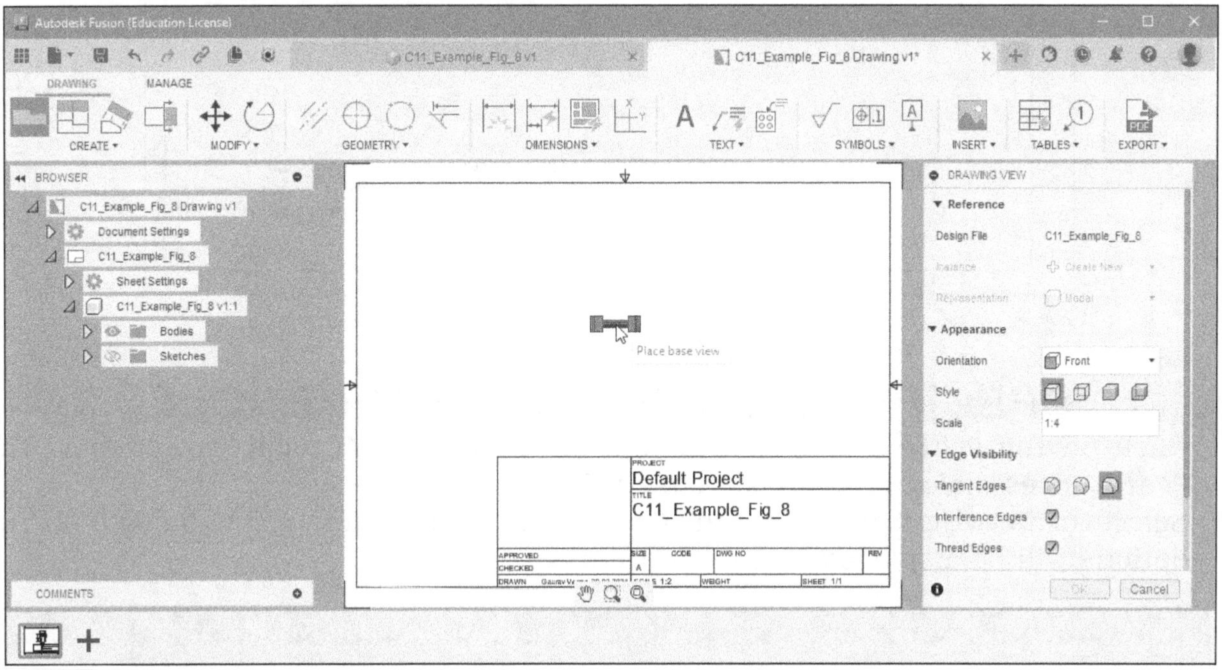

Figure-2. DRAWING workspace

- The model will be attached to the cursor. Click on the drawing sheet to place the base view.

Parameters in DRAWING VIEW dialog box

- Click on the **Orientation** drop-down and select the base view of model. Here, **Front** view is default option. When you change the view from **Front** to **Top**, the view of model will automatically changed.
- Select the style of model from the **Style** section.
- Click in the **Scale** drop-down and select required scaling factor for model.
- Select required option from **Tangent Edges** section to apply the edges with the selected view.
- Select the **Interference Edges** check box if you want to keep interfering edges within the selected view. Interfering edges are overlapping edges from two features of the model.
- Select the **Thread Edges** check box if you want to display the threads of model in current view.
- After specifying the parameters in **DRAWING VIEW** dialog box, click on **OK** button. The selected view of model will be placed; refer to Figure-3.

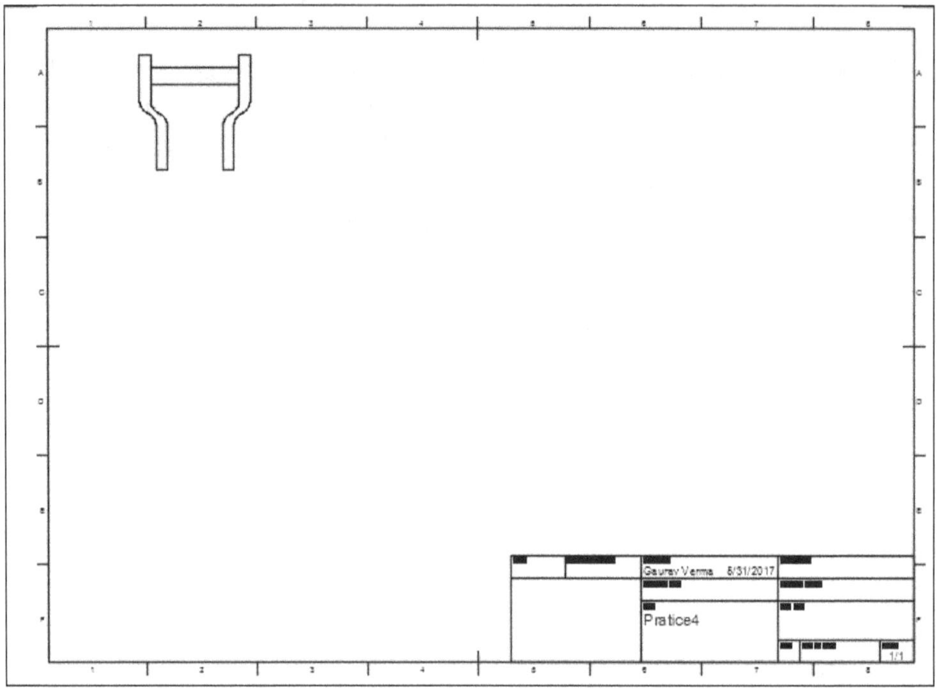

Figure-3. Top view of model

SPECIFYING DRAWING PREFERENCES

- Click on the **Preferences** option from the **Autodesk Account** drop-down. The **Preferences** dialog box will be displayed.
- Select the **Drawing** option from the **General** node at the left in the dialog box. The options will be displayed as shown in Figure-4.

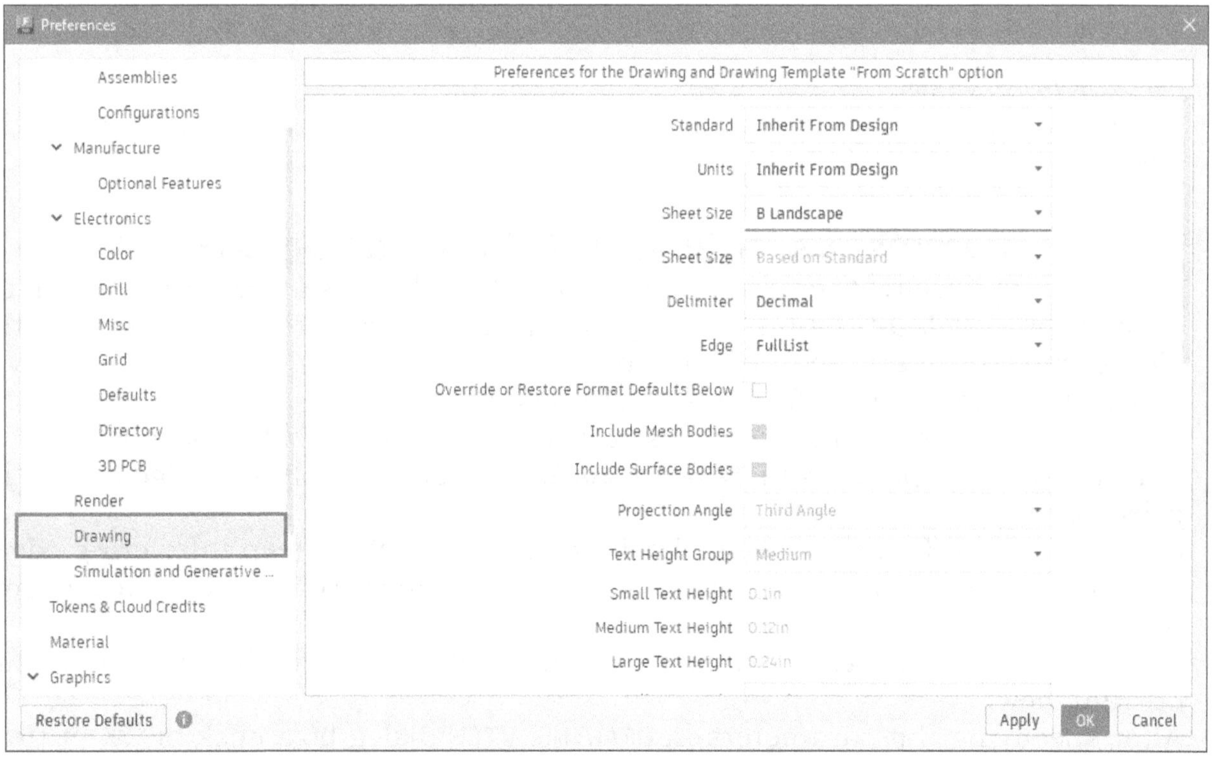

Figure-4. Drawing node in Preferences dialog box

- Select desired option from the **Standard** drop-down to define which standard to use for drafting. You can select **ASME** or **ISO** option from the drop-down to set it default for drafting or you can select the **Inherit From Design** to define the standard by 3D Model.
- Select desired unit of length from the **Units** drop-down. You can select inch or mm as unit.
- Select desired default size of sheet from the **Sheet Size** drop-down.
- Select desired delimiter from **Delimiter** drop-down to be used for numerical values in the drawing. You can use comma or decimal as delimiter.
- Select desired edge majority symbol type from the **Edge** drop-down.
- Select the **Override or Restore Format Defaults Below** check box if you want to use parameters different from selected standard. The options below this check box will be activated; refer to Figure-5.

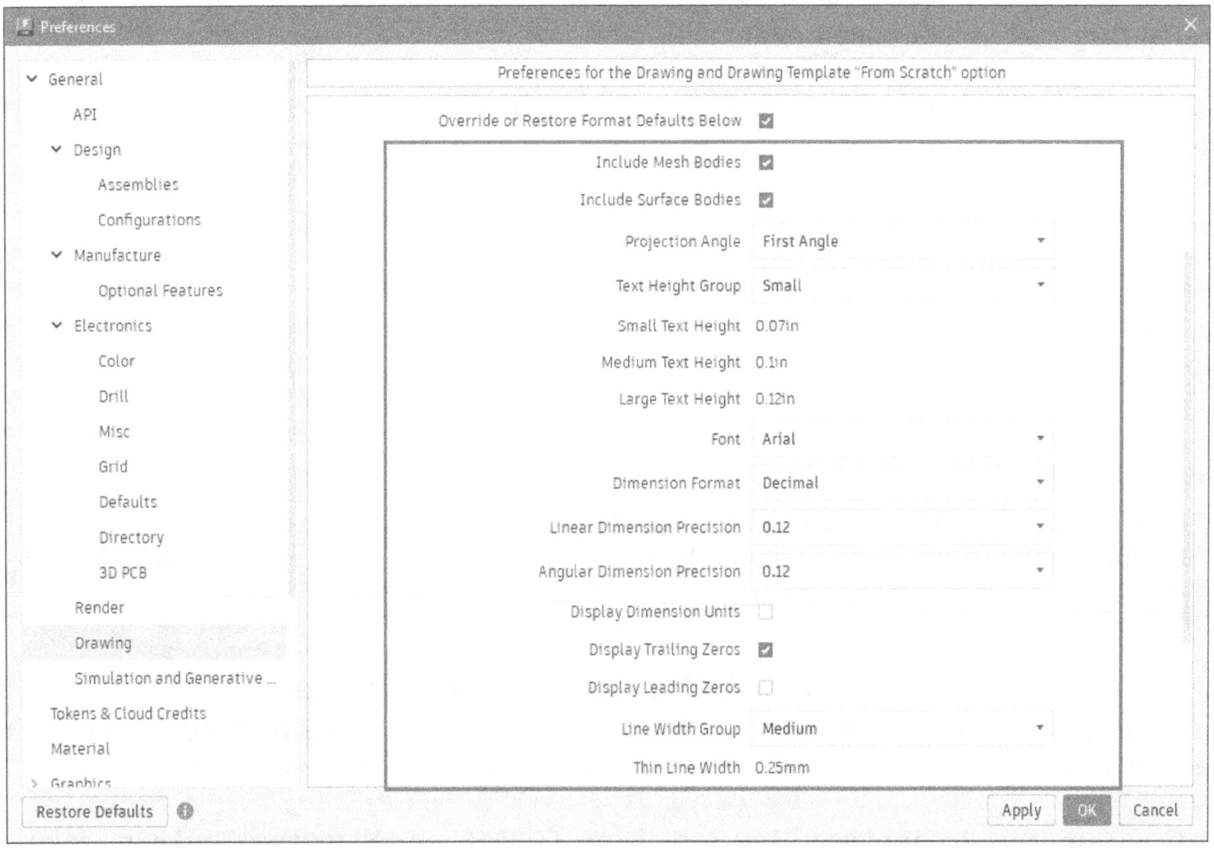

Figure-5. Override options

- Select **Include Mesh Bodies** check box to include mesh in drawings.
- Select **Include Surface Bodies** check box to include surface in drawings.
- Select desired option from the **Projection Angle** drop-down to define the view projection method for drawing.
- Select desired value for height of annotations in **Text Height Group** drop-down.
- Select desired font from **Font** drop-down to define font of all the annotations in drawing area.
- Select desired dimension format for the drawings from the **Dimension Format** drop-down.
- Select desired precision level for linear and angular dimensions in the **Linear Dimension Precision** and **Angular Dimension Precision** drop-downs, respectively.
- Select the **Display Dimension Units** check box to display unit of annotation in drawing.

- Select the **Display Trailing Zeros** check box to display zeros after decimal places if the dimension is not up to specified precision level.
- Select the **Display Leading Zeros** check box if you want to display zeros before the dimension values in the annotations.
- Select desired value for line width for drawings in **Line Width Group** drop-down.
- Select the **Display Line Widths** check box if you want to display lines in drawing by their specified widths rather than using same width for all lines.
- Click on the **OK** button from the **Preferences** dialog box.

CREATING BASE VIEW

The **Base View** tool is used to create base view derived directly from a 3D model. You can create various views of your model using this view. Note that you should have only one base view and other views should be projection of that view. The procedure to use this tool is discussed next.

- Click on the **Base View** tool from **CREATE** panel; refer to Figure-6. The **DRAWING VIEW** dialog box will be displayed.

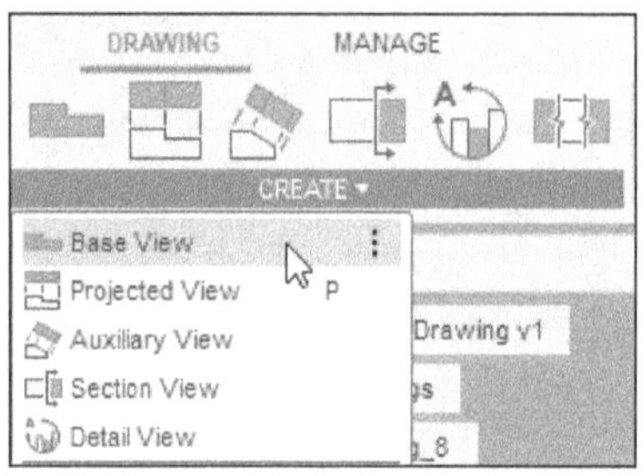

Figure-6. Base View tool

- Click at desired location to place the view and specify desired parameters in the dialog box. The options of **DRAWING VIEW** dialog box have been discussed earlier.
- Click on the **OK** button from the dialog box to generate the view.

CREATING PROJECTED VIEW

The **Projected View** tool is used to create drawing views generated from an existing base or drawing view. The procedure to use this tool is discussed next.

- Click on the **Projected View** tool from **CREATE** panel in the **Toolbar**; refer to Figure-7. The tool will be activated.

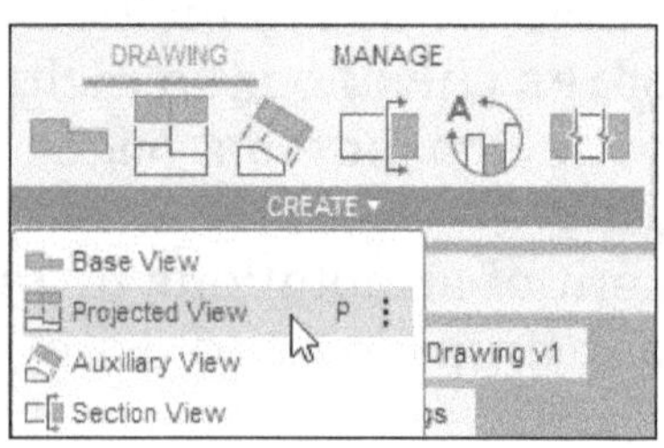

Figure-7. Projected View tool

- Click on the pre-existing base view from drawing sheet to select the view as parent view; refer to Figure-8. The projected view will be attached to the cursor; refer to Figure-9.

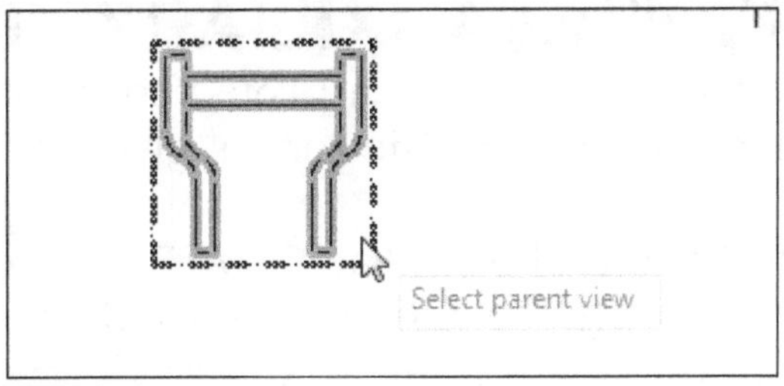

Figure-8. Selecting parent view

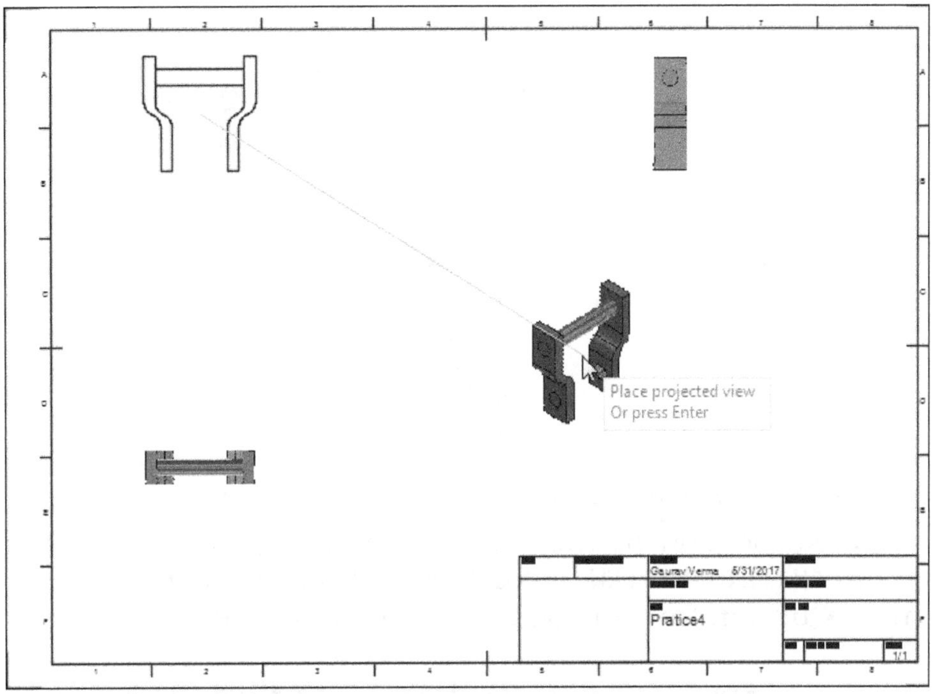

Figure-9. Placing projected view

- Place the projected views of model at desired locations and press **ENTER**. The projected view(s) are created on drawing sheet; refer to Figure-10.

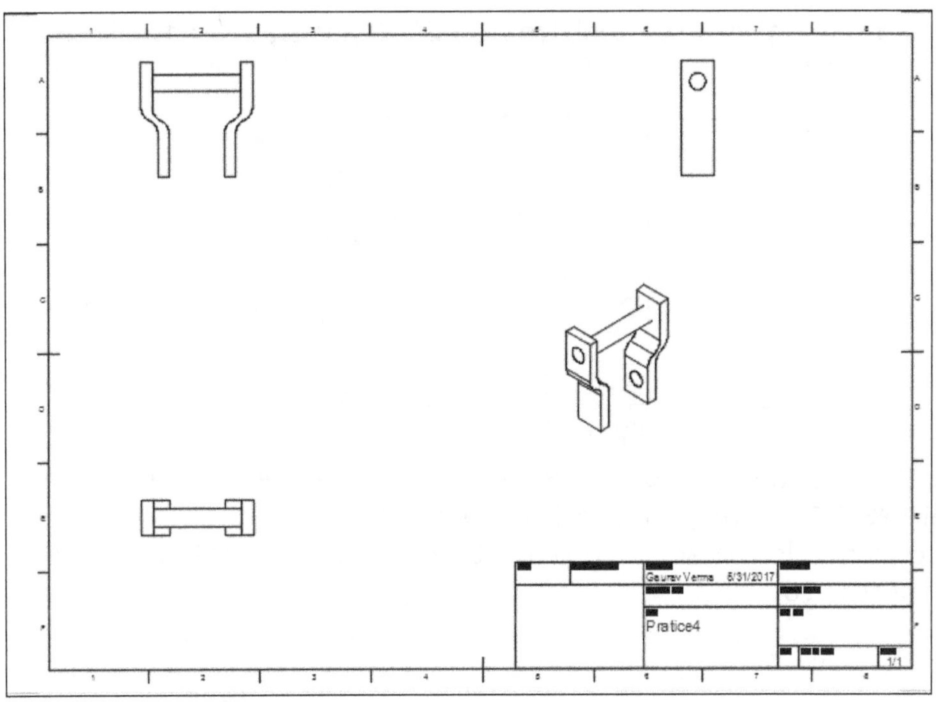

Figure-10. Projected views created

CREATING AUXILIARY VIEW

The **Auxiliary View** tool is used to create a projected view using view point normal to selected edge. The procedure to use this tool is given next.

- Click on the **Auxiliary View** tool from the **CREATE** drop-down in the **Toolbar**. You will be asked to select the edge for generating auxiliary view.
- Select desired edge from the model. The auxiliary view will get attached to cursor; refer to Figure-11.

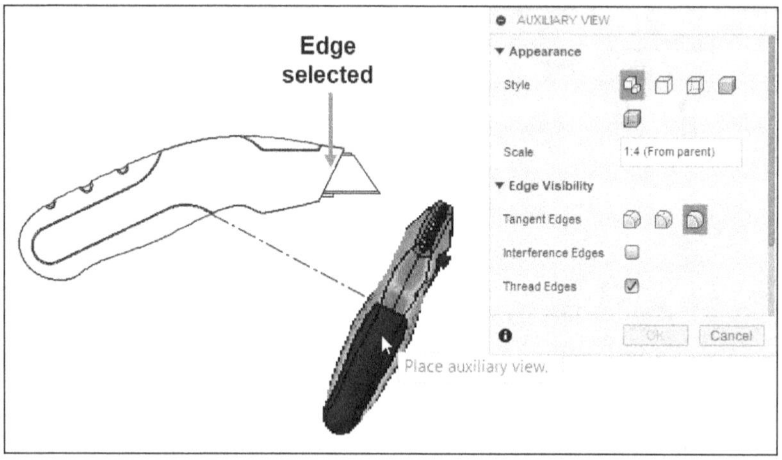

Figure-11. Auxiliary view attached to cursor

- Click at desired location in the drawing area to place the view and set the parameters in **AUXILIARY VIEW** dialog box as discussed earlier.
- Click on the **OK** button from dialog box to create the view.

CREATING SECTION VIEW

The **Section View** tool is used to create full, half, offset, or aligned section views. The procedure to use this tool is discussed next.

- Click on the **Section View** tool from **CREATE** panel; refer to Figure-12. The tool will be activated.

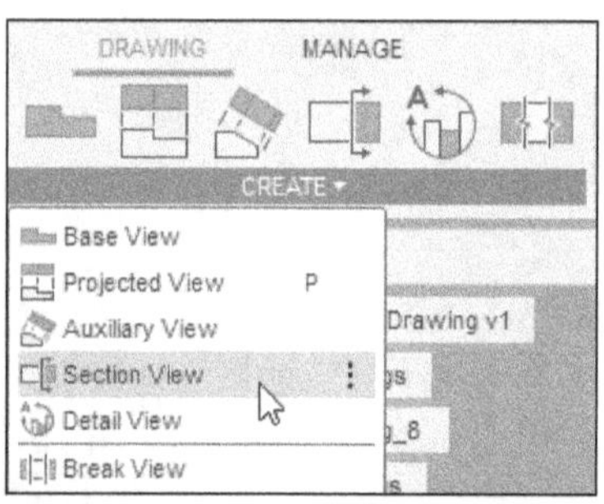

Figure-12. Section View tool

- Click on the projected or base view from drawing sheet to be used for section view. The **DRAWING VIEW** dialog box will be displayed.
- You need to divide the selected parent view into two parts to create half section; refer to Figure-13.

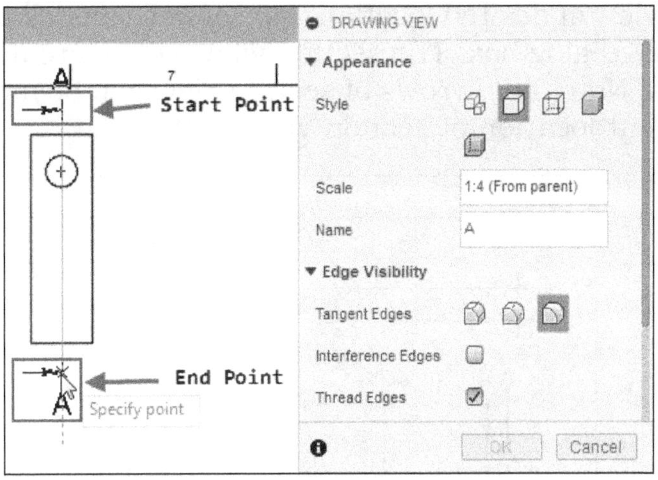

Figure-13. Creating section view

- Click on the parent view to specify the start point and end point. You can create different shape of section line to create desired type of section. Note that you can use snap point in right-click shortcut menu to select points for section line; refer to Figure-14. After specifying the start point, intermediate points, and end point, click on **ENTER** key. The section view will be created and attached to the cursor; refer to Figure-15.

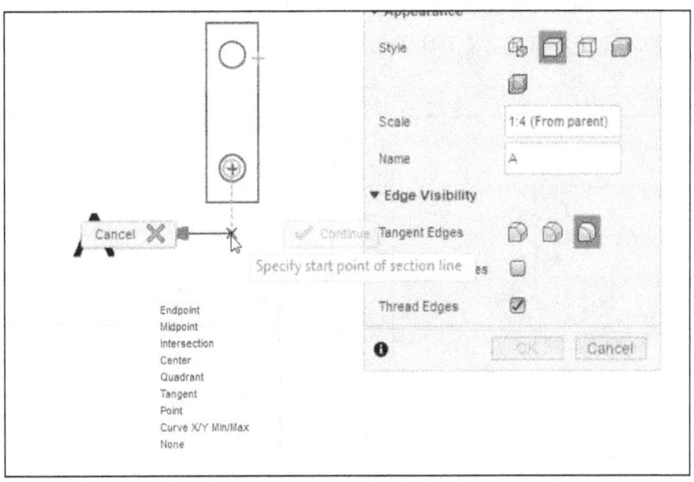

Figure-14. Shortcut menu for snap points

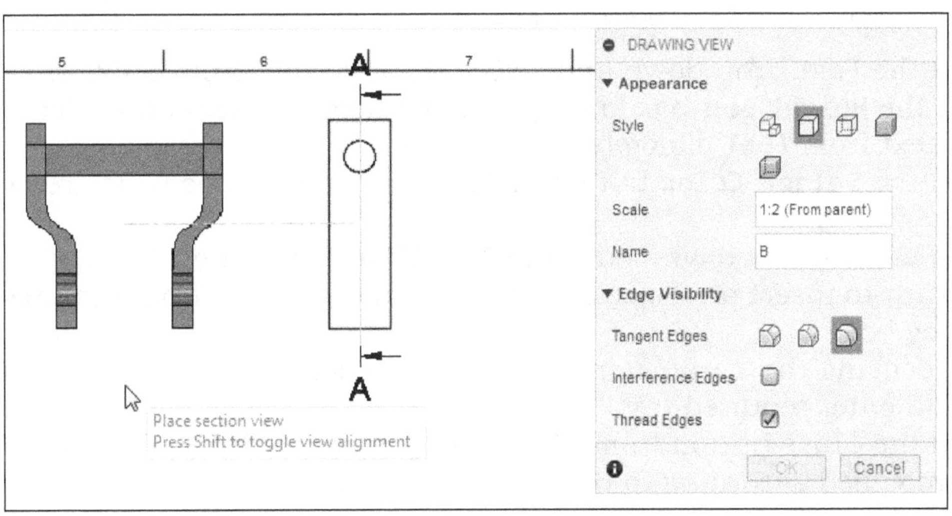

Figure-15. Section view attached to the cursor

- Place the section view at desired location/side of base model and click on **OK** button from **DRAWING VIEW** dialog box. The section view will be created on drawing sheet; refer to Figure-16. Note that arrows of section view will be modified automatically based on placement location of section view.

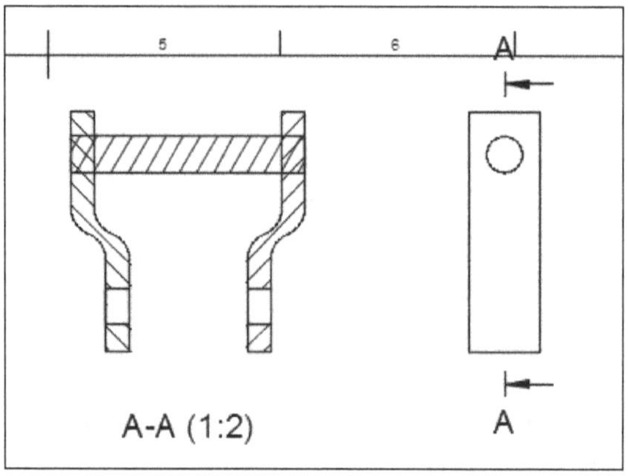

Figure-16. Section View created

- Note that the hatching is created automatically in the section view. To edit hatching, double-click on it. The **HATCH** dialog box will be displayed. Specify desired values and click on the **Close** button.
- If you want to edit the section annotation then double-click on it. The **TEXT** dialog box will be displayed; refer to Figure-17.

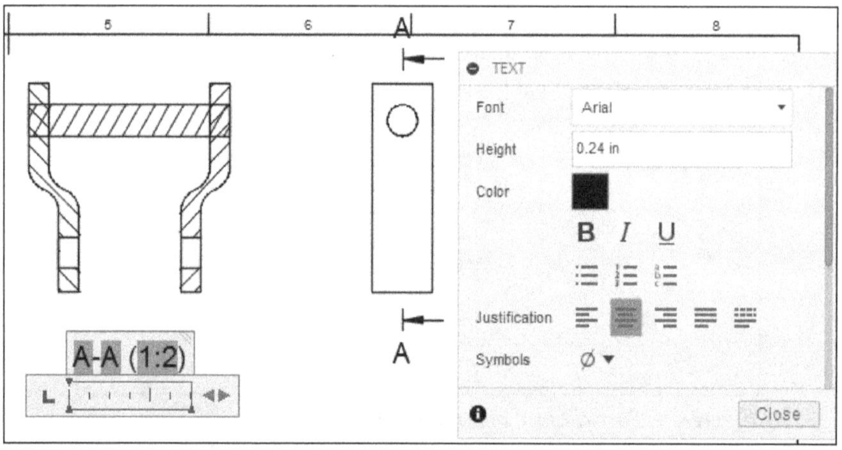

Figure-17. TEXT dialog box for annotation

- Click on the **Font** drop-down and select required font from the list.
- Click in the **Height** edit box and specify the height of text and select the writing style of text from **TEXT** dialog box.
- Click on the **Select Color** button of **Color** section to specify desired color of the text.
- Click on desired text alignment from **Justification** section.
- If you want to insert any special symbol then click on it from **Symbols** section of the dialog box.
- After specifying the parameters for the text, click in the text box from drawing sheet and enter required text.
- Click on the **Close** button from **TEXT** dialog box to complete the process. The text will be modified according to parameters specified.

CREATING DETAIL VIEW

The **Detail View** tool is used to create detail view from any projected or base view. The procedure to use this tool is discussed next.

- Click on the **Detail View** tool from **CREATE** panel; refer to Figure-18. The tool will be activated and you will be asked to select a view whose selected section is to be included in detail view.

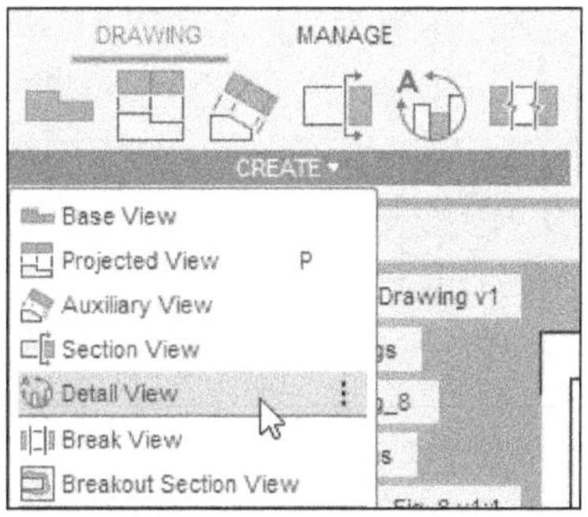

Figure-18. Detail View tool

- Select desired view from drawing sheet; refer to Figure-19. The **DRAWING VIEW** dialog box will be displayed.

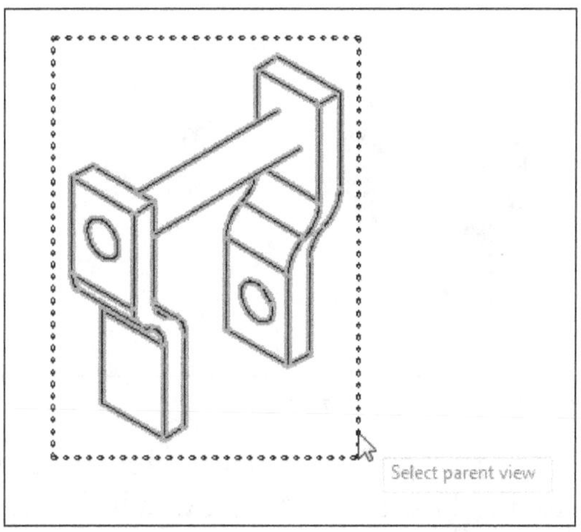

Figure-19. Selecting parent view for detail view

- Click at desired location to specify the center point for boundaries of detail view; refer to Figure-20.

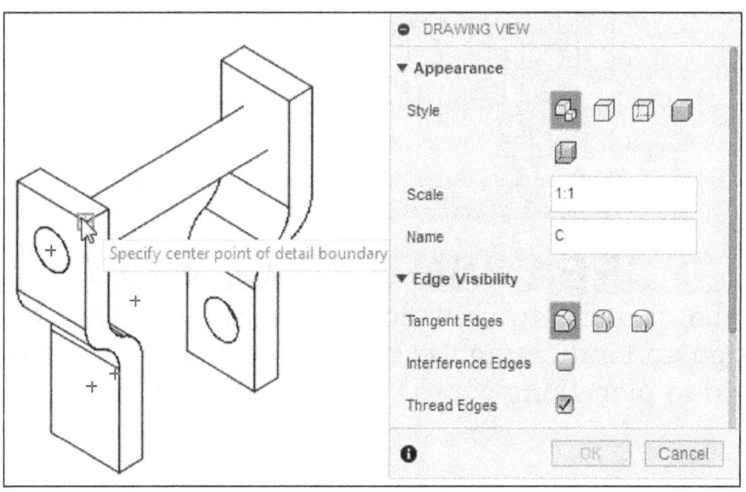

Figure-20. Specifying center point for boundary

- Create the boundary on parent view as required; refer to Figure-21.

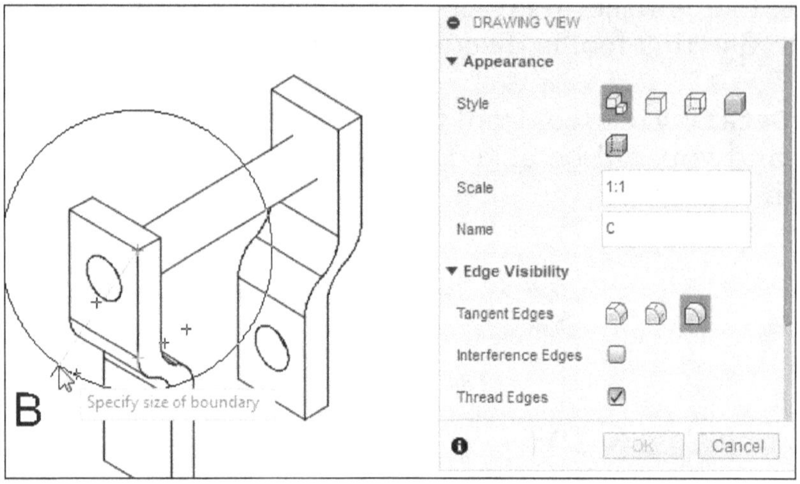

Figure-21. Creating boundary

- On creating the circular boundary, the detail view of model will be attached to the cursor; refer to Figure-22. Place it as desired.

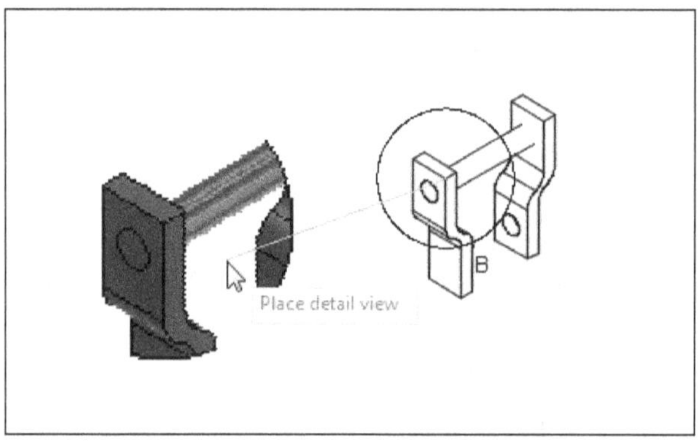

Figure-22. Placing detail view

- After placing the view, set the parameters of detail view in **DRAWING VIEW** dialog box and click on **OK** button. The detailed view will be created; refer to Figure-23.

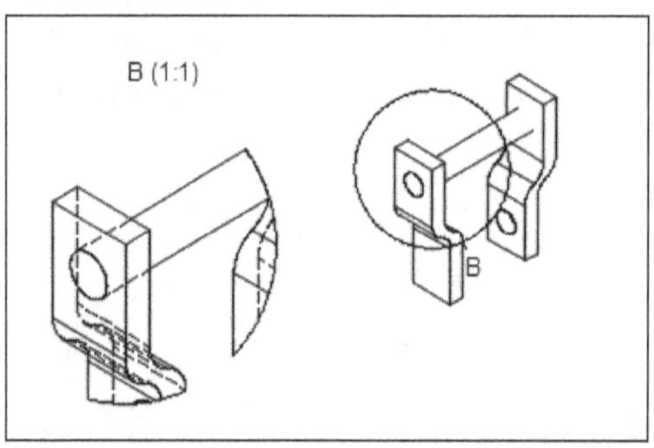

Figure-23. Detailed view created

CREATING BREAK VIEW

The **Break View** tool is used to shorten an existing drawing view by removing a portion of the design and indicating the missing section in the drawing. Broken view is generally created to place long views. The procedure to use this tool is discussed next.

- Click on the **Break View** tool from **CREATE** panel; refer to Figure-24. The **BREAK VIEW** dialog box will be displayed and you will be asked to select the drawing view to be broken; refer to Figure-25.

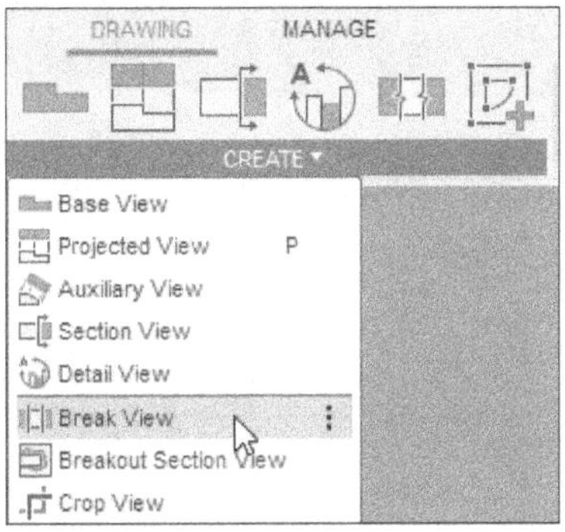

Figure-24. Break View tool

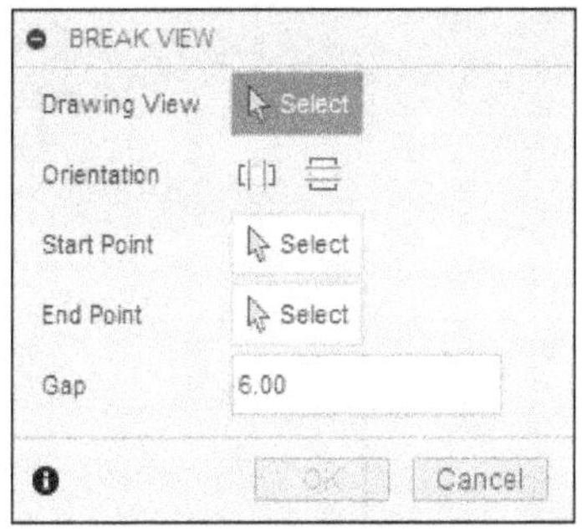

Figure-25. BREAK VIEW dialog box

- The **Select** button of **Drawing View** section is active by default. Select desired view from drawing sheet which you want to break; refer to Figure-26. You will be asked to select break position.

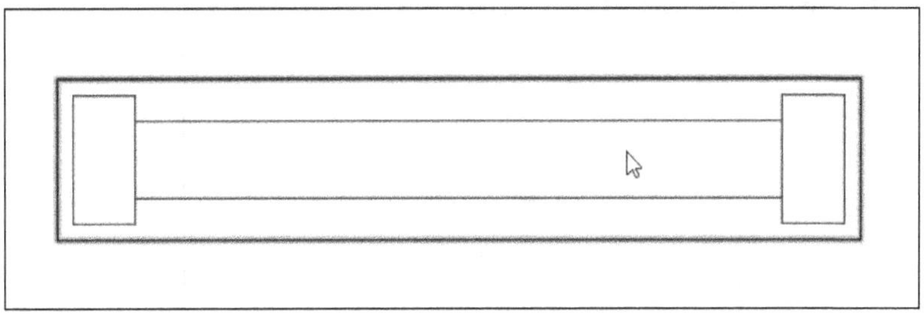

Figure-26. Selecting drawing view for broken view

- Select the start point of break position using the **Start Point** selection button; refer to Figure-27. You will be asked to select end point of break position.

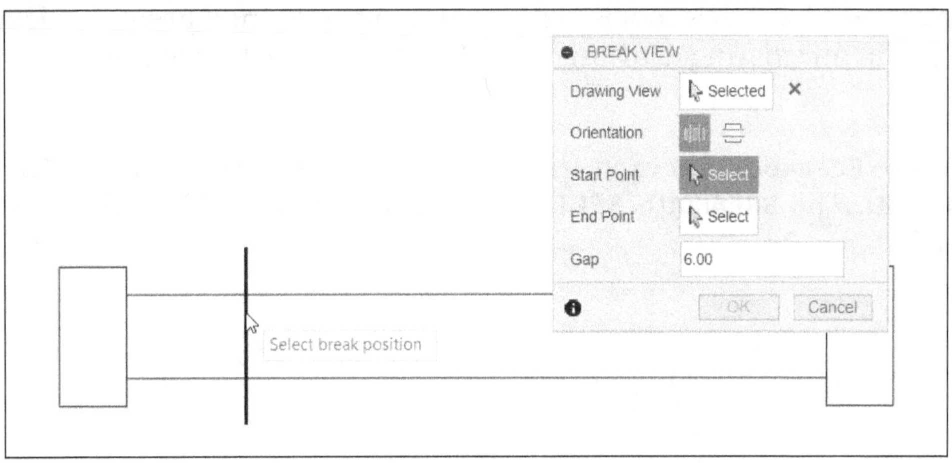

Figure-27. Selecting start point of break position

- Move the cursor away and click at desired location to specify end position of break position in the **End Point** selection button; refer to Figure-28.

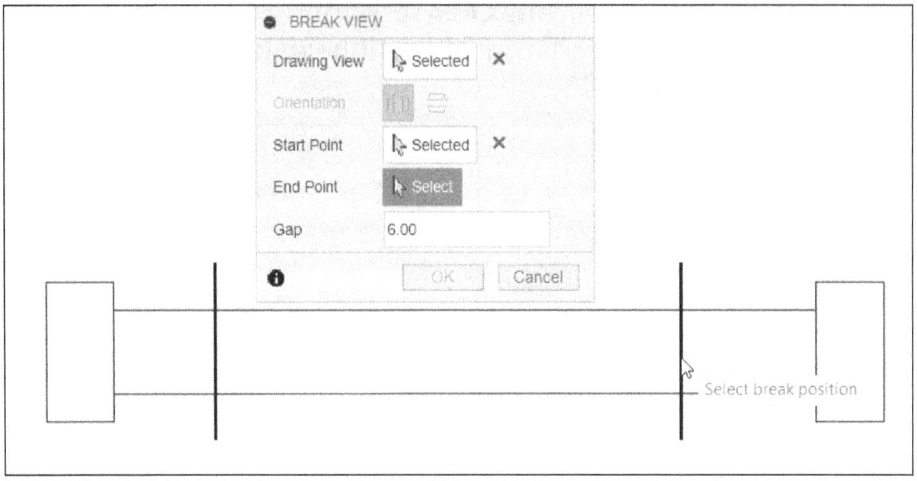

Figure-28. Selecting end point of break position

- Specify desired value in **Gap** edit box of the dialog box to specify distance for the gap between the two sections.
- After specifying parameters for break view, click on the **OK** button from the dialog box. The broken view will be created; refer to Figure-29.

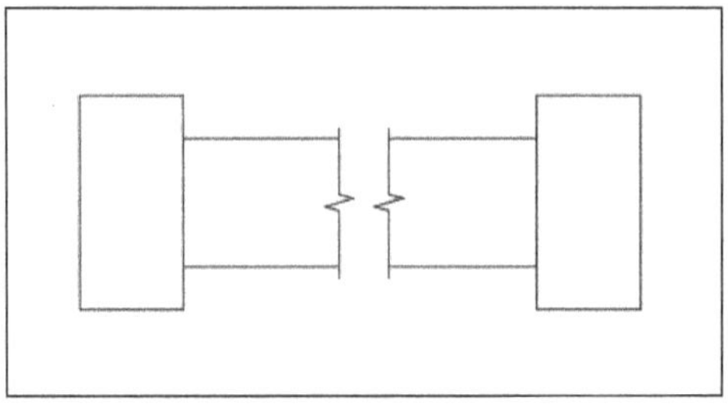

Figure-29. Broken view created

BREAKOUT SECTION VIEW

The **Breakout Section View** tool is used to remove a defined area of object to expose inner features in an existing drawing view. The procedure to use this tool is discussed next.

- Click on the **Breakout Section View** tool from **CREATE** panel in the **Toolbar**; refer to Figure-30. The **BREAKOUT SECTION VIEW** dialog box will be displayed; refer to Figure-31.

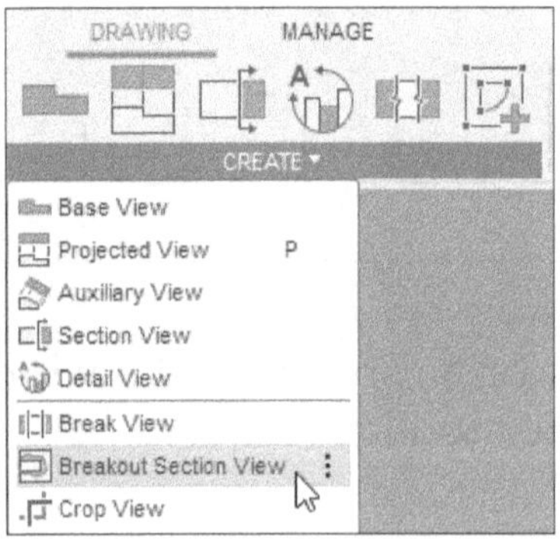

Figure-30. Breakout Section View tool

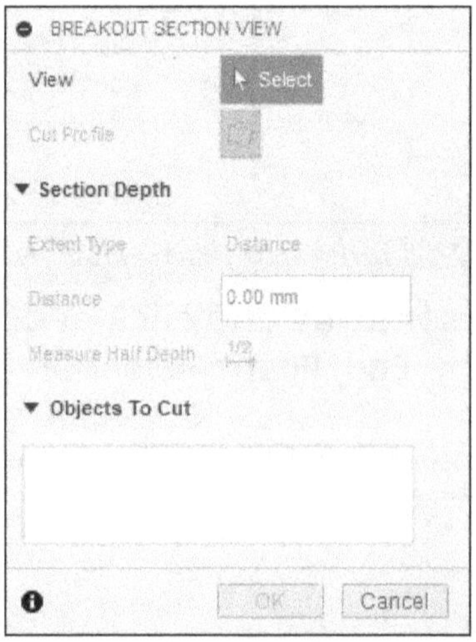

Figure-31. BREAKOUT SECTION VIEW dialog box

- The **Select** button of **View** section is active by default. Select desired view from drawing sheet in which you want to display breakout; refer to Figure-32. The Cut Profile selection will become active and you will be asked to specify the start point.

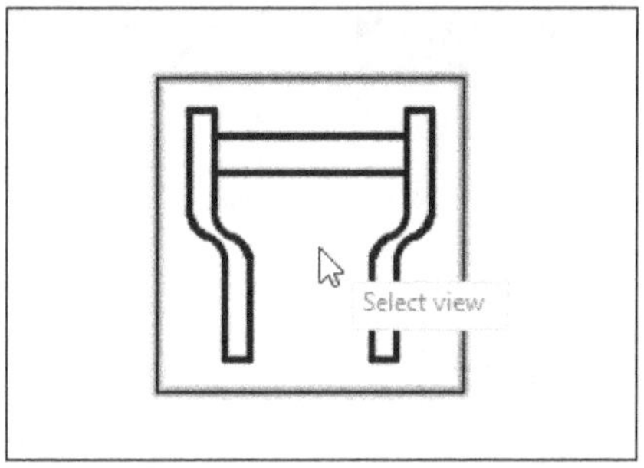

Figure-32. Selecting the view for breakout

- Click in the view at desired location to specify start point of the section. You will be asked to specify the next point.
- Move the cursor away and click at desired locations to specify next consecutive point(s).
- After specifying desired points, press **Enter**. The breakout section view will be created and other sections of the dialog box will be activated; refer to Figure-33.

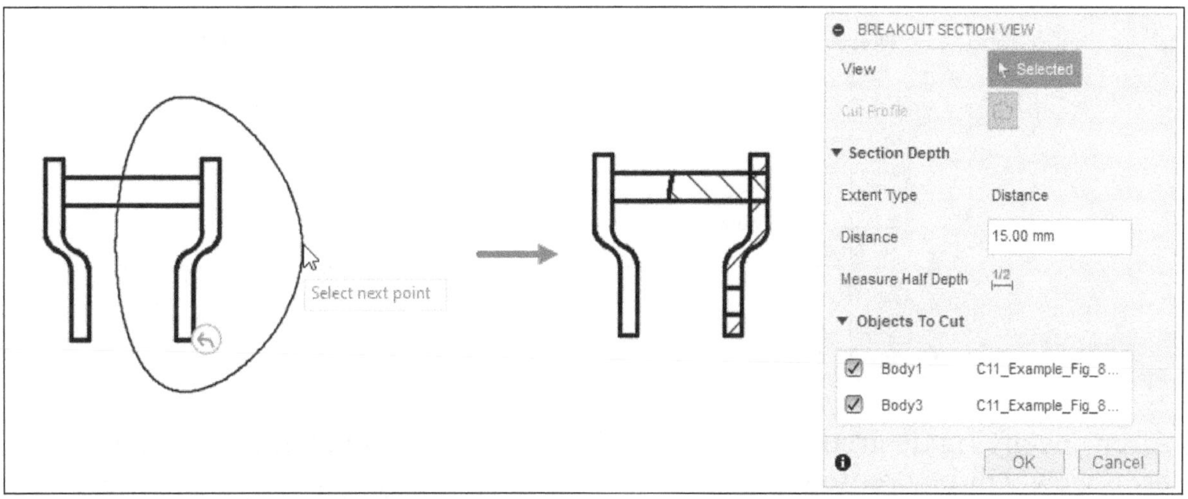

Figure-33. Breakout section view created

- The **Distance** section displays the half of the design's depth by default. You can specify desired depth value in the edit box at which section will be created.
- Click on the **Measure Half Length** button to go back to the default depth distance.
- Clear check boxes for components from **Objects To Cut** section of the dialog box to exclude them from creating breakout section view.
- After specifying desired parameters, click on the **OK** button from the dialog box.

CROP VIEW

The **Crop View** tool is used to remove unnecessary portion of the drawing view image. The procedure to use this tool is discussed next.

- Click on the **Crop View** tool from **CREATE** panel in the **Toolbar**; refer to Figure-34. The **CROP VIEW** dialog box will be displayed; refer to Figure-35.

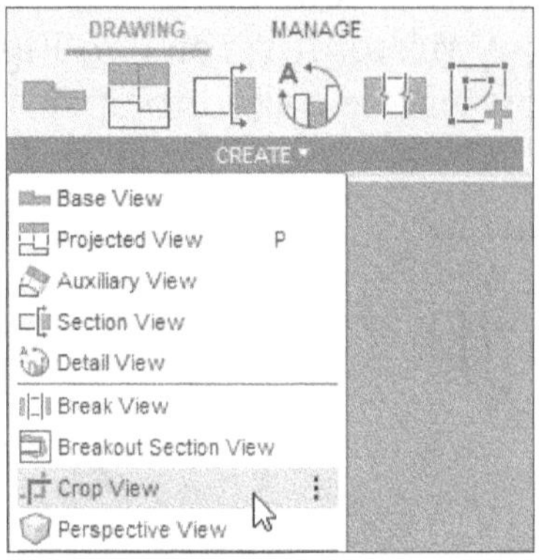

Figure-34. Crop View tool

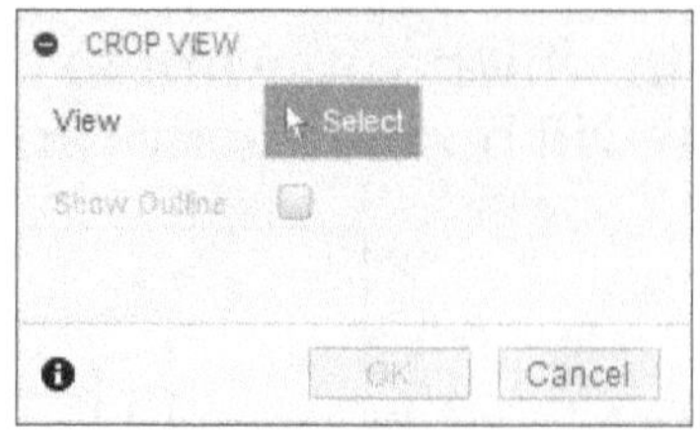

Figure-35. CROP VIEW dialog box

- Select desired view from the drawing area. You will be asked to specify the first corner.
- Click in the drawing area at desired location to specify the first corner of crop window. You will be asked to specify the second corner.
- Move the cursor away and click at desired location to specify the second corner of crop window; refer to Figure-36.
- Select the **Show Outline** check box to display the crop window outline; refer to Figure-37.

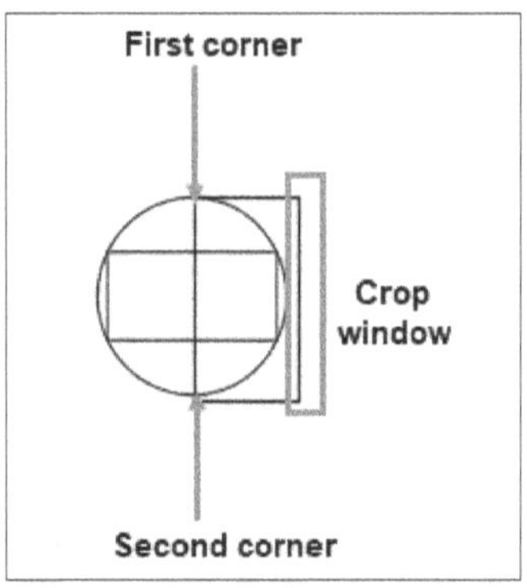

Figure-36. Selecting the first and second crop window

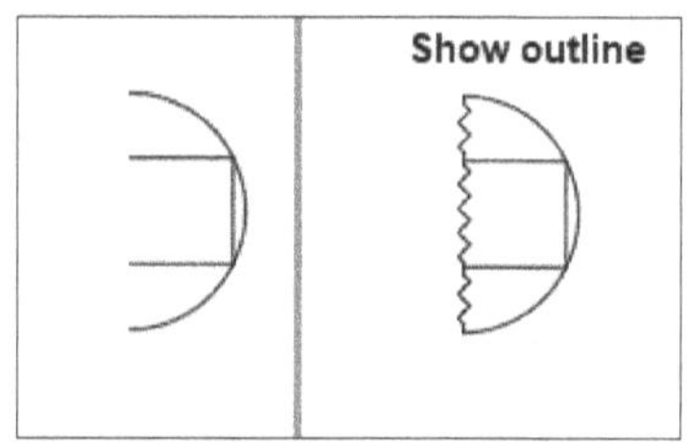

Figure-37. Showing outline of crop view

- After specifying desired parameters, click on **OK** button from the dialog box. The crop view will be created.

PERSPECTIVE VIEW

The **Perspective View** tool is used to create perspective view of the design i.e., design in a three-point perspective. The procedure to use this tool is discussed next.

- Click on the **Perspective View** tool from **CREATE** panel in the **Toolbar**; refer to Figure-38. The **DRAWING VIEW** dialog box will be displayed as discussed earlier and you will be asked to place the perspective view.

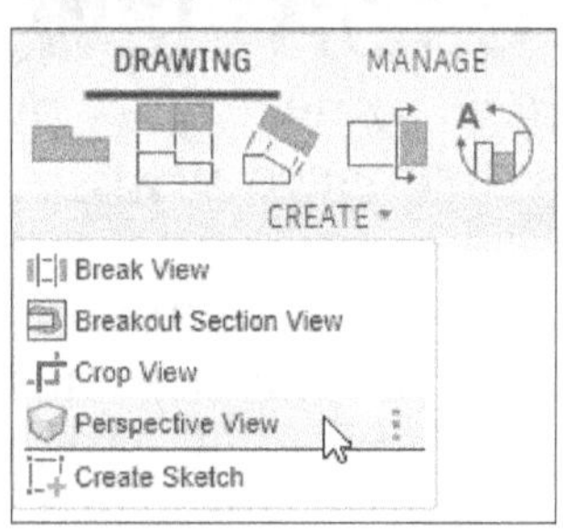

Figure-38. Perspective View tool

- Click in the drawing area at desired location to place the perspective view and specify desired parameters in the **DRAWING VIEW** dialog box as discussed earlier.
- After specifying desired parameters, click on the **OK** button from the dialog box. The perspective view will be placed; refer to Figure-39.

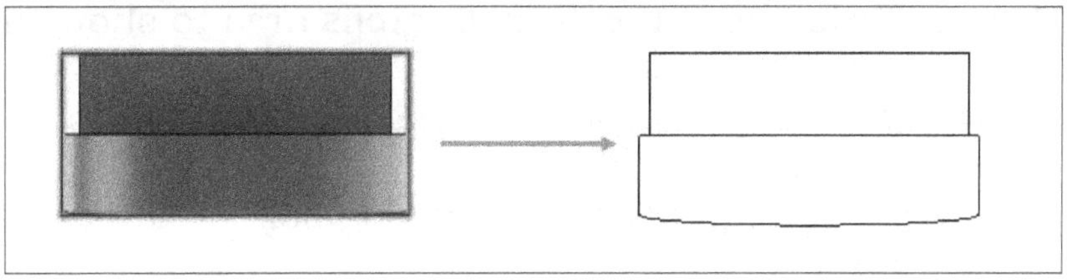

Figure-39. Perspective view created

CREATING SKETCH

The **Create Sketch** tool is used to the sketch mode and create a new sketch on the current sheet. The procedure to use this tool is discussed next.

- Click on the **Create Sketch** tool from **CREATE** panel in the **Toolbar**; refer to Figure-40. The **SKETCH** contextual tab will be displayed along with **SKETCH** dialog box; refer to Figure-41.

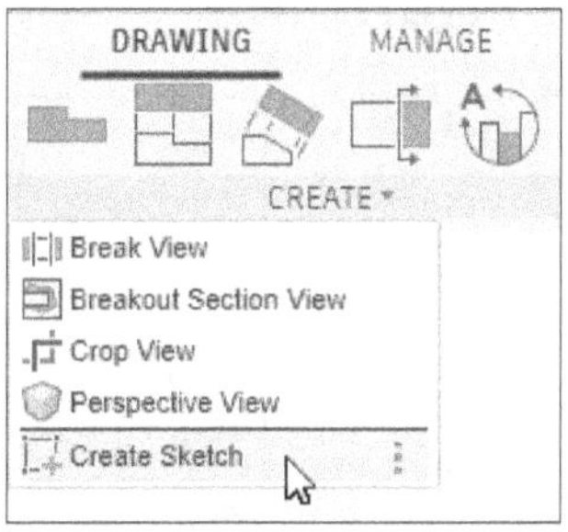

Figure-40. Create Sketch tool

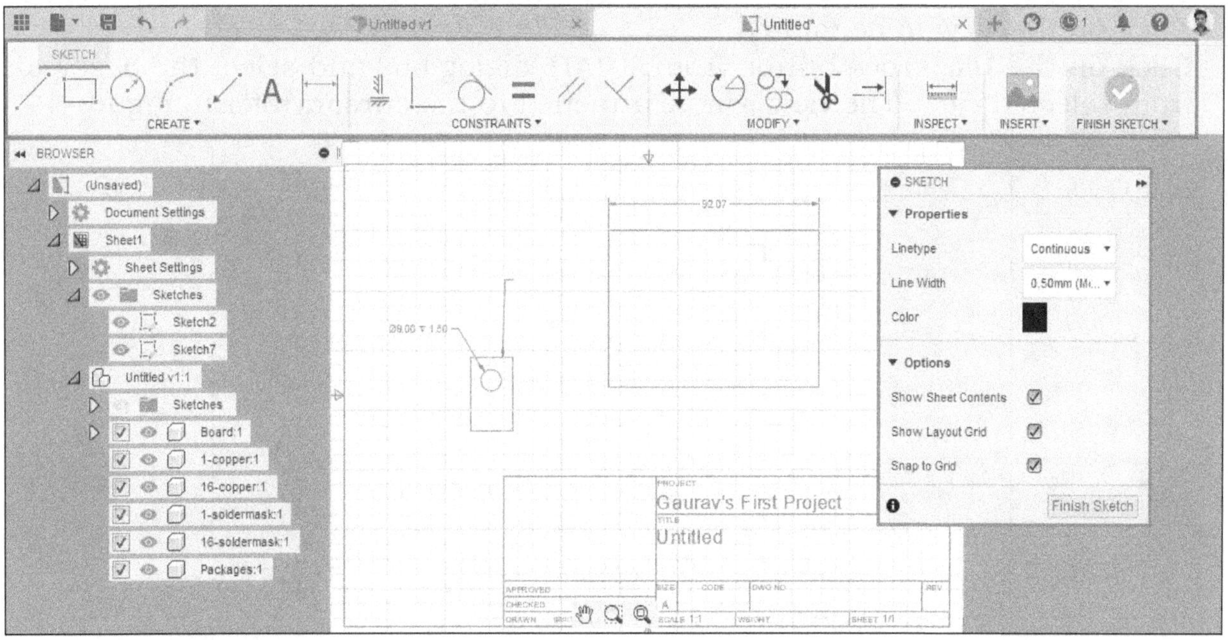

Figure-41. SKETCH contextual tab with SKETCH dialog box

- Select desired option from **Linetype** drop-down of **Properties** area in the dialog box to change the linetype of new or selected sketch geometry.

- Select desired option from **Line Width** drop-down of **Properties** area in the dialog box to change the line width of new or selected sketch geometry.
- Select **Show Sheet Contents** check box from **Options** area to show the contents of the sheet as you edit the sketch.
- Select **Show Layout Grid** check box from **Options** area to show the layout grid in the canvas as you edit the sketch.
- Select **Snap to Grid** check box from **Options** area to snap to the layout grid in the canvas as you edit the sketch.
- After specifying parameters in the **SKETCH** dialog box, create desired sketch from **SKETCH** tab in the **Toolbar**.
- After creating the sketch, click on **Finish Sketch** button from **Toolbar** or from the dialog box to exit the tab.

ROTATING VIEWS

The **Rotate** tool is used to rotate selected view as desired. The procedure to use this tool is discussed next.

- Click on the **Rotate** tool from **MODIFY** panel; refer to Figure-42. The **ROTATE** dialog box will be displayed; refer to Figure-43.

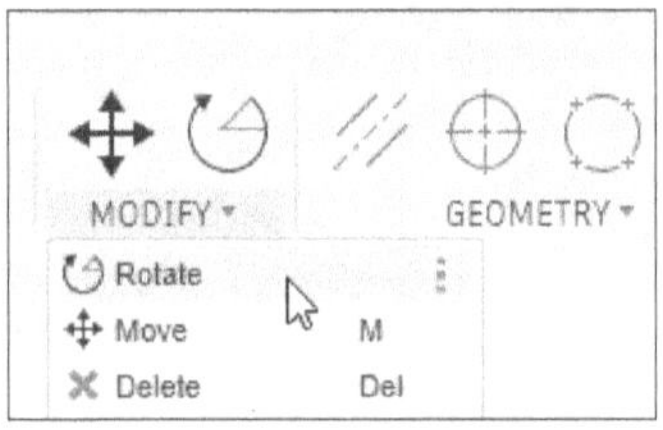

Figure-42. Rotate tool

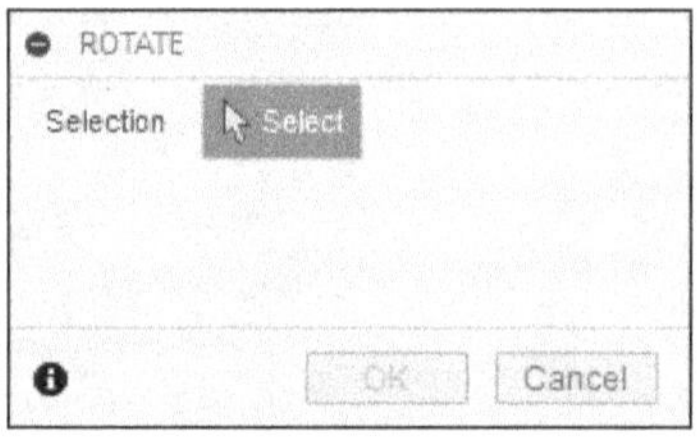

Figure-43. ROTATE dialog box

- The **Select** button of **Selection** section in **ROTATE** dialog box is active by default. Click on the view to be rotated.
- Click on the **Transform** button from **ROTATE** dialog box and select the base point from selected view. The view will be attached to the cursor; refer to Figure-44.

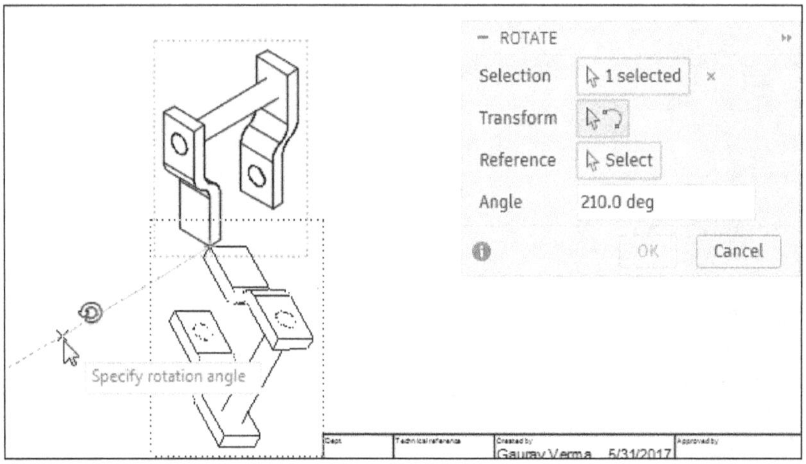

Figure-44. Rotating view

- You can adjust the angle of rotation of view by moving the cursor around parent view and place as required. If you want to specify the value of rotation then click in the **Angle** edit box of **ROTATE** dialog box and specify the value.

- You can also set the reference for rotation by clicking on **Select** button of **Reference** section and selecting the reference point from parent view.
- After specifying the parameters, click on **OK** button from **ROTATE** dialog box to complete the process.

MOVING VIEWS

The **Move** tool is used to move selected view from one place to another. The procedure to use this tool is discussed next.

- Click on the **Move** tool from **MODIFY** drop-down; refer to Figure-45. The **MOVE** dialog box will be displayed; refer to Figure-46.

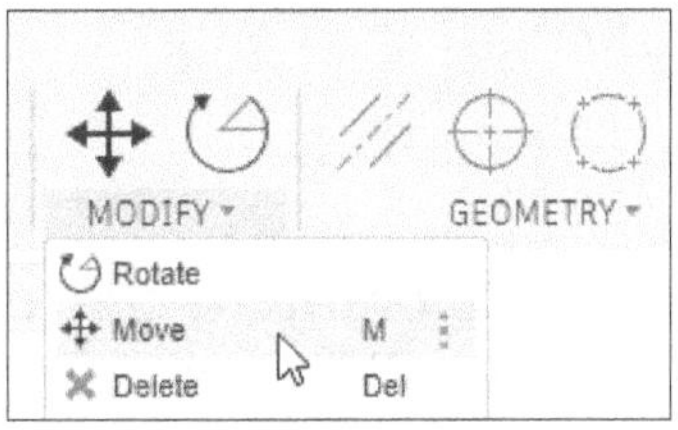

Figure-45. Move tool

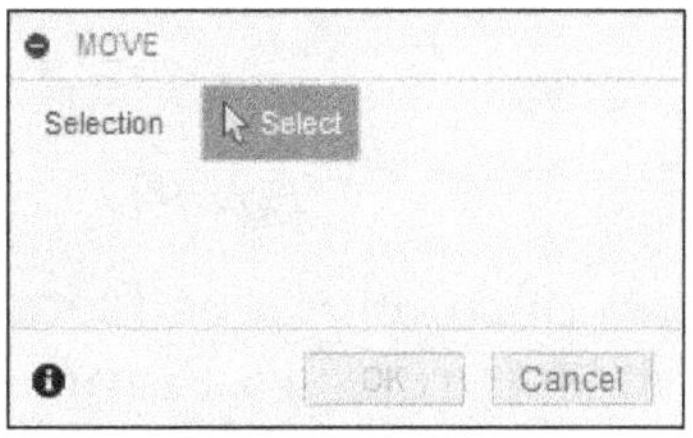

Figure-46. MOVE dialog box

- The **Select** button of **Selection** section in **MOVE** dialog box is active by default. Click on the view to select the view to be moved. The updated **MOVE** dialog box will be displayed; refer to Figure-47.

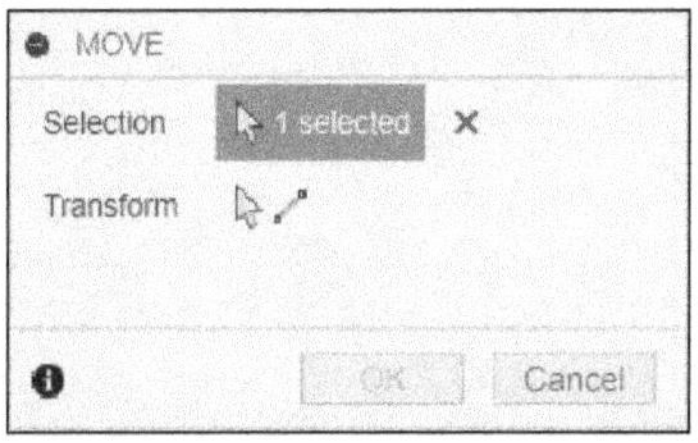

Figure-47. Updated MOVE dialog box

- Click on **Transform** button from **MOVE** dialog box and select a base point from the selected view. The selected view will get attached to the cursor to move the view from one place to another; refer to Figure-48.

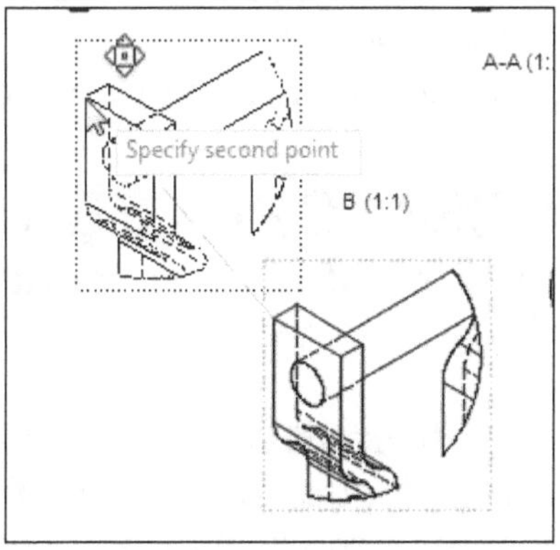

Figure-48. Specifying second point

- Click on the sheet to place the view. The view will be moved from previous position to new position.
- Click on the **OK** button from **MOVE** dialog box to complete the process.

CREATING CENTER LINE

The **Center Line** tool is used to create centerline. The procedure to use this tool is discussed next.

- Click on the **Center Line** tool from **GEOMETRY** panel; refer to Figure-49. The tool will be activated.

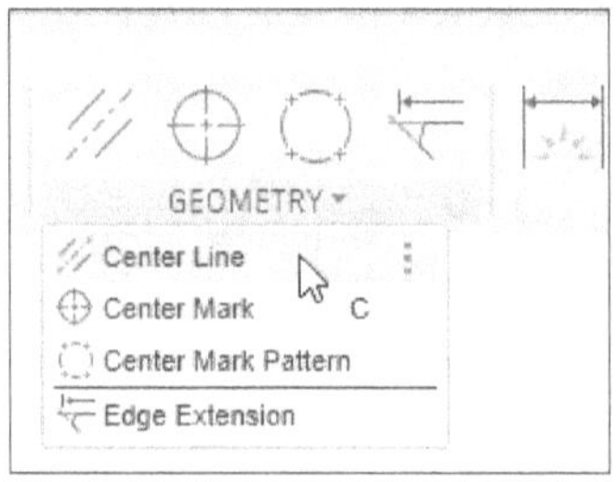

Figure-49. Center Line tool

- You need to select parallel edges from a view to create a center line. Click on the desired edge to select; refer to Figure-50. You will be asked to select the second edge.

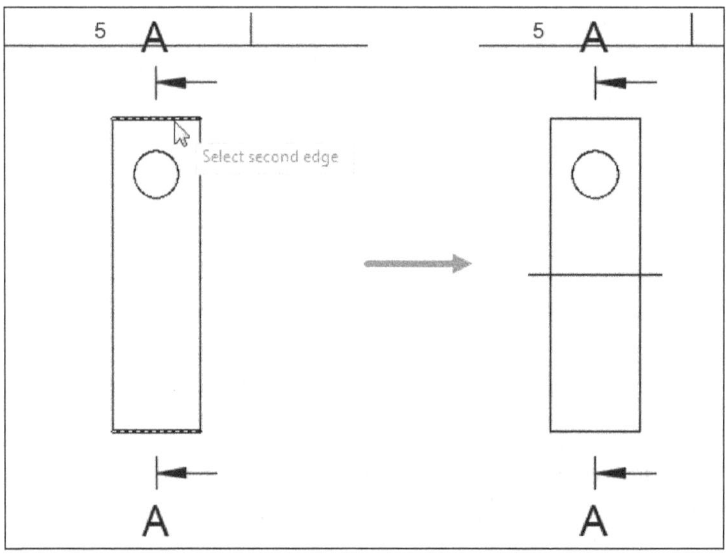

Figure-50. Creating centerline

- On selecting second edge, the center line will be created.

CREATING CENTER MARK

The **Center Mark** tool is used to create center mark for rounds and circles. The procedure to use this tool is discussed next.

- Click on the **Center Mark** tool from **GEOMETRY** panel; refer to Figure-51. The tool will be activated. You need to select a round edge from any view.
- On selecting the edge, the center mark will be created for selected round edge; refer to Figure-52.

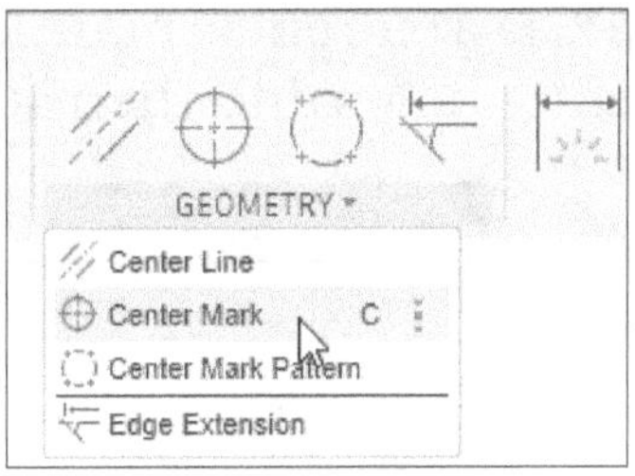

Figure-51. Center Mark tool

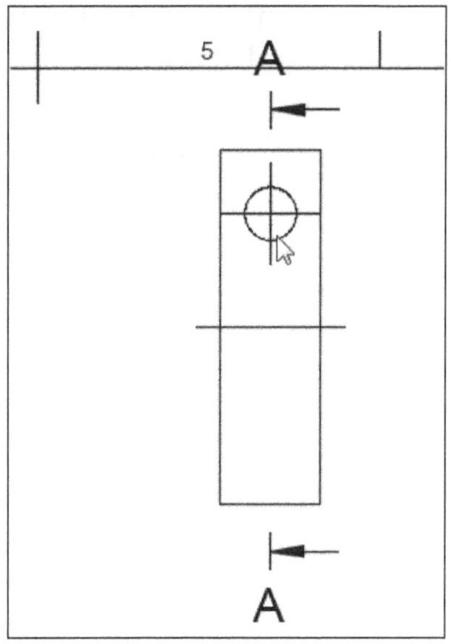

Figure-52. Creating center mark

CREATING CENTER MARK PATTERN

The **Center Mark Pattern** tool is used to generate pattern of center marks in the drawing view. The procedure to use this tool is given next.

- Click on the **Center Mark Pattern** tool from the **GEOMETRY** panel in the **Toolbar**; refer to Figure-53. The **CENTER MARK PATTERN** dialog box will be displayed; refer to Figure-54. You will be asked to select a hole or round edge whose center mark is to be created.

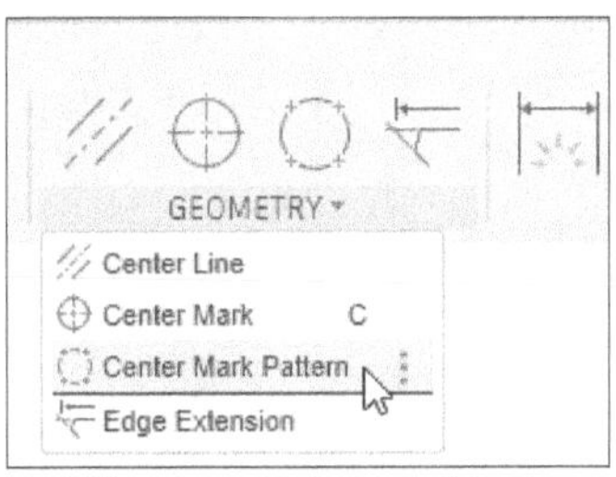

Figure-53. Center Mark Pattern tool

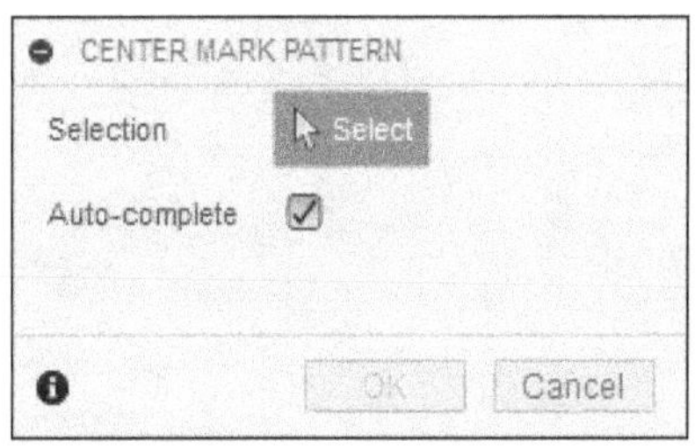

Figure-54. CENTER MARK PATTERN dialog box

- Click on desired holes one by one. If the holes are in circular pattern then the dialog box will be displayed as shown in Figure-55. Select the **Center Mark** check box to generate center mark for pitch circle. Click on the **OK** button to generate center marks.

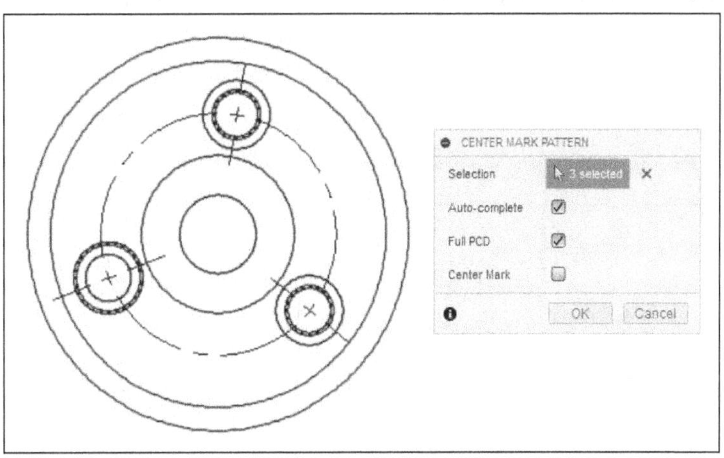

Figure-55. Holes selected in circular pattern

- In cases where you want to specify the PCD reference manually, click on the **Reference Edge** selection button after selecting holes and then select the reference edge; refer to Figure-56.

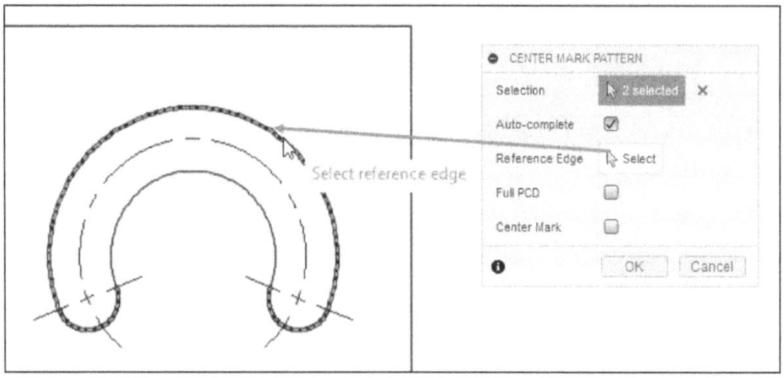

Figure-56. Selecting reference edge

- In case of selecting holes in linear direction, you can select maximum 3 holes for center mark.

EDGE EXTENSION

The **Edge Extension** tool is used to create an extension of associative edge for two intersecting (unequal) edges within an existing drawing view. The procedure to use this tool is discussed next.

- Click on the **Edge Extension** tool from **GEOMETRY** panel; refer to Figure-57. The tool will be activated.

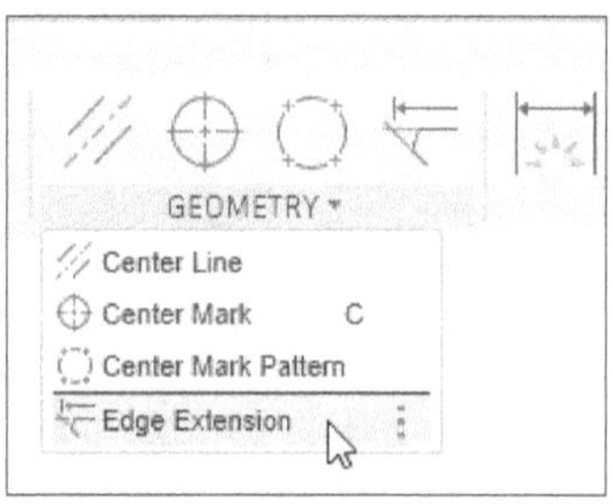

Figure-57. Edge Extension tool

- You need to select the two non-parallel (going to intersect) edges to create the extension. Click on the edge to select; refer to Figure-58.
- On selecting the second edge, the extended edge will be displayed; refer to Figure-59.

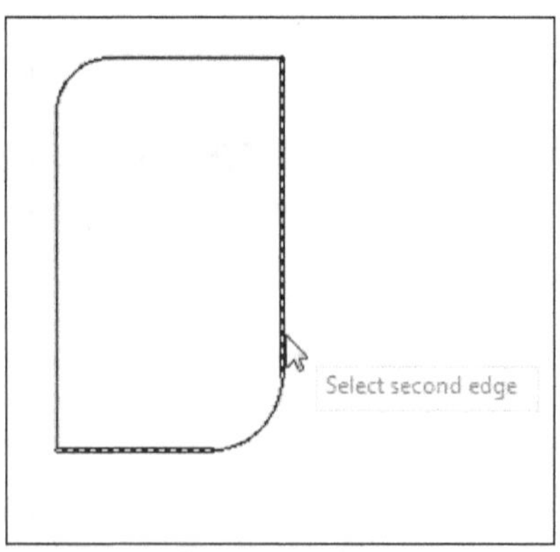

Figure-58. Selecting second edge

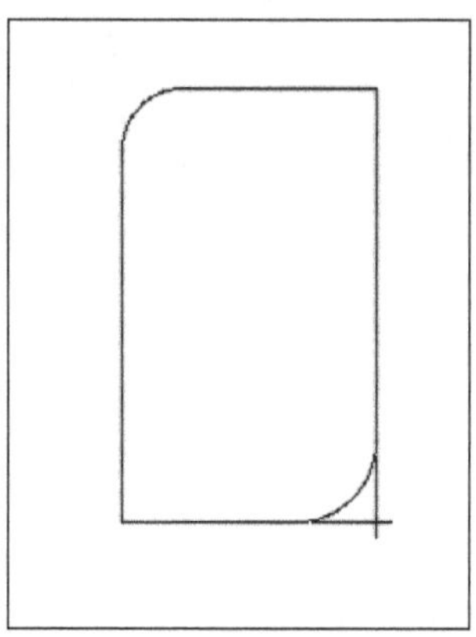

Figure-59. Edge extension created

DIMENSIONING

The **Dimension** tool is used to apply dimension to model. The procedure to use this tool is discussed next.

- Click on the **Dimension** tool from **DIMENSIONS** panel; refer to Figure-60. The tool will be activated.
- When you hover the cursor over on any geometry, the measurement of that dimension will be displayed; refer to Figure-61.

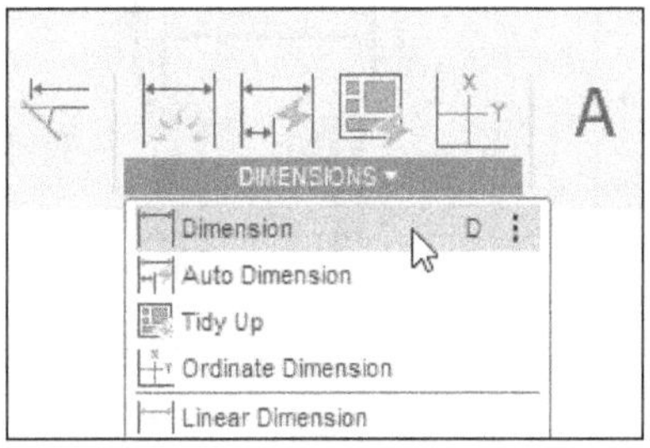

Figure-60. Dimension tool

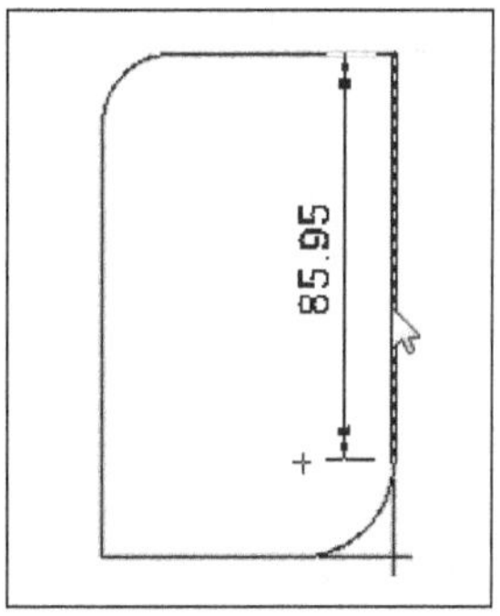

Figure-61. Checking dimension

- If you want to mention that dimension then click on the line. The dimension will be attached to the cursor.
- Place the dimension at desired distance by clicking.

Automatic Dimensioning

The **Auto Dimension** tool is used to create and customize the dimensions automatically. The procedure to use this tool is discussed next.

- Click on the **Auto Dimension** tool from **DIMENSIONS** panel; refer to Figure-62. The **AUTO DIMENSION** dialog box will be displayed; refer to Figure-63.

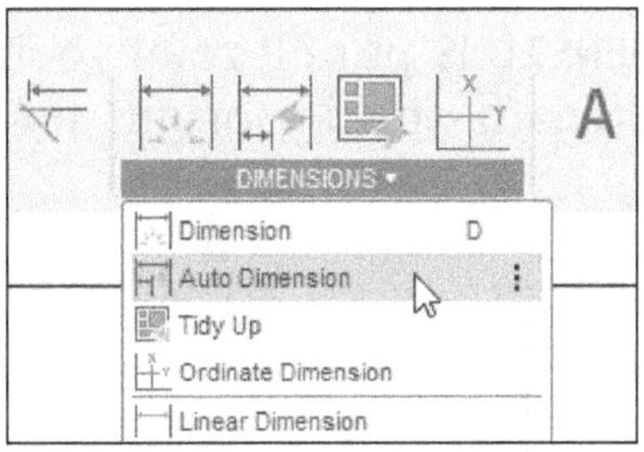

Figure-62. Auto Dimension tool

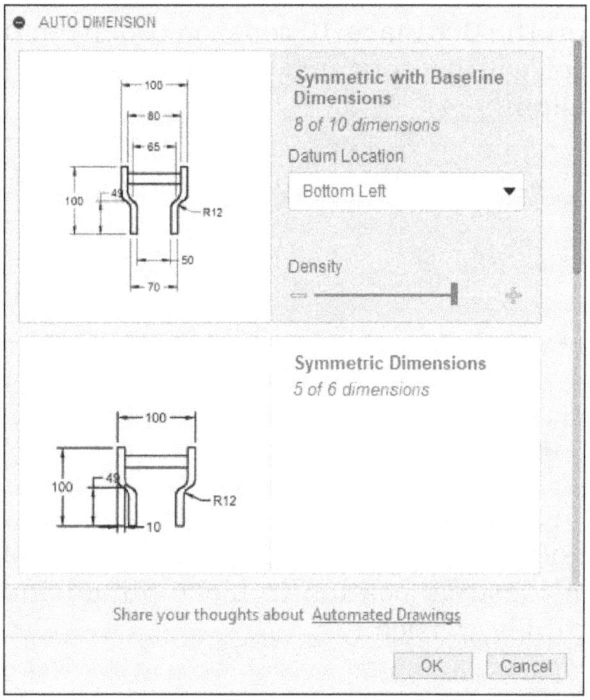

Figure-63. AUTO DIMENSION dialog box

- Select desired dimension layout from the dialog box to be applied. The dimension will be applied to the drawing; refer to Figure-64.

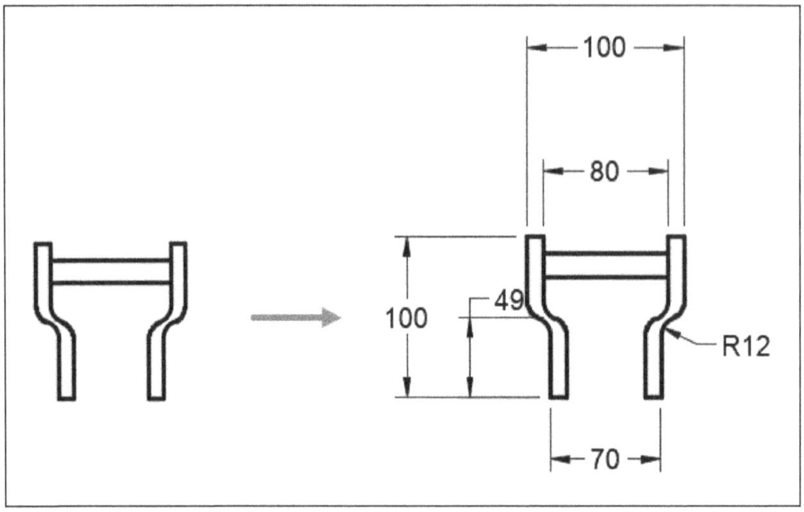

Figure-64. Dimension layout applied

- Select desired option from **Datum Location** drop-down to specify the location of dimensions.
- Drag the **Density** manipulator to specify the density of dimensions.
- After specifying desired parameters, click on **OK** button from the dialog box.

Tidy Up

The **Tidy Up** tool is used to automatically move dimensions that are overlapping. It also rearranges, re-sorts, and re-sizes objects in the sheet to keep the layout tidy.

Ordinate Dimensioning

The **Ordinate Dimension** tool is used to apply ordinate dimensioning. The procedure to use this tool is discussed next.

- Click on the **Ordinate Dimension** tool from **DIMENSIONS** panel; refer to Figure-65. The tool will be activated and you will be asked to specify origin for ordinate dimensioning.

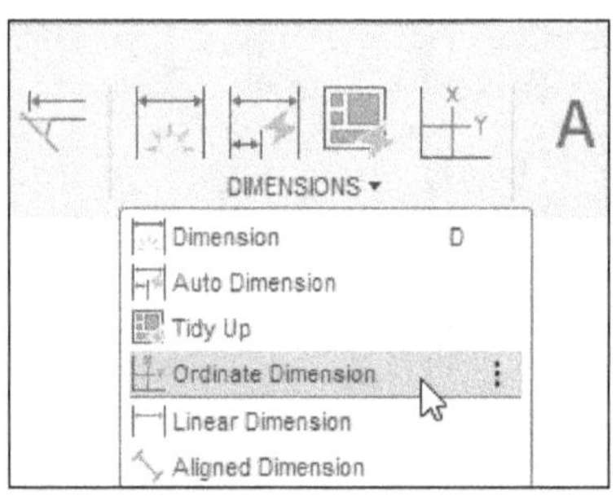

Figure-65. Ordinate Dimension tool

- Click at desired location to place origin of ordinate dimensioning. The ordinate dimension will be attached to the cursor; refer to Figure-66.
- Click at desired location to place dimension text. Similarly, you can dimension horizontally/vertically.

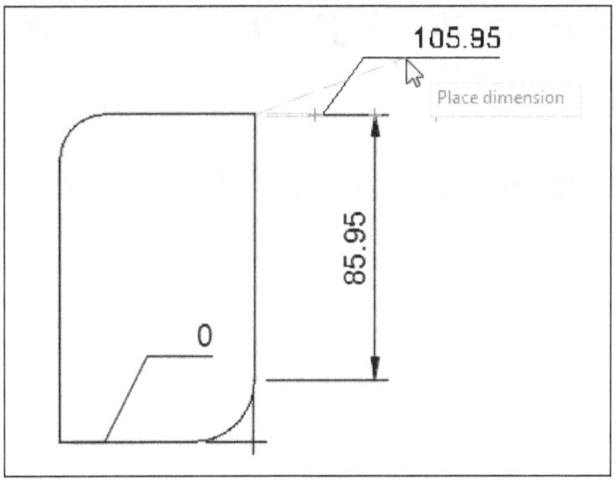

Figure-66. Calculating ordinate dimension

Creating Linear Dimension

The **Linear Dimension** tool is used to create linear dimensions in horizontal/vertical directions. The procedure to use this tool is given next.

- Click on the **Linear Dimension** tool from the **DIMENSIONS** panel in the **Toolbar**; refer to Figure-67. You will be asked to select points.

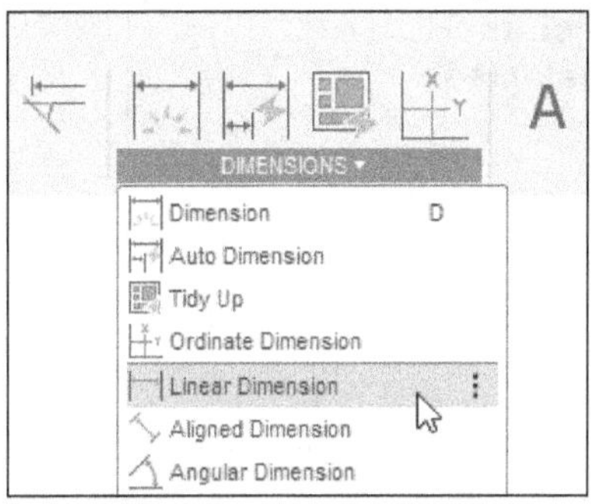

Figure-67. Linear Dimension tool

- Select the two points one by one to create horizontal/vertical distance dimension. The dimension will get attached to cursor.
- Move the cursor in desired direction to create vertical or horizontal dimension if the two points are not in aligned vertically/horizontally; refer to Figure-68.

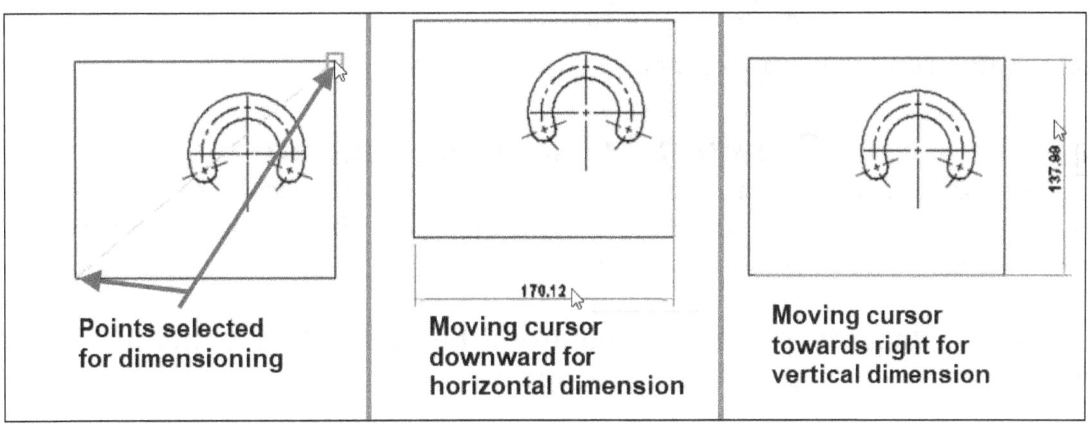

Figure-68. Creating linear dimension

- Click at desired location to place the dimension.

Creating Aligned Dimension

The **Aligned Dimension** tool is used to create aligned dimension between two selected points. The procedure is given next.

- Click on the **Aligned Dimension** tool from **DIMENSIONS** panel in the **Toolbar**; refer to Figure-69. You will be asked to select points.

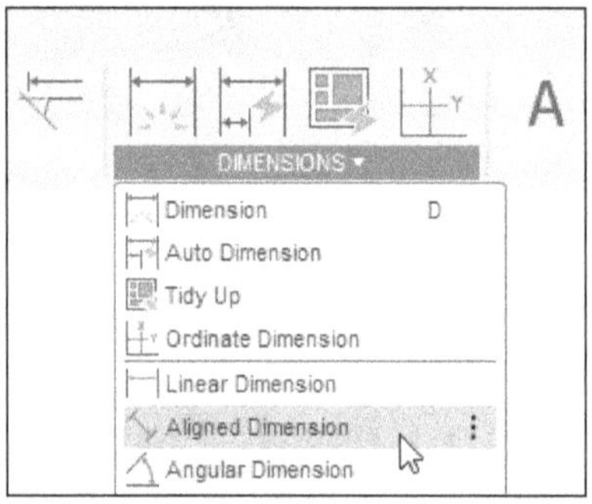

Figure-69. Aligned Dimension tool

- Click at desired two points. The distance dimension between two selected points will get attached to cursor; refer to Figure-70.

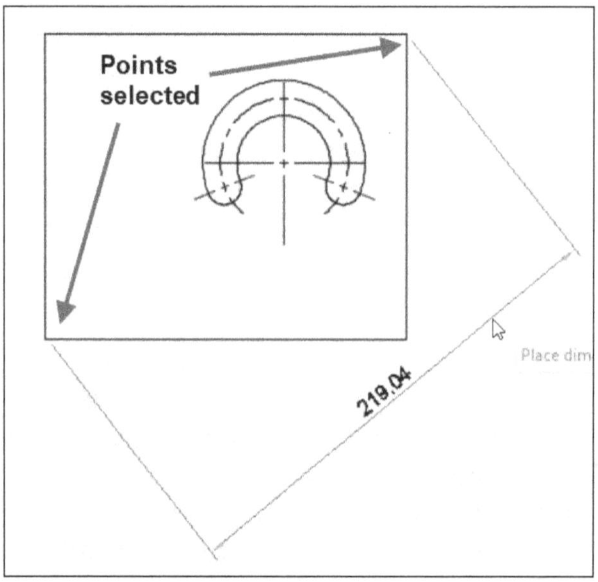

Figure-70. Placing Aligned dimension

- Click at desired location to place the dimension.

Creating Angular Dimension

The **Angular Dimension** tool is used to create angle dimension between two selected lines/edges. If you select an arc then its angular span is created as dimension. The procedure to use this tool is given next.

- Click on the **Angular Dimension** tool from the **DIMENSIONS** panel in the **Toolbar**; refer to Figure-71. You will be asked to select entities.

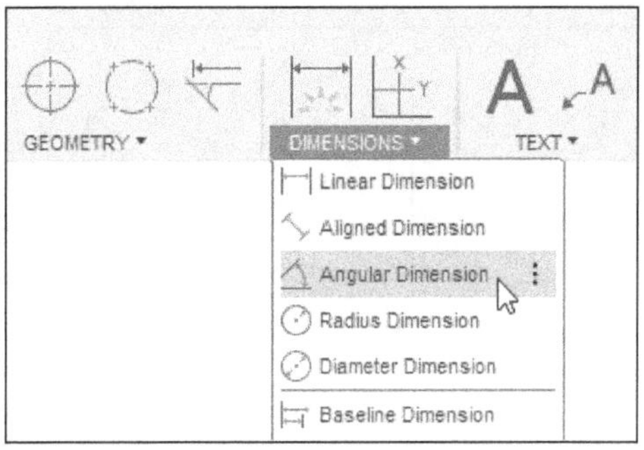

Figure-71. Angular Dimension tool

- Select two lines between which you want to create angular dimension or select an arc whose angular dimension is to be created. The dimension will get attached to cursor; refer to Figure-72.

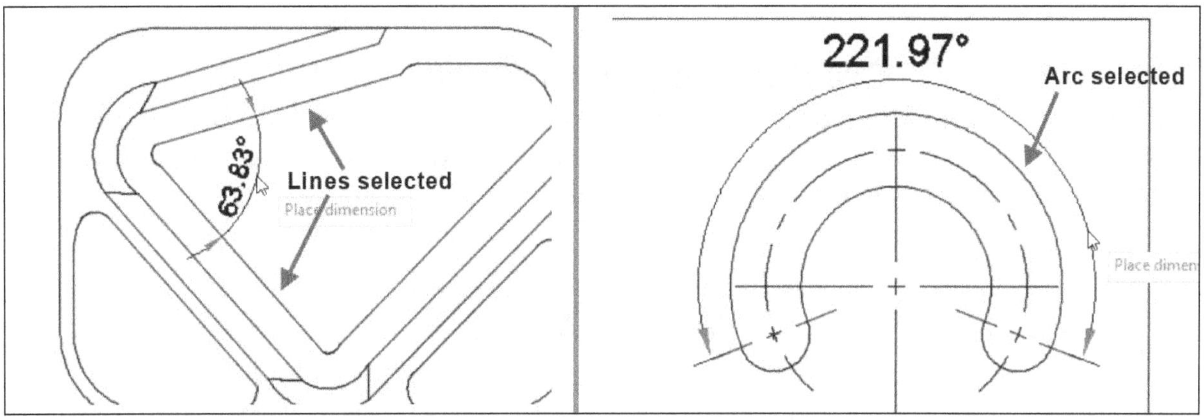

Figure-72. Creating angular dimension

- Click at desired location to place the dimension.

Creating Radius Dimension

The **Radius Dimension** tool is used to apply radius dimension to selected arc, circle, and circular edges. The procedure to use this tool is given next.

- Click on the **Radius Dimension** tool from **DIMENSIONS** panel in the **Toolbar**; refer to Figure-73. You will be asked to select circular edge or circle in the drawing.

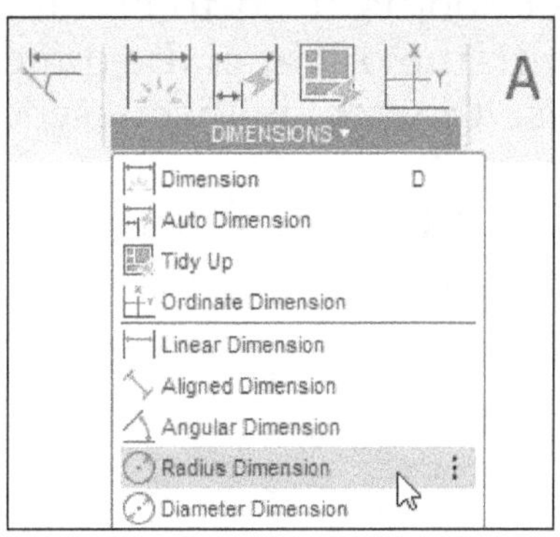

Figure-73. Radius Dimension tool

- Click at desired entity. The radius dimension will get attached to cursor; refer to Figure-74.

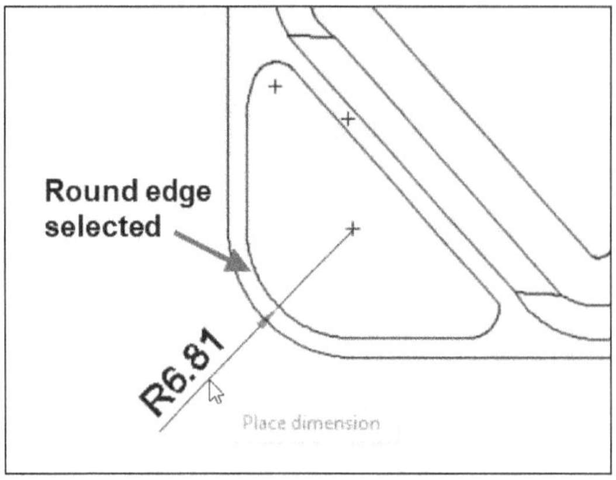

Figure-74. Creating radius dimension

- Click at desired location to place the dimension.

Creating Diameter Dimension

The **Diameter Dimension** tool is used to create diameter dimension for selected round edges, circles, and fillets in the drawing; refer to Figure-75. The procedure to use this tool is similar to **Radius Dimension** tool.

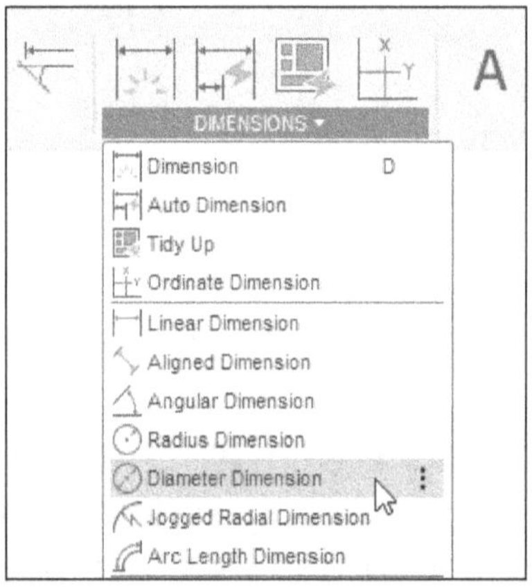

Figure-75. Diameter Dimension tool

Jogged Radial Dimension

The **Jogged Radial Dimension** tool is used to create radius dimension of a circle, arc, or polyline arc segment with the origin of the dimension and a jog at convenient locations. The procedure to use this tool is discussed next.

- Click on the **Jogged Radial Dimension** tool from the **DIMENSIONS** panel in the **Toolbar**; refer to Figure-76. You will be asked to select an arc or circle.

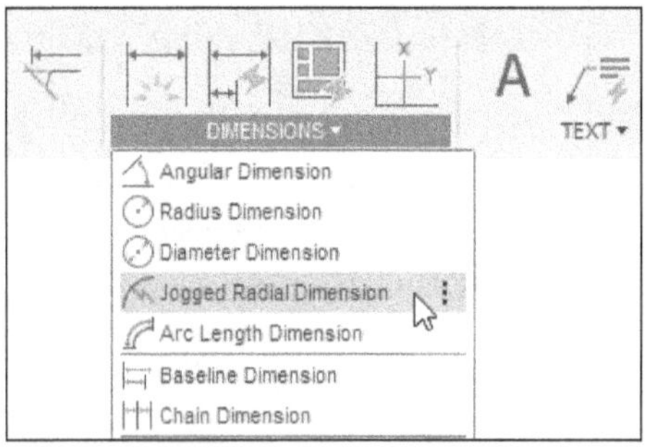

Figure-76. Jogged Radial Dimension tool

- Select desired arc or circle in the drawing. You will asked to specify center location.
- Select center location for the dimension. The jogged radial dimension will get attached to the cursor; refer to Figure-77.

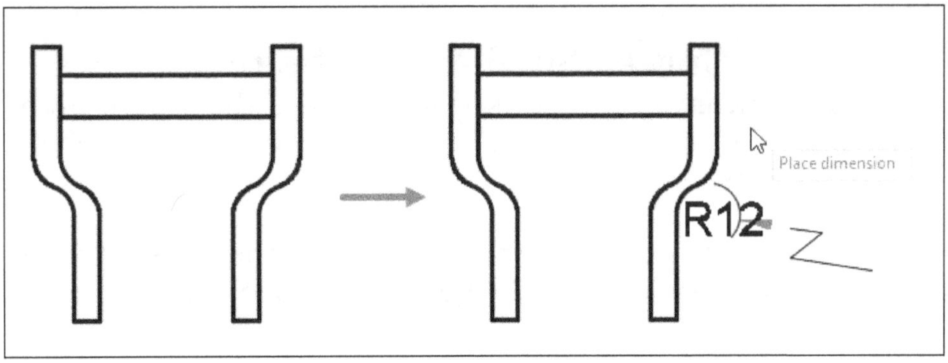

Figure-77. Radial jogged dimension attached to cursor

- Click at desired location to specify the jog location. The jogged radial dimension will be created.

Arc Length Dimension

The **Arc Length Dimension** tool is used to measure the distance along an arc or a polyline arc segment. The procedure to use this tool is discussed next.

- Click on the **Arc Length Dimension** tool from **DIMENSIONS** panel in the **Toolbar**; refer to Figure-78. You will be asked to select an arc or polyline arc segment.

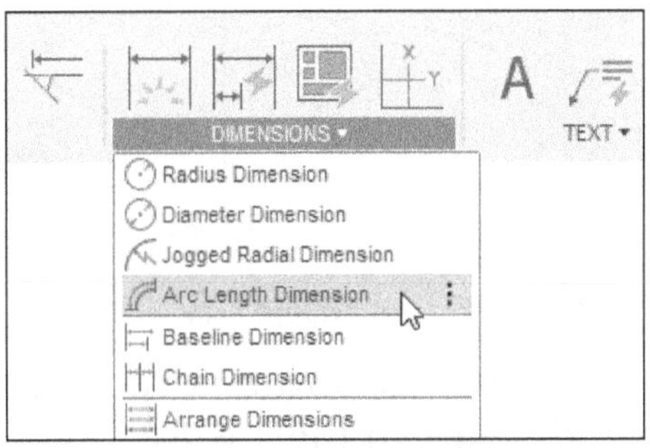

Figure-78. Arc Length Dimension tool

- Select desired arc in the drawing. The distance dimension will get attached to the cursor; refer to Figure-79.

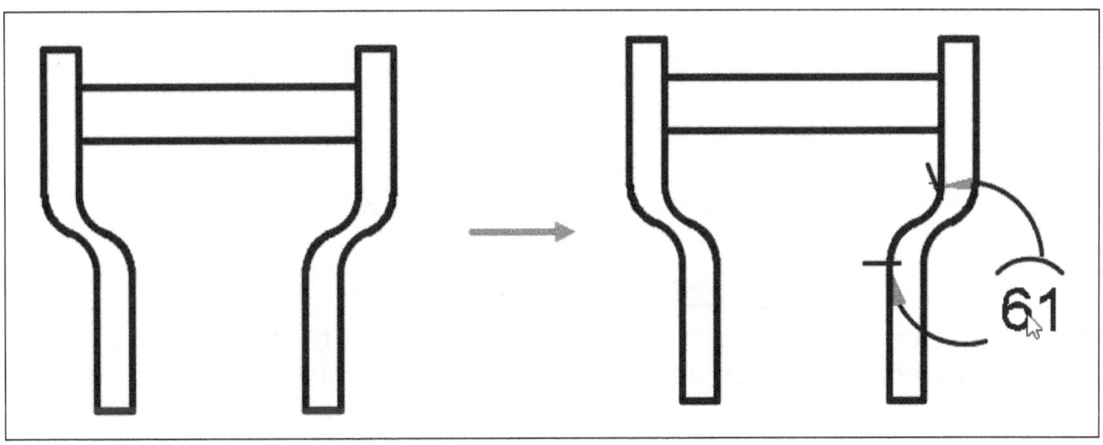

Figure-79. Arc distance measured

- Click at desired location to place the dimension or right click to select to select **Full Arc Dimension** or **Partial** option from the context menu to specify full or partial length of the arc, respectively.

Curve Min Max Dimension

The **Curve Min Max Dimension** tool is used to measure the minimum or maximum distance between an edge and a curve or between two curves. The procedure to use this tool is discussed next.

- Click on the **Curve Min Max Dimension** tool from the **DIMENSIONS** panel in the **Toolbar**; refer to Figure-80. You will be asked to select the first edge or curve.

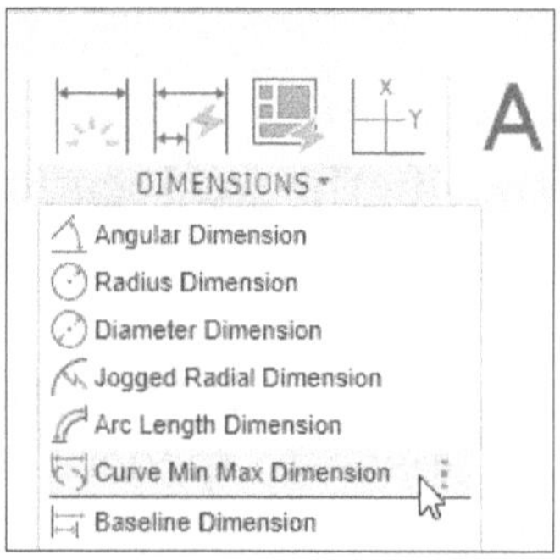

Figure-80. Curve Min Max Dimension tool

- Select first desired edge or curve from the drawing area; refer to Figure-81. You will be asked to select the second curve.

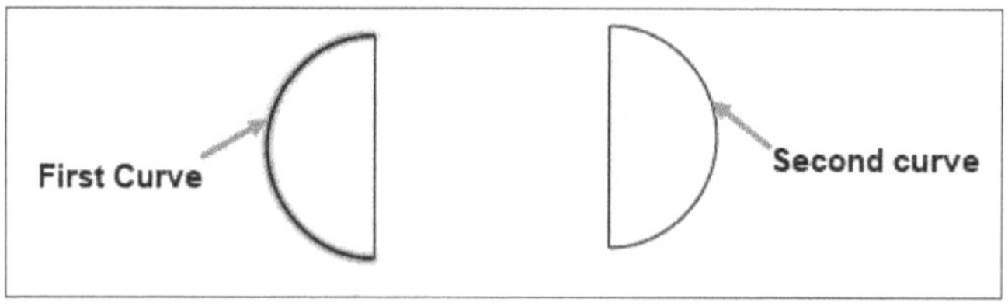

Figure-81. Selecting the curve on min max dimension

- Move the cursor away and select second desired curve. The dimension between the curves will be measured; refer to Figure-82.

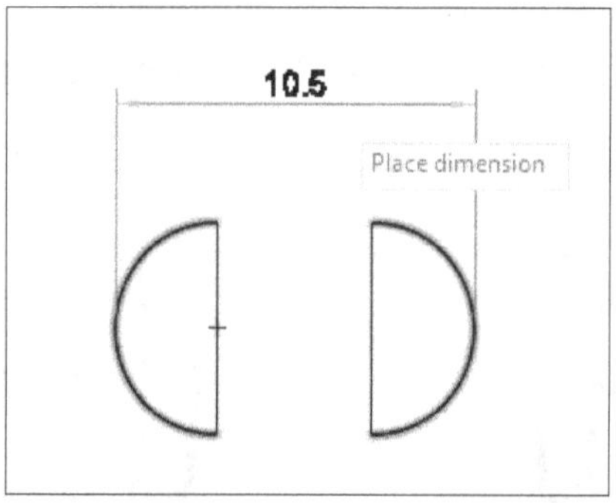

Figure-82. Min Max dimension created

Baseline Dimensioning

The baseline dimensioning is performed when you want to create linear dimensions with respect to one common base reference. The procedure to create baseline dimensions is given next.

- Click on the **Linear Dimension** tool from **DIMENSIONS** panel in the **Toolbar**; refer to Figure-83, and create a linear dimension which will be used as base line; refer to Figure-84.

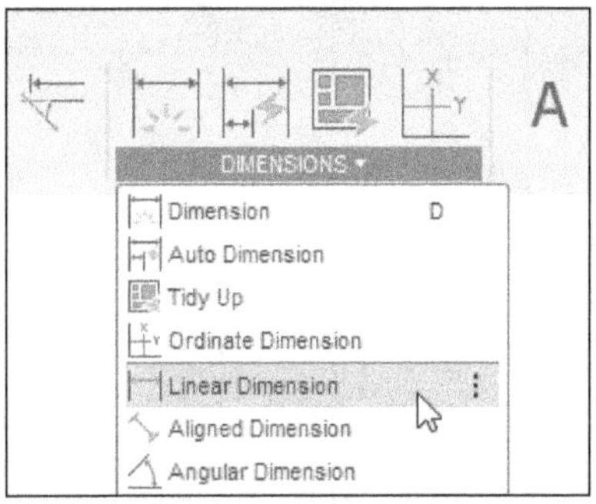

Figure-83. Linear Dimension tool

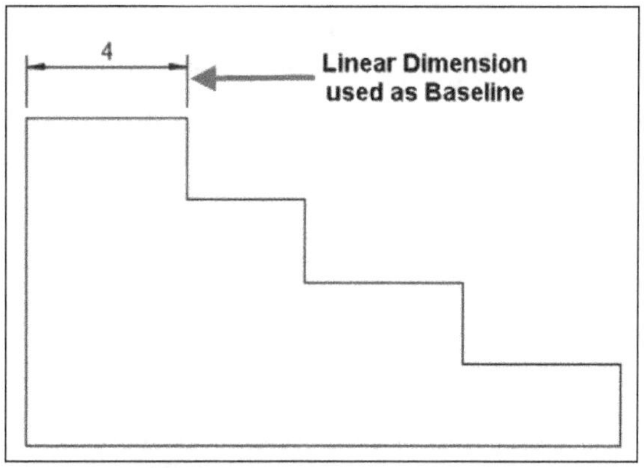

Figure-84. Linear dimension used as baseline

- Click on the **Baseline Dimension** tool from **DIMENSIONS** panel in the **Toolbar**; refer to Figure-85, and select one of the leg of base dimension.

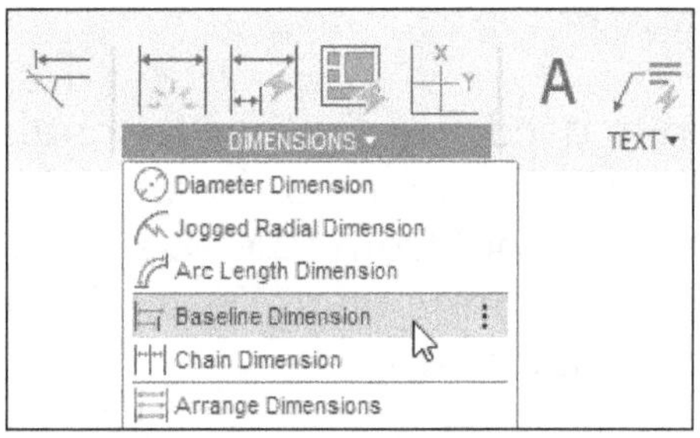

Figure-85. Baseline Dimension tool

- A new dimension will be generated with one end point fixed to selected leg and other end point of dimension attached to cursor; refer to Figure-86.

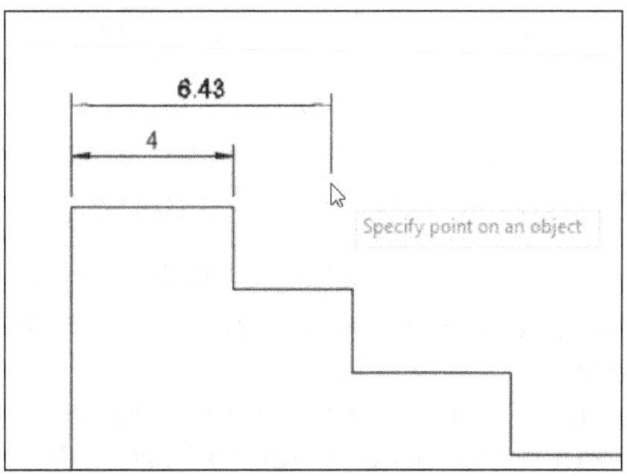

Figure-86. Placing baseline dimension

- Select desired point of sketch to create the dimension. You will be asked to specify end point for another dimension. Select desired points to create required dimensions. Once you have created required dimensions, press **ENTER** from keyboard to complete the process. The dimensions will be generated; refer to Figure-87.

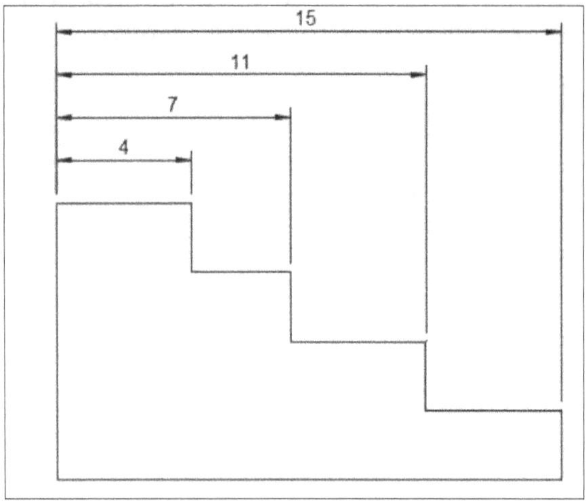

Figure-87. Baseline dimension created

Chain Dimensioning

In chain dimensioning, all the linear dimensions are placed side by side. The procedure to use this tool is given next.

- Create a linear dimension to used as reference for chain dimensioning as discussed in previous section for baseline dimensioning.
- Click on the **Chain Dimension** tool from **DIMENSIONS** panel in the **Toolbar**; refer to Figure-88, and select the base dimension. You will be asked to specify end point of new dimension; refer to Figure-89.

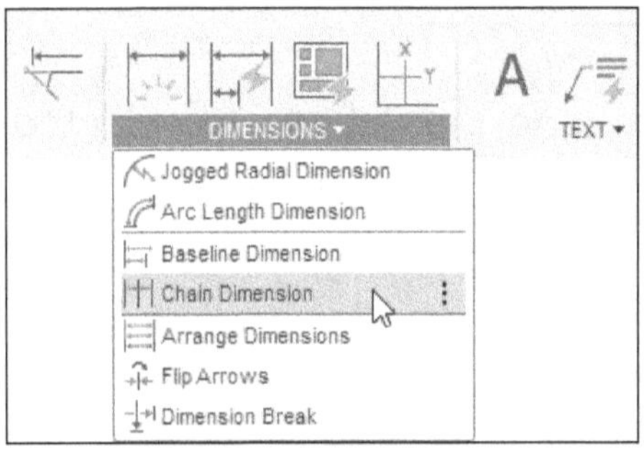

Figure-88. Chain Dimension tool

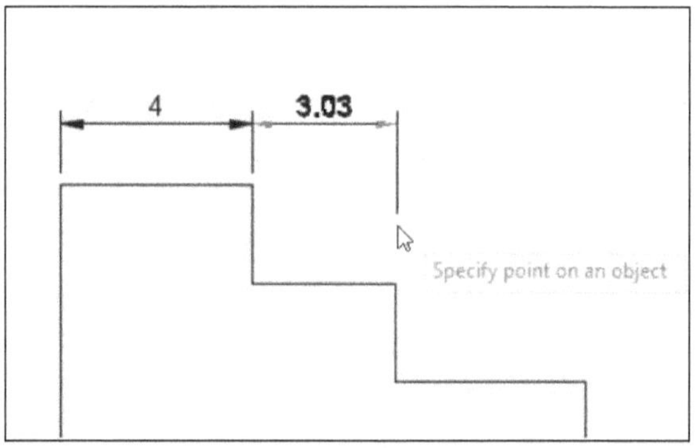

Figure-89. Placing chain dimensions

- Click at desired location to specify end point. You will be asked to specify end point of another dimension.
- Click at desired locations to create required dimensions and then press **ENTER** to exit. The dimensions will be created; refer to Figure-90.

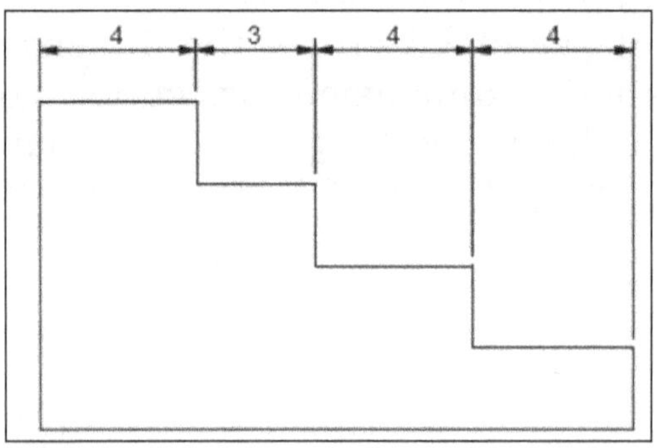

Figure-90. Chain dimensions created

Arrange Dimensions

The **Arrange Dimension** tool is used to stack or align linear or angular dimensions in the **DRAWING** workspace. The procedure to use this tool is discussed next.

- Click on the **Arrange Dimensions** tool from **DIMENSIONS** panel in the **Toolbar**; refer to Figure-91. The **ARRANGE DIMENSIONS** dialog box will be displayed; refer to Figure-92.

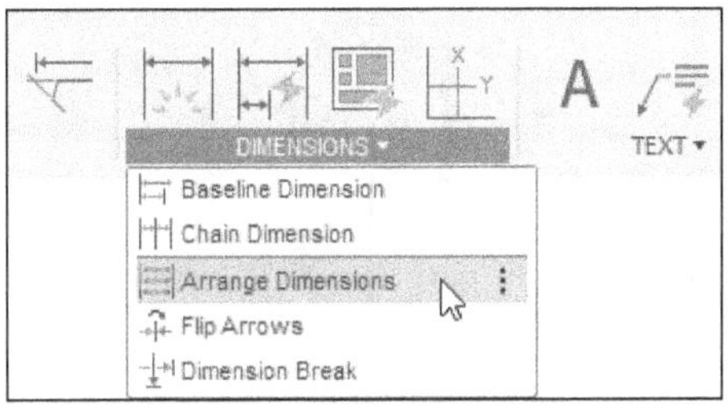

Figure-91. Arrange Dimensions tool

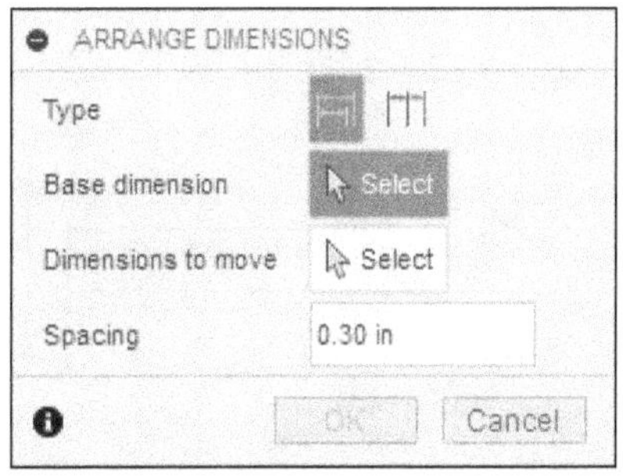

Figure-92. ARRANGE DIMENSIONS dialog box

- Select **Stack** or **Align** option from **Type** section of the dialog box to create the dimension.
- The **Base dimension** selection option is active by default. Select the base dimension that all other dimensions will be stacked above/below; refer to Figure-93.

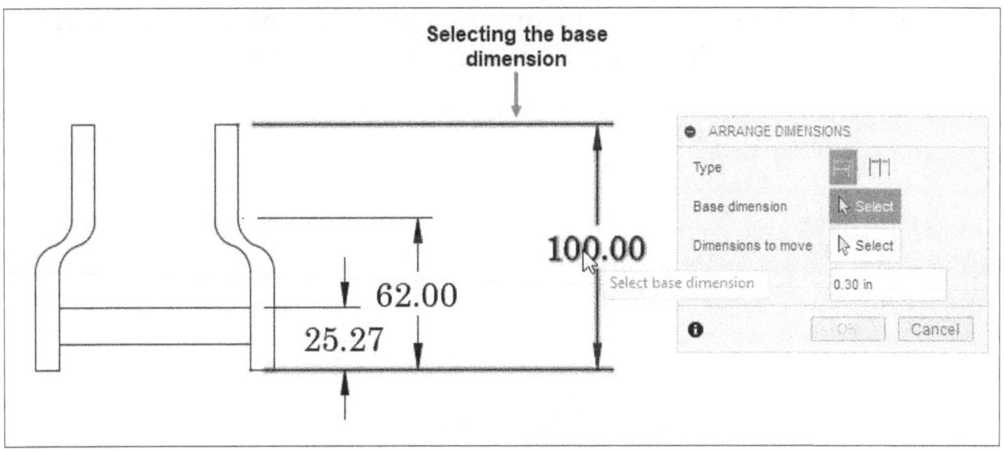

Figure-93. Selecting the base dimension

- After selecting the base dimension, select the other dimensions that you want to stack; refer to Figure-94.

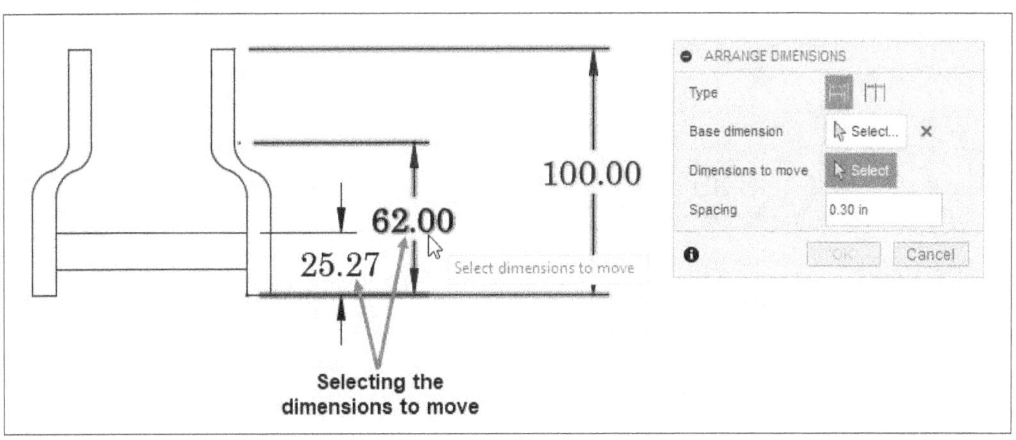

Figure-94. Selecting the dimensions to move

- Specify desired spacing between stacked dimensions in the **Spacing** edit box of the dialog box.
- After specifying desired parameters, click on the **OK** button from the dialog box. The dimensions will be arranged; refer to Figure-95.

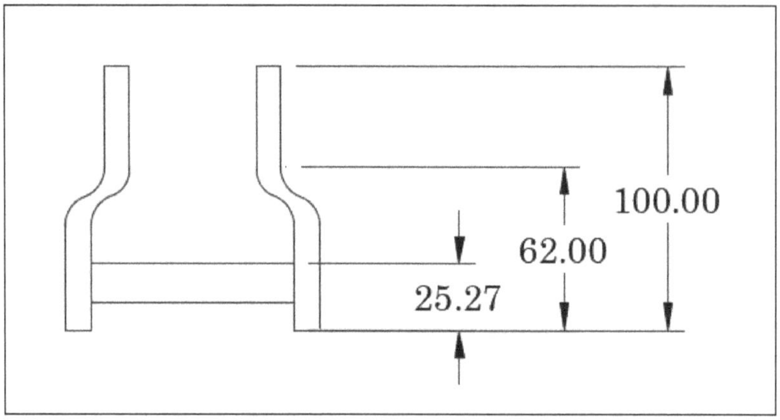

Figure-95. Dimensions arranged

Match Dimension

The **Match Dimension** tool is used to replicate the format of the selected dimension in the drawing workspace in Fusion. The procedure to use this tool is discussed next.

- Click on the **Match Dimension** tool from **DIMENSIONS** panel in the **Toolbar**; refer to Figure-96. You will be asked to select the source dimension.

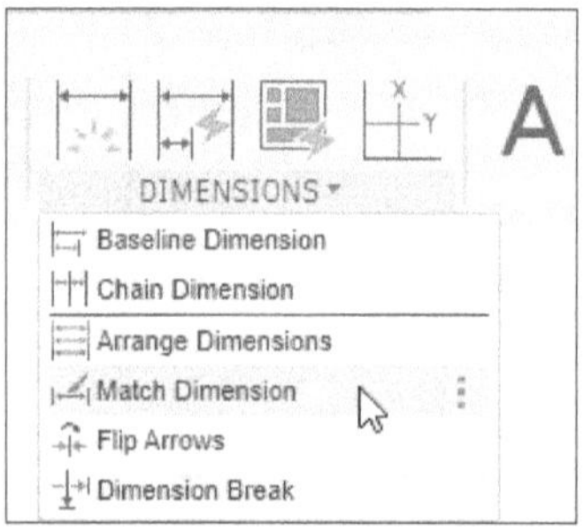

Figure-96. Match Dimension tool

- Select desired source dimension from the drawing area; refer to Figure-97. You will be asked to select the destination dimension.

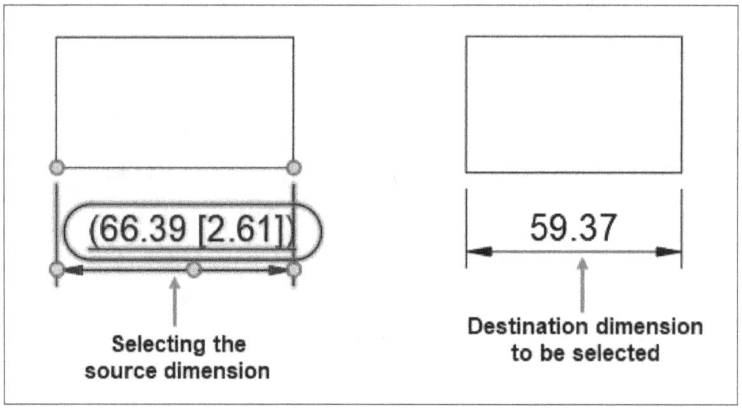

Figure-97. Selecting the source dimension

- Select desired destination dimension to be matched from the drawing area. The dimensions will be matched; refer to Figure-98.

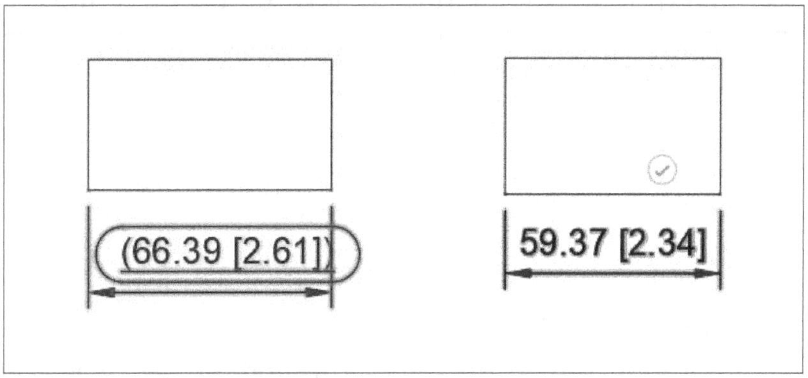

Figure-98. Dimensions matched

Flip Arrows

The **Flip Arrows** tool is used to flip the direction of the selected dimension arrow. The procedure to use this tool is discussed next.

- Click on the **Flip Arrow** tool from **DIMENSIONS** panel in the **Toolbar**; refer to Figure-99. You will be asked to select the dimension.

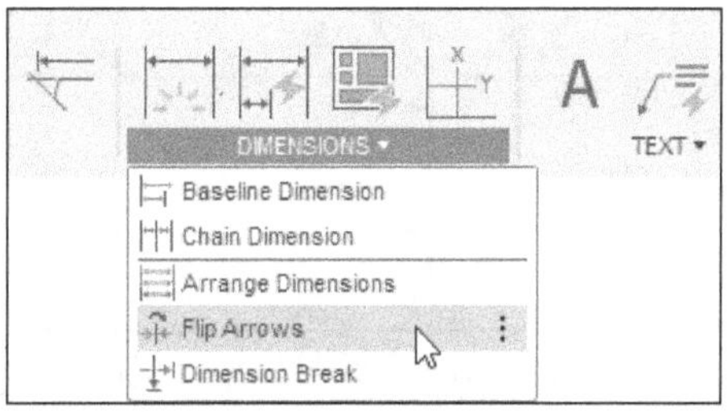

Figure-99. Flip Arrows tool

- Select desired dimension to flip the arrow direction. The arrow direction will be flipped; refer to Figure-100.

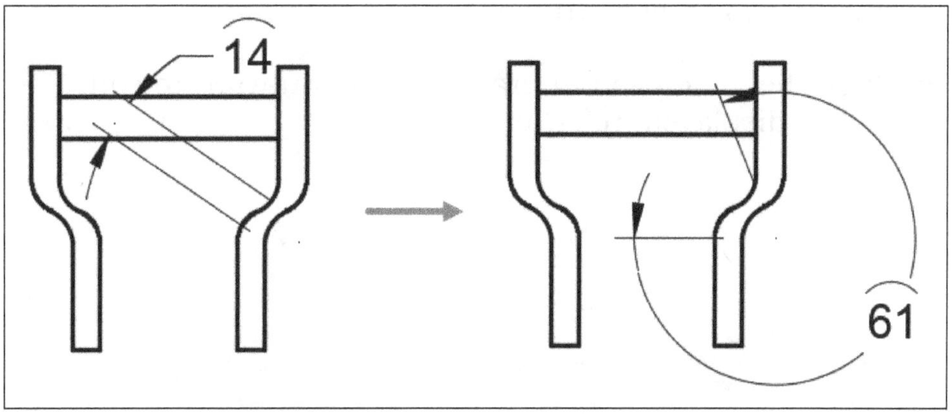

Figure-100. Arrow direction flipped

Dimension Break

The **Dimension Break** tool is used to resolve intersecting dimensions in the drawing. This tool adds/removes break in selected dimension. The procedure to use this tool is given next.

- Click on the **Dimension Break** tool from **DIMENSIONS** panel in the **Toolbar**; refer to Figure-101. The **DIMENSION BREAK** dialog box will be displayed; refer to Figure-102, and you will be asked to select the dimension to add or remove break.

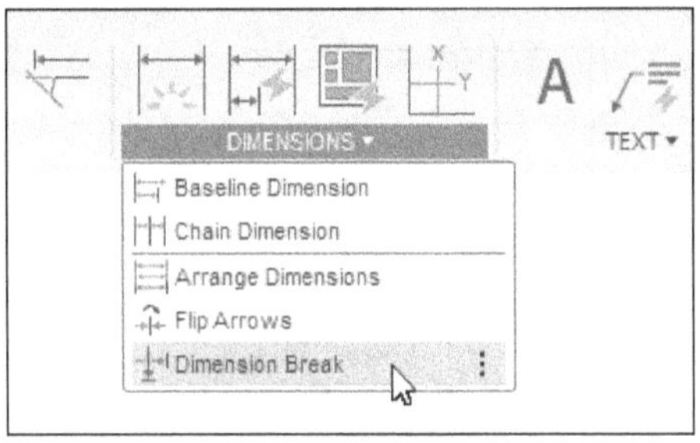

Figure-101. Dimension Break tool

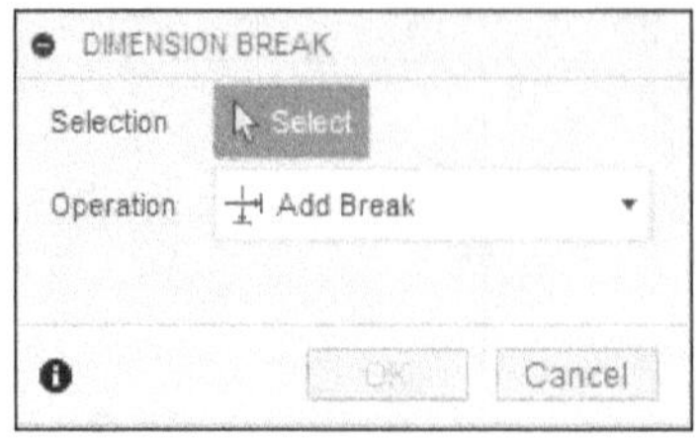

Figure-102. DIMENSION BREAK dialog box

- Select desired dimension and then select the **Add Break** or **Remove Break** option from the **Operation** drop-down to perform respective action. In our case, we are selecting **Add Break** option from the drop-down to add break in intersecting dimension.
- Click on the **OK** button from the dialog box. The selected operation will be performed on the dimension; refer to Figure-103.

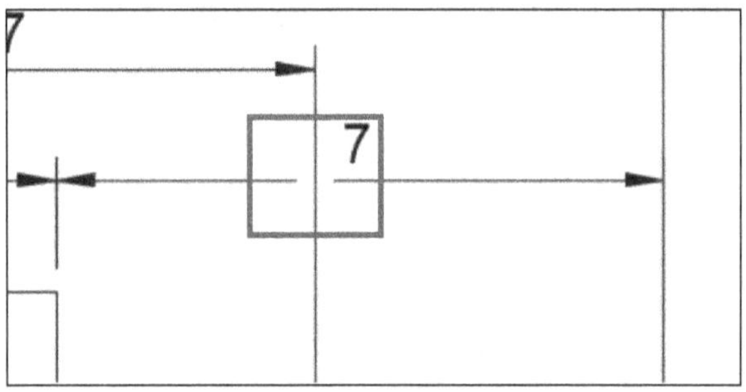

Figure-103. Dimension after applying Add Break

EDITING DIMENSIONS

Once you have generated dimensions, there are some cases where you need to provide special symbols with dimensions or you want to modify the value of dimension. The procedure to edit dimension is given next.

- Double-click on the dimension in drawing that you want to edit. The **DIMENSION** dialog box will be displayed; refer to Figure-104.

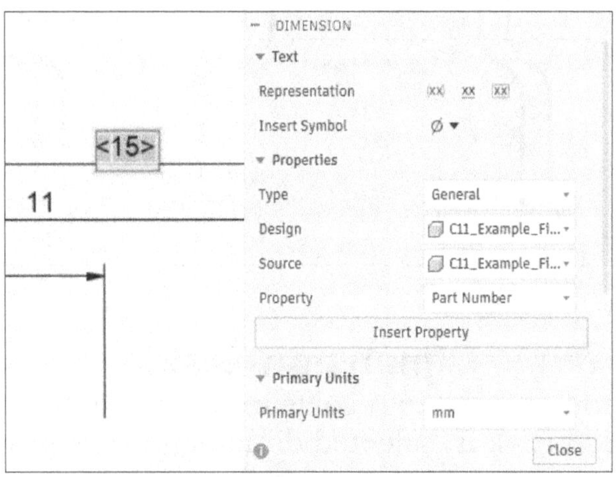

Figure-104. DIMENSION dialog box

- Select desired button from **Representation** section in the **Text** node to make the dimension as reference dimension, not to scale, and theoretically exact; refer to Figure-105.

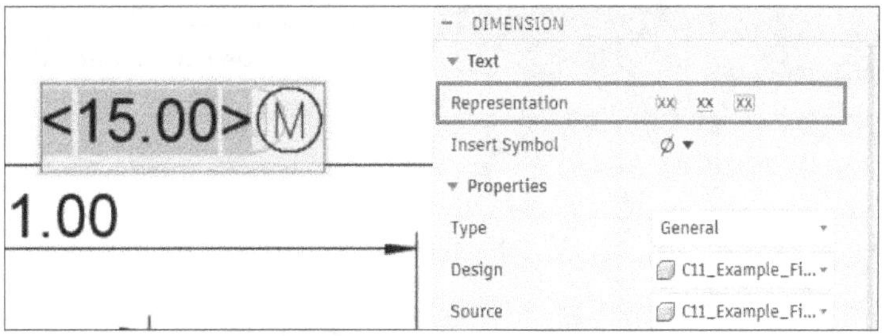

Figure-105. Representation options

- Click at desired place in dimension box and select desired symbol to be inserted. The symbol will be added to dimension; refer to Figure-106.

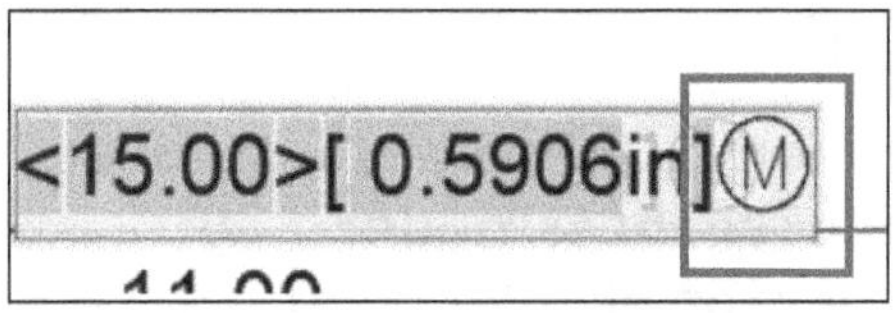

Figure-106. Symbol added to dimension

- Select desired option from **Type** drop-down in the **Properties** section to define type of dimension to be assigned. Select the **General** option from drop-down if the dimension falls in general category, select the **Physical** option from drop-down if it is a physical property like mass, or select the **Parameter** option if it is a parameter like diameter, length,angle etc.
- Select desired option from the **Source** drop-down to define the hierarchy level in model from which you want to link the source of dimension in assembly.
- Select desired option in **Property** drop-down to define the type for selected property and click on the **Insert Property** button to insert property as text in the dimension.
- Select desired unit from **Primary Units** drop-down in the **Primary Units** node.
- Select desired precision level and tolerance precision level from **Linear Precision** and **Linear Tolerance Precision** drop-downs, respectively.
- Select desired option from **Zeros/Units** section to add/remove zeros and units to/from the dimension.
- Select the **Alternate Units** check box to also display dimensions in inches if they are in mm and vice-versa; refer to Figure-107.

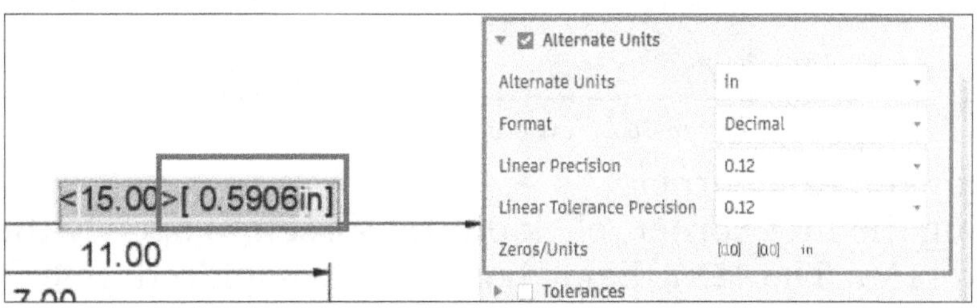

Figure-107. Alternate units

- Select the **Tolerances** check box and select desired type of tolerance from the **Type** drop-down to apply tolerance to dimension. Select the **Symmetrical** option if tolerance is equal in both negative and positive directions. Select the **Deviation** option if tolerance is different in positive and negative directions. Select the **Limit** option if you want to display upper and lower limit of dimension. Select the **Fit** option to apply standard Hole-Shaft tolerances; refer to Figure-108.

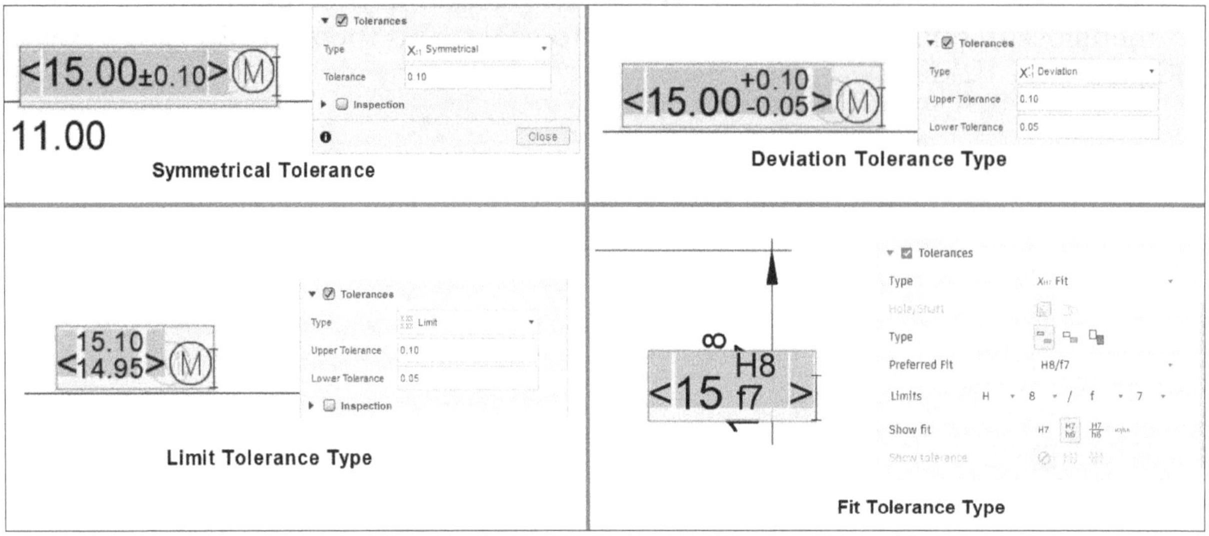

Figure-108. Tolerance types

- After selecting desired option from drop-down, specify desired value of tolerance in edit boxes below it in **Tolerances** node.
- Similarly, select the **Inspection** check box and set desired parameters if you want to define inspection rate of current dimension.
- After specifying parameters, click on the **Close** button or click anywhere in blank space of drawing to exit the tool.

CREATING TEXT

The **Text** tool is used to insert text into the active drawing. The procedure to use this tool is discussed next.

- Click on the **Text** tool from **TEXT** panel; refer to Figure-109. The **Text** tool is activated and you will be asked to draw a text box.

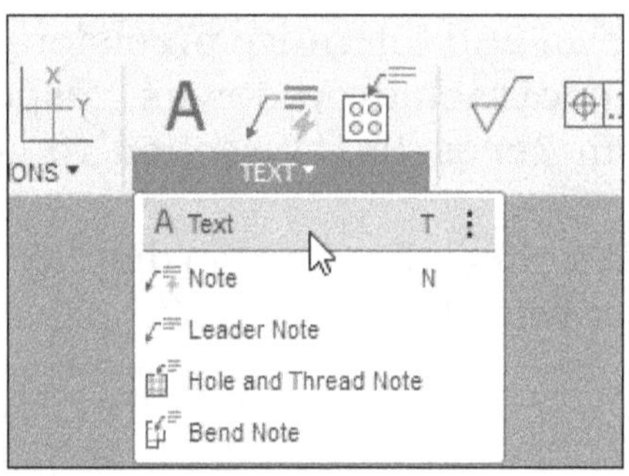

Figure-109. Text tool

- Click to specify the first corner.
- After specifying the first corner, click on the screen to specify the second corner; refer to Figure-110. The **TEXT** dialog box will be displayed; refer to Figure-111.

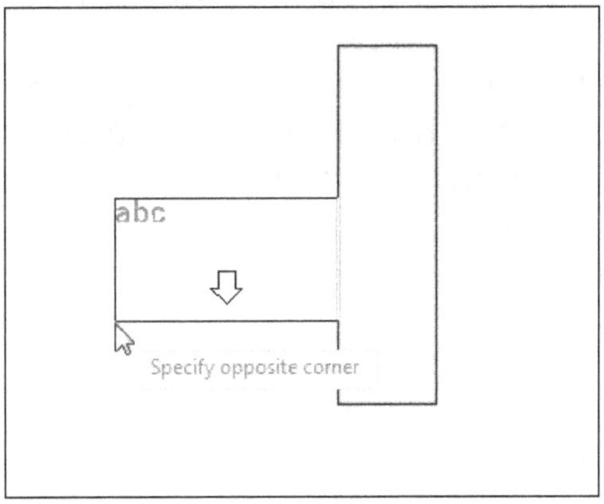

Figure-110. Specifying second corner

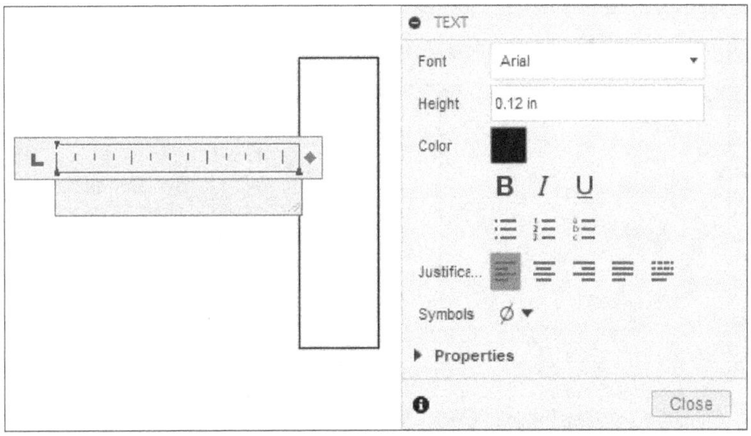

Figure-111. TEXT dialog box displayed

- Click on the **Font** drop-down and select required font for text.
- Click in the **Height** edit box and specify the height of text.
- Click on the **Select Color** button from **Color** section. The **Color Picker** dialog box will be displayed from which you can select desired color for the text.
- Set the other parameters and type desired text in the **Text** box.
- Click on **Close** button. The text will be added in drawing sheet.

CREATING NOTE

The **Note** tool automatically creates different type of note based on the type of object you select on the current sheet. The procedure to use this tool is discussed next.

- Click on the **Note** tool from **TEXT** panel in the **Toolbar**; refer to Figure-112. The **NOTE** dialog box will be displayed; refer to Figure-113.

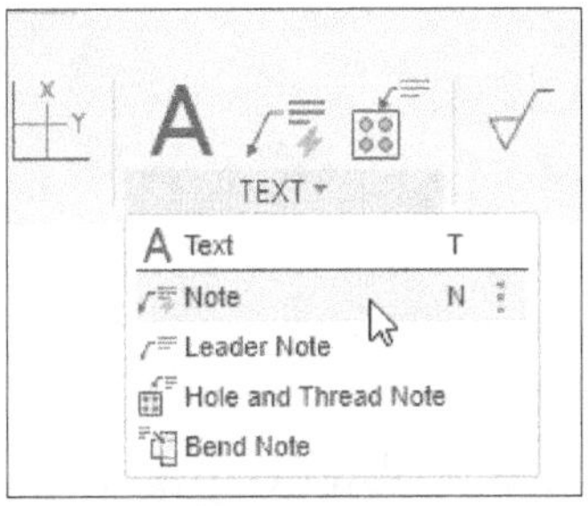

Figure-112. Note tool

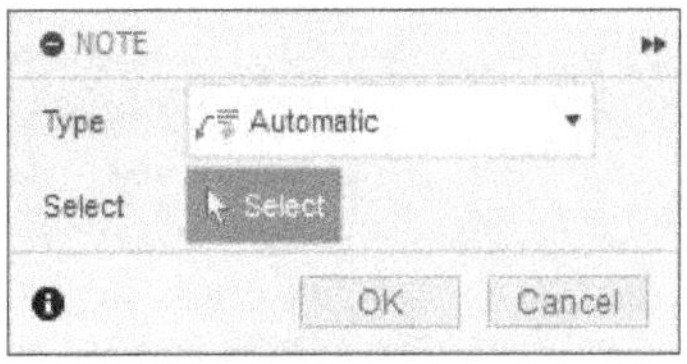

Figure-113. NOTE dialog box

- The **Automatic** option in **Type** drop-down of **NOTE** dialog box is selected by default.

- Select **Leader Note** option from **Type** drop-down to create a multiline text object with a leader that associates the note to a component or feature.
- Select **Hole and Thread Note** option from **Type** drop-down to create a hole or thread note associated with a hole or thread feature.
- Select **Bend Note** option from **Type** drop-down to create a bend note associated with a sheet metal flat pattern bend.
- Here, we selected **Leader Note** option in **Type** drop-down of dialog box or click on **Leader Note** tool from **TEXT** panel of **Toolbar**; refer to Figure-112. The tool will be activated.
- The **Select** button of **Select** section is active by default. Click on the drawing to select the start point. An arrow will be attached to the cursor.
- Click on the screen to place text box. The text box will be displayed along with **TEXT** dialog box; refer to Figure-114.

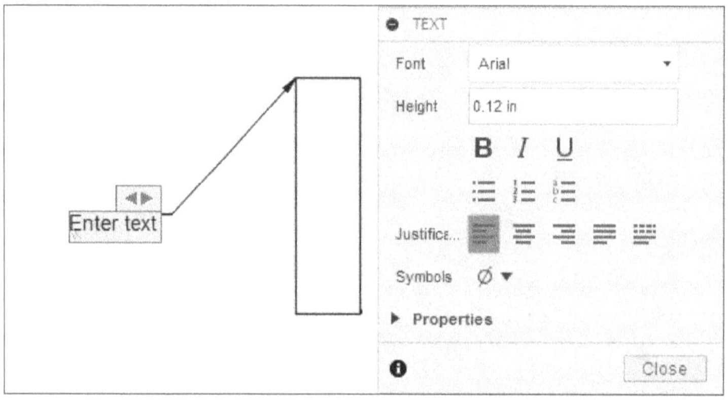

Figure-114. Leader text box

- Set desired parameter in **TEXT** dialog box and type the text in text box.
- After specifying the parameters, click on **Close** button from **TEXT** dialog box.

Similarly, you can use the **Hole and Thread Note** tool and **Bend Note** tool.

APPLYING SURFACE TEXTURE

The **Surface Texture** tool is used to apply surface finish symbol to objects in drawing. The procedure to use this tool is discussed next.

- Click on the **Surface Texture** tool from **SYMBOLS** panel in the **Toolbar**; refer to Figure-115. The tool will be activated.

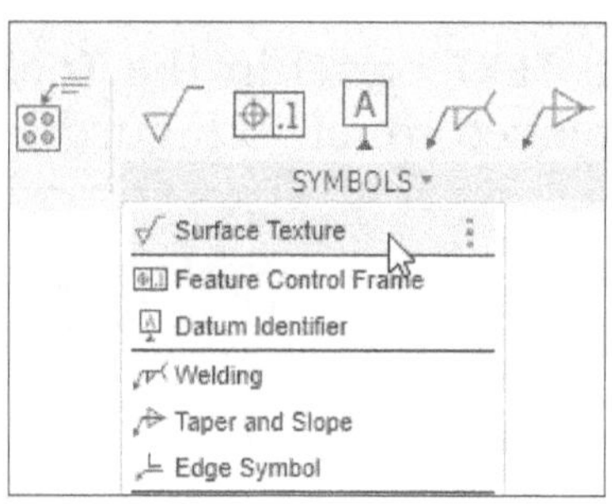

Figure-115. Surface Texture tool

- Click on the model in drawing view to select object. An arrow will be displayed on the selected part.

- Click to select the second point for leader or press **ENTER** key to place the symbol directly on selected face. The **SURFACE TEXTURE** dialog box will be displayed; refer to Figure-116.

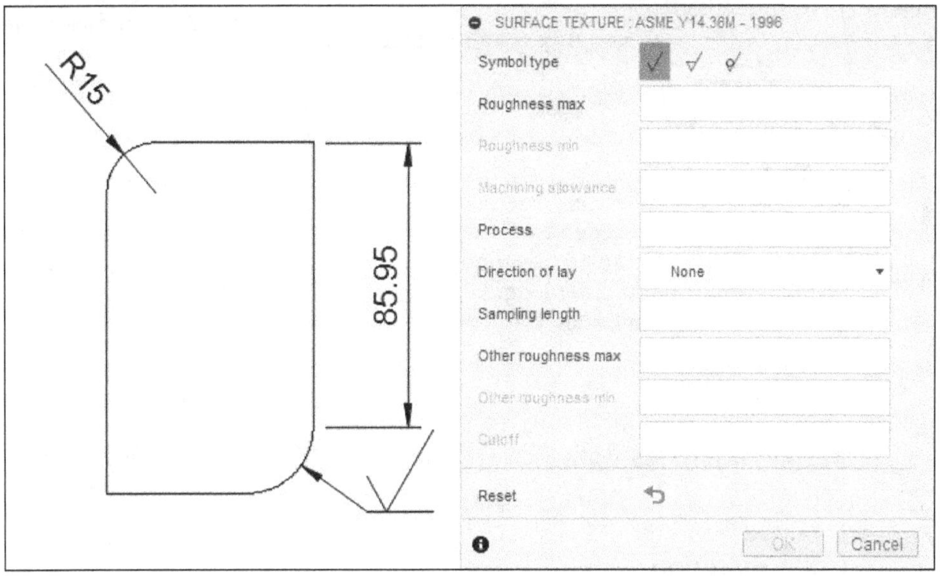

Figure-116. SURFACE TEXTURE dialog box

- Select desired surface finish symbol button from **Symbol type** section.
- Specify the maximum and minimum roughness of surface texture in the **Roughness max** and **Roughness min** edit boxes of the dialog box, respectively.
- Specify desired values in the **Machining allowance** and **Process** edit boxes.
- Select the lay direction option as desired from **Direction of lay** drop-down.
- Specify the other parameters in the dialog box as desired.
- Click on the **Reset** button to reset all the properties to default values.
- After specifying desired parameters, click on the **OK** button from **SURFACE TEXTURE** dialog box; refer to Figure-117.

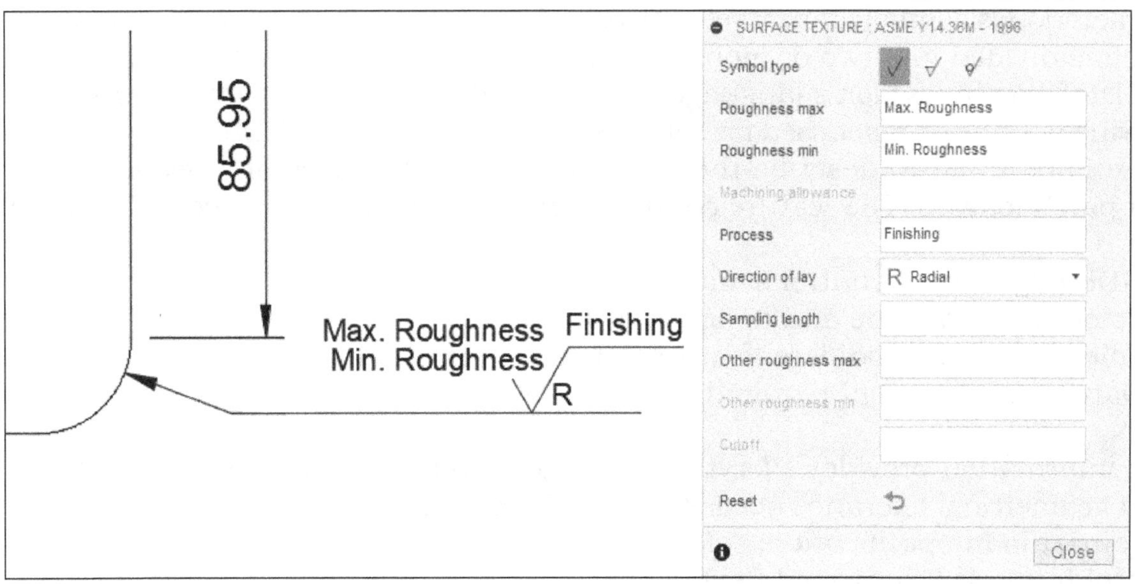

Figure-117. Applying Surface Texture

Surface Texture Symbols or Surface Roughness Symbols

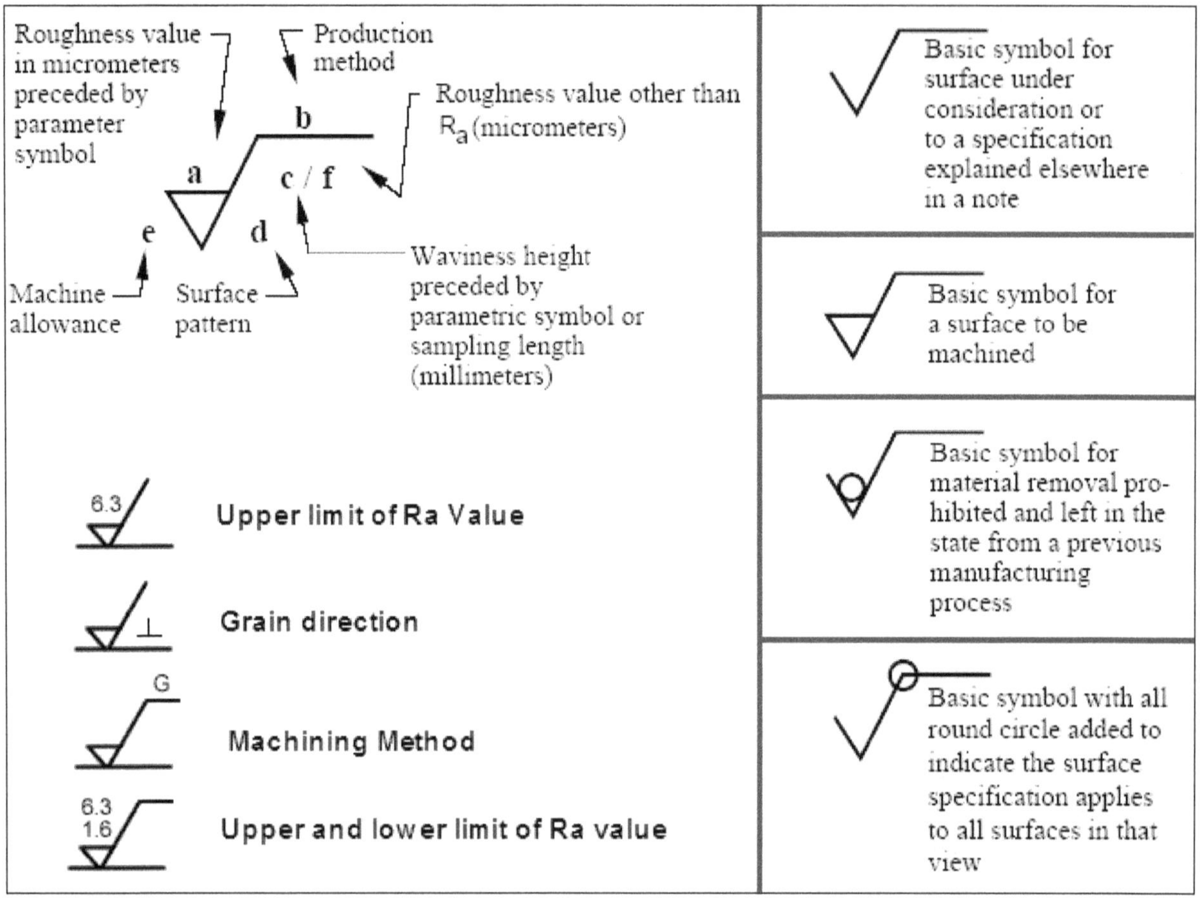

CREATING FEATURE CONTROL FRAME

The **Feature Control Frame** contains data for controlled specifications. It shows the characteristics symbol, datum reference, and tolerance value. It is a rectangular frame which is divided into two or more sections. The feature control frame is also known as GD&T box in laymen's language. The method to insert Feature Control Frame in drawing is same as discussed for **Surface Texture** symbol. In GD&T, a feature control frame is required to describe the conditions and tolerances of a geometric control on a part's feature. The feature control frame consists of four pieces of information:

1. GD&T symbol or control symbol
2. Tolerance zone type and dimensions
3. Tolerance zone modifiers: features of size, projections...
4. Datum references (if required by the GD&T symbol)

This information provides everything you need to know about geometry of part like what geometrical tolerance needs to be on the part and how to measure or determine if the part is in specification; refer to Figure-118. The common elements of feature control frame are discussed next.

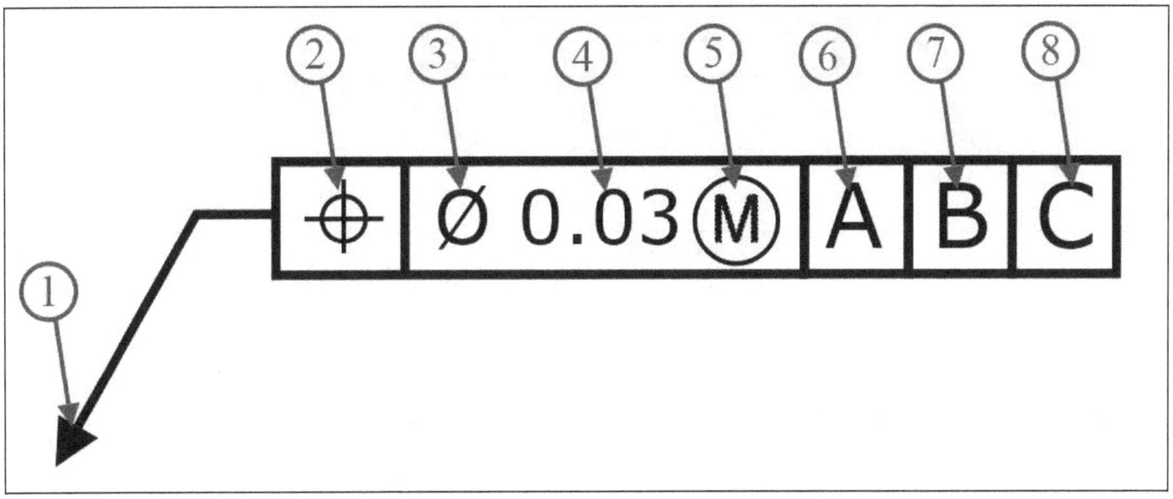

Figure-118. Feature control frame

1. **Leader Arrow** – This arrow points to the feature then the geometric control is placed on. If the arrow points to a surface then the surface is controlled by the GD&T. If it points to a diametric dimension then the axis is controlled by GD&T. The arrow is optional but helps clarify the feature being controlled.
2. **Geometric Symbol** – This is where your geometric control is specified.
3. **Diameter Symbol (if required)** – If the geometric control is a diametrical tolerance then the diameter symbol (Ø) will be in front of the tolerance value.
4. **Tolerance Value** – If the tolerance is a diameter you will see the Ø symbol next to the dimension signifying a diametric tolerance zone. The tolerance of the GD&T is in same unit of measure that the drawing is written in.
5. **Feature of Size or Tolerance Modifiers (if required)** – This is where you call out max material condition or a projected tolerance in the feature control frame.
6. **Primary Datum (if required)** – If a datum is required, this is the main datum used for the GD&T control. The letter corresponds to a feature somewhere on the part which will be marked with the same letter. This is the datum that must be constrained first when measuring the part. Note: The order of the datum is important for measurement of the part. The primary datum is usually held in three places to fix 3 degrees of freedom.
7. **Secondary Datum (if required)** – If a secondary datum is required, it will be to the right of the primary datum. This letter corresponds to a feature somewhere on the part which will be marked with the same letter. During measurement, this is the datum fixated after the primary datum.
8. **Tertiary Datum (if required)** – If a third datum is required, it will be to the right of the secondary datum. This letter corresponds to a feature somewhere on the part which will be marked with the same letter. During measurement, this is the datum fixated last.

Reading Feature Control Frame

The feature control frame forms a kind of sentence when you read it. Below is how you would read the frame in order to describe the feature.

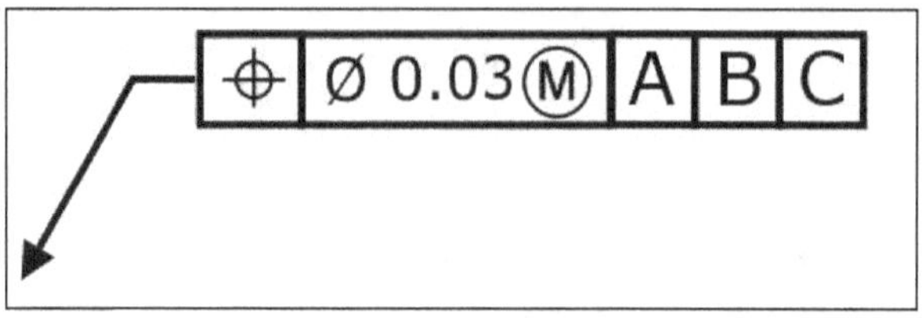

gives meaning of

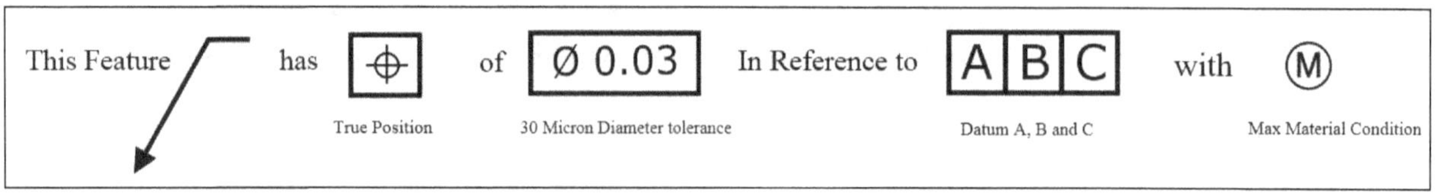

Meaning of various geometric symbols are given in Figure-119.

SYMBOL	CHARACTERISTICS	CATEGORY
—	Straightness	Form
⏥	Flatness	
○	Circulatity	
⌭	Cylindricity	
⌒	Profile of a Line	Profile
⌓	Profile of Surface	
∠	Angularity	Orientation
⊥	Perpendicularity	
//	Parallelism	
⌖	Position	Location
◎	Concentricity	
⌯	Symmetry	
↗	Circular Runout	Runout
⌰	Total Runout	

Figure-119. Geometric Symbols

Figure-120 and Figure-121 shows the use of geometric tolerances in real-world.

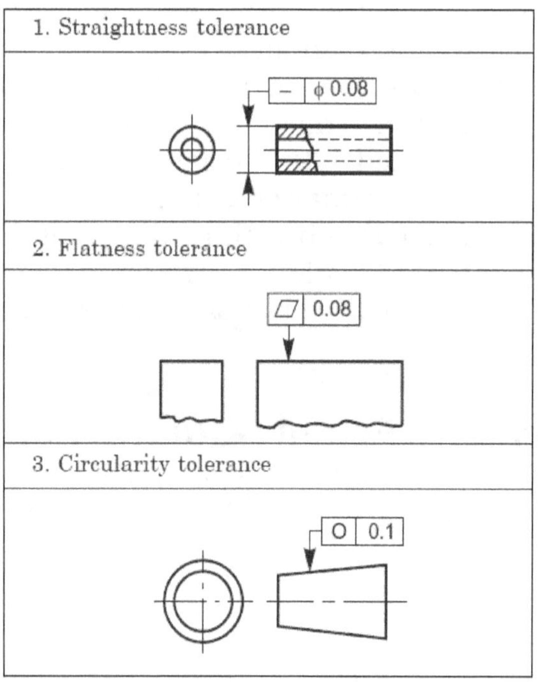

Figure-120. Use of geometric tolerance 1

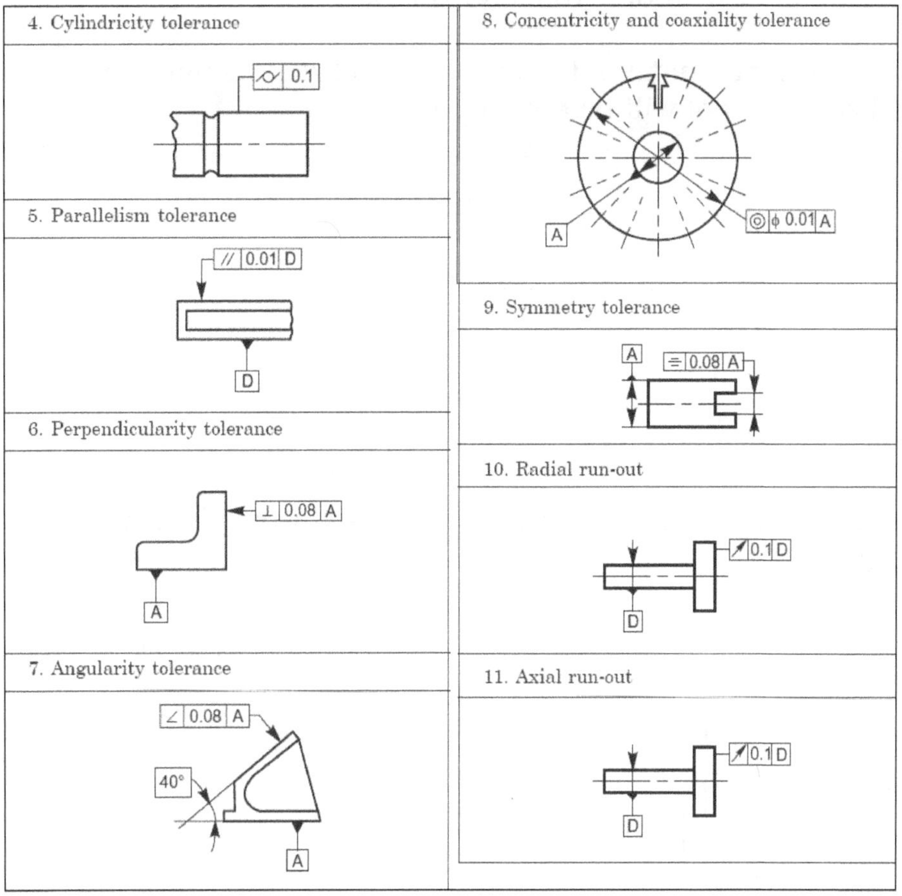

Figure-121. Use of geometric tolerance 2

Note that in applying most of the geometrical tolerances, you need to define a datum plane like in Perpendicularity, Parallelism, and so on. There are a few dimensioning symbols also used in geometric dimensioning and tolerances, which are given in Figure-122.

Symbol	Meaning	Symbol	Meaning
Ⓛ	LMC – Least Material Condition	⌖	Dimension Origin
Ⓜ	MMC – Maximum Material Condition	⌴	Counterbore
Ⓣ	Tangent Plane	⌵	Countersink
Ⓟ	Projected Tolerance Zone	↧	Depth
Ⓕ	Free State	⌓	All Around
∅	Diameter	↔	Between
R	Radius	✕	Target Point
SR	Spherical Radius	⌲	Conical Taper
S∅	Spherical Diameter	⌳	Slope
CR	Controlled Radius	□	Square
⟨ST⟩	Statistical Tolerance		
[77]	Basic Dimension		
(77)	Reference Dimension		
5X	Places		

Figure-122. Dimensioning symbols

The procedure to use this tool is discussed next.

- Click on the **Feature Control Frame** tool from **SYMBOLS** panel in the **Toolbar**; refer to Figure-123. The tool will be activated.

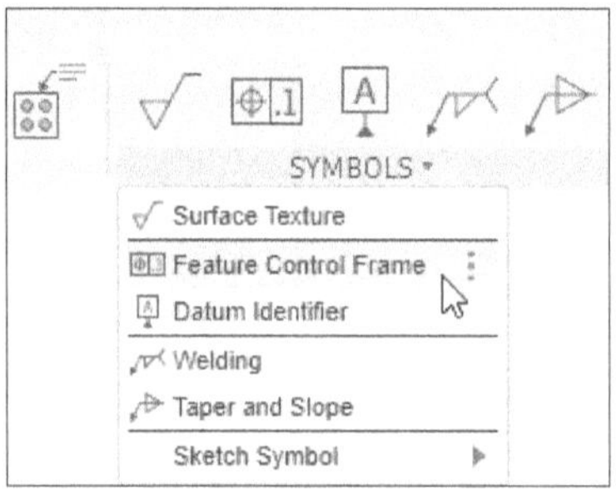

Figure-123. Feature Control Frame tool

- Click on the drawing to select the object. An arrow will be attached to the cursor; refer to Figure-124.

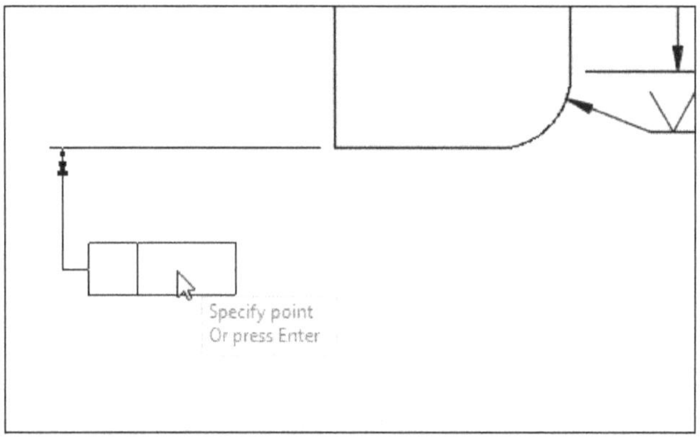

Figure-124. Placing the rectangular box

- Click on the screen to place the rectangular box and press **ENTER** key. The **FEATURE CONTROL FRAME** dialog box will be displayed; refer to Figure-125.

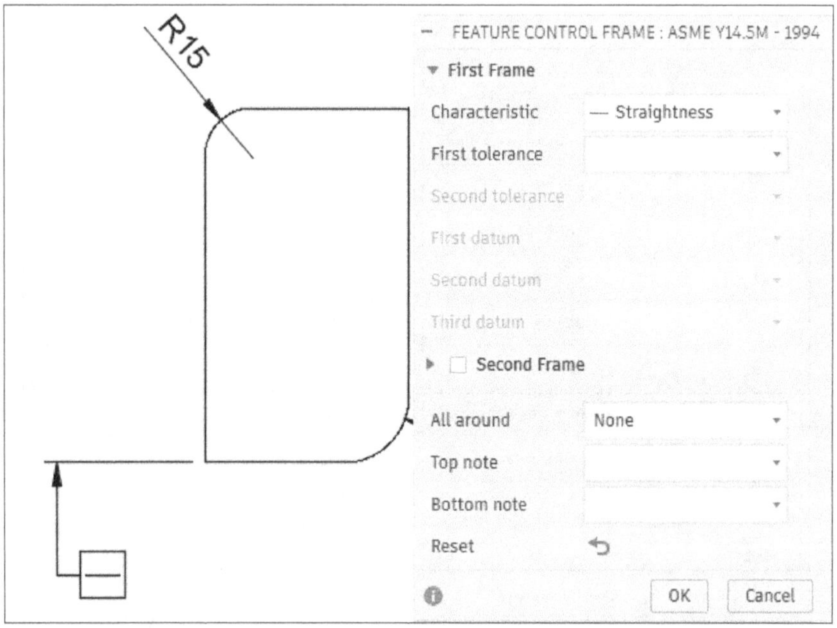

Figure-125. FEATURE CONTROL FRAME dialog box

- Expand the **First Frame** node and select required symbol from **Characteristic** drop-down. The selected symbol will be displayed in the feature frame rectangular box.
- Click in the **First tolerance** edit box and enter the value of tolerance. You can also add the required symbol; refer to Figure-126.

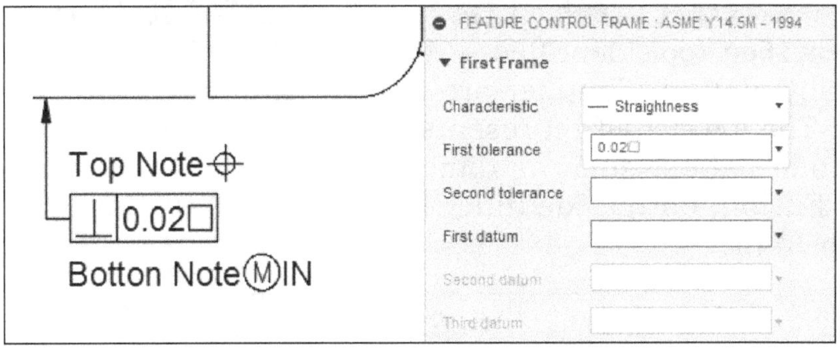

Figure-126. Adding tolerance

- Click on the **First datum** edit box and enter the value of datum as required; refer to Figure-127.

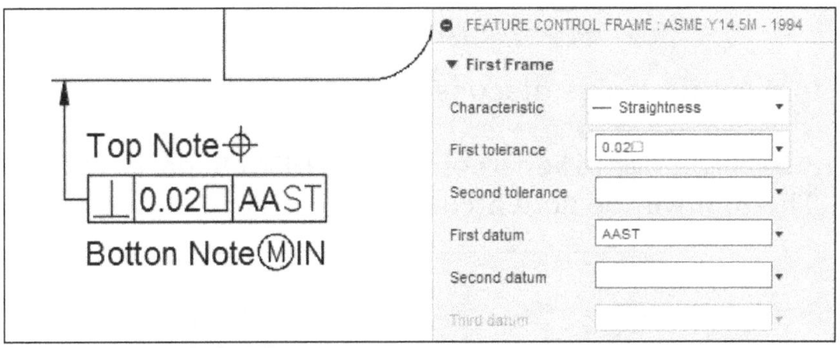

Figure-127. Specifying datum value

- Similarly enter the remaining parameters in respective edit boxes.
- Select the **Second Frame** check box of **FEATURE CONTROL FRAME** dialog box if you want to add second frame for the drawing. Feature Control Frames with two frames is also called Composite Feature Control Frame.
- Click in the **Top Note** edit box and enter the note. If you want to add any symbol then click on the drop-down button. A list of symbols will be displayed; refer to Figure-128.

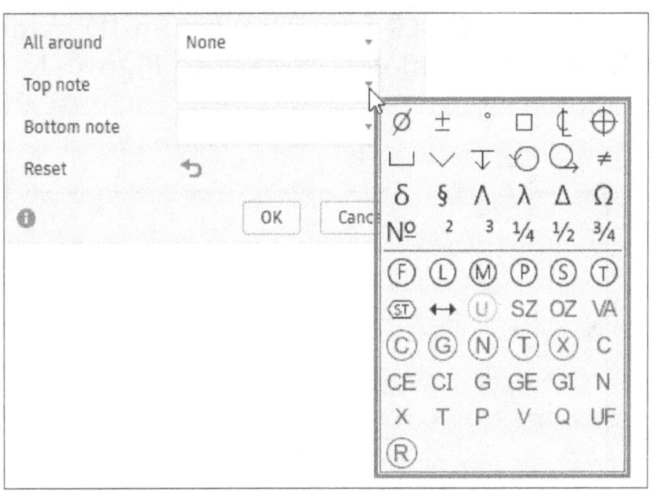

Figure-128. Adding symbols

- Click on required symbol. The selected symbol will be added over the feature control frame box. Similarly, you can set the symbol for **Bottom Note** edit box.
- After specifying the parameters, click on the **OK** button from **FEATURE CONTROL FRAME** dialog box to complete the process.

CREATING DATUM IDENTIFIER

The **Datum Identifier** tool identifies a datum feature for a feature control frame symbol. Generally, datum identifier are circular frames divided in two parts by a horizontal line. The lower half represents the datum feature and the upper half is for additional information, such as dimensions of the datum target area; refer to Figure-129. In Fusion, datum identifier is represented by datum identifying letter in a rectangular frame.

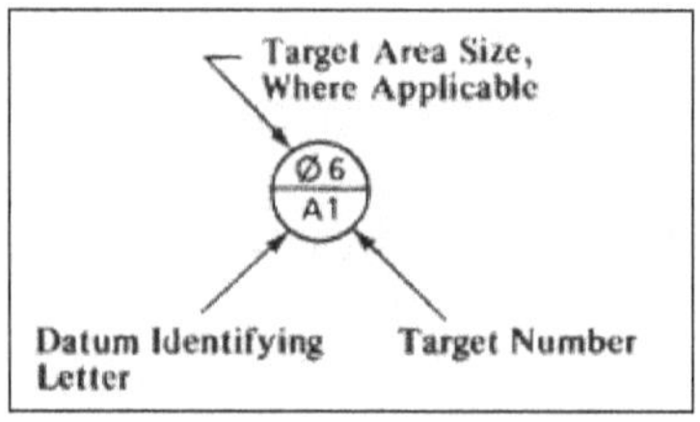

Figure-129. Datum target area

The procedure to use this tool is discussed next.

- Click on the **Datum Identifier** tool from **SYMBOLS** panel of **Toolbar**; refer to Figure-130. The tool will be activated.

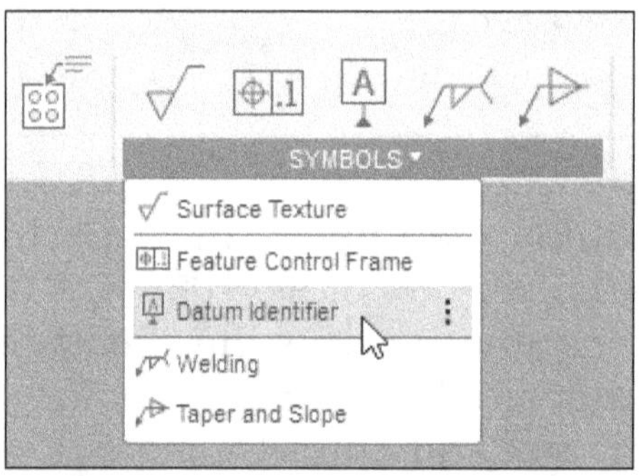

Figure-130. Datum Identifier tool

- Click on the drawing to select object. An arrow will be attached to the cursor.
- Specify the point and press **ENTER** key. The datum ID symbol will be displayed along with **DATUM IDENTIFIER** dialog box; refer to Figure-131.

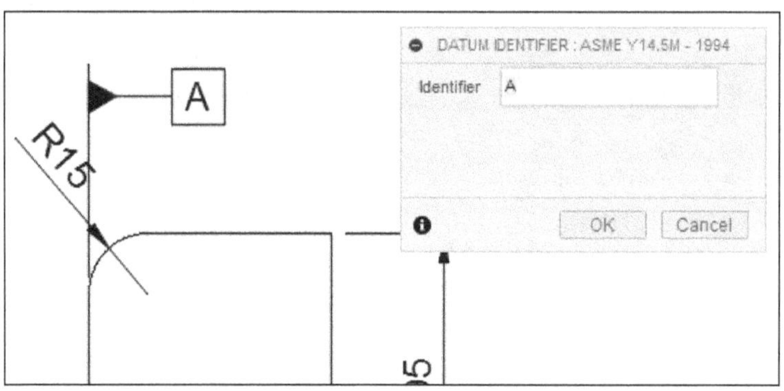

Figure-131. DATUM IDENTIFIER dialog box

- Modify the identifier as desired and click on the **OK** button from **DATUM IDENTIFIER** dialog box.

CREATING WELDING SYMBOL AND OTHER SYMBOLS

The **Welding** tool in **SYMBOLS** drop-down of **Ribbon** is used to insert welding symbols applied to selected edge/face. Using this tool, you can apply annotation to the edges where weld is to be performed. The procedure to place a weld symbol is similar to placing Feature Control Frame discussed earlier. Similarly, you can use the **Taper and Slope** tool from the **SYMBOLS** drop-down in the **DRAWING** tab of **Ribbon** to apply symbol defining taper/slope on selected edge.

GENERATING TABLES

The **Table** tool is used to generate empty table, parts list, and bend table of the assembly model linked with drawing. The procedure to use this tool is discussed next.

- Click on the **Table** tool from **TABLES** drop-down in the **Toolbar**; refer to Figure-132. The **TABLE** dialog box will be displayed along with attached empty table; refer to Figure-133.

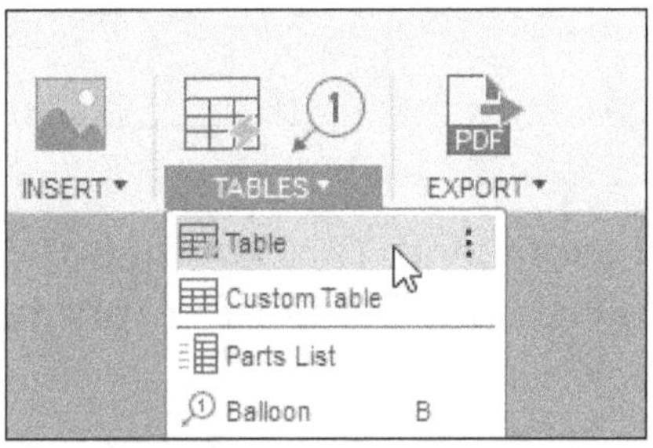

Figure-132. Table tool

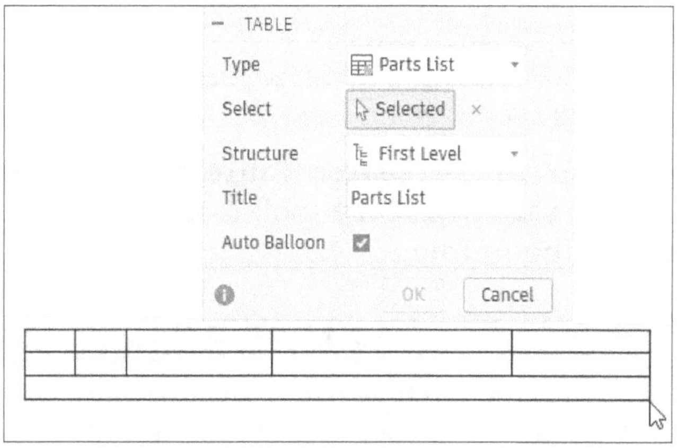

Figure-133. TABLE dialog box along with empty table

- The **Automatic** option in **Type** drop-down of **TABLE** dialog box is selected by default. The **Automatic** option automatically creates a parts list or bend table, based on the contents of the current sheet.
- Select **Custom Table** option from **Type** drop-down to create an empty table.
- Select **Parts List** option from **Type** drop-down to create a parts list based on an assembly, storyboard, component, or sheet metal component reference. Note that Parts list is also called Bill of Materials or BOM.
- Select **Bend Table** option from **Type** drop-down to create a bend table based on a sheet metal flat pattern reference.
- Select **Hole Table** option from **Type** drop-down to create a hole table based on the origin you place in a drawing view.
- Select **Revision History** option from **Type** drop-down to create a revision history for the active sheet.
- Here, we are selecting the **Parts List** option from **Type** drop-down of dialog box or click **Parts List** tool from **TABLES** drop-down in the **Toolbar**; refer to Figure-132.

- The **Select** button of **Select** section is active by default. Select desired view on the current sheet.
- Select **First Level** option from **Structure** drop-down to include first level components only.
- Select **All Level** option from **Structure** drop-down to include all components in the assembly.
- Select **Auto Balloon** check box to create balloon automatically to identify components in an assembly.
- Click at desired location in the drawing to place the parts list. Parts list will be generated with balloons; refer to Figure-134.

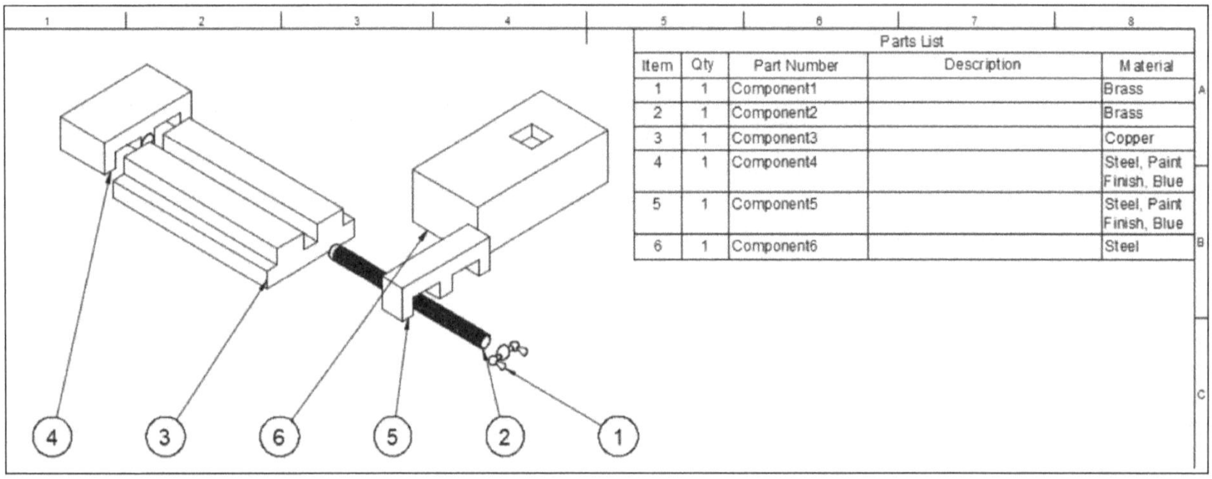

Figure-134. Parts List of assembly

Similarly, you can use **Custom Table (Empty Table)** tool, **Bend Table** tool, **Hole Table** tool, and **Revision History** tool. Note that you can edit the fields of empty table by double-clicking in them.

GENERATING BALLOON

The **Balloon** tool is used to generate balloons for components in drawing. The procedure to use this tool is discussed next.

- Click on the **Balloon** tool from **TABLES** drop-down; refer to Figure-135. The **BALLOON** dialog box will be displayed; refer to Figure-136 and you will be asked to select the component.

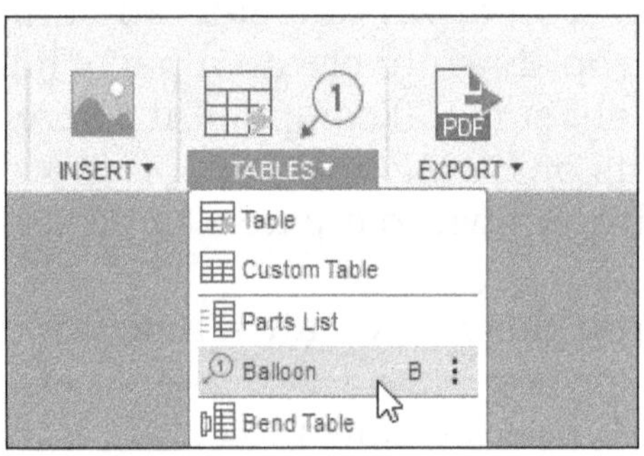

Figure-135. Balloon tool

Figure-136. BALLOON dialog box

- By default, the **Standard** option is selected in the dialog box, so straight lines are created with balloon. If you want to create spline attached to balloon in place of line then select the **Patent** option from the **Type** drop-down.

- Click on desired edge of component. On selection of edge, an arrow will be attached to the cursor.
- Click at desired location to place the balloon; refer to Figure-137 and Figure-138.

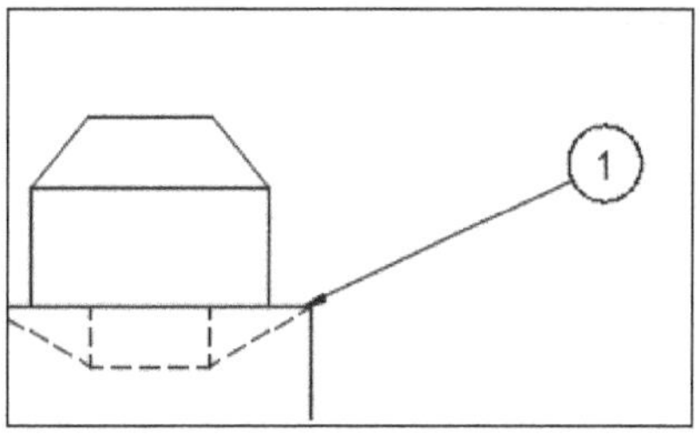

Figure-137. Placing balloon with Standard option

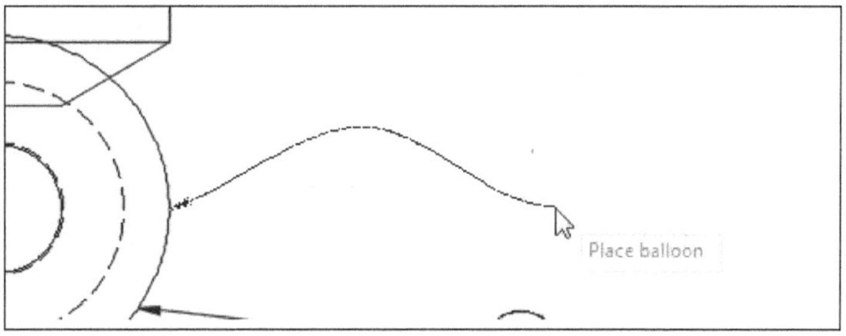

Figure-138. Placing balloon with Patent option

BEND IDENTIFIER AND TABLE

The **Table** tool discussed earlier works in a different way for sheet metal component. If you are generating drawing for a sheetmetal part then **Table** tool will generate bend table for the part and like balloons in assembly, bend identifiers are used to identify bends as per the table. The process is given next.

- After starting drawing environment, using flat pattern of a sheet metal part, click on the **Bend Identifier** tool from the **TABLES** drop-down in the **Toolbar**; refer to Figure-139. You will be asked to select the bends in flat pattern.
- Click on the sheet metal bends in drawing one by one. Bend identifiers will be assigned to the bends; refer to Figure-140.

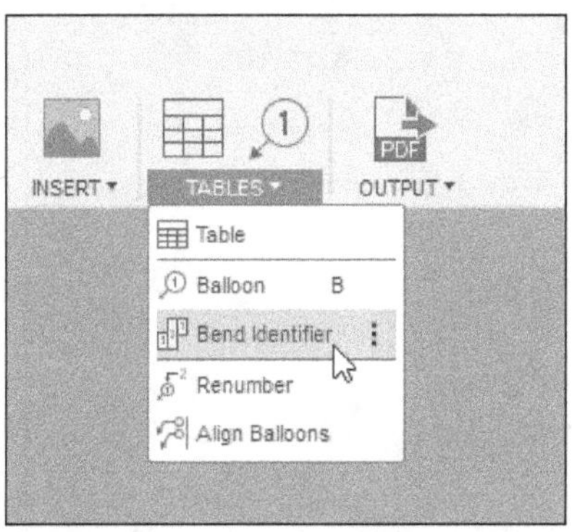

Figure-139. Bend Identifier tool

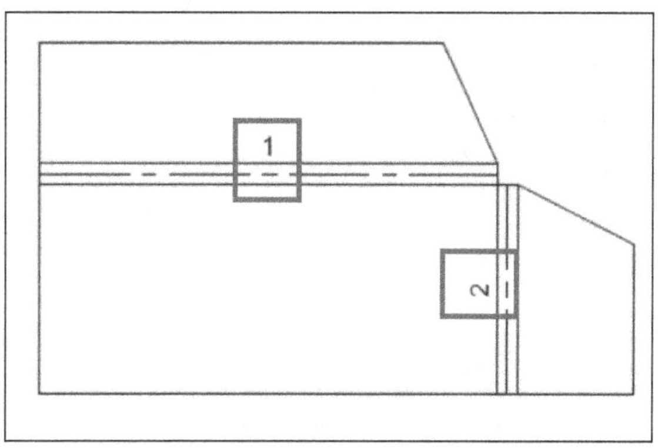

Figure-140. Bend identifier assigned

- Press **ESC** to exit the tool.
- Click on the **Table** tool from **TABLES** drop-down in the **Toolbar** and place the bend table at desired location; refer to Figure-141.

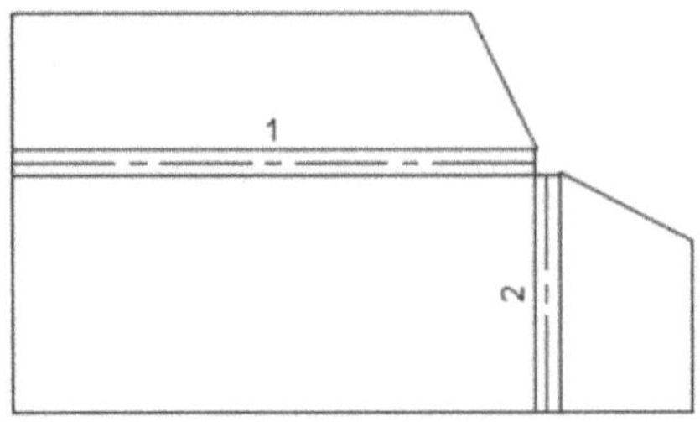

Bend Table			
ID	Direction	Angle	Radius
1	Up	120.00	2.50
2	Up	120.00	2.50

Figure-141. Flat pattern with bend table

REVISION MARKER

The **Revision Marker** tool is used to create non-associative and associative revision markers with and without a leader in a **DRAWING** workspace. The procedure to use this tool is discussed next.

- Click on the **Revision Marker** tool from **TABLES** panel in the **Toolbar**; refer to Figure-142. The **REVISION MARKER** dialog box will be displayed; refer to Figure-143.

Figure-142. Revision Marker tool

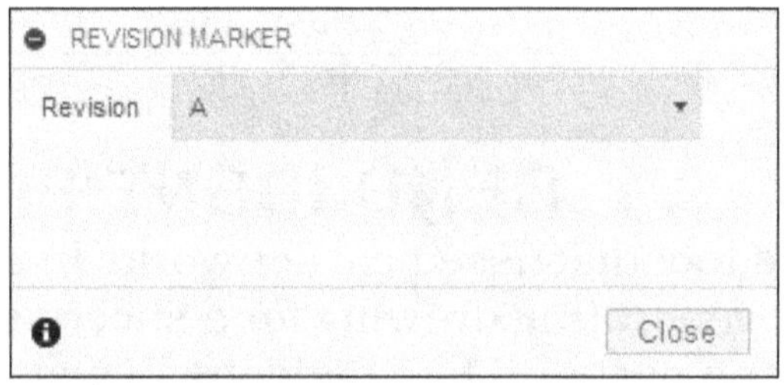

Figure-143. REVISION MARKER dialog box

- Select desired revision from **Revision** drop-down, if more revisions are available.
- Select an object or specify a point to place the revision marker; refer to Figure-144.

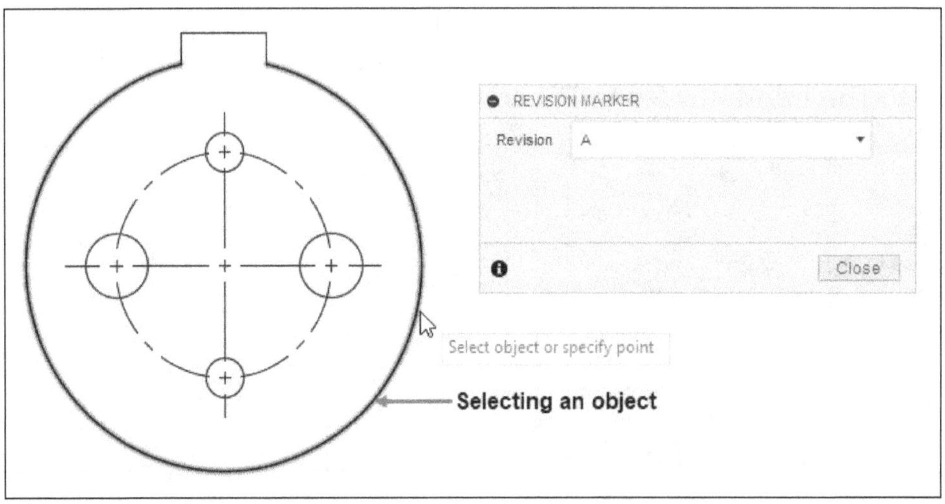

Figure-144. Selecting an object

- After selecting the object, an arrow will be attached to the cursor.
- Click at desired location to place the revision marker; refer to Figure-145.

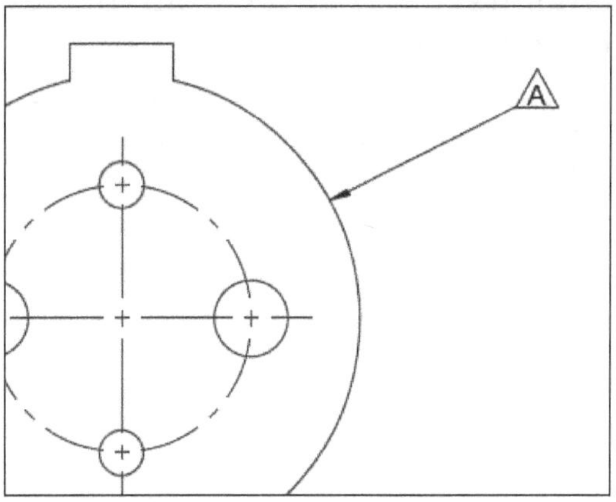

Figure-145. Revision marker placed

- Click on the **Close** button from the dialog box to exit the tool.

REVISION CLOUD

The **Revision Cloud** tool is used to create cloud-shaped objects to call attention to specific changes or portions of each drawing in the **DRAWING** workspace. The procedure to use this tool is discussed next.

- Click on the **Revision Cloud** tool from the **TABLES** panel in the **Toolbar**; refer to Figure-146. You will be asked to specify the first point.

Figure-146. Revision Cloud tool

- Click in the canvas at desired location to specify the first point of the revision cloud.
- Move the cursor away and click at desired location to specify the next point of the revision cloud; refer to Figure-147. Optionally, you can specify the more points of the revision cloud.

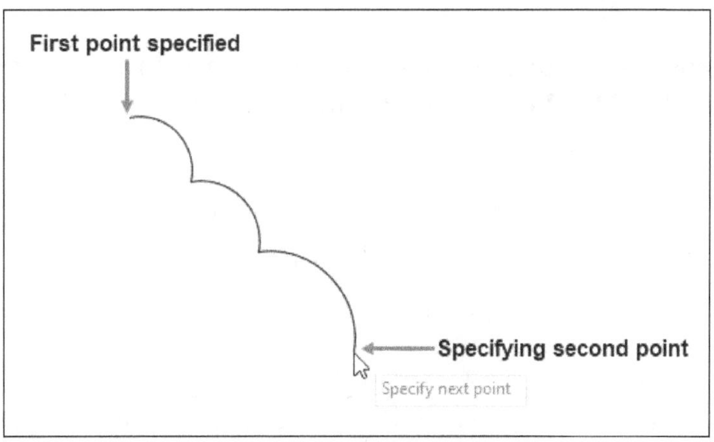

Figure-147. Specifying points of revision cloud

- After specifying desired points, press **Enter** from the keyboard. The revision cloud will be created; refer to Figure-148.

Figure-148. Revision cloud created

REVISION HISTORY

The **Revision History** tool is used to generate a table of list of revisions in the drawing. After performing revisions then generating revision markers, click on the **Revision History** tool from the **TABLES** drop-down in **Toolbar**. The revision history table will be created; refer to Figure-149.

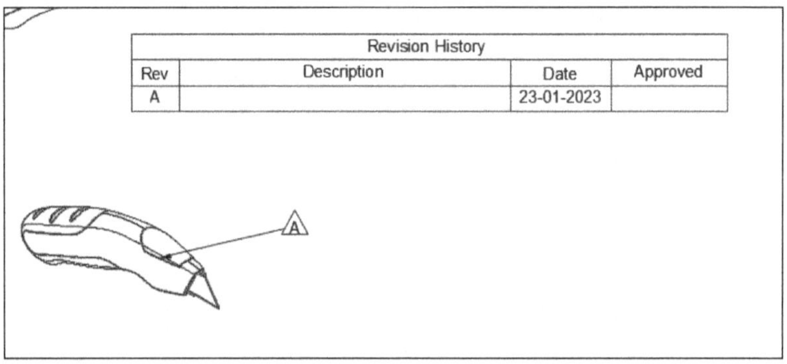

Figure-149. Revision History table

RENUMBERING

The **Renumber** tool is used to renumber the existing balloons. The procedure to use this tool is discussed next.

- Click on the **Renumber** tool from the **TABLES** drop-down in the **Toolbar**; refer to Figure-150. The **RENUMBER** dialog box will be displayed; refer to Figure-151.

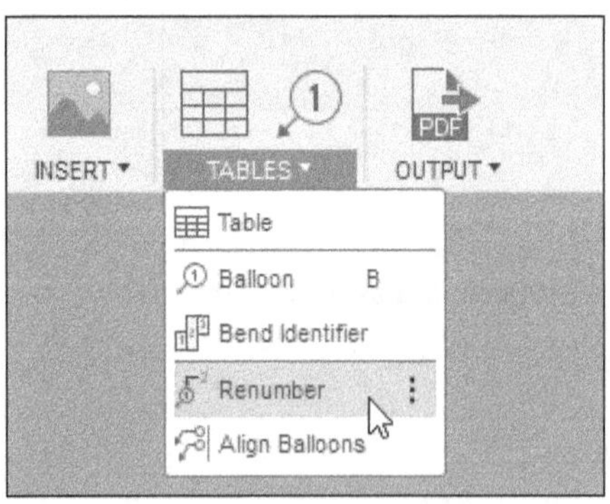

Figure-150. Renumber tool

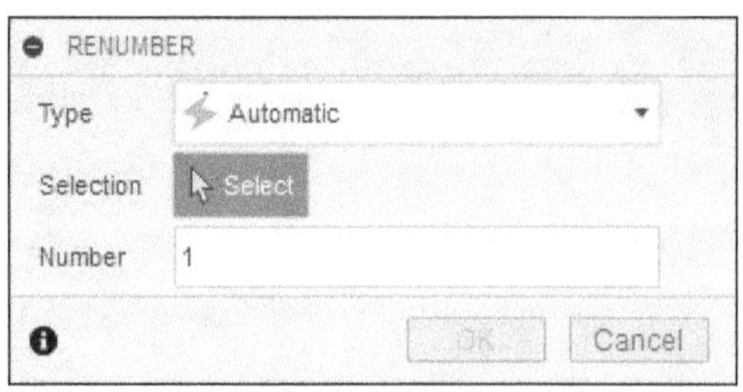

Figure-151. RENUMBER dialog box

- Select **Automatic** option from **Type** drop-down to renumber the balloons or bend identifiers, based on the selection. Select **Balloon** option from **Type** drop-down to renumber the balloons for components in a parts list. Select **Bend Identifier** option from **Type** drop-down to renumber the bend identifiers for sheet metal bends in a bend table.
- Click in the **Number** edit box and enter desired number.
- Click on **Select** button from **Selection** section and click on the balloons as per their sequences to renumber them. The balloon numbers will be changed; refer to Figure-152.

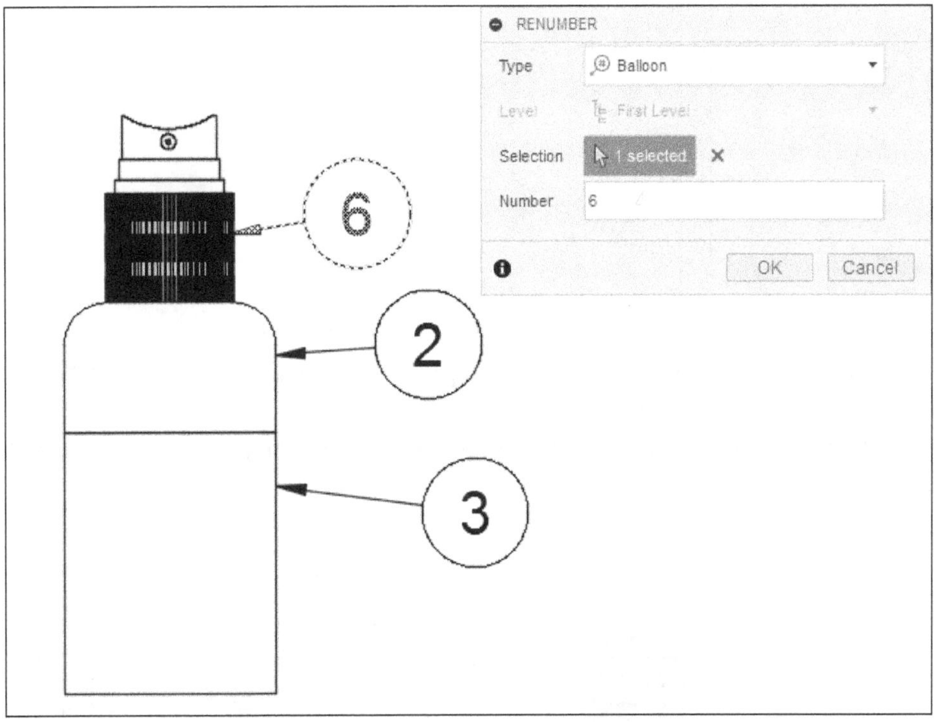

Figure-152. Changed balloon number

- After specifying the parameters, click on **OK** button from **RENUMBER** dialog box to complete the process.

ALIGNING BALLOONS

The **Align Balloons** tool is used to align all the pre-existing balloons. The procedure to use this tool is discussed next.

- Click on the **Align Balloons** tool from **TABLES** drop-down in **Toolbar**; refer to Figure-153. The tool will be activated.

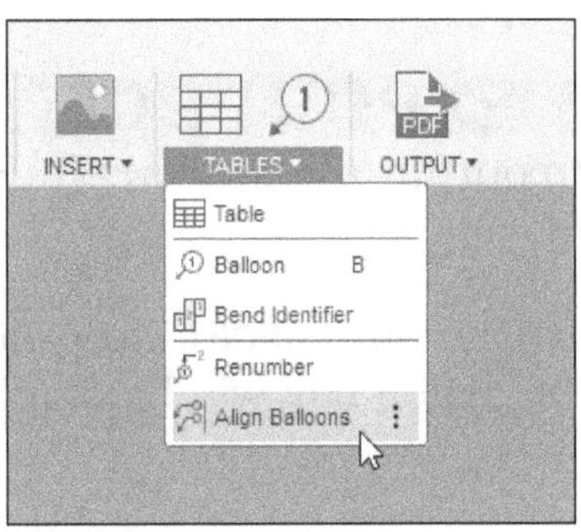

Figure-153. Align Balloons tool

- Click to select all the balloons to aligned; refer to Figure-154 and press **ENTER**. You will be asked to specify starting point of line to be used for alignment of balloons.

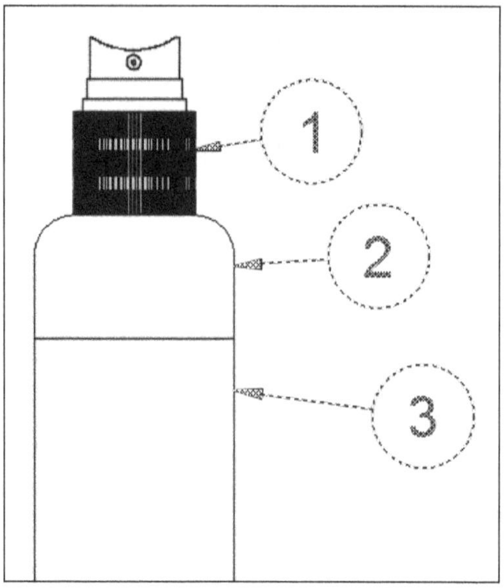

Figure-154. Selection of balloons for alignment

- Click on the screen to specify the start point. End point of alignment line will be attached to cursor.
- Click on the screen at desired location to define alignment of balloons; refer to Figure-155.

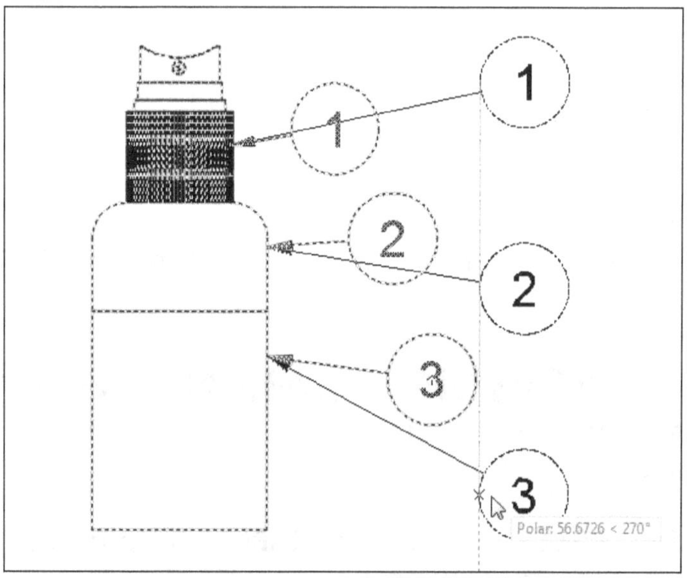

Figure-155. Performing alignment process

EXPORT PDF

The **Export PDF** tool is used to output the drawing in PDF format. The procedure to use this tool is discussed next.

- Click on the **Export PDF** tool from **EXPORT** drop-down in the **Toolbar**; refer to Figure-156. The **EXPORT PDF** dialog box will be displayed; refer to Figure-157.

Figure-156. Export PDF tool

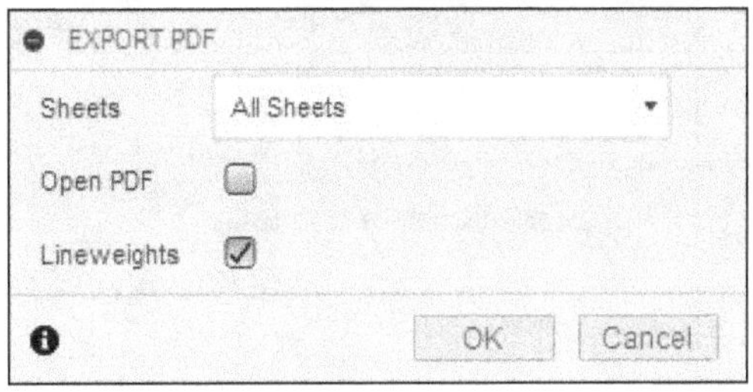

Figure-157. EXPORT PDF dialog box

- Click on the **Sheets** drop-down from the **EXPORT PDF** dialog box and select required sheet for output. You can also use **SHIFT** key or **CTRL** key to select multiple sheets.
- Select the **Open PDF** check box if you want to open the output PDF file.
- Select the **Lineweights** check box if you want to make bold lines of drawing otherwise, clear it.
- After specifying the parameters, click on the **OK** button from **EXPORT PDF** dialog box. The **Export PDF** dialog box will be displayed to save the file; refer to Figure-158.

Figure-158. Export PDF dialog box for saving file

- Click in the **Name** edit box and specify desired name for pdf file.
- Specify desired location of file in the **Default Project** section and click on **Save** button to save the file.
- Or, select **Save to my computer** check box and click on the [...] button. The **Select Location** dialog box will be displayed; refer to Figure-159.

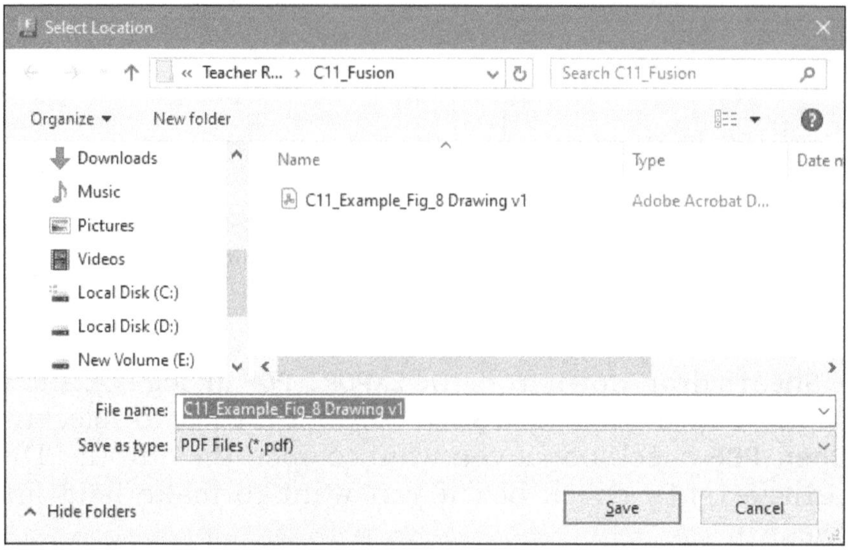

Figure-159. Select Location dialog box

- Browse to desired location where you want to save the file and specify desired file name in the **File name** edit box.
- Click on the **Save** button. The PDF file will be created.

EXPORTING DWG

The **Export DWG** tool is used to create an output file of drawing in **DWG** format. The procedure to use this tool is discussed next.

- Click on the **Export DWG** tool from **EXPORT** drop-down in the **Toolbar**; refer to Figure-160. The **EXPORT DWG** dialog box will be displayed to save the file; refer to Figure-161.

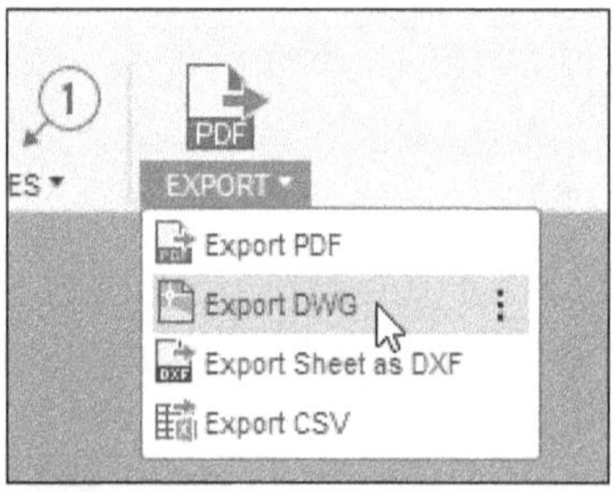

Figure-160. Export DWG tool

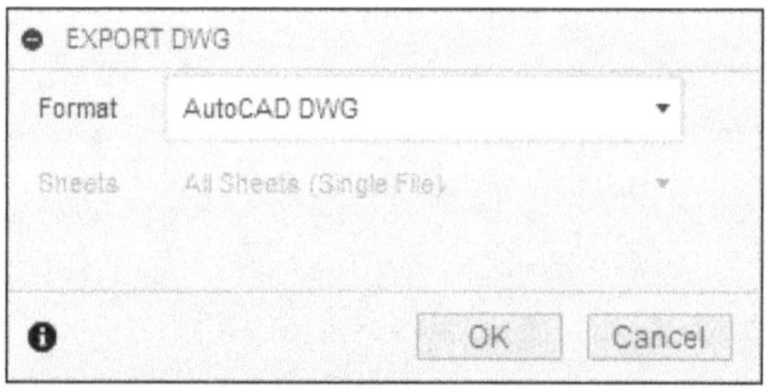

Figure-161. EXPORT DWG dialog box

- Select **Simplified DWG** option from **Format** drop-down of dialog box to export the contents of the current sheet as a DWG file, including views, title block, border, and all annotations as 2D geometry in Model Space.
- Select **AutoCAD DWG** option from **Format** drop-down to export the contents of all sheets to a DWG file. Each sheet is exported as a separate Layout tab.
- Click on the **Sheets** drop-down from **EXPORT DWG** dialog box and select required sheet for output. You can also use **SHIFT** key or **CTRL** key to select multiple sheets.
- After specifying the parameters, click on the **OK** button from **EXPORT DWG** dialog box. The **Output DWG** dialog box will be displayed to save the file; refer to Figure-162.

Figure-162. Output DWG dialog box for saving the file

- Rest of the procedure is same as discussed for previous tool.

EXPORTING DXF FILE

The **Export Sheet as DXF** tool from **EXPORT** drop-down in the **Toolbar** exports the sheets in a drawing as a DXF file. The procedure to use this tool is similar to the **Simplified DWG** option in the **Format** drop-down of **EXPORT DWG** dialog box.

EXPORTING CSV FILE

The **Export CSV** tool is used to create the output of the current file in CSV format. CSV is a format used by database management software and point cloud software. The procedure to use this tool is discussed next.

- Click on the **Export CSV** tool from **EXPORT** drop-down in the **Toolbar**; refer to Figure-163.

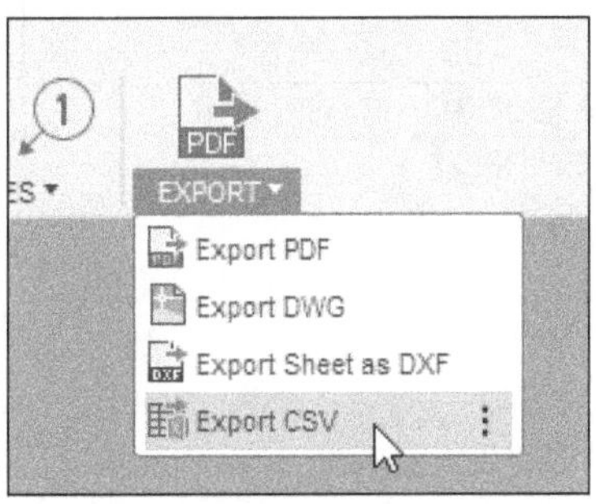

Figure-163. Export CSV tool

- Select the table, parts list, or bend table in the Model Space. The **Output Table** dialog box will be displayed; refer to Figure-164.

Figure-164. Output Parts List or Table dialog box

- Rest of the procedure is same as discussed for previous tool.

PRACTICAL 1

Generating part drawing for the model as shown in Figure-165.

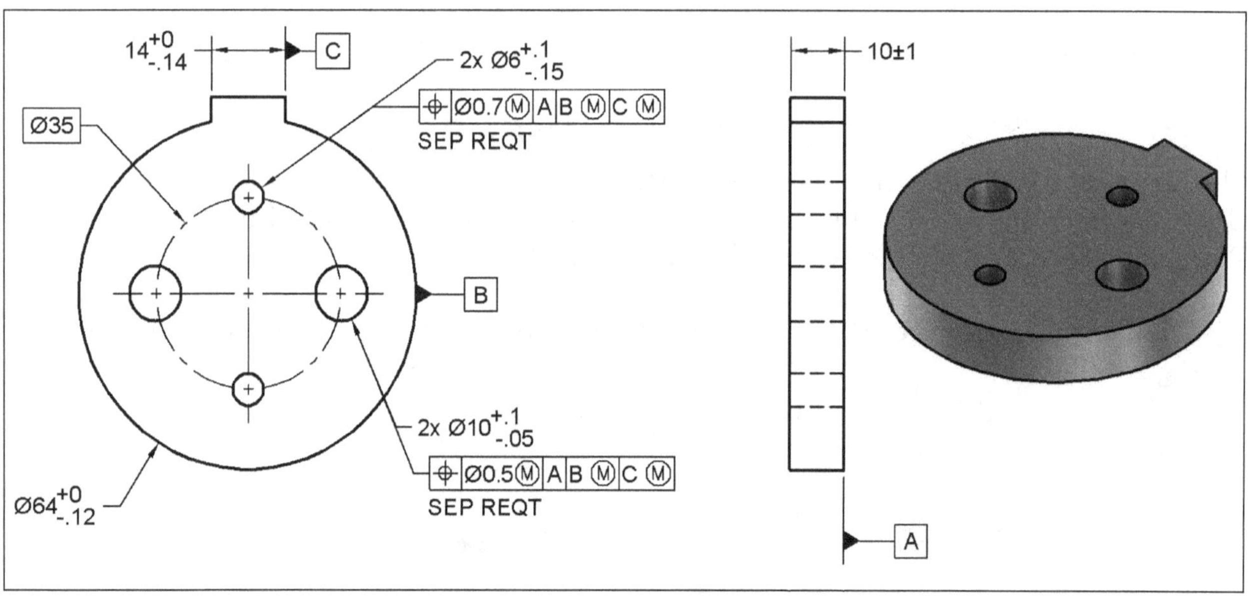

Figure-165. Practical 1 Drawing

Starting a New Drawing using Part

- Set the parameters as shown in Figure-166 for preference.

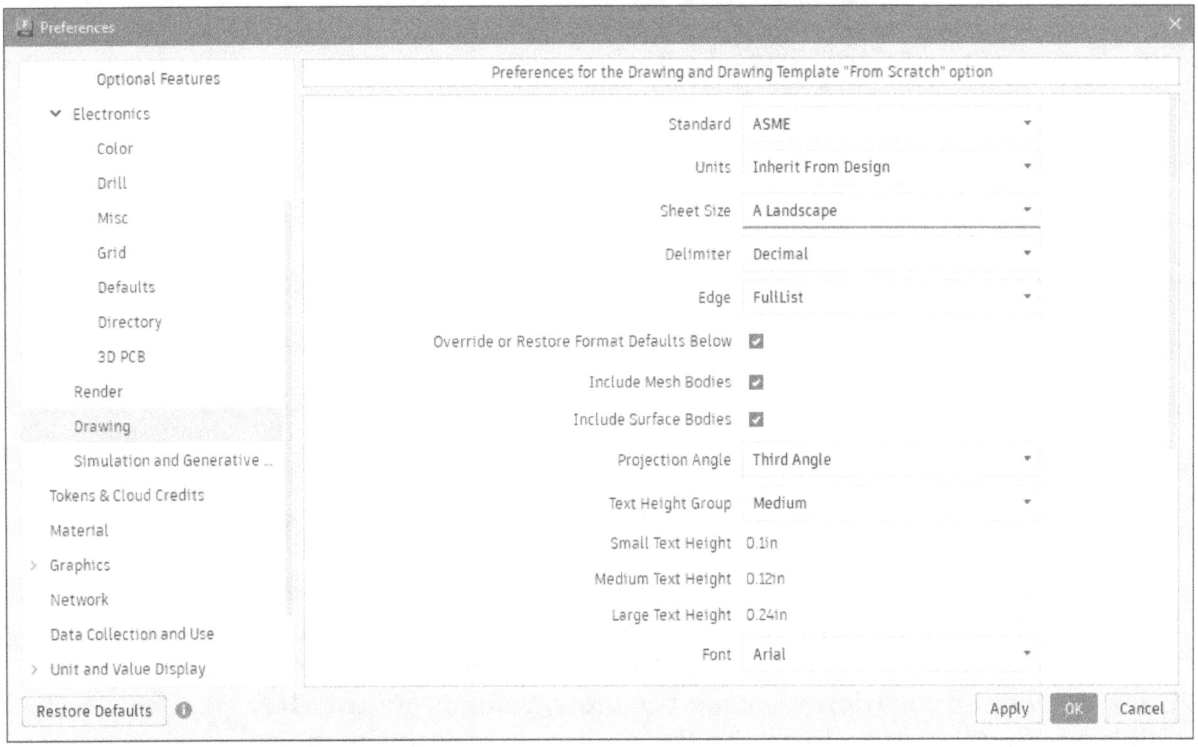

Figure-166. Specifying drawing preferences

- Open the model file for Practical 1 of Chapter 11 in the resource kit. The model will be displayed in the canvas.
- Click on the **From Design** option from **DRAWING** cascading menu in the **Change Workspace** drop-down; refer to Figure-167. The **CREATE DRAWING** dialog box will be displayed.

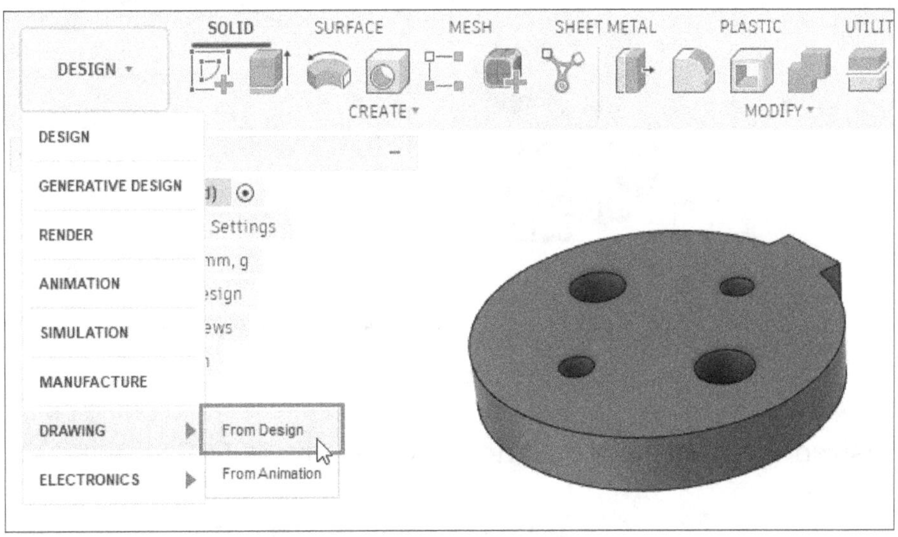

Figure-167. Starting new drawing

- Make sure **ASME** is selected in the **Standard** drop-down of **CREATE DRAWING** dialog box and click on the **OK** button. The **DRAWING VIEW** dialog box will be displayed with preview of drawing view; refer to Figure-168.

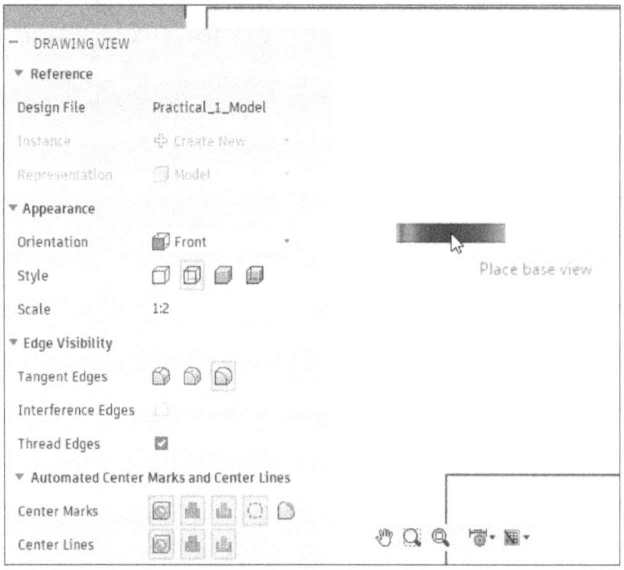

Figure-168. Preview of drawing view

Placing Views

- Select the **Top** option from the **Orientation** drop-down, **Visible and Hidden Edges** button from **Style** section, and **1:1** in **Scale** drop-down from the dialog box.
- Click at desired location to place the view; refer to Figure-169.
- Click on the **OK** button from the dialog box to create the view.
- Click on the **Projected View** tool from the **CREATE** panel in the **Toolbar**. You will be asked to select the base view.
- Select the view earlier placed and move the cursor towards right. The view will get attached to the cursor; refer to Figure-170.

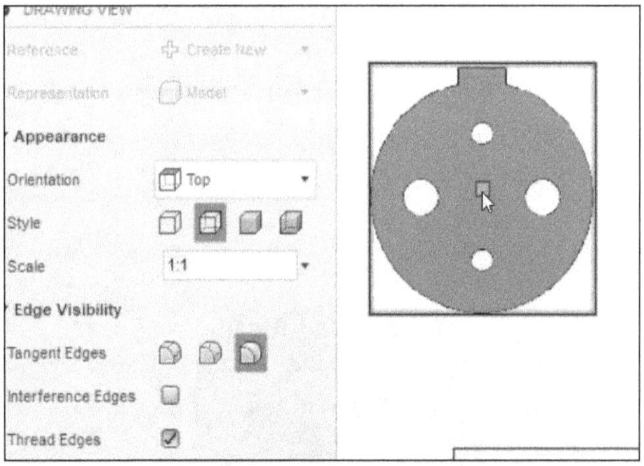

Figure-169. Placing base view

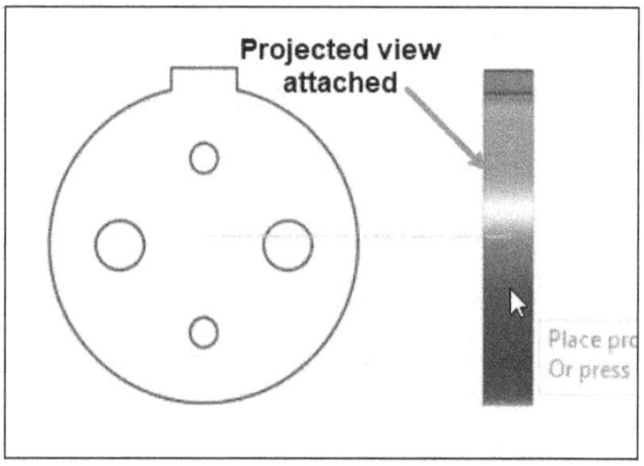

Figure-170. Projected view attached to cursor

- Click at desired location to place the view and press **ESC** to exit.

Applying Annotations

- Click on the **Center Mark Pattern** tool from the **GEOMETRY** panel in the **Toolbar**. The **CENTER MARK PATTERN** dialog box will be displayed.
- Click on one of the holes in the base view and select the **Center Mark** check box. The preview of center mark pattern will be displayed; refer to Figure-171.

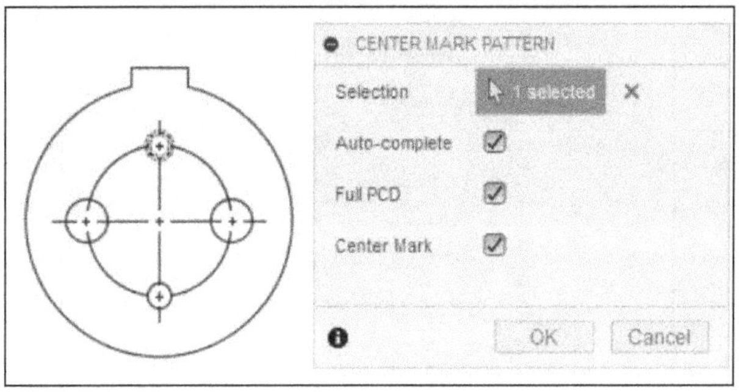

Figure-171. Preview of center mark pattern

- Click on the **OK** button from the dialog box.
- Click on the **Dimension** tool from the **DIMENSIONS** panel in the **Toolbar** and apply dimensions as shown in Figure-172.
- Click on the **Datum Identifier** tool from the **SYMBOLS** panel in the **Toolbar** and place the datum identifiers as shown in Figure-173.

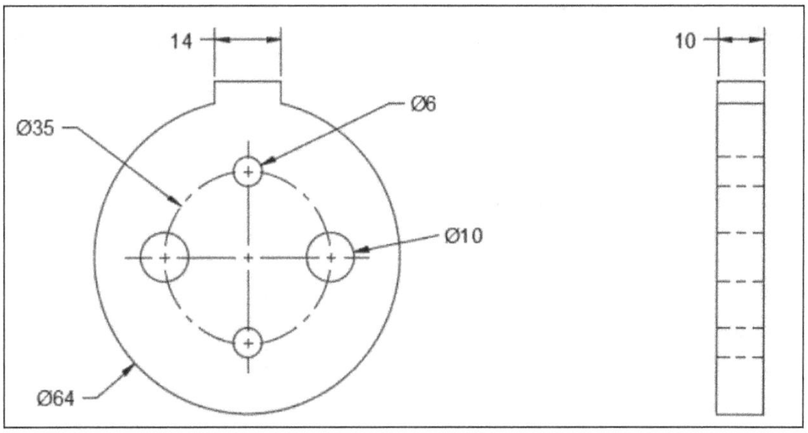

Figure-172. Applying dimensions

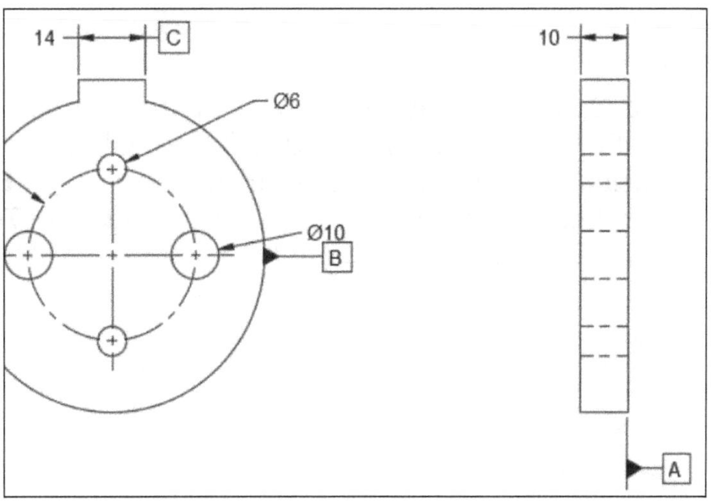

Figure-173. Applying datum identifier

Adding Tolerances to Dimension

- Double-click on the dimension with **10** value. The **DIMENSION** dialog box will be displayed; refer to Figure-174.

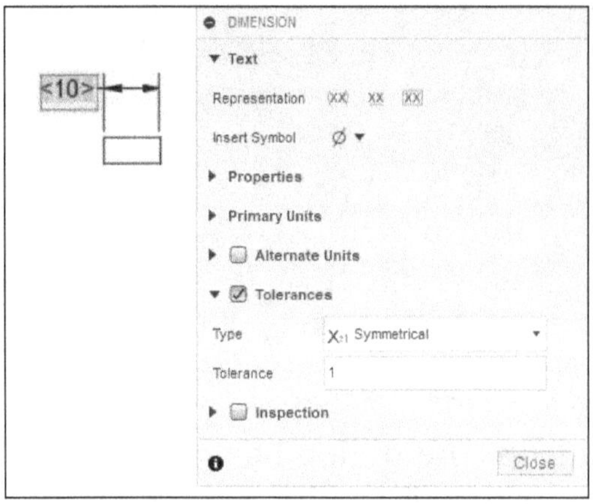

Figure-174. DIMENSION dialog box

- Select the **Symmetrical** option from the **Type** drop-down in **Tolerances** node of dialog box and specify the value as **1** in **Tolerance** edit box. Click on the **Close** button to exit the dialog box.
- Similarly, set the tolerances for other dimensions; refer to Figure-175.

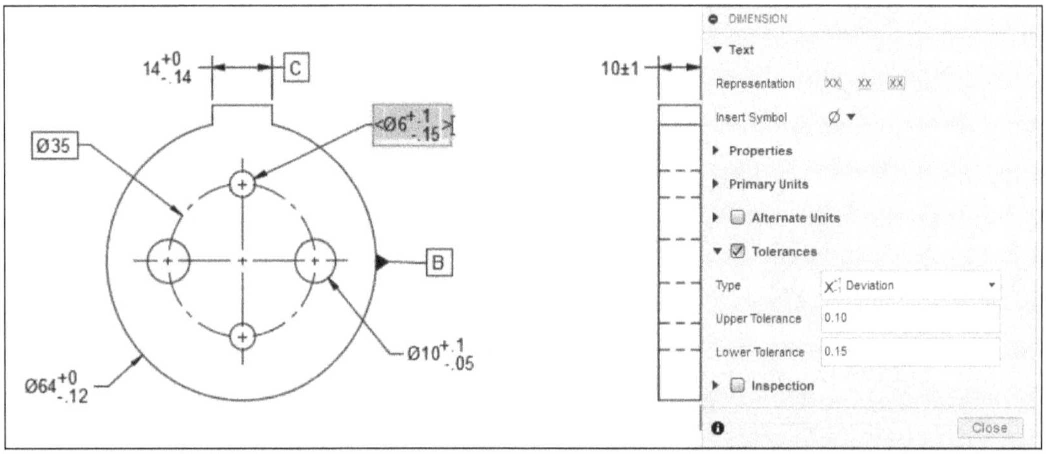

Figure-175. Applying tolerances

- Click on the **Feature Control Frame** tool from the **SYMBOLS** panel in the **Toolbar** and select the hole of diameter **6**. The control frame will get attached to cursor.
- Click at desired location to place the control frame and press **ENTER**. The **FEATURE CONTROL FRAME** dialog box will be displayed; refer to Figure-176.

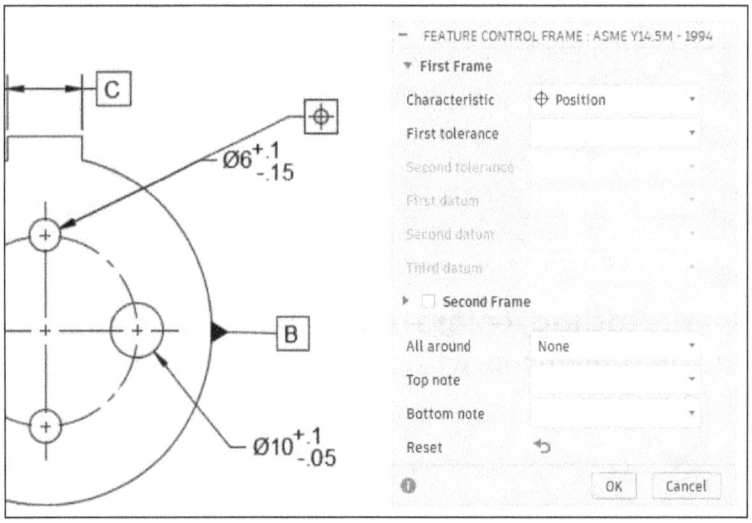

Figure-176. Placing feature control frame

- Specify the parameters as shown in Figure-177 and click on the **Close** button.

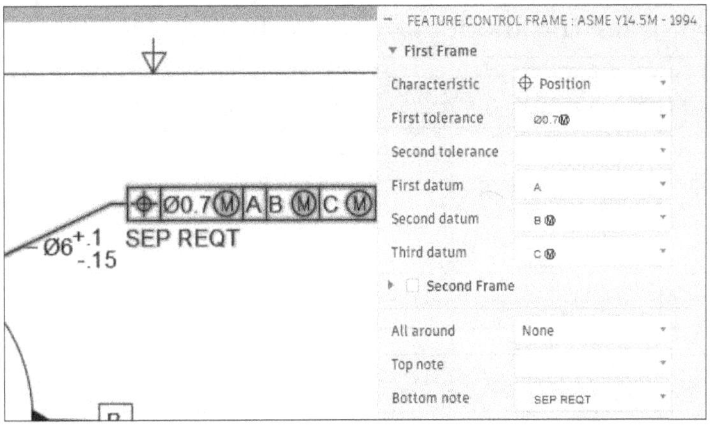

Figure-177. Creating feature control frame

Similarly, define position feature control frame for other hole and place another base view as 3D NE Isometric view; refer to Figure-178.

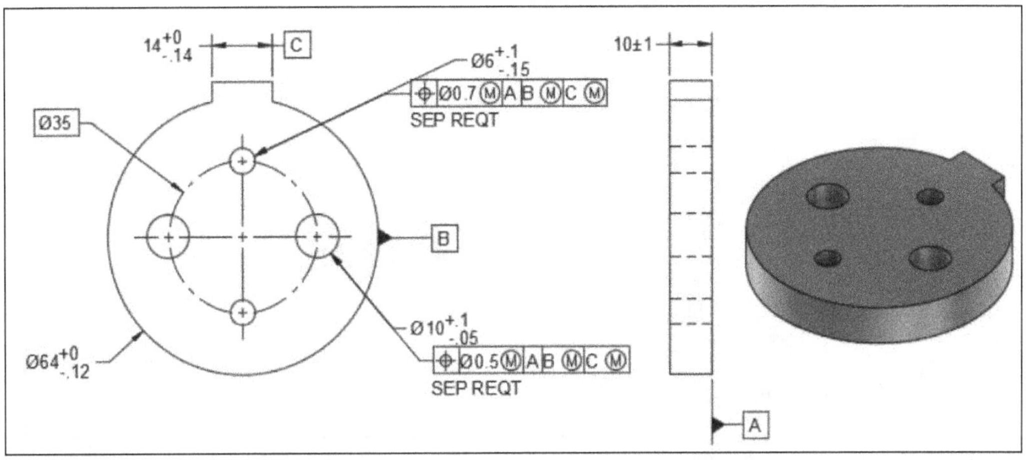

Figure-178. Completed drawing

PRACTICAL 2

Generate part drawing for the model as shown in Figure-179.

PARTS LIST				
ITEM	QTY	PART NUMBER	DESCRIPTION	MATERIAL
1	1	LEADSCREW		STEEL
2	1	SCREWLINK		STEEL
3	1	RODENDBEARINGBALLF RONT		STEEL
4	1	MASTERCYLINDERFRON T		STEEL
5	1	CENTRALLINK		STEEL
6	1	RESORVOIRFRONT		STEEL
7	1	BASEGROUND		STEEL
8	1	90037A102		STEEL
9	1	90037A102(1)		STEEL
10	1	PISTONFRONT		STEEL

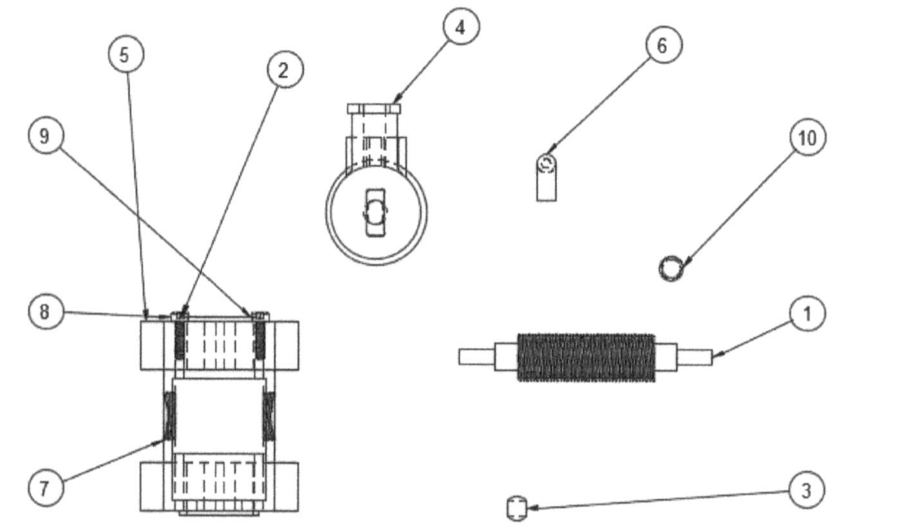

Figure-179. Practical 2 drawing

- Open the model file for Practical 2 of Chapter 11 in the resource kit. The model will be displayed in the canvas.
- Click on the **From Design** option from **DRAWING** cascading menu in the **Change Workspace** drop-down; refer to Figure-180. The **CREATE DRAWING** dialog box will be displayed.

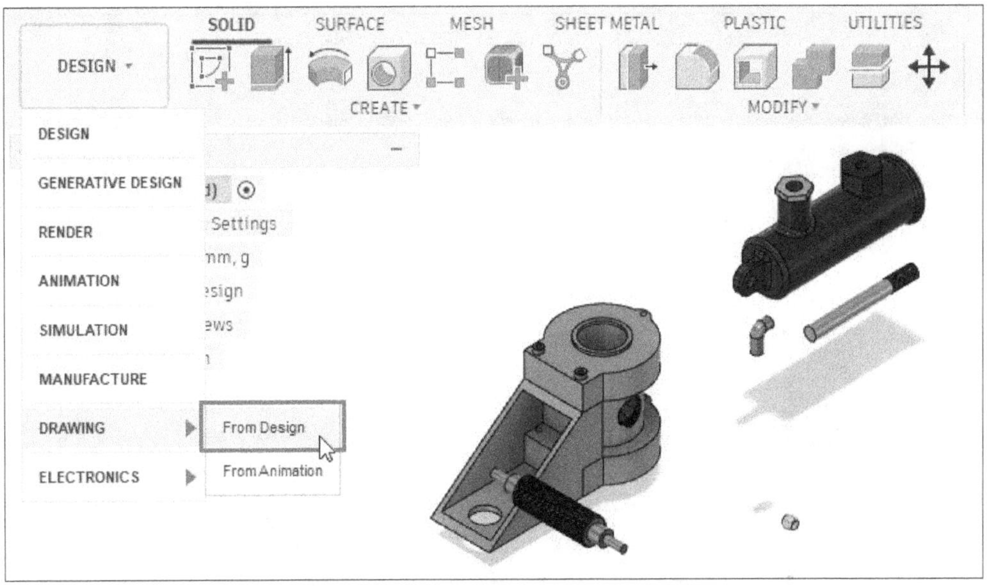

Figure-180. Starting new drawing

- Make sure **ASME** is selected in the **Standard** drop-down of **CREATE DRAWING** dialog box and click on the **OK** button. The **DRAWING VIEW** dialog box will be displayed with preview of drawing view; refer to Figure-181.

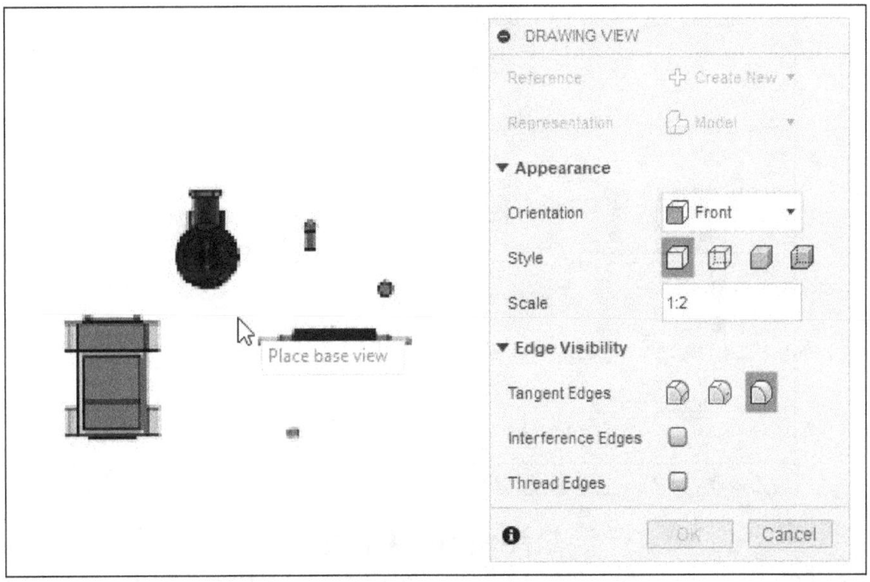

Figure-181. Preview of drawing view

Placing Views

- Select the **Front** option from the **Orientation** drop-down, **Visible and Hidden Edges** button from **Style** section, and **1:1** in **Scale** drop-down from the dialog box.
- Click at desired location to place the view; refer to Figure-182.

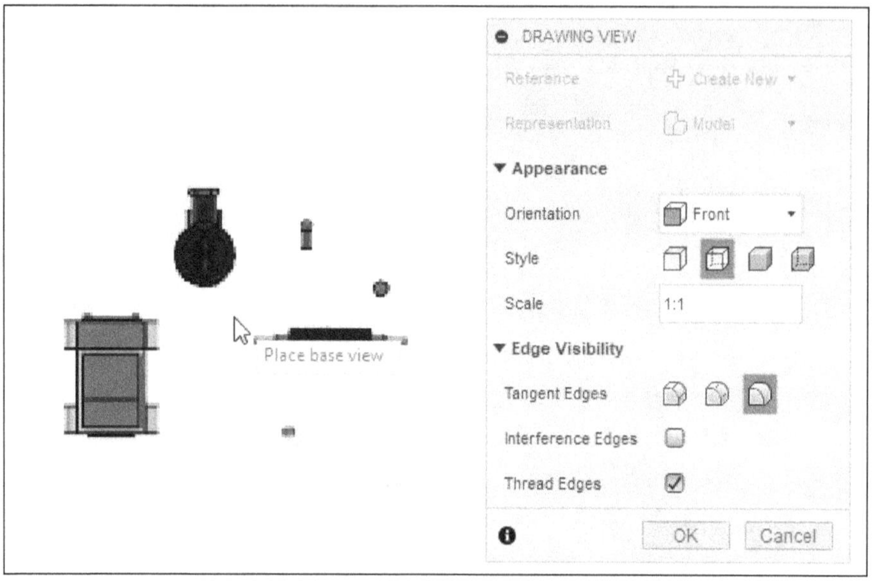

Figure-182. Placing base view

- Click on the **OK** button from the dialog box to create the view; refer to Figure-183.

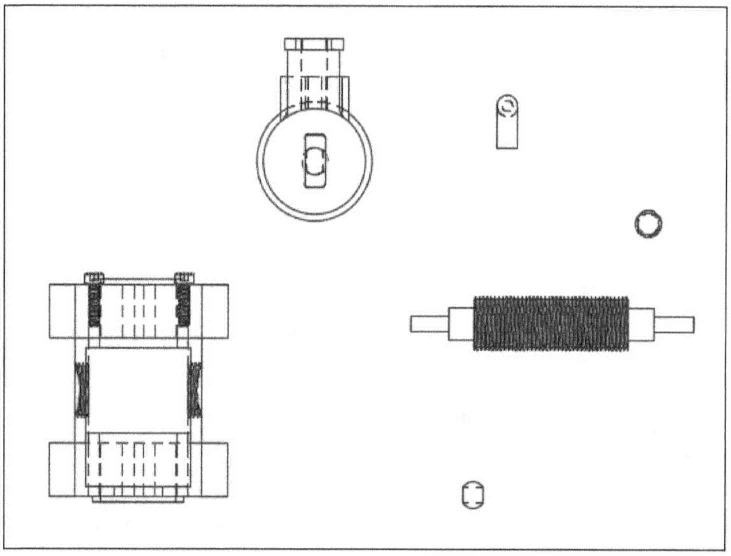

Figure-183. Base view created

Creating Table

- Click on the **Table** tool from **TABLES** drop-down in the **Toolbar**. The **TABLE** dialog box will be displayed along with attached empty table; refer to Figure-184.

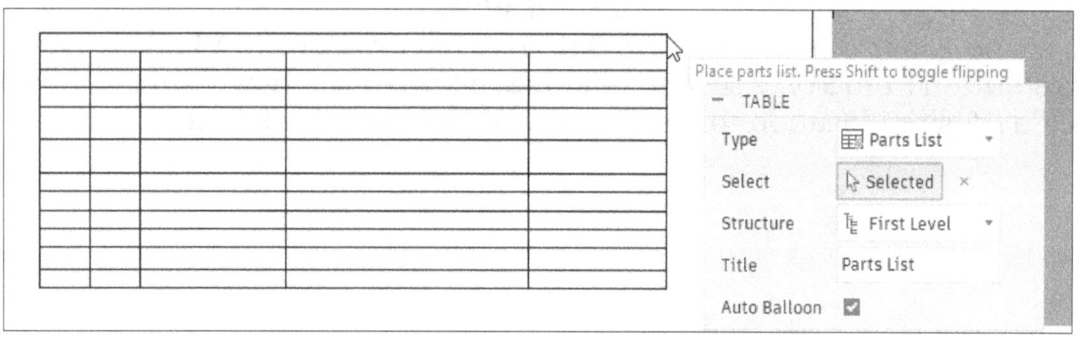

Figure-184. TABLE dialog box along with empty table

- Select **Parts List** option from **Type** drop-down in the dialog box and the current drawing view will be selected automatically.
- Click at desired location in the drawing sheet to place the parts list. Parts list will be generated with balloons; refer to Figure-185.

PARTS LIST				
ITEM	QTY	PART NUMBER	DESCRIPTION	MATERIAL
1	1	LEADSCREW		STEEL
2	1	SCREWLINK		STEEL
3	1	RODENDBEARINGBALLFRONT		STEEL
4	1	MASTERCYLINDERFRONT		STEEL
5	1	CENTRALLINK		STEEL
6	1	RESORVOIRFRONT		STEEL
7	1	BASEGROUND		STEEL
8	1	90037A102		STEEL
9	1	90037A102(1)		STEEL
10	1	PISTONFRONT		STEEL

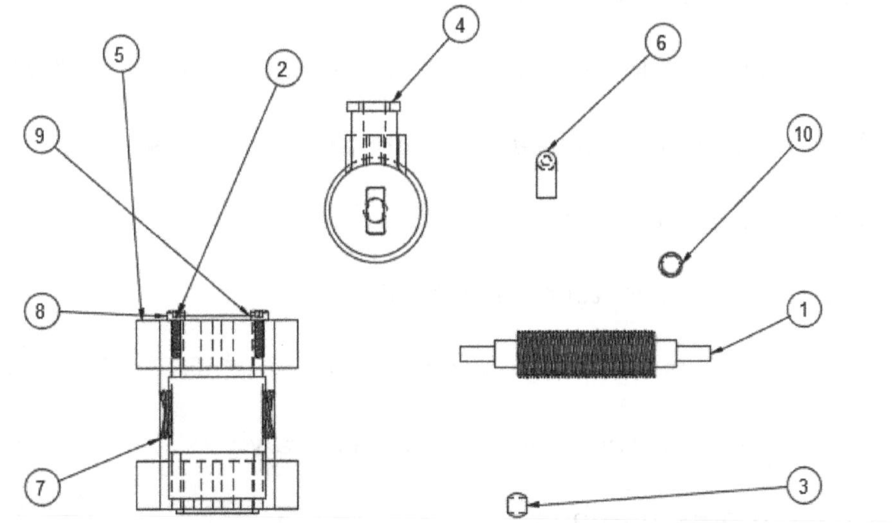

Figure-185. Parts list of assembly generated

PRACTICE

Create drawings for the models discussed in practical and practice sections of Chapter 5 of this book.

SELF ASSESSMENT

Q1. The .... tool is used to create drawing views generated from an existing base or drawing view.

Q2. What is the difference between **ASME** and **ISO** option in **CREATE DRAWING** dialog box?

Q3. In which view of drawing, hatching is automatically created?

Q4. Text can be aligned by **Justification** section. (T/F)

Q5. The drawing view can be move from one place to another with the help of **Move** button. (T/F)

Q6. What is the use of **Edge extension** tool?

Q7. Two parallel edges should be selected to create the extension. (T/F)

Q8. When is the baseline dimensioning required?

Q9. What is Feature Control Frame?

Q10. What is the use of **Datum Identifier** tool?

Q11. The .... tool is used to create an output file of drawing in DWG format.

Q12. What is the primary purpose of engineering drawings?

A. To create artistic representations
B. To guide manufacturing processes
C. To perform mathematical calculations
D. To enhance 3D models

Q13. In Autodesk Fusion, which workspace is used to create drawings?

A. MODEL workspace
B. RENDER workspace
C. DRAWING workspace
D. SIMULATION workspace

Q14. What happens when the "Automatic" radio button is selected in the CREATE DRAWING dialog box?

A. Manually inserts views and dimensions
B. Automatically generates standard views and design dimensions
C. Allows for detailed annotations
D. Saves the file automatically

Q15. Which option in the Contents drop-down is used to create a drawing of only visible components?

A. Full Assembly
B. Visible Only
C. Select
D. Manual

Q16. What is the default projection method used by the ISO standard in the CREATE DRAWING dialog box?

A. Third angle projection
B. First angle projection
C. Orthogonal projection
D. Axonometric projection

Q17. How does selecting "A (8.5x11)" differ from "A (11x8.5)" in sheet size?

A. It creates a Landscape sheet instead of a Portrait sheet
B. It creates a Portrait sheet instead of a Landscape sheet
C. Both create identical sheets
D. It affects only the scaling

Q18. Which option in the Preferences dialog box allows inclusion of mesh in drawings?

A. Include Surface Bodies
B. Include Mesh Bodies
C. Display Trailing Zeros
D. Override Format Defaults

Q19. What is the role of the Base View tool?

A. To create auxiliary views
B. To create the first view derived directly from a 3D model
C. To create section views
D. To add annotations

Q20. What is the purpose of the Auxiliary View tool?

A. To create views normal to a selected edge
B. To add text annotations
C. To edit base views
D. To specify dimensions

Q21. Which tool is used to create a shortened view by removing a portion of the design?

A. Break View
B. Section View
C. Projected View
D. Detail View

Q22. What does the Breakout Section View tool expose in a drawing?

A. Outer dimensions
B. Annotations and text
C. Inner features of a specific area
D. Material tolerances

Q23. Which tool is used to enter the sketch mode and create a new sketch on the current sheet?

A. Move
B. Create Sketch
C. Rotate
D. Centerline

Q24. What is displayed when the Create Sketch tool is selected from the CREATE panel?

A. MOVE dialog box
B. ROTATE dialog box
C. SKETCH contextual tab and SKETCH dialog box
D. GEOMETRY panel

Q25. How can you change the linetype of the sketch geometry?

A. Using Line Width drop-down
B. Using Linetype drop-down in the Properties area
C. By selecting the Layout Grid
D. By selecting the Snap to Grid option

Q26. What is the function of the Show Layout Grid checkbox in the SKETCH dialog box?

A. To display the layout grid in the canvas
B. To display the contents of the sheet
C. To snap the sketch to the grid
D. To finish the sketch

Q27. Which tool is used to move a selected view from one place to another?

A. Rotate
B. Move
C. Centerline
D. Dimension

Q28. What happens when you click the Transform button in the MOVE dialog box?

A. The view is rotated
B. The selected view gets attached to the cursor for movement
C. The base point for rotation is selected
D. The view is deleted

Q29. How can you specify the angle of rotation while using the Rotate tool?

A. By moving the cursor around the parent view
B. By selecting an option from the Linetype drop-down
C. By entering the value in the Angle edit box of the ROTATE dialog box
D. By checking the Snap to Grid checkbox

Q30. What is the function of the Centerline tool?

A. To create centerlines between parallel edges
B. To create center marks for circles
C. To create center marks for patterns
D. To extend intersecting edges

Q31. How many holes can be selected in a linear direction for center mark creation?

A. Two
B. Three
C. Four
D. Unlimited

Q32. What does the Tidy Up tool do?

A. Automatically applies dimensions
B. Rearranges, re-sorts, and resizes objects to keep the layout tidy
C. Moves dimensions to a new position
D. Specifies the datum location

Q33. What is required to create a Baseline Dimension?

A. A linear dimension to be used as a base reference
B. A circular dimension
C. A chain of dimensions
D. A jogged radial dimension

Q34. In chain dimensioning, how are dimensions placed?

A. Overlapping
B. At a 45-degree angle
C. Side by side
D. Randomly

Q35. What is the primary function of the Arrange Dimension tool?

A. To measure dimensions
B. To align or stack dimensions
C. To delete dimensions
D. To change the color of dimensions

Q36. Which option must be selected to create a dimension in the Arrange Dimension tool dialog box?

A. Flip
B. Break
C. Stack or Align
D. Edit

Q37. What does the Flip Arrows tool do?

A. Changes the size of dimension arrows
B. Flips the direction of selected dimension arrows
C. Deletes dimension arrows
D. Adds new dimension arrows

Q38. What must be selected in the Dimension Break tool to add or remove a break in a dimension?

A. The Spacing edit box
B. The desired dimension and operation type
C. The Font drop-down
D. The Alternate Units check box

Q39. Which drop-down in the Editing Dimensions tool allows you to define the hierarchy level in a model?

A. Text
B. Source
C. Type
D. Primary Units

Q40. How can you display dimensions in both inches and millimeters in the Editing Dimensions tool?

A. Select the Alternate Units check box
B. Click the Font drop-down
C. Use the Linear Precision drop-down
D. Select the Zeros/Units section

Q41. What does the Note tool allow users to do?

A. Modify surface textures
B. Insert text into an active drawing
C. Create geometric symbols
D. Arrange dimensions

Q42. What parameter in the Surface Texture tool allows specifying the maximum surface roughness?

A. Machining allowance
B. Roughness max
C. Direction of lay
D. Process edit box

Q43. Which element in a Feature Control Frame identifies the surface or axis being controlled?

A. Geometric Symbol
B. Datum Reference
C. Leader Arrow
D. Tolerance Value

Q44. What symbol is used in a Feature Control Frame to indicate a diametrical tolerance?

A. #
B. %
C. Ø
D. @

Q45. What is the purpose of the Datum Identifier tool?

A. To apply surface textures
B. To identify a datum feature for a feature control frame symbol
C. To arrange dimensions
D. To edit the dimension value

Q46. How do you activate the Text tool?

A. Click the Arrange Dimensions tool
B. Select the Text tool from the TEXT panel
C. Use the Flip Arrows tool
D. Select the Primary Units drop-down

Q47. What can be modified in the DATUM IDENTIFIER dialog box?

A. The length of the arrow
B. The identifier value
C. The dimension font
D. The dimension alignment

FOR STUDENT NOTES

Index

Ethics of an Engineer

- Engineers shall hold paramount the safety, health and welfare of the public and shall strive to comply with the principles of sustainable development in the performance of their professional duties.
- Engineers shall perform services only in areas of their competence.
- Engineers shall issue public statements only in an objective and truthful manner.
- Engineers shall act in professional manners for each employer or client as faithful agents or trustees, and shall avoid conflicts of interest.
- Engineers shall build their professional reputation on the merit of their services and shall not compete unfairly with others.
- Engineers shall act in such a manner as to uphold and enhance the honor, integrity, and dignity of the engineering profession and shall act with zero-tolerance for bribery, fraud, and corruption.
- Engineers shall continue their professional development throughout their careers, and shall provide opportunities for the professional development of those engineers under their supervision.

OTHER BOOKS BY CADCAMCAE WORKS

Autodesk Revit 2026 Black Book
Autodesk Revit 2025 Black Book
Autodesk Revit 2024 Black Book
Autodesk Revit 2023 Black Book

Autodesk Inventor 2026 Black Book
Autodesk Inventor 2025 Black Book
Autodesk Inventor 2024 Black Book
Autodesk Inventor 2023 Black Book

Autodesk Fusion Black Book (V 2701.1.18)
Autodesk Fusion PCB Black Book (V 2701.1.18)

AutoCAD Electrical 2026 Black Book
AutoCAD Electrical 2025 Black Book
AutoCAD Electrical 2024 Black Book
AutoCAD Electrical 2023 Black Book

Basics of Autodesk Inventor Nastran 2026
Basics of Autodesk Inventor Nastran 2025

Autodesk CFD 2026 Black Book
Autodesk CFD 2024 Black Book

Tinkercad Black Book: (2nd Edition)

SolidWorks 2026 Black Book
SolidWorks 2025 Black Book
SolidWorks 2024 Black Book
SolidWorks 2023 Black Book

SolidWorks Simulation 2026 Black Book
SolidWorks Simulation 2025 Black Book
SolidWorks Simulation 2024 Black Book
SolidWorks Simulation 2023 Black Book

SolidWorks Flow Simulation 2026 Black Book
SolidWorks Flow Simulation 2025 Black Book
SolidWorks Flow Simulation 2024 Black Book

SolidWorks CAM 2026 Black Book
SolidWorks CAM 2025 Black Book
SolidWorks CAM 2024 Black Book
SolidWorks CAM 2023 Black Book

SolidWorks Electrical 2026 Black Book
SolidWorks Electrical 2025 Black Book
SolidWorks Electrical 2024 Black Book

SolidWorks Workbook 2022

Mastercam 2023 for SolidWorks Black Book
Mastercam 2022 for SolidWorks Black Book
Mastercam 2017 for SolidWorks Black Book

Mastercam 2026 Black Book
Mastercam 2025 Black Book
Mastercam 2024 Black Book
Mastercam 2023 Black Book

Creo Parametric 12.0 Black Book
Creo Parametric 11.0 Black Book
Creo Parametric 10.0 Black Book
Creo Parametric 9.0 Black Book
Creo Parametric 8.0 Black Book

Creo Manufacturing 12.0 Black Book
Creo Manufacturing 11.0 Black Book
Creo Manufacturing 10.0 Black Book
Creo Manufacturing 9.0 Black Book

ETABS V22 Black Book
ETABS V21 Black Book
ETABS V20 Black Book
ETABS V19 Black Book

FreeCAD 1.0 Black Book
FreeCAD 0.21 Black Book
FreeCAD 0.20 Black Book
FreeCAD 0.19 Black Book

LibreCAD 2.2 Black Book

Ansys Discovery 2025 Black Book

www.ingramcontent.com/pod-product-compliance
Lightning Source LLC
LaVergne TN
LVHW082007200926
848481LV00010B/2820
9781774592045